P9-CRP-409

History of the Theatre

HISTORY OF

NINTH EDITION

PN
2101
.B68
2003

THE THEATRE

OSCAR G. BROCKETT

University of Texas at Austin

Franklin J. Hildy

University of Maryland

Allyn and Bacon

BOSTON   NEW YORK   SAN FRANCISCO
MEXICO CITY   MONTREAL   TORONTO   LONDON   MADRID   MUNICH   PARIS
HONG KONG   SINGAPORE   TOKYO   CAPE TOWN   SYDNEY

Editor in Chief: Karen Hanson
Senior Editor: Molly Taylor
Editorial Assistant: Michael Kish
Marketing Manager: Mandee Eckersley
Editorial-Production Service: Chestnut Hill Enterprises, Inc.
Manufacturing Buyer: Chris Marson
Cover Administrator: Linda Knowles

492766632

For related titles and support materials, visit our online catalog at
www.ablongman.com

Copyright © 2003 Pearson Education Group, Inc.
All rights reserved. No part of the material protected by this copyright
notice may be reproduced or utilized in any form or by any means,
electronic or mechanical, including photocopying, recording, or by any
information storage and retrieval system, without written permission
from the copyright owner.

To obtain permission(s) to use material from this work, please submit
a written request to Allyn and Bacon, Permissions Department,
75 Arlington Street, Boston, MA 02116 or fax your request to
617-848-7320.

Previous editions were published copyright © 1999, 1995, 1991, 1987,
1982, 1977, 1974, 1968 by Allyn & Bacon

Between the time Website information is gathered and published,
some sites may have closed. Also, the transcription of URLs can
result in typographical errors. The publishers would appreciate
notification where these occur so that they may be corrected
in subsequent editions.

Library of Congress Cataloging-in-Publication Data

Brockett, Oscar Gross, 1923–
    History of the theatre / Oscar G. Brockett, Franklin J. Hildy. — 9th ed.
      p. cm.
    Includes bibliographical references and index.
    ISBN 0-205-35878-0
    1. Theater—History. 2. Drama—History and criticism.   I. Hildy, Franklin J. (Franklin
Joseph), 1953–   . II. Title.

PN2101 .B68   2003
792'.09—dc21

2002025352

Printed in the United States of America

10 9 8 7 6 5   CIN   07 06 05

WITHDRAWN

Contents

DUCKWORTH LIBRARIES
YOUNG HARRIS COLLEGE

www.ablongman.com/brockett9e

For the Appendix *The Nature
and Scope of Theatre History* go to
www.ablongman.com/brockett9e

Preface

This book has already gone through eight editions since its publication in 1968. The ninth edition tracks the theatre from its beginnings until 2001. Its primary emphasis continues to be the European tradition, with a secondary emphasis on the traditions of Africa and Asia. Despite its scope, the book is not all-inclusive, but in it an effort has been made to describe and trace the major trends and examine the principal characteristics of what are generally recognized as the major components of those traditions. The goal has been to provide a chronological survey of the theatre's history as a cultural institution rather than an exhaustive treatment of any one of its parts. Historical accounts are a mixture of evidence and interpretation, and consequently scholars often differ markedly in the conclusions they reach, even when they use the same pieces of evidence. Therefore, this book tries to alert readers to significant differences in scholarly opinion and to encourage them to read several accounts before accepting any as being adequate.

This ninth edition includes numerous changes, undertaken to update the account, sharpen points, reinterpret information, and take note of current controversies. The most prominent changes have to do with the reorganization of the book. Instead of the previous 19 chapters, there are now 26. Primarily, these changes are intended to make the chapters more uniform in length and, in some cases, to stimulate an alternative way of looking at the development of theatre. The first of the organizational changes divides Greek theatre, with Chapter 2 being devoted to Classical Greece, and Chapter 3 combining the Hellenistic Greek with Roman and Byzantine developments to give greater emphasis to the evolution of theatre in the Greco-Roman world. The order of Chapters 5, 6, and 7 has been changed to foreground the continuation of medieval practices and influences in England and Spain before taking up the Italian innovations that were to dominate all European theatre thereafter. Perhaps the most noticeable changes begin with Chapter 11, where, because of excessive length in earlier editions, it and all subsequent chapters through 23 have been divided into two, generally one dealing with Continental European theatre and the other with English-language theatre. These are divisions of organizational convenience, which we hope will not obscure the enormous influences that the theatre of Continental Europe and the theatre of the English-language countries had on one another. These divisions have, however, made it possible to add new material on the history of theatre in Latin America, Canada, Australia, and New Zealand. The exceptions are Chapters 16 and 17 where the development of realism and nonrealism, which used to be the topic of Chapter 14, have now been examined separately. Chapter 24, on Contemporary Theatre, is almost entirely new. The chapters on African theatre (formerly Chapter 19) and Asian theatre (formerly Chapter 18) have been renumbered, becoming Chapters 25 and 26, respectively. We have continued to provide these histories as separate chapters because integrating them into the larger narrative seemed to obscure their development without providing greater insight into the development of theatre as a whole.

Despite the changes made in the new edition, the basic format and approach remains unchanged. The Appendix (on the nature, scope and methods of theatre history) has been moved to the book's Website: http://www.ablongman.com/brockett9e. This Website provides updated information, corrections, and a place where readers may raise issues and suggest future changes. It also includes links to Websites that provide additional information about various aspects of theatre history.

We have attempted to examine the full complexity of theatre as an art form from its function in a given culture to its many component parts including acting, audiences, theatrical space, texts (whether written or not), playwriting, costume, makeup/masks, scenery, lighting, properties, machinery, special effects, music, dancing, singing, directing, management, criticism, and more. All of these topics are addressed, but not every chapter addresses every topic, and the space devoted to each topic varies from one chapter to the next. Although this book includes abundant information, its major concern is the characteristic practices that give the theatre its flavor in each era, as well as those features that apparently have contributed to later eras.

A book of this scope obviously depends heavily on the work of many scholars. It is impossible to acknowledge each debt within the text, since to do so would double its length. But at the end of the book, there are chapter-by-chapter bibliographies, both as an acknowledgement of the principal sources used in writing the book and as a guide to reading in greater depth. (Additional bibliographic information is provided on the Website.) Since the theatre can at times best be understood through visual materials, many illustrations are included in each chapter, both to clarify the written text and to suggest the visual characteristics of the theatre in that era.

The assistance of many other people in the preparation of this edition is gratefully acknowledged. In addition to the scholars whose works are listed in the Bibliography, we are also indebted to countless students who have contributed to our knowledge in classes and seminars. Indebtedness to individuals, publishers, libraries, and collections for permission to reprint materials is acknowledged in the credits accompanying the illustrations and source materials. We would especially like to acknowledge the extensive and thoughtful suggestions made by Denise Corte, Sandra M. Cypess, Elizabeth Vandiver and Gary J. Williams, along with the valuable assistance in preparing the manuscript provided by Carrie Cole, Brett Crawford, and Donna Trieschmann. We gratefully acknowledge the contribution of the following reviewers: Anthony Hill, The Ohio State University; Barbara Burgess-LeFebvre, West Virginia Wesleyan College; Kim Christison, Snow College; E. Rodney Peterson, Fort Scott Community College; Ronald O. West, Southern Illinois University. We also want to thank Molly Taylor and Michael Kish, at Allyn and Bacon, for their editorial assistance as well as Marjorie Payne (Marbern House) and Cynthia Newby (Chestnut Hill Enterprises) for their work during the production process. They have been generous with their help, expertise, and patience.

1
The Origins of Theatre

Performative elements (including dramatic and theatrical) are present in every society, no matter how complex or how unsophisticated the culture may be. These elements are evident in our political campaigns, holiday celebrations, sports events, religious ceremonies, and children's make-believe, just as they are in the dances and rituals of primitive peoples. Nevertheless, most participants in these activities do not consider them to be primarily theatrical, even when spectacle, dialogue, and conflict play large roles. Consequently, it is usual to acknowledge a distinction between *theatre* (as a form of art and entertainment) and the presence of *theatrical* or *performative elements* in other activities. This distinction is crucial here, since it would be virtually impossible to write a coherent history of all the human activities that through the ages have made use of performative conventions. Therefore, this book is concerned primarily with the origin and subsequent development of the theatre as an autonomous activity.

THE THEORY OF RITUAL ORIGIN

But how did theatre originate?

In seeking to describe its origin, one must rely primarily on speculation, since there is little concrete evidence on which to draw. The most widely ac-cepted theory, championed by anthropologists in the late nineteenth and early twentieth centuries, envisions theatre as emerging out of myth and ritual. The process perceived by these anthropologists may be summarized briefly. During the early stage of its development, a society becomes aware of forces that appear to influence or control its food supply and well-being. Having little understanding of natural causes, its members attribute both desirable and undesirable occurrences to supernatural or magical forces, and they search for means to win the favor of these forces. Perceiving an apparent connection between certain actions performed by the group (or its shamans) and the results it desires, the group repeats, refines, and formalizes those actions into fixed ceremonies, or rituals.

Stories (myths), which explain, disguise, or idealize, may then grow up around a ritual. Frequently the myths include representatives of those supernatural forces that the rites celebrate or hope to influence. Performers may wear costumes and masks to represent the mythical characters or supernatural forces in the rituals or in accompanying celebrations. As a people becomes more sophisticated, its conceptions of supernatural forces and causal relationships may change. As a result, it may abandon or modify some rites. But the myths that have grown up around the rites may continue as part of the group's oral tradition and may even come to be acted out under conditions divorced from ritualistic concerns. When this occurs, the first step has been taken toward theatre as an autonomous activity, and thereafter entertainment and esthetic values may gradually replace the former mystical and socially efficacious concerns. This, in brief summary, is the traditional view of how theatre developed out of ritual.

A few points need to be made about those who formulated this theory. First, their views were grounded in "cultural Darwinism"—that is, they extended Darwin's theory about the evolution of biological species to include cultural phenomena—and consequently they assumed that human institutions (including theatre) evolved through a process in which there was a steady development from the simple to the complex. Second, they assumed that societies that had evolved such autonomous arts as theatre were superior to those in which the arts had not been separated from ritual. Therefore, their accounts of primitive cultures were written with the unconscious (but nevertheless condescending) assumption that the European was the cultural model toward which all lesser societies would evolve, although local conditions might inhibit or stall that evolution. Third, they believed that, since all societies evolve through the same stages, those still-existing primitive or less advanced societies can serve as valid evidence about how European culture had developed during its prehistoric phase.

FIG. 1.1
Bull dance of the Mandan Peoples of North America. Note the figures at center-front wearing buffalo headdresses and skins. George Catlin, *Bull Dance*, Mandan O-Kee-Pa Ceremony, 1832. Oil on canvas, 24¼ × 28 in. (59.0 × 71.1 cm.) L.1965.1.505, National Museum of American Art, Washington, DC/Art Resource, NY.

After World War II, doubts grew about the superiority of a technologically based society (which had created the atomic bomb, seriously threatened the planet's ecological balance, and been divided into alienated and violent factions). Primitive, less "advanced" societies, because of their cohesiveness, came to be seen by many as embodying alternative social models, different from but perhaps more effective than the European that had long served as the standard. Consequently, several of these societies (including their myths and rituals) were studied more to uncover their modes of thought, communication, and social structuring than to define their developmental stage in relation to a supposed evolutionary model. Myth and ritual came to be looked upon as tools, comparable to language, through which a group discovers, promulgates, and reaffirms its values, expectations, and societal relationships. A number of anthropologists argued that patterns comparable to those found in primitive societies were also still evident in advanced societies (including our own), especially in secular rituals. Thus, all societies came to be seen as developing sets of conventions (or rituals) which enact relationships and serve as unconscious guidelines for behavior. As examples, wedding rituals redefine relationships between two people, between two extended families, and within the society at large; and criminal trial rituals, through which decisions about guilt and innocence are reached, redefine the accused person's place within society. Although we may think of these two examples as legal proceedings rather than as rituals, we do so only because their conventions are so embedded in our consciousness as to have become societal guidelines about certain relationships, whereas our lack of familiarity with the wedding conventions or modes of determining guilt and innocence in other societies may make them seem to us merely bizarre and irrational. Thus, each society develops numerous conventions that may be viewed as rituals that define societal relationships, and it seeks validation of these conventions through religion, morality, law, or social utility.

Ultimately, many post-World War II anthropologists tended to see almost all human transactions as basically performative—as enactments of relationships with specific purposes—involving a number of elements (which are also those found in ritual and theatre). Thus, the earlier concern for the relationship between ritual and theatre was transformed. Both ritual and theatre came to be seen as merely different ways of organizing and using elements that are basic in almost all human activity. Therefore, theatre was not seen as necessarily originating in ritual; rather ritual and theatre were viewed as coexisting modes in which the same elements might be used for differing functions within the same society.

PERFORMATIVE ELEMENTS AND FUNCTIONS

Performative activities (which encompass most human transactions) make use of a number of common elements: time, place, participants (players/audience), scenario (agenda/goal/text/rules), clothing (uniform/costume/mask/makeup), sound (speech/music), movement (gesture/pantomime/dance), and function or purpose. How each of these elements is treated, combined with others, and for what ultimate purpose distinguishes one kind of transaction from another. Although not all of these can be examined at length here, a few examples may clarify the flexible interrelationships within and among these elements.

On one level, all transactions occur in clock time—the amount of actual time it takes to complete an event. But within the event itself, time may be manipulated in many different ways. In most religious ceremonies, time has at least two dimensions: time as immediate (the length of the ceremony) and time as eternal (the never-ending relationship between the human and the divine). In drama, time is fictional, allowing months or years to be telescoped into the couple of hours required by the performance. In many games, strict time limits may be among the most important rules; contrarily, in jury deliberations, time is extendable until a verdict is reached. Time is significant in still other ways, since by convention some events occur in the morning, others at night, some on certain days of the week, or during particular seasons of the year. Similarly, place may vary from spaces designed to meet the specific needs of one type of event, or it may be adaptable to multiple needs. Events, such as a ritual, might take place in one space, or they might involve a procession with portions of the ritual being performed at various places along the way; the place may be arranged to keep the performers and spectators wholly separated or to intermingle them.

It should be clear, without discussing them separately, that each element of a ritual can vary widely and can be combined with others in many ways. It should also be clear that almost any event involving societal interaction can be viewed as manipulating the same basic set of performative elements. A business conference, for example, is scheduled for a particular time in a particular place; there is an agenda that sets forth the scope of the discussions; those asked to participate know what dress is appropriate, what type of behavior is acceptable, and what the

FIG. 1.2
Costume and mask made of bark cloth and used for a jaguar dance. From the Amazon River region of Brazil. Neg. #319672. Courtesy Department of Library Services, American Museum of Natural History, New York.

cerns, and the rituals of each tribe differ in specific content and focus from those of other tribes. Many primitive tribes (meaning those that have not yet developed a written language) use initiation rites, some occupying only a few days and others extending over years, to acquaint the young with the tribe's sacred beliefs, taboos, mores, and history. Such rites are still common in Australia and Africa and were once traditional among Native Americans. Rituals may also be intended to influence or control events. A fundamental premise of many rituals is that a desired result—such as success in battle, adequate rainfall, or the favor of a god—can be achieved by acting it out. Masks and costumes are often used to represent supernatural powers in the belief that a spirit is attracted by and enters into its likeness. Masks or body paint may also be used to represent an animal to be killed or as an aid in bringing about desired events. Other rites are related to the seasonal and life cycles of birth, growth, maturity, death, and rebirth. The myth of the god-as-human who is killed and resurrected occurs in almost every society. Most societies also have rituals that glorify—a supernatural power, victories in hunt or war, the society's past, a hero, or a totem (that is, an animal, plant, or natural element with which the group thinks itself closely related). All rituals reflect in some way the society's understanding of its relationship to the powers that govern its well-being and its own interrelationships. Ultimately, rituals also include elements that entertain and give pleasure. Even the most solemn ceremony may give pleasure through spectacle, the repetition of familiar patterns, and the skill of the participants. Pantomimic dances and rhythmical musical accompaniment are often primary means in ritual, as are imaginative costumes and masks.

As should be evident, much that is found in ritual is also present in theatre. In ritual, beyond those elements already mentioned, there must be "actors"—those who enact the rites or stories—and those who exercise control over the performance ("directorial" functions often undertaken in rites by initiates, elders, or priests). Both theatre and ritual also use an "acting area" and an "auditorium," the shape, size, and organization of which may vary considerably from one society or period to another.

But, though ritual and theatre may use many of the same elements, the distinction between them ultimately depends on their functions. Perceptions about the function of an event may vary widely, depending on one's relationship to the event and familiarity with its conventions. As members of our own society, we may easily recognize the distinctions among church services, theatrical events, athletic games, and political rallies, but someone wholly un-

hierarchy within the group is; and they know what the purpose of the conference is. Thus, the event is governed by a set of conventions that the participants understand and adhere to; failure to adhere to them usually results in some type of sanction. Ritual and theatre employ the same basic elements as other human activities do but, having different purposes in mind, choose the particular form needed for each element and then organize these elements to achieve the purposes of ritual or theatre.

According to Joseph Campbell, most rituals are related to one of three basic concerns: pleasure (food, shelter, sex, children); power (conquest, aggrandizement of self or tribe); and duty (to the gods, the tribe, or the mores and values of society). Together, these concerns include sustenance, continuation of the family and tribe, prestige, defense against enemies, integration of the individual into society, and the good will of supernatural powers. Individual rituals are concerned with only some portion of these con-

FIG. 1.3
Horned god (or a man disguised as an animal). Drawing from a prehistoric cave in the Volp River region of France. The figure has been redrawn by the Abbé H. Breuil. From Henri Begouen and l'Abbé H. Breuil, *Les Cavernes du Volp* (1958). Courtesy Arts et Métiers Graphiques, Paris.

familiar with our cultural conventions might perceive all of these as essentially theatrical, just as we might those of some African tribe about whose religious and cultural conventions we are entirely uninformed.

It is probably true that ritual preceded theatre as autonomous activity, since it seems unlikely that the earliest societies made clear distinctions among the functions of their activities. As societies became more complex, activities became more specialized and distinctions among functions became clearer. The recognition of specialized function seems a necessary condition for the separation of ritual and theatre, but where the line between them is to be drawn is difficult to specify since it depends primarily on our perception of the function of an event or activity.

OTHER THEORIES OF ORIGIN

Although origin in ritual has long been the most popular, it is by no means the only theory about how the theatre came into being. Storytelling has been proposed as one alternative. Under this theory, re-

lating and listening to stories are seen as fundamental human pleasures. Thus, the recalling of an event (a hunt, battle, or other feat) is elaborated through the narrator's pantomime and impersonation and eventually through each role being assumed by a different person.

A closely related theory sees theatre as evolving out of dances that are primarily pantomimic, rhythmical or gymnastic, or from imitations of animal noises and sounds. Admiration for the performers' skill, virtuosity, and grace is seen as motivation for elaborating the activities into fully realized theatrical performances.

In addition to exploring the possible antecedents of theatre, scholars have also theorized about the motives that led people to develop theatre. Why did theatre develop, and why was it valued after it ceased to fulfill the functions of ritual? Most answers fall back on theories about the human mind and basic human needs. One, set forth by Aristotle in the fourth century B.C.E., sees humans as naturally imitative—as taking pleasure in imitating persons, things, and actions and in seeing such imitations. Another, advanced in the twentieth century, suggests that humans have a gift for fantasy, through which they seek to reshape reality into more satisfying forms than those encountered in daily life. Thus, fantasy or fiction (of which drama is one form) permits people to objectify their anxieties and fears, confront them, and fulfill their hopes in fiction if not in fact. The theatre, then, is one tool whereby people define and understand their world or escape from unpleasant realities.

But neither the human imitative instinct nor penchant for fantasy invariably leads to an autonomous theatre. Therefore, additional explanations are needed. One necessary condition seems to be a somewhat detached view of human problems. For example, one sign of this condition is the appearance of the comic vision, since it requires sufficient detachment to view deviations from norms as ridiculous rather than as serious threats to the welfare of the entire group. Another sign is the development of the esthetic sense. For example, some early societies ceased to consider certain rites essential to their wellbeing and abandoned them; nevertheless, they retained as parts of their oral tradition the myths that had grown up around the rites and admired them for their artistic qualities rather than for their religious usefulness. Two other conditions are also important: the appearance of people who can organize performative elements into theatrical experiences of a high order, and a society that acknowledges the value of theatre as an autonomous activity.

Another perspective on theatre history is provided by the notion of static and dynamic societies. In every society some forces seek to maintain the status quo, while others promote change. Usually one tendency is dominant in a given society or during a particular time span. A society may also be dynamic for a time and then become static. Those societies called primitive are ones that became static at an early stage of development. But some advanced societies, such as ancient Egypt or Japan from the fourteenth to the nineteenth century, become relatively static after a period of dynamism. These societies tend to establish and perpetuate ritualized conventions that alter little over centuries of time. Still other societies, such as those of western Europe, emphasize progress and view stasis as an invitation to decay and dissolution. Their dramatic and performance conventions are always in flux.

Joseph Campbell's analysis of the differences between Western and Eastern thought throws some light on these contrasting conditions. In Western myths, the dominant concern is the relationship between two types of beings—gods and humans—and the tension between the roles assigned to each. The roles, which are not fixed, vary considerably from one period and group to another. Sometimes major emphasis has been placed on the supreme power of one or more gods, with humans relegated to a position of total dependence. This, in essence, is the religious view. At other times primary stress has been given to the ability of human beings to manage their own affairs—the humanistic view. Primitive, ancient Near Eastern, and Egyptian peoples tended to emphasize the religious view and to see the world as controlled by divine will emanating from some eternal, unchanging realm. The Greeks first enlarged the human role and established the dominant strain of Western thought, in which humans (sometimes as agents of the gods but often quite independently) are assigned a major share in action and control. After the Renaissance the humanistic view was increasingly accepted and the notion of divine interference steadily diminished. Thus, in Western thought the world came to be seen primarily from the human point of view—as a place of conflict, change, and progress—with humanity as the principal agent both for good and evil.

On the other hand, the dominant strain in Eastern thought recognizes no basic dichotomy between god and human. In Eastern myths, people seek to transcend temporal limitations and achieve oneness with the mystery of being, in which all divisions—including human and divine—disappear. Although on the surface everything may seem tempestuous and ever-changing, behind this apparent flux lies a harmony so complete as to defy all attempts to define it. The Eastern view encourages a conception of world order in which all duties, roles, and possibilities are fixed; it does not see reality as a series of constantly changing relationships (as does the West) but as a fixed state of being. Humanity cannot influence this being; it can only seek to become one with it. Consequently, to the traditional Eastern mind change and progress seem illusions, whereas to the Western mind they seem inevitable.

These differences help to explain why the theatrical traditions of Asia and Africa have in the past been most attuned to tradition and stasis, whereas those of Europe and America have been dominated by change and progress, and why, as electronic media have disseminated much the same ideas throughout the world, the former differences between East and West have lessened. This book deals primarily with the Western tradition. Before taking up that history, however, it should be helpful to look briefly at conditions in Egypt and the Near East, where civilization is usually thought to have begun.

ANCIENT EGYPT AND THE NEAR EAST

Recent studies of artifacts from the Ice Age have indicated that people may already have been performing rituals some 30,000 years ago. Several centuries later (about 20,000 years ago) humanity began to leave somewhat more definite records in the form of paintings on the walls of caves in Africa, France, and Spain that seem to show rituals related to hunting. Our interpretations of these early records remain tentative, however, because we lack sufficient information to clarify them. The picture becomes somewhat clearer when we reach the period in which humans began to develop the skills and habits that made civilization possible: the domestication of animals (by *c.* 9000 B.C.E.); the cultivation of grain (*c.* 7000 B.C.E.); the invention of pottery (*c.* 6500 B.C.E.); and the abandonment of a nomadic existence as hunters and food-gatherers to become fixed residents raising animals and food. The earliest permanent settlements appear to have been established in that part of the Near East called Mesopotamia (present-day Iraq) sometime around 8000 B.C.E. Evidence from that time shows that fertility rites were then already common.

By 3500 to 3000 B.C.E., cities had grown up in both Mesopotamia and Egypt, and by 3000 Egypt had formed an effective central government. For 2500 years thereafter, Egypt and the Near East were to be the major centers of civilization. Forms of writing were devised and elaborate monuments were erected. Although Egypt and the Near East developed more or less simultaneously, in the brief overview that follows Egypt will be given primary emphasis, since it was more stable than the Near East, where numerous empires (Sumerian, Babylonian, Hittite, Assyrian, Chaldean, Canaanite, and Persian) flourished and declined.

Archeological discoveries in recent years seem to establish that human beings evolved first in the Rift Valley of eastern Africa. Thus, the oldest humans and the first rulers of Egypt may have been black—information which some recent scholars see as having been deemphasized because of racial prejudice.

Most of the information used in studies of ancient Egypt comes from the hieroglyphics, decorations, and artifacts preserved in the great pyramids built as tombs for the pharaohs and in the temples dedicated to the numerous Egyptian gods. Many of these remains relate in some way to Egyptian myths about seasonal and life cycles—birth, maturity, death, and rebirth. These patterns are embodied in stories of gods who engage each other in battles, are killed, and resurrected. These stories of the gods are, in turn, associated with the pharaoh, the gods' representative on earth. Thus, though one pharaoh might die, another took his place, just as one season followed another. Overall, the myths show the triumph of continuity and order over chaos and disruption in both the divine and human realms.

Egyptian myths provide a basis for speculation about the performative aspects of those rituals with which they were associated, but they do not provide specific information about the rites themselves. Consequently, scholars disagree violently over the degree to which these texts should be considered dramatic. For example, hieroglyphic scenes, depicting the trials through which the spirit must pass before being admitted to an honorable place in afterlife, appear on the walls of many pyramids. The more than fifty surviving "pyramid texts" date from 2800 to 2400 B.C.E., although certain passages may have been traditional by that time and may have originated 1000 years earlier. Some scholars have argued that these texts are dramas and were enacted by priests at regular intervals to ensure the well-being of the dead pharaoh and to show the continuity of life and power. Their view is based principally on the presence of occasional passages of dialogue and indications of action. But there is no definitive evidence that they were intended to be acted out or that they ever were. Consequently, equally reputable scholars have denied that these texts were performed, pointing out that such nondramatic works as epic poems and the Bible also contain passages in dialogue and indications of action.

Other similarly contested texts relate to the coronation of pharaohs. One of the few remaining fragments has been interpreted by some scholars as a series of ritualistic scenes performed at various places in Egypt, with the new ruler thereby symbolically taking possession of his kingdom. In this text, the pharaoh is associated with Horus, who in mythology succeeded his father, Osiris, as ruler.

Another text, sometimes called the Memphite Drama, appears to have been performed each year on the first day of spring. It dates from about 2500 B.C.E. and tells of the death and resurrection of Osiris and the coronation of Horus. Some historians interpret this as a drama in which Horus, symbolizing the regenerated year spirit, was impersonated by the pharaoh.

The most important performative event is often referred to by modern scholars as the Abydos Passion Play, a title which deliberately links it to European religious dramas of the Middle Ages. This event concerns the death and resurrection of the god Osiris. In Egyptian myth, Osiris, son of Geb (the earth) and Nut (the sky), succeeded his father as ruler

FIG. 1.4

Egyptian acrobatic dancers. Note how the hair is weighted and how the figures at left seem to be providing a clapping accompaniment. Relief sculpture from a tomb at Saqqara, Egypt.

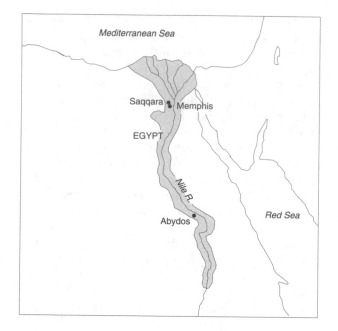

FIG. 1.5
Ancient Egypt.

of Osiris was reenacted. They see the event as a ritual commemorating all the dead pharaohs, each of whom was symbolized in Osiris. They argue that the basic premise of the event was that Osiris is dead and that consequently the ritual took on the characteristics of a royal funeral. Information sufficient to resolve this dispute is not presently available, although all apparently agree that some type of performative event took place.

In addition to Egyptian texts, others from the Near East—Sumerian, Babylonian, Hittite, Canaanite, and so on—date from *c.* 2500 B.C.E. onward and show that the number of gods worshipped by the people of that region was enormous. The texts are for the most part concerned with the seasonal patterns of birth, growth, maturity, death, and resurrection. (Translations and discussions of selected Near

and married his sister, Isis. His brother, Set, jealous of Osiris' power, killed Osiris and buried parts of the body at various spots in Egypt. Isis found the pieces and, with the aid of Anubis, later the jackal-god of embalming, revived Osiris. Unable to remain on earth, Osiris, after his body was buried at Abydos, went to dwell in the afterworld, where be became the judge of souls. Horus, son of Osiris, fought with Set and won back his father's kingdom. This was the most revered of all Egyptian myths.

At Abydos, the most sacred spot in Egypt, some kind of performance relating to Osiris (the one often referred to as the Abydos Passion Play) occurred annually from about 2500 until about 550 B.C.E. In spite of this long history, no part of the text remains. What we know of it is deduced from an account left by Ikhernofret, a participant sometime between 1887 and 1849 B.C.E., in which he tells what he did during one of the celebrations. Again, however, scholars disagree markedly in their interpretations of Ikhernofret's account. Some have argued that the major events of Osiris' life were reenacted with much spectacle (including battles, processions, and burial ceremonies), the principal roles being taken by priests and the crowds being portrayed by the people. Furthermore, they suggest that each section of the play was performed at a different location and perhaps over several weeks or months. As they see it, this was one of the most elaborate dramatic spectacles ever staged. Contrarily, other scholars have vigorously objected to the designation of this event as a "passion play" and have denied that the life or death

FIG. 1.6
The Ikhernofret stone (dated about 1868 B.C.E.), the primary evidence concerning the so-called Abydos Passion Play. At right, the events have been divided into acts by a modern scholar. From Schaefer, *Untersuchungen zur Geschichte und Altertumskunde Aegyptens,* IV (1904).

Eastern and Egyptian texts can be found in Theodor Gaster's *Thespis,* in which the author seeks to establish that these were full-fledged dramas.)

As this brief summary suggests, the difficulty in studying these early years lies not in establishing that numerous performances occurred but in determining the nature of the performances. Present-day religious services offer little help in envisioning rituals of those earlier times. In Egypt and the Near East a temple was usually considered the private residence of the god, to which admission was granted to no one other than those (priests) appointed, usually by the ruler, to act as the god's servants. These priests dressed the god's image, served it food, and treated it as they might the king himself, who was often considered to be a god or a god's earthly manifestation. Through much of the year, then, the ordinary people participated in major religious rites only at second hand through the ruler and his priest-assistants. On a few occasions each year, the god's image was taken from the temple in a procession over some prescribed route where at certain stations rites were performed in the presence of (and perhaps with limited participation by) the general populace. Thus, the majority of people were allowed only occasional glimpses of their earthly and heavenly rulers. It seems likely that the rites, both those performed within and without the temples, were elaborate, lavish, and precise, since nothing less would have been considered suitable. Such ceremonies both validated and reaffirmed the existing order. Their function was religious, social, and political rather than theatrical.

A question inevitably arises about the influence of Egypt and the Near East on Greece, where Western theatre is usually thought to have begun. Contacts among the civilizations of the eastern Mediterranean were constant, and the Greeks themselves acknowledged considerable indebtedness to the Egyptians, Phoenicians (from whom they borrowed the alphabet), and others. The Greek historian Herodotus (*c.* 484–425 B.C.E.), after visiting Egypt around 450, noted two performances there and commented that Dionysus, the god in whose honor plays were presented in Greece, was another version of Osiris. Nevertheless, since the early nineteenth century most historians have minimized the influence of Egypt and the Near East on Greece. Some present-day historians charge that such attempts to diminish the contributions of Africa and Asia Minor to Greek civilization were motivated by racism and anti-Semitism, and by the desire to maintain the superiority of European over other cultures by denying its indebtedness to peoples who by the nineteenth century had come to be looked upon as inferior. Thus, Greece came to be treated as the originator of those values and institutions considered to be the hallmarks of the European tradition.

Although the influence of Egypt on Greece apparently was considerable, one important difference remains between their performance traditions. The Egyptians maintained an advanced civilization for some 3000 years (a period longer than the one that separates us from the beginnings of Greek drama) and never developed theatrically beyond ritualized performances, repeating the same ceremonies year after year for centuries. Theirs was a society that resisted changes that might have led to an autonomous theatre, whereas the Greeks went on to a theatre in which new plays were presented each year. Thus, despite the achievements of the Egyptians, it appears that Greece took the decisive step toward an autonomous theatre.

LOOKING AT THEATRE HISTORY

Among the first problems faced by the historian is the amount of information that has survived (and is available) about the topic being studied. The more one is removed from an event in time, the more apt evidence is to be scarce. But it is not merely the ravages of time that cause information to be lacking. It may be difficult to find materials relating to certain conditions that existed as recently as 50 or 100 years ago because no one considered them sufficiently important to record. In most past eras, records were systematically maintained only about those things officially sanctioned by state and religious authority. Consequently, we tend to know much more about rulers, wars, political and religious controversies, and similar matters than we do about the lives of ordinary people, the activities and contributions of women and ethnic minorities, or about popular culture (the entertainments of the common people as opposed to the "high" art favored by rulers or a cultural elite). Thus, the kinds of things a society thought important to record tell much about its values. Similarly, the major monumental structures erected by a society also indicate priorities in its values—the pyramids of Egypt, the temples of Greece, the cathedrals of Medieval Europe, the palaces of the Renaissance, the government buildings of the nineteenth century, the office skyscrapers of the twentieth century—just as differences in types of monumental structures from one period to another help us see how priorities may vary.

Even if information has survived, it must be interpreted. Although historians have usually proclaimed their objectivity, they have inevitably brought to their work a set of beliefs and assumptions—that is, an ideology—that predisposes them to find some parts of the surviving evidence significant and other parts unimportant. Thus, they interpret events from a particular point of view, even when they try to avoid bias. Consequently, it can be revealing to ask about historical treatises what assumptions or ideological stances have shaped the authors' interpretations of the evidence they have used. To identify an author's stance does not necessarily invalidate an interpretation, but it does help us understand that this is only one among the possible interpretations that might emerge if the material were viewed from other perspectives.

Martin Bernal has argued extensively that the contributions of Egypt, black Africa, and the Near East to European culture were distorted during the nineteenth century by racial attitudes of that period. Here is one brief excerpt:

> The paradigm of 'races' that were intrinsically unequal in physical and mental endowment was applied to all human studies, but especially to history. . . . To be creative, a civilization needed to be 'racially pure.' Thus it became increasingly intolerable that Greece—which was seen by the Romantics not merely as the epitome of Europe but also of its pure childhood—could be the result of the mixture of native Europeans and colonizing Africans and Semitics.

Martin Bernal, *Black Athena: The Afroasiatic Roots of Classical Civilization*, vol. I (London: Free Association Books, 1987), 29.

One difficulty encountered by a present-day historian seeking to deal with Egyptian texts can be seen in this translation of Ikhernofret's account of his participation in the ceremonies at Abydos. [The dashes indicate gaps in the surviving Egyptian text.]:

> I celebrated the [feast of] "Going Forth" of Upwawet, when he proceeded to champion his father. I repelled the foe from the sacred barque. I overthrew the enemies of Osiris. I celebrated the "Great-Going-Forth," following the god at his going. I sailed the divine boat of Thoth upon _____. I equipped the barque (called) "Shining-in-Truth" of the lord of Abydos, with a chapel. [I] put on his regalia when he went forth to ____ Peker; I led the way of the god to his tomb before Peker; I championed Wennofer at "That Day of the Great Conflict"; I slew all the enemies upon the flats of Nedyt. I conveyed him into the barque [called] "The Great," when it bore his beauty; I gladdened the heart of the eastern highlands; I ___ed the rejoicing in the western highlands. When they saw the beauty of the sacred barge, as it landed at Abydos, they brought [Osiris, First of the Westerners, lord] of Abydos to his palace, and I followed the god into his house, to attend to his ____, when he resumed his seat. I loosed the knot in the midst of his attendants, among his courtiers.

Translation from James Henry Breasted, *Ancient Records of Egypt*, vol. I (Chicago: University of Chicago Press, 1906), 300.

In recent years, theorists have sought to articulate a unifying theory that encompasses all types of performance:

> Performance is an inclusive term. Theater is only one node on a continuum that reaches from the ritualizations of animals (including humans) through performances in everyday life—greetings, displays of emotion, family scenes, professional roles, and so on— through to play, sports, theater, dance, ceremonies, rites, and performances of great magnitude [xiii]. . . . Whether one calls a specific performance "ritual" or "theater" depends mostly on context and function. A performance is called theater or ritual because of where it is performed, by whom, and under what circumstances. If the performance's purpose is to effect transformations—to be efficacious—the performance is a ritual. . . . No performance is pure efficacy or pure "entertainment." The matter is complicated because one can look at specific performances from several vantages; changing perspectives changes classification [120].

Richard Schechner, *Performance Theory*, rev. and expanded ed. (New York: Routledge, 1988.)

2
Theatre and Drama in Ancient Greece

While the civilizations of the Near East and Egypt were flourishing, others were maturing in neighboring areas. For our purposes, the most important were the Aegean forerunners of the Greeks. The Minoan culture flourished on Crete and the nearby islands from about 2500 to 1400 B.C.E. The Minoans had a highly advanced civilization and built three-story palaces decorated throughout with frescos and featuring such amenities as working sewers that would not be seen elsewhere in Europe for 1500 years. Excavations at the palaces of Knossos, Phaistos, Gournia, and Amnisos have revealed stone "theatral areas," but nothing is known about their function. The Mycenaeans, a Helladic culture on the Greek mainland, flourished from around 1600 to 1100 B.C.E. These were the Greeks who fought the famous war with Troy, a major city in Asia Minor near the entrance to the Hellespont, in the thirteenth century B.C.E. Shortly afterwards, Mycenaean civilization began to decline. These early Aegean civilizations had little to do directly with the development of the theatre, but their indirect influence was enormous, for their gods, heroes, and history supplied the material for Homer's (eighth century B.C.E.) *Iliad* and *Odyssey* and for most Greek drama. Thus, these civilizations are in many ways the fountainhead of Western literature.

The Greek civilization that was to produce the first great era of the theatre took shape between the eighth and sixth centuries. The major political unit came to be the *polis* (or city-state, composed of a town and its surrounding countryside). The most important of these city-states were Attica (Athens), Sparta, Corinth, Thebes, Megara, and Argos, but there were others on the coast of Asia Minor and on the Aegean islands. In addition, after 750 B.C.E., numerous colonies were founded in places ranging from the Black Sea in Asia to the coasts of Africa, Spain, and France, although the most important were those in Sicily and southern Italy (Magna Graecia). All of these Greeks acknowledged their kinship, but they also insisted on differences among themselves based primarily on dialect. The primary divisions were Dorian (with Sparta and Corinth as the major cities) and Ionian (represented by Athens and the cities of Asia Minor). Most of these states depended on control of the seas (as the major avenue of trade) for their wealth, power, and well-being. Consequently, rivalries for dominance motivated them to form leagues or to wage war with each other or with non-Greek states.

For some time, the city-states were ruled by kings, but after 800 B.C.E. nobles were able to assume considerable power. The more ambitious nobles soon

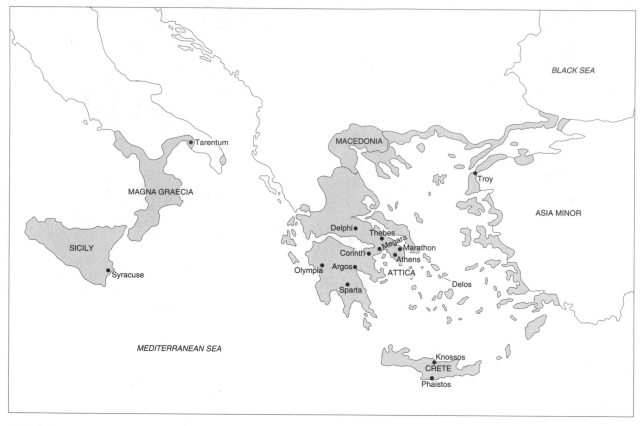

FIG. 2.1
The Greek world during the classical period.

learned they could win support through promises of improved rights for tradesmen and farmers, who had few privileges. Through such means, a number of "tyrants" won control of states between 650 and 500 B.C.E. Many of these tyrants did much to improve social conditions and to promote the arts. For example, Peisistratus, who dominated Athens from 560 to 510, redistributed land, promoted farming and foreign trade, made Athens the leading center of the arts, and established or enlarged numerous festivals, including the City Dionysia, which was to be the major home of drama. But by the late sixth century Greeks were weary of tyrants and found means to prevent them from assuming power. Athens' solution was to found the world's first democracy (around 508 B.C.E.).

Although by 500 B.C.E. Athens was the artistic center of Greece, Sparta was the major power and the head of an alliance that encompassed most of the city-states, including Athens. War with Persia soon altered this arrangement. At the beginning of the fifth century, Persia, already the most extensive empire of the time, sought to expand into Europe. In 490 the Greeks defeated the Persians at Marathon, and in 480–479 the Athenians dealt the Persians a mortal

blow by destroying their fleet. Because of troubles at home, in 477 Sparta withdrew from further involvement in the conflict (which continued for many years as Greek cities in Asia Minor rebelled against Persia). Consequently, Athens rapidly became the major force in the Mediterranean, and in return for protecting others it exacted payments and gained other rights that brought it great wealth and power. In effect, Athens ruled an empire during the remainder of the fifth century. Under the leadership of Pericles (c. 495–430 B.C.E.), Athens built numerous temples and public buildings (among them the Parthenon). Athens' political power was broken in 404, when it was defeated in the Peloponnesian War, but throughout the fifth century it enjoyed a privileged place both politically and artistically.

No doubt the Athenians' confidence in their strength and worth did much to motivate artistic expression during the fifth century. Equally important, however, was the Greek view of human beings and the gods, never a wholly coherent view since it was composed of diverse elements (some derived from the earlier Helladic civilization, some from more recent times, and others from Egypt and the Near East). For the most part, the Greeks conceived of their gods in human terms. Zeus presided over a number of other deities who were as unpredictable as their human counterparts. If wooed with prayers and sacrifices, the gods might help people, but they were just as apt to take offense and hold grudges. Furthermore, they often differed among themselves, and some assisted and others opposed the same people or undertakings. In addition, the gods themselves were not immune to Fate, which lurked behind all Greek thought and made all destiny, both human and divine, uncertain.

Perhaps the most important aspect of Greek culture, unlike that of any people who preceded them, was its concern with humanity. The Greeks systematically raised and sought answers to almost all issues, including the nature of the gods and the universe. As time went by, they became increasingly skeptical about Greek myths. Before the end of the fifth century B.C.E. Protagoras proclaimed, "Man is the measure of all things."

Nevertheless, the Greeks never ceased to set limits on what humans can know, and they always acknowledged the unpredictability of fate. Thus, Greek thought is characterized by a tension between belief in human rationality and acknowledgement of unpredictability. That the Greeks established democracy tells much about their faith in humanity, although even here they were not wholly consistent, for they did not hesitate to enslave others or severely restrict the role of women. Overall, in Greek thought humans were elevated to a place of great prominence, but happiness still depended on a conjunction of human and superhuman forces; when the two were in harmony, life could be peaceful, but the truce was always fragile and could be broken without warning. Such a view promoted a drama that centers on human struggles, but one in which the supernatural element is always strong.

THE ORIGIN OF TRAGEDY

As in all emerging societies, records relating to the beginnings of theatre and drama in Greece are scarce. The Greeks learned to write sometime after 700 B.C.E., when they borrowed the alphabet from their Near Eastern Phoenician neighbors and adapted it to their own use. Thereafter, written records increase, but those relating to performative activities continue to be rare until the Athenian government accorded official sanction and financial support to theatre. This connection between theatre and state is usually said to have begun in 534 B.C.E., at which time Athens apparently instituted a contest for the best tragedy presented at the City Dionysia, a major religious festival. It should be noted, h[...] some scholars have argued recently tha[...] not introduced until 501, when the C[...] was reorganized, and that earlier perfo[...] were essentially choral. Others sugg[...] merely the date when official records beg[...] there is no reason to reject 534 as the beginning of the tragic contests. The debate serves as a reminder that few facts about Greek theatre history can be clearly established.

Although tradition credits Thespis (the alleged winner of the first contest) with the invention of drama, some ancient accounts place him as late as sixteenth in the line of tragic poets. The disparity is probably owing to impreciseness in the original meaning of *tragoidia* (literally, "goat song," from which we get the word tragedy), a term now thought to date from a time when the chorus danced either for a goat as a prize or around a goat which was then sacrificed. Unfortunately, none of the theories about how the term *tragedy* originated (and there are many) provides important clues as to how the dramatic form we call tragedy developed.

The earliest still-extant account of how Greek drama originated—a chapter in Aristotle's *Poetics* (c. 335–323 B.C.E.)—states that tragedy emerged out of improvisations by the leaders of dithyrambs. Consequently, it may be helpful to look briefly at the dithyrambic form, a hymn sung and danced in honor of Dionysus, the Greek god of wine and fertility. Originally the dithyramb probably consisted of an improvised story (sung by a choral leader) and a traditional refrain (sung by the chorus). It was transformed into a literary composition by Arion (c. 625–585 B.C.E.), allegedly the first to record (in writing) dithyrambs on well-defined, heroic subjects and to give them titles. Arion is sometimes associated with the beginnings of tragedy because his performers were called *tragoidoi* and their songs *tragikon drama*. Furthermore, Arion lived at Corinth, a major center of the Dorian Greeks, who later claimed to have invented tragedy. Although this claim is unjustified (insofar as a dramatic form is concerned), the Dorians did develop to a high degree certain elements—lyric poetry, choral singing and dancing, and mythological subjects—that were later emphasized in dramatic tragedy. That the Dorians considered Arion's compositions to be tragedy probably explains why some ancient writers placed Thespis so late in the line of tragic writers.

Exactly how dithyrambic improvisations led to tragedy or over how long a period is unclear, but the final step has long been attributed to Thespis. His innovation probably involved the addition of a prologue and lines (spoken by an actor impersonating aracters) to what had previously been a wholly narrative work sung and danced by a chorus and its leader. This change did not come about by enlarging the role of the chorus leader (the *koryphaios*), for he continued his original function after the introduction of an actor (the Greek term for which was *hypokrites*, meaning "interpreter" or "answerer"). Virtually nothing is known of Thespis. It is possible that as early as 560 B.C.E. he was performing in Icaria, a subdivision of Attica. Horace, writing some 500 years later, declares that Thespis traveled about on a cart with plays. If that is true, Thespis probably performed in several Greek towns other than Athens.

Not all scholars believe that Greek drama developed out of dithyramb. Alternate theories are too numerous to summarize here. One theory argues that drama evolved from rites performed at the tombs of heroes, and almost all depict drama as having emerged gradually out of rituals of one kind or another. In a quite different vein, Gerald Else has advanced the theory that drama was a deliberate rather than a gradual creation. As he sees it, for some time prior to 534 B.C.E. certain festivals had featured recitations (by rhapsodes) of passages from such epic poems as the *Iliad* and *Odyssey*. In addition, Athenian poets (especially Solon) had written verse in which characters were impersonated. In 534 then, according to Else, Thespis merely joined these elements with a chorus to create a primitive drama that could be developed fully only after Aeschylus' addition of a second actor (around 490 B.C.E.) permitted face-to-face conflict on stage. Else more or less reverses the dithyrambic theory, for he believes that the individual performer (the rhapsode) linked his work to a chorus rather than emerging from it.

All theories of origin are in part conjectural, since evidence to substantiate any of them definitively is lacking. Whatever its origin, the major step toward drama seemingly was taken during the late sixth century, when it was accorded official recognition. At this time an association with Dionysus was also established, one that was to continue, for thereafter all state-sponsored dramatic productions in Athens were given at festivals in honor of that god.

THE CITY DIONYSIA IN THE SIXTH CENTURY

The worship of Dionysus probably originated in the Near East and was only later imported into Greece, perhaps as early as the thirteenth century B.C.E. At first the cult met considerable resistance because of its ecstatic nature: its celebrations often involved in-

FIG. 2.2

Men dancing dressed in bird costumes. Note the flute player at the extreme left. A Greek vase of the late sixth or early fifth century B.C.E. Courtesy British Museum.

toxication, sexual orgy, and the rending and devouring of sacrificial victims (including humans). In spite of all resistance, however, worship of Dionysus was eventually accepted throughout Greece. In some places he displaced other gods, whose attributes were then assigned to him. The orgiastic aspects of the Dionysian rites eventually abated and by the sixth century they had largely disappeared.

According to myth, Dionysus was the son of Zeus (the greatest of Greek gods) and Semele (a mortal). Reared by satyrs (who are often associated with him in dithyramb, drama, and art), he was killed, dismembered, and resurrected. As a god, he was associated with fertility, wine, and revelry, while the events of his life linked him with the year-spirit found in other early religions—that is, the cycle of the seasons and the recurring pattern of birth, maturity, death, and rebirth. Through their rites, Dionysian worshippers sought a mystical union with the primal creative urge. On a more practical level, they sought to promote fertility: to guarantee the return of spring, the productivity of both human beings and the land, and ample harvests. The rites were also intended to ward off evil.

The Greeks honored each of their gods through one or more annual festivals. In Attica, where Athens was the principal town, four festivals were held each year in honor of Dionysus, and it was at one of these—the City (or Great) Dionysia—that drama was first presented. Although the City Dionysia was the last of the four festivals to be inaugurated, it rapidly became the most important after it was reorganized in the late sixth century.

From time to time the events that made up the City Dionysia were altered to meet changing conditions. Around 508 Athenian democracy was created and, in order to break up the family loyalties that had been at the root of past rivalries, all the inhabitants of Attica were divided into ten tribes. It may have been out of the desire to stimulate loyalty to the recently created tribes that about this time a new contest—for dithyrambic performance—was inaugurated at the City Dionysia. Each tribe, in competition with the other nine, presented two dithyrambs each year, one for men and one for boys. Around 501 reorganization of the City Dionysia added a contest for satyr plays. After this time, each dramatist was required to present three tragedies and a satyr play each time he entered the competition. Thus, by 500 the City Dionysia had become relatively complex.

Other than Thespis, only three dramatists of the sixth century are known to us: Choerilus, Pratinas, and Phrynichus. Choerilus, who began his career between 523 and 520 and continued into the fifth century, is said to have written 160 plays, to have won thirteen contests, and to have made unspecified innovations in costumes and masks. Pratinas, who wrote about fifty dramas, was especially noted for satyr plays, a form he is sometimes said to have invented. Phrynichus (*fl.* 511–476), the first author known to have written on contemporary subjects, is also credited with introducing female characters into drama. He was noted for the beauty of his choral lyrics and for inventing new varieties of choral dance.

No drama from the sixth century has survived. The scraps of information that have come down to us suggest that in these early years experimentation with forms and conventions was common, that the lyrical and choral elements were dominant and highly developed, that all characters were played by a single actor (the author), and that subject matter was drawn primarily from recent history.

TRAGEDY IN THE FIFTH CENTURY

Our knowledge of Greek tragedy is based almost entirely on the work of three playwrights of the fifth century: Aeschylus, Sophocles, and Euripides. His-torians usually assume that the surviving [p]representative, but it is perhaps well to reme[mber] only thirty-one tragedies by three author[s (or four) remain from the more than 1000 tha[t] written by numerous playwrights between 500 and 400 B.C.E.

The surviving plays use a number of recurring structural features. Most of the tragedies begin with a *prologue* which provides information about events that have occurred prior to the opening of the play. Next comes the *parodos,* or entrance of the chorus; if there is no prologue, the *parodos* begins the play. The *parodoi* of extant plays vary in length from twenty to two hundred lines; they introduce the chorus, give exposition, and establish the proper mood. Following the *parodos,* a series of episodes, varying in number from three to six and separated by choral dance songs (or *stasima*), develop the main action. The *exodos,* or concluding scene, includes the departure of all the characters and the chorus.

The point of attack in the plays is late—that is, the story is usually taken up just prior to the climactic moment, and only the final part is dramatized. Thus, considerable exposition of earlier events is required. Most of the tragedies but not all (for example, Sophocles' *Ajax*) place scenes of death and physical violence offstage; this convention requires the frequent use of messengers to relate what has occurred elsewhere. In most of the plays, the time of the action is continuous, but there are notable exceptions (as in Aeschylus' *Agamemnon*). Similarly, most of the tragedies occur in a single place, but again some works (among them Aeschylus' *Eumenides*) deviate from the typical pattern.

All extant Greek tragedies are based on myth or history. Each writer was free, however, to alter the stories and to invent motivations (which are often not provided in myth) for characters and actions. Thus, though dramatists might begin with the same basic story, they ended with widely different interpretations of it. Agathon, writing at the end of the fifth century, was supposedly the first to invent stories for tragedy, but his example was never widely followed and none of his plays has survived.

Greek dramatists were very economical in the number of events and character traits they included, preferring a few broad strokes to multiplicity of detail. They paid little attention to the physical and sociological aspects of characterization, concentrating instead on the psychological and ethical attributes of their personages.

The oldest surviving Greek plays are by Aeschylus (*c.* 523–456), who began competing at the City Dionysia about 499 B.C.E. and is credited with thirteen victories. Although about eighty titles are known, the only ones to have survived are: *The Persians* (472), *Seven Against Thebes* (467), the *Oresteia*, a trilogy of plays made up of *Agamemnon, Libation Bearers,* and *Eumenides* (458), *The Suppliants,* and *Prometheus Bound* (exact dates unknown but probably after 468). His authorship of the latter play, however, has been disputed by some modern scholars, who believe it may be the work of an unidentified author. The major innovation attributed to Aeschylus is the introduction of the second actor. It is usually assumed that this occurred early in his career, but no date can be fixed for it. After about 468, when Sophocles reputedly introduced the third actor, Aeschylus made use of this additional performer.

Most scholars have argued that all of Aeschylus' extant plays, with the exception of *The Persians,* formed parts of trilogies (three plays based on a single story or common theme). That Aeschylus often needed three plays to encompass his tragic idea indicates his interests and method. For example, the *Oresteia* (the only surviving Greek trilogy) is usually interpreted as showing the evolution of the concept of justice, with the impersonal power of the state eventually replacing personal revenge, which up to the final play creates an endless chain of private guilt and punishment. Reconciling the conflicting claims in an all-encompassing principle allows Aeschylus to resolve the action happily. This pattern (pitting one principle against another and then reconciling them through some larger principle) apparently characterized several of his works, and seems to indicate that Aeschylus was interested in philosophical issues quite different from those pursued by Sophocles and Euripides.

Because Aeschylus' characters embody cosmic conflicts, they are sometimes said to be superhuman. They usually have a limited number of traits, but these are incisive, powerful, and entirely appropriate to the action. Although Aeschylus is essentially a philosophical and religious dramatist, he is also the most theatrical of the Greek tragedians, for he makes great demands on the theatre's resources. His plays often call for spectacle on a monumental scale: second choruses and numerous attendants; chariots drawn by horses; picturesque and sometimes frightening mythological characters; and so on. He also makes considerable use of visual symbolism, unusual choral dances, and lavish costumes. The grandeur of his conceptions has seldom been surpassed.

Sophocles (c. 496–406) is thought to have written more than 120 plays, but only seven have survived: *Ajax* (between 450 and 440), *Antigone* (c. 441), *Oedipus the King* (c. 430–425), *Electra* (c. 418–410), *Trachiniae* (c. 413), *Philoctetes* (409), and *Oedipus at Colonus* (406). A substantial portion of one satyr play, *The Trackers,* is also extant. Sophocles is said to have won twenty-four contests, the first in 468 when he defeated Aeschylus, and he never placed lower than second. He is credited with the introduction of the third actor, with fixing the size of the chorus at fifteen members, and with the first use of scene painting.

In comparison with Aeschylus, Sophocles placed increased emphasis on individual characters and reduced the role of the chorus. His personages are complex and psychologically well motivated. The protagonists, noble but not faultless, are usually subjected to a terrible crisis that leads to suffering and self-understanding, including the perception of a higher than human law behind events.

Sophocles is the most skillful of Greek dramatists in mastery of dramatic structure: his *Oedipus the King* is often called the most perfect of Greek tragedies (though it won only the second prize when it was first performed). In his plays, exposition is carefully motivated; scenes are built through suspense to a climax; the action is clear and logical throughout. His poetry has been universally admired for its beauty and clarity of expression. There are no elaborate visual effects; the impact derives almost entirely from the force of the dramatic action itself.

Euripides (c. 480–406) wrote about ninety plays, of which eighteen have survived: *Alcestis* (438), *Medea* (431), *Hippolytus* (428), *The Children of Heracles, Andromache, Hecuba, Heracles, The Suppliants, Ion* (dates unknown, but probably between 417 and 415), *The Trojan Women* (415), *Electra, Iphigenia in Tauris* (dates unknown, but probably between 417 and 408), *Helen* (412), *The Phoenician Women* (c. 409), *Orestes* (408), *The Bacchae, Iphigenia in Aulis* (produced after Euripides' death), and *Cyclops,* a satyr play (date unknown). The relatively large number of extant plays by Euripides is explained by his enormous popularity in later periods, although he was not highly appreciated during his lifetime, winning only four contests.

There are at least two reasons for the adverse judgment of Euripides by his contemporaries. First, he often introduced subjects thought unsuited to the stage and questioned traditional values. His use of Phaedra's love for her stepson, Medea's murder of her children, and Pasiphae's passion for a bull were denounced for their abnormality, and his realistic exploration of psychological motivations was sometimes thought too undignified for tragedy. Euripides' characters often questioned the gods' sense of justice, since they seemed sources of misery as often as of happiness. At times Euripides suggested that chance rules the world, and that human beings are more concerned with moral values than are the gods—at least as depicted in myths. Second, his dramatic method was not always clear. Because his basic themes are not always readily grasped, the significance of the dramatic action is sometimes obscure. His techniques, growing out of this thematic concern, often seem inadequate when compared with those of Sophocles. For example, many of his plays begin with a monologue-prologue baldly summarizing past events; the episodes are not always causally related and some may even appear superfluous; speeches often resemble forensic addresses; choral passages are at times only tenuously related to the dramatic action; and gods are frequently used to resolve conflicts and to foretell the future. Thus, Euripides was thought dangerous because of his ideas and artistically inferior because of his dramatic techniques. But, if Euripides' techniques call attention to themselves, they are counterbalanced by realistic strokes in characterization, dialogue, and costuming.

Euripides began many dramatic practices that were developed more fully in the fourth century. He often turned to minor myths for his subjects or severely altered the major ones. Such works as *Ion, Helen,* and *Iphigenia in Tauris,* which pass over into tragicomedy and melodrama, are often cited as signs that the late fifth-century Greek tragedy was already abandoning profundity for intrigue and startling reversals. As Euripides' popularity rose in succeeding centuries, it was the sentimental and melodramatic aspects of his work that were most often imitated.

THE SATYR PLAY

The tragic dramatist of the fifth century also had to master one kind of comic writing since he was required to supply a satyr play each time he competed at the City Dionysia (though exceptions were apparently made, as Euripides is said to have substituted *Alcestis* for a satyr play in 438). As with tragedy, little is known of the origin of the satyr play. Some historians have argued that it was the first form of drama and that gradually both tragedy and comedy emerged from it. But most of the evidence credits Pratinas with having invented this form sometime before 501 B.C.E.

Out of the hundreds of satyr plays written, the only complete example to survive is Euripides' *Cyclops.* It is based on an episode from the *Odyssey* in which Odysseus and his crew are captured by and escape from the Cyclops. In addition, a large part of Sophocles' *The Trackers* is extant. It tells of Apollo's attempt to find a herd of cattle stolen by Hermes, the god of thieves. Because of the limited evidence available to us, it is difficult to generalize about the form, although we may speculate about its typical features.

The satyr play takes its name from the chorus, which was made up of the half-beast, half-human companions of Dionysus. The leader of the chorus was Silenus, the father of the satyrs. Sometimes the story of a satyr play connected it in theme or subject with the tragedies it accompanied, but more often it was entirely independent. Essentially a burlesque treatment of mythology (often ridiculing gods or heroes and their adventures), the boisterous action occurred in a rural setting and included vigorous dancing, as well as indecent language and gestures. In structure, the plays resembled tragedy, since the action was divided into a series of episodes separated by choral odes. Language and meter deviated from those typical of tragedy by tending toward the everyday and colloquial. Serving as afterpieces to the tragedies, the

FIG. 2.3
The so-called Pronomos vase from the late fifth century B.C.E. showing actors of a satyr play. Note the masks and various kinds of garments. From Baumeister, *Denkmaler des Klassischen Altertums* (1888).

satyr plays provided a kind of comic relief from the serious plays that had gone before.

GREEK COMEDY IN THE FIFTH CENTURY

Comedy (*komoidia*) was the last of the major dramatic forms to receive official recognition in Athens, not being accepted into the City Dionysia until 487–486 B.C.E. Its history prior to that time is largely conjectural.

Aristotle says that comedy grew out of the improvisations of the leaders of phallic songs but, because there were many phallic rites, it is unclear which he had in mind. Some of the predramatic ceremonies were performed by a dancing chorus who at times masqueraded as animals, rode on animals, or carried an animal as a representative; there were also choruses of fat men, satyrs, and men on stilts. The rites often included a procession with a chorus who sang and danced as they carried large phallic symbols (representations of male sexual organs) aloft on poles. These ceremonies provided opportunity for considerable byplay and mockery between participants and spectators. All of these elements have their parallels in early comic drama.

None of the phallic rites was dramatic, however, and the process by which they achieved comic form is uncertain. As with tragedy, the Dorians claimed to have invented comedy; Aristotle associates the decisive step with Epicharmus, who lived at Syracuse, a Dorian colony on the island of Sicily. Little is known about Epicharmus except that he was certainly writing plays between 485 and 467 B.C.E. The extant fragments of his works show these characteristics: some scenes have as many as three speakers, but there is no evidence of a chorus; elaborate word play, parody, "patter" speeches, and farcical situations abound. The relationship of these plays to the comedies performed in Athens is unclear, however, since comedy had been recognized at the City Dionysia before the first known work of Epicharmus was written. A direct influence might have been exerted, nevertheless, since Epicharmus may have been writing as early as 500 B.C.E., and the first Athenian comedies, the nature of which is unknown, may have been patterned after those of Epicharmus.

Another possible source of Dorian influence on Athenian comedy is the mime, which supposedly first appeared in Megara (a city some twenty-five miles from Athens) shortly after 581 B.C.E. No mimes from this early period survive, but later ones are short satirical treatments of everyday domestic situations or are burlesqued versions of the myths with titles

FIG. 2.4

Statuette representing an Old Comedy character. From Robert, *Die Masken der Neueren Attischen Komoedie* (1911).

such as *The Women Visitors to Isthmia* and *Dionysus and Ariadne*. It is possible that the Athenians borrowed mimic scenes and combined them with their own phallic choruses. Some of the lively dances in Athenian comedy—such as the *kordax* and *mothon*— also were Dorian in origin.

Regardless of its origin and early history, comedy was sufficiently developed by 487 to be accorded a place at the City Dionysia. (It had probably been performed earlier without official sanction or financial aid.) The names of a few early comic dramatists have been recorded: Chionides, who supposedly won the prize at the first contest; Magnes, who won eleven victories with such plays as *Birds, Fig-flies,* and *Frogs;* Ecphantides, who is said to have written a more refined comedy than that of his predecessors; Cratinus (*fl.* 450–422), credited with twenty-one plays and thought to have been the first truly outstanding comic writer; Crates (*fl.* 449–425), who dropped personal satire, which had previously been typical of comedy, in favor of more general subjects; and Eupolis (*fl.* 429–411), Aristophanes' chief rival, noted for his witty satire and inventiveness.

All of the extant comedies of the fifth century, however, are by a single author, Aristophanes (c. 448– c. 380). He is thought to have written about forty plays, of which eleven survive: *Acharnians* (425), *Knights* (424), *Clouds* (423), *Wasps* (422), *Peace* (421), *Birds* (414), *Lysistrata* (411), *Women at the Thesmophoria* (411), *Frogs* (405), *Assembly Women* (392/391), and *Plutus* (388). Although it is usual to treat Aristophanes' first nine compositions as typical of Old Comedy (as the plays of this period are called), it is unclear how his works compare with those of his predecessors and contemporaries. Nevertheless, generalizations about Old Comedy are necessarily based primarily on Aristophanes' practice.

Probably the most noteworthy characteristic of Aristophanic comedy is its commentary on contemporary society, politics, theatre, and above all the Peloponnesian War. The plays are organized around a ruling theme, embodied in a rather farfetched "happy idea" (such as a private peace with a warring power, or a sex strike to bring an end to war). Although the events of most Old Comedies could not occur in everyday life, parallels with real events are abundantly clear, the fantastic exaggerations serving to point up the absurdity of their real-life counterparts. In addition to fantasy, farcical situations are typical, and considerable emphasis is placed on the pleasures of eating, drinking, sex, wealth, and leisure. Coupled with the comic elements are some of the most beautiful lyrics and some of the most obscene passages in Greek literature.

Although there are many variants, the basic structural pattern of Aristophanic comedy is simple. A prologue establishes the mood and sets forth the "happy idea"; the chorus enters, and there follows a debate (or *agon*) over the merits of the idea and a decision is reached to try the scheme. A *parabasis* (or choral ode in which the audience is addressed directly) divides the play into two parts. In the *parabasis,* some social or political problem is often discussed and a line of action advocated. At times, however, the *parabasis* is used to praise the author of the play, to plead for the audience's favor, or for similar purposes. The second part of the play shows, in a series of loosely connected scenes, the results of adopting the happy idea. The final scene (or *komos*) usually concludes with the reconciliation of all the characters and their exit to a feast or revels. These features of comic structure are sometimes rearranged but are almost always present.

After 404, when Athens was defeated in the Peloponnesian War, political and social satire gradually disappeared from comedy and new types evolved. The quality of tragedy also declined after this time. Thus the world's first great age of dramatic writing was largely over by 400 B.C.E.

THE DRAMATIC FESTIVALS OF THE FIFTH CENTURY

Although in Athens four annual festivals (Rural Dionysia, Lenaia, Anthesteria, and City Dionysia) were held in honor of Dionysus, plays were presented only at one—the City Dionysia—prior to 442, almost a century after the first dramatic contests were introduced. At the Anthesteria, entire plays were seldom produced. But by the late fifth century drama was important at the Lenaia and the Rural Dionysia, although the City Dionysia continued to command the greatest prestige. In Athens, drama was not part of the many festivals held in honor of other gods, although performative elements were prominent in almost all festivals.

The City Dionysia, which commemorated the coming of Dionysus to Athens, was held each year at the end of March or early April and extended over several days. Both a civic and religious festival, it was open to the whole Greek world and during the fifth century served as a showcase for Athenian wealth and culture. It was under the general supervision of the *archon eponymos,* the principal civil magistrate of Athens.

FIG. 2.5
Old woman holding a child. Terracotta statuette of an actor from Old or Middle Comedy. Courtesy Metropolitan Museum of Art, Rogers Fund, 1913.

A few days before the festival began, each dramatist appeared with his actors at a *proagon* and announced the subject of his plays. After another preliminary event (the reenactment of Dionysus' coming to Athens), there was a procession, which included public officials, the *choregoi* (sponsors of the plays), and many others, who carried gifts or escorted sacrificial animals for the god. This procession wound through much of Athens, stopped for dances and sacrifices at various altars, and ended with the presentation of offerings and the sacrifice of a bull at the altar of Dionysus Eleuthereus. The sacrificial animals, except for portions reserved for the god, were consumed at a public feast.

Before the plays were performed, the blood of young pigs was sprinkled around the theatre to purify it. During the fifth century, five days were devoted to performances. Precisely what was presented on each day is a matter of some disagreement. On each of three days, one dramatist presented three tragedies and one satyr play. The other two days probably were devoted primarily to dithyrambic contests, one day to ten choruses of adult males, the other to ten choruses of boys (each of Attica's ten tribes supplying one chorus of each type). After 487, each of five comic writers presented a single play (except during the Peloponnesian War, when the number was reduced to three). One comedy may have been presented on each of the five days, but the precise arrangement is uncertain. Until 449, prizes were offered only for plays; after that time prizes were also given to actors. Two days after the festival ended, an assembly was convened to consider the conduct of the officials in charge of it and to receive complaints about misconduct by citizens during the festival.

The Lenaia was celebrated near the end of January under the supervision of the *archon basileus,* the principal religious official of Athens. It has been suggested that originally the Lenaia was identical with the Rural Dionysia, and that its date and nature were changed only after Athens lost its rural character. No deme (or subdivision) of Attica celebrated both the Lenaia and Rural Dionysia, and the Lenaia was observed only in the city. As the seas were considered unsafe in January, the Lenaia was primarily a local festival. Consequently, more freedom of expression was permitted, and the Lenaia came to be associated especially with comedy, in which Athenian officials and political affairs were often severely ridiculed.

Dramatic activities were not officially recognized at the Lenaia until about 442, although plays may have been presented there on an informal basis before that date. By the late fifth century the plays were being performed in the Theatre of Dionysus (Athens' major theatrical structure) but when they were first given there is unclear. Originally the Lenaia may have been held elsewhere, for Dionysus was worshipped under a number of guises, and each cult had its own sacred area, just as Christian sects do today. The City Dionysia was presented in honor of Dionysus Eleuthereus and the Theatre of Dionysus was erected within his sacred precinct, whereas the Lenaia was held in honor of Dionysus Lenaios, whose sanctuary's location is now unknown. Today, many scholars assume that originally there was a performance area in the Agora (the principal marketplace) and that

FIG. 2.6
The so-called Andromeda vase, dating from the late fifth century B.C.E. The figure at center and those in the upper corners are often cited as examples of tragic costuming, although there is little evidence to connect this vase with theatrical performance. Note also that some figures are nude. From Engelmann, *Archaeologische Studien zu den Tragikern* (1900).

the Lenaia plays were at first performed there. Some historians have suggested that the plays continued to be presented in the Agora until they were given official sanction in 442 and at that time they were transferred to the Theatre of Dionysus.

Contests at the Lenaia were at first only for comic dramatists and actors, but in 432 other competitions were added for tragic playwrights and actors. As at the City Dionysia, five comic writers competed each year (except during the Peloponnesian War), but only two tragic dramatists (who offered two plays each) participated. Satyr plays and dithyrambs were never presented.

The Rural Dionysia was celebrated in December, although not on the same day in all demes. It was under the supervision of the *demarchos* (principal magistrate) of each deme. The major feature of the festival was a procession in which a giant phallus was carried aloft on a pole, apparently with the purpose of reviving fertility at a time when the sun was at its weakest. It is unclear when dramatic performances became a part of this festival. It is unlikely that all of the more than 100 Attic demes included plays in their celebrations, but drama may have appeared in some of them before it was recognized at the Lenaia. It is certain that plays were being performed in a number of demes before the end of the fifth century, and the custom seems to have been widely adopted during the fourth century. Plato (*c.* 427–347 B.C.E.) wrote that in his time the Rural Dionysia was held on different days in different demes so that people might travel from one to the other to see plays presented by troupes of traveling actors. The demes in which dramatic production was most important were Piraeus (where Euripides is said to have presented at least one play), Icaria, Salamis, Trachones, and Eleusis. Many of the rural demes built their own permanent theatres.

Most of our information about the Rural Dionysia dates from the fourth century or later. By that time actors were reviving works already produced elsewhere, but the source of plays presented in the fifth century is unknown. The Rural Dionysia may have served as an outlet for plays not accepted for the City Dionysia or Lenaia, or as a place where works already seen in the city were revived. While the Rural Dionysia probably had little effect on the development of Greek drama, its activities suggest how intense the interest in drama was and show that the theatre was not confined to Athens.

PLAY SELECTION AND FINANCING

Each author wishing to have his plays produced at a festival had to apply to the *archon* for a chorus. It is not known how this official chose the plays to be presented, but it has been suggested that each dramatist recited parts of his work before a committee. The choices of the next year's plays were made approximately one month after the end of each festival. Although this would have left about eleven months until performance, it is unknown how much of this time was actually used for rehearsals.

After about 501, a large share of the expense of play production was borne by the *choregoi* (singular is *choregos*), chosen by the *archon* from wealthy citizens who performed this duty in rotation as a part of their civic and religious responsibilities. The *choregos* (one was appointed for each author and for each dithyrambic chorus) underwrote the training and costuming of the chorus and probably paid the musicians. In addition, he may have supplied properties and supernumerary actors and may have met other demands (such as a second chorus required by some plays) not provided by the state. The responsibility of the state seems to have been restricted to the theatre building, prizes (for authors, *choregoi,* and actors), and payments to actors and, possibly, to dramatists. Because he bore the major financial burden, a *choregos* could do much to help or hinder the playwright. Most *choregoi* seem to have been generous, perhaps because prizes for plays were awarded to them and the author jointly.

Nearly all tragic dramatists directed their own works, but it was not unusual for comic playwrights to turn this task over to someone else. In Aeschylus' time, the author acted in his plays, trained the chorus, composed the music and dances, and supervised every aspect of production. Thus the primary source of unity was the playwright-director, whose task was as complex as that of any director today. The playwright-director's key role is indicated by the term applied to him, *didaskalos* (teacher), for he was considered to be the instructor of both the performers (during the process of play production) and the audience (through the finished product).

ACTORS AND ACTING

Originally the actor and the dramatist were one. Separation of the two functions did not begin until early in the fifth century when Aeschylus introduced a second actor. Playwrights continued to act in their own plays, however, until the time of Sophocles, who abandoned this practice about 468 and introduced a third actor. It seems likely that when the contest for tragic actors was inaugurated (around 449) the separation of actor from playwright was complete. Nevertheless, in the fifth century actors were at best semiprofessionals, for there was as yet no demand for full-time performers and they must have supplemented their income through other activities.

After about 468, the number of actors available to each tragic playwright was fixed at three, who had to perform all the roles in all three plays plus the satyr play, so each had to impersonate a number of characters. The "three-actor rule" was softened somewhat by allowing supernumeraries to assume nonspeaking roles or to speak a very limited number of lines. Still, Sophocles' *Oedipus at Colonus* could have been performed by three actors only if the same character was played by different actors in successive scenes. The difficulties presented by this three-actor convention (at least by modern standards) have led many scholars to question whether such a rule ever existed. Nevertheless, there seems to be sufficient evidence to verify that it was observed.

In comedy most scenes could have been acted by three actors, but several require four and at least one would have required five. Some historians have argued that all extant plays could have been acted by three actors if a single role was sometimes divided among more than one actor. Since restrictions were probably established in order to make the contest fair, the rules at the Lenaia may have differed from those at the City Dionysia, since other conditions differed at the two festivals.

Before about 449 (that is, up until the inauguration of contests for actors), each playwright probably selected his own cast, but after that time the leading actors were assigned by lot to the competing dramatists. This procedure was probably adopted to ensure that no writer had an unfair advantage over his rivals. The other two actors allotted to each dramatist were probably selected jointly by the playwright and his leading actor. Although all of the actors were paid by the state, only the leading actor could compete for the prize, which could be awarded for a performance in a non-prize-winning play.

The Greeks seem to have placed considerable emphasis on the voice, for they judged actors above all by beauty of vocal tone and ability to adapt manner of speaking to mood and character. Nevertheless, the delivery was probably more declamatory than realistic, for actors did not attempt to reproduce the attributes of age or sex so much as to project the appropriate emotional tone. Furthermore, the plays demanded three kinds of delivery: speech, recitative, and song. As the primary means of expression, the voice was trained and exercised by the actor much as it might be by an opera singer today. While the best actors attained high standards of vocal excellence, others apparently ranted and roared.

Facial expression was of no importance to Greek actors, since they were always masked. In tragedy, gesture and movement appear to have been simplified and broadened; in comedy, everyday actions—running the gamut from the commonplace to the bizarre—were exaggerated in the direction of the farcical and ludicrous. It is sometimes suggested that movement tended toward a set of conventionalized, stylized, or symbolic gestures like those used in mimetic dance.

It is now impossible to determine precisely the style of acting seen in fifth-century Greece, but several conventions, all leading away from realism, can be listed: the same actor usually had to play more than one role in a play; men played all roles, including those of women; and song, recitative, choral passages, dance, and masks were common features. Still, the exaggeration which characterized tragic acting in late Greece was probably not typical of the fifth century. Both tragic and comic acting undoubtedly departed from the everyday—tragedy in the direction of idealization, comedy in the direction of burlesque—but they remained sufficiently recognizable to link the dramatic events to the spectator's own world.

Several additional elements influenced the overall effect: the chorus, music and dance, costumes and masks, and theatre architecture. An examination of these elements should help to clarify the total impression created by productions in the fifth century.

THE CHORUS

In the early tragedies the chorus was dominant, since there was only one actor, who left the stage often to change roles. In Aeschylus' plays, although a second actor was available, the chorus was still given as many as one-half of the lines. Furthermore, in *The Suppliants* the chorus serves as protagonist, while in *The Eumenides* it is the antagonist. After Aeschylus' time the role of the chorus diminished progressively until in the plays of Euripides it is often only tenuously related to the dramatic action.

Historians disagree about the size of the tragic chorus. One view holds that the number was originally fifty, but that it was reduced to twelve during the career of Aeschylus and was then raised to fifteen by Sophocles. There is no clear evidence to support any of these figures. The arguments for a fifty-member chorus are deduced primarily from two sources. First, there is Aristotle's statement that tragedy developed out of improvisations by leaders of dithyrambic choruses. With this can be grouped the assertions of later classical writers who fix the size of the early tragic chorus at fifty largely because that was the size of the dithyrambic chorus. Although this early testimony must be respected, it cannot be verified, for we do not know how large the dithyrambic chorus was before its size was fixed at fifty, probably around 508 B.C.E., and thus after tragedy presumably was well established. The second major source of evidence for a fifty-member chorus is Aeschylus' *The Suppliants,* in which the chorus is composed of the daughters of Danaus, who in mythology numbered fifty. Aeschylus does not state how many daughters there are in his play. Furthermore, evidence discovered in the 1950s has redated this play (formerly thought to have been written *c.* 490) as having been produced after Sophocles began to compete (that is, after 468) and thus within the period when some scholars maintain that the chorus numbered only twelve or fifteen. Thus, there is much testimony that the chorus originally numbered fifty, but there is also much skepticism about this testimony.

The evidence to support the idea of a twelve-member chorus is based primarily on a twelve-line choral passage in the *Agamemnon* which, according to some critics, was divided among the individual members of the chorus. That the lines were assigned to individuals, however, is pure conjecture. Those who support the theory of a twelve-member chorus usually argue that at some time during Aeschylus' career the chorus was divided to assign an equal number of the original fifty to each of the four plays an author presented when he competed. The reason given for this change is usually economic—that is, to reduce the expenses of production.

The evidence for a chorus of fifteen is found in the commentaries of authors writing several centuries after Sophocles' lifetime. They cite no authority for their statements. Nevertheless, it has long been accepted that the probable size of the chorus was fifteen in all the extant plays of Sophocles and Euripides. In later times, the chorus diminished in size, sometimes having no more than three members.

Some Greek tragedies require a second chorus, essentially mute though sometimes provided with a few lines. Aeschylus' *The Suppliants* includes a chorus of attendants on the daughters of Danaus, while Euripides' *Hippolytus* has two quite distinct choruses.

As a rule, the tragic chorus entered with a stately march, but occasionally members came in singly or in small groups from various directions. The basic choral formation is thought to have been rectangular, composed of three five-member files. Most choral passages were sung and danced in unison, but at times the chorus was divided into two groups who performed in turn. Sometimes the chorus exchanged spoken dialogue with a character, and, in rare instances, individual members may have spoken single lines. As for acting, it is assumed that all members responded appropriately to the situations, but it is unknown how they were grouped or placed during episodes or how their formations changed during choral odes.

The chorus of Old Comedy was composed of twenty-four members. Sometimes it was divided into two semi-choruses, as in *Lysistrata* where the two are of opposite sexes. Comedy seems to have enjoyed much more freedom than tragedy, and consequently the entrances, dances, and uses of the chorus were more varied. The texts of the plays suggest that the chorus was extremely active throughout the performance of the play.

In each dramatic form, the chorus normally made its entrance after the prologue and remained until the end of the play. In a few instances, however, it was present at the opening and occasionally it left and returned during the action.

The chorus serves several functions in Greek drama. First, it is a character in the play; it gives advice, expresses opinions, asks questions, and sometimes takes an active part in the action. Second, it often establishes the ethical or social framework of the events and sets up a standard against which the action may be judged. Third, it frequently serves as an ideal spectator, reacting to the events and characters as the dramatist might hope the audience would. Fourth, the chorus helps to set the overall mood of the play and of individual scenes and to heighten dramatic effects. Fifth, it adds movement, spectacle, song and dance, and thus contributes much to theatrical effectiveness. Sixth, the choral passages serve an important rhythmical function, creating intervals or retardations during which the audience may reflect upon what has happened and what is to come.

In the fifth century, the members of the chorus were amateurs. Nevertheless, they probably were not inexperienced, since choral dancing was so common in Greece and since there were at least one thousand participants each year in the dithyrambic contests at the City Dionysia. Some historians now maintain that the dances were based on military formations, with which all adult male citizens would have been familiar. Because choruses were usually awarded to playwrights approximately eleven months prior to performance, training was probably spread over a long period. In the beginning, the playwright choreographed and trained the chorus, but these tasks were later taken over by professionals. Most of the information that has survived about choral training concerns dithyrambs, but historians usually assume that the same practices were used with drama. This information suggests that training, like that of athletes, was long and arduous, involving diet, exercise, and disciplined practice under the watchful supervision of several persons. It also indicates that choruses were often pampered and given special treatment. Training and outfitting the chorus were the most important and expensive parts of the *choregos'* duties. For tragedy, each chorus assigned to a playwright had to learn all the dances and songs for all three tragedies and the satyr play and they required a different set of costumes for each. In the *Oresteia,* they performed as old men in the first play, young slave women in the second, furies and townswomen in the third, and satyrs in the satyr play. They were judged on the artistry and skill with which they performed the wide variety of dances and music associated with these very different roles.

MUSIC AND DANCE

Music was an integral part of Greek drama. It accompanied the passages of recitative and was an inseparable part of the choral odes. Only rarely was it used apart from words, and then only for special effects. In the beginning, the musical accompaniment was probably subordinated to ensure that the words would be understood. By the time of Euripides, however, the accompaniment had become more elaborate, and lengthy trills prolonged some syllables. As a result, some passages were probably unintelligible. Critics have suggested that this may be one reason for the decline in importance of choral odes.

The musical accompaniment for drama was played on a "flute" (*aulos*) with tonal qualities resembling those of a modern oboe or clarinet. Other instruments, including the lyre, the trumpet, and various forms of percussion, were used occasionally for special effects. The flute player preceded the chorus into the orchestra, but his placement thereafter is uncertain. Some historians maintain that he wore a wooden shoe with which he marked the beat. Occasionally an actor used the lyre to accompany his own recitative or song.

It is unclear who composed the music. At first the playwright may have done so, but later this was probably the responsibility of the flute player. Flute players were considered so important to the success of a production that they were assigned to the *choregoi* by lot to insure fairness, a practice later adopted for assigning the lead actor to a playwright.

So little Greek music has survived that no comprehensive reconstruction of it is possible. The Greeks believed that music had ethical qualities. This suggests that they associated particular kinds of music with particular emotions or ideas. They recognized a large number of *modes,* which differed from each other in tonality and in sequence of intervals. The tones of the various modes were not always equal in value, however, some of the intervals being as small as quarter-tones. In quality, Greek music probably resembled Middle Eastern more than modern Western music. The principal modes were the Dorian, Ionian, Phrygian, Aeolian, and Lydian, but there were many variations on these, such as Hypodorian or Myxolydian. Each had qualities which associated it with a particular range of feeling. (The use of music in Greek theatre seems analogous to that in twentieth-century film.) Some modes were thought suitable to tragedy, others to comedy, and some unsuited to any form of drama.

Like music, dance was considered to have ethical qualities. The Greeks defined dance as any expressive rhythmical movement; thus dance did not necessarily mean patterns created by footwork, since gestures or pantomime, if rhythmical, might qualify as dance. Most Greek dance was mimetic (expressive of a particular kind of character or situation). In theatrical performances, dance seems to have been closely related to the words through a set of moment-by-moment symbolic gestures (or *cheironomia*).

By the fourth century the dances of tragedy had come to be called *emmeleia* (a term that signifies harmony, grace, and dignity). This classification obviously was broad, for the choral passages range from religious processions to wedding dances, ecstatic frenzies, and many other types.

The dances of comedy were less dignified than those of tragedy. Many were intentionally ridiculous. Often at the end of plays the chorus exited dancing wildly. Comic choral dances were derived from many sources: animal movements, religious ceremonies, victory celebrations, and various other activities and rites. The individual actors performed dances that involved kicking the buttocks, slapping the chest or thighs, leaping, performing high kicks, spinning like a top, or beating other actors. The most common term for the comic dances is *kordax*.

The basic dance of the satyr play was the *sikinnis,* which probably involved vigorous leaping, horseplay, and lewd pantomime. Often it burlesqued the tragic dances.

COSTUMES AND MASKS

The overall visual style of a Greek theatrical production was greatly influenced by costumes and masks. Several historians have argued that the standard costume for all tragic actors was a sleeved, highly decorated tunic, usually full-length, although sometimes shorter. This garment is said either to have been

FIG. 2.7

Fragment of a vase from about 470 B.C.E. showing a mask, presumably an actor's. This is often cited as the oldest extant visual evidence concerning theatrical masks. Note the garment on the right (also supposedly theatrical) and the lack of foot covering. Courtesy the American School of Classical Studies at Athens.

cles' *Oedipus at Colonus* and *Philoctetes* refer to their torn clothing. Although some lines may merely be included to justify departures from standard practice, they suggest that costume was not rigidly prescribed. It has also been suggested that costumes may at first have been highly formal and that they became more realistic toward the end of the fifth century or that they reflect a stylistic conflict.

The plays also give some information about the dress of the chorus. In Aeschylus' *The Suppliants* the chorus is said to be wearing non-Greek garments, while in Sophocles' *Philoctetes* the opposite point is made. An oft-repeated (and very late) account of the first performance of Aeschylus' *Eumenides* states that the chorus of Furies was so frightening in appearance that several women in the audience miscarried. Other textual evidence suggests a wide variety of costumes for the chorus. As a result, historians, even those who argue for a standardized costume for actors, have

derived from the robes of the Dionysian priests (thus indicating the actor's sacred and ceremonial function) or to have been invented by Aeschylus early in the fifth century. That the actor wore a standardized garment, however, is far from certain. Its presumed appearance is derived almost entirely from figures depicted on vase paintings. But this evidence is open to doubt for several reasons: (1) most of the vases are from a period later than the fifth century; (2) the relation of most paintings to actual theatrical practice is unclear; (3) most important, other vase paintings, usually ignored by those who argue for a standardized garment, show figures in quite different costumes, and even those vases showing the presumed standard often depict deviations from it, including complete nudity. Other evidence cited for a conventionalized garment is the statement of several ancient commentators (writing long after the fifth century) that robes designed by Aeschylus for his actors were later adopted by the priests at Eleusis. Aristophanes' *Frogs*, on the other hand, merely credits Aeschylus with clothing tragic actors in garments more dignified than those worn by ordinary persons. Thus, though the sleeved, decorated tunic apparently was used, there are many reasons for questioning whether it was standardized and worn by all actors.

The plays surviving from this period contain few references to costume. Some indicate that the characters are in mourning, for which black was the usual color in Greek daily life. In Euripides' *Alcestis,* Death is said to be clothed in a black and "terrifying" garment. That characters in several of Euripides' plays wore ragged costumes seems to be borne out by Aristophanes' *Acharnians.* The protagonists of Sopho-

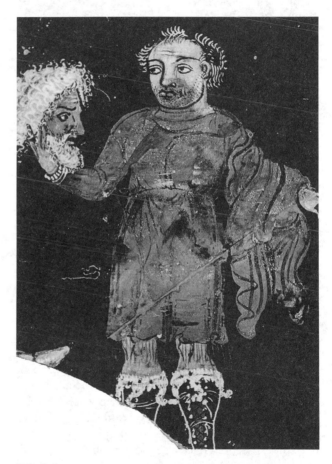

FIG. 2.8

Fragment of a vase from Tarentum showing a tragic actor holding a mask. Note the short fringed tunic and the tasseled boots. This fragment probably dates from the fourth century B.C.E. Courtesy Martin von Wagner Museum of the University of Würzburg.

FIG. 2.9

Greek Actor of South Italy. *c.* 360–350 B.C.E. The actor stands next to Dionysus (not shown) and the costume suggests an actor in tragedy. The mask, however, looks comic. © Virginia Museum of Fine Arts, Richmond. The Adolph D. and Wilkins C. Williams Fund.

spear, the suppliant by his branch, the herald by his wreath, and so on.

Footwear in tragedy varied. The usual foot covering seems to have been a soft shoe or boot, often reaching to the calf. In later times this was called a *kothornos* and was given a thick sole, but neither the name nor the elevation seems to have been used in the fifth century. In vase paintings, figures are shown in a wide variety of footwear, or even as barefoot.

Fortunately, there is more agreement among scholars about comic costuming, although the available evidence is no more reliable than that for tragedy. Most agree that costumes were adapted from those worn in everyday Greek life. For theatrical purposes, the *chiton* was frequently made too short and too tight so as to emphasize comic nudity. It was worn over flesh-colored tights, which were often padded. Male characters, but not the chorus, wore the *phallus.*

This costume, shown in much of the extant pictorial evidence, was probably that of the comic slaves and ridiculous old men. But it was not likely to have

FIG. 2.10

Greek tragic actor of the mid fourth century. Photo by F. J.Hildy ©. Used by permission of the Aphrodisias, Turkey, Excavations, New York University.

suggested that the dress of the chorus was determined by relatively realistic criteria (such as sex, age, nationality, and social status). Did, then, one principle govern the costume of the chorus and a quite different one that of the actors? Although this seems unlikely, it is not impossible, since the state or the performers may have supplied the actors' costumes, while the *choregoi* supplied those for the choruses. A uniform principle would seem more logical, nevertheless, and it is possible that such characters as foreigners, gods, and other supernatural beings wore the sleeved, decorated tunic, for which there was no precedent in native Greek dress, while the more familiar personages wore some variation on Greek garments.

In addition to the tunic (or *chiton*), both actors and chorus might wear a short cloak (*chlamys*) or a long one (*himation*). The identity of both actors and chorus might be established in part by symbolic properties: the king by his scepter, the warrior by his

FIG. 2.11
Greek comic actors of Southern Italy c. 380 B.C.E., just shortly after Aristophanes wrote the last of his Middle Comedies. Actor on left is in padded "nude" costume with comic phallus attached. Note raised stage. © Virginia Museum of Fine Arts, Richmond. The Adolph D. and Wilkins C. Williams Fund.

been the universal costume, for the plays also include many young men who are ridiculed only slightly. Probably the comically grotesque costume was considerably modified toward typical daily dress for these characters. Similarly, there is a wide range of female characters, whose sexual attributes were also emphasized through costume. Since some comedies parodied scenes from well-known tragedies, it may be that tragic costume was sometimes adapted and ridiculed.

Relatively little attention has been paid by historians to the costuming of satyr plays. The satyrs are thought to have worn goatskin loincloths, to which were attached the phallus in front and a horse-like tail in the rear; other parts of the body appeared to be nude, but in the theatre this probably meant some kind of flesh-colored garment. (See Fig. 2.3.) Silenus, the leader of the chorus, is usually depicted as wearing shaggy or fleecy tights under an animal-skin cloak. Since the characters in satyr plays are usually mythological personages, the costumes probably were somewhat ridiculous variations on tragic costumes.

All performers during the fifth century, with the possible exception of flute players, wore masks. According to ancient commentators, Thespis experimented with several types of disguise for the face—such as smearing it with wine dregs and dangling leaves in front of it—before adopting the mask. Tradition has it that Phrynichus was the first to introduce female masks and that Aeschylus was the first to use painted masks. No masks used by actors have survived, since they were made of perishable linen, cork, or lightweight wood. Masks covered the entire head and thus included the appropriate hairstyle, beard, ornaments, and other features. Although in later periods the masks seem to have been considerably larger than the face and to have had exaggerated features, in the fifth century neither the size nor the expression seems to have been unduly enlarged.

It is impossible to determine whether masks for tragedy were restricted to a few conventionalized types during the fifth century. Some historians have argued that they were, but others have suggested that experimentation was encouraged. The masks for the characters of a single play must have been sufficiently differentiated to make the frequent change of roles readily apparent. On the other hand, chorus members in tragedy were always identical in appearance.

The masks for comedy were extremely varied. The choruses often represented birds, animals, or insects, all of which were identified by appropriate, though not necessarily realistic, masks. The masks of human characters often exaggerated those attributes, such as baldness or ugliness, considered to be ridiculous. Although all of the members of some choruses wore identical masks, others were individualized (as in *The Birds*). When actors portrayed well-known Athenians, such as Socrates in *The Clouds,* "portrait masks" were used.

Members of the satyr chorus are usually depicted as snub-nosed, with dark, unkempt hair and beards, and pointed, horse-like ears. Sometimes they are shown as partially bald and at others they are given horns. Silenus is portrayed as having gray hair and beard. The actors probably wore masks similar to those used in tragedy.

The great importance of costumes and masks in the Greek theatre means that the costumer and mask maker were crucial. Nevertheless, virtually nothing is known about them or their working methods.

THEATRE ARCHITECTURE

In Greece, places of performance were constructed on public land, either in the parks associated with major temples or in the central marketplaces (the *agora*). The oldest known "theatral area" is at the Minoan palaces at Phaistos, which dates to about 2000 B.C.E. It has stone risers for a standing audience of about 500 arranged on two sides of a rectangular performance area approximately forty by thirty-five feet

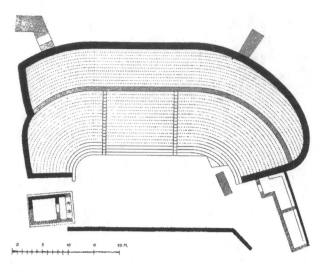

FIG. 2.12

Plan of the theatre at Thorikos, at least part of which dates from the sixth century B.C.E. Note the modified rectangular shape. From Dörpfeld, *Griechische Theater* (1896).

in size. The Minoan theatres are assumed to have been used for dances, ceremonies, and bull-leaping but no one really knows. The last of these theatres, the one at Knossos, would have disappeared by 1300 B.C.E., nearly 600 years before the emergence of theatres on mainland Greece. Early theatrical performance spaces on the Greek mainland, however, were also rectangular. The theatres at Thorikos (the oldest theatre in Greece), Trachones, and Isthmia in Attica and the first theatre at Syracuse in Sicily, among others, still show this rectilinear origin. It is now thought possible that the circular orchestra traditionally associated with Greek theatres was not developed until the mid fourth century.

Although there were many theatres in Greece, major interest centers on the Theatre of Dionysus in Athens, for the surviving Greek plays were first presented there. The earliest feature of the Theatre of Dionysus (located in the precinct of Dionysus Eleuthereus on the southeast slope of the hill below the Acropolis) was the *orchestra* (or dancing place). Originally it was the only essential feature, since the audience sat or stood on the hillside to watch the choral performances which predated tragedy. Sometime during the sixth century a terrace was formed at the foot of the hill, and on it an *orchestra* was laid out. Since its excavation in 1886, scholars had accepted the view that this orchestra was circular, approximately sixty-six feet in diameter, and remained essentially unchanged until the Christian era. In recent years, however, archeologists have reexamined the ruins of this theatre and many have argued that the original orchestra was rectangular and remained

so until the fourth century (that is, throughout the period during which the extant plays were written and performed). A table or altar (*thymele*) was located in the orchestra, but its location, whether in the center or off to one side, has been debated.

The scene building (or *skene*) is of later origin than the orchestra. Since *skene* means "hut" or "tent," the scene house probably developed out of some temporary structure intended originally as a dressing room but later incorporated into the action by some imaginative playwright. Aeschylus' *Oresteia* (produced in 458 B.C.E.) is the first extant play to require a building as a background. Since virtually all parts of the early scene house have long since vanished, its appearance cannot be determined. Some of the many possible arrangements are shown in the accompanying illustrations (see Fig. 2.14).

Extensive changes were made in the Theatre of Dionysus when Pericles built the Odeion (or music hall) adjoining it, probably in the 440s. Until recently, it was accepted that the old curved retaining wall of the orchestra terrace was replaced with a straight one at this time, but the existence of a previous curved wall is now questioned. Ten grooves were cut on the inner face of this wall (facing the auditorium). The most common interpretation is that these cuts were designed to hold the heavy wooden posts used to support a temporary scene house. In addition, a stone-surfaced area or terrace jutted from the wall toward the orchestra. Although the purpose of this area is unknown, it may have served as a foundation for theatrical machinery or as the base for a low, raised platform or porticoed entry. It was also long accepted that these sketchy physical remnants were all that now remain from the fifth-century structure.

FIG. 2.13

The Theatre of Dionysus as it may have looked in the late sixth century B.C.E. From Fiechter, *Antike Griechische Theaterbauten.* Courtesy Verlag W. Kohlhammer GmbH, Stuttgart and Dr. Charlotte Fiechter.

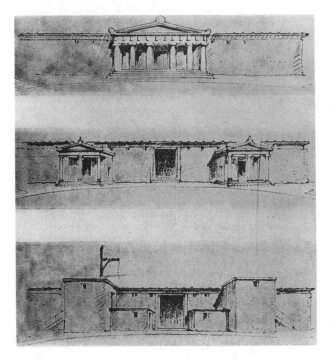

FIG. 2.14

Three reconstructions showing possible appearances of the stage house of the Theatre of Dionysus in the fifth century B.C.E. From Fiechter, *Das Dionysostheater in Athen.* Courtesy Verlag W. Kohlhammr GmbH, Stuttgart and Dr. Charlotte Fiechter.

Although all these features still exist, some archeologists have now concluded that they were not added until the fourth century. If so, there are no identifiable physical remains from the fifth-century theatre.

Historians usually assume that in the fifth century a temporary scene house was erected for each festival—at least from 458 onward. The features of the *skene* required by the extant plays are few: one or more doors (opening onto an acting area) and an upper level (either the roof or a platform on a second level) used primarily for the appearance of gods or to represent high places. A few historians have argued that one door is sufficient to accommodate the needs of all the extant plays; they have also suggested that there may have been one or more windows considerably above ground level, as the action of some comedies seem to demand them. Although some scholars in the past argued that a stone scene building had been built by the late fifth century, most now date the permanent *skene* from the fourth century and thus after the era of great drama was over.

Questions relating to the *skene* are closely bound up with others about scenery. Was the background for all plays the scene house's conventional facade, or was some type of scenery used to suggest locale

more specifically? Although these questions cannot be answered definitively, they can be illuminated.

It is important to distinguish between scenic practices before and after the scene building was introduced, for they probably changed when the *skene* became the background for the action. The challenges posed in the period before a *skene* was clearly available are well illustrated by *Prometheus Bound,* in which a rugged mountainous locale is supposedly engulfed in an earthquake during the final scene. Some commentators have argued that for this play a set piece representing a mountain cliff was erected at the edge of the orchestra terrace and that during the supposed earthquake it was tipped over the embankment. (The scenic requirements of this play are the primary reason that some scholars now think it was written at a later date by an author other than Aeschylus.) Others have countered that the whole performance was highly conventionalized and that the idea of an earthquake was conveyed entirely by the lines. Still others have insisted that a fully developed stage house was already in use and that for this play it was disguised to represent the mountainous terrain. None of these theories can be verified, but they illustrate some possible approaches to staging in the early period.

It is widely assumed that after 458 all plays used the *skene* as a background (an assumption that may be incorrect if the *skene* was a temporary structure). A *skene* could easily meet the demands of most plays since the majority are set before a temple, palace, or some other type of building. But what of those works set before caves (as are *Philoctetes* and numerous satyr plays), in groves of trees (*Oedipus at Colonus*), or in army camps (*Ajax*)? Answers to this question have varied. Some historians have argued that a few stock sets, designed to meet the range of possible locales, were used. Others have argued that a few symbolic properties (such as shields to identify an army camp, or shells and rocks to indicate a seashore, or a single tree to suggest a grove) were merely added to the otherwise undisguised scene house. Still others have suggested that the spoken lines provided the necessary indications of locale and that the facade of the *skene* served as a conventionalized background for all plays.

This controversy is closely allied with another concerning scene painting. Aristotle (writing in the late fourth century) credits Sophocles with introducing the decoration of the *skene,* while Vitruvius (first century B.C.E.) states that it originated in the time of Aeschylus. In seeking to reconcile these two statements, some historians have placed the beginnings of *skene* decoration (sometimes interpreted as scene painting) between 468 and 456, that is, during the years when the careers of Aeschylus and Sophocles overlapped. Vitruvius' description of the first painting on the *skene* suggests that it was an architectural design on a flat surface; this has been interpreted variously to mean that an attempt was made to create the illusion of real architectural details or, conversely, that a previously undecorated surface was now given some schematic but nonillusionistic pattern.

The issue of conventionalization versus illusionism is an important one, for, if illusion was attempted, then a single background could not have met the demands of all plays without changes of some kind. Consequently, those who have argued for a degree of representationalism have also had to suggest means whereby the appearance of the *skene* could have been altered. Two major devices have been proposed: *pinakes* (or painted panels similar to modern flats), and *periaktoi* (or triangular prisms with a different scene painted on each of their three sides). *Pinakes* supposedly could be attached to the scene building and changed as needed. But, though the use of *pinakes* in the fifth century is well documented, the practice of changing them for different plays is not. It is possible that painted panels were used to create the visible exterior of a temporary *skene*. In later periods, a series of *periaktoi* were mounted on pivots and revolved to show the appropriate side, but the use of this device during the fifth century has not been established.

Most Greek tragedies occur in a single locale, but the successive plays offered on the same day were often set in different locations. Thus, if scene changes were attempted, they could have been made between plays in most instances. On the other hand, some tragedies (such as Aeschylus' *Eumenides* and Sophocles' *Ajax*) and numerous comedies change place during the action. How could these changes have been handled? *Pinakes* and *periaktoi* offer a representational solution to this problem, but several nonrepresentational solutions, like those found in many early forms of theatre in Asia, have been suggested as well. In some instances, the actors and chorus may have left the scene and then returned, thus indicating a change in the place of the action (as was later to be the practice in Shakespeare's theatre). In comedies, a trip around the orchestra probably accomplished the same result. It also seems likely that in comedy individual doors or sections of the *skene* were sometimes used to represent widely separated places; it is possible that this convention was also used in tragedy.

Enough has been said to demonstrate that the evidence concerning scenic practices in the fifth century is inconclusive. Nevertheless, it appears unlikely that illusionism was ever attempted to any marked degree. The use of a few symbolic properties or set pieces would not have been out of keeping with other Greek artistic conventions of the period, and the eventual erection of a permanent stone *skene* suggests that conventionalization predominated over illusionism.

Inconclusive evidence has also led to disagreement over whether the Theatre of Dionysus had a stage during the fifth century. Those who believe, as A. W. Pickard-Cambridge did, that there was not one, argue: (1) that during the fifth century there was no Greek word for stage (*logeion* was not adopted until later) and that there are no archaeological remains of a stage from this period; (2) that the choral performances which preceded the invention of drama did not use a stage and thus would have provided no precedents for one; and (3) that no extant plays require a stage but do require the free mingling of actors and chorus, which a raised stage would have prevented. On the other hand, those who follow Peter Arnott in arguing for a stage note: (1) that all ancient commentators, though they originally lived much later, unanimously believed that there was a raised stage in the fifth century, (2) that a number of extant plays indicate that actors were on a higher level than the orchestra; and (3) that the intermingling of actors and chorus was not often required so a low raised stage (four feet or less) with steps to the orchestra was quite workable. Pickard-Cambridge was concerned primarily with refuting the idea of an eight- to thirteen-foot-high platform, and he admits that there may have been a stage one or two feet in height.

In the fifth century, a limited amount of machinery was available for special effects. The most important devices were the *ekkyklema* and the *mechane* or *machina*. The *ekkyklema* (a device for revealing tableaux, most often the bodies of characters killed offstage) was probably a platform that could be rolled out through the central doorway of the *skene*. On the other hand, some ancient accounts state that it was revolved or turned, while others associate it with the upper story of the scene house or with the side doors. The *mechane*, or crane, was used to show characters in flight or suspended above the earth. Occasionally characters are said to be in chariots or on the backs of birds, insects, or animals, while at other times actors seem to have been suspended by a harness. The crane was probably situated so that an actor could be attached to it out of sight of the audience (behind either the scene house or some part of an upper level) and then raised in the air and swung out over the acting area. The crane was most often used for the appearance of gods, but certain human characters in tragedy might require it (for example, Bellerophon on his flying horse). In comedy, it was often used to parody tragedy or to ridicule human pretensions. It is difficult to establish the use of the crane prior to about 430, but it may have been available much earlier. Its overuse in the last part of the century (especially by Euripides, who often employed gods to resolve his plots) led to the term *deus ex machina,* god from the machine, to describe any contrived ending.

Although stage properties were not numerous, they were essential elements of the productions. In several plays, characters sacrifice to a god or take refuge at an altar. Some scholars have argued that an altar in the center of the orchestra was used at these times; others have questioned the existence of such an altar and argued that if it did exist, it would have been dedicated to Dionysus so its use as a stage property would have been considered sacrilegious. Arnott suggests that there was a low structure in front of the central doorway that could be used either as altar or tomb. Other essential properties included chariots drawn by horses, biers for dead bodies, statues of various gods, and torches and lamps to indicate night scenes. Furniture was rarely required in tragedy and was restricted to couches for persons too ill or weak to stand. On the other hand, both furniture and other common domestic articles were numerous in comedy. In neither comedy nor tragedy were properties used to create the illusion of reality; they served instead to make some dramatic point.

AUDITORIUM AND AUDIENCE

Thus far, only those elements relating to the acting areas and performers have been considered. But the auditorium and audience were also important ingredients of a performance. The spectators, standing or seated on the slope of the Acropolis, commanded a view that included not only the performers but also a panoramic landscape that extended to the sea in the distance. The eye was not restricted to the interior of the theatre but rather was situated to see the theatre as part of that larger world whose drama was symbolically played out on the stage.

In Greek theatres, the auditorium and scene house were always separate architectural units. Between the scene house and the auditorium lay the orchestra and the *parodoi* (or entrances into the orchestra at either end of the stage house). The *parodoi* were used primarily by the chorus, although actors might enter there as well. The *parodoi* may also have been used by spectators as auditorium entrances and exits (although not the only ones).

The first *theatron* (or "seeing place," as the auditorium was termed by the Greeks) of the Theatre of Dionysus was the hillside that sloped down from the southeast corner of the Acropolis. Originally, spectators probably stood to watch performances, but wooden stadium–like seating may have been erected during the late sixth century, for the first major re-

modeling of the auditorium, undertaken shortly after 500, is thought to have been motivated by the collapse there of wooden seats. At this time, the hillside was regraded to change the slope, and a series of terraces, on which rested wooden benches, was probably laid out. When the Odeion was built in the 440s, the slope was changed again. The seats seem to have remained temporary, for Aristophanes refers to them as *ikria,* a term normally reserved for wooden benches. Stone seats may have been introduced gradually, but the stone auditorium was not completed until some time between 338 and 326 B.C.E. (A plan of the first stone theatre is shown in Fig. 2.16.)

The completed stone auditorium seated 14,000 to 17,000 persons. Nevertheless, only a small portion of the population could have attended the theatre at any one time. This may explain the introduction of tickets and an admission fee around the middle of the fifth century (although it is possible that admission was charged from the very beginning). To equalize the opportunity to attend, Pericles established a "theoric fund" around 450 to provide tickets for the poor. He also may have specified the price to be charged, but there is no definite record of admission costs until the late fourth century, when all seats not reserved by the state were sold at a uniform charge (the nominal sum of two obols). This money seems to have gone for the upkeep of the theatre, which was leased to a manager.

Tickets admitted holders to a section of the theatre rather than to specific seats. Each tribe may have had its own section. The audience certainly included men and boys, but there is considerable scholarly debate as to whether it included women or slaves. The central seat in the front row was reserved for the priest of Dionysus. Seats were also reserved for other

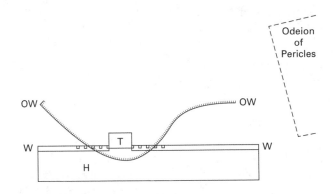

FIG. 2.15
Plan showing changes thought to have been made in the Theatre in Dionysus in the 440s. W = the new retaining wall with slots for timbers; OW = original retaining wall; T = stone terrace at orchestra level; H = the hall later built below the retaining wall. Drawing by Douglas Hubbell.

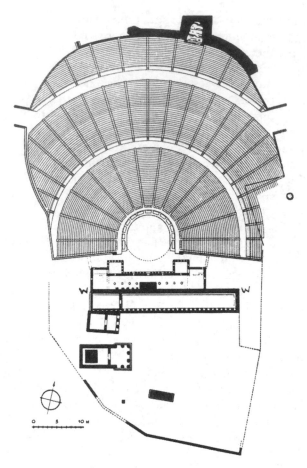

FIG. 2.16

Plan of the Theatre of Dionysus as it probably appeared when completed in the late fourth century B.C.E. The wall supposedly erected in the 440s is indicted by W-W. The square notches at the wall's front edge represent the slots allegedly used to hold the timbers of temporary stage houses. Below the wall is the hall, perhaps used for storage, and touching the wall at the left is the old temple of Dionysus; the new temple and the sacrificial altar are shown in the lower part of the plan. The *skene* and *paraskenia* are shown immediately above W-W. The upper crosswalk of the auditorium incorporated a public road. At the extreme top, a monument is set into the supporting walls of the Acropolis. O indicates the location of the Odeion, built in the 440s. From Dörpfeld, *Griechische Theater* (1896).

priests and perhaps for priestesses, for certain state officials, visiting ambassadors, and persons the state wished to honor. Officials were responsible for keeping order and for checking tickets to see that their holders sat in the correct section. Violence in the theatre was punishable by death.

Performances probably lasted all day, since a number of plays were presented in sequence. If so, there must have been much coming and going and considerable eating and drinking in the theatre. The au-

dience expressed its opinions noisily and at times hissed actors off the stage; tradition has it that Aeschylus once had to take refuge on the altar to escape the wrath of the spectators. Some ancient writers damned the audience as debased, but others praised it as discriminating. Probably the spectators represented a cross-section of tastes as well as of society.

One of the high points of each festival was the awarding of prizes. Although not all of the details are clear, these are the probable procedures: at some time prior to the festival, a list of potential judges (one list for each of the ten tribes) was drawn up; all of the names from the same tribe were placed in a single urn; the ten urns were then sealed and placed under guard until the beginning of the contest, when they were brought into the theatre, where the *archon* drew one name from each urn; these men then served as judges for the contest. (An alternative account, apparently reporting an exception to the usual practice, suggests that the judges were ten of the most powerful political and military leaders.) After witnessing the plays, each judge placed his vote in an urn, from which the *archon* drew five. On the basis of these five votes, the winner was declared. In the case of a tie, additional votes could be counted until the tie was broken.

The nature of the prizes is unclear, but they may have included money. Certainly the honor was great; victorious *choregoi* often erected monuments to commemorate victories, and state records were kept of the winners.

Although there are many unresolved questions about the theatre in the fifth century, we can be reasonably sure that it was a vigorous institution, in high repute both with the general populace and with civil and religious authorities. Drama was the most prized form of literature and the theatre the most popular of the arts.

ATHENIAN THEATRE AFTER THE FIFTH CENTURY

Following the Peloponnesian War, economic prosperity returned and the old forms of government continued for a time, but loyalty to the *polis* had been severely undermined and internal dissensions greatly increased thereafter. Sparta's domination of Greece passed to Thebes in 371 and then in 338 to Macedonia, which made the Greek city-states dependencies. Nevertheless, the outward changes in Greek life were not extreme, and Athens actually gained in reputation as a cultural center. Thus, it is usual to consider the first three-quarters of the fourth century a continuation of the classical age. Records indicate that in quantity artistic activity in the fourth century exceeded that in the fifth. Unfortunately, so few dramatic works have survived that we are unable to judge them fairly.

Theatre had never been confined to Attica, but Athens had always been the most important center. Before the end of the fifth century, plays by Athenian dramatists were in demand elsewhere (Aeschylus had twice visited Sicily and produced plays there, and Euripides had written plays while in Macedonia). After 400 B.C.E. tragic output continued unabated. Many writers who are no longer remembered, such as Theodectes, Astydamas, and Chaeremon, ranked at the forefront of dramatists in their day. But of fourth-century tragedies, only one—*Rhesus,* sometimes attributed to Euripides—has survived. Based on the tenth book of the *Iliad,* it is noteworthy primarily for its simulation of night, during which the entire action occurs.

During the fourth century, writers began to turn to the lesser myths, especially those of a slightly sensational nature, and to employ forensic elements and melodramatic devices with increasing frequency. Some of these changes may have come about because of Euripides' growing influence. Many of the ear-

lier dramatists were greatly admired, and after about 341 B.C.E. at least one old tragedy was presented each year at the City Dionysia.

Little is known of the satyr play after the fifth century. It must have declined in popularity, however, for beginning around 341 only one satyr play was produced each year.

On the other hand, comedy increased in popularity after the fifth century. Later commentators divided Greek comic writing into three periods: Old, dating from the beginning of the form until the end of the Peloponnesian War in 404; and Middle, from 404 until 336 (when Alexander the Great came to power); followed by the New Comedy of the Hellenistic period. Middle Comedy is essentially a transitional type, moving away from personal invective and political and social satire toward events based on contemporary life and manners or, alternatively, on mythological burlesque. Although we know the names of about fifty writers and have a number of fragments of Middle Comedy, the only complete plays that have survived are Aristophanes' *Assembly Women* (392–391) and *Plutus* (388). Both lack the political satire and the parabasis of Old Comedy, and the role of the chorus has been

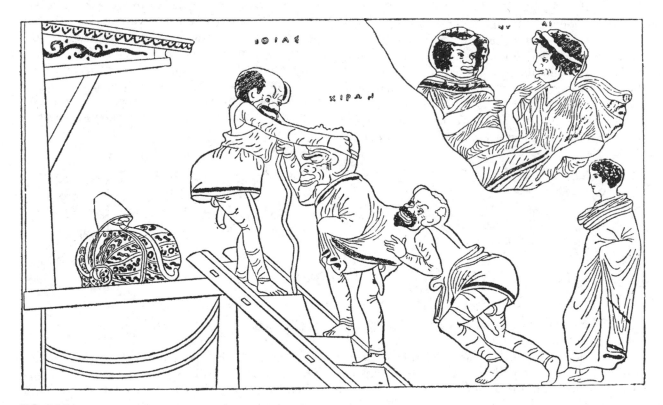

FIG. 2.17
Scene from a misnamed *phlyax* vase of the fourth century B.C.E. possibly depicting a scene from middle comedy. Note the portico, steps, raised stage, and costumes. From Baumeister, *Denkmaler des Klassichen Altertums* (1889).

FIG. 2.18
The remains of the Hellenistic theatre at Epidaurus. This is the best preserved of all the ancient Greek theatres. The stage house at left is a temporary structure erected for performances at a modern festival. Courtesy Greek Embassy.

contests for the production of old plays were instituted in the last part of the century, a practice seemingly never permitted at the Lenaia. The increased popularity of comedy was reflected in the institution of a contest for comic actors at the City Dionysia.

By about 350, professional singer-dancers, who appeared in both comic and tragic choruses, were replacing amateurs used in earlier times, and they were being rehearsed by professional trainers. Acting also grew in importance and came to overshadow playwriting. Probably as a result, around 350 the rules governing tragic performers at the City Dionysia were changed to require each of the three leading actors to appear in one play by each of the competing dramatists. Many actors might rightfully be termed stars, for the fame of Polus, Theodorus, Thettalus, Neoptolemus, Athenodorus, Aristodemus, and others spread throughout the Greek world.

It is ironic that the Theatre of Dionysus was not given its permanent stone form until about 325, by which time the Athenian theatre was already losing its privileged position. This permanent structure is important, nevertheless, since its archeological remains have served as the primary basis for most conjectures about theatre architecture in the fifth century. (It has usually been assumed that the stone theatre was merely a more permanent version of earlier temporary structures, but this assumption is questioned by many archeologists.) After 300, Athens was no longer in the forefront of developments, and its theatre building eventually came to seem outmoded, since it did not have the high raised stage and *thyromata* that were characteristic of Hellenistic theatres.

markedly reduced. Play fragments from this period show that many playwrights stopped writing choruses completely, simply inserting the equivalent of "a chorus goes here" into the play. Other than Aristophanes, the most famous writers of Middle Comedy were Antiphanes, Alexis, Anaxandrides, and Eubulus.

During the fourth century many changes were made in the dramatic festivals. At the City Dionysia,

LOOKING AT THEATRE HISTORY

One of the primary ways of approaching the Greek theatre is through archeology, the systematic study of material remains such as architecture, inscriptions, sculpture, vase painting, and other forms of decorative art. About the contributions of archeology to our knowledge of ancient civilizations, it has been said: "The recovery of these long-forgotten episodes in human history has been an astonishing performance—as remarkable . . . as . . . reaching the moon. As a result . . . our own generation is aware

of more aspects of the distant past than were dreamed of by our great-grandfathers."

Serious on-site excavations began in Greece around 1870, but W. Dörpfeld did not begin the first extensive study of the Theatre of Dionysus until 1886. Since that time, more than 167 other Greek theatres have been identified and many of them have been excavated. These excavations have revealed much that was previously unknown, especially about the dimensions and layout of theatres. Nevertheless, they still do not permit us to describe the precise appearance of the *skene* (illustrations printed in books are conjectural reconstructions), since many pieces are irrevocably lost because the buildings in later periods became sources of stone for other projects and what remains is usually broken and scattered. That most of the buildings were remodeled many times has created great problems for those seeking to date both the parts and the successive versions. Despite these drawbacks, archeology provides the most concrete evidence we have about the theatre structures of ancient Greece. But, if they have told us much, archeologists have not completed their work, and many sites have scarcely been touched.

Perhaps the most controversial use of archeological evidence in theatre history is vase paintings, thousands of which have survived from ancient Greece. (Most of those used by theatre scholars are reproduced in Margarete Bieber's *The History of the Greek and Roman Theater.*) Depicting scenes from mythology and daily life, the vases are the most graphic pictorial evidence we have. But they are also easy to misinterpret. Some scholars have considered any vase that depicts a subject treated in a surviving drama or any scene showing masks, flute players, or ceremonials to be valid evidence of theatrical practice. This is a highly questionable assumption, since the Greeks made widespread use of masks, dances, and music outside the theatre and since the myths on which dramatists drew were known to everyone, including vase painters, who might well depict the same subjects as dramatists without being indebted to them. Those vases showing scenes unquestionably theatrical are few in number.

Written evidence about ancient Greek theatre is often treated as less reliable than archeological evidence because most written accounts are separated so far in time from the events they describe and because they provide no information about their own sources. Of the written evidence, the surviving plays are usually treated as the most reliable. But the oldest surviving manuscripts of Greek plays date from around the tenth century, C.E., some 1500 years after they were first performed. Since printing did not exist during this time span, copies of plays had to be made by hand, and therefore the possibility of textual errors creeping in was magnified. Nevertheless, the scripts offer us our readiest access to the cultural and theatrical conditions out of which they came. But these scripts, like other kinds of evidence, are subject to varying interpretations. Certainly performances embodied a male perspective, for example, since the plays were written, selected, staged, and acted by men. Yet the existing plays feature numerous choruses of women and many feature strong female characters. Because these characters often seem victims of their own powerlessness and appear to be governed, especially in the comedies, by sexual desire, some critics have seen these plays as rationalizations by the male-dominated culture for keeping women segregated and cloistered. Other critics, however, have seen in these same plays an attempt by male authors to force their male audiences to examine and call into question this segregation and cloistering of Athenian women.

By far the majority of written references to Greek theatre date from several hundred years after the events they report. The writers seldom mention their sources of evidence, and thus we do not know what credence to give them. In the absence of material nearer in time to the events, however, historians have used the accounts and have been grateful to have them. Overall, historical treatment of the Greek theatre is something like assembling a jigsaw puzzle of which many pieces are missing: historians arrange what they have and imagine (with the aid of the remaining evidence and logic) what has been lost. As a result, though the broad outlines of Greek theatre history are reasonably clear, many of the details remain open to doubt.

One good example of the type of written evidence available to historians is *The Deipnosophists,* compiled by Athenaeus in Egypt around 200 C.E. In the following passage, he writes about events in Greece some 600 years earlier. Much of what he says is consistent with other reports, and his testimony has been repeated so often that it has been accorded the status of fact, but its reliability cannot be firmly established. It is amusing (and cautionary) to note, however, that his final statement is almost never quoted, although it is difficult to see why Chamaeleon should be considered an unreliable witness on this point if he is to be believed on others.

> *Aeschylus was not only the inventor of becoming and dignified dress, which the hierophants and torchbearers of the sacred festivals imitated; but he also invented many figures in dancing, and taught them to the dancers of the chorus. And Chamaeleon states that he first arranged the choruses, not using the ordinary dancing-masters, but himself arranging the figures of the dancers for the chorus; and altogether that he took the whole arrangement of his tragedies on himself. And he himself acted in his own plays very fairly. . . . But Aeschylus was often drunk when he wrote his tragedies, if we may trust Chamaeleon: and accordingly Sophocles reproached him, saying, that even when he did what was right he did not know that he was doing so.*

Athenaeus, *The Deipnosophists, or Banquet of the Learned,* trans. C. D. Yonge, 3 vols. (London: H. G. Bohn, 1854), bk. I, ch. 39.

3
Hellenistic, Roman, and Byzantine Theatre

Theatre as an autonomous activity first developed in classical Greece (*c.* 500–336), but it spread throughout the Mediterranean world in the time of the European empires. During the Hellenistic period (336–*c.* 31 B.C.E.) Greek theatre was introduced to cultures throughout the eastern Mediterranean and all the way to India. During the later years of the Roman Republic (509–27 B.C.E.) and especially during the Roman Empire (27 B.C.E.–476 C.E.), theatre spread to the western Mediterranean and as far as England. The subsequent Byzantine Empire (476–1453 C.E.) was Christian and did not encourage the development or spread of theatre, but it did preserve much of the information and some of the traditions of Greco-Roman theatre that would allow Western Europe to rediscover the classical theatre during the Renaissance.

THE HELLENISTIC THEATRE

Between 336 B.C.E. and his death in 323, Alexander the Great, ruler of mainland Greece, conquered the Persian Empire and extended his realm into present-day India and Egypt, creating the first great empire to be launched from Europe. Wherever he went he built new cities and promoted Greek culture and learning. As a result, the entire eastern Mediterranean

was "Hellenized." (A Greek theatre still exists as far east as Ai Khanoum in central Afghanistan.) Athens continued to be a major cultural center, even after the loss of its democracy in 322, but its preeminence was challenged in the third century by Pergamum (in Asia Minor) and especially by Alexandria (in Egypt), which became the literary capital of the Greek world because of its library and institute for literary research.

Alexander's empire disintegrated after his death, but major parts were maintained by his followers. Mainland Greece regained a precarious independence, but it was so lacking in unity that it could put up no effective resistance to Rome and became a Roman province in 146 B.C.E. Egypt, which had been ruled by the descendants of Alexander's general, Ptolemy, since 305, fell to the Romans with the defeat of Cleopatra's forces in 31 B.C.E. bringing to an end the last of the Hellenistic states.

DRAMATIC THEORY

During the fourth century, Greek thought became increasingly secularized. Religious worship and festivals continued, but belief in their efficacy was seriously undermined by the intellectual scrutiny to which the gods and myths were subjected during this great age of Greek philosophy, epitomized above all by the work of Plato (*c.* 427–347) and Aristotle (384–322). During this time philosophers inquired into every aspect of Greek life, including the theatre. Plato argued for censorship and strict state control over drama, whose powerful influence he feared. Aristotle referred to the theatre in several of his works, but his major ideas are set forth in the *Poetics* (*c.* 335–323), the first systematic treatise on drama. In addition to its discussion of tragedy, the *Poetics* contains in its early chapters the oldest surviving history of dramatic forms. While preparing this work, Aristotle is said to have compiled a record of the plays and winners at all the festivals, a major source of information for subsequent Greek and Roman historians; only fragments of his list now survive.

Aristotle's influence has been especially great on critical theory, for his *Poetics* has been crucial in practically all discussions of tragedy since the sixteenth century, when it first became widely known. Because many of Aristotle's ideas are stated cryptically, however, the *Poetics* has been interpreted variously. It must be read with great care if it is to be helpful. Aristotle states in the *Poetics* that every drama has six parts: plot, character, thought, diction, music, and spectacle. He discusses unity of action, probability, the requirements of plot, characteristics of the tragic hero, problems of diction, and many other topics. His conclusions continue to be informative and controversial.

FIG. 3.1
Terracotta statuette of an old woman from New Comedy. Courtesy British Museum.

NEW COMEDY

Hellenistic writers favored a form of domestic, middle-class comedy that is commonly identified as New Comedy. Unlike Old Comedy, New Comedy ignored political issues and favored a more generalized concern for love, financial worries, and familial or societal relationships. New Comedy eventually became repetitious both in terms of situation and dramatic devices (especially concealed identity, coincidence, and recognition). Many plays were essentially character studies, and others were based on myths. But a typical plot revolved around a young man who, against the strong opposition of his father, seeks to marry a girl, frequently a slave about to be forced into prostitution; after many comically unsuccessful attempts to circumvent the father's wrath, the son achieves his goal when it is discovered that the girl is the long-lost daughter of some wealthy Athenian. The entire action, then, rests on a misunderstanding, which, when cleared up, resolves the conflict. But in recent years some critics have come to view these plays as works that questioned and then reaffirmed certain societal conventions during a period when values and mores were being challenged. Thus, they treat the plays as reflections of prevailing ideology rather than merely frivolous, diversionary entertainment.

Several plays of Euripides, most notably *Ion, Helen, Iphigenia at Tauris,* and *Alcestis* (staged in place of a satyr play in 438), are tragicomic and make use of such plot devices as long-lost children and scenes of recognition. These were very popular and may well have set the pattern for the structure of New Comedy, with a prologue followed by a series of episodes separated by choral passages that usually had little connection with the incidents. In many New Comedies the chorus appeared onstage only during the interludes between episodes. New Comedy was also mixed in tone, for in many plays pathetic and moral elements injected a serious note. Other plays, however, were primarily farcical. The language reflected everyday usage but was not extremely colloquial, for dialogue was still cast in verse.

Characters may have gradually become conventionalized into a restricted number of types. Pollux (a Greek lexicographer of the second century C.E.) lists the common characters in New Comedy as: nine types of old men, four of young men, seven of slaves, five of young women, and various soldiers, parasites,

FIG. 3.2
Statuette of a slave from New Comedy. From Robert, *Die Masken der Neueren Attischen Komoedie* (1911).

ers of New Comedy include Diphilus, Philemon, and Apollodorus.

After the third century B.C.E., comedy began to decline, just as tragedy had a century earlier. New Comedy was the last vital expression of Greek drama.

ACTORS AND ACTING

Alexander is said to have assembled more than 3000 performers from across the Greek world for a victory festival, and thereafter the occasions on which plays might be presented were numerous, especially since rulers began to encourage worship of themselves as gods and to establish festivals in their own honor or for primarily secular purposes. Consequently, plays were no longer performed exclusively at Dionysian festivals.

The rapid expansion in the number of festivals created a demand for qualified performers, and perhaps as a result the theatre of the Hellenistic period became almost totally professional. By 300 well-known actors were touring everywhere. Actors had also gained such ascendancy over dramatists that they changed texts to suit their talents. Acting competitions were no longer restricted to performances in plays but could involve the performance of scenes from plays or even just speeches from them. Actors were judged on the elaborate displays of vocal virtuosity and the ability to convey emotion.

and others. Pollux differentiates each subtype within these broad groupings by some distinctive quality in both mask and costume.

Although the names of sixty-four writers of New Comedy are known and about 1400 plays of this type were probably produced, only one complete work—*Dyskolos* (*The Grouch*) by Menander—has survived, and it was not rediscovered until 1957. Menander (342–291 B.C.E.), who wrote more than one hundred plays after 321, is by far the most important author of New Comedy. In addition to *The Grouch,* a comedy of character about an irascible old man, Menander's works are now known from lengthy fragments of *The Arbitration, The Girl from Samos,* and *The Shorn Girl,* and lesser fragments of about eighty-five other plays. Fragments continue to be discovered. In the ancient world, Menander was celebrated for his varied and sympathetic characterizations, his easy, natural style, his ability to adapt sentiment to character, and his ingenuity in constructing plots. In Rome, where his plays were frequently adapted, Menander's reputation was higher than that of any Greek author except Homer. Other important writ-

FIG. 3.3
A bas-relief from Naples of a scene from New Comedy: two old men at the left, the flute player at center, and a youth and slave at the right. From Robert, *Die Masken der Neueren Attischen Komoedie* (1911).

During this period theatre professionals formed a guild, usually referred to as the Artists of Dionysus. Although the date of its formation is uncertain, it was clearly in existence by 277 B.C.E., for it was given official sanction in a decree of that year. During the first century C.E., the Roman emperor Claudius (reigned 41–54 C.E.) addressed a decree to the World Artists of Dionysus, and by the time of the emperor Hadrian (reigned 117–138 C.E.) the world headquarters was located in Rome.

The Artists of Dionysus included among its members poets (dramatic, epic, and lyric), actors, chorus members, trainers, musicians, and costumers—all the personnel needed to produce plays and to give recitations at festivals. Mime performers and other popular entertainers were never admitted to this guild (although eventually they had their own).

As the name of the guild suggests, the performers retained their connection with Dionysus, even though they produced plays and acted at many non-Dionysian festivals. When planning a festival, a city apparently negotiated a contract with the nearest branch of the guild. The obligations of each party were clearly specified in the agreements. Because of the importance of the festivals and because following the death of Alexander the Hellenic world had broken up into a number of states, international agreements were reached under which the safety of the guild's members was guaranteed even in times of war.

COSTUMES

Tragic costumes and masks changed considerably after the fifth century. Although the progressive changes cannot be dated, it is reasonably clear that by the first century B.C.E. a tragic actor wore a padded costume, thick-soled boots (*kothornoi*), and a high headdress (*onkos*), all intended to increase the actor's apparent size. The facial features of the masks were also enlarged and exaggerated. In other words, tragic actors were now made larger than life and their overall appearance was distorted and conventionalized. In New Comedy, costume, although somewhat conventionalized, was based on the dress of ordinary life. The character types of comedy apparently were considerably more extensive than those of tragedy. Most comic masks probably were realistic, but some, such as those for slaves and certain old men and ridiculous characters, were still caricatured. Hair color was also conventionalized. Most slaves, for example, had red hair, while courtesans usually had yellow.

FIG. 3.4
Marble relief sculpture, often said to represent Menander with three masks: in his hand, the mask of a youth; on the table, masks of a young woman and a man. First–second century C.E. copy of a third century B.C.E. work. Courtesy the Art Museum, Princeton University.

THEATRE ARCHITECTURE

Theatre architecture also underwent considerable change in the Hellenistic period. Between the middle of the fourth century and the first century B.C.E., a theatre structure quite unlike that of the Theatre of Dionysus evolved. Important examples were built at Priene, Oropus, Ephesus, Delos, Epidaurus, Oeniadae, Sicyon, Pergamum, Corinth, and Alexandria. Of the 167 known Greek theatres, the vast majority are of the Hellenistic type.

Although the basic features of the Hellenistic theatre are reasonably well established, the date and place of origin are disputed. Some scholars argue that drastic deviations from the Athenian plan were made as early as the fourth century, but others date them from the second century B.C.E. The evidence is hopelessly confused, primarily because archeologists cannot agree on the dates when the original structures were built or when they underwent the various remodelings to which all were subjected. The details of this controversy are unimportant here; it is sufficient to note that the basic structural features of the Hellenistic theatre

FIG. 3.6

The Hellenistic theatre at Eretria. The upper view shows an early phase in the stage building's evolution, while the lower shows fully developed *thyromata*. From Fiechter, *Antike Griechische Theaterbauten*. Courtesy Verlag W. Kohlhammer GmbH, Stuttgart and Dr. Charlotte Fiechter.

may have been present as early as 300 B.C.E. or may have taken shape over a period of 150 years. Almost all scholars agree that the Hellenistic theatre building was fully developed by 150 B.C.E.

Probably the most important Hellenistic innovation was the high raised stage. Varying from 8 to 13 feet in height, it was sometimes as long as 140 feet, although it was only from 6½ to 14 feet deep. Since *paraskenia* (or side wings of the scene house) were eliminated, this long, narrow platform was open at both ends. In some theatres, ramps parallel to the *parodoi* led up to the stage; in others, steps to the orchestra were provided at the ends of the stage; in still others, the stage could be entered only from the scene house. The front edge of the stage was supported by the *proskenion* (or facade of the lower story), while the *episkenion* (or facade of the second story) rose at the back of the raised stage. Often the two facades were approximately equal in height. In some theatres, the *proskenion* overlapped the outer rim of the orchestra circle by a few feet, although in others the full circle of the orchestra remained entirely visible. The auditoriums underwent no significant changes, but they varied widely in seating capacity, ranging from 3000 at Oropus to 24,000 at Ephesus.

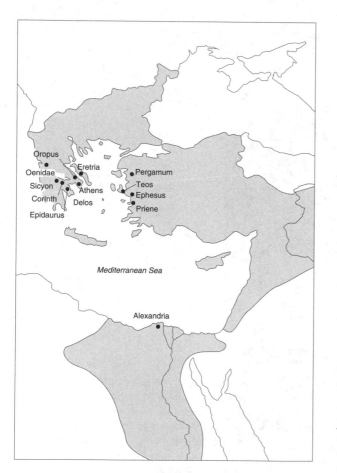

FIG. 3.5

Hellenistic Greece and the Near East.

The alterations in the *skene* raise many questions about staging. Was the orchestra used by all performers when old plays requiring a large chorus were revived, and was the raised stage reserved for those newer plays in which the chorus was small or incidental? Did the actors use the stage and the chorus the orchestra? Was the upper stage at first used only for gods and special scenes and only later transformed into the usual acting area for all scenes? Was the orchestra used only for nondramatic performances (such as dithyrambic choruses)? Was the orchestra merely a vestigial structural feature that no longer served any necessary function? Each of these questions has received both affirmative and negative answers, none of which can be accepted with certainty. What is certain is that these buildings were multipurpose structures. They represented too large an investment to be used only for an occasional theatrical performance and served as general meeting places for many kinds of civic activities.

Many problems also arise in relation to scenic practices. For example, in the early Hellenistic theatre the *proskenion* was composed of pillars spaced several feet apart; often these pillars were notched so as to hold *pinakes* (painted panels) inserted from the rear. In many theatres dating from later than the second century B.C.E., however, the pillars are no longer notched. On this basis, some historians have argued that as long as performances occurred in the orchestra a scenic background was provided; whereas later, when all action was transferred to the stage, the *proskenion* became merely an open colonnade, since *pinakes* were no longer needed at the orchestra level.

As time passed, the facade of the second story also underwent a number of changes. During the second century B.C.E., the *episkenion*, which originally had been fitted with from one to three doors, was converted into a series of sizable openings (or *thyromata*) varying in number from one to seven. These *thyromata*, averaging about 10 to 12 feet in width and extending upward as high as the roof would permit, were separated from each other by narrow upright supports. Thus, on the upper level there was now a long shallow forestage backed by a rear stage equally as deep or deeper.

FIG. 3.7
Reconstruction of the Hellenistic theatre at Ephesus. Note the *thyromata* treated as though each was a miniature proscenium stage. From Frickenhaus, *Die Altgriechische Bühne (1917)*.

This change is usually associated with the decline of the chorus and the increased use of the high platform for the action. Some scholars have also assumed that *thyromata* were created to permit greater scenic illusion, and have suggested that each opening served as a miniature proscenium arch behind which individual settings could be erected. This theory (as well as all others about the *thyromata*) is entirely conjectural.

Vitruvius, writing in the first century B.C.E., describes the facade as providing spaces for *periaktoi*. Possibly *periaktoi* were set up in *thyromata*. Vitruvius also says that there were three kinds of backgrounds: one each for tragedy, comedy, and satyr plays. Though some historians have interpreted this passage to mean that illusionistic scenery was used, others have argued that it merely suggests some type of conventionalized painting on the *periaktoi*.

Although the Greek theatre continued until after 500 C.E., its vitality declined rapidly after the first century B.C.E. Beginning in the second century B.C.E., the Romans gradually gained power over all the eastern Mediterranean and, though Greek ideals persisted, Roman standards eventually altered them. After the first century C.E., most of the theatres were remodeled to conform more nearly to the Roman ideal of theatre architecture. These remodeled structures are usually called Greco-Roman, since they have some features characteristic of each type. Many purely Roman theatres were also erected in Greek territories.

The theatre in Athens was not immune to these changes, although it long resisted them. The Theatre of Dionysus retained its classical form until sometime between the third and first centuries B.C.E., when it was remodeled along more fashionable Hellenistic lines. Other extensive changes were made in the first century C.E., when the stage was extended forward over part of the orchestra to make it conform more nearly to the Roman ideal. After this time, gladiatorial contests were sometimes staged in the orchestra (which was by then fenced in with a stone barricade); about the fourth century C.E. the orchestra was sealed so that water spectacles could be given in it.

It is not clear when the Athenian dramatic contests ceased. A decline in personal wealth among Athenians led (sometime between 317 and 307) to the discontinuance of the practice of appointing *choregoi,* a step that was also made practical by the declining use of choruses in plays. After this time an elected official, the *agonothetes,* was given a state appropriation out of which to finance all theatrical productions. The records of the City Dionysia continue until the first century C.E., while those of the Lenaia can be traced

FIG. 3.8

The "golden courtesan" of New Comedy. From Robert, *Die Masken der Neueren Attischen Komoedie* (1911).

only until about 150 B.C.E. Nevertheless, the contests may have gone on for some time after the records stop. The Theatre of Dionysus was used for various kinds of spectacles until at least the fourth century C.E. and perhaps longer. It had a truly remarkable history of nearly 1000 years of continuous use.

GREEK MIMES

We know the most about the comic and tragic performances given at official festivals in Greece because these generated the kinds of records and commentary that get preserved for later study. But Greece had numerous forms of popular entertainment that, while they left fewer records, were certainly a greater part of the lives of the average person in the Hellenistic age.

Many types of popular entertainment are often grouped under the heading of "mime," a term applied indiscriminately both to scripts and performers. Mime was a variety entertainment that could include short playlets, mimetic dance, imitations of animals and birds, singing, acrobatics, juggling, and more. Small troupes of mimes may have performed at banquets, at market fairs (on temporary stages), and on other occasions as early as the fifth century B.C.E. Thus, mimes were probably the first professional entertainers. As far as we can determine, mimes were the first theatrical performers to include women among their ranks and the first to perform regularly without masks, though some mime forms certainly did employ masks.

Short mime playlets seem to have originated in Megara in the sixth century B.C.E. Troupes of "masked men" performed in Sparta, while "improvisers" performed works like *The Quack Doctor, Dionysus and Ariadne,* or *The Woman Visitor to Isthmia* throughout Greece perhaps as early as the fifth century. The Greek colonies of southern Italy and Sicily favored mime during the fifth century, but not until Hellenistic times did it flourish throughout the eastern Mediterranean. Mime "plays" ranged from improvised skits, to sung dialogues, to danced stories (like the jig of Shakespeare's day). After 300 B.C.E., mime performers increasingly appeared at festivals, although they were never admitted to membership in the Artists of Dionysus.

In southern Italy, mimes were called *phlyakes.* Rhinthon, who lived at Tarentum in the first half of the third century B.C.E., is said to have formalized this type. Of the thirty-eight plays attributed to him, most are *hilarotragoidiai,* or burlesques of tragedy, but only a few fragments survive. Although mimes were popular throughout the Hellenic world, *phlyakes* have received the most attention because a series of vases from southern Italy were once thought to depict scenes from this form. These vases have now been redated to 400–325 B.C.E., about a century before any known *phlyax* plays were written, but they are still often called *phlyax* vases, even though their connection with mime performances is uncertain. (Historians now argue that the scenes they depict are from Middle Comedy.) The characters wear padded tights, short chitons, and the phallus. The subjects range from mythological burlesque (the adventures of Heracles is a favorite) to daily life. Lovemaking, gluttony, beatings, thievery, and trickery are popular motifs.

Probably of greatest interest is the representation of the stage. The paintings show a raised platform varying in height and resting on posts or decorative columns, between which are draperies or painted panels. Steps, often being used by actors, lead up from the ground level to the stage. The facade at the back of the stage varies: sometimes it is composed of a portico and door; other times there are columns and decorative motifs; sometimes there is a window or gallery

on an upper level. Trees, altars, thrones, chests, and tables appear among the properties. Some scholars have interpreted the paintings as evidence that performers used a temporary stage that could be erected as needed by traveling troupes; others have suggested that the vases show the stages of permanent theatres depicted in a simplified manner because of the limited space available to the vase painters. (See Fig.2.17.)

Regardless of how the vases are interpreted, it is clear that the theatre flourished in southern Italy. It was there, in the third century B.C.E., that the Romans first encountered Greek culture. After this time historical interest shifts to Rome, where Greek forms and practices were adopted and transformed, though it should not be forgotten that the Greek theatre continued throughout the Roman era.

THE ROMAN THEATRE

According to tradition, Rome was founded in 753 B.C.E. (about the time the Greeks were colonizing southern Italy and Sicily). It remained an insignificant town under the domination of neighboring Etruria, the home of several of its early rulers, until it expelled its last Etruscan king and founded a republic in 509 (just as Athens was becoming a democracy). During the fourth century, Rome began to expand and by 265 controlled the entire Italian peninsula, including the Etruscan areas to the north and the Greek territories to the south. Next, following the first Punic War with Carthage (264–241), Rome acquired Sicily. As a result of its expansion between 270 and 240, Rome took over several Greek territories in which the theatre had long flourished. By 240, a sufficiently large number of Romans were familiar with Greek art and theatre that regular drama (either translations or imitations of Greek plays) was introduced into Rome. Consequently, the year 240 B.C.E. is often said to mark the beginning of Roman theatre. But while this date may establish when regular Roman drama began, it does not mark the beginning of Rome's theatrical activity, which can be traced back more than a century prior to that time.

If we are to understand Roman theatre, it is essential to recognize from the outset that drama in the Greek sense played only a small role in it, since it was always dominated by variety entertainment more closely related to the Greek mimes. We can probably grasp the essence of Roman theatre more readily by comparing it with American television programming, for it encompassed acrobatics, trained animals, jugglers, athletic events, music and dance, dramatic skits, short farces, and full-length dramas. The Roman public was as fickle as our own: like channel-switchers, they frequently left one event for another and demanded diversions capable of withstanding all competition. From time to time new forms of entertainment were introduced to Rome; some of these were retained for several centuries, whereas others lost their popularity more quickly and were either discarded or relegated to a minor role. Regular drama must be included among the forms that flourished for a time and then declined.

ETRUSCAN ANTECEDENTS

During Rome's early history, Etruria was the dominant influence on Roman theatrical activities, although it is difficult to assess the Etruscan contributions fully. Nevertheless, it was probably from Etruria that Rome inherited many features of its religious festivals (the principal occasions on which theatrical performances were given in Rome). Just as Rome's sacred festivals eventually would, Etruria's included acting, dancing, flute playing, juggling, prizefighting, horseracing, acrobatics, and competitive sports. The Etruscans also believed that the religious portions of their festivals must be performed precisely and without error, a belief which the Romans shared and which often led them to repeat entire festivals when mistakes were made. Some Etruscan festivals also had a commercial element, being held in conjunction with fairs to which people came from faraway places. All these attributes help to explain the nature of Roman festivals, which mingled diverse activities in an atmosphere partly religious, partly secular, even carnival-like. Other Etruscan practices also probably influenced Roman theatre. Among these was the extensive use of music and dance in almost all ceremonies; music was especially important in

FIG. 3.9
Etruscan musician playing the double flute. From the tomb of the Leopards, Tarquinii. From *Jahrbuch des Deutschen Archäologischen Instituts,* 31 (1916).

Etruria, for it accompanied activities ranging from sacrifices to boxing matches to daily work. The Etruscans also originated gladiatorial contests, although as funeral ceremonies rather than as the form of entertainment they became in later Rome.

The influence of Etruria on Roman theatre is attested by many ancient sources. The Roman poet Horace (65–8 B.C.E.) states that Latin drama originated in the Fescennine Verses (a name thought by some to be derived from Fescennium, a town on the Etruscan border), compositions consisting of improvised, abusive, and often obscene dialogue exchanged

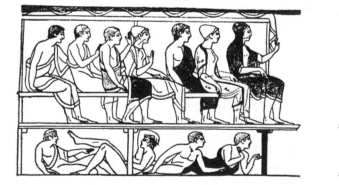
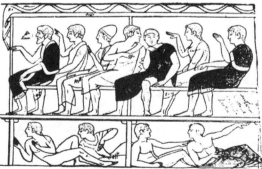

FIG. 3.10
Stands for audiences at an Etruscan entertainment. Wall painting from a tomb at Corneto. From *Jahrbuch des Deutschen Archäologischen Instituts,* 31 (1916).

FIG. 3.11
The Italian peninsula c. 500 B.C.E. before Rome began to expand.

between masked clowns at harvest and wedding celebrations. On the other hand, Livy (59 B.C.E.–17 C.E.), the Roman historian, dates the first theatrical performances in Rome at 364 B.C.E., when musical and dancing performers were imported from Etruria in an effort to appease the gods when plague was ravishing the city. Rome derived its term for actors (*histriones*) from these professional performers (called *ister* by the Etruscans). Subsequently, according to Livy, improvised dialogue was added to the music and dance to create a new type, performed at first by amateurs but later by professionals. It was also an Etruscan ruler of Rome, the elder Tarquin (616–579 B.C.E.), who established the *ludi Romani* (the festival at which Greek drama was later first presented) with its chariot races, boxing contests, and other entertainments. Since Etruscan tomb paintings show grandstands for spectators at festivals, stadium-like seating was probably used in Rome long before the Greek theatre was known there.

In addition to Etruria, southern Italy contributed to Rome's early theatre. The primary influence came from the Atellan farce (*fabula Atellana*), which takes its name from the Oscan town of Atella (near what is now Naples). Farce was probably imported to Rome during the first half of the third century, for by 275 B.C.E. the Romans had become undisputed masters of the Oscan region. Little is known of the early Atellan farce. Some scholars argue that it was derived from the *phlyakes* or other mimes of southern Italy. It was probably short, largely improvised, and based on domestic situations or mythological burlesque. Type characters, each with its own fixed costume and mask, seem also to have been characteristic.

Thus, by 240, when Greek drama was imported into Rome, various kinds of entertainments (music, dance, farce, chariot races, and boxing) were already well established at Roman festivals. Regular drama was merely added to them.

THE ROMAN CONTEXT

By 146 B.C.E., Rome had conquered Greece and thereafter it gradually absorbed the entire Hellenic world. In turn, Rome was heavily influenced by Greek culture. From the third century onward, Greek tutors were in demand in Rome, and many Romans went to study in Greece. Furthermore, much Roman art and literature after 240 B.C.E. borrowed from Greek models.

As a people, the Romans are noted for adopting the ideas and practices of others. But they were neither indiscriminate nor unintelligent borrowers, for of all the people who came into contact with the Greeks, the Romans embraced Greek artistic forms most fully. Nevertheless, Romans should not be viewed as mere extensions of the Greeks, for their own character made them reject much that was distinctively Greek.

The Romans had little of the philosophical bent so characteristic of the Greeks. A practical people, they were for the most part uninterested in theoretical questions. Though they were among the greatest engineers, military tacticians, and administrators the world has known, they speculated little about these subjects. They were content to discover how things worked without asking why. Where Aristotle had invented dramatic criticism with *Poetics* (c. 335–323), the Roman writer Horace would be content to provide a manual for the writing of good plays in his *The Art of Poetry* (c. 19 B.C.E.). These traits also affected their art, which tended to be grandiose, sentimental, or diversionary rather than, as with the Greeks, a serious exploration of the human condition.

Rome's history can best be understood by dividing it into two phases: the republic (509–27 B.C.E.) and the empire (27 B.C.E.–c. 476 C.E.). It was the "republican virtues"—discipline, economy, endurance, military precision, and loyalty to family and state—that made it possible for Rome to become a world power. The Romans were noted for their

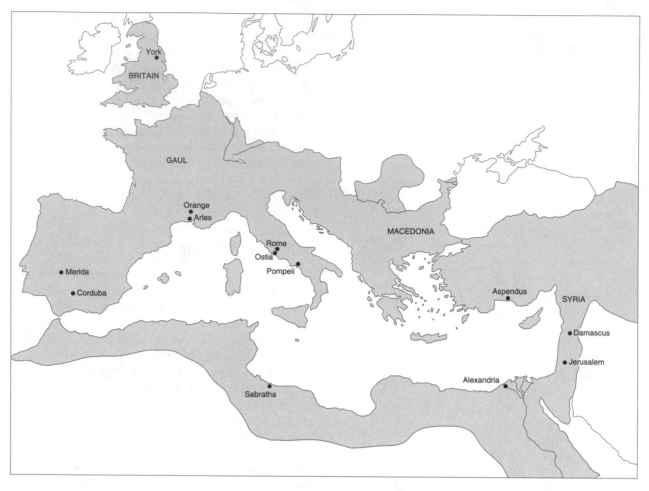

FIG. 3.12
The Roman Empire at its height.

incorruptibility, their sense of duty to the republic, and their faith in law and order.

By the first century B.C.E., Rome ruled a vast territory that poured wealth into the capitol. Roman citizens were receiving grain free of charge, the army had become professionalized, and the government was bureaucratized. In 27 B.C.E., power passed from representative bodies to the emperor. Thereafter, the virtues that had built Rome lessened. The basic problem became how to maintain and administer Rome's far-flung territories. That the empire endured so long is a testament to the Roman genius for organization.

Similar elements of change can be noted in the theatre. Under the republic, regular drama prospered for a time: tragedy's appeal probably lay in its echo of republican sentiments about virtue, honor, and loyalty, whereas comedy's was in the lighthearted treatment of domestic complications that were resolved happily. Neither form seems to have reflected any profound philosophical concerns or to have seriously questioned Roman values. Under the em-

pire, regular drama was largely abandoned in favor of variety entertainment; the theatre became increasingly diversionary, with novelties of all kinds demanded and offered—new types of entertainments, ever-increasing lavishness and elaborateness of spectacle, thrills of all sorts (nudity, sex, violence, and bloodshed among them).

Nevertheless, it should not be forgotten that the theatre in Rome almost always was associated with festivals, most of them religious, especially during the republic. Thus, theatrical offerings (regardless of content) were long thought to be pleasing to (or capable of propitiating) the gods. Not only were Roman counterparts of the Greek gods worshipped, but household spirits and animistic forces were venerated as well; as Rome expanded, new gods were continually added to the list, for the Romans were a superstitious people fearful of offending any supernatural power. The Romans seem to have placed as much or more emphasis on the form as on the substance of religious ceremonies.

Perhaps this explains why at the festivals honoring the gods the content of theatrical entertainments mattered less than the fact that the entertainments were offered.

Overall, it seems clear that Roman drama did not reach a level comparable to that of fifth-century Greece. But it is equally true that in Rome the theatre was far more highly developed, varied, and extensive than in any earlier culture.

ROMAN FESTIVALS

Most state-sponsored theatrical performances in republican Rome were given at official religious festivals, or *ludi,* honoring various gods and were preceded by a religious procession (*pompa*). A number of other "extraordinary," "honorary," or "donated" festivals (*munera*) were given on special occasions (such as after major victories in war, at the dedication of public buildings or monuments, at the funerals of important personages, or when an individual or politician wished to curry favor), and many of these included theatrical performances.

The oldest of the official festivals was the *ludi Romani,* given in honor of Jupiter each September. Established in the sixth century B.C.E., it included various types of performance beginning in 364 and regular comedy and tragedy beginning in 240. Eventually five additional festivals granted theatrical entertainments a major role: *ludi plebeii,* held in November, and with plays by 200; *ludi Apollinares,* begun in 212 and held in July; *ludi Megalenses,* with theatrical entertainment after 194; *ludi Florales,* celebrated in April/May, and with performances, especially of mimes, after 194; and *ludi Ceriales,* founded in 202 and celebrated in April (it is not known when performances first became part of this festival). Still other festivals included theatrical events from time to time. None of the festivals at which plays were performed honored Dionysus (or Bacchus, his Roman counterpart).

It is difficult to estimate how many days the Romans devoted to theatrical performances annually, since the number of official festival days differed from year to year and "donated festivals" were frequent. Furthermore, festivals were sometimes repeated, because when irregularities in the rituals occurred the entire festival, including, it seems, even the plays, had to be redone. (Such repetition was labeled *instauratio.*) That *instauratio* was not uncommon is shown by the repetition of the *ludi Romani* in eleven of the years between 214 and 200 and of the *ludi plebeii* seven times in one year. It should be noted, however, that there is no record of *instauratio* occurring at any festivals other than the *ludi Romani* and the *ludi plebeii.*

Although the precise number of performances in any given year cannot be determined, they increased steadily after 240 B.C.E. By 200 B.C.E. the number had grown to between four and eleven, by 190 to between seven and seventeen, by 150 to about twenty-five, and by the beginning of the Christian era to about forty. Under the empire, the number of performances was greatly inflated. The motive for providing public performances became increasingly political as emperors used free "bread and circuses" to court a populace that was at loose ends. In 354 C.E., one hundred days were devoted to theatrical entertainments and another seventy-five to such events as chariot races and gladiatorial contests. After 400 C.E., as the empire began to disintegrate, the number seems to have varied considerably from one reign to another, but performances continued into the sixth century. In addition to the state and "donated" festivals, both under the republic and the empire, there probably were privately arranged indoor performances and even some public performances given for paying audiences by traveling troupes.

DRAMA UNDER THE ROMANS

By the time Rome ceased to be a republic in 27 B.C.E., regular drama had already declined markedly and the minor forms had become dominant. Of the more than 900 years over which the history of Roman theatre extends, only about 200 are of much importance for drama because it was during this time that most of the plays intended for performance were written.

Roman literature is usually said to have begun with Livius Andronicus (*fl.* 240–204 B.C.E.), for the comedies and tragedies that he wrote, translated, or adapted were the first important literary works in Latin. Little is known of Andronicus. He may have come to Rome as a prisoner of war, but, if so, he was later freed. Apparently he was from Tarentum (located in the Greek territories of southern Italy). The first native-born dramatist was Gnaeus Naevius (*c.* 270–*c.* 201 B.C.E.), who began writing about 235. He excelled at comedy, although like Andronicus, who was best at tragedy, he wrote both types. Naevius did much to naturalize the drama by introducing many Roman allusions into the Greek originals and by writing plays on Roman stories. By the time Andronicus and Naevius died, drama was well established in Rome. Since each of their successors tended to specialize in a single form, the development of tragedy and comedy followed separate paths thereafter. By this time also, a guild of writers (*collegium poetarum*) seems to have been established.

The names of many comic writers have come down to us. Two of these—Plautus and Terence—are of principal interest because they are the authors of the only surviving Roman comedies. Titus Maccius Plautus (*c.* 254–*c.* 184 B.C.E.) was the first important successor to Livius Andronicus and Naevius in comedy. His popularity was so great that after his death as many as 130 plays came to be attributed to him. In seeking to resolve the question of authorship, the Roman scholar Varro (116–27 B.C.E.) divided the plays into those certainly by Plautus, those possibly by Plautus, and those clearly not by Plautus. In the first group he placed twenty-one works, twenty of which have survived and are still credited to Plautus: *The Comedy of Asses, The Merchant, The Braggart Warrior, The Casket, Pot of Gold, Stichus, Pseudolus, Curculio, The Two Bacchides, Casina, Amphitryon, The Captives, Epidicus, The Menaechmi, The Haunted House, The Persian, The Carthaginian, The Rope, Three-Bob Day,* and *The Churl*. The twenty-first play, *Vidularia*, survives only in fragments. (*Querolus*, a comedy of the fifth century C.E., was once credited to Plautus but is now thought to be based on his *Pot of Gold*.) Few of these plays can be dated with certainty, although all were probably written between 205 and 184. Plautus was much admired for his Latin dialogue, his varied poetic meters, and his witty jokes. Although his plays show a wide range of comic powers, he is best known for his farce.

Publius Terentius Afer (195 or 185–159 B.C.E.) is said to have been born in Carthage, brought to Rome as a slave when a boy, educated, and freed. He wrote six plays, all of which have survived: *Andria* (166), *Mother-in-Law* (165), *Self-Tormentor* (163), *Eunuch* (161), *Phormio* (161), and *The Brothers* (160). Terence's plots are more complex than those of his predecessors, for he adapted and combined in a single play more than one Greek original, a practice for which he was often denounced. The chief interest in his works, however, does not lie in intrigue but in character and the double plots that provided him with opportunities for showing contrasts in human behavior. His sympathetic treatment of characters moves his plays toward romantic or sentimental comedy. Since he strove for consistency, he avoided inserting Roman allusions into the Greek plots upon which he drew. His language, that of everyday polite conversation, lacks the great metrical variety found in Plautus' plays. Terence was much more conscious of artistic principles than was Plautus, but he never equaled the latter's popularity.

FIG. 3.13
Wall painting from the Casa di Casca in Herculaneum showing a comic scene. At left a priestess and in the background an altar. First century C.E. From Baumeister, *Denkmaler des Klassischen Altertums* (1889).

Of the other comic writers, the most important was Caecilius Statius (c. 219–168 B.C.E.), the principal dramatist in the years between Plautus and Terence and considered by many Roman critics the greatest of all comic authors. Unfortunately, none of his plays survives. His work is thought to have combined characteristics of both Plautus' and Terence's plays and to form a transition between them. Other comic writers were Marcus Atilius, Aquilius, Lucius Lanuvinus, and Sextus Turpilius. Turpilius (d. 103 B.C.E.) is the last known writer of *fabula palliata* (comedy based on Greek originals), although his works and those by earlier playwrights continued to be performed for some time.

It is customary to distinguish comedies based on Greek subjects (*fabula palliata*) from those based on Roman materials (*fabula togata*). No plays of the latter type have survived, and only three authors—Titinius, Afranius, and Atta—are known to have written this form. Except in subject matter, the *fabula togata* seems to have differed in no important respect from the *fabula palliata;* it never attained the popularity accorded the *palliata.*

Comedy ceased to be a vital form after about 100 B.C.E., but the works of Plautus and Terence survived, even after the decline of Rome, perhaps because they were valued as models of spoken Latin. Since later critics turned to them as the foremost examples of comic drama, the plays of Plautus and Terence exerted enormous influence on Renaissance comedy. All of the extant Roman comedies are adaptations of Greek plays. It was long usual to declare (on no solid evidence) that Plautus and Terence departed little from the structure of the originals and that whatever changes they made were minor. We now know that this is untrue. A lengthy fragment of Menander's *The Double Deceiver,* on which Plautus' *The Two Bacchides* is based, has been discovered, permitting direct comparison between Plautus' source and his adaptation. As a result, critics have come to acknowledge that Plautus (along with Terence) was a creative adapter rather than merely a translator. Some of the changes made by the Roman dramatists are significant. They eliminated the chorus, which in Greek New Comedy divided the plays into episodes. (The division into acts found in most present-day editions of the Roman comedies was made by later editors.) Another important change is the addition of musical accompaniment to the dialogue, a feature probably reflecting the Etruscan heritage. In Plautus' plays, about two-thirds and in Terence's about one-half of the lines were accompanied by music. All of the action takes place in the street, with the result that scenes that logically would occur inside are

FIG. 3.14

A bas-relief allegedly showing a scene from a Roman comedy. From Dörpfeld, *Griechische Theater* (1896).

placed out of doors. Eavesdropping is common and many complications turn on overheard conversations.

Although Roman tragedy is treated condescendingly today, it was highly regarded by critics and audiences of the time. Nevertheless, the names of only three tragic writers between 200 and 75 B.C.E. are known: Quintus Ennius (239–169), Marcus Pacuvius (c. 220–c. 130), and Lucius Accius (170–c. 86). It is difficult to generalize about this early tragedy, since no plays survive. Judging from fragments, titles, and contemporary comments, however, the majority of the plays were adapted from Greek originals (a type labeled *fabula crepidata*), while a smaller number were based on Roman subjects (called *fabula praetexta*). They probably did not depart structurally in any important way from Greek tragedies, but they seem to have emphasized bolder effects (such as extremes of virtue, vice, horror, and noble deeds, melodramatic plots, and rhetorical and spectacular display). Although tragedy was regularly performed into the Christian era, the last tragedy clearly written with production in mind was *Thyestes* by Varius Rufus, presented in 29 B.C.E. at a festival celebrating the Roman victory at Actium.

Historians speculate that public taste coarsened to such an extent under the empire that tragedy could no longer hold its own and that complete plays ceased to be performed at the festivals, although excerpts or shortened versions continued to be presented. Nevertheless, closet dramas were written, such as *Medea* by Ovid (43 B.C.E.–c. 17 C.E.). It is possible that scenes from these later plays were recited at banquets.

FIG. 3.15
Scene from a Roman tragedy. A wall painting in Pompeii of the first
century C.E. or earlier. From Dieterich, *Pulcinella* (1897).

The only Roman tragedies that have survived are
from this later period. Of these, all but one are by
Lucius Annaeus Seneca (5 or 4 B.C.E.–65 C.E.). Born
in Spain and educated in Rome, Seneca was famous
for his works on rhetoric and philosophy and became
one of the most influential men in Rome after his
pupil Nero was named emperor in 54 C.E. He subsequently declined in favor and committed suicide
in 65 C.E.

Nine of Seneca's plays survive: *The Trojan Women,
Medea, Oedipus, Phaedra, Thyestes, Hercules on Oeta, The
Mad Hercules, The Phoenician Women,* and *Agamemnon.*
All are adapted from Greek originals. *Octavia,* sometimes mistakenly attributed to Seneca, is the sole surviving example of *fabula praetexta,* or tragedy on
Roman themes. It deals with the death of Nero's
wife, and in it Seneca appears as a character, but the
author is unknown.

Although it is not clear whether Seneca's plays
were presented in Rome's public theatres, they were
destined to become major influences in the Renaissance. Since they helped shape tragedy in the age of
Shakespeare, their characteristics are important. First,
Seneca's plays are divided into five episodes by choral
interludes only loosely related to the action. In the
Renaissance, the five-act form was to become standard, while the chorus, though reduced to a single

character, often commented on the action. Second,
Seneca's elaborate speeches, often resembling forensic addresses, were imitated by later writers. Third,
Seneca's interest in morality, reflected through sensational deeds that illustrate the evils of unrestrained
emotion and in *sententiae* (or pithy, proverbial generalizations about the human condition), is paralleled
in Renaissance drama by the use of horrifying examples of evil behavior and in moralizing ruminations on humanity. Fourth, Seneca's scenes of
violence and horror (for example, in *Oedipus* Jocasta
rips open her womb and in *Thyestes* the bodies of
children are served at a banquet) were imitated by
later writers. Fifth, Seneca's preoccupation with
magic, death, and the interpenetration of the human
and superhuman worlds paralleled a major interest of
the Renaissance. Sixth, Seneca's creation of characters who are dominated by a single obsessive passion
(such as revenge) that drives them to their doom provided Renaissance dramatists valuable lessons in establishing psychological motivations and in creating
unified characters. Seventh, many of Seneca's technical devices, such as soliloquies, asides, and confidantes, were taken over by later authors. Thus, even
though his plays may not have been performed in
Roman theatres, Seneca was to exert enormous influence in later times.

If regular comedy and tragedy had diminished in popularity by the first century C.E., this was certainly not true with the minor forms that dominated the Roman repertory from the first century B.C.E. onward. The Atellan farce and mime performances were chief among these minor forms. Both had been presented at festivals since the third century B.C.E., although little is known of their early history, since they remained nonliterary types until the first century B.C.E. It was not until the major forms began to decline that the *fabula Atellana* and the mime were first written down.

Pomponius and Novius (writing between 100 and 75 B.C.E.) are credited with making the Atellan farce literary. At this time, the *fabulae Atellanae* seem to have been short, perhaps 300–400 lines, and to have served as *exodia,* or afterpieces, to regular drama. The Atellana emphasized rural settings, characters, and speech, while its subject matter most often involved cheating, gluttony, fighting, or sexual exploits. Its rustic atmosphere and its use as an afterpiece led many Romans to associate it with the satyr play, and Roman references to the latter form may be to the Atellan farce.

Four stock characters appeared in the *fabula Atellana*: Bucco, a vivacious, boisterous braggart; Pappus, a comic old man; Maccus, a gluttonous fool; and Dossenus, a hunchback of frightening appearance. Standardized costumes were probably worn by these figures. Consequently, many historians have traced the similar conventions of the *commedia dell'arte* of sixteenth-century Italy back to the Atellan farce. The peak of popularity for the *fabula Atellana* was reached during the first century B.C.E., and after the second century C.E. there are no direct references to it. Its place was usurped by the mime.

The first clear reference to the mime, or *fabula riciniata,* is found in Rome in 211 B.C.E., although it probably had been performed there much earlier. Under the republic, mime was associated especially with the *ludi Florales,* which honored one of the fertility goddesses and was noted for nudity and licentiousness. This festival was especially popular with the common people. Like the *Atellana,* mime was transformed into a literary type in the first century B.C.E. Decimus Laberius (106–43 B.C.E.) and his contemporary, Publilius Syrus, are usually credited with this development. Under the empire, the mime appears to have reverted to a nonliterary type, although its popularity increased until it virtually drove all other forms from the stage. The term *mime* seems also to have been used in this period to designate almost any kind of entertainment offered in the theatre. Basically, however, the mime was a dramatic form, usually short, but sometimes quite elaborate and complex in its use of spectacle and large casts. It might treat almost any subject and could be either serious or comic, but usually it dealt with some aspect of everyday life seen from a comic or satiric point of view. Scholars have tended to discuss these mimes almost wholly in terms of obscene and violent examples, although it is far from certain that these were typical. There seems little reason to doubt that extramarital affairs were frequent subjects, but some historians have assumed that because one of Rome's more depraved emperors, Heliogabalus (ruled 218–222 C.E.), ordered sexual acts to be performed realistically, this was typical throughout the empire. It is true that the mimes reflected the taste of the period, as can be seen from the numerous beatings, fights, deaths, and other forms of violence included in them. But many of the examples often cited to illustrate the depravity of the theatre actually occurred in the amphitheatres, which were always more bloodthirsty than the theatres. The mimes were especially disliked by the Christians, whose sacraments and beliefs were often ridiculed on stage. Much of the testimony about the depravity and excesses of mime comes from Christian writers seeking to undermine the theatre's appeal.

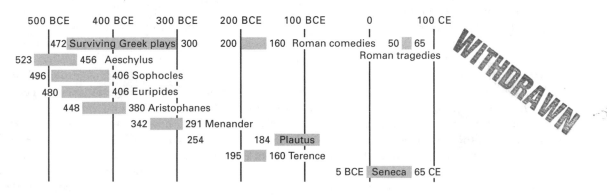

FIG. 3.16
Greek and Roman dramatists and their surviving plays.

DUCKWORTH LIBRARIES
YOUNG HARRIS COLLEGE

FIG. 3.17
Dossenus of the *fabula Atellana,* a mimic fool, or a grotesque actor of farce. Graeco-Roman bronze statuette found in southern Italy. It has been dated 300–100 B.C.E. Courtesy Metropolitan Museum of Art, Rogers Fund, 1912.

In addition to dramatic pieces, mime troupes also presented a wide range of incidental entertainment, including various feats performed on tightropes and trapezes, fire spitting, sword swallowing, juggling with balls, daggers, and other objects, stilt walking, trained animals (who sometimes performed in dramatic pieces), singing (sometimes approaching the operatic), dancing, and so on. In seeking to feed the audience's appetite for the novel and unusual, mime came to include an extremely wide range of offerings.

Under the empire, pantomime (or *fabula saltica*) was also popular. Roman pantomime was a forerunner of modern ballet for it was essentially a storytelling dance. As a form it was known in Greece as early as the fifth century, although there it usually involved two or more dancers. In Rome, it was essentially a solo dance, although there might be an assistant who was kept very much subordinate. Pantomimic plots were usually taken from mythology or history. The action of the silent dancer was accompanied by a chorus (who sang an explanatory text) and an orchestra of flutes, pipes, and cymbals. This form of pantomime

seems to have been introduced at Rome in 22 B.C.E. by Pylades and Bathyllus. Characteristically it was serious, but occasionally it was comic (a type in which Bathyllus excelled). Although the comic mode soon declined in popularity, the serious form of pantomime usurped the position formerly held by tragedy. Emperors and nobles often kept their own pantomime performers, and intense rivalries developed over the relative merits of dancers. Pantomime was also a favorite with the common people, although less so than mime, especially in late Rome.

Comedy and tragedy (or perhaps only scenes) continued to be performed during the empire, although they were less popular or frequent than mime and pantomime.

One Roman critic, Horace, was to exert influence on later theory and practice second only to Aristotle. His *The Art of Poetry (c.* 19 B.C.E.) contains advice on subject matter, characterization, language, and style. He insists that plays must be written in five acts and that they should teach and please. He especially encouraged writers to revise and polish their works to insure unity, grace, and decorum. He was to be especially influential during the Renaissance.

OTHER ENTERTAINMENTS

The theatre had to compete with several other kinds of entertainments. The oldest and most popular of these was chariot racing, supposedly introduced by the Etruscan king, the elder Tarquin (616–578 B.C.E.). These races were included among the events of several religious festivals during both the republic and the empire. Their popularity was enormous during the empire, when four main factions (or bands of supporters) engendered bitter rivalries. This pastime of the Romans continued until at least 549 C.E. Several other entertainments were given in the circuses built to accommodate chariot races. These included horseracing (sometimes with trick riding), mock cavalry battles, footraces, acrobatics, prizefighting, wrestling, exhibitions of wild and trained animals, and fights between animals or between animals and men.

Gladiatorial contests provided another kind of popular entertainment. Introduced into Rome in 264 B.C.E. as funeral games given by private individuals, they did not become a part of official state festivals until 105 B.C.E., and then only irregularly until the first century C.E. when contests were established throughout the empire. The number of combatants steadily increased. In 109 C.E. 5000 pairs were said to have appeared at one festival following a military victory. It was primarily as a place for glad-

FIG. 3.18
Terracotta plaque showing a charioteer about to round one end of the race track in a Roman circus. Courtesy British Museum.

iatorial contests that amphitheatres were built, the first in Pompeii in 75 B.C.E., and subsequently throughout the empire. As time went by, the contests became more and more elaborate; often they were accompanied by mood music and sound effects and even costume and scenic elements. Special schools trained the gladiators, most of whom were slaves. As in the mimes, novelty was demanded and captives from faraway Britain fought others from Africa or Asia. Various types of weapons and combat techniques were employed. Romans seem to have taken special delight in this game of life and death in which at least one member of each pair was always doomed unless he won the crowd's favor.

The *venationes,* or wild animal fights, were closely related to the gladiatorial contests and were also staged in amphitheatres. Wild animals seem to have been exhibited first at the Circus Maximus in 186 B.C.E., and soon afterwards they were being used to fight each other or human beings. By the middle of the first century B.C.E., *venationes* had become very elaborate. Still, such entertainments were not frequent until the Colosseum was opened in 80 C.E., when 9000 animals were killed during the 100-day inaugural program. Many of the animals seen in the arena were trained beasts who performed but did not fight. Most, however, were used in one of two ways: in wild beast hunts, during which armed bands were allowed to track down and kill animals in the arena; or as man-killers who stalked human prey. As with other entertainments during the empire, the desire for novelty led to the importation of animals from all over the world; in addition, the arenas were often fitted out with trees, hillocks, and other scenic ele-

ments to simulate some environment and the victims were often costumed accordingly. Above all other forms of entertainment, these gladiatorial contests and *venationes* earned late Rome its reputation for bloodthirstiness.

Perhaps the most spectacular of all the entertainments were the *naumachiae,* or sea battles. The first was given in 46 B.C.E. by Julius Caesar on a lake dug for the occasion; it featured a battle involving 2000 marines and 6000 oarsmen. Later the amphitheatres were sometimes flooded for such events. By far the most ambitious of all the *naumachiae* was given in 52 C.E. on the Fucine Lake east of Rome to celebrate the completion of a water conduit. On that occasion, 19,000 participants fought and many perished.

Occasionally, pale imitations of such entertainments were given in theatres, where the orchestra was flooded for miniature sea battles or water ballets, or where a few gladiators fought in the orchestra or on stage. But the theatre was ill equipped to compete with the vast arenas available in most cities. On the other hand, theatrical spectacle seems to have been imported increasingly into amphitheatres, where machinery for raising and lowering scenic elements and performers became highly developed. Furthermore, the gladiatorial contests and *venationes* seem to have been given novelty occasionally by the inclusion of entertainments approximating modern ballets with large casts and elaborate scenic effects.

Although many of the entertainments described here were not technically theatrical, they cannot be ignored in a study of the Roman theatre. Such spectacles frequently were presented in festivals alongside plays, and actors often had to compete with them. Thus it is often said that the necessity of holding an audience's attention under such circumstances

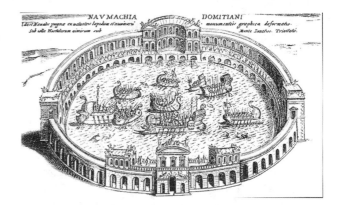

FIG. 3.19
A conjectural reconstruction made in the Renaissance of a *naumachia* of the reign of Domitian (late first century C.E.). From Laumann, *La Machinerie au Théâtre* (1897).

led to the general coarsening of theatrical fare during the empire. That the theatre was partially successful in this contest is shown by the fact that as late as the mid fourth century C.E. one hundred days were devoted to theatrical fare as compared to seventy-five days for all other types of entertainments (although it should be remembered that all the theatres in Rome combined did not hold as many spectators as the Circus Maximus alone).

PRODUCTION ARRANGEMENTS

The state festivals at which entertainments were given were under the jurisdiction of magistrates, who received a grant to cover expenses. These sums were insufficient, however, and the magistrates and their political allies usually supplied additional funds, since a well-received festival had considerable potential to forward the political careers of the magistrates. Dramatists (or their patrons) seem to have negotiated with the magistrates to get their plays selected for production. The magistrates then contracted with managers (*domini*) of acting troupes (*greges,* singular *grex*) to produce the plays that had been chosen. Under the empire, middlemen (or agents) seem to have been involved in this process. The leader of each troupe arranged for music, properties, and costumes. The plays may have been performed before the magistrates prior to public viewing, both for purposes of censorship and to ensure a high quality of performance. It is not clear whether during the republic any public notice of plays was given, but during the empire posters listed the various attractions.

Several companies normally presented plays at a festival. Each received a basic fee, but additional prizes or payments were made to companies, individual actors, and authors who especially pleased the audience. Occasional references are found to claques (people paid to respond positively or negatively to a play) and attempted bribery of audiences and officials in awarding favors. During the empire, rulers sometimes exerted considerable power over the plays, their content, and the awarding of prizes; they also often granted or withheld favors to actors. Ordinarily, however, it was the popular audience who most influenced theatrical performances. Each play was given without intermissions. Even the intervals between plays were usually filled with incidental entertainment or short mimes; consequently, performances were continuous throughout each day devoted to *ludi scaenici.*

Admission to state-supported performances was always free, and all classes attended. In his prologues, Plautus refers to women, magistrates, attendants, slaves, nurses with children, and prostitutes as being in the audience, and he indicates that there was considerable jostling for places. In some periods, special seats in the orchestra were reserved for the senators and designated rows of seats were held for the wealthy. Some tickets dating from the empire have survived, but it is not clear whether they were for the privileged few for whom seats were reserved, or whether they were required of everyone to prevent overcrowding in the theatre. The surviving tickets are quite precise in their indication of the entrance to be used and the section and level of the seat's location within the theatre.

The theatres seated thousands of persons. The capacity of the early temporary structures is unknown, but the first permanent theatre held approximately 17,500 persons. Obviously, only a fraction of Rome's population could be accommodated in the theatre at a given time, for Rome grew in size from about 215,000 persons in 200 B.C.E. to about 1,000,000 during the empire. Ordinarily, all of the plays for a festival were presented in the same theatre, but for one elaborate celebration in 17 B.C.E., three different theatres were used continuously for three consecutive days and nights.

Many spectators, though not necessarily all, were interested primarily in entertainment, and though special officials maintained order, the audience was free to come and go during a performance. Furthermore, other attractions competed for the audience's favor. The first two productions of Terence's *Mother-in-Law* were failures because at the first the audience left to see a rope dancer and at the second to watch gladiators. Spectators might also leave to buy food and drink, which were sold just outside the theatre. The audience seems to have been quick to express praise or condemnation, and since its response determined whether a troupe received additional payments, its favor was constantly sought.

ROMAN THEATRE ARCHITECTURE

The first permanent theatre building in Rome (the Theatre of Pompey) was not constructed until 55 B.C.E., almost 200 years after the introduction of regular drama, and over 100 years after the last surviving comedy was written. Consequently, as in Greece, the permanent structures date from a considerably later time than the period of significant dramatic writing.

In the third century B.C.E. there were several architectural precedents upon which the Romans could have drawn: (1) the Etruscan, (2) the Atellan, and (3) the Greek. Which of these, if any, they chose is unknown, but it seems likely that Livius Andronicus would have adapted the Greek structure for his plays, since he was most familiar with it. On the other hand, since many types of entertainment were given and a new temporary structure was supposedly erected for each festival, considerable experimentation would have been possible.

The problem is complicated by the relationship between theatrical performances and religious rites. Unlike the early Greeks, the Romans presented plays in honor of many gods, each of whom had his or her own sacred precinct in which it was considered unsuitable to dedicate offerings to any other god. J. A. Hanson, in *Roman Theatre-Temples,* concludes that "all sites for *ludi scaenici* which can be located with certainty or probability before the erection of a permanent theatre in Rome are not only connected with a temple but are further specified as in front of a temple." He also suggests that performances were always given "in sight of the god" to whom they were dedicated, and that consequently the stage was erected facing the temple, where the image of the god was set up to view the performances; but not all scholars agree with his conclusions.

The first permanent theatre in Rome had a temple dedicated to Venus at the top of the auditorium. Many historians have seen this as a sly trick to overcome the objections of the Senate to building a permanent theatre. Although this interpretation may be correct, it is also possible that Pompey (the official in charge) was following a tradition. On the other hand, there was always a group in Rome who objected to theatrical performances on grounds of decadence and expense. Some historians believe that it was as a concession to this group that no permanent theatres were erected prior to 55 B.C.E. Again, however, it may be that before this time the Senate thought it unwise to build a theatre dedicated to one god unless they were to honor equally the other gods to whom plays were dedicated, and that it was too costly to build so many permanent theatres. In any case, the permanent theatres which were begun in 179, 174, and 155 B.C.E. were never completed. Perhaps under the empire the claims of many gods and goddesses could be met by placing altars dedicated to them in the theatre, and by bringing the effigy of the one being honored into the theatre during his or her festival. It also appears that religious aspects of festivals became less important as time went by. Regardless of the reasons for the change from temporary to permanent structures, the distinctions between them should be noted.

With six festivals, each with on average 150 years of experience with staging plays by 55 B.C.E., the Romans had over 900 examples on which to base their first theatre building. It seems improbable that they were uniform in size or design. Their general characteristics are at best conjectural, but scholars who have attempted to reconstruct the temporary stages have usually made them merely flimsier and somewhat simpler versions of the later stone theatres. Disagreements among historians about the details of the temporary theatres center around such matters as the elaborateness of the stage background, the size of the stage, and the extent to which seating was provided for the audiences, none of which can be resolved.

The structures appear to have become progressively more sumptuous and detailed. In 99 B.C.E. Claudius Pulcher is said to have erected a theatre with such realistically painted details that birds tried to perch on them. Pliny the Elder (23–79 C.E.) states that Marcus Aemilius Scaurus built a theatre in 58 B.C.E. with a stage of three stories, the first of marble, the second of glass, and the third of gilded wood, the whole being decorated with 360 columns and 3000 bronze statues; the auditorium supposedly accommodated 80,000 people. Pliny also states that in 50 B.C.E., Gaius Scribonius Curio built two theatres, each on a central pivot; while the audience remained seated, the two parts were supposedly revolved to form an amphitheatre. Although modern historians seriously question their reliability, Pliny's accounts are indicative of structures sufficiently unusual and sumptuous to have become legendary by Pliny's time.

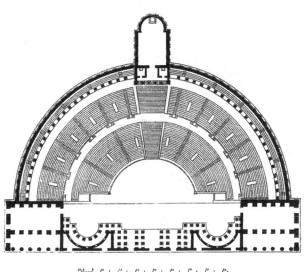

FIG. 3.20
Plan (made in late Roman times) of the Theatre of Pompey. Note the temple of Venus at top and the elaborate *scaena frons* at bottom. From Streit, *Das Theater* (1903).

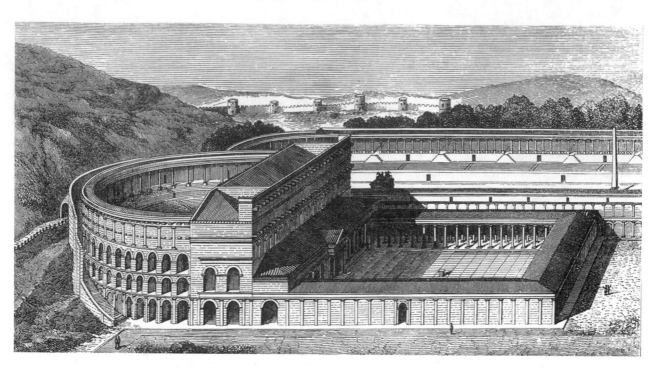

FIG. 3.21
The theatre at Orange (at left front). Note the elaborate forecourt adjoining the stage house. Note also that the theatre is built into a hillside and takes advantage of it for some entrances. Beyond the theatre is the circus. From Caristie, *Monuments Antiques à Orange* (1856). Courtesy Boston Public Library.

Considering the elaborateness of temporary theatres, it is not surprising that Pompey was allowed to erect a permanent theatre in 55 B.C.E. This theatre, which had a diameter of 500 feet, seated approximately 17,500 and had a stage 300 feet wide (the length of a football field). Before the end of the century, two others had been built in Rome: the theatre of Balbus in 13 B.C.E. (seating approximately 8000), and the theatre of Marcellus in 11 B.C.E. (seating approximately 14,000). A fourth theatre was built by the emperor Trajan (reigned 53–117 C.E.) but it was taken down by Hadrian (76–138). No other permanent theatres were ever built in Rome, although temporary structures continued to be used there and elsewhere. The empire included approximately 1000 cities, most of which had theatres, either permanent or temporary.

The permanent theatres of the empire are sufficiently similar in design to allow generalizations about their basic characteristics. Many were built on level ground, though those that are best preserved today were built at least partially on a slope as the Greek theatres were. Corridors and stairways around and beneath the auditorium allowed an efficient flow of traffic. When theatres utilized natural slopes, corridors were cut into the hillsides. A number of vertical aisles divided the auditorium (or *cavea*) into sections, while at least one broad aisle about halfway up the slope and a covered portico at the top permitted horizontal movement.

The stage house (or *scaena*) and the auditorium were joined to form a single architectural unit the same height all the way round. Thus, unlike in the Greek theatre, the spectator's view was confined within the structure. The passages corresponding to the *parodoi* were roofed over to provide corridors (or *vomitoria*) into the orchestra and auditorium. Over each there was sometimes a box reserved for the emperor or the magistrates responsible for the festival. The orchestra, an exact half circle, was usually used for seating privileged groups, especially senators, although at times it accommodated dancing, animal fights, gladiatorial contests, or water ballets.

The stage (or *pulpitum*) was raised about five feet. Its front was placed on the diameter of the orchestra circle. In theatres built before 100 C.E., a slot was provided for the curtain near the front edge of the stage; after the second century, when other means of handling the curtain were developed, the slots were filled in. The size of the stage was determined by that of the theatre, but most were very large by modern standards, being from 20 to 40 feet in depth and from 100 to more than 300 feet in length. There were from three to five doors in the rear wall, and at least one door in the wings (or *versurae*) which enclosed the ends of the stage. The plays make frequent reference to the *angiportum*, a passageway (or street) behind the facade, used to explain the offstage movement of characters.

The facade (or *scaenae frons*) of the stage house was decorated with columns, niches, porticos, and statues, and was often painted or gilded. The stage was covered by a roof which probably improved acoustics and protected the elaborate *scaenae frons*. Most of the early permanent theatres probably had straight, painted facades; but after the second century C.E., curved niches, forming deep vestibules and alcoves, were usual. This later arrangement cut into the backstage space until little more than a corridor remained. Dressing rooms and other work spaces were housed in the side wings.

The Romans were concerned with the comfort of audiences. Under the empire they perfected a system of cooling based on air blowing over streams of water. To protect the audience from the sun, awnings (or *vela*) were introduced around 78 B.C.E. Attached to masts set in two rows of corbels (or supporting projections) around the top edge of the auditorium, the awnings were brightly colored and occasionally had a scene painted on the visible surfaces. (For example, Nero had himself depicted on an awning as the Sun God driving a chariot.)

An archeological survey done in the early 1990s identified 790 known classical theatres. Three hundred and eleven were Roman theatres, 123 unclassified (the majority of which are almost certainly Roman), sixteen Greco-Roman, and 89 Gallo-Roman theatres, plus another 62 odea, most of which are also Roman. These permanent theatres were built throughout Europe, in North Africa, and in Asia Minor. A few purely Roman theatres were built in Greek areas of the empire, but the usual practice was to remodel existing Greek structures along Roman lines. In some, the *thyromata* were replaced by a Roman *scaenae frons;* some retained the high stage, but in others it was only three to five feet. To increase the depth, the Greek stage was often extended forward into the orchestra as much as twenty feet. Since many of the Greek structures had no side wings, an extra door was often placed in the rear facade at the extreme ends to give a total of five to seven doors.

OTHER STRUCTURES FOR ENTERTAINMENTS

In addition to theatres, structures were erected in Rome and elsewhere to meet the demands of other

FIG. 3.22
Reconstruction of the Roman theatre at Ostia, built between 30 and 12 B.C.E. and remodeled *c.* 200 C.E. From d'Espouy, *Fragments d'Architecture Antique,* 2 (1902).

types of entertainment. The Circus Maximus, designed for chariot races, was the oldest and largest of these structures. Laid out originally around 600 B.C.E., it was approximately 2000 feet long by 650 feet wide. At the beginning of the empire, its stadium seating accommodated some 60,000 spectators, but it was later enlarged. Its primary feature was the track that permitted twelve chariots to race abreast at the same time. But, though designed for chariots, the Circus Maximus also housed other circus games (*ludi circenses*) such as horseracing, prizefighting, wrestling, wild animals, and so on. Eventually three other smaller circuses were built in Rome, the last in 309 C.E.

The other principal type of structure was the amphitheatre, designed primarily to house gladiatorial contests and *venationes,* although occasionally *naumachiae* may have been held there. The first amphitheatre in Rome was built in 46 B.C.E., but this and its two successors were temporary structures. In 80 C.E., the Flavian amphitheatre (now called the Colosseum) was completed. Originally three stories high, it was increased to four in the third century C.E. It was then 157 feet tall, 620 feet long, and 513 feet wide and seated approximately 50,000 persons. The arena measured 287 by 180 feet. The space beneath the arena is of special interest: it housed elevators capable of raising scenic elements, wild beasts, and combatants to the arena level through an extensive system of trap doors.

SCENERY

The basic scenic background in the Roman theatre was the *scaenae frons*. In comedy, this facade was treated as a series of houses opening onto a city street, represented by the stage. In tragedy, the facade normally represented a palace or temple. Although some plays are set in the country or other open places devoid of buildings, there was probably little attempt to change the visual appearance of the stage from one play to another. As the Prologue of *The Menaechmi* says: "This city is Epidamnus during the performance of this play; when another play is performed it will become another city." The audience probably depended primarily upon the dramatists' words to locate the action. Richard Beacham has argued that several surviving wall paintings from Pompeii and elsewhere depict the stages of temporary theatres, each of which could differ in appearance.

There are, notwithstanding, a number of problems relating to the scenic background. One concerns the amount and kind of three-dimensional detail required by the plays of Plautus and Terence, whose works predate the oldest surviving theatres by over one hundred years. The question has arisen largely because of the many scenes in comedies involving eavesdropping or the failure of one character to see others who are on stage at the same time. One group of historians has insisted that three-dimensional structures would have been necessary to stage the scenes convincingly, while another insists that the conventions of the Roman stage permitted characters to see each other or not as the dramatic situation dictated. Overall, it seems likely that convention was stronger than realism in the time of Plautus and Terence.

The doors of the *scaenae frons* are of considerable scenic importance, since in comedy each may represent a different house, and since they are referred to so frequently by the characters. In tragedy, all of the doors in the *scaenae frons* were probably treated as entrances to the same building; some ancient commentators state that the central doorway was reserved for the principal personage, while the side doors were used by the lesser characters. If so, staging must have been highly conventionalized. The doors leading into the wings (*versurae*) may also have had conventionalized uses, for many ancient writers declare that one was understood to lead to the forum or city and the other to the harbor or country.

For the most part, *periaktoi* seem to have been the chief means of differentiating place. Vitruvius, writing about 15 B.C.E., states: "The *scaena* itself displays the following scheme. In the center are double doors decorated like those of a royal palace. At the right and left are the doors of the guest chambers. Beyond are

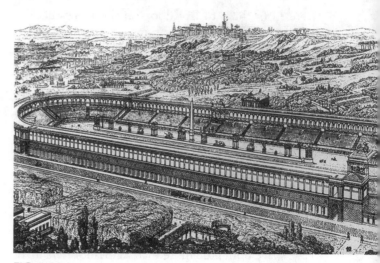

FIG. 3.23
Reconstruction of the Roman circus of Caligula and Nero, built in the first century C.E. From Durm, *Handbuch der Architektur* (1905).

the spaces provided for the decoration—places that the Greeks call *periaktoi*, because in these places are triangular pieces of machinery which revolve, each having three decorated faces." As to what was painted on the *periaktoi*, Vitruvius adds: "There are three kinds of scenes, one called the tragic, second, the comic, third, the satyric. Their decorations are different and unlike each other in scheme. Tragic scenes are delineated with columns, pediments, statues, and other objects suited to kings; comic scenes exhibit private dwellings, with balconies and views representing rows of windows, after the manner of ordinary dwellings; satyric scenes are decorated with trees, caverns, mountains, and other rustic objects delineated in landscape style." The meaning of this passage has been the subject of endless debate. The most sensible interpretation seems to be that the decoration for each type of play was conventionalized and painted on *periaktoi* placed near each end of the stage. In any case, the *periaktoi* could not have covered more than a very small portion of the vast *scaenae frons*, most of which would have remained visible. Other Roman commentators refer to sliding scenery (*scaenae ductilis*), apparently painted panels that could be moved to change the setting. It is not clear where these were mounted or how extensively they were used.

Most discussions of the stage background concentrate on the requirements for regular drama, but the permanent theatres were built after the rise to prominence of the minor dramatic forms, some of which placed considerable emphasis on spectacle. Nevertheless, we know little of the scenic conventions of these lesser types. Perhaps some clues are offered by the uses made of two types of curtains: the *auleum*,

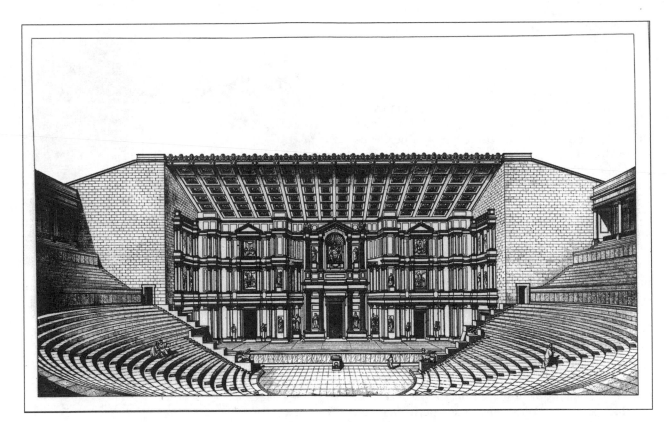

FIG. 3.24
Scaenae frons and interior of the theatre at Orange; a reconstruction of what the theatre supposedly looked like in its original state. From Caristie, *Monuments Antique à Orange* (1856). Courtesy Boston Public Library.

or front curtain; and the *siparium*, or background curtain. The *auleum* may have been introduced as early as 133 B.C.E. and was certainly in use by 56 B.C.E. Originally, it was lowered into a slot at the front of the stage by means of a series of telescoped poles. Extending the poles upward to their full height raised the curtain, while the reverse process lowered it. After the second century C.E., the curtain was suspended from overhead and raised by ropes. The front curtain was important to spectacle, for it permitted the sudden revelation of a scene or the rapid concealment of a striking tableau. Before its introduction, all characters had to be brought on and gotten offstage in full view of the audience. After its introduction, producers seem to have capitalized on the surprises and striking effects it made possible.

The *siparium* probably came into the theatre with the mime. Originally a small curtain, it may have been hung at the rear of an improvised platform to serve both as background for the action and as masking for the offstage space. Entrances were probably made through slits cut in it. As the mime grew in importance, the *siparium* increased in size and was often hung against the *scaenae frons* in the man-

ner of a backdrop. Some scholars suggest that the *siparium* was sometimes used to mask changes of painted panels set into the *scaenae frons* or erected behind door openings. They could, however, simply have served to focus audience attention on a performance that might otherwise have been lost on these enormous stages. Overall, there appear to have been simultaneous and contradictory trends toward more elaborate curtains and more elaborate permanent facades.

Many spectacular effects were achieved through the use of large numbers of supernumeraries in dances, battles, and processions. This trend toward mass effects had begun as early as the first century B.C.E., for Cicero states that at the dedication of the Theatre of Pompey in 52 B.C.E., 600 mules crossed the stage in one play and that 3000 bowls were displayed in another. Such excesses increased under the empire, when spectacle and sensationalism seem to have been among the primary goals of the theatre.

Although intricate machinery is seldom mentioned in ancient accounts, the Romans knew how to achieve mechanical scenic marvels. This machinery seems to have been developed in the amphitheatres, especially in the Colosseum, during the first century C.E., to lift the animals from subterranean spaces to the arena level. A special ministry (the *summum choregium*) was created around 100 C.E. to serve the spectacles, and a building was erected near the Colosseum to house scenic elements and properties, which could be transported as needed to the Colosseum's basement, some twenty-one feet beneath the arena, or to other sites of entertainments. Martial (c. 40–c. 102 C.E.) speaks of intricate spectacles in the Colosseum, including "sliding cliffs and a miraculous and moving wood." On another occasion, the ground repeatedly opened and a magic wood with fountains appeared and was immediately filled with exotic animals from foreign places.

Sometimes plays or pantomimes were acted out in the arenas. In one instance, a criminal impersonating Orpheus appeared from below the arena level as if coming from Hades. He played music which enchanted rocks and trees so that they moved to greet him and animals crouched at his feet; then, at the end of this display, he was torn to pieces by a bear.

In the eastern part of the empire, where spectacles were less bloody, more emphasis was placed on Pyrrhic dances (or ballet-like performances). Apuleius (second century C.E.), in his novel *Metamorphoses,* describes such a performance in the amphitheatre at Corinth in Greece. The scenery seems to have been three-dimensional and practicable, for it represented a mountain on which were shrubs, trees, a stream, grazing goats, and a shepherd. An entertainment based on the story of Paris' judgment on the beauty of Hera, Athena, and Aphrodite was enacted on the mountain. At the end, a fountain of wine sprang out of the mountain's top and the entire structure sank out of sight. There are also references to devices (*pegmata*) for flying characters or objects, but it is not clear where these were located or operated.

Although these accounts concern amphitheatres, they make it clear that Roman engineers had developed scenic devices as complex as any that would be introduced into the theatre prior to modern times.

ACTORS AND ACTING

The usual term for actors in Rome was *histriones*, although *cantores* (or declaimers) was also used. At first a clear distinction was made between the actors of regular dramas and the performer of mimes (the *mimus* or *saltator*), the latter being considered inferior. In late Rome, however, the term *histriones* came to be applied to all actors. The majority of per-

FIG. 3.25
Two Roman comic actors. Bronze figures on the cover of a third century B.C.E. box or chest found at Praeneste, near Rome. Courtesy British Museum.

formers were male, for only in mimes did women appear on stage.

The social status of the Roman actor has been much disputed. Some historians have suggested that all actors were slaves owned by company managers. Although this arrangement may have been used in some cases, it was by no means universal. Roscius (131–63 B.C.E.), the most famous of Roman actors, was certainly never a slave and was eventually raised to the nobility. Similarly, Aesopus, a contemporary of Roscius, was a member of the Optimates, a group that exercised considerable control over public affairs because of its wealth, influence, and ability. On the other hand, mime actors appear always to have been considered infamous, and many of them certainly were slaves. Occasionally emperors forced noblemen to appear on stage as a form of punishment and degradation. Overall, it seems likely that, though the social status of actors could vary considerably, the majority always ranked low in public esteem.

Little is known about the professional performers in Rome prior to the introduction of comedy and tragedy in 240 B.C.E. by Livius Andronicus, who acted in his own plays. Succeeding dramatists, however, seldom followed his practice and instead left production entirely to the professional managers. Thus, in Rome there was not the intimate connection between playwriting and performance found in early Greece. At least some Roman actors belonged to a worldwide guild, especially as the number of festivals increased in the far-flung cities of the empire, but it is not clear what the performance arrangements were.

Although there apparently were no restrictions on the number of actors that could be used on the Roman stage, the extant plays could have been performed by a company of five or six actors, if doubling was practiced and supernumeraries used occasionally. Troupes may have been much larger, however, for no information about their size during the republic has survived. In the first century B.C.E., as the regular drama declined, emphasis shifted to the "star" performer. Many stars amassed fortunes, and under the empire they had followings not unlike those of

FIG. 3.26
Female mime performer or dancer. In her hands she holds clappers and on her left foot she wears a footclapper. Bells are attached to her cap, skirt, and ankle. Bronze statuette, late second century C.E. Courtesy Art Museum, Princeton University.

a modern movie star. In late Rome, many of the most popular performers were tightrope walkers, trapeze artists, jugglers, sword-swallowers, fire-eaters, and dancers.

Acting style probably varied according to the dramatic form. In comedy and tragedy, the actors were male, wore masks, and probably doubled in roles as the Greeks had done. In tragedy, delivery seems to have been slow, stately, and declamatory; in comedy, it was conversational. Most roles required proficiency in speaking, singing, and dancing. Contemporary writers also made it clear that expressive pantomimic gesture (perhaps heavily dependent on stock attitudes and poses) was a prominent ingredient in every performance. In tragedy, movement seems to have been slow and dignified, but in comedy it was more lively, for running, beatings, and farcical horseplay of all sorts were common. Since the theatres sometimes seated as many as 17,000 persons, the actors' gestures and movements probably were considerably enlarged. They were not greatly exaggerated, however, since Roman teachers of oratory suggested actors as suitable models for imitation by public speakers. Typical human movement, gesture, and intonation appear to have been reduced to their essentials, then enlarged and conventionalized for stage use. For the most part, actors specialized in one type of drama, although Andronicus and Roscius departed from the usual practice by performing in both comedy and tragedy.

In the mimes, masks usually were not worn and consequently facial expression was important. Through much of its history, mime was in part improvised, and therefore it required a talent for the invention of dialogue, business, and movement. Mime actors seem to have been selected either for their physical beauty or comic ugliness, for the plots most typically revolved around sexual desirability or some grotesquerie. In the second century B.C.E., the companies were probably very small, with perhaps no more than three or four members; but under the empire they included as many as sixty performers, although many of these were acrobats and variety entertainers. In the first century B.C.E., a school for mime actors was operating in Rome.

In pantomime, the emphasis was on the solo performer. Noted for their handsomeness and athletic qualities, these actors depended entirely upon gesture and movement to portray a series of characters and situations. Many were renowned for the subtlety and complexity of their portrayals at a time when tragic acting had become increasingly exaggerated.

In addition to the public performers, there were a number of private troupes in late Rome. These were probably composed of slaves kept by emperors and rich men to provide entertainment for their households and friends.

MASKS AND COSTUMES

Masks apparently were used in the Roman theatre from the very beginning. All of the cultures that influenced Rome—Etruria, Greece, southern Italy—had used masks in their entertainments, and thus it seems unlikely that the Romans would have rejected an accepted convention of the forms they borrowed—Greek comedy and tragedy, Atellan farce, and Etruscan dances. The use of masks also made the doubling of roles much easier and simplified the problem of casting characters of identical appearance, as in Plautus' *Menaechmi* and *Amphitryon*.

Masks were made of linen and, with the attached wig, formed a complete covering for the head. It is usually assumed that Roman masks for comedy and tragedy resembled those used in the Hellenistic theatre. The masks for pantomime had closed mouths and according to Lucian (second century C.E.) were much more natural than those for tragedy, which were much exaggerated. Quintilian, writing in the first century C.E., refers to masks with one cheerful and one serious side, apparently an attempt to indicate a change of emotion without a change of mask.

FIG. 3.28
Ivory statuette showing a tragic actor, c. second century C.E. Note the distorted mask, high headdress, and thick-soled boots. Some scholars believe it represents a Greek actor of the Hellenistic period, but it is more likely Roman. From Baumeister, *Denkmaler des Klassischen Altertums* (1889).

FIG. 3.27
Masks for Terence's *Andria*. From a ninth century C.E. manuscript now in the Vatican. Courtesy Biblioteca Vaticana.

Mime actors did not usually wear masks, and, as mime increased in popularity under the empire, the use of masks in the theatre became less common.

Costumes varied with the type of play. Comedy based on Greek life (the *fabula palliata*) followed the costuming conventions of Greek New Comedy, for which everyday Athenian dress was adapted. Similar principles probably governed the costumes for comedies based on Roman life (the *fabula togata*), in which Roman garments were substituted for Greek. In this case, the Roman tunic was the usual garment over which the cloak, or toga, was worn.

The costume for tragedy was also based upon Greek practice. The *fabula crepidata* (or tragedies on Greek themes) probably followed the conventions of the Hellenistic Greek theatre, although some scholars have suggested that it was Roman influence that led to the extreme stylization of dress in late Greece. Regardless of the direction of influence, it seems likely that Greek and Roman tragic costumes were similar. For the *fabula praetexta* (or tragedies on Roman subjects), costumes probably followed the conventions of the *fabula crepidata*, except that Roman garments were used as a basis. The toga with a purple border (the *toga praetexta*) was sufficiently typical that the dramatic form took its name from it.

It is usually assumed that each of the four stock characters of the *fabula Atellana* had his own standardized mask and costume and that these remained the same from one play to another. Since most of the other characters were rustics, their costumes were probably exaggerated versions of country dress. Some of the known titles of Atellan farces refer to doctors, musicians, painters, fortune tellers, and fishermen, each of whom may have been indicated by costume.

The pantomime performer wore a long tunic and cloak that allowed freedom of movement. As a variation on tragedy, pantomime probably used a less exaggerated version of tragic dress. Nothing is known of the costume for comic pantomime, the popularity of which was short-lived.

Mime actors wore the tunic as a basic garment, but their most distinctive accessory was the *ricinium*, or hood, frequently used for purposes of disguise. Some mime characters, probably the fools, wore the *centunculus*, or patchwork jacket, and had shaven heads. Others represented fashionable and sophisticated men and women who, like modern film stars, were dressed lavishly in the latest fashions.

MUSIC

Although music was not highly valued by the Romans, it was used, perhaps because of Etruscan influence, more extensively in Latin than in Greek plays. Up to two-thirds of the lines of Plautus' plays were accompanied by music, and it figured only slightly less prominently in the works of other authors.

As with Greek music, we know little of the Roman modes. The accompaniment used in the theatre seems to have been composed by each troupe's own flute player, although probably he merely played suitable mood music. One reference from the first century B.C.E. suggests that the accompaniment was so conventionalized that the audience could tell what kind of character was to appear by listening to the music. Thus, it may have resembled the more trite musical scores of our motion pictures. That the musicians were valued, however, is indicated by records

FIG. 3.29
Musicians shown on a mosaic in a villa in Pompeii. Some scholars interpret it as a choral interlude in Greek New Comedy but it is as likely an entertainment of another type. The musicians perform on double flute and percussion instruments. From Fiechter, *Die Baugeschichte des Antike Theaters* (1917).

which list their names immediately after that of the principal actor.

The music for plays was performed on a "flute" with two pipes, each about 20 inches long, that was bound to the performer's head to leave his hands free to work the stops. The flute player was on stage throughout performances and supposedly moved about to accompany first one character and then another.

The musical element in pantomime was more elaborate than that for regular drama, for it required an orchestra of flutes, pipes, cymbals, and other percussion instruments. It is also likely that the music for mimes became more extensive during the late empire as the performances became more spectacular and ornate.

THE DECLINE OF THE THEATRE IN ROME

In terms of numbers of performances, theatres, and spectacular display, the Roman theatre reached its height during the fourth century C.E. Although it continued as a publicly supported institution for another two hundred years, it had already encountered difficulties that were eventually to overwhelm it.

One source of opposition was the rising Christian church. At first the new sect was very weak and, as it came to popular attention, met considerable opposition on political as well as religious grounds. Its adherents refused to place allegiance to the state

FIG. 3.30
The division of the Roman Empire into East and West.

285 Empire first divided East/West by Diocletian

307 Empire reunited under Constantine

331 Capital moved to Constantinople

395 East/West division becomes permanent after several attempts at reunification

above the dictates of religious teachings, insisted that other gods were false despite the Roman tradition of accepting all gods out of a desire to offend none, and perhaps more importantly, refused to worship the emperor as a god. Romans, on the other hand, were willing to accept the Judeo-Christian god as another deity but were unwilling to abandon all others. The intractability of the Christians resulted in the decision of the emperor to stamp out the new religion as a subversive element in the state.

In spite of persecution, the power of Christianity gradually increased. Constantine (emperor, 324–337) first made Christianity lawful, and in 393 Theodosius I made the profession of any religion other than Christianity unlawful. After about 400 C.E., therefore, some of the excesses of the theatre abated and state festivals ceased to be given in honor of the pagan gods, but by that time the Roman populace considered theatrical entertainments one of its fundamental rights and thereby ensured their continuance. Gladiatorial contests were abolished in 404, however, and *venationes* in 523 C.E.

The theatre was a favorite target of the Christians for at least three reasons. First, it was associated with the festivals of pagan gods. Second, the licentiousness of the mimes offended the moral sense of the church leaders. Third, the mimes often ridiculed such Christian practices as baptism and the sacrament of bread and wine. As a result, the break between church and theatre was inevitable. Tertullian (*c.* 150–*c.* 220 C.E.), the North African theologian, denounced the theatre in his *De Spectaculis,* arguing that Christians forswore the theatre when they were baptized. From about 300 C.E. on, church councils sought to dissuade Christians from attending performances, and in 398 the Council of Carthage decreed excommunication for any Christian who went to the theatre rather than to church on holy days. Actors were forbidden the sacraments of the church unless they forswore their profession, a decree not rescinded in many places until the eighteenth century.

But church opposition seems to have had no decisive effect on the Roman theatre. Alone, the Christians perhaps would not have succeeded in prohibiting performances. But two other forces were at work: the decay of the Roman Empire from within, and pressures from barbarian tribes from without. The sense of loyalty to the state which had been the strength of the Roman Republic was increasingly undermined after the second century C.E. as military and governmental bureaucracies took over all functions and made citizen concern irrelevant. Furthermore, the soldiers and bureaucrats were increasingly recruited from remote provinces that had little interest in the capital city. To simplify administering its vast territories, the empire was also divided into two parts which by 400 C.E. were almost completely independent of each other; Rome remained the capital in the West, but Constantinople had become even more powerful as the center of the eastern empire, which was more stable and wealthier than the West.

The internal weakness of the West made it difficult to withstand invasions by barbarian tribes there, and by 410 C.E. the Visigoths had sacked Rome itself. When the capital was taken again in 476, the last emperor to hold Roman citizenship was deposed, and thereafter it was ruled by foreigners. Consequently, some historians use 476 to mark the end of the western empire, although the conquerors sought to continue it, for they were not so much interested in destroying as controlling it. Nevertheless, the Roman Empire rapidly disintegrated, and by the sixth century C.E. its western half had lost all semblance of unity.

During the fifth and sixth centuries, however, the foreign rulers, like their predecessors, found it expedient to support the theatre, and after each upheaval theatrical performances were resumed. Theodoric (the Ostrogoth who ruled Italy from 493 to 526) even restored the Theatre of Pompey. But during the sixth century order crumbled. The last definite record of a performance in Rome is dated 549. The theatre may have persisted, but it does not seem to have survived the Lombard invasion of 568, after which state recognition and support of theatrical performances definitely ceased. Thereafter, the theatre in the western territories returned to the obscurity out of which it had emerged some 900 years earlier.

THEATRE IN THE EASTERN EMPIRE, BYZANTIUM

Although by the sixth century C.E. the western Roman Empire had disintegrated, the eastern part remained and flourished. Thus, after the fall of Rome the center of power shifted once more to the Hellenized areas of the eastern Mediterranean. In actuality, these areas had always been the most sophisticated parts of the empire, for though Rome was the center of power, the Hellenic territories were more advanced in terms of culture, manufacture, and trade, and Rome depended much on the East for its learning, luxuries, and crafts.

The East began to assume a dominant role politically in the early fourth century C.E. after Diocletian divided the empire into two parts to simplify its administration. In 330, the Emperor Constantine moved the capital of the entire empire to a city he had built on the Bosporus, Constantinople. After 395 the division of the empire into East and West became permanent. Consequently, the Byzantine Empire (as the eastern part came to be called) is considered by

FIG. 3.31
Eastern mimes of the eleventh century. Fresco in St. Sophia in Kiev (Ukraine). Redrawn and published in *Sapeski Emperatorskago Archaeologishago Obshchestva*, n.s. 3 (1903).

many historians to date from this time, though others prefer to identify its beginnings with the fall of the western half of the empire in 476.

The rulers of the Byzantine Empire thought of themselves as Romans and considered their government a continuation of the Roman Empire. They viewed the territories in the West as temporarily lost to invaders or usurpers, and from time to time sought to regain them. Under Justinian (527–565) much of the West was retaken, but Byzantium became and remained primarily an eastern Mediterranean power. Justinian was also the last of the emperors to speak Latin, and thereafter the official language of the empire was Greek.

Between the time of Constantine and Justinian, the empire was converted into a Christian state. In Byzantium the emperor assumed leadership in religious as well as secular affairs and came to be considered God's regent on earth. He appointed all major church officials and took an active part in settling doctrinal differences, which were numerous and intense. This subordination of church to state (especially during times when the Byzantine Empire was ruled by empresses), along with disputes over the authority of the Bishop of Rome (the Pope), became a source of controversy so great that after 1054 the church permanently broke into two parts: Roman Catholic and Eastern Orthodox. The latter prevailed in most of Eastern Europe, Russia, and Asia Minor, and the former in the rest of Europe. To this schism can be attributed many of the differences in outlook and culture between Eastern and Western Europe down to the present time.

The Byzantines considered themselves the defenders of Christian territories from the encroachment of others. With Islam's rise and territorial expansion from the seventh century onward, the Byzantine Empire came under increasing pressure. Eventually Byzantium appealed to western Christians to aid in holding or recapturing the holy lands of the eastern Mediterranean. To meet this challenge, the West launched six "crusades" between 1096 and 1229. Unfortunately, the Westerners respected Byzantine Christians no more than they did Muslims, and in 1204 they took Constantinople itself and divided its territories. Although the empire was reestablished in 1261, it never regained its former strength, and in 1453 it fell to the Turks, who refashioned Constantinople into their own capital, the present-day Istanbul.

THE BYZANTINE THEATRE

Byzantium was merely another phase in a continuous history reaching back through the Romans and Alexander the Great to the world of classical Greece. Although it was self-consciously Christian, the Byzantine Empire was also proud of its Greek heritage, which it sought to preserve even as it denied the pagan gods and myths that had shaped it. The results were a paradoxical mixture of cultures, for though Christianity was intertwined with almost every aspect of religious and civic life, Byzantine popular entertainments resembled those of late Rome. In turn, Byzantine scholars scorned the popular theatre and devoted their attention to the drama of classical Greece. Thus, Byzantine theatre has three main aspects: popular, religious, and scholarly.

It is difficult to assess the extent and nature of Byzantine theatre because the surviving evidence is so slight and historians cannot agree on how the evidence should be interpreted. Nevertheless, it is probable that theatrical performances continued throughout the Byzantine period.

Originally, Constantinople is said to have had two theatres of the Roman type, and at least one survived into late Byzantine times. The empire also included most of those eastern Mediterranean territories in which Hellenistic and Greco-Roman theatres had been built. Unfortunately, we know little about what went on in these theatres. According to one account, the comedies of Menander were still being performed at Antioch (in Syria) as late as the fifth century C.E. Most records, however, suggest that the fare resembled that of late Rome: mime, pantomime, scenes or recitations from tragedies and comedies, dances, and variety entertainment of all sorts. It is not always clear if the performances being referred to took place in theatres or in circuses or amphitheatres.

The center of secular entertainment in Constantinople was the Hippodrome, modeled after the Circus Maximus in Rome and designed primarily for chariot races. Two factions much like modern political parties grew up around the races there. Perhaps this explains why the Hippodrome was also used as a forum, for the emperor often addressed the people and issued proclamations there. It was, in effect, the city's chief place of assembly. Entrance to the Hippodrome was open to all male inhabitants regardless of class or occupation; a token was required for entrance but no charge was made. Estimates of the Hippodrome's capacity range from 40,000 to 80,000. In addition to chariot races, *venationes* were also held there, and sometimes political prisoners were tortured, executed, or forced to fight in gladiatorial contests. Religious processions, such as the major one on Palm Sunday, also made use of the Hippodrome. Theatrical entertainments can be added to these activities, for the intervals between chariot races were filled with perfor-

FIG. 3.32
Ivory diptych *c.* 517 C.E. showing Byzantine entertainments. At left, trained horses (above) and mime scenes (below); at right, animal baiting. Courtesy Bibliothéque Nationale, Paris.

mances by mimes, acrobats, dancers, and miscellaneous acts of all sorts. Some festivals were devoted entirely to team sports intermingled with variety performers.

Entertainments were also given in places other than the Hippodrome or theatre. Mimes, acrobats, and ceremonial dancers appeared at banquets given by the emperor on state occasions; revels of various sorts were features of urban festivals; and wandering performers played at rural festivals and wine harvests. Foreign visitors to Byzantium often reported their amazement and delight at the variety and skill of its entertainments, which exceeded anything then known in Western Europe.

But though performers may have been plentiful, they seem to have been considered disreputable. The state denied actors many civil rights. Churchmen often denounced them, and in 692 the Trullan Synod sought to have all mimes and theatrical performances banned. According to ecclesiastical rules, both professional entertainers and anyone who married them were to be expelled from the church. The ambivalent attitude toward the theatre is perhaps best summed up by noting that, despite all reservations, performances were included in state festivals, and the emperor, who was head both of state and church, blessed the participants with the sign of the cross from his box in the Hippodrome. After a time, the church seems to have ceased trying to abolish theatrical entertainments and contented itself with prohibiting them on Saturdays and Sundays and denying performers the church's sacraments.

Some have suggested that the theatrical impulse in Byzantium was satisfied by the numerous church ceremonies with their rich vestments and accessories. Religious celebrations were especially elaborate during the Easter season, when the events of Christ's last days were recalled in processions that wound through the streets from one church to another to the accompaniment of responsive singing.

Where scholarly opinion divides, however, is on the question as to whether the Byzantines developed a liturgical drama. The view that drama was sometimes performed as a part of church services is based on a number of surviving homilies (or sermons) with dialogue sections (always involving episodes from the life of Christ or the Virgin Mary). Those favoring dramatic performance argue that some of these dialogues were so long (about thirty lines) that it would have been difficult for one person to deliver them effectively and that they must either have been acted or chanted responsively. Since they date from the period prior to the ninth century, some scholars think these homilies exerted direct influence on Western liturgical drama, which emerged in the tenth century. Such views remain theories, however, for there is no evidence to show how or if the dialogues were performed or that they influenced Western practices.

In addition to homilies, a few other pieces of evidence relating to religious drama have survived. One is a play, the *Christos Paschon* (or *Christus Patiens*), formerly thought to date from the fourth century C.E. but now assigned to the eleventh or twelfth

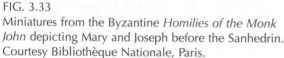

FIG. 3.33
Miniatures from the Byzantine *Homilies of the Monk John* depicting Mary and Joseph before the Sanhedrin. Courtesy Bibliothèque Nationale, Paris.

century. Most scholars agree that it is a closet drama not intended for performance. Mingling material about Christ's death with classical elements, it begins: "Now in the manner of Euripides, I will the Passion tell which saved the world." About one-third of the 2640 lines are paraphrased from Euripides' tragedies. Overall, the play is perhaps most interesting as a demonstration of the Byzantine desire to reconcile Christianity with the classical heritage.

Another drama from the East, a passion play in ten scenes or episodes, has also survived. Estimates of when it was written range from the tenth to the fourteenth century. There seems little doubt that it was staged, but the manuscript comes from Cyprus during the period when it was governed by Westerners, and therefore many scholars argue that it was imported from Europe, where religious drama was by then flourishing.

Still another argument that religious plays were staged in Byzantium is based on a tenth-century account by Liudprand of Cremona, a bishop sent by the German ruler Otto as an ambassador to the Byzantines. In his report, Liudprand tells of performances he saw in Constantinople. It is often stated

that he describes a play in which the prophet Elijah was flown up to heaven, thus proving that religious drama was highly developed in Constantinople. But other scholars now argue that Liudprand's account has been misinterpreted and that he was objecting to the performance of mimes during a religious festival honoring the ascent of Elijah to heaven. On the basis of such evidence, it is impossible to know whether the Byzantines had a religious drama.

Regardless of what one concludes about Byzantine performances, Constantinople is important in theatre history for another reason: its preservation of classical Greek manuscripts. Byzantine scholars were interested in classical drama, especially during the final centuries of the empire. When Western powers ruled Constantinople itself from 1204 to 1261, many important manuscripts were sent to Europe. When Constantinople fell in 1453, many of the remaining scholars fled to the West taking with them the last of the manuscripts on which our texts of the Greek plays are based. Without the efforts of these scholars, many Greek plays would have been lost forever.

To sum up, then, it seems clear that theatrical entertainments persisted throughout the 1000-year history of the Byzantine Empire. Nevertheless, no indisputably Byzantine plays intended for performance have survived and our records concerning entertainments are so sparse that they render suspect any firm conclusions about the nature and extent of Byzantine theatre. Still, from what remains we gain glimpses that suggest a rich theatrical life and even more intriguing possibilities that Byzantine practices may have played a role in the revival of Western drama. That it would have been possible for Byzantium to influence Western Europe is clear, for communication and trade between the two never ceased. Without question, Byzantine art influenced Western church architecture and motifs in the early ninth century. The Crusades also increased contacts between East and West beginning in the eleventh century. But despite the obvious opportunities, it is impossible to prove direct influence on Western theatre. Nevertheless, Byzantium probably kept alive a theatrical tradition, and some parts of it may have affected later artists.

THE RISE OF ISLAM

The Byzantine Empire finally succumbed to the forces of Islam (the Muslims or Mohammedans). The Moslem world had expanded rapidly after the

FIG. 3.34
Turkish shadow puppets. Courtesy Puppentheatersammlung,
Munich Stadtmuseum.

teachings of Mohammed (570–632 C.E.) began to
be accepted around 622. In the century following
his death, Mohammed's followers conquered all of
North Africa and penetrated into Europe through
Spain as far as France before they were finally halted
in a battle at Tours in 732. They also spread
eastward into Persia and northern India, and
eventually as far as present day Indonesia and the
Philippines.

The early Muslims had great respect for learning:
they founded many universities; they preserved and
transmitted much of the heritage from Greece, Persia, and Egypt to succeeding generations; and they
made many contributions of their own to medicine,
philosophy, mathematics, and geography. Because of
their far-flung territories, they were the medium
through which many oriental inventions—such as
paper and the magnetic compass—reached the West.
They created a brilliant and graceful civilization be-
side which Western Europe in the eighth and ninth
centuries seemed barbarous and Byzantium backward.

In a history of theatre, however, Islam is largely a
negative force. It forbade artists to make images of
living things because Allah was said to be the only
creator of life and to compete with him was considered a mortal sin. Thus, Islamic art remained primarily decorative rather than representational. The
prohibitions extended to the theatre, and consequently in those areas where Islam became dominant

advanced theatrical forms were stifled. Storytelling
survived almost everywhere, and in some places a
crude folk drama persisted. In other areas, especially
India, Indonesia, Turkey, and Greece, shadow puppets became popular. But these puppets were kept
as nonrepresentational as possible. They were two-
dimensional cut-outs made of translucent leather and
manipulated with sticks. Furthermore, usually only
their shadows—projected on a cloth by the light of
lanterns or torches—were actually seen. In several
countries shadow puppetry became a highly developed art.

In Turkey, shadow puppets seem to have been introduced around the fourteenth century. After the
fall of Byzantium, they became the principal theatrical form in areas that had formerly seen performances in the great classical, Hellenistic, and
Greco-Roman theatres. In these areas, the puppet
plays revolved around Karagoz and his farcical adventures (which could be pointedly satirical and topical). Eventually these entertainments came to be
called Karagoz, and have survived under that name
to the present day.

In other areas, still other means were found to circumvent the prohibitions, but all tended to avoid direct representationalism. Thus, while the Moslems did
not obliterate theatrical activities in their territories,
they did discourage them and in most instances succeeded in confining them to minor forms.

LOOKING AT THEATRE HISTORY

Since the interests or unconscious assumptions of writers inevitably influence their view of events, students of history should learn to recognize the biases of historical accounts. The theatre during the Roman era, more so than in most periods, has been especially subject to prejudicial views, partially because since the early nineteenth century there has been a tendency to praise the Greeks at the expense of the Romans. Thus, the Greeks are almost always treated reverently and seldom are their shortcomings acknowledged; on the other hand, the Romans are usually treated condescendingly and their strengths acknowledged only grudgingly. For example, Roman comic dramatists were long treated as mere adapters of Greek works (which were almost invariably pronounced superior to the Roman adaptations), although, since so few fragments of the Greek comedies adapted by Romans survive, it may well be that the Romans improved on the originals. Such prejudices are so deeply ingrained in modern thought that it is difficult to obtain a balanced view of Roman theatre from works written during the past two centuries. This problem is not confined to treatments of Greece and Rome, for there is a widespread tendency to take some aspect (often the sensational or what is so out of the ordinary as to stand out) and convert it into the typical. In this way, the best or most unusual or most shocking may be converted into the representative.

The following excerpts are from two accounts written about the Roman theatre in the second century C.E. In the first the author, seeking to persuade Christians to avoid the theatre, makes all that he dislikes typical. In the second, the author, concerned with showing the superiority of pantomime as a theatrical form, makes all that he likes typical. Both eventually acknowledge that there is another side, but each dismisses the deviations as insignificant or insidious.

> . . . [D]emons, . . . with the purpose of attracting man away from his Lord and binding him to their own service, achieved their purpose by granting him the artistic talents required by the shows.
> . . . Christians are forbidden the theatre . . . where . . . the best path to its god's favor is

the vileness of the Atellan gestures or the buffoon in woman's clothing . . . in His law it is stated that the man is cursed who attires himself in female garments; what then must be his judgment on the pantomime, who is trained up to play the woman! . . . Granted you have in the theatre pleasant things both agreeable and innocent in themselves, even some excellent things . . . , [for to accomplish his purposes] the devil puts into his deadly draught things most pleasant and acceptable stolen from God. . . .

From Tertullian, *On the Spectacles*, c. 200 C.E.

Other entertainments of eye or ear are but manifestations of a single art. . . . The pantomime is all-embracing. . . . The performer's art is as much intellectual as physical: there is meaning in his movements; every gesture has its significance . . . he must be a critic of poetry and song, capable of discerning good music and rejecting bad. . . . So potent is his art that the licentious spectator is cured of his infirmity by seeing the evil effects of passion, and he who enters the theatre in sorrow leaves it serenely. . . . Pantomimes cannot all be artists; there are ignorant performers who badly bungle their work.

From *The Works of Lucian of Samosta*, c. 125–180 C.E.

One of the difficulties facing anyone seeking to envision a performance in a Roman or Greek theatre is that of scale. For the most part, we are used to relatively small theatres and tend to place considerable value on intimacy between actor and audience. But to get some sense of a Greek or Roman performance, we would do well to think of the performance space in terms of a football stadium or sports arena rather than the indoor theatres we know. Even a very large indoor theatre in our time usually holds no more than 3500 people, whereas a Greek or Roman theatre might be five times as large. This difference in scale is crucial, since it cannot help but affect conventions and performance modes.

Students can learn a great deal about interpreting historical evidence by examining personally some of the primary sources on which certain interpretations have been based. When they do, they often find that some interpretations are very questionable. One good example of how sources can be used to extend conclusions beyond those supported by the evidence is found in interpretations of the following passage:

Also on the twentieth [of July] on which day the capricious Greeks celebrate the ascension of the Prophet Elijah with scenic plays, he [the emperor] ordered me to come to him . . .

From *Legatio Liudprandi ad Nicephorum Phocam,* trans. Barbara Spear. (The date referred to by Liudprand is 968 C.E.)

Some scholars have seen in this sentence a clear indication that dramas were staged inside Byzantine churches (even though the place of performance is not mentioned) and that elaborate machinery was used to fly Elijah up to the church's dome (even though neither the content of the plays nor their staging is described). The most that one can reasonably conclude, however, is that on Elijah's feast day plays were performed.

4
European Theatre in the Middle Ages

Beginning in the fourth century C.E., general disorder increased in Western Europe, and gradually towns and industry decayed and long-distance trade diminished to a trickle. Wars, famine, and disease depopulated many areas and large tracts of tilled land returned to forest. As civil authority decreased, the church began to fill the gap with its own hierarchically organized bureaucracy. From the fourth century onward, the Bishop of Rome, claiming to be the successor to St. Peter, asserted his precedence over all other church officials in the West, and gradually Rome's primacy was acknowledged both in church governance and in doctrinal matters. But during the sixth and seventh centuries the church's power decayed considerably as education declined and as formerly pagan groups (who clung to many of their beliefs and rites) were incorporated into it. By this time, European society consisted primarily of three groups: a great mass of peasants who tilled the soil, and over them two kinds of lords, secular and ecclesiastical.

The arts held a precarious foothold in this insecure world. Building in stone almost ceased, and art objects were intentionally kept small so they might be transported easily in times of upheaval. Illuminated manuscripts, containers to hold the remains of saints or other sacred objects, articles used in church ceremonies, and various kinds of jewelry were the prin-

cipal outlets for artistic expression. The writings of the period were primarily hymns, sermons, and similar theologically oriented works. Latin became merely a literary and ecclesiastical medium, whereas in everyday life local dialects, the forerunners of the modern European languages, were the norm.

The major preservers of learning in this period were the monasteries. From the beginning of Christianity, those seeking to lead especially holy lives had abandoned society to live under the simplest possible conditions. In Europe such people often banded together, and eventually buildings (or monasteries) were constructed for them. Because they were looked upon as especially holy places, monasteries were relatively immune from the violence of the times. As oases in a turbulent world, they became the primary repositories of manuscripts and learning. For several centuries the monastic schools were the only ones of consequence in Western Europe.

In the eighth century, Europe returned to greater stability under the Carolingian kings. The progenitor of this line, Charles Martel, defeated the Muslims at Tours in 732, primarily through his innovative use of armored horsemen as the principal military force (thus initiating what would develop into the tradition of knighthood). The most important ruler from this line was Charlemagne (reigned 768–814), who extended his realm eastward into Slavic territories (forcibly converting non-Christians on the way) and southward to Spain and into Italy. In Rome on Christmas Day in 800, Charlemagne was crowned by the Pope, who pronounced him the legitimate successor to Constantine. This was the first attempt to establish what would later (from 962 to 1806) be called the Holy Roman Empire, ostensibly the continuation of the original Roman Empire. As the one who bestowed the crown, the Pope also asserted his precedence over all secular princes.

The arts revived somewhat under the reign of Charlemagne. He promoted learning and sought to increase literacy among the clergy. His palace school was the first major center of learning outside of monasteries. While in Italy, Charlemagne visited the Byzantine churches that had been built by Justinian at Ravenna, and upon his return to Aachen (Aix-la-Chapelle) erected a chapel modeled on one of them. This was one of the first important stone structures built in Western Europe after the fall of Rome. It also opened a period of Byzantine influence on Western religious art.

Unfortunately, Charlemagne's empire rapidly disintegrated following his death in 814. Not only did his descendants fight among themselves, but they were also unable to withstand a new menace from

FIG. 4.1
Europe in 1096 C.E.

the north: the still-pagan Vikings (later Normans). Just as the Muslims had come to control the Mediterranean, the Vikings controlled the northern seas, from which they launched devastating raids. Once more Europe broke into small units isolated from each other and the world at large. Gradually a system took shape that is usually called feudalism, the societal pattern that underlay early medieval culture.

Historians usually divide the Middle Ages into stages. In the earliest of these (*c.* 900–*c.* 1050) life was still relatively simple, for towns and industry had not yet revived. During these years two patterns were established. Under manoralism, the basic unit was the *manor* (or large estate) whose owner assumed absolute authority over the serfs or peasants who worked his land collectively. Under feudalism, the lords of manors were usually the *vassals* (or subjects) of some greater lord, and he in his turn was the vassal of a king or ruler of a state. Vassals were bound to supply their lords a specified number of knights upon demand, and the lords in return were bound to protect their vassals. This arrangement was the origin of the various ranks and titles of nobility, many of which persist to the present day.

THE THEATRE, 500 TO 900 C.E.

The theatre also began to revive during the early Middle Ages. Following the disintegration of the Roman Empire, organized theatrical activities had virtually disappeared in Western Europe as conditions returned to a state similar to the period that preceded the emergence of drama in the sixth century B.C.E. Nevertheless, theatrical elements survived in at least four different kinds of activities: the remnants of the Roman mimes; Teutonic minstrelsy; popular festivals and pagan rites; and Christian ceremonies. The theatre was to emerge again from these wellsprings during the early Middle Ages.

After the Western Roman Empire crumbled and the state ceased to finance performances, the mime troupes had broken up. Small nomadic bands seem to have traveled about thereafter, performing wherever they could find an audience. For the most part they became storytellers, jesters, tumblers, jugglers, rope dancers, and exhibitors of trained animals. None of the surviving records indicate that they were giving dramatic pieces, although it is possible that they presented crude sketches. Such performers were most common in southern Europe, which had been most fully Romanized. From the beginning they were denounced by the church, which branded them infamous and sought to make them outcasts. In the ninth

FIG. 4.2

Miniature showing a trained horse. From *Li Romans d'Alixandre,* a manuscript from *c.* 1340. Courtesy the Curators of the Bodleian Library, Oxford.

century they seem to have been especially active, for the number of church edicts against *mimi, histriones,* and *ioculatores*—terms used interchangeably for all secular performers—are most numerous at the time.

In northern Europe (in Germanic or Teutonic territories) where Roman influence had been slight, another type of performer—the *scop*—flourished from the fifth to the seventh or eight centuries. The *scop* was a singer and teller of tales about the deeds of Teutonic heroes. As the principal preserver of the tribe's history and chronology, he was prized and awarded a place of honor in society. His songs and stories were major features of feasts and other great occasions. After the Teutonic tribes were converted to Christianity during the seventh and eight centuries, however, the scop was denounced by the church. From the eighth century onward, the once honored scop was classed with mimes and like them was branded infamous.

There were also numerous festivals throughout Western Europe. Itinerant, as well as local, entertainers often came to these celebrations and took their place among other events. Most of these festivals were outgrowths of centuries-old pagan rites. The church made slow headway against such festivals, for many of the people were only nominally Christian, having been forcibly converted or merely enrolled as Christians when their rulers were converted. Not surprisingly, many pagan rites persisted, and some of their elements found their way into Christian ceremonies.

Some of the pagan rites were related to the midwinter solstice and sought to revive the year spirit or the waning sun by bringing evergreens indoors, by lighting bonfires or torches, or by wild, ecstatic dancing (often involving costumed demon figures who were routed). Perhaps even more common were the spring fertility rites. They might involve dancing around the phallic maypole or going about fields with ceremonial carts carrying fertility symbols, statues of gods, or young men and women crowned with flowers. Many of the ceremonies symbolized the struggle between life and death or summer and winter, and often took the form of fights with swords or staffs, wrestling, racing, or other athletic events. Overall, there were a large number of strongly entrenched festivals with many performative elements.

The church, in seeking to convert Western Europe to Christianity, usurped many of the existing festivals. For example, the date of Christ's birth was not fixed as December 25 until the fourth century. Some historians argue that this date was chosen to displace the pagan winter festivals that clustered around that time of the year. Similarly, Easter is said to have been located to replace the spring fertility festivals. Other festivals may have been created to replace those honoring local pagan deities; often a festival was assigned by the church to that area's patron saint and a church honoring him or her was built on a site previously dedicated to some pagan god. Thus, existing festivals were permitted to continue but were reoriented. Nevertheless, some pagan rites survived and some eventually became entertainments after their religious significance was forgotten. For example, the sword dance and the Morris dance, popular entertainments in the sixteenth and seventeenth centuries, appear to be secularizations of rituals relating to the year spirit.

As time went by, the rites of the Christian church also became more elaborate, and liturgical drama was

FIG. 4.3
Figures wearing animal masks suggestive of rituals or entertainments of the early Middle Ages. Miniatures from *Li Romans d'Alixandre, c.* 1340. Courtesy the Curators of the Bodleian Library, Oxford.

ultimately to emerge out of these elaborations—and within the church itself—during the tenth century. This final step, however, was merely a culmination of innovations that can be traced back into preceding centuries.

THE LITURGICAL DRAMA

By the early Middle Ages the church had two kinds of services: the Mass and Hours. The Mass was divided into two parts: the introduction and the sacrament of bread and wine. The introduction was largely devotional and included readings from the Bible, prayers, sermons, and psalms; it varied from day to day according to the church calendar. The second part, the sacrament of bread and wine, varied little, for it was the central and unchanging focus of worship. The importance of the Mass discouraged innovations; consequently, few dramatic episodes were ever attached to it. (It is perhaps worth noting, however, that some scholars have argued that the Mass itself is a drama.) The services of the Hours were far more significant in the revival of drama, for they included no indispensable act. Since they were variable in content from day to day, the Hours could accommodate drama more easily than the Mass, and most church playlets eventually were performed at these services. By the tenth century there were eight Hours services each day: Matins, Lauds, Prime, Terce, Sext, Nones, Vespers, and Compline. Since lay Christians could not attend nine church services daily, the Hours were associated primarily with monastic orders.

The church calendar also provided an incentive toward dramatization because it commemorated particular biblical events on specific days of the year. By the tenth century a number of theatrical elements had been incorporated into these annual celebrations in an attempt to vivify them. For example, Palm Sunday was usually observed with an elaborate procession in which a figure representing Christ riding on an ass moved from outside the city to a church. On Good Friday, a cross was often wrapped in burial clothes and placed in a symbolic tomb, from which it was raised on Easter Sunday. Similar ceremonies commemorated other events of the Christian year.

Symbolic objects and actions—church vestments, altars, censers, and the pantomime of the priests—constantly recalled the events which Christian ritual celebrates. Certain emblems had also come to be associated with specific biblical characters (such as "the keys of the kingdom" with Saint Peter and the dove with the Virgin Mary), making it easy to identify these characters and also providing a basis for conventionalized costumes in the plays. Thus, there were extensive sets of visual signs that could be used to communicate with an audience that was largely illiterate.

In addition, a type of dialogue existed in the church's antiphonal songs, whose responses were divided between two groups or between an individual and a group. By the end of the sixth century these choral portions of the services had been arranged in Pope Gregory the Great's *Antiphonarium* according to their appropriateness for specific days of the church calendar.

By the ninth century, the musical portion of church services had become extremely complex and had motivated the introduction of tropes (or interpolations into an existing text). These first took the form of lengthened musical passages, originally of the final syllable of Alleluia. Eventually these extended melodies became so elaborate that words were added, one syllable for each note, as an aid to memory. Although the origin of this practice is obscure, it is associated especially with the monastery at St. Gall (in Switzerland) under Notker Balbulus (*c.* 840–912). By the early tenth century tropes were being used in many choral passages.

Liturgical drama has traditionally been traced to tropes inserted into the Easter service. The oldest extant Easter trope dates from about 925. It reads in its entirety:

Angels:	Whom seek ye in the tomb, O Christians?
The three Marys:	Jesus of Nazareth, the crucified, O Heavenly Beings.
Angels:	He is not here, he is risen as he foretold. Go and announce that he is risen from the tomb.

This text, found in the introductory portion of the Easter Mass, was probably merely antiphonal (that is, sung responsively by two groups) and probably did not involve actors impersonating the characters.

It is unclear just where church music-drama first appeared. Monasteries at Fleury and Limoges in France are often suggested as likely places of origin. But the earliest extant playlet, complete with directions for its performance, is found in the *Regularis Concordia* (or *Monastic Agreement*) compiled between 965 and 975 by Ethelwold, Bishop of Winchester (England). Although it has usually been assumed that Ethelwold was merely adopting practices already established on the continent, this is by no means certain. At this time, monasteries were being revived in

FIG. 4.4
The three Marys encounter the angel at the tomb. From the *Benedictional* (*c.* 965–975) of Ethelwold, Bishop of Winchester, England. Courtesy Trustees of the British Museum.

England after a long period of civil disorders, and the *Regularis Concordia* was designed to establish uniform practices and to encourage a sense of purpose and order in England's monasteries. Ethelwold probably introduced liturgical drama as a device to stimulate and educate the monks. Regardless of where liturgical drama originated, it was widespread before the end of the tenth century.

In addition to liturgical dramas, a few nonliturgical plays have survived from this period. At about the time when liturgical drama was coming into being, Hrosvitha (*c.* 935–973), a canoness at the monastery of Gandersheim in northern Germany, wrote six plays modeled after Terence's comedies but using religious subjects. According to her own account, she was drawn to Terence because of his style, but fearing the adverse influence of these pagan works, she set out to provide a suitable alternative. There has been considerable disagreement over whether her plays—*Abraham, Callimachus, Dulcitius, Gallicanus, Paphnutius,* and *Sapientia*—were performed in her time. They were first published in 1501 and subsequently had considerable influence on religious and didactic plays of the sixteenth century. These

plays have a special place in theatre history for a number of reasons: Hrosvitha is the first known female dramatist; she is the first identifiable Western dramatist of the postclassical era; and she provides us with the oldest extant feminist perspective in drama. She was followed by Hildegard of Bingen (d. 1179), a Benedictine abbess, who wrote a Latin play, *Ordo Virtutum* (*c.* 1155), featuring a struggle between personified virtues and forces of evil. Nuns continued to contribute to theatre throughout the period (Katherine de Sutton, abbess of Barking, was producing theatre in England in the late fourteenth century), but most restricted themselves to more traditionally religious plays.

It was the emerging liturgical drama, nevertheless, that set the tone for what was to follow. In the beginning, liturgical plays were performed almost entirely in the Benedictine monasteries. They flourished especially at Limoges and Fleury (in France), St. Gall (in Switzerland), Richenau (in Germany), and Ripoll (in Spain).

The full development of liturgical drama, however, did not occur until the second phase of medieval civilization (*c.* 1050–*c.* 1300). By the middle of the eleventh century the Vikings had been converted to Christianity and had ceased their plundering. Conditions had become sufficiently stable that town life began to revive and industry and trade were able to flourish. This revival was rapid and felt throughout Europe. Sizable cities arose, many of them independently governed, and as they gained power manorial feudalism declined. Contacts with the Byzantines and Arabs greatly increased because of trade and the six crusades that were launched between 1096 and 1229. These contacts greatly enlarged political, intellectual, and artistic horizons.

As confidence grew, monumentally scaled buildings increased in number. Earlier, fortified castles had begun to be built, and a few sizable churches had been erected. But large-scale buildings did not become common again until the eleventh century. Churches erected prior to about 1150 were in the Romanesque style, using the Roman arch as the primary form. Perhaps the most famous church of this type was at Cluny (France), completed around 1100 and measuring 415 feet by 119 feet. In the middle of the twelfth century the Gothic mode, with its pointed arches and buttressed walls, came into being, first with the church of St. Denis, just outside Paris, in 1144. Thereafter the Gothic style rapidly replaced the Romanesque, and by 1300 monumental churches, richly decorated with statuary, carvings and stained glass, had been built throughout Western Europe.

Schools grew up around these cathedrals and, along with universities, which began to be created in the twelfth century, soon displaced monasteries as the primary seats of learning. After the cathedrals were built, liturgical dramas also began to be performed in them, and thus they became more accessible to laymen than when they had been performed in monasteries. Religious drama continued to be performed primarily within churches—whether cathedrals or monasteries—until about 1200, when occasionally it began to be presented out of doors. Although liturgical plays continued to be performed in some churches until the sixteenth century, after 1200 they ceased to play a significant role in the development of the theatre.

Liturgical drama spread as far east as Russia and from Scandinavia in the north to Italy in the south. The most prolific areas were France and Germany. In Spain (except in the northern part which had been liberated about 800) the Muslim occupation prevented the spread of drama there. Because the number of surviving liturgical plays is so great, it is sometimes forgotten that a single church probably performed no more than one or two each year and that many never performed plays. Therefore, though a dramatic revival was underway, plays remained rarities almost everywhere.

The length and complexity of liturgical plays differed considerably from one area to another. Some of the simplest extant works date from the fifteenth century, while some of the most elaborate had been written by the eleventh century. Consequently, no clear pattern of development can be traced. Although several historians have argued that the plays grew in length and complexity through the gradual addition of new episodes, this is not necessarily true, for complex plays may have been written as soon as the desirability of dramatization was accepted.

The oldest and most numerous of existing plays (more than 400) deal with the visit of the three Marys to the tomb of Christ. The most elaborate Easter dramas date from the thirteenth century. One of these, found at Klosterneuberg in Germany, includes the following episodes: after the burial of Christ, Jewish high priests ask Pilate to set a watch over the tomb; Pilate agrees and the priests lead Roman soldiers to the tomb and give them money; while the soldiers are keeping guard, an Angel appears and strikes them to the ground; the Marys stop at a perfume seller's stall to purchase ointments and then proceed to the tomb, where they discover that Christ has risen; the soldiers revive and report the news to the priests, who bribe them to declare that the body has been stolen; Mary Magdalene reports the news to Peter and John, who rush to the tomb; Mary Magdalene meets Christ disguised as a gardener; Christ is led by two Angels to the gates of Hell, which he forces open to free the imprisoned souls; the Marys and apostles proclaim the resurrection of Christ. Despite the number of events, there are only about 200 lines of dialogue in this play. It is long, nevertheless, in comparison with most liturgical dramas.

The crucifixion was rarely dramatized. Only a few plays on this subject have survived. The earliest comes from Montecassino (Italy) around 1150. It begins with Judas' betrayal of Christ and continues through the crucifixion. As it has survived, it includes twelve scenes (320 lines of dialogue), but apparently other scenes are now missing. Two other crucifixion plays are contained in the *Carmina Burana,* a thirteenth-century manuscript collection of plays and poems discovered at the monastery of Benediktbeuern in Germany. The longest treats several events in the life of Christ and ends following the crucifixion, the point at which most Easter plays begin.

Next to Easter, the Christmas season prompted the greatest number of dramas. Few, however, treat the nativity itself; those which do are simple. On the other hand, there are many plays about the Three Kings (performed on January 6), some of which include Herod's rage and his massacre of the children. A few separate plays dramatize this "slaughter of the Innocents," commemorated on December 28.

FIG. 4.5
Hrosvitha's *Abraham and Maria*. From the first published edition of her plays (1501).

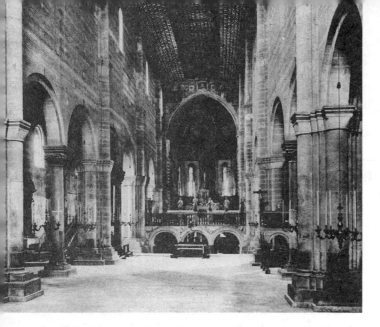

FIG. 4.6
Interior of St. Zeno's, a Romanesque church built in Verona (Italy) in the twelfth century. Note the raised apse and the crypt beneath it. This photograph was made around 1910. From *Romanesque Art in Italy* (1913).

Another popular drama of the Christmas season was the Prophets play. Unlike other liturgical plays, it was derived from a nonbiblical source, a sermon of the fifth or sixth century (inaccurately attributed to St. Augustine throughout the Middle Ages) that sought to convict the Jews of error in their dealing with Christ by summoning their own prophets. The witnesses were called one by one, each speaking his prophecy concerning Christ. In the extant plays of this type, the number of characters vary from two to twenty-eight, and in some plays such pagan figures as Virgil and the Sybil appear. Most of these Christmas plays were short and most were associated with particular days of the church calendar. Only one surviving work, found in the *Carmina Burana,* unites all of the episodes of the Christmas story into a single drama.

Although Easter and Christmas plays are by far the most numerous, others dramatized a wide range of biblical materials: the Raising of Lazarus, the Conversion of St. Paul, the Wise and Foolish Virgins, Pentecost, Isaac and Rebecca, Joseph and his Brethren, Daniel in the Lion's Den, and various events in the life of the Virgin Mary. The most elaborate play of all is the *Antichrist,* dating from the twelfth century. Based upon the prediction that before the second coming of Christ a deceiver will appear and attempt to subvert Christ's mission, its scenes are set at places ranging over the known world, and its battles and other complex episodes are so nu-

merous that some scholars have doubted that it was ever performed.

THE STAGING OF LITURGICAL DRAMA

A number of staging conventions used in the church would remain standard throughout the Middle Ages. The playing area had two basic components: small scenic structures (variously called mansions, *sedes, loci,* or *domi*) and a generalized acting area (the *platea,* playne, or place). The mansions served to locate the scene and housed any properties required. But since the action could not be performed within the limited space provided by the typically small mansions, the actors appropriated as much of the adjacent floor area (the *platea*) as they needed. Mansions were arranged around or along this neutral floor space, and the performers moved from one mansion to another as the action demanded.

The earliest liturgical plays required only one mansion, but more complex plays used many mansions dispersed about the church. The individual mansions varied considerably in size and complexity. For example, a simple altar sometimes represented the tomb of Christ, but in some of the great cathedrals imitations of the "true sepulchre" in Jerusalem, large enough for several persons to enter at once, were used. A few mansions housed elaborate and numerous properties (especially those for the Last Supper, Nebuchadnezzar's fiery furnace, Daniel's lion den, and Isaac and Rebecca's kitchen), and some had curtains so that characters or objects might be revealed at the right moment or concealed at the end of an episode. The choir loft was sometimes used to represent high places or Heaven, while the crypt (usually located beneath the main floor) often served for low places or Hell. Flying machinery was also used at times to pull the star ahead of the Three Kings, to lower a dove for the Annunciation, or to create flames for Pentecost. That this machinery grew to be extremely elaborate in some churches is established by Bishop Abraham of Souzdal's account of liturgical plays he saw performed in Florence (Italy) in 1439. In one, showing Christ's Ascension into Heaven, the actor portraying Christ was raised upward by means of ropes and pulleys to be engulfed in simulated clouds and then united with God and the Angels in Heaven (a platform located some 50 feet above the church floor).

The costumes for these dramas were usually church vestments, to which were added realistic or symbolic accessories. Female characters usually wore dalmatics (a type of enveloping robe) with the hoods pulled up to cover their heads. Angels were signified by wings attached to the church vestments. The prophets and the Three Kings were sometimes given elaborate nonclerical garments, and symbolic properties were often used to identify personages.

In most cases, the actors were members of the clergy or choir boys, although in the thirteenth century some roles may have been taken by wandering scholars or schoolboys. Much of our knowledge about the staging of plays comes from the rather detailed prescriptions contained in the church manuals of the period. More space in these manuals is often taken up with stage directions, especially those concerning movement, pantomime, and tone of voice, than with lines of dialogue. As long as the plays were performed in the church, the majority of lines (all in Latin) were chanted rather than spoken, and the acting in general was probably more schematic than realistic.

THE FEAST OF FOOLS

Although most of the performances in the church were serious and devotional, an element of buffoonery crept into some plays associated with Christmas. During this season a number of days were assigned to the minor clergy, who conducted the church services, staged processions through the town, and often collected gifts or exacted payments. St. Stephen's Day (December 26) was given over to the deacons; the Feast of the Holy Innocents (December 28) to the choir boys; and the Feast of the Circumcision (January 1 or alternatively January 6 or 13) to the subdeacons.

One of these festivals—the subdeacons' revelries, commonly called the Feast of Fools—was especially important in the development of comedy. The festival's appeal lay in the inversion of status that allowed the lesser clergy to ridicule their superiors and the routine of church life. Much of this is reminiscent of earlier pagan festivals, and many scholars have linked the Feast of Fools with pagan rites. Although such practices may not have been typical, at times during this feast the celebrants rang the church bells improperly, sang out of tune, wore strange garments and masks, and used puddings, sausages, and old shoes as censers. The Feast of Fools was presided over by a "bishop fool" who assumed ecclesiastical authority on festival days. It is not clear when this celebration began, but it was well established by the end of the twelfth century, and efforts to suppress it were not wholly successful until the sixteenth century. The festivities were accompanied by much revelry, some of which passed over into licentiousness. Sometimes plays were staged as a part of the occasion and a certain amount of burlesque and comedy probably crept into the liturgical plays in this manner. Although extensive development of comic episodes had to await the separation of drama from the liturgy, the Feast of Fools undoubtedly influenced the development of comedy both in religious and secular plays.

The choir boys' celebrations, commonly known as the Feast of the Boy Bishop, included some of the same inversion of status found in the Feast of Fools, but it was much more sedate and restrained. Perhaps for that reason, it encountered little opposition. On the other hand, it probably had little influence on the development of drama.

By 1300 liturgical drama seemingly had developed as far as it could within the confines of the church, and consequently plays began to be given out-of-doors. Although liturgical plays would continue to be presented in some churches for another 300 years, they would undergo no significant change. However, innovations were to come in nonliturgical drama.

THE LATE MIDDLE AGES

Not until the late Middle Ages (c. 1300–1500) were performances of religious plays commonly given outside of churches. But once the innovation was made, many productions became extremely elaborate, often extending over several days and drawing on the re-

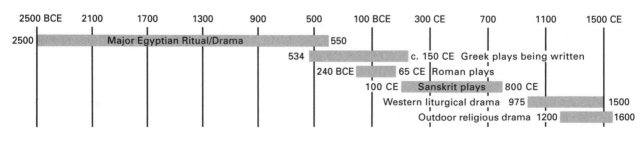

FIG. 4.7
Major periods of drama, 2500 B.C.E.–1500 C.E.

FIG. 4.8
Europe during the late Middle Ages.

sources of the entire community. As in Greece and Rome, the theatre became once more a cooperative effort of church, state, and citizens.

The flowering of drama in the late Middle Ages can be traced in part to economic and political changes that had occurred during the high Middle Ages (*c.* 1050–1300), especially the formation of guilds and the growth of towns. Guilds originated during the eleventh and twelfth centuries as protective organizations against local feudal lords and for merchants when traveling. By the thirteenth century, many craftsmen—bakers, brewers, goldsmiths, tailors, and so on—had formed organizations to regulate working conditions, wages, the quality of products, and other matters affecting their well-being. These guilds were organized hierarchically. Each was governed by a council of masters (those who owned their own shops and supervised the work of others); under each master were one or more jour-

neymen (those skilled in the trade but who worked for wages); and below the journeymen were apprentices (young men and boys who received room and board while learning a trade, usually over a period of seven years).

The rise of guilds was paralleled by the growth of towns. Originally towns were under the jurisdiction of local feudal lords, but as trade and manufacture grew the towns became sufficiently strong to win concessions, and eventually most of them became self-governing. Thereafter power resided primarily in the guilds, since they usually elected the mayor and the council from among their members.

The growth of guilds and towns brought a corresponding decline in feudalism. Kings and princes began to gain more control over subject lords, and as they did so the nations of modern Europe began to take shape. Princes were aided in this process by townsmen who contributed taxes in return for the ruler's protection and his maintenance of conditions favorable to manufacture and commerce.

The universities also played a significant part in shaping the late Middle Ages. Universities came into being during the twelfth century and soon replaced monasteries as the major seats of learning. Although not opposed to the church, universities stimulated interest in secular learning.

By 1300 the church's dominant role in society was being challenged, and throughout the late Middle Ages it had increasingly to share its position of authority with other institutions. The trend toward secular concerns was gradual but continuous. It was a time of transition and change during which medieval ideas and practices coexisted with others that would give rise to the Renaissance.

As groups other than the church gained in prominence, it was probably inevitable that they should come to participate in and eventually to dominate theatrical production. Nevertheless, throughout the late Middle Ages drama continued to be primarily religious, and the major theatrical conventions were those that had been employed within the church.

PERFORMANCES OUTSIDE THE CHURCH

Performances of religious plays outside the church seem to have begun during the twelfth century. Before the end of the fourteenth century, lengthy vernacular religious cycles (composed of many short plays or episodes) had come into being. It is usual, therefore, to consider the years between 1200 and 1350 as a time of transition during which vernacular plays assumed the position of dominance previously held by liturgical drama. We know little about the transition since so little evidence has survived. The long-accepted view was that vernacular drama came into existence through a gradual process in which individual short liturgical plays, having first been moved out of doors, were brought together to form long plays which were then translated into the vernacular tongues and performed by laymen.

Major support for this view, apart from assumptions grounded in cultural Darwinism, is *The Mystery of Adam,* a play usually dated around 1150. Its detailed stage directions suggest that it was staged outdoors but adjacent to the church (although some historians argue strongly for indoor performance). The text has three main parts: the first section concerns Adam and Eve; the second Cain and Abel; and the third is a traditional Prophet's play, in which a number of figures from the Old Testament foretell the coming of Christ. In the first two sections, the dialogue is in French, but the stage directions and choral songs are in Latin; in the final section, the scriptural passages spoken by the Prophets are given first in Latin and then paraphrased in the vernacular. It is unclear whether the actors were clergy or laymen, or where and when the play was produced. This work seems to look both backward to liturgical drama and forward to the vernacular cycles and has been used to support the theory of gradual evolution. A few other plays and fragments using vernacular languages (among them *La Seinte Resurrection,* an Anglo-Norman play of the late twelfth century; the Spanish *The Play of the Magi Kings;* and the French *Sponsus* using Provencal) have survived, but they offer scant evidence on which to base an account of theatrical tradition over a 150-year period. This lack of information is perhaps explained by conditions under which productions were no longer integral parts of church services but had not yet been taken over by secular organizations.

The traditional view of evolutionary development has been challenged by Glynne Wickham, V. A. Kolve, and many others who argue that the vernacular plays developed quite independently of the liturgical drama and that the similarity between the two types is attributable not to direct descent but to common sources—the Bible and other religious and devotional literature. Wickham believes that vernacular plays were intended to emphasize Christ's humanity in the world.

Whatever the causes, a number of significant changes occurred in the years between 1200 and 1400. First, many plays came to be staged outdoors primarily during the spring and summer months, in part because of the favorable weather but also because of the newly created feast of Corpus Christi. This festival was conceived by Pope Urban IV in 1264, was given official sanction in 1311, and was being celebrated almost everywhere by 1350. Observed on the Thursday following Trinity Sunday, it varies in date from May 21 to June 24. Corpus Christi was instituted out of a desire to give special emphasis to the redemptive power of the consecrated bread and wine. Since it honored that mystery which to the medieval mind gave meaning to existence (the union of the human and divine in the person of Christ and the promise of redemption through his sacrifice), all biblical events could be related to it without anachronism. Furthermore, if the meaning of Christ was to be made clear through drama, it seemed essential to include many events preceding Christ's birth, as well as those relating to his life, death, and resurrection. Often the Last Judgment (in which the ultimate human outcome is demonstrated) was also included. Thus, there grew up around Corpus Christi a cosmic drama which encompassed events ranging from the creation to the destruction of the world.

Obviously plays of such scope made demands in excess of those found in liturgical drama. Not bound by the restrictions of church architecture and church liturgy, the producers of the outdoor plays were able to experiment. The result was great diversity in staging during the two hundred years between 1350 and 1550.

The feast of Corpus Christi was also motivated in part by the desire to make the church more relevant to the ordinary people and their lives. Therefore, secular groups were given a role in the celebrations. Representatives of all ranks and professions (nobles, merchants, craftsmen, and churchmen) were included among those who participated in the central feature of the Corpus Christi festival: a procession through the town with the consecrated Host. Many scholars have seen in this cooperative venture the beginning of layman involvement that would eventually lead to its predominance in the staging of outdoor plays.

But if Corpus Christi supplied the impetus for presenting cyclical dramas, once established the plays did not always continue to be associated with that festival. They were given at other times, perhaps most often at Easter or Whitsuntide (seven weeks after Easter). In addition, a city might stage plays on the feast day of its patron saint, and occasionally cities gave elaborate productions out of gratitude for deliverance from a plague, drought, or other disaster.

One of the most important innovations was the abandonment of Latin in favor of the vernacular tongues. This change, in turn, led to the substitution of spoken for chanted dialogue and facilitated the transition from clerical to nonclerical actors. The adoption of vernacular languages also indicated a major step toward national and away from international drama (which Latin had encouraged).

THE VERNACULAR RELIGIOUS DRAMA

It is impossible to determine when each change in dramatic practice first occurred, but it is clear that by the late fourteenth century lengthy vernacular religious plays were coming into being. Between 1350 and 1550 the medieval theatre reached its peak. Our knowledge of it is most extensive in the late fifteenth and especially the sixteenth century, for most of the surviving evidence dates from those years. Vernacular religious drama was performed throughout Western Europe.

In the British Isles, plays were produced in 127 different towns at some time during the Middle Ages.

Nevertheless, only a few texts survive. Most of the extant English works are parts of four cycles: York (48 plays), Chester (24), Wakefield (sometimes called the Towneley Plays; 32), and the N____ town Plays (place unknown; 42). The last-named cycle is made up of three distinguishable groups of plays and perhaps were never performed together. It is often assumed that these four cycles typify English practice, but such cosmic dramas can be clearly established in only twelve English towns. It is certain that many cities never developed cycles.

The earliest English cycle dates from about 1375; others apparently date from the fifteenth century. All were performed until the mid sixteenth century. During the active life of the cycles, many individual plays were rewritten, some new ones were added, and others were dropped; consequently, the plays vary widely in dates of composition, as well as in quality. The surviving texts show the cycles as they existed at a specific time in their active production lives. In addition to these cycle plays, ten other dramas in English and three in Cornish have survived from the British Isles.

A much larger number of plays from France are extant. They range from short works to those requiring twenty-five or more days to perform. Rather than covering material from the Creation to the Last Judgment, as most of the English cycles did, the French plays are usually more restricted in time. Most end with the death and resurrection of Christ. In Germanic territories, major plays were staged at Frankfurt, Madgeburg, Tergensee, Lucerne, Alsfeld, Donaueschingen, Villengen, Bozen, and elsewhere. Spain was also very rich in vernacular religious plays. In Italy, a type of devotional drama called *laudi* developed out of a penitential and flagellant movement in the thirteenth century. Jacopore da Todi (*c.* 1236–1306) wrote more than 90 *laudi*. Originally, *laudi* were essentially narrative but became dramatic, although they included choral portions, an element that distinguishes them from their successor, the *sacre rappresentazioni,* which resembled other European religious plays and which flourished especially in Florence. Although religious drama was infrequently performed elsewhere than in England, France, Germany, Italy, and Switzerland, there is scarcely any European country in which it was unknown.

The length and scope of the dramas varied widely, but they all dealt with the same basic subject matter: God's ordering of existence as revealed in the Bible, the Apocrypha, legends about biblical figures and saints, writings of the church fathers, and collections of sermons. Consequently, regardless of where they were written, the medieval plays drew on the same subject matter.

The dramas seldom observe a clear-cut, cause-to-effect relationship among incidents. They are episodic, and there is little attempt to bridge the gaps between the short plays that make up long cycles. This loose structure probably did not bother the medieval audience, who believed that events occur because God wills them. The dramas display little sense of precise chronology, as can be seen in frequent references by biblical characters to things that happened long after their own time. Again, however, to medieval audiences temporal existence was merely a short preface to eternity, and the telescoping of past events only served to make the dramatic characters contemporary and to reinforce the message of the plays.

The religious dramas combine stylization with realism. Stylization is seen in the rhymed-verse dialogue, schematized action, minimal characterization, and mansion-settings. This stylization gives way to realism in most of the incidents that deal with miraculous occurrences, which usually depend on convincingly illusionistic details. These realistic scenes serve two purposes: they reinforce faith through their convincing actualism, and they establish the relevance of the events to the medieval world.

In spite of their essentially religious purpose, many plays contain extended comic scenes, usually involving devils, villains, or buffoons. Most of the comic episodes show human failings set against the larger framework of divine commandments, and thus they reinforce rather than distract from the plays' didactic purposes, just as they help to make the productions highly effective theatrical entertainments.

The authors of these religious plays are for the most part anonymous (as are most medieval artists). Most of those we can identify are French: Jean Bodel, author of *The Play of Saint Nicolas* (*c.* 1200); Rutebeuf, author of *The Miracle of Theophile* (*c.* 1261); Arnoul Greban, author of *The Mystery of the Passion* (*c.* 1450); and Jean Michel, author of another passion play (*c.* 1486) which incorporated parts of Greban's. (The passion play presented at Mons in 1501 was an adaptation and amalgamation of Greban's and Michel's plays.) Michel's passion play, published in 1490, was so popular that it had gone through fifteen editions by 1542. Greban (along with his brother Simon) is sometimes credited with *The Acts of the Apostles* (*c.* 1452–1478), which is said to have required forty days to perform when it was presented at Bourges in 1536.

PRODUCTION ARRANGEMENTS

Before the end of the fourteenth century, the production of plays had in most places passed out of the control of the church, although the scripts were still acceptable to church officials and were performed at religious festivals. Thus, though in most places the church gave up its direct participation, it kept an eye on the contents of the plays and their presentation.

There were many kinds of producing organizations in the late Middle Ages. On the continent, religious guilds, or confraternities, were typical producers. The members of these groups, which began to appear about 1300, were mostly laymen, although some were clergymen. These guilds undertook charitable deeds, and many presented plays.

In many parts of Britain confraternities also produced plays, but discussions of production usually concentrate on a few towns in northern England where trade or craft guilds assumed most of the responsibility. While the trade guilds were primarily designed to protect the interests of craftsmen, they retained many religious connections: each helped to support a chapel, each had a chaplain and a patron saint, and, like the confraternities, the guilds undertook charitable deeds and sometimes presented plays as their contribution to religious festivals.

Other arrangements for theatrical productions include those in which responsibility was assumed by a town, a group of neighboring towns, the clergy, an individual, jointly by town and clergy, or by a temporary society formed for the express purpose of presenting a play. Thus, arrangements differed widely, but all involved many persons working together.

The complex motives and arrangements for presenting plays are best summed up at Lucerne (Switzerland), where a passion play was presented at intervals for more than a century. Here the play was said to honor God, edify humanity, and glorify the city. The division of authority in Lucerne is revealed in these procedures: the proposal that the play be given came from the Brotherhood of the Crown of Thorns; after ratification by the city council, a public proclamation was made from the pulpit; the production was then placed under the supervision of a committee appointed jointly by the brotherhood and the city council, while the church reserved the right to approve the script.

The delegation of responsibilities and the methods of financing productions depended upon the type of organization. In northern England, the town council and trade guilds often shared the responsibilities. The council decided whether performances would be given in a particular year; it also assigned the plays to individual guilds, and demanded faithful adherence to the script; it specified fines for guilds that did not produce their plays or did not perform them well; and it chose the playing places. The majority of the work and expense fell to the guilds. The plays were supposedly assigned on the basis of appropriateness: Dramas about Noah were given variously to the shipwrights, watermen, and fishers, while the plays about the Three Kings were assigned to the goldsmiths, those showing the Last Supper to the bakers, and so on. Each guild was then responsible for providing a pageant wagon, scenery, costumes, properties, special effects, actors, and supervisors. Two small or poor guilds might be given a joint assignment. Since each play was a distinct unit and since the individual plays were performed in sequence, the entire cycle could be coordinated without difficulty.

When all episodes were performed on the same platform and when all were presented by a single organization, an entire cycle often came under the direction of one person or a small committee. Double casting, crowd scenes, and elaborate scenery and special effects also were facilitated by the fixed stage. Such centralization, however, often led to complex financial arrangements. Sometimes a city corporation might make a grant; often those cast in the play were required to pay a fee and to furnish their own costumes and properties; sometimes the local chapter of clergy might provide part of the money. In some instances, admission was charged and salvaged materials were sold after the performances as a means of recovering expenses. At Valenciennes (France) in 1547, where a cooperative society was formed to produce a play, the members raised the money and shared the considerable profits. In the East Anglia area of England, admission was almost always charged, and the profits were used for community projects.

THE DIRECTOR

Such complex productions required careful organization, since the handling of casts that sometimes included as many as 300 actors, complex special effects, and large sums of money could not be left to chance. Consequently, the director (or stage manager, or pageant master) was of considerable importance.

Still, the director's duties varied considerably from one locale to another. In the guilds of northern England, the wardens of each company were responsible to the town council for the proper staging of the plays, and they controlled finances and paid all bills. The wardens seldom did the actual work of play production, however, for normally each guild hired or appointed someone to do this job. Often this position was given to a member of the guild, but in some instances a "pageant master" was put

FIG. 4.9

The Martyrdom of St. Apollonia. A miniature by Jean Fouquet, c. 1460. The figure at center right is often said to represent the director. Note the audience and raised mansions. Courtesy Musée Condé, Chantilly.

under contract for a number of years at an annual salary. For example, at Coventry in 1454 the Smiths contracted for a period of twelve years with Thomas Colclow, who was to supply everything needed except the wagon and costumes. The pageant master secured actors, arranged rehearsals, and took charge of every phase of production. In addition, where processional staging was used, he supplied the men to move the pageant wagon from one location to another and to control crowds during the procession and the performance.

If one person directed an entire cycle on a fixed stage, he needed even more skills. Technically, a committee of supervisors (often with as many as twelve members) was usually in charge of the plays staged by confraternities, but it normally delegated its authority to one person or to a small group. At Lucerne in 1583 the committee turned over all details to the city clerk, Renward Cysat. At Vienna in 1505 much the same arrangement seems to have been used, since there Wilhelm Rollinger took complete charge. At Mons (Belgium) in 1501, four actor-managers, each with one assistant, were employed to stage the play. Some directors became sufficiently famous to be sought by many towns. After staging a cycle at Poitiers (France) in 1508, Jean Bouchet was still in demand as late as 1532. In Spain, Lope de Rueda, a professional actor-manager, was put under contract by the city of Valladolid in 1552 to serve as pageant master for the Corpus Christi festivities. In the Tyrol region of Austria and Switzerland, Vigil Raber staged plays in a number of towns during the early sixteenth century.

The director's duties were outlined by Jean Bouchet: he must oversee the erection of a stage and the placement of scenery and machines; he must find persons to build and paint scenery and to construct seating for the audience; he must ensure that all goods delivered are of the proper amount and quality; he must cast and rehearse the actors; he must discipline the actors and establish a scale of fines for those who infringe rules; he may act some roles himself; he must assign persons to take money at the entrances; he must address the audience at the beginning of the play and, after each intermission, give a resume of previous happenings and promise greater marvels in the portions yet to come. Although not all directors had to cope with so many problems, many did. Consequently, the men given such positions had to be versed in every aspect of theatrical production.

Some historians have argued that the director was always on stage during performances, following the actors about, whispering their lines to them, and giving them directions. This notion, which seems most unlikely, is based almost entirely upon one anecdote of doubtful authenticity and a painting seemingly depicting a play about St. Apollonia in which a figure with a book and staff stands in the middle of the stage. Some scholars identify this figure as the stage manager, although there seems no good reason to assume that he is not a character in the play. Considering the emphasis placed on learning lines and the fines levied against those who neglected to do so, it seems improbable that actors would have depended on the stage manager to supply each speech. On the other hand, the director or an assistant was probably in a position to give cues to actors and machinists and to prompt in an emergency.

A few records kept by directors in the Middle Ages have survived. From a play staged at Frankfurt-am-Main around 1350 we have the director's scroll (some 14 feet long) giving all the actors' cues and complete stage directions. In addition, some detailed prompt books are extant. Those most readily available are from Mons (1501) and Lucerne (1583). Nothing in these books is left to chance; every detail has been prepared and recorded. They are the work of men who were stage directors in the modern sense.

ACTORS AND ACTING

The number of actors required for productions varied considerably. In the guild cycles of northern England, many of the individual plays include no more than five to ten characters. Thus, each guild needed only a few actors, but the total number of performers in the entire cycle was considerable. When plays were mounted on fixed stages under the supervision of a single organization, casting was more complicated. For *The Acts of the Apostles,* presented at Bourges in 1536, the 494 roles were distributed among 300 actors. Most plays of this scope date from the sixteenth century and seem to mark a considerable increase in numbers of roles over earlier works.

The majority of actors were drawn from the local population. Only in a few cases can we tell how they were selected. At York in 1476, the city council decreed that four of "the most cunning, discreet, and able players within this city" were to audition all persons who wished to act. No one was to appear in more than two plays. These provisions seem to indicate that guilds did not confine casting to their own members, and that actors might perform for two different guilds. At Seurre in 1496, the mayor, assisted by three other persons, cast the play. In 1540, heralds rode through the streets of Paris appealing for volunteers. At Lucerne in 1583, requests were made from the pulpit that all those interested in acting register with the city clerk, who then chose the cast with the aid of a committee. In those instances when plays were revived, an actor might play the same role many times over a period of years.

The majority of actors were chosen from the merchant or working classes, although members of the clergy and the nobility sometimes participated. Most were men or boys, but women and girls appeared occasionally. Doubling was a common practice. At Valenciennes in 1547 the more than 100 roles were assigned to 72 actors, and at Mons in 1501 about 350 roles were cast with approximately 150 players. On the other hand, sometimes a single role required more than one actor, as when a character grew from childhood to adulthood. For scenes of violence, such as beheadings and burnings at the stake, realistic effigies were substituted for live actors.

The good faith and discipline of the actors were ensured by a number of devices. At Lucerne in 1583, actors were allowed fourteen days in which to decide if they wished to accept roles; once committed, they were bound by oath to continue. At

Valenciennes in 1547 actors were required to take an oath before a notary, in which they agreed to appear on the days of performance. Other provisions of the Valenciennes agreement are also revealing: All actors were required to accept the roles assigned them and to attend rehearsals at the specified times; each agreed not to meddle in the affairs of the supervisory committee or to grumble against their decisions. There was also a schedule of fines for missing rehearsals or for other infringements of rules. Agreements from other towns indicate that jealousies, bickering, and resignations were common, and that producers had learned by the sixteenth century to guard against them.

The time devoted to rehearsals was not great by modern standards. For example, although the play given at Mons in 1501 required four full days to perform, there were only forty-eight rehearsals. Two to five rehearsals were considered sufficient for the individual plays in the English cycles.

Something of the overall process can be inferred from the detailed records preserved from Lucerne in 1583 for a play that required twenty-four hours to perform in its entirety. Prior to the first rehearsals, a general meeting of the entire cast was held; the script was divided into twelve units for rehearsal; in addition to the regularly scheduled sessions, actors were urged to arrange other opportunities for working together privately; when the action presented unusual problems, extra rehearsals were called; changes in dialogue, action, and properties were frequently made during the preparatory period. Although the performances were given out-of-doors, rehearsals were held in a large hall. About eighty days elapsed between the first rehearsal and the performance of the play, but the total number of rehearsals is unclear.

The sponsoring organization supplied the actors with food and drink at rehearsals. If participants had to miss work, someone was paid to replace them on the job. This expense usually fell to the actors, but if they were too poor the producing group absorbed the cost.

It is uncertain whether dress rehearsals were customary. Each episode was probably prepared separately; but some plays were so long (as for example the one at Bourges, France, in 1536 which required forty days to perform) that a dress rehearsal in the modern sense would have been impossible. On the other hand, at Romans (France) in 1509, after the dress rehearsal revealed that the playing time was much too long, extensive cuts were made. At Valenciennes in 1547, in a production taking up the afternoons of twenty-five days, the actors were required to report at 7 A.M. each morning for what was obviously a rehearsal of that day's episodes.

For the long plays given on fixed stages, actors assembled as a group and then went in procession to the site of the performance. Upon arrival, they marched around the playing area before taking their places inside or near the appropriate mansions. In many instances, the actors remained visible throughout, coming forward when needed and retiring to their places when no longer required. At Lucerne, elaborate plans were made so that the actors might slip away to change costumes and to eat during the two twelve-hour performances. At Valenciennes, the players agreed not to leave the stage during the performances without permission and to accept whatever food and drink might be passed to them there. At the end of the day's performance, the actors returned in procession to the place of assembly, where they were often served a banquet.

Undoubtedly the quality of acting varied considerably. Many contemporary accounts praise certain actors lavishly, but others condemn the performers. In acting, voice seems to have been valued above all else. The chanting that had been typical in liturgical drama was abandoned in the vernacular plays in favor of a delivery based on everyday speech but formalized by rhymed verse. Since characters in the extant plays are lacking in subtlety, they did not require highly versatile performers. Most characters are stereotyped with a few clear-cut actions and emotions (such as adoration, joy, anger, or grief). Serious characters are usually restrained, but the comic roles allow much scope for improvisation and pantomime.

Attempts to be realistic occasionally exposed performers to considerable danger. At Metz (France) in 1437, the actor playing Judas almost died while being hanged; at Seurre (France) in 1496, Satan's costume caught fire. Actors in Hell scenes were often injured by the cannons and other devices used to create noise, fire, and smoke.

By the sixteenth century, a number of actors were sufficiently skilled to be employed as coaches. The extent to which professionalism had arrived is a matter of controversy. Although the majority of players were clearly amateurs, a few were paid well for performing, although even they usually had other regular trades. Nevertheless, by the end of the Middle Ages, the professional actor was beginning to be in evidence.

COSTUMES

Most characters were dressed in garments resembling those worn by their counterparts in medieval life. For example, Roman soldiers were attired in medieval armor, and Jewish high priests wore robes that recalled those of Catholic prelates. Many of the biblical characters closely associated with orthodox Christianity, though historically Jews, were dressed in Catholic clerical garb, but most other Jews normally wore clothing typical of the medieval Jew. Often, however, exotic details were added to the costumes of these historical characters to set them apart from contemporary persons. God was costumed as an emperor or pope, and angels wore church robes to which wings were attached. Supernatural characters also usually wore masks. If associated with Heaven, the masks were usually gilded. The devils were conceived most imaginatively, for they were made to resemble great birds of prey, monsters with animal heads, or creatures with scales, tails, horns, or claws. Any important character, human or divine, might carry an identifying emblem (the Archangel Michael, for instance, always wielded a flaming sword).

In most instances, actors had to supply their own costumes, unless these differed markedly from those available in daily life. Consequently, the records of producing organizations show payments only for such exceptional garments as those of devils and effigies or for accessories and emblems. Actors often incurred heavy expenses, especially when playing wealthy personages. Double casting increased the outlay, particularly in the sixteenth century when stage costumes, even for lower-class characters, were often made of rich fabrics. Occasionally, as at Chalons-sur-Marne (France) in 1507, nonparticipating wealthy citizens were required to buy costumes for actors unable to furnish their own. Other sources of supply included the clergy (who loaned or rented garments), other groups that regularly produced plays, and individuals (who occasionally contracted to outfit an entire production).

Because actors usually supplied their own costumes, supervision and coordination were needed. At Lucerne, the director gave performers detailed descriptions of the appropriate costumes for their roles. It seems likely that similar procedures were followed elsewhere. Many of these practices extended to hand properties as well. Unless an item was not readily available, it was supplied by the actor who used it. Unusual articles were made at the expense of the producers.

THE STAGES

The stages upon which the vernacular plays were performed might be fixed or movable. Fixed stages were most common, but in some parts of England, Spain, Italy, Belgium, the Netherlands, and a few other places movable stages were used. Nevertheless, because some of the extant English plays were

FIG. 4.10
Reconstruction of a performance on a pageant wagon. From Sharp, *A Dissertation on the Pageants or Dramatic Mysteries . . . at Coventry . . .* (1825).

originally related to Corpus Christi processions which made use of pageant wagons, the movable stage is often treated as typical in English staging. The traditional view has been that each play in a cycle was mounted on a wagon and on the days of performance all were presented in succession at a number of different places in the town.

This view has been challenged by scholars who have argued that the plays themselves were not presented at various places but that the wagons in the procession served much the same function as modern "floats" and that costumed characters rode on the wagons and tried in a brief pantomime to convey the essence of each play at the various stations set up for viewers. Following the procession, they argue, the plays in their entirety were presented at a single location, where the wagons served as mansions for the plays. New evidence concerning the York cycle has rather convincingly shown that processional staging was used. It is possible, nevertheless, that fixed stages may have been used for some cycle plays staged elsewhere.

No one questions that in some English towns pageant wagons played a part in the Corpus Christi (or in some places Whitsun) celebrations. Nevertheless, the appearance of an English pageant wagon is the subject of much controversy. Most modern

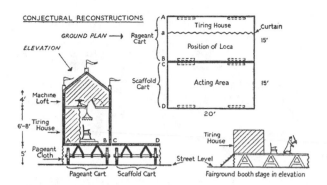

FIG. 4.11
A reconstruction of an English pageant wagon and a ground plan of the overall playing arrangement. From Wickham, *Early English Stages,* 1. Courtesy Columbia University Press and Routledge & Kegan Paul Ltd.

higher room they performed. (Another surviving version of his account states that the wagons had four wheels.)

Rogers's account, long accepted as accurate, is now questioned for two principal reasons. First, it is not certain that Rogers ever saw the plays performed. Second, the wagons, as he describes them, would be extremely cumbersome. They would be at least 15 feet tall (allowing for the wagon wheels, the dressing room space, and the scenery on the top level), but relatively narrow, since they had to be moved through alley-like streets. With the top level divided between the mansions and the playing space, the actors would have had to perform on a narrow ledge about nine feet above the street. Considering that a play such as the Chester cycle's "Last Judgment" depicts Heaven, Earth, and Hell, and includes more than twenty characters, this arrangement has been challenged as impractical. For these and other reasons, Glynne Wickham has argued in *Early English Stages* that the pageant wagon was a one-leveled structure taken up entirely by the mansions and "off-stage" space. The wagon served, he suggests, merely to provide a scenic background and dressing rooms, while the acting took place on a scaffold cart

discussions are based upon the account given by David Rogers in *A Breviarye, or Some Few Recollections of the City of Chester* (a manuscript of the late sixteenth or early seventeenth century). Rogers states that a pageant wagon was a structure with two rooms, a higher and a lower, mounted on six wheels and that in the lower room they dressed, and in the

FIG. 4.12
Denis van Alsloot's "The Triumph of Isabella," 1615. These wagons may have been similar to those used for English cycle plays. Courtesy of the Board of Trustees of the Victoria and Albert Museum.

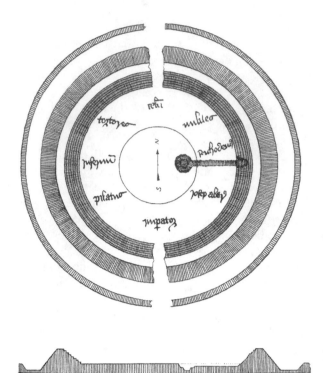

FIG. 4.13
Plan (above) and section (below) of a "round" at Perranzabuloe in Cornwall (England). This structure, which resembles those built by Vikings in Scandinavia, may have been used for dramatic performances. Superimposed on it is a circular arrangement of the mansions needed for staging one of the surviving Cornish plays. From Albright, *The Shakespearian Stage* (1909).

alongside which the wagon was drawn up. From stage directions, we know that characters sometimes used the street as a playing space.

Other evidence seems to support some parts of Rogers' description of the pageant wagon. An inventory from Norwich around 1565 includes: "A pageant, that is to say, a house of wainscot painted and built on a cart with four wheels. A square top to set over the said house." Several experiments with reconstructing performances on pageant wagons have shown that the plays can be staged effectively with scenery and acting confined to the wagon. The experiments also suggest that the most effective use of the space places the scenery at one end, using the length of the wagon as playing area in the manner of a thrust stage.

The pageant wagons were not necessarily uniform in size or design. Since a guild always performed the same play, its wagon could be built to meet its special requirements. In those rare instances when the same wagon was used by more than one

guild, the scenic needs of the plays using that wagon were very similar.

"Processional" staging was not confined to England; it seems to have been used in Belgium, the Netherlands, and especially in Spain. Apparently wagons were in use in those countries by about 1450, and they remained features of the Corpus Christi festivals through the seventeenth century. In Spain, at each playing site in a town, a platform was available, and the wagons, or *carros,* were drawn up with the narrow side touching this platform, which served as additional acting space. The scenic investiture of these plays was relatively complex, and consequently from two to four wagons were required for each of the plays. (See the chapter on Spanish theatre to 1700.)

In Europe as a whole, however, fixed stages were certainly more common than wagons. The sites of fixed stages varied considerably. At Bourges and Rome, the ancient Roman amphitheatres were

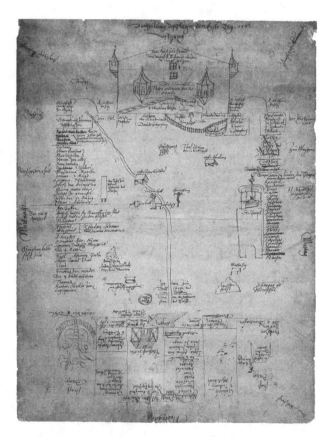

FIG. 4.14
Renward Cysat's plan for the first day's performance of the Lucerne Passion Play, 1583. At the top is the building that served as Paradise, with, at its base, the Garden of Eden. Down either side are mansions, each with a list of the characters assigned to it; at lower left is the Hell Mouth. Courtesy Bürgerbibliothek, Lucerne.

used. In Cornwall (southwest England), the "Cornish rounds" offered similar playing arrangements. (These circular earthen embankments, enclosing areas up to 120 feet in diameter, are very similar to Viking fortifications found in Scandinavia. Apparently they were not constructed specifically for the performance of plays.) Sometimes stages were erected in cemeteries adjoining churches. Courtyards of private residences (as at Valenciennes in 1547) or of monasteries (as at Romans in 1509) were used. Most typical, however, were stages set up in large public squares, as at Frankfurt-am-Main around 1350, at Mons in 1501, and at Lucerne in 1583. As these variations indicate, stages might be viewed from all sides, from two or three sides, or from one side only.

Perhaps the most typical fixed stage was a long rectangular platform set against a building or row of houses, although sometimes the stage extended down the middle of a square. Occasionally there was no platform, and the mansions were placed directly on the ground. The size of the stages also varied. At Autun (France) in 1516 the platform was about 200 feet long and 60 feet deep. At Lucerne, the playing space was irregularly shaped, being about 125 feet long but varying in depth from 80 to 60 feet.

In addition to outdoor stages, indoor platforms were used occasionally. For example, the Confrérie de la Passion in Paris played for more than one hundred years indoors at the Hôpital de la Trinité, where the stage was only about 40 feet wide.

SCENERY

As in the church, the playing space was composed of two basic elements, the mansions and the *platea,* and as in liturgical drama, the locale of a scene was established by relating it to a mansion and then extending it to include as much of the adjoining stage space as was needed by the action. This convention was observed regardless of the type of stage.

Most pageant wagons carried only one mansion, although occasionally there might be as many as three. But, though the scenic investiture of individual wagons was limited, an entire cycle demanded considerable variety, for taken altogether the wagons sometimes added up to more than one hundred mansions.

To spectators, a fixed stage undoubtedly was more impressive visually than the movable ones, because on the former all of the scenery was visible simultaneously. This convention was somewhat modified, however, by other practices. Because of their scope, many of the plays were divided into parts (or *journées*), separated by intermissions varying in length from one

FIG. 4.15
Model showing Albert Koster's reconstruction of Renward Cysat's plan for the Lucerne Passion Play, 1583. Not shown, at bottom, is another section of bleacher seating. Courtesy Theatermuseum, Munich.

to twenty-four hours. During these intervals, mansions were changed as needed; furthermore, the identity of a mansion might be altered so that during the course of a production it represented more than one location. Consequently, it is difficult to know how many mansions were actually used to depict the places named in a script. In the play presented at Lucerne in 1583, about seventy different locales are indicated, but there seem to have been only thirty-two mansions.

The scenic complexity of a production might vary daily. For a passion play at Arras (France) in the early fifteenth century, the number of mansions required by each of the four *journées* ranged from eight to fifteen. Other plays might require twenty or more mansions for a single *journée*. It was not taken for granted that the identity of mansions would be clearly evident. Therefore, the director usually appeared at the beginning of each *journée* and indicated (among other relevant information) what each structure represented. At times, descriptive labels were suspended above mansions. The stage was unframed, and one place flowed into another. Encompassing Heaven, Earth, and Hell, the medieval stage symbolized the entire universe.

The two places most often represented on the fixed stages were Heaven and Hell. Characteristically, Heaven was placed at one end of the platform and Hell at the other. It has been suggested that when an arena was used, Heaven was placed at the east and

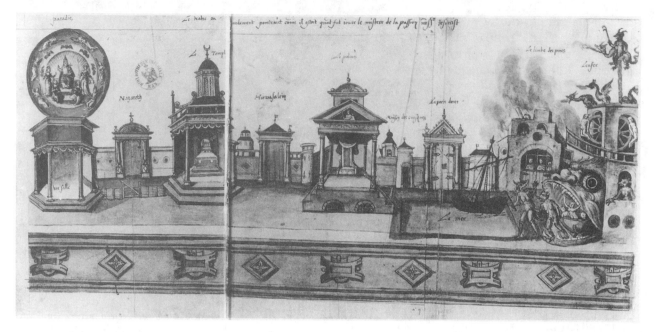

FIG. 4.16

The stage of the Valenciennes Passion Play, 1547. Note the Heaven mansion at the left and the Hell mansion (with Hell mouth) at right. The mansions between these two were changed each day as needed. Twenty-five days were required to perform the entire work. Courtesy Bibliothèque Nationale, Paris.

Hell at the west end of an axis. The earthly scenes were located between Heaven and Hell, which symbolized people's dual nature and the choices that faced them. Since Heaven and Hell were both the most important and most permanent structures, not being replaced each day, they were also the most complex.

Of all mansions, Heaven is the most difficult to reconstruct from the available evidence, for it seems to have impressed audiences with its splendor and magnificence, qualities not always evident in surviving illustrations. In the fifteenth and sixteenth centuries Heaven was usually raised above the level of the other mansions. As a rule, it was supported structurally by an "earthly paradise" (the Garden of Eden), or a room beneath it at stage level. The size of Heaven was probably large, for it often accommodated many characters. At Rouen (France) in 1474, God was accompanied by Peace, Mercy, Justice, Truth, and nine orders of angels. Sometimes Heaven included a series of intricately contrived turning spheres, and the whole was often gilded and brightly lighted with concealed torches to give the effect that golden light was emanating from it. In some instances, Heaven would open and close, and often machinery permitted angels to "fly" between Heaven and Earth, although stairs, either visible or concealed, were used in less elaborate productions. Above all, Heaven was made as inviting or awe-inspiring as possible.

Conversely, Hell was made as terrifying as possible. Just as Heaven was raised above the level of the stage, some portions of Hell were lower. At times Hell was treated as a fortified town, an especially effective device in those productions in which Christ forced open the gates of Hell to free the captive souls within. Hell was frequently divided into four parts: the Limbo of biblical prophets and others who, according to medieval doctrine, were forced to languish there until Christ's redemptive power freed them; the Limbo of infants; Purgatory; and the pit of Hell, usually placed below stage level. The entrance to Hell was at times represented by the head of a monster (the "Hell mouth") that seemed to swallow those who entered there. Fire, smoke, noise, and the cries of the damned issued from Hell, and devils sallied forth from it to seize sinners and thrust them into eternal damnation.

The mansions representing earthly places were less elaborately depicted, although their complexity varied with dramatic need. Many were equipped with curtains that could be drawn to conceal or reveal interior scenes. The structures were of many sizes and shapes. Some were hexagonal, others were square or rectangular. Some were elevated a few steps above the stage floor. Often they were furnished with beds, tables, benches, altars, or thrones. Sometimes, as at Mons in 1501, they were lavishly outfitted with tapestries borrowed from wealthy families and

FIG. 4.17
Hell mouth and the interior of hell as conceived by a medieval artist. Redrawing of a fresco in the Chapel of the Holy Cross, Stratford-on-Avon (England). From Sharp, *A Dissertation on the Pageants or Dramatic Mysteries.* (1825).

churches. A curtain representing the sky (sometimes complete with sun, moon, and stars) was often hung at the rear of the stage. Painted cloths representing clouds frequently concealed the overhead flying equipment and other devices for special effects.

Although a number of persons were required to build and paint the settings, few records pertaining to them have survived. Sometimes master artists were imported for the occasion, as at Mons in 1501. At Romans in 1509, the carpenters began work about four and one-half months prior to the performance. At Lucerne, the director of the play supervised the labor of city-employed workmen, who built the mansions, and of skilled artists, who painted the mansions, curtains, and effigies. Many other persons were required to operate the scenic effects during performances.

SPECIAL EFFECTS AND MACHINERY

Most of the realistic touches in medieval productions involved special effects. These grew in number and

complexity during the fifteenth and sixteenth centuries as the machinists' abilities to contrive seemingly miraculous events increased.

Many special effects involved "flying." The fixed stages often were set against buildings so that pulleys and windlasses could be installed on the roofs and concealed with painted clouds or sky cloths. Additional flying machinery was concealed within the Heaven mansion. Using such devices, angels passed between Heaven and Earth; Lucifer lifted Christ to the top of the temple (a distance of up to forty feet); the souls released from Limbo floated up to Heaven; and devils and fire-spitting monsters flew about the stage. In some instances, characters rose to or descended from the heavens on platforms disguised as clouds.

Other effects depended upon devices operated from beneath the stage. Trapdoors permitted sudden appearances, disappearances, and the skilful substitution of effigies for live actors in scenes of violence. In such episodes as the feeding of the multitudes through the miracle of the loaves and fish, the baskets could be replenished from beneath the stage. Concealed mechanisms allowed the fig tree cursed by Christ to wither, and fountains to spring up at a magical touch.

Water was important in many plays. One of the most notable examples is the staging of Noah's flood. For this scene at Mons in 1501 sufficient water was stored in wine barrels on the roofs of adjoining houses to produce a continuous rain of five minutes. Other scenes included Christ walking on the sea and the apostles pulling in their nets filled with fish.

In the frequent scenes of torture and executions effigies were usually substituted for live actors. In a production showing Barnabas burned at the stake, an effigy was filled with bones and animal entrails to give a properly realistic smell. In another, showing the decapitation of St. Paul, the severed head bounced three times, and at each spot a well flowed: one with milk, one with blood, and the third with water.

Many animals were required. While some could be live, others had to be impersonated by actors or by effigies. Lions kneeled to St. Denis and tigers to St. Andrew. In one play, tigers sprang up out of the earth, pursued the apostles, and eventually were turned into sheep. The Serpent appeared in the Garden of Eden to tempt Eve. In other plays there were dragons, wolves, and wild or fanciful creatures.

Transformation scenes were popular. Moses' staff changed into a snake, Lot's wife into a pillar of salt, water into wine. Light also was treated as a special effect. As a nimbus or halo, it sometimes surrounded God, Christ, and saints. Normally this was achieved by reflecting the rays of concealed torches off of gilded or highly polished surfaces. Sometimes a change from light to darkness was indicated by substituting a painted cloth depicting the sun for another showing the moon and stars. In a few plays, buildings were burned. For these, wicker structures covered with cloth were actually set on fire.

Many of the special effects required enormous skill and ingenuity. Thus, it is not surprising that by the sixteenth century accomplished machinists were in great demand. At Mons in 1501, two directors of "secrets" (as special effects were sometimes called) were imported from Chauny (France); eight master machinists were employed for a passion play at Vienna in the early sixteenth century. These persons were aided by numerous assistants who operated the effects during the performance; at Mons, seventeen were required for the Hell scenes alone.

During the sixteenth century the machinists were second only to the director in importance. They made detailed cue sheets and planned the operation of the effects as carefully as the director planned other parts of the production. The ultimate success of the plays depended much upon their skills.

MUSIC

Music was prominent in most medieval productions. Frequently it was played until the actors were ready to begin. During the plays, a chorus of angels (composed of choir boys and usually visible in the Heaven mansion) sang hymns. Angels played fanfares on trumpets to introduce God's proclamations, and the transitions between scenes were bridged with instrumental or vocal music. Most plays included a number of songs ranging from popular secular tunes sung by individual actors to religious hymns sung by groups. The names and contents of songs, however, are seldom indicated in the scripts. Singing was usually done by choir boys or actors, whereas instrumental music was played by professional musicians. At least forty minstrels were hired at Chelmsford (England) in 1562, and 156 musicians were employed at Lucerne in 1571. The musicians also kept the populace amused during the intermissions and in the evenings after the performances had ended.

Some plays (or stage directions) indicate that dance sometimes played a prominent role, but little is known about the specific dances.

AUDIENCES AND AUDITORIUMS

In most places, plays were not given every year. Even where the plays were well established, the interval between productions ranged from one to ten years.

Some of the most elaborate performances were never repeated. In those years when plays were to be given, preparations extended over a period of months, and the days of playing were holidays.

Prior to performances, various devices acquainted the public with upcoming events. Invitations were usually sent to all the surrounding towns, posters were set up at the city gates, and a few days before the performance a procession, often with actors in costume, went about the town. On the days of performance a herald rode through the city sounding a trumpet and summoning people to the play. The audiences were drawn from all classes and from both local and neighboring areas. In some places, work was forbidden during the hours of performance, and special guards were sent to protect homes and businesses against robbery.

The provisions made for spectators varied widely. In those parts of England where pageant wagons were used, a number of different viewing places were established. At York there were twelve to fifteen, at Beverley six. In most towns, performances lasted for several days. At Chester three days were required, and while York allotted only one, the performances there began at 4:30 A.M. Some scholars have argued that at York, where the cycle included some fifty plays, it would have been impossible to perform all these plays at all the stations within a single day. Not all the plays may have been presented at each festival, however, and two or more plays may have been presented as a single unit, thereby lessening the lapse of time between plays. In any case, the available evidence suggests that the presentation was completed in one day.

Spectators were probably admitted free to most English plays, but there are clear instances of fees being collected at Leicester in 1477 and a number of East Anglian locations. It has been suggested that at York charges may have been made by the persons who controlled the viewing places along the processional route, since these were assigned according to bids received. It is possible, therefore, that successful bidders erected some kind of barrier and charged admissions. Distinguished citizens probably watched from the windows of surrounding houses and scaffold seating may have been erected for lesser personages, but the lower orders probably stood. These details are entirely conjectural, however, for there is no concrete evidence about how audiences were handled for the English pageant processions.

When a fixed stage was used, all spectators had to be accommodated in one place. Structures such as Roman amphitheatres or Cornish rounds provided ready-made seating; but in courtyards or city squares temporary auditoriums had to be improvised. In some instances, arrangements not unlike those that became typical in later professional theatres were used. For example, at Romans in 1509 standing room was available near the stage, and behind this there was scaffold seating which in turn was surmounted by a series of eighty-four boxes. At Vienna in 1560, private boxes could be rented for performances which extended over several days. At Lucerne, scaffold seating surrounded three sides of the playing area, and the owners of adjacent houses probably rented space to spectators in their windows and on their roofs.

Entrance fees were not charged for many of the municipally sponsored productions. On the other hand, some productions were designed (in part) to make money. At Valenciennes in 1547, the members of the organization that produced the play divided the profits. Municipalities also sometimes charged fees in order to recover their outlay. Except when fees were charged, it is difficult to estimate attendance. If the available figures are typical, attendance was large. At Reims in 1490, 5616 persons paid admissions; at Romans in 1509, 4780 attended the first day, 4420 the second, and 4947 the third.

The hours of performance varied. In some cases, plays began about 7 A.M. and ran until 11; after an hour's intermission, they continued until about 6 P.M. In others, plays were presented in a series of afternoon performances; in still others, a production might proceed uninterrupted for as long as twelve hours. Often spectators began to take their places as early as 4 A.M., for usually seats were not reserved, except for officials, clergy, and important visitors. Sometimes children, elderly persons, and pregnant women were forbidden entry. A barrier of some kind (a ditch, a fence, water, or guards) was used to prevent the audience from getting too near the stage. Guards were posted at night to protect the stage and its furnishings.

It is clear that by the sixteenth century the producers of plays had learned to cope with many problems. They had achieved a high level of technical excellence, as well as considerable sophistication in organizing and producing plays of great scope.

SECULAR DRAMATIC FORMS

Alongside the religious stage, a less elaborate secular theatre existed and grew steadily. It emerged from many sources: mimes and entertainers of all sorts, *jongleurs* with their stories and songs, and pagan rituals. Such antecedents seem to have existed throughout Europe, but a secular drama is not evident until the thirteenth century, at about the time that religious plays were first being performed outdoors.

Among the oldest extant medieval secular drama is *The Play of the Greenwood,* written by Adam de la Halle (1240–1288) of Arras (France) in 1276/77. It mingles satirical scenes about the residents of Arras with such folk material as fairies and supernatural occurrences. Folk materials are even more evident in Adam's other work, *The Play of Robin and Marion* (c. 1283), a pastoral tale of the wooing of a shepherdess by a knight, the objections of her shepherd lover, and the eventual resolution of the conflict, followed by dances and games. Other secular plays include the English *Dame Sirith* (c. 1275–1300) and *The Interlude of the Clerk and the Girl* (c. 1300), both of which show an old woman convincing a young girl to succumb to a would-be lover.

From the thirteenth century onward, the number of secular dramas grew steadily. But, as with religious plays, the majority of the works that have survived were written after 1400. The secular entertainments of the late Middle Ages were of many types: farces, moralities, plays of the Chambers of Rhetoric, interludes, mummings and disguisings, tournaments, and royal entries.

FARCE

If the religious plays treat the triumph of virtue and the punishment of vice within an eternal order, the farces show imperfect humanity within the social order. Marital infidelity, quarreling, cheating, hypocrisy, and other human failings are the typical subjects. The clever man, even if a sinner, is usually the hero; the dupes deserve their fates because they are stupid or gullible. Sentiment is almost totally absent.

Farce can first be found in the thirteenth century. One of the oldest to survive, *The Boy and the Blind Man* (c. 1280), written in a Flemish dialect, shows how a rogue deceives a blind man through ventriloquism, then robs and beats him. The cynical tone typical of medieval farce is already fully developed in this work.

The majority of extant farces are from France and Germany. Most of them are similar in tone and form. Typically they are short (no longer than a few hundred lines), in verse, and emphasize sex and bodily excretions. The rapid and simple action uses few characters and no complicated exposition. Most of the extant French farces are mere dramatized anecdotes, but one—*Pierre Pathelin* (c. 1470)—is now considered a minor masterpiece. It tells how a lawyer tricks a merchant out of a piece of cloth and is in turn cheated out of his fee by a supposedly stupid peasant, whom he has defended on a charge of stealing

FIG. 4.18

Pierre Pathelin and his wife. Woodcut from the edition of
the play published in 1490.

sheep. The play was so popular that it had gone
through thirty editions by 1600.

Two variations on farce—*sotties* and *sermons joyeux*—
also became popular in France. Both may have appeared because of the church's attempts to suppress
the Feast of Fools, many features of which were expropriated in the fifteenth century by secular guilds
or "companies of fools" called *sociétés joyeuses.* In
some places the celebrations were taken over by the
basoches, or society of lawyers, as one of their social
activities. At other times, student groups staged a
"festival of fools," but moved from Christmas to
Mardi Gras, May Day, or the summer months. The
sermon joyeuse was a burlesque sermon, while the *sotties* were only thinly disguised political, social, or religious satires in which all the characters were fools.
The characters wore variations on the fool's traditional parti-colored garments, including a hood with
ass's ears or a cock's comb. In Paris the *sotties* were
made famous by two groups: the Basoche du Palais
and les Enfants sans Souci. Pierre Gringoire (1475–*c.*
1539) wrote the most celebrated *sotties,* among them
The Prince of Fools (1512), a satire on a quarrel between France's Louis XII and Pope Julius II.

In Germany, farce seems to have grown out of folk
festivals, especially the revels preceding Lent (thus
early German farces are often called "Shrovetide"
plays). Such plays can be found in southern Germany,
Austria, Switzerland, and Holland. But most of the
surviving farces are from Nuremberg. There plays
came to be associated with the apprentices' revels (or
Schembartlaufen) during the pre-Lenten carnival season. By around 1450 these revels, which centered
around an elaborate and often riotous procession, had
become an accepted part of Nuremberg life. As a
part of the procession, the apprentices performed
short plays that required so little background they
could be presented anywhere and repeated at various places along the way. Early writers of Shrovetide plays include Hans Rosenplüt and Hanz Folz.
By far the best known of the authors is Hans Sachs
(1494–1576).

Sachs was a shoemaker but also a master singer, a
form of artistry cultivated by the German trade
guilds. As a singer, Sachs traveled widely and learned
much about the poetry and drama of other areas.
He was the author of 198 dramatic works, of which
he classified only sixty-four as Shrovetide plays. Nevertheless, his reputation now rests almost entirely upon
his farces. Of these, one of the best is *The Wandering Scholar and Exorcist,* in which a student convinces
a man that he can call up the Devil, whom he forces
a priest to impersonate as a price for concealing his
illicit relationship with the man's wife; all bestow
money on the student—the man to reward him for
skill in exorcism, the priest and the wife to bribe him
to remain silent about their adultery.

Sachs was also able to improve the quality of performances by removing the plays from the *Schembartlaufen*. With a company of amateur actors, he

FIG. 4.19

Schembart revelers as depicted in a Schembart book of
the sixteenth century. From Vogt and Koch, *Geschichte
der Deutschen Literatur,* 1 (1887).

presented plays twice a week between Twelfth Night and Lent each year. His work marked the culmination of the medieval secular drama in Germany and established a foundation upon which a strong national tradition might have been built, had not political and religious wars interfered.

In England, farce developed within the religious plays. For example, *The Second Shepherd's Play* of the Wakefield cycle includes a fully developed farce within the framework of a nativity play. As an independent form, however, farce did not emerge in England until the sixteenth century with the work of John Heywood (*c.* 1497–*c.* 1580), whose most famous play, *Johan, Johan* (1533), tells the story of a henpecked husband who, when ridiculed by his wife and her lover, a priest, drives them both from his house, only to worry about what they may be doing elsewhere.

In all countries, the conventions used in the staging of farces deviated in no important respect from those used for religious plays. Perhaps the most notable difference lay in the economy of means demanded by the farces, for rarely do they require more than two mansions or employ any complex special effects.

THE MORALITY PLAY

The morality play is the secular form closest in tone to the cycle plays. These didactic dramas first appeared in the fourteenth century as religious plays, but were later secularized and became one of the principal links between the religious and the professional stages.

The origin of the morality play can be traced to a number of influences. First, "Pater Noster" prayers, which were divided into seven petitions, each relating to the seven cardinal virtues (prudence, justice, temperance, fortitude, faith, hope, and charity) and seven deadly sins (pride, covetousness, lust, anger, gluttony, envy, and sloth), had established a framework of continual struggle between good and evil to possess man's soul. Second, popular outdoor preachers, in applying biblical teachings to the problems of daily living, also adopted the concepts of the seven virtues and vices as a scheme for depicting the choices required of humanity. Third, literature, both religious and secular, had popularized allegory. One of the most influential of medieval works was the thirteenth century *Romance of the Rose,* a love story that included such allegorical characters as Slander, Danger, and Fair Welcome. Fourth, Christianity had become increasingly concerned with death and afterlife and was constantly admonishing people to "think upon their last

ending." In the visual arts, death's heads, skeletons, and similar devices were prominent; in drama this theme was epitomized in "The Dance of Death," in which Death summons representatives of all ranks and professions, from the pope to the lowest of peasants, in a demonstration that death is the lot of all humans, whose only hope lies in salvation.

The immediate dramatic ancestors of the moralities are probably the Pater Noster plays performed in England at York, Lincoln, Beverley, and elsewhere, although these continued to be staged long after morality plays were well developed. Many of the Pater Noster plays were presented by municipalities and trade guilds under the same general arrangements as those used for the religious cycles. At Beverley in 1469 there were eight pageant wagons, seven of which transported plays about the seven deadly sins. Unfortunately, no Pater Noster plays have survived and consequently their precise relationship to the moralities cannot be determined.

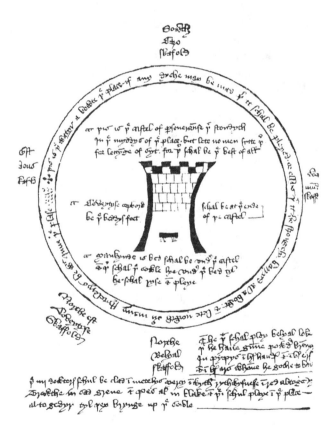

FIG. 4.20

Plan of the mansions and playing area for the *Castle of Perseverance.* In the middle is the tower of Mankind. The legend enclosed within the circles reads: "This is the water about the place, if any ditch be made where it shall be played, or else let it be strongly barred all about." The location of five mansions is indicated outside the circles.

As a distinct form, the morality play flourished between about 1400 and 1550. Although some examples have been found elsewhere, the morality was for the most part an English and French phenomenon. The oldest extant morality is a fragment of *The Pride of Life* (c. 1350), in which the King of Life displays an overweening pride, from which he cannot be dissuaded. No doubt the lost portions showed his humiliation and repentance.

In terms of staging, the most interesting morality is *The Castle of Perseverance* (c. 1400–1425), which depicts Mankind's progress from birth to death and shows the final judgment on his soul. The play is long (more than 3600 lines) and includes thirty-six characters. The manuscript provides some information about its performance. In a prologue, two heralds outline the action and declare that the play will be presented "on the green" beginning at 9 A.M. one week following the announcement. A diagram of the suggested playing arrangement is also included. It shows a circular area around the perimeter of which are placed five mansions; Mankind's castle is set in the center of the circle. Concerning the circle, a note declares: "This is the water about the place, if any ditch be made where it shall be played, or else let it be strongly barred all about." It used to be thought that the water or fence referred to here was meant to enclose all of the mansions and audience areas and was intended to keep out nonpaying spectators at a performance given by professional actors. Recently, however, it has been argued that the water or fence is meant only to enclose Mankind's castle and that it is a scenic element rather than a device for controlling crowds.

Another play, *Mankind* (c. 1465), of which only part survives, may originally have been a completely serious work, but if so it was later altered to include comic interludes and a number of songs and dances. In the version that has survived, the play's action is also interrupted to permit the actors to collect money from the audience. There are only seven roles and no scenery or complex properties. Thus *Mankind* demonstrates how the morality play was adapted to the needs of professional players and how the original didactic intention was altered to include various types of popular entertainment out of a desire to attract a paying audience.

In France, moralities seem to have remained closer to the vernacular religious cycles both in terms of length and in approach to production. For example, *Well-Advised, Ill-Advised,* presented at Rennes in 1439, is some 8000 lines long (about three times as long as Shakespeare's plays) with sixty characters and elaborate spectacle. As its title suggests, it contrasts the behavior of the well-advised and the ill-advised

FIG. 4.21
Everyman. Frontispiece to the edition published by John Sklot, *c.* 1530.

man. In its spectacular ending, Well-Advised is carried off to Heaven by Angels, while Ill-Advised is consigned to Hell.

A similar contrast forms the basis for *The Just Man and the Worldly Man,* written by Simon Bougoin (a member of Louis XII's household) and staged at Tarascon in 1476. Unlike most French but like English moralities, *Man the Sinner,* a play performed at Tours in 1494, develops the story of a single central figure in a relatively simple plot, demonstrating human frailty in the face of temptation and the eventual recognition that true happiness lies in obedience to God.

Perhaps the best know of all moralities is *Everyman* (c. 1510), seemingly an English translation of the Dutch *Elkerlyc* (c. 1495) by Peter Dorlant. More restricted in its subject than most dramatic allegories of the time, in it Everyman receives Death's summons, struggles to escape, and finally resigns himself to necessity. Seeking companions to accompany him on his journey, Everyman is quickly deserted by such former associates as Kindred, Goods, and Fellowship. Eventually only Good Deeds goes with him into the grave.

In the sixteenth century the morality play underwent many changes. In some instances, it was used to treat almost wholly secular subjects, as in John Skelton's *Magnificence* (*c.* 1520), which describes the lifestyle appropriate to a ruler, or in Nicolas de la Chesnaye's *Condemnation of the Banquet* (1507), which treats both mental and physical health and warns especially against the dangers of overeating. In other instances, the morality play was adapted as a weapon in the religious controversies that swept Europe during the sixteenth century. Perhaps the best of these plays is John Bale's (1495–1563) *King John* (1538), in which the English ruler holds out against the evil forces of the pope. Here historical personages and events are integrated with the allegorical figures and struggles typical of the original moralities. Bale's drama is often said to mark a major step toward the English chronicle play.

As religious controversy grew, doctrinal plays also began to be written in northern Europe. The first great stimulus to this movement came in 1501 with the publication of the previously unknown plays of Hrosvitha, the tenth-century German canoness who had sought to write dramas in the manner of Terence but to tell stories about the "chastity of Christian virgins." Her works exerted considerable influence throughout the sixteenth century on a movement best summed up in the collective title used for Cornelius Schonaeus's plays, *Christian Terence,* or *Sacred Comedies* (1592).

During the sixteenth century these north European dramatists were divided between those who supported Protestantism and those committed to Catholicism. Among the Protestant dramatists, perhaps the most influential was Gnapheus, whose play on the prodigal son, *Acolastus* (1582), stimulated many other works on the same theme: the reclamation of those who have strayed from the paths of virtue. Many of the Protestant plays denounced Catholicism. Perhaps the most forceful of these was Thomas Naogeorgus's *Pammachius* (1538), which treats the struggle against Antichrist over a period of almost 1000 years, ending with the glorification of Martin Luther as a major target of antichristian forces, epitomized in Bishop Pammachius.

Other changes in the morality play can be attributed to the introduction of classical subjects when interest in Greece and Rome and in learning for its own sake revived. This resulted in plays that were primarily philosophical, informative, and educational, best

exemplified in Henry Medwall's *Nature* (*c.* 1500) and John Rastell's *The Four Elements* (*c.* 1518).

By the early sixteenth century, then, the morality play had become extremely diversified, and all of the various strains were to be continued into Shakespeare's time. As the morality was increasingly secularized, the distinctions vanished between it and the type of play commonly labeled "interlude."

At first, morality plays were probably performed by amateurs, but gradually they were taken over by professionals. The basic conventions of the religious drama were followed in staging, although as professionalism increased, the number of actors and scenic elements declined. The emphasis on allegory was reflected in the costuming of such characters as Mercy, Kindred, and Good Deeds, abstractions that had seldom been seen in the cycle plays. The dress of allegorical figures was often very imaginative. The costume for Fame had eyes, ears, and tongues painted on it, while that for Vanity was covered with feathers of many hues, and that for Wealth was decorated with gold and silver coins. In the plays of religious controversy, each side drew on allegorical conventions and dressed its adherents as the Virtues and its opponents as the Deadly Sins; such figures as Flattery and Ignorance were often costumed as priests of the opposing sect.

As dramas, the moralities mark a movement away from Biblical characters and events to ordinary humans in their everyday surroundings. Consequently, they paved the way for the great secular plays of the succeeding period.

CHAMBERS OF RHETORIC

Closely related to the moralities are the plays performed by the Chambers of Rhetoric in the Low Countries. Originating in the fourteenth century, these societies were concerned with poetry, music, and drama. By 1500 there were about 160 societies spread throughout the Netherlands; Ghent had five. Competitions among societies were being held by 1413 and were especially popular in the period from 1493 to 1570. Typically a question was posed (such as "What is the greatest consolation to a person who is dying?"), to which the various Chambers composed and performed answers in the form of allegorical dramas. Prizes were given for those judged the best. These plays constituted the major (though not the sole) dramatic expression of the Low Countries.

Most plays were given outdoors on a stage which anticipated many features of the Elizabethan public theatre. At the back of a large platform, a fixed facade was erected. At the stage level there were normally

FIG. 4.22
Rhetoric stage at Antwerp, 1561. This type of stage may have influenced the layout of the Elizabethan public stage. From Wilhelm Creizenach, *The English Drama in the Age of Shakespeare* (1916).

three openings which could be closed with curtains or opened to reveal interior scenes. A second level included similar openings, while on the third level there was a throne for the figure (such as Wisdom, Lady Rhetoric, or the Virgin) in whose honor the festival was held. At the end of the contest, this figure was often flown to stage level to distribute the prizes.

The productions became increasingly lavish. The peak was reached in 1561 at a contest in Antwerp which lasted for one month. The nine competing societies made elaborate processional entries into the city using a total of twenty-three triumphal chariots and 197 pageant wagons. Plays were given over a period of fifteen days. To finance this festival, the city spent the enormous sum of 100,000 guilders, in addition to the funds provided by the competing societies.

Until the sixteenth century the Chamber plays often sought to convey theological messages. But in 1516 Spain gained control of the Low Countries just as the Protestant movement was gaining force

there. In an attempt to control the content of the plays presented by the Chambers of Rhetoric, an edict was issued in 1539 forbidding publication of the plays. Many groups insisted on their right to express their views, but others turned increasingly to less controversial subjects. After 1625 the Chambers declined rapidly and were eventually replaced by professional companies.

INTERLUDES

Interlude is an imprecise term, since it was at various times applied to almost every type of play presented in the Middle Ages. Today it is normally used to designate the plays first presented indoors as a part of the entertainments of rulers, nobles, rich merchants, and schools. The label probably derives from the practice of presenting entertainment between the parts of some other event, such as the courses of a banquet. The interlude might be of any type: religious, moral, farcical, historical. Often there was singing and dancing as well. Since they were often given in crowded banquet halls, the interludes used little (often no) scenery and few characters.

Like the morality play, the interlude was associated with the rise of the professional actor. From the eleventh century onward, most professional entertainers were grouped under the general heading of "minstrels," and various accounts speak of their popularity among the nobility and clergy throughout Europe. During the fourteenth century, as wealthy merchants began to emulate the nobility, demand for the services of minstrels increased, and some took up permanent residence in larger towns. By 1350 many nobles were retaining their own companies of performers. As early as the thirteenth century, there had been attempts to classify minstrels according to their specialties, but not until the late fifteenth century did acting begin to be recognized as a distinct activity separate from minstrelsy, a term which thereafter came to be associated almost entirely with musical performances.

Since actors were more assured of a livelihood if they were attached to a noble household, many troupes became servants to kings or great lords. In England Richard III (reigned 1483–1485) and Henry VII (reigned 1485–1509) each maintained a small company. There were many similar troupes by 1500, and they proliferated rapidly during the sixteenth century as more and more nobles acquired their own companies. Most troupes were permitted to tour under the names of their patrons when their services were not required at home. When they toured, the troupes presented their credentials to the mayor of a town, gave a performance before him and the aldermen, and, if approved, then gave other performances for a paying public in the town hall, an inn, or "on the green." In spite of their rising importance, however, professional players remained secondary to amateur performers until religious drama declined during the last half of the sixteenth century.

That professional actors were only beginning to appear in the late fifteenth century may explain why there are so few interludes prior to 1500. The oldest extant English play of this type, *Fulgens and Lucrece* by Henry Medwall, dates from 1497. A total of about seventy interludes survive, most from the sixteenth century.

The typical place for performing interludes was the "great hall" (or chief room) of a nobleman's residence, a university, a guild, or other organizations. These large rooms were constructed after a standard pattern: at one end was a raised platform reserved for the persons in authority and their favored associates or friends; at the opposite end was the "screen," a wall with two or three openings used as entryways for visitors and which provided access to the kitchen; above the screen there was sometimes a gallery for musicians. Many of the halls were vast in size (one was *c.* 240 by 68 feet), others more modest (among the smallest was one 47 by 23 feet). The great hall was used for various kinds of official business and social activities. For banquets, tables were erected on the platform as well as on the floor of the room; the closer one was to the "high table," the higher one's status. Such an arrangement of tables would have been typical when performances were given at banquets. On other occasions, the tables might be replaced by scaffold seating or standing room for spectators.

In staging the interludes, elaborate mansions were sometimes built for court performances, but more typically no scenery was used. At times, the screen, each of whose openings could serve to represent a separate mansion or as an entrance, may have been used as scenic background. If there was a musicians' gallery, it might also have been incorporated into the action. But most plays seem to have been staged in the midst of the audience, where the acting space

FIG. 4.23
Scene from a tournament. Miniature from a wedding chest. Painting by Domenico Morone (fifteenth century). Courtesy The National Gallery, London.

was small and, as the lines of several plays attest, the audience often encroached upon it and was asked to make room for the performers or to assist in some way. Because so much of the action occurred in the midst of the audience, scholarly opinion now downplays the role of the screen in the staging of interludes. Variations in the size of the hall must have influenced acoustics and other performance conditions.

Most interludes were written for small troupes. In England, the title page of Phillip's *Patient Grissell* states that it may be played by eight persons. The printed versions of Lewis Wager's *Mary Magdalene* and *Wealth and Health* are said to be suitable for a company of four, and the title page of Preston's *Cambises* shows how the thirty-eight roles may be distributed among eight actors.

TOURNAMENTS, MUMMINGS, AND DISGUISINGS

Alongside the interludes, other entertainments grew up around tournaments, mummings, and disguisings. Tournaments began in the tenth century as a means of training knights in warfare. During the thirteenth century, because a number of contestants had been killed, reforms in the conduct of tournaments were introduced, and by 1300 dramatic elements had begun to creep in. Soon, instead of merely seeking to unseat each other, knights were fighting to capture mansions representing such allegorical conceits as the Castle of Love inhabited by suitably costumed ladies and attendants.

At the most elaborate of the tournaments (the *pas d'armes*), spectators were carefully segregated according to sex and rank in galleries that surrounded the field of combat. At various points around this field were placed the elaborate mansions that established the allegorical context of the tournament. Among the favorite emblematic devices were mountains, castles, woods, fountains, ships, and chapels. For the most part, tournaments used the same visual symbolism found in the religious plays but often gave it a secular turn.

Tournaments were essentially noble or royal entertainments. Some were international events for which royal heralds were sent to foreign courts to issue challenges. In addition to the combats, there were elaborate processions, and in the evenings various forms of entertainments, including banquets during which interludes were presented.

Many of these indoor celebrations were also closely related to mumming and disguising. Although by 1500 mummings and disguisings were principally court entertainments, they may have had their ori-

FIG. 4.24

Mummers play in the banqueting hall of Haddon Hall, Derbyshire, England. A nineteenth-century reconstruction. Note the hall screen in the background with the balcony above. The hall screen is sometimes considered a possible source for the facade of the Elizabethan public stage. From Joseph Nash, *The Mansions of England in Olden Times,* 1 (1869).

gins in such pagan ceremonies as sword and Morris dances. The sword dance may have been military in origin, but by the fourteenth century minstrels were performing it at weddings and other festivities. Sometimes it was called "the dance of the buffoons," for it usually included one or more comic dancers. In the similar Morris dance, the participants wore bells, and some blackened their faces (Morris may be a corruption of Moorish).

Some scholars have argued that *mummers' plays* (derived from a French word meaning to play in dumb show, mask, or disguise) were performed during the Christmas season with Father Christmas as master of ceremonies or "presenter." Usually in these plays at least one character was killed in combat, after which a doctor arrived and brought the dead back to life through some grotesque device. Among the characters associated with these plays are a clown, a fool, a hobby horse, a man dressed as Maid Marian, St. George, and a dragon. Although the oldest surviving text of a mummer's play dates from the eighteenth century, there are many references during the late Middle Ages to such plays. There were many types of disguisings. Throughout the Christmas and carnival season preceding Lent, costumed and masked revelers of various sorts took to the streets. Some went from house to house presenting plays, songs, and dances. Most took up collections, but some, wishing to show gratitude or respect to the king or other official, used this opportunity to offer gifts. Because such disguisings came to be used as a cover for criminal behavior, they were suppressed in England (except at court) in the fourteenth and fifteenth centuries. Elsewhere disguisings of various sorts continued among the common people; in many places they have persisted to the present day, especially in pre-Lenten carnival celebrations (such as those associated today with *mardi gras*). In theatre, however, the most important offshoots of mummings and disguisings were such courtly entertainments as English masques, Italian *intermezzi*, and French *ballets de cour*.

The disguisings given at court might be arranged for any special occasion. They were performed at banquets following tournaments, for visits of royalty, at weddings, and on a variety of other occasions. Eventually they developed into complex spectacles. The first record of a courtly entertainment with elaborate scenic structures dates from 1377, when Charles V of France entertained the Holy Roman Emperor Charles IV. In England, disguisings were very popular under Henry VII (reigned 1485–1509) and Henry VIII (reigned 1509–1547). Scenic units were usually mounted on wheels so they could be brought into a hall between the courses of a banquet and removed for the dancing that followed; thus, they were somewhat similar to the pageant wagons of religious cycles. The playlets were largely pantomimic, and were intended above all as ingenious allegorical compliments to the persons being honored.

Characteristically, the entertainments concluded in a dance. In England, performers did not at first mingle with the audience, but beginning in 1513 the dancers chose partners from among the spectators. Since this practice was borrowed from the Italian courts, productions after this time were called "masques after the manner of Italy." In the English masques, courtiers served as actors and dancers, and professional musicians provided music and song. Since they required elaborate scenery and costumes, masques were far more costly to produce than were interludes, and the outlay increased steadily as time passed. Henry VIII was especially fond of court entertainments and in 1527 had a House of Revels built in which to stage them. In 1545, in order to centralize control over court entertainments, he also created an Office of Revels. Under Elizabeth I, the authority of this office was to be extended to cover all professional acting troupes in England.

Such court entertainments reached their peak in Italy and France during the sixteenth and seventeenth centuries and in England between 1603 and 1640. As integral parts of the Renaissance theatre, these descendants of medieval forms are treated at greater length in subsequent chapters.

ROYAL ENTRIES AND STREET PAGEANTS

Theatrical productions also came to be incorporated into the street pageants given by municipalities in honor of coronations, royal weddings, military victories, or visiting rulers. These celebrations followed a basic pattern: Civic officials and representatives of the clergy and trade guilds met the person to be honored at a prearranged place outside the city; then they escorted the visitor along a carefully planned route through the town to the cathedral

FIG. 4.25
Arch erected in Gracechurch Street for the entry of James I into London in 1604. Frontispiece to Vol. I of John Nichols, *The Progresses, Processions and Magnificent Festivities of James the First . . .* (1828).

for a religious service, after which the visitor was taken to a place of residence. It was an occasion upon which the city could demonstrate its loyalty, respect, or gratitude.

At first there was merely a procession, but gradually plays were added. These may have appeared as early as 1236, but were definitely being used by 1298, when the city of London honored Edward I's victory over the Scots. In Paris, the first clear record of plays as features of royal entries is found in 1313, when Edward II of England visited France. Gradually such celebrations spread throughout Europe. Although they still persist in a modified form, they largely ceased to be occasions for dramatic performances after the seventeenth century.

Plays were added to the entries at about the same time that religious dramas were first performed outdoors, and in the early years the subjects were almost identical with those at religious festivals. Beginning in the fifteenth century, the plays became increasingly allegorical or historical. These later works might take the form of elaborate lessons to a ruler on his duty to his subjects. Since they exploited

the Bible, history, mythology, and allegory, the plays might resemble any of the major types of medieval drama: religious plays, morality plays, tournament plays, disguisings, or serious interludes. Despite these similarities, there was one major difference: Most of these plays were pantomimic. Consequently, they are often called *tableaux vivants* (or living pictures).

In the beginning only a single tableau was mounted for an entry, but by the mid fifteenth century there were often as many as six or more, and narration might be added to clarify the allegory. Each play was complete in itself but all were connected by a common theme. In England during the sixteenth and seventeenth centuries, major dramatists (among them Nicholas Udall, John Lyly, Ben Jonson, Thomas Dekker, and John Webster) were commissioned to write them.

Each play was mounted on its own separate stage; the procession halted at each stage to view the performance and then moved on to the next. The stages erected for the tableaux varied in size and complexity; many were multistoried. In equipment and conventions, they were similar in all important respects to those used for other dramatic types of the period. The primary audience for the plays was the visitor and his party. On the other hand, for the city's populace, who lined the route, stood on housetops, or watched from windows, the attraction was the procession and the visitor.

Throughout Europe the planning and financing of these pageants were undertaken jointly by the city council and trade guilds. For example, at the entry of Katherine of Aragon into London in 1501, each tableau was assigned to a city alderman, who engaged workmen, obtained actors, and supervised all arrangements. The money was raised through taxes levied on the citizens. This method, or some variation on it, seems to have been typical.

FIG. 4.26
Scene staged for the royal entry of Charles V into Bruges, 1514. King Solomon's court is shown. From Bapst, *Essai sur l'Histoire du Théâtre* (1893).

THE END OF MEDIEVAL DRAMA

In the 600 years during which it existed, the medieval theatre became increasingly complex and diverse. From the simple liturgical plays and popular entertainments of the tenth century, it flowered into the great cycles, civic and court pageants, and secular plays of the sixteenth century. Yet during the sixteenth century the religious theatre that had been typical of the Middle Ages almost completely disappeared despite its obvious popularity and broad-based support. The reasons for this change were numerous, but a few were of special importance.

Perhaps most significantly, the church had been weakened by internal conflicts. It had reached the peak of its power around 1200, when the pope's supremacy in both religious and secular matters was almost universally accepted. But as nations began to take shape, princes sought ways of gaining control over religious affairs within their own territories. It soon became evident that the most effective means of control lay in the election of the pope, and rulers began intriguing to influence the choice; those elected often proved not to be immune from corruption. Between 1305 and 1377 the seat of the church was moved from Rome to Avignon, and the pope became a virtual captive of the French. Between 1378 and 1417 there were rival popes: at one time three claimed the papacy. By the fifteenth century, therefore, the church had been greatly weakened and many of its practices, perhaps most notoriously the selling of indulgences (or spiritual pardons), had led to demands for reform. Furthermore, as learning had revived with the rise of universities, a new spirit of questioning had been fostered throughout Europe. The Black Death, which killed much as a quarter of Europe's population in the fifty years following its introduction (c.1347), also caused people to question the church and its ability to protect them. (On the other hand the lack of labor pushed wages up significantly in many parts of Europe, thereby making it possible for more communities to afford theatre.)

The elements in this ferment eventually came together in the sixteenth century in the Reformation, as dissident groups challenged the Catholic church's authority and set out to reform religious practice. Princes were drawn into the conflict, since they were called on by the church to enforce its decrees. Some heeded the pope's demand but others refused or were in the vanguard of dissidence. The civil wars and the political and religious realignments that resulted did much to shape modern Europe.

Obviously the theatre could not remain aloof from these events. In England, Henry VIII's break with the church of Rome in 1534 led to bitter controversies in which drama was used as a weapon to attack or defend particular dogmas. In an attempt to still the conflict, Elizabeth I, upon coming to the throne in 1558, forbade all religious plays. Although not immediately successful, Elizabeth's edict, except in rare instances, had silenced the cycles by the 1570s.

Parallel events were underway in other countries. In the Netherlands the production of religious plays ran into trouble with church officials after 1539, with the result that religious subject matter was largely abandoned. The many Protestant secessions led the Catholic church to convene the Council of Trent (1545–1563) to cope with the issues and to reassert its control over all expressions of church doctrine. Medieval religious plays, though at the height of their popularity, came to be viewed as provocations to controversy, and consequently they were discouraged almost everywhere. Production of religious plays had virtually ceased in Italy by 1547, and in 1548 they were forbidden in Paris. In some Germanic areas they continued into the seventeenth century, but in most of Europe the religious drama had been abandoned by 1600. Only in Spain, where the Inquisition had established its unquestioned control over theology and drama, did they continue.

The abandonment of religious subject matter led to other changes. First, dramatists had to turn to secular subjects. In doing so, they took advantage of the reviving interest in Greek and Roman works, and in the process gained a new appreciation of dramatic form. The resulting blend of classical and medieval heritages did much to create the great secular drama of the Renaissance. Second, the abandonment of religious subject matter destroyed the last remaining basis for an international drama. Henceforth, each country developed its own national interests and characteristic style. Third, when the religious cycles were forbidden, the active support of the clergy, town councils, and merchant class, who had previously sanctioned and financed the most elaborate theatrical performances, was withdrawn. These groups made a clear distinction between productions motivated by religious and civic pride and the work of professional actors seeking to entertain for pay. The church had never rescinded the condemnation of professional actors pronounced in Roman times, and the censure was now reiterated.

Perhaps most important of all, the relationship of theatre to society underwent a drastic change at this time. In Rome, and medieval Europe, the theatre, in its most characteristic form, had enjoyed the active support of governmental and religious bodies. Theatre had been ceremonial and occasional, for it was essentially a community offering used to celebrate special events considered significant to all. Beginning in the sixteenth century, however, it was deprived of its religious and civic functions and henceforth it had to wage a fight for recognition on purely commercial and artistic grounds. In the beginning, it was sustained by noblemen and rulers, who continued the system of private patronage that had grown up in medieval times. With this help, the professional theatre gradually established itself throughout Europe, although in some countries the process was not to be completed for some 200 years.

LOOKING AT THEATRE HISTORY

Definition is crucial in historical study, for we must be able to establish the limits of a subject before we can determine what materials constitute appropriate evidence. At times definitions are relatively easy to arrive at, but at others they involve fundamental conflicts. Nowhere is this more evident than in conclusions about the beginnings of liturgical drama. Following are two major scholarly points of view. One rules out the Mass as a liturgical drama, the other insists that the Mass is an archetypal play.

> By some criterion we must be able to discriminate between what is merely dramatic or theatrical, because of its similarity to things familiar upon the stage, and what is authentically a play. No one can have failed to observe that in its external resemblances to stage-performances the Roman liturgy is abundantly dramatic. . . . Dramatic externalities of this kind, however, must not be mistaken for genuine drama itself, in which the essential element is not forms of speech and movement, but impersonation. . . . [79–80]. The Mass, then, has never been a drama, nor did it ever directly give rise to drama. The dramatic features of this service, . . . may have contributed suggestions as to the possibility of inventing drama, and may, indirectly, have encouraged it; but the liturgy itself, in its ordinary observances, remained always merely worship. [85]

Karl Young, *The Drama of the Medieval Church,* I (Oxford: at the Clarendon Press, 1933).

> The conclusion seems inescapable that the "dramatic instinct" of European man did not "die out" during the earlier Middle Ages, as historians of drama have asserted. Instead, it found expression in the central ceremony of Christian worship, the Mass, [41]. Just as the Mass is a sacred drama encompassing all history and embodying in its structure the central pattern of Christian life on which all Christian drama must draw, the celebration of the Mass contains all elements necessary to secular performance. [79]

O. B. Hardison, Jr., *Christian Rite and Christian Drama in the Middle Ages* (Baltimore: The Johns Hopkins Press, 1965).

Stage directions are often one of the historian's most useful sources. Those included in some church manuals when dramatic episodes began to be performed in the churches of the West are very precise. In fact, they provide directions that permit many liturgical performances to be reconstructed more accurately than any earlier theatrical pieces can. The following is an excerpt from the oldest surviving instructions for presenting a liturgical play:

> While the third lesson is being read, four brethren shall dress, one of whom, wearing an alb as if for some other reason, shall enter and go secretly to the site of the sepulchre, and holding a palm in his hand shall sit there quietly. And while the third respond is being pronounced, the remaining three shall follow, all wearing hoods and bearing censers with incense in hand, step by step as though looking for something, shall come to the sepulchre. These things are done in imitation of the angel sitting on the tomb, and of the women coming with perfumes to anoint the body of Jesus. When, therefore, the one seated shall see the three approach as if wandering and seeking something, he shall begin to sing in a sweet modulated voice Quem Quaeritis? *With this sung to its end, the three shall answer, with one voice.* Ihesum Nazarenum. *The former shall respond:* Non est hic. Surrexit sicut praedixerat. Ite, nuntiate quia surrexit a mortuis. *At this command the three shall turn to the choir saying,* Alleluia. Resurrexit Dominus. *With this sung, the one seated, as if calling the other back, shall say the antiphon* Venite et videte locum. *Then he shall rise and raise the veil and show them the place, empty of the cross but with the linen in which the cross was wrapped; at this sight they shall set down their censers in that same sepulchre, and shall take up the linen and hold it before the clergy and, as if showing that the Lord had risen and was no longer wrapped in it, they shall sing this antiphon:* Surrexit Dominus de sepulcro, *and shall then place the linen on the altar.*

From Ethelwold, Bishop of Winchester, *The Monastic Agreement of the Monks and Nuns of the English Nation,* trans. Barbara Spear.

The stage directions in *The Mystery of Adam* (*c.* 1150) provide evidence suggesting that plays were by that time being staged out-of-doors. Here is one of the crucial passages:

> Then let God go to the church, and let Adam and Eve walk about, innocently delighting in the Garden of Eden. Meanwhile, let demons run back and forth through the square, making suitable gestures. . . .

Other major sources for the historian of medieval theatre are the municipal records kept by towns that were directly involved in the production of plays. One of the most complete accounts can be deduced from the records of the city of Mons (Belgium), which sponsored a passion play in 1501. Here is an excerpt from which we learn how many rehearsals were held, where they were held, and how the actors were notified:

> To Jehan Billet, for the 48 days of summoning he had carried out in having assembled the players at all the rehearsals held since the beginning of the said play at the City Hall, as agreed upon, 6.1.

> Translation by Lenyth Brockett. All of the accounts of this production can be found (in French) in Gustave Cohen, *Le Livre de Conduite du Regisseur . . . pour le Mystère . . . à Mons en 1501* (Paris, 1925).

There appear to have been a variety of professional entertainers during the middle Ages and an equally varied moral response to them. Here is one account written by the Bishop of Salisbury (England) in the first half of the fourteenth century:

> There are three kinds of histriones. Some metamorphose and transform their bodies through unseemly leaps and foul gestures, either exposing themselves shamefully or donning fearful masks, but surely all are damned unless they abandon their employment. Likewise there are others who work at nothing, . . . but follow after assemblies of great men and tell of disgraces and scandals so as to please others. They are also surely damned, for the Apostle forbids us to take food with such men. There is also a third kind of histriones who have musical instruments for delighting men, and of these there are two kinds. Some

> frequent public drinking bouts and licentious societies, and there they sing various songs so that men are moved to wantonness; these are to be damned as are the others. But there are also others, who are called jesters, who sing the deeds of rulers and the lives of the saints, and provide solace for men whether in their sicknesses or in low spirits, and they do not invent countless infamies as do the dancers and dancing girls and the others who play in shameful representations and cause apparitions to be seen through enchantments or by another method. But these . . . bring comfort to men. . . .

> Thomas de Cabham, *Penetential*, trans. Barbara Spear.

A major controversy has raged around David Rogers' account of the staging of the Chester cycle. Not only is his account important in discussions of the construction of the pageant wagons, but in the concern over whether the plays were actually performed on the wagons or whether they merely transported the actors who, during a procession, gave some brief indication of the longer play that was later seen at a fixed location:

> They were divided into 24 pageants or parts, and every Company brought forth their pageant which was the carriage or place which they played in. . . . they began at the Abbey gates and when the first pageant was played at the Abbey gates then it was wheeled from thence to the pentice at the high cross before the Mayor, and before that was done the second came, and the first went into the Watergate street and from thence unto the Bridge street and so all one after an other till all the pageants were played. . . . These pageants or carriage was a high place made like a house with two rooms being open on the top. [In] the lower room they apparelled and dressed themselves, and in the higher room they played, and they stood upon 6 wheels.

> David Rogers, *A Breviarye, or Some Few Recollections of the City of Chester* (Harley Manuscript 1944, fol. 21–22). The spelling and punctuation have been modernized to facilitate reading.

5
English Theatre to 1642

Because of wars and internal strife, England was scarcely affected by the Renaissance until the late fifteenth century. Since the Norman Conquest in 1066, England's kings had also controlled extensive territories in France and had intermarried with French ruling families. In 1337 England laid claim to the French throne, thereby precipitating a lengthy conflict (often called the Hundred Years' War) that continued until 1453. For a time England seemed to be winning the struggle, especially after 1420 when Henry V (reigned 1413–1422) was named regent and heir to the French throne. But after his death and Joan of Arc's victory at Orleans in 1429, the English rapidly lost control. By 1453 England held only Calais in France. At about the same time a struggle for the throne of England (the War of the Roses) began between the rival houses of York and Lancaster. The conflict continued until 1485 when Richard III was defeated by the Earl of Richmond, who united the dissident factions and as Henry VII (reigned 1485–1509) founded the Tudor line that ruled England until the death of Elizabeth I in 1603. The Tudors played a major role in the religious conflicts that were to dominate Europe in the sixteenth century, but they also brought a strong central government to England and despite continued internal

and external conflicts made it a major international power.

EARLY TUDOR DRAMA

Although medieval theatrical practices continued to be dominant, the spirit of the Renaissance began to be felt in England during the reign of Henry VII. Erasmus and other continental humanists came to England; Colet and other English humanists studied in Italy. These men taught at both Oxford and Cambridge, giving English scholars and writers an interest in ancient literature. The court saw the first influences of humanism on drama in 1497, with the performance of Medwall's *Fulgens and Lucrece,* and it saw this influence grow in the morality plays of Medwall, Skelton, Rastell, and Bale (discussed in Chapter 4). The didactic nature of these works provided the models for the propaganda plays written during Henry VIII's (reigned 1509–1547) break with the Catholic Church.

Oxford graduates were the early leaders in spreading the new approaches to learning into the schools. William Lily (1468–1522) studied the staging of Latin comedy with Pomponius Laetus in Rome before becoming first headmaster of St. Paul's grammar school.

John Heywood (*c.* 1497–*c.* 1578) was a court musician and author of the first nondidactic interludes in England. Nicholas Udall (1505–1566) became headmaster of Eton (and later of Westminster) and wrote one of the best-known early Tudor comedies, *Ralph Roister Doister* (*c.* 1534–1541). Heavily indebted to Plautus' *Braggart Warrior*, Udall's play shows the foolish posturings of a boastful coward and his discomfiture in his courtship of a widow. Richard Edwards (1524–1566) worked with the children of the Chapel Royal and wrote *Damon and Pythias* (1564), the first English play with a complex plot.

Humanist performances were flourishing at Cambridge University by the 1520s. In 1546 Queen's College at Cambridge mandated the yearly performance of plays and constructed a removable theatre structure for its main hall (this remained in service until at least 1640 and may have influenced the design of the London playhouses). Students performed plays, many in Latin but others in English, for members of the university and invited guests. The best known of the plays in English was *Gammer Gurton's Needle,* written by "Mr. S." and acted at Christ's College sometime between 1552 and 1563. This play fuses subject matter and characters similar to those typical of medieval farce with techniques borrowed from Roman comedy. It develops a series of comic misunderstandings (most of them initiated by Diccon, the "bedlam" or fool) between two neighboring households over the loss of a needle.

The humanist influences seen in schools and universities were carried to London's Inns of Court: Gray's Inn, Lincoln's Inn, the Inner Temple, and the Middle Temple. Principally places of residence and training for lawyers, the Inns admitted young men, generally recent graduates of Oxford and Cambridge, for further legal education. These wealthy and aristocratic students were taught music, dancing, and other graces, which were practiced in part through the presentation of plays. Most performances came during the Christmas "revels," which extended over a period of four weeks. But the Inns also mounted many other elaborate entertainments to celebrate special occasions. The audiences were aristocratic, well educated, and interested in the latest fashions in drama, both at home and abroad.

In 1561, the Inner Temple presented what is usually said to be the first English tragedy, *Gorboduc* or *Ferrex and Porrex,* written by Thomas Sackville and Thomas Norton. The following year it was presented at Whitehall with Queen Elizabeth in attendance. The subject, chosen from the legendary history of England, was developed in a pseudo-Senecan manner. The action is divided into five acts and treats the jealousy aroused between Ferrex and Porrex when their father, Gorboduc, decides to divide his kingdom between them. All the principal characters eventually are killed, and their fate is used to point a lesson for England about the dangers of leaving uncertain the order of succession to the throne. Although the play now seems weak, it made such a deep impression that it had been printed five times by 1590. It established the fashion for modeling tragedies on the works of Seneca, and its use of blank verse, instead of the traditional rhymed verse, was to have a profound influence on subsequent playwriting. Gray's Inn presented George Gascoigne's (*c.* 1542–1578) *Supposes* in 1566. This adaptation of Ariosto's *I Suppositi* (*The Substitutes,* 1509) tells the story of a young nobleman who poses as a servant in the household of a well-to-do widower in order to win the love of the widower's daughter. Its success established prose as the medium for English comedy and set a fashion for Italian plots and settings.

Despite the humanist influence, medieval practices and conventions continued to dominate English theatre through most of the sixteenth century. Entertainers of all sorts traveled the country and local communities continued to produce mummings, farce comedies, and other kinds of amateur performances. Aiming to attract a wide audience, professional actors combined elements of popular entertainment with subjects drawn from many sources. Biblical stories were mingled with adaptations of foreign novels and chivalric tales, and classical myths with English historical and low-comedy figures. The entire popular tradition is probably best summed up in Thomas Preston's (1537–1598) *A Lamentable Tragedy Mixed Full of Pleasant Mirth, Containing the Life of Cambises, King of Persia, from the beginning of his Kingdom, Unto his Death, His One Good Deed of Execution, after that Many Wicked Deeds and Tyrannous Murders, Committed by and Through Him, and Last of All, His Odious Death by God's Justice Appointed* (*c.* 1561). Although the play is set in Persia, many of the characters are mythological (Cupid and Venus), allegorical (Shame, Diligence, Trial, and Proof), or English (Hob, Lob, and Marian-May-Be-Good). It freely mingles the comic and the serious, ranges over a considerable period of time, and changes place with bewildering rapidity. The numerous bloody deeds, such as beheadings, flayings, and murders, are all shown on stage. And all of this, according to the printed version of *c.* 1569, could be performed by eight actors playing thirty-eight roles. As one of the most popular plays of the day, *Cambises* reveals much about the tastes of the audience that made a public theatre feasible. Its variety also illustrates the need for dramatists capable of unifying the diverse elements out of which the plays were compounded.

Many forces eventually shaped the great English drama of the late sixteenth century. Among the most important of these were the religious and political controversies that led up to and followed Henry VIII's break with the Catholic church (1529–1536). While Henry's actions were arguably more political than religious, their effect was to make England the first major nation to embrace the Protestant Reformation Luther had begun in 1517. Henry's policy of forced conversion caused deep divisions within the country. His dissolution of the monasteries (1536–1540) and distribution of the resulting wealth among his followers further polarized those on both sides. The early death of Henry's only son Edward VI (ruled 1547–1553) brought Henry's oldest daughter Mary to the throne as England's first ruling Queen in 400 years. She sought to return England to Catholicism, and during her reign as Mary I (1553–1558) more than 300 persons were executed for heresy or sedition. She also married a Catholic, Philip II of Spain, and when Mary died in 1558 Philip considered it a duty to remove Henry's second daughter, the Protestant Elizabeth I (reigned 1558–1603), from the throne. This religious animosity was compounded by England's challenging of Spain in the New World and aiding of the Netherlands in its attempts to throw off Spanish rule.

By the 1580s the ongoing religious and political intrigues had become focused around Mary, Queen of Scots. Mary (1542–1587) had been queen of Scotland from the time she was one week old and, as wife of Francis II (reigned 1559–1560), was briefly Queen of France. She was coerced by Protestant forces to abdicate the Scottish throne and fled to England in 1568. Many of Elizabeth's opponents, including Philip II, thought that, as grandniece to Henry VIII, the Catholic Mary of Scotland was the true heir to the throne of England. Eventually Mary was implicated in a plot to overthrow Elizabeth and was executed in 1587. In 1588 Philip II sent an invasion fleet to England. The decisive victory of Elizabeth's navy over this seemingly invincible Spanish Armada established England as a major maritime power and left English Protestantism relatively secure. The resulting upsurge of England's national confidence in the late sixteenth century seems to parallel a remarkable growth in its professional theatre. But problems continued at home and abroad. The war with Spain went on until 1604, rapid economic change led to serious food shortages, especially in London, the plague was an ever-present killer, and Protestant security was compromised by factionalism.

During Elizabeth's reign, interest at universities and schools expanded beyond classical drama to plays based on English history or recent Italian works. By 1600 the influence schools, universities, and Inns of Court had on professional theatre was waning. But they had performed a crucial role by familiarizing students with effective dramatic techniques. When school-educated writers began to work for the professional troupes, English drama entered an era of greatness.

THE UNIVERSITY WITS

During the 1580s all the strands of drama began to coalesce, primarily because of Thomas Kyd and a group of educated men, commonly called "the University Wits," who turned to writing for the public stage. The most important of these writers were John Lyly from Oxford and Robert Greene and Christopher Marlowe from Cambridge.

Thomas Kyd (1558–1594) is remembered primarily for *The Spanish Tragedy* (*c.* 1587), the most popular play of the sixteenth century. In telling his sensational story of murder and revenge, Kyd places all the important events on stage, lets the action range freely through time and place, and uses such Senecan devices as ghosts, a chorus (one person), soliloquies, confidants, and division into acts. Yet Kyd manages to construct a well-articulated plot with rapid, clear, and absorbing action. Although lacking in depth of characterization or thought, *The Spanish Tragedy* is a remarkable advance over preceding plays and established the vogue for "revenge" tragedy, of which *Hamlet* was to be the most lasting example.

John Lyly (*c.* 1554–1606) wrote primarily for boys' companies catering to aristocratic audiences. His most characteristic works are pastoral comedies that mingle classical mythology with English subjects. His

FIG. 5.1

Illustration from an edition of Marlowe's *Doctor Faustus* published about 1620.

is a fairy-tale world in which troubles vanish at the wave of a magic wand. All but one of Lyly's plays were written in the carefully balanced, refined, and somewhat artificial prose for which he was famous. Among his characteristic works are *Campaspe* (1584), *Endimion* (c. 1588), and *Love's Metamorphosis* (c. 1590). These delicate pastoral works established the tradition upon which Shakespeare built in *As You Like It*.

Robert Greene (1560–1592) also wrote pastoral and romantic comedies, but for the adult companies. The works of his short career are more varied than Lyly's, since he crowded many diverse elements into a single play. In his *Friar Bacon and Friar Bungay* (c. 1589) and *James IV* (c. 1591), stories of love and pastoral adventures are mingled with historical materials. Greene is especially noted for his charming and resourceful heroines, who, after wandering in disguise through a series of temptations, are rewarded with the fulfillment of their fondest desires.

Christopher Marlowe (1564–1593) was by far the most influential of this group. Among the plays he wrote for the public theatre are *Tamburlaine*, Parts 1 and 2 (1587–1588), *Doctor Faustus* (c. 1588), *The Jew of Malta* (c. 1589), and *Edward II* (c. 1592). Marlowe's plays focus on the protagonist, whose complex motivations are illuminated by an episodic story. *Edward II* was especially important in the development of the chronicle play, for with it Marlowe demonstrated how to rearrange, telescope, and alter diverse historical events to create a sense of causal relationships and thus a coherent story, but *Doctor Faustus* has been his most influential work. When he was killed in 1593 he and Shakespeare had written about the same number of plays, but many critics believe that Marlowe had the better command of blank verse.

The University Wits bridged the gap between the learned and popular audiences. Their successful blending of classical and medieval devices with compelling stories drawn from many sources dominated the stage during Shakespeare's early years as a dramatist and established the foundations upon which Shakespeare and his contemporaries built.

SHAKESPEARE AND HIS CONTEMPORARIES

William Shakespeare (1564–1616) is frequently said to be the greatest dramatist of all time. He entered the world of the London theatre as an actor sometime between 1585 and 1592. Andrew Gurr has noted that if Shakespeare acted for the companies who performed his plays, he must have worked for Strange's Men, Pembroke's Men, and Sussex's Men before becoming a shareholder in the Chamberlain's

Men in 1594. He remained with them for the rest of his career, becoming a householder (part owner) in the Globe playhouse in 1598 and in the second Blackfriars playhouse in 1608. Shakespeare, then, was directly involved in more aspects of the theatre than any other writer of his day.

Shakespeare is generally thought to have taken up playwriting between 1589 and 1592, with *Henry VI* Parts 1, 2, and 3 (though some scholars believe that *Two Gentlemen of Verona* and *Taming of the Shrew* may be his earliest works). He wrote the very popular tragedies *Titus Andronicus* and *Richard III* and an adaptation of a Roman comedy, *Comedy of Errors*, before joining the Chamberlain's Men. For the next ten years he wrote roughly one comedy and one tragedy per season, including many of his best-known plays: *Love's Labour's Lost* and *Romeo and Juliet* (1594–1595); *A Midsummer Night's Dream* and *Richard II* (1595–1596); *The Merchant of Venice* and *King John* (1596–1597); *Henry IV,* Parts 1 and 2 (1597–1598); *Much Ado About Nothing* and *Henry V* (1598–1599); *As You Like It* and *Julius Caesar* (1599–1600); *Twelfth Night* and *Hamlet* (1600–1601); *The Merry Wives of Windsor* and *Troilus and Cressida* (1601–1602); *All's Well That Ends Well* and *Measure for Measure* (1602–1603). His output was lower for the remaining ten years of his career; he wrote only tragedies and tragicomedies, several in partnership with other playwrights. The plays of this period include: *Othello* (1604–1605); *King Lear* and *Macbeth,* the latter probably revised by Thomas Middleton (1605–1606); *Antony and Cleopatra* (1606–1607); *Coriolanus* and *Timon of Athens,* the latter possibly written with Thomas Middleton (1607–1608); *Pericles,* possibly written with George Wilkins (1608–1609), *Cymbeline* (1609–1610); *A Winter's Tale* (1610–1611); *The Tempest* (1611–1612); and *Henry VIII* and *Two Noble Kinsmen,* both written with John Fletcher (1612–1613). Along with these thirty-eight plays he wrote an early lost play *Love's Labour's Won* (though this may be an alternative title for *Taming of the Shrew*), and a late lost play *Cardenio* (1612–1614), written with John Fletcher. Some scholars believe he had a hand in several other plays as well. Sixteen of his plays were published in quarto versions before his death, but the survival of his work can be credited in large part to the First Folio (1623), a collection of thirty-six of his plays edited by his fellow actors Henry Condell and John Heminges.

It is impossible to do justice to Shakespeare in a short space, for no playwright's work has been more fully studied. Only a few characteristics of his dramaturgy can be reviewed here. Shakespeare borrowed stories from many sources (history, mythology, legend, fiction, plays) but reworked them until they became distinctively his own. Typically, situations and characters are clearly established in the opening scenes, and the action develops logically out of this exposition. A number of plots are usually interwoven, at first proceeding somewhat independently of each other but eventually coming together as the denouement approaches, so that the resolution of one leads to that of the others; in this way apparent diversity is given unity. The action normally encompasses months or years and occurs in widely separated places. This broad canvas creates a sense of ongoing life behind the scenes.

Shakespeare's large casts are composed of well-rounded characters who run the gamut from the inept and ridiculous to the commanding and heroic, from the young and innocent to the old and corrupt. Despite the enormous range of his characters, Shakespeare entered into most of them sympathetically and made them appear to be living individuals rather than mere stage figures. His penetrating insights into human behavior have remained valid.

No playwright uses language as effectively as Shakespeare. His poetic and figurative dialogue not only arouses specific emotions, moods, and ideas, it creates a network of complex associations and connotations that transcends the immediate dramatic situation.

Shakespeare was by far the most comprehensive, sensitive, and dramatically effective playwright of his time. He attempted almost all the popular dramatic types and subjects of his age, and in each instance gave them their most effective expression. In his own day, Shakespeare's critical reputation was lower than Jonson's or Fletcher's, but his fame began to grow in the late seventeenth century and reached its peak in the nineteenth century.

Except for Shakespeare, Ben Jonson (1572–1637) is usually considered the finest Elizabethan playwright. An actor for a time, Jonson began writing plays in the mid-1590s and went to prison several times for his contributions to politically satiric comedies. He was the acknowledged leader of those authors who favored conscious artistry (that is, writing according to a set of principles or rules). More than any other English dramatist, Jonson turned attention to the classical precepts as a way of tempering the excesses of native playwrights, though he frequently deviated from or altered those classical principles in his own works. Jonson gained the favor of James I, for whom he wrote more masques than any other dramatist. His receipt of a royal pension in 1616 made him the first "poet laureate" of England. When he published a carefully edited collection of his own plays that same year, he gave a new respectability to drama, which had long been seen as mere diversionary entertainment (much like television dramas are today).

Of Jonson's twenty-eight plays, the comedies, especially *Every Man in His Humour* (1598), *Volpone* (1606), *Epicoene, or the Silent Woman* (1609), *The Alchemist* (1610), and *Bartholomew Fair* (1614), are now best known. Jonson was concerned primarily with reforming human behavior and concentrated upon the foibles of contemporary types. Jonson's comedy is often described as realistic and "corrective" since the characters are supposedly based upon direct observation and are castigated for their shortcomings. Because Jonson does not arouse sympathy for most of his characters, the plays appear more harshly moralistic than do Shakespeare's. Jonson popularized the "comedy of humours." Since classical times medical theory had posited four bodily "humours" (blood, phlegm, yellow bile, and black bile). Health supposedly depended upon a proper balance among them. By Jonson's day humours were seen as determinants of basic temperaments, and in his plays eccentricities of behavior are attributed to the imbalance of humours. He created a wide range of character types based upon this scheme. Although the self-conscious use of humours waned after 1603, it continued as one basis for characterization until about 1700. Jonson also wrote two tragedies, *Sejanus* (1603) and *Catiline* (1611), both of which were among the most respected plays of the century (although they failed in the theatre).

Shakespeare and Jonson were surrounded by a host of less-celebrated figures. Among the more important of these were Chapman, Dekker, Marston, Heywood, Middleton, and Tourneur. George Chapman (c. 1560– 1634) wrote twenty-one plays between 1595 and 1613, concentrating first on comedy in the vein of Jonson and then on tragedy in the manner of Marlowe. In such plays as *May Day* (c. 1600) and *Sir Giles Goosecap* (1603), he mingled satirical and romantic elements with "humours" psychology to produce a moral comedy less biting than Jonson's. His most famous tragedies, *Bussy D'Ambois* (c. 1604) and *The Revenge of Bussy D'Ambois* (c. 1610), center around strong men of action who seem doomed to fail.

Thomas Dekker (c. 1570–1632) wrote at least sixty-five plays, on many of which he collaborated with other leading dramatists of the day. His most famous work, *The Shoemaker's Holiday* (1599), depicts the unsophisticated world of apprentices and tradesmen, emphasizing only its pleasant aspects, in the story of an industrious tradesman who becomes Lord Mayor of London. Like many of Dekker's plays, it appears to much better advantage on the stage than on the printed page.

John Marston (1576–1634) wrote or collaborated on twelve plays between 1599 and 1608. He wrote for the boys' companies, which gives a perplexing context to his preoccupation with human imperfections as reflected in such comedies as *Histriomastix* (*c.* 1600) and *What You Will* (*c.* 1601), and such serious plays as *The Dutch Courtesan* (*c.* 1603–1605) and *The Malcontent* (1605). All his works lash out at a world in which people have substituted their own desires for the Christian virtues, but *The Malcontent,* in which the discontent of the central character provides effective motivation for such attacks, is his most successful. Marston is also noted for his violent and original imagery, which influenced many of his successors.

Thomas Heywood (*c.* 1574–1641) claimed to have had a hand in more than 220 plays. He was especially good at arousing the pathetic emotions, but he seldom rose to those of tragedy. Today he is remembered primarily for *A Woman Killed with Kindness* (1603). This domestic tragedy tells the story of a good wife caught in an adulterous affair with her husband's trusted friend. Rather than take revenge on the pair, the husband banishes his wife from home and children, after which she dies of grief for her transgression and he realizes too late the value of Christian forgiveness.

Thomas Middleton (1580–1627) wrote or collaborated on at least two dozen plays, covering a range of moods and subjects second in diversity only to Shakespeare's. Like Shakespeare, he could enter into all characters and situations, but unlike Shakespeare, Middleton seems lacking in strong feeling or original insight. In plays such as *Michaelmas Term* (1604–1606), *A Trick to Catch the Old One* (1604–1607), and *A Chaste Maid in Cheapside* (1611), he creates a vivid view of capitalist London and demonstrates a remarkable facility for inventiveness and verbal wit. His later work features more tragedy. With William Rowley (*c.* 1585–after 1625) he wrote *The Changeling* (1622) and *The Spanish Gypsy* (1623); his other works include the political satire *A Game at Chess* (1624) and the sinister *Women Beware Women* (1625). Middleton's serious plays tend to show the destruction of a potentially great person through gradual corruption, but the tragic effect is blunted because the characters do not progress significantly in self-knowledge. In recent years scholars have become increasingly convinced that Middleton is also the author of *The Revenger's Tragedy* (*c.* 1606), one of the darkest dramas of the period. Traditionally, however, this play has been assigned to Cyril Tourneur (*c.* 1575–1626), who wrote the almost equally dark *The Atheist's Tragedy* (1611) and *The Nobleman* (1611–1612).

The plays of Shakespeare and his contemporaries display many technical similarities. Almost all use an early point of attack and follow a chronological organization with all important episodes shown on stage. In most plays, the short scene is the basic structural unit. Because they were written for a nonillusionistic stage, the plays are essentially placeless, although the locale is always specified in the dialogue when it is important to the action. The major concern is for developing action, in which time and place often shift rapidly. Tone also may vary frequently from serious to comic. Most of the plays are shaped in part by the belief in a moral order that allows us free will, but holds us responsible for the choices we make. Although less obviously than in medieval drama, the characters are still caught in a struggle between good and evil. Much of this moral tone is established through poetic imagery, soliloquies, and observations, although the lesser writers resort to straightforward statements of moral lessons.

JACOBEAN AND CAROLINE DRAMATISTS

Critics have traditionally identified a subtle change in English drama during the first decade of the reign of James I, though some argue that this may not be as clear as it once seemed. Increasing numbers of plays during this period do appear to reflect cynicism and doubt, however. Tragicomedies, with their contrived happy endings for otherwise serious plays, were increasingly popular, encouraging the pathetic or sensational as substitutes for the more genuinely tragic emotions. Thrills and excitement took precedence over significant insights or complex characterization more often than they had done before. Yet at the same time, technical skill increased. The playwrights handled exposition more adroitly, compressed the action into fewer episodes, built complications to startling climaxes, and alternated quiet with tumultuous scenes. As a result, the plays of this later period are more skillfully contrived than those written earlier, but they are often lacking in profundity. Much of this is evident in the plays of Tourneur and in the late collaborations of Middleton. Of the many other dramatists who worked between 1610 and 1642 the most important are Webster, Beaumont, Fletcher, Massinger, Shirley, and Ford.

John Webster (*c.* 1580–1634) wrote about fourteen plays, some in collaboration with Dekker, Heywood, Middleton, Rowley, and others. He is remembered chiefly for *The White Devil* (1609–1612) and *The Duchess of Malfi* (1613/14), the Jacobean tragedies that rank closest to Shakespeare's in modern estimation. His plays are admired for their well-drawn characters and powerful dramatic poetry, but criticized for the obscurity of their action. His protagonists are surrounded by corruption, which inevitably destroys them, but they do not themselves achieve any deep new insights. Webster's plays lack that sense of affirmation found in Shakespeare's tragedies and manage only to raise important issues without illuminating them. Francis Beaumont (c. 1584–1616) is best known today for *The Knight of the Burning Pestle* (c. 1607), his burlesque of middle-class taste in theatre. But his name is inextricably linked with that of John Fletcher (1579–1625) because a collection of about fifty plays, published in 1647 and 1679, was attributed to their joint authorship. Actually they collaborated on only few of these works, among them *The Maid's Tragedy, Philaster,* and *A King and No King,* all written between 1608 and 1613. But these works did much to establish the tone and technique of Jacobean drama. *A King and No King* is typical of the trend toward sensationalism in its depiction of a brother and sister caught up in an apparently incestuous love, only to have their moral problem resolved by the discovery that they are not related.

Fletcher was one of the most successful dramatists of his day and probably replaced Shakespeare as principal dramatist for the King's Men, the leading theatrical company of the time. He knew how to shape every element in terms of dramatic effectiveness, and his dialogue was especially admired by aristocratic theatregoers, who saw in it the epitome of the way they would like to speak. During the Restoration, Fletcher's plays were more frequently performed than those of either Shakespeare or Jonson. His *The Scornful Lady* (1616), *The Chances* (1617), *The Spanish Curate* (1622), *A Wife for a Month* (1624), and *Rule a Wife and Have a Wife* (1624) were especially popular and were performed regularly into the nineteenth century.

Philip Massinger (1583–1640) often collaborated with Fletcher, and he later revised many of Fletcher's plays. Consequently, it is difficult to distinguish their individual contributions. After 1625, Massinger replaced Fletcher as the chief dramatist to the King's Men, for whom he wrote all or parts of at least fifty-five plays. Of these, *A New Way to Pay Old Debts* (1621/22) is by far the best known, since the role of Sir Giles Overreach, whose villainy eventually leads him to madness and death, was a favorite with leading actors for over two hundred years.

James Shirley (1596–1666) succeeded Massinger as principal dramatist for the King's Men. He wrote about thirty-six plays and is known especially for his comedies, such as *Hyde Park* (1623) and *The Lady of Pleasure* (1635), which depict the manners and fashions of aristocratic London society. Shirley considered his best work to be *The Cardinal* (1641), a tragedy similar to *The Duchess of Malfi.*

The plays of John Ford (1586–c. 1639) are usually cited as exemplifying the decadence that character-

ized Caroline drama, since *'Tis Pity She's a Whore* (1629–1633) treats with apparent sympathy a love affair between brother and sister and ends with the destruction of nearly everyone in the play. Other significant plays among the seventeen attributed to Ford are *The Lover's Melancholy* (c. 1628) and *The Broken Heart* (c. 1627–1631). Scarcely noted in his own day, Ford is now admired for his ability to illuminate evil by associating it with ordinary human beings.

These are only a few of the dramatists who were active between 1590 and 1642, a period during which Gerald Eades Bentley estimates that about 2000 plays were written by more than 250 dramatists, although the majority of the plays performed in public theatres were written by about 50 authors. It is also well to remember that the precise authorship of most plays from this period is difficult to determine because collaboration was so common (at times each act was written by a different author), and plays were frequently revised by persons other than the original writer. Thus, we can seldom establish the relationship of a surviving script to the playwright's original text.

GOVERNMENT REGULATION OF THE THEATRE

The development of playwriting as a profession was made possible by the emergence of a public theatre that constantly required new plays. In turn, the stability of the theatre was heavily dependent on government regulations. When she succeeded to the throne, Elizabeth was faced with the challenge of gaining effective control over the numerous forces that made for divisiveness in England. During her reign she slowly consolidated her power to such an extent that her successors, the Stuart kings (beginning with James I, son of Mary of Scotland), were able for a time to rule almost as absolute monarchs. The theatre was among those activities over which the crown gained control, and since the court was always more favorable to professional actors than local governments were, the growth of the theatre paralleled the central government's assumption of authority over professional performances.

When Elizabeth came to the throne in 1558, any gentleman could maintain a troupe of actors. Any actor not employed by a gentleman was classed as a vagabond and was subject to severe penalties. Since the troupes patronized by gentlemen were permitted to tour when not needed at home, actors were not always closely supervised, and many illegal companies falsely claimed patronage or performed partisan plays that aggravated religious controversy. These conditions led Elizabeth to take a number of measures designed to bring order out of the chaos. In 1559 she banned plays on religious or political subjects, and made local officials responsible for licensing all public performances in their areas.

Since these regulations were not entirely effective, new measures were taken in the 1570s. The religious cycles were now systematically suppressed, a process that was completed with the closure of the Coventry cycle in 1581. At the same time, actors were brought under closer supervision. In 1572 it was declared illegal for anyone below the rank of baron to maintain a troupe or to authorize one to tour. (The ranks, from lowest to highest, were baron, viscount, earl, marquis, and duke. Noble women were not excluded as the Duchess of Suffolk and the Countess of Essex, among others, maintained companies.) Other companies could perform by obtaining a license from two Justices of the Peace, but since this license was good only in the locality where the Justices resided, a new one had to be secured in each town when troupes toured. On the other hand, the law specifically absolved authorized actors of vagabondage, the charge previously used against them. The overall effect of the law was to reduce the number of troupes but to extend firm legal protections to those that remained. The authority of the crown was extended much farther in 1574 when the first royal patent was granted to Leicester's Men, a company headed by James Burbage (1530– 1597), one of the earliest builders of playhouses in England. The patent transferred the power to license this company's plays from local authorities to the Master of Revels, the official who, since 1545, had been responsible for the monarch's entertainment and who served under the manager of all royal household affairs, the Lord Chamberlain.

The rapid expansion of London's population and the increasing amount of time the patrons of acting troupes spent there brought more troupes to London for longer periods of time. This probably explains the boom in theatre building, five being opened between 1575 and 1577. Critics of the theatre responded forcefully to this marked increase in professional theatre activity. The first major assault came in John Northbrooke's *A Treatise Against Dicing, Dancing, Plays, and Interludes* (1577). This was soon followed by former playwright Stephen Gosson's *The School of Abuse* (1579) and *Plays Confuted in Five Actions* (1582). These works railed in the harshest terms against the theatre as an instrument used by the Devil to encourage vice and to take people away from honest work and other useful pursuits. The attacks were answered by Thomas Lodge in *A Defence of Poetry, Music, and Stage Plays* (1579), and especially by Sir Philip Sidney in *The Defence of Poesy* (c. 1580), which argued that literature is the most effective instrument for teaching morality and moving people to virtuous action. This was the first major statement of the neoclassical ideal in English and exerted a strong influence on the next generation of writers, especially Ben Jonson. Although they were not able to suppress the theatre, the critics voiced the ideas that dominated the governing councils of many English towns, which opposed the professional players.

The controversy encouraged the Queen's government to take further control of the professional theatre. In 1581 the Master of the Revels, Sir Edmund Tilney (served 1579–1610), was granted a special commission to license all plays (not just those for Leicester's Men), and this authority was expanded to include the licensing of playhouses in 1598. The same powers were granted to his successors: Sir George Buck (served 1610–1622), who was also granted the authority to license plays for publication, and Sir John Astley (served 1622–1623), who received the additional authority of licensing acting companies. Fees paid for these licenses made the office a lucrative one, especially under Sir Henry Herbert (served 1623–1642 and 1660–1673). Many local officials, however, believed that the crown was usurping authority which should reside with them, since they were responsible for health, conduct, and morals in their communities. The Common Council of the City of London was especially adamant in asserting its own authority on this matter.

In 1583 the Crown attempted a compromise by establishing the Queen's Men, granting them a monopoly to perform in London and stipulating the Inns they could use for performance. This put crown support behind the city's attempt to limit the number of professional companies performing within the city of London, but the arrangement broke down as the Queen's Men declined after 1588. A new accommodation was made in 1594 when the Lord Chamberlain and the Lord Admiral replaced the monopoly held by the Queen's Men with what they intended to be dual monopolies held by their own troupes, the Admiral's Men and the Chamberlain's Men, playing in the London suburbs.

The first serious threat to these new companies came in 1597, when several members of the Admiral's Men illegally formed a third company at the Swan playhouse. This brought a surprisingly harsh order from the Queen's Privy Council that all the playhouses around London were to be pulled down. For reasons that remain unclear the order was not carried out, and the following year (1598) the monopoly status of the Admiral's and Chamberlain's companies was officially recognized.

The Stuart monarchs, who succeeded the Tudor line in 1603, were strong believers in the divine right of kings and insisted on exerting authority more blatantly than Elizabeth had thought wise. During the reign of James I (1603–1625), only companies with a royal patent assigning them to members of the royal family were allowed to reside in the London area. Under Charles I (reigned 1625–1649), the patent for the King's Men continued, and one was issued for Prince Charles' Men in 1631, but all other companies were licensed by the Master of the Revels. This two-patent system was to be revived in the Restoration.

ACTING TROUPES

There were many acting troupes in England during the reigns of the early Tudor monarchs, but their activities are hard to trace before 1572, when they were required to have noble patrons. From 1572 to 1642 we know the names of over 100 companies that toured England, though few have long histories. Many did nothing but tour, while others, especially after the 1580s, were London-based companies on occasional tours or offshoots of London companies using "exemplifications" (a duplicate copy of a license), while still others were illegal companies traveling with expired or forged licenses. A number of troupes also toured on the continent, and it is from those itinerant English companies that the professional theatre in Germany is descended.

There were two types of professional companies during this period: adult companies, which were organized on the sharing system, and boys' companies, which, when they became professional, were led by an adult impresario. From the 1570s on, companies of both types sought to focus their activities in London, and the best companies eventually resided there. Of the many adult companies of the day, the Queen's Men, the Admiral's Men, and the Chamberlain's Men were the most influential. Of the boys' companies, Paul's Boys and Blackfriars Boys had the greatest influence.

The Queen's Men were established in 1583, when the Master of Revels was ordered to form an all-star company to perform for the Queen and to give that company a monopoly on playing within the city of London. With twelve shareholders this was the largest company in England; it started the vogue for large cast plays and pioneered the practice of dividing into two units by using a copy of its license. It raised the standards for acting in England until deaths and dissensions among its members caused it to go into decline after 1588.

The failure of the Queen's Men led to the formation, in 1594, of the two most famous companies of the age: the Admiral's Men, under the leadership of the actor Edward Alleyn and with the financial backing of the important theatre entrepreneur, Philip Henslowe; and the Chamberlain's Men, a cooperative venture of the Burbage family and a group of actors, including William Shakespeare. Like the Queen's Men, both these companies were formed from players recruited from existing companies. These companies vied for prominence in the London market for the next twenty years, and they were the first to acquire their own playhouses. When James I came to the throne in 1603, the Chamberlain's company was renamed the King's Men, a title it retained until the closing of the theatres in 1642. (This title was renewed in 1660 for a company formed by Thomas Killigrew.) The Lord Admiral's Men became Prince Henry's Men (1604–1613) and were the Elector Palatine's Men (the king's son-in-law) when they disbanded in 1625.

Like all the adult companies of the day these companies were organized on the sharing plan, under which financial risks and profits were divided among those actors who had become part-owners of the company by buying shares in it. To become a shareholder, an actor had to put up a sizable sum of money and commit himself to the company for a minimum of three years. The companies bought back and resold the shares of those who left. Not all actors were shareholders, and not all owned equal shares. The number of shareholders in the London-based companies could be as high as twelve, while the touring companies generally had six. The shareholders formed a self-governing, democratic body that selected and produced plays. In addition to acting the major roles in the company's repertory, each shareholder generally had additional responsibilities such as business management, playwriting, or the supervision of costumes and properties. It is difficult to estimate their income because financial practices were so varied. But after meeting all expenses (which included payments to authors, "hired men," and the fund out of which the "common stock" of costumes, properties, and other materials was purchased), the shareholders divided the company's portion of the house receipts. In a court suit of 1635 one witness stated that shareholders in the King's Men earned about £180 annually, although the actors themselves estimated their earnings at £50. Even the latter figure, however, is about twice the amount earned by schoolmasters at this time. Undoubtedly the King's Men was the most affluent of the companies, but so long as performances were not interrupted by forced closures, the sharing actors in all companies were reasonably well off.

The nonsharing adult members of the company, the "hired men," worked under contracts paying from five to ten shillings per week. Records show, however, that they frequently were not paid the full amount. Hired men performed supporting roles, and served as prompters, wardrobe keepers, stage keepers, musicians, and janitors. Those who developed a good reputation as actors were eventually offered the opportunity to buy any available shares, and many borrowed money to do so.

Companies were further augmented by four to six boys apprenticed to well-established adult actors. Apprenticeship could last from three to twelve years. Some boys may have begun as early as age ten, and others remained apprentices into their early twenties. Boys played all of the women's roles, although older women's roles, especially the comic ones, may have occasionally been played by men. The apprentices lived with their masters, who trained, fed, and clothed them. The masters were paid by the company for the boys' services. Some of the apprentices went on to become adult actors, but many followed other professions upon reaching maturity.

Each company had rules of conduct and fines for their infringement. In 1614 Lady Elizabeth's Men agreed to this schedule of fines, for example: one shilling (twelve pence) for lateness to rehearsals; three shillings for lateness to performance; ten shillings for being intoxicated during performance; one pound (twenty shillings) for missing a performance; and forty pounds (more than a year's income for many actors) for wearing a costume outside the theatre or for taking company property.

With few exceptions, all acting companies toured, since not even London had a sufficient audience base for all of them. Touring entailed many problems, however. Until 1620, permission to perform was based on a preview performance given to city officials, and some cities insisted on this kind of preview throughout the period. If the play was approved, the company would be paid for its performance and authorized to give several more within the city. If the play was rejected, the company might be paid to move on or, in extreme cases, could end up in jail. After 1620, if a city declined a preview and accepted the Master of the Revels' license on a play, that did not insure that a company could perform. Bristol was the only city outside London with a permanent theatre (first the Playhouse in Wine Street c. 1605–1625, owned by Nicholas Woolfe, and later one in Redcliffe Hill, purpose-built by Richard Barker), so a company could be denied permission to perform on the grounds that there was no suitable space. Permission could also be denied based on the fear of spreading plague or because of public unrest, or for many other reasons. When they were allowed to perform, the companies had to be able to adapt to a wide variety of performance conditions from fairgrounds to manor-house halls.

Those few companies with a base in London could tour less often and were the beneficiaries of generous royal patronage. The number of such companies went from just one in 1583, to two in 1594, to three in 1602, to a high point of six in 1611, and four or five thereafter. Elizabeth saw an average of five professional productions each year, for each of which she paid a fee of about ten pounds. The Stuart kings, on the other hand, paid the same fees but saw many more productions: James I saw an average of seventeen plays each year, while Charles I saw an average of twenty-five. In addition, the Stuarts put the London companies under royal patronage. Shareholders in the royal companies were paid a yearly fee and given allowances for food, light, and fuel. Occasionally they received additional sums to buy new costumes or to tide them over when the plague closed the theatres. In return, these actors were called upon to help with court masques, and to perform on special state occasions. Court performances were held at night and so rarely conflicted with public performances, and since the plays given at court were usually those played for the general public, they did not overburden the actors with additional preparation.

The boys' companies were as likely to be seen at court as the adult troupes up until 1610. Originally these companies were formed in the choir schools, where the boys were given a good education and performed in plays to learn elocution and deportment. They were especially popular at court in the 1560s and 1570s, and some choir masters exploited their talents by staging plays to which they charged admission. After 1600 these companies became fully professional, but the boys were treated like apprentices, not shareholders. The Children of Paul's, or Paul's Boys, was the first to achieve prominence. This company ran public performances at its own St. Paul's playhouse from 1575 to 1590 and again from 1599 to 1606. It was best known for its citizens' comedies, written by Middleton, Chapman, Beaumont, and other outstanding dramatists of the day.

The Blackfriars Boys, also known as The Children of (Her Majesty's) Chapel, or the Chapel Boys, was the most famous of the boys' companies, however. It was the resident troupe for the first Blackfriars playhouse in 1576 and operated the second Blackfriars theatre from 1600 to 1608. This troupe was a special favorite of Queen Anne, who had it designated Children of the Queen's Revels in 1604 and gave it the privilege of not having its plays licensed by the Master of the Revels. Most of the greatest writers of the day, including Ben Jonson, wrote for this troupe. It was known for its "railing" comedies, which satirized just about everything, but in 1608 two of those satires so enraged the king that he ordered the company disbanded. The company was allowed to reform in 1609 but was forced to move outside the city to the Whitefriars Playhouse, where it continued performing until 1613. Its name and license was used by touring companies until at least 1635. This was the last of the great boys' companies. (The Caroline Young Company and Beeston's Boys of later decades were companies of young men.)

Companies needed a sizable repertory so they could change their bills daily to keep the audiences coming. A writer, or group of writers, seeking to sell a play would be asked to read part or all of it to the shareholders. Once purchased and produced, plays were retained as long as they drew audiences and might be revised when they declined in popularity. The demand for new works made companies seek liaisons with dependable dramatists, some of whom worked under contract. Until about 1603 the average payment for a play was six pounds, but by 1613 the price had risen to ten or twelve pounds. Playwrights were sometimes also given all the receipts (minus the company's expenses) at the second performance, thus beginning the benefit system that was to be especially important to English theatre in the next century. In the 1630s, at least one writer (and perhaps others) was being paid a weekly salary, in addition to a benefit performance for each play he supplied the company. Writers were also paid to revise old plays and to write new scenes, prologues, or epilogues.

Once the playwright's fees had been paid, the play generally belonged to the troupe, though if the writer were also a shareholder in the company he might retain more control. Since there were no copyright laws, however, companies had no means of maintaining exclusive performance rights except by keeping plays out of the hands of others. The more popular works were often pirated by printers, and troupes sometimes sold publication rights during times of financial stress. Playwrights who had no ongoing contract with a company sometimes sold plays to printers after they had collected their fees from the actors, a practice which, though perhaps unethical, was not illegal. When a company disbanded, the distribution of its stock of plays was always of the greatest concern to the shareholders.

Legally, every play had to be submitted to the Master of Revels for licensing before performance. The principal result was the elimination of passages thought to be morally, religiously, or politically ob-jectionable, though it is clear that those who worked for the Master of Revels were relatively liberal-minded about such things. The licensed script was the company's official copy of the play. Actors were merely supplied "sides," which included only their own lines and three-word cues.

On average, only three weeks transpired from the purchase of a play to its first performance. Since that included the time for licensing and copying out of the actors' sides, rehearsals could not have been extensive. As a rule, playwrights knew which troupe they were writing for, however, and could tailor their work to the size of the company and to the skills of individual actors. The prompter (sometimes called the bookholder or bookkeeper) was responsible for copying out the sides, posting the platt (an outline of the scenes with a list of the actors involved in each), making lists of the necessary properties, costumes, and music, and finally for running the performances.

We know the names of more than 1000 actors, or "players," from this period, but we have cast lists for only 43 plays (and these may not be for the original performances). Few performers achieved lasting renown. Richard Tarleton (?–1588) and Robert Wilson (?–1600) were both members of the Queen's Men. They were accomplished comic performers who also wrote plays and won wide followings. The first great tragic actor was Edward Alleyn (1566–1626), who created Marlowe's Faustus and Tamburlaine and Kyd's Hieronimo. He gave up acting in 1597 but returned to the stage when the Admiral's Men moved to the Fortune in 1600. He finally retired in 1604, but continued in management with his father-in-law, Philip Henslowe.

The members of the Chamberlain's (later King's) Men gained more lasting fame because Shakespeare was one of their fellow players. The leading performer was Richard Burbage (c. 1567–1619), who created such roles as Richard III, Hamlet, Lear, and Othello, and was generally acknowledged to be the greatest actor of his age. Other members of the company included William Kempe (?–c. 1603), noted for his low comedy acting and dances; John Heminges (1556–1630), the business manager; Robert Armin (c. 1568–1615), a celebrated clown; John Lowin (c. 1576–c. 1659), noted for his Falstaff and Henry VIII and company manager after Heminges's retirement; Joseph Taylor (c. 1585–1652), who replaced Burbage when he died and who shared in the company management; and Nathan Field (1587–1620), considered by many second only to Burbage. Another company member, Christopher Beeston (c. 1580–1639), became the most successful theatrical impresario under the Stuarts.

The acting style of the Elizabethan performer can only be guessed at. Some scholars insist that double casting, the performance of female roles by male actors, the nonrealistic nature of the scripts, the conventionalized stage background, the large repertory, which would have made detailed individualized characterizations difficult, and limited rehearsal time would have made the acting style "formal." Others argue for a relatively realistic style, based on Shakespeare's "advice to the players" in *Hamlet;* contemporary references to the convincing characterizations given by such actors as Burbage; the emphasis on contemporary life and manners in many comedies; the truthfulness of human psychology portrayed in the serious plays; and the proximity of spectators to actors during performances. Judging by contemporary accounts, many actors moved audiences with the power and "truth" of their playing, but this tells little about acceptable conventions, for what is considered "truth in acting" varies markedly from one period to another. The most that one can say is that the better actors represented well contemporary conceptions of artistic excellence.

THE PUBLIC THEATRES

By 1560 there were two well-established traditions in staging: the outdoor and the indoor. The religious cycles, street pageants, tournaments, and morality plays had been given out-of-doors, and the companies attached to noble houses often played outside when on tour. On the other hand, mummings, disguisings, interludes, academic plays, and special entertainments were normally given indoors; touring players often performed in town halls, guild halls, manor houses, or inns. Consequently, there were many precedents upon which the Elizabethan troupes could draw when building permanent theatres. In London those permanent theatres were of two types. One was an open-air structure designed for a general public; the other was a smaller roofed structure which catered to a more aristocratic audience. It is customary to call structures of the first type "public" and those of the second type "private." Both types were in use by 1575.

Thirteen public open-air playhouses were built near London between 1567 and 1623. They were: The Red Lion (1567–?); The Theatre (1576–1598); The Playhouse at Newington Butts (c. 1576–1594); The Curtain (c. 1577–c. 1627); The Rose (1587–c. 1606, remodeled in 1592); The Swan (c. 1595–c. 1632); The Boar's Head, Whitechapel (1598–c. 1616); The Globe (1599–1613); The Fortune (1600–1621); The Red Bull (1605–1663, remodeled in 1625);

FIG. 5.2
Yard of the Tabard Inn, London. This sketch was made just before the inn was destroyed in the nineteenth century. Supposedly the yard had remained unchanged since the time of Elizabeth I. Although the Tabard was probably not used for plays, it illustrates the arrangement that made inns usable as theatres in Elizabethan times. From Thornbury, *Old and New London.*

The Second Globe (1614–?1644); The Hope (1614–1656), and The Second Fortune (1623–1662).

The Red Lion was built about a mile east of the City of London. We know from historic documents published in 1983 that "scaffolds" were built for audience seating and that the stage was 5 feet high, 40 feet wide, and 30 feet deep. Attached to the stage was a "turret" 30 feet high. Beyond this basic information, however, we know little about the building. We can only speculate on its shape and size; on how the scaffolds, stage, and turret might have been linked together; or on how permanent the theatre was intended to be. But this playhouse, the first known in England, was built by John Brayne, the brother-in-law of James Burbage, the man who seems to have headed Leicester's company in 1572. We do not know what became of The Red Lion but in 1576, with the financial backing of Brayne, Burbage built the far more famous playhouse called "The Theatre."

The Theatre was located on leased land in the popular recreational area of Shoreditch, just outside the northeastern limits of the city. It was a large, polygonal building with three levels of roofed audience galleries enclosing a yard which was open to the sky. Into this yard, presumably, a raised stage was thrust out from one wall. The audience in the yard stood around three sides while the audience in the galleries watched from at least three sides and perhaps four. The Theatre has long been thought to have served as the model for subsequent public playhouses, largely because when its property lease expired in 1597, the same year James Burbage died, his sons had it dismantled and used its timbers in the building of The Globe. We do not know how much the design of The Theatre was influenced by The Red Lion; how The Theatre compared to The Playhouse at Newington Butts, which William Ingram has argued was also built in 1576 (about a mile south of the city); or whether The Curtain (built nearby The Theatre) was an improvement. But the inspiration for the design of these unroofed public theatres has usually been traced from two sources: innyards and gaming arenas.

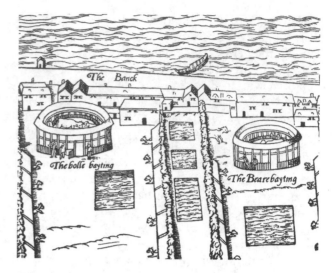

FIG. 5.4

A portion of the Agas map of London (the sketches for which were made between 1569 and 1590 but not printed until 1631). Note that the bull- and bear-baiting rings appear more nearly corrals than three-tiered galleried structures.

It is certain that many troupes played in inns both before and after permanent theatres were built. At least six inns in London were used as theatres, including The Bull, The Bell, The Bel Savage, and the Cross Keys inns. The usual reconstructions of innyard theatres ignore the irregular shape of most such spaces and show a booth-like stage set up at one side of a courtyard, with the inn's permanent outside galleries providing seating on a raised level and the yard serving as a place where spectators could stand. The permanent theatre structures are then said to be a formalization of this arrangement. But scholars now question the widespread use of innyards for playing. Performances in an innyard would have seriously disrupted an inn's normal activities, and The Records of Early English Drama (REED) project has found that when troupes performed at inns, they generally performed indoors. Known innyard theatres like The Boar's Head were built long after public theatres were established and after the buildings they occupied no longer functioned as working inns. Nevertheless, innyards may provide a precedent for the structure of the permanent open-air theatres.

The arenas used for bull or bear baiting, fencing matches, and wrestling have also been cited as possible prototypes for the unroofed structures. Some scholars have argued that the theatres were formed merely by setting up a removable booth stage in such an arena. But early map views of these baiting rings show them as little more than corrals. They are not shown with multileveled galleries for spectators until

FIG. 5.3

A Renaissance conception of the Roman theatre. Note the polygonal shape, the galleries, and the label "Theatrum." This illustration is from an edition of Terence's plays published in Lyon in 1493; it could have been an influence on Burbage's *The Theatre* (1576). From Bapst, *Essai sur l'Histoire du Théâtre* (1893).

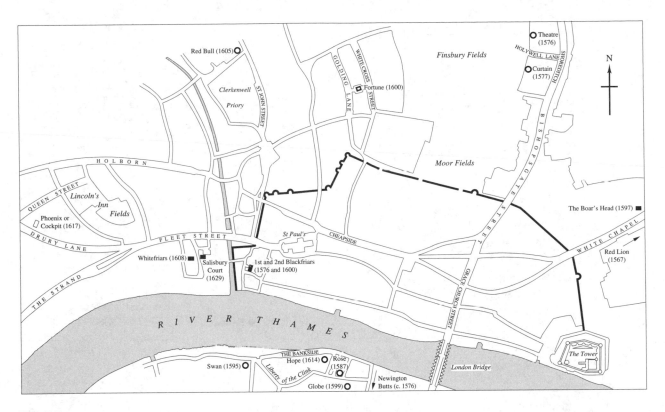

FIG. 5.5

Map showing the location of London's playhouses. From Andrew Gurr, *The Shakespearean Stage, 1574–1642* (1970). The location of the Red Lion has been added. Courtesy Cambridge University Press.

after several playhouses were built, so the direction of influence is unclear.

Other possible sources, less frequently cited, are illustrations published in editions of Terence's works. Some of these show circular, open-air structures with galleries labeled *"Theatrum."* Perhaps this explains where Burbage got the idea for calling his playhouse "The Theatre," a term not in common use at that time. Unfortunately, this cannot be proven.

The stage itself is thought to have been derived from such diverse sources as the pageant wagons and fixed platforms of the religious plays, the booth stages of traveling players, and the hall stages of the universities. The facade erected at the rear of the stage has been compared to the Rhetoric stages used in the Netherlands, to the triumphal arches used in civic pageants, and to the "screen" found in manor halls where actors are known to have performed. But what links there may be between any of these elements and the building of the theatres in London remains unclear. The possible influences on the public theatres are therefore numerous, but direct connections are difficult to establish.

After The Curtain, there was a ten-year break before The Rose playhouse was built by the theatrical

entrepreneur Philip Henslowe, whose careful records of his financial transactions are the principal source of information about the operation of these theatres. The Rose was located south of the city, just across the river, and, as the first home of the Admiral's Men, was one of the most successful theatres of its day. In 1988–1989, archaeologists discovered the foundations of this playhouse, and their excavations of it have provided some of the most reliable information available (see Fig. 5.6). The Rose was originally a fourteen-sided polygon with an outside diameter of about 72 feet. The foundations supported galleries which were 11½ feet deep, so the inner yard, where about one third of the audience stood for performances, must have measured roughly 49 feet across. The yard was sloped down toward the stage and paved with a surface made of cinders and nutshells. The stage thrust out into the yard about 16 feet 5 inches. (It was 36 feet 9 inches wide where it intersected the galleries and tapered to 26 feet 10 inches at the front.) In 1592 this building was enlarged, the stage thrust was increased to 18 feet 4 inches, and the yard was leveled. A roof seems to have been erected over the stage at this time as well, and three years later Henslowe paid to have flying machinery installed there. But foundations do not, of

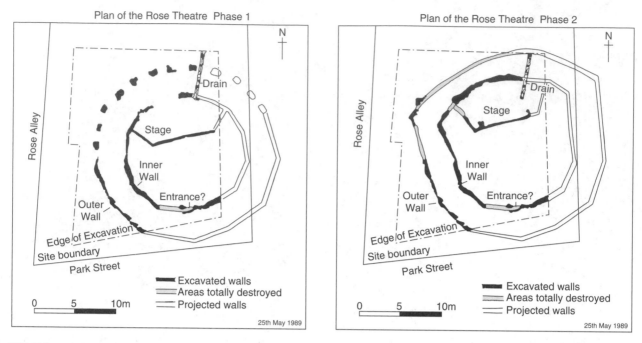

Plan of the Rose Theatre Phase 1

Rose Alley

Drain

Stage

Inner
Wall

Outer
Wall

Entrance?

Edge of Excavation

Site boundary

Park Street

N

0   5   10m

Excavated walls
Areas totally destroyed
Projected walls

25th May 1989

Plan of the Rose Theatre Phase 2

Rose Alley

Drain

Stage

Inner
Wall

Outer
Wall

Entrance?

Edge of Excavation

Site boundary

Park Street

N

0   5   10m

Excavated walls
Areas totally destroyed
Projected walls

25th May 1989

FIG. 5.6

Ground plan of the first Rose Theatre as revealed by excavations in 1989.
Phase 1 shows the layout of the theatre when it was built in 1587; phase 2
shows the layout following alterations in 1592. Courtesy Museum of London.

course, provide any information on the heights of
these structures, so that information must be gleaned
from other sources (see Fig. 5.7).

The Rose was a smaller building than most scholars had expected for a public theatre of this period.
The tapered stage was also something of a surprise,
since other evidence had indicated that a rectangular shape was more likely. What was most unex-

pected, however, was the relatively small size of the
stage, which is known to have supported some of the
most spectacular large-cast plays of the period. While
it corresponds well with the known dimensions for
stages in the indoor theatres, this stage is substantially
shallower than stages were thought to be in the outdoor playhouses.

The Swan Playhouse was built west of The Rose
in 1585. It is of special importance because of The
Swan drawing (often called the de Witt drawing),
which is the only contemporary image we have of
the interior of one of these open-air playhouses (see
Fig. 5.8). The distorted scale makes it difficult to determine the dimensions of the building, the yard, or
even the stage. But the drawing does provide our
only record of a "tiring house" facade, which it
shows having two doors leading onto the rear of the
stage with a balcony above. A letter attached to this
drawing praised the decoration of The Swan, but
there is little sign of such ornateness in the drawing
itself. What has proven more troubling for scholars,
however, is that what is shown in the drawing does
not seem sufficient for staging the plays of the period. About 500 plays still survive from the 1056 Alfred Harbage has recorded as being performed during
this time. They occasionally provide stage directions
and if we take only one of those plays, Middleton's
A Chaste Maid in Cheapside (performed at the Swan
between 1611 and 1613), we find that it calls for "a

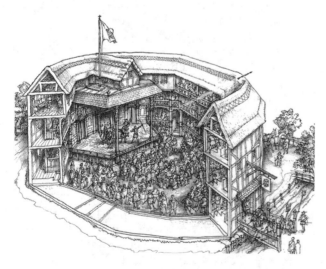

FIG. 5.7

A reconstruction by C. Walter Hodges depicting a 1594
performance at the Rose Theatre. Courtesy Mr. Hodges.

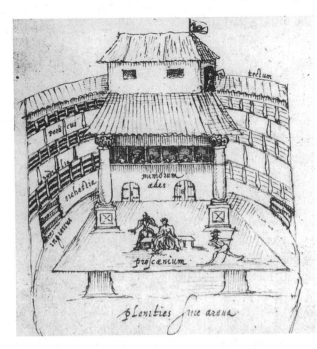

FIG. 5.8

Interior of The Swan Theatre, 1596. The original drawing, made by a Dutch visitor, Johannes de Witt, has not survived; this is a copy made of it by Arend van Buchell. The drawing is accompanied by a descriptive passage which reads in part: "Of all the theatres, . . . the largest and most magnificent is . . . the Swan; for it accommodates . . . three thousand persons. . . . [It is] supported by wooden columns painted in such excellent imitation of marble that it is able to deceive even the most observant . . . its form resembles that of a Roman work . . . " Note the absence of a central discovery space and the human figures in the gallery above the stage. From Bapst, *Essai sur l'Histoire du Théâtre* (1893).

FIG. 5.9

J. C. Adams's reconstruction of The Globe theatre. Note the inner stages both on the first and second levels and the "musicians' gallery" on the third level. Courtesy Folger Library and Mr. Adams.

Shop being discovered," "a bed thrust out upon the Stage, Allwit's Wife in it," and "a sad song in the Music Room."

The music room is now generally thought to have been in one section of the tiring-house balcony, with the other sections being "Lords' Rooms," the most expensive seats in the theatres. But this raises another issue. A certain number of plays seem to require scenes to be performed at windows, balconies, battlements, or other high places, the balcony scene of *Romeo and Juliet* being the best-known example. It is not clear how those scenes could be staged in this space. Many present-day historians have argued that such scenes do not occur often, are not long, and generally involve few characters, so the actors could simply have used the music room for the duration of such scenes. Historians in past decades, however, most notably J. C. Adams, have offered far more complex solutions (see Fig. 5.9).

Either of the two doors shown at The Swan would provide enough space for a bed to be thrust out in Middleton's play. But there seems to be no facility for a shop "being discovered," yet discoveries are called for in a number of plays. One possibility, proposed by Richard Southern, is that there was a central opening in The Swan tiring house but it was covered by a curtain hanging from the balcony when de Witt made his drawing. This central opening could have provided the necessary discovery space, though any characters revealed there would have to move onto the main stage quickly in order to be seen by the entire audience. This is a solution common to the "Terence stage" of the continent (see Chapter 7) and the corral theatres of Spain. References to curtains and hangings are sufficiently common to give this solution credence, and a central discovery space would also provide a third entrance onto the stage, something we know existed in the indoor theatres. Another possibility, proposed by C. Walter Hodges, is that theatres owned a "pavilion" that could be set up in front of the tiring house as needed (see Fig. 5.10). This arrangement's advantage is that the pavilion opens on three sides, so everyone in the audience could see. There are references to pavilions in some of the plays, but it is not

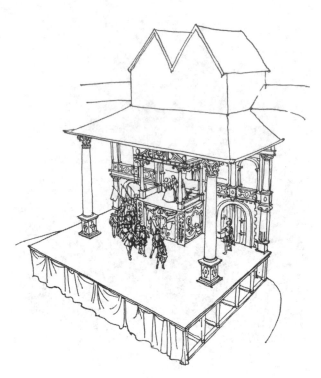

FIG. 5.10
C. W. Hodges's reconstruction of the Elizabethan stage showing a pavilion at the rear. From Hodges, *The Globe Restored.* Courtesy Mr. Hodges.

clear that they were used in this manner. A third possibility, proposed by Richard Hosley, is that the discovery was made behind one of the two doorways, a solution that allows for two separate discoveries. All three theories and more are possible; none has been entirely persuasive.

When The Globe opened across the street from The Rose, Henslowe and Alleyn had The Fortune theatre built north of the city for the Admiral's Men. Before the recent archaeological discoveries, a builder's contract for The Fortune playhouse was the primary source of information about these theatres. From this contract we learn that The Fortune was a timber-frame structure, 80 feet square. Its roofed galleries were three stories high, surrounding an open yard that was 55 feet square. The contract gives heights for the galleries like those seen in The Swan drawing: 12 feet high for the first, 11 feet high for the second, and 9 feet high for the third. It also states that the first gallery depth was 12½ feet, about what was found at The Rose. Somewhere within these galleries were "gentlemen's rooms" and "two penny rooms" (other documents mention spaces for "quiet standing"), but their exact locations are unknown. The stage was 43 feet wide (leaving 6 feet between it and the galleries on either side), and it extended to

the middle of the 55-foot yard. The contract calls for the stage and tiring house to be erected "within the frame," and recently scholars have been debating precisely what this means. It has generally been taken to mean that the tiring house occupied the galleries behind the stage; this would make the stage 27½ feet deep, giving it dimensions which compare well to the stages at The Red Lion (40 feet wide by 30 feet deep) and The Boar's Head (40 feet wide by 23 feet deep). But all these stages are substantially bigger than the stage found at The Rose. If the dimensions for these larger stages include space for the tiring house, however, their open area available for performance would have a depth closer to that found at The Rose. The issue is important, since the depth of a stage has major implications for staging, but the existing evidence does not allow for any clear resolution. When The Fortune was destroyed by fire in 1621, it was immediately replaced, but The Second Fortune seems to have been round and built of stone.

An even shorter contract exists for The Hope playhouse of 1614. It was designed to house plays and animal baitings on alternating days. The contract instructs the builder to model this theatre on The Swan, except that the roof which protected the stage (called "the heavens" here but "the shadow" in The Fortune contract) was not to be supported by stage posts. Both the stage and tiring house had to be removable for bear baiting, so the heavens had to be self-supporting. (The fact that the tiring house was removable would suggest that it was not built into the galleries.) Evidence from other sources suggests that the underside of the heavens may have been painted with the signs of the zodiac or some other representations of sky, sun, and moon. Some plays refer to flying effects and sound effects like thunder, alarm bells, and cannonades, which would seem to require machinery in the attic space above the heavens. We do not know if The Hope heavens was capable of supporting such equipment.

Historians have paid relatively little attention to the backstage space and have little to say about dressing rooms or storage space for the wardrobe, furniture, properties, and other equipment. Some companies owned adjoining structures that may have been used for these purposes. When The Globe burned in 1613, there are no reports of major additional losses, but when The Fortune burned in 1621 the company was said to be undone by the loss of its wardrobe and playbooks. In general, however, little is known about the space used for preparing and maintaining productions.

These theatres were owned by "householders" who held shares in the building. Most were entrepreneurs like Philip Henslowe, a householder for

The Rose, Fortune, and Hope, or Francis Langley, a householder for The Swan and Boar's Head. But others were actors such as James Burbage, Edward Alleyn, Richard Burbage, and William Shakespeare. Householders paid the expenses for maintaining these buildings and rented them out to the professional acting companies, amateur actors, fencers, tumblers, and miscellaneous entertainers. Arrangements varied, but generally the householders received half the take from the galleries. They may also have received fees from the sale of food, drink, and other items on their property.

The first Globe playhouse has always received the greatest attention because of its association with Shakespeare, who owned a one-eighth share in the venture and saw most of his greatest plays performed there. Contemporary maps of London provide small and generally contradictory images of its exterior, but beyond that scholars have had little direct evidence to go on. The Chamberlain's Men (King's Men after 1603) performed there and used it as a summer home even after they began performing in the private Second Blackfriars playhouse. When The Globe was destroyed by fire in 1613, it was im-mediately rebuilt, grander than before; that building was reported as "pulled down" in 1644; that report is suspect, but tenements occupied the site by 1655.

In 1989 archaeologists discovered a small part of its foundations (perhaps less than 8 percent of the total), and these show that the first-level galleries at The Globe were about the same depth as those at The Rose and Fortune, but this is all that can be said with confidence. Using a geometric analysis of the remains, John Orrell has argued that The Globe was a twenty-sided structure (circular in appearance) and that the remains confirm his earlier conclusions, based on a meticulous examination of the 1644 Hollar map of London, that the Globe had an exterior diameter of approximately 99 feet and a yard diameter of 74 feet. Others have concluded that the remains show an eighteen-sided structure with an outside diameter of 90 feet and a yard diameter of 66 feet or even a sixteen-sided building with an outside diameter of 86 feet and a yard of 61 feet. Orrell's interpretation has been the basis for the full-scale reconstruction called Shakespeare's Globe, which opened in London in 1997 (Fig. 5.11).

FIG. 5.11
Shakespeare's Globe, London. This highly ornate simulation of an Elizabethan public playhouse opened in 1997 and was adjusted in 1999.
Photo by F. J. Hildy ©.

THE PRIVATE THEATRES

Although historians have usually treated the public theatres as those most typical of pre-Commonwealth England, it is likely that more performances were given indoors than outdoors in the years between 1558 and 1642. Many of these indoor productions were staged in manor houses, town halls, inns, or at court, but those at "private" theatres are of primary interest.

The term "private" is not used until 1600 in relation to theatres that were actually open to the public. It is then applied to indoor theatres being used by two boys' companies who had started performing in London in direct violation of the monopolies held by the Admiral's and Chamberlain's Men. It looks suspiciously as though the term was adopted as a ploy, since private performances were not covered by the laws which required companies to have a patron and to have their plays and buildings licensed. But whatever the reason for the term's original use, it is now applied to the roofed theatres of the period. These theatres differ from the public theatres in that they were smaller (accommodating about one-fourth as many spectators), they charged considerably higher admission prices, they provided seats for all spectators, and they depended on candles (supplemented by windows) for illumination.

Nine "private" theatres were built in and around London between 1575 and 1635: St. Paul's (c. 1575–

1590, 1599–c. 1608); First Blackfriars, at the Old Buttery (1576–1584); Second Blackfriars, at Upper Frater Hall (1596–1655); Whitefriars (?1580–1596 and c. 1606–1629); Porter's Hall (1615–1616); The Cockpit/ Phoenix in Drury Lane (1616–c. 1667); Salisbury Court (1629–1658 and 1660–1666); the Cockpit-in-Court (1629–c. 1666); and the French Theatre at Le Fevre's Riding Academy (1635–1636). All these theatres (with the exception of Porter's Hall and possibly Salisbury Court) were built into existing buildings.

Little is known about the St. Paul's playhouse of 1575 except that it must have been located on church property or it would not have been allowed in London. It is assumed to have used an arrangement similar to those for performance in university halls, since the Paul's Boys' repertory consisted of the same kind of plays. This theatre closed in 1590 but was reopened in 1599. It closed again in 1606, and the Whitefriars playhouse (built west of the city) was apparently intended to replace it.

The first and second Blackfriars were also built within the City of London, but they were in a "liberty," property under the direct control of the Crown, and therefore exempt from city regulations. The Blackfriars, like the Whitefriars, was one of 376 religious properties confiscated by the Crown between 1536 and 1540. Although much of the property was later ceded to private individuals, the Crown retained jurisdiction over the London liberties until 1608. The first Blackfriars was opened in 1576. When Richard Farrant, choirmaster of the Chapel Royal at Windsor, leased the property, he stated that it would be used in preparing the children for their appearances before the queen; no mention was made of public performances. Farrant's concealment of his real intentions led to a series of lawsuits that put an end to the theatre in 1584. By that time, a number of children's companies had played there. The theatre is thought to have measured only 46½ feet by 26 feet with an audience capacity of 100.

The second Blackfriars was built by James Burbage in 1596. It was located in a large second-story hall, but before it could open the residents of Blackfriars secured an injunction against its use. When Burbage died in 1597, he willed the Blackfriars to his sons, who, unable to use it, leased it for twenty-one years to Henry Evans. Evans installed the Blackfriars Boys there, and between 1600 and 1608 they became one of the most popular and successful troupes in London, seriously challenging the adult companies.

The private theatres, then, were used exclusively by boys until 1609. The boys' standing as amateurs, the privileged nature of their audiences, and the location of their theatres on church or crown controlled property made London officials slightly less diligent

FIG. 5.12
A reconstruction of the second Blackfriars Theatre, 1597. Note the curtained inner stages on both levels and the audience seated at the sides of the main platform. Drawing by J. H. Farrar. Courtesy the Architect of the Greater London Council.

in trying to get them closed down. After 1609, however, the popularity of the children faded, and the private theatres passed to adult troupes. The first important change came when the Burbages reclaimed the Blackfriars in 1608. James I authorized the King's Men to play there, although an outbreak of plague delayed their opening until December 1609. City officials did not attempt to block the move, though they now had jurisdiction over the liberties.

Because of its length of service and its association with Shakespeare's company, the second Blackfriars is by far the most important of the private theatres, and until recently was the subject of most extensive study. This theatre was created within a room measuring approximately 46 feet wide by 66 feet long. The theatre had two or three galleries, some private boxes, and a pit with seats. Estimates for its audience capacity range from 500 to 1000. The stage platform was raised (estimates range from 4 to 4½ feet above the pit floor). The stage was open, having neither a proscenium arch nor a front curtain. Three doors led onto the stage from the tiring house. Estimates of the dimensions of the stage range from 30 feet wide by 23 feet deep to 46 feet wide by 18½ feet deep, although the first set of dimensions is now favored. The stages in private theatres were quite likely smaller than those in the public playhouses, but most scholars, though they differ on details, agree that they were otherwise similar in all important respects, since the companies moved productions freely from one type of theatre to the other. The King's Men played at Blackfriars from mid-October to mid-May and at The Globe for the remaining five months. The Blackfriars brought the company twice the income it got from The Globe.

The financial success of the King's Men encouraged others to acquire private playhouses. In 1615 Edward Alleyn joined a group of investors to build Porter's Hall near the second Blackfriars. But Blackfriars was no longer a liberty, and London officials forced it to close. From that time on all private theatres were built in the fashionable western suburbs. In 1616 Christopher Beeston converted a cockpit in Drury Lane into a private theatre and moved Queen Anne's Men there from The Red Bull. A riot by apprentices, upset over the loss of their Red Bull company, destroyed The Cockpit shortly after it opened. It was rebuilt as The Phoenix and was occupied successively by Queen Anne's Men, the Prince's Men, Lady Elizabeth's Men, Queen Henrietta's Men, and Beeston's Boys. For some years now a set of plans by Inigo Jones (Fig. 5.13 A, B) has been conjecturally identified as those for this theatre, but since the 1989

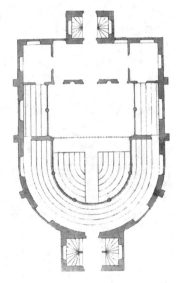

FIG. 5.13A
Exterior and floor plan of a theatre, possibly The Phoenix/Cockpit in Drury Lane, but now thought to be an unrealized project designed by Inigo Jones for William Davenant in 1639. Courtesy Worcester College, Oxford.

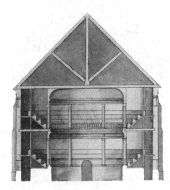
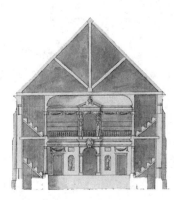

FIG. 5.13B
Cross-section of the auditorium and stage of the same theatre. Courtesy Worcester College, Oxford.

exhibition of Jones' architectural drawings a strong case has been made for their belonging to an unrealized project begun by William Davenant in 1639. They seem likely, however, to reflect the standards for private theatres of the time. The plans show the dimension of the proposed theatre to be 37 feet wide by 52 feet long externally. The stage, raised 4 feet, is 23½ feet wide and 15 feet deep. The stage background shows three doors on the stage level (a large central doorway and two smaller side doors). On the second level, there is one central opening with audience seating on either side. The auditorium, containing two levels of galleries, is elliptical in shape with seating continuing all the way to the stage facade on either side of the playing area.

The Salisbury Court Theatre, built in 1629, was used by the King's Revels, Prince Charles's Men, and the Queen's Men. The interior was destroyed by Parliamentary troops in 1649 and not rebuilt until 1660. It was 40 feet wide, but beyond that nothing is known. In that same year, however, Charles I had Inigo Jones convert the Royal Cockpit at Whitehall into a permanent theatre for the use of professional companies when they played at court. Most scholars now accept that an existing set of plans (Figs. 5.14 A, B) are those

made by John Webb in preparation for his repairs to the building in 1660–1662, though some have argued for their being the original plans by Jones. The Cockpit-in-Court was approximately 58 feet square; inside, the gaming area was octagon-shaped (about 28 feet on a side), and three sides of this octagon were converted into the stage. The king's box was located directly opposite the center door of the facade; other seats were placed in the pit and in two galleries shaped to follow the octagon. The stage was a semicircle, approximately 35 feet wide by 16 feet deep. It was backed by a two-storied facade stylistically reminiscent of Teatro Olimpico, designed by Palladio, an architect much admired by Jones. At stage level, there were five entrances; the largest, located upstage center, was arched and about 4 feet wide. None could be characterized as an "inner stage," although all could have served as "discovery spaces" from which properties or relatively small set pieces could be thrust out. The second level had only one central opening that could be used as an

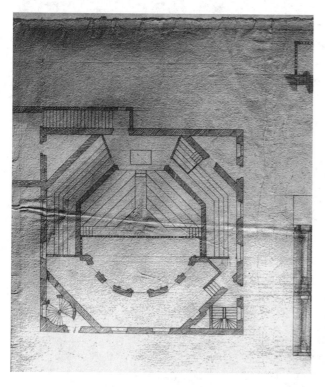

FIG. 5.14A
Floor plan of The Cockpit in Court designed by Inigo Jones, 1629–1631. The King's chair faces the stage. Drawing by John Webb, 1660–1661. Courtesy Worcester College, Oxford.

FIG. 5.14B
Facade and plan of the stage of The Cockpit in Court. An existing building was remodeled into a theatre for use by the public troupes when they played at court. Drawing by John Webb. Courtesy Worcester College, Oxford.

acting space. The private theatres depicted in these drawings represent theatres that were, or were intended to be, capable of mounting productions imported from the public theatres. Consequently, some scholars have argued that these drawings are among the most reliable evidence we have for the stage practices of the period. If this is the case, they constitute a serious argument against the notion that the Elizabethan theatre had deep stages, an inner stage, or sizable acting areas on the stage balcony level.

The French Theatre at Le Fevre's Riding Academy (1635–1636) was built into a gaming house and was just 31 feet wide by 40 feet long. Its significance is that it was built for a French company of actors (and actresses) on the site of what is now The Theatre Royal, Drury Lane. The venture was cut short when plague closed the theatres from May 1636 to October 1637.

SCENERY, PROPERTIES, SPECIAL EFFECTS, AND MUSIC

Although historians usually assume that the stage facade provided the background for all plays in this period, scenic practices are by no means clear. The principal sources of information about scenery are the play scripts, the accounts of the Master of Revels, and Henslowe's papers.

A number of scholars have analyzed the plays for scenic requirements, but their results conflict because they begin with different premises. One group assumes that the players relied primarily upon "spoken decor" (that is, they believe that places are mentioned only when dramatically relevant and because they were not scenically represented). Another group assumes that the audience would expect the things mentioned in the dialogue to be physically represented by some scenic piece. Probably neither of these views is correct. Reynolds's study of staging at The Red Bull concludes that the troupes were very inconsistent in their practices and varied them in accordance with available means rather than consistent theory. Nevertheless, all scholars agree that if scenic devices were used, they more nearly resembled medieval mansions than Italian perspective settings.

A study made by T. J. King of all plays staged between 1599 and 1642 shows that the following items were used on stage: tables, chairs, and stools; beds; carpets and cushions; hangings, curtains, and traverses; thrones; tents and canopies; altars and pulpits; stocks, scaffolds, and gibbets; biers, coffins, dead bodies, and litters; barriers and lists; chariots and vaulting horses; banks and caves; and arbors, trees, bushes, boughs, and flowers.

The Master of Revels' accounts of the late sixteenth century record items used for performances at court. When professional troupes played before the queen, the Revels office prepared a hall and supplied the necessary scenery. The items listed in the accounts include rocks, mountains, battlements, trees, and houses, all of which suggest that medieval-like mansions were in use. Numerous hangings, cloths, and curtains are also mentioned, although the majority of these were probably used to decorate the hall. Thus, it appears that staging at court was probably more elaborate than in the public theatres, but the specific differences between them are unclear.

From the available evidence, however, it seems probable that Elizabethan scenic practices were adapted from medieval conventions. The main acting area was essentially a *platea,* the identity of which could be altered by several devices. As much as 80 percent of the scenes in Shakespeare's plays can be done on a bare stage, suggesting that the stage was most often treated as a neutral space. If it needed to be localized, this could be done either by the dialogue or by the use of set pieces such as arbors, tents, tombs, prison bars, beds, and thrones. It is possible that some scenic devices were so cumbersome that they were set up on the main stage, where they remained throughout the performance, ignored except when relevant to the action. Other heavy pieces could be revealed in, or thrust out from, the doorways, or from some sort of discovery space. Smaller articles were brought on and off stage as needed. Reynolds suggests that the number of set pieces employed in each play depended both upon the company's stock and the sequence of scenes, for the troupes suited their practice more to convenience than to principle. Neither audiences nor actors seem to have been bothered by inconsistencies.

The theatres retained and stored all scenic pieces, most of which could be used in a number of plays. Henslowe's accounts show no regular payments to painters or carpenters, which would indicate that there was no systematic attempt to increase the stock, articles being added at random. The scene stock was looked after by "stage keepers" who were also responsible for the scenery, properties, and sound for each production. As the lowliest of the hired men, the stage keepers performed many miscellaneous functions as janitors, bill posters, and extras.

Emphasis on spectacle increased after 1603 as the influence of the court grew. The boys' companies began to emphasize masque-like elements around 1605, and the adult troupes continued this trend when they took over the private theatres. Elaborate set pieces became more frequent during this period, and there is a marked increase in the use of flying effects, pyrotechnic displays, magic tricks, and displays of swordsmanship. Music, dance, the use of gorgeous costumes, and the appearance of characters from classical mythology also became more common. But neither the public nor the private theatres seem to have attempted to copy the perspective settings used for the masques.

Music played a very large part in English theatrical production from the beginning and was especially prominent in this period. Boys' companies, having originated as choirs, were famous for their music and offered concerts up to an hour in length before performances, a practice taken over by the adult troupes when they moved to the private theatre. Most adult actors had to be able to sing, and the number of incidental songs in plays was large. Most theatres seem to have had an orchestra composed of about six instrumentalists. In addition, there were trumpeters and drummers who provided flourishes before entrances or to introduce proclamations and provide sounds for battle scenes. Dance had a similar history. In the early days it was designed to appeal primarily to the popular audiences, but it became more sophisticated as the influence of aristocratic audiences increased. At the public theatres, performances often ended with a "jig" or other display of dancing skill and musical ability.

COSTUMES

Because scenery and properties were used sparingly and because the actor was always of primary concern, costume was the most important visual element in the Elizabethan performance. Contemporary accounts mention the costliness and elegance of the players' costumes, and Henslowe's papers record numerous loans for the purchase of costumes, such as seven pounds for "a doublet of white satin laid thick with gold lace" and nineteen pounds for a cloak. It was not unusual for Henslowe to pay more for a woman's costume in a play than he had paid for the play itself. It is little wonder that the most costly fine an actor could incur was the fine for wearing a costume outside the playhouse. The sumptuousness of the costumes worn by English actors was often praised by foreigners and condemned by English conservatives.

The conventions that governed costuming between 1567 and 1642 differed little from those in effect during the Middle Ages. Most characters, regardless of the historical era in which they supposedly lived, were clothed in Elizabethan fashion. The deviations from contemporary dress may be divided into five categories: (1) "ancient," or out-of-style clothing, used to indicate unfashionableness, or occasionally, to suggest

FIG. 5.15
A sketch, allegedly made in 1595, of a scene from Shakespeare's *Titus Andronicus*. Some scholars argue that this is a nineteenth-century forgery. Courtesy Marquess of Bath.

another period; (2) "antique," consisting of drapery or greaves added to contemporary garments, used for certain classical figures; (3) fanciful garments used for ghosts, witches, fairies, gods, and allegorical characters; (4) traditional costumes, associated with a few specific characters such as Robin Hood, Henry V, Tamburlaine, Falstaff, and Richard III; and (5) national or racial costumes, used to set off Turks, Indians, Jews, and Spaniards. Although some of these costumes were conventionalized versions of garments from past periods, they were not historically accurate. With rare exceptions, even the "history plays" were costumed in Elizabethan dress.

The troupes bought most of their costumes. Sometimes noblemen gave them garments, and frequently servants who had been willed their masters' wardrobe sold it to the actors. Actors were sometimes given the costumes they wore for performances before the nobility, and occasionally the royal family made grants to the troupes to replenish their wardrobes. It was also possible to rent costumes, either from the Revels Office or from enterprising businessmen. Once a costume was acquired, it was used over and over again. Since the actors relied heavily upon costumes, the acquisition and maintenance of a sizable wardrobe were important. A few records from the period refer to tiremen and tirewomen (wardrobe keepers), some of whom apparently had been trained as tailors, although there is little specific information about what they did for the companies.

AUDIENCES

The period from 1567 to 1642 was a time of great social, economic, intellectual, religious, and political change in England. London was the only city large enough to sustain a professional acting company for more than a few days of performances, and during this time its population increased considerably—from about 100,000 to around 400,000. Scholars estimate that only 10 to 20 percent of the greater London population could have been regular playgoers, so competition for audiences was intense, and the acting companies had to adapt to the rapidly changing times.

Numerous devices were used to advertise plays. Posters appeared in London as early as 1563, and handbills were in use by the seventeenth century. Occasionally a procession with drums and trumpets advertised performances, but this practice was largely restricted to touring outside London. Flags were flown above the roofs of London's theatres on the days when performances were to be given, and announcements of coming attractions were made from the stage during performances.

We do not know the capacity of the six or so London inns that were used for performance. Of the indoor theatres, the first Blackfriars may have seated as few as 100, while the second Blackfriars may have seated up to 1000. The capacity of the larger public theatres was perhaps as high as 3000. Several book-length studies have been done on the composition of these audiences. They agree that the cost of admission kept the poorer classes out of the private theatres. They disagree, however, on the composition of the audiences in the public theatres, some arguing for a predominantly working-class audience, while others see these audiences as predominantly upper middle class, even at the public playhouses. It may even be true that different public playhouses attracted different sorts of audiences; audiences at The Red Bull, for example, were known for their rowdy behavior, while audiences at The Fortune appear to have been reserved. Audiences of the period seemed to have behaved in their playhouses more as we might at a sporting event than as we do in our theatres.

During Elizabeth's reign it was possible to see a play in London on any day of the week, except during Lent and periods, which occurred nearly every year, when the weekly deaths due to plague exceeded fifty (plague closed the theatres for 18 months in 1582–1583, 11 months in 1593, 13 months in 1603–1604, and 17 months in 1636–1637). The crown had authorized daily playing in 1574, but the city always protested playing on Sunday, and James I made it illegal (though this law does not seem always to have been obeyed). At best a company might perform 214 times a year, but they generally performed much less.

A visit to a public playhouse involved going to a recreational district outside the city. As much as a third of the audience in these theatres stood in the yard, around three sides of the stage. It was possible to pay an additional penny to sit in the galleries, and a third penny for a cushioned seat in a box, or to spend six pennies for a seat in the Lords' Rooms. For a new play all the fees might be doubled. There were no restrictions on women in these theatres, but it does appear that it was detrimental to a woman's reputation to stand in the yard for a performance.

THE STUART COURT MASQUES

In addition to the public performances given for the paying patrons, many others, open only to invited audiences, were given at court and in the homes of the nobility. Most of the plays seen at court were presented by professional troupes who, though they might make use of scenery and costumes from the Master of Revels' stock, probably deviated little from the conventions they followed in the public playhouses. The court masques, on the other hand, introduced Italian ideals of staging into England and began the trend toward the proscenium-arch theatre that was to triumph after 1660.

Although masques had been popular at the court of Henry VIII (the term was first used *c.* 1512), they were infrequently given during the reign of Elizabeth, who contented herself with elaborate entertainments given by others in her honor. When James I came to the throne, masques were revived with ever-increasing splendor. Under James I an average of one masque was performed each year; under Charles I this number was increased to two, typically one at Twelfth Night and another at Mardi Gras. The Carolinian masques were usually planned in pairs, one given by the king and the gentlemen and the other by the queen and the ladies of the court. In addition, the Inns of Court produced masques, usually in honor of the royal family or an important visitor or on some special occasion.

In *Splendor at Court,* Roy Strong uses such terms as "the theatre of power" and "the politics of spectacle" to describe the masque and other comparable forms produced at courts throughout Europe during the sixteenth and seventeenth centuries. In many ways, these productions were attempts to justify the concentration of power in the hands of monarchs, who were depicted as ruling by merit and divine right. Thus, an idealized vision of monarchy lay at the heart of the masques, and the movement of the masque was from disorder to order with the ruler as transforming agent.

In England, as elsewhere, great sums of money were lavished on these productions and rationalized as demonstrations of kingly virtue and magnanimity.

FIG. 5.16

Entertainment given for Queen Elizabeth by the Earl of Hertford in 1591 at Elvetham in Hampshire. This is the second day's entertainment for a four-day visit. A crescent-shaped lake was dug especially for the water pageant. Queen Elizabeth's chair is at upper left. From John Nichols's *The Progresses and Public Processions of Queen Elizabeth*, 2 (1788).

In 1618 James I spent £4000 on a single production, considerably more than on all the performances of plays given by professional companies at court during his entire reign. The most costly of all masques, however, was given jointly by the four Inns of Court in 1634 to demonstrate their loyalty after a member of Lincoln's Inn, William Prynne, attacked the theatre, and indirectly the crown, in *Histriomastix*. This masque, *The Triumph of Peace,* written by James Shirley with scenery by Inigo Jones, cost £21,000. One of the participants, Bulstrode Whitlocke, preserved an account of this production so complete that it could still be reconstructed in all important details.

Considering the rewards both in prestige and money, it is not surprising that many leading dramatists (among them Marston, Chapman, Beaumont, Middleton, Daniel, Milton, and Davenant) wrote masques. The majority of the masques presented at the Stuart court, however, were written by Ben Jonson and designed by Inigo Jones. Eventually, Jonson objected to the dominant role given to spectacle and, after an open break with Jones in 1631, he was replaced by other writers.

Music played a major part in the masques. Unfortunately, no complete musical score for a masque has survived, but we do have the music for about 50 songs and some 250 dances, although it is not always possible to assign them to specific masques.

The masque was similar to the Italian *intermezzo,* since it presented an allegorical story which suggested parallels between the person being honored or the occasion being celebrated and some mythological personage or event. The story and symbolism were conveyed primarily through visual means: scenery, costumes, properties, pantomime, and dance. Narrative and dialogue (spoken or sung) were used primarily to clarify what could not be conveyed through visual means.

The serious speaking and singing roles were assumed by professional musicians, while the comic or grotesque roles were played by professional actors. The major emphasis, however, was upon dance, which was performed by courtiers. This division in casting tells much about then-current attitudes toward actors: the courtiers did not speak lines because they wished to maintain their amateur (and idealized) status.

Embedded in the masque's allegorical plot were usually three "grand masquing dances": an entry dance; a main dance, during which the performers usually went down into the hall to dance with selected

FIG. 5.17
Jones's costume for a Fiery Spirit in *The Temple of Love,* 1635. Devonshire Collection, Chatsworth. Reproduced by permission of the Trustees of the Chatsworth Settlement.

productions, but the court dancing masters also invented elaborate symbolic formations. The dancers in a masque were all of one sex, except in those occasional double masques in which equally balanced groups of men and women were used. Each dancer was usually accompanied by a "torchbearer" (that is, the carrier of a candelabrum) when the dancing took place in the auditorium. The torchbearers, usually young noblemen or children, often performed a special dance of their own. After 1608, Jonson introduced the "anti-masques" designed to provide a contrast with the main story. Anti-masques introduced humorous or grotesque characters and dances. They also provided ample opportunity for the scenic designer to contrive striking transformations from ugliness to beauty, or from chaos to order.

The characters of the masques were usually either allegorical or mythological. The women might be goddesses, nymphs, queens, "The Beauties," or "The Graces." The men might be gods, ancient heroes, Signs of the Zodiac, "Sons of Peace, Love, and Justice," or representatives of various countries. The torchbearers might represent fiery spirits, Indians, Oceanae, or "antique" Britons. The anti-masques included satyrs, drunkards, gypsies, sailors, beggars, fools, or animals.

The majority of Stuart masques were staged in banqueting houses at Whitehall Palace. The physical arrangement was much the same for most of the masques. Tiers of seats were set up along the sides and across the back of the hall. The royal dais was

spectators; and a "going out" dance. Many social dances of the period were incorporated into these

FIG. 5.18
Jones's setting for Act V of *Salmacida Spolia,* 1640. Note the "glory." Devonshire Collection, Chatsworth. Courtesy Trustees of the Chatsworth Settlement.

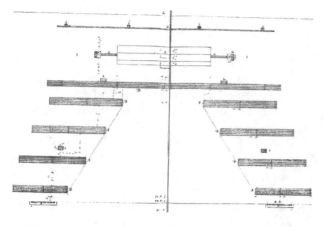

FIG. 5.19
Jones's floor plan of the setting for *Salmacida Spolia*. Note the use of nested wings and back shutters, all of which could be changed by sliding them in grooves. This may be the first example of a completely changeable setting in England. Courtesy Trustees of the British Museum.

well back in the auditorium to provide the best view of the stage and to leave room forward of it for the dancers. Steps connected the hall with the stage.

The stages varied in size, but the average dimensions were about 40 feet wide by 27 feet deep. The platform, raised about 6 feet above the hall floor, sloped upward toward the rear. It was used primarily for scenic effect, because most of the action and dancing took place at the front of the stage or on the floor of the hall.

The scenery, costumes, and special effects for most of the masques were by Inigo Jones (1573–1652), the first important English scene designer. Born in London, Jones went to Italy about 1600 to study, after which he worked for a time at the court of Denmark before returning to England around 1604. He designed his first masque for James I in 1605. He may have visited Italy again in 1607–1608, and certainly did in 1613–1615. In 1615 he was appointed Surveyor of His Majesty's Works, a post which he held until dismissed in 1643.

Jones was thoroughly familiar with Italian artistic movements. At the court of Florence he obviously studied the work of Giulio Parigi, for almost all of his designs after 1630 are copied directly from Parigi's *intermezzi*. His surviving copy of Palladio's treatise on architecture contains notes comparing Palladio's ideas with those of Serlio, Scamozzi, Vignola, and others. As the court architect and designer, Jones was the most influential English artist of his day. At his death, he willed his papers to his pupil and assistant, John Webb, who was to be a leading architect and scene designer of the Restoration. Since William Davenant, one of the principal theatre managers of the Restora-

tion, had written several of the last masques designed by Jones, and since Webb worked closely with Davenant after 1656, Jones also exerted considerable influence on Restoration scene design. To Jones, more than to any other artist, can be attributed the naturalization of the Italian ideal in England.

Jones's innovations were not all evident in his early designs; some of the most important did not appear until 1640, so it is useful to examine the evolution of his techniques. The nature of his contributions can be seen by comparing his designs with those used for the masques before he began his work at the Stuart court. The earlier masques had been staged with "dispersed decor" (that is, with mansion-like structures scattered around the hall). Jones ushered in a new era in 1605 when, for Jonson's *The Masque of Blackness,* he erected a stage at one end of the hall and placed all the scenery on it. Furthermore, instead of mansions, he employed a perspective setting composed of angled wings and a backscene, all concealed until the beginning of the masque and then revealed suddenly by dropping a front curtain.

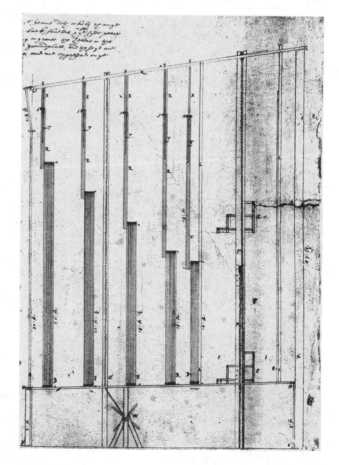

FIG. 5.20
Sectional plan for *Salmacida Spolia*. Courtesy Trustees of the British Museum.

Between 1605 and 1610 Jones made other innovations. In 1606, for *The Masque of Hymen,* the principle of the *periaktoi* was used to create a globe with no visible axle, which revolved to reveal eight dancers seated inside a "mine of several metals." In the same production, Jones suspended eight dancers in a cloud machine that moved from upstage to downstage. In 1608, for *The Hue and Cry After Cupid,* Jones made his first known use of the proscenium arch and of scenery that parted in the middle to reveal another scene behind it. In the *Masque of Oberon* (1610) two sets of shutters were worked in grooves to reveal three successive scenes. After 1610 Jones tended to repeat the devices he had already perfected.

In the 1630s, however, he began to experiment once more. Perhaps because of Parigi's influence, Jones's use of flying machinery increased considerably. But the most important change was the abandonment of angled for flat wings. This innovation may have been made as early as 1634, but clearly was used in 1635 when Jones designed settings for Davenant's *The Temple of Love.* Jones's experiments reached their culmination in 1640 with Davenant's *Salmacida Spolia,* the last of the pre-Commonwealth masques. He put four sets of flat wings and several back shutters in grooves so that the settings could be changed rapidly. So by 1640, Jones had introduced into England all the features then characteristic of the Italianate stage. When the English theatres reopened in 1660, Jones's practices were to triumph over those that had characterized the pre-Commonwealth public stage.

In addition to designing the masques, Jones staged them. He also designed scenery for about twelve plays presented after 1626 by the courtiers for court audiences. At least some of these plays were performed at The Cockpit-in-Court; Strong and Orgel have published designs by Jones depicting that theatre with a proscenium arch and Italianate scenery, which they believe were used for one or more of these productions. Orrell believes these designs were intended for The Phoenix/Cockpit in Drury Lane.

Unlike the masques, the plays staged by the court used amateurs, including the queen and other women, in speaking roles. The presence of women in speaking roles was so unusual at this time, and knowledge of the court performances sufficiently well known, that when William Prynne in *Histriomastix* (1633), a 1000-page work attacking the growing influence of Catholicism, listed "women actors, notorious whores" in the index, he was fined £5000, expelled from the legal profession, deprived of his academic degree, had his ears cut off, and was sentenced to life imprisonment.

These productions and the extravagance of the court masques were some among many factors that led to the eventual downfall of Charles I. Like his father, Charles I quarreled often with Parliament because he wanted to rule as an absolute monarch. From 1629 until 1640 he ruled without Parliament. When financial difficulties forced him to call a session, Parliament declined to authorize any new taxes until the king agreed to have limits set on his power. Charles refused, and in 1642 civil war broke out. Eventually Charles was defeated and in 1649 was beheaded.

The war rekindled religious opposition to the theatre. The antipathy was intensified because of the close association between the theatre and members of the royal family. In September 1642 Parliament used the disturbed state of the country as an excuse for closing the theatres for five years. When that time expired, the Puritans were in control of the government, and they declared the closure to be permanent. Thus ended one of the most brilliant and productive periods the theatre has known.

LOOKING AT THEATRE HISTORY

One of the most revealing approaches to theatre history in any period can be made through reconstructions of its theatre buildings, either in drawings or scale models. Such an approach requires that decisions be made about the size, shape, and principal features of the structures. It also reveals what we do not know, for in seeking to convert the available evidence into concrete visual detail, we quickly learn that much information about the overall appearance, decorative detail, dimensions, and even the precise location of machinery and workspace is often mere conjecture. Still, unless we can visualize the space in which plays were performed, it is difficult to understand the theatrical practices of an age. In many ways, then, the attempt to reconstruct theatre buildings epitomizes the problem of the historian: how to create a defensible whole out of the fragmentary remains of the past.

Because of the great interest in Shakespeare's plays and how they were originally staged, historians have been especially interested in reconstructing the theatre buildings of the era 1567–1642. Three examples of these efforts can be seen in Figs. 5.7, 5.9, and 5.11. In 1997 a structure simulating the first Globe Playhouse was built near the original location south of the Thames river in London (Fig. 5.11). It is a 20-sided polygon 100 feet in diameter with a yard 73 feet 9 inches across. The stage is 44 feet wide by 24 feet 9 inches deep, and the stage posts are set 27 feet 6 inches apart. A private theatre based on the drawings shown in Figs. 5.13A and 5.13B is planned for the same location. Much of the surviving visual evidence relating to English theatres prior to 1642 is reproduced in Figs. 5.6, 5.8, 5.13, and 5.14. In addition, short building contracts for The Fortune (1600) and The Hope (1614) have survived. Here is an excerpt from The Fortune contract describing the stage:

> With a Stage and Tyring house to be made, erected & set up within the said frame, with a shadow or cover over the Stage, which Stage shall be placed & set, as also the stair cases of the said frame, in such sort as is prefigured in a plot there of drawn, and which Stage shall contain in length Forty and Three foot of lawful assize and in breadth to extend to the middle of the yard of the said house.

These excerpts from The Hope contract describe the multipurpose nature of that structure:

> [The builder shall] set up one other Game place or Playhouse fit and convenient in all things, both for players to play in, and for the game of Bears and Bulls to be baited in the same, and also a fit and convenient tyre house and a stage to be carried or taken away, and to stand upon trestles good substantial and sufficient for the carrying and bearing of such a stage. . . . [He] shall also build the Heavens all over the said stage to be borne or carried without any posts or supporters to be fixed or set upon the said stage.

Shakespeare is considered one of the world's greatest dramatists, but we know little about his life or his approach to writing. His fellow playwright Ben Jonson gives us one of the few contemporary glimpses into Shakespeare's qualities as writer and man:

> I remember that the players have often mentioned it as an honor to Shakespeare, that in his writing, whatsoever he penned, he never blotted out a line. . . . He was

> . . . honest, and of an open and free nature; had an excellent fancy, brave notions, and gentle expressions, wherein he flowed with that facility that sometime it was necessary he should be stopped. . . . Many times he fell into those things could not escape laughter. . . . But he redeemed his vices with his virtues. There was ever more in him to be praised than to be pardoned.

Ben Jonson, *Timber; or Discoveries Made Upon Men and Matter* (1620–1635?).

Because it was so controversial, the theatre motivated numerous decrees, proclamations, petitions, and other documents during the reign of Elizabeth I. These public documents are among our important sources of information about the theatre of that age. Many of the documents are reprinted in two readily available sources: E. K. Chambers, *The Elizabethan Stage,* 4 vols. (London, 1923), and Glynne Wickham, *Early English Stages,* 1300–1600, 2 vols. (New York, 1959, 1972).

On May 16, 1559, Elizabeth issued a proclamation that effectively outlawed religious and political subject matter. In part it read:

> her majestie doth likewise charge every [official] . . . that they permit [no interludes] to be played wherein either matters of religion or of the governance of the estate of the common weale shall be handled or treated . . .

Foreign visitors often provide important information about the theatre, especially when what they see differs markedly from what they are used to in their own country. One particularly helpful description is provided by Thomas Platter, a Swiss who visited London in 1599:

> Thus daily at two in the afternoons, London has two, sometimes three plays running in different places. . . . The playhouses are so constructed that they play on a raised platform, so that everyone has a good view. There are different galleries and places, however, where the seating is better and more comfortable and therefore more expensive. For whoever cares to stand below only pays one English penny, but if he wishes to sit he enters by another door, and pays another penny, while if he desires to sit in the most comfortable seats, which are cushioned . . . then he pays another English penny at another door. And during the performance food and drink are carried round the audience. . . . The actors are most expensively and elaborately costumed; for it is the English usage for eminent lords or knights at their decease to bequeath and leave almost the best of their clothes to their serving men, which it is unseemly for the latter to wear, so they offer them for sale for a small sum to the actors. . . .

Thomas Platter, *Travels to England* (1599).

Salmacida Spolia (performed at Whitehall in January 1640), the last of the great Stuart Masques, illustrates well the characteristic masque form. The subject was allegorical, as this summary by the author, William Davenant, indicates:

Discord, a malicious fury, appears in a storm, and by the invocation of malignant spirits, . . . endeavors to disturb these parts [England], envying the blessings and tranquility we have long enjoyed. These incantations are expressed by those spirits in an Antimasque: who on a sudden are surprised, and stopt in their motion by a secret power [Wisdom]. . . . This secret Wisdom, in the person of the King and attended by his nobles, and under the name of Philogenes or Lover of his people, hath his appearance prepared by a Chorus. . . . Then the Queen personating the chief heroine, with her martial ladies, is sent down from Heaven by Pallas as a reward of his prudence, for reducing the threatening storm into the following calm.

The final scene is depicted in Fig. 5.18. D'Avenant describes it thus:

. . . The scene was changed into magnificent buildings composed of several selected pieces of architecture: in the furthest part was a bridge over a river, where many people, coaches, horses, and such like were seen to pass to and fro: beyond this, on the shore were buildings in prospective, which . . . showed as the suburbs of a great city. From the highest part of the heavens came forth a cloud far in the scene, in which were eight persons richly attired representing the spheres; this, joining with two other clouds which appeared at that instant full of music, covered all the upper part of the scene, and, at that instant beyond all these, a heaven opened full of deities, which celestial prospect with the Chorus below filled all the whole scene with apparitions and harmony.

The Dramatic Works of Sir William D'Avenant, 2 (London, 1872).

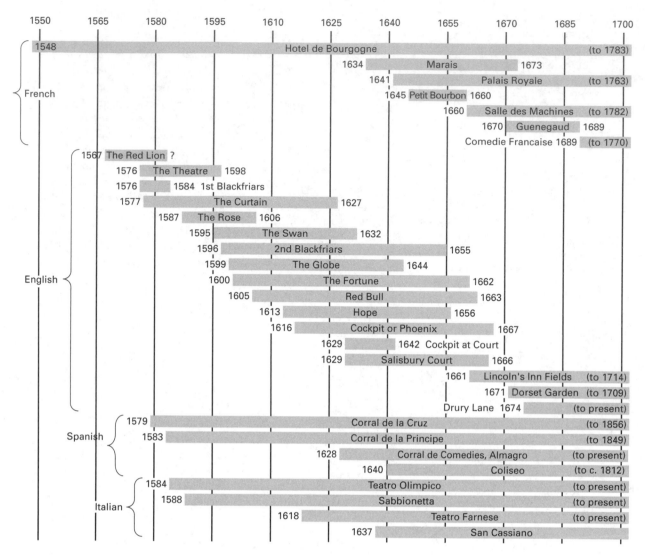

FIG. 5.21
Major permanent theatres of Europe, 1548–1700.

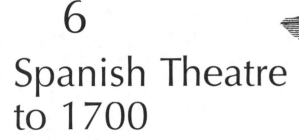

6
Spanish Theatre
to 1700

As in England, the theatre in Spain flourished during the sixteenth and seventeenth centuries. The period of 1580–1680 was so productive it is called the Golden Age (*Siglo de Oro*) of Spanish drama. But the influences on Spanish and English drama differed markedly. In Spain, many of the influences were related to the Moorish culture that had supplanted the Visigoths on the Iberian Peninsula by 711. For nearly 500 years the Muslims ruled all of Spain except for a small northern portion. Moorish Spain was the most prosperous region in the Mediterranean and far more advanced culturally than feudal Europe. Its philosophers and scholars exerted strong influence on medieval universities and its craftsmen were the envy of Europe. Around 1200 the Christian kingdoms of northern Spain united against the Moors, and by 1276 had driven them from all but the southeastern portion. Spain was not to become a major power, however, until after 1479, when Aragon and Castile united under Ferdinand and Isabella. By 1492, these rulers had conquered all of the peninsula except for Portugal and united it into a single nation. To insure Christian purity in the new kingdom, the Inquisition was established in 1480 to hunt down and punish heretics. Moors and Jews who would not convert were expelled from the country. Spain, therefore, avoided the challenges to Roman Catholicism that were spreading over the rest of Europe.

Another important influence on drama was Spain's sense of its own position as a world power. Following Columbus's first voyage in 1492, Spain rapidly became the dominant force in the New World, and in 1519 its king, Charles I, became the Holy Roman Emperor. Under Philip II (reigned 1556–1598), Portugal, Sicily, the Kingdom of Naples, Milan, the Netherlands, and parts of northern Africa were all brought under Spanish control, making it the most powerful nation in the Western world. The drama of the Golden Age was dominated by a sense of confidence in the state, energy, expansiveness, faith in God and church, and a Moorish concern for honor and the separation of public spheres for men and women. By 1640 the decline of its empire had already begun, but this was not fully evident until the end of the seventeenth century.

THE RELIGIOUS DRAMA

Because of the Islamic disapproval of theatre, only the Christian portions of Spain developed medieval drama. As the Christian forces conquered Moorish territory, theatre was introduced as a form of religious teaching. Until the mid-sixteenth century, however, the Spanish religious plays were similar to those performed throughout medieval Europe, but after 1500

FIG. 6.1
The Spanish peninsula *c.* 1700.

they assumed distinctive traits which they retained until religious performances were prohibited in 1765.

Perhaps because of the church's firm control over its content, Spanish religious drama grew in importance at the very time when it was being suppressed in other countries. During the last half of the sixteenth century plays came to be closely associated with Corpus Christi, the festival that emphasizes the power of the church's sacraments. Probably for this reason, the plays were labeled *autos sacramentales.*

An *auto* combined characteristics of the morality and cycle plays. Human and supernatural characters were mingled with such allegorical figures as Sin, Grace, Pleasure, Grief, and Beauty. Stories could be drawn from any source, even completely secular ones, as long as they illustrated the efficacy of the sacraments and the validity of church dogma.

Although production arrangements varied somewhat from one area to another, those in the capital city of Valladolid, and afterwards in Madrid (the new capital after 1561), were sufficiently typical to stand for all. Until 1550 trade guilds were responsible for staging the plays, but at some time between 1551 and 1558 the City Council assumed control. Professional troupes were then employed to produce the plays, which were written by Spain's finest dramatists. Thus, after the mid-sixteenth century the connection between the public and religious stages was close.

By the end of the sixteenth century production procedures had assumed the pattern that (with minor exceptions) was to be followed until 1705. Three *autos,* sometimes new, sometimes old, were presented by a single company each year until 1592, after which four were presented by two troupes until 1647. In that year, Madrid reduced the number of *autos* to two and Calderón was hired to write them, which he did until his death in 1681. Troupes were chosen during Lent. In addition to being paid a sizable fee, these companies were awarded exclusive rights to give public performances in Madrid between Easter and Corpus Christi. After Corpus Christi, the actors toured the *autos* to neighboring towns and performed them in the public theatres of Madrid as well. Thus, there were many incentives for the actors to participate in the festivals.

The plays were mounted on *carros,* or wagons, supplied by the city, which also furnished everything needed for the productions except the costumes and hand properties. Two *carros* were used for each play until Calderón started writing the plays in 1647, when the number was increased to four. The two-storied carros were made of wooden frames covered with painted canvas and equipped according to instructions supplied by the dramatists. There is little information about the size of the wagons until the mid-1630s, when they were about 20 feet long by 10 feet wide.

The facade of the upper story was often hinged so that it might open to reveal something within. Scenic devices might also rise out of the lower story, and many of the wagons included machinery for flying actors or objects. The *carros* served as entrances to the stage and as dressing rooms for the actors.

Until 1647 a portable stage (in the form of another wagon) accompanied the *carros* as an acting area. After 1647, when four wagons began to be used for each play, fixed platforms were erected at each playing place. Two *carros* were now drawn up at the back and one at either end of the stage, which was bare but equipped with trapdoors for special effects. The awkwardness of taking away the four *carros* used for one *auto* and bringing in four others for the next led, in 1692, to arranging all eight wagons around the platform throughout the performance. The resulting stage area may have been as large as 45 to 50 feet wide and 36 feet deep.

Between eight and twenty days before Corpus Christi, the actors were required to give a preview performance before the City Council. In some towns the first official performance was given inside the cathedral but this practice had largely been discon-

tinued by the seventeenth century, although in places the first performance was still given just outside a church. There is no evidence that the plays were ever performed inside the churches of Madrid, and by the early seventeenth century even performances in front of the churches there had been discontinued. Nevertheless, the *carros* were still included in the procession of the Host through the streets, and the plays remained an accepted part of the festival.

The City Council specified the playing places, often establishing so many that the performances extended over several days. After 1600, the first performance was usually given before the king in a palace courtyard. The plays were then presented in the square before the city hall, on one day for the Council of Castile (the most powerful of governmental groups), and on the next for the City Council. Several other state councils were also entitled to special showings, and at least two performances were given for the general public. The *carros* were pulled from place to place by bullocks with gilded horns.

In addition to the *autos,* the actors performed short farcical interludes and dances. Other performers were employed by the city to carry large carnival figures of giants and dragons about the streets and to perform the traditional dances. When the *autos* were finally forbidden in 1765, the reasons given were the predominance of the carnival spirit, the objectionable content of the farces and dances, and the undesirability of having religious plays performed by actors of questionable morality. All these complaints had been voiced since the sixteenth century, however, and other reasons must have been equally important. Certainly interest had been declining since the death of Calderón in 1681, after which the *autos* became merely imitative of older works. The general loss of interest is probably also indicated by the abandonment of processional staging in 1705, after which the *autos* were performed only in the public theatres. Regardless of the reason for their decline and prohibition, *autos* were an important supplement to the professional stage for more than 200 years.

FIG. 6.2
Reconstruction by Richard Southern of an *auto sacramental* performed in the Plaza Mayor, Madrid. It is based on a ground plan of 1644. Note the two *carros* alongside a platform and the boxlike seating provided for the City Council and the Council of Castile. From *Le Lieu Théâtrale à là Renaissance.* Courtesy Centre National de la Recherche Scientifique, Paris.

SECULAR DRAMA

From about 1470 the connections between Spain and Italy were close, and the awakening interest in classical learning found its way into Spanish intellectual circles. Printing was introduced to Spain in 1473, and over the next century many Latin and Greek works were translated into Spanish and widely disseminated. In 1508 a university was founded at Alcala de Henares to encourage the study of Latin, Greek, and Hebrew, and this study soon led to an interest in classical

FIG. 6.3
Frontispiece to an edition of *Calisto and Melibea*
published in Toledo in 1538.

drama. The performance of plays by Plautus and Terence was mandated at Salamanca University in 1538, and Jesuit schools, which spread rapidly throughout Spain in the 1540s, used drama as an important component of their teaching system.

It was during this period that a Spanish secular drama began to emerge. Perhaps the most important early work is *The Comedy of Calisto and Melibea,* a novel in dialogue rather than a true play. The first edition in 1500 consisted of sixteen acts, but these were increased to twenty-one in the edition of 1502. Usually attributed to Fernando de Rojas (*c.* 1465–*c.* 1541), the novel may contain sections written by others. Although *Calisto and Melibea* was not performed, it was so widely read that it influenced later writers through its depictions of conflict between idealized and realistic behavior. Especially famous were the low-life scenes portraying La Celestina, who served as go-between for the lovers, Calisto and Melibea.

Juan del Encina (1469–1529) is often called the founder of Spanish drama, since his early works predate *Calisto and Melibea.* After studying with the great Spanish humanist, Nebrija, Encina turned to writing "eclogues" in the manner of the Italian pastoral drama, which he also acted in. But his early plays, dating from the 1490s, were still essentially religious, and it was not until he went to live in Rome that he turned to more purely secular works, such as *The Eclogue of Placida and Victoriano* (1513). His relatively simple plays were the first Spanish secular dramas to be performed. Bartolomé de Torres Naharro (*c.* 1485–*c.* 1520) at first imitated Encina's work but went on to write much more sophisticated farces and comedies. Like Encina,

he lived for a time in Italy, where his plays were performed before being published in 1517 under the title *Propalladia*. His preface to this collection provides one of the first contributions to dramatic theory in Europe, and his most famous play, *Comedia Himenea* (*c.* 1516), established the honor-vengeance theme that was to be a major influence on later dramatists. The structure of Naharro's plays is primitive, for without the prologues the action of many would be unintelligible. His fluent verse and topical satire, however, won him a wide reading public. Gil Vicente (*c.* 1453–*c.* 1537) wrote primarily for the Portuguese court, but many of his plays were in Spanish. He is generally considered superior to his contemporaries because of his considerable lyrical gift, great range, comic sense, and spontaneity. In addition to these native works, Italian plays were being performed at the Spanish court by 1548.

All the early secular drama in Spain was aimed at an aristocratic audience, and its influence on the professional theatre was negligible. Nevertheless, these plays established a foundation which later Spanish dramatists recognized as the source of their own practice.

EARLY PROFESSIONAL THEATRE

As in other countries, the early history of professional playing in Spain is obscure. Records show that by 1454 actors were being paid to perform at Corpus Christi, and that in 1539 six men were employed to perform farces at the Cathedral in Toledo. But it is not until the 1540s that notices concerning professional actors become common. Although most of these relate to Corpus Christi festivities, they show that by 1550 a number of troupes were in existence. In 1548, the first important Italian company appeared at Valladolid, and for the next fifty-five years Italian troupes provided a significant source of competition and influence for the Spanish companies (though scholars do not agree on the extent of that influence).

The first important figure of the Spanish professional theatre is Lope de Rueda (*c.* 1510–*c.* 1565), of whom the first notice as a performer is found in 1542, when he appeared in religious plays at Seville. By 1551 he was sufficiently well known to be summoned by the governors of Valladolid, then the capital of Spain, to perform for the king. From 1552 until 1558, Rueda was employed there at a considerable annual salary to supervise the Corpus Christi festivities. In addition, he performed frequently at court and toured widely. Rueda was also the first successful writer of plays for popular audiences. A number of his full-length works have survived, including *The Frauds, Medora, Armelina,* and *Eufemia.* But he is best known for his farce sketches (*pasos*), of which *The Mask* and *The Olives* are probably the most famous. The plots serve primarily as an excuse for the earthy humor and picturesque dialogue. Fools and simpletons (roles played by Rueda) are the most fully developed characters.

Cervantes states that Rueda's stage consisted of four or five boards set on benches backed with a blanket and that his costumes were "four white sheepskins trimmed with gilded leather." This statement has often been accepted as an accurate description of the professional theatre during Rueda's time. Even a cursory examination of contemporary records, however, will show that Cervantes oversimplified the situation, not surprisingly since he was recalling after fifty years a performance that he had seen as a boy. Rueda's contracts required him to supply costumes of silk and velvet for Corpus Christi productions, and it seems unlikely that he did not use them at other times. Probably Cervantes saw one of Rueda's pasos, for which sheepskins and a crude background would have been appropriate.

Rueda proposed to build a theatre in Valladolid as early as 1558, but there is no evidence of its having actually been built. Like his English and Italian counterparts, he had to adapt to many conditions, acting in city squares, courtyards, and great halls at court or in houses of the nobility. Although Rueda is now almost universally considered the founder of the Spanish professional theatre, in actuality he was merely the most successful actor-manager of his day.

The popularity of the theatre mushroomed in the 1570s. Actors were welcomed throughout the country and permanent theatres began to appear in Seville, Toledo, Valencia, Granada, Cordova, and other cities. By 1585, however, Madrid had emerged as the dominant theatrical center of Spain.

Although the demand for new plays increased rapidly, no writer of true importance appeared until the late 1580s, when Lope de Vega began to write regularly for the stage. Between 1565 and 1590 plays were contrived primarily by the actor-managers of theatrical companies, a fact which led to the continuing designation of managers throughout the seventeenth century as *autores de comedias* (authors of plays). In the last quarter of the sixteenth century, two authors—Cueva and Cervantes—achieved a measure of fame as dramatists. Juan de la Cueva (1550–1610), working in Seville, wrote fourteen plays. He was one of the first dramatists to draw on Spanish history in plays such as *The Seven Children of Lara.* He also wrote on classical subjects and on themes from everyday life, but his most important contribution was his popularizing of polymetry, using different meters to fit the needs of different characters and situations within a single play. Miguel de Cervantes (1547–1616), remembered principally for his novel *Don Quixote* (1605–1615), also wrote about thirty plays, of which ten comedias and eight *entermeses* survive. The best of these are *The Siege of Numancia,* about a Roman attack on a Spanish town in 134 B.C.E.; *The Traffic of Argel,* a semi-autobiographical drama of his own years of slavery after being captured by Algerian pirates; and *The Fortunate Ruffian,* a play of contemporary Spanish life. Cervantes's plays, many of which were written between 1580 and 1587, came to seem stilted after Lope de Vega's works appeared. Yet, like the University Wits in England, Cueva, Cervantes, and other educated dramatists of the 1580s provided the link between academic drama and the professional stage.

By the end of the sixteenth century, several dramatic types had become popular. Since Spanish terminology is unique, a brief summary will facilitate later discussions. *Comedia* was used to describe any full-length play, whether serious or comic. Most were divided into three acts (the five-act form was used by some authors but was never widely adopted in Spain). There were many types of *comedia,* among them *comedias de capa y espada* (cape and sword plays, named for the dress of gentlemen of minor ranks about whom these plays revolve); *comedias de costumbres* (comedies of manners); *comedias de santos* (saints plays); *comedias mitológicas* (mythological plays); *comedias pastoriles* (pastoral plays); and plays that required stage machinery for the desired effects, among them *comedias de teatro, comedias de cuerpo* (corpse), and *comedias de ruido* (situation plays). The most common characters in these plays were the *cabellero* (gentleman), *galán* (young cavalier), *dama* (lady), *gracioso* (comic character, usually servant to the *galán*), and the *criada* (lady's maid), although these were supplemented by many other character types. The most common subjects were honor, love, patriotism, and religion.

Until about 1615, every performance began with a *loa* (compliment), or prologue, either a monologue or a dialogue. It was designed to gain the good will of the audience, and was usually preceded by singing and dancing. Although it declined in popularity after 1615, the *loa* was not abandoned for many years. *Entremeses* ("interludes"), or short topical sketches, were performed in the intervals between the acts of plays. Some *entremeses* were sung, others were spoken, and still others mingled speech and song. Around 1650, the term *sainete* came into use for many short farces which earlier would have been called *entremeses* or *pasos*. Most Spanish dramatists wrote all these forms.

LOPE DE VEGA AND HIS CONTEMPORARIES

By far the most prolific Spanish playwright was Lope Félix de Vega Carpio (1562–1635), whose personal life was as flamboyant as the plays he wrote. He sailed with the Spanish Armada in 1588, was secretary to a nobleman and participant in many business and love affairs, and, after 1614, became a priest. In spite of his many activities, he declared in 1609 that he had written 483 *comedias*. Estimates of his total output run as high as 1800 plays, although 800 is probably more nearly accurate. Of these, 331 have survived, with another 200 surviving plays being attributed to him. He also found time to write on dramatic theory in *The New Art of Writing Plays for Our Time* (1609). He was the first Spanish dramatist to make his living as a playwright, and no other dramatist has so dominated the professional theatre of any period.

It is difficult to assess the quality of Lope's work because of its quantity, but some broad generalizations are possible. Above all, his plays are notable for clearly defined actions which arouse and maintain suspense. Many revolve around the conflicting claims of love and honor, a theme which Lope popularized and bequeathed to virtually all succeeding Spanish drama. Since he disliked unhappy endings, Lope usually found means for resolving conflicts on an optimistic note. His characters include representatives of practically every rank and condition, into all of whom Lope entered sympathetically. The female roles are among his best. He also extended the scope of the *gracioso*, or simpleton, a standard character in the plays of the day. Lope's dialogue is natural, lively, and appropriate; it ranges through many verse forms, for Spanish dramatists never developed an equivalent to English blank verse. Lope is often compared to Shakespeare, and some critics have suggested that if only his best thirty-eight plays are considered, Lope's work is superior in its depiction of romantic passion and the mastery it shows of a variety of verse forms. But most critics agree that Lope does not penetrate as deeply into human nature as Shakespeare was able to do, and that his optimistic endings gloss over the darker side of life. Although the plays produce many surprises, they offer few insights; they celebrate the variety of life without significantly illuminating it.

Lope was by far the most popular writer of his age. To modern audiences, his most appealing work is perhaps *The Sheep Well* (*Fuente Ovejuna*, c. 1614), in which a tyrannous feudal lord is killed by villagers, who refuse to confess even under torture and are saved by the intervention of the king. Many critics have seen revolutionary sentiments in the play, but it is more likely that Lope was praising the king for abolishing the feudal system. Others among his best-known plays are *The Foolish Lady* (1613), *Finding Truth through Doubt* (1620–1624), *The Knight from Olmeda* (1622), and *Punishment without Revenge* (1631).

Although Lope is now acknowledged as perhaps the greatest of all Spanish playwrights, he was surrounded by a host of other writers. The most important of these were Guillén de Castro, Tirso de Molina, and Juan Ruiz de Alarcón. Guillén de Castro (1569–1631), a friend and follower of Lope, wrote forty-three plays but is now remembered almost entirely for his *The Youthful Adventures of the Cid* (*Las Mocedades del Cid,* 1612–1618), which was to serve as the basis for the French playwright Corneille's controversial *Le Cid* in 1637. Tirso de Molina (*c.* 1584–1648) wrote a wide variety of *comedias,* including tragedies based on biblical stories and comedies dealing with contemporary political issues. The latter got him into trouble with the Council of Castile in 1625, and he was exiled from Madrid, after which his dramatic output decreased significantly. He is said to have written about 400 plays, of which eighty survive. He is known for creating intelligent, determined, and daring heroines, though by far the most famous of his plays today is *El Burlador de Sevilla* (*The Trickster of Seville,* 1616–1630), the first dramatic treatment of the Don Juan story. Juan Ruiz de Alarcón (*c.* 1581–1639), born in Mexico and educated in Spain, where he worked for the government, wrote about twenty-five plays, the best of which center around court life in Madrid. The finest is *The Suspicious Truth* (1619), which explores the consequences arising from the inability of a young man to tell the truth. In his plays, Alarcón makes characterization and subtle moral sentiments the bases of dramatic action.

CALDERÓN AND HIS CONTEMPORARIES

Before Lope de Vega died, his preeminence had been challenged by another writer, Calderón, who was to be ranked above Lope by many critics. Unlike Lope and his contemporaries, who were associated principally with the public theatres, Calderón and the best dramatists of his time wrote primarily for the court theatre. In this shift, many historians have seen a major cause of the decline of Spanish drama.

Pedro Calderón de la Barca (1600–1681), the son of a court official, received a university education and then entered the service of a nobleman. In 1651, after a series of personal disasters, Calderón became a priest, although he continued to write *autos* for the city of Madrid and occasional plays for the court. Of his approximately 200 plays, about 100 have survived. Eighty of these are *autos*.

Calderón wrote practically all of his best secular plays between 1622 and 1640. These fall into two major categories: the "cape and sword" comedies, such as *The Phantom Lady* (1629), which depend on happily resolved love intrigues and misunderstandings; and the serious plays, many of which explore jealousy and honor. Of the latter type, one of the best known is *The Physician to His Own Honor* (1635) in which a man, suspecting that his wife is unfaithful, kills her in a manner that will avoid scandal. Although the play on the surface seems to treat the man's action sympathetically, some critics insist that it is intended to make audiences aware of a practice of which Calderón disapproved.

Calderón's most famous secular play, *Life Is a Dream* (c. 1636), is a philosophical allegory about the human situation and the mystery of life. The main character, Segismundo, a prince by birth, is reared in anonymity, taken to court while unconscious, and returned to his former state after being found unworthy; when he awakens, he believes that the interlude at court was a dream. Eventually, after he comes to understand that life is a dream from which only death awakens us, he takes the throne in a civil war and becomes a wise ruler. In the chaotic years following 1640, when Catalonia and Portugal revolted against Spain, Calderón wrote only one outstanding *comedia, The Mayor of Zalamea* (c. 1642), the story of a peasant who exacts revenge for the violation of his daughter by an army officer. After 1652, all of Calderón's secular plays were written on demand for the court. They are short and light, often based on classical myths or pastoral subjects, with choral passages and much of the dialogue set to music. Because so many of them were performed at the royal hunting lodge, La Zarzuela, this type of musical play, which later was to be (and still remains) one of the most popular of Spanish dramatic forms, came to be called the *zarzuela*.

Above all, Calderón is noted for his *autos,* for he perfected the form. In his *autos,* Calderón effectively embodied Catholic dogma in symbolic stories told in lyrical dialogue of great beauty. Although he had written *autos* from the beginning of his career, he turned to them especially after 1647, writing two each year for the city of Madrid until his death. Nevertheless, his finest *autos, The Constant Prince* (1629) and *Devotion to the Cross* (1633), were written before he became a priest.

Of Calderón's contemporaries, two—Rojas Zorilla and Moreto—stand out. Francisco de Rojas Zorilla (1607–1648) lived chiefly in Madrid, where he held a position at court and wrote primarily for the royal theatre. Of his 70 plays, the best-known, *All Equal below the King* (*Del Rey abajo Ninguno,* 1651), tells the story of a nobleman who is forgiven by the king for killing a man who sought to seduce his wife. In light comedy Rojas Zorilla broke new ground with such works as *The Fools' Sport* (1638) and *What Women Are* (1645), in which a variety of pompous characters replace the traditional *gracioso* as the principal source of humor. Unfortunately, since Rojas Zorilla had no real followers, his breaks with tradition had little effect in Spain. His plays were greatly admired in France, however, and were adapted by Scarron, Thomas Corneille, and LeSage.

Augustín Moreto y Cabaña (1618–1669) was born in Madrid and spent most of his life at court, for which he principally wrote. The best-known of his fifty plays is *Scorn for Scorn* (1654), which served as the basis for Molière's *La Princesse d'Elide.* It tells the story of a woman who scorns all her lovers, only to be captured by one who pretends to scorn her. Moreto's delicate poetry, elegant and subtle wit, and interesting character portraits won him a wide following among aristocratic audiences. Most of his plays are adaptations of *comedias* by Lope de Vega and others.

The output of the Golden Age was phenomenal. Estimates of the total number of plays written prior to 1700 range from 10,000 to 30,000. In quantity, the drama of Spain greatly exceeded that of England between 1590 and 1642. On the other hand, its failure to probe deeply into human destiny and its preoccupation with a narrow code of honor are limitations which make it less universal than the best English work. Nevertheless, many of the plays were widely known and imitated outside of Spain, and at home they established a lasting standard.

ACTING COMPANIES

It is difficult to estimate the number of acting companies in Spain between 1550 and 1600, for many lasted only a single season and mergers or separations were frequent. In addition to the Spanish troupes, Italian *commedia dell'arte* companies frequently visited during this time. The troupe led by Alberto Naselli (1574–1584), who used the stage name Ganassa, seems to have been influential in the early creation of the theatres (*corrales*) in Madrid, while among the many other Italian troupes those led by Estefanelo

Botarga, Maximiliano Milanino, and Tristano Martinelli were especially popular. The number of Spanish troupes increased rapidly after permanent theatres were built, so in 1603 the government sought to regulate them by severely restricting the Italian companies and reducing the number of Spanish troupes to eight licensed companies. In 1615 the number of licenses was raised to twelve.

There were two kinds of licensed companies: sharing troupes (*compañías de parte*) and salaried actors working for a manager under one- or two-year contracts. Companies licensed by the Royal Council could be contracted to do the *auto sacramentales* for a city, for which the companies received relatively high fees. Licensed companies could also be contracted to perform in the *corrales*. Generally only one licensed company at a time would perform in a city, but in Seville and Madrid there could be as many as four. Payments to companies varied widely. Usually a troupe was given a fixed sum for each performance, and a percentage of the receipts was sometimes added. Occasionally companies were paid entirely through a fixed percentage of receipts. If a company had to travel a long distance to keep an engagement, it might receive additional payments since traveling from one engagement to the next was time-consuming and costly. In 1586, for example, it took one company thirteen days to travel the 270 miles between Madrid and Seville. The mode of transportation, depending upon the company's finances, ranged from walking to using carts, pack animals, and coaches. Contracts often specified allowances for travel, as well as the type of lodging and food to be provided on the road.

Between 1610 and 1640, the period of the theatre's greatest popularity, the average licensed company consisted of sixteen to twenty actors and included men, women, and apprentices performing a repertory of up to sixty plays. In addition companies generally had their own prompter, wardrobe keepers, stage hands, and money collectors. Little is known of individual companies, although the names of many actor-managers have survived. Among the most famous were Alonso Riquelme (*fl.* 1602–1621), Cristobal Ortiz (*fl.* 1613–1626), Roque di Figueroa (*fl.* 1612–1650), and Antonio de Rueda (*fl.* 1628–1662).

Each play in a company's repertory had to be licensed separately. After 1600 all plays were subject to censorship, and dramatists could be excommunicated if they did not comply with recommendations. Before 1590, many playwrights were attached to troupes as actors. After 1590, such close connections were unusual, though company managers generally commissioned new plays so the playwrights still wrote their *comedias* with a specific company in mind. At the height of his career Lope de Vega received about 500 reals for each play, at a time when an actor's average annual salary was about 6000 reals. This disparity in income may explain why dramatists were so prolific. By the 1650s the payment had increased somewhat—to about 800 reals—for works by the best writers. Plays commissioned for the court paid two to three times that amount.

Actors not contracted to licensed companies often joined "companies of the road" (*compañías de la legua*) which performed anywhere they could and shared the takings for each performance. Since there were no copyright laws, a play could be performed by any company that could obtain a copy and its license, and it was common practice for the licensed companies to lease licensed plays to these unlicensed troupes (which were not above stealing such plays when necessary). The size of these companies varied considerably. Augustín de Rojas Villandrando's fictional *Entertaining Journey* (1604) describes troupes ranging in size from the single performer, who recited monologues or scenes from plays, to those with sixteen members. During the long closure of the theatres from 1646 to 1651 the "companies of the road" seem to have continued in operation (even though they had been made illegal in 1644), while the licensed companies disbanded. When the theatres reopened, only eight companies were licensed and their energies were focused increasingly on the court.

ACTORS AND ACTING

The position of the professional performer in Spain was ambiguous. Since Roman times actors had been forbidden the sacraments of the church, and Alfonso X (1221–1284) declared that all actors were to be branded infamous. These strictures were not officially removed in Spain until the twentieth century. During the Golden Age the usual attitude was one of tolerance, however, so long as actors did not perform plays that contradicted church teachings; certainly many actors, especially those in licensed troupes, were married and buried in the church. They were employed by city officials to produce the *autos* at Corpus Christi and their work was essential to the funding of many charities. Nevertheless, many churchmen were opposed to the theatre, especially to the use of professional actors in religious plays. They often petitioned the king to ban professional theatre, and while such petitions were rarely granted, they did result in a very close supervision of the theatre by government officials.

A major concern of those opposed to theatre was the presence of professional actresses. Professional female performers in Spain can be traced back as far as the fifteenth century, and by the mid-sixteenth century, they were included in several acting troupes. Nevertheless, most women's roles were played by boys or men until 1587, when women were first licensed to appear on the stage. Churchmen secured a royal decree banning actresses in 1596, but it seems never to have been enforced. After a bitter controversy in 1598 and 1599, the royal council declared that no actresses were to perform unless their husbands or fathers were in the company, and that neither sex might appear in the dress of the other. This decree too, however, especially the later portion of it, seems not to have been enforced. Further attempts to still criticism probably lay behind the decree of 1608, which stated that only actors were to go backstage, forbade friars to attend the theatre, and banned the presentation of secular plays in churches or religious houses. At this time strict censorship was established over plays, and in 1615 it was extended to dancing, about which there had been many complaints.

Dance played an important role in both the *comedias* and the *autos*. Most actresses danced as well as acted, and the contracts of many actors specified that they must dance and sing. Many complaints against the theatre cited the *zarabanda,* introduced about 1588, as licentious and voluptuous. In addition, *bayles* (dances accompanied by couplets) were considered morally questionable by many persons. After the decree of 1615, dances became more sedate.

In 1631 the actors were allowed to form a guild similar to those of other recognized trades. Called the Cofradía de la Novena, it still exists and is open to all theatrical personnel. It did much to raise the social status of the actor.

The Biographical Dictionary of Actors in Spanish Classical Theater database now being developed by the University of Valencia contains the names of over 6500 professional actors who worked in the theatre prior to 1700. Most performers were recruited from the common people, although occasionally members of the minor aristocracy went on the stage. The best known of these actors include Damien Arias de Peñafiel (*fl.* 1617–1643), who, with his "pure, clear voice, vivacious manner, and excellent memory," was universally regarded as the finest actor of his time. Other outstanding performers included Cosme Perez (*c.* 1585–1673), the most famous comic actor of the age, and Jusepa Vaca (*fl.* 1602–1634), the most celebrated actress.

In his *Entertaining Journey,* Rojas Villandrando describes the actor's life around 1600: Performers must rise early and study their roles from 2 until 9 A.M., and then attend rehearsals until noon; after eating, they go to the theatre to perform, completing their work about 7 P.M.; if they are summoned by officials or nobles to perform, they may work well into the night. Under Philip IV (reigned 1621–1665), the actors were much in demand at court, and Philip's practice of sending for companies on such short notice that they had to cancel public performances is sometimes cited as a reason for the decline of public interest in theatre, though the long closure of the theatre from 1646–1651 is undoubtedly a larger factor in this.

The actors were usually paid after each performance. In sharing companies, the receipts were divided after all expenses were subtracted. Salaried actors were paid by the day, and since the number of performances might vary widely from one year and troupe to another, it is difficult to calculate the average income. One historian has estimated it at about 6000 reals per year, a rather liberal sum for the time. Most salaries were supplemented by a daily maintenance allowance, and additional payments might be made for traveling expenses and costumes. Thus, though actors did not rank high in the social scale, they were in many ways better off than their French contemporaries, who were denied religious rights, or English actors, who were always at odds with the civic authorities.

COSTUMES

The costume practices of the Spanish stage were similar to those of England during the same period. Expensive contemporary clothing served in most cases, although historical and legendary figures were sometimes differentiated by outmoded or fanciful dress. Moors, toward whom the Spaniards felt a special antipathy, were always clearly distinguished from other characters.

Contracts for the *autos* specified costumes of silk and velvet. Often the actors petitioned civic officials for additional funds to pay for unexpectedly expensive garments, and their requests were frequently granted. In addition, towns voted special prizes to companies or actors who had distinguished themselves in the *autos* either through acting or costuming. These costumes were then reused by the companies in their performances at the *corrales.*

Although a sharing company usually maintained a wardrobe that was available to all its members, many actors supplied their own costumes. Actors' contracts often specified allowances for costumes. The manager was responsible for the wardrobes of apprentices.

In most cases, actors seem to have dressed as lavishly as finances permitted. In 1653 actresses were forbidden to wear strange headdresses, decolleté necklines, wide hooped skirts, or dresses not reaching the floor. In addition, they were restricted to one costume for each play unless the scripts clearly demanded a change. Records of extravagance are numerous. In 1589 an actor paid 1100 reals and in 1619 another paid 2400 reals for a single costume, sums equivalent to about one-fifth to one-half of a typical actor's annual income. No doubt the minor performers were less richly dressed. A good wardrobe was considered one of the actor's greatest assets, for it helped secure employment and could be pawned in bad times.

THE CORRALES

Early acting companies performed in the courtyards (*corrales*) that are a distinctive feature of Spanish urban architecture. City blocks are organized around a series of such courtyards. The term *corral*, therefore, came to be used for theatre. The first public theatre structure in Spain was built by the Italian architect Juan (Giovanni) Marin Modeñin Bellini in Seville in 1574. The last one was built at Almagro in 1628 for Don Leonardo de Oviedo, a priest who had it purposely built within the courtyard of his inn, The Bull. (This is the only Golden Age theatre that still exists.) Between these two dates, *corral* theatres (and often more than one) were built in at least eighteen other cities in Spain and four in the Americas, and probably many more besides. Most of what we know about *corral* theatres concerns Madrid, however, and the account that follows is primarily about that city, although it is unclear to what extent Madrid's practices were typical. In Madrid, the *corrales* were at first under the direct control of three charitable "confraternities" like those which had presented religious plays throughout Europe during the Middle Ages. The Cofradía de la Pasión y Sangre de Jesucristo, founded in 1565 to feed and clothe the poor and support a hospital, was the first to be granted the privilege of operating a theatre as a means of raising money. By 1568 it was using a rented courtyard in the Calle de Sol for performances and soon added two others. In 1574 the Confradía de la Soledad de Nuestra Señora, founded in 1567, petitioned to have one of the existing courtyards placed under its control, a move which led to a sharing of revenues and expenses by the two *cofradías*. In 1583 the General Hospital of Madrid was also given a share in the revenues. These three organizations controlled the public theatres of Madrid until 1615. This made the theatre a means of raising money for charity, which helped to isolate it from public criticism.

FIG. 6.4
The *corral* theatre of Almagro (near Ciudad Real), Spain. Built in 1628, it was restored in 1953–1954. The stage is 28 feet wide and 13 feet deep to the row of posts at the rear, where a curtain would have hung from the gallery. It is another 2 feet 8 inches from the posts to the doors in the rear wall. Photo by F. J. Hildy.

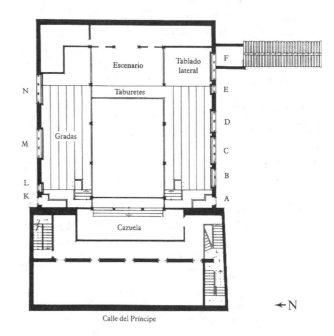

FIG. 6.5
Plan by J. J. Allen and Carlos Dorremochea of the second level of the Corral del Príncipe, c. 1697. The letters at the sides indicate boxes. The stage (*escenario*) and side stages (*tablado lateral*) are shown at top. Benches (*taburetes*) for seating in the *patio* are forward of the stage. Courtesy the University Presses of Florida and Mr. Allen.

A new phase in the career of the theatres began in 1615 when the City of Madrid was ordered to pay the hospitals an annual subsidy. After this time, the *cofradías* gave up direct control over theatrical management and leased the theatres to entrepreneurs, normally for four-year periods. In 1638 control of the *corrales* passed to the city, and two commissioners were appointed to oversee them, although the theatres continued to be leased. Despite some alterations in the system during the eighteenth century, the theatres were used to finance charities until the mid-nineteenth century. At no time during the Golden Age did the actors control the *corrales,* which were occupied by them merely for short-term engagements under contracts with the theatres' lessees.

At first the *corrales* were temporary, at least five different ones being used in Madrid during the 1570s. The desirability of permanent theatres became evident after one was built in Seville in 1574, however, and in 1579 the Corral de la Cruz, the first permanent theatre in the capital, was opened in Madrid. It was followed by the Corral del Príncipe in 1583. After 1585 these were to be the only public theatres for drama in Madrid until the mid-eighteenth century.

Madrid's *corrales* were built around a square or rectangular courtyard (unroofed until the eighteenth century). Adjustable awnings were used to shade the audience and provide some lighting effects, an innovation introduced by the Italian Ganassa company in 1574. A stage (*encenario*) with a tiring house (*vestuario*) behind it, occupied one end of the courtyard. The Madrid *corrales* had discovery spaces in the *vestuario* and side stages that could be used for medieval style mansions or for extra audience seating. These features were shared by some, but not all, of the *corrales* outside the capital.

The large central courtyard (*patio*) was occupied primarily by standing spectators, although by the mid-seventeenth century a row of benches (*taburetes*) had been set up immediately in front of the stage. Along each side of the *patio* was bleacher-style seating (*gradas*), divided from the *patio* by a railing and protected from the weather by an overhanging roof.

FIG. 6.6
Interior of the Corral del Príncipe, c. 1697. At center left is the main stage, and to the right of it one of the side stages (occupied by spectators). At bottom left is the *patio,* and at bottom right the *gradas* backed by the grated windows of the first level of boxes; at top right are the *desvánes* and below them a row of open boxes. Drawing by Carlos Dorremochea. From John J. Allen, *The Reconstruction of a Spanish Golden Age Playhouse* (1983). Courtesy the University Presses of Florida and Mr. Allen.

The *gradas* extended up to the second-story level of the four-story houses that surrounded the *patio*. Each window in a house served as a theatre box (*aposento*), and those on the second floor were fitted with grilles to prevent climbing into the theatre. The fourth-floor boxes were often called *desvanes* (attics) because of their location and cramped space.

At the rear of the *patio* was a refreshment booth (*alojeria*), above which was the gallery for unaccompanied women (the *cazuela*). Strict segregation of men and women was enforced by an *alcalde* (Justice of the Peace). Women were forbidden the *patio* and men the *cazuela*. Women could, however, sit in boxes if accompanied by an adult male member of their own family.

Above the *cazuela* were two other galleries, the first divided into boxes (two of which were assigned to the City of Madrid and the Council of Castile), and the other used at different stages of the theatre's development as a seating area for clergymen and intellectuals (*tertulia*) or as an upper *cazuela*.

Some of the theatres outside of Madrid deviated from this typical pattern. Some were roofed from the beginning. Some were purposely built as theatres and did not have to contend with surrounding houses. Many were only three-story rather than four. In most of these, the *aposentos* were replaced by open galleries divided into compartments like those later used in the Italian public opera houses; others had one row of *aposentos*, above which there were open galleries. Nevertheless, the basic arrangement—an enclosed courtyard—was the same everywhere.

Madrid's two theatres had several entrances; at each entrance there were two money takers, since two entrance fees were paid, one to the lessee and one to a representative of the charities. About three-fifths of the combined total income went to the lessee and the actors. The entrance fee admitted women to the *cazuela* and men to the *patio*. Additional fees were collected from the men if they wished to sit on the *gradas*, *taburetes*, or side stages. The theatre controlled all the boxes facing the stage, but the arrangement with the boxes located in the side houses varied. Some homeowners collected entrance fees for their boxes on certain days and the theatre lessee collected the fees on other days; some owners had sole rights to their boxes in return for allowing passageways through their property to other boxes; and some owners paid the theatre an annual fee for the right to watch the plays. (The problems created by such arrangements was a primary motivation for tearing down the *corrales* in the mid-eighteenth century and building self-contained theatres on the same sites.)

Until the 1580s performances were confined to Sundays and feast days. But in 1579 the Italian Ganassa

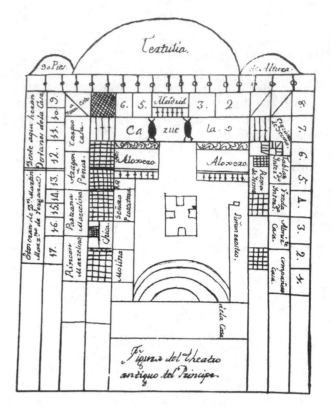

FIG. 6.7
A rough plan of the Corral del Príncipe made about 1730. The stage is shown at the bottom, and the refreshment booth, *cazuela*, and *tertulia* at the top; the side walls, showing the boxes, are drawn as though the various levels were side by side. From a plan published in 1881.

troupe was permitted to play on a weekday, and this privilege was soon extended to Spanish companies. By the seventeenth century performances were allowed daily except on Saturdays. The theatrical season ran from September to Lent and from just after Easter until July. About 198 days each year were devoted to performances, but the theatres were often closed for periods of official mourning, plagues, and wars.

The Madrid *corrales* probably had a capacity of about 1000 when they opened, but this had increased to about 2000 by the 1630s, when Madrid's population stood at about 150,000. It has been estimated that roughly 350 places were reserved for unaccompanied women in the *cazuela*, but it is not known how many more may have been in the boxes at any one time. Performances began at 2 P.M. in the fall and winter season and at 3 to 4 P.M. during the spring; they were required to end at least one hour before nightfall. The daily bill began with music, singing, and dancing; next came the *loa*, or prologue, which was followed by another dance; then came the *comedia*, the acts of which were separated by *entremeses;* a dance concluded the performance.

Spectators, especially those in the *patio* and *cazuela,* were often noisy. The *mosqueteros* in the courtyard were usually the most unruly, but the women sometimes threw fruit at the actors, and both men and women carried such noisemakers as whistles, rattles, and bunches of keys. They were equally voluble in approval, which they demonstrated by applauding and shouting "Victor!" Refreshments, such as fruit, wafers, and drinks, were sold throughout performances. On any occasion when a full house was expected, the *alcalde* was seated on one side of the stage as a visual reminder that order would be enforced. He had a number of attendants (*alguaciles*) to assist him in case disturbances broke out.

THE STAGE AND SCENERY

Like the costuming and the theatres themselves, the stage and scenery of the Spanish public theatre were in many ways similar to those of England. The stage was a raised platform without a proscenium arch and was bounded at the back by a permanent façade. Since side-stage seating and *aposentos* extended up to that façade, the action was viewed from three sides, though the majority of spectators sat or stood in front of the stage.

Although the dimensions of the Corral de la Cruz are uncertain, its stage was probably about 26 feet wide by 16 feet deep. At each side of the stage were lateral platforms that could serve as additional seating for *capa y espada* plays and as space for scenic units, such as the commonly referred to "mountain" in *comedias de fábrica.* The stage at the Corral del Príncipe was about 28 feet wide by 14½ feet deep. (A semicircular extension about 5 feet deep was added to the front in the eighteenth century.) It too had lateral platforms for additional seating or special scenic pieces. At both theaters, the stage was raised about 5 to 6 feet above the *patio.* All *corrales* for which we have information on stage size roughly share these measurements (the smallest is 20 feet by

FIG. 6.8
Setting for *Los Celos hacen estrellas* by Juan Velez de Guevara at the court in 1672. Courtesy Bildarchiv, Osterreichische Nationalbibliothek, Vienna.

11½ feet). This open platform was backed by a facade of two or three levels. The lower level had three openings, those at the sides serving as entrances and the larger central space primarily as a place for "discoveries." The discovery space was about 13 feet deep at the Corral de la Cruz and about 8½ feet deep at the Príncipe. The upper levels, essentially galleries, could be used in a variety of ways, but normally represented towers, city walls, or hills. At times, discoveries were also made there by drawing curtains. It was sometimes necessary to go from the stage to an upper level in full view of the audience, and to meet this need portable stairs were brought on and then removed when no longer required.

For the most part, the simple staging conventions resembled those of the Elizabethan theatre. An exit and reentry was sufficient to mark a change of place. In addition, three different kinds of scenic background might be used. First, the facade often served as the sole background for the action. Second, curtains were drawn aside to reveal properties or scenic pieces set up in the discovery space when localization of the action was required. Third, medieval-like mansions were sometimes set up on the lateral platforms at the sides of the stage. Surviving scripts clearly show that scenic pieces were used at times to represent gardens, fountains, mountains, rocks, trees, forts, and castles. Sometimes they are specified when not strictly required by the action, while in other instances the spectators are requested to imagine some place not shown. It seems likely that practice was inconsistent and was guided more by the availability of scenic pieces than by any conscious theory of stage decoration. On the other hand, as spectacle increased after 1650, painted flats and practicable windows and doors began to be set into the facade in lieu of curtains. Except in rare instances, however, there was no attempt to use perspective painting. The stage was equipped with several trapdoors, while the roof over the stage housed machinery for flying, which was increasingly popular after 1650. Essentially, however, scenic practices changed little during the course of the Golden Age.

THEATRE IN THE AMERICAS

Once the voyages of Columbus brought the Americas into European consciousness, the Spanish set about to conquer this territory just as they had done the Iberian Peninsula. By 1519 they had conquered the Bahamas, the Caribbean islands, and Cuba; by 1522 the Aztec empire of Mexico and Central America; by 1533 the Inca Empire of western South America. Florida came under their control by 1565. In 1581 Spain gained control of Portugal and along with it came Brazil (until 1668). Southeastern South America was added about the same time.

Among the hundreds of cultures they conquered, there were certainly traditions of storytelling, narrative dance, epic songs, rituals, ceremonies, and popular entertainment that would be of great interest to the study of theatre. Unfortunately the conquistadors had little interest in such things. By the time the Dominican and Franciscan friars recorded their observations of these cultures in the mid to late sixteenth century, much had already changed. As early as 1512 Europeans began to insert Christian elements into native performance traditions. By 1523 the Spanish were introducing large numbers of African slaves into the region, and their performance traditions soon merged with those of the native peoples. The Maya were already a fading culture before the Spanish arrived, and they, along with the other major cultures of the Americas, were soon experiencing near total collapse as European disease and constant warfare (with both Europeans and other indigenous peoples) destroyed an estimated 92 percent of the native populations within just thirty years of colonization. Smaller cultures simply disappeared. With the exception of the Maya and Aztecs (whose records were systematically destroyed), the cultures of the Americas were nonliterate and had not recorded their own traditions. It is therefore difficult to assess the remaining evidence for pre-Columbian performance traditions.

The Spanish recorded a type of farce called *baldzamil* among the Maya and described stages with staircases used for these performances. There is also a Mayan dramatic text from Guatemala for the epic dance-drama, *The Rabinal Warrior* (*Rabinal Achí*) or the *Dance of the Tun*. It was not recorded until 1855 (from the memory of a performer who had appeared in the work several times before 1820), but some scholars believe that it reflects performance traditions that go back to the thirteenth century. The play tells the story of an unnamed Queché warrior who is captured by the Rabinal Warrior and taken before the Rabinal ruler named Five Rains. It ends with the ritual slaying of the captured warrior by a group of twelve eagles and twelve jaguars. Though as many as a hundred performers were involved in the production, there are only three speaking roles. In Nicaragua sometime in the sixteenth or seventeenth centuries, a comedy called *The Old Man* (*El Güegüence*) was composed incorporating what are thought to be pre-Columbian traditions of a comic buffoon character, but this play was not transcribed until 1883. A similar "buffoon" tradition was noted in conjunction with the ceremonial *kachina* dances of the Pueblo peoples when the Spanish encountered them in what is now the Southwestern United States around 1540. The Spanish observed, as well, a thriving performance tradition of social satire among communities subjugated by the Incas in Peru. In the 1780s Antonio Valdés produced *Ollantay*, an epic drama he claimed was of pre-Columbian origin, which he had transcribed from the oral tradition of these people, but its authenticity is questioned by many scholars.

The earliest known performance of a European play in the Americas took place at a seminary in Puerto Rico in 1510. But the Dominican and Franciscan friars who set out to Christianize the Americas were soon adapting local performance traditions to Christian purposes just as had been done in Europe in the Middle Ages. They wrote numerous *autos,* generally in the local language, to be performed by those they were converting. Native dance, music, and costuming were incorporated into many of these. By 1539 the *autos* of New Spain (Mexico) had gained political overtones with *The Conquest of Rhodes* and *The Conquest of Jerusalem* being performed by rival groups in two different cities. Over 1000 Indians were used as musicians and extras in these plays. In 1544 the archbishop of New Spain ordered an end to this kind of activity. But the evangelical use of theatre simply moved on to Peru in 1546 and Brazil by the 1570s, and it never really stopped even in New Spain.

México (Mexico City) established a prize for the best play at Corpus Christi in 1565. But the real turning point for theatre in the Americas came in 1574. At the consecration of the new archbishop, the first Spanish-language play to be written by a native-born dramatist was performed: *Spiritual Contract between the Shepard Peter and the Mexican Church* by Juan Pérez Ramires (1545–?). The first plays of the first major dramatist of the New World, Spanish-born dramatist Fernán Gonzáles de Eslava (1534–c. 1601), were also performed for this event, which in addition is celebrated for the appearance of the first professional actor of the Americas.

In 1586 *autor* Alonso de Buenrostro brought his acting troupe from Spain, and by 1601 there were three acting companies based in Mexico City. In 1597 Francisco de León built the first *corral* theatre there. A second was built sometime before 1602, and others were built at Pueblo de Los Angeles, Lima (Peru), and New Veracruz. Throughout the seventeenth century theatre was performed in many parts of the Spanish territories, but New Spain, and especially Mexico City, continued to be the focal point.

Three volumes of religious *comedias* attributed to Juan Bautista were published in New Spain in 1599. The Mexican nun Sor Juana Inés de la Cruz (*c.* 1648–1695), a towering intellect of the period and one of the most admired women of her day, wrote her first play, *The Second Celestina,* in 1676. She also wrote *The Trials of a Noble House* (1683), which was thought to have achieved a lyric beauty matched only by Calderón. In the 1680s Juan del Valle y Caviedas (1652–1694) become the first playwright in Peru. His fame was quickly eclipsed, however, by Pedro de Peralta Barnuevo (1664–1743), who wrote full-length plays on French and Greek themes. These New World dramatists and the many others who surrounded them wrote fairly typical Spanish Golden Age plays of all types, but the local color and native characters they included made their works distinctive.

COURT ENTERTAINMENTS

Although court entertainments like those found elsewhere in Europe had been seen in Spain since the thirteenth century, it was not until the reign of Philip III (1598–1621) that theatrical performances were given regularly at court. Philip's queen was especially fond of the theatre, and both professional productions and masques performed by courtiers were frequent until her death in 1611.

The court theatre reached its height during the reign of Philip IV (1621–1665), who between 1623 and 1653 saw about 300 different plays at court. Although Italianate scenery had been used occasionally since the sixteenth century, it did not become common until Cosme Lotti (?–1643), a student of the great Italian designer, Alfonso Parigi, was brought from Florence in 1626. Until the 1630s most of the court entertainments were staged in a large hall at the Alcázar or in the gardens at Aranjuez; after 1633 the new palace in Madrid, the Buen Retiro, became the center of court entertainments. With the opening of Buen Retiro, performances by professional troupes replaced the amateur performances of the courtiers.

Many lavish outdoor productions were staged on the palace grounds. One of the most famous of these was Calderón's *The Greatest Enchantment Is Love* (1635), which treated Ulysses' encounter with the enchantress Circe. For this production Lotti built a floating stage on a lake. The special effects included a shipwreck, a triumphal chariot drawn across the water by dolphins, and the destruction of Circe's palace. The whole was lit by 3000 lanterns, and the king and his retinue watched from gondolas. In 1636 the three acts of Calderón's *The Three Great Prodigies* were given on three separate stages, each act being performed by a different professional troupe. In addition, there were many lavish masquerades, tournaments, and machine plays. For a carnival in 1637, Lotti designed huge wheeled structures measuring 22 feet in width, 32 feet in length, and 46 feet in height.

In 1640 a permanent theatre, the Coliseo, was constructed by Lotti in the Buen Retiro. This theatre seems to have resembled the public *corrales,* for it had a *patio,* three levels of *aposentos,* and a *cazuela.* The royal box was situated above the *cazuela.* It differed from the *corrales* in being roofed and probably in having a proscenium arch, often said to be the first in Spain. The Coliseo was frequently open to the public, who paid the same entrance fees as at the public *corrales.* Furthermore, the same percentage of the receipts was given to charities. The plays were performed by troupes that normally appeared in the *corrales,* and the scenic demands for most of the plays were similar to those written for the public theatres. Other plays, however, were machine plays; spectacular pieces that required Italianate scenery and special effects. Sometimes private performances for the court preceded those open to the public. More intimate entertainments were

FIG. 6.10

An opera at court, *c.* 1680. The suspended figures on stage indicate that the theatre was equipped with Italianate machinery. From *Histoire de France.* Courtesy Bibliothèque Nationale, Paris.

given in other rooms or in one of the courtyards in the palace.

The 1640s saw a marked decline in theatrical activities, both at court and in the public theatres. The Catalan and Portuguese rebellions of 1640 ushered in a period of uncertainty, and, following the deaths of Lotti in 1643 and of the queen in 1644, court theatricals virtually came to an end. Between 1646 and 1651 the public theatres were closed.

By 1650 Philip had remarried and had settled many of his political problems; consequently, the Coliseo was reopened to the public in 1651, the same year in which the public theatres were permitted to resume performances. Another Italian designer, Baccio del Bianco (?–1657), was imported in 1652, and the use of spectacular scenery increased markedly. Court performances were frequent until Philip's death in 1665. They were resumed about 1670, and the old practices were continued. In these years, a Spaniard, José Caudi, who replaced the Italians, became the first native scene designer of note. After the death of Carlos II in 1700, the court theatre declined rapidly.

By the late seventeenth century, the financial resources of Spain were virtually exhausted, and Spain's political power was rapidly declining. The great dramatic impulse was also over, for after the death of Calderón in 1681 new writers sought primarily to recapture a past glory instead of exploring new paths. As a consequence, the most vital and productive period of Spanish theatre had ended by 1700.

FIG. 6.9

A play at the court of Carlos II, *c.* 1680. The king is seated on a dais at lower right. Note the proscenium arch and the perspective scenery. From *Histoire de France,* published at Antwerp by Philibert Buttats the Younger. Courtesy Bibliothèque Nationale, Paris.

LOOKING AT THEATRE HISTORY

Public archives often contain some of the most valuable information concerning the theatre. This is especially true for a study of *autos sacramentales:* The Municipal Archives in Madrid contain numerous documents relating to the preparation and performance of Corpus Christi celebrations there. Many of the pertinent documents have been published by N. D. Shergold and J. E. Varey in an ongoing series of volumes under the collective title *Fuentes para la Historia del Teatro en España.*

Other major sources of information are accounts written by visitors from other countries. Often they provide more graphic details of theatrical conditions than native writers who are so familiar with local situations that they consider it unnecessary to record them. One of the best descriptions of the Corpus Christi festivals in Madrid is found in an account written by the Dutchman Francis van Aerssen, who visited Spain in 1654–1655. His account was published in French in 1666 and in English in 1670.

> . . . they begin by a procession, whose first ranks include several [musicians]; a great many habited in parti-colored clothes, skip and frolic as extravagantly as in a Morris dance. The king . . . after Mass, returns with a torch in his hand, following a silver Tabernacle, in which is the Holy wafer, attended by the Grandees of Spain and his several Councils. . . . Before these . . . move Machines, representing Giants; these are Statues of Pasteboard carried by men concealed under them. . . . The Tarasca is a Serpent of enormous greatness in form of a Woman, moving on wheels, the body covered with scales, a vast belly, long tail, short feet, sharp talons, fiery eyes, gaping mouth, out of which extend three tongues, and long tusks. This Bulbeggar stalks up and down . . . and sometimes lays hold on Country fellows, whose fright moves laughter amongst the people. . . . The Procession having filed to the Piazza, returns by the . . . Calle Mayor, adorned by many tapestries waving on the balconies filled with men and women of all conditions. . . . In the afternoon about five o'clock, Autos are represented. . . . The two companies of Players that belong to Madrid at this time,

shut their theatres, and for a month represent these Holy Poems: this they do every evening in public on scaffolds erected to that purpose in the streets before the houses of the Presidents of several Councils. They begin at Court the day of the Solemnity. . . . The stage is at the foot of these Scaffolds, and little painted booths are rolled to it, . . . and serve as tiring houses.

A Journey into Spain (London, 1670), 118–124.

In his account of a visit to Spain in 1659, François Bertaut describes the theatres:

> . . . there are troupes of players in nearly all the towns, and they are better, in comparison, than our own [the French], but there are none in the pay of the King. They perform in a courtyard, where a number of private houses join together, so that the windows of the rooms . . . do not belong to the players but to the owners of the houses. They perform by day and without torches, and their theatres . . . have not such fine decorations as ours. . . . There are two places . . . in Madrid, which they call Corrales, and which are always filled with merchants and artisans, who leave their shops and repair thither. . . . Some of the spectators have seats close to the stage. . . . The women all sit together in a gallery at one end, which the men are not allowed to enter.

Relation de l'Estat et Gouvernement d'Espagne (Cologne, 1666), 59–60.

In 1679 the Comtesse D'Aulnoy wrote a number of letters recording her impressions of her travels in Spain. In one she describes her visit to an opera (*Alcina*) at the court theatre located in the Buen Retiro palace:

> I never saw such wretched machinery. The gods descended on horseback upon a beam which extended from one end of the stage to the other; the sun was lighted up by means of a dozen lanterns of oiled paper in each of which was a lamp. When Alcina practiced her enchantments and evoked the demons, the latter arose leisurely out of hell upon ladders. . . . The building is certainly very beautiful and handsomely painted and gilded; the boxes are furnished with

blinds . . . [which] reach from top to bottom, so that they seem to form a kind of room.

Relation du Voyage d'Espagne (The Hague, 1693), 10th letter.

Considerable information about the sharing companies of the seventeenth century can be gleaned from the contractual agreements made when the companies were formed. One contract dated June 1614 sets forth the agreement between Andrés de Claramonte and eleven other actors. Some of the provisions are these:

Andrés de Claramonte binds himself to furnish . . . as many as forty comedias and such others as the said company may require, besides the necessary entreméses, letras, *and* bailes.

Item: *. . . the various roles in the comedias shall be assigned amongst the members . . . in such manner as shall seem most suitable to each in the opinion of the said company.*

Item: *. . . members . . . are bound to attend with care and punctuality the rehearsals of all the comedias to be represented each day, at nine o'clock, at the house of . . . Andrés de Claramonte, where rehearsals are ordinarily to take place, and shall not fail to be present at any of the said rehearsals, under penalty of two reals. . . .*

Item: *. . . if, during the said time, any member of the . . . company shall absent himself from it, he shall lose all that would have fallen to his share. . . .*

Hugo A. Rennert, *The Spanish Stage in the Time of Lope de Vega* (New York, 1909), 147–149.

Although the neoclassical mode never made a marked impact in Spain, its precepts were not unknown there. Lope de Vega, writing in 1609, made it clear that he was familiar with the neoclassical rules. After setting forth these rules, Lope goes on to explain the precepts he has followed in writing his plays and then concludes with these reflections:

These things you may regard as aphorisms which you get not from the ancient art. . . . Nobody can I call more barbarous than myself, since in defiance of art I dare to lay down precepts, and I allow myself to be borne along in the vulgar current, wherefore Italy and France call me ignorant. But what can I do if I have written 483 plays . . . ? For all of these, except six, gravely sin against art. Yet, in fine, I defend what I have written, and I know that, though they might have been better in another manner, they would not have had the vogue which they have had; for sometimes that which is contrary to what is just, for that very reason, pleases the taste.

Lope de Vega, *The New Art of Writing Plays in This Age* (1609), trans. William T. Brewster.

7
Italian Theatre to 1700

Long before the medieval theatre came to an end in the late sixteenth century, the ideas and practices associated with the Renaissance had already taken shape. In fact, the late Middle Ages and the early Renaissance coexisted, for historians usually date both from about 1300, although they recognize that medieval elements remained dominant until around 1500. In addition, the same forces that undermined medieval culture were crucial in creating the culture of the Renaissance, for both the waning of the Middle Ages and the emergence of the Renaissance can be attributed in part to the decline of feudalism, the growth of cities, the increased power of princes, and challenges to church dominance over learning and life.

Perhaps most of all, the Renaissance is associated with a revived interest in the humanist ideals of the classical world. Humanism, as the name implies, marked a return to concern for the worth of humanity and earthly life, not merely as preparation for eternity but as valuable in themselves. Nevertheless, the humanists were not irreligious, for they championed human virtues and ideals grounded in Christian as well as classical teachings: justice, courtesy, magnanimity, integrity, loyalty, courage, and duty to self and others, including developing one's potentials to the fullest. They established as ideals those qualities they thought humans at their best ca-

pable of; these ideals were to dominate Western thought into the twentieth century. Still, the humanists were not ascetics. They acknowledged the pleasures of the flesh and the proneness of humans to temptation and error, but they also, explicitly or implicitly, judged all behavior by the standards of the humanist ideal. As the first champions of humanism, the classical world of Greece and Rome provided inspiration for Western Europe as its own interest in humanism revived.

As these new concerns grew, so did curiosity and the spirit of adventure. The Renaissance was an era of expansion, through geographical exploration, scientific experimentation, philosophical inquiry, and artistic creativity. In education the goal became the development of the universal human being skilled in many fields: science, politics, sports, and art.

There are many reasons why the Renaissance emerged first in Italy, causing its theatre to develop quite differently from that of England and Spain. As the major terminus of trade routes to Asia and Africa, Italy was more strategically placed than the rest of Europe to absorb ideas from Byzantium, Islam, and other cultures. Trade with the eastern Mediterranean also produced the wealth needed by Italy to support the arts and learning. Additionally, Italy, as the seat of the Roman Catholic Church, was strongly affected by the controversies that afflicted the papacy beginning

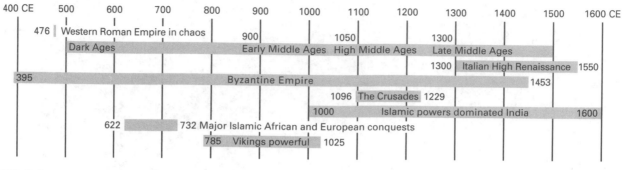

FIG. 7.1

From late Rome to the Renaissance, 400–1600 C.E.

in the late thirteenth century. The removal of the papal seat to Avignon in 1305 (it returned to Rome in 1377) and the intrigues among rival popes from 1378 to 1417 created skepticism about the integrity of the church. The corruption of the papacy also made the church itself subject to numerous secular influences. Since the fourth century the church had argued that the pope was the legitimate successor to the Roman emperors, and consequently it was not difficult in the early Renaissance to revive interest in the Roman Empire and its secular accomplishments. The years of papal exile afforded rulers of the numerous Italian city-states an excuse for seeking to fill the gap created by the pope's absence, and they vied with each other for power and prestige. One mark of a state's enlightenment was support of scholars, writers, and artists, and, as patronage increased, the Renaissance flourished.

As appreciation for individual potential grew, the anonymous craftsmen and writers of the Middle Ages gave way to artists whose personal accomplishments were honored. In this new art, Biblical and theological subjects were often supplanted by classical myths, history, and invented stories. Renaissance art began in Italy around 1300 with Dante (1265–1321) who—though he treated a theological subject—took the Roman poet Virgil for his guide in *The Divine Comedy,* the first major literary work written in a modern vernacular language. In painting, Giotto (1266–1337) explored new paths after breaking with the stiff decorative style of medieval art. The Renaissance spirit was still more evident in the writings of Petrarch (1304–1374), who collected ancient manuscripts, urged scholars to study ancient Greece, modeled his style after Cicero and Seneca, and championed human over theological subjects. Boccaccio (1313–1375) too urged the study of the classics, compiled information about classical myths, wrote a spirited defense of secular authors, and celebrated the human lust for life in his collection of bawdy tales, *The Decameron.* But it was Manuel Chrysoloras

(c. 1350–1415), a Byzantine diplomat who taught the Greek language in Florence in the late 1390s, who made it possible for European humanists to finally read Greek texts.

RENAISSANCE DRAMA

In drama, the first sign of change was a new awareness of dramatic form that came from the study of Roman plays. The study of Latin plays had never been completely out of favor, but Seneca's tragedies had been read principally as illustrations of moral lessons or rhetorical display and the comedies of Terence and Plautus as models of oral style. But during the fourteenth century a few persons began to appreciate the plays for their dramatic values and to compose imitations of them. The earliest tragedy, Albertino Mussato's *Eccerinus* (c. 1315), used a modified Senecan form but drew its subject matter from Christian doctrine. Beginning with *Achilles* (c. 1390) by Antonio Laschi, however, classical form and subject were united. Therefore, *Achilles* is frequently called the first Renaissance tragedy. Comedy in the classical mold also began to appear during the fourteenth century. The oldest known example is Pier Paolo Vergerio's *Paulus* (1390), a satire on contemporary student life. During the fifteenth century, a number of leading humanists wrote comedies, although none of lasting interest.

All of these early comedies and tragedies were written in Latin, and none apparently was performed. Drama written in the vernacular did not appear until the early sixteenth century. By that time, other events had accelerated classical influence: In 1429, twelve of Plautus' lost plays were rediscovered; in 1453, the fall of Constantinople brought many scholars, along with manuscripts of Greek plays, to Italy; in 1465, the introduction of the printing press into Italy made the wide dissemination of classical texts possible, and between 1472 and 1518 all of the then-known Greek and Roman plays were published. During this period, interest in classical drama, which until the late fifteenth century had been confined principally to scholars, spread to the courts of the many small states into which Italy was then divided. Around 1485, Italian rulers began to finance productions of Roman plays. (Twenty-two of Plautus's and Terence's plays were produced in Ferrara alone between 1486 and 1505.) The desire to make the plays more accessible to courtly readers and spectators was probably the major motivation for translating the Roman plays into Italian and eventually for writing new plays in the vernacular.

New vernacular drama had been launched by 1508 with a production at the court of Ferrara of *La Cassaria (The Casket)* by Lodovico Ariosto (1474–1533). In this comedy, a favorite Roman plot (in which lovers are united following the discovery that the girl is the long-lost child of a rich father) is given a contemporary Italian setting. The development

FIG 7.2
The Italian states, showing places that figured prominently in theatrical development during the Renaissance.

FIG. 7.3

Frontispiece to an edition of Ariosto's plays published in Rome, 1535.

of vernacular comedy was also encouraged by Bernardo Dovizi da Bibbiena's *La Calandria* (1513), a successful blending of Roman and contemporary elements. Based in part upon Plautus's *Menaechmi*, Bibbiena's play uses twins of different sexes and reunites them only after subjecting them to a complicated intrigue based on disguises and illicit love affairs. This combination of traditional and contemporary materials served as a model for those who came after. Another significant strain of comedy is exemplified by Niccolò Machiavelli's (1469–1527) *The Mandrake* (*c.* 1518), in which the subject matter is invented but the form borrowed from Roman comedy. Showing how a clever lover overcomes the hesitations of a virtuous young wife and cuckolds her overcredulous husband, the play is similar in tone to medieval farce. By 1540 a native comedy was well established in Italy. Although few are now remembered, these dramatists (among them Pietro Aretino, Giovan Maria Cecchi, Anton Francesco Grazzini, Andrea Calmo, Lodovico Dolce, and Girolamo Parabosco) were the first in Renaissance Europe to mas-

ter the techniques of Latin comedy and to adapt them to contemporary taste. After 1550 Italian plays were read and translated with increasing frequency in France and England, and consequently they exerted considerable influence on the emerging drama of those countries.

The first important vernacular tragedy was *Sofonisba* (1515) by Giangiorgio Trissino (1478–1550). Following the example of the Greek tragedians, Trissino used a chorus of fifteen and avoided the division into acts. Trissino, with his deliberate attempt to counteract the pervasive influence of Seneca, launched a controversy that was to last for many years over the relative merits of Greek and Roman drama as suitable models for Italian authors. That this struggle was eventually won by the partisans of Rome was due in large part to the popularity of one author— Giambattista Giraldi Cinthio (1504–1574), whose *Orbecche* (1541), a tale of revenge in the Senecan manner, was the first tragedy written in Italian to be produced. After writing two other tragedies, *Dido* and *Cleopatra,* Cinthio turned to serious plays with happy endings because he found that audiences preferred this kind of plot. As a result, his late plays are essentially melodramas. Nevertheless, Cinthio influenced almost all of his successors, even those who avoided happy resolutions. No other serious dramatist rivaled Cinthio in popularity, but several were admired both at home and abroad (Shakespeare's *Othello* is based on a novella by Cinthio) and did much to reestablish the tragic mode which had languished since Roman times.

In addition to comedy and tragedy, pastoral drama also thrived in Renaissance Italy. This form perhaps developed out of the interest in the satyr plays of antiquity, although in the Renaissance the boisterous and licentious world of Greek satyrs gave way to an idyllic society of shepherds and nymphs. The principal subject was love, which usually triumphed over the many obstacles placed in its path. The first pastoral appeared in 1471, and the form reached a peak of popularity in the late sixteenth century with Torquato Tasso's *Aminta* (1573) and Giambattista Guarini's *The Faithful Shepherd* (1590), both of which were admired and imitated throughout Europe.

During the 200-year period, then, between the late fourteenth and the late sixteenth centuries, Renaissance drama developed in Italy. Today these Italian plays are considered artistically inferior and are seldom read or performed. They are valued primarily because they marked the first clear break with medieval practices and because they served as models for dramatists in other countries (especially England and France) where drama of more lasting value would be written. But it should be remembered that these plays were only parts, often very minor parts, of a larger artistic and political context. A dramatic performance was only one among many events offered at festivals and celebrations mounted to mark some special occasion. Thus, plays and the conditions under which they were performed had much more in common with Roman practices than with those of the modern era.

MANNERISM AND THE BEGINNINGS OF THE BAROQUE

Around the middle of the sixteenth century the Italian Renaissance entered a new phase as its original vitality waned under the impact of the same forces that brought an end to medieval theatre. A new sense of purpose for the Catholic church had come out of the Council of Trent, which met between 1545 and 1563 to deal with the challenges posed by Protestant secessions and during which the church approved means to discourage dissident opinion and to ensure orthodoxy. Among these means were the reinstitution of the Inquisition and the compilation of the *Index Expurgatorius* (a list of works the church sought to suppress by declaring it a sin to print, disseminate, or possess them). Thus, freedom of thought and conscience were curtailed. Italy also was forced to reassess its economic position. The fall of Constantinople had closed many trade routes to the East, and the geographical explorations undertaken by Spain, Portugal, and other nations from the late fifteenth century onward increasingly threatened Italy's primacy in trade and wealth.

For these and other reasons the second half of the sixteenth century was a time of anxiety for Italy. Art historians now use the term *mannerist* to describe the self-conscious and artificial visual style of that period. They also use the term *baroque* to describe the style that came into being around 1600 and continued until about 1750. They consider the baroque to be in part an expression of the church's new self-confidence which took the form of monumental architecture and elaborate decoration. Historians also relate these changes in style to the marked growth of princely power that found expression in grandiose palaces and other trappings of authority. The classical architectural forms that had been revived in the Renaissance lost their clean lines and static quality under baroque elaborations of S-curves and infinite decorative features which created a sense of restlessness and movement. In music, melodic lines were embroidered with complex details and striking contrasts. In all the arts, the movement was toward grandeur, richness, movement, and monumentality. Most of these characteristics can be seen in the theatre, although their impact was not fully evident until around 1700.

THE NEOCLASSICAL IDEAL

In drama the new concern for authority was first felt through the formulation of the neoclassical ideal. This had been given full expression in Italy by 1570, and thereafter it spread to the rest of Europe, where it was to dominate criticism from the mid-seventeenth until the late eighteenth century.

Prior to 1550, interest in literary theory developed slowly and was concerned above all with two classical treatises: Horace's *Art of Poetry* and Aristotle's *Poetics*. Although Horace's work had never been lost sight of since it was written in the first century B.C.E., Aristotle's was little known prior to 1498, when it was published in Italy in a Latin translation, but during the sixteenth century, it came to be considered the supreme authority on literary matters. In 1548 the first commentary (by Robortello) on the *Poetics* was published, and in 1549 an Italian translation of Aristotle's treatise appeared.

Aristotle's authority was greatly increased when the Council of Trent adopted the teachings of St. Thomas Aquinas (1225–1274), who had drawn heavily on Aristotle's works, as the official position of the church. Thereafter, most commentators tended to accept Aristotle as the primary authority on all literary questions. Of the many treatises written on drama after 1550, the most influential were those by three men: Antonio Minturno (?–1574), Julius Caesar Scaliger (1494–1558), and Lodovico Castelvetro (1501–1571). Although these and other writers differed on details, they were in general agreement on the basic precepts that constituted the neoclassical ideal.

In neoclassical doctrine, the fundamental demand was for verisimilitude, or the appearance of truth. A complex concept, verisimilitude may be divided into three subsidiary goals: reality, morality, and universality. In relation to reality, critics urged dramatists to confine their subjects to events that could happen in real life. Consequently, in neoclassical plays, fantasy and supernatural events were usually avoided unless they were integral parts of some received story from myth, history, or the Bible, and even in these instances they were minimized as much as possible. Furthermore, such devices as the soliloquy and the chorus were discouraged on the grounds that it is unnatural for characters to speak aloud while alone or to discuss private matters in the presence of a group so large as the chorus. These devices were replaced by others, of which the most typical was *confidants* (or trusted companions) to whom the principal characters could believably reveal their inmost secrets. The demand for reality also led dramatists to keep battles, crowd scenes, violence, and deaths offstage on the premise that it was too difficult to represent such occurrences convincingly onstage.

Faithfulness to reality was considerably modified by another demand—that drama teach moral lessons. Consequently, the dramatist was asked not merely to copy life but to reveal its ideal moral patterns. Since God was said to be both omnipotent and just, it seemed only logical that the world over which God reigns should be represented in drama in such a way as to reveal His power and justice. This, in turn, meant showing wickedness punished and good rewarded. Those instances in life in which justice seemingly did not prevail were explained away as some part of God's long-range plans not fully comprehended by humans but in which justice is certain eventually to prevail. Therefore, apparent aberrations in the workings of justice were thought unsuitable subjects for drama, which should depict that ultimate truth which is inseparable from morality and justice.

Both reality and morality were further modified by still another demand—for universality as the key to truth. Rather than seeking truth in a welter of surface details, the neoclassicist located it in attributes that are common to all phenomena in a particular category. Those characteristics that vary from one example to another were considered accidental and therefore not essential parts of truth. Thus, truth was defined as those typical and normative traits that are discoverable through the rational and systematic examination of phenomena, whether natural or man-made. Since these norms were considered to embody truth in its most essential form—one that remains unchanged regardless of historical period or geographical location—they were declared the foundation upon which all literary creation and criticism should rest.

The concept of verisimilitude, then, represents an attempt to define the reality that playwrights should seek to mirror in their works. Out of this basic view developed a number of lesser principles, for the idea that truth is to be found in universal norms was extended to almost every aspect of dramatic composition. All "regular" drama was reduced to two basic forms, comedy and tragedy, and other types were considered inferior because they were "mixed." Consequently, purity of dramatic form—that is, no intermingling of comic and serious elements—was demanded. "Irregular" forms were usually ignored in critical writing.

Comedy and tragedy were thought to have their own normative patterns. Comedy was said to draw its characters from the middle or lower classes, to base its stories on domestic and private affairs, to have happy endings, and to imitate the style of everyday speech. Tragedy was said to draw its characters from the ruling classes, to base its stories on history or mythology, to have unhappy endings, and to employ a lofty and poetic style. These norms mark several departures from Greek practice, but perhaps the most significant is the substitution of social rank for moral qualities in the description of character.

The concept of norms was also extended to characterization, since the dramatist was expected to write about the permanent aspects of human nature rather than those peculiar to one time and place. In establishing norms (or the proper *decorum* for characters), all humanity was categorized according to age, rank, sex, profession, and predispositions, and the attributes of each were described. As a result, neoclassical drama tended to depict types, who prosper if they observe the appropriate decorum and who are punished when they deviate from it.

All plays were said to have as their main functions "to teach and to please." Although the didactic ideal had often been stated in classical times, it was not given primary emphasis until the humanists of the Renaissance found it necessary to justify the study and writing of literature at a time when learning was moving away from purely theological concerns. Because they wished to depict drama as a useful tool, they tended to emphasize the instructional over the pleasurable potentials of literature. Comedy was said to teach by ridiculing behavior that should be avoided and tragedy to show the horrifying results of mistakes and misdeeds. These ideas about the functions of drama were to dominate critical thought until the end of the eighteenth century.

The "three unities" of action, time, and place were also formulated during the sixteenth century. Unified action had been declared an ideal by Aristotle, but unity of time was first advocated around 1543 and unity of place in 1570. It was Castelvetro who in 1570 first stated all three as essential rules. He argued that since an audience knows that it has been in the theatre for only a few hours, it cannot be convinced that long periods of time have elapsed. Likewise, since the audience knows that it has been in only one place, it cannot accept any change of locale. After the 1570s, most Italian critics demanded that a play have a single plot, take place in twenty-four hours or less, and be confined to one place, although the latter rule was often extended to include additional places if they could easily be reached without violating the twenty-four-hour rule. The division into five acts was also considered essential to regular drama. Horace had first stated this rule in Roman times, and it was adopted in the Renaissance as a norm for all regular drama.

Although many of the neoclassical principles now seem arbitrary and restrictive, they were accepted as reasonable and desirable among critics and scholars from about 1570 until after 1750. As the neoclassical ideal took shape in Italy, academic drama became increasingly regular. Although some plays deviated from the rules, they were usually denounced as inferior and as unworthy of serious consideration.

During the sixteenth century the neoclassical rules were little known outside of educated circles (or outside of Italy), however, and the plays written in accordance with them did not reach large audiences. Tragedy met a mixed reception even with educated groups, and comedy, which was produced primarily at court, was popular in part because of the *intermezzi* inserted between the acts.

INTERMEZZI AND OPERA

Intermezzi were descended from the *mascherata* of carnival time and the entertainments given at court on special occasions. (For a discussion of their early history, see Chapter 4.) They were first coupled with comedies in the late fifteenth century. The principal appeal of *intermezzi* lay in their scenery, costumes, lights, special effects, music, and dance: Dialogue was used only when the allegorical plots had to be explained. Since entertainments were given at court almost solely on such special occasions as betrothals, weddings, births, and state visits, *intermezzi* were often used to pay elaborate compliments to those being honored by drawing parallels between mythological figures and contemporary persons. Thus, not only were they stunning as spectacle, they were instruments of power, politics, and diplomacy.

Six *intermezzi* became typical—one used as a prologue, four to fill the intervals between the five acts of a regular drama, and one as an afterpiece. At first this interruption of a dramatic action with allegorical spectacle met considerable opposition, but the *intermezzi* soon become more popular than the plays they accompanied. Originally, the various *intermezzi* seen on a single occasion had no connection with each other or with the play being performed. Gradually, however, they were often related both to each other and to the theme of the main drama. Critics became fond of likening *intermezzi* to the choral interludes of Greek drama.

Since the *intermezzi* depended upon spectacle, they motivated many experiments with scenery. Fur-

thermore, the need to change settings rapidly for the alternating segments of plays and *intermezzi* encouraged the development of new devices for shifting scenery. In the seventeenth century, the *intermezzi* were gradually absorbed into opera, although for a time they were performed between the acts of this new form as they had been with comedy. By 1650, they had virtually disappeared.

Opera was destined to become the most popular dramatic form in Italy. During the Renaissance, Italy had many "academies," or associations of men with common intellectual or artistic interests, and it was out of one of these, the Camerata of Florence, that opera came, although it built on the interests and experiments of earlier groups. Members of the Camerata, who in this instance were concerned with Greek music and its relation to drama, sought to create plays similar to ancient Greek tragedies. Their first full-length work, and the first "opera," was *Dafne* (1594), with text by Ottavio Rinuccini and Giulio Caccini and music by Jacopo Peri. The dialogue and choral passages were recited or chanted to a musical accompaniment, which served merely to enhance the dramatic effectiveness of the dialogue. From this simple beginning, opera grew into one of the major art forms of the baroque era and in Italy displaced interest in spoken drama.

Until 1637, however, opera remained principally an entertainment of the courts and academies. In that year, the opening of an opera house in Venice made

FIG. 7.4
Costume designs by Bernardo Buontalenti for an *intermezzo* at the Uffizi palace, Florence, 1589. Courtesy Theatre Museum, Victoria and Albert Museum.

the form available to the general public on a continuing basis. So successful was this venture that between 1640 and 1700 four opera houses operated regularly in Venice, a city of about 140,000 people. From Venice, opera spread throughout Italy and then to the rest of Europe.

The first great operatic composer was Claudio Monteverdi (1567–1643), whose *Orfeo* (1607) enlarged the role of instrumental music and began the shift in interest from dramatic to musical values. Other composers continued these trends. The melodious songs, or arias, increased in number as passages of recitative and choral songs declined. Nevertheless, the playwright remained dominant until about 1675, after which the composer gained ascendancy. As singers achieved stardom, they began to demand that arias written to display their virtuosity be inserted into already existing operas. Partially as a result, the plots became so baffling that printed librettos were sold in theatres so the audience could follow the action. Happy endings became typical and all of the scenic wonders of the court *intermezzi* were incorporated and elaborated. Consequently, when opera was imported into other countries, so were Italian scenic practices.

THE DEVELOPMENT OF NEW SCENIC PRACTICES

Although interest in classical drama revived in the fourteenth century, no ancient play was performed until 1486, when the Roman Academy began its experiments. At about the same time the court at Ferrara also began presenting plays, and soon other courts and academies were competing for preeminence in staging. By the early sixteenth century, plays were considered suitable entertainment for almost all court celebrations as well as for those presented by academies for their members and guests. Members of the wealthy middle class also occasionally staged private performances.

The production of plays was motivated in part by interest in Vitruvius' treatise on Roman architecture. Rediscovered in 1414 and printed in 1486, *De Architectura* had by 1500 assumed the position of authority on all matters relating to architecture and staging that Aristotle's *Poetics* was to gain in literature. Since the early producers wished to duplicate authentic Roman practices, they turned to Vitruvius for information about the auditorium and stage, about the appropriate scenery for tragedy, comedy, and satyr (or pastoral) drama, and for justification of productions financed by rulers and wealthy citizens. But Vitruvius's somewhat cryptic remarks were eas-

FIG. 7.5
The "Terence Stage." Note the several doors, with the names of characters above them, an arrangement characteristic of this type of stage. From the edition of Terence's plays published at Lyon (France) in 1493.

ily misinterpreted, especially since his verbal descriptions were not accompanied by visual plans. Because it was so ambiguous, *De Architectura* prompted many commentaries and critical editions, the most influential of which were those by Jocundus (1511) and Philander (1544). It was first translated into Italian in 1521.

When members of the Roman Academy began staging plays around 1486, they turned to Vitruvius for guidance. Under the leadership of Pomponius Laetus (1424–1498), they sought to reconstruct the features of the Roman theatre for their productions. Young men from all over Europe came to study with Laetus and took many of his ideas back to their native lands.

From his study of Vitruvius, Laetus may have arrived at a stage similar to that shown in late fifteenth-century illustrated editions of Terence's plays. In these illustrations, a platform is backed by a continuous facade, either straight or angled and divided into a series of curtained openings, each representing the house of a different character. The first edition of Terence's plays to show this stage was printed at Lyon in 1493 by Johannes Treschel. The illustrations for this edition were made under the supervision of Jodius Bodius Ascensius (1462–1535), who had been involved in performances of Terence's plays in Ferrara in the 1480s. These illustrations were imitated in a Venetian edition of Terence's comedies in 1497 and thereafter became current throughout Europe. Some scholars have argued that during the sixteenth century this "Terence stage" was in use almost everywhere, especially in schools. Contrarily, others have denied that its use was ever widespread.

If Pomponius and others did employ a stage of this type, their practice was soon modified by the addition of perspective painting, whose influence was to outdistance that of Vitruvius. Although perspective developed over a long period, its systemization is usually credited to the architect, Filippo Brunelleschi (1377–1446) and the painter Masaccio (1401–1428) around 1425. But it was Leon Battista Alberti's *Della Pittura* (1435), the first treatise on the subject, that disseminated practical directions for making perspective drawings. Alberti's understanding of perspective was limited, however, for with his method all objects had to be drawn as if parallel to the picture plane. It was not until the time of Leonardo da Vinci (1452–1519) that space was perceived as spherical, curving away from the viewer in all directions. Even then, techniques had not yet been devised for

FIG. 7.7
The ancient theatre according to fifteenth-century humanists. Frontispiece to an edition of Plautus's plays published in Venice, 1511.

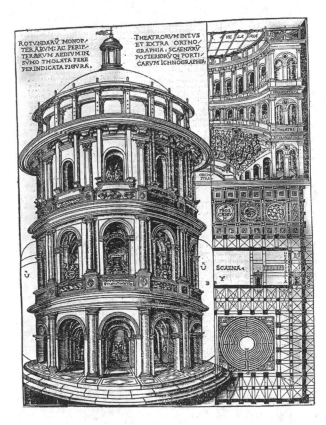

FIG. 7.6
A Renaissance conception of the Roman theatre as a fully circular structure. From an edition of Vitruvius's *Architectura* published in 1521. Courtesy Lilly Library, Indiana University.

transferring objects so perceived to the various flat surfaces of a stage setting, and many of the later developments in scene design became practical only after much experimentation.

It is difficult now to appreciate the fascination that perspective drawing exerted on the Renaissance mind, for it seemed almost magical in its ability to manipulate illusion. Consequently, it is not surprising that perspective should soon find its way into the theatre, especially since scenery was usually designed by the leading painters and architects of the day. Although perspective settings may have been used as early as the 1480s, the first certain example is that by Pellegrino da San Daniele for Ariosto's *The Casket* at Ferrara in 1508. The first perspective settings were merely painted on flat surfaces at the back of the performance space—in other words, they were primarily backdrops. Around 1513, a single set of wings was added forward of the back scene, and shortly thereafter additional wings were added. By the 1540s the arrangement of wings and backdrop that had developed had set the standard that, though it might be elaborated, was not to be changed essentially during the next 250 years. Originally one goal was to capture Vitruvius's description of theatrical settings: "Tragic scenes are delineated with columns, pediments, statues, and other objects suited to kings; comic scenes exhibit private dwellings with balconies and views representing rows of windows after the manner of ordinary dwellings; satyric scenes are decorated with trees, caverns, mountains, and other rustic objects delineated in landscape style." It also embodied another Renaissance interest derived from Vitruvius: the "ideal city." Vitruvius's overall purpose was to provide a guide for laying out towns. Renaissance artists, fascinated by the concept of the ideal city, sought in their stage settings to embody various aspects of it by depicting in the tragic scene the royal and ceremonial sections, and in the comic scene those occupied by ordinary citizens.

The practices of the early sixteenth century are best summed up in Sebastiano Serlio's (1475–1554) *Architettura*, the second part of which was published in 1545. It was the first Renaissance work on architecture to devote a section to the theatre. It also includes illustrations of the tragic, comic, and satyric scenes, based on Vitruvius's descriptions. Serlio was heavily indebted to other artists, especially Baldassare Peruzzi (1481–1537), with whom he had studied and who was a major designer of perspective settings. In his book, Serlio seems to be describing practices typical of his time, and, since this treatise was circulated

FIG. 7.9
Serlio's comic scene. From Serlio's *Architettura*, book 2, 1569 edition. Courtesy Fine Arts Library, Indiana University.

throughout Europe, it was a prime disseminator of Italian ideas abroad. Furthermore, after 1547 Serlio's perspective sketches of the tragic, comic, and

FIG. 7.8
Serlio's tragic scene. From Serlio's *Architettura*, book 2, 1569 edition. Courtesy Fine Arts Library, Indiana University.

FIG. 7.10
Serlio's pastoral scene. From Serlio's *Architettura*, book 2, 1569 edition. Courtesy Fine Arts Library, Indiana University.

FIG. 7.11
Cross-section of Serlio's hall stage.

satyric scenes were often reprinted in editions of Vitruvius's *De Architectura,* a practice that encouraged readers to transpose Vitruvius's descriptions into perspective settings.

In *Architettura,* Serlio took for granted that theatres would be set up in already existing rooms, for in his day halls of state in palaces had become the usual places for staging plays. Thus, he fitted Vitruvius's semicircular auditorium into a rectangular space by constructing stadium-like seating around an orchestra (used almost exclusively to seat the ruler and his attendants). The stage was raised to accord with the eye level of the ruler and the perspective scenery was designed so that the ideal view of it was seen from his chair. The front portion of the stage floor was level, since it was intended for use by the actors, but back of this the floor sloped upward at a sharp angle so as to increase the illusion of distance. All scenery was placed on this raked portion.

Serlio considered his renderings of Vitruvius's three scenes adequate to meet the needs of all plays. Each of his three sets used the same basic floor plan, for all required four sets of wings (the first three angled and the fourth flat) and a backdrop. The wings closest to the audience were given many three-dimensional details and some even had open arcades and galleries. Although Serlio mentioned no framing device for his stage pictures, the downstage wings probably extended to the walls of the hall, and a valance probably limited the overhead view to preserve the illusion.

Serlio's settings were conceived in architectural terms and were not meant to be changed. When *intermezzi* were performed, pageant wagons were drawn into the space just forward of the stage or portable set pieces were carried onto the platform. Shortly after Serlio's treatise was published, however, interest in spectacle had increased sufficiently that there arose a demand for settings that could be changed during performances.

The shifting solution first adopted involved *periaktoi* (as described by Vitruvius and Pollux). It is not clear when *periaktoi* were first used in the Renaissance, but among the earliest was by Aristotile

de San Gallo (1481–1551) at Castro in 1543. They were in use at Florence by 1569, and in 1583 Giacomo Barozzi da Vignola (1507–1573), in his *The Two Rules of Perspective Practice,* recommended structures with from two to six sides as means of changing scenes.

Nicola Sabbattini's (1574–1654) *Manual for Constructing Theatrical Scenes and Machines* (1638), a major source of information about seventeenth-century practices, listed three principal methods of changing scenery. One required *periaktoi,* but the other two were devices for changing the angled wings. In the first of these two methods, new wings were maneuvered around those already in place, and in the second, new painted canvas coverings were pulled quickly around the wings to conceal the previously visible scene. In addition, Sabbattini explained how to change the flat wings used near the back of the stage by sliding them in grooves or by mounting several in such a way that they could be turned like pages in a book. All these devices demonstrate that wings had been considerably simplified during the century that separates Sabbattini's from Serlio's treatise, for by

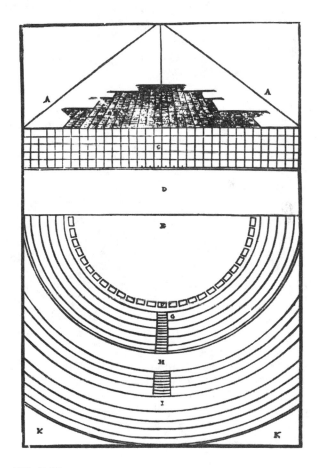

FIG. 7.12
Ground plan of Serlio's hall stage.

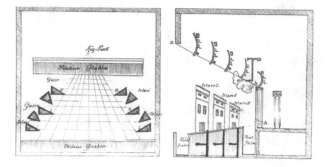

FIG. 7.13

Joseph Furttenbach's plan and section of a stage showing the use of *periaktoi,* bow-shaped borders, and a rear pit for special effects. From *Die Theater Weins* (1899).

1638 the three-dimensional details used by Serlio had been replaced almost completely by painted details.

The ultimate solution to scene shifting required that all angled wings be replaced with flat wings, but this change had to await new developments in perspective drawing. Throughout the sixteenth century, the angled wings had been painted in position: The vanishing point was established on the back wall of the stage and a cord was anchored there; this cord was then stretched downstage and used to determine the relative height and size of all the details to be painted on the angled wings. Drawing, therefore, was relatively simple, for the two faces of each wing were treated as different sides of a single structure, one parallel and the other at an angle to the picture plane. On flat wings, however, all details had to be depicted on a series of surfaces set parallel to the picture plane. The problems of transferring a perspective picture to a series of flat wings were not adequately solved until 1600, when Guido Ubaldus's *Six Books of Perspective* was published. The first application of Ubaldus's principles to stage settings composed entirely of flat wings has been attributed to Giovan Battista Aleotti (1546– 1636) at Ferrara in 1606, but flat-wing settings were probably in use elsewhere prior to this time. By 1650 angled wings were considered to be outmoded.

Using flat wings, any number of settings could be easily shifted. At each wing position as many flats were set up, one immediately behind the other, as there were settings. Changes were accomplished simply by withdrawing the set of visible wings to reveal another set behind them. To support the flats and to permit their easy movement on and off stage, grooves were installed on the stage floor and overhead. The back scene was normally painted on two flats (or shutters) which met at the center of the stage, although cloths that could be rolled up would eventually be used.

Until about 1650, most scenes, following classical practice, showed exteriors. Consequently, overhead masking was usually painted to represent the sky or clouds. Sometimes an unbroken canvas was mounted to curve over the entire setting, but as flying machinery of various sorts became common, a bow-shaped border was hung above each set of wings. When interior settings were introduced, the borders were painted to represent ceilings, beams, domes, or other appropriate details.

By the early seventeenth century, then, the three basic elements of every setting were the side wings, back shutters, and overhead borders, and all could be changed simultaneously. At first, many stagehands were utilized to make quick changes, but the results were not entirely satisfactory, since it was difficult to synchronize the movements of so many persons precisely.

The next significant step is usually attributed to Giacomo Torelli (1608–1678), who perfected the chariot-and-pole system of scene shifting at the Teatro Novissimo in Venice between 1641 and 1645 (see Fig. 7.14). Torelli cut slots through the stage floor so that upright supports (or poles) could pass through. These poles, on which flats were mounted above the floor level, were attached beneath the stage to "chariots" that ran in tracks parallel to the front of the stage. As the chariots rolled toward the center of the stage they carried flats into view, while the opposite movement took them out of sight. By

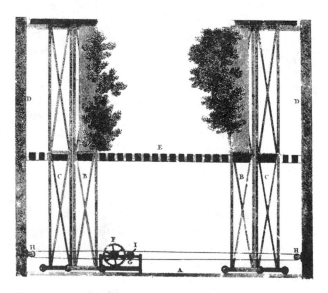

FIG. 7.14

Diagram of chariot-and-pole shifting mechanism. A = the tracks in which the chariots ride; B and C = chariots; D = the stage walls; E = the stage floor; F, G, H, and I = the lines, pulleys, and levers that operate the system. From Rees, *Cyclopedia,* 20 (1803).

FIG. 7.15
Torelli's setting for Act III of Strozzi's opera, *La Finta Pazza,* the work that launched Torelli's career in Venice in the early 1640s. Courtesy Theatersammlung, Osterreichische Nationalbibliothek, Vienna.

atres and Theatrical Machinery (1668) by Fabrizio Carini Motta (1627–1699), director of theatrical activities in Mantua for almost thirty years. Motta describes how box settings are to be created by mounting two-part flats on each chariot, one part attached to the pole, the other hinged so it can be folded out to fill in the space between the wings. Motta also provides a rather full description of the stage house, its equipment and machinery (including the chariots and flying apparatus), and stage lighting. Motta seems to sum up stage practice as it had developed up to that time, although the box set was not to be used extensively until the nineteenth century.

Since scenic design was long an adjunct of architecture or painting, many of Italy's finest artists designed scenery in the years between 1475 and 1650. Because designers moved about frequently, essentially the same scenic conventions were current throughout Italy. The prestige to be gained through lavish productions encouraged many rulers, notably those of Ferrara, Florence, Mantua, Urbino, Milan, and

means of an elaborate system of ropes and pulleys, every part of a setting could be attached to a single winch which, when turned, changed all of the elements simultaneously. This innovation, which at first seemed magical in its ability to produce transformations, was soon adopted almost universally in Europe, where it was to be the standard method of shifting scenery until the late nineteenth century. The older and simpler groove system would persist principally in England, Holland, and America.

The advent of the flat wing coincided with and probably facilitated the development of the baroque visual style that began to take shape around 1600. As long as angled wings had predominated, each wing usually represented a separate building, a tradition that persisted for a time with flat wings. But this convention did not lend itself to effects of grandeur and, as the taste for monumentality grew during the seventeenth century, the former series of buildings gave way to a sequence of columns, porticos, or other architectural features that were treated as parts of a single structure. This change increased both the unity and the apparent size of stage settings. These trends toward monumentality were not completed until the eighteenth century, when the baroque style in scene design reached its fullest expression.

By the late seventeenth century, the box setting (enclosed on three sides and with a ceiling) seems already to have been developed in Italy. Orville Larson has called attention to a manuscript, *Construction of The-*

FIG. 7.16
First *intermezzo* of an evening's entertainment entitled *The Liberation of Tyrrhenus,* performed in Florence at the Medici court at carnival time, 1616. The setting is by Guilio Parigi. Etching by Jacques Callot.

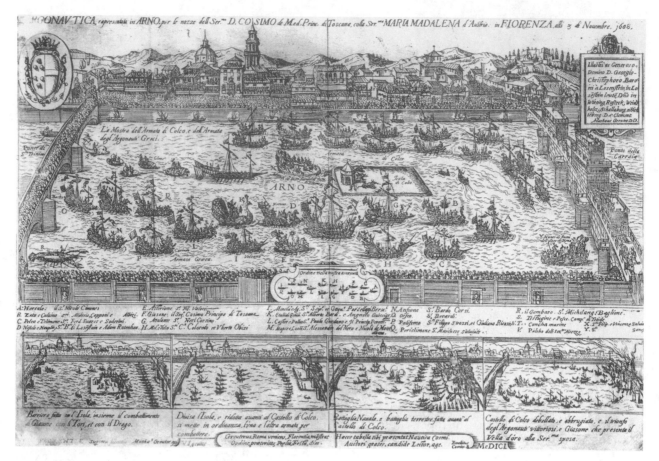

FIG. 7.17

A *naumachia* on the Arno River in Florence given in honor of the marriage of Cosimo de'Medici to Maria Madalena of Austria in 1608. This *naumachia* was based on the story of Jason and the Golden Fleece. Engraving by Mathias Greuter. Courtesy Theatermuseum, Munich.

Rome, to patronize the theatre. Scenic grandeur was especially highly developed under the Medicis at Florence, and reached its peak there in the work of Bernardo Buontalenti (1536–1608), who served as architect and supervisor of entertainments at the Medici court for nearly sixty years. Buontalenti's work foreshadowed and probably helped create the visual style that was to become so elaborate during the baroque era. His finest work was done in 1589 in connection with the festivities honoring the marriage of the Grand Duke Ferdinand I, when three weeks were devoted to masquerades, animal hunts, a *naumachia*, comedies with *intermezzi*, and numerous other events. Buontalenti's fertile genius enriched the court spectacles with highly imaginative costumes, scenery, machinery, and special effects. He was succeeded by his pupil Giulio Parigi (*c.* 1570–1635), who designed major festivals in 1606, 1608, and 1616, of which many engravings have survived. It was from Parigi that Inigo Jones learned much that he applied in stag-

ing English masques between 1605 and 1640, and Cosmi Lotti learned what he took to the court of Spain from 1626 to 1643. It was also from Parigi that Joseph Furttenbach (1591–1667) absorbed many of the ideas that he was to take back to Germany and disseminate through his books, *Civil Architecture* (1628), *Recreational Architecture* (1640), and *The Noble Mirror of Art* (1663). Scenic marvels continued at the Medici court throughout the seventeenth century under Parigi's son Alfonso (1606–1656) and later under Ferdinando Tacca (1619–1686).

With the opening of the Venetian public opera houses beginning in 1637, scenic splendor was made available to the general public. From opera it spread to the other dramatic forms and to the public playhouses. By the end of the seventeenth century, Italian scenic practices had been adopted almost everywhere in Europe. By that time also, scene design had become more nearly the province of the painter than of the architect.

DEVELOPMENT OF THEATRE ARCHITECTURE

In spite of the great interest in theatrical production, plays were presented by courts and academies only on special occasions. Therefore, the need for permanent theatres was slow in arising. Many early productions were given out-of-doors in courtyards or gardens, but during the sixteenth century banqueting halls or other large rooms became the typical sites. These temporary theatres were usually arranged in the manner described by Serlio.

Some permanent theatres were built during the sixteenth century (allegedly a theatre at Ferrara burned in 1532), and an elaborate theatre was created within Florence's Uffizi palace in 1586. The oldest surviving Renaissance theatre, however, is the Teatro Olimpico, built between 1580 and 1584 by the Olympic Academy of Vicenza. Founded in 1555 to study Greek tragedy, this academy at first used temporary stages for its occasional productions. When the members decided to build a permanent theatre, Andrea Palladio (1518–1580), eminent architect, student of Vitruvius and of Roman ruins, and a member of the academy, undertook to reproduce a classical theatre inside a preexisting building. In the Teatro Olimpico, semi-elliptical seating curves around a small orchestra. The rectangular stage, 82 feet wide by 25 feet deep, is enclosed at the back and ends by a facade decorated with pillars, niches, statues, and bas-reliefs. Five openings pierce the facade, one at either end and three at the back. The

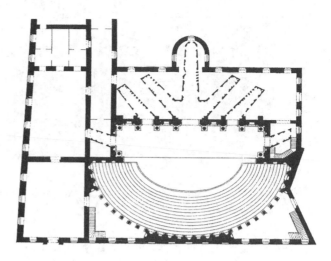

FIG. 7.19
Ground plan of the Teatro Olimpico. From Streit, *Das Theater* (1903).

overall effect is that of a miniature Roman odeon. Palladio died before the theatre was completed, and his work was finished by Vincenzo Scamozzi (1552–1616), who added (as Palladio seems to have intended) street scenes built in perspective behind each of the stage openings to create the impression that the stage is a city square into which a number of streets lead. Each spectator has a view down at least one of the streets. These vistas still remain as permanent parts of the stage. The theatre opened in 1585 with a production of *Oedipus Rex,* about which so much information has been preserved that it could be recreated today with considerable accuracy. It was staged by Angelo Ingegneri (*c.* 1550–*c.* 1613), who was later to write an important treatise on staging, *Discourse on Representational Poetry and the Manner of Presenting Stage Plays* (1598).

The Teatro Olimpico was not, however, in the main line of development, and after a few productions was virtually abandoned. Nevertheless, it probably was the inspiration for the small theatre built by Scamozzi at Sabbioneta in 1588. Here a complete theatre building was designed as a unit, although the interior still essentially followed Serlio's plan. Semicircular seating faces a stage without a proscenium arch, upon which angled wings are used for settings. As one of the few surviving Renaissance theatres, it is of considerable importance in showing the evolution of theatre architecture, although it too was soon abandoned.

The prototype of the modern stage is usually considered to be that of the Teatro Farnese at Parma (designed by Giovan Battista Aleotti, completed in 1618 and first used in 1628), since it is the oldest surviving structure with a permanent proscenium arch. But

FIG. 7.18
Interior of the Teatro Olimpico as it appears today.

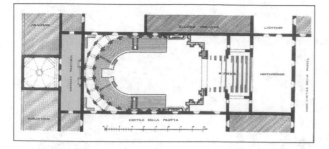

FIG. 7.20
Ground plan of the Teatro Farnese, Parma. From Streit, *Das Theater* (1903).

FIG. 7.22
Auditorium of the Teatro Farnese. The floor is left free for dancing, water ballets, and other uses. The ducal box is located above the entrance at center left. From Streit, *Das Theater* (1903).

that stage was certainly not the first to use a proscenium arch. The oldest extant depiction of a proscenium arch is found in a drawing made around 1560 by Bartolomeo Neroni (*c.* 1500–1571), but that arch was probably temporary. The theatre built by Buontalenti in the Uffizi palace in Florence in 1586, however, certainly had a structurally permanent proscenium arch (see Figure 7.16), perhaps Europe's first. The destruction of the Uffizi theatre in the eighteenth century left the Teatro Farnese our oldest surviving example of the picture-frame stage, although it is in part a reconstruction, having been heavily damaged during World War II.

The origins of the proscenium arch are obscure. Some scholars have suggested that the doorways of the Roman or "Terence" stages were gradually enlarged to permit playing scenes inside the openings, and that eventually all were merged into a single arch. Others have argued for a similar evolution out of

the triumphal arches used in street pageants. Still others believe that the proscenium frame was borrowed from perspective painting, in which a central view was often framed by architectural side units (much as in Serlio's stage settings).

Any or all of these practices may have contributed to the proscenium arch, which was adopted to fill a need first clearly felt in the Renaissance. In the medieval theatre, Heaven, Hell, and Earth were shown simultaneously, since space was treated as unbounded and infinite. Contrarily, Renaissance artists sought to depict only objects that could be seen from one fixed point; when multiple locales were required, they were sequential rather than simultaneous. Because space was now treated as finite, a framing device was needed to restrict the view of the audience. The proscenium arch, then, helped both to create the illusion of reality and to mask the mechanisms upon which it depended.

The proscenium came into use only gradually. In early sixteenth-century settings, the first pair of wings and an overhead valance provided sufficient masking. But as the desire to change settings increased, so did the need for downstage masking to conceal the changes. For a time, the first set of angle wings was neutralized to blend with the various settings; in some temporary theatres, an appropriate proscenium arch was erected for each new production. But in permanent theatres the desirability of a permanent framing device was clear, especially after the flat wing was adopted. Consequently, during the seventeenth century the architectural proscenium arch became standard.

FIG. 7.21
Proscenium wall of the Teatro Farnese, 1618. From Streit, *Das Theater* (1903).

The usefulness of an arch was not restricted to the front of the stage; the Teatro Farnese (as well as many later theatres) had two additional frames further back on the stage. This feature encouraged the use of settings of varying depths, since the openings made it easy to increase or restrict the visible stage space. The concept of internal arches increased in importance as the desire for grandeur and monumentality grew during the baroque era. The opening between the last set of wings came to serve as a second frame behind which a deep perspective vista was placed. Sometimes barriers were erected to prevent actors from moving too near the perspective backdrops and thereby destroying the illusion of distance, but with increasing frequency stages of great depth were also built to accommodate scenes of true immensity.

Although the stage of the Teatro Farnese may serve as the prototype of virtually all those that were to follow during the next 300 years, its auditorium was still that of a conventional court theatre. In it, U-shaped, stadium-like seating surrounded a large open space that could be used for dancing or for other forms of spectacle. (During the initial production, this space was even flooded for a *naumachia*.) The prototype of the later auditorium, therefore, is not found in the court but in the public theatres.

The professional public theatre began to emerge in Italy during the second half of the sixteenth century. The first record of an Italian public theatre building is found in 1565 at Venice. By the early seventeenth century there were a number of public theatre buildings, although none was elaborate. Major architectural innovations did not come until opera began to be performed professionally in 1637.

Venice was the logical place for the public theatre to develop, for it was one of only a few Italian states not ruled by a monarch. Since its wealth depended upon commerce, it had a strong middle class capable of supporting a public theatre.

The auditorium of the Venetian public opera house was arranged to encourage attendance by all classes while permitting relative privacy for those who wished it. The success of the San Cassiano, the first to be built, was so great that by 1641 three other theatres had been opened, and the public performance of opera (and its attendant auditorium design) spread from Venice to other cities in Italy and elsewhere throughout Europe.

The only extant seventeenth-century plan of a Venetian opera house is that for the SS. Giovanni e Paolo, built in 1639. It shows five balconies, each with twenty-nine boxes. The first two levels, the most expensive, were patronized by the wealthier classes; the upper three were used by persons of lesser rank and wealth; the open area on the ground floor (the pit or *parterre*) attracted those to whom propriety was unimportant. The arrangement of tiers, one above the other, permitted large numbers of persons to be accommodated in a restricted space, and the division of the tiers into boxes permitted small groups or families to attend the theatre without mingling with the general public.

Although the Venetian opera houses established one prototype of the "pit, box, and gallery" auditorium, they were not without precedents, for many of the theatres erected for the religious plays of the Middle Ages had employed variations on this arrangement, and less elaborate versions of it were used for the public theatres of Paris, London, and Madrid before opera houses were opened in Venice. Nevertheless, the prestige of opera gave approval to the pattern that was to dominate auditorium design until the end of the nineteenth century. Furthermore, since the Venetian opera houses also incorporated the proscenium arch, elaborate machines, and perspective scenery, they were the first public theatres to include all of the features that were to be most characteristic of the picture-frame stage.

MACHINERY AND SPECIAL EFFECTS

Much of the wonder inspired by the productions at courts and academies resulted from special effects.

FIG. 7.23

A public theatre of the early seventeenth century, thought to be in Centro (Italy). Drawing by G. F. B. Guercino. Courtesy British Museum.

FIG. 7.24
Design by Bernardo Buontalenti for the *Harmony of the Spheres,* an *intermezzo* given at the Uffizi palace in Florence, 1589. The design also illustrates the use of "glories." Courtesy Theatre Museum, Victoria and Albert Museum, London.

Continuing and elaborating on medieval practice, the Renaissance machinists arranged seemingly magical transformations, and made gods, monsters, and mythological creatures appear on the sea, in the air, in Heaven, or in Hades. Just as playwrights turned to classical subjects, the machinists found justification for their work in Pollux's list of machines and Aristotle's inclusion of spectacle as one of the six basic parts of drama. Even in plays that observed unity of place, spectacle was often introduced to reduce the austerity imposed by a single setting. Typically, however, elaborate special effects were reserved for *intermezzi* or operas.

Much of the spectacle depended upon machinery for "flying." Gods appeared frequently to resolve the dramatic action, and these and other mythological characters were suspended above the stage in chariots, on clouds, or on the backs of animals or birds. From one to fifty figures might be shown in "the glory" of a brightly lighted paradise formed of clouds. To achieve these effects, appropriately shaped figures, such as chariots, horses, or clouds, were made of wood and canvas and then painted. Since the overhead space was limited in theatres of this period, beams with tracks for casters overhead, in combination with fulcrums, ropes, and pulleys at the sides of the stage, allowed objects or characters to be flown into and out of view. Some structures were hinged to fold up in the overhead space and to unfold as they descended. Ingenious riggings were devised for moving objects up and down stage while they were suspended in the air. In many productions transformations were masked by clouds that engulfed the stage (as painted cloths or flats were lowered from above or moved on from the sides); the transformed scene was then revealed as the clouds dissipated.

Other effects depended on trapdoors in the stage floor. Since the temporary theatres used platforms only about four to six feet high, the working space beneath the stage was restricted. Nevertheless, the effects were elaborate: mountains, rocks, trees, and other objects rose and sank. Most of these objects were painted on cloths or were hinged so they might collapse into the limited below-stage space. To create the effect of a ghost rising through the floor, for example, a figure was painted on cloth, attached to a pole, and elevated through a slot in the floor. Through traps characters appeared or disappeared, and objects and persons were transformed through substitutions from beneath the stage.

Fire and smoke were common. Sabbattini describes a device for making flames seem to rise out of the earth, and an arrangement of fire in front and in back of actors to make it appear that they are dancing in flames.

The popularity of sea scenes motivated the invention of several devices for simulating waves. In one, a large sheet of painted cloth was moved up and down rhythmically by means of cords attached to its underside; in another, a series of two-dimensional pieces shaped like waves as seen from the front were moved in such a way that as one line of waves rose, another lowered to simulate the movement of the sea; in a third, a series of long, spiral cylinders was rotated one behind the other to create the sense of waves swelling and falling. Sometimes a sufficient number of units were utilized so that changes from calm to storm, from darkness to light, and various other conditions at sea could be simulated.

Ships, whales, and dolphins moved through the waves. To create the proper illusion, miniatures were usually mounted on poles and operated from beneath the stage. When ships had to accommodate a number of people, they were mounted on casters and pulled across the stage by means of concealed ropes. One of the *intermezzi* designed by Buontalenti at Florence in 1589 showed Amphitrite moving through the waves on a shell accompanied by dolphins and Tritons; then a ship bearing twenty men sailed into view as a watchman in the crow's nest sang a song and a dolphin danced in the waves below.

Sometimes spectacles demanded that walls, fortified castles, or other buildings collapse. In these instances, the scenery was constructed in sections (like building blocks) and held together by concealed bars; when the bars were removed, the structures fell.

Sound was also important. Thunder was created by rolling cannon balls or stones down a rough channel; wind was simulated by whirling thin-layered strips of wood through the air rapidly.

The front curtain might also be considered a special effect, since it was used to conceal the scenic wonders and to increase amazement when they were suddenly revealed. It was used only to begin performances and never to divide them into acts. At first, the curtain was dropped; but, since this created too many hazards, the roll curtain (which wound the curtain into the space above the proscenium), or the divided curtain (that could be pulled to the side), was eventually adopted.

MUSIC AND DANCE

Music and dance were integral parts of Italian ceremonies, festivals, and theatrical presentations. They are referred to so often in accounts of performances that both obviously were used liberally. Music often continued throughout a procession, pageant, ceremony, or other theatrical event. It might be vocal or instrumental, solo or in various combinations. Before 1600, it figured most prominently in the *intermezzi*, in which it accompanied the numerous songs and dances and much of the primarily pantomimic action. It was also played during scene shifts to bridge scenes and to disguise unwanted noise.

With the coming of opera, music played an even more prominent role. A considerable amount of music has survived from this period, but unfortunately we can associate very few of these pieces with particular performances. Even with opera, few libretti can be assigned to specific musical scores. Thus, our understanding of the musical element in theatrical entertainments of this period is more general than precise.

This conclusion is even more applicable to dance, since for dance there was no equivalent of a musical score or dramatic text to record it. What remains are some pictorial illustrations and verbal descriptions. Nevertheless, we know that dance contributed much to theatrical entertainments and that in this period the foundations of ballet were laid (to be more fully exploited in the *ballet de cour,* the French variation on the *intermezzi*).

THE FESTIVAL CONTEXT

The majority of the information we have about Italian theatrical performances in the sixteenth and seventeenth centuries has survived because the performances were included in festivals conceived to commemorate some important occasion, which was then memorialized in engravings and descriptions of the total festival. All the elements that made up a festival were treated as parts of an overall design and all were related to some theme, usually one that suggested parallels between the occasion being celebrated and some significant story drawn from classical mythology. Overall, the plays and *intermezzi* occurred

FIG. 7.25

An outdoor carnival pageant, *The War of Love,* at the Medici court, 1615. The procession includes pageant wagons representing Africa and Asia. Etching by Jacques Callot.

within a festival context much as performances had in Rome.

For these festivals, the Italian courts revived many of the spectacles of the Roman Empire and continued others from the Middle Ages. Roman triumphal entries were transformed into *trionfi:* elaborate processions with pageant wagons, costumed classical or allegorical figures, and choreographed patterns. Like other spectacles, they were also a symbol of power, wealth, and enlightenment. These *trionfi* were usually viewed from balconies and galleries of palaces, courtyards, or town squares. One of the most elaborate of these processions was mounted in Florence in 1566 as *A Masque of the Genealogy of the Gods* with twentyone pageant wagons and 392 costumed mythological figures, all designed by Giorgio Vasari (1511–1574), many of whose drawings for this pageant still survive. *Naumachiae* were also revived. Usually they were presented on rivers, but at times flooded courtyards and other structures were used. Perhaps the most elaborate *naumachia* was *The Battle of the Argonauts,* given on the Arno River in Florence in 1608 (see Fig. 7.17) as one event among others for a court festival. After 1600, the kind of spectacle developed earlier in *intermezzi* began to be staged quite apart from plays. There were various other kinds of processions, street revels, masquerades, carnivals, tournaments, and animal baitings. Several festivals are described in detail by A. M. Nagler in his *Theatre Festivals of the Medici, 1539–1637.*

Each festival was usually under the overall supervision of one person, often the court architect whose responsibilities included the design and staging of court entertainments. Persons other than architects might serve this function, as for example at Mantua in the mid-sixteenth century where Leone di Somi (1527–1592) was in charge of theatrical entertainments. We are also indebted to di Somi for a treatise on production and staging, *Four Dialogues Concerning Theatrical Performance* (*c.* 1556), in which he gives advice about playwriting, acting, costuming, and staging.

STAGE LIGHTING

When performances moved indoors, stage lighting became an important element of theatrical production for the first time. Although some of the medieval courtly entertainments had been performed indoors, it was not until the sixteenth century that indoor productions were common. At that time, techniques for lighting the auditorium and the stage had to be devised.

The illuminants available were candles and oil lamps. Candles were preferred for the auditorium because they smoked less and had a more pleasant odor than oil. Usually the auditorium was lighted by chan-

FIG. 7.26

Device for dimming candles. The hollow pipes could be lowered to obscure the light or raised to brighten it. From Sabbattini, *Manual for Constructing Theatrical Scenes and Machines* (1638).

deliers hung just in front of the stage, illuminating both the auditorium and a portion of the platform.

The downstage acting area was also lighted by footlights, often mounted behind a parapet placed a short distance in front of the stage. Sabbattini states that the smoke from footlights and chandeliers often created a haze, and other writers comment upon the heat and fumes. The lights mounted on stage were usually concealed behind overhead or side masking pieces. Several oil lamps were placed in evenly spaced rings attached to vertical poles set up behind the proscenium and each of the wing positions. Other lamps were mounted on horizontal battens in back of the front valance and each of the borders. To increase efficiency, reflectors made from tinsel, mica, or polished basins were placed behind the lamps.

At least three methods of darkening the stage were used: Lamps were extinguished (although this was awkward if the lights had to brighten again); open cylinders were suspended above the lamps and lowered over them to darken the stage or raised to brighten it; or all lamps might be mounted on rotating poles that could be turned either toward or away from the visible portions of the stage. When exceptionally bright light was required, some scenic device such as a cloud, shell, or grotto was equipped with a downstage rim inside which lamps could be concealed and directed toward persons or objects inside the structure.

Sometimes the sun, moon, or lightning was shown. At Florence in 1539, San Gallo filled a crystal sphere with water and lighted it from behind with candles to form a sun that rose at the beginning of the play, moved across the sky, and set as the action closed. The moon was often represented in similar fashion. Bolts of lightning were made from jagged pieces of wood covered with tinsel and shot across the stage on wires. Occasionally attempts were made to color the light by placing containers filled with tinted liquids between the lamps and the stage. Since this reduced intensity markedly, it was normally reserved for such decorative devices as jeweled windows or festive lights mounted on top of buildings.

Since the intensity of lamps and candles was so limited, providing an adequate level of illumination took precedence over the other functions of stage lighting. Nevertheless, Renaissance theorists formulated several artistic principles similar to those advocated in modern times. Leone di Somi argued that tragedy benefits from a lower level of illumination than that needed for comedy, and both he and Ingegneri stated that the stage will appear brighter if it can be contrasted with a darkened auditorium. Sabbattini

suggested that lighting the stage primarily from one side gives a more pleasing effect than even lighting from the front. For the most part, however, Renaissance artists had to depend upon general illumination, for they had only limited control over color, distribution, and intensity. Nevertheless, they mastered most of the techniques that were to be typical until the late eighteenth century.

COMMEDIA DELL'ARTE

Productions at courts and academies were given for aristocratic audiences on special occasions. The plays were usually written by court poets and the scenery and costumes designed by court architects and painters. Acting was done by courtiers and music was supplied by court musicians, and productions usually received only one performance. Thus, in spite of the high visual quality of the productions and their influence on later theatrical practice, they were essentially coterie performances. The development of a public, professional theatre in Italy was to come primarily from another source—*commedia dell'arte*.

Commedia dell'arte (comedy of professional players), *commedia all'improviso* (improvised comedy), and *commedia a soggetto* (comedy developed from a plot, theme, or subject) are terms used to distinguish the plays performed by professional troupes from those (*commedia erudita* or learned comedy) presented by

FIG. 7.27
Scene from an Italian comedy of the early seventeenth century. From Rasi, *I Comici Italiana* (1895–1905).

the amateur actors at courts, academies, and in residences of prosperous citizens. Historians do not know when the *commedia dell'arte* came into being. A contract dated 1545 appears to be that for a *commedia* troupe, but the first clear reference to a *commedia* performance is found in 1568.

Several theories have been advanced to explain the origin of *commedia*. One school seeks to trace it from the Atellan farce of Rome as preserved by wandering mimes during the Middle Ages. The principal evidence for this view is the similarity of stock characters in the two forms. A variation on this theory traces the *commedia* from troupes of Byzantine mimes who supposedly fled to the West when Constantinople fell in 1453. Other scholars have argued that it evolved out of improvisations on the comedies of Plautus and Terence or on Italian *commedia erudita*.

Still others have traced it to the Italian farce of the early sixteenth century. Farce had appeared in Italy, as elsewhere, during the late Middle Ages, but its first extensive development came between 1500 and 1550, when it was especially popular with the general public; after this time, written farce declined as *commedia dell'arte* rose in esteem. Written farce reached its height in the work of Angelo Beolco (*c.*

1495–1542), who began writing and acting around 1520, roughly the time when *commedia erudita* was developing. Disliking the formality of *commedia erudita,* he turned for inspiration to the everyday life and natural speech of northern Italy. Many of his plays center around the peasant Ruzzante, a role played by Beolco. The continuance of Ruzzante through several plays has been cited as a forerunner of the *commedia's* use of stock characters.

None of the theories about the origin of *commedia* can be confirmed or refuted. Many influences probably contributed to its development. Regardless of its source, before 1600 it had spread throughout Europe, where it was a typical and popular form of entertainment into the eighteenth century.

The two fundamental characteristics of *commedia dell'arte* were improvisation and stock characters: the actors worked from a plot outline, on the basis of which they improvised dialogue and action, and each performer always played the same character with its fixed attributes and costume.

The earliest clear reference to improvisational playing is found in 1568, but, if it was new at that time, it soon became common. Historians have disagreed over the extent to which improvisation was

FIG. 7.28

Two *commedia* figures. From Jacques Callot's *Balli di Sfessania,* a series of twenty-four etchings made *c.* 1621–1622. The figures are considerably exaggerated.

used in performances. Certainly, several factors worked to reduce it. Each actor usually played the same character throughout his career, and this practice must have encouraged the repetition of lines or stage business that had been well received by audiences. Many comic bits (*lazzi,* singular *lazzo*) were sufficiently standardized to be indicated in plot outlines as *lazzo* of fear, hat *lazzo,* and so on. The rhymed couplets used to close scenes were probably memorized, and the actors playing the fashionable young lovers were encouraged to keep notebooks in which to record appropriate sentiments of poetry and popular literature. Consequently, most of the actors probably stored up lines and action which they repeated frequently. On the other hand, no actor could be sure what the others would say or do and thus had to concentrate upon the unfolding action. As a result, performances must have created the impression of spontaneity.

The scenarios were refined over a period of time and passed down from one troupe to another. More than 1000 have been preserved; the oldest fifty were published by Flaminio Scala (*fl.* 1600–1621) in 1611. By far the greatest number of scripts were comic, although a few were serious and many were melodramatic. The popularity of the troupes, however, rested primarily upon comedies revolving around love and intrigue, disguises, and cross-purposes. The *commedia* actors also performed occasionally in written plays and at court; consequently, they may have been influenced by the *erudita.*

Every troupe had its own set of fixed characters, each with a name and traits that set each off from similar characters in other companies. Nevertheless, the same character types tended to be repeated from one troupe to another. Consequently, although variations were numerous, the basic outlines remained relatively constant.

The character types in *commedia* can be divided into two general categories: the unmasked and the masked. The unmasked roles were those of the young lovers, who usually served as a norm against which the peculiarities of other characters were seen. Typically they were depicted as witty, handsome, well-educated young men and women, but they might also be characterized as naive, even not-too-bright. They dressed in the fashionable garments of the day. Each company had one or two pairs of lovers. The young man, the *innamorato* or *amoroso,* was often opposed in his love affairs by an older man, sometimes even his father. The young woman, or *innamorata,* was usually a young lady courted by both young and old. When there were two pairs of lovers, the contrasts between them were usually emphasized.

FIG. 7.29
The lover of *commedia dell'arte.* Etching by Jacques Callot.

The masked roles can be divided into masters and servants. Of the masters, three recurred most frequently: the Capitano, Pantalone, and Dottore. Originally the Capitano was one of the lovers and unexaggerated in manners and dress. Eventually, however, he was transformed into a braggart and coward who boasted of his great prowess in love and battle, only to be completely discredited in both. The sword, cape, and feathered headdress were standard features of his costume, though the degree of exaggeration varied considerably. He was often given such fanciful names as Spavento da Vall'Inferno, Coccodrillo, Rinocorente, or Matamoros. He frequently figured in the action as an unwelcome suitor to one of the young women, and his discomfiture was often a high point of the comedy.

Pantalone was always a middle-aged or elderly merchant. He spoke in a Venetian dialect, was fond of proverbs, and, in spite of his age, often posed as a young man and courted one of the young women. Typically, his costume included a tight-fitting red male servants. Occasionally, they were older and might be the hostess of an inn, wife to a servant, or the object of an old man's affection.

Of the *zanni,* Arlecchino (Harlequin) was by far the most popular after the mid-seventeenth century, although he did not figure prominently in the early scripts. He was a mixture of cunning and stupidity and was an accomplished acrobat and dancer. He was usually at the center of any intrigue. His costume underwent many changes. Originally, it was a suit with many irregularly placed patches, but these were gradually formalized into the diamond-shaped red, blue, and green pattern now associated with Harlequin. On his shaven head Harlequin wore a rakish hat above a black mask, and at his side he carried a wooden sword, or "slapstick," that figured prominently in the many fights and beatings of the *commedia.* Other related characters are Truffaldino and Trivellino.

Harlequin's most frequent companion was a cruel, libidinous, cynically witty servant who went by a variety of names. He was often called Brighella in

FIG. 7.30

The Capitano of the *commedia dell'arte.* From Sand, *Masques et Bouffons* (1859).

vest, red breeches and stockings, soft slippers, a black, ankle-length coat, a soft brimless cap with trailing wisps of hair, a brown mask with a large hooked nose, and a scraggly gray beard.

Dottore was usually Pantalone's friend or rival and, like Pantalone, held an established place in society. He was a pedant, usually a doctor of law or medicine, who spoke in a Bolognese dialect interlarded with Latin words and phrases. He loved to show off his spurious learning, but was often tricked by others because of his extreme credulousness. His dress was the academic cap and gown. He was a jealous husband, but was often cuckolded.

The most varied of all the *commedia* types were the servants, or *zanni.* Most scripts required at least two of these characters, one clever and the other stupid, but the number might vary from one to four. They usually figured prominently in the intrigues, and their machinations kept the plots moving as they sought to help or thwart their masters. Most of the servants were male, but there might be one or more maids, or *fantesca,* who served the *innamorata.* Typically young, coarsely witty, and always ready for an intrigue, they carried on their own love affairs with the

FIG. 7.31

Zanni, or Scapino. Etching by Jacques Callot, 1618–1619. Note the audience and performers in the background.

FIG. 7.32
In the foreground, characters of *commedia dell'arte* and in the background members of the French royal family. Seen at right are Pantalone and Harlequin. Painting attributed to Paul and Frans Porbus, 1572. Courtesy Bayeux Museum.

the plays were actually rehearsed, pains were taken to see that each actor understood what was expected.

Most companies were organized on a sharing plan (under which the members assumed the financial risk and divided the profits), although some of the younger actors may have been salaried until they were granted full membership. The troupes traveled frequently, and at each new town they had to petition for the right to perform, a favor not always granted. Usually they hired large rooms in which to play, but they were equally at home on improvised outdoor stages and on indoor court stages. When perspective settings and elaborate effects were available, they were used, but the actors could perform

the eighteenth century, when his mask had a hooked nose and mustache, and his trousers and jacket were ornamented with green braid. Other variations on this character included Buffetto, Flautino, Scapino, and Mezzetino. Scaramuccia, another popular character, varied considerably in his attributes, sometimes resembling Harlequin, at others Brighella or the Capitano.

Pulcinello was always a Neapolitan, but his function in the plays varied. Sometimes he was a servant, or he could be the host of an inn or a merchant. He was a mixture of foolishness and shrewdness, villainy and love, wit and dullness. He had an enormous hooked nose, a humpback, and wore a long pointed cap. He was the ancestor of the English puppet character, Punch. In addition to these common types, many other servants and incidental characters are listed in the scripts, since each troupe tended to develop its own variations on the traditional character types.

In size, the troupes averaged ten to twelve members: seven or eight men and three or four women. A typical troupe included two sets of lovers, a servant girl, a Capitano, two *zanni*, and two old men (Pantalone and Dottore), but this pattern might be augmented or reduced according to the financial state of the group.

Productions were supervised by the leader or most respected member of a troupe. It was the leader's responsibility to explain the character relationships, clarify the action, enumerate the *lazzi*, and acquire the properties needed. Although it is not clear whether

FIG. 7.33
Scene from a *commedia* play, *The Fairies, or the Tales of Mother Goose,* first performed at the Hôtel de Bourgogne, Paris, 1697. Harlequin is depicted at center. From Gherardi, *Le Théâtre Italien,* 6 (1741).

just as easily with no scenery at all. Adaptability was one key to their success.

The *commedia* was most vigorous between 1570 and 1650, the period of the most famous troupes. The history of these companies is often difficult to trace because of scanty records, frequent mergers and separations, and the similarity of names adopted by the troupes.

The first company of note was that of Alberto Naselli (known as Zan Ganassa), which played in such diverse places as Mantua, Ferrara, Paris, and Madrid between 1568 and 1583. Eventually it was eclipsed in fame by the Gelosi ("zealous") troupe, which performed between 1568 and 1604. The outstanding members of the Gelosi were Francesco Andreini (1548–1624), originally an *innamorato* and later a Capitano, and his wife, Isabella (1562–1604), the most renowned *innamorata* of her day and a poet as well. They joined the Gelosi in 1583, later replaced Flaminio Scala as leaders of the company, and made it fashionable throughout Italy and France. They performed at the elaborate wedding celebrations in Florence of Ferdinando I in 1589 and were invited to France by Henri IV. The troupe disbanded upon the death of Isabella in 1604.

The Confidenti troupe performed between 1574 and 1639. Like others, it traveled widely, appearing throughout Italy, Spain, and France. Its many fine actors included Flaminio Scala, who published the oldest collection of *commedia* scripts and eventually became head of the company. The Desiosi ("desirous") company played between 1581 and 1599. In spite of references to its high quality, we know little of its work. The Accesi ("flashing" or "inspired") troupe performed between 1590 and 1628, although its best work was done between 1600 and 1609 under the leadership of Pier Maria Cecchini (1575–1645), who played Fritellino. For a time, Cecchini shared leadership with Tristano Martinelli (c. 1557–1630), the first famous Arlecchino. The Accesi played in Italy, France, Austria, and Germany. The Fideli ("faithful") company was active from about 1601 until 1652. Its principal actors were Giambattista Andreini (c. 1578–1654), son of Francesco and Isabella Andreini, and his wife Virginia (1583–c. 1627/30). They made at least four trips to France and played as far north as Prague. In addition to these important troupes, others were patronized by the Dukes of Mantua throughout the seventeenth century. The most important troupes between 1650 and 1700 were attached to the courts of Parma and Modena.

The *commedia dell'arte* continued until about 1775, but never regained the prestige it commanded prior to 1650. Although it was always most popular in Italy, France was a second home, and troupes often traveled in Spain, Germany, Austria, England, and elsewhere in Europe. Wherever they went, they influenced native actors and writers.

THE DECLINE OF ITALY

By 1650 Italy had developed the dramatic types, critical principles, and theatrical practices that were to dominate the European theatre for the next 150 years. The neoclassical ideal, classically inspired comedy and tragedy, opera, *commedia dell'arte,* theatre architecture, perspective scenery, indoor lighting techniques, complex special effects and stage machinery—all of these were to find their way to other countries, where they would be mingled with native practices and adapted to local needs.

Despite these achievements, by 1650 Italy had lost its privileged position in Europe. As the seat of the Catholic church, it had exerted profound influence on other Western countries during the preceding 1000 years. Furthermore, its location had made it the bridgehead for trade with the East, and in turn this trade had brought it wealth and sophistication. In addition, under feudalism the small states into which it was divided could compete effectively with those elsewhere in Europe.

But during the Renaissance all this began to change. The schisms in the church weakened the position of Italy, especially during the time when the seat of the church was Avignon and after the many Protestant secessions began. Although the papacy regained much of its prestige after 1550, its authority never equaled its influence of earlier centuries. In addition, as Mediterranean trade routes to the East were disrupted after 1453 and as new ocean routes were subsequently opened, Italy declined as a center of trade. With this decline went the basis of the wealth that had encouraged Italy's ruling classes to patronize the arts and learning. This decline was not immediately evident, since Italy long remained a major banking center of Europe because of the capital it had accumulated through trade. Nevertheless, by 1700 Italy had been reduced economically to secondary status.

Italy also declined in political importance. In the tenth century the Holy Roman Empire had been revived as a confederation of German and Italian states. At times the emperor had attained effective control over subject princes, but during the fourteenth and fifteenth centuries the Italian states were almost totally independent of outside interference. Then, during the sixteenth century, Italy became a source of contention among such strong nations as Spain, France, and Austria. For a time Spain gained dominance, and its troupes even sacked Rome in

1527. After 1559 Austria became the major force; many Italian states remained dependencies of Austria until the mid-nineteenth century.

In the century following the Council of Trent the spirit of the counter-Reformation motivated a final burst of creativity in church architecture and painting that produced the great baroque churches of Italy, including St. Peter's in Rome. In the theatre, the greatest of baroque creations was opera, which permitted Italy to remain a strong force in Europe's artistic life even after its drama had ceased to be significant. For the most part, however, by the late seventeenth century Italy was no longer important either politically or economically. Thereafter, it was forced to defer culturally to France.

LOOKING AT THEATRE HISTORY

One hazard in historical study is the necessity of dividing the whole into segments, since not everything can be examined simultaneously. Common ways of dividing history are by period, country, topic, artistic or political movement, or theme. Each of these can be justified, but all have their shortcomings. When divisions are made according to country, the interconnections among events occurring in two or more countries may go unnoticed or remain unexplored. Division into time periods may interrupt or obscure ongoing developments, or may give undue emphasis to some event or type of activity (especially war or politics) as crucial in marking the end or beginning of a period or movement. Therefore, students should be aware that in theatre history what is selected for inclusion and how it is interpreted are influenced in part by the system of segmentation being used, and that another way of dividing the whole would likely yield a somewhat different view of the same historical events or processes. In this book, for example, the division into Medieval and Renaissance periods separates many simultaneous and interconnected developments; through the choice of what is included (and excluded) in each of the chapters, lines of development and directions of change are made to seem clearer than they might were all of the material treated together. Nevertheless, each historian must choose some scheme of division, even though each scheme encourages some form of oversimplification. No historical work can ever convey the "whole" truth.

In theatre history, the context in which we place events is crucial to our vision of their significance. This is well illustrated in Roy Strong's study of Renaissance courtly theatrical activities and festivals as reflections of royal power.

Through [festivals] the prince was able to manifest himself at his most magnificent in the sight of his subjects. By means of myth and allegory, sign and symbol, gesture and movement, festival found a means to exalt the glory of the wearer of the Crown. In such a way the truths of sacred monarchy could be propagated to the court and a tamed nobility take its place in the round of ritual. [21]

For the modern reader the central thought tenet that motivated Renaissance court fetes is the least interesting one. We can see them in retrospect for what they were: extravagant assertions of a mirage of power. They retain their fascination 350 years later only because through this alliance of art and power arose our modern opera and ballet and the theatre of illusion. In this century festivals have been studied seriously mostly as a curious ancestor of theatre, but they are in reality much more a branch of political history and thought. [247–248]

Roy Strong, *Splendor at Court: Renaissance Spectacle and Illusion* (Boston: Houghton Mifflin, 1973).

Accounts of ceremonies were often written to record the magnificence of court festivals. Much of our information comes from these books. Here are a few excerpts from Pavoni's account of the festivities accompanying the wedding of Christine of Lorraine to the Grand Duke Ferdinand I in 1589. This section describes a mock sea battle staged in the courtyard of the Pitti Palace in Florence:

The courtyard was filled with water to a height of some five feet by means of underground water conduits . . . and . . . there entered . . . eighteen vessels. [Pavoni describes a sea battle between Christians and Turks, with the Turks defeated; then the Christians, still on their ships, attacked a Turkish castle at one end of the courtyard.] At last . . . rope ladders were attached to the walls by means of hooks . . . and other devices; and indeed many fell into the water . . . [Finally] the Christians . . . won possession of the walls and the castle. And there, with many indications of happiness, songs, and dancing, . . . they finished the festivities.

Giuseppe Pavoni, *Diario descritto da Giuseppe Pavoni delle Feste Celebrate nella solenissime Nozze dell Serenissimi Sposi, il Sig. Gran Duchi di Toscanna* (Bologna, 1589).

Serlio combines praise for the ruler with concern for the relationship of his work both to antiquity and perspective:

Although halls (however large they may be) could not accommodate theatres such as the ancients had, nevertheless in order to follow the ancients as closely as possible, I have included in my plan such parts of the ancient theatre as a great hall might contain . . . The greater the hall, the more nearly will the theatre assume its perfect form.

Sebastiano Serlio, *The Second Book of Architecture* (1545), trans. by Allardyce Nicoll in *The Renaissance Stage*, ed. Barnard Hewitt (Coral Gables, Fla.: University of Miami Press, 1958), 24–32.

By the late sixteenth century, Italian critics had set forth the basic tenets of neoclassicism. Minturno stated the fundamental concept that truth is unchanging, that it remains constant in all times and in all places:

[Some contemporary critics] are seeking to set forth a new art of poetry. . . . But if [Aristotle and Horace] have taught a true art, I do not see how another different from it can be established, for truth is single and what is once true must necessarily be true in every age . . . in everything Art abides by a law with which it is regulated and by which it directs everything.

Antonio Minturno, *L'Arte Poetica* (1564), Book I, sections 32–33.

In 1571 Castelvetro reduced to strict rules many of the tenets that were to dominate critical thought for the next 200 years. Here are a few key excerpts from his lengthy treatise:

Dramas do not show on the stage murders and other things that are difficult to represent with dignity, . . . such deeds should be done off stage and then narrated by a messenger. . . . A drama spends as many hours in performing things as was taken by the actions themselves . . . therefore tragedy and comedy . . . cannot last longer than the time permitted by the convenience of the audience, nor include more things than can occur in the space of time that the comedies and tragedies require in performance. . . . It is not possible to make the audience believe that several days and nights have passed when they have the evidence of their senses that only a few hours have gone by.

Lodovico Castelvetro, *The Poetics of Aristotle Translated and Annotated* (1571), sections 57 and 109.

One of the major sources of information about the *commedia dell'arte* is Perrucci's description of all aspects of the form. Here are some excerpts from his account of rehearsal practices:

The scenario is no more than the fabric of scenes woven from a plot, with brief hints of the action, divided into acts and scenes, which are to be acted extemporaneously by the performers. In the margins are indications as to where each character is to enter and . . . exit.

The manager or more experienced actor rehearses the scenario before it is acted, so the actors know the contents of the play, where the dialogue should end, and where new lazzi can be inserted . . . he will plant the lazzi, . . . giving attention to the things needed in the play, such as letters, purses, daggers, and other properties. . . .

After the actors have been told what they must do . . . , they will be able to go through the scenes and rehearse new lazzi or material of their own invention. It is wise, however, not to depart from the plot so far that . . . the audience will lose the thread of the plot. . . . [Then] the actors ought to think about bringing in something . . . they have memorized for use in any play.

Andrea Perrucci, *Dell'arte rappresentativa, premeditata, ed all' improvviso* (1699).

8
French Theatre
to 1700

France began to feel the effects of the Renaissance in the late fifteenth century. From 1494 on it maintained close relationships with Italy, and in the early sixteenth century controlled parts of it. Francis I (reigned 1515–1547) was especially interested in the new artistic and literary movements and invited several Italian artists and scholars to his court, where they developed the style called the School of Fontainebleau. In 1546 Francis commissioned Pierre Lescot to rebuild the Louvre in Renaissance style, and during his reign the great chateaux of the Loire region began to be built.

Medieval influences in France continued throughout the sixteenth century. Some of the most elaborate outdoor religious dramas were staged in France between 1500 and 1550, and farces and *sotties* were among the most popular of dramatic types. Thus, medieval and Renaissance elements existed side by side and were mutually influential.

THEATRE AT COURT AND IN SCHOOLS PRIOR TO 1600

Before the end of Francis I's reign, Renaissance drama had made an impact both on schools and at court. As in other countries, the trend began with the study of Roman plays, continued with imita-

tions in Latin of classical works, and progressed to plays in French. It was in France (at Lyons) in 1493 that the first illustrated edition of Terence's plays was published, and the "Terence Stage" depicted in that edition may have provided the model for the staging of plays in French schools and at court until after the mid-sixteenth century.

Some French authors also began to write plays in the classical manner. Between 1501 and 1524 Revisius Textor composed a number of Latin *Dialogi* which were performed by students at the University of Paris, and in 1536 Roilletus published three Latin tragedies that had been acted by his students in Paris. Around 1540, classical plays and critical treatises began to be translated into French. Plays by Sophocles, Euripides, Aristophanes, Seneca, Plautus, and Terence and critical works by Aristotle and Horace were printed before 1550. Recent Italian plays also were translated, as were Italian commentaries on Aristotle's *Poetics*.

Renaissance influence accelerated after Henri II (reigned 1547–1559), who had married Catherine de' Medici (1519–1589), succeeded to the throne. By 1550 a group of seven French writers, led by Pierre de Ronsard and known as the Pléiade, had come to the fore. Seeking to develop French as the medium for a literature modeled on classical works, they formulated rules of grammar and prosody, enriched the language by inventing new words, and illustrated their ideals in their own literary works. Of necessity, the Pléiade addressed itself primarily to the educated classes.

The first plays in French modeled on classical forms were written by a member of the Pléiade, Etienne Jodelle (1523–1573), who in 1552 composed *Cléopâtre Captive,* a tragedy, and *Eugène,* a comedy. Other playwrights soon followed Jodelle's example, and like him most wrote both comedies and tragedies. Among these authors were Jacques Grévin, Jean-Antoine de Baïf, Jean de la Taille, and Robert Garnier. The comedies, though classical in form, resemble medieval farces in their subjects. They deal primarily with urban, amoral, middle-class characters motivated primarily by sex and money. The tragedies treat classical or biblical subjects. In most there is little dramatic tension because the emphasis is on the suffering of the characters who are the victims of fate and who describe their suffering in a series of set rhetorical speeches. By modern standards these tragedies seem uninteresting, but they were much admired at the time, probably because moral tone, displays of erudition, and dignity of expression were considered more important than suspense or psychological motivation.

In the late sixteenth century, Pierre de Larivey (*c.* 1540–1619) moved comedy away from the mixture of medieval subject and classical form. He modeled his works on Italian *commedia erudita* but adapted them to French locales and manners. His comedies were the most popular of the French plays that have come down to us from the period prior to 1630.

By 1572, when Jean de la Taille published a work advocating the three unities, the neoclassical ideal had been fully set forth in France. The French playwrights of the late sixteenth century adhered to these rules only sporadically, however, perhaps because, as in England and Spain, medieval influence was still potent and because playwrights considered it more important to please audiences than to adhere strictly to the rules. Whatever the reasons, the works of this period display considerable variety of form and style.

Most of the plays about which information has survived were performed in colleges or at court. Jodelle's *Cléopâtre* was presented at court to an audience that included Henri II. The setting was described as "antique," but it is not clear whether this was a "Terence Stage" or a perspective setting. At this time either could have been used. Vitruvius's treatise on architecture was translated into French in 1547, and perspective scenery had certainly been used in Lyons in 1548 for a production of Bibbiena's *La Calandria* given in honor of Henri II and Catherine. But, though the French obviously knew about Italian scenic practices, most of the spectacles at court used "dispersed decors," medieval-like scenic elements scattered around a hall rather than concentrated in a single, unified setting.

Among the most characteristic entertainments of this period were the court festivals, which were especially popular after 1553. Both Francis I and Henri II were fond of tournaments, and Henri II met his death in 1559 while participating in one. His death left Catherine de' Medici in a position of power that was to last throughout the lives of her three sons: Francis II, husband of Mary of Scotland (reigned 1559– 1560), Charles IX (reigned 1560–1574), and Henri III (reigned 1574–1589). Catherine was especially fond of royal entries and festivals of various sorts, which she used to illustrate France's power and to encourage alliances or reconciliations. The festivals arranged by Catherine began at Chenonceaux in 1563 and Fontainebleau in 1564; they were followed by a two-year ceremonial progress of the court through the various provinces of France, where every major town mounted a royal entry. An especially elaborate festival was held at Bayonne in 1565, when the main attraction was a water pageant offered by Catherine. These festivals were designed in part by France's foremost mannerist artist, Antoine Caron (*c.*

FIG. 8.1
Catherine de' Medici's water fête given during the Festival at Bayonne, 1565. Drawing by Antoine Caron, who also probably designed the fête. Courtesy Pierpont Morgan Library, New York.

FIG. 8.2
Ballet Comique de la Reyne as given at the Petit Bourbon in 1581. Note the dispersed decor and the placement of spectators. The king and his retinue are in the foreground. Courtesy Bibliothèque Nationale, Paris.

1527–1599), several of whose designs have survived. Other important celebrations were mounted for the entry of Charles IX into Paris in 1571; for the marriage of Catherine's daughter to Henri of Navarre in 1572; and for the visit of the Polish Ambassadors in 1573.

Through such spectacles, the *ballet de cour* (the French variation on Italian *intermezzi* and English masques) evolved. Their creators sought to unite dramatic plot, song, dance, and spectacle in the "antique manner." These experiments culminated in 1581 in the *Ballet Comique de la Reyne* with text by LaChesnaye, music by the Sieur de Beaulieu, scenery by Jacques Patin, and the whole planned and directed by Baltasar de Beaujoyeulx. It was based on the myth of Circe, who lures men into a life of vice and transforms them into beasts. The action was treated as a moral struggle between virtue and vice, with the King depicted as the deliverer. This story was developed through a series of *entrées* by various allegorical and mythological figures and ended with the triumph of reason and virtue and with praise for the wisdom of the kings of France. It was staged in the Salle du Petit Bourbon (located in the palace adjacent to the Louvre), which was to be one of the important court theatres of the seventeenth century. It measured about 49 feet wide by 177 feet long, with an apse extending another 44 feet. The king and courtiers sat at one end, while other spectators occupied two balconies extending around the side walls. The *Ballet Comique de la Reyne* is often said to be the first full expression of the *ballet de cour,* which was to be revived and extended in the seventeenth century. In the meantime, however, further developments were to be delayed by civil war.

THE PUBLIC THEATRE IN PARIS BEFORE 1595

While court spectacles and neoclassical plays were gaining in strength, the French public stage was at a low ebb. This was due, at least in part, to the Confrérie de la Passion, a confraternity that had a monopoly on theatrical production in Paris. Organized in 1402 to produce religious drama, the Confrérie presented its occasional productions in a large hall at the Hôpital de la Trinité for many years. Forced to move in 1539, it had settled in the Hôtel de Flandres until that building was torn down in 1543. In 1548, after a series of relocations, the Confrérie began construction of a new building, probably the first permanent public theatre to be built in Europe since Roman times. Because it was located on land formerly owned by the Dukes of Burgundy, the theatre was called the Hôtel de Bourgogne. Before the theater was completed, however, religious plays were banned. Nevertheless, the Confrérie's monopoly on all theatrical production in Paris was reconfirmed. Thus, while the traditional justification for the group's productions—the presentation of devotional dramas—had been removed, the Confrérie now gained control over the secular theatre. Few records of performances between 1548 and 1575 have survived. The Confrérie probably played at irregular intervals, but its popularity waned with its new repertory, principally farces and other secular works in the medieval mode but with a sprinkling of plays in the new Renaissance style.

Numerous professional companies had developed outside of Paris by the mid sixteenth century, possibly as offshoots of the confraternities formed to produce religious plays. Few played in Paris, however, because of the Confrérie's monopoly. But in the 1570s visiting companies from the provinces began to lease the Hôtel de Bourgogne for short periods, and thereafter the theatre was used increasingly by temporary occupants. Not all visiting companies played at the Hôtel de Bourgogne, but all had to pay fees to the Confrérie no matter where they performed within the city.

By the 1570s both the public theatre and the court entertainments were being affected by the civil disturbances growing out of the struggle between Catholics and Huguenots (Protestants). Persecution of Huguenots had begun about 1540 but did not assume major proportions until 1572, when thousands of Protestants were murdered in the Massacre of St. Bartholomew's Day. Subsequently, as the Catholics gained strength under the leadership of the Duke of Guise, Henri III began to fear them and eventually had the Duke assassinated. In turn, Henri III was killed in 1589, and since he left no heir, Henri of Navarre, a Protestant who had married Henri III's sister, succeeded to the throne as Henri IV (reigned 1589–1610). Open civil war followed and did not cease until Henri IV converted to Catholicism. Unable to enter Paris until 1594, Henri was not able to restore peace fully until after 1598 when he issued the Edict of Nantes granting almost complete autonomy to Protestants. During the disturbances, court entertainments were greatly curtailed, and public performances in Paris almost totally ceased. As a result, French theatre did not revive until the late 1590s.

THE PUBLIC THEATRE, 1595–1629

In 1595 public theatrical performances resumed at the fairs of St. Germain and St. Laurent. French drama was still of little consequence, however, as the neoclassical dramatists had catered to aristocratic audiences and failed to produce any plays of lasting public interest. Although a few of the learned dramas had been presented in the public theatres, the usual popular fare was farce, much of which was improvised under the influence of the *commedia dell'arte* troupes, which had played sporadically in Paris between 1571 and 1588 and were to return frequently after 1599.

These conditions began to change around 1597, when the Confrérie gave up active participation in production and more skilled companies and playwrights began to appear in Paris. In the final years of the century, Antoine de Montchrestien (c. 1575–1621) wrote five tragedies that are recognized as the best of their time. One of these, *L'Escossoise,* about Mary of Scotland, created considerable friction between the governments of France and England.

Around 1597, Alexandre Hardy (c. 1572–1632), France's first professional dramatist, also began his career. Hardy was inspired by the Spanish dramatists and, like them, wrote an exceptional number of plays. He claimed to have written over 500, but only thirty-four have survived. Working for a popular audience, Hardy adapted his plays to its tastes. So while he used such neoclassical devices as the five-act form, poetic dialogue, messengers, and the chorus, he did not permit reverence for antiquity to interfere with his primary aim of telling an interesting story. He seldom observed the unities of time and place, and he put all important episodes, no matter how violent, on stage. At first he wrote tragedies, but since these did not please, he turned to tragicomedy and pastoral. Because he worked under contract to acting companies who retained ownership of the plays he wrote for them, Hardy was unable to publish any of his work until 1624. Five volumes were in print by 1628, but scholars debate the extent to which these plays were changed for publication and how much they actually reflect the original texts used by the actors.

Although Hardy never achieved greatness, his accomplishment was considerable. Coming to the theatre when farce reigned, he paved the way for subsequent tragedy with his tragicomedies and for comedy with his pastorals. His success encouraged others to write for the stage. Not until after 1625, however, did any plays equal Hardy's in popularity.

Hardy's early work was done primarily for Valleran LeComte (*fl.* 1592–1613), the first important French theatrical manager. Although a number of itinerant companies played in Paris after 1595, Valleran's (which first appeared in Paris in 1598) was by far the best. By 1598, Valleran's company was well established, having performed since 1592 in major provincial cities, and was already being called *Les Comédiens du Roi* (The King's Players), probably because it had at some time performed before Henri IV. The title, however, carried with it no special privileges or subsidy. Between 1598 and 1612, Valleran's company, which had to be disbanded and reformed several times because of constant financial difficulties, was the most important company in Paris, although, like its competitors, it also toured elsewhere. Throughout the seventeenth century, the number of French companies outside of Paris was great. We can identify about 400 between 1590 and 1710, although we know little about them. No company, however, was allowed to settle in Paris permanently until 1629.

In the early seventeenth century, acting companies were bound together by two- or three-year contracts. All were organized on the sharing plan, under which profits were divided after each performance. The manager normally received two shares, while lesser actors might be allotted less than a full share. Companies ranged in size from eight to twelve members, sometimes supplemented by "hired men" and apprentices. By 1607, a few women were included in the companies, but some comic roles continued to be played by men. Marie Vernier (*fl.* 1590–1619) is one of the few actresses known to us from this period. But if acting gained steadily in popularity between 1595 and 1629, the social and religious stigma attached to it led most performers to assume stage names when they went into the theatre.

Farce continued to be the most popular dramatic form, and between 1610 and 1629 the most famous actors in Paris were the players of the farcical types, Turlupin, Gaultier-Garguille, and Gros-Guillaume. Turlupin, acted by Henri LeGrand (*c.* 1587–*c.* 1637), who used the name Belleville in serious roles, was a rascally servant similar to Brighella of the *commedia dell'arte*. Gaultier-Garguille, acted by Hugues Guéru (*c.* 1573–1633), who played as Fleschelles in serious drama, was a tall, thin, bow-legged creature who could contort his body like a marionette. Gros-Guillaume, acted by Robert Guérin (*c.* 1554–*c.* 1634), who used the name LaFleur in serious roles, had a flour-whitened face and an obese body, emphasized by a belt above and below his enormous stomach. The practice of playing fixed characters with stock costumes and makeup suggests how close French farce of this period was to *commedia dell'arte*, a similarity which may have extended to improvisational playing. When Valleran's troupe left Paris in 1612, Gros-Guillaume formed his own company, probably with Gaultier-Garguille, and Turlupin seems to have joined them two years later. When not on tour they rented the Hôtel de Bourgogne and their success was probably key to the building of an audience for professional theatre in the city.

The usual place for performances between 1595 and 1629 was the Hôtel de Bourgogne, since it was the only permanent theatre in Paris. Even though this building was used from 1548 to 1783, its dimensions are uncertain; the most reliable estimate indicates that it was about 40 feet wide and 105 feet long. The first floor was taken up entirely by the pit, or *parterre*, in which there were no permanent seats (with the possible exception of a bench running along each of the side walls). Around the auditorium ran two or three galleries, portions of which were divided into boxes, or *loges*. That part of the first gallery facing the stage was left undivided so as to form the *amphitheatre*. The total capacity of the auditorium was about 1600.

The stage was raised about 6 feet above the pit. Although there was no proscenium arch, the side galleries, which extended to the stage, created a frame. The stage occupied the full width of the building, but the visible space was probably no wider than 25 feet. The depth of the stage is unknown, but estimates range from 17 to 35 feet.

Although the Confrérie probably had used medieval mansions on this stage, the little that is known of scenic practices before 1629 can be summarized briefly: the Confrérie may have owned scenery which it rented with the theatre; Valleran's records show that he sometimes paid painters for scenic pieces; Hardy's extant plays require from three to seven locations, each probably represented by a separate mansion and all arranged around the periphery of the stage as they were to be in the 1630s; the few extant illustrations of farces show a stage with a compartment on either side, and either a cloth or doors at the back (see Fig. 8.3). Since all of the troupes were itinerant, none probably attempted elaborate settings.

For those who did not play at the Bourgogne, the usual choice was a tennis court. Since the Middle Ages, tennis (or *jeu de paume*) had been a favorite European game, and by the sixteenth century many courts were enclosed and roofed. Estimates of the number of courts in Paris in the seventeenth century range from 250 to 1,800. By 1600, the measurements of tennis courts were standardized at about 90 by 30 feet. Thus, they did not differ markedly in size from the Hôtel de Bourgogne. A number of features recommended the use of tennis courts as theatres: the presence of a gallery for spectators along one side or end; the large open floor space; and the row of windows just below the roof which provided ample light. To convert a tennis court into a theatre, therefore,

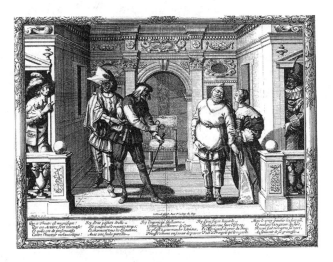

FIG. 8.3
Farce actors at the Hôtel de Bourgogne, c. 1630. On stage are Turlupin, Gaultier-Garguille, and Gros-Guillaume. Engraving by Abraham Bosse. Courtesy Bibliothèque Nationale, Paris.

required primarily the addition of a platform, an operation so simple that it was often done for a single performance. For more permanent conversions, the galleries were extended around the other walls and divided into boxes. Throughout Europe, the tennis court became the first choice of actors seeking buildings to convert into theatres.

In Paris, performances were given two or three times a week during the early seventeenth century. By 1600, posters were being used to advertise productions, and announcements of coming attractions were made from the stage. The starting times varied, but official regulations required that performances end sufficiently early that spectators might reach home before dark. Because the starting time was indefinite and spectators came early to secure good places, each company employed a "prologuist" to entertain the audience until the performance began. Bruscambille (*fl.* 1610–1634) was famous in this role. The daily bill might include a long play followed by a farce, although an entire program might be made up of short plays and variety entertainment. Music was a part of all performances.

The audience was drawn from all classes, but prior to 1629 it was largely undiscriminating in its search for entertainment. Many spectators wore swords or daggers, and fights in the pit were common. Probably there was much jostling and moving about by the up to 1000 persons who might be standing in the pit. The confusion was increased by the sale during performances of food, drink, and other articles.

In 1629 for the first time a company was permitted to settle permanently in Paris. Up to this time, the French theatre fared poorly when compared with the theatres of Italy, Spain, or England, but soon it was to undergo changes that would elevate it above all others in the critical estimate of the time.

THE TRIUMPH OF THE NEOCLASSICAL IDEAL

The stabilization and growth of the theatre paralleled political changes. Under Henri IV, order had been restored but, like his predecessor, Henri was assassinated in 1610, bringing to the throne Louis XIII (reigned 1610–1643), then only nine years old. His mother and her ministers followed policies that stirred up trouble, and the Huguenot question resurfaced because Protestant towns had become so independent as to constitute a nation within the nation. Beginning in the 1620s, the real power behind the throne was Cardinal Richelieu (1586–1642), who, following new civil wars, was able to wrest power from the Protestants and nobles and concentrate it in the crown.

With the return of stability in the 1620s came a resurgence of interest in literature and theatrical performance at court. This renewal had begun somewhat tentatively in the early years of Louis XIII's reign, when in 1610 the *ballet de cour* was revived with *Alcine,* performed in an Italianate perspective setting. During the next ten years, largely due to the importation of such designers as Tomaso Francini (1571–1648), most of the Italian scenic innovations were seen at the French court. At first, sets were composed of painted cloths which could be dropped to reveal others. But in 1617 angled side wings and back shutters were introduced for *The Deliverance of Renaud.* By 1620, perspective scenery, unified settings, the raked stage, and scene shifting were in use at court.

During the 1620s, rekindled interest in neoclassical principles began to affect playwriting. Of the dramatists who began their careers in the late 1620s, four were to be of special importance: Mairet, du Ryer, Rotrou, and Corneille. Jean de Mairet (1604–1686) came to Paris in 1625, the year in which his first play, *Chryséide and Arimand,* a tragicomedy, was performed. In 1626 he turned to writing pastorals, which he helped to popularize through such works as *Sylvie* (1628) and *La Sylvanire* (1631). Soon recognized as the leading dramatist of his day, he confirmed his reputation with *Sophonisba* (1634), the first tragedy of the new age to observe the neoclassical rules. It did much to revive interest in tragedy, which had been dormant since the first years of the century. Although Mairet's reputation has suffered because of his intemperate attack upon Corneille's *Le Cid,* he was as successful and often more highly regarded than Corneille in the 1630s. By the time he retired in 1640, he had probably done more than any other writer of his day to set drama on its new path.

Pierre du Ryer (*c.* 1600–1658), a well-educated government official, wrote prolifically in an attempt to overcome his perennial poverty. His early works were either irregular tragicomedies, such as *Clitophon* (*c.* 1629) and *Argenis and Poliarque* (1631), or farce vehicles for Gros-Guillaume. After coming under Mairet's influence about 1634, however, he turned to tragedy in the neoclassical mode. Of these later works, the best is *Scévole* (1644), which remained in the repertory for more than a century. Along with Mairet and Corneille, du Ryer established tragedy as a popular form.

Jean de Rotrou (1609–1650) began writing plays in 1628, and eventually succeeded Hardy as principal dramatist to the Hôtel de Bourgogne. Through Rotrou's adaptations of Spanish drama, the theme of love versus honor became a staple of the French stage. Interested primarily in rapid and absorbing actions, Rotrou failed to create characters

FIG. 8.4
A tennis court of the type used for remodeling into theatres. Redrawing by Michael Heil from a sixteenth-century French engraving.

of depth. Consequently, his plays now seem shallow, although in their day they did much to extend public interest in drama and offered Corneille his severest competition.

Despite the accomplishments of his contemporaries, Pierre Corneille (1606–1684) is the dramatist most often linked to the triumph of the neoclassical mode in France. Born in Rouen and educated for the law, he began to write plays after seeing the Montdory-LeNoir troupe perform in his hometown. The result was *Mélite* (1629), a comedy unlike either farce or pastoral, the major comic forms of the time. Consequently, *Mélite* is often said to have set French comedy on a new path, one in which the intrigues and misunderstandings of lovers replaced the earlier emphasis on comic servants or sentimental love affairs. Until 1636, most of Corneille's plays were comedies and, though much admired, they served only to establish his reputation as a promising writer.

Le Cid (1636–1637) marked the turning point in Corneille's career and in French drama, for it pre-

cipitated a battle destined to clarify the conflict between the old and new ideals. Based upon Guillén de Castro's *The Youthful Adventures of the Cid,* a play in six acts treating events occurring over eleven years and in many places, Corneille's play compresses the events into five acts, twenty-four hours, and four locations in a single town. Revolving around the theme of love versus honor, the action forces both the hero, Roderigue, and the heroine, Chimène, to choose between their love for each other and their duty to family and state. Although an enormously popular success, it was attacked by several critics, including Mairet and Georges de Scudéry (1601–1667), another leading playwright.

Several issues were raised by *Le Cid*. While the unity of time had been observed, verisimilitude had been strained by crowding numerous and complex incidents (including a war) into one day. Furthermore, Chimène's apparent agreement to marry Roderigue, who has killed her father less than twenty-four hours earlier, violated the neoclassical notion of decorum. The play did not fit any recognized dramatic type: It resembled tragicomedy in the number and variety of incidents, in the perils overcome by the hero, and in the happy ending; it resembled pastoral in the love story; and it resembled tragedy in its narrative and lyrical passages. The bitterness of the controversy prompted Cardinal Richelieu to request a verdict on the play from the newly formed French Academy. The results were destined to focus public attention on the neoclassical ideal.

After his rise to power, Richelieu had used his position to encourage the development of French literature and the arts so that France might become the cultural leader of Europe. Since to Richelieu greatness seemed most likely to be achieved through following the Italian ideals of writing and staging, he encouraged, through financial support and other incentives, those authors who sought to implement the neoclassical ideal. Furthermore, in his own palace he built the first Italianate theatre in France. Perhaps most important, he promoted the formation of the French Academy as an arbiter of literary taste.

The French Academy originated in 1629 when a small group of men began meeting to discuss literature. Hearing of their work, Richelieu urged them to form an organization modeled after the Italian academies. In 1636 they reluctantly did as he wished, and in 1637 the French Academy received the state charter under which it still operates. Membership in the Academy was (and continues to be) restricted to forty, presumably the most eminent literary figures of the age. Upon its formation, the Academy took as its primary task the study and codification of French language and style.

FIG. 8.5
The second scene, "Garden of Delights," from *The Deliverance of Renaud,* produced at the French court in 1617. This seems to have been the first production in France to use angled side wings and back shutters. Courtesy Bibliothèque Nationale, Paris.

It was to this newly formed group that Richelieu referred the controversy over *Le Cid.* The verdict, written principally by the group's leader, Jean Chapelain (1595–1674), was contained in *The Judgment of the Academy on Le Cid* (1638). In it, Chapelain praised *Le Cid* insofar as it adhered to neoclassical doctrine and censured it for all deviations. He also restated the neoclassical ideal and urged its universal adoption.

Although Corneille later embraced neoclassical doctrine, he was stung by the reactions to *Le Cid* and wrote no more plays until 1640. Between 1640 and 1644, however, he produced the works now considered most characteristic of his style: *Horace* (1640), *Cinna* (1640), *Polyeucte* (1642–1643), and *The Death of Pompey* (1643). Each centers around a hero of indomitable will who chooses death rather than dishonor. Since Corneille's protagonists are never in doubt about their goals, they often appear one-sided; never divided within themselves, they are revealed in a series of episodes showing their reactions to external obstacles. Consequently, Corneille's characters are simple, but his plots complex. Beginning with *Rodogune* (1644), Corneille's stories often became so involved that they were difficult to follow. This trend toward complexity was not unique to Corneille's plays, for most dramatists of the time followed the same path until the 1660s when Racine's simplicity began a reaction against it.

Corneille set the standard in comedy as well. His *The Liar* (1643), adapted from Alarcón's *The Suspicious Truth,* is considered the finest French comedy before Molière. Only one other comic writer, Paul Scarron (1610–1660), challenged Corneille's supremacy. Scarron paved the way for Molière by combining the comedy of intrigue, in which Corneille excelled, with farce, most notably in *Jodelet,* or *The Servant The Master* (1643) and *Jodelet Insulted* (1645), both written for the farceur Jodelet. In *The Scholar of Salamanca* (1654) Scarron introduced the character Crispin, who became so popular that other dramatists incorporated him into their plays. Scarron's novel, *A Comical Tale* (1651), is also noteworthy for its depiction of the life of touring actors.

The vigor of the 1640s was followed by a decline in the 1650s. Tragedy lost its appeal and, after the failure of his *Pertharite* in 1652, Corneille gave up writing for many years. (He wrote his last play, *Suréa,* in 1674.) The decline can also be attributed in part to another civil war. Richelieu died in 1642 and Louis XIII in 1643. When Louis XIV (reigned 1643–1715) succeeded to the throne he was only five years old and his mother was named regent, although the major force was Cardinal Mazarin (1602–1661), her chief minister. Mazarin was unpopular not only because he used his position to enrich himself but because he was Italian. The nobility, sensing a chance to regain its old rights, joined together in a movement called La Fronde ("the sling") which developed into open rebellion in 1648. By 1652 the resistance of the nobility had been completely broken and thereafter those of the highest rank were forced to live at court where they could be watched. As a result, all authority was concentrated in the crown, where it was to remain until the Revolution of 1789.

ACTING COMPANIES, 1629–1660

The new vigor in playwriting after 1625 was paralleled by increased stability in acting companies. In contrast with the preceding period, when no troupe was allowed to remain permanently in Paris, a company was permitted to settle in the Hôtel de Bourgogne in 1629, and in 1634 a second company obtained permission to settle in the Théâtre du Marais. Thereafter, Paris continued to have at least two companies competing with one another.

The Bourgogne's troupe was the one established by Gros-Guillaume when Valleran left Paris in 1612. Gaultier-Garguille and Turlupin had joined the company early, and Bellerose (Pierre le Messier, c. 1592–1670), the company's rising star, became a member in 1622. Bellerose had begun as an apprentice in Valleran's company in 1609. After Valleran's death in about 1613 he toured, establishing his own company in Marseille about 1620 before he joined the Gros-Guillaume's troupe. Bellerose was a fine actor in both comedy and tragedy. He brought dignity to the theatre just as the new drama was achieving greater subtlety and as the taste for farce was declining. Noted for his natural style, he was nevertheless accused of affectation by some critics. He became the company leader in 1634 and his supremacy in the troupe remained unchallenged until his retirement in 1647.

The rival troupe was headed by Montdory (Guillaume des Gilleberts, 1594–1654) and Charles LeNoir (fl. 1610–1637). Montdory began his career about 1612 in Valleran's company, and, upon Valleran's death, joined the Prince of Orange's Players. In the late 1620s he formed a company with Charles LeNoir, another actor-manager who had performed in Paris intermittently since 1610. After touring the provinces, they returned to Paris in 1629, bringing with them Corneille's first play, *Mélite*. Because of his preference for the new drama, Montdory soon won the favor of Cardinal Richelieu, who awarded him a subsidy and established the company in the newly converted tennis court, the Théâtre du Marais, in 1634. This was the first serious rival to the Hôtel de Bourgogne.

Le Cid and many of the other outstanding plays of the 1630s were first played by the Montdory company. Sometimes called the first great French actor, Montdory was at his best in the roles of tragic heroes. Although a declamatory actor, he was capable of great emotion and is said to have brought conviction to all his parts. Under Montdory's leadership, the Marais became the leading theatre of Paris, a position which it was to hold until 1647. Unfortunately, Montdory suffered a partial paralysis in 1637 and was forced to retire.

Montdory was replaced at the Marais by Floridor (Josias de Soulas, 1608–1672), an aristocrat who had played in a touring company for many years. Upon Montdory's retirement, Floridor joined the Marais troupe as its leading actor until 1647, when he went to the Bourgogne to replace Bellerose. After Floridor's departure, the Marais declined, for Corneille and other leading dramatists now gave their plays to the Bourgogne. Floridor continued as the leading serious actor of Paris until his retirement in 1671. Floridor shared tragic roles with Montfleury

(Zacharie Jacob, 1600–1667), who joined the Bourgogne company in 1639 and rose rapidly to a position second only to that of Bellerose. Although he was enormously fat and employed a pompous delivery, he had a large following.

The farce tradition was continued by Jodelet and Guillot-Gorju. Jodelet (Julien Bedeau, c. 1600–1660) was a member of Montdory's troupe until ordered by Louis XIII to transfer to the Bourgogne in 1634. In the early 1640s he returned to the Marais, where he was so popular that a number of dramatists wrote plays especially for him. In 1659 he joined Molière, who created some roles for him, although Jodelet's death in 1660 made their association brief. Playing with a flour-whitened face in the manner of Gros-Guillaume, Jodelet was especially noted as the comic valet, a role which he raised to great popularity. Guillot-Gorju (Bertrand Hardouin de St. Jacques, 1600–1648) joined the Bourgogne troupe in 1633 upon the death of Gaultier-Garguille. In the role of the ridiculous doctor, he was famous for his witty repartee. He retired in 1641 to practice medicine, which he had studied prior to going on the stage.

After 1647, the Bourgogne troupe gained the ascendancy that it was to maintain until 1680. Meanwhile, the Marais, in an attempt to retain its popularity, turned increasingly to spectacle. Under the management of Laroque (Pierre Regnault Petit-Jean, c. 1595–1676), it fought a losing battle from 1647 to 1673, when the theatre was closed.

Both the financial and social position of the actor improved between 1629 and 1660. When Richelieu and others began to patronize the Marais troupe in the 1630s, Louis XIII granted the Comédiens du Roi a subsidy. All major troupes after this time received subsidies. Concern for the actor's dignity also began to grow around 1630. Gougenot's *La Comédie des Comédiens* (c. 1631), a play depicting a rehearsal, defends actors from the charge of immorality, and Georges de Scudéry's play of the same title, performed in 1632, takes the same position. Scudéry argues that actors, like the members of other professions, vary and that each should be judged on merit. Scudéry also lists the characteristics of the good actor: appropriate facial expression, impressive bearing, unconstrained movement, absence of extravagant posturing and provincial accent, a good memory, and sound judgment.

In 1641 Louis XIII sought to remove the stigma attached to acting by issuing a decree stating his desire that "the actors' profession . . . not be considered worthy of blame nor prejudicial to their reputation in society." But though it abolished certain legal restrictions, this decree did not alter the church's decrees, under which actors were supposed to be denied the sacraments—including baptism, marriage, and death rites. But whether these decrees were enforced depended much on actors' moral reputations in their own parishes and the judgment of the parish priest.

THE PUBLIC THEATRES, 1629–1660

The major public theatres of Paris between 1629 and 1660 were the Hôtel de Bourgogne and the Théâtre du Marais. Presumably the physical attributes of the Bourgogne (already described) remained relatively unchanged from 1548 until 1647, when, by order of the King's Council, it was remodeled, probably in order to compete more effectively with the Marais.

Almost nothing is known of the first Théâtre du Marais, which was converted from a tennis court in 1634. When it burned in 1644, it was replaced immediately with a more elaborate structure that remained in use until 1673. The new Marais measured about 115 feet in length, 38 feet in width, and 52 feet in height. The pit, for standing spectators, was about 61 feet by 38 feet; the side walls had three galleries, the first two divided into boxes, the third given over to an undivided space, the *paradis;* at the rear of

FIG. 8.6
Pierre Corneille's *Polyeucte*. In this scene pagan statues are being thrown down and destroyed. From the first edition of the play, 1643. Courtesy Lilly Library, Indiana University.

the auditorium, the first two galleries were divided into boxes, and above them rose the amphitheatre with its stadium-like seating. The capacity of the auditorium was about 1500 persons.

The stage, raised about 6 feet above the *parterre*, sloped upward toward the back. It occupied the full width of the building and had a proscenium opening 25 feet wide. There was also a *théâtre supérieure*, or second stage, raised almost 13 feet above the main platform. Semicircular, it curved upstage 6 feet at its center. But though documents clearly show that the Marais had a *théâtre supérieure*, scholars disagree about its size and placement. The reconstruction of the stage made by Deierkauf-Holsboer had the second stage begin only 6 feet in back of the front edge of the main platform and consequently she shows the lower stage as being only about 13 feet deep at its center. Bjurstrom, on the other hand, suggests that the lower stage was about 29 feet deep at its center, and Golder argues for 19½ feet. Bjurstrom and Golder's reconstructions seem more logical than Deierkauf-Holsboer's, especially in light of the Marais's emphasis upon spectacle. On the other hand, much of the spectacle may have depended upon the upper stage. Since it might represent the "heavens," flying objects could rest on the upper stage in back of clouds used to conceal the platform. It is clear from many scripts, however, that not all flying was handled in this manner, and some scholars have questioned whether it was ever the usual method. Scholars also disagree about the use made of the second stage. Some argue that it was essential to almost every play, while others state it was rarely employed. Although its precise use cannot be established, the *théâtre supérieure* was unquestionably available at both the Marais and the Bourgogne, although in the latter theatre it may have been removable.

It was probably the need to compete more effectively with the new Marais that led to the remodeling of the Bourgogne in 1647. The imprecise contract for the changes still exists. It specifies that the stage is to be some 45 feet deep and "as wide as the building" (about 40 feet). The floor was raked upward toward the back and beams were installed at the front, probably to accommodate a curtain and to form a proscenium arch, neither of which apparently was used earlier. The stage opening was about 25 feet wide. In the auditorium, the galleries were curved into a U-shape to eliminate the former sharp angles at the rear corners. In spite of the remodeling, the Hôtel de Bourgogne remained the Parisian theatre least concerned with spectacle. Additional changes were made in 1656 to allow for increased spectacle and special effects.

SCENIC PRACTICES IN THE PUBLIC THEATRES, 1629–1660

The scenic practices of the early 1630s are well documented in *Le Mémoire de Mahelot, Laurent, et d'Autres Décorateurs,* . . . one of the most valuable theatrical records of the seventeenth century. This document is divided into three parts, each relating to widely separated years. The first part ends in 1635. Some scholars assume that it summarizes only the season of 1634–1635, while others argue that it records usage from about 1622 to 1635. It consists of seventy-one notices (that is, summaries of the scenic requirements) and forty-seven designs for plays in the repertory of the Hôtel de Bourgogne. Most scholars believe that the designs are by the compiler, Laurent Mahelot, although others have suggested that Mahelot was merely the theatre's machinist and that the designs are by George Buffequin, the major scenic designer of the period.

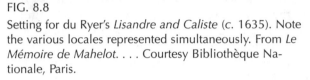

FIG. 8.8
Setting for du Ryer's *Lisandre and Caliste* (c. 1635). Note the various locales represented simultaneously. From *Le Mémoire de Mahelot.* . . . Courtesy Bibliothèque Nationale, Paris.

Mahelot's compilation demonstrates clearly that in 1635 scenic practices in the public theatres were still essentially medieval. Since the unity of place was not yet common, most plays required a number of locales, each of which was represented by a mansion. All mansions were present simultaneously, arranged along the sides and across the back of the stage to leave the center free for the actors. The back scene usually represented a single place, but typically there were two mansions on each side. Many of the mansions were of such a general nature—a house, a wood, a palace, a grotto, a cave, a tomb, a prison, a tent, a seacoast—that they reappeared in a number of different plays. When a play required more mansions than could be accommodated on stage at once, units were converted by removing painted canvas coverings or by opening curtains to reveal an interior.

A few visual characteristics relate these simultaneous settings to Italian perspective scenery: Some of the backcloths are painted in perspective; balanced pairs of mansions sometimes resemble Serlio's arrangement of angled wings; in some settings decorative details are repeated from one mansion to another to give greater unity to the whole. In spite of these superficial similarities, however, the effect is clearly more medieval than Italianate.

A few machines and special effects are mentioned by Mahelot: Gods and other supernatural characters appear above the stage; boats with passengers move from one side of the stage to the other; clouds, fire, smoke, and sound effects are specified. Properties, such as human heads and sponges filled with blood, are noted. Furniture seems to have been restricted to an occasional throne or stool.

FIG. 8.7
Setting for Act V of *Le Martyre de Sainte Catherine* by Jean Puget de la Serre, produced at the Hôtel de Bourgogne, 1643. In this production the basic structure remained fixed, while the view behind the central doorway and on the upper level changed with each act. The scene on the upper level apparently made use of the *théâtre supérieure*. From the original edition of the play. Courtesy Bibliothèque Nationale, Paris.

Le Mémoire also gives some information about costumes, since it lists all items supplied by the company. It reveals that actors supplied their own garments except for the roles of devils, ghosts, monks, coachmen, and valets, or when a number of identical costumes were required. The governing principle seems to have been that the company supplied those costumes that an actor could not reasonably be expected to own.

The second part of the *Mémoire* lists seventy-one titles of works in the repertory of the Hôtel de Bourgogne in 1646–1647, but unfortunately it includes neither "notices" nor designs. It may be assumed that by this time scenic practices had moved from simultaneous to unified settings as unity of place was adopted following the controversy over *Le Cid*. Certainly by 1680 settings were appreciably simpler than in 1635.

THE TRIUMPH OF THE ITALIAN IDEAL IN SCENERY, 1640–1660

Although Italianate scenery had been introduced at court before 1625, its use did not become a matter of artistic principle until after 1640. Perhaps to provide a model, Cardinal Richelieu had the architect LeMercier construct in his palace the first theatre in France with a permanent proscenium arch and a stage designed to use flat wings. This theatre, commonly called the Palais Cardinal, had a stage 59 feet wide by 46 feet deep, and an auditorium 59 feet wide by 65 feet deep. Two undivided galleries surrounded the hall, while most of the ground floor was taken up by an amphitheatre that rose in broad steps from a small pit. Since the theatre was intended only for invited guests, the auditorium did not follow the arrangement used in the public theatres.

The Palais Cardinal was opened in January 1641 with *Mirame,* scenery and special effects for which were designed by Georges Buffequin. Since *Mirame* required only one setting, the potentialities of the theatre were not fully displayed until later in 1641 when the *Ballet de la Prospérité des Armes de la France,* with nine settings, was produced. When Richelieu died in 1642, the theatre came under the control of the crown and thereafter was called the Palais Royal.

Richelieu's successor as Chief Minister, Cardinal Mazarin, had a taste for opera, a form that he sought to promote in France. His first production, in 1645, set in motion a series of events that were to bring Giacomo Torelli to Paris. A visiting *commedia dell'arte* troupe, fearing the power of opera, became so anxious over Mazarin's plans that it begged the queen to import a designer and choreographer from Italy

FIG. 8.9
Theatre built by Cardinal Richelieu in his palace in 1641. Seen in the foreground (right to left) are Richelieu, Louis XIII, and the Queen. After Richelieu's death, this theatre was called the Palais Royal.

to ensure the appeal of its own productions. Consequently, the queen wrote to the Duke of Parma, who sent Torelli in response to her request.

By 1645, Torelli was probably the most famous scene designer in Italy because of his productions at the Teatro Novissimo in Venice. Torelli accepted the royal summons without realizing that he was to work with *commedia dell'arte* players. Upon learning the truth, he at first refused to cooperate, but eventually he agreed upon the condition that he be allowed to design operatic productions as well. For his first opera

FIG. 8.10
La Prospérité des Armes de la France as performed at Cardinal Richelieu's new theatre in 1641. Note the figures atop the walls and the chariot in the sky. Courtesy Theatre Museum, Drottningholm.

FIG. 8.11
Giacomo Torelli's setting for Act II of Pierre Corneille's *Andromède* at the Petit Bourbon, 1650. Engraving by François Chauveau. Courtesy Bibliothèque Nationale, Paris.

in Paris, in 1645, he chose *La Finta Pazza,* the work that had made him famous in Venice. To house this opera, Torelli converted the Petit Bourbon into an Italianate theatre. He erected a platform 6 feet high to make a stage about 49 feet wide by 48 feet deep, somewhat larger than the one he had used in Venice. He also installed his chariot-and-pole system of scene shifting, probably his only major improvement over Richelieu's theatre. Performed for the court, the opera was a complete success. Most historians date the full triumph of the Italian ideal in France from this production.

In 1646 Torelli remodeled the Palais Royal to accommodate the chariot-and-pole method of shifting, and in 1647 *Orphée* was staged there at a tremendous cost, which Mazarin paid for out of state funds. The presence of so many Italians, the hostility which the French nobles felt against Mazarin, and the use of state money to finance operas aroused considerable resentment. Mazarin, seeking works more compatible with French taste, then commissioned Corneille to write *Andromède,* which when finished was labeled a "play with machines" since it differed considerably from Italian opera. *Andromède* was like regular drama in that its story progressed through spoken episodes, but resembled opera in that each act provided an excuse to introduce elaborate machinery and special effects during a pantomimic episode accompanied by music. Most of the scenery

and machinery used for Corneille's play had already appeared in *Orphée*. Staged at the Petit Bourbon in 1650, *Andromède* was successful enough to begin a vogue for "machine" plays, one that the Marais sought to meet with such productions as *The Golden Fleece, The Loves of Jupiter and Semele, The Loves of Venus and Adonis,* and *The Marriage of Bacchus and Ariadne.* Eventually the Marais was virtually bankrupted by the sums required to mount these spectacles.

In the late 1640s ballet began to recapture the popularity it had enjoyed at court before 1620. It was especially prominent between 1651 and 1660, when Louis XIV appeared in many of the productions. Called *ballets d'entrées,* these entertainments did not require the proficiency in dance technique needed for modern ballet. They were allegorical stories, explained by a spoken libretto and pantomimed by performers in movements based upon ballroom dances of the time, although these dances were often given elaborate choreographic patterns. One of the most characteristic works, *The Ballet of the Night* (1653), was divided into forty-three "entries," featuring such groups as hunters, bandits, shepherds, gypsies, astrologers, the Four Elements, Venus, and Aurora, each related to a different phase of the night. Finally, the Sun, danced by Louis XIV, appeared to disperse the darkness. This piece of transparent flattery was one of many works that helped to create the image of Louis XIV as the "Sun King" (around which everything revolves), a symbol promoted assiduously throughout his reign.

In 1654 Mazarin, seeking once more to adapt opera to French taste, commissioned Isaac Bensérade (1613–1691), who had composed the librettos for the majority of the court ballets, to write an opera with ballets interspersed between the acts. For this production, *The Marriage of Peleus and Thetis,* Torelli designed seven sets and a number of spectacular special effects. Louis XIV appeared in six roles. Thus, opera and ballet were joined in a relationship that would continue thereafter. After Louis gave up performing around 1660, dance was professionalized, especially after Louis established the Royal Academy of Dance in 1661.

THE NATURALIZATION OF THE ITALIAN IDEAL, 1660–1700

In 1660 Louis XIV married Marie Thérèse of Spain, and in 1661 Mazarin died. These two events mark the coming of age of Louis, who thereafter assumed complete control over governmental affairs. By this time, the crown's power was so firmly established that Louis could convincingly declare, "I am the State."

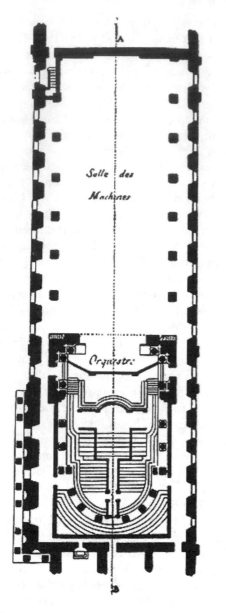

FIG. 8.12

Plan of the Salle des Machines designed by Gaspare Vigarani and first used in 1662. From L. P. de la Guepière, *Théâtre et Machine* (1888).

During the years that followed, French artists developed their own distinctive version of the baroque visual style, appropriately called Louis Quatorze.

The innovations in scenic practice that had been introduced by Torelli were strengthened by the preparations made for the marriage of Louis XIV. In 1659 Mazarin sent to Italy for Gaspare Vigarani (1586–1663), famous at this time as a scenic designer and builder of theatres. The Petit Bourbon was torn down, and a new wing was added to the Tuileries Palace. Within this wing Vigarani constructed the largest theatre in Europe, the Salle des Machines. Al-

though only 52 feet wide, the new theatre was 232 feet long; of this length, only 92 feet were occupied by the auditorium, leaving 140 feet of depth for a stage which had a proscenium arch only 32 feet wide. This enormous depth is symptomatic of the trend then underway toward settings of ever-increasing size. Completed in 1660, the Salle des Machines was inaugurated in 1662 with the opera *Hercules in Love*, a transparent compliment to the king. Interlayered with ballets, the opera featured Vigarani's scenery and machines, on one of which, 60 feet deep by 45 feet wide, the entire royal family and their attendants were flown. This machine was used again in *Psyché* (1671) to display 300 deities surrounded by clouds. Despite this auspicious beginning, the Salle des Machines was seldom used after the 1660s because of its size and poor acoustics.

When Mazarin imported Vigarani, he had not intended to exclude Torelli, but the latter's enemies rallied around Vigarani, and after Mazarin died in 1661 Torelli was ordered to leave France. He returned to his native Fano, where he later built a theatre. There he staged his last production in 1677, the year before he died. Although Torelli left Paris under a cloud, the primary credit for establishing the Italian ideal in France must go to him. When Vigarani died in 1663, his post as court designer was given to his son, Carlo (1623–1713), who retained it until 1680. Carlo Vigarani's principal work was done at the opera in Paris and at the court at Versailles.

After 1660 Louis XIV's attention turned increasingly to the palace he was building at Versailles twelve miles outside of Paris. Eventually this palace would be more than a half mile long with several wings and hundreds of rooms. While it was being built, Louis staged several festivals there, using temporary theatres set up at various spots in the palace grounds. One of the most spectacular of the celebrations was that of 1664, called "The Pleasures of the Enchanted Island," which extended over three days, and included processions, tournaments, ballets, and plays.

Throughout the 1660s, "comedy ballets," in which scenes in dialogue alternate with ballet entries, were a favorite with Louis. Many of these were written by Molière and Jean-Baptiste Lully (1632–1687), destined to become the founder of French opera. Lully was born in Italy, but came to France when only twelve years old. Appointed a court musician in 1653, by 1661 he was superintendent of all court music. In this capacity, he worked closely with Molière and others on court entertainment, and his experience with ballets, machine plays, and other forms familiarized him with French musical taste. In 1672 he obtained a monopoly on musical per-

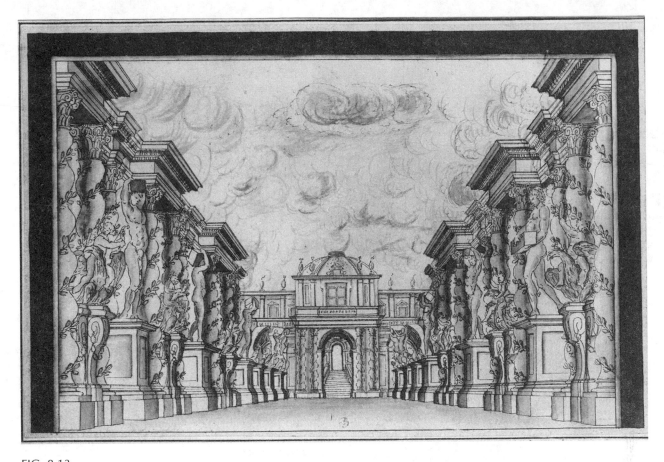

FIG. 8.13
Design by Vigarani, c. 1660. Courtesy National Museum, Stockholm.

formances in Paris from Louis XIV, and in 1673 after Molière's death, he wrested control of the Palais Royal from Molière's widow to use as the home of his Royal Academy of Music and Dance (created in 1672 by the amalgamation of the Royal Academy of Dance and the Royal Academy of Music), more commonly called simply the Opéra. Although the terms of Lully's monopoly were vague, he interpreted them to cover any performance that required more than six instruments, two trained singers, or elaborate spectacle. The latter provision is indicative of the period's association of spectacle with opera, for, as the neoclassical ideal triumphed in drama, staging had become increasingly simple. Lully's monopoly put an end to the "machine plays" at the Marais and thus further weakened that company, which had steadily declined since 1647.

Between 1672 and 1687 Lully created a series of works considered to mark the beginnings of French opera. His principal collaborator was Phillippe Quinault (1635–1688), author of fourteen librettos, of which the most famous are *Atys* (1676) and *Armide* (1686). Until 1680, when he returned to Italy, Vigarani designed the scenery for these operas.

Vigarani was succeeded by Jean Berain *père* (1637–1711). Educated entirely in France, Berain is credited with the first complete realization of the visual style associated with the reign of Louis XIV. Employed at court in 1671 to design embroidery, tapestry, woodcarving, and furniture, he succeeded Henri Gissey as "Designer of the Cabinet of the King" in 1674. Since Gissey had customarily designed costumes for the opera, Berain also assumed this job. After 1680, Berain was principal designer for the court and the opera until his death, when he was succeeded by his son, Jean Berain *fils* (1678–1726), who held the posts until 1721. To the Berains goes the credit for establishing a distinctively French style of design emphasizing heavy line, reverse curves, and encrusted ornamentation. Most of the operas designed by Berain required only one set but many machines and special effects for each act. This combination of static scenery and dynamic machinery was to remain typical of French operatic design through the eighteenth century.

In 1682 Louis moved the seat of government to Versailles, and forced all of France's leading noblemen to live there so he might keep an eye on them.

FIG. 8.14

One of the entertainments from the first day of "Pleasures of the Enchanted Island," given by Louis XIV at Versailles in 1664. The stage in the middle of a lake represents the palace of Alcine; after an elaborate ballet was performed there, the palace was destroyed by fire. A contemporary engraving by Israel Silvestre.

FIG. 8.16

Berain's costume design for an Indian in *The Triumph of Love*, 1681. From Adolphe Jullien, *Histoire du Costume au Thèâtre* (1880).

By this time the nobility had become relatively powerless, though it had been deprived of none of its major privileges. Forced to live at court, the nobles lost touch with lesser ranks, especially those in the provinces. Versailles not only became the symbol of the king's absolute power, but also of the conditions that led to the French Revolution a century later.

By the time the court moved to Versailles, the Italian ideals of staging had been completely naturalized, and France had replaced Italy as the cultural center of Europe. Court taste had been decisive in this process. After 1682, however, the influence of the court on the Parisian stage declined, no doubt because after the move to Versailles courtiers no longer made up such a significant part of the audience.

FIG. 8.15

Jean Berain's design for Lully's opera, *Armide* (1686). Courtesy National Museum, Stockholm.

FRENCH DRAMA, 1660–1700

Court taste played a crucial role in the development of French drama. Following its decline during the Fronde rebellion, drama began to recover in the late 1650s. Tragedy returned to favor with *Timocrate* (1656) by Thomas Corneille (1625–1709), younger brother of Pierre Corneille. Author of more than forty plays, the best of which are *Ariane* (1672), *The Statue's Banquet* (1673), and *The Count of Essex* (1678), Thomas Corneille was one of the most successful dramatists of his time, although his reputation has suffered by comparison with that of his

200   CHAPTER 8

FIG. 8.17
Scene from Racine's *Bérénice,* first performed in 1670 at the Hôtel de Bourgogne with Mlle Champmeslé in the title role. Engraving from the edition of Racine's plays published in 1676.

brother. Pierre Corneille also returned to writing in 1659 with *Oedipe* and continued until 1674.

Although many of Pierre Corneille's late works are of unquestioned merit, they are overshadowed by Jean Racine's (1639–1699) plays, with which French tragedy reached its peak. Racine received an excellent education which instilled in him a lasting admiration of the Greek dramatists, whose example he sought to follow. His first tragedy, *La Thébaide,* was produced in 1664 by Molière, who, in spite of the financial failure of the play, also produced Racine's second work, *Alexander the Great* (1665). Dissatisfied with the production, Racine permitted the Hôtel de Bourgogne to present the same play two weeks later, an unprecedented breach of contract. Furthermore, Racine allegedly induced Mlle Du-Parc, Molière's principal tragic actress, to join the Hôtel de Bourgogne troupe. This double treachery led to a permanent rupture between the two men.

Racine's reputation, established by *Andromaque* in 1667, grew steadily during the next ten years with *Britannicus* (1669), *Bérénice* (1670) *Bajazet* (1672), *Mithridate* (1673), *Iphigénie* (1674), and *Phèdre* (1677). After *Phèdre,* Racine gave up playwriting, in part because his enemies had contrived to make a success of Jacques Pradon's (1632–1698) *Phèdre,* produced simultaneously with Racine's play, and his own a relative failure. At this time, Racine was appointed historiographer to

Louis XIV and abandoned his literary life. Some years later he wrote *Esther* (1689) and *Athalie* (1691) for Mme de Maintenon's (Louis XIV's second wife) school for girls at St. Cyr. Neither play was performed professionally during his lifetime. In addition to his tragedies, Racine wrote one comedy, *The Litigants* (1668), based in part on Aristophanes' *The Wasps.*

Racine's reputation is based on the tragedies written between 1667 and 1677, of which *Phèdre* (whose uncontrollable passion for her stepson Hippolyte brings disaster) is the acknowledged masterpiece. Racine's greatness stems from his ability to develop compelling dramatic actions out of the internal conflicts of his protagonists. In contrast with Corneille's use of simple characters and complex plots, Racine constructed simple plots and complex characters. Because Racine's protagonists vacillate between two courses of action, torn between their sense of duty and their uncontrollable desires, dramatic interest is centered on the inner struggle rather than on the external events, which are important only as they contribute to the inner crisis. The plays usually begin some time after the protagonists have become aware of a dilemma. In a state of high emotion, they usually lay their souls bare to *confidants* during the opening scene. Although no information is withheld, neither the audience nor the characters can foresee the outcome. The protagonist's psychological struggle makes up the dramatic action. Therefore, Racine was able to express his tragic vision adequately within the confines of the neoclassical ideal. Upon Racine's retirement, tragedy began a long decline, although this was not immediately apparent, since at the time other writers seemed worthy successors.

Like tragedy, comedy reached its peak in the 1660s and 1670s. As Racine represents the summit in tragic writing, so Molière epitomizes comic dramaturgy. Building upon the comedy of intrigue popularized by Corneille and Scarron, Molière added new interest through characterization. With his work, comedy was raised to a level equaling tragedy.

Molière (Jean-Baptiste Poquelin, 1622–1673), the son of a prosperous upholsterer and furniture maker, was given an excellent education and was destined for a court position until he joined with nine other young people to form the Théâtre Illustre in 1643. Having failed in Paris, the troupe set off on a tour of the provinces in 1646, which lasted until 1658. At this time, numerous companies were touring France, and Molière's company soon joined with that of Charles Dufresne (*c.* 1611–*c.* 1684). By 1651, Molière was head of the troupe. He then turned to writing plays, his first important work being *The Blunderer,* performed at Lyons in 1655.

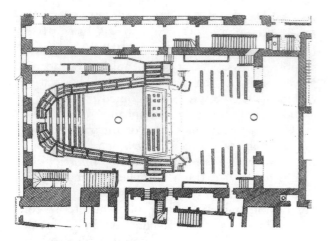

FIG. 8.18

Plan of the Palais Royal. This theatre was built by Richelieu and remodeled by Torelli. It served as the home of Molière's company from 1660 until 1673, and was used by the Opéra from 1673 until 1763, when it was destroyed by fire. Note the seatless pit (marked O at left). From Blondel, *Architecture Française* (1754).

"comedy ballets," such as *The Bores* (1661), *The Forced Marriage* (1664), *The Princess of Elide* (1664), and *Monsieur de Pourceaugnac* (1669). Others, such as *Amphitryon* (1668) and *Psyché* (1671) were "machine plays" with much spectacle. On most of the court plays, Molière collaborated with Lully, who provided the music. Molière attempted serious drama, as in *Don Garcie de Navarre* (1661), but with little success.

Molière's great achievements are his comedies of character and manners, such as *The School for Husbands* (1661), *The School for Wives* (1662), *Tartuffe* (1664, 1667, 1669), *The Misanthrope* (1666), *The Miser* (1668), *The Learned Ladies* (1672), and *The Imaginary Invalid* (1673). His observations on contemporary manners and character types in these works embroiled him in much controversy. The first important battle was precipitated by *The School for Wives* (1662), which treated the upbringing appropriate to young girls who are to be faithful wives. Although enormously popular, the play was attacked

The turning point in the troupe's fortunes came in 1658 when it was invited to court by the king's brother, who had seen it perform in the provinces. The company was sufficiently well received to be granted permission to settle in Paris, the title Troupe de Monsieur, and the use of the Petit Bourbon for public performances.

The company was not very successful with the public, however, until it presented Molière's *Les Précieuses Ridicules* (*The Affected Ladies,* 1659), a satire on contemporary affectations. After this production, its fortunes were assured. When the Petit Bourbon was torn down, Molière was allowed to use the Palais Royal, built by Richelieu and remodeled by Torelli. Here the company played from 1660 until 1673, enjoying a position of preeminence in comedy similar to that attained by the Bourgogne in tragedy. In 1665 they were granted an annual subsidy and the title "The King's Troupe." The Marais, meanwhile, was relegated to the third rank.

The reputation of the Palais Royal troupe derived primarily from Molière's plays, the core of its repertory. Now remembered principally for his comedies of character, Molière wrote other kinds of plays as well. Many of his works are farces in the manner of the *commedia dell'arte,* by which he was much influenced. Some of the most popular of these were *Sganarelle,* or *The Imaginary Cuckold* (1660), *The Doctor in Spite of Himself* (1666), and *The Tricks of Scapin* (1671). Other works were written especially for court festivities, although most were later performed for the general public. A large number of these were

FIG. 8.19

Scene from Molière's *The Learned Ladies,* first performed at the Palais Royal in 1672 with Molière in the role of Chrysale (at left). From the edition of Molière's plays published in 1682.

on both artistic and moral grounds. Molière answered in two plays: *The Critique of The School for Wives* (1663) and *The Rehearsal at Versailles* (1663). By far the bitterest controversy centered around *Tartuffe*, a play in which the title character is exposed as a religious hypocrite. Many saw this as a condemnation of all religion when it was performed at court in 1664, and Molière had to rewrite it twice (in 1667 and 1669) before it was authorized for performance. The 1669 production ran for thirty-three performances, a record for the time.

These quarrels clearly indicate that Molière had made comedy a vital reflection of contemporary life and manners. Still, there is little bitterness in his plays, for though he ridiculed customs and character types, he did not believe that humans could be changed. He shows human nature being deformed by various kinds of deviant behavior but he does not imply that it can be perfected. Consequently, his characters remain much the same (though often having exchanged one extreme position for another) at the end of the plays as at the beginning. This probably explains why his resolutions, usually brought about by some external force, are often criticized. When, as in *The Misanthrope*, no external power intervenes, the action remains unresolved.

In his long plays, Molière usually conforms to the neoclassical ideal of five acts and the unities. Some of the plays are written in verse, others in prose. Although his language is varied, it is rarely witty for its own sake; aptness to character and situation is the secret of his dialogue. Many of his plays are set in drawing rooms, a clear departure from previous comedy, which had usually been placed out of doors in the manner of Roman comedy. With Molière, the settings are a reflection of the manners and characters depicted, and his example did much to popularize the interior setting for comedy. Molière wrote for his own company and knew who would play each character. Furthermore, he directed his own plays and often played the leading role himself. Hence, details were probably added during rehearsals that are not explicitly stated in the scripts.

ACTING COMPANIES, 1660–1700

When Molière died in 1673, Paris had five professional troupes: Molière's, Lully's opera company, a *commedia dell'arte* troupe, and the companies at the Hôtel de Bourgogne and at the Marais. All received some financial assistance from the crown. By 1700, only two would remain.

At Molière's death, many doubted his company's ability to continue. To allay anxieties, the troupe

FIG. 8.20
Angelo Constantini receiving Arlequin's mask and baton from Columbine. In the background are seen the figure and tomb of Domenico Biancolelli, the Arlequin who has died. This is the *commedia dell'arte* company that played in France from 1661 until 1697. Watercolor by Lichery, 1688. Courtesy Bibliothèque Nationale, Paris.

resumed performances after one week. Soon, however, a number of actors seceded, and Lully was able to evict the troupe from the Palais Royal. The company sought control of the theatre in the rue Guénégaud, which had housed Lully's troupe, but the Marais company also was vying for it. Louis XIV intervened by ordering the closing of the Marais and the amalgamation of the two companies. The combined groups opened at the Guénégaud in July 1673.

This situation continued until 1679, when Mlle Champmeslé, the Bourgogne's principal tragic actress, left that company to join the troupe at the Guénégaud and the Bourgogne's leading tragic actor, LaThorillière, died. This crisis was also resolved by a crown order joining the two companies. Thus came

FIG. 8.21

The expulsion of the Italian actors from Paris in 1697. An engraving based on a painting by Watteau. Courtesy British Museum.

into existence the Comédie Française, the world's first national theatre. The new company gave its first performance on August 25, 1680, at the theatre in the rue Guénégaud.

Upon its formation, the Comédie Française was given a monopoly on the performance of all spoken drama in French. (The Confrérie de la Passion had been dissolved in 1677.) Almost immediately, however, an exception to this monopoly was granted the *commedia dell'arte* troupe headed by Tiberio Fiorillo (1608–1694) that had made Paris its permanent home since 1661 and had begun to perform in French. Other famous actors in this company were Domenico Biancolelli (*c.* 1637–1688), a favorite of Louis XIV and the popularizer of Arlequin in France; Marc'Antonio Romagnesi (*c.* 1633–1706), who at first played the lover and later Dottore; and Angelo Costantini, who made many innovations in the character Mezzetin. When the Comédie Française was installed at the rue Guénégaud in 1680, the *commedia* troupe was assigned the Hôtel de Bourgogne, which it refurbished, adding a third level of *loges,* remodeling the stage, and installing machinery that permitted the use of complex spectacle.

During the 1690s, as the *commedia* troupe's popularity increased with the middle classes it declined with the court, with which it was often in trouble because of the audacity of its plays. Nevertheless, it overcame all difficulties until 1697, when it was expelled from France. The reason for this expulsion is not entirely clear, although most often it is attributed to the troupe's alleged performance of *The False Prude,* a supposed satire on Mme de Maintenon, Louis XIV's second wife. Other factors may have

been involved, among them intrigues by the Comédie Française to be rid of competition, and the crown's desire to cease its financial support to the Italians at a time when the government was heavily in debt. Whatever the reasons, there were to be no more Italian troupes in Paris until 1716. Thus, in 1697 the Parisian companies were reduced to two: the Comédie Française and the Opéra.

THE ORGANIZATION OF FRENCH ACTING COMPANIES

All of the French acting companies of the seventeenth century were organized on the sharing plan, under which all regular members participated in the management and divided the profits. The number of members varied with the company's prosperity. Before 1650, there were usually eight to twelve; when Molière returned to Paris in 1658, his troupe included ten members, but was increased to twelve (seven men and five women) in 1659. When the Comédie Française was formed in 1680, 21¼ shares were divided among twenty-seven members (17 full shares, 7 one-half shares, and 3 one-quarter shares). Thus, an actor's share varied according to his or her importance in the company.

Since the number of shares in the Comédie Française was fixed by the First Gentlemen of the Chamber (the court officials who superintended the troupe), not all the actors were sharing members (or *sociétaires*). No new member could be admitted as a sharer until an actor resigned, retired, or died. When a vacancy occurred, the *sociétaires* elected a new member, usually from among the *pensionnaires* (the actors who worked for the troupe on salary). To obtain a position with the Comédie Française, actors were required to play a series of roles in regular public performances; if the troupe wished to retain them, they placed them on salary until a vacancy in membership occurred, although many *pensionnaires* never became *sociétaires*. When they became *sociétaires*, actors bound themselves to the company for twenty years and made themselves liable to a heavy fine if they quit. The *sociétaires* had a voice in all matters of policy, including the acceptance of new plays. The actor with the longest service acted as head (or *doyen*) of the troupe. The Comédie Française also continued the pension system that had evolved among the earlier troupes. Under it, actors could retire after twenty years of service with an annual pension. The government also continued to provide the troupe with an annual subsidy.

A member of the Comédie Française had considerable security, but an assured position as a *socié-*

204 CHAPTER 8

www.ablongman.com/brockett9e

taire sometimes led to complacency and arrogance. The opportunities for employment had also been considerably restricted, since after 1680 Paris had only one troupe for French spoken drama.

Of the actors who achieved fame in the years between 1660 and 1700, several were associated with Molière. Madeleine Béjart (1618–1672) was already an established provincial actress when Molière met her. She is credited with inducing him to become an actor and was intimately involved in his work until her death. In the early years she often played tragic heroines, but later she was best as the saucy maids of Molière's comedies. Geneviève (*c.* 1622–1675); Joseph (*c.* 1620–1659), who played young lovers; and Louis Béjart (1625–1678), who played comic valets, were also members of the troupe. Armande Béjart (1642–1700), who became Molière's wife in 1662, made her debut in 1663 and thereafter played the heroines in his plays. A versatile actress, she did much to hold the company together after her husband's death. In 1677 she married Isaac François Guérin d'Etriché (*c.* 1636–1728), who acted until he was past eighty and had become *doyen* of the Comédie Française.

Along with Molière's wife, LaGrange (Charles Varlet, *c.* 1639–1692) was responsible for the continuation of Molière's company. Employed in 1659 to replace Joseph Béjart, he played a variety of roles (including young lovers) and also kept the company's records until 1685. His *Registre,* which records receipts, performances, and all deliberations, is the principal source of information about Molière's troupe and the early years of the Comédie Française. LaGrange also wrote the only contemporary biography of Molière, published in 1682 in the first edition of Molière's works.

Of tragic performers, the most important were Mlle DuParc, Mlle Champmeslé, and Michel Baron. Mlle DuParc (1633–1668) joined Molière's troupe in the provinces and remained with him until 1666, when Racine is said to have lured her to the Bourgogne, where she became the leading tragic actress. Mlle Champmeslé (1642–1698) came to the Marais in 1669, also after a career in the provinces. Within six months she was considered the finest tragic actress in Paris and had moved to the Bourgogne. She retained her position of supremacy until her death, creating such great tragic roles as Phèdre. Supposedly her desertion of the Bourgogne motivated the formation of the Comédie Française. She passed on her declamatory style to two of her pupils, Mlle Desmares and Mlle Duclos, the leading tragic actresses of the early eighteenth century.

The void left at the Bourgogne by the death of Montfleury in 1667 and the retirement of Floridor in 1671 was not filled until Michel Baron (1653–1729) deserted Molière's troupe in 1673. Baron had been a child actor even before Molière took him into his home in 1666 and trained him further. His adult career began in 1670 as Domitien in Corneille's *Titus and Bérénice.* By the time of Molière's death, Baron was noted as a fine actor of the natural school; soon after he joined the Bourgogne in 1673, he was recognized as the leading tragic actor of the day and continued to be so regarded until he retired in 1691. (His return to the stage in 1720 will be considered later.) To many, Baron was the epitome of great acting and the finest serious actor of the seventeenth century.

Actors were not as yet employed to play a specified range of character types, as they were to be in the eighteenth century, although type casting seems often to have been used. A new play was cast by the author, and actors were forbidden to refuse a role. Old plays were cast by the company in consultation. Rehearsals, perfunctory by modern standards, were held in the late morning. Although authors allegedly staged their own plays, they probably relied heavily upon the advice of a leading actor. Once a play had been performed, the actors were considered ready to present it at any time thereafter. There were usually about seventy plays in the active repertory, and these plays were rotated in a daily change of bill.

Until the 1650s, authors were paid a fixed sum for each play. Subsequently they were assigned two shares for the initial run, after which there were no further payments. As long as the play remained unpublished, it was considered the exclusive property of the company that had bought it; after publication, any company could produce it without paying a fee.

The expenses of a company were subtracted before the sharing actors were paid. The troupe did not supply costumes. Although most characters were dressed in contemporary garments, others, especially classical, Near Eastern, and Native American figures, were usually played in elaborate and costly costumes quite unlike those worn in daily life. The typical dress of classical heroes, the *habit à la romaine,* an adaptation of Roman armor, tunic, and boots, accompanied by a full-bottomed wig and plumed headdress, cost about 2000 livres, a sum roughly equivalent to one-third of the actor's annual income. This financial burden was somewhat relieved by the royal practice of paying actors 400 livres for each costume they provided in plays mounted especially for court. In spite of the expenses, the sharing actor in the Comédie Française was well paid by the standards of the time.

Until 1680, the troupes played only three or four days each week, the preferred days being Tuesday, Friday, and Sunday. After 1680, the troupes began to play daily; in the 1682–1683 season the Comédie Française gave 352 performances. After 1680, the usual starting time was about 5 P.M. Although the population of Paris was about 500,000, the average attendance at the Comédie Française between 1680 and 1700 was only about 450 persons in theatres designed to hold 1500 to 2000. Spectators still stood in the pit and moved about freely. Others sat on the stage, a practice which some scholars date from the first production of *Le Cid* in 1636. By the late seventeenth century, there were occasionally as many as 150 spectators on the stage during a performance, a condition that undoubtedly affected acting style and the sense of illusion.

THEATRE ARCHITECTURE AND SCENIC PRACTICES, 1660–1700

The public theatres of Paris remained relatively unchanged from the 1640s until after Molière's death. In 1673 the Marais was abandoned, and the Palais Royal was refurbished for the Opéra. Little is known of the theatre in the rue Guénégaud, occupied by the Marais-Molière troupe from 1673 to 1680 and by the Comédie Française from 1680 until 1689. Built in 1670 by the Marquis de Sourdéac, it housed Lully's operatic productions from 1671 until 1673, when he gained control of the Palais Royal.

The Comédie Française was ordered to leave the rue Guénégaud in 1687, when the Sorbonne decided to build a new college nearby. Not until 1689 was it able to acquire a new home, the Etoile tennis court in the rue Neuve-des-Fossés in the St. Germain-des-Prés quarter of Paris. Remodeled by the architect François d'Orbay at a cost of 200,000 livres, it put the company in debt for many years. It was to be the home of the Comédie Française until 1770.

D'Orbay ignored the exterior walls of the tennis court and constructed inside them a U-shaped auditorium. On the ground floor, a standing pit was backed by an amphitheatre raised about 6 feet above it. Along the walls, two levels of nineteen boxes were surmounted by an undivided gallery. The total capacity of the auditorium was about 2000.

The stage was about 41 feet deep by 54 feet wide, but the available acting area was considerably restricted by spectators on the stage. A few benches were placed in the orchestra pit, which was not used by the musicians because of objections raised by the

FIG. 8.22
Theatre in the rue Guénégaud, built in 1670, and used by the Opéra, the Molière-Marais company, and the Comédie Française successively. Note the chandeliers over the stage and the spectators on the stage and in the boxes. Courtesy Bibliothèque Nationale, Paris.

Opéra. When musicians were needed, they were placed in a box at the rear of the auditorium. The stage was equipped for flat wings and shutters, but since changes of scene were seldom required, the machinery was minimal.

This stage reflects the changes which had occurred in scenic practices since the 1630s. *Le Mémoire de Mahelot, Laurent, et d'Autres Décorateurs,* the last part of which was compiled between 1678 and 1686, contains notices of fifty-four plays performed at the Hôtel de Bourgogne between 1678 and 1680, and sixty-nine notices of plays staged at the rue Guénégaud between 1680 and 1686. Most of these notices were written by Michel Laurent.

The principal change indicated by Laurent's notices of 1678 to 1686, in comparison with those by Mahelot in 1634 and 1635, is the trend toward simplicity. By Laurent's time, most settings represented a single place and were composed of flat wings. The rear shutters may have been pierced by doors, since entrances from the sides were impeded by onstage spectators.

The typical, though not invariable, background for tragedies was the *palais à volonté,* a neutral setting suited to the action but without particularizing details. Consequently, it could serve as a background for all scenes in the same town without any changes, for it was usually so anonymous that it might represent a street, a square, a vestibule, or a palace. A variation showed tents near a battlefield, often with a sea or city in the background. For comedy, the *chambre à quartre portes* (a room with four doors) was typical. It differed in no important way from the *palais à volonté,* except that it depicted domestic architecture, usually an interior, whereas the *palais à volonté* was more formal. The unity of place was never completely adopted, however, for in some plays the settings changed with each act. In others, a shutter or curtain was opened to reveal another place behind the one previously shown. By the end of the seventeenth century, the typical setting at the Comédie Française supplied a suitable, though neutral, background which placed little emphasis upon illusion and concentrated attention upon the actor.

THE CLOSE OF THE SEVENTEENTH CENTURY

By 1700, then, two Parisian troupes with monopolistic privileges divided the whole range of drama between them. The Opéra depended much on Italianate scenery and machines for the effectiveness of its musical dramas and ballets. The Comédie Française relied little on spectacle, although it too had adopted the Italian mode in scenery modified by the neoclassical ideal in drama.

The vigor of earlier years had been replaced by a spirit of conservatism. Rather than searching for new horizons, dramatists looked to the past for standards. The prevailing mood can be seen in the "Battle of the Ancients and Moderns" which raged in the French Academy and elsewhere after 1688 over the relative merits of classical and seventeenth-century French writers. The battle had many political overtones as well, since Louis XIV could not help

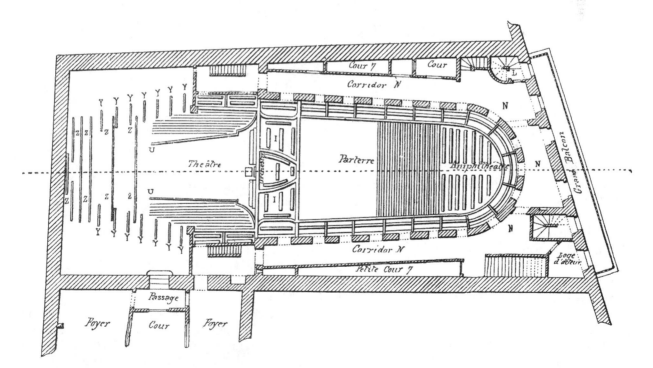

FIG. 8.23
Plan of the theatre used by the Comédie Française from 1689 until 1770. It opened 18 April 1689 with *Phèdre* and *The Doctor in Spite of Himself.* The benches for spectators on stage were added in the eighteenth century. From Adolphe Jullien, *Les Spectateurs sur le Théâtre* (1875).

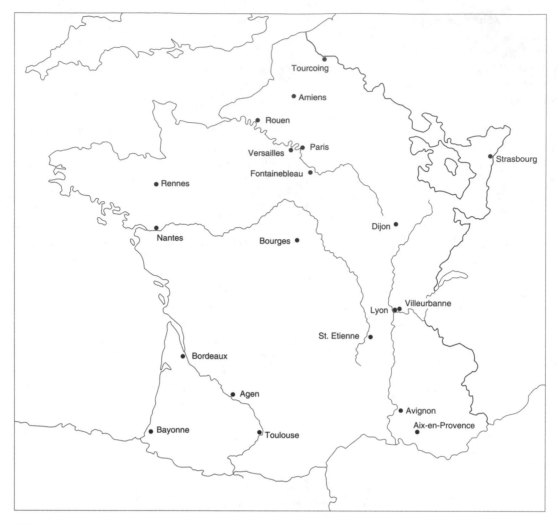

FIG. 8.24

Map of France showing cities that have played an important role (past and present) in French theatre.

being flattered if the cultural level of his reign was declared superior to that of Greece and Rome. Perhaps it is not surprising, then, that in general the battle, which continued into the eighteenth century, was decided in favor of French authors. In practice, this meant that Corneille and Racine replaced the Greek tragedians as standards for tragedy and that Molière replaced Plautus and Terence as models for comedy.

It is worth noting that just as the crown established its absolute authority during the course of the seventeenth century, it also established its control over the theatre through institutions licensed and supported by the crown, among them the French Academy, the Academy of Music and Dance, and the Comédie Française. Rules were established for drama, and the theatre's operation was governed by regulations supervised by committees appointed by the king. Attempts to maintain the status quo achieved during the seventeenth century would lead to stagnation and decline in mainstream theatre during the eighteenth century. Although French drama long continued to set the standard for Europe, its period of greatest vitality, like the Golden Age of Spanish Theatre, was over by 1700.

The stagnation that was becoming evident by the end of the seventeenth century reflected political and social developments. In 1685 Louis XIV revoked the Edict of Nantes that had guaranteed freedom of conscience, and subsequent persecutions led some 200,000 Huguenots to emigrate, a serious loss to the nation in wealth and talent. Louis also became increasingly puritanical. He gave up attending the theatre altogether, and this no doubt helped to provoke a number of attacks on the theatre as immoral. The enormous sums expended on building Versailles and conducting a series of wars had depleted the country's resources and left the country with a considerable deficit. In addition, Louis's attempts to extend his power throughout Europe had been checked by alliances among other countries. In 1700 France was the most powerful country in Europe, both politically and culturally, but thereafter its energies would be devoted more to maintaining the status quo than to seeking new paths.

LOOKING AT THEATRE HISTORY

One may sometimes gain additional insight into theatre history by reading novels and plays that have theatrical backgrounds, since they often give details and provide local color that are missing from presumably factual accounts. A number of such fictional works were written in France during the seventeenth century. Le Sieur Gougenot's *The Comedy of the Comedians* (c. 1631) depicts Gros-Guillaume, Turlupin, Bellerose, and other actors as they prepare a play for presentation at the Hôtel de Bourgogne. Similarly, Georges de Scudéry's play of the same title (1632) depicts the performers at the Marais (thinly disguised under other names) and provides considerable information about contemporary theatrical conditions. Later in the century, Molière treated the critical attitudes of his day in *The Critique of The School for Wives* (1663), written in answer to the storm of protest raised by his play, and in *Rehearsal at Versailles* (1663) he reveals much about his approach to rehearsals and about his ideas on acting. Paul Scarron's novel, *A Comical Romance* (1651, 1657), follows the fortunes of a band of strolling actors as they travel through France. In the opening chapters, the company sets up a stage in a tennis court and gives a performance. Its subsequent adventures are detailed in the course of the two-volume work.

From France in the seventeenth century we also have one of the earliest nonfictional attempts to describe how a company functioned. Written by a playwright, Samuel Chappuzeau (1625–1701), it treats almost all aspects of theatrical production in the 1670s. Here is his summary of rehearsal practices:

The roles being duly distributed, each actor goes off to memorize his part, and if time is pressing and a special effort is made, a full length play can be memorized in a week. . . . When they feel themselves secure in their parts, they gather for the first rehearsal, which serves only to give a rough sketch of the whole, and it is not until the second or third rehearsal that it is possible to judge what success the play may have. They do not risk producing a play until it has been perfectly memorized and well staged, and the final rehearsal ought to be exactly like a regular performance. Ordinarily the author attends these rehearsals and instructs the actor if he falls into some error, if he fails to grasp the sense, if he fails to be natural in voice and gesture, if he expresses more or less emotion than the action demands. Intelligent actors are allowed to give their opinions in these rehearsals, without offending their comrades, since it is a question of the common good.

Le Théâtre Français (Paris, 1674), book II, ch. 17.

By the mid-seventeenth century, the neoclassical ideal had triumphed in France. In passing judgment on Corneille's *Le Cid*, the French Academy provided a rationale for its point of view, even though it contradicted that of the majority of playgoers:

Nature and Truth have put a certain value to things, which cannot be altered by what chance or opinion set up. . . . We must not say with the crowd that a play is good merely because it pleases, unless the learned and the expert are also pleased. . . . If it happens that irregular plays sometimes please, it is only by reason of what is regular in them. . . . And on the other hand, if certain regularly-constructed plays give little pleasure, it must not be thought that this is the fault of the rules, but of the author, whose sterile wit was unable to exercise his art upon sufficiently rich material.

Opinions of the French Academy on the Tragicomedy "The Cid" (1637).

During the seventeenth century French scenic conventions underwent a complete transformation. The scenic practices of the Hôtel de Bourgogne are well documented in *Le Mémoire de Mahelot, Laurent, et d'Autres Décorateurs*, . . . the first part of which ends in 1635. Here is Mahelot's summary of the requirements for du Ryer's *Lisandre and Caliste*. (The sketch of this simultaneous setting is reproduced in Fig. 8.8.)

It requires at the center of the stage the little castle of Saint Jacques and a street where the butchers are located, and in one of the butcher's houses a window which is directly across from the grilled window of the prison, from which Lisandre can speak to Caliste. This must be hidden during the first act, and it should be made to appear during the second act and to close again during the same act; in closed position it serves as the palace. At one side of the stage a hermitage on a mountain and a cavern below from which a hermit enters. On the other side of the stage, there should be a room into which one enters from behind, raised by two or three steps. Some helmets, bucklers, shields, trumpets, and an unsheathed sword. It is also necessary in one scene for it to be night.

By the mid-century the Italian scenic ideal had triumphed, largely because of Torelli's work after 1645. Torelli's settings for Corneille's *Andromède* (presented at the Petit Bourbon in 1650) are described in the playwright's script and are depicted in a series of contemporary engravings. Here are the descriptive passages for Act II. The engraving of this setting is shown in Fig. 8.11.

The public square vanishes in an instant to give way to a delightful garden; and the great palaces are changed into so many white marble vases, which alternately bear statues from which jets of water spring, others blossoming with jasmine, and other plants of that nature. On each side stands a line of orange trees in similar vases, which form an admirable bower in the middle of the stage, and separates it into three paths, which the ingenious art of perspective makes appear more than a thousand feet deep. . . .

Here thunder commences to sound with so great a noise with lightning redoubled so quickly that it arouses astonishment with its naturalness. Meantime one sees Eolus descend with eight winds, of which four are at either side. . . . Two [winds] . . . descend, seize Andromède by the arms and lift her into the clouds.

Oeuvres de Pierre Corneille, vol. VI (Paris, 1821).

When Molière died without having renounced his profession as actor, he was denied a Christian burial in part, no doubt, because of the enemies he had made during the controversy over *Tartuffe*. Louis XIV intervened, but even then the Archbishop of Paris authorized only the minimal service:

We authorize the vicar of St. Eustache to give ecclesiastical burial to the body of the deceased Molière in the cemetery of the parish on condition that there shall be no ceremony, with two priests only, after nightfall, and that there shall be no solemn service for him either in the parish of St. Eustache or elsewhere, in any church of the regular clergy.

9
English Theatre to 1800

Because of the civil war between the Royalists (Cavaliers) and Parliamentarians (Roundheads or Puritans), life in England was very unsettled during the 1640s. England did not return to peace until Charles I had been captured, tried, and beheaded by the Puritans in 1649. For a time England was governed by a committee appointed by Parliament, but after 1653 Oliver Cromwell was a virtual dictator. When he died in 1658, his son was chosen as his successor, but he could not maintain control. In 1660 the Stuarts were restored to the throne.

THEATRICAL ACTIVITY, 1642–1660

During the eighteen years between 1642 and 1660, the Puritans sought to stop all theatrical activity. As a result, few records relating to performance have survived, although playing certainly continued intermittently. At first the actors complied with the law passed in 1642 suspending performances for a period of five years. The King's Men sold its wardrobe, and its Globe Theatre was torn down. Actors soon began to perform surreptitiously, however, and performances were given at the Fortune, Phoenix/Cockpit, and Salisbury Court theatres. Although Parliament ordered officials to halt the violations, suppression was sporadic and ineffectual. When the law prohibiting performances expired in 1647, open playing was immediately resumed. But in 1649, Parliament passed a new law ordering that all actors be apprehended as rogues and that the interiors of the Fortune, Phoenix/Cockpit, and Salisbury Court be dismantled. The actors continued to perform, nevertheless, using The Red Bull, which had escaped demolition, or, when that appeared too dangerous, private houses, tennis courts, or inns. Often officials were bribed to ignore violations. In these years, the usual form of entertainment seems to have been the "droll," a short play condensed from a longer work.

Apparently, the actors believed that the theatre would eventually be legalized. Around 1650, William Beeston (c. 1606–1682) acquired The Salisbury Court, and John Rhodes bought The Phoenix/Cockpit. Perhaps most significantly, William Davenant, who in the 1630s had succeeded Jonson as the principal writer of court masques and received a theatre patent in 1639, began openly to stage what have been called England's first operatic productions. His initial offering, *The First Day's Entertainment at Rutland House,* was presented in May 1656.

The production of *The Siege of Rhodes,* also in 1656, is a far more important event, however, for it marks the first clear use in England of Italianate scenery for a public performance. Designed by John Webb (1611–1672), pupil of Inigo Jones, the settings were

211

FIG. 9.1
England, Scotland, and Ireland, 1642–1800.

mounted on a stage measuring only 22 feet in width, 18 feet in depth, and 11 feet in height. Behind the proscenium, a series of fixed wings, painted to represent rocky cliffs, terminated in movable shutters which, in combination with set pieces, depicted the various locales required by the action.

These first entertainments were given in Rutland House, Davenant's residence, but in 1658 and 1659 Davenant presented at least three others at The Phoenix/Cockpit, in which a proscenium arch was erected. Although some opposition was expressed, by this time the restoration of the monarchy was

FIG. 9.2
A composite drawing of the stages used during the Commonwealth for "drolls." Note that characters from several plays are included. Note also the chandeliers and footlights. From Kirkman, *The Wits,* a collection of drolls, published in 1672.

imminent and no action was taken. On the other hand, Davenant was not violating any law, for his pieces were "musical entertainments," which had not been forbidden.

THE REESTABLISHMENT OF THE THEATRE

The restoration of the monarchy occurred in 1660 when Charles II (reigned 1660–1685) was restored to the throne. The period we call Restoration theatre extends to 1700 because about that time a significant change in the drama can be identified. Under Charles, England rejected the strict Puritanism of the Commonwealth, so much so that the Restoration became noted for its permissiveness, even libertinism. Charles maintained an uneasy political truce with Parliament, since neither wished to give up any rights

FIG. 9.3
The proscenium and side wings for *The Seige of Rhodes* as designed by John Webb and presented by William Davenant at Rutland House in 1656. The wings, representing cliffs, remained fixed throughout, and scenic units were changed behind them. This perspective setting with movable units is the first known use of Italianate scenery on a public stage in England. Devonshire Collection, Chatsworth. Reproduced by permission of the Trustees of the Chatsworth Settlement.

or engage in another open conflict. Charles's belief in his rights as a monarch are nowhere more evident than in his relation to the theatre, which he treated as a royal property to dispose of as he saw fit.

As soon as it became evident that the monarchy would be restored, the reopening of the theatres began. John Rhodes opened The Phoenix/Cockpit

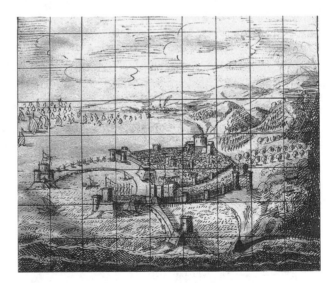

FIG. 9.4
The first background for *The Seige of Rhodes,* a distant view of Rhodes and the harbor. The drawing is divided into squares to facilitate transfer to the shutters. Devonshire Collection, Chatsworth. Reproduced by permission of the Trustees of the Chatsworth Settlement.

under license from General Monk. Michael Mohun reformed what was left of the prewar King's Men and began to play at The Red Bull. Sir Henry Herbert resumed the position of Master of Revels, which he had held since 1623, and licensed a company under William Beeston at The Salisbury Court. Upon his arrival Charles II issued a warrant giving exclusive rights to open theatres, hire actors, and perform plays in London to Killigrew and Davenant, who soon set to work closing down their competitors. The issue was not resolved until 1662/63, however, when the king reissued the two patents that had existed before the war. The one that had belonged to the King's Men went to Thomas Killigrew (1612–1683), who had grown up in the English court, had been a successful playwright before 1642, and had been with the royal family throughout its exile. The second pre-civil war patent was granted to Davenant for a company to be sponsored by the king's brother James, Duke of York.

Henry Herbert was deprived of the right to license theatres and companies in London, but his authority to license companies outside of London and to collect fees for licensing plays was confirmed. (When Herbert died in 1673, Killigrew became Master of the Revels, followed by his son, Charles, who held the post until 1725.) The actors from the rival companies soon signed contracts with the new patent holders.

Meanwhile, in late 1660, George Jolly (*fl.* 1648–1673) was granted a license by the king to perform in London. During the Commonwealth years, Jolly had headed a touring company in northern Europe which had performed for the future Charles II in 1655. Apparently Jolly had received some kind of commitment from Charles about the future.

In 1662, Davenant and Killigrew leased Jolly's license while he went on a tour. During his absence, the two managers convinced the king to revoke it. When Jolly attempted to return to London after the long plague closure in 1665 (during which London lost one-fifth of its population) and the great fire of 1666, Davenant and Killigrew were able to prevent his company from performing, but, to avoid legal challenges, Jolly was hired to manage a Nursery company to train young actors. After 1673 no more is heard of him.

Thus, Davenant and Killigrew established complete control over theatrical performances in London. The patents issued to them by Charles II were to remain in effect until 1843, seriously hampering the growth of the British theatre.

fessionals before the civil war, while Davenant's Duke's Company was left with younger performers. Although Killigrew began with the advantage of experienced actors, his company did not prosper. He devoted little attention to the theatre, delegating authority to three of his actors. Perhaps as a result, the company was wracked by constant dissension. Davenant, on the other hand, supervised his theatre closely until his death in 1668, after which the actors Thomas Betterton and Henry Harris (the latter succeeded by William Smith in 1677) assumed artistic direction under the control of the Davenant family. By 1682 Killigrew's company was in such serious financial difficulties that the two troupes were merged.

The arrangement reached in 1682 lasted until 1695, when several actors seceded to form another troupe after a series of events had placed them in an untenable position. Alexander Davenant, who had controlling interest in the Davenant patent, fled England to escape his creditors in 1693. His financial support had come from Christopher Rich and Sir Thomas Skipworth; Rich, a lawyer without any theatrical experience, seized control of the company. He proved himself so unpleasant, by withholding salaries and favoring those actors who catered to his whims, that the major performers, under Betterton's leadership, secured a license from William III to form a second troupe. This separation was to last from 1695 until 1708.

In addition to the London companies, a number of troupes were licensed to perform in the provinces. The most important provincial center was Dublin, perhaps because it had its own Master of Revels. In 1637 John Ogilby (1600–1676) had been given a license to open a theatre in Dublin and was named Master of Revels for Ireland. Ogilby's patent, dormant after 1641, was renewed in 1661, and in 1662 he opened the Smock Alley, the first theatre built in Great Britain after the Restoration. Upon Ogilby's death, the patent passed to Joseph Ashbury, who maintained the finest company outside of London for the next forty-five years.

Many other types of performance took place outside of theatres and were not subject to the same restraints. These included the Lord Mayor's Show, entertainments at fairs, holiday processions and ceremonies, and many others. These were often quite topical and political in their implications.

ACTING COMPANIES, 1600–1700

Killigrew, as manager of the King's Company, recruited older actors, many of whom had been pro-

ENGLISH DRAMA, 1660–1700

One of the problems facing managers in 1660 was a suitable repertory. At first they depended on pre-

Commonwealth plays, which the Master of Revels divided between the companies. Of these, the works of Beaumont and Fletcher were the most popular; Jonson's, though much admired, were seldom produced. Several of Shakespeare's plays were revised to bring them into line with contemporary tastes. Many of the older works soon proved too outmoded, and they were dropped from the repertory as soon as new ones were available. Others, however, remained favorites.

Several types of serious plays were written between 1660 and 1700. Until 1680 the dominant mode was "heroic" tragedy, which, heavily indebted to Spanish and French authors and set in exotic locales, emphasized stories centering around the rival claims of love and honor. This type first reached popularity through the works of John Dryden (1631–1700) with *The Indian Queen* (1664), *The Indian Emperor* (1665), *The Conquest of Granada,* parts 1 and 2 (1669–1670), and *Aureng-Zebe* (1675) and through the works of Roger Boyle, Earl of Orrery (1621–1679), especially *The Tragedy of Mustapha* (1665), *The Black Prince* (1667), and *Tryphon* (1668). Other popular writers of this genre were Elkanah Settle (1648–1724), author of *Cambyses, King of Persia* (1671), and *The Empress of Morocco* (1673); and Nathaniel Lee (1653–1692), author of *The Rival Queens* (1677).

In these works, typically an idealistic hero and a beautiful heroine are faced with a situation in which the fulfillment of their mutual love will precipitate other events apt to bring ruin or dishonor to themselves, their families, or country. Often the background is martial, and frequently a happy ending is contrived. Filled with ranting speeches in rhymed couplets, the plays now seem hopelessly stilted. The genre was dealt a heavy blow in 1671 by *The Rehearsal,* written by George Villiers, second Duke of Buckingham (1628–1687), which burlesqued the typical themes, plot devices, and staging conventions of heroic tragedy. Buckingham's play outlived its target, remaining in the repertory until the late eighteenth century.

As the heroic mode declined, it was replaced by tragedy written in blank verse and according to the neoclassical rules. Using relatively simple plots and observing the three unities, the form first gained popularity through Dryden's *All for Love* (1677), a "regularized" reworking of Shakespeare's *Antony and Cleopatra*. It was to remain the dominant mode through the remainder of the century. English neoclassicism was always more liberal than the version that prevailed on the continent. Unity of action was interpreted to permit a number of related subplots, and the unity of place was thought to have been adequately observed if the characters could move easily between the various locales without violating the 24-hour time limit.

FIG. 9.5
Dryden's *All for Love*. From Dryden's *Dramatick Works,* 4 (1735).

The combined influence of neoclassicism and of Shakespeare is evident in the work of the best serious playwright of the age, Thomas Otway (1652–1685), whose *The Orphan* (1680) and *Venice Preserv'd* (1682) remained in the repertory until the late nineteenth century. The first of these plays focuses on a woman who is loved by two brothers, one of whom she marries secretly, upon which the other brother, suspecting an illicit relationship, brings ruin to them all. *Venice Preserv'd* deals with a conspiracy to overthrow the government of Venice and ends in death for the three principal characters, Pierre, Jaffier, and Belvidera. But though in Otway's plays pathos has not yet replaced tragic pity, a trend toward the tearful was already evident and would thereafter accelerate.

Building upon Davenant's Commonwealth "entertainments," opera also flourished during the

Restoration. It differed from heroic tragedy primarily in the addition of music, song, and spectacle, and it departed from the conventions of Italian opera by substituting spoken passages for recitative. Not only were Shakespeare's *Macbeth, The Tempest,* and *A Midsummer Night's Dream* adapted to the operatic mode, but such original works as Dryden's *Albion and Albianus* (1685) and *King Arthur* (1692) also achieved considerable popularity. This English strain of opera was to decline rapidly after the vogue for Italian opera began in England around 1705.

But the Restoration is noted above all for its diverse comic drama: comedies of "humours," comedies of intrigue, farces, and comedies of manners. Because of Jonson's reputation, "humours" were much exploited during the Restoration. Of the major authors, Thomas Shadwell (1642–1692) was the most successful writer of humours comedy with *The Sullen Lovers* (1668), *The Humourists* (1670), *The*

FIG. 9.6
Congreve's *The Way of the World.* At center is Lady Wishfort and her nephew from the country. From an edition of Congreve's plays published in 1753.

Squire of Alsatia (1688), and *Bury Fair* (1689). Each of these plays introduces a series of eccentric characters in a story of contemporary life, told with frank and outspoken dialogue.

Perhaps because of the influence of Corneille and the Spanish dramatists, the comedy of intrigue was also popular in these years. The best exemplar of this genre was Aphra Behn (1640–1689), the first woman known to have made her living as a playwright. She wrote at least 17 plays along with a comic opera and a novel, and is best know for *The Rover,* parts 1 and 2 (1677–1680). Farce reached its height in the works of Edward Ravenscroft (*fl.* 1671–1697), whose *London Cuckolds* (1681) and *The Anatomist* (1697) were played throughout the eighteenth century.

Above all, however, the Restoration is noted for its sprightly comedy of manners. John Dryden, the most versatile dramatist of the age, contributed to its formation with such works as *Sir Martin Mar-All* (1667), *The Mock Astrologer* (1668), and *Marriage à la Mode* (1672), each of which includes a pair of carefree, witty lovers. The fully developed comedy of manners, however, is usually traced to the plays of Sir George Etherege (*c.* 1634–1691), who, after a somewhat erratic beginning in *Love in a Tub* (1664), set the pattern for later writers with *She Would If She Could* (1668) and *The Man of Mode* (1676). Here for the first time we find the elements that were to be typical of the type: characters drawn from the upper classes and preoccupation with seduction, arranged marriages, the latest fashions, and witty repartee.

Of the later writers in this vein, Wycherley and Congreve were of special importance. William Wycherley (1640–1715) began writing for the stage in 1671 with *Love in a Wood,* and continued with *The Gentleman Dancing Master* (1672), *The Country Wife* (1675), and *The Plain Dealer* (1676). Although these plays are well constructed and present subtly depicted characters, their moral tone has offended many critics. *The Country Wife,* in which the hero circulates the rumor that he is sexually impotent in order to facilitate his seductions, is often cited as evidence of the moral laxity of Restoration comedy. The comedy of manners reached its peak in the plays of William Congreve (1670–1729), whose *Love for Love* (1695) and *The Way of the World* (1700) are still considered masterpieces because of their brilliant scenes, sparkling dialogue, and clear-cut characterizations. *The Way of the World,* in which the witty lovers Millamant and Mirabell reach their own unique marital agreement based on their knowledge of the ways of their world, inhabited primarily by intriguers, fops, and fools, is usually thought to be one of the best of all English comedies.

FIG. 9.7
Scene from Farquhar's *The Beaux' Stratagem*. From an edition of the play published in 1733.

The subject matter and tone of the Restoration comedies of manners have led to much debate over their moral viewpoint. In them the wise are rewarded, the foolish are duped, and virtue consists of unsentimental self-knowledge. The self-deceived are ridiculed and gulled, often by protagonists who use their own superior (if sometimes cynical) insights to justify their treatment of the fools. Discussions about the acceptability of these standards of behavior have often obscured the remarkable accomplishments of the Restoration dramatists.

By 1700 changes in English life and drama were becoming evident. When Charles II died, he was succeeded by his brother James II (reigned 1685–1688), who was suspected of plotting to reestablish Catholicism. He was tolerated until his son was born, raising the threat that his policies would be perpetuated. A group of leading politicians then invited James's Protestant daughter Mary and her husband William of Orange, ruler of the Netherlands, to assume the throne. William invaded England; James fled; and Parliament declared Mary II (reigned 1689–1694) and William III (reigned 1689–1702) co-rulers of England. Parliament passed and the new rulers accepted a bill requiring Parliament's consent on all important matters and giving it the right to determine the succession to the throne, which went to Mary's sister, Anne (reigned 1702–1724). The new rulers were sympathetic to the mercantile class, which was rapidly becoming the major source of England's wealth and power, as its fleet of merchant ships and overseas enterprises steadily increased. In effect, the legislation that brought William and Mary to the throne put an end to absolute monarchy in England, thereby resolving the major cause of the dissension that had plagued England throughout the century. But in overthrowing James II and denying the succession to his son, it set in motion the Jacobite rebellions that would plague the country for the next half century.

Still, it is not surprising that the middle class should begin to make its tastes felt in the theatre or, since it was morally conservative, that, when it did, Puritan sentiment would surface again. This reawakened conservatism was expressed through several attacks on the theatre during the 1690s, but none was truly effective until Jeremy Collier's *A Short View of the Immorality and Profaneness of the English Stage* (1698) appeared. Collier succeeded where others had failed because he began with the accepted neoclassical doctrine that the purpose of drama is to teach and to please and went on to show the disparity between theory and practice. Most dramatists found it impossible to answer Collier effectively, since they too had accepted moral teaching as the basic aim of drama. A few playwrights, among them Dryden, made public recantations; Congreve at first protested and then gave up playwriting altogether. Even as the controversy raged, English drama began to move in new directions.

ENGLISH DRAMA, 1700–1750

The transition toward a new approach is best seen in the plays of Cibber and Farquhar, in which the characteristics of the established comic types are modified considerably by a more conservative moral outlook and by greater sentimentality. In Colley Cibber's (1671–1757) *Love's Last Shift* (1696), *The Careless Husband* (1704), *The Double Gallant* (1707), and *The Lady's Stake* (1707), profligate characters pursue their fashionable follies until the fifth act, when they undergo rapid and sentimentalized conversions. George Farquhar (1678–1707) preserved much of Congreve's wit, but set his plays in the country and resolved them in a manner that removed moral obstacles. His best plays are *The Constant Couple* (1699), which introduced Sir Harry Wildair, one of the most popular characters of the eighteenth century, *The Recruiting Officer* (1706), and *The Beaux' Stratagem* (1707), the latter two still perennial favorites.

This transition period is also significant for its large number of female playwrights (more than at any time until the present). Between 1695 and 1715, thirty-seven new plays by women were produced on London's stages. Although these writers, including Mary Pix (1666–1706), Delariviere Manley (*c.* 1672–1724), Catharine Trotter (1679–1749), and Susanna Centlivre (*c.* 1670–1723), were among the most successful dramatists of their time, they have, with the exception of Centlivre, largely been ignored in accounts of the period. Some of Centlivre's plays, such as *The Busy Body* (1709) and *The Wonder* (1714), were to hold the stage until well into the nineteenth century.

The trend in comedy toward sentimentality and toward protagonists drawn from the middle class first reached full expression in *The Conscious Lovers* (1722) by Sir Richard Steele (1672–1729). Based on Terence's *Andria,* Steele's play transfers the action to eighteenth-century London. The play's penniless heroine, Indiana, after withstanding many trials of her virtue, is discovered to be the daughter of a rich merchant, thus making a suitable marriage possible. The few humorous scenes fall to the servants. In Steele's play the purpose of comedy has been seriously altered: Rather than seeking to arouse laughter or ridicule, it sought to arouse noble sentiments through the depiction of trials bravely borne by sympathetic characters who are rescued from their sufferings and handsomely rewarded. As Steele put it, he wished to arouse "a pleasure too exquisite for laughter."

Today much of the drama of the eighteenth century is called "sentimental" because so many of the characters appear unnaturally good and their problems seem too easily overcome. These plays were accepted in the eighteenth century, nevertheless, as truthful representations of human nature. The disparity in attitude is explained by our changed view. Eighteenth-century philosophers conceived of humanity as good by nature, a state which individuals could retain by following their instincts, but from which bad examples might divert them. Consequently, it was thought possible to reclaim people from vice by appealing to those virtuous human feelings that had been glossed over by thoughtless or callous behavior. For this reason, characters could be reformed quickly if their "hearts" could be touched. Pathetic situations were also considered to be useful devices because they demonstrated the goodness of the characters who withstood all trials and because they provided spectators with an occasion for displaying their own goodness, since to be moved by the sight of virtue in distress was a sign of a properly sensitive and moral nature.

Although Richard Steele was to have no important successors in comedy until after 1750, this new vein in drama was exploited effectively in tragedy. In the early eighteenth century, Nicholas Rowe (1674–1718) had written a number of tragedies, featuring pathetic heroines, as in *The Ambitious Step-Mother* (1701), *Tamerlane* (1701), *The Fair Penitent* (1703), and *The Tragedy of Jane Shore* (1714), which were to hold the stage until the nineteenth century. Other important serious playwrights included Ambrose Philips (1675–1749), whose *The Distrest Mother* (1712), based upon Racine's *Andromaque,* remained a popular vehicle for actresses for over a century, and Joseph Addison (1672–1719), whose *Cato* (1713) was considered a masterpiece. These tragedies, however, were all based upon historical or mythological subjects and drew their characters from the ruling classes. A significant new direction was taken in 1731 when George Lillo (1693–1739) wrote *The London Merchant,* in which the hero-apprentice, George Barnwell, is led astray by a prostitute, kills his kind uncle, and ends on the gallows in spite of his abject repentance. Lillo chose his subject from everyday life because he believed that the lessons of traditional tragedy, with characters drawn from the nobility, were not sufficiently applicable to the ordinary person. It is clear that he was considered successful, for until well into the nineteenth century the apprentices of London were sent each year during the Christmas season to see this play as a warning against going astray. Lillo had many imitators, but none achieved his success.

Although during the eighteenth century neoclassicism remained the dominant mode, a number of minor dramatic types (pantomime, ballad opera, comic opera, and burlesque) undermined its authority. Pantomime combined elements from *commedia dell'arte* and farce with topical satire and stories drawn from classical mythology. *Commedia dell'arte* troupes had appeared occasionally in England since the sixteenth century, and *commedia* types had been incorporated into the dances and entr'acte entertainments of English performers since the late seventeenth century. In 1702 John Weaver became the first to organize the dances into a connected story, but it remained for John Rich (1692–1761), son of Christopher Rich and manager of Lincoln's Inn Fields and Covent Garden theatres, to establish the accepted pattern of English pantomime with such works as *Harlequin Executed* (produced during the season of 1716–1717) and *Amadis, or the Loves of Harlequin and Columbine* (1718). In Rich's pantomimes, serious scenes based on classical mythology alternated with comic episodes featuring *commedia* characters. The comic scenes were mute, but the serious plot used dialogue and song. Music accompanied much of the action. But the dominant feature was spectacle, motivated by Harlequin's acquisition of a magic wand that could transform places or characters. Unlike most pantomimes, Rich's were long-lived. In forty-five years he created only about twenty, thirteen of which were first performed between 1717 and 1732. Nine pantomimes became mainstays in his repertory, were refurbished at regular intervals, and were alternated from season to season. Under the name Lun, Rich was also the most famous and the most accomplished English pantomimist of the eighteenth century.

By 1723, pantomime was the most popular form of theatrical entertainment. Although pantomimes served only as afterpieces, many were more popular than the plays they accompanied. Prices were always raised for new pantomimes, several of which had initial runs of forty to fifty performances. Rich trained a number of other pantomime players, of whom the most famous was Harry Woodward (1717–1777), who deserted Rich in 1738 and for the next twenty years mounted pantomimes at Drury Lane in competition with his teacher.

Rich is also associated with the rise of ballad opera, since he produced the first one, *The Beggar's Opera* (1728) by John Gay (1685–1732), after it had been refused by Drury Lane. Ballad opera emerged in part out of the vogue for Italian opera, which began around 1705 and accelerated in 1710 with the arrival in England of George Frideric Handel (1685–1759). In 1719 the Royal Academy of Music was founded as the home of opera. Although always in financial difficulties after 1730, the opera continued to enjoy great prestige with the aristocracy

FIG. 9.8
A pantomine at the Haymarket Theatre in the late eighteenth century. Note also the theatre's architecture: proscenium doors, wide apron, stage box, and backless benches in the pit. From Wilkinson, *Londina Illustrata* (1825).

FIG. 9.9

Gay's *The Beggar's Opera*. Polly and Lucy are pleading for Macheath's life. Note the spectators on the stage. An engraving by William Blake after William Hogarth's painting of 1729. Courtesy Harvard Theatre Collection.

through the remainder of the century. Gay's ballad opera drew upon many operatic conventions (even as it satirized them) but it departed from them by alternating spoken dialogue with lyrics set to popular tunes. Gay's work was more than popularized opera, however, for its story of London low-life commented satirically on the political situation of the time and set the tone for much of the minor drama of the next ten years. No subsequent ballad opera, however, achieved the popularity of the first one.

The satirical burlesque, which differed from ballad opera principally in the absence of sung portions, appeared in the 1730s. The finest writer of this form was Henry Fielding (1707–1754), who began his dramatic career with adaptations of Molière and then turned to topical satire in his burlesque of contemporary tragedy, *Tom Thumb, or the Tragedy of Tragedies* (1730). His later plays, such as *Pasquin* (1736), *Tumble-Down Dick* (1736), and *The Historical Register of 1736* (1737), burlesqued the major figures and events of the day. Like ballad opera, burlesque waned after the passage of the Licensing Act in 1737.

GOVERNMENTAL REGULATION OF THE THEATRE

The Licensing Act of 1737 was an outgrowth of both political and theatrical conditions. During the reign of Queen Anne, political parties became more important as the role of Parliament increased. Her successor, George I (reigned 1714–1727), was a German prince who spoke no English and permitted his chief minister, Sir Robert Walpole (usually said to be Britain's first prime minister), to run the government. George I's practice was continued by his son, George II (reigned 1727–1760). Thus, after 1714 political factions and government officials and policies provided fertile ground for satire. Dramatists did not fail to capitalize on this opportunity, especially during the 1720s and 1730s.

By this time, the legal status of the patents issued by Charles II was also being debated. William III had raised the question in 1695 when he granted Betterton's troupe a license, and Queen Anne had caused further confusion by licensing the eminent architect and playwright, Sir John Vanbrugh (1664–1726), to build the Queen's Theatre in the Haymarket in 1705. The two companies in existence after 1695 continued in opposition until 1708, when they were reunited by crown action. When Rich immediately returned to his oppressive policies and ignored orders to meet his actors' demands, he was banned from Drury Lane in 1709. But he still held controlling interest in the Davenant patent, which he used to open Lincoln's Inn Fields Theatre in 1714. His son used it to open Covent Garden in 1732.

Drury Lane retained the Killigrew patent, but its validity seems to have been questioned (the patents had never been confirmed by Parliament). Drury Lane management secured a license to operate, and with the exception of the years between 1715 and 1719 when a patent was granted to Sir Richard Steele, it operated under renewable licenses thereafter. Questions concerning the patents led several men to defy them.

The first serious challenge came from John Potter, who opened the Haymarket Theatre in 1720. By the 1730s four unlicensed theatres were operating in London. The confusion was compounded in 1733 when the courts dismissed the legal actions brought by the two patent theatres against actors who had seceded from Drury Lane to act elsewhere. Since this decision seemed to deny the validity of the patents, clarification was needed.

The immediate motivation for the Licensing Act, however, was Prime Minister Walpole's sensitivity to the political satires being offered at unlicensed theatres. Following a particularly scurrilous attack on Walpole in a play by Fielding, a bill was rushed through Parliament. Since it was not thoughtfully devised, it created as many problems as it solved. The main provisions of this bill, the Licensing Act of 1737, were simple: (1) it prohibited the acting for "gain, hire, or reward" of any play not previously li-

FIG. 9.10
Strolling players dressing in a barn. Note the many stage props, bits of scenery, costumes, and the preparations for performance. An engraving by William Hogarth. Courtesy Indiana University Libraries.

censed by the Lord Chamberlain, and (2) it restricted authorized theatres to the City of Westminster (the official seat of government). The Drury Lane and Covent Garden thus were confirmed as the only legitimate theatres in England, for no provisions were made for troupes in any other city. This law had an immediate and lasting effect both on drama and theatrical activity.

At first the law was obeyed, but in 1740 Henry Giffard, who had managed the best of the unlicensed troupes between 1731 and 1737, reopened the Goodman's Fields Theatre. Ostensibly charging admission only for concerts, to which plays were added free, Giffard sought to evade the Licensing Act by interpreting literally the prohibition against unauthorized acting for "gain, hire, or reward." The attention drawn to this theatre by David Garrick's debut there in 1741 soon brought its closure. Others were to use similar ruses; Samuel Foote, for example, offered his "free" entertainments to those who paid for a "Dish of Chocolate" or to attend an "Auction of Pictures." Such ventures were tolerated for a time, but most were eventually forbidden. It was the closure of the New Wells Theatre that prompted William Hallam to send a troupe to America in 1752, an event usually said to mark the beginning of the American professional theatre.

Other public entertainments did not require licensing until 1752, when abuses led to the passage of a new bill. Under this legislation all places of entertainment within a twenty-mile radius of London were required to secure licenses from local magistrates. Although regular drama was expressly forbidden, the permissible kinds of entertainment were left undefined.

No law as yet provided for theatrical entertainments outside of the area adjacent to London. Nevertheless, the provincial theatre had continued to operate (either by ignoring the law or by using various ruses to circumvent it), and a number of regular circuits had grown up. By the 1760s, the larger towns were objecting to being denied lawful theatres. As a result, Parliament began to authorize theatres in specific towns: in Bath and Norwich in 1768, in York and Hull in 1769, in Liverpool in 1771, and in Chester in 1777. By the end of the century, almost every major town had a "theatre royal," or crown-authorized theatre.

In London no exception to the monopoly held by Drury Lane and Covent Garden was made until 1766, when, in recompense for having been crippled by a prank instigated by the Duke of York, Samuel Foote was granted a license to present plays at the Haymarket Theatre between May 15 and September 15, a period during which the patent houses normally closed. Although Foote's license was granted only for his lifetime, he sold it to George Colman in 1777 and it was renewed thereafter until 1843. Thus, the Haymarket became a third legitimate theatre, though it was restricted to playing during the summer months.

Still another bill was passed in 1788 that permitted magistrates outside the twenty-mile radius of London to license theatres for legitimate drama. As a result, the theatre was once again legitimized throughout the British Isles. After the act of 1788, the possibilities of confusion were almost as great as before 1737, for there were now four distinct licensing authorities: (1) the Lord Chamberlain, who licensed all plays performed in Britain and all theatres in the city of Westminster; (2) local magistrates within twenty miles of London, who licensed places of minor entertainment; (3) local magistrates outside the twenty-mile radius, who licensed legitimate theatres in their districts; and (4) Parliament, who authorized "theatres royal" in specific towns. The confusion was not to be exploited until the nineteenth century, when changing conditions led managers to search for ways to evade the legal restrictions.

ENGLISH DRAMA, 1750–1800

Drama was seriously affected by the Licensing Act of 1737, since thereafter it had to pass the scrutiny of a censor. The minor forms suffered most, for topical and political satire were strongly discouraged. Consequently, both ballad opera and burlesque declined rapidly. Ballad opera was replaced by a new musical type, comic opera, that had sentimental plots and original music. The most famous writer of the new type was Isaac Bickerstaffe (1735–1812), with such works as *The Maid of the Mill* (1765) and *Lionel and Clarissa* (1768). Other works in this vein include Richard Brinsley Sheridan's (1751–1816) *The Duenna* (1775), John O'Keeffe's (1747–1833) *The Poor Soldier* (1783), and George Colman the Younger's (1762–1836) *Inkle and Yarico* (1787).

Few burlesques were written in the last half of the eighteenth century, and in those few the targets were literary and dramatic works rather than politics. By far the best of the burlesques was Sheridan's *The Critic* (1781), a satire on tragedy, critics, authors, and the vogue of spectacle. It replaced Buckingham's *The Rehearsal* and was regularly performed until the end of the nineteenth century.

Pantomime was little affected by the Licensing Act, but no devisor of this form stands out in the last half of the century. The major change is seen after 1760 in the waning popularity of Harlequin and the rise of the more sentimentalized clown. Still, pantomime continued to be the most popular of all theatrical entertainments.

After 1750 domestic tragedy declined in favor. The only work of this type to win continuing fame was Edward Moore's (1712–1757) *The Gamester* (1753), which depicted the downward career of a gambler. As domestic tragedy declined in popularity, sentimental comedy flourished, perhaps because audiences preferred to see characters rescued from misfortune rather than punished for mistakes. The most important later writers were Hugh Kelly (1739–1777), whose *False Delicacy* (1768) treats the disentanglement of three pairs of unsuited lovers; Richard Cumberland (1732–1811), whose *The West Indian* (1771) tells the story of a young rake who, after being reformed by marriage, is rewarded by the discovery that his wife is an heiress; and Thomas Holcroft (1745–1809), whose *The Road to Ruin* (1792) shows a gambler so touched by his father's shame that he is restored to virtue. Such sentimental drama, with its emphasis upon moral teaching through poetic justice, was to develop into melodrama in the nineteenth century.

Robust comedy did not altogether die out. Between 1720 and 1760, however, "laughing" comedy was restricted primarily to farce, usually short plays performed as afterpieces. Samuel Foote (1720–1777) did much to keep the comic spirit alive through such works as *The Knights* (1749), *The Orators* (1762), *The Minor* (1760), and *The Maid of Bath* (1771), for all

FIG. 9.11
Isaac Bickerstaffe's *The Maid of the Mill*. The setting is by Inigo Richards, one of the major scene designers of the late eighteenth century. From *The Magazine of Art* (1895).

combine farcical wit and situations with satire on such contemporary targets as the rising Methodist religion.

After 1760 a few writers began to oppose sentimentalism. George Colman the Elder (1732–1794) approached the spirit of Restoration comedy in *The Jealous Wife* (1761) and other plays. The most im-

FIG. 9.12
She Stoops to Conquer as produced at Covent Garden in 1773. Shown here are Edward Shuter and Mr. Green as Mr. and Mrs. Hardcastle and John Quick as Tony Lumpkin. Painting by Parkinson. Courtesy Theatre Museum, Victoria and Albert Museum, London.

portant of the later comic writers, however, were Goldsmith and Sheridan. Oliver Goldsmith's (1730?-1774) *The Good Natur'd Man* (1768), an attack upon the style of Kelly, Cumberland, and others, is somewhat stilted and structurally weak, but *She Stoops to Conquer* (1773) is a comic masterpiece. Subtitled *The Mistakes of a Night,* it shows how two young men are duped into mistaking the home of a country gentleman for an inn, their consequent ill-mannered treatment of their host, and the misunderstandings, intrigues, and discoveries that eventually lead to the satisfactory conclusion of the love affairs of the principal characters. Its skillful manipulation of an amusing and rapid action was an effective argument in favor of a return to "laughing comedy."

Richard Brinsley Sheridan (1751–1816) is noted primarily for *The Rivals* (1775) and *The School for Scandal* (1777), which recall Congreve's comedies of manners with their sparkling and witty dialogue and their vivid pictures of the fashionable society of the day. But Sheridan's morality is more conventional than was Congreve's, for he always made true virtue triumphant. In *The School for Scandal,* for example, though he permitted his scandalmongers to murder reputations through witty gossip and comic intrigue and to promote the sentiment-spouting but hypocritical Joseph Surface at the expense of his rakish but open-hearted brother Charles, eventually Joseph is exposed, Charles is united with the virtuous Maria,

and the strong-willed but naive Lady Teazle is recalled to her duty to her elderly and comically crotchety husband, Sir Peter.

Goldsmith and Sheridan did much to recapture the brilliance of English drama, and, with the exception of Shakespeare's, their plays have held the stage more consistently than have those by any other English dramatists. Unfortunately, Goldsmith and Sheridan had no successful emulators, and after 1780 English drama moved steadily toward melodrama.

The eighteenth-century theatre was by no means restricted to production of contemporary plays. The pattern followed throughout the eighteenth century had been set during the Restoration, when a company's repertory of thirty-five to forty plays was divided about equally between pre-Commonwealth plays and new plays or successes from recent seasons. By the early eighteenth century, the repertory had increased to forty to seventy-five plays, and by the last quarter of the century had increased to about ninety works. After 1750, about one-third of the repertory was drawn from Shakespearean and other pre-Commonwealth plays, another third was made up of Restoration or early eighteenth-century works, and the remaining third was composed of recent successes or new plays. Consequently, new plays constituted the smallest portion of the repertory.

THE PLAYWRIGHT

The greatest demand for new plays came during the ten years preceding the passage of the Licensing Act in 1737, for during this time a number of minor theatres were open, some of them specializing in new plays. After 1737 the demand for new plays was minimal. The opportunities for production were few, and as a consequence the financial rewards to the playwright were uncertain. For a time during the Restoration, a few playwrights were attached to companies at a fixed salary or as a shareholder. Dryden, for example, held a share in the King's Company from 1668 until 1678, in return for providing three plays each year. But as the supply of plays began to exceed the demand, other financial arrangements were made. After 1680, dramatists were paid by the "benefit" system, under which they received the proceeds (less house expenses) of the third night of the initial run. After 1690, they might also be given a benefit on the sixth night, if the play ran so long, and in the eighteenth century on every third night of the original run. Few plays ran beyond the third night, however, and some did not run that long. Once a play's initial run was over, the playwright received no further payments from the company, even though the

FIG. 9.13
The "screen scene" from Sheridan's *The School for Scandal* at Drury Lane in 1777. A contemporary print.

play might be placed in the repertory and remain there for many years.

Normally, playwrights were able to increase their income by selling the copyrights to their plays. After 1709 works could be copyrighted for a period of fourteen years. Usually the theatre bought the copyright to protect its investment, for once a play was printed any other theatre could produce it. Occasionally playwrights sold the copyright to a publisher. In either case, they were paid no royalty beyond the initial sum. After fourteen years (if they were still alive) the copyright reverted to the authors and could be renewed for an additional fourteen years.

Although occasionally they were paid set sums by theatres for their plays, throughout the eighteenth century dramatists depended primarily upon benefit performances for their income, since copyright payments were relatively small. A few plays brought their authors considerable financial rewards, but these were exceptional.

FINANCIAL POLICIES

By 1700 theatre managers had evolved most of the financial policies that were to remain in use in England for the next 150 years. In these policies, shares played a heavy role. There were two kinds of shares: in buildings and in companies.

From the Restoration on, theatres in England were normally erected on leased land with money obtained by the sale of shares in the buildings. In return for their investment, shareholders were paid a fixed sum for each day the theatre was used for performances. Often they also had the right to attend the theatre free of charge.

The second type of sharing involved an investment in a company and its productions. For a time after 1660, the old system under which actors shared in the company's risks and profits was revived, but as the theatre declined in prosperity actors came to prefer a fixed salary to the indefinite income derived from sharing. Consequently, by 1690 the sharing arrangement had been abandoned in London. It was revived by Betterton's troupe from 1695 to 1708, but after that time it disappeared almost altogether in London, although it continued to be used in most provincial theatres until well into the nineteenth century.

As the actors' control declined, the power of outside investors increased. Davenant and Killigrew established the pattern that eventually prevailed when they mortgaged their patents, scenery, and costumes in order to raise capital. When the mortgages were not redeemed, partial ownership of the companies passed to persons who had little or no interest in the theatre except as a commercial investment. The danger of this system first became evident in 1693 when Christopher Rich, ostensibly to protect the investors, assumed control of the United Companies, even though he had had no theatrical experience of any kind. He was merely the first of many similar persons who were to gain control over theatres in London and elsewhere.

Although there might be many investors in a company, the financial risk fell almost entirely on the man who leased the theatre and ran the company (that is, on the manager of the troupe). Few managements survived long, and consequently few in the eighteenth century are significant. Among the most important were those of the Rich family. Although Christopher Rich was evicted from Drury Lane in 1709, his son John managed Lincoln's Inn Fields from 1714 to 1732 and Covent Garden from 1732 to 1761. Thus, from 1693 until 1761, the Rich family played a crucial role in London's theatrical life. After 1767, when Rich's heirs sold their interest, Covent Garden was weakened by dissensions among the owners. Then, in 1771, control passed to Thomas Harris, who retained it into the nineteenth century.

Between 1710 and 1733 the Drury Lane was very successful because of the policies of the "triumvirate" of actor-managers, Colley Cibber, Robert Wilks, and Thomas Doggett (replaced after 1713 by Barton Booth). After 1733, however, Drury Lane was in grave financial difficulty until 1747, when stability was restored under David Garrick and John Lacy. With Garrick assuming responsibility for staging and Lacy for finances, this management was to be the most admired of the eighteenth century. After Garrick's retirement in 1776, control passed to a group under the leadership of Richard Brinsley Sheridan. Most of the production duties, however, fell to Thomas King, an actor. King was given so little authority, however, that the theatre had declined considerably by 1788, when John Philip Kemble replaced him.

The Haymarket Theatre was under many short-lived managements until 1766, when it became the third licensed house. From 1766 until 1777 it was managed by Samuel Foote, and after 1777 by George Colman. Both men supervised their companies closely.

Out of the many failures of those managers who knew too little about the theatre came the actor-manager system. Betterton and Garrick had lead the way, but it did not become common until near the end of the century, after which it dominated British theatre until the First World War.

Despite occasional retrenchments, the trend between 1660 and 1800 was toward larger companies and more carefully mounted productions, both of which demanded greater financial resources. Whereas the typical company of the Restoration had included thirty-five to forty persons, the troupe of 1800 had about eighty. In addition to actors, each company employed a treasurer, ticket takers, "numberers" (people who counted spectators as a check on the ticket takers), prompters, dancers, musicians, bill distributors, scene painters, candle snuffers, stagehands, wardrobe keepers, dressers, laundresses, and maintenance personnel. In the late eighteenth century the major troupes were employing more than 200 people.

Expenses were calculated in terms of a single playing day. This was necessary in part because by the eighteenth century benefits were an important feature of theatrical life and a manager had to state the amount to be deducted from the receipts as the theatre's expenses on these occasions. In the early eighteenth century the average daily expenses were about £40; by 1735 they had risen to £50, and by 1790 to £105.

Since managers depended primarily upon ticket sales for income, only two paths were open to them as expenses increased: to raise the price of tickets or to increase attendance. Although at times they did both, they were cautious about raising prices. Consequently, the scale of entrance fees did not change markedly. During the Restoration the basic charges were: boxes, 4 shillings; pit, 2 shillings 6 pence; middle gallery, 1 shilling 6 pence; upper gallery, 1 shilling. In the late eighteenth century the comparable prices were 5 shillings, 3 shillings, 2 shillings and 1 shilling. The normal prices were raised for premieres, or when expenditures for new costumes or scenery were thought to justify a temporary increase. On special occasions, such as a benefit for a particularly popular actor, portions of the pit were converted into boxes and additional seating was erected on the stage. Such alterations were also accompanied by a considerable increase in the prices charged for those sections, although little of the additional income went to the manager.

Beginning in the 1690s spectators were allowed to enter at the end of the third act at "half price," except when a new pantomime or other attraction was to be given as an afterpiece. On the other hand, if prices were raised because of the afterpiece, the spectator who left at the end of the main piece was refunded the additional charge. Besides tickets, the managers realized some income from the lease of concessions to those who hawked food, drink, playbooks, and playbills in the theatre.

Steadily increasing expense, however, forced most managers to enlarge their theatres to accommodate additional spectators. Most of the changes in theatre auditoriums were motivated by this need, whereas alterations of the stage resulted from changing fashions in spectacle.

THEATRE ARCHITECTURE

Although following the Restoration the Salisbury Court, Phoenix/Cockpit, and Red Bull theatres were used for a short time, none was thought sufficiently suited to the Italianate scenery which was then coming into vogue. Killigrew used Gibbon's Tennis Court until his Theatre Royal in Bridges Street was ready for occupancy in 1663. Little is known of the latter building, which burned in 1672. Another structure, usually called the Drury Lane Theatre, was erected on the same site. Opened in 1674 and used until 1791, it measured 58 feet by 140 feet.

In 1661 Davenant converted Lisle's Tennis Court into the Lincoln's Inn Fields Theatre. Measuring only about 30 by 75 feet, it became increasingly inadequate for the operatic spectacles that Davenant favored. Consequently, in 1671 it was replaced by the Dorset Garden Theatre, a structure measuring 57 by 140 feet, designed by Christopher Wren. The Dorset Garden was seldom used after the troupes were united in 1682 and was torn down in 1709. When Betterton's company was licensed in 1695, it reopened the old Lincoln's Inn Fields Theatre.

Thus, in London between 1660 and 1700, there were three theatres of importance: Drury Lane, Lincoln's Inn Fields, and Dorset Garden. They varied in size and detail, but they shared common features that established the pattern for English playhouses until the nineteenth century.

In those theatres the auditorium was divided into pit, boxes, and galleries. Unlike its French equivalent, the English pit was raked to improve sightlines and equipped with eight to ten rows of backless benches for all spectators. There were two or three galleries. The first was partitioned into boxes; the uppermost

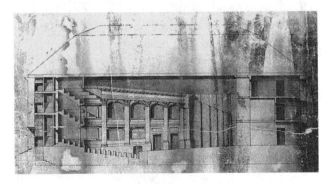

FIG. 9.14
Sectional plan of a theatre, believed to be Drury Lane, as designed by Christopher Wren in 1674. The auditorium is at left. Note the backless benches in the raked pit; the deep apron with two proscenium doors; and the relatively shallow stage behind the proscenium. Copyright the Warden and Fellows of All Souls College, Oxford.

FIG. 9.15
Stage of the Dorset Garden Theatre. The proscenium
doors can be glimpsed at the extreme sides. The scene is
from Settle's *The Empress of Morocco,* produced in 1673.
From Wilkinson, *Londina Illustrata* (1825).

change of place. Thus, the forestage thrust the action into the auditorium, rather than confining it behind the picture frame. In its combination of features of the pre-Commonwealth and Italianate stages, it foreshadowed in many respects the thrust stage of the twentieth century.

The floor of the stage sloped upward from the front of the forestage to the back wall of the stagehouse. Behind the proscenium, grooves were installed to accommodate wings and shutters, while trapdoors and flying machinery provided for special effects. With minor changes, these basic characteristics were to continue through the eighteenth century.

Between 1700 and 1800 only a few theatres were important: Drury Lane, Lincoln's Inn Fields, the King's Theatre, the Haymarket, and Covent Garden. The Drury Lane, which originally seated about 650, was renovated in 1775 to accommodate 2,300, then torn down and rebuilt in 1794 to increase the capacity to 3,611. When Lincoln's Inn Fields was abandoned in 1705, Christopher Rich razed it and erected a new theatre on the site. This building, which seated about 1,400, was used from 1714 until 1732, when Covent Garden opened. The King's Theatre (until 1714 called the Haymarket or Queen's Theatre), built in 1705, was devoted entirely to opera from 1707 until 1789, when it was gutted by fire. At the time of its destruction it had a capacity of more than 3,000 persons. The Haymarket, built in 1720, was used by unlicensed companies until 1766, after which it took its place as a major theatre. In the late eighteenth century it held about 1,500. The Covent Garden, built in 1732 to replace Lincoln's Inn Fields, remained in use until 1808. Originally it seated just under 1,400, but in 1784 it was enlarged to hold 2,500 and in 1792 it was rebuilt to accommodate 3,000. (This renovation was made in part because Drury Lane was being rebuilt at that time to hold 3,600.) Thus, the size of auditoriums increased throughout the eighteenth century, although the trend toward largeness did not accelerate until after 1760. In spite of the increase in size, however, the basic arrangement remained constant. All the theatres continued to be divided into pit, boxes, and galleries, and until the 1790s none had more than three levels of galleries.

As the auditorium grew in size, so did the stage. Around 1700 the stage behind the proscenium at Drury Lane was increased to about 30 feet, and by 1790 some theatres had stages more than 50 feet deep. At the same time, the forestage dwindled. Around 1700 Rich removed one set of proscenium doors and shortened the forestage to make room for more seats in the pit. Consequently, throughout the eighteenth century there was usually only one proscenium door on either side of the stage. The forestage, now re-

was undivided and equipped with benches; the middle gallery, when present, might be partially devoted to boxes and the remainder to benches. The early theatres were small. At the Drury Lane, for example, the distance from the front of the stage to the back of the auditorium was only about 36 feet. Seating capacity was limited. In the seventeenth century, the Drury Lane held only about 650 persons and Lincoln's Inn Fields even fewer. Thus, these were relatively intimate theatres.

If the auditorium resembled that of the continental theatres, the stage differed, for it included both a proscenium arch and an open platform forward of the proscenium. The Drury Lane of 1674 had a stage about 34 feet deep, divided into two roughly equal parts by the proscenium. Two (and in one theatre three) doors, surmounted by balconies, opened onto the forestage at either side. These doors were the customary entrances for all characters, since most of the action took place on the forestage. As in Elizabethan times, an exit through one door and reentry through another were sufficient to indicate a

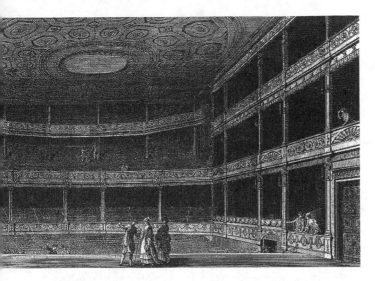

FIG. 9.16
The auditorium of the Drury Lane Theatre after it was remodeled and redecorated in 1775. Engraving by R. and J. Adams. Courtesy Theatre Museum, Victoria and Albert Museum, London.

duced to about 12 feet in depth, remained the favorite playing area, however, until at least 1765, after which it was used less extensively.

The work areas needed for production were also enlarged during the eighteenth century by remodeling the existing structure or by acquiring or constructing smaller buildings adjoining it. These spaces included dressing rooms, greenrooms, storage of various kinds, areas used in the construction of scenery and for costumes and properties. In spite of all additions and alterations, by 1790 most of the theatres were considered inadequate, and soon after they were to be replaced by larger, more elaborate buildings.

SCENIC PRACTICES

After 1661 the scenic practices of the English stage differed little from those then in use in Italy and France. Wings, borders, and shutters were the standard units, although after 1690 roll drops were sometimes used in the place of shutters. Sets were shifted by means of grooves installed on the stage floor and overhead. Stagehands made the necessary changes upon a whistled signal from the prompter. (For reasons that are unclear, the chariot-and-pole system, the standard method of shifting scenery in continental theatres, was seldom used in England, except at the opera house.) Since the front curtain was raised after the prologue was spoken and not lowered until the end of the performance, all changes were made in full view of the audience. Even entr'acte enter-

tainments were given in front of a full stage setting until about 1750, after which an "act drop" was used as a background. Heavy properties or furniture could be set up and removed behind the shutters or the act drop. Occasionally they were brought on by servants in full view of the audience.

Between 1660 and 1800 each theatre accumulated a stock of scenery that was reused often. When a new theatre was built, settings were commissioned even before the repertory was fixed. This practice was made possible by the neoclassical attitude that specific times and places are irrelevant in drama, and that attempts to particularize only diminish universality. The aim was to capture the essence of a type of place rather than to re-create the features of a particular place. Thus, settings were so anonymous that they could be used in many different plays. One author, writing about 1750, lists the necessary scenes as: (1) temples, (2) tombs, (3) city walls and gates, (4) palace exteriors, (5) palace interiors, (6) streets, (7) chambers, (8) prisons, (9) gardens, and (10) rural prospects. He adds that other settings are needed only occasionally. During the Restoration, a few comedies depicted well-known places in London, but this type of particularity diminished markedly during the eighteenth century, except in those minor dramatic types, such as pantomime, in which spectacle played a major role. Even in these instances, however, the scenery created for them was reused extensively in other plays.

The development of spectacle was retarded by the presence of spectators on the stage. Although well established before 1642, this practice was not revived until about 1690, and was not usual until about 1700. It continued until 1762, when Garrick banished the audience from the stage. Between 1700 and 1762, rows of benches extended upstage from the proscenium, and at benefits additional amphitheatrical seating often was erected across the back of the stage. On the other hand, the audience was sometimes forbidden to sit on the stage if a production depended heavily on spectacle.

Because most plays were performed in stock scenery, ticket prices were raised when new sets were introduced. The additional revenue that this provided may be one reason why spectacle increased, for Rich's successful exploitation of spectacle in pantomimes led him to experiment with it in regular drama. In the 1730s he added a procession and coronation scene to *Henry VIII,* in 1750 a funeral procession to *Romeo and Juliet,* and in 1761 the coronation of George III to several of Shakespeare's history plays. Elaborate spectacle was ordinarily reserved for the minor genres, however, until about 1765, when Garrick returned from the continent with new ideas of staging. Through the remainder of the century, scenery was to become more particularized and new settings more common. Of the thirty-seven new plays presented at Drury Lane between 1765 and 1776, nineteen were given entirely new scenery.

The increasing interest in spectacle was accompanied by a change in the status of the scene painter. From 1660 until about 1735, no theatre had a scene painter on its regular staff; settings were usually commissioned as needed from easel painters. But by the late eighteenth century, two or more scene painters were attached to each major theatre. This probably explains why so little is known of English scene designers before 1760. During the Restoration John Webb (1611–1672) worked with Davenant, and Samuel Towers (*fl.* 1676–1682), Robert Robinson (*c.* 1653–1706), and Robert Streeter (1624–1680) painted settings for Killigrew. Scene painting was apparently still a fledgling art in England, and consequently complex designs were costly. In 1669 Killigrew was sued by Isaac Fuller (1606–1672), who claimed that he had not been paid for one setting, which he testified had taken him six weeks to paint; the court awarded him 335 pounds for his work (at a time when a leading actor was paid about 2 ½

pounds per week). In 1674–1675, another painter was paid 800 pounds to do settings for one play. By the early eighteenth century, however, payments were considerably less, perhaps because the painters now had greater facility. Since before 1760 scenery was commissioned only sporadically, the average yearly expenditure for settings was small. Covent Garden spent only 253 pounds in the season of 1746–1747, and until after 1750 only about one-tenth of a company's budget was ever spent on settings.

From occasional references we know the names of many scene painters of the first half of the eighteenth century. Some of the more important are James Thornhill (1675–1734), who flourished in the early years of the century; John DeVoto (*fl.* 1708–1752), who worked between 1719 and 1744; George Lambert (*c.* 1699–1765), a landscape painter who did settings for Rich at Lincoln's Inn Fields and Covent Garden and some of whose settings remained in use until 1808; and Francis Hayman (1708–1776), who painted settings for Drury Lane in the 1730s and 1740s.

The situation began to change in 1749, when Rich imported designers from the continent. The

FIG. 9.17
Setting for Act 1, scene 1 of *Arsinoe*. Design by James Thornhill. Courtesy Theatre Museum, Victoria and Albert Museum, London.

most significant of these was Jean-Nicolas Servandoni (1695–1766), famous for his work at the Paris Opéra and elsewhere in Europe. Rich seems to have had Servandoni paint some settings for which he had no immediate use, for one was introduced at Covent Garden as late as 1773 as never having been used before. Other important artists who worked at Covent Garden include Giovanni Battista Cipriani (1727–1785), a Florentine painter who came to London in 1755; Nicholas Thomas Dall (?–1776), a Dane who settled in England around 1750, considered one of the finest painters of his age; and John Inigo Richards (c. 1729–1810), a distinguished English painter noted especially for his picturesque landscapes.

The most important designer of the late eighteenth century, however, was Philippe Jacques De-Loutherbourg (1740–1812), a French artist who had studied with Boucher and Boquet of the Paris Opéra. Engaged by Garrick in 1771 to oversee all elements of spectacle, he continued in this position until 1781, when he resigned because Sheridan proposed to cut his salary of 500 pounds. DeLoutherbourg continued to design settings occasionally until 1785. Between 1771 and 1785 he prepared more than thirty productions, of which a few are of special importance: *A Christmas Tale* (1773), with its subtle lighting effects; *The Wonders of Derbyshire* (1779), which depicted actual places in England and established the vogue for "local color"; and *Omai, or a Trip Around The World* (1785), a "travelogue" based on Captain Cook's voyage. In other productions, DeLoutherbourg re-created such recent events as the Portsmouth Naval Review (1773) and a fashionable outdoor festival (1774). From 1781 to 1786 he maintained a miniature theatre, the Eidophusikon, where, on a stage 6 by 8 feet, he created remarkable illusions of specific places and weather conditions through painting, lighting, sound effects, and music.

DeLoutherbourg's contributions were many. He popularized reproductions of real places on the stage. To increase illusion, he broke up the stage picture with ground rows and set pieces to gain a greater sense of depth and to avoid the symmetrical composition imposed by parallel wings and shutters. He used miniature figures at the rear of the stage to depict battles, marching armies, and sailing vessels; and sound effects, such as waves, rain, hail, and distant guns, to increase the illusion. He revamped the lighting system, installing overhead battens, using silk screens and gauze curtains to gain subtle variations in color and to simulate various weather conditions and times of day. Perhaps most important of all, DeLoutherbourg achieved unity of design by overseeing all the visual elements of productions. Before

FIG. 9.18

A sketch by DeLoutherbourg for the battle scenes in Shakespeare's *Richard III*. Note the tent at left and others in the background. From *The Magazine of Art* (1895).

DeLoutherbourg's time, the various settings for a single play were often done by different painters. Furthermore, a play might be given one new set and have others taken from stock. Thus, although a manager probably had a vague agreement with his painters about the kind of scenes to be provided, there seems to have been little attempt to coordinate efforts. DeLoutherbourg's practices established a standard that was not to be fully achieved by his successors until well into the nineteenth century.

The work of DeLoutherbourg and others reflects the growing interest in both local color and history. The rediscovery of Herculaneum in 1709 aroused public curiosity about past civilizations, and gradually an interest in picturesque places and customs began to replace the neoclassical preoccupation with generalized, universalized times and places. Settings became more specific, and composition began to move away from the symmetrically balanced settings typical of the preceding period. These new interests were not fully exploited, however, until after 1800.

Little is known of lighting practices during the Restoration. Performances were given in the afternoon, and windows probably provided some illumination. Chandeliers hung above the apron and behind the proscenium. Pepys, in his *Diary*, often complains of headaches caused by looking into the candles. Footlights were certainly in use by 1672, for they are depicted in an illustration printed in that year. (See Fig. 9.2.) Since most of the action occurred on the apron, both auditorium and stage were illuminated throughout performances.

FIG. 9.19
A riot at Covent Garden in 1763. Dressed for Arne's *Artaxerxes,* the actors wear Near Eastern dress while the actresses wear fashionable English clothing. Note also the chandeliers hanging over the stage. Courtesy Theatre Museum, Victoria and Albert Museum, London.

By 1744, lights were apparently being mounted on vertical "ladders" behind each wing and dimmed by "scene blinds" (that is, by shields that could be manipulated to intervene between the light source and the stage), for an inventory made at Covent Garden in that year lists twelve pairs of "scene ladders," twenty-four "scene blinds," and 192 tin candlesticks. Footlights were mounted on pivots which allowed them to be lowered below the stage level for dimming. Lamps were used in some positions, since reflectors made candles wilt. It is difficult to say when these arrangements began. Possibly they date from the Restoration, for similar practices were clearly in use on the continent by that time.

Although Garrick is credited with reforming stage lighting in 1765, the nature of his reforms is unclear. He seems to have removed all visible light sources from the stage and to have increased brightness, perhaps with improved lamps and reflectors. He also popularized the continental system of making the light ladders rotate so that they could be made to reflect light toward or away from the stage. During the 1770s DeLoutherbourg made other changes. Using silk screens to reflect light, and perhaps transparent silk filters, he gained considerable control over color for the first time. This increased concern for lighting is reflected in the costs: In 1745 theatres were spending about 340 pounds a year on lighting, while during the 1770s expenses rose to 1,970 pounds.

Lighting further improved after the introduction in 1785 of the Argand, or "patent," lamp. Using a cylindrical wick and glass chimney to control the relative proportions of oxygen and oil, this lamp produced a much brighter and steadier light than earlier instruments had. After this time, oil largely superseded candles for stage lighting. Since the chimneys could be colored, experimentation with color effects also increased.

Improvements in lighting and increased emphasis upon illusion encouraged managers to place more of the action behind the proscenium arch. This trend was not fully completed during the eighteenth century, however, and the auditorium continued to be lighted as a part of the total picture.

COSTUME PRACTICES

For the most part, the principles governing costume between 1660 and 1800 differed little from those of pre-Commonwealth times or from those of seventeenth-century France. Since time and place were considered unimportant, most characters wore contemporary garments. Furthermore, since neoclassicism tended to idealize nature, most actors dressed their characters as sumptuously as possible. As in the earlier period, however, some deviations from contemporary dress were usual. Classical heroes wore the *habit à la romaine,* while Near Eastern characters were identified by turbans, baggy trousers, and long fur-trimmed robes. On the other hand, actresses playing classical or Near Eastern roles merely added feathered headdresses or a few exotic

FIG. 9.20
Whitehead's *The Roman Father* at Drury Lane in 1750. At center is Garrick. Note the *habit à la romaine* worn by the men and the few exotic touches at the shoulder and waist of the women's dresses. Courtesy the Folger Shakespeare Library, Washington, D.C.

touches to otherwise contemporary dress. Until about 1750, actresses often wore black velvet in tragedy, but after that time they appeared increasingly in the latest fashions.

Conventionalized costumes continued for a few characters, notably Falstaff (played in ruff and Cavalier boots), Richard III (dressed in Elizabethan pumpkin hose), and Henry VIII (clothed after the manner of Holbein's portrait). Other conventions included costuming Hamlet in black, adding ermine trim to Lear's otherwise contemporary dress, and playing Macbeth in the uniform of a British army officer.

Concern for greater realism and appropriateness began in the 1740s. In 1741 Charles Macklin clothed Shylock in a black gabardine gown, long trousers, and red hat (which he considered realistic Jewish dress). After 1750, Garrick occasionally attempted to costume pre-Commonwealth plays in Elizabethan garments, although he continued to perform all those written after 1660 in eighteenth-century dress. Garrick's costumes were neither historically accurate nor consistent, but his concern indicates the awakening interest in history and the desire to reflect it in costuming. At first, there were no guides to historical costume, but in 1757 there appeared in London *Recueil des Habillements,* a collection of designs taken from paintings by Holbein, Van Dyke, Hollar, and others, "to which are added the habits of the principal characters on the English stage." In 1775 Joseph Strutt was to provide more accurate information in *The Dress and Habits of the Peoples of England.* As with scenery, however, costuming was not significantly altered by these trends until the nineteenth century.

Between 1660 and 1800 the principal sources for costumes were the company's wardrobe and the actor's own garments. Each company maintained a "common stock" of costumes, which was preserved and added to regularly. Throughout the eighteenth century, companies always spent more on costumes than on scenery and in time wardrobes became extremely large, since nothing was thrown away and costumes were frequently refurbished. In staging a coronation scene in 1761, Garrick is said to have used garments that had been in stock since 1727. In the late 1760s the Covent Garden wardrobe had grown so large that it had to be moved to an adjoining house.

At a glance, these practices suggest that a company provided adequate costumes for its repertory, but this is not completely true. In the second half of the eighteenth century a company added to its stock only an average of about twelve new women's and twelve new men's outfits each year. Since an acting company included seventy to eighty plays, this rate of acquisition would probably have left most actors rather shabbily dressed if all had depended on the company's wardrobe.

FIG. 9.21

The play-within-the-play from *Hamlet* as shown in a painting by Francis Hayman, who also painted scenery for the Drury Lane Theatre in the 1730s. At center, Claudius is rising from his seat; Hamlet is seated on the floor in the lower right corner. Note the costumes. Courtesy the Folger Shakespeare Library, Washington, D.C.

It is probably for this reason that actors with sufficient means supplied most of their own costumes. Some demanded and received a special allowance from the manager for this purpose. The actors' desire to dress as sumptuously as possible led to intense rivalries. As a result, costumes often reflected the actor's purse rather than the character's position, and a queen played by a poor actress might appear shabby alongside an attendant played by a performer of greater means.

Nevertheless, the company's wardrobe was available to all actors. Wardrobe keepers checked out costumes to players, who were free to select whatever they wished to wear. In the late eighteenth century this freedom of choice was considerably curtailed as concern for appropriateness grew and as managers began to give wardrobe keepers more authority to decide what garments should be worn. Nevertheless, by modern standards the costume practices of the eighteenth century were at best haphazard.

In addition to looking after the costumes, wardrobe keepers made and altered garments, purchased supplies, and took an inventory annually. Laundresses to keep the clothes clean and "dressers" to assist the actors during performances were also employed.

ACTORS AND ACTING, 1660–1800

A major innovation of the Restoration was the introduction of women into acting companies. By 1661 both Davenant and Killigrew had a full complement of actresses, and within a short time men appeared only in such female roles as witches and comic old women, a practice that persisted through the eighteenth century.

Between 1660 and 1800 beginning actors usually entered a company on a probationary status and learned by observing established performers. In the 1660s and 1670s Davenant and Killigrew maintained a training company, and in the 1740s Macklin ran an acting school, as did Thomas Sheridan somewhat later, but none of these operations was a marked success. At Drury Lane between 1710 and 1730, the young actors had to attend three sessions a week to learn singing and dancing, and the established actors in that company were sometimes paid to teach the beginners. After 1750 Garrick instructed his young actors, and Rich trained several pantomime players. Such attempts were sporadic, however, and most performers learned through trial and error.

The beginners, or "utility," actors played an enormous number of small roles each season and eventually discovered the types for which they were best suited. After a few years, they advanced into a "line of business" (a limited range of character types) in which they usually remained for the rest of their careers. It is impossible to determine when lines of business were first recognized, for they may extend back to pre-Commonwealth times. By the late eighteenth century four clearly distinguishable ranks existed: (1) players of leading roles, (2) players of secondary roles, (3) players of third-line parts (often called "walking ladies" or "walking gentlemen"), and (4) general utility performers. The first rank was usually restricted to players of heroes and heroines of tragedy and light comedy, although an unusually popular performer in another line might command a salary of the highest rank. The lesser ranks included specialists in such lines as low comedy roles, "singing chambermaids," fathers and elderly men, eccentric types, witches, and hags.

The extent to which actors specialized depended upon both their versatility and the size of the company in which they performed. A small, provincial company required its actors to play a wider range of parts than did the large London troupes. Most actors had a serious and a comic line, although they

were seldom equally good in both. Lines of business led to the "possession of parts," since once actors were cast in roles they continued to play them as long as they remained in the company (though those who started with young lover roles generally moved into more mature parts). Under the repertory system, actors were assigned a large number of roles, each of which, once learned, they were supposedly able to perform on 24-hour notice. Actors jealously guarded their parts, and crises often developed when established actors were brought into a company and roles had to be redistributed as a consequence. This problem increased in the late eighteenth century, when troupes began to employ multiple performers in the same line of business. The number of parts that leading actors had in their active repertory varied. Mrs. Oldfield had an average of about twenty-six, Barton Booth about thirty-five, and Garrick, ninety-six.

The lesser actors in a company were employed by the season, but leading actors were usually put under contract for a longer period, although almost never exceeding five years. On the other hand, after 1743 Macklin usually performed only under short-term engagements, a practice which foreshadowed the "starring" arrangements which dominated the nineteenth-century theatre. The concept of starring engagements also received considerable impetus from those eighteenth-century performers who made brief appearances with provincial troupes during the summer months when the major theatres in London were closed.

The income of actors varied considerably. Salaries, though quoted by the week, were paid only for those days upon which the theatres were open; and closure brought a proportionate deduction from the actors' pay. Except for leading performers, little is known about actors' salaries prior to 1750. In the 1690s Mrs. Barry received about £70 a year; by the 1740s a top-ranking actor earned about £180; in the 1760s the four ranks of actors were paid £287, £148, £70, and £42 per year; by 1790 several leading performers were receiving well above £300 per year.

This stated salary, however, was usually augmented by at least one benefit annually. Benefit performances for groups of actors were instituted in the 1660s and were first accorded to individuals in the late 1680s. After 1695 Betterton began offering benefits as inducements to actors to remain with his company, and this custom was gradually extended until it included every employee of the playhouse. Major performers had separate benefits, but lesser actors and most of the nonperforming personnel usually shared benefits. Typically the beneficiaries received all the receipts in excess of house expenses, although there were many variations on this arrangement. At first the benefits were scattered throughout the season, but after 1712 they were normally concentrated in the period between March and the summer closing.

A well-attended benefit might bring a performer more income in a single evening than was made throughout the rest of the year, especially since spectators often voluntarily paid higher admission fees and presented gifts of money or jewelry to popular performers. On the other hand, the receipts sometimes did not meet the house expenses and the actor lost money. The lure of a profitable benefit, however, probably permitted managers to pay actors considerably less than might otherwise have been demanded.

Usually an experienced actor was appointed to stage the plays (and was given the title "acting manager") when the theatre manager was not qualified for this task. Betterton was acting manager of the companies in which he worked for most of the years between 1668 and 1709; at Drury Lane between 1710 and 1732, the triumvirate of actor-managers divided the rehearsal duties; John Rich staged pantomimes and spectacles, but employed such actors as James Quin, Lacy Ryan, and James Lacy to rehearse the regular drama; Charles Macklin was acting manager at Drury Lane from 1734 to 1743, and Garrick was in charge of the repertory and staging at that theatre from 1747 until 1776.

The first three rehearsals of a new play fell to the dramatist, who presumably helped the actors with interpretation. The acting manager was responsible for revivals. Rehearsals were few by modern standards; they were held from about 10 A.M. until 1 P.M. and seldom extended beyond two weeks. Garrick was sometimes more meticulous and occasionally prolonged rehearsal to eight weeks. Little time was spent on blocking or movement patterns. Actors learned by experience how to move about the stage and when to give the dominant positions to the major performers. Most scenes were played on the forestage or near the front of the main stage, and lines were addressed to the audience as much as to the other characters. Since furniture was seldom used, actors usually stood throughout and gave little thought to creating realistic stage pictures. During rehearsals the players seldom attempted to give full portrayals. Consequently, innovations conceived by an actor were usually not revealed until the first performance, when they surprised fellow actors as much as the audience. The typical brief rehearsals usually meant that on opening night actors were often still uncertain of their lines and depended much on improvisation. Furthermore, their relatively secure positions seem to have made many actors neglectful. As a result, managers sought to impose discipline through an elaborate system of fines for such faults

as tardiness at rehearsals, failure to learn lines, refusal of roles, and a variety of other lapses.

The orderly operation of a company depended much upon the prompter, whose duties included securing licenses for the plays, copying out the actors' "sides," holding rehearsals when requested to do so, and assessing fines. During performances the prompter gave cues for scene shifts and music, dispatched call boys for actors, and prompted as necessary. Some of these prompters, notably John Downes, William Chetwood, and Richard Cross, have left invaluable records of the theatres in which they served.

Acting was a mixture of tradition and innovation. Roles were passed down from one generation to the next, and with them went the traditional interpretation. When one actor succeeded another, he or she was expected to learn the business used in that company, since the repertory could not be restaged to suit one actor. Because so much of playing became traditional, new conceptions of characters, or even new line readings, often produced sensations. Thus, Charles Macklin greatly altered the conception of Shylock in 1741 by departing from the traditional low-comedy interpretation. On the other hand, Garrick built his reputation through the unique qualities he was able to achieve without altering the basic tradition of his roles.

The style of acting varied from formal to realistic. Until about 1750, the dominant approach was oratorical, as epitomized in the playing of Betterton, Booth, and Quin. Then Macklin and Garrick urged the adoption of a style based upon direct observation of life, although they too probably idealized reality. The two styles came into direct conflict in the 1740s when Quin and Garrick were the leading performers of London. Garrick's ultimate victory parallels the changes evident in the other theatre arts, since it marks a movement away from the idealized generality of neoclassicism, which Quin favored, to a more specific and individualized characterization. The neoclassical and oratorical style persisted, however, even among Garrick's troupe, and two rather distinct modes were often seen in the same production.

Despite changes, however, some conventions remained relatively constant, and clearly distinguish the "realism" of the eighteenth century from that of today. First, whenever possible, actors played at the front of the stage. Furthermore, as one reporter stated: "They never turn their backs on the public, and seldom show their faces in profile." They seem also to have exchanged stage positions after each speech. As one observer put it, "An actor passes invariably to the right as his interlocutor passes to the left, and vice versa." Other customs included "affected prolongation of certain cries and exclamations,

FIG. 9.22

Charles Macklin as Shylock and Mrs. Pope as Portia in the trial scene of *The Merchant of Venice*. Macklin's manner of playing and dressing the part created a sensation because it departed so markedly from earlier treatments. Note the contemporary garments worn by the other characters. Courtesy the Folger Shakespeare Library, Washington, D.C.

the sort of 'organ-point' by which all of the oh's and ah's are emphasized; the frequent transports in which the actors feel compelled to precipitate themselves full length to the floor, and the frightful noise of these oft-repeated plunges."

During the early part of the century, actors seem to have observed the meter of verse in a long intoned chant, but from Garrick's time onward they attempted to disguise the verse so as to make it sound as "natural" as possible. Throughout the century actors seem in speaking to have distinguished between less important passages and high points by delivering the former in a manner called "level speaking" and the latter with great vehemence. Actors sought and expected to receive applause as they made "points" throughout the play. (Since there were not curtain calls at the end of the play, this applause had to suffice.) Taken altogether, the performance style of the eighteenth-century actor probably resembled what we now see in conventional opera productions.

The period between 1660 and 1800 is noted above all for its actors. In fact, so many outstanding

performers appeared during this time that only a few can be noted here. By far the most important actor of the Restoration was Thomas Betterton (*c.* 1635–1710). On the stage from 1660 to 1709, he excelled in heroic and tragic parts and was universally considered the greatest actor of his day. Betterton performed a wide range of roles, both comic and serious, although he was probably best in such parts as Hamlet, Othello, Hotspur, and Brutus. He remained completely in character throughout a performance and commanded attention with his restrained but powerful action and speech. His somewhat formal and elocutionary style established the model for others. Three of the actresses were outstanding: Nell Gwynn, Mrs. Barry, and Mrs. Bracegirdle. Nell Gwynn's (1650–1687) acting career was brief, 1665 to 1669, but sufficient to establish her fame as a comedian (especially in roles requiring male attire), dancer, and speaker of witty prologues and epilogues. Elizabeth Barry (1658–1713) played leading tragic roles opposite Betterton. Ann Bracegirdle (*c.* 1663–1748), trained by Betterton, excelled in comedies of manners from 1680 until 1707, when she retired at the height of her career. Other important actors of the Restoration included Charles Hart (*c.* 1630–1683), Edward Kynaston (1643–1712), John Lacy (*c.* 1615–1681), Michael Mohun (*c.* 1616–1684), and Cave Underhill (*c.* 1634–1710).

Between 1710 and 1735 the outstanding actors were Colley Cibber, Robert Wilks, Thomas Doggett, Barton Booth, and Anne Oldfield. Cibber (1671–1757) began his acting career in 1690. Remaining with Rich when the more experienced actors seceded in 1695, he was soon playing leading roles and writing popular plays. From 1710 until 1733 he was one of the managers and leading performers of Drury Lane. In 1740 he published his autobiography, a principal source of information about the English theatre between 1690 and 1735. As an actor, Cibber was best in the roles of fops. Robert Wilks (*c.* 1665–1732), who began his acting career in Ireland in 1691, was well established at Drury Lane by 1698, where he played leading roles and served as acting manager. From 1710 until his death he was one of the managers of Drury Lane. Successful in tragedy, he was even more admired as the dashing young hero of comedy. Thomas Doggett (*c.* 1670–1721) was considered the finest low comedian of his day. He began his career in Dublin and worked in several provincial companies before coming to London in 1691. Taken into the management of Drury Lane in 1710, he resigned in 1713 and seldom acted afterward. Barton Booth (1681–1733) began his career in Dublin about 1698 and came to London in 1700. He played secondary roles until 1713, when he made a great sensation in Addison's *Cato*. By royal order, he was admitted to the management of Drury Lane. From 1713 to 1727, when ill health forced him to retire, he was considered the finest tragic actor of London and Betterton's true successor. Anne Oldfield (1683–1730) went on the stage in 1700 and achieved her first success about 1704. After the retirement of Mrs. Barry and Mrs. Bracegirdle, she was considered the finest actress of her time. She played both comic and serious roles, but was especially admired in high comedy. Her burial in Westminster Abbey is an indication of the respect in which she was held.

By 1733 these actors were either dead or retired. During the next ten years there was a dearth of outstanding performers. The leading actor was James

Quin (1693–1766), who began his career in Dublin in 1712, came to Drury Lane in 1714, and in 1718 joined John Rich, for whom he worked as acting manager. He returned to Drury Lane in 1734 and retired in 1751. Although his declamatory style in tragedy led to unfavorable comparisons with Garrick, he was universally admired in such comic roles as Falstaff. Despite Garrick's reforms, Quin was still at the height of his popularity when he retired.

Although Garrick is often credited with inaugurating the more natural style of acting, he was anticipated by Charles Macklin (1699–1797). Born in Ireland, Macklin began acting about 1719 and continued until 1789. He first came to London about 1725, but his style was considered too prosaic, and he returned to the provinces until 1730. He served as acting manager at Drury Lane from 1734 until 1743, when he and other actors, including Garrick, seceded. Refused a license, they capitulated, but the manager would not employ Macklin again. For a time he ran an acting school, and thereafter for the most part played short engagements in London and elsewhere. Macklin's reputation was based primarily upon a few roles, especially Shylock and the protagonists of his own comedies, such as *Love à la Mode* (1759) and *The Man of the World* (1781). Although he was more devoted to naturalistic acting than Garrick was, Macklin's limited range as an actor and his quarrelsome nature restricted his success. He specialized in bluff, hearty old men, and eccentric characters.

From the 1740s until 1776 David Garrick (1717–1779) dominated the English stage. After making his London debut at Goodman's Fields Theatre in 1741, he alternated between Drury Lane and Covent Garden until 1747, when he became joint manager of Drury Lane, a position which he held until his retirement in 1776. Garrick influenced the theatre through his managerial policies as much as through his acting, for in addition to being a careful and devoted director, he was responsible for several significant innovations. As an actor, he had an extremely wide range, playing almost every kind of character, although he was considered best as Lear, Macbeth, and Hamlet. He had a mobile face, piercing eyes, and expressive body, all of which he used to great effect in the pantomimic byplay for which he was famous. His agreeable and well-controlled voice was somewhat lacking in fullness. Through intense concentration upon the immediate situation, Garrick made whatever he did seem compellingly real. Above all, he seemed to grasp the complexities of each role, and he gave them fuller expression than did any of his contemporaries. Garrick is often said to have been the greatest English actor of all times.

FIG. 9.23
The closet scene from *Hamlet* as performed in the early eighteenth century. Note the contemporary dress worn by Hamlet and the Queen. From Rowe's edition of Shakespeare's plays, 5 (1709).

Garrick's fame has overshadowed the many other fine performers of the late eighteenth century. Among the actresses who worked with him were Peg Woffington (c. 1714–1760), noted especially for her portrayal of spirited heroines of comedy and for "breeches" parts (roles played in male attire); Kitty Clive (1711– 1785), who began her career in 1728 and remained a favorite with audiences in farce and spirited comedy; and Frances Abington (1737–1815), noted for high comedy roles. Equally important were Mrs. Cibber and Mrs. Pritchard. Susanna Cibber (1714–1766), daughter-in-law of Colley Cibber, began her career as a singer but turned to acting in 1736. Appearing almost entirely in tragedy, she modified her declamatory style somewhat after joining Garrick in 1753. Mrs. Hannah Pritchard (1711–1768) was universally considered the finest tragic actress of her time. So thoroughly did she make Lady Macbeth her own that Garrick never appeared in the play after she died.

Garrick's greatest rival was Spranger Barry (1719–1777), who began his career in Ireland in 1743 and came to London in 1746. From 1750 to 1758 he played at Covent Garden in competition with Garrick. Although Garrick outshone him in most roles, Barry was considered superior as the romantic lover.

FIG. 9.24
David Garrick as Macbeth and Mrs. Pritchard as Lady Macbeth just prior to the murder of Duncan. Note that Macbeth is costumed as a British army officer, while Lady Macbeth wears eighteenth-century fashionable garments. Courtesy Theatre Museum, Victoria and Albert Museum, London.

From 1766 until his death, he often appeared with Garrick at Drury Lane.

Other performers of note include: George Ann Bellamy (c. 1727–1788), remembered principally as Garrick's Juliet; Mary Ann Yates (1728–1787), who replaced Mrs. Cibber in tragedy; Edward Shuter (1728–1776), famous for his comic old men and for his entr'acte entertainments; Richard Yates (1706–1796), a low comedian and Harlequin; Thomas King (1730–1805), a player of comic old men and acting manager under Sheridan at Drury Lane; John Henderson (1747–1785), considered Garrick's successor, but whose early death prevented him from establishing a lasting reputation; and Elizabeth Farren (1759–1829), an outstanding actress of fine ladies, who left the stage to marry the Earl of Derby in 1797. By the 1790s the leadership in acting was passing to the Kemble family, who were to dominate the next generation.

AUDIENCES AND PERFORMANCES

During the Restoration the theatrical season ran from October to June; in the eighteenth century it opened in mid-September and continued until the end of May or early June. After about 1750, the theatres played two or three times a week in the fall until mid-October, after which they performed daily except Sundays. All theatres were closed on certain specified occasions: Christmas Eve, Christmas night, January 30 (the anniversary of the death of Charles I), Ash Wednesday, Holy Week, and Whitsun Eve. Plays were also forbidden on Wednesdays and Fridays during Lent, but after 1740 oratorios were permitted on those days. Other closures were decreed on days of national thanksgiving or during periods of mourning. Thus, the number of annual performances during the regular season might vary considerably, but the average was between 170 and 200.

Playing in the summer only gradually came into vogue. During the Restoration it was restricted almost altogether to occasional programs given by apprentice actors. In the 1740s several illegal companies gave summer performances, but these were usually not allowed to continue for long. It was only after 1766, when the Haymarket was licensed to perform from May 15 to September 15, that London regularly had a summer season.

Performances were advertised in various ways: posters set up around the city; handbills distributed at coffee houses, private homes, and elsewhere; advertisements in newspapers, after these began to appear in the early eighteenth century; and announcements made from the stage each evening.

The performance time was gradually moved from midafternoon to early evening. During the early Restoration, the beginning time was 3 or 3:30 P.M.; before 1700, it had been moved to 4 or 5; between 1700 and 1710, the time varied from 5 to 5:30 to 6; after 1710, the usual hour was 6 P.M.; by the last quarter of the eighteenth century it had become 6:15 or 6:30. The unauthorized theatres, however, often played at other hours. The doors of the theatres were usually opened long before performances began and, since seats were not reserved, many persons came early or sent servants to hold seats. By the 1730s tickets for boxes could be bought in advance, but specific seats were not reserved. Each part of the house—boxes, pit, and galleries—had its own entrance, ticket sellers, and ticket takers. Since seats were unnumbered, squabbles over places often occurred.

The evening's bill was complex. In the Restoration, it consisted of a full-length play, with singing and dancing between the acts. Around 1700, Christopher Rich added acrobats, trained animals, and other circus-like performers in an attempt to compete more effectively with Betterton's troupe; this kind of entertainment was never completely absent from the theatre thereafter. Around 1715 the afterpiece was introduced and soon became standard. Thus, after 1720 a typical evening's bill was arranged in this way: approximately one-half hour of music preceded the performance; then came the prologue, followed by a full-length play; the intervals between acts were filled with miscellaneous variety entertainment; following the main play, an afterpiece (a pantomime, farce, or comic opera, all usually in two acts) was performed; and the evening concluded with a song and dance. Performances lasted from three to five hours.

The relationship between audience and performers was close. Actors often took their grievances to the spectators, who sometimes refused to let performances proceed until explanations from alleged offenders were forthcoming. Riots, precipitated by changes in casting, in the evening's bill, or well-established customs, were not uncommon. Thus, spectators believed firmly in their rights and did not hesitate to exert their power to correct any grievance, actual or supposed.

Throughout the eighteenth century the theatre gained steadily in popularity as commercial prosperity enlarged the potential playgoing public. Consequently, by the 1790s the theatre buildings had grown too small to accommodate all those who wished to attend. Also by this time new values had undermined neoclassicism. England was on the threshold of new developments in both its theatre and drama.

THE PROVINCIAL THEATRE

During the eighteenth century, theatre in the British Isles was not confined to London. Dublin was especially important as a theatrical center; it not only supported thriving companies but also supplied London with many of its most prominent playwrights and actors. The theatre in Dublin prospered in part because Ireland was exempted from the provisions of the Licensing Act of 1737, and consequently until the 1760s it maintained the only legitimate theatres in the British Isles outside of London.

Nevertheless, though they lacked legal sanction, companies continued to perform throughout England and Scotland after 1737. They evaded the law by advertising their programs as medleys of songs, dances, and dramatic scenes. Provincial officials ignored the infringements of the law, except on those rare occasions when citizens instituted legal proceedings against the actors. After the 1760s, when Parliament began to authorize provincial troupes, the theatre outside of London prospered. The best companies were those of Edinburgh, Bath, York, Norwich, Liverpool, Manchester, Bristol, Newcastle, and Brighton. They were the training ground for most of Britain's actors, and they offered a steady supply of new talent to London's companies. But no city outside London was able to fully support a professional company, so touring circuits were developed, with companies spending from a few days to a few weeks in each of the several towns that made up their circuit. Together, the provincial troupes provided entertainment for virtually the whole of the British Isles.

THEATRE OF COLONIAL NORTH AMERICA

British attempts to establish a colony at Roanoke (1585) failed, so it was not until the founding of Jamestown (1607) that any permanent British colonies were established in North America. As colonization spread, the British came into contact with a great diversity of distinctive American peoples from the Iroquois Confederacy and the Algonquian-speaking peoples in the northeast and mid-Atlantic region to the Cherokee, Creek, Choctaw, and Chickasaw nations of the southeast. But these cultures were already under stress from the devastation of epidemics introduced and reintroduced by Europeans since 1514. As native groups fought Europeans and each other, their cultures declined further. We know little, therefore, about the pre-Columbian performance traditions of these preliterate peoples. Many certainly had a sophisticated tradition of narrative dance. Others had complex ceremonies and rituals that were theatrical in nature. But if they had the kinds of epic dance drama found in the Spanish occupied territories, few records remain of it. Early Jesuits saw dramatic elements to the masked "False Face" dances of some of the Iroquois peoples. Paul Radin transcribed the text for a ritual drama of the Winnebago people, *The Road of Life and Death,* but this is unlikely to represent traditions from earlier than the eighteenth century (the transcription did not occur until 1908). Europeans would not be exposed to native theatre on the scale found in New Spain until they encountered the highly elaborate *potlatch* ceremonies of the peoples of the Pacific Northwest.

The first play written and performed in North America was Marc Lescarbot's *The Theatre of Neptune in New France* in 1606, in the French colony of Nova Scotia. A number of other plays were presented by amateurs there before a controversy over *Tartuffe* brought a prohibition in 1694. But by this time England was already winning its competition with other European countries for control of North America, and by 1763, when Canada came into its possession, England was the dominant power (until it lost the American Revolution of 1775–1783).

The earliest record of a performance in British held territories is not found until 1665, when three men in Virginia were hauled into court for performing a playlet, *The Bear and the Cub.* No other instances are noted until the end of the century, when students presented plays in the colleges at Harvard and William and Mary. In New York sometime between 1699 and 1702, Richard Hunter obtained permission to give theatrical entertainments, but it is not certain that he did so. In 1703 Anthony Aston (?1682–1753), the first professional actor to arrive in North America, gave a few performances in Charleston and New York to earn money for his return passage to England. *Androboros* (or "Maneater") by Robert Hunter, governor of New York, became the first extant American play when it was published in 1714. A rather crude satire, it ridiculed Hunter's political opponents.

Between 1715 and 1735, however, theatrical activities increased. In 1716 William Levingston of Williamsburg, Virginia, built the first theatre in what was to become the United States, and here until about 1732 Charles and Mary Stagg arranged entertainments, the precise nature of which is uncertain. The theatre operated until 1745 and was torn down by 1770. In Philadelphia strolling players performed in 1723 and 1724; in Lancaster performances were given irregularly between 1730 and 1742; and in New York amateur players staged plays and fitted out a theatre between 1730 and 1733. In

Charleston, South Carolina, amateurs gave a season of three plays in 1735 and built a theatre for performances in 1736 and 1737. This flurry of activity came to an end in the late 1730s, however, probably because of the religious fervor that accompanied the appearances of George Whitefield and John Wesley in the colonies.

A significant new beginning was made in 1749, when a company under the leadership of Walter Murray and Thomas Kean made its initial appearance in Philadelphia. Almost nothing is known about the origin or qualifications of the actors in this company. Most of the players probably were amateurs. This troupe played in a converted warehouse on Water Street in Philadelphia until 1750, when it toured New York and various towns in Virginia and Maryland. Nothing is heard of it after 1752. Regardless of its artistic stature, the Murray-Kean company was the first to present seasons of some length in several towns. It established a precedent that was to be followed by its more important successor, the Hallam troupe.

Before turning to the Hallams, however, it is necessary to glance briefly at Jamaica, which had been seized from Spain by the English in 1655. Theatrical performances had been given sporadically there since about 1680 and a playhouse was built in 1682. The arrival in 1745 of John Moody (?–1812), an Irish actor, marked a significant change. After playing with an amateur group, he returned to England to recruit professional actors, among them David Douglass (?–1786), who became head of the company after Moody left Jamaica permanently in 1749. It may have been Moody who alerted English actors to opportunities in the colonies at a time when the Licensing Act had seriously curtailed the theatre in England. His news came at an especially crucial moment in the career of the Hallams.

William Hallam (?–c. 1758), one of a large family of actors, had opened the New Wells Theatre in Goodman's Fields, London, in 1740. At first he presented only minor entertainments, but in 1744 turned to more ambitious works in spite of the Licensing Act. Although he prospered for several years, in 1751 his theatre was closed. It was at this time that Hallam conceived the idea of sending a troupe to America. The new company was headed by his brother, Lewis Hallam (1714–1755), an actor of secondary roles, with Mrs. Lewis Hallam (?–1773) as the leading actress. Consisting of twelve adults and Hallam's three children, the troupe was organized on the sharing plan, which was then still typical of English provincial troupes. In America, they fitted out a theatre at Williamsburg and opened in September, 1752. From this date can be traced the effective beginning of the professional theatre in America.

In addition to Williamsburg, the Hallams played in New York, Philadelphia, and Charleston before sailing to Jamaica in 1755. When they arrived, David Douglass was preparing to leave for England to recruit new actors, and the amalgamation of the troupes solved difficulties for both companies. Lewis Hallam died in 1755, and in 1758 Mrs. Hallam married Douglass, who remained head of the troupe until the Revolution. From 1758 to 1764 Douglass' company played in the mainland colonies. During these years Mrs. Douglass continued as the leading actress, while Lewis Hallam, Jr. (c. 1740–1808) was now the leading man. Between 1759 and 1761, the troupe performed in New York, Philadelphia, Annapolis, Williamsburg, and elsewhere, and in 1761–1762 in Rhode Island, where his company gave the first professional performances in New England.

After another interval in Jamaica, Douglass returned to the mainland from 1766 to 1775. By now, he had developed considerable optimism about the future and began to build substantial permanent playhouses. The first, the Southwark Theatre in Philadelphia, was opened in 1766. In 1767 he built the John Street Theatre in New York, and thereafter erected theatres in major towns between New York and Charleston. During these years Douglass also performed the first American play to be given a professional production, Thomas Godfrey's (1736–1763) *The Prince of Parthia*. A neoclassical tragedy with echoes of many Shakespearean works, it was given in Philadelphia in 1767. At the outbreak of the Revolution in 1774, the Continental Congress called for the cessation of theatrical entertainment. In 1775 Douglass sailed for Jamaica. Although many members of his company were to return after the war, Douglass' theatrical career soon ended.

The colonial theatre between 1752 and 1774 differed little from the English provincial theatre of the day. The Hallam-Douglass company had to tour, for as yet there was no center capable of supporting a permanent theatre. The expense and inconvenience of travel made it necessary to keep the troupe small and the scenic investiture simple. The performers were at best third-rate; they doubled in roles and appeared in entr'acte entertainments as well. But while the artistic level may not have been high, the company established the foundations upon which later and more substantial companies would build. During the Revolution there were few professional performances, although British soldiers presented numerous plays in Boston, New York, and Philadelphia, and American troops performed on a much less ambitious scale.

In Canada, performances by soldiers were common, and these garrison companies revived the tradition of having female roles played by men, though many eventually used local women in their casts. A professional company with the borrowed title of the "American Company of Comedians," led by Mr. Mills (with Henry Giffard as the leading man), came from Brunswick, North Carolina to perform in Halifax, Nova Scotia, in 1768. The garrison began regular performances by 1773, and in 1774 they produced *Acadius, or Love in a Calm,* a romantic comedy with an antislavery slant set in Boston. The author is unknown, but the play is generally considered to be the first English-language play written in Canada. The Halifax garrison built Canada's first purpose-built theatre in 1789, the 500-seat Grand. Charles Stuart Powell arrived with a company, recruited from Boston's Federal Street Theatre, in 1795 and ran a professional theatre in Halifax for twelve years.

The garrison at Montreal was also quite active, producing several seasons of plays between 1774 and 1790 (in both English and French). The first professional company of English actors played there in 1786. William Moore, Edward Allen, and John Bentley had left the John Street Theatre in New York to form this company, which also toured to Québec City where the restrictions on theatre established by the French during the *Tartuffe* incident of 1694 were gradually being relaxed.

A few American playwrights were active. Mercy Otis Warren (1728–1814) satirized British sympathizers in *The Adulateur* (1772) and *The Group* (1775), Hugh Henry Brackenridge (1748–1815) wrote a blank verse play, *The Battle of Bunker's Hill* (1776), and to John (or Joseph) Leacock is attributed the five-act prose work, *The Fall of British Tyranny* (1776). The most effective play of the period was Robert Munford's (1737–1783) *The Patriots* (1779), a satire on "super patriots" who label all opponents enemy agents. Although the literary output of the period is slight, it is still significant as the first flurry of dramatic writing in America.

When the peace treaty that made the United States fully independent was ratified in 1783, the British territories in North America were permanently divided, although relations between the theatres of the United States and Canada remained close. Theatrical activity in the United States began to revive in the early 1780s. Thereafter, it would grow steadily and spread widely as new territories were opened up. But, it would be many years before North American theatre would deviate significantly from English patterns.

LOOKING AT THEATRE HISTORY

The versions of plays performed in the theatre are not necessarily those now commonly available for reading. This is especially true in dealing with Shakespeare's plays. Restoration and eighteenth-century audiences found many of Shakespeare's scripts unacceptable and preferred adaptations of them. Thus, when eighteenth-century actors appeared in *King Lear* (to name only one conspicuous example), they did not perform the text we know. The student can gain considerable insight into eighteenth-century taste from reading the *King Lear* that held the stage through that century. Written by Nahum Tate and first performed in 1681, it has Cordelia and Edgar in love with each other, and omits the Fool altogether. At the end, Lear is restored to the throne, Goneril and Regan die of poison, and Cordelia and Edgar are united in marriage. Thus, the neoclassical demand for poetic justice was upheld.

Neoclassicism also motivated the use of generalized scenery, as this passage makes clear:

The stage should be furnished with a competent Number of painted scenes sufficient to answer the Purposes of all the Plays in the Stock, in which there is no great variety, being easily reduced to the following classes. 1st. Temples 2ndly. Tombs 3rdly. City Walls and Gates 4thly. Outsides of Palaces 5thly. Insides of Palaces 6thly. Streets 7thly. Chambers 8thly. Prisons 9thly. Gardens and 10thly. Rural prospects of Groves, Forests, Desarts, &c. All these should be done by a Master, if such can be found: otherwise they should be as simple and unaffected as possible to avoid offending a judicious eye. If for some particular purpose, any other Scene is necessary, it can be got up occasionally.

The Case of the Stage in Ireland (Dublin, 1758).

During the course of the eighteenth century, pantomime did much to cultivate a taste for more spectacular scenery as can be seen from this stage direction in *Harlequin a Sorcerer* (one of John Rich's pantomimes, first presented in 1725 and revived often thereafter):

The Curtain rises, and discovers dark rocky Caverns, by the Side of a Wood, illumin'd by the Moon: Birds of Omen promiscuously flying, Flashes of Lightning faintly striking.

Under his stage name of Lun, Rich also perfected pantomimic acting. Here is a description of his portrayal of the scene in *Harlequin a Sorcerer* in which Harlequin is hatched from an egg:

This certainly was a masterpiece in dumb show. From the first chipping of the egg, his receiving motion, his feeling the ground, his standing upright, to his quick Harlequin trip around the empty Shell, through the whole progression every limb had its tongue, and every motion a voice, which "spoke with most miraculous organ" to the understandings and sensations of the observers.

John Jackson, *The History of the Scottish Stage* (Edinburgh, 1793), 367–368.

Probably the most important first-hand account of the English theatre between 1690 and 1740 is that written by Colley Cibber. He covers almost all important topics, and is especially helpful in describing the qualities of the principal actors of the period. Here is a passage about Thomas Betterton:

Betterton had so just a sense of what was true or false applause, that I have heard him say he never thought any kind of it equal to an attentive silence; that there were many ways of deceiving an audience into a loud one; but to keep them hushed and quiet was an applause which only truth and merit could arrive at: of which art, there never was an equal master to himself. . . . In all his soliloquies of moment, the strong intelligence of his attitude and aspect, drew you into such an impatient gaze, and eager expectation, that you almost imbibed the sentiment with your eye, before the ear could reach it.

Colley Cibber, *Apology for His Life* (London, 1740).

By the mid-eighteenth century, ideas about acting and costuming began to change. Here is a description of a performance in which both Quin (the major exponent of the older school) and Garrick (the major exponent of the newer school) appeared:

Quin presented himself . . . in a green velvet coat embroidered down the seams, an enormous full bottomed periwig, rolled stockings and high-heeled square-toed shoes, with very little variation in cadence, and in a deep full tone, accompanied by a sawing kind of action, which had more of the senate than of the stage in it, he rolled out his heroics with an air of dignified indifference. . . . Garrick, then young and light and alive in every muscle and in every feature, came bounding on the stage . . . it seemed as if a whole century had been stept over in the transition of a single scene; old things were done away, and a new order at once brought forward, bright and luminous, and clearly destined to dispel the barbarisms and bigotry of a tasteless age, . . . superstitiously devoted to the illusions of imposing declamation. . . . Yet in general [the audience] seemed to love darkness better than light, and . . . bestowed far the greater show of hands upon the master of the old school than upon the founder of the new.

Richard Cumberland, *Memoirs* (London, 1806), 59–60.

Before the end of the century, dissatisfaction with anachronistic costuming was becoming more intense. Here is one complaint about the mixture of modes in *Richard III*:

King Richard's troops appear in the present uniform of the soldiers in St. James's park, with short jackets and cocked-up hats. King Richard wears indeed the habiliments of his time, but Richmond is dressed à la vraie moderne; . . . The Lord Mayor . . . figures in his own character, but the other attendants in the play not so. . . . How is it possible to reconcile Macbeth or Hamlet dressed in our fashionable short coats, with the idea of habits of ages so far anterior?

Gentleman's Magazine (May, 1789).

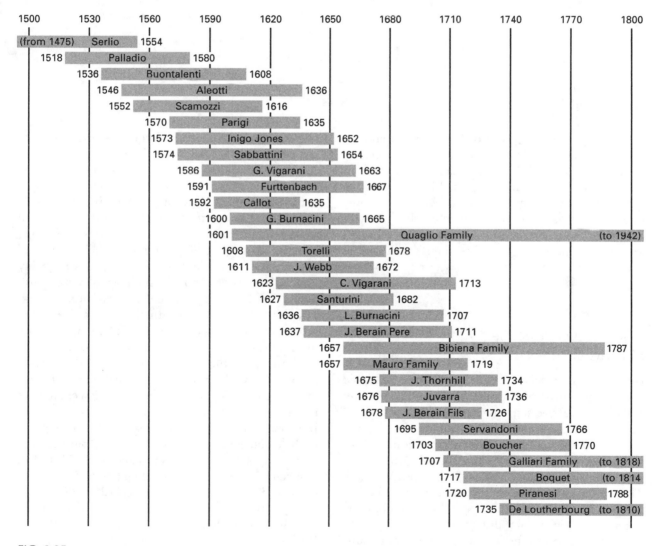

FIG. 9.25

Major scene designers of Europe, 1500–1800.

10
Italy and France to 1800

By 1700, Italy was of little consequence in European politics. Many of its several states were included within the Holy Roman Empire, which from 1559 until 1806 was always headed by a member of the Hapsburg family that ruled Austria. Consequently, Austria came to dominate northern Italy. It controlled some parts directly and others through local princes loyal to it. In effect, then, much of Italy was a dependency of Austria.

THE EVOLUTION OF ITALIAN SCENIC DESIGN

By 1700 Italian scenic practices had been adopted throughout most of Western Europe. Proscenium arches, perspective settings (composed of flat wings, shutters, and borders), rapid shifts of scenery, and spectacular special effects had become common almost everywhere. In 1700 the visual conventions were still those popularized by Torelli and Vigarani. Thus, typically, settings were symmetrically arranged perspective alleys depicting a series of buildings terminating in a view of a distant prospect.

Through most of the seventeenth century the important centers for theatrical design were Venice, Parma, Bologna, Florence, Milan, Turin, Rome, and

Naples. But after 1650 the Imperial court at Vienna challenged the Italian cities for supremacy, since it could provide significant rewards both in money and prestige for outstanding designers. Here between 1652 and 1707, Giovanni Burnacini (1600–1665) and Ludovico Ottavio Burnacini (1636–1707) staged some of the most lavish entertainments in Europe and gained international renown. Of their more than 115 productions, the most elaborate was probably *The Golden Apple* (1668), which opened the lavish new opera house. It required twenty-three settings and thirty-five machines; in the final scene, three groups of dancers performed simultaneously—one in the sky, one on the sea, and one on land.

Throughout the seventeenth century there was a noticeable trend toward increased size and splendor in stage settings. These and other changes seem to have reached their fullest expression in the work of the Bibiena family, perhaps the most influential designers of the eighteenth century. Of the many Bibienas, the most important were Ferdinando (1657–1743), Francesco (1659–1739), Giuseppe (1696–1757), Antonio (1700–1774), and Carlo (1728–1787). The family's reputation was first established widely through Ferdinando's work at Bologna and Parma. By 1708 he was sufficiently famous to be summoned to Barcelona, where he staged the festivities for the marriage of the future Emperor Charles VI, and in

FIG. 10.1

Design by Ludovico Burnacini for *The Golden Apple*, Act 1, scene 2: The Palace of Paris. Above the stage area are seen the goddesses who insist that Paris judge their beauty. This production opened the new opera house in Vienna in 1668. Courtesy Theatersammlung, Osterreichische Nationalbibliothek, Vienna.

1711 Charles VI appointed him court architect at Vienna to succeed Burnacini. Thereafter the Bibienas were in demand wherever an interest in opera developed. During the eighteenth century they were employed in such major cities as Paris, Lisbon, London, Stockholm, Berlin, Dresden, and St. Petersburg. The Bibienas were also among the leading architects of the eighteenth century, and they designed theatres in France, Italy, Austria, and Germany.

The contributions of the Bibiena family to scenic design were numerous. Ferdinando worked with Torelli before becoming court architect at Parma. He is credited with the introduction of angle perspective (*scena per angolo*), perhaps his most significant innovation. Rather than a single vanishing point located at the rear of a setting, Bibiena used two or more vanishing points at the sides. Whereas previous designers emphasized a central vista, Bibiena (while he did not give up the earlier practice) characteristically placed buildings, walls, statues, or courtyards at the center of the picture and relegated vistas to the sides.

Bibiena also altered the scale of settings. Before his time, the stage had been treated as an extension of the auditorium, and the scenery had been proportioned accordingly. Thus, in Torelli's settings the tops of the buildings were always visible. Furthermore, the rectangular alignment of the auditorium was continued by the central perspective alley created by the scenery. Bibiena, on the other hand, divorced his settings from the auditorium both in angle

and scale. Consequently, since a scene could now be depicted from varying eye points, the former symmetrical arrangement was no longer necessary. Furthermore, the wings near the front of the stage often were treated as though they were merely the lower portion of a building too vast to be contained in the narrow confines of the proscenium.

In spite of its apparent size, a setting using angle perspective might require less space than one with a central alley, for the effect of vastness was created in part by side vistas not fully shown. Most of Bibiena's settings divided the stage into a forward section (where the acting usually occurred) and a background section (which might extend the view almost to infinity). The forward section was composed of wings mounted as dictated by the chariot-and-pole machinery, but upstage numerous flats were placed wherever needed to create the receding planes demanded by the perspective. These upstage flats, the positions of which were often unrelated to the chariot-and-pole machinery, made for some difficulty in shifting (requiring the manual handling of some pieces), but the pictorial effects justified the additional effort. (This way of handling the upstage scenery was one of the Bibienas' major innovations.)

The surviving engravings often show stairs and multiple levels (sometimes with human figures on the upper levels). This has led some scholars to assume

FIG. 10.2

Design by Giuseppe Galli Bibiena for *Costanza e Fortezza* as presented at the royal palace in Prague, 1723. Courtesy Theatermuseum, Munich.

FIG. 10.3
Stage setting by Giuseppe Galli Bibiena for an opera given at the betrothal of members of the ruling houses of Poland and Saxony in 1719. Courtesy Metropolitan Museum of Art. The Elisha Whittelsey Collection, The Elisha Whittelsey Fund, 1951.

that the sets included practicable units. Actually, most of these details were accomplished by painting. Only rarely were practicable stairs used and these never included more than a few steps; the presence of painted human figures on background scenery was an accepted convention of the period. The engravings idealize the settings and tend to obscure the actual floorplans (how the picture was divided up when transferred to flats, drops, and borders). Fortunately, a number of the Bibienas's floorplans have survived to clarify their scenography. They reveal that, despite the many diagonals, drops were never hung diagonally. Flats were placed parallel to the picture plane, and effects were created primarily through painting.

Virtually all of the practices for which the Bibienas are now noted were extensions of the baroque style, which had begun to appear in the late sixteenth century. The baroque marks a departure from the dominant mode of the Renaissance, which was characterized by restraint, order, symmetrical balance, and rectangular space. Baroque art was extravagant, asymmetrical, and mingled rectangular and curvilinear space. While, as in the Renaissance, the principal architectural elements in the baroque era continued to be columns, arches, and pediments, these were modified by twisting the columns, entwining them with garlands and incorporating S-curved supports, carving, statuary, and painting. By a careful juxtaposition of mass and space, by using such new materials as stucco and plaster out of which to create swirling details, and by such devices as foreshortening and forced perspective, the whole structure was given a sense of

activity and movement. The overall effect was one of restlessness, monumentality, grandeur, and richness. It is these qualities, which were so typical in architecture by 1700, that the Bibienas exploited in their scenic designs.

Although the *scena per angolo* was popularized by Ferdinando Bibiena, it was also exploited by Filippo Juvarra (1678–1737), who adopted angle perspective in Naples around 1706. After working in Rome, Juvarra went to Turin (which rivaled Vienna as an artistic center), where he became the leading architect of northwestern Italy. Juvarra's settings differ from Bibiena's in being essentially curvilinear (rather than rectilinear). Thus, the eye of the observer is led in a circle and always back to the foreground rather than off to the sides, as was often the case with Bibiena's

FIG. 10.4
Design by Filippo Juvarra. At the bottom are two variants on the setting, probably indicating that this is a permanent setting with changeable back scenes. Courtesy Theatre Museum, Victoria and Albert Museum, London.

side alleys. It may be for this reason that Juvarra's settings also seem less monumental and fantastic than do Bibiena's.

Juvarra did considerable experimentation in settings, sometimes using unit settings in which the background elements were altered behind a fixed foreground. He also created some settings entirely of draperies, and in others he included what were then very exotic elements, such as tropical foliage and Near Eastern architectural forms. In designing his settings, Juvarra appears to have worked from floor plans, for they are often included at the bottom of his drawings.

In addition to the Bibienas, several other families of scenic designers were active in the eighteenth century. Members of the Mauro family worked in the principal theatrical centers of Italy and Germany from the seventeenth century until 1820. Beginning with Gaspare Mauro (*fl.* 1657–1719), the family designed settings in Venice, Turin, Parma, Monaco, Milan, Dresden, Vienna, and elsewhere. The Quaglio family, beginning with Giulio (1601–1658) and ending with Eugen (1857–1942), continued as designers through six generations. Although of Italian origin, they worked principally in Austria and Germany. From 1778 until 1917 they maintained headquarters at Monaco, where the museum now preserves many of their designs. The Galliari family, whose most famous members were Bernardino (1707–1794) and Fabrizio (1709–1790), were active from the early eighteenth century until 1823. Although they worked in many cities, they were associated primarily with Milan and Turin, where they succeeded Juvarra.

The visual style established between 1700 and 1750 underwent many changes in the late eighteenth century as new interests emerged. As comic opera, *opera buffa,* grew in popularity, domestic and rustic settings became common. By the late eighteenth century Paolo Landriani, working at the Teatro alla Scala in Milan, was reviving the use of box sets to better represent these settings. Comic opera evolved out of the *intermezzi* often performed with serious operas in Italy. The first Italian comic opera to achieve widespread fame was Pergolesi's *The Servant the Mistress* (1733). Variations on comic opera appeared throughout Europe (in England the ballad opera, in Germany the *singspiele,* in France the *opéra comique*). The type was so popular by the late eighteenth century that many of the larger opera houses were maintaining what amounted to two separate troupes, one for comic and one for serious opera.

An increased interest in history also affected scenic design during the late eighteenth century. The rediscovery of Herculaneum in 1709 and of Pompeii in 1748 captured the imagination of Europeans and

FIG. 10.5
Design dating from about 1780 by Giuseppino Galliari. Note the classical forms in a state of picturesque ruin. Courtesy Museo Civico, Turin.

called attention to the "pastness" of classical civilizations. Engravings of classical ruins were widely circulated, and many aristocrats had ruins constructed in their gardens as visual focal points. Similarly, scenic designers began to show classical structures in various stages of deterioration, with shrubs and vines growing from fissures. This renewed interest in history also stimulated the writing of works based on the postclassical national past and on folk materials. Many of these works were set in the Middle Ages and thus they brought Gothic architecture into the theatre.

The late eighteenth century also brought a rebellion against baroque music and art with all its ornamentation and nonfunctional details. This reaction was perhaps best captured in the work of the composer Christoph Willibald Gluck (1714–1787), who through such works as *Orpheus and Eurydice* (1762) sought to recapture the simplicity of early Florentine opera and to synthesize action and music. The popularity of his works helped to initiate a new "classical" era in music during the last quarter of the eighteenth century, known today above all through the works of Wolfgang Amadeus Mozart. This trend was paralleled in architecture and scenic design by an attempt to return to pure classical forms devoid of extraneous ornament and detail.

But perhaps the most important innovation of the late eighteenth century was the introduction of "mood" into design. Before the late eighteenth century, settings were for the most part painted so that every detail was depicted clearly. Now designers began to emphasize the atmospheric values of light and shadow. The key figure in this trend probably was Giovanni Battista Piranesi (1720–1778). Although he was not a scene designer, Piranesi adopted many scenographic conventions in the more than 1,000 engravings of Roman ruins and contemporary prisons he published between 1745 and 1778. His drawings of ruins contributed much to the interest in "ruined" antiquity, and his prisons, with their marked contrasts in light and shadow, accelerated interest in atmospheric qualities. Scenic designers began to depict picturesque places as seen by moonlight or interiors illuminated by a few shafts of light. Color played only a minor role in this trend, for the palette was limited. Settings were painted in sepia or pastel shades of green, yellow, and lavender. Mood, therefore, was achieved primarily through the juxtaposition of painted masses of light and shadow.

These concerns for greater realism and appropriate mood probably stimulated Pierre Patte to experiment with lighting instruments equipped with lenses and reflectors and mounted on the side boxes of the auditorium as a device for eliminating footlights. His experiments were not to bear fruit, however, for another century.

In spite of the trend toward greater visual variety, the types of places represented in late eighteenth-

century operas can be reduced to about twelve. Because each locale was idealized, settings could be reused for a number of different works. The basic compositional techniques remained unchanged, however, for the *scena per angolo* continued to dominate. The many innovations after 1750, especially in new visual content and the increased concern for mood, are indicative of the dissatisfaction with the strictures that had been imposed by the neoclassical outlook. Perhaps more important, they are harbingers of romanticism, which soon was to become the dominant mode.

ITALIAN DRAMA OF THE EIGHTEENTH CENTURY

If Italy's designers dominated the theatre of Europe, the same cannot be said for its dramatists. Because of the prestige of opera, most Italian playwrights were content to compose libretti. An estimated 20,000 opera libretti were written in the seventeenth and eighteenth centuries. The two most honored Italian dramatists of the period, Apostolo Zeno (1668–1750) and Metastasio (Pietro Trapassi, 1698–1782), both became poets to the Imperial Court at Vienna largely because of their opera libretti.

Serious spoken drama was not popular in eighteenth-century Italy. Prior to 1750, the only tragedy of note was *Merope* (1713) by Francesco Scipione di Maffei (1675–1765). It is based on the classical story of Merope, who, on the verge of slaying her long-lost son, discovers the truth and is able to effect revenge upon the real cause of her misery. Italy's most famous tragedian, Vittorio Alfieri (1749–1803), came to the fore around 1775. Alfieri sought to present the most powerful emotions in the simplest possible dramatic form. In his plays everything not essential is pared away. As a result, his tragedies are closer to those of Racine than to typical eighteenth-century works. Of his dramas, which include *Oreste* (1776), *Antigone* (1783), and *Mirra* (1789), the acknowledged masterpiece is *Saul* (1782). In it, attention is concentrated upon the Biblical king Saul, the remnant of a powerful leader now vacillating between madness and sanity, petty tyranny and greatness as he watches David grow in esteem as his own influence wanes. Most of Alfieri's works are marked by his strong political interest in independence for Italy, which sometimes led him to place too great an emphasis upon doctrinal messages. But it was his political ideas that influenced his successors, though none rose to his artistic level.

Comedy fared somewhat better than tragedy. Until 1750, the comic impulse was largely channeled into

FIG. 10.6
Piranesi's engraving of the Forum of Nerva. Note the emphasis on light and shadow. From Giovanni Battista Piranesi, *Le Antichita Romane Opera* (1765). Courtesy Lilly Library, Indiana University.

FIG. 10.7
Scene from Alfieri's *Saul*. From an edition published in Florence in 1824.

the *commedia dell'arte*. Unfortunately, after 1700 this formerly vital form grew repetitious. Minor characters, music, and spectacle were added to increase its variety, but, as sentimentalism in other forms grew, *commedia* came to seem crude and unfeeling. In Venice, where there was the largest middle class audience in Italy, there was a growing interest in the sentimental comedies of England and France. In the 1740s, Carlo Goldoni (1707–1793), who began his career in 1734 by writing scenarios for *commedia* troupes there, began to write plays and pamphlets that championed the new drama and proposed changes that would bring *commedia* more in line with the new style. This set off a public debate, first with Jesuit turned dramatist Pietro Chiari (1712–1785), and then with nobleman turned dramatist Carlo Gozzi (1720–1806), that was to make Venice the most vibrant theatre center in Italy and produce the most significant Italian comedies of the period.

Goldoni's interests were by no means restricted to *commedia* or even to comedy. One of the most prolific dramatists of the century, he wrote 10 tragedies,

83 musical dramas, and about 150 comedies. Many of these are mere trifles, but others are among the finest works of the age. He is credited with making *opera buffa* acceptable to the major opera companies. Although Goldoni depicted almost every profession and class, he idealized the middle and lower classes, and often characterized the nobility as decadent and useless. Above all he idealized his female characters, as his most famous play *The Mistress of the Inn* (1753) illustrates. In this play, Mirandolina is wooed by three nobles, each representing an aspect of that class that Goldoni found repugnant. In the end she chooses her honest, resourceful servant Fabrizio. There is a sentimental strain in this play that is found throughout Goldoni's work, but there is sufficient wit, charm, and vivacity to avoid the cloying sentimentality that afflicts most plays of the era.

Goldoni began his program for reforming the *commedia* by writing out the principal role in *Man of the World* (1738). By the time he wrote his most successful

FIG. 10.8
Goldoni's *The Servant of Two Masters,* Act 1, scene 7. From Carlo Goldoni, *Commedie* 14 (1824).

FIG. 10.9

Performance in the Roman ampitheatre in Verona. In his *Memoirs*, Goldoni writes: "Spectacles of all kinds are given [in the amphitheatre]: courses, jousts, bull-fights; and in summer, plays are even represented. . . . For this purpose . . . there is erected, on very strong supports, a theatre in boards, which is taken down every winter and refitted again in the fine season." Painted by Marco Marcola, Italian (Veronese), *c. 1740–1793*, *An Italian Comedy in Verona*, oil on canvas, 1772, 115.3 × 84.2 cm (oval). Gift of Emily Crane Chadbourne, 1922. 4790. Photograph © 1993, The Art Institute of Chicago. All rights reserved.

commedia play, *The Servant of Two Masters* (1743), only the part of the comic servant hero, Truffaldino, was left to be improvised as it was played by Italy's greatest comic actor, Antonio Sacchi (1708–1788). When the play was published in 1753, however, even this role was fully scripted. Goldoni joined the company of Girolamo Medebach (1706–1790) at the Teatro Sant' Angelo in 1748 and quickly eliminated all improvisation from his *commedia* plays. He was also calling for even more radical changes to the traditional form.

By this time Pietro Chiari was becoming famous for his parodies of Goldoni's plays and was especially successful with *The School for Widows* (1749). Goldoni responded with *The Comic Theatre* (1750) in which he argued that the methods of the *commedia* were antiquated. He called for abandoning masks (because they prevented subtle facial expression), adopting better stage speech (he used the Venetian dialect because it was closer to the audience's experience), and substituting subjects based on real life for the conventionalized situations of *commedia*. Since he had already abolished improvisation, he was calling for the elimination of virtually all of *commedia's* essential characteristics. These innovations won him an invitation to write for the acclaimed Vendramin company at the San Luca theatre in 1753 and to go to Paris (where he remained until his death) to write for the Comédie Italienne in 1762. By that time Goldoni had done much to banish fantasy, vulgarity, and nonrealistic devices from the *commedia*. He had also humanized and softened the stock characters, making the ridiculous, miserly, and lecherous old Pantalone of the traditional scenarios, for example, into an honest merchant, good father, and solid citizen. But in making these changes, he also removed the distinctions between *commedia* and regular comedy.

Carlo Gozzi strongly objected to Goldoni's alterations of the *commedia,* to his sentimentalism, and to his denigration of the upper classes. In *The Love for Three Oranges* (1761), *King Stag* (1762), *Turandot* (1762), and *The Magic Bird* (1765), Gozzi emphasized the elements that Goldoni sought most to suppress: fantasy, enchantment, masked characters and improvisation. He called these plays *fiabe* and chose his subjects from fairy tales or legends (which provided many opportunities for spectacular effects). Gozzi satirized the sentimental trends Goldoni championed, and this topicality, along with a dependence on improvisation, makes the plays difficult to comprehend fully today. But they were very popular at the time and have remained important because they were an inspiration to the later German romantics and the nonrealists of the twentieth century. Gozzi brought a new life to the *commedia,* but his work was soon eclipsed by Elisabetta Carminer (1751–1796), who wrote adaptations of French sentimental plays, most notably *The Honest Criminal* (1770). Gozzi tried to respond with adaptations of Spanish *capa y espada* plays, but these never had the success of his *fiabe*. For the next century Italian drama confined itself to the types of drama found elsewhere in Europe.

FRENCH DRAMA OF THE EIGHTEENTH CENTURY

Throughout the eighteenth century, France remained a major power, but its former position of dominance was considerably weakened by a series of wars and by disastrous economic policies. The War of Spanish Succession, which resulted when Louis XIV sought to unite France and Spain by placing his grandson on the Spanish throne, pitted France against most of the rest of Europe between 1701 and 1713. The proposed succession was eventually permitted after France agreed that Spain and France would never be united, but France had suffered a number of humiliating defeats by England and Austria, who thereafter kept France in check. After 1750 France also lost its major territories in the New World to England. These wars put a heavy strain on France's economy, with the burden falling on the middle and lower classes, since the nobility and clergy were exempted from taxation. Such conditions created increasing unhappiness, which eventually erupted in the Revolution of 1789.

Despite France's problems, Paris continued to be the major cultural center of Europe throughout the eighteenth century, and its drama was the standard against which all others were judged. Yet French drama tended to be backward-looking, taking its standards from the seventeenth century. Most eighteenth-century tragic writers sought to follow in Racine's footsteps, but perhaps because they substituted involved plots and complex character relationships for his emphasis upon internal conflicts, their work failed to achieve lasting fame. The major trends can be seen in the work of LaGrange-Chancel, Crébillon, and Voltaire.

Joseph de LaGrange-Chancel (1677–1758) wrote fourteen plays after 1694. The most popular, *Ino and Mélicerte* (1713), tells the story of Ino, now a slave in the household of her former husband, the king, who believes her to be dead. The present queen is plotting to kill Ino's son, Mélicerte, who is unaware of his own identity. A number of other complex relationships are clarified in a series of recognition scenes, which thwart the evil queen and restore Ino to happiness. The trend toward melodrama, evident in this plot, was accelerated by Prosper Jolyot Crébillon (1674–1762). Many of Crébillon's extremely complex dramas were designed to arouse horror in the spectator, as in *Atreus and Thyestes* (1707), in which Thyestes is served a drink concocted from the blood of his sons. Crébillon's preference for complex plots is well illustrated by *Electre* (1707), in which Aegisthus is provided with a son and daughter to motivate complications based on the love of Aegisthus' children for Electra and Orestes. Crébillon's best play is *Rhadamisthe and Zénobie* (1711), in which the unrecognized heroine is loved by Rhadamisthe (her cruel husband, who is present in disguise although he is presumed to be dead), her unscrupulous father-in-law, and her brother-in-law Arsames. After numerous recognition scenes and the death of Rhadamisthe, Zenobie finds happiness in marriage to the virtuous Arsames. This play, considered one of the finest of the eighteenth century, held the stage until 1830.

Voltaire (François-Marie Arouet, 1694–1778) dominated tragedy in the eighteenth century, as he did virtually all French literature and thought. Beginning with *Oedipe* (1718), he wrote fifty-three plays, more than half of them tragedies. Although superior in many respects, Voltaire's tragedies continue the trend toward complex plots, involved character relationships, and sudden reversals based upon recognitions.

One of Voltaire's best works, *Zaïre* (1732), is set in the Middle East at the time of the Crusades and tells the story of the slave, Zaïre, who is loved by her master, the Sultan Osman. Her discovery that she is the daughter of Lusignan, the Christian former king of the area and a fellow-slave, is kept from the sultan, who grows insanely jealous of her meetings with Nerestan, Zaïre's recently discovered brother, and kills them both before he discovers the truth. Voltaire's philosophical interests are reflected in many of his plays. For example, *Alzire* (1736), a complex story about the Spaniards in Peru, argues that a religion should be valued only to the extent that it produces humanitarian results. The trend toward sentimentalism is reflected in Voltaire's frequent use of the *voix du sang* (an instinctive attraction to unknown blood relatives) as a dramatic device to foreshadow recognition scenes.

After living in England from 1726 to 1729, Voltaire came to consider the French neoclassical ideal overly restrictive and sought thereafter to liberalize it. His reforms, however, were confined to introducing ghosts and a limited amount of violence onto the stage, to widening the range of permissible subjects, and to increasing spectacle. But Voltaire's attempts to use spectacle more effectively were frustrated by the presence of spectators on the stage, and it was largely due to his influence that the practice was abolished in 1759. This innovation, coming at just the time when public interest in history and local color was growing, encouraged the exploitation of spectacle in the regular drama. For example, Voltaire's *Tancrède* (1760) turned attention to the Middle Ages and began a vogue for plays about the French national past, which was exploited in numerous popular works.

Comedy, perhaps because of its less-privileged position, underwent more changes than did tragedy. The influence of Molière, dominant until about 1720, is seen in the comedies of Dancourt, Regnard, and LeSage, the major comic authors of the early eighteenth century. Florent-Carton Dancourt (1661–1725) made his debut as an actor at the Comédie Française in 1685 and eventually became the leader

FIG. 10.10

Scene from Regnard's *The Universal Heir* at the Comédie Française, 1708. From the original edition of the play.

of the troupe. Of his more than fifty comedies, two are of special importance, *The Fashionable Gentlemen* (1687) and *The Fashionable Middle-Class Women* (1692). The first introduces a type that was to be prominent in later plays, the *chevalier d'industrie* or gigolo, while the second satirizes the attempts of merchants' wives to become ladies of fashion. In such plays, Dancourt reflects the rise (much as in England at this time) of an ambitious mercantile class. His other plays, most of them comedies of manners, treat a wide range of character types and social customs of his day. From 1688 to 1694, Jean-François Regnard (1655–1709) wrote for the *commedia* troupe then resident in Paris. His later plays were intended for the Comédie Française. His finest works are *The Gambler* (1696), a comic portrait of a compulsive gambler, and *The Universal Heir* (1708), a farce about a valet who schemes to make his master heir to an irascible old uncle. Alain-René LeSage (1668– 1747), after adapting plays by Lope de Vega, Rojas Zorilla, and Calderón, launched a remorseless attack upon contemporary tax collectors in

Turcaret (1709). Often called the first great French comedy of manners, it depicts a world of clever rascals who prey upon each other. Under the surface lurked a thinly disguised criticism of Louis XIV's economic policies, which permitted the privileged and unscrupulous to thrive at the expense of lesser and more honest citizens. The controversy aroused by the play left LeSage estranged from the Comédie Française. As a result, he confined himself thereafter to novels and comic operas, which were produced by the illegitimate theatres at the Parisian fairs.

The trend toward sentimentalism, which, as in England, began around 1720, is most evident in the works of Marivaux and LaChaussée. Pierre Carlet de Chamblain de Marivaux (1688–1763) came to prominence in 1720 with *Arlequin Refined by Love*. This play was presented by the Italian troupe that had been readmitted to France in 1716 following the death of Louis XIV. The majority of Marivaux's thirty-five plays were produced by this company, whose acting style was much better suited than that of the Comédie Française to Marivaux's subtle presentation of emotion. Most of Marivaux's plays are concerned with awakening love. Unlike earlier comedies, in which lovers are kept apart by some external force (usually parents or guardians), the obstacles in Marivaux's plays arise from the inner conflicts of the characters. For example, in *The Game of Love and Chance* (1730) two friends arrange a marriage between their children, but only on the condition that the boy and girl are willing to accept each other; the young couple, who have never met, are skeptical about the match and each hits upon the idea of changing places with a servant to observe the other; then, each irresistibly and unwillingly falls in love with a supposed servant. Here, as in most of Marivaux's plays, interest is focused on subtle changes in feelings within characters rather than upon external intrigue. Consequently, Marivaux is sometimes likened to Racine. He is also noted for his distinctive prose style, often labeled *marivaudage*. With his emphasis on feeling, Marivaux contributed significantly to the development of sentimentalism, but his charm and wit raise him far above his contemporaries. Because of his interest in inner psychological conflicts, his critical stature has grown steadily since the late nineteenth century.

With *False Antipathy* (1733) and *The Fashionable Prejudice* (1735), Pierre Claude Nivelle de LaChaussée (1692–1754) established the *comédie larmoyante,* or tearful comedy, perhaps the most popular dramatic type in France from the 1730s until about 1750. In LaChaussée's works, virtuous protagonists are faced with obstacles designed to arouse sympathy and compassion and from which they are rescued by the revelation of previously unknown facts and rewarded for their constancy. Thus, his plays resemble contemporary tragedy in their plots based on concealed information and in their verse dialogue, and comedy in their happy endings. The overall effect was one of considerable refinement and delicacy. Several other authors, among them Voltaire with such works as *The Prodigal Son* (1736) and *Nanine* (1749), also contributed significantly to the development of sentimental comedy.

After 1750, *comédie larmoyante* was absorbed into other types as a few writers, most notably Denis Diderot (1713–1784), demonstrated and sought to win acceptance for an enlarged range of dramatic genres. At this time virtually all traditional concepts, including those about drama, were being reevaluated by a group of advanced thinkers (the *philosophers*) through controversial essays in the *Encyclopédie,* edited by Diderot and published in twenty-eight volumes between 1748 and 1772. Diderot's own ideas about drama are expressed primarily in a few dialogues and in two plays, *The Illegitimate Son* (1757) and *The Father of a Family* (1758). Diderot argued that neoclassicism was too narrow in restricting the acceptable dramatic types to traditional comedy and tragedy, and that additional "middle" genres—the *drame* (or domestic tragedy) and a comedy concerned with virtue—should be added. He also suggested many innovations in staging, for he believed that drama would move an audience profoundly only if it created an illusion of reality. Consequently, he advocated subject matter chosen from everyday life and presented in settings that duplicated real rooms. He urged the use of prose dialogue, detailed pantomime, and the "fourth wall" convention in acting (that is, behavior which takes no cognizance of the audience). Diderot's ideas on staging foreshadowed some aspects of realism, but they had little effect on the theatre of his time and, even if they had, would have produced effects quite unlike those of late-nineteenth-century realism. His theories on acting as expressed in such works as *Observations on Garrick* (1770) and *The Paradox of the Actor* (published 1830) were more immediately influential.

Diderot did inspire a number of disciples who sought additional inspiration in English sentimental drama. Bernard-Joseph Suarin (1706–1781) adapted Moore's *The Gamester* as *Beverlei* (1768), and Louis-Sebastian Mercier (1740–1814) adapted *The London Merchant* as *Jenneval* (1769), as well as writing such original works as *The Judge* and *The Indigent Man.* The best of the *drames* was *A Philosopher without Knowing It* (1765) by Michel-Jean Sédaine (1719–1797). Its subject, the story of a young man who survives an unwanted duel to become the friend of his former enemy, is a typical one, but the play rises above other *drames* because of its superior characterization and less

FIG. 10.11
Final act of Beaumarchais's *The Marriage of Figaro.* From the 1785 edition of the play. Courtesy Lilly Library, Indiana University.

obvious didacticism. Since the Comédie Française did not encourage it, the *drame* had little chance to develop, except in the minor theatres, where it was to mingle with pantomime and music and emerge in the nineteenth century as melodrama.

The late eighteenth century produced only one major French dramatist, Beaumarchais (Pierre-Augustin Caron, 1732–1799). Now remembered chiefly for his comedies, Beaumarchais also wrote a number of *drames,* such as *Eugénie* (1767) and *The Two Friends* (1770). But his assured fame rests on *The Barber of Seville* (1775) and *The Marriage of Figaro* (1783). The former, a comedy of intrigue in which an elderly guardian's plans to marry his young ward are thwarted, introduces Figaro, the culmination of all the comic servants of French drama. Although *The Marriage of Figaro* includes many of the characters found in the earlier play, its tone is quite different, for intrigue is now subordinated to commentary upon society and class relationships. It is a far more complex play than *The Barber of Seville.* Although the setting ostensibly is Spain, *The Marriage of Figaro* clearly reflects contemporary France, for by this time the nobility had become superfluous and Louis XVI's (reigned 1774–1793) attempts to curb its privileges had proven wholly ineffectual, much to the chagrin of the middle and lower classes who bore the burden of taxation, even though they enjoyed few civil rights. Beaumarchais recaptured the spirit of "laughing" comedy, much as Goldsmith and Sheridan had done in England, but he added to it a sense of political and sociological concern that made his plays quite controversial.

By 1790, then, French drama had taken a few tentative steps away from neoclassicism. Nevertheless, though the typical subject matter and treatment often differed considerably from those of 1700, no startling innovations had been made before the Revolution inaugurated a new era in France.

THE DRAMATIST

In the eighteenth century, the payment of authors was regulated by the government. After a dramatic troupe's daily expenses and a poor tax (ranging from 1/6 to 5/18) had been deducted from receipts, the author was paid 1/9 (after 1781, 1/7) of the revenue for a long play and 1/18 (after 1760, 1/12) for a short play. This arrangement continued until the receipts fell below a prescribed amount, after which the dramatist received no further payment. Since the Opéra sought long runs, its scheme of payments differed. For long works, the librettist and composer each were paid 100 francs for the first ten performances and 50 francs for the next twenty; for short pieces, 60 francs for the first ten and 30 francs for the next twenty.

Although this scheme guaranteed the playwright an income, the actors found ways of decreasing it. The most significant was the exclusion from their calculations of income from annual box rentals. Beaumarchais's objections to this practice led him in 1777 to found the Bureau Dramatique (the origin of France's present-day Society of Authors) to represent dramatists. Largely because of this organization's efforts, the National Assembly in 1791 passed the world's first law relating to royalty payments. It secured to authors and their heirs complete control over dramatic works until five years after the author's death and made it possible for playwrights to collect fees for each performance of their works.

PARISIAN ACTING TROUPES

In 1700 there were only two legitimate troupes in Paris, the Opéra and the Comédie Française, each with monopolistic privileges. These companies were

FIG. 10.12

Scene from a fair-theatre play, *The Quarrel of the Theatres,* satirizing the Comédie Française (represented by the figure on the right) and the Comédie Italienne (represented by the figure on the left) for plundering the fair theatres of their stock in trade. From *Le Théâtre de la Foire, ou l'Opéra Comique* by LeSage and D'Orneval 3 (1723).

to remain the major ones throughout the century, although they were to encounter considerable competition. The first challenge came from the illegitimate theatres at the fairs, especially those of St. Germain, which ran from February 3 until Easter, and St. Laurent, which ran from the end of June until near the end of October. Together they were open about six months each year. Since the sixteenth century the fairs had featured entertainers, such as acrobats, dancers, and exhibitors of trained animals and freaks. In the late seventeenth century they introduced crude dramatic skits and *commedia dell'arte* plays, and, when the Italian company was expelled from France in 1697, they seized the opportunity to enlarge their activities. After 1698, the Opéra and the Comédie Française strove continuously to suppress these troupes, which used various ruses to evade the monopolies. Because of their desire to offer entertainments not prohibited by the monopolies, the fair companies experimented continuously with dramatic forms, and the popularity of their "irregular" plays did much to undermine the neoclassical ideal in France.

The first significant minor form to emerge was comic opera. Forbidden to use dialogue, the fair troupes condensed the necessary exposition and speech into couplets, which were printed on placards held by small boys dressed as cupids and suspended above the stage; the couplets, set to popular tunes, were then sung by confederates planted in the audience. By 1714, the Opéra was in such financial difficulties that, in return for a sizable fee, it authorized one of the fair troupes to use music, dance, and spectacle. After this time, the entertainments were called *opéras comiques.* Between 1713 and 1730, LeSage, who gave up writing for the Comédie Française after the

controversy over *Turcaret,* exploited this form so successfully that he is often called the founder of French comic opera. In his works, spoken dialogue alternates with verses set to popular tunes much as in English ballad opera. Featuring *commedia* characters, these short pieces parodied tragedies and operas and satirized current events and fashions. The fair companies' bills, which always included sideshow variety acts, contrasted sharply with the staid performances of the Comédie Française and the fashionable offerings of the Opéra.

The Parisian theatre was further diversified in 1716, when the Duc d'Orleans, Louis XIV's libertine brother and Regent for the young Louis XV (reigned 1715–1774), invited a *commedia dell'arte* troupe back to France. Installed in the Hôtel de Bourgogne, the Italians were led by Luigi Riccoboni (c. 1676–1753), who in 1713 had attempted unsuccessfully to establish a national theatre in Italy. By 1716 Riccoboni had already recognized that *commedia* was declining, and he sought to diversify his offerings. Thus, when the company's initial popularity in Paris slackened, he began to perform such works

FIG. 10.13
Painting by Antoine Watteau, possibly showing the Italian company of actors, *c.* 1720. Courtesy National Gallery of Art, Washington; Samuel H. Kress Collection.

as Maffei's *Merope* and Italian translations of French tragedies and tragicomedies. In 1718 he added a few works in French, and in 1719 he began to present parodies in the manner of the fair troupes. By 1721, Riccoboni had added four French actors to his company and had induced such authors as Marivaux to write plays for him.

The turning point in the company's fortunes came in 1723, when it was made a state theatre with the official title Comédiens Ordinaires du Roi (although it was almost always referred to as the Comédie Italienne). At the same time the company was granted an annual subsidy and placed under a set of governing rules similar to those of the Comédie Française. At this time its repertory was restricted to *commedia dell'arte* scripts, irregular comedies, and parodies.

The fair companies, which had been suppressed in 1718, although they had continued to perform surreptitiously, resumed open playing in 1723, after Louis XV (who that year had been declared of age) attended a performance. This apparent sanction won them many years of unmolested prosperity. After 1723, then, Paris had three legitimate troupes, plus a number of semilegitimate fair companies.

FIG. 10.14
Charles-Simon Favart in the role of a shepherd in a sentimental *opéra-comique*. From *Die Theater Wiens 2, 1* (1899).

In the 1740s *opéra comique* began to drop its farcical and satirical subject matter in favor of more sentimental stories. Charles-Simon Favart (1710–1792) was especially successful with the new type. His *Acajou* (1744) was so popular that the Opéra suspended the fair troupe's right to use music and spectacle, which it had granted the minor company in return for an annual fee, and sought to take control of *opéra comique*. This led to such a violent controversy that the crown issued an injunction against all performances of comic opera. Between 1745 and 1751, the years during which the injunction was in effect, English pantomime was introduced to fill the void. It was received so enthusiastically that it remained a staple of the Parisian minor theatres for the rest of the century.

Two significant innovations were made in *opéra comique* after its revival in 1751. First, ordinary characters began to replace the *commedia* figures. As a part of this shift, local color, in the form of picturesque characters, places, and customs, came into the minor theatres long before it was common at the major houses. Second, following the great success in Paris of Pergolesi's *The Servant the Mistress* (1752), original music began to replace the popular tunes to which couplets had been sung prior to that time. Possibly because these innovations brought the form greatly increased popularity, the Comédie Italienne was awarded a monopoly on *opéra comique* in 1762. At the same time, Goldoni was imported from Italy to write for the troupe. *Opéra comique* and Goldoni's comedies proved so popular that between 1769 and 1780 French plays were dropped altogether from the Comédie Italienne's repertory.

When the fair troupes were deprived of *opéra comique,* they returned to the original form of comic opera, in which songs were set to popular tunes. Now called *comédies-en-vaudevilles,* plays of this type were to retain their appeal until well into the nineteenth century. Pantomime also increased in popularity as it became more melodramatic with mood music underscoring emotional scenes of innocence persecuted and rescued from villainy. By 1780, dialogue had been introduced into this previously silent form and such anachronistic labels as *pantomimes dialoguées et parlées* (with dialogue and speaking) had become common. After 1769, when the Comédie Italienne dropped its French repertory, the minor companies also began to perform *drames* and irregular comedies, perhaps because French playwrights now had no other market if their works were refused by the Comédie Française.

After 1760 the fair troupes began to relocate on the Boulevard du Temple, a fashionable recreational spot, although they continued to play part of each

FIG. 10.15

Booth theatres at the Fair of St. Ovid (one of the lesser Parisian fairs). On the right, Nicolet's booth. Note the balconies on which *parades* (brief skits used to entice customers inside) were performed. From Pougin, *Dictionnaire du Théâtre* (1885).

year at the fairs. Thus, they became year-round companies. Of the troupes that moved to the Boulevard, four were especially important: Audinot's, Nicolet's, the Théâtre des Associés, and the Variétés Amusantes. (The location of these theatres was to supply the term still applied to Parisian companies catering to popular audiences—boulevard theatres.)

During the 1780s the minor theatres had to make a number of adjustments, primarily because of actions taken by the major companies. Some changes were initiated by the Comédie Italienne, which after Goldoni's retirement in 1773 had declined in popularity. Consequently, in 1780 it was reorganized once more and both its Italian plays and performers were dropped, thus severing its last connections with Italy. At this time, irregular French comedies and *drames* were returned to the repertory. Since the boulevard theatres were not allowed to compete directly with the state companies, they had to adjust their offerings; the result was an increased emphasis on pantomime. Other changes were initiated by the Opéra. Seeking to solve its perennial financial problems, in 1784 it petitioned for and was granted authority over the minor companies. Those agreeing to pay a substantial yearly fee were permitted to continue performances, but those who defied the grant were expropriated or suppressed.

This situation continued up to the time of the Revolution. Then, in 1791 the National Assembly abolished all monopolies, thus freeing the theatres from former restraints. Although other restrictions were soon to be imposed, the act of 1791 marks the end of an era.

Throughout all the controversies of the eighteenth century, the Comédie Française maintained its monopoly on tragedy and "regular" comedy (defined primarily by its five acts). Consequently, most of the major playwrights wrote for it, since only the lesser and "irregular" forms were permitted at the Comédie Italienne and the fairs. These restrictions often meant that a play refused by one company had to be rewritten to meet the genre restrictions placed on another troupe. Furthermore, the limited demand for new works sometimes led to the acceptance of plays years before they were produced. It is probably for this reason that in the late eighteenth century the Comédie Française was required to produce one new play or revival each month.

Of all the troupes, the Opéra enjoyed the greatest prestige. For this reason, it was allowed to exploit other companies. After 1714 it collected considerable revenue by licensing other theatres to use music, dance, or elaborate spectacle. After 1762 the Comédie Italienne paid the Opéra from 20,000 to 54,000 francs yearly for the right to present musical plays, and after 1784 the boulevard theatres were subsidiaries of the Opéra.

The Comédie Française and the Comédie Italienne were organized as sharing companies. When the Comédie Italienne became a state troupe in 1723, it was placed under the supervision of the Gentlemen

FIG. 10.16

Various kinds of acrobatic entertainments used as incidental diversions at Nicolet's theatre on the Boulevard du Temple in the late eighteenth century. From Pougin, *Dictionnaire du Théâtre* (1885).

of the Chamber, who also oversaw the Comédie Française, and under regulations similar to those governing the older company. Ostensibly all decisions were made at weekly meetings of the actors. After 1759 even the *pensionnaires* were included in deliberations. On the other hand, the Gentlemen of the Chamber had to ratify all decisions, including the choice of plays and actors, changes in financial procedures, and alterations in the theatre buildings. They sometimes ordered the admission of actors as *sociétaires* (even if this forced others to retire), redistributed shares, and interfered in other ways.

The Opéra was organized along entirely different lines. Although the crown provided a subsidy and laid down the rules under which it functioned, the management was farmed out to an entrepreneur. Because of its large expenses, the Opéra was always in financial difficulties, and by 1749 had accumulated a debt of more than one million francs. In that year, it was ceded to the City of Paris. Having failed to achieve a sound fiscal policy, the city also farmed out the management after 1757. By 1780 the situation was so chaotic that the crown resumed control. This arrangement continued until the Revolution. In spite of its abysmal financial and managerial record, the Opéra was the favored troupe with aristocratic audiences throughout the century. It presented the most spectacular productions in Paris, and after 1775 was considered the finest opera company in Europe.

The fair and boulevard theatres were run entirely as private ventures. Each was operated by a manager who assumed both risks and profits.

FIG. 10.17
Pen drawing by Boquet of costumes for a *pas de deux* at the Opéra, danced by M Gardel as Hippomene and Mlle Asselin as Atalanta, 1769. From Adolphe Jullien, *Histoire du Costume au Théâtre* (1880).

The troupes increased in size during the century. In 1713 the Opéra had 121 performers (singers, dancers, and musicians), but by 1778 there were 228. By the 1770s, the Comédie Française included about 50 actors and the Comédie Italienne about 70. Although it brought increased expenses, growth was probably less responsible for the troupes' constant financial difficulties than were their strange fiscal policies. Both the Comédie Française and the Comédie Italienne received subsidies (ranging from 12,000 to 15,000 francs), required each new *sociétaire* to invest from 8,000 to 15,000 francs in the company, and collected large sums in annual rentals for private boxes. Most of this money, however, was divided among the *sociétaires* rather than going into a common fund, with the result that the troupes were never able to meet unexpected expenses. Consequently, the Comédie Française owed 487,000 francs in 1757 and the Comédie Italienne 400,000 in 1762, even though *sociétaires* were sometimes receiving as much as 30,000 francs a year, as compared to a *pensionnaire's* salary of less than 2,000 francs. Thus, while the troupes in theory were sharing companies, they appear to have shared income rather than expenses. Occasionally the crown made special grants or ordered economies to reduce indebtedness, but no effort was made to reform fiscal policies.

The dramatic troupes played daily. At first the season extended from November 2 until Easter, but after 1766 it ran from November 15 until May 15. In 1700 the curtain time was 5 P.M.; it later changed to 5:15 or 5:30. Each theatre was required to list its bill two weeks in advance. Normally a different play was offered each day, except when a popular new piece was produced. At the Opéra, performances were given only three days a week. Its season was divided in two parts: October to Lent, and Easter to mid-May. In 1700 performances began at 4 P.M., but after 1714 at 5:15. The Opéra ran each production as long as it drew an audience and sometimes performed no more than four or five works in a season.

The evening's bill was simpler than in a London theatre. The Comédie Française normally presented a long play and an afterpiece. After 1757 ballets were given as entr'actes. The Comédie Italienne often gave programs made up of several short pieces, and its bills were organized to reserve certain days of the week for each of the genres it was permitted to perform. In the 1740s it added a dance troupe, and after 1750 pantomimes and displays of fireworks became typical offerings. The Opéra normally presented one major work along with incidental ballets. After the 1770s, when Jean-Georges Noverre (1727–1810) became the ballet master, ballet increased in importance at the Opéra. (Noverre began his career in 1743 in *opéra comique* and later worked in several major European cities. In 1760 he published his revolutionary work, *Letters on the Dance and Ballet,* which was instrumental in transforming ornamental and spectacular dances into storytelling works that were the forerunners of modern ballets.) At the fair theatres, variety was the key, for there the carnival atmosphere predominated. Thus, the Parisian theatre included as wide a range of entertainment as the English, but the restrictions on the French companies led to more specialization by each troupe.

During the second half of the eighteenth century, theatre also flourished in the provinces, where at least twenty-three cities built new theatres between 1750 and 1773. These companies offered little that was new, emulating instead Parisian trends in repertory and staging.

ACTORS AND ACTING

The eighteenth century also brought the first successful attempt to establish an orderly system for training actors. Until the 1780s, most French actors received their training while playing utility roles in a provincial troupe. A few beginners were accepted into the Parisian companies after being coached by leading actors (who were paid 500 francs for each pupil taken into the company). These methods were eventually judged insufficient, however, and in 1786 the Royal Dramatic School, forerunner of the present Conservatoire, was founded as an adjunct to the Comédie Française.

Gaining admission to the major Parisian troupes was difficult. Applicants had first to be approved by a committee of actors; they then played at least three roles in public performances; if deemed successful, they were accepted as *pensionnaires* until a vacancy occurred among the *sociétaires*. By the late eighteenth century, a *pensionnaire* had to be either admitted as a *sociétaire* or released by the end of the second year with the troupe. This rule often led to reassignments of shares or forced retirements in order to make room among the *sociétaires* for desirable performers.

A young actor often began as understudy, or *double,* to a major performer. As in England, most casting was governed by "lines of business." The major lines in tragedy were kings, tyrants, lovers, princesses, mothers, and female lovers, while the major lines in comedy were old men, lovers, valets, peasants, old women, coquettes, and soubrettes. In addition, there were a number of secondary lines, and the bottom rank was made up of general utility players. Certain tragic and comic lines were usually filled by the same actors. For example, the *jeune premier* (or leading male

performer) played the lover in both comedy and tragedy, while the actress who played princesses in tragedy normally assumed the roles of coquettes in comedy. As a rule, actors remained in the same line of business throughout their careers.

The eighteenth century produced many distinguished performers, most of them members of the Comédie Française. Between 1700 and 1720, a period noted for its formal and oratorical style, the major actors were Mlle Desmares, Mlle Duclos, and Beaubour. Charlotte Desmares (1682–1753) succeeded Mlle Champmeslé, her aunt, as leading actress of the Comédie Française in 1698 and retained that position until she retired in 1721. Her principal rival was Mlle Duclos (Marie-Anne de Chateauneuf, 1668–1748), Mlle Champmeslé's understudy and pupil. After the vogue in acting style changed around 1720, she lost most of her following; by the time she retired in 1736, she was judged very old-fashioned. Pierre-Trochon de Beaubour (1662–1725) replaced Baron at the Comédie Française in 1691. His good looks and excellent declamation assured him the position of leading actor until he retired in 1718.

Around 1720 the performance style became more realistic, partially because of Michel Baron's return to the stage from 1720 to 1729. The trend toward realism was also strengthened by Adrienne Lecouvreur (1692–1730), who made her debut in 1717 and became the leading actress of the company after

FIG. 10.18
Painting by Antoine Watteau, probably showing actors of the Comédie Française, c. 1720. Note the *habit à la romaine* worn by the actor in the foreground. At right rear, a figure dressed as one of Molière's characters, some of whom continued to be costumed in seventeeth-century dress. Courtesy Metropolitan Museum of Art, Jules S. Bache Collection, 1949.

the retirement of Mlle Desmares in 1721. She died suddenly in 1730 and was refused Christian burial, being interred in some unknown spot in the same year that Mrs. Oldfield was buried in Westminster Abbey. Aside from Baron, the leading actor of this period was Quinault-Dufrense (1693–1767), admitted to the Comédie Française in 1712 as understudy to Beaubour, whose roles he inherited in 1718 and retained until his retirement in 1741.

In the succeeding period, the leading performers were Mlle LaGaussin, Grandval, and Mlle Dangeville. Mlle LaGaussin (Jeanne-Catherine Gaussens, 1711–1767), daughter of Baron's valet, was accepted into the Comédie Française in 1731 and was its leading actress until overshadowed by Mlle Dumesnil and Clairon. Her ability to express tenderness and grief made her especially effective in "tearful comedy." Charles-François de Grandval (1710–1784) began in 1729 as understudy to Quinault-Dufresne, whole roles he inherited in 1741. He remained the company's leading actor until 1768. Marie-Anne-Botot Dangeville (1714–1796) was admitted to the Comédie Française in 1730 and was its principal comedienne until her retirement in 1763. Garrick thought her the finest actress on the French stage.

Perhaps the most famous players of the eighteenth century were Mlle Dumesnil, Mlle Clairon, and Lekain. Mlle Dumesnil (Marie-Françoise Marchand, 1713–1803) began her acting career in the provinces around 1733. Accepted as an understudy at the Comédie Française in 1737, she became a *sociétaire* in 1738 and was soon the leading performer of such strong tragic roles as Clytemnestra and Medea. In his *Paradox of the Actor,* Diderot depicts her as an erratic performer dependent on inspiration and thus sometimes magnificent and at others mediocre. She retired in 1776. Mlle Clairon (Claire-Josèphe-Hippolyte Léris de la Tude, 1723–1803) began her career in 1736 at the Comédie Italienne and, after performing in the provinces and at the Opéra, was admitted to the Comédie Française in 1743 as understudy to Dumesnil. Diderot idealizes her as an artist conscious of every detail in performance. Voltaire and Garrick also considered her superior to Dumesnil. At first declamatory in style, Clairon was persuaded by the critic Marmontel in 1753 to assume a more conversational tone. This change made her question the old traditions of costuming, and in 1755 she began to adopt more realistic and historically accurate stage dress. She retired in 1766 at the height of her career. Mlle Clairon's reforms were supported by Henri-Louis Lekain (1729–1778), who was admitted to the Comédie Française in 1750 largely because of Voltaire's influence. He worked hard to overcome his vocal and physical shortcomings, but was not awarded

FIG. 10.19

Crowning a bust of Voltaire during a performance of his *Irène* at the Comédie Française, 1778. At this time the Comédie was performing in the Théâtre des Tuileries. From Pougin, *Dictionnaire du Théâtre* (1885).

a full share in the company until 1758. His talents were not fully recognized until after Grandval's retirement in 1768. Thereafter, Lekain was considered the greatest tragic actor of his age. Together he and Mlle Clairon did much to bring greater realism to the acting of the time.

Lekain's principal successors were Larive and Molé. Larive (Jean Mauduit, 1747–1827) was appointed understudy to Lekain in 1775 and succeeded to many of his roles in 1778. But in spite of his handsomeness and fine voice, he never achieved Lekain's reputation. He retired in 1788. François-Rene Molé (1734–1802), after several years in the provinces, was admitted to the Comédie Française in 1760. Thereafter he was the leading player of young comic heroes and inherited as well several of Lekain's serious roles. He left the troupe in 1791.

The principal tragic actresses of the late eighteenth century were Mme Vestris and Mlle Raucourt. Mme Vestris (François-Marie-Rosette Gourgaud, 1743–1804), after studying with Lekain, was admitted to the company after the retirement of Clairon and Dumesnil. Mlle Raucourt (1756–1815) made her debut in 1772 as understudy to Mme Vestris. Dismissed in 1776 following a scandal, she was readmitted in 1779. She was excellent in stern tragic roles but lacking in tenderness.

The finest comic actor of the late eighteenth century was Préville (Pierre-Louis Dubus, 1721–1799), who played in the provinces before joining the Comédie Française in 1753. Préville revolutionized the playing of low comedy roles, which had previously been treated as fat and alcoholic bunglers. Préville, who was handsome, slender, and graceful, used these qualities in his carefully differentiated characterizations. He retired in 1786.

As this brief survey indicates, the most potent influences on acting during the eighteenth century were tradition, learning by observation and imitation, and an orderly system of passing along lines of business and roles.

Although most of the famous actors were associated with the Comédie Française, a few achieved fame at the Comédie Italienne. Luigi Riccoboni, leader of the original troupe, was excellent as the "first lover," and Giovanna Benozzi, the second *amoureuse*, was the inspiration for many of Marivaux's heroines. Perhaps the most famous performer of the Comédie Italienne was Marie-Justine Favart (1727–1772), wife of Charles-Simon Favart. After playing at the fairs, she joined the Comédie Italienne in 1749 and continued there until 1771. A performer of great versatility, she was also a leader in costume reform. But the restriction of the Comédie Italienne to minor forms and the frequent reorganization of the company prevented the development of strong traditions and an outstanding ensemble.

With the coming of the Revolution, French actors achieved full civil and religious rights. The National Assembly forbade discrimination against players and, though this act did not make performers entirely socially acceptable, it removed the legal grounds that had encouraged prejudice in the past.

COSTUME PRACTICES

Costume practices in France differed little from those of England. Most characters were dressed in contemporary garments and as sumptuously as the performers could afford. Ordinarily, fashionable garments were used in both comedy and tragedy until 1727, when Adrienne Lecouvreur adopted the much more elaborate and formal court dress for tragedy. Her practice soon became standard for all tragic heroines. The actors also adopted court dress for tragedy except in classical roles, for which the *habit à la romaine* was retained, although it, too, grew more elaborate and conventionalized; the plumed helmet was often replaced by a three-cornered hat and the skirt of the tunic was frequently hooped. The use of traditional costumes for a few roles continued through the eighteenth century. Molière's ridiculous characters, such as Harpagon, Sganarelle, Scapin, and Gros-René, were most subject to this treatment, for all continued to be costumed in the style of the mid-seventeenth century when the plays were written.

As in England, costumes came from two sources: the company's wardrobe and the actor's privately

FIG. 10.20
Mme Favart in the costume she supposedly imported from Istanbul to ensure authenticity of dress in *The Three Sultans,* 1761. From *Costumes et Annales des Grand Théâtres de Paris* (1786–1789).

owned garments. Each company owned an extensive wardrobe, but since it was reused constantly, the costumes were often threadbare. As a result, it was used primarily by the lesser performers. By 1730 the major actors were engaging in bitter competition to outdo each other in the lavishness of their stage dress. When Adrienne Lecouvreur died, her wardrobe was sold for 40,000 francs, and Mlle Raucourt was given a wardrobe valued at 20,000 francs when she made her debut in 1772.

The ideal of lavishness began to be challenged in the 1750s. The first significant change came in 1753, when Mme Favart wore an authentic peasant dress as the heroine of *The Loves of Bastien and Bastienne.* In 1761 she supposedly sent to Constantinople for an authentic dress to wear in *The Three Sultans.* The new trend came to the Comédie Française also in the 1750s, under the leadership of Mlle Clairon and Lekain. For his *The Orphan of China* (1755), Voltaire asked the artist Joseph Vernet to design clothing which, though based on Chinese dress, would not

FIG. 10.21
Lekain and Dumesnil in Voltaire's *Sémiramis,* 1756. Although the play is set in ancient Assyria, Mlle Dumesnil wears an elaborate court dress of the eighteenth century and Lekain a formalized costume similar to that used for classical heroes. An English print of 1772.

provoke laughter. The results were more nearly Turkish than Chinese in appearance. The innovation was favorably received, nevertheless, and thereafter Clairon and Lekain sought to dress each role appropriately. In 1756 Lekain outraged audiences by appearing in *Sémiramis* with bare arms, disarrayed hair, and bloody hands. Voltaire disapproved of so much realism, calling it "too English." Voltaire's *Tancrède* (1760) introduced medieval costumes, and thereafter other periods and locales were occasionally represented in costumes. The increased concern for costume is seen at its peak perhaps with Beaumarchais, who described in detail the dress for each of his characters, even when the plays had contemporary settings.

None of these reforms had far-reaching effects. Many of the actors refused to accept the changes, and others were inconsistent in their use of them. By 1790 the reforms had amounted to little more than the abandonment of hooped petticoats for classical figures and plumed headdresses for all characters, and the adoption of sixteenth-century garments for all historical periods other than classical or contemporary. Since, with rare exceptions, actors chose their own costumes, inconsistencies abounded. The deviations from historical accuracy in costuming are well illustrated in Levacher de Charnois' *Costumes et Annales des Grand Théâtres de Paris* (1786–1789), in which pictures of actors in their costumes are followed by historically accurate drawings of the same garments.

Nevertheless, the seeds of change had been planted. The conflict between the old outlook, in which art was expected to idealize, and the new, in which art was expected to copy life, had begun. As yet, neoclassicism still reigned, but its foundations had been undermined.

FIG. 10.22
Mlle Clairon's costume for the *Orphan of China,* 1755. Although it marked a change to more accurate costuming, this costume fell considerably short of authenticity. From a contemporary print.

THEATRE ARCHITECTURE

The major theatre buildings of Paris remained virtually unchanged until after 1750, when interest in theatre architecture increased. Articles appeared in Diderot's *Encyclopédie,* and Dumont's *Comparison of the Most Beautiful Theatres of Italy and France* (1763) contrasted the outmoded French structures with their newer Italian counterparts. Perhaps as a result, the new buildings followed the Italian trends toward the ovoid auditorium and the enlarged stage.

The first major change in the Parisian theatres came in 1763 when the Palais Royal (home of the Opéra) burned. From 1763 until 1769, the opera company performed in the Théâtre des Tuileries, converted from the stage (an area 52 by 140 feet) of the disused Salle des Machines. With its three tiers of boxes, it recreated the principal features of the Palais Royal. The Opéra's new theatre opened in 1769 and burned in 1781. The troupe then moved

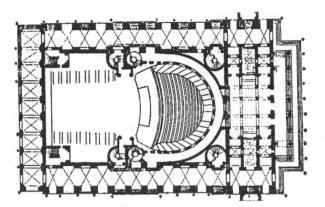

FIG. 10.23
Plan of the theatre built for the Comédie Française in 1782. It later became the Odéon. Note the horseshoe-shaped auditorium; also the seated pit, an innovation in France. Note too that the stage is deeper than the auditorium. From Donnet and Kaufmann, *Architectonographie des Théâtres* (1836–1857).

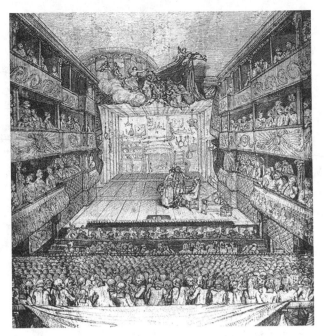

FIG. 10.25
The Hôtel de Bourgogne in 1769 when the repertory of the Comédie Italienne was restricted to *opéra-comique* and Italian comedies. On stage is a scene from an *opéra-comique*. Note the footlights, prompter's box at front-center of the stage, and the orchestra. Note also that most of the action is placed on the platform forward of the proscenium. There are a few benches at the front of the auditorium but the remainder of the spectators in the pit are standing. Drawing by P. A. Wille the Younger. Courtesy Bibliothèque Nationale, Paris.

to the new Porte-Saint-Martin Theatre, where it remained until 1794.

The Comédie Française continued to use its converted tennis court until 1770. Alterations to it were minor. Around 1716, five benches, holding about 140 persons, were permanently installed on either side of

FIG. 10.24
Theatre designed by Victor Louis in 1785 for the Opéra, but never used by that company. When this engraving was made c. 1790 it was the home of the Variétés Amusantes. Note the emphasis on spectacle with the practicable suspended bridge. This theatre was to be the home of the Comédie Française after 1799. Courtesy Bibliothèque Nationale, Paris.

the stage. In 1759, when spectators were banished from the stage, these benches were removed, but seating for about 180 persons was provided at the front of the pit. At the same time, in order not to diminish the space allotted to standing spectators, the amphitheatre was reduced in size. In 1770 the troupe moved to the Théâtre des Tuileries, recently vacated by the Opéra, until its new theatre, on the site of the present-day Odéon, was opened in 1782. The new building provided seats for all spectators and wholly abolished the standing pit for the first time in a Parisian theatre devoted to nonoperatic performances. The auditorium was ovoid in shape, and the stage much better equipped than that of its predecessor.

The Comédie Italienne played in the Hôtel de Bourgogne from 1716 until 1783, when this theatre, built in 1548, was abandoned. Changes in the Bourgogne during the eighteenth century paralleled those made at the Comédie Française. A number of large boxes were subdivided in 1760, and in 1765 benches were installed at the front of the pit to accommodate the spectators who were banished from the stage at that time. Perhaps out of a desire to compete with the Comédie Française, the Comédie Italienne moved into a new building in 1783. It, too, incorporated the latest Italian features, but it retained a "standing pit" sufficiently large to hold 650 spectators. In 1788 the attempt to furnish this area with benches was met with such opposition that the plan was abandoned. Not until the early nineteenth century was seating in the pit fully accepted in Paris.

The boulevard theatres also began to acquire elaborate buildings in the late eighteenth century. The Variétés Amusantes, designed by Victor Louis and originally intended for the Opéra, opened in 1785. It was modeled on an earlier structure designed by Louis, the Grand Theatre in Bordeaux, built between 1773 and 1780, one of the most influential theatre buildings of its time. When the Variétés Amusantes opened, it was the finest theatre in Paris and after 1799 was to be the home of the Comédie Française.

By the time the Revolution began, all the major theaters of Paris had been modernized. The changes appear to have been motivated by the desire to improve sightlines, to provide better facilities for spectacle, and to increase seating capacity.

SCENIC PRACTICES

Although as early as the 1730s Voltaire had urged the use of more appropriate spectacle, little could be done to implement his suggestions in nonoperatic productions until 1759, when spectators were banished from the stage. Thus, until about 1760 the *palais à volonté* and the *chambre à quatre portes* continued to be the usual settings.

The removal of spectators from the stage was motivated primarily by the desire to use more elaborate settings. An important turning point in the attitude toward spectacle can be seen in the Comédie Française's production of Voltaire's *The Orphan of China* (1755), which was billed as having new and accurate Oriental costumes and settings. During the 1750s the Comédie Italienne also began to introduce local color and, as soon as spectators were removed from the stage, both companies markedly increased their use of spectacle. In 1760 Voltaire's *Tancrède* directed attention to the Middle Ages, and soon other plays were being set in such locales as Norway, Russia, Spain, America, and the Near East and in many different periods. Diderot's plea (made in the 1750s) for greater fidelity to everyday life was also met in a few plays, such as Voltaire's *The Scots Girl* (1760), set in the common room of an inn, and Beaumarchais's *Eugénie* (1767), which sought to reproduce a domestic background in all its details. In spite of these

innovations, however, the majority of plays continued to be presented in stock scenery.

At the Opéra considerable emphasis was placed on spectacle throughout the century. After the retirement of Jean Bérain in 1721, the most important designer was Jean-Nicolas Servandoni (1695–1766), a Florentine who worked for the Opéra from about 1728 to 1746. His principal contributions to French design were the *scena per angolo* and monumentality in the manner of the Bibienas. Servandoni is also noted for his "mute spectacles," mounted in the Salle des Machines between 1738 and 1742 and again from 1754 to 1758. In these, he recreated faithfully a number of well-known places, and the naturalism of these actorless spectacles probably did much to motivate the other theatres of Paris to improve their settings.

Servandoni's successors at the Opéra changed so rapidly that none was able to establish a dominant style. Among the later designers the most important were François Boucher (1703–1770), who worked for a number of theatres after 1740 and who was noted for his idyllic landscapes; Louis-René Boquet (1717–1814), famous for ballet costumes as well as scenery in which Chinese decorative motifs were prominent; and Pietro Algieri, who designed settings from about 1748 to 1761 and turned attention away from the fantasies of Boucher and Boquet to more formal architectural settings. Many of the best-known French painters, such as Charles Gillot, Saint-Aubin, Charles de Wailly, and P. L. Moreau the Younger, also designed settings. Nevertheless, scenic design in France seldom rose to the level achieved by the Italian designers of

FIG. 10.26

The auditorium of the Comédie Française, 1726. Note the audience on stage peering through and around the curtain. Note also the standing pit. From Adolphe Jullien, *Les Spectateurs sur le Théâtre* (1875).

FIG. 10.27
Stage setting by Jean-Nicolas Servandoni, who popularized the *scena per angolo* in France. From Bapst, *Essai sur l'Histoire du Théâtre* (1893).

the period. The frequent changes in management and the constant financial difficulties at the Opéra, the continued adherence to the neoclassical ideal, and the reticence of the actors to authorize large expenditures for scenery at the Comédie Française did much to keep scenic practices in old paths. Although new directions had been suggested before the Revolution, they had not yet been fully exploited.

By 1790 France was involved in radical change of a more fundamental sort. In 1789 the country was in such financial distress that Louis XVI was forced to call a meeting of the States-General (the French national assembly) for the first time since 1614. When one group within the assembly demanded a constitution and basic social reforms, Louis attempted to disband the States-General, thereby precipitating a reaction that led to the fall of the Bastille, which initiated the French Revolution. Ultimately the conflict was over the divine right of kings versus equality among people. At stake was the class system that had existed since the Middle Ages. The new doctrine of equality and of government as a social contract had been forcefully stated by the American Declaration of Independence in 1776, but its impact was to be far more radical in France, which was still governed as an absolute monarchy. But the true revolution lay not so much in the violent events of the 1790s as in the ideas about social organization and human rights, for they gave the common people a new vision of themselves and their worth, the effects of which are still being felt today.

LOOKING AT THEATRE HISTORY

The theatre may be viewed as an autonomous art, but it may also be seen as one among several related arts. Familiarity with the painting, music, and literature of a period can clarify much about the theatre of the age, especially its stylistic qualities and conventions. Thus, the more fully one knows the other arts, the more insights one gains into the theatre. This is true in part because the arts of an age are usually based in shared theoretical and cultural assumptions. For example, Arnold Hauser in *The Social History of Art* argues that all baroque art has common characteristics that grow out of an uneasy world view brought about by Copernicus's discovery that the earth (and therefore humanity) is not the center of the universe. "The whole of the art of the baroque is full of this shudder. . . . The impetuous diagonals, the sudden foreshortenings, the exaggerated light and shade effects,

everything is the expression of an overwhelming unquenchable yearning for infinity."

A. Hyatt Mayor theorizes that stage design offered an ideal outlet for the baroque imagination, whose conceptions were so grandiose that few of its architectural fancies could be realized in stone. "The wise heads of the time must have seen that the new visions of space and grandeur . . . remained uninhabitable dream palaces . . . the Bibienas, in designs as arbitrary as the mandate of the autocrats they served, summed up the great emotional architecture of the baroque." (*The Bibiena Family*, 27–28)

As a branch of theatre, opera is especially important in the study of scenic design and theatre architecture. In fact, the majority of extant pictorial evidence about scenery between the Renaissance and the nineteenth century is from opera, and thus studies of scenic design emphasize musical more than non-musical production. This is especially true of the eighteenth century, during which the Bibiena family dominated operatic design. In 1785 Stefano Arteaga wrote of Ferdinando Bibiena's contributions:

> The art of making tiny space seem vast, the ease and speed of changing sets in a twinkling of an eye, . . . and above all buildings seen at an angle brought the science of illusion to the highest possible pitch . . . the change from perspectives that limit sight and imagination by running to a central vanishing point was like opening a new world to busy the imagination . . . and could represent and ennoble the real things of this world. . . .

> From A. Hyatt Mayor, *The Bibiena Family* (New York: H. Bittner and Co., 1945), 24.

Italy was the traditional home of opera and *commedia dell'arte*. But before the middle of the eighteenth century the *commedia* was beginning to be out of tune with the sentimental tastes of the age. In his *Memoirs*, Goldoni tells of his attempts to reform it:

> The mask must always be very prejudicial to the action of the performer . . . and however he may gesticulate and vary the tone, he can never convey by the countenance . . . the different passions. . . . [For this and other reasons, I attempted] the reform of the Italian Theatre, and to supply the place of farces with comedies. . . . I undertook to produce a few pieces merely sketched, without ceasing to give comedies of character. I employed the masks [in some] and I displayed a more noble and interesting comic humor in the others. . . . with time and patience I brought about a reconciliation [of the two]; and I had the satisfaction, at length, to see . . . my own taste [become] in a few years the most general and prevailing in Italy.

> Carlo Goldoni, *Memoirs,* trans. John Black (London, 1814), II, 56–57.

Diderot did not find the two forms of drama sanctioned by neoclassicism sufficient, and he proposed two "middle genres" to enlarge the range to four types:

> Laughing comedy, whose purpose is to ridicule vice; serious comedy, whose function is to depict virtue and duty; the kind of tragedy that is concerned with domestic troubles; and finally, the kind of tragedy that deals with public catastrophes and the misfortunes of the mighty.

In addition, Diderot wished to reform theatrical production to make it as illusionistic as possible. He became the first to propose the "fourth wall" conception of the stage:

> Regardless of whether you are writing or acting, think no more about the audience than if it did not exist. Imagine a wall across the front of the stage, dividing you from the audience, and act precisely as if the curtain had not risen.

> Denis Diderot, *On Dramatic Poetry* (1758).

In France in the 1750s reforms began to be made in acting and costume to achieve greater naturalness. Here is a brief comment by Marmontel on one of the first attempts:

> I went to see [Mlle Clairon] in her dressing room, and, for the first time, I found her dressed in the habit of a sultana; without hoop, her arms half-naked, and in the truth of Oriental costume. . . . The event surpassed her expectation and mine. It was no longer the actress, it was Roxanne herself. . . . The astonishment, the illusion, the enchantment, was extreme. . . . [The audience] had heard nothing like it. I saw her after the play. . . . "Don't you see that it ruins me? In all my characters, the costume must now be observed; the truth of declamation requires that of dress; all my rich stage-wardrobe is from this moment rejected. . . ."

> Jean François Marmontel, *Memoirs* (London, 1805), 44–45.

11

Northern and Eastern European Theatre to 1800

Although by 1700 the professional theatre was firmly established in England, France, Italy, and Spain, it had scarcely begun in Northern and Eastern Europe. The slowness of Northern Europe to develop a professional theatre can be attributed in large part to unsettled religious and political conditions dating back to the early sixteenth century. The conflict between Protestants and Catholics had led to the Treaty of Augsburg in 1555, but the results were never wholly satisfactory, and in 1618 open warfare broke out again. Usually called the Thirty Years War, this conflict continued until 1648. By 1635 it had become more political than religious, as France, under Cardinal Richelieu's guidance, actively aided the Protestant faction out of a desire to curb the power of Austria. By the time of the Peace of Westphalia (1648), the population and resources of Germanic territories had been so seriously depleted that it would take almost 150 years for full recovery. In addition, the area was divided into more than 300 independent units, some large but others only a few square miles in size, making "Germany" the designation of a region, not a reference to a nation-state. Under these political, economic, and religious conditions, an adequate professional theatre could come into existence only gradually. In this struggle for survival, professional troupes received little encouragement, since the policies of both court and church discouraged rather than assisted native spoken drama.

THE COURT THEATRES OF THE GERMAN STATES

France's decisive role in negotiating an end to the Thirty Years War gave it considerable prestige throughout the German states, where soon rulers were seeking to create their own versions of the French court. As a result, opera, ballet, and theatrical spectacles of all sorts became a regular part of court life. The more affluent rulers imported Italian or French designers, musicians, and performers, but the less prosperous had to rely on native Germans to copy the foreign models.

Austria set the pattern when in 1652 the emperor imported Ludovico Burnacini from Venice to stage court entertainments. At Vienna an elaborate court theatre was opened in 1668. To serve it, the most famous composers and librettists of the age were brought from Italy. As a result, Vienna was to be the most important center for operatic production in Europe from about 1660 to 1740. It was in Vienna that the Bibienas mounted some of their most sumptuous productions during the eighteenth century.

Other German rulers followed the Austrian example. At Munich, a court theatre opened in 1654 and there Francesco Santurini, one of Italy's most outstanding designers, mounted numerous lavish spectacles. An opera house was built in Dresden sometime between 1664 and 1667 and another in Gotha about 1683. By the end of the seventeenth century, opera and Italianate scenery were to be seen at numerous courts in Germany. During the eighteenth century these court theatres vied for the services of members of the Quaglio, Mauro, and Bibiena families of scene designers. Although rulers oc-

casionally witnessed spoken drama, they confined their financial support for the most part to opera, ballet, and foreign troupes.

Considering its favored position with the ruling class, it is not surprising that opera also became the most admired form with the prosperous middle class. Before the end of the seventeenth century, some of the populous commercial centers had been able to establish public opera houses. Hamburg had an opera company from 1678 until 1738 and Leipzig from 1693 until 1720, although both performed only sporadically. Nevertheless, with both the aristocracy and the bourgeoisie, opera was the favorite form until well after 1750, and spoken drama only gradually won their support.

FIG. 11.1

Northern and Eastern Europe during the eighteenth century. The Holy Roman Empire was divided into many small states, the borders of which are not shown here.

FIG. 11.2
The court theatre at Vienna designed by Ludovico Burnacini and opened in 1668.
On stage is seen part of *The Golden Apple,* the opera which opened the theatre.
On the dais are the Emperor Leopold I and his retinue. Engraving by Franz Geffels,
1668. Courtesy Bildarchiv, Osterreichische Nationalbibliothek, Vienna.

THE JESUIT THEATRE

In the seventeenth century numerous German schools,
both Protestant and Catholic, presented plays, since
drama was thought effective not only for teaching
doctrine but also for training students in speaking and
deportment. Many plays were presented in Latin,
others in the vernacular.

The school drama reached its peak in the Catholic
schools run by the Jesuits. The Society of Jesus, an outgrowth of the Counter-Reformation, was founded in
1534 (given papal sanction in 1540) to combat heresy
and to strengthen the authority of the church. It
viewed education as a primary tool whereby to influence those most likely to become the future leaders of church and state. By 1600 it had established
200 schools, universities, and seminaries, and by 1706
the number had increased to 769. In some parts of
Europe it achieved a virtual monopoly over education. It was especially successful in France, Austria,
and southern Germany.

FIG. 11.3
Setting by Francesco Santurini for *Antiopa Justificata* as
presented in Munich, 1662. Courtesy Theatermuseum,
Munich.

With the Jesuits the educational theatre reached its highest peak prior to modern times. The first recorded Jesuit production occurred in 1551, but soon almost every Jesuit school was performing at least one play a year and often more. Students made up the casts; often the plays were written by professors of rhetoric; and the audiences were composed of members of the courts, municipal authorities, church dignitaries, parents, and others.

At first the plays were presented in Latin and kept by piety within narrow confines, but gradually some vernacular and low comedy, as well as considerable spectacle, music, and ballet, crept in. The Terence stage, used in the beginning, gave way in the seventeenth century to well-equipped proscenium theatres, complete with perspective scenery, machinery, and elaborate special effects. Out of the Jesuit schools came many of the most important works on theatrical practice published in the seventeenth and eighteenth centuries, among them Dubreuil's *Treatise on Perspective* (1649), Pozzo's *Pictorial and Architectural Perspective* (1693–1700), and Lang's *Dissertation on Stage Acting* (1727). The height of the Jesuit theatre was reached during the seventeenth century. By the eighteenth century a decline in vigor was apparent, and the order had begun to make powerful enemies because of its political intrigues and attempts to gain a monopoly on education. As a result, in 1773 it was suppressed. Although later revived, it never regained its former power.

In the seventeenth and eighteenth centuries the Jesuit theatre could be found wherever the order established schools, but it was especially highly developed in Austria and southern Germany, where it gave the most elaborate productions to be seen in those areas outside the courts. There through such plays as Jakob Bidermann's (1578–1639) *Cenodoxus* (1602) and Jakob Masen's (1606–1681) *Androphilus* (1647), it sought to teach the vanity of worldly pursuits and the certainty of divine retribution.

The Jesuit theatre probably reached its peak in Vienna with Nikolaus of Avancini's (1612–1686) *Pietas Victrix* (1659), presented before Leopold I, whom it glorified by associating him with the subject of the play, the victory of the Christian Emperor Constantine over the pagan Emperor Maxentius. This production included battles on land and sea, visions, angels and spirits of hell, and the eventual enthronement of Constantine as an angel hovered overhead on a cloud. On the frame of the proscenium the Hapsburg emblem was prominently displayed, thus making it clear that the Austrian Empire rested on Constantine's victory for the Christian faith. *Pietas Victrix* was staged with money provided by the court and was designed by Giovanni Burnacini, the

FIG. 11.4
Scene from Nikolaus of Avancini's *Pietas Victrix*, a Jesuit play performed before the emperor in Vienna in 1659. The setting is by Giovanni Burnacini. From *Die Theater Wiens* (1899).

court architect and one of the leading scenic designers of Europe.

Despite their theatrical sophistication, the Jesuits did not encourage the professional theatre, which, in their view, all too often led the faithful astray. Consequently, they contributed little to its development. In fact, by setting high standards in production and by demanding a high moral tone, they probably did much to deter attendance at performances given by German professional troupes, who in their use of music and spectacle fell far short of the standards set by the Jesuit theatres.

THE EARLY PUBLIC THEATRE IN THE GERMAN STATES

If the Jesuit and court theatres prospered after 1650, the same cannot be said for the troupes of professional actors, who had to depend primarily upon unsophisticated playgoers for their support. This had not always been true, for prior to 1650 several companies had been patronized by rulers, especially Duke Heinrich Julius of Braunschweig (1564–1613) and the Landgrave Moritz of Hessen (1572–1632). These early troupes were English in origin, and consequently the German professional theatre can be said to descend from those Elizabethan actors who began to tour widely on the continent around 1586. Among these early companies the most important were those of Robert Browne (from about 1590 to 1606), John Spencer (from 1605 to 1623), and John Green (from 1606 to 1628). These troupes often moved from one German court to another, taking with them letters of recommendation. Some enjoyed considerable reputation with the ruling classes. These companies were considerably affected by the Thirty Years War. Nevertheless, until after 1650, the designation of a company as "English" was synonymous with high quality.

Still, the lot of these troupes was not always easy. To attract a German-speaking audience when not performing at court, the English-speaking actors had to adapt their plays (most of them drawn from the London public theatres) by simplifying plots and by adding low comedy elements, pantomime, music, song, and dance. Perhaps because they depended little on language, clowns became a special favorite with audiences, and English actors developed such stock comic fools as Johan Posset, Stockfish, and Pickelherring. In seeking to increase their appeal, the English actors had by 1600 added German phrases, speeches, and entire scenes, and by 1626 had begun to include German actors in their troupes. By 1650 a few companies were composed entirely of Germans. The last important English group was that headed by George Jolly, who performed in German states during the 1650s when the English theatre was closed. By 1660 English actors had virtually disappeared from the continent. After this time, German rulers seldom patronized the German-speaking troupes.

The first German troupe of note was that managed by Carl Andreas Paulsen from 1650 to 1687. More significant was that of Johannes Velten (1640–1695), a well-educated man who sought to raise the level of the German theatre by adapting the plays of Corneille, Molière, and others for his company. He could accomplish little, however, under the existing theatrical conditions. Since there were no cities of any size, troupes were forced to travel constantly in search of new audiences. They competed especially vigorously for the right to perform at fairs held annually in the major towns, since it was here that the largest crowds assembled. Wherever they played, they were required to contribute up to one-fourth of their receipts to local charities. Since there were no permanent theatres available to the traveling companies, the actors set up their stages in town squares, riding schools, inns, fencing grounds, rooms above markets, and tennis courts. They had to change their bills daily and replenish their repertories often in order to attract the small potential audience. Velten's troupe usually had eighty-five to ninety plays in its repertory.

At the end of the seventeenth century, a program was made up of a long play and an afterpiece, both of which might include such incidental entertainment as songs, dances, and acrobatic feats. The main offering, called the *Hauptaktion* (chief play) or *Haupt-und-Staatsaktion* (chief and state play), might be either

FIG. 11.5
Strolling players performing on the Anger in Munich in the eighteenth century.
A painting by Joseph Stephan, c. 1770. Courtesy Theatermuseum, Munich.

FIG. 11.6

Stranitzky (foreground) as Hanswurst. From *Die Theater Wiens* (1899).

FIG. 11.7

Gottsched's pastoral drama, *Atalanta, or the Disdainful One Defeated by Disdain*. Frontispiece to the printed edition of the play.

serious or comic. The afterpiece, or *Nachspiel,* was usually a farce. It is unclear who wrote most of these plays. Many of the long works were hodgepodges of serious and comic scenes, of bombast and violence, villainous machinations, and fortunate escapes. No matter how serious the play, the clown was usually the most prominent figure.

By 1707 all of the earlier clowns had coalesced in the character Hanswurst. Given his distinctive traits by Joseph Anton Stranitzky (1676–1726), Hanswurst was compounded of many elements: Harlequin, familiar to German audiences from touring *commedia dell'arte* troupes; the medieval fool; and the various clowns introduced by English actors. Stranitzky's Hanswurst was a jolly, beer-drinking peasant with a Bavarian accent. His costume consisted of a green pointed hat, red jacket, long yellow trousers, and white neck ruff. Although Hanswurst's attributes and dress varied somewhat from one part of Germany to another, the broad outlines of the character established by Stranitzky were retained.

Stranitzky worked primarily in Vienna, where he virtually created the public theatre. Until his death he was the mainstay of the Karntnertor, Vienna's first permanent public theatre, built by the town council in 1708. Here Stranitzky established such a vigorous tradition of improvisation that written drama made little headway in Austria until after 1750.

In the early eighteenth century, then, several factors contributed to the theatre's low state: a repertory designed to attract an unsophisticated audience; the uneducated actors, who were little better than sideshow performers; and conditions which made it impossible to rehearse and mount plays with care. Under the circumstances, it is not surprising that aristocrats and churchmen held the professional theatre in contempt.

THE REFORMS OF GOTTSCHED AND NEUBER

The first significant steps toward reform were taken in the 1720s by Johann Christoph Gottsched (1700–1766), who, after being educated at the University of

FIG. 11.8
A company believed to be that of Caroline Neuber in Nuremberg, c. 1730. Note the heroic figures at center flanked on either side by clownish figures. Courtesy Theatermuseum, Munich.

Königsberg, rapidly became the intellectual leader of Germany. The development of German as a medium for literary expression ranked high among his many interests, for Latin was still the language of the universities (the first lecture in the vernacular had not been given until 1687), while French was favored by the aristocracy. Above all, Gottsched was interested in raising the moral level and refining the artistic taste of Germans, not only of the educated and aristocratic but also of the common people. The theatre attracted him because he saw in it a means of reaching the masses who could not read.

Gottsched was not the first well-educated German dramatist, for the schools had produced many. A few of their plays, among them some by Andreas Gryphius (1616–1664) and Daniel Caspar von Lohenstein (1635–1683), had been performed by professional troupes. But these earlier writers had no close connections with professional actors and many would have thought it immoral to do so. Gottsched, on the other hand, actively sought liaisons with those professional companies that came to play in Leipzig, where he lived. His overtures were unsuccessful until 1727, when he met the Neubers.

The daughter of a lawyer and government official, Caroline Neuber (1697–1760) had run away from home in 1717 with Johann Neuber, whom she married in 1718 after joining an acting troupe. For a time they were members of the troupe headed by Johann Caspar Haacke and Karl Ludwig Hoffman, but they formed their own company in 1727. They also acquired the title "Royal Polish and Electoral Saxon Court Comedians," which brought with it the right to play during the annual fair at Leipzig, then the intellectual capital of Germany, and Gottsched's home.

In 1727 the Neubers and Gottsched agreed to work together toward the reform of the theatre. This liaison, which was to last until 1739, is significant as the first alliance between a leading literary figure and a professional acting company in Germany. Unfortunately, it was easier to formulate high ideals than to achieve them. First, a new repertory had to be obtained, for Gottsched wished to eliminate *Haupt-und-Staatsaktion* plays, improvisation, burlesque afterpieces, and Hanswurst. Gottsched and his circle set out to supply the new works, principally by translating or imitating French neoclassical plays, which to them represented the ideal form of drama. The most famous of the new works was Gottsched's *The Dying Cato* (1731), reprinted ten times before 1756; adaptations of plays by Destouches, LaChaussée, Voltaire, and others also were translated and performed.

As her contribution, Neuber sought to raise the level of theatrical performances. She insisted upon careful rehearsals and the abandonment of improvisation; she assigned each actor additional duties, such as painting scenery, making handbills, or sewing costumes; and she policed the performers' personal lives in an attempt to overcome moral prejudices against actors. She was doomed to disappointment, however, for it was impossible to attract a new kind of spectator rapidly enough to replace those alienated by the new drama. In order to survive, she was forced to compromise, much to the impatience of Gottsched. In 1735 more than half of her afterpieces still included Hanswurst and, although in 1737 she banished him from the stage in a short play of her own composition, by 1738 he had crept back into many productions under another name and in different garb. Furthermore, the company still had to tour, for the audience was too small to support a year-round theatre in Leipzig, and elsewhere enthusiasm for the reforms was not yet strong. Her problems are illustrated by an eight-month season in Hamburg, second only to Leipzig as a cultural center, where in 1735 her 203 performances included 75 full-length and 93 one-act plays. Considering the problems of maintaining such a large repertory, it is not surprising that her performances did not always achieve the polish she so optimistically promised.

Although Neuber attracted some powerful supporters, notably the ruler of Schleswig-Holstein, she did not succeed as she had hoped, and after 1735 began to rebuke audiences publicly for their lack of taste. She alienated many of her supporters in Hamburg and Leipzig, and in 1739 broke with Gottsched. Thereafter, her career declined. In 1740 she was invited to St. Petersburg, but the death of the Empress Anna six months after her arrival led to the closure of her theatre. Returning to Leipzig in 1741, she found one of her former actors established in her theatre. There followed a pitched battle, in the course of which Neuber satirized Gottsched and his ideas. Although her attack signaled the end of Gottsched's leadership, it did not aid her. She remained in Leipzig for a few years, then moved on to Vienna and elsewhere until her death in 1760.

Although Gottsched and Neuber were not always successful, neither were they failures. By the 1740s regular drama was in the repertory of all German companies, much of it from the six volumes of plays published by Gottsched between 1740 and 1745 under the title, *The German Stage*. Furthermore, Neuber's production techniques were being adopted by other troupes. Thus, though Gottsched and Neuber were often ridiculed by later dramatists and actors, they made the future gains possible.

ACTING TROUPES, 1740–1770

Between 1740 and 1770, Neuber's principles were perpetuated and extended by a number of troupes. The earliest of these was formed in 1740 by Johann Friederich Schönemann (1704–1782), who had entered the Neuber troupe in 1730. Originally a clown, Schönemann played comic valets in Neuber's company. When he formed his own group, he borrowed Neuber's methods and repertory. The vitality and refinement of his young and relatively well-educated actors attracted much support in the towns of north and east Germany. Three of his performers—Sophia Carlotta Schröder, Konrad Ackermann, and Konrad Ekhof—were to become famous. Sophia Carlotta Schröder (1714–1793), a well-educated woman in need of employment after leaving her husband, was persuaded by Ekhof to take up acting. Although she had no theatrical experience, she immediately became the leading actress of the Schönemann company. Her career is thereafter inextricably tied to that of Konrad Ackermann (1712–1771), whom she was to marry in 1749. Ackermann, although he did not begin acting until he was almost thirty years old, achieved success quickly, perhaps because his family background and fine education encouraged in him that stately presence for which he was noted. If Schröder and Ackermann prospered immediately, the same cannot be said for Konrad Ekhof (1720–1778), who, short and homely, had to work hard to win acceptance. Schröder and Ackermann left Schönemann after one season, but Ekhof remained with him for seventeen years. By 1752 Ekhof was the company's leading man. He was also the first important theorist of the German stage, and in 1753 sought to establish a school in Schwerin to train actors. Although he was able to institute his plan (which he described in twenty-four articles), classes were soon abandoned because of the indifference and mockery of fellow actors.

After Schönemann's troupe was given the title "Court Comedians to the Duke of Schwerin" in 1751, it divided its time between Schwerin and Hamburg. This comparative stability, however, encouraged Schönemann to pursue his mania for horse-trading, with the result that the company declined. In 1757, after Ekhof had resigned in protest, the company collapsed and Schönemann retired. Ekhof was induced to return, but having little interest in management, he requested Heinrich Koch to take charge. New friction caused Ekhof to join Ackermann's troupe in 1764.

Heinrich Koch (1703–1775) entered Neuber's company in 1728 and remained with her until she left Leipzig in 1739. Obtaining her former license, he toured in that area until he assumed control of the Schönemann troupe in 1758. Between 1758 and 1763, Koch succeeded in playing most of each year in one city, Hamburg, a feat not yet accomplished by any troupe. In 1766, following the Seven Years War, he returned to Leipzig, where he built that city's first permanent theatre. (In spite of the city's importance as the cultural center of Germany, all previous public theatres had been temporary.) Koch played at the court theatre in Weimar from 1768 to 1771 and in Berlin from 1771 until his death in 1775. He was probably the first German manager fully to achieve Neuber's ideals. Paying careful attention both to staging and to public taste, he was eventually able to abandon touring and establish a company in one location.

FIG. 11.9
Exterior view of the building, constructed by Konrad Ackermann in 1765, that served as home to the Hamburg National Theatre, 1767–1769. A nineteenth-century print.

The third major company was that of Konrad Ackermann. With Sophia Carlotta Schröder, he worked in a number of companies, touring as far afield as Russia, before establishing a more stable organization in 1753. In 1755 he built a permanent theatre in Königsberg (in East Prussia, now Kaliningrad in Russia), perhaps the first in Germany intended for sole use by a dramatic company. Unfortunately, in 1756 the Seven Years War (in which between 1756 and 1763 Prussia and Austria fought for supremacy, with Prussia emerging as leader of the German states) forced Ackermann to flee west, where he played in Switzerland, Alsace, and elsewhere before coming to Hamburg in 1764. In that year Ekhof joined the company. Because of the Ackermanns, Ekhof, Sophie Hensel (1738–1789), and young Friedrich Schröder, the troupe was probably the finest in the German states at this time. In 1765 Ackermann built Hamburg's first permanent theatre. Unfortunately, rivalries within the company led to friction. It was probably for this reason that Ackermann agreed to give up his company and rent his theatre to the newly created Hamburg National Theatre.

The Hamburg National Theatre grew out of ideas set forth by Johann Friedrich Löwen (1729–1771), Schönemann's son-in-law and author of the first history of German theatre (published in 1766). Löwen blamed the low repute of the theatre on uncultivated managers and actors, the profit motive, the lack of state support, the necessity of touring, and the shortage of German dramatists. To remedy the situation, he proposed the establishment of a permanent, subsidized, nonprofit theatre, run by a salaried manager. He advocated establishing an academy to train actors, high salaries and a pension system to attract the best performers, and prizes to encourage dramatists. Löwen persuaded twelve businessmen to back his venture; he was to be the artistic director and Abel Seyler (1730–1801), a businessman and friend of Sophie Hensel, the business manager. The actors, with a few exceptions, were drawn from Ackermann's company. G. E. Lessing, by this time considered the finest German playwright, was induced to become resident critic and advisor to the company and to edit a theatrical journal designed to create interest in the repertory and to educate the public. Because of the functions he served, Lessing is now considered to have been the first *dramaturg* (that is, literary and artistic advisor, reader of plays and recommender of repertory, and in-house critic), a position now considered essential in most major European companies.

The Hamburg National Theatre was opened with high hopes in April 1767. Löwen soon lost authority over the actors, however, and only Ekhof could maintain some discipline. Furthermore, in spite of the stated goal of presenting drama of higher quality than had previously been seen, the theatre was forced to add variety acts to keep up attendance. The venture came to an inglorious end in 1769. Its most lasting achievement was Lessing's theatrical journal, *Hamburg Dramaturgy*, now considered one of the major critical works of the eighteenth century. Although it accomplished little, the Hamburg National Theatre remains a landmark as the first German attempt to establish a theatre on noncommercial lines. It was not truly a "national" theatre; however, it popularized the notion that the German states needed such theatres and paved the way for those that were soon to appear.

GERMAN DRAMA, 1740–1787

By the 1740s Gottsched and his circle had laid the foundations for a new repertory but had provided no plays of lasting value. As their influence waned, a new group of dramatists appeared. Among the most important of these were Johann Elias Schlegel (1719–1749), who wrote a number of comedies and tragedies, of which probably the best is *Hermann* (1743), a tragedy based on the conflict of German tribes with the Romans in the first century C.E., and C. F. Gellert (1715–1769), who championed tearful comedy and domestic tragedy.

But the finest playwright of this period was Gotthold Ephraim Lessing (1729–1781), the first truly significant German dramatist. Lessing began his career in 1748 with *The Young Scholar,* performed by the Neuber troupe, and won his first widespread fame in 1755 with *Miss Sara Sampson,* a domestic tragedy that swept Germany and won a resounding triumph for sentimental drama. The way for Lessing's tragedy had been paved not only by Gellert's works but by translations of such English plays as Lillo's *The London Merchant* and Moore's *The Gamester.* In writing *Miss Sara Sampson,* Lessing drew upon the Medea myth but set it in contemporary England. He also changed the focus of the story by making the victim of Medea's wrath the central figure. His play tells the story of a naive and loving young girl who is persuaded by a rakish young man to run away with him; when the young man's mistress learns that she has been deserted, she contrives to poison Sara and to escape across the English channel. First performed by Ackermann's troupe, *Miss Sara Sampson* was soon the most popular play in the German states and the most widely imitated. Such drama, given still further impetus when Lessing translated Diderot's works, was able to attract a large middle-class audience to the theatre for the first time in Germany. Because Lessing had only gradually come to believe that English

FIG. 11.10
Lessing's *Minna von Barnhelm*. Engravings by Daniel Chodowiecki.
Courtesy Theatermuseum, Munich.

drama was the most suitable model for German writers, it was not until about 1760 that he broke completely with Gottsched's emphasis upon French models. Thereafter, Lessing sought to discredit Gottsched and the French neoclassicists and to elevate English drama both through his plays and criticism, especially in the *Hamburg Dramaturgy* (1767–1769).

Lessing's second influential play, *Minna von Barnhelm* (1767), is often called Germany's first national comedy. Treating events immediately following the Seven Years War, the play presents lovers drawn from opposing sides who symbolize problems and divisions within Germany. The union of the lovers at the end of the play, therefore, had a significance beyond the literal. In spite of its topical subject, it is one of the most durable of eighteenth-century comedies, for, though the play is sentimental, Minna's resourcefulness and humor give it freshness. Like *Miss Sara Sampson, Minna von Barnhelm* became exceptionally popular and stimulated numerous imitations.

Lessing's third influential drama, *Emilia Galotti* (1772), adapts the classical story of Appius and Virginia to an eighteenth-century background. Lessing's depiction of virtuous citizens at the mercy of the despotic ruler of a small state led many to interpret his work as an attack on the morality of the aristocracy. Lessing's last important work, *Nathan the Wise* (1779), a dramatic poem not intended for the stage, is considered by many the greatest philosophical drama of the eighteenth century. In it, he depicts characters representing Judaism, Islam, and Christianity to demonstrate that universal love is the only fruitful doctrine. Probably because it was not written for performance, its structure is much freer than that of Lessing's other plays. It is also the first major German work to be written in blank verse (previously plays had been cast either in the alexandrine or in prose). Following Goethe's experiments with verse drama at Weimar, blank verse became standard in German tragedy. *Nathan the Wise* was soon performed and has continued to be one of the most frequently produced German works.

Thus, Lessing, through his plays and criticism, established a new standard by leading drama away from Gottsched's narrow path and by demonstrating that a native playwright could attract a wide following. It would be a mistake, however, to assume that the repertory had been transformed by the time Lessing died in 1781. The majority of plays continued to be adaptations or close imitations of foreign works. Nevertheless, the hold of French drama had been broken, and the English drama had replaced it as a model.

In spite of Lessing's reforms, he had remained within the mainstream of eighteenth-century rationalism, which viewed the universe as ruled by a benevolent god, man as essentially good, and the human mind as capable of solving all important problems through the exercise of reason. His own plays, while freer in structure than the French dramas of the period, merely represent a "revised classicism" rather than a markedly new approach. His criticism, however, had served to undermine the hold of neoclassicism. Consequently, before Lessing died a new and more radical group of dramatists had appeared.

The revolt of dramatists against the past was centered in the *Sturm und Drang* (Storm and Stress) school of writers. Traditionally dated 1767–1787, the Storm-and-Stress movement reached its peak in the 1770s. Among it major writers and works are Goethe's *Goetz von Berlichingen* (1773), Jacob M. R. Lenz's (1751–1792) *The Tutor* (1774) and *The Soldiers* (1776), Heinrich Leopold Wagner's (1747–1779) *The Child Murderess* (1776), Johann Anton Leisewitz's (1752–1806) *Julius von Tarent* (1776), Friedrich Maximilian Klinger's (1752–1831) *Storm and Stress* (1776), and Friedrich Schiller's *The Robbers* (1782), *Fiesko* (1782), and *Intrigue and Love* (1783).

The Storm-and-Stress plays have often been described as completely formless rebellions against neo-classicism, primarily because *Goetz von Berlichingen*, with its fifty-four scenes and tangle of plots, and *Storm and Stress*, with its rhapsodic emotionalism, have been taken as typical of the plays. In actuality, most of the plays are written in five acts, and as many observe the unities of time and place as violate them. Storm-and-Stress was a frankly experimental movement of young men in revolt against eighteenth-century rationalism. Since they agreed upon no alternative philosophy, the plays show wide variations both in thought and expression. *The Robbers* displays a liberal, democratic outlook, while *The Soldiers* upholds the need for class distinctions; *Julius von Tarent* is written in a strict neo-classical form, while *Goetz von Berlichingen* uses a loose, episodic structure; the naturalistic subject matter of *The Child Murderess* contrasts sharply with the lyrical subjectivism of *Storm and Stress;* and the diction ranges from the formal verse of *Julius von Tarent,* through the staccato, expressionistic outbursts of *Storm and Stress,* to the conversational prose of *The Tutor.* The very diversity of the plays was bewildering to audiences, for the young authors seemed to be challenging all artistic and social values. The subject matter was often shocking. *The Soldiers* proposes a state-sponsored system of prostitution so as to protect respectable young women from seduction by soldiers, while in *The Child Murderess* a rape occurs just off stage and a baby is killed on stage by thrusting a hatpin into its brain. The plays made many new demands on staging. For example, *Goetz von Berlichingen* moves from one place to another as rapidly as any screenplay does, and other plays call for detailed settings, clearly described in lengthy stage directions.

Few Storm-and-Stress plays were produced, and even fewer were well received. The major exceptions were *Goetz von Berlichingen* and Schiller's early works. Nevertheless, Storm-and-Stress plays were widely read and discussed. Consequently, they helped to break down old barriers and to pave the way for other writers who adapted many of the new ideas and techniques to popular tastes. They also probably aided in gaining acceptance for Shakespeare's plays, then being introduced on the German stage, since to many critics they seemed similar in structure and outlook. Out of these beginnings, a more mature drama was to come between 1785 and 1805.

FIG. 11.11
Klinger's *The Twins,* a Storm-and-Stress play. Engraving by Albrecht. Courtesy Österreichische Nationalbibliothek, Vienna.

THE ESTABLISHMENT OF NATIONAL THEATRES, 1770–1800

While the drama was breaking new ground in the 1770s, the theatre was consolidating its former gains. Several periodicals kept the scattered troupes in touch with each other and helped to create shared

FIG. 11.12
Konrad Ekhof and Hensel in *School for Fathers* by Romanus as presented at the Gotha Court Theatre in 1776. Engraving by Liebe after a painting by G. M. Kraus. Courtesy Theatersammlung, University of Hamburg.

production ideals. The number of troupes also increased. From about six in Neuber's time, they had grown to about fourteen in 1776. Most important, state-supported theatres were founded.

The first state theatre was established at Gotha in 1775 from the remnants of the Hamburg National Theatre troupe. When the Hamburg theatre closed in 1769, Abel Seyler formed a new company, including Sophie Hensel and Ekhof, which, after touring for a time, settled in Weimar between 1772 and 1774. When the Weimar theatre burned, Seyler moved to Gotha. There in 1775 a scheme for the formation of a state theatre was proposed and carried out. Although Seyler left, Ekhof and the better actors remained.

The Gotha Court Theatre was a nonprofit organization, in which each member was a state employee with pension rights. Ekhof, who was responsible for staging the plays, was at this time the most respected actor in Germany. He brought to Gotha a number of talented young people who received fine training and later became the leading actors of Germany after Ekhof's death. Ekhof was very conservative in his tastes, however, and did nothing to forward the new drama. In 1779, upon Ekhof's death, the theatre was closed.

Before the Gotha venture ended, a far more important state theatre was founded in Vienna. Although it had always been the most powerful Germanic city, Vienna had lagged behind the others in the development of a public theatre. The court had spent lavishly on opera, but it had almost completely ignored German drama, considered so inferior that the Empress Maria Theresa (1717–1780) did not see a German play until she was more than fifty years old. Dramas at court were usually given by French actors, who performed in the Burgtheater, converted from a tennis court in 1741.

The general public had been served by the Karntnertor theatre since 1708, but because of the traditions established by Stranitzky and his successors, Gottfried Prehouser (1699–1769) and Felix Kurz-Bernadon (1717–1783), improvised drama had been the usual fare until about 1750. Written drama began to gain a foothold after Koch appeared in Vienna in 1748, but it was not until the 1760s, when Josef von Sonnenfels (1733–1817) waged a campaign in its favor, that regular drama was widely accepted and performed in German year-round at the Karntnertor. In 1776, these developments culminated in the Emperor Joseph II's establishment of the Imperial and National Theater (more commonly called the Burgtheater after the building in which it performed). Its organization and procedures were modeled after those of the Comédie Française. Although the Burgtheater encountered many difficulties in its early years, it gradually moved to the forefront of German-language theatres because generous state support permitted it to assemble a fine company. By 1825 it was considered the best of all the German-language troupes.

A third state theatre was founded at Mannheim in 1779, when the ruler, Karl Theodor, succeeded to the Electorate of Bavaria and moved his court to Munich. As a gift to compensate his subjects in Mannheim, he created the Court and National Theater. Under the supervision of Baron Heribert von Dalberg (1749–1806), the company was an amalgamation of Seyler's troupe and the recently disbanded Gotha company. At first, Seyler had primary responsibility for production, but after 1781 Dalberg took charge and made the theatre one of the finest in Germany, especially between 1784 and 1795.

After 1780 state theatres were established throughout German-speaking areas. Among the best were those at Cologne, Mainz, Salzburg, Weimar, and Passau, but the theatre founded in Berlin in 1786 was destined to become the most important. As in other states, drama had been given little encouragement in Prussia during the early eighteenth century, although Frederick the Great (reigned 1740–1786), who was devoted to French culture, had engaged a French troupe for his private theatre and had supported lavish operatic productions. Neither Schönemann nor Koch received any recognition from the court when they played in Berlin. A new era did not begin until 1786 when Frederick William II (reigned 1786–1797) established a subsidized state troupe. Prussia's position of leadership in Germany made its theatre especially influential after 1800.

Thus, in the years between 1775 and 1800 far-reaching changes occurred in German theatre. In contrast with the period between 1725 and 1740, when troupes were virtually ignored by the aristocracy, rulers now vied with each other in establishing theatres, much as they had formerly competed in supporting opera. The theatre was now viewed as a cultural institution that should serve as an instrument for unifying Germany. Perhaps fortunately, the continued division of Germany into many states perpetuated a decentralized theatre with excellent resident companies scattered throughout Germanic territories.

The establishment of state theatres was paralleled in the same period by the building of permanent theatres in towns other than the seats of state governments. Before 1800 there were permanent theatres in Linz, Innsbruck, Brunn, Frankfort-am-Main,

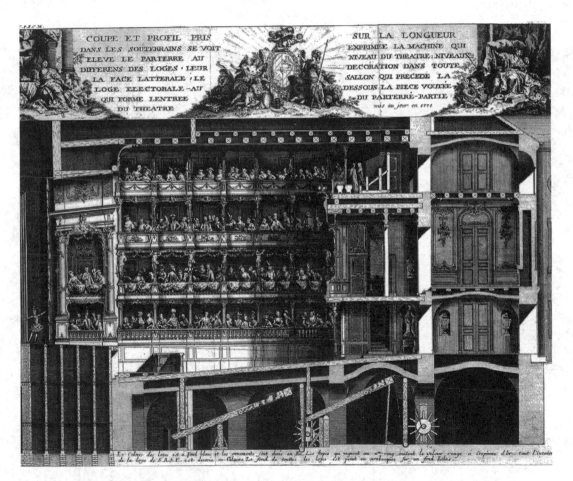

FIG. 11.13
Cross section of the Residenztheater, Munich, 1771, designed by François de Cuvillié *père*. The forward part of the stage and space beneath it are at the left. The pit floor could be raised so that it was level with the stage for balls and similar events. The machinery used to lower and raise the floor is seen at bottom center. The ruler's box is at center right. Engraving by Valerian Funck. Courtesy Theatermuseum, Munich.

Augsburg, Nürnberg, Altona, Breslau, Riga, and elsewhere. By the 1790s there were more than seventy Germanic companies, over half of them permanently located. Touring was now restricted to minor troupes.

EVOLUTION OF STAGING IN THE EIGHTEENTH CENTURY

The trend during the eighteenth century toward greater security is reflected in every aspect of the theatre. As audiences increased in size, the companies could reduce the number of plays in the repertory. This change, in turn, permitted more careful preparation. Nevertheless, not until the last part of the century was ensemble playing achieved, as managers demanded strict order and punctuality at all rehearsals and performances.

So long as there were no permanent theaters, spectacle was not extensively developed. Furthermore, during the early years the necessity of touring forced companies to rely upon a few settings which might be adapted for almost any play. Before 1725, three sets were considered sufficient: a wood for all exterior scenes, a hall for palaces, and a cottage room for domestic interiors. After 1750 the typical stock settings were somewhat more numerous: a Prachtsaal (or *palais à volonté*), a street, a village, several middle-class rooms, a prison, and a scene depicting several hills and shrubs. Changes of place were difficult to handle before permanent theatres were built. Consequently, up to the 1770s many companies hung a curtain about half way back on the stage so that shallow and full stage scenes could be alternated and changes made behind the curtain.

The 1770s brought significant innovations in spectacle. Permanent theatres introduced the chariot-

FIG. 11.14
The Margrave's Opera House, Bayreuth, designed by Guiseppe and Carlo Galli Bibiena, 1748. This theatre captures baroque splendor at its height. Gouache by Gustave Bauernfeind, 1879. Courtesy Theatermuseum, Munich.

FIG. 11.15

Hamlet as performed in Berlin, 1778. J. F. H. Brockmann is seen as Hamlet seated on the floor at right. In the background is the play within the play. Engraving by Daniel Chodowiecki. From *Die Theater Wiens* (1899).

and-pole system of scene shifting just when changing standards created a demand for more appropriate, varied, and detailed settings. The success of *Minna von Barnhelm* (1767) and the subsequent vogue for plays with war backgrounds brought the first attempts to create authentic settings and costumes. For these productions, managers often sought the cooperation of local army garrisons, borrowing soldiers to use as supernumeraries in productions with military backgrounds.

Concern for historical accuracy was initiated by *Goetz von Berlichingen* and the series of chivalric plays (or *Ritterstücke*) that it stimulated. The production of *Goetz* in Hamburg in 1774 was seemingly the first to use scenery and costumes intended to evoke a historical milieu. Although inaccurate in detail, they were sufficiently effective to make a semblance of historical spectacle standard for plays in the Ritterstücke tradition.

By the 1790s dramatists were writing plays that demanded the use of practical bridges, walls, and other complex set pieces. Doors and windows began to be set up between wings, thus marking the first steps in Germany toward the box set. As elsewhere, however, the trends toward greater realism and accuracy of detail were not to be fully exploited until the nineteenth century.

Costumes followed the same general trends. Before 1725, extreme simplicity was the rule. Each actor was expected to own a pair of black breeches, while the manager supplied a coat and waistcoat. The basic costume, used in numerous roles, was altered by the addition of simple accessories; a king carried a scepter and wore a feathered headdress; a classical hero draped a scarf diagonally across his chest and wore a helmet. Actresses wore the most fashionable garments they could afford. Lace was often made from cut paper.

As the influence of French drama increased, the costuming conventions of the Parisian troupes were adopted. Most tragic heroes and heroines were played

FIG. 11.16

A German theatre in the second half of the eighteenth century. Note the pit, boxes, footlights, prompter's box, and wings of the interior setting. Note also that upstage a door has been set between the wing and backshutter, a practice that prefigured the fully developed box set. Courtesy Theatermuseum, Munich.

in French court dress, while classical heroes wore the *habit à la romaine,* and Near Eastern characters adopted baggy trousers and turbans. Performers sought to accumulate their own wardrobes, and managers to increase the common stock.

Beginning with Gottsched, intermittent attempts were made to introduce a measure of historical accuracy. Gottsched recommended the use of Roman togas in classical plays and, after their break, Neuber revenged herself on him by following his prescriptions for costuming *The Dying Cato,* much to the amusement of audiences who were reduced to uncontrollable laughter. In 1766 Koch created a considerable stir when he opened his new theatre in Leipzig with Schlegel's *Hermann* done in period dress. It was not until the 1770s, however, that historical costumes became common. For his production of *Goetz* in 1774, F. L. Schröder dressed the knights in armor, the monks and bishops in appropriate ecclesiastical garments, and the courtiers, citizens, and gypsies in allegedly accurate clothing. This is the feature of the production, considered a major innovation, that seems to have most impressed critics of the day. Thereafter the Ritterstücke plays accepted some attempt at historical costuming as necessary. Nevertheless, all of these Ritterstücke plays used garments of a single period—the sixteenth century—no matter the supposed time of the action. In 1776 Roman dress was adapted for some classical plays at Gotha, and in the 1780s Dalberg introduced it at Mannheim.

In the 1770s authors of domestic plays began to prescribe the costumes to be worn by their characters, often enumerating the colors and details at length. Thus, by 1800 managers were becoming aware of the need for individualized costumes, although earlier practices probably continued to dominate.

Other theatrical customs also changed. Through much of the eighteenth century, performances were not permitted on Saturdays, Sundays, holidays, or during Lent and Advent. Gradually the strictures were relaxed, but it was not until about 1800 that daily playing throughout the year was permitted. As in other countries, the starting time was moved to later hours. The Neubers' performances began at 4 or 4:30 P.M.; by the 1770s the usual hour was 5, and by 1800, 5:30 P.M.

F. L. SCHRÖDER

Probably the most influential troupe in the years between 1770 and 1800 was that of Friedrich Ludwig Schröder (1744–1816). The son of Sophia Carlotta Schröder, he was on the stage from the time he was three years old. Separated from the Ackermanns at

FIG. 11.17
Schröder as Falstaff. From *Literatur und Theaterzeitung* (1780).

the time of the Seven Years War, he learned to fend for himself by joining with itinerant performers, who taught him acrobatics and dancing. Later, he rejoined his parents and came into contact with Ekhof, who first made him realize what great acting might be. When the Hamburg National Theatre was formed in 1767, Schröder left the company and performed for a time with Kurz-Bernadon, from whom he learned improvisational playing. Schröder returned to Ackermann's Hamburg troupe in 1769 and became artistic director of the company when his stepfather died in 1771.

The challenge of management seems to have transformed Schröder. Previously a careless performer who could scarcely be induced to rehearse, he now became a firm disciplinarian who insisted upon perfection in every detail. Consequently, his was perhaps the first German company to become a truly integrated ensemble. Furthermore, he produced a distinguished repertory. Not only did he perform Lessing's works, but he was the first manager to champion Shakespeare and the Storm-and-Stress writers. In 1774 he gave the premier of *Goetz von Berlichingen,* a play which most managers considered unproducible. Beginning in 1776 with *Hamlet,* Schröder had by 1779 performed eleven of Shakespeare's plays, although in severely adapted versions.

In addition to his managerial duties, Schröder performed about thirty-nine new roles each year, and between 1771 and 1780 he translated, adapted, or wrote twenty-eight plays. Although he remained a versatile actor, he gradually moved away from light comedy to tragic roles. By 1780 he was generally recognized as Germany's greatest actor.

Despite his success, Schröder remained merely the employee of his mother, who retained complete financial control over the company. In 1780 she was still paying him the same salary as in 1771. For this and other reasons, Schröder resigned his post in 1780 and for the next six years played at leading theatres elsewhere, especially in Vienna between 1781 and 1785. Meanwhile, the Hamburg company rapidly declined. Thus, when in 1786 Schröder returned, he assumed complete control of the company. For the next twelve years he made it one of the most respected troupes in Germany. In spite of continuing acclaim, however, his major contributions had already been made, for now Schröder seemed content merely to repeat his earlier successes. He retired in 1798 while at the height of his career.

Schröder is considered by many the greatest actor Germany has known. In his lifetime he played more than 700 roles. Historically, he is perhaps most important for creating what came to be called the "Hamburg school" of acting and production (a precursor of the romantic mode) in which character, emotion, and setting were carefully delineated and differentiated.

FIG. 11.18
Iffland and Mme Bethmann in a scene from Iffland's *The Family Friend*. Contemporary engraving.

IFFLAND AND KOTZEBUE

In the years between 1775 and 1800, German drama attained maturity. In these years the theatre attracted audiences from every class, in large part because of the plays of Iffland and Kotzebue, although true distinction was reserved for Goethe and Schiller.

August Wilhelm Iffland (1759–1814) began his acting career in the Gotha company under Ekhof and joined the newly created Mannheim state theatre in 1779. During Iffland's tenure, the Mannheim theatre was one of the most vital in Germany. Schröder played there in 1780 and introduced Shakespeare into the repertory; Schiller's first three plays were first produced there and for a time Schiller was the resident dramatist; and Dalberg made numerous innovations in theatrical practice.

Iffland rapidly came to the fore, both as actor and dramatist. From 1784, when his *Crimes of Ambition* established his fame as a writer, until 1796, when he left the troupe, Iffland was the most influential member of the Mannheim company. Thirty-seven of his plays were first performed by this theatre, and Iffland's enormous reputation, which extended throughout Germany, served to elevate this theatre in public esteem. As Iffland's plays became widely known, he began to be in great demand for starring engagements, and thereafter he traveled extensively. From 1796 until 1814 he was head of the Berlin state theatre, which he welded into one of the finest ensembles of his time.

Iffland was considered by many Schröder's equal or superior in acting. As a performer, he depended especially upon his expressive body and face, for his voice was weak. His major appeal lay in his ability to humanize all roles, making his characters seem naturally noble but average human beings. His Mannheim school of acting is often said to form a bridge between Schröder's romantic–realistic mode and the Weimar classical mode.

Iffland's own plays provided him with his best acting vehicles. Offering idealized portraits of ordinary men and women, their touching situations tended to

FIG. 11.19
Kotzebue's *Misanthropy and Repentance* (or *The Stranger*). The final scene of reunion as shown in the edition of the play published in 1790. Courtesy Österreichische Nationalbibliothek, Vienna.

Kotzebue's success can probably be explained by his ability to adapt new trends to public tastes. Thus, while he used many of the themes and devices introduced by Storm-and-Stress dramatists, he was successful where they had failed. He knew how to titillate audiences without shocking them and how far he could depart from accepted conventions without confusing unsophisticated spectators. He combined sensational subjects, striking spectacle, and humanitarian sentiments so successfully that he helped to create the vogue for melodrama that was to dominate the nineteenth-century stage. Largely because of Kotzebue's plays, German drama was by 1800 considered the most vital and popular in the world.

GOETHE, SCHILLER, AND WEIMAR CLASSICISM

If Iffland and Kotzebue raised German drama to the peak of its popularity with the theatre-going public, Goethe and Schiller were to be numbered among Germany's greatest playwrights. In their joint work at Weimar, they also created a distinctive style of production that was to dominate the German theatre throughout much of the nineteenth century.

Johann Wolfgang von Goethe (1749–1832) is usually considered the greatest literary figure Germany has known. A "universal genius," Goethe's interests ranged through almost every field, and to most he made significant contributions. He began his literary career at a very early age, but it was his play *Goetz von Berlichingen* (1773) and his novel *The Sorrows of Young Werther* (1774) that made him the most famous young writer of his time and the center of the Storm-and-Stress school. Throughout Europe, Goethe's *Werther* came to epitomize the longings of the new generation.

In 1775, at the request of the young ruler, Duke Karl August, Goethe settled in Weimar, which he helped to make one of the cultural centers of Germany. Arriving shortly after Seyler and Ekhof had departed, Goethe became a leader in the amateur group that provided the town's only theatrical entertainment. After the enthusiasm of the amateurs waned, the ducal theatre, which had been built in 1780, was leased in 1784 to a professional troupe under the direction of Joseph Bellomo. Given a small subsidy and a limited supply of scenery and costumes, Bellomo's troupe remained in Weimar until 1791.

Goethe's visit to Italy from 1786 to 1788 marks a turning point to his outlook. His new appreciation of the classical past made him reject his former Storm-and-Stress period in favor of the classical mode. His *Iphigenia in Tauris* (1787) is often consid-

romanticize the simple life, as in *The Huntsmen* (1785), which contrasts virtuous middle-class persons with oppressive aristocrats. Although some aspects of his work seemed to anticipate romanticism, Iffland opposed the new movement and sought to keep the romantic drama out of the repertory at Berlin.

August Friedrich von Kotzebue (1761–1819) was even more popular than Iffland as a playwright. From 1787, when he won his first success with *Misanthropy and Repentance* until his death, he was the most popular playwright in the world. Between 1787 and 1867, one-fourth of all the Burgtheater's performances were of Kotzebue's plays; at other theatres the proportion was often higher. Thirty-six of the plays were translated into English, and several remained starring vehicles throughout the nineteenth century. Kotzebue's more than 200 plays range through domestic drama, historical spectacle, verse plays, and farces.

FIG. 11.20
The Court Theater at Weimar. A contemporary engraving.

ered one of his greatest achievements. Within the framework of the ancient myth, it depicts humanity's ethical evolution from a narrow concern for self to an awareness of broader claims.

In 1791 Karl August dismissed Bellomo's troupe and established a subsidized theatre like those that had been appearing elsewhere. But, since the population of the city of Weimar was only 6,000, the duke could not afford a first-rate company. Failing to attract a suitable director, he appointed Goethe to the post. The Weimar Court Theatre opened in 1791 with a mediocre company under the artistic direction of Franz Fischer, an actor. Goethe took little interest in the theatre until 1796, when a visit from Iffland gave him a vision of what the troupe might become if given sufficient guidance. This interest was deepened by Schiller, who stimulated Goethe to take a more active part in the company's work.

Friedrich Schiller's (1759–1805) career had developed along quite different lines than Goethe's. The son of an army officer, Schiller had been forced by the Duke of Wüttemberg to enter military school. When, following the success of his first play, *The Robbers* (1782), Schiller was forbidden to write, he fled to Mannheim; there he was appointed resident dramatist to the state theatre and wrote for it *Fiesko* (1783) and *Intrigue and Love* (1784), in both of which Iffland played the leading role.

Like Goethe, Schiller underwent a significant change during the 1780s. While working on *Don Carlos* (1787), he began to reassess his values in the light of his study of history. He wrote no plays between 1787 and 1798, devoting himself instead to historical studies. His *The Revolt of the Netherlands* and *A History of the Thirty Years War* won him fame as a historian, and in 1789 he was appointed professor of history at the University of Jena, only twelve miles from Weimar. In 1794, Goethe and Schiller established a close friendship and began to exert a strong influence on each other. In 1799, Schiller took up residence in Weimar, where he was intimately involved in the theatre's operation. Between 1797 and 1805 Schiller wrote his mature works, and he and Goethe made the Weimar theatre one of the most famous in Germany.

Although Goethe and Schiller were almost opposite in temperament, they were united by a common artistic view. Goethe, under the impact of his visit to Italy, and Schiller, after his study of history and philosophy, sought to counter the major artistic trends of their day. Although both wrote some plays in the classical style, it was not the formal characteristics of ancient drama that attracted them so much as its spirit. For them, the formal conventions of Greek tragedy served merely as devices to "distance" the spectators from the play's events so they might perceive the ideal patterns behind everyday reality. Thus, Goethe and Schiller argued that drama should transform ordinary experience rather than create an illusion of real life. Consequently, they adopted verse, conventionalized structural patterns, simple but harmonious settings and costumes, and precise rhythmic speech in an attempt to lead spectators beyond their normal perceptions into the realm of ideal truth. Out of these views came "Weimar classicism."

Schiller's late plays are extremely complex works in which philosophical, historical, and individual conflicts are interwoven. For most, Schiller chose subjects that represent turning points in history. *Wallenstein's Camp* (1798), *The Piccolomini* (1799), and *Wallenstein's Death* (1799) form a trilogy on the Thirty Years War conceived on a vaster scale than any dramas between Schiller's and Shakespeare's. *Mary Stuart* (1800), *The Maid of Orleans* (1801), and *William Tell* (1804) treat decisive events in English, French, and Swiss history.

Goethe turned his attention to transforming the second-rate Weimar troupe into a true ensemble. The actors' varied regional origins and lack of education were evident in performance because of the wide range of accents and stage behavior. Since they had so many roles to learn, most of them had come to depend upon improvisation. To remedy this situation, Goethe evolved a set of rules (later recorded by two members of Goethe's company) which, without a knowledge of the actors' problems, might seem elementary. They cover proper enunciation, ways of overcoming regional dialects, control of tempo and tone, principles of movement and grouping, posture and stance, and social behavior. All aim at achieving grace, dignity, and ease.

At Weimar, the number of rehearsals for a play did not differ markedly from typical practice elsewhere—usually no more than six to ten. Unlike other managers, however, Goethe worked with individual actors, sometimes over several months, on the interpretation of their roles prior to the first company rehearsal. Group preparations began with a series of reading rehearsals during which Goethe corrected line readings and interpretation, with special attention to the proper speaking of verse and to rhythmic patterns. He was so concerned with rhythm and cadence that he sometimes beat time like a music conductor. (Other companies assimilated verse and rhythm into a conversational mode.) At the same time, Goethe sought to make his actors so comfortable with these patterns that on stage they would seem natural rather than artificial. The number of on-stage rehearsals were few and did not begin until the actors knew their lines. To aid blocking, Goethe divided the stage into squares and specified the actors' movements in relation to them, and drew on his knowledge of painting to achieve the most pleasing pictorial composition. He did not always attend all stage rehearsals, leaving the execution of his design

FIG. 11.21
Schiller's *Fiesko* as performed at Weimar in 1805. Aquatint by J. C. E. Müller after a painting by G. E. Opitz. Courtesy Theatermuseum, Munich.

to others, but he did attend almost all performances and made his reactions known.

Rather than seeking to create the illusion of reality, Goethe attempted to achieve a harmonious and graceful picture which, in combination with intelligent and euphonious line readings, would attune the spectator to an ideal beauty. By requiring strict adherence to his directions, Goethe achieved the most integrated ensemble of his day. Because of his working methods, he must be considered one of the first directors in the modern sense. At the time, however, critics varied widely in their opinions about the theatrical effectiveness of Goethe's productions. His numerous admirers praised the results extravagantly; others found the performers so uniform that they might exchange roles without any noticeable effect.

The remodeled Weimar theatre, which opened in 1798 with the premiere of Schiller's *Wallenstein's Camp*, was small and minimally equipped for Schiller's large-scale dramas. The proscenium opening was about 27 feet wide and the stage was slightly more than 30 feet deep. The auditorium held about 500 persons; there was a pit fitted out with benches, a row of boxes on the second level (with the royal box facing the stage), and an undivided gallery on the third level.

The combined fame of Goethe and Schiller attracted many visitors, and soon "Weimar classicism" was famous throughout Germany. Despite Goethe's ideals, the repertory was not confined to plays of the type that he and Schiller admired. Since the court subsidy covered only about one-third of the company's expenses, Goethe had to arrange the repertory so as to ensure popular support. Consequently, of the three weekly performances, one was usually devoted to musical plays or opera, one to popular drama (especially by Kotzebue and Iffland), and the third to plays that Goethe admired. The actors complained, probably with good cause, that Goethe devoted two-thirds of the preparation time to plays of the last type. Goethe often experimented with unusual production devices or plays. He used half-masks in Terence's *The Brothers,* revived some *commedia dell'arte* scripts, and presented plays by Shakespeare, Calderón, and other authors not normally found in the repertories of the period.

Through this unusual repertory, Goethe sought to enlarge the experience of both his actors and his audience. He treated the audience as autocratically as he did the actors and sometimes reprimanded them in the theatre if they responded in ways he considered inappropriate.

After Schiller died in 1805, Goethe's interest in the theatre was sporadic. He eventually lost control of the Weimar troupe to Caroline Jagemann (1777–1848), an actress and the duke's mistress, and he resigned his post in 1817. By that time his actors were in great demand and, joining other troupes, they disseminated the Weimar approach widely. The German stage was caught between the demands of the Weimar and Hamburg schools. In this struggle, the Weimar mode was usually triumphant and tended to dominate until the late nineteenth century.

Of Goethe's later dramatic works, the most famous is *Faust,* the first part of which was published in 1808 and the second in 1831. Not intended for the stage, this dramatic poem seeks to depict the human search for fulfillment, and it suggests that people find salvation through such striving. Its episodic structure and philosophical viewpoint are similar in all important respects to the work of the romantic playwrights. Thus, while Goethe stands as the culmination of German classicism, he also contributed much to romanticism, which came to the fore after 1798.

THEATRE IN OTHER COUNTRIES OF NORTHERN EUROPE

By 1800 the German states had assumed a position of leadership in the European theatre, but other countries of Northern Europe continued to play a subordinate role. Nevertheless, the theatres of the Low Countries could boast a continuous history

FIG. 11.22
Interior of the Schouwburg, Amsterdam, built in 1638. Engraving by S. Savry, 1658. Courtesy Toneelmuseum, Amsterdam.

since the Middle Ages, when spectacular religious dramas and Chambers of Rhetoric had flourished.

The Flemish and Dutch areas of the Low Countries were especially prosperous during the seventeenth century. They had declared their independence from Spain in 1581, although their new status was not recognized by treaty until 1648. During the last half of the seventeenth century, the Netherlands became the world's greatest maritime power and Amsterdam the world's major commercial city, the center of an empire that reached into the New World and the Far East.

By the beginning of the seventeenth century, the Chambers of Rhetoric were in decline, and in 1617 the only two remaining societies in Amsterdam were united under the more fashionable name, The Academy. In 1618 the city of Amsterdam gave The Academy a building which was soon christened the Schouwburg (Playhouse). In 1638, the Academy's home was replaced by a new building. Designed by Jacob von Campen (1595–1659), who had studied in Italy, the stage of the new Schouwburg was a compromise between those used by the Rhetoric and Italian theatres. Raised about 7 feet above the auditorium floor, the stage had no proscenium arch or front curtain. Along the sides and across the back there were pilasters at intervals with space between them to mount flats, each of which might represent a different locale or, less frequently, parts of a single place. At times the pilasters across the back were used to form an open colonnade. The stage picture,

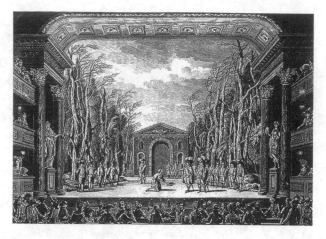

FIG. 11.23

Scene from *Gysbrecht van Aemstel* as presented in 1775. Setting by A. van der Groen. This illustration also shows the interior of the Nieuwe Schouwburg shortly after it was rebuilt in 1774. Courtesy Toneelmuseum, Amsterdam.

therefore, varied from multiple settings similar to those used at the Hôtel de Bourgogne in the early 1630s to modified perspective settings in the Italian manner. Some of the flats were double-sided to permit quick changes. When needed, the central portion of the rear facade could be used as an inner stage. The main stage was divided into two parts by a curtain hung about halfway back; this curtain could be closed to permit quick changes behind it or opened to indicate a shift in locale. At times mansion-like structures were set up on the stage. There was also a permanent upper stage in the form of a balcony extending across the back and partway down the sides. Like the *théâtre supérieure* of the Théâtre du Marais in Paris, the upper stage might be treated as part of a unified setting or used to represent one or more separate locales. The ovoid auditorium consisted of a standing pit, 46 feet wide by 23 feet deep, surrounded by two levels of raised boxes and, above the boxes, an open gallery.

In this period the major Dutch dramatist was Joost van den Vondel (1587–1679), author of thirty-two plays, many of them imitations of Plautus and Terence but others on biblical or historical subjects, such as *Lucifer, Jeftha,* and *Maria Stuart.* His best-known play is *Gysbrecht van Aemstel,* a glorification of the city of Amsterdam, played annually on New Year's Day until 1969.

In 1664 the old theatre was torn down and replaced by the Nieuwe Schouwburg, a wholly Italianate structure. This building burned in 1772 but was rebuilt in 1774. During the eighteenth century the Netherlands declined as a world power, but it remained prosperous and its theatre thrived, although

for the most part thereafter it merely reflected major trends current elsewhere in Europe.

Farther north, the professional theatre was slower in appearing. Until the eighteenth century, Norway and Denmark (unified as a single country until 1814) were dependent upon French, English, and German troupes. Beginning in the late seventeenth century, the court maintained a French troupe, but the general populace had to content itself with traveling companies of the type then common in Germany.

The turning point came in 1720, when Frederick IV dismissed his French company. Its leader, René Magnon de Montaigu, had been in Denmark since 1686 and wished to remain. Consequently, he joined with Etienne Capion, another Frenchman and former actor, in a petition to the king asking permission to open a public theatre. Upon receiving a favorable response, they built a small theatre (seating about 400) and opened it in 1722. This venture ended in bank-

FIG. 11.24

Scene from Holberg's *The Busy Man.* From an eighteenth-century edition of the play. Courtesy Teaterhistorisk Museum, Christiansborg.

FIG. 11.25
Interior view of the theatre at Drottningholm as it appears today. On stage is a *palais à volonté* setting designed by Carlo Bibiena in 1774. Note the wave machine in the background. Courtesy Drottningholm Theatermuseum, Stockholm.

ruptcy in 1727. Montaigu then received permission to use the court theatre and was given a small subsidy. But in 1730, under pressure from puritan forces, all theatrical activity was banned.

In spite of these difficulties, native drama dates from these years during which Ludwig Holberg (1684–1754) became the first dramatist to write plays in the Danish language. Not only was Holberg well educated, he had traveled throughout Europe and had seen the best companies of England, France, and Italy. In 1718 he was appointed a professor at the University of Copenhagen. Soon afterwards he began his literary career with *Peder Paars,* a literary satire usually considered to mark the beginnings of literature in Danish. To write in the vernacular was revolutionary, for Latin was still the accepted medium for scholars and French for the court.

Since Holberg was the only writer to have used the vernacular successfully, it is only natural that Montaigu and Capion should commission him to supply their newly created company with dramas suited to a Danish audience. Between 1722 and 1727, Holberg wrote twenty-six plays. Of these, *Jeppe of the Hill* (1722) and *Erasmus Montanus* (printed 1731) are probably the best known. Many of Holberg's plays resemble robust medieval farces, although he always

appended moral lessons to them. For example, *Jeppe of the Hill* tells the story of a henpecked peasant who is kidnapped while in a drunken stupor and is then led to believe that he is a great lord before being returned to his village during another bout of drunkenness. This comic story concludes with the argument that class barriers must be maintained, since, as Jeppe has shown, the lower classes would become tyrannical if given power. But not all of Holberg's comedies are medieval in tone, for he borrowed freely from Plautus, Molière, and *commedia dell'arte,* although he always recast his borrowings until they seemed native in their origins. Holberg's works were to be the backbone of the Danish repertory, but they also were extremely popular throughout Northern Europe.

When Frederick V came to the throne in 1746, he lifted the ban against playing, and in 1748 a new theatre was opened. At this time Holberg wrote seven additional plays, but they lacked the vitality of his earlier work. The fortunes of the new theatre were as uncertain as those of the old until 1772, when the Royal Danish Theatre, still the national theatre of Denmark, was created.

The bulk of the late eighteenth-century repertory was foreign, for Holberg had few successors. Johan Herman Wessel (1742–1785), a prolific translator, also wrote numerous parodies of foreign works. Johannes Ewald (1743–1781), Denmark's first important serious playwright as well as one of its greatest lyric poets, provided *Rolf Krage* (1770), the first significant Danish tragedy, and *The Fisherman* (1780), the first serious Danish play to treat ordinary people sympathetically. Ewald also called attention to the rich heritage of North European folklore and legend and laid the foundations for the succeeding romantic movement.

In Sweden, school plays were being written in the vernacular by about 1550, but they did not lead to significant developments, perhaps because Sweden was involved in a series of conflicts (including the Thirty Years War). In 1667 the first permanent theatre was opened in Stockholm. In 1737 the first theatre under royal patronage was founded. It performed a mixture of French, Swedish and *commedia* plays before being transformed into a national theatre in 1773.

During the eighteenth century, the Swedish theatre received considerable impetus during the reign (1771–1792) of Gustav III, who established a Swedish academy, wrote plays, encouraged native writers and performers, and in general sought to reshape native arts along French lines. Unfortunately, the results were for the most part mere imitations of foreign models.

Despite its considerable accomplishments, Gustav's reign is now remembered in theatre history primarily because of the theatre at Drottningholm, a royal residence near Stockholm. Erected between 1764 and 1766, this theatre was used extensively during the late eighteenth century but was closed upon Gustav's death in 1792. Until 1921, when it was rediscovered, it remained untouched and virtually forgotten. As a result, the stage and its machinery, thirty stage settings, and the auditorium survived intact. As one of the few truly authentic eighteenth-century theatres still in existence, it has become one of the world's major theatrical museums. It is now used frequently for performances of eighteenth-century works. The theatre at the royal residence at Gripsholm has also survived, but it is smaller and less typical of its age.

THEATRE IN RUSSIA TO 1800

The eighteenth century also saw the establishment of theatre and drama in Russia. As in other parts of Europe, folk and ritual drama in Russia can be found from the earliest times and wandering entertainers can be traced back as far as the tenth century. If an extensive liturgical drama ever existed there, however, few traces of it have survived. In the seventeenth century drama was introduced into the Jesuit schools of the Ukraine, and until the eighteenth century students from these schools toured plays as far east as Siberia.

The first clear record of theatre in Moscow is found in 1672 during the reign of Alexis (1645–1676), who persuaded Johann Gottfried Gregory, a Lutheran minister and schoolteacher in the resident German colony, to produce plays for the theatre that Alexis had built in one of his residences. Upon Alexis's death in 1676, this theatre was abandoned.

The theatre then lay fallow until Peter the Great (reigned 1682–1725) decided to use it in his campaign to westernize Russia. In 1702 he imported Johann Kunst's company from Gdansk and installed it in a theatre on what is now Red Square. But Peter was too preoccupied with wars and building his new capital city, St. Petersburg, to devote much attention to the theatre, and consequently it did not prosper.

Between 1725 and 1750 theatrical activities were largely confined to the court. For the coronation of the Empress Anna (reigned 1730–1740), the Polish king sent a *commedia dell'arte* troupe. Their success led to the demand for other Western forms, and consequently Francesco Araia, a Neapolitan opera composer, was imported in 1735 and Jean-Baptiste Landet, a French dancing master and founder of Russian ballet, in 1738. In 1740 the Neuber troupe was invited to St. Petersburg, but their engagement was cut short by the death of the Empress Anna.

Under the Empress Elizabeth (reigned 1741–1762), the Italians and French struggled for supremacy in the court theatre. Eventually a French company was employed to perform plays twice a week, while the Italians continued their spectacular operatic productions. By 1750 the Russian court was conscious of the latest Western trends in opera, dance, and theatre. There was as yet, however, neither a public theatre nor a native Russian repertory.

Around 1750 a number of developments began a new era in the Russian theatre. First, a talented Russian dramatist, Alexander Sumarokov (1717–1777), began to write plays on Russian subjects but cast in French neoclassical form. His tragedies and satirical comedies mark the beginning of the Russian classical school. In 1749 the success of the cadets at the Academy of the Nobility with Sumarokov's first play, *Khorev* (1747), induced them to present other works by Sumarokov.

Another major train of events was set in motion around 1750 when Fyodor Volkov (1729–1763), a merchant's son who had seen theatrical performances by foreign companies in St. Petersburg, decided to present plays in his native Yaroslavl. Assembling a troupe from among his family and friends, Volkov fitted up a barn as a theatre. Enthusiasm was so great that he had moved into more adequate quarters before being summoned to play for the empress in 1752. Impressed by their work, the empress sent some of the actors to the Academy of the Nobility for further education and permitted them to give performances for the general public. Thus, Volkov is usually considered the founder of the Russian professional theatre.

The next significant development came in 1756, when the empress established a state theatre for Russian plays. The troupe, made up primarily of Volkov's actors, was placed under the direction of Sumarokov, although ultimate authority resided in a court official. The relatively slight value placed on this Russian company, however, is indicated by its subsidy of 5,000 rubles as compared with the 20,000 given the French actors and the 30,000 granted the Italian opera troupe. The Russian plays, treated condescendingly by the court, were attended primarily by the middle class.

Under Catherine II (reigned 1762–1796) the theatre spread to many parts of Russia. Playwrights increased, although few won lasting fame. Leadership passed from Sumarokov to his son-in-law, Yakov Kniazhnin (1742–1791), who after 1769 wrote seven tragedies and a number of comedies in the neoclassical style. But the best of the eighteenth-century Russian dramatists was Denis Fonvizin (1745–1792), who began writing in 1761 and achieved his first significant success in 1766 with *The Brigadier General,* a satire on the newly rich and on the Russian tendency to praise everything from Western Europe and to disparage everything Russian. His lasting reputation rests principally on *The Minor* (1781), a satirical picture of the brutish, uneducated, rural gentry.

The majority of the plays in the repertory, however, were translations, and, after the 1760s, as the works of Diderot, Destouches, Mercier, Lillo, Lessing, and Beaumarchais were imported, domestic tragedy and sentimental comedy were the most popular types. Musical plays in the manner of ballad opera or *opéra comique* also gained an enormous following. The most popular of these works was A. Ablesimov's (1742–1783) *The Miller, the Witchdoctor, the Cheater and the Matchmaker* (1779), which held the stage through the nineteenth century.

Under Catherine, the state continued its firm control over the theatre. All plays were subject to strict censorship, and the court- and state-subsidized theatres operated under regulations established by the crown. Although opera continued to be the favored form with the aristocracy, the dramatic troupes achieved increased security. In 1776 a pension system was inaugurated, and after 1789 the companies were allowed four annual benefit performances, the proceeds of which were divided among all the actors.

In 1779 an acting school was established, and in the 1790s a second state theatre was opened in St. Petersburg. In general, acting companies followed "lines of business" similar to those current in France. A state document of 1766 lists the lines as follows: first, second, and third comic and tragic lovers, noble fathers, comic fathers, first and second domestics, moralizers, clerks, confidants, first and second tragic and comic female lovers, first and second chambermaids, old women, and confidantes.

After the death of Volkov in 1763, the most famous actor was Ivan Dmitrevsky (1734–1821), who began his career in Volkov's Yaroslavl troupe. In 1765 and 1767 he went abroad, where he is said to have studied the acting of Clairon, Lekain, and Garrick. He acted only rarely after 1787, but became an influential teacher. In 1791 he was appointed supervisor of all performances in the state dramatic troupes. A carefully controlled performer who planned every effect, Dmitrevsky was best in the classical repertory. Yakov Shusherin (1753–1813), on the other hand, was famous for his portrayal of sentimental roles. Between 1787 and 1810 he was the most popular actor on the St. Petersburg stage.

By the end of the eighteenth century, itinerant companies were touring to the principal cities of Russia. Many privately owned theatres also had appeared; some gave public performances, while others were maintained by nobles for private entertainments. Few of those giving public performances were successful. In Moscow, for example, the public theatre was open

FIG. 11.26

Interior of the Bolshoi Theatre, St. Petersburg, in the late eighteenth century. A contemporary engraving.

only sporadically. When one venture failed, after lasting only from 1759 to 1761, there was no professional troupe there until 1786, when M. E. Medox's company opened and struggled along until 1796. Moscow was not to be given a state-supported theatre until the nineteenth century.

By far the majority of the privately owned theatres were maintained by the great landowners. With the encouragement of Catherine II, the aristocracy began to patronize the arts as a sign of their enlightenment, and many nobles established small courts of their own. Many maintained theatrical troupes composed of their serfs.

Unlike the rest of Europe, where it had largely disappeared during the Renaissance, in Russia serfdom was not established until the late sixteenth century, when a series of decrees bound the peasants to the land. Thereafter, serfdom became the principal basis of the Russian economy, and a landowner's wealth was measured primarily in terms of the number of serfs bound to his estate. During the late eighteenth century many nobles began to select serfs and train them as performers. Thus, they owned their own troupes. In 1797 in Moscow alone there were fifteen serf the-

atres, many of which rivaled in quality the court and state theatres of St. Petersburg. Prince Yusopov, owner of 21,000 serfs, established separate ballet, opera, and dramatic companies and a training school. Count Peter Sheremetyev built three separate theatres, one of which had three tiers of boxes. His principal troupe had 230 members. He retained an agent in Paris to keep him abreast of all the latest developments in Western Europe, and his productions, famous for their lavishness, were attended by the royal family, important nobles, and foreign dignitaries. Sometimes landowners sold entire companies or rented them out for public performances. The most important serf companies operated between 1790 and 1810, but some continued to operate until serfdom was abolished in 1861.

By 1800, then, Russian theatre and drama had gained a relatively firm foothold. Few important dramatists had appeared and the theatre was still largely imitative of French and Italian practices, but the basis for future developments was clearly evident. The Russian situation also shows that by 1800 the professional theatre had spread throughout Europe. It remained for the nineteenth century to bring it to full flower.

LOOKING AT THEATRE HISTORY

The study of theatre history can be enhanced by a knowledge of geography, which is concerned, among other things, with configurations of the land (such as rivers, plains, and mountains) and with conditions that affect economic life (such as the soil, climate, and natural resources). These factors are important in theatre history, since the division of territory into political units, the distribution of population and wealth, and physical hazards of travel seriously affect theatrical conditions. Perhaps at no time have geographical considerations been so crucial to the theatre as in eighteenth-century German states. Bruford observes:

> Germany was not at this time . . . a single national state, but . . . a loose confederation of states, the boundaries and authority of which were so ill-defined that it is for many purposes misleading to speak of the "Germany" of that age. . . . Many general causes have

> been suggested for the [overall divisiveness]. . . . The one least in dispute is the geography of the country. The abundance of barriers in the interior and the absence of clearly marked natural boundaries on its borders made the centralisation of authority much more difficult in Germany than it was in either England or France. . . . [There were] kings of European importance like those of Austria and Prussia, the electoral princes, 94 spiritual and lay princes, 103 counts, 40 prelates, 51 Free Towns, in all some 300 separate "Territories," each jealous of its time-honoured privileges and little affected by any memories of a common inheritance. [1–2 and 7]

W. H. Bruford, *Germany in the Eighteenth Century* (Cambridge: University Press, 1965).

In the early eighteenth century, when Germanic rulers disdained the native drama, the theatre was at a low ebb, as this account by Konrad Ekhof testifies:

Travelling troupes of mountebanks, going from one fair to another all over Germany, amused the mob with low farces. . . . The performance of the plays was just as ridiculous as their plots. One very frequently presented everywhere was entitled Adam and Eve, or the Fall of the First Men. *. . . . I remember seeing it acted at Strasbourg. You saw a fat Eve, in tights made of coarse flesh-colored linen, to which a narrow girdle of figleaves was attached. The costume of Adam was equally ridiculous, while God the Father appeared in an old dressing gown. . . . The comic element was provided by the devils . . . the old German plays . . . were not written out in full. The actors usually had just a scenario and played everything extempore. Hanswurst above all found abundant scope for his sallies. . . . A miserable wooden hut served as playhouse; the scenery was lamentable. . . . In a word, the theatre was an amusement for the mob.*

Quoted in F. J. von Reden-Esbeck, *Caroline Neuber und ihre Zeitgenossen* (Leipzig, 1881), 37.

Meantime, Germanic rulers were presenting some of the most lavish operatic spectacles to be seen in all Europe. In 1716, the Emperor Charles VI, on the occasion of his son's birth, presented *Angelica, Vincitrice di Alcina* out of doors at night in the Favorite Park, Vienna. The settings were by Ferdinando and Giuseppe Bibiena. Here is an eyewitness account from a letter written by Lady Mary Wortley Montagu:

The stage was built over a large canal, and, at the beginning of the second act, divided into two parts, discovering the water, on which there immediately came, from different parts, two fleets of little gilded vessels, that gave the representation of a naval fight. . . . The story of the opera is the Enchantments of Alcina, which gives opportunity for a great variety of machines, and changes of scene, which are performed with a surprising swiftness. The theatre is so large, that it is hard to carry the eye to the end of it; and the habits in the utmost magnificence, to the number of one hundred and eight. No house could hold such large decorations.

The Letters of Lady Mary Wortley Montagu (London, 1861), I, letter to Alexander Pope, dated 14 September 1716.

Lessing, the first major German critic and playwright, more than any one else was responsible for turning German taste away from the French neoclassical ideal championed by Gottsched and his circle. In the final numbers of his *Hamburg Dramaturgy* (1767–1769), he sums up his fundamental views:

I set myself the task of judging . . . some of the most celebrated models of the French stage. For this stage is said to be formed quite in accordance with the rules of Aristotle, and it has been particularly attempted to persuade us Germans that only by these rules have the French attained to the degree of perfection from which they can look down on all the stages of modern peoples. We have long so firmly believed this, that with our poets, to imitate the French was regarded as much as to work according to the rules of the ancients.

Nevertheless this prejudice could not eternally stand against our feelings. These were fortunately roused from their slumbers by some English plays, and we at last experienced that tragedy was capable of another quite different effect from that accorded by Corneille and Racine. . . . No nation has more misapprehended the rules of ancient drama than the French.

Gotthold Ephraim Lessing, *Hamburg Dramaturgy*, trans. Helen Zimmern (New York: Bohn's Standard Library, 1890).

By the end of the eighteenth century Weimar's theatre was one of the best known in Germany because of Goethe and Schiller. In one of his many conversations with J. P. Eckermann, Goethe describes some of his methods for achieving what came to be called Weimar classicism:

I did not look to magnificent scenery and a brilliant wardrobe, but . . . to good pieces. . . . By means of good pieces I educated the actors. . . . I was, also, constantly in personal contact with the actors. I attended the readings of the plays, and explained to every one his part; I was present at the chief rehearsals, and talked with the actors as to any improvement that might be made; I was never absent from a performance, and pointed out the next day anything which did not appear to me to be right.

Conversations of Goethe with Eckermann and Soret, trans. John Oxenford (London, 1874), conversation of 22 March 1825.

Two actors who were coached by Goethe, Pius Alexander Wolff and Karl Franz Grüner, set down precepts they learned from their teacher. These were later arranged by Eckermann and published as Goethe's "rules for actors." Here are a few of the ninety-one rules:

35. . . . the actor must understand that he not only should imitate nature but present it ideally . . . uniting the true with the beautiful.

36. . . . the actor must gain complete control over every part of his body so that he may use each part freely, harmoniously and gracefully as expression demands.

39. *The actors should not out of a mistaken idea of naturalness play to each other as if no third person were present. They should never play in profile or turn their backs to the audience. . . .*

91. *These rules are to be observed primarily when noble and worthy characters are to be represented.*

Johann Wolfgang von Goethe, *Werke*, 40

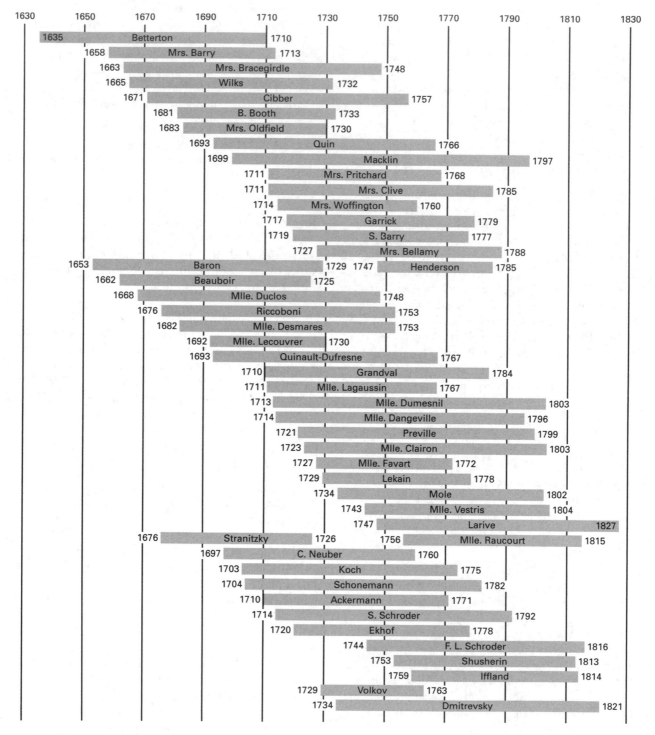

FIG. 11.27
Major European actors, 1700–1800.

12
Continental European Theatre in the Early Nineteenth Century

The nineteenth century was to bring the most radical social and political changes since the Renaissance. Most of the period from 1790 to 1850 was taken up with a struggle between those seeking to maintain the *status quo* and those working for a more equitable society. France played the key role in this struggle since the French Revolution was the principal motivating force.

What had begun in France in 1789 as a relatively modest demand for a constitutional monarchy soon became more radical, especially after other countries, worried that the Revolution might spread, declared war on France, and its royal family was accused of aiding the enemy. By 1792 France had been declared a republic, and in 1793 Louis XVI was guillotined. There followed the "reign of terror" during which thousands of persons were executed, many on mere suspicion of treason or lack of sympathy with the Revolution. This bloodbath finally ended in 1795, but by then most of the Revolution's major leaders had themselves been executed. Thereafter revolutionary fervor abated, but France's affairs, both internal and external, continued in disarray until Napoleon (1769–1821) came to power in 1799 and brought order out of chaos. In 1804 Napoleon named himself emperor, and between 1805 and 1812 gradually became master of practically all of Europe, placing members of his family or army on the thrones of

Spain, Holland, and many German and Italian states. Thus, he assembled the most extensive European empire since Roman times. Within this empire he made many reforms. He abolished the Holy Roman Empire in 1806, reduced the number of German states to less than forty, and put an end to serfdom in parts of Eastern Europe.

By 1810 the vision of a democratic order that had blossomed around 1790 had degenerated into dreams of empire. Many who originally had considered Napoleon a deliverer abandoned this view and championed nationalist sentiments that were to dominate Europe and Latin America throughout the nineteenth century.

In 1812 the tide began to turn against Napoleon. In 1814 he was deposed; in 1815 he made a brief comeback but was defeated at the Battle of Waterloo and was then permanently exiled. The aftermath was a blow to liberal sentiments, for the Congress of Vienna (1814–1815) sought above all to restore the sociopolitical conditions that had existed before 1789, although it did not hesitate to alter national boundaries or to award territory to its major participants. As a result, after 1815 repressive regimes returned to power throughout Europe, and most of them sought to ensure that the French experience would not be repeated. For Spain, however, it was already too late. Wars of independence broke out among its North,

Central, and South American colonies in 1810, and by 1828 it had lost all of them, retaining only its Caribbean holdings. Portugal lost Brazil in 1822.

The period after 1815 was one of great economic hardship. The Napoleonic wars had severely depleted Europe's resources, and the wars of independence in Latin America were followed by territorial conflicts among the new nations. Industrialization (which had been spurred on by the military needs created by war) accelerated as such inventions as the power loom, the steamship, and the locomotive promoted the factory system over individual craftsmen. Factories forced people to move into towns in order to be near their work. With urbanization came wretched living conditions that cried out for social legislation at a time when conservative governments viewed any request for reform as a prelude to revolution. Therefore, it is not surprising that around 1830 frustrations boiled over into a series of uprisings throughout Europe. Most were unsuccessful, and in many instances even more intense repression resulted. Not until after another series of revolutions in 1848 and 1849 did significant change begin. Industrialization, which led to competition among nations for raw materials and markets, fueled the desire to acquire additional overseas territories. Thus, the nineteenth century brought increased nationalism and imperialism.

It is within this context that the theatre operated during the first half of the nineteenth century. Until about 1840 the movement called romanticism, with its idealistic views and yearnings for natural man and equality, dominated both artistic and social thought. But the failure of the 1830 uprisings in Europe, and the lack of stability in the new Latin American nations, gradually turned this idealism, already weakened by earlier events, into disillusionment. Thereafter pessimism grew. Around 1850 a new movement—realism—began to replace the romantic vision. Still, between 1800 and 1850 romanticism was the dominant mode, even though it varied considerably from one country to another and from one decade to the next.

THEORETICAL FOUNDATIONS OF ROMANTICISM

The eighteenth century had witnessed the gradual decline of the neoclassical ideal as the former emphasis upon human beings as rational creatures was undermined by a growing faith in feeling and instinct as guides to moral behavior. Writers began to idealize the distant past when people allegedly had lived in a natural state, free from the shackles of despotic rulers. These changes contributed to shaping a new view of human nature, political theory, and literary forms. Most of these trends came together around 1800 under the label romanticism.

As a conscious movement, romanticism began in Germany, although many of its concepts had been developing there and elsewhere for some time. Ultimately it affected all the Western world in varying degrees. Romanticism was first used as a descriptive term by a group of writers in Berlin in their literary journal, *Das Athenaeum* (1798–1800). These German romantics were not in revolt against a stagnating drama, as their French counterparts were later to be, for they appeared at the very time when Goethe and Schiller were at the peak of their creativity. Rather, they saw themselves as clarifying and developing concepts derived from the Storm-and-Stress school of writers and from Goethe and Schiller. They also borrowed liberally from the writings of Immanuel Kant (1742–1804) and other idealist philosophers in formulating the theoretical bases of a "romantic" art.

The philosophical foundations of romanticism are complex, but the fundamental tenets can be summarized briefly. First, the romantics (especially in Germany) argued that beyond earthly existence there is a higher truth than that of everyday social forms and natural phenomena, for all that exists has been created by an absolute being (variously called God, Spirit, Idea, Ego). Consequently, all creation participates in eternal truth, and all things are part of the whole and of each other. Truth, then, is viewed in relation to infinite variety, rather than to observable norms, as the neoclassicist had held.

Second, since all creation has a common origin, a thorough and careful observation of any part may give insights into the whole (essentially a democratic idea). The less spoiled a thing is—that is, the less it deviates from its natural state—the more likely it is to embody some fundamental truth. Hence, the romantic writer preferred as topics untamed nature and unspoiled natural people or people in rebellion against the unnatural restraints of a highly structured and bureaucratic society.

Third, the romantics saw human existence as compounded of dualities: the body and the soul, the physical and the spiritual, the temporal and the eternal, the finite and the infinite. Because of its own dual nature, humanity is divided against itself, for it must live in the physical world although its spirit strives to transcend this limitation. Thus, humanity longs for some ideal existence or society but is kept from achieving it by circumstances or human limitations. In this scheme, art is of enormous significance, for it is one of the few means of making human beings "whole again," since during an aesthetic experience people are freed momentarily from the divisive forces of everyday existence. Art also makes the "supersensuous sensuous" by giving a higher, eternal truth concrete, material form so that it can be apprehended by the limited human sensory apparatus; through the glimpses of ultimate truth provided by art, people become more fully aware of their potential—artistically, socially, and politically.

Fourth, to perceive the final unity behind the apparently endless diversity of existence requires an exceptional imagination, one found fully active only in the artist-genius and the philosopher. Thus, art like philosophy, is a superior form of knowledge and the artist a truly superior being capable of providing guidance for others willing to listen.

Romantic theory implies that complete happiness and truth are to be found only in the spiritual realm and thus that they are impossible to attain fully during earthly existence. Furthermore, since spirit, as a part of the absolute, is eternal and infinite, human beings, held back by their physical limitations, can never grasp truth in its totality. Therefore, the romantic playwrights were faced with an impossible task, for not only was the highest truth always just beyond their grasp, but also the profound intuitions granted the playwright as a genius could never be embodied adequately because the means were necessarily too limited. (Similarly, the ideal society and state remained more nearly visions than attainable goals because of human weaknesses.) The demands of the physical stage were often viewed as too restrictive, and many dramatists refused to write with them in mind, preferring instead the freedom for imaginative flights permitted by "closet" drama.

Given these conceptions, it is not surprising that the romantics rejected the unities of time and place, the strict separation of drama into genres, the rationalistic outlook, and narrow didacticism. To them, Shakespeare's plays seemed most nearly to approach the desired goal; consequently, they accepted them as models to be followed in writing. For many writers, however, Shakespeare merely meant freedom from restraint, and they justified their own disorganized and episodic works by his example. This subjectivity and lack of discipline alienated Goethe, who in other respects had much in common with the romantic authors, for even though late in life Goethe called romanticism "sickly," his *Faust,* with its enormous scope, its picture of eternal human striving, and its attempt to encompass the infinite variety of existence, epitomizes much of romantic thought and sums up much of his own and German literary experience between 1770 and 1830.

The ideas of the German romantics were eventually disseminated throughout Europe and the Americas (where it encouraged the idealization of lost native cultures), although seldom were they articulated so completely or consciously. But everywhere playwriting and production were gradually altered by these views, which for the most part undergirded dramatic and theatrical practice in the years between 1800 and 1850.

ROMANTIC DRAMA IN GERMANY

In Germany, among those who called themselves romantics, only two, Schlegel and Tieck, were deeply concerned with drama. August Wilhelm Schlegel (1767–1845) formulated and disseminated romantic theory in Germany and elsewhere through his lectures and essays. In England Samuel Taylor Coleridge adapted Schlegel's ideas, and Mme de Staël popularized his views in France and Italy through her *Of Germany.* Schlegel was perhaps the first critic to use classicism and romanticism as polar terms, and it was largely through his influence that they passed into currency almost everywhere. Schlegel considered Shakespeare to be the greatest of all dramatists, and he translated seventeen of the plays. His translations, and those of Shakespeare's other plays made by members of the Tieck-Schlegel circle, were mainstays of the German repertory until well into the twentieth century. In his criticism Schlegel paid little attention to dramatic form, preferring instead to discuss tragic and comic "moods" as states of perception out of which differing types of drama come. Thus, mood, emotion, and character were for him the main ingredients of drama, while plot was treated as a contrivance used especially by lesser playwrights to keep a story moving. This conception of dramatic elements dominated much critical thought after Schlegel's time and served to divert attention from structure to vision.

Ludwig Tieck (1773–1853) had already developed a profound interest in Elizabethan drama before he met the other early romantics. This interest continued throughout his life, and, perhaps more than anyone else, he was responsible for familiarizing Germans with the works of Shakespeare and his contemporaries. Among his own dramatic works were a number of "fantastic comedies" in the manner of Gozzi's *fiabe,* based on such fairy tales as "Little Red Riding Hood" and "Puss in Boots" but serving as springboards for his satirical comments on eighteenth-century rationalism and theatrical practices. These comedies are surprisingly modern in tone, for they break dramatic illusion frequently and call attention to the theatrical medium and contemporary artistic taste. Tieck also wrote tragedies. Of these, *Kaiser Octavianus* (1802) is perhaps the best known. Set in the Middle Ages, its basic subject is the development of

Christianity and the union of all humanity in a universal church. Its extremely episodic plot is held together primarily by the allegorical figure, Romance. The prologue to this play became famous for its evocation of twilight as that time when the logic of daylight meets the mystery and magic of night. Tieck's contemporaries considered this passage so characteristic of the romantics that they dubbed them the "twilight men."

The early romantics were held together by close personal ties, but as their ideas spread and as they separated, the movement became increasingly diverse. Consequently, literary historians now divide the German romantics into groups, such as the Heidelberg Romantics, the Berlin Romantics, and so on. Few of their plays were produced, and even fewer found favor with the German public. The movement made an impact on the ordinary theatregoer primarily through the work of such popularizers as Kotzebue or through the writers of "fate tragedy," which was in great vogue between 1810 and 1820. Fate tragedy was initiated by Zacharias Werner's (1768–1823) *The Twenty-Fourth of February* (1809), which tells of a series of widely separated tragic events, all stemming from a curse and all occurring on the 24th of February. This play (first produced in Weimar) also spread the influence of Schiller, who previously had been derided by the romantics because of his attempt to unite literature and the theatre, a task which they thought impossible because of the limitations that production placed upon the playwright's genius. The phenomenal success of Werner, who had taken his inspiration from Schiller's *The Bride of Messina,* wrought a change of attitude and led to many imitations of Schiller's plays. Other popular writers of fate tragedy include Gottfried Müllner (1774–1829) with *Guilt* (1814), and Ernst von Houwald (1778–1845) with *The Portrait* (1820).

The best German dramatist of the early nineteenth century, Heinrich von Kleist (1777–1811), had little direct connection with the romantics. Receiving little encouragement during his lifetime, he remained virtually unknown until Tieck published his collected works in 1821. But by 1900 his reputation far exceeded that of any of the romantics, and his plays, among them *The Broken Jug* (1808) and *Penthiselea* (1808), still figure prominently in the German repertory. *The Prince of Homburg* (1811), Kleist's masterpiece, depicts a young army officer who is sentenced to die even though his disobedience of an order has led to a military victory. Following a scene in which he begs for his life and admits that his action was motivated by ambition, he is pardoned. Kleist here seems to be concerned with the conflict between selfishness and selflessness. Kleist probably failed to achieve recognition in his own time because, unlike the self-conscious romantics, he often emphasized people's sensual (rather than spiritual) nature.

POSTROMANTIC GERMAN-LANGUAGE DRAMA

A change in the German consciousness began to be evident around 1805–1806 as Germany and Austria came under Napoleonic dominance. Thereafter, rebelling against foreign influence, the Germanic people began to develop a sense of nationalism and an interest in their Teutonic past. Nevertheless, little nationalistic drama of importance was written, perhaps because censorship was so strict both during and following the Napoleonic years. Because innovation was frowned upon, the repertory came to be made up of classics (including works by Lessing, Goethe, Schiller, and Shakespeare) and innocuous dramas by such writers as Kotzebue, who lived until 1819.

In the rather fallow years between 1815 and 1830, two dramatists—Grabbe and Grillparzer—stand out. Christian Dietrich Grabbe (1801–1836), virtually ignored during his lifetime, is now recognized as a precursor of expressionism, epic theatre, and absurdism. In revolt against the optimism of the preceding years, Grabbe used a chaotic structure in *Comedy, Satire, Irony, and Deeper Meaning* (1822) to depict his own views of society as a tangle of selfish interests, outworn clichés, and static conventions; in the final

FIG. 12.1
Werner's *The Twenty-Fourth of February,* Act V. From *Le Monde Dramatique.*

FIG. 12.2

Grillparzer's *The Dream of Life,* Act IV. Engraving by Andreas Geiger. Courtesy Bildarchiv, Osterreichische Nationalbibliothek, Vienna.

scene he appears as a character. In *Don Juan and Faust* (1829), Grabbe uses the principal figures to symbolize such contemporary polarizations as the masses and the intellectuals, the sensual and the spiritual. Most of Grabbe's plays are difficult to stage; for example, *Napoleon, or the One Hundred Days* (1831) demands the European continent as a stage and has the populace as protagonist. Only one of Grabbe's plays was produced during his lifetime, and his fame did not begin to grow until after 1875.

Franz Grillparzer (1791–1872) was Austria's first important serious playwright. He began his career in 1817 with *The Ancestress* (a melodramatic work likened by critics to the fate tragedy then in vogue) and thereafter wrote regularly for the stage (despite almost continuous difficulty with the censor) until 1838, when a ban on one of his works led him to withhold his plays from production. Consequently, many were not staged until after his death. His plays range through classical subjects, as in *Sappho* (1818) and a trilogy, *The Golden Fleece* (1821); history, as in *The Luck and Fall of King Ottokars* (1824) and *The Jewess of Toledo* (1837); and philosophical fantasy, as in *The Dream of Life* (1834) inspired by Calderón's *Life is a Dream.* Grillparzer was the first significant playwright to express the sense of disillusionment that followed the Congress of Vienna. In his plays, the protagonists usually are rootless or alienated from their society. Motivated by some high ideal, they strive for reconciliation with others or with themselves but usually end in disaster. More than any other writer of his time, Grillparzer captured in his poetic works the prevailing sense that idealism is ineffectual against the forces of society and destiny.

The Austrian temperament found more characteristic expression, however, in the folk and peasant play, which had been the dominant dramatic type since Stranitzky had developed Hanswurst. This long tradition culminated in the nineteenth century in the plays of Raimund and Nestroy. Beginning in 1823, Ferdinand Raimund (1790–1836) wrote a series of plays for the Leopoldstadter Theater (founded in 1781), where he acted from 1817 until 1830. In these works realistic scenes of peasant life are interwoven with fantasy and fairy-tale elements. Regional dialects, folklore, allegory, and farce are the major ingredients of such plays as *The Barometer-Maker on the Magic Island* (1823) and *The Alpenking and the Misanthrope* (1828). Johann Nepomuk Nestroy (1801–1862), a comic actor and singer, began writing plays about 1832, most of them (with leading roles for himself) for Karl Carl's (1782–1854) company at the Theater an der Wien, where he worked for almost thirty years. His early work, such as *The Evil Spirit Lumpazivagabundus* (1833), resembled traditional folk drama in its use of fantasy, but his subsequent plays abandoned the fantastic for more realistic subjects treated satirically. Typical of the later works is *The House of Temperaments* (1837), which uses four apartments simultaneously to show four families headed by fathers of different temperaments. Nestroy also wrote farces and parodies. His *Out for a Lark* (1842) was to serve as the basis for Thornton Wilder's *The Matchmaker* (1954) and Tom Stoppard's *On the Razzle* (1981). After about 1835 Nestroy was the most popular Viennese playwright of his day.

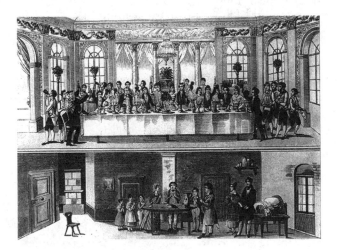

FIG. 12.3

Nestroy's *The Ground Floor and the First Floor,* showing the use of two settings simultaneously, one above the other. Engraving from *Theaterzeitung.* Courtesy Bildarchiv, Osterreichische Nationalbibliothek, Vienna.

FIG. 12.4
Scene from Nestroy's *Lumpazivagabundus* (roughly *Rascal Vagabond*) in 1833; Nestroy is at left, and the actor-manager Karl Carl at center. The exaggerated comic costumes are typical of the period. From *Schriften der Gesellschaft für Theatergeschichte* (1908).

FIG. 12.5
Hebbel's *Agnes Bernauer* at the Burgtheater, Vienna, 1868. The performers are Friedrich Krastel as Albrecht and Friederike Bognar as Agnes. Courtesy Osterreichische Nationalbibliothek, Vienna.

Following the abortive revolutions of 1830 a new movement—Young Germany—came to the fore and provided some of the most controversial plays of the 1830s and 1840s. In many ways quite diverse, its members were united by their scorn for abstraction and romantic idealism. They championed social awareness and the relevance of ideas to contemporary affairs. In drama the leaders were Gutzkow and Laube. Karl Gutzkow (1811–1878) began writing plays in 1835 but had no work produced until 1839 when *Richard Savage,* in which a poet struggles with class prejudice, was given in Frankfurt. His most enduring play is *Uriel Acosta* (1846), which treats a conflict of conscience in a young Jewish heretic. Heinrich Laube (1806–1884) began writing plays in 1841 with *Mondaleschi.* His best work probably is *The Karls Schoolboy* (1846), concerning Schiller's conflict with the Duke of Württemberg (who forbade him to write). In these and other Young German works the concern for contemporary problems was only feebly masked under stories from other times and places. Consequently, the writers were often in trouble with the censor, and only after the revolution of 1848 were their works widely produced. But Young Germany plays were so firmly tied to the contemporary situation that they were soon dropped from the repertory.

Far more enduring fame was won by Georg Büchner (1813–1837), a writer somewhat tenuously re-

lated to Young Germany. Büchner wrote only three plays, *Danton's Death* (1835), *Leonce and Lena* (1836), an ironic comedy, and the uncompleted *Woyzeck* (1836). *Danton's Death,* an episodic drama set during the "reign of terror" following the French Revolution, has as its central character an idealist who, seeing his highest aims wrecked by pettiness, comes to suspect that his ideals were merely a disguise for sensual appetites. His superior sensitivity, which causes him to question the meaning of existence, will permit no resolution of his doubts, and he ends in despair and death. *Woyzeck,* one of the first plays to treat a lower-class protagonist sympathetically, shows the gradual degradation of a man trapped by heredity and environment. The play foreshadows naturalism in its subject matter and expressionism in its structural devices and dialogue. Because his outlook and techniques were considerably in advance of his time, Büchner seemed very modern when his plays were rediscovered by Max Reinhardt around 1913. Since then Büchner has been considered one of the major dramatists of the nineteenth century.

After 1840 the German playwright most praised by contemporary critics is Friedrich Hebbel (1813–1863). Largely self-educated, Hebbel began his playwriting career in 1840 with *Judith*. Among his most important works are *Genoveva* (1842), *Maria Magdalena* (1844), *Herod and Miriamne* (1849), *Agnes Bernauer* (1853), and the trilogy *The Niebelung* (1855–1862). Like many of his contemporaries, Hebbel underwent a serious crisis in belief after first accepting the romantic outlook. Unlike Büchner, who never passed beyond pessimism, Hebbel found consolation in his own version of G. W. F. Hegel's philosophical position. Thus, he came to view society as a reflection of Absolute Spirit, which lies behind human existence and works out its own perfection through humanity. In Hebbel's view, the most significant human problems arise because values tend to harden into conventional patterns rather than remaining flexible to meet changing situations. Consequently, advances in morality are accomplished only after a violent conflict has destroyed worthwhile human beings seeking a better way of life; death serves to raise doubts about the old patterns, however, and to make way for new ones. Since the new values will rigidify in their turn, the process must be repeated. Thus, Hebbel viewed history as a series of conflicts, and his plays reflect his preoccupation with moral evolution. Most of his protagonists are female.

In Hebbel's principal works the main characters are representative of the old and the new orders. Since the old has the power of established authority behind it, the new, which can rely only upon faith or love, is usually destroyed. This destruction, however, foreshadows the triumph of the position that has seemingly been defeated. Through such views, Hebbel reconciled his sense of the world's current imperfections with the possibility of improvement. His most famous play, *Maria Magdalena,* is now usually studied as a forerunner of realism because its characters are drawn from ordinary life, its dialogue is in prose, and its story ends in the suicide of the heroine, a victim of society's narrow-mindedness. Thus, the play can be viewed as a realistic depiction of nineteenth-century German life. Nevertheless, like Hebbel's other plays, it too embodies the conflict between old and new values, and the heroine's death serves to make way for the new by raising serious doubts about the old. After Hebbel's death in 1863, German drama entered a period of decline while the Germanic states were formed into a united Germany, which finally occurred in 1871. Drama, however, did not recover until the 1890s.

THEATRICAL CONDITIONS IN GERMAN-LANGUAGE THEATRES

The vitality of the German theatre between 1805 and 1815 was curtailed by the French occupation, during which many state troupes lost their subsidies. While the downfall of Napoleon brought the reinstatement of financial aid, it also brought greater political control. Government officials, many with no theatrical experience, were appointed as superintendents of state theatres on the grounds that they could mediate between the public good and the sometimes self-serving practices of theatre workers. As a result, the manager's authority was undermined, and a bureaucratic organization was imposed on each company. Initiative soon declined and routine efficiency tended to replace innovation. New theatres could only be opened with government permission. Censorship,

FIG. 12.6

The coronation procession from Schiller's *The Maid of Orleans* as staged by Iffland at the Berlin National Theater in 1801. This production was one of the first anywhere to emphasize historical accuracy in costumes and scenery, although many elements were more nearly sixteenth than fifteenth century, the time of the action. From Weddigen, *Geschichte der Theater Deutschlands* (1904).

which in many states was quite severe, also discouraged anything considered potentially offensive or dangerous. As a result, the German theatre of the early nineteenth century tended to be competent but rarely inspired.

If few companies were truly outstanding, the theatre in general prospered. In subsidized troupes actors were relatively secure because they were civil servants with pension rights; company deficits were made up by governments, which also supplied buildings with good facilities. By 1842 the German states had sixty-five permanent theatres employing about 5,000 actors, singers, and musicians. By 1850 both state and municipal governments took it for granted that they should support the theatre, and because of this attitude each sizable city had a troupe of reasonably good quality. On the other hand, decentralization made it difficult for any theatre to become dominant.

Nevertheless, two cities—Berlin and Vienna—stood out above the others during these years. In the beginning, Berlin was dominant, perhaps because of Iffland, who ruled over the National Theater there until his death in 1814. Iffland mounted the most sumptuous productions (primarily of Schiller's works, sentimental plays and operas) to be seen in Germany.

FIG. 12.7
Ludwig Devrient as King Lear in the storm scene. From Weddigen, *Gerschichte der Theater Deutschlands* (1904).

These productions, designed by Bartolomeo Verona, accelerated the trend toward historical accuracy. Iffland's production of Schiller's *The Maid of Orleans* (1801), for example, featured a coronation procession with over 200 extras in period dress before a Gothic cathedral setting. Iffland was succeeded from 1814 to 1828 by Count Karl Bruhl (1772–1837), a court official who was even more insistent upon accuracy in costumes and settings, although he was not insistent upon ensemble acting. After 1816 his principal designer was Karl Friedrich Schinkel (1781–1841), a leader in the classical revival then underway. It was also Schinkel who designed the company's new theatre, opened in 1820 and used until 1944, which, with its half-circle auditorium and extensive work space, influenced almost all subsequent theatre architecture in Germany. Schinkel exerted considerable influence as well through his books on scene design.

After 1815 primacy passed to the Burgtheater in Vienna, largely because of Josef Schreyvogel's (1768–1832) leadership between 1814 and 1832. Schreyvogel was a friend and admirer of Goethe and Schiller and a champion of Grillparzer. The Burgtheater's eminence was stimulated in part by being the first German-language state theatre to restrict its repertory (beginning in 1810) to spoken drama. (Others continued to mingle spoken and musical drama.) He also popularized the idea that a theatre's repertory should reflect the nation's culture. Despite strict censorship, Schreyvogel was able to build the finest repertory and the best ensemble of any German theatre. His outstanding company included Sophie Schröder (1781–1868), the greatest tragic actress of her day; Heinrich Anschütz (1785–1865), noted for heroic roles in middle-class comedy, drama, and tragedy; and Ludwig Costenoble (1769–1837), one of the most versatile comic and character actors of the time. In production, Schreyvogel sought a middle ground between Weimar's spare, declamatory mode and Berlin's sumptuous, spectacular style. Consequently, he emphasized beauty and grace in acting and pictorial composition but he did not stint on decor and costumes. Between 1810 and 1848 the Burgtheater's decor was under the supervision of Philip von Stubenrauch, an expert on all historical periods, who did much to ensure accuracy in both costumes and settings.

A similar trend toward historical accuracy was evident in virtually all the theatres of Germany at this time. Nevertheless, in costuming, five generalized periods were considered sufficient for all plays set in past eras: classical, medieval, sixteenth century, seventeenth century, and mid-eighteenth century. More precise treatment was not to come until after 1850, when additional information became readily available in Jakob Weiss's authoritative histories of costume (published between 1856 and 1872).

While most settings continued to be composed of wings and drops, the box set was used occasionally for interiors. A semblance of the box set was evident in the late eighteenth century when a door or window was set up between two wings. Gradually other units were added, until the acting area was completely enclosed. The first fully developed box set in Berlin was used in 1826. By the 1830s Nestroy, in his *The House of Temperaments,* could demand a setting that showed two rooms on the stage level and two above. Nevertheless, the box set did not become usual for interior scenes until about 1875.

The kind of ensemble attained by Schröder and Goethe seems to have declined after 1830 as emphasis shifted to starring performers, perhaps because of the romantic glorification of individual genius. Starring engagements, popularized in the eighteenth century by Schröder and Iffland, grew in number during the nineteenth century, especially after the opening of the first railroad in 1835. Managers thought it necessary to engage a series of stars, for, while the theatre was the favorite form of entertainment, the German public was not attracted by the standard repertory unless performed by noted actors. Since the visitors seldom rehearsed extensively with the local companies and often insisted that other roles be curtailed so as not to detract from their own, ensemble effect was difficult to attain.

During the first half of the nineteenth century Germany produced many outstanding actors. Its greatest romantic actor was Ludwig Devrient (1784–1832), who made his debut in 1804 and achieved his greatest success in character roles. He performed over 500 roles, for each of which he achieved a sense of intense individuality, but he was especially noted for his Shylock, Falstaff, Lear, and Franz Moor (in Schiller's *The Robbers*). Devrient came to Berlin in 1815, but because of conflict with the company's leading tragic actor, Pius A. Wolff (1782–1828), who had been trained by Goethe, Bruhl appointed Devrient stage manager for comedy. Thus, after his initial season in Berlin Devrient was confined primarily to acting comic roles at the very time when he was at the height of his powers. In 1828 he went to the Burgtheater and for the next four years electrified Viennese playgoers with his passionate and versatile acting. Unfortunately, his powers were soon exhausted, and he died at the age of forty-eight.

Throughout this period the conflict between acting styles, often within the same company, was evident. This conflict is epitomized in the acting of Bogumil Dawison (1818–1872) and Emil Devrient (1803–1872), nephew of Ludwig Devrient. The Polish-born Dawison, both as a touring star and as a member of companies in Vienna, Dresden and elsewhere, created tormented portraits, filled with raw emotion, of such characters as Richard III, Iago, and Shylock. Emil Devrient, a disciple of Weimar classicism and a supreme virtuoso whose acting often outshone the plays in which he appeared, was noted for his sensitive voice and heroic gestures, especially in the works of Goethe and Schiller. Other major performers included Ferdinand Esslair (1772–1840), after 1820 the leading actor in Munich, although he spent much of his time touring in his heroic interpretations of Schiller's protagonists; and Karl Seydelmann (1793–1843), who made his reputation in Kassel between 1822 and 1828 and then toured extensively in such roles as Iago, Shylock, and Mephistopheles before joining the Berlin company in 1838.

Not everyone was content with the prevailing conditions. Among those who sought reform, the most important were Tieck and Immermann. Ludwig Tieck's interests extended far beyond the playwriting which had first introduced him to the theatre. By the 1820s he was considered Germany's leading authority on the theatre because of his critical essays and his performances as a platform reader. Nevertheless, his ideas about production were

FIG. 12.8
Ludwig Tieck's production of *A Midsummer Night's Dream* in Berlin, 1843. Note the tapestries downstage on either side; note also the steps that curve up to form an inner stage between them. A contemporary lithograph.

FIG. 12.9
Immermann's stage for Shakespeare's *Twelfth Night*, 1840. The forestage and facade remained unchanged but some scenic pieces were changed within or behind the openings at rear. Courtesy Theatermuseum, Munich.

considered impractical, and, though he served as literary advisor (or *Dramaturg*) to the Dresden troupe from 1824 until 1842, his influence was restricted to improvements in the repertory. It was not until 1841, when he was sixty-four years old, that Tieck was given a chance to implement his ideas about staging.

The difficulties that Tieck encountered are explained by the dominance of Weimar classicism and realistic spectacle in German theatres of the period. Since Tieck advocated psychologically realistic acting on a simple platform stage, he called for an approach at variance with the two dominant styles of the time. Many of Tieck's ideas stemmed from his intensive study of Shakespeare. In 1836, with the architect Gottfried Semper (1803–1879), he reconstructed (on paper) The Fortune Theatre, the first attempt of this kind. In his novel, *The Young Master Cabinetmaker* (1837) Tieck described a performance of *Twelfth Night* on an Elizabethan public stage. Believing that true illusion results from convincing acting and is destroyed by pictorial realism, Tieck was the first modern critic to advocate a return to the open stage. He also believed that every element of a production should be supervised by a single and autocratic director.

Tieck's chance to try out his ideas came in 1841 when William IV of Prussia decided to devote his court theatre at Potsdam to experimental productions. He summoned Tieck to stage Sophocles' *Antigone*, an innovation in itself, since professional productions of Greek tragedies were practically unknown at this time. Tieck was given complete authority over the production. He extended the apron

over the orchestra pit in a semicircle and constructed a Greek *skene,* which served as the only background for the action. After its success at Potsdam, the production was moved to the state theatre in Berlin and was soon adapted by companies at Dresden, Leipzig, Mannheim, Munich, and Karlsruhe.

Tieck's most famous production was of Shakespeare's *A Midsummer Night's Dream,* presented in 1843 with incidental music by Felix Mendelssohn. For it, Tieck adapted Elizabethan conventions to the proscenium theatre. Letting the forward part of the stage form a large open space, he constructed a unit at the rear, with curving stairs leading to an acting area 8 feet above the main stage with another beneath it at stage level. The sides of the stage were masked by tapestries hung at right angles to the proscenium. This production was repeated forty times at the Berlin theatre during the first season and was imitated by numerous troupes throughout Germany. Because of illness, Tieck was never able to complete production of *Henry V,* which he planned to do without any set changes.

Tieck's work was made possible only because William IV ordered all theatrical personnel to follow Tieck's orders. Bypassing the permanent managers created considerable friction, and after Tieck's retirement the old methods were resumed. Nevertheless, Tieck's ideas were to be revived and pursued more consistently at the end of the century.

Karl Immermann (1796–1840) combined the ideas of Goethe and Tieck, for while he advocated a declamatory acting style, he accepted many of Tieck's theories about spectacle. Immermann believed that the salvation of the theatre lay in drama of high quality and productions controlled by a single artistic consciousness. Originally a law-court official, he began his theatrical work around 1829 with amateurs. In 1834 he took over the management of the Düsseldorf Municipal Theatre, where he presented plays by Calderón, Goethe, Schiller, Lessing, Kleist, and others, although the majority of the works were light, ephemeral pieces. For a time, Grabbe served as his dramaturg. Despite Immermann's high ideals, he was forced by economic pressures to give up management in 1837, although his theatre was long considered a model of ensemble work.

Ironically, Immermann is now remembered primarily for a single private production of Shakespeare's *Twelfth Night* given in 1840. The architect Wiegman designed a special stage for this production with a fixed facade around three sides of an open space. At each end were entrances and across the back an inner stage and other smaller openings. Historically it is significant as the first important attempt to return to a stage like that for which Shakespeare wrote, even if the results more nearly resemble the Teatro Olimpico than the Globe.

Throughout the first half of the nineteenth century the German-language theatre enjoyed considerable popularity. In general it was prosperous, and the number of companies steadily increased. Not only were theatres opened in cities previously without them, but in such major centers as Vienna and Berlin several theatres were in operation simultaneously before 1850. They would continue to grow in number during the second half of the century.

THE FRENCH THEATRE, 1789–1815

During the period of political uncertainty in France following the fall of the Bastille in 1789, the minor theatres grew ever bolder in their encroachments on the privileges of the major troupes, who protested in vain. After the monopolies were abolished in 1791, numerous new companies were formed in Paris. It is difficult to chronicle their development, for many soon expired, and others adopted new names with bewildering frequency in the desire to reflect changing political currents and to remain in favor with various factions. Between 1791 and 1800 more than fifty troupes can be identified.

Most of the theatres catered to mob tastes by offering a wide range of popular entertainments combined with appeal to patriotic sentiment. The first burst of freedom, during which censorship was lifted, gave way during the "reign of terror" to repressive measures and severe punishments for any alleged opposition to the Revolution. Consequently, little drama of merit appeared. By far the most popular playwright of the Revolution was Marie-Joseph Chénier (1764–1811), whose *Charles IX* (1789) and *Henri VIII* (1791) set the political tone for others. In spite of their revolutionary sentiments, however, Chénier's plays remained clearly within the neoclassical tradition.

During the 1790s the former crown theatres lost much of their prestige. In 1791 the Comédie

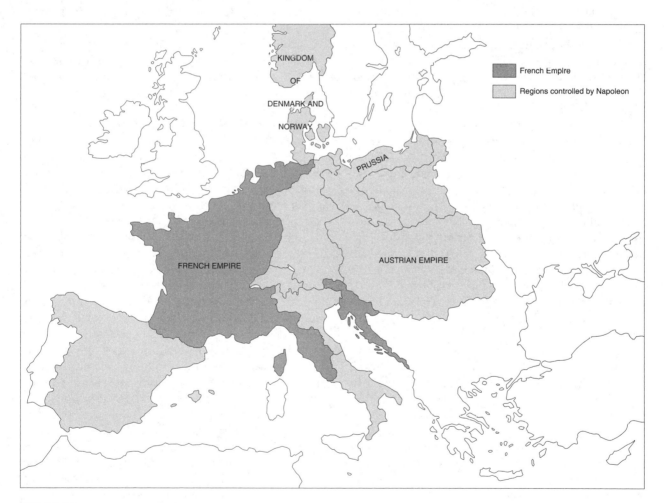

FIG. 12.10
The expansion of France under Napoleon.

Française, already weakened by internal strife, split into two troupes. The actors sympathetic to the Revolution, including Talma and Mlle Desgarcins, joined those of the Variétés Amusantes to form the Théâtre de la République in 1792. After 1793, when the actors at the Comédie Française were imprisoned, the Théâtre de la République was considered the finest in Paris. The Comédie Italienne, renamed the Théâtre Favart, was dangerously weakened by its fierce competition with the Théâtre Feydeau, and the Opéra survived only because it was taken over by the city of Paris.

By 1799, when Napoleon came to power, France was weary of intrigues and fanaticism. Napoleon immediately made clear his opposition to partisan drama by suppressing several plays favorable to his own cause. As a result, the theatre began to turn away from partisan subjects.

The changed atmosphere also brought renewed stability to the major troupes. In 1799 the fragments of the Comédie Française were reunited; the next year its theatre was declared state property and its use ceded to the troupe; in 1801 its pensions and subsidies, interrupted in 1791, were reinstated. In 1801 the Théâtre Feydeau and the Théâtre Favart were united in the state-subsidized Théâtre National de l'Opéra-Comique. In 1802 the Opéra was brought under state control once more, and in 1803 it was granted a subsidy.

The favors shown the major troupes were paralleled by repressions of minor theatres, for which Napoleon had little respect. In 1806 he decreed that works in the repertories of the state troupes could not be performed by any other theatres, that all plays must be approved by a censor and that no new theatres might be established without state permission. The next year he took more drastic measures. First, he authorized four state-supported theatres: The Comédie Française (for regular comedy and tragedy); the Théâtre de l'Impératrice, usually called the Odéon (for lesser drama); the Opéra (for grand opera and serious ballet); and the Opéra-Comique (for light opera and comic ballet). These troupes (in varying guises) were to continue into the twentieth century. Second, he ordered the closure of all minor theatres except four: the Théâtre de la Gaîté and the Ambigu-Comique (both to perform melodramas and pantomimes); and the Théâtre des Variétés and the Vaudeville (both to perform short plays, parodies, and *comédies-en-vaudevilles*). Other theatres, such as the Porte-Saint-Martin and the Cirque Olympique, were eventually allowed to reopen, but they too were restricted to minor genres. Napoleon's strictures were continued under the restored monarchy from 1815 until 1831, when a new uprising brought a change.

Between 1807 and 1831 the number of theatres in Paris was controlled and each was restricted to entertainments of specific types. Thus, theatrical conditions differed little from those of the 1780s. As before the Revolution, the principal innovations were to come from the boulevard theatres.

FRENCH DRAMA TO THE 1850s

Just as Napoleon sought to pattern his empire after Rome, so too he favored a classical drama. It is often said that in return for supporting the theatre he expected a new masterpiece each year. Beginning in 1804 he annually offered prizes of 10,000 and 5,000 francs for the best tragedy and the best comedy performed at the Comédie Française. Unfortunately, few of the prize works found lasting favor. Probably the best playwright of the time was Népomucène Lemercier (1771–1840), author of *Pinto* (1800) and *Christophe Colomb* (1809), but the latter work was performed at the Odéon billed as a "Shakespearean tragedy" because of its defiance of the unities and its mixture of genres.

Ironically, it was the boulevard theatres that produced the only truly popular plays, and these were melodramas rather than the tragedies for which Napoleon longed. Although melodramatic works, most often in the guise of tragicomedy or pastoral, can be traced back to classical Greece, the term *melodrama* did not come into widespread use until after 1800. While all of the characteristic elements of melodrama had long been present in many boulevard theatres, it was René Charles Guilbert de Pixérécourt (1773–1844), in *Victor, or The Child of the Forest* (1798), *Coelina* (1800), and other works, who gave them their typical form. The popularity of Pixérécourt's works (in combination with Kotzebue's) established melodrama as the dominant dramatic type of the nineteenth century.

The basic characteristics of melodrama can be summarized briefly: a virtuous hero (or heroine) is relentlessly hounded by a villain and is rescued from seemingly insurmountable difficulties only after undergoing a series of threats to life, reputation, or happiness; an episodic story unfolds rapidly after a short expository scene; each act ends with a strong climax; all important events occur on stage and often involve elaborate spectacle (such as battles, floods, or earthquakes) and local color (such as festivals, dances, or picturesque working conditions); the typical plot devices include disguise, abduction, concealed identity, and fortunate coincidence; strict poetic justice is meted out, for, although they may succeed until the final scene, the villains are always defeated; comic

FIG. 12.11
Pixérécourt's *The Marseilles Plague*, Act III, at the Théâtre de la Gâité, Paris, 1828. Setting by Gué. Note the various levels and numerous entrances and places of concealment. Courtesy Bibliothèque de l'Arsenal, Paris.

relief is provided by a servant or companion to one of the principal characters; song, dance, and music provide additional entertainment or underscore the emotional values of scenes. Melodrama, with its simple, powerful stories, unequivocal moral tone, and elements drawn from popular entertainment, could be understood and enjoyed by the least sophisticated of theatregoers. Probably for this reason, melodrama was largely responsible for bringing into the nineteenth-century theatre a large popular audience comparable to that of motion pictures and television in the twentieth century.

Although Pixérécourt, with his more than 120 works, was the most successful writer of the melodramas, he had many competitors. Of these, the most influential were Victor Ducange, author of such plays as *Thirty Years, or the Life of a Gambler* (1827), and Louis Caigniez (1762–1842), author of such plays as *The Hermit of Mont-Pausilyse* and *Child of Love*.

Melodrama paved the way for French romantic drama by popularizing departures from neoclassical precepts and by creating a large potential audience for a new kind of play. Furthermore, melodrama's plot devices were taken over by the French romantics to such an extent that many of their plays can be distinguished from melodrama because of only a few differences: romantic drama was divided into five acts (melodrama into three); it avoided happy endings; and it was more dependent on poetic diction. In broad outline, nevertheless, the characteristic French romantic dramas were often merely elevated melodramas.

The romantic movement was slow in getting underway in France because of political conditions. Its first important impetus came with the publication of Mme de Staël's *Of Germany*. Born Germaine Necker, Mme de Staël (1766–1817) was the daughter of Louis XVI's minister of finance and wife to the Swedish ambassador to France. A bitter enemy of Napoleon, she spent the years of his reign in Germany, where she became familiar with romanticism, especially through her acquaintance with A. W. Schlegel, who for a time was tutor to her children. *Of Germany*, which described the romantic movement, was published in France in 1810 but was immediately suppressed. Following Napoleon's downfall in 1814, it was quickly reissued. The notoriety of Mme de Staël's feud with Napoleon brought the book much publicity and gave its ideas wide currency. Thereafter debate over the relative merits of neoclassicism and romanticism raged in earnest.

Stendhal (Marie-Henri Beyle, 1783–1842) contributed to the controversy with *Racine and Shakespeare* (1823–1825), in which he declared Shakespeare's plays to be more suitable as models for dramatists than those of Racine. But the major French statement of romantic doctrine came in Hugo's preface to his play *Cromwell* (1827). Victor Hugo (1802–1885) set forth few ideas not already current in Germany, England, and elsewhere. He called for the abandonment of the unities of time and place, denounced the strict separation of genres, and advocated placing dramatic actions within specific historical milieus. Perhaps most important, he insisted that art should go beyond the neoclassicist's "idealized nature" to one that included both the sublime and the grotesque. Since for Hugo the sublime was related to spiritual qualities and the grotesque to animal nature, he argued that a truthful depiction of humanity requires that both be represented in literary works.

The culmination of the debate came in 1830 with the production of Hugo's *Hernani* at the Comédie Française. A pitched battle between the romantics and traditionalists, during which the actors were scarcely heard, raged for several nights. The bitterness of the contest is probably explained by the feeling on both sides that principles involving the future course of the theatre were at stake. Several events had accelerated the trend toward romanticism in France after 1827: Charles Kemble's troupe of English actors had performed Shakespeare's plays to admiring Parisian audiences in 1827; W. C. Macready had appeared in Paris in English romantic plays in 1828; Sir Walter Scott's novels were attracting an ever-wider reading public throughout France; and Shakespeare's plays were being read and produced in France with increasing frequency. Furthermore, by 1829 French romantic plays were making their way into the repertory of the Comédie Française: Alexandre Dumas *père's Henri III and His Court,* Casimir Delavigne's

FIG. 12.12
The battle over *Hernani,* 1830. Onstage is the final scene. From Grand Carteret, *XIXe Siècle* (1892).

Marino Faliero, and Alfred de Vigny's adaptation of *Othello* as *The Moor of Venice* were all produced in 1829. By opposing *Hernani,* the conservative audience hoped to halt this trend.

In *Hernani* Hugo deliberately violated many of the rules that the advocates of neoclassicism sought to retain. First, he made innovations in the alexandrine, which had been the accepted verse form for tragedy since the seventeenth century. Second, he used many words that had long been considered beneath the dignity of tragedy. Third, he broke the unities of time and place. Fourth, he showed deaths and violence on stage. Fifth, he shifted the mood of his scenes frequently and mixed humor with seriousness.

Hernani is essentially a melodrama with an unhappy ending. It tells the story of the noble outlaw Hernani and his attempt to wed Dona Sol over the opposition of the king and her guardian, both of whom also love her. Eventually he succeeds, and a happy future seems to lie ahead when he is reminded of a pledge made to the guardian earlier in a moment of crisis—that Hernani would give his life if the guardian ever demanded it. When the vindictive guardian asks that the pledge be redeemed, the couple choose suicide above a dishonored oath.

It is usual to date French romanticism from the triumph of *Hernani.* The upsurge in the production of romantic plays is probably also explained by the lifting of censorship (later reimposed) and the easing of genre restrictions following the Revolution of 1830. In addition to Hugo, whose popularity continued to increase with such plays as *Marion Delorme* (1831), *The King Amuses Himself* (1832), and *Ruy Blas* (1838), other important dramatists of the school include Dumas *père* and Musset.

The plays of Alexandre Dumas *père* (1802–1870) are of two types: historical spectacles, such as *Henri III and His Court, Christine* (1829), and his dramatization of *The Three Musketeers;* and domestic dramas, such as *Antony* (1831). Although Dumas had a surer sense of dramatic situation than did Hugo, he lacked Hugo's poetic gift, and, when he attempted to express profound emotion or significant thought, often sounded sophomoric.

Of French romantic dramas, those by Alfred de Musset (1810–1857) have fared best, although originally they were virtually ignored. After the failure of his first play, *A Venetian Night* (1830), Musset ceased writing with production in mind. Consequently, his later works shift time and place freely and depend little upon spectacle. Like Racine and Marivaux, Musset is primarily concerned with the inner feelings of his characters, especially their inability to resist love's compelling force. Musset's characters are essentially selfish, however, and seek desperately to protect their egos by forcing others to reveal their feelings first. But since the others also are loathe to lay themselves open to hurt or rejection, the participants indulge in a series of ploys and counterploys. Sometimes the results are happy, as in *A Door Should Either Be Shut or Open,* and sometimes tragic, as in *No Trifling with Love* (1834). Musset seldom strayed from his preoccupation with love, but his *Lorenzaccio* (1834), the story of a Hamlet-like character who seeks to right the Florentine state, is one of the finest historical dramas of the nineteenth century. Musset's plays, most of which were written between 1830 and 1840, did not begin to be produced until 1847. Since that time, they have never been absent from the French repertory.

George Sand (Aurore Dupin Dudevant, 1804–76) was one of the few women who made an impact as a dramatist in this period, although she was better known as a novelist. Some twenty-five of her plays were performed in Paris between 1840 and 1872. Her first produced play, *Cosima* (1840), concerns a married woman who enters into a love affair largely out of boredom. *Francois le Champi* (1849), a realistic folk play, was a great success and was revived often. Others of her plays include *Claudie* (1851), *Victorine's Marriage* (1851), and *If It Will Please You* (1856). Like those of many female dramatists, Sand's plays were largely ignored after her death, and interest in them has only recently revived.

Following the easing of genre restrictions, romantic drama found a ready home in the boulevard theatres. There it mingled with melodrama and absorbed still more melodramatic traits even as it helped to elevate melodrama. But by the 1840s the enthusiasm for romantic drama had waned. The failure of Hugo's *Les Burgraves* in 1843 is usually considered to mark the end of the romantic era in France.

Romanticism was succeeded by the "Theatre of Common Sense," which sought a middle ground between neoclassicism and romanticism. The leader of the new group was François Ponsard (1814–1867), who came to prominence in 1843 with *Lucrèce*. But, as with most compromises, the Theatre of Common Sense soon lost its appeal. By the 1850s it was giving way to still another movement—realism.

THEATRICAL CONDITIONS
IN FRANCE TO THE 1850s

The number of theatres in Paris grew steadily during the first half of the nineteenth century. Although the government retained firm control over licensing, the eight companies authorized by Napoleon in 1807 had grown to twenty-eight by 1855. Of these, the four state-supported troupes commanded the greatest prestige. After genre restrictions were eased in 1831, the Odéon and Opéra-Comique often rivaled the Comédie Française and Opéra in the quality of works presented and in the mounting of their productions. Throughout the century, the boulevard theatres were the most experimental, often championing new playwrights or methods of production long before they were accepted by the state troupes. Of the secondary theatres, the most influential were the Vaudeville, Gymnase, Porte-Saint-Martin, Gâité, and Ambigu-Comique.

Apart from the Comédie Française, all the Parisian troupes (with a few minor exceptions) were run by managers who hired actors on contract. The Comédie Française, on the other hand, continued to be a sharing company, operating under rules much like those in effect before the Revolution. The new regulations, established by Napoleon in 1812 by the "Decree of Moscow," sought through 101 articles to correct some of the earlier problems. A reserve fund was established to ensure pensions and to take care of deficits. *Sociétaires* were guaranteed a minimum annual wage and, in addition, were paid a small fee for each day they performed. As in earlier years, the government provided a generous subsidy. Ostensibly the actors were responsible for all policy decisions, but the supervisor, who replaced the Gentlemen of the Chamber, often assumed considerable authority. Furthermore, in the 1830s problems became so pressing that the actors were forced to cede much of their authority to a manager.

The other state theatres were let (under renewable contracts) to managers who had full control over the performers and the repertory, although their work was subject to close governmental scrutiny. The Opéra continued to be the favored troupe. Not only was its subsidy often four times as great as that of the Comédie Française, but between 1811 and 1831 it was allotted up to 1/20 of the receipts of all private theatres.

All the Parisian theatres retained the repertory system until after 1850, although the long run began to alter the old patterns. In the early years of the century only unusually popular plays were performed for a number of consecutive evenings; typically the bill was changed every day. But as early as 1835 a run of one hundred nights had been achieved, although this was not to be common until the 1870s.

Spectators at Parisian theatres had to present their tickets to three persons: the theatre's official ticket taker; the government employee, who made a record of the poor tax; and a representative of the Society of Dramatic Authors, who calculated royalties. The Society of Dramatic Authors, which succeeded the Bureau Dramatique in 1829, was a "closed shop" that boycotted any theatre refusing to accept its authority over contracts. The standard contract specified the maximum permissible delay between the acceptance and production of a play, required that each play be performed at least three times, and allowed a cessation of rehearsals for ten days so that authors might revise their work. Dramatists received from 10 to 15 percent of each performance's receipts. The society also established a pension fund for playwrights who had been members for more than twenty years and who had had more than a minimum number of plays produced. French playwrights were the first in the world to collect a royalty for each performance of their works and to achieve the financial security of a pension fund.

Every theatre had a claque to ensure correct and adequate response. Some actors even specified in their contracts the amount of applause they were to receive at their first entrance in each play. As a result of this prearranged approval, other spectators often restricted overt response to disapproval.

DIRECTING AND ACTING
IN FRANCE TO THE 1850s

In France melodrama initiated a concern for "directing," for much of its effect depended upon the precise manipulation of coincidence and spectacle.

Plots often evolved around overheard conversations, fortunate entrances, and spectacular feats of physical courage, and the resolutions often saw the villain foiled by an earthquake, a volcanic eruption, or some other fortuitous cataclysm. The effectiveness of many melodramas, therefore, depended upon the precise coordination of many elements. It was for this reason that Pixérécourt insisted upon absolute control over the staging of his works. He later declared that his preeminence as a dramatist was due to his care in production.

Pixérécourt's example was followed by several of the romantics, and above all by Hugo and Dumas. But, whereas Pixérécourt had been concerned primarily with the coordination of special effects, Hugo was additionally concerned with the actor's stage positions and the overall composition. Prior to 1830, French actors tended to form a straight line or semicircle at the front of the stage near the prompter's box, for though the amount of stage furniture had begun to increase by the 1820s, it was seldom used by the actors and was treated primarily as decoration. Contrary to earlier practices, Hugo utilized the entire stage space, replaced the usual long diagonal movements with short curved movements, and even occasionally had an actor play a scene with his back to the audience. By 1835 critics were noting that in the boulevard theatres actors sometimes sat on the arms of chairs, leaned on tables, or remained seated while speaking. Still, most directors were more concerned with picturesque local color, historical accuracy, or precision of stage business than with creating an illusion of real life. Those who did move toward greater lifelikeness met considerable opposition from critics, who argued that art should idealize rather than copy life. Even those who approved of the trend usually denounced any attempt to represent sordidness on the stage.

Throughout the first half of the nineteenth century French actors continued to be employed according to lines of business. But, as elsewhere, there was a trend toward stars. Even at the Comédie Française leading actors were listed on the bills after 1805 as a means of stimulating audience interest.

Between 1790 and 1850 France produced a number of outstanding actors. Prior to 1825 the leading performers were Talma, Mlle Duchenois, Mlle Mars, Fleury, and Mlle George. François-Joseph Talma (1763–1826), often called the greatest of all French actors, spent much of his youth in England, but returned to France in 1785 and was one of the first students at the École Royale Dramatique when it opened in 1786. Entering the Comédie Française in 1787, he was a constant source of friction because of his dissatisfaction with the troupe's acting style,

FIG. 12.13
Talma as Titus in Voltaire's *Brutus* in 1791. From Adolphe Jullien, *Histoire du Costume au Théâtre* (1880).

costuming practices, and politics. He attained his first success in 1789 in Chénier's *Charles IX,* a work which contributed to the separation of the company in 1791. After the troupe was reunited in 1799, Talma became and remained its acknowledged leader until his death. He was a favorite of Napoleon, who summoned him to play before the rulers of Europe. Talma was devoted to authenticity in costume (at least for classical roles) and to detailed study of every role. To this care, he joined intense feeling and vigor. It is sometimes said that he was by temperament a romantic but by circumstance doomed to perform in neoclassical plays.

Mlle Duchenois (c. 1777–1835) was Talma's usual companion in tragedy. In 1802 her debut as Phèdre was so successful that the play was repeated for eight nights. Her ability to play "profound tenderness and melodious sorrow" won her a devoted following. She seldom played after Talma's death and retired altogether in 1830.

While Talma and Mlle Duchenois dominated tragic acting, Mlle Mars and Fleury were the most famous performers of comedy. Mlle Mars (1779–1847), on the stage from childhood, joined the Comédie

Française in 1799 and after 1805 was the idol of Paris. She created Dona Sol in *Hernani* and all critics spoke of her in glowing terms. When the Comédie Française began to go into debt in the 1830s, she resigned as a *sociétaire* so that she might demand an exorbitant salary as a *pensionnaire,* thus setting a precedent that was to plague the troupe through much of the century. She continued to play young heroines until her retirement at the age of 62.

Abraham-Joseph Fleury (1750–1822) joined the Comédie Française in 1778 and taught at the Conservatoire from its founding in 1786. His elegant manner in comedy made him a fit companion for Mlle Mars. He retired in 1818.

Mlle George (1787–1867), daughter of a provincial manager, made her debut at the Comédie Française in 1802 at the age of fifteen. Her rivalry with Mlle Duchenois was intensified when Napoleon took her as his mistress, and the Empress Josephine retaliated by taking Mlle Duchenois under her protection. In 1808 Mlle George left Paris to play in St. Petersburg, Stockholm, and elsewhere before returning in 1813. After Napoleon's downfall, she fled France once more until 1822. After this time her career was bound up with that of Jean-Charles Harel, manager of the Porte-Saint-Martin and Odéon theatres. Harel was very sympathetic to the romantics and in the 1830s produced many of their plays. In these, Mlle George

FIG. 12.14
Rachel's farewell appearance during a highly successful engagement at Her Majesty's Theatre in London, 1841. Courtesy Theatre Museum, Victoria and Albert Museum, London.

played the heroines and did much to popularize the new drama.

Melodrama and romantic plays brought many boulevard actors to the fore. Of these, the most popular were Mme Dorval, Bocage, and Deburau. Mme Dorval (1798–1849), after studying at the Conservatoire, played for a time in the provinces before joining the Porte-Saint-Martin troupe in 1818. Here she played in melodrama until the theatre was permitted to perform other genres. An intuitive actress, she was best at portraying vehement emotion and seductive charm. From 1835 to 1837 she played at the Comédie Française, but she encountered so much opposition (primarily from the partisans of Mlle Mars) that she returned to the more compatible boulevard theatres.

Bocage (1797–1863) was refused an engagement at the Comédie Française in 1821, so he turned to the boulevards, where he was soon regarded as the greatest stage lover of his day. He appeared at the Comédie Française briefly in the 1830s but found the atmosphere so hostile that he soon left. After 1845 he served as manager of the Odéon.

Jean-Baptiste Deburau (1796–1846) was born into a family of touring acrobats. In 1811 he settled in Paris, where he was associated principally with the Théâtre des Funambules. His fame came after 1825 as he developed the character Pierrot, a pale, lovesick, ever-hopeful seeker after happiness. In this role he became one of the most popular performers in Paris.

The most renowned romantic actor of France, Frédérick Lemaître (1800–1876), entered the Conservatoire at the age of fifteen, and performed at the circus in pantomime and melodrama while still undergoing this rigorous classical training. In 1823 he achieved renown by turning the villain of a melodrama into a comic caricature. Thereafter he took considerable liberties with his roles until he was employed by Harel at the Odéon and Porte-Saint-Martin, where he became a dedicated performer. Lemaître was the most versatile actor of his day, for he refused to be bound by the usual lines of business. He delighted in astonishing audiences by novel interpretations and passionate outbursts. The peak of his popularity was reached between 1830 and 1850, but he went on acting until his death, long after his popularity had waned.

Of similar temperament but performing an entirely different kind of repertory, Rachel (1821–1858) made her professional debut in 1837 at the Gymnase. In 1838 she was engaged at the Comédie Française, where she soon became its major attraction. She insisted on an enormous salary (sometimes equaling that of France's prime minister). Her performances revived the popularity of the classical repertory, which had declined markedly after romanticism came to the fore. While she filled the Comédie Française on the nights when she played, she impoverished the company by taking most of the receipts and by going on extended tours. Largely because of this experience, the Comédie has since that time refused to give any performer star billing and has listed all actors according to seniority.

Rachel's repertory was not large, and only one of her major roles, Scribe's Adrienne Lecouvreur, was from a contemporary play. She was unsuited to comedy and could not portray convincingly tenderness, gaiety, or heartiness; her strength lay in scorn, triumph, rage, malignity, and lust. Within her range, however, she had no peers. Her death throes as Adrienne aroused both admiration and horror because of their lifelikeness. By 1841 she was in demand for foreign tours and began to play throughout Europe; in 1855 she appeared in America. Tuberculosis brought a decline in her powers, and in her last years she conserved her strength for the great moments and rushed through other scenes. Nevertheless, her intensity and power established a standard remembered through the rest of the century.

SCENERY, COSTUME, AND LIGHTING IN FRANCE TO THE 1850s

Although local color and historically accurate motifs had been introduced before the Revolution, they were not exploited fully until the nineteenth century. During the 1790s many managers sought to re-create actual places and real events, but a consistent emphasis upon spectacle first became evident in the boulevard theatres between 1800 and 1830. Here it served at least two major functions: as a plot device in dramatic action and as a novelty designed to attract audiences. Both promoted the increased use of detailed settings and special effects.

Early nineteenth-century melodramas often depended upon natural disasters to forward the plot. For example, Pixérécourt's *The Exile's Daughter* shows a flood uprooting trees, inundating the stage, and carrying the heroine away on a plank. Similarly, his *Death's Head* uses a volcanic eruption to engulf the stage and foil the villain. The Cirque Olympique, under the direction of Laurent Franconi, re-created famous battles, using more than one hundred persons and thirty horses, in which a troupe of cavalry not uncommonly arrived at the crucial moment. Thus, many of the boulevard plays depended heavily upon spectacle to keep plots moving or to resolve them.

Emphasis was also placed on the novelty of the spectacle. Playwrights sought to include new places or examples of local color never before represented on the stage. Consequently, a variety of historical periods, exotic locales, and fantastic settings was introduced. Spectacle was so highly developed by 1828 that the new Ambigu-Comique opened with a play in which the "Muse of the Mise-en-Scène" demanded admission to Mount Parnassus. As evidence of her worth, she displayed all the scenic marvels of the theatre and so impressed the other Muses that she was granted admission to their ranks. Nevertheless, spectacle did little to enrich characterization, for usually it merely gave variety to an otherwise routine story.

During this period two designers, Daguerre and Ciceri, laid the foundations for many later developments. Daguerre is especially important for his work with the panorama and diorama, which brought illusion ever closer to reality. The panorama, invented and patented by Robert Barker in 1787, was first seen in Edinburgh in 1788 and in London in 1792. Robert Fulton (1765–1815), an associate of Barker and later the inventor of the steamboat, secured a French patent on the panorama in 1799. He then sold it to an American, James Thayer, who opened two panoramas in Paris in 1800. Panoramas were displayed in circular buildings in which the audience, occupying a central platform, was completely surrounded by a continuous painting. To the spectators, the total effect was that of being set down at a spot from which they had a commanding view in every direction.

Louis-Jacques Daguerre (1787–1851) began his career as a scene painter at the Opéra and apparently also worked as an assistant to Pierre Prévost (1764–1823), one of the first painters of panoramas. Daguerre's interest in optics, which was to culminate in his invention of the first effective form of photography (the daguerreotype) in 1839, led him to experiment with variations on the panorama. Thus, in 1822 he began to display his diorama. Here the spectator was not surrounded by the painting, but rather sat on a platform which revolved every 15 minutes to reveal one of two different paintings, each about 71 feet wide by 45 feet high, on proscenium-like stages. Daguerre's improvement lay in his ability to create the illusion of constant change. While Daguerre's partially transparent scenery remained stationary, he varied its appearance by manipulating (with a system of screens and shutters) the direction, intensity, and color of the natural light which entered through overhead openings. By controlling light, he was able to depict the gradual change from fair weather to storm, from day to night, and other conditions. Daguerre was not long content with his accomplishment, and soon perfected the *diorama à double effet*. Here some details were painted on the front and some on the rear of a translucent cloth. Through changes of light, Daguerre could make details visible or invisible. One of his most famous dioramas, "Midnight Mass at St. Etienne-du-Mont," showed, all through painting and light, the church empty by day, then gradually filling with people for midnight mass, and finally returning to emptiness.

Panoramas were displayed throughout the Western world during the nineteenth century and were soon adapted to theatrical uses. The panorama was always more useful in the theatre than the diorama because it did not depend upon the manipulation of stage lighting. On the other hand, the panorama had to be altered considerably for stage purposes, since it could no longer surround the audience; thus, it assumed the shape that Daguerre adopted for his dioramas. Perhaps for this reason, after the 1820s the terms *panorama* and *diorama* were often used interchangeably.

Moving panoramas were introduced into the theatre in the early nineteenth century. A continuous scene was painted on a cloth of enormous length, suspended from an overhead track, and attached at either end to an upright roller, or "spool." When the spools were turned, the cloth moved across the stage. In this way, characters, ships, horses, and carriages, while remaining in full view, apparently moved from one place to another without any abrupt change in

FIG. 12.15
Setting by Daguerre for the third act of *Elodie* as produced at the Théâtre de l'Ambigu Comique, Paris. Courtesy Bibliothèque Nationale, Paris.

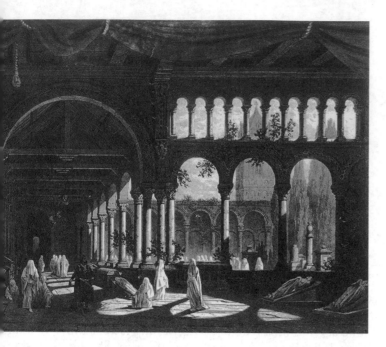

FIG. 12.16
Design by Ciceri for Meyerbeer's *Robert le Diable* at the Paris Opera in 1831. Seen here is a cloister in which was danced the ballet of dead nuns. Courtesy Bibliothèque Nationale, Paris.

the setting, as would have been necessary had wings and drops been used.

The panorama and diorama also permitted designers to dispense with sky borders, which by the early nineteenth century were considered unsatisfactory, since they destroyed illusion by making breaks in the sky. Panoramas permitted a new arrangement. Flats representing architectural units or natural objects were erected near the front of the stage to form an arch, through which was seen a distant view painted on a panorama curving across the back and down the sides of the stage. Not only did this eliminate sky borders, but an entire scene, with the exception of the downstage masking pieces, could be painted on a continuous surface. This practice would eventually lead to the development of the neutral cyclorama to surround the acting area.

The panorama and diorama, then, contributed in many ways to illusionism. In Paris their theatrical uses were first fully exploited at the Panorama-Dramatique where, between 1821 and 1823, panoramic spectacles with only two characters made up the entire repertory.

In addition to his work with panoramas and dioramas, Daguerre became one of the major scene designers of his day. After serving an apprenticeship as a scene painter from 1810 to 1816, he was principal

designer at the Ambigu-Comique from 1816 to 1822. After 1822 he virtually abandoned the stage.

Pierre-Luc-Charles Ciceri (1782–1868) was the most admired designer of the period, probably because of his ability to depict the favorite visual themes of the time: quaint local color, nostalgic ruins, and picturesque historical milieus. From about 1810, Ciceri was the Opéra's principal designer, but he also worked for the Opéra-Comique, Comédie Française, Porte-Saint-Martin, Panorama-Dramatique, and other theatres. After 1822, he was in such demand that he opened one of the first scenic studios in Paris, where he eventually employed specialists (one for architectural details, another for landscapes, and so on), a practice which was to prolong the use of different designers for a single production. From Ciceri's time, the independent scenic studio began to replace those maintained by individual theatres. Ciceri's students were to dominate stage design in France for the rest of the century.

Interest in spectacle accelerated after 1820. The new Opéra, opened in 1822, incorporated all of the latest developments, including gas lighting and a water system for creating realistic fountains and waterfalls. After 1825, when Baron Taylor was appointed its supervisor, even the Comédie Française began to follow the new trends. Taylor, previously director of the Panorama-Dramatique, employed Ciceri in 1826 to provide historically accurate settings for a number of plays, among them *Hernani*.

After 1828 the increased interest in spectacle led to the publication of *livrets scéniques,* or promptbooks, describing in detail the scenery and special effects

FIG. 12.17
Opening performance at Alexandre Dumas *père's* Théâtre Historique, Paris, 1847. From *The Illustrated London News* (1847).

FIG. 12.18
Costumes for Dumas's *Don Juan de Marana,* 1836. From *Revue du Théâtre* (1836).

used in the Parisian theatres, with suggestions for simplifying spectacle in less well equipped theatres. After 1830 concern for historical accuracy also increased, for the romantic playwrights were scornful of the inconsistencies often seen in productions of melodramas. Hugo consulted the Commission on Historical Monuments and other sources before making the sketches that he provided for productions of his plays. Dumas *père* often publicly castigated those producers who failed to provide sufficiently accurate spectacle for his works. From 1847 to 1850 he headed his own Théâtre Historique where he staged productions so lavish they almost bankrupted him.

By 1840 dramatic critics were writing detailed accounts of scenery, costumes, and lighting and often even criticized fairy-tale pantomimes for alleged inaccuracies. The classical repertory, for which the *palais à volonté* had continued in use, largely escaped the trend toward historical accuracy until 1842, when the revival of *Le Cid* with six settings established a new pattern.

Although local color and historical accuracy were the most popular forms of scenic illusionism, realism of daily life also made headway. Under its impact, the box set, complete with ceiling, gradually came into use for interior scenes. It is impossible to say when the box set was first used in France, but by the 1820s it was no longer unusual. Only gradually, however, was it furnished with complete realism, for until 1850 most of the properties and furniture were mere painted cut-outs. In 1846 *Pierre Fevrier* created a sensation with its real furnishings and its decorated floor cloth, simulating black-and-white marble squares, the first seen in Paris.

As with scenery, costumes between 1790 and 1850 became increasingly realistic. In the early years Talma did much to popularize historical accuracy in tragic costuming. As early as 1787 he startled audiences by appearing in a toga and with bare arms and legs, the first attempt in France to achieve true authenticity

in classical dress. Although a consistent approach was long in developing, progress was steady, especially in serious plays. Comedy continued to be performed in contemporary dress until 1815. Then, seventeenth-century garments began to be adopted for Molière's plays, although Mlle Mars refused to accept the changes and continued to wear the latest fashions. Baron Taylor, who became superintendent of the Comédie Française in 1825, placed considerable emphasis on accuracy of spectacle, a view which the romantic dramatists strongly favored. Consequently, by 1840 critics were almost universally scornful of anachronisms in dress.

In lighting, eighteenth-century practices were continued until 1822, when the Opéra introduced gas. The flexibility and greater intensity of gaslight soon led other theatres to adopt it, although the Comédie Française did not install it until 1843. Even then, the Comédie retained its oil footlights because the actresses considered gas light too harsh. Allowing greater control over intensity and direction, gas encouraged more realistic lighting effects. Since spotlights had not yet been invented, however, stage lighting still consisted primarily of general illumination.

RUSSIAN DRAMA AND THEATRE TO THE 1850s

From 1805 onward, Russia was one of France's major foes during the Napoleonic era, and it was during his Russian campaign that Napoleon suffered his first major defeat. As elsewhere, nationalist sentiment steadily grew in Russia during these years. The most popular playwright of the time was Vladislav Ozerov (1770–1816), probably because his works appealed to patriotic sentiment at a time when Russia was endangered by France. Written in the neoclassical style, his plays, most notably *Dmitri Donskoi* (1807), were extravagantly praised but soon forgotten.

As in other countries of Europe, in Russia the end of the Napoleonic era brought new repressions. Alexander I (ruled 1801–1825) talked of freeing the serfs and making other reforms, but when it became evident that nothing would be done, revolutionary groups began to organize. After Nicholas I (ruled 1825–1855) came to the throne in 1825 this dissatisfaction boiled over into open rebellion. The revolt was quickly put down, and to prevent recurrences the czar established a secret police force and the most stringent censorship in Europe. Although his reign was one of great creativity, the best plays were almost always severely mutilated before they were licensed for production.

FIG. 12.19

Griboyedov's *Woe from Wit.* At center, Mikhail Shchepkin as Famusov. From Komissarzhevsky, *Moscow Theatres* (1959).

The most accomplished playwrights of the period were Griboyedov, Pushkin, and Lermontov. Alexander Griboyedov (1795–1829) is remembered primarily for *Woe from Wit* (1822–1825), one of the masterpieces of Russian drama and sometimes said to be the only significant Russian play in the neoclassical style. As in Molière's *The Misanthrope,* the disillusioned hero of *Woe from Wit* seeks to make others aware of the shortcomings of a materialistic and hypocritical society. To demonstrate his point, Griboyedov brings together a gallery of character types representative of Moscow life. Unfortunately, it was completed just as censorship was tightened following the revolt of 1825. As a result, it was long kept from the stage. The complete version was not seen until 1869; since then, it has never been absent from the Russian repertory.

By the time Griboyedov's play was written, romanticism was emerging. Alexander Pushkin (1799–1837) is usually given major credit for establishing the new style. His *Boris Godunov* (1825), with its variety, magnitude, poetic strength, and historical subject, marks the first victory in Russia of romanticism over neoclassicism. Sometimes called the first Russian play on a political theme, it deals with the relationship of a ruler to his subjects. Censorship kept the play out of print until 1831 and from production until 1870. Mussorgsky's operatic version, presented in 1873, has largely supplanted the original text in the theatre. Mikhail Lermontov (1814–1841), one of Russia's finest romantic poets, also wrote a few plays after 1830, beginning with *The Spaniards.* He is now remembered primarily for *Masquerade* (1835), in which corrupt society is blamed for a man's murder of his wife. Censorship kept this play from the stage until 1852.

Given the severity of censorship, it is not surprising that most Russian plays were either innocuous or flattering to the ruler. Consequently, romanticism flourished primarily in the patriotic spectacles encouraged by Nicholas I. One of the most successful writers of such plays was Nestor Kukolnik (1809–1868), whose *The Almighty's Hand the Fatherland Has Saved* (1834) depicts the election of Michael Romanov, Nicholas I's ancestor, to the throne. Nikolai Polevoy (1796–1846) exploited the same vein, although he achieved his greatest success with melodrama, which had become popular in Russia following the production in 1829 of Ducange's *Thirty Years.* Polevoy's greatest contribution, however, was the introduction of Shakespeare to the Russian stage through his translation of *Hamlet* in 1837. Thereafter, the works of Shakespeare became increasingly prominent.

As elsewhere, the repertory in Russia was dominated by melodrama and musical plays. A large number were translations, especially of French works, but native writers cultivated the genre. The *comédie-en-vaudevilles,* a one-act comedy with couplets sung to familiar tunes, was especially popular. It reached its high point in the work of Alexander Pisarev (1803–1828), but many other writers followed his example through the remainder of the century.

A more realistic drama began to appear in the 1830s with the work of Nikolai Gogol (1809–1852). As a playwright Gogol is now remembered primarily for *The Inspector General* (1836), the story of a young man mistaken for an official from St. Petersburg. Satirizing the corruption and boorishness of provincial officials, the play was original for its time, since it included neither a love story nor sympathetic characters. Its claim to realism lies almost entirely in its grotesque characters and its preoccupation with pettiness, hypocrisy, and corruption. Its production, allegedly after the personal approval of the czar, encouraged other authors to turn to more realistic portraiture.

During the nineteenth century the Russian theatre expanded constantly, but always under close government supervision. Prince Alexander Shakhovskoy (1777–1846), Director of Repertory in the Imperial Theatres from 1801 to 1826, initiated several important changes. In 1805 a state theatre was opened in Moscow, for which the crown purchased a company of seventy-four serf actors. In 1809 a training school was added; gradually, the Moscow troupes grew in theatrical importance, although the companies in the Russian capital, St. Petersburg, continued to receive favored treatment and higher subsidies. Shakhovskoy, after visiting Paris and other Western theatrical centers, also attempted to raise the level of production, and worked out regulations for governing the troupes which were to remain in effect from 1825 until 1917.

Throughout this period the imperial theatres had a total monopoly on theatrical production in St. Petersburg and Moscow. St. Petersburg had three theatres: the Bolshoi for ballet and opera; the Maly (replaced by the Alexandrinsky in 1832) for drama; and the Mikhailovsky for foreign works. Moscow had two theatres, one for opera and ballet and the other for drama. Both Moscow companies were originally housed in temporary buildings, but in 1824 a permanent home for spoken drama, the Maly, was opened; it remains in use. In 1825 the Bolshoi was inaugurated for opera and ballet; after it burned in 1853, it was replaced in 1856 with the present building. Because of their prestige, the state troupes set the standard for all Russia, which for the most part depended upon touring companies of poor quality.

Between 1800 and 1850, actors in the state troupes were still hired according to lines of business adopted from French usage. State-approved rules governed rehearsals, the behavior of actors, and every aspect of their lives. In 1839 they were placed under civil service and divided into three ranks according to length of service.

The actors in the St. Petersburg troupes were long considered superior to those in Moscow. Semyonova and Yakovlev were especially admired. Yekaterina Semyonova (1786–1839), trained by Dimitrevsky, played leading roles in both comedy and tragedy, although she excelled in the latter; she was unsuited to domestic drama. Because of her popularity, she was paid considerably more than other performers and given a special allowance for costumes. Aleksey Yakovlev (1773–1817), also trained by Dimitrevsky, made his debut in 1799. An impulsive actor who depended primarily upon inspiration, Yakovlev was especially popular in Ozerov's tragedies, then at the height of their vogue. During the second quarter of the nineteenth century, the St. Petersburg stage was dominated by Vassily Karatygin (1802–1853). Tall, handsome, and vocally gifted, he played roles of almost every type. He was a master technician who paid careful attention to costume, makeup, and every detail of his performances.

After 1825, however, the lead gradually passed to Moscow. Among the early performers there the most important were Mochalov and Shchepkin. Pavel Mochalov (1800–1848) was on the stage from the age of seventeen. An uneven, emotional actor, he swept audiences away when he was at his best. He was especially admired in melodrama and in such roles as Richard III and Hamlet. According to Stanislavsky, Mikhail Shchepkin (1788–1863) was the first great Russian actor. Shchepkin spent his early career in a serf troupe but began to travel with a professional company in 1808, obtaining his freedom in 1821. By 1823 he was a member of the Maly troupe in Moscow, with which he remained the rest of his life. After 1832 he taught at the dramatic school and toured frequently throughout Russia. Shchepkin was a painstaking technician who strove for naturalness in acting. Because of his influence, ensemble effects were achieved at the Maly long before they were usual elsewhere in Russia. He initiated the practice of reading the play to the company before the roles were cast and guided other actors in their characterizations. He excelled in Gogol's comedy, and his natural style is said to have encouraged playwrights to draw more realistic characters.

In general the Russian theatre was very conservative in its scenic practices, and for the most part it continued to depend on a limited range of stock settings made up of wings and drops. The box set was introduced in the 1830s but it found little favor until much later in the century.

Opera, which had been primarily an aristocratic entertainment, began to win a wider following in the 1830s, when Mikhail Glinka (1804–1857) initiated the Russian school of composers. Nevertheless, foreign influence remained dominant throughout the century. Ballet was also under foreign influence. Between 1801 and 1829, Charles Didelot, a Frenchman, introduced Noverre's reforms into Russia. He emphasized vertical movement, replaced the soft shoe with one permitting difficult turns, introduced leotards, and shortened skirts. Foreign stars, such as Marie Taglioni (1804–1884), the most celebrated ballerina of her day, were imported beginning in the 1830s and gave further emphasis to technical excellence. Not until the late nineteenth century, however, was Russian ballet to be given its distinctive form.

FIG. 12.20
Interior of the Bolshoi Theatre, Moscow. From Barkhin, *Architektura Teatra* (Moscow, 1947).

LOOKING AT THEATRE HISTORY

Melodrama, like pantomime before it, brought to drama the kind of spectacular effects that since the Renaissance had been associated primarily with opera. Pixérécourt, the "father of melodrama," was a master of spectacle. The second act of his *Daughter of the Exile*, for example, includes a flood in which the heroine escapes by floating away on a plank. Here is a contemporary review of the production:

> The scenery of the second act must be considered a marvel of perspective and mechanics. The progressive heightening of the waves, the falling of snow and of rocks, the uprooting of trees, the balancing of the plank on the surface of the waters, all is a striking and realistic imitation.

Journal des Debats, March 16, 1810.

Spectacle became even more realistic with the introduction of moving panoramas and dioramas. Daguerre's dioramas *à double effet,* especially, created a great sensation, since on a single canvas, through the manipulation of painting and lighting, more than one picture could be made to appear and to change before one's eyes. These dioramas marked one step toward the development of the motion picture. Daguerre has left a detailed description of the process he used in creating these dioramas, of which only a few excerpts are given here. Other passages tell precisely how both painting and lighting were controlled:

> One indispensable essential is to employ [cloth] which is exceedingly transparent . . . it is necessary to prime it, on both sides, with at least two coats of parchment size. The first effect, which ought to be the clearer of the two, is executed on the right side of the canvas. . . . The second effect is painted on the wrong side of the canvas. . . . The first effect . . . is lighted . . . only by a light which comes from the front, while the second effect . . . receives its light . . . from behind only. . . . We may employ both lights at once, in order to modify certain portions of the picture.

L. J. M. Daguerre, *An Historical and Descriptive Account of the Various Processes of the Daguerreotype and the Diorama* (London, 1839), 81–86.

This was also an era of great actors, many of whom developed international followings much like those of movie stars today. One of the most famous was the French actress, Rachel. Here is a review of her performance in Racine's *Phaedra:*

> Her entrance as she appeared, wasting away with the fire that consumed her, standing on the verge of the grave, her face pallid, her eyes hot, her arms and hands emaciated, filled us with a ghastly horror. . . . In the second act, where she declares her passion, Rachel was transcendent. There was a subtle indication of the diseased passion, of its fiery but unhealthy—irresistible and yet odious—character, in the febrile energy with which she portrayed it. It was terrible in its vehemence and abandonment . . . when she left the scene our nerves were quivering with excitement almost unsupportable.

J. Foster and G. H. Lewes, *Dramatic Essays* (London, 1896), 84–85.

The fame of such actors created a desire to see them in person, and extensive tours were arranged for them. Soon lesser actors were emulating them, much to the detriment of resident companies, which began to disintegrate. Here are the American manager William Wood's comments on this situation:

> When the performance of great leading parts were claimed by Cooke or Kean as stars, the regulars [in the resident company] never, in my experience, showed dissatisfaction. . . . But when we had cast upon us, as stars . . . actors of all grades, the case became widely different. The companies here found, night after night, some new person they had never before heard of, announced in big letters—all their own plans deranged, themselves forced into extraordinary and severe study, and their whole time absorbed . . . merely that they might act as subsidiaries . . . to some foreign adventurer, who possessed no merit half so great as their own; while he took away in one night twice as much as they could earn as their whole weekly wages. . . . Accordingly men who, up to this time, had been perfectly contented with their wages, and with their home reputation of clever stock actors . . . now abandoned that safe position for the attractive honors of the star.

William B. Wood, *Personal Recollections of the Stage* (Philadelphia, 1855), 446–447.

13
English-Language Theatre in the Early Nineteenth Century

George III (reigned 1760–1820) had overseen perhaps the most remarkable period in British history. Under his rule the British consolidated the control they had had on India (since 1757), and added Canada (1763), Australia (1788), South Africa (1814), and a host of smaller territories to their overseas empire. George III also saw the American Revolution, the French Revolution, the Napoleonic Wars, and a host of revolutions that would lead, during the reign of George IV (1820–1830), to the independence of all Spanish colonies on the American continents.

TRENDS IN ENGLISH THEATRE, 1800–1843

In the years between 1790 and 1815, England, more than any other country, opposed France. (Its attempt to interrupt all shipping to France precipitated the War of 1812 with the United States.) The Industrial Revolution, which began in the late eighteenth century, had made England the leading manufacturing and trading nation of the world by the early nineteenth century. Nevertheless, the Napoleonic Wars severely strained English resources and thereby emphasized the long-standing need for social and political reforms. But as elsewhere, the post-Napoleonic

era was one of governmental conservatism. As a result, England underwent financial stress and social upheaval during the 1820s and 1830s. Fortunately, Britain was more flexible than other European countries, and made a number of significant parliamentary and labor reforms. Nevertheless, from the 1790s until about 1840 England was almost always in a state of unrest because of war, economic instability, urbanization, and social displacements.

Under William IV (reigned 1830–1837) the rapid construction of railroads and steamships, combined with improvements in road construction and the advent of the first working telegraph (1833), led to improvements in transportation and communication that were to have far-reaching effects on theatre. But it was under Victoria (reigned 1837–1901) that Britain developed the most extensive modern empire in the world.

The United States continued to be the destination for large numbers of English-speaking immigrants, and it experienced its greatest period of territorial expansion during this time. The Louisiana Purchase was made in 1803; Florida and the Oregon Territories were acquired from Spain in 1818, the Republic of Texas in 1845, and California, New Mexico, and Arizona in 1848. Except for a small portion of Arizona and New Mexico, all the contiguous territory it now possesses had been acquired by

FIG. 13.1

One of the many theatres built in London between 1810 and 1840, the Royal Coburg, as it looked when it opened in May 1818. Later called the Old Vic, it is still in use. From Wilkinson, *Londina Illustrata* (1825).

1850, more than tripling the nation's size. Politically, the country struggled to define the exact nature of republicanism, however, and the issue of slavery was the constant focal point in that struggle.

By 1800 London was the world's largest city, and by 1843 its population had doubled, to two million. During these years the working classes began to attend the theatre in large numbers for the first time and to exert important influences on it. The results were several.

First, the patent theatres were enlarged. The seating capacity of Covent Garden was increased in 1792 to about 3,000, and in 1794 Drury Lane was rebuilt to accommodate more than 3,600. Second, minor theatres were opened. The first were licensed in the 1780s by magistrates outside the City of Westminster (the official seat of government) under the provisions of the law of 1752. After 1804, when the Earl of Dartmouth became Lord Chamberlain, an impor-

tant change occurred. He interpreted the Licensing Act as authorizing minor theatres within the City of Westminster, so long as they did not infringe upon the rights of the patent houses. Consequently, beginning in 1807 he issued a number of permits for new theatres. By 1843 there were twenty-one theatres in the London area, as compared to six in 1800. Furthermore, the Lord Chamberlain authorized longer seasons for the Haymarket, originally restricted to five months during the summer. By 1812 it was open seven months, and by 1840 ten months. Third, the repertory was affected. While only the major houses (Covent Garden, Drury Lane, and the Haymarket) were authorized to perform regular drama, other theatres were restricted to the lesser forms and incidental entertainment. In an attempt to retain audiences in the face of the new competition, the patent theatres increased their offerings of minor drama. Furthermore, in seeking to cater to all tastes, the evening's bill was extended until it lasted five or six hours. Sometimes as many as three plays were performed on the same evening; a bill composed of two full-length plays, an afterpiece, and numerous variety acts was not unusual between 1820 and 1843. Many persons felt that the patent theatres had abdicated their responsibility for producing regular drama by adopting a repertory not unlike that seen in the minor houses. Consequently, around 1810 and again in the 1830s, attempts were made to establish a "third theatre" which would be devoted entirely to the standard repertory. Although nothing came of these efforts, they focused attention upon the need for reform. As the repertory of the major theatres changed, especially after 1810, a number of the former spectators deserted the drama for opera at the King's Theatre, where even the frequenters of the pit were required to wear formal evening dress. Much of the audience that remained faithful to drama seemed to care little for poetic plays, and by 1843 it was widely believed that Shakespeare's plays brought ruin at the box office.

Although the patent houses were free to perform the minor genres, other theatres could not play regular drama. Consequently, they sought loopholes in the Licensing Act which would allow them to compete more effectively with the major theatres. Two dramatic types, burletta and melodrama, provided a loophole. By 1800 burletta, imported into England in the mid-eighteenth century as a type of comic opera, had become such an ambiguous label that the Lord Chamberlain accepted as a burletta any work that had no more than three acts, each of which included at least five songs. This ambiguity was first exploited by Robert Elliston, manager of the Surrey Theatre. One of the finest actors of his day, Elliston was not content to perform in the usual fare of the minor theatres. Consequently, in 1809 he transformed Farquhar's *The Beaux' Stratagem* into a burletta and followed it with *Macbeth* presented as a "ballet of action." Thereafter, almost any work might be altered to meet the licensing requirements.

Melodrama, which most minor theatres were allowed to perform, offered a similar loophole. Characteristically it was written in three acts and was accompanied by a musical score. Thus, regular plays could be billed as melodramas if they were divided into three acts and if musical accompaniment was added. This ruse became so perfunctory that *Othello* is said to have been performed as a melodrama with the mere addition of a chord struck on the piano every five minutes.

Although minor theatres were occasionally penalized for such evasions, the distinctions between patent and minor theatres became increasingly blurred. The demand for reform became so insistent that action was at last taken by Parliament. In 1843 the Theatre Regulation Act abolished the privileges of the patent houses that had been in effect since the 1660s. Thereafter any licensed theatre could perform works of any type. The new law did not affect the demand that plays be licensed in advance by the Lord Chamberlain. This form of censorship was to remain in effect until 1968.

ENGLISH DRAMA TO THE 1850s

While most of the major English poets of the early nineteenth century wrote plays, few of their works were intended for production, and few had any success when presented. Most of the poetic plays written between 1800 and 1850 were neo-Elizabethan in subject matter and approach and sought to recapture Shakespeare's glory. Samuel Taylor Coleridge (1772–1834), the major theorist of romanticism in England, wrote *Remorse* (1813), William Wordsworth (1770–1850) *The Borderers* (1796), and John Keats (1795–1821) *Otho the Great* (1819). Percy Bysshe Shelley (1792–1822) was probably the best poetic dramatist of the time, but his plays *The Cenci* and *Prometheus Unbound* were not acted until much later in the century. *The Cenci* (1819), which tells of Beatrice Cenci's revenge upon her father for his inhuman behavior, comes closer to Jacobean drama than does any play of its period. George Gordon, Lord Byron (1788–1824), was the most successful of the romantic poets in the theatre. Not only did he write more plays, but more were suited to the stage. As a member of the governing committee of Drury Lane, Byron probably had more knowledge and interest in production than did his contemporaries. Nevertheless, only *Marino Faliero* (1821) was acted during his lifetime (and that over his objections), but all of his plays were eventually performed. *Sardanapalus* (1821) offered such later producers as Charles Kean irresistible opportunities for historical spectacle, while *Werner* (acted 1830), the story of a man destroyed by his obsession with revenge, became one of Macready's vehicles. Joanna Baillie's (1762–1851) poetic dramas, each focused on a specific passion such as jealousy or pride, were published in three volumes, *Plays on the Passions* (1798, 1802, 1812). Only one, *De Mountfort* (1800) won success on the stage.

Although Sir Walter Scott (1771–1832) had an abiding interest in the theatre and wrote several plays, his influence came primarily through his novels, most of which were adapted by others for performance. With their emphasis on local color and history, they helped to establish the vogue for the historical romance. Robert Browning (1812–1889), author of many "dramatic" poems, seemed ideally fitted for writing dramas and, at Macready's urging, he accepted the challenge. But *Stafford* (1837), *A Blot on the 'Scutcheon* (1843), and *Colombe's Birthday* (1853) gained no marked success.

If tragedy did not fare well, melodrama did. Thirty-six of Kotzebue's plays were translated into English, and *The Stranger* and *Pizarro* remained in the repertory throughout the nineteenth century. Melodrama also received considerable impetus from native playwrights, especially Matthew Gregory Lewis (1775– 1818), usually called "Monk" Lewis because of his famous novel, *Ambrosio, or the Monk* (1795). Dramatized many times, this novel and *The Castle Spectre* (1797) began a vogue for "Gothic" melodrama. Set in the Middle Ages, such plays often transpired in mysterious ruined castles or abbeys and featured outcasts, ghosts, long-lost relatives, and long-concealed crimes. In 1802 Thomas Holcroft (1745–1809) gave the trend toward melodrama new strength with *A Tale of Mystery* (an adaptation of Pixérécourt's *Coelina*), the first play in English to be labeled a melodrama. Soon this new form was attracting large audiences and thereafter they were a mainstay of the minor theatres.

The majority of melodramas were rather exotic, either because they were set in some remote time or place, or because they featured the supernatural or highly unusual. Astley's and the Royal Circus featured melodramas which incorporated daring feats of horsemanship. Dog dramas, featuring trained canines performing heroic acts, were also popular (though they

FIG. 13.3
An aquatic spectacle at Sadler's Wells Theatre where the stage was equipped with a water tank. From *Microcosm of London,* 3 (1902).

did not reach their peak until mid-century). The Sadler's Wells Theatre had a water tank installed in 1804 so that it might perform "aquatic" plays featuring sea battles and rescues from drowning. But Pierce Egan's *Tom and Jerry, or Life in London* (1821) began a trend toward melodramas of contemporary life and local color. Egan's work featured a number of well-known places in London and told a story based on contemporary events.

The trend begun by Egan was developed by Jerrold, Fitzball, and Buckstone. Douglas William Jerrold (1803–1857) began his playwriting career in 1821 and gained his greatest success with a series of "nautical" melodramas; *Black-Eyed Susan* (1829) was to become one of the most popular plays of the century. Although remembered primarily for his melodramas, Jerrold wrote many kinds of plays, including blank verse tragedy. Edward Fitzball (1792–1873) had dramatized a number of Scott's novels before turning to original compositions; soon his nautical melodramas rivaled those of Jerrold. One of the most prolific playwrights of the century, he is now remembered for initiating the vogue for melodramas based on actual crimes. His *Jonathan Bradford or the Murder at the Roadside Inn* (1833) had an initial run of 160 nights, a record not surpassed until 1860. Fitzball continued to turn out plays until his death. John Baldwin Buckstone (1802–1879), a popular

FIG. 13.2
An equestrian melodrama at Astley's Amphitheatre. Both the ring and the stage could be used for dramatic performances. From Wilkinson, *Londina Illustrata* (1825).

actor-manager, wrote or adapted more than 200 plays between the 1820s and the 1870s. His early work, especially *Luke the Laborer* (1826), helped to popularize "domestic" melodrama. Many of Buckstone's later plays were farces, pantomimes, or dramatizations of recent novels. Although the older exotic melodrama continued, domestic themes began to dominate after 1830.

While most melodrama made its greatest appeal to the unsophisticated theatregoer, the plays of Knowles and Bulwer-Lytton attracted a more discriminating audience with works that were both theatrically effective and critically acceptable. Actor-dramatist James Sheridan Knowles (1784–1862) first gained renown with *Virginius* (1820), soon a standard play in theatres throughout England and North America. Knowles consolidated his fame with *William Tell* (1825), *The Wife* (1833), and *The Hunchback* (1832). His success stemmed from a skillful blending of melodramatic stories with a pseudo-Shakespearean form. For many years he enjoyed a considerable critical and popular following. His successor was Edward George Bulwer-Lytton (1803–1873), who established "gentlemanly" melodrama as a recognizable form. Already noted for his novels, Bulwer-Lytton was persuaded by Macready to turn to playwriting. Three of his works, *The Lady of Lyons* (1838), *Richelieu* (1839), and *Money* (1840), which owe much to Macready's suggestions, held the stage throughout the nineteenth century. With "gentlemanly" melodrama, the theatre began to regain its former prestige with the upper classes.

ENGLISH THEATRICAL CONDITIONS, 1800–1843

Between 1800 and 1817, the English theatre maintained its stability largely because of the work of John Philip Kemble (1757–1823). When Kemble became acting manager of Drury Lane in 1788, it had fallen considerably from the height to which Garrick had lifted it. Richard Brinsley Sheridan, the manager, had devoted himself increasingly to politics but had failed to delegate sufficient authority to Thomas King, who ran the theatre in his absence. Although Kemble did much to reestablish the reputation of the Drury Lane, he tired of coping with crises induced by Sheridan's frequent financial difficulties, and in 1803 he moved to Covent Garden, where he remained until his retirement in 1817. During his tenure, Covent Garden became the leading theatre of the English-speaking world. Kemble's greatest trial as a manager came in 1809 at the opening of the newly completed Covent Garden (rebuilt at great expense after its destruction by fire in 1808). Kemble's

attempt to recover costs by raising entrance fees precipitated the "Old Price" riots that continued for sixty-one nights, despite the attempt of police and soldiers to intervene. The riots ended only after Kemble capitulated to the audience's demands.

By the time Kemble retired, England, as a result of the Napoleonic Wars, was in a financial crisis that was to last until 1840. Scarcely a theatrical management escaped bankruptcy between 1817 and 1843. The rapid decrease in income can be seen at Drury Lane, where receipts diminished from £80,000 in 1812–1813 to £43,000 in 1817–1818. Nevertheless, the owners of theatres were slow to lower their rental charges. At Drury Lane between 1819 and 1827, Robert Elliston paid £10,000 annually for his lease, and it was only in 1832, after Elliston and several of his successors had failed, that the rent was lowed to £6,000. Pressure on the managers was reduced somewhat by a decline in other expenses. At Covent Garden, nightly expenses fell from £300 in 1809 to £154 in 1836. Still between 1833 and 1835 the major theatres were in such straits that Alfred Bunn (1798–1860) was able to lease both Drury Lane and Covent Garden and run them with a single company. Of the patent houses, only the Haymarket, a small theatre free from major competition during the summer months, remained relatively prosperous.

Some of the difficulties during these years are explained by the greater financial outlay required by the increasingly elaborate spectacle. It is sometimes suggested that the enormous auditoriums made subtlety in acting impossible and shifted emphasis to visual effects. Covent Garden was destroyed by fire in 1808 and Drury Lane in 1809. In the new Covent Garden (1809) the distance from the stage to the back of the upper gallery was 104 feet, and at the new Drury Lane (1812) only slightly less. Such size, coupled with the growing interest in melodrama, local color, and history, undoubtedly encouraged greater emphasis upon the visual elements.

Increased concern for spectacle was evident as early as the 1790s, when Kemble began to mount Shakespearean revivals with the same care previously lavished upon minor drama by Garrick and De-Loutherbourg. The major designer of the Kemble era was William Capon (1757–1827), who came to the fore when the Drury Lane was reconstructed in 1794. This theatre had a stage 85 feet wide and 92 feet deep, with a proscenium opening 43 feet wide by 38 feet high. One of Capon's sets in 1799 showed the nave, choir, and side aisles of a fourteenth-century cathedral; it measured 36 feet in width, 52 feet in depth, and 37 feet in height. Capon continued as principal designer at Drury Lane until it burned in 1809, after which he worked at Covent Garden.

FIG. 13.4
Interior of Drury Lane as it appeared before it was destroyed by fire in 1809. From *Microcosm of London,* 1 (1902).

Some of his scenery was in use as late as 1840. Unlike DeLoutherbourg, Capon designed primarily for regular drama and was one of the first important advocates in England of historical accuracy in scenery. Nevertheless, consistency had not yet been attained, for often several different designers, each working independently, provided settings for a single play, and frequently one act was newly mounted while the others were performed in stock scenery.

Kemble's attitude toward scenery and costumes marks an important transition from the "generality" favored by the neoclassicists to the "individuality" advocated by the romantics. He advocated historical accuracy and individualizing detail, but applied it sporadically and inconsistently. Although he often clothed the major characters in pseudo-historical garments, for example, the minor personages usually wore stock costumes from the company's wardrobe. While his leading actress, Mrs. Siddons, was persuaded to discard her fashionable dress for tragedy, conventionalized "draperies" of no particular era were substituted for it. Kemble also always put theatrical effectiveness above archaeological accuracy. He set *Coriolanus* in the late Roman period because he thought audiences were unprepared to accept the architecture of early Rome, and for *King Lear* the costumes were given merely a "Saxon tendency."

During Kemble's lifetime, complex practical scenic pieces also increased markedly in number. Sheridan's *Pizarro* (1799), for example, required a gorge spanned by a bridge, which could be cut loose so that the hero

might escape from his would-be killers. Such devices became common as melodrama grew in popularity. In 1811, under the influence of equestrian drama, Kemble even employed a troupe of mounted cavalry. He also made increased use of processions, coronations, and other mass effects. By the time he retired in 1817, it was accepted that all drama should be "illustrated" as completely as possible.

Robert Elliston (1774–1831), manager of Drury Lane from 1819 to 1826, continued the emphasis on spectacle. His *King Lear* (1820) featured trees that actually bent in the wind and storm noises so realistic that Lear could not be heard. Elliston installed a water system to achieve greater illusion of fountains and waterfalls, and one of his principal designers, Clarkson Stanfield (1793–1867), introduced moving dioramas (stationary panoramas had been used in London theatres since about 1800).

Charles Kemble (1775–1854), brother of John Philip Kemble, managed Covent Garden from 1817 to 1832. A major step toward antiquarianism was taken when James Robinson Planché (1796–1880) persuaded him to use historically accurate costumes for every role in his 1823 production of Shakespeare's *King John*. Although the actors feared that they would be laughed at, the audience apparently welcomed the innovation, and in 1824 both historically accurate costumes and scenery were used for *Henry IV, Part I.* But in spite of the success of these productions, Kemble did not repeat the experiment until 1827, and it was not until Macready accepted it in 1837 that authenticity was consistently exploited. Thus, while Planché's work in 1823 must be considered a landmark, it did not bring an immediate revolution in theatrical practice.

FIG. 13.5
Setting by William Capon for J. P. Kemble's Shakespearean revivals at Covent Garden after 1809. From *The Magazine of Art* (1895).

FIG. 13.6
Costume design by J. R. Planché for Henry IV in Charles Kemble's production of 1824. From J. R. Planché, *Costume of Shakespeare's King Henry IV, Parts 1 and 2* (1824). Courtesy Lilly Library, Indiana University.

Planché continued to be a leader in the movement toward antiquarianism. Finding it difficult to obtain information for his costume designs, he undertook extensive research which resulted in his *History of British Costume* (1834), long the standard English work in this field. He continued his study of heraldry and was frequently consulted by producers. Thus, Planché not only provided impetus to authentic staging, but also supplied the information that made it possible.

By the 1830s it was assumed that each theatre would prepare a number of handsomely mounted productions each season. The increased financial outlay meant, however, that longer runs were required to justify the investment. Consequently, from this time the trend toward long runs accelerated, although it was not to be widely exploited until after 1850.

Between 1800 and 1843 a number of important actors appeared on the English stage. Until 1815 it was dominated by the Kemble family. Almost all of the twelve children of Roger Kemble (1721–1802), a provincial actor-manager, became actors, but major fame was achieved only by John Philip and Sarah Kemble Siddons (1755–1831). As an adult, John Philip Kemble was on the stage from 1776. After coming to London in 1783, he only gradually gained favor, but from 1790 until his retirement he was considered to be the leading actor of the English-speaking world.

Mrs. Siddons was on the stage from childhood; attaining no success at Drury Lane in 1775, she returned to the provinces until 1782. From her reappearance in London until her retirement in 1812, she was recognized as the greatest tragic actress of her day.

Kemble and Mrs. Siddons established a style usually called "classical" because of its emphasis upon stateliness, dignity, and grace. (In its major outlines, it resembled Weimar classicism.) In Kemble, this style often gave the impression of coldness, and he was truly excellent only in such roles as Cato, Coriolanus, Cardinal Wolsey, Brutus, Rolla, and the Stranger. His characterizations were always worked out studiously and sustained with care. As a result, he was often accused of self-consciousness. Mrs. Siddons, while attaining a comparable dignity, rose far above her brother because of her greater emotional intensity. She was especially noted for her playing of Lady Macbeth, Queen Katharine (in *Henry VIII*), Volumnia (in *Coriolanus*), and Mrs. Haller (in *The Stranger*).

Other members of the Kemble family included Stephen (1758–1822), who acted primarily in the provinces but became famous in London for his

FIG. 13.7
Engraving based on a painting by G. H. Harlow (1819) showing various members of the Kemble family in Shakespeare's *Henry VIII*, although they probably never appeared together in the play. Front right, Mrs. Siddons as Queen Katherine; at left John Philip Kemble as Cardinal Wolsey; seated at table center Charles Kemble as Cromwell; upstage center Stephen Kemble as Henry VIII. Courtesy Theatre Museum, Victoria and Albert Museum, London.

Falstaff; Eliza Kemble Whitlock (1761–1836), who, after performing in the provinces, migrated to the United States in 1794 to become one of the most noted actresses in the new country; and Charles, who excelled as the young heroes of John Philip Kemble's productions and later managed the Covent Garden theatre. Much of Charles Kemble's later fame was linked to his daughter Frances Anne Kemble (1809–1893), a popular leading lady from her debut in 1829 until her retirement in 1834. Charles Kemble retired in 1836 and later served as Examiner of Plays for the Lord Chamberlain.

The Kemble school of acting was continued by Charles Mayne Young (1777–1856), who succeeded to many of John Philip Kemble's roles until his retirement in 1832; J. W. Wallack (1791–1864), who became a leading figure in the American theatre; and Eliza O'Neill (1791–1827), considered by many to be Mrs. Siddon's true successor.

The classical approach was challenged after 1814 by the romantic school. Although Edmund Kean was the greatest exponent of the new style, he was preceded in it by George Frederick Cooke (1756–1812). On the stage from 1776, Cooke did not appear in London until 1800 when his powers were already declining. Addicted to alcohol, Cooke was unreliable and sometimes disappeared for long periods but, when in full possession of his powers, no one could so captivate an audience. At his best in villainous roles such as Richard III and Iago, he cared little for grace or nobility but was unequaled in portraying hypocrisy and evil. He favored realistic acting and even wrote out poetic dialogue as prose so as to avoid emphasizing rhythm or rhyme. His last years, 1810 to 1812, were spent in the United States; as the first major English actor to undertake a starring tour of the United States, he established a precedent that was to have far-reaching consequences.

If Cooke prepared the way for romantic acting, Edmund Kean (1787–1833) perfected the style. On the stage as the child prodigy Master Carey, Kean began his adult career at fourteen in a provincial company. He did not appear in London until he was twenty-seven, but from his debut there in 1814 he was considered a major star and, after Kemble's retirement, the foremost actor of his day. Like Cooke, he excelled in somewhat villainous roles, such as Richard III, Shylock, Sir Giles Overreach (in *A New Way to Pay Old Debts*), and Barabas (in *The Jew of Malta*); he seldom appeared in comedy. He worked out every movement and intonation with care. Once set, a role was much the same at every performance, although Kean sometimes revised a characterization, and his intentions were often subverted by his alcoholism. In later years, he was inclined to save his strength for great moments and to slight the remainder of a role. Unlike Kemble, Kean did not value grace and dignity; he was willing to cringe or crawl on the floor if he thought it necessary to convey the proper effect. Thus, he tended to emphasize realism of emotion, whereas Kemble had sought to convey an ideal nobility. Kean's style pleased the new audiences, but his erratic behavior had lowered his popularity considerably before his death in 1833.

Largely because of Kean's example, starring engagements became the norm for major performers after 1815. In London, Kean was never a regular member of an acting company after the early 1820s. Instead, he frequently demanded £50 or more for each time he performed. (Kemble had never received more than £36 a week, and Mrs. Siddons never rose above £30 pounds a week.) His demonstration that a star could command a high salary with a limited repertory established a precedent followed by many of his successors.

Although no comic actors achieved the lasting fame enjoyed by Kemble and Kean, many won popular acclaim. In addition to his importance as a manager, Robert Elliston was universally admired as the

FIG. 13.8
Edmund Kean as Richard III. A contemporary engraving.

FIG. 13.9
A poorly attended benefit performance in an English provincial theatre.
Note the many architectural and staging features of the early nineteenth
century theatre. From Pierce Egan, *The Life of an Actor* (1825).

young hero of comedy and later in such character
roles as Falstaff. Charles Mathews the Elder (1776–
1835) was noted especially for his "At Homes," in
which he portrayed a succession of character types
based upon observation. Beginning around 1808, this
superior kind of mimicry made him a leading attraction throughout England and took him to the
United States for tours in 1822 and 1834. Above all,
however, it was the era of the low comedian. For
the first time, such performers as Joseph Munden
(1758–1832), John Liston (1776–1846), and Robert
Keeley (1793–1869) commanded salaries equaling
or exceeding those of major serious actors. Other
outstanding stars included Tyrone Power (1795–
1841), noted for his comic Irish portrayals, and T. P.
Cooke (1786–1864), famous as the hero of nautical
melodramas.

Audiences were also attracted by the eccentric and
unusual, and the early nineteenth century brought a
craze for child actors, of which the most famous was
William Henry West Betty (1791–1874), often called
the Young Roscius. When Master Betty came to
London in 1804 after winning fame in the provinces,
his following became so great that Kemble and Mrs.
Siddons gave up playing for a time. On one occasion, Parliament was adjourned so that its members

might see him perform. Betty's fame soon passed,
and after 1811 he sank into obscurity.

Except during starring engagements, actors were
still employed by the season at a weekly salary and a
yearly benefit. Although "lines of business" continued to be the norm, specialization increased. After
1809, Kemble employed the equivalent of three
troupes, one for serious drama, one for comedy, and
one for music and dance. Thereafter, the trend in
large companies was to hire actors who were outstanding in a limited range, whereas diversity was
achieved because each troupe included so many specialized performers.

Rehearsals were still perfunctory. Although Kemble aimed at ensemble effects, he did little beyond
holding line rehearsals, probably because by this time
conventional groupings and movement served in
most instances. It was customary for actors to space
themselves an arm's length apart so as not to inhibit
gestures. Because the footlights had a large cluster at
center stage ("the rose"), actors moved to this bright
spot each time they had an important speech. After
delivering the speech, they then moved three steps
to the left or right to make way for the next speaker.
This continuous shifting of places was typical of acting through most of the early nineteenth century.

MACREADY AND VESTRIS

In the 1830s two English managers, Macready and Vestris, began to bring order out of the near-chaos that had reigned since about 1815 and to lay the foundations for the recovery of the theatre.

William Charles Macready (1793–1873) had no intention of going on the stage until a financial crisis in his father's theatre at Birmingham forced him to leave school in 1810. By 1816 he was playing in London, where he was soon considered a serious rival to Kean, although it was not until Kean's death that he was acclaimed England's foremost actor. As a performer, Macready combined much of Kemble's dignity and studiousness with Kean's fire. Unlike Kemble, however, he sought to give an illusion of everyday life and included many domestic and familiar details in his stage business. He was famous for his lengthy pauses, during which he seemed to reflect and compose his responses.

Macready's profound dissatisfaction with theatrical conditions eventually led him into management as the only effective means of reforming them. From 1837 to 1839 he managed Covent Garden and from 1841 to 1843 Drury Lane, each with more artistic than financial success. In spite of difficulties, however, Macready introduced many innovations which were to form the basis of later practices.

Macready was one of the early directors in the modern sense. He did not allow actors to choose their own stage positions, but sought instead to prescribe positions for them. He was often derided and defied, but he did not give up. Furthermore, Macready insisted upon acting during rehearsals rather than "saving himself" for performances, the usual practice of the day. While he did not convert all of his company, his superior success as a performer and director won many converts.

Macready paid attention to every detail of his productions. Although he presented stock plays which were repeated many times each season, he introduced and lavished attention upon a few new productions each year. He was the first English director who consistently sought historical accuracy in both costumes and scenery. His usual designer was Charles Marshall (1806–1880), one of the finest landscape artists of the day, but he also employed many other noted designers. For *Henry V,* Clarkson Stanfield designed a moving diorama to illustrate the sea voyage from Southampton to Harfleur, and Col. Hamilton Smith (1776–1859), a noted antiquarian, was often consulted on costumes.

Macready sought to improve the repertory. He placed considerable emphasis upon Shakespeare's plays and claimed much credit for restoring the original texts, although he was not always scrupulous in this matter. He persuaded some of the foremost literary figures of his time to write for the stage and from these efforts came "gentlemanly" melodrama. Macready also considered it important to perform no work more than three times a week, regardless of its popularity. (From this policy stemmed many of his financial difficulties.)

Macready maintained a company of high quality. Helen Faucit (1817–1898), an actress of the Kemble school who made her London debut in 1836, was generally considered the finest actress of the day. Mrs. Mary Warner (1804–1854) was recognized as the leading performer of such mature roles as Lady Macbeth, and Samuel Phelps, soon to attain fame as a manager, was second only to Macready in the company.

Continually disappointed in his efforts to achieve a stable theatre of high quality, Macready gave up management in 1843 and thereafter was a touring star. His last appearance in the United States in 1849 was marred by the Astor Place Riot, stemming from his rivalry with Edwin Forrest, during which twenty-two people were killed. Macready retired in 1851.

Whereas Macready's influence came through his productions of regular drama, Vestris's most significant work was done with minor forms. Born Lucia Elizabetta Bartolozzi (1797–1856), in 1813 she married Armand Vestris (1788–1825), a famous dancer of the time. In 1815 she went on the stage, playing in both London and Paris. She achieved her first outstanding success in a "breeches role" in *Giovanni in London* (1820), a burlesque of Mozart's *Don Giovanni.* She remained one of the most popular per-

FIG. 13.10

Macready's production of *King Lear,* 1838. Macready at center as Lear; to his left Priscilla Horton as the Fool (often played by women in the nineteenth century). From George Scharf, *Recollections of the Scenic Effects of Covent Garden Theatre, 1838–1839* (1839).

FIG. 13.11

Mme Vestris and Charles Mathews the Younger (both at left) in W. B. Bernard's *The Conquering Game* at the Olympic Theatre, 1832. The set is considered to be one of the first box sets on the English stage. Drawing from the title page of the acting edition, *Duncombe's British Theatre,* 35 (c. 1865).

formers of light comedy and burlesque until her retirement in 1854.

Vestris's importance, however, stems from her work as a manager, notably at the Olympic Theatre from 1831 to 1839. Here she had the assistance of J. R. Planché, who wrote many of the plays in her repertory, which was restricted to burlesques, extravaganzas, and similar minor types. At this time, the burlesque was a broad caricature of popular drama, myth, or current events. In its original form the extravaganza was a whimsical treatment of a myth or fairy tale placing special emphasis upon dance and spectacle. Both burlesque and extravaganza usually made considerable use of music. Because of their common characteristics, they were eventually intermingled and the type designations lost their specificity. Burlesque seems to have appealed to the nineteenth-century taste for broad humor, while extravaganza was a precursor of musical comedy. Both were extremely popular, especially between 1830 and 1870. Planché, one of the most prolific writers of these forms, turned out about 175. With their whimsy and wordplay, Planché's works were to be a major influence on the comic operas of Gilbert and Sullivan.

As a manager, Vestris is important for several reasons. First, she paid close attention to all elements of production and coordinated them into an integrated whole. Second, she gave special consideration to spectacle and is usually credited with introducing the box set into England. Although some versions of it had been used previously, Vestris was probably the first English producer to use this type of setting with some consistency; she may also have been the first to enclose the acting area completely. There is much dispute over the date when the box set was introduced at the Olympic, but 1832 seems most likely. By 1834 it had been seen at Drury Lane and by 1837 was in use at Covent Garden. Nevertheless, the box set remained something of a novelty and was not widely adopted until after 1870.

Not only did Vestris use box sets, she equipped them like rooms in real life. Rugs were laid on the floor, knobs were attached to doors, and bookcases, books, and bric-a-brac were included to give the appearance of reality. This care extended to costumes. With Planché's encouragement, Vestris substituted garments like those worn in real life for the ridiculously exaggerated costumes that had been typical in burlesque. Thus, she was the first producer to treat minor drama with the respect formerly reserved for the classics.

Vestris was also instrumental in simplifying the evening's bill when she curtailed her offerings so that the program ended no later than 11 P.M., a drastic measure since programs at this time usually lasted until 1 or 2 A.M. The popularity of the innovation began the trend that eventually led to the one-play bill.

In 1838 Vestris gave up the Olympic Theatre and married Charles Mathews the Younger (1803–1878), a performer of light comedy roles in her company. Together they managed Covent Garden from 1839 to 1842. Now able to present regular drama, Vestris staged a number of influential Shakespearean productions using virtually uncut texts. Her *A Midsummer Night's Dream,* with sets by John Grieve, was especially influential, in part because she cast herself as Oberon, thus beginning a long tradition of having that role played by a woman. From 1847 to 1856, she and her husband managed the Lyceum, where they were assisted by William Roxby Beverley (c. 1814–1889), one of the finest designers of the day. Their insistence on the highest quality in every detail created financial difficulties, and both managerial ventures ended in bankruptcy. Nevertheless, Vestris' reforms were to inspire others and to produce important results in the 1860s.

Thus, by 1850 the English theatre was in a state of transition. The Theatre Regulation Act of 1843 had removed many obstacles to initiative and innovation, and a marked change was becoming evident.

THEATRE IN NORTH AMERICA, 1781–1815

In the United States, theatrical performances resumed as soon as the Revolutionary War fighting ended in 1781 (the war officially ended in 1783). The first professional performances, after hostilities ceased, were given in 1781 at Annapolis and Baltimore by Thomas Wall, a former member of Douglass's troupe. Irish actors Dennis Ryan and his wife joined Wall's company in 1782. By 1783 Ryan had assumed control of the "American Company of Comedians," which played between New York and Charleston until 1785. In that year, another former member of Douglass's players, John Henry (1738–1794), who had returned from Jamaica in 1782, formed the "Old American Company" with Lewis Hallam, Jr., who had returned from Jamaica in 1784. They performed at the John Street Theatre in New York, where until 1794 they were the new country's major troupe and the nucleus of a permanent theatre in that city.

Between 1794 and 1815, however, Philadelphia was to be the dominant theatrical center. It began with little promise, for the prohibition against acting, instituted in 1774, was not rescinded until 1789. In 1791 Thomas Wignell (1753–1803), Hallam and Henry's principal low comedian, and Alexander Reinagle, a musician, set out to establish a company there. Desiring to create a theatre of high quality, they erected the Chestnut Street Theatre, the finest in North America. Designed by Inigo Richards, one of England's leading scene designers and Wignell's brother-in-law, it seated about 1,200 and had a stage 71 feet deep with a proscenium opening about 36 feet wide. While it was being built, Wignell sailed for England, where he engaged the best company yet seen in America. Among his recruits were Eliza Kemble Whitlock, sister of John Philip Kemble and Mrs. Siddons; Mrs. Oldmixon (?–1835/36), a favorite singer at Covent Garden; and James Fennell (1766–1816), an actor of enviable reputation both in Edinburgh and London.

The troupe was further strengthened in 1796 with the addition of Mrs. Merry, Warren, and Cooper. Anne Brunton Merry (1768–1808) had been the leading actress at Covent Garden before retiring on her marriage in 1792. Financial reverses soon made it necessary for her to return to the stage, but the unavailability of a suitable engagement in England brought her to the United States, where she remained at the head of her profession until her death at the age of forty. After her first husband died, she

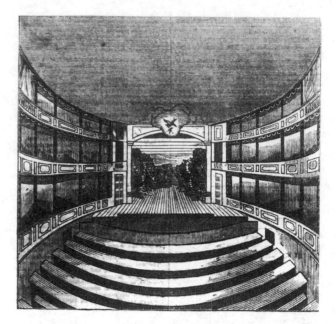

FIG. 13.12
Chestnut Street Theatre, Philadelphia, 1794. A plate published in *New York Magazine*, 1794. Courtesy Hoblitzelle Theatre Arts Collection, University of Texas at Austin.

married successively Wignell and then William Warren (1767–1832), an actor of old men's roles, who was connected with the Chestnut Street Theatre from 1796 until 1829 and who from 1806 until 1827 shared in its management. Thomas Abthorpe Cooper (1776–1849), one of England's most promising young actors, came to the United States in 1796 because he was unable to find a suitable engagement at home. Within a few years he was considered North America's leading actor. Essentially a tragic performer, he popularized the Kemble style in the United States. In 1797 Wignell added John Bernard (1756–1828) to his troupe. A performer of heroes in high comedy, Bernard had played at Covent Garden and elsewhere before coming to the United States. In Philadelphia, Boston, New York, and Montreal, Bernard did much to raise the level of performance before returning to England in 1819. With this superior company and under sound management, the Chestnut Street Theatre forged to the front. Its high standards were maintained by Wignell and Reinagle's successors, Warren and William Wood (1779–1861), joint managers of the company from 1810 to 1826.

The secondary position of the New York theatre between 1794 and 1815 is explained in part by dissensions within its company. In 1792 John Hodgkinson (c. 1765–1805), a versatile and ambitious English provincial actor, joined the troupe, and by 1794 he had replaced Henry in the management. By this time,

Hallam's popularity was declining, and his jealousy of Hodgkinson seems to have interfered with the orderly operation of the theatre. Perhaps for this reason, William Dunlap (1766–1839), the leading American playwright of the period, was induced to join the management. Shortly afterward, Hallam gave up his share, as did Hodgkinson in 1798, although both continued to act with the company and to create dissension. Thus, by the time Dunlap became sole manager in 1798, the troupe was in serious difficulty despite attempts to strengthen it with new talent. In 1793 Mrs. Charlotte Melmoth (1749–1823), an actress who had won considerable fame at Covent Garden and Drury Lane, had arrived to play principal tragic roles, and in 1795, Joseph Jefferson I (1774–1832), a popular comic actor who was to found an important theatrical family, joined the company. In spite of these and other additions, factions within the troupe made it difficult to maintain discipline and to achieve high artistic standards.

The New York theatre had also been weakened financially by Hodgkinson's insistence upon taking the company to play in New England and by competition from the Chestnut Street troupe, which still made occasional visits to New York. Furthermore, the John Street Theatre was inadequate and a new home had to be built. In 1798 the Park Theatre, destined to be New York's leading theatre until the 1840s, was opened. As sole manager, Dunlap struggled along until 1805, when bankruptcy overtook him. In 1807 Thomas A. Cooper became manager, and the Park entered a period of prosperity, especially after 1808–1809 when Cooper sold a share in the company to Stephen Price (1783–1840), a lawyer and businessman who proved to be a skillful manager. After Price demonstrated his abilities, Cooper spent an increasing amount of time on starring tours, and by 1815 had given up management altogether.

It was Cooper and Price who did most to popularize tours by starring actors, a practice that would eventually undermine resident troupes. Although leading actors had played short engagements with companies other than their own since about 1800, it was Cooper and Price's importation of George Frederick Cooke in 1810 that created a demand for stars of the first magnitude. Cooper and Price served as Cooke's agents in the United States and arranged engagements in Boston, Philadelphia, and Baltimore. This tour was so profitable that others were inevitable, although the War of 1812 (the American portion of the Napoleonic conflicts then underway in Europe) prevented immediate successors.

The 1790s also introduced the professional theatre in Boston where the Puritan outlook until that time had been able to outlaw it. Performances seem to have begun in 1792, although the prohibition against acting was not actually lifted until 1793 when the Federal Street Theatre was erected and Charles Stuart Powell (1748–1811) assembled an inferior company for it in England. Managements changed often and conditions remained unsettled until 1802, when Snelling Powell (1774–1843) assumed control. The company was especially strong between 1806 and 1811, when John Bernard shared in the management and attracted a number of outstanding players.

Charleston emerged as the fourth important theatrical center of the 1790s. While the Ryan-Wall troupe had played in Charleston as early as 1785, no continuing company settled there until 1795, when John Joseph Sollee assumed control of the City Theatre. Much of the vitality of the Charleston theatre came from the influx of French refugees, both at the time of the French Revolution and following the slave uprising in Santo Domingo in 1793. In the 1790s many plays were performed in French, and

FIG. 13.13
Final scene of Tyler's *The Contrast* (1787). The Yankee character Jonathan is seen at center. From the first edition of the play (1790). Courtesy Humanities Research Center, University of Texas at Austin.

many outstanding actors were of French origin. Perhaps the most important French artist was Alexandre Placide (c. 1750–1812), a dancer, acrobat, and pantomimist from the Parisian fair and boulevard theatres, who appeared with all of the major troupes in America before becoming manager of the Charleston theatre from 1798 until 1812.

By the 1790s, then, the theatre was firmly established along the Atlantic seaboard, where most of the nation's four million inhabitants were concentrated. Four main circuits were established: the Charleston troupe controlled all of the towns northward to Richmond; the Philadelphia troupe controlled Baltimore, Annapolis, and later Washington; the New York company toured for a time in the adjacent area, but after 1800 tended to remain fixed; and the Boston troupe dominated New England. While there were other lesser ones, these were the principal companies until 1815.

After 1790, the major troupes abandoned the sharing arrangement in favor of salaries and a yearly benefit, although lesser groups continued the older tradition through much of the nineteenth century. Performances were still given only three times a week, and the length of seasons in each town was variable, since most troupes toured and yellow fever and the discomfort of winter cold and summer heat often required the suspension of playing.

For the most part the repertory was English. Nevertheless, American playwrights, notably Tyler, Dunlap, and Payne, laid the foundations for a native drama. Royall Tyler (1757–1826) is remembered now primarily for *The Contrast* (1787), the first American comedy to be professionally produced. Owing much to Sheridan's plays, it is saved from mere imitativeness by the Yankee servant, Jonathan, whose frank and naive responses to New York social life illuminate the manners of the period.

Tyler's success may have inspired William Dunlap to turn to playwriting. Dunlap had spent the years between 1784 and 1787 in England and had seen most of the important performers and plays of the time. After the success of *The Father* (1789), he went on to write some sixty plays, at least thirteen of which were adapted from works by Kotzebue. His most famous original drama, *André* (1798), is based on a true incident involving a British spy during the Revolutionary War. The majority of Dunlap's plays were written before 1812, after which he devoted his time primarily to painting. Dunlap is also important for his *History of the American Theatre* (1832) and the first history of American art (1834).

John Howard Payne (1791–1852) came to public attention when only fourteen years old as the publisher of *The Thespian Mirror,* a critical journal. In the following year, his first play, *Julia* (1806), was acted at the Park Theatre, and in 1809 he made his acting debut, billed as a child prodigy. With Stephen Price as his manager, he enjoyed a considerable vogue for a short time, but by 1811 his popularity had waned. In 1813 he went to England, where he spent the next twenty years as dramatist and critic. Payne wrote or adapted between fifty and sixty plays. His best-known plays were *Brutus* (played by Edmund Kean in 1818), *Charles II* (performed by Charles Kemble in 1824), and *Clari* (1823), famous for the song, "Home, Sweet Home." Payne was America's first internationally successful dramatist. After 1832, he ceased writing for the stage.

THE EXPANDING AMERICAN THEATRE, 1815–1850

Following the War of 1812 the westward movement of American settlement accelerated. As the United States acquired the territories that would soon link it to the Pacific Ocean, settlers began to move into this new territory and the theatre followed. The first theatres were community theatres with performances by local amateurs. But the French had established a significant professional theatre in New Orleans by 1791. In 1810 the James Douglass company came to Lexington, Kentucky, from Montreal, and the William Turner troupe split off from this organization to establish a theatre in Cincinnati, Ohio, shortly thereafter.

But the first major step toward establishing a professional theatre in the "West" came in 1815 when Samuel Drake (1769–1854) took a company overland from Albany to Pittsburgh and down the Ohio River to Kentucky. Here Drake established a circuit, including Lexington, Louisville, and Frankfort, although he ventured at times into Ohio, Indiana, Tennessee, and Missouri. His scenery was designed to meet all situations. An adjustable cut-drop served as a proscenium that could be erected in any large room; a roll drop served as a front curtain; three sets of wings (one for exteriors, one for fancy interiors, and a third for plain interiors) and six roll drops (garden, street, wood, palace, parlor, and kitchen) served all scenic demands. Plays were altered so that they could be performed by his company of ten actors, who also doubled in backstage capacities. Drake's work is typical of all the pioneers who came after him, for like the Hallams he improvised to meet whatever situation he encountered and remained in each town as long as attendance permitted. Typically, troupes began by touring over a large area and, as the population increased, confined themselves to an ever smaller territory until touring could be given up altogether.

Drake soon had a number of competitors. The most important between 1820 and 1840 was James H. Caldwell (1793–1863), an English light comedian who came to America in 1816. Appearing first in Charleston and Richmond, he moved to New Orleans in 1820. Between 1825 and 1835, Caldwell dominated the theatre in the Mississippi Valley, for he controlled theatres in Natchez, St. Louis, Nashville, and elsewhere. Thus, Caldwell could offer attractive contracts to touring stars as they came to include the West in their tours around 1830. After suffering serious financial losses during the depression of 1837, he gave up his theatrical interests in 1843.

Caldwell was succeeded by Ludlow and Smith. Noah Ludlow (1795–1886) came west with Drake, and in 1817 set off to tour through Tennessee, Alabama, and elsewhere, giving the first theatrical performances ever seen in many areas. He alternated between management and acting engagements until 1835, when he formed a partnership with Solomon Smith (1801–1869), who had begun his acting career in 1823 and had played for a number of managers in the West before joining Ludlow. Between 1835 and 1853 they dominated the St. Louis theatre, controlled the Mobile theatre until 1840, and from 1843 to 1853 succeeded to Caldwell's position

of preeminence in New Orleans. Thus, during the 1840s they were the most powerful managers in the West. Ludlow and Smith are also important for having written accounts of their experiences, major sources of information about the "frontier" theatre.

This westward expansion was facilitated by improvements in transportation. During the early nineteenth century canals and toll roads were constructed; in 1830 the first railroad began operation, and others soon followed. But during this period the most common mode of travel was by water. The steamboat was invented in 1807, and by 1846 some 1,200 steamboats were in operation on the Mississippi and its tributaries alone.

Most theatres in the West were situated on rivers easily reached by boat. Few were located north of the Ohio River. Chicago did not see a professional production until 1833 and had no permanent theatre until 1847. Small itinerant companies were to be found almost anywhere, however, for just as the new territory provided a buffer against financial crises and overpopulation in the East, so too it offered a chance to actors who had been unsuccessful in the major theatrical centers. Most itinerant companies set up temporary theatres in each town they visited. In the 1830s, however, a new answer, the showboat, was conceived. While actors had long traveled by water, no one seems to have thought of fitting out a boat as a theatre until 1831, when William Chapman (1764–1839), an English actor who had come to the United States in 1827, converted a flatboat and gave performances on it while floating downstream from Pittsburgh to New Orleans. Unfortunately, flatboats had to be abandoned when they reached the end of the trip, and it was not until 1836 that a steamboat, which could return up-river, was used to tow showboats both up and down stream. Showboats were eminently practical, for they allowed traveling companies to take well-equipped theatres wherever there was a navigable river. Interrupted by the Civil War, showboating resumed immediately afterward. The most lavish "floating palaces" were in service between 1875 and 1900, when A. B. French, E. A. Price, and E. E. Eisenbarth dominated the river. Showboats continued in regular use until about 1925, after which they became quaint relics.

While the frontier was being settled, the eastern cities continued to grow. The population of New York increased from 60,000 in 1800 to 312,710 in 1840, and Philadelphia grew from 41,000 in 1800 to 93,665 in 1840. Much of this growth can be attributed to the rapid industrialization of the eastern United States after 1820.

The demand for theatrical entertainment resulting from this growth was met in several ways. Existing

FIG. 13.14

Advertisement for a showboat circus in 1853. From Hulbert, *The Ohio River* (1906).

FIG. 13.15
Auditorium of a showboat, the Dixiana, c. 1920 at the end of the showboating era. From the Robert Downing Collection, Hoblitzelle Theatre Arts Collection, University of Texas at Austin.

theatres were enlarged. In Philadelphia the Chestnut Street Theatre, which originally seated 1,200, was remodeled in 1805 to hold 2,000, and the Park Theatre in New York was enlarged in 1807 to accommodate 2,372. After both theatres burned in 1820, they were rebuilt for audiences of between 2,000 and 2,500. In New York the Bowery Theatre, built in 1826, seated 3,000. The number of weekly performances was also increased. In 1820 the Park Theatre began to play six times a week, a move which was adopted in 1823 by the Chestnut Street Theatre. Others soon accepted the new trend.

New companies were also established. By 1825 there were about twenty resident troupes in the United States, and by 1850 about thirty-five. In addition, there were countless temporary or itinerant groups. In the major cities of the East, expansion followed a typical pattern. Usually a second theatre began as an amphitheatre or circus, which occasionally added a theatrical production to its offering, and then progressed to a full season of plays. New York gained its second theatre in 1812, when a circus was converted into the Olympic Theatre (later called the Anthony Street and then Pavilion Theatre). By the 1830s New York had four theatres, and the number increased steadily thereafter. In spite of competition, the Park Theatre retained its preeminence. By 1815 the management had passed to Stephen Price and Edmund Simpson (1784–1848), an English actor who came to New York in 1809. After 1840 Simpson was sole manager until 1848, the year in which the Park Theatre burned, thus ending its dominance of New York theatrical life. One of the most ambitious of the Park's competitors was the Bowery The-

atre, the largest in the country when it opened in 1826. It soon turned to melodramas so gory that it came to be called the "slaughter house." When it was rebuilt in 1845 it could seat 4,000 persons.

A similar pattern can be seen in Philadelphia. In 1812 a former circus began to offer occasional dramatic entertainments and later became the Walnut Street Theatre. When the Arch Street Theatre opened in 1828, a three-way struggle for supremacy left all of the companies weakened. William Wood, who had left the Chestnut Street Theatre in 1826, headed the Arch Street Theatre, but both he and Warren, who had continued to manage the Chestnut Street, were bankrupt before the season of 1828–1829 ended. Both then retired. Nevertheless, after 1828 Philadelphia usually had at least three theatres in operation. The Chestnut Street's preeminence passed to the Arch Street during the 1830s, and after 1850 the Walnut Street came to the fore. The Chestnut Street was closed in 1855.

In Boston the Federal Street Theatre encountered its first competition in 1827 when the Tremont Street Theatre was opened. The two companies were amalgamated in 1829, but new competition appeared in

FIG. 13.16
The Park Theatre, New York, 1822. On stage are Charles Mathews the Elder and Ellen Johnson in *Monsieur Tonson*. Courtesy of the New York Historical Society, New York.

1832 with the opening of the National Theatre. Thereafter, Boston always had more than one troupe. The most important company was to be that of the Boston Museum. Opened in 1841 as a collection of sideshow exhibits, the Museum included a music salon in which short entertainments were given. By 1843 regular plays were being offered, and in 1846, following the enormous popularity of *The Drunkard* (1844), a melodrama written by the company's stage manager, William H. Smith (1806–1872), a regular theatre was erected. This was to house one of North America's leading companies until 1893.

In New Orleans, English-language companies usually performed at the Orleans Theatre, home of the French troupe, and alternated performance nights with that company until 1824, when the American (or Camp Street) Theatre opened. This new theatre, which was equipped with gas lighting two years earlier than any theatre in New York, was to have a major rival after 1835, when the St. Charles Theatre was completed. Perhaps the most magnificent theatre in America at that time, the St. Charles certainly had the largest stage (90 by 95 feet). After 1835 the rivalry between companies in New Orleans was intense.

During this period the theatre in Canada slowly built on the success of the garrison theatres of the late eighteenth century. A company headed by the Scottish actor known only as Mr. Ormsby built the first theatre in Montreal in 1804. In 1807 the 600 seat New Theatre was built there by an English actor, Mr. Prigmore. In 1810 many of the best actors in the city were recruited for a company headed by English actor James Douglass to start a theatre in Lexington, Kentucky, apparently the first professional company west of the Alleghenies. This troupe included William Turner, who soon formed a second troupe in Cincinnati. Royal circuses were built in both Montreal and Quebec in 1824 for the exhibition of trick riding and hot-air ballooning, but both were often used as theatres in the evenings, and the first professional French company to tour these cities (headed by Scévola Vistor) played these circuses in 1827. Toronto (called York until 1834) recorded its first theatrical performances in 1809. But it was not until the Erie Canal opened in 1825, providing a direct link to New York, that touring companies and star performers from England, France, and the United States began to include regular stops in Canada. The Theatre Royal, Montreal, with an audience capacity of over 1,000, marked the coming of age for Canadian theatre when it opened in 1825. It had an American company (supplemented by local talent) under the management of Fredrick Brown (*c.* 1794–1838). Edmund Kean played there in 1826, Charles Kean and Edwin Forest in

1831, Charles and Fanny Kemble in 1833, and William Charles Macready in 1844. This theatre was replaced by a new Theatre Royal in 1847 with seating for 2,400 and a stage that was 76 feet wide by 110 feet deep. But this theatre proved too large for the needs of drama and was used primarily for opera and musical extravaganzas. The Royal Circus in Quebec was converted to the Theatre Royal in 1832. Toronto built its first important theatre in 1834 and added the Royal Lyceum in 1848. To a great extent, however, professional theatre in Canada was treated as an extension of theatre in the United States. It was not until the construction of a substantial railway system in the 1850s that Canada began to develop its own theatre identity.

THEATRICAL CONDITIONS IN THE UNITED STATES AND CANADA

The rapid expansion of the theatre during a period of financial crisis brought many bankruptcies and frequent changes of management. The battle for audiences was reflected in many ways, but perhaps most importantly in the increased use of visiting stars after Edmund Kean's visit to the United States in 1820–1821. Then considered the finest actor of the English-speaking world, Kean set an example that made it easy to persuade other major actors to cross the Atlantic. After 1820 Price spent much of his time in London recruiting performers for American tours. Stars came with ever-increasing frequency: Charles Mathews the Elder in 1822 and 1833–1835; Macready in 1826–1827, 1843–1845, and 1849; Charles Kean in 1830, 1839, and 1845–1847; Charles and Fanny Kemble in 1832–1834; Mme Vestris and Charles Mathews the Younger in 1838. At first, tours were restricted to the Atlantic Coast and Canada, but as transportation improved, stars ventured to New Orleans and up the Mississippi River.

In the beginning, visits from major actors served to elevate the quality of local companies, but after 1830, as starring engagements came to be a mark of distinction, lesser actors began to tour. Consequently, few good actors were content to remain within the confines of a local troupe. The quality of performances also began to suffer, for stars usually arrived too late for adequate rehearsals, performed only in vehicles adapted to their talents, and relegated local leading actors to secondary roles. Often stars demanded enormous salaries and one or more benefits, leaving the managers with little profit from their visits. Nevertheless, managers were soon trapped by the system, for audiences were loathe to attend unless some novelty was offered.

The struggle for survival was also reflected in the repertory. Entr'acte entertainments increased in number and variety, novelties (such as child actors, animals, and specialty performers) abounded, and melodrama and minor forms composed an ever-larger part of the repertory. While this pattern did not differ markedly from that current in England, it was complicated by the American ambivalence toward foreign plays and performers. As Americans developed a national consciousness, especially after the War of 1812, the mass audience tended to be suspicious of anything foreign, while the better-educated and more sophisticated groups looked to Europe for their standards and gave only condescending attention to native talent. Consequently, after 1815 American dramatists and performers gained recognition only gradually and were usually accepted by the mass audience before winning critical approval. Acceptance was won more easily after 1830 as "Jacksonian democracy" encouraged faith in the tastes of the common man and native institutions.

Until around 1830 the majority of actors, both major and minor, were English-born and English-trained. The dominant performer up to 1825 was Cooper, but his "classical" style was less admired as Kean's approach triumphed. Of the new school, perhaps the most important was Junius Brutus Booth (1796–1852). On the stage from 1813, Booth came to the United States in 1821 and remained for the rest of his life. Although he managed theatres for brief intervals, he was essentially a touring star, one of the first to appear in the Mississippi Valley and the first major actor to play in California. It is sometimes said that Booth did more than any other performer to create America's taste for tragic acting. His erratic behavior made him undependable, however, and lessened his potential influence in the major theatrical centers. Another English actor who contributed significantly to the American stage in this period was Mary Ann Duff (1794–1857). When Mrs. Duff came to the United States in 1810, she had had little experience or training, and did not emerge as a leading player until 1818. Edmund Kean, Forrest, and Cooper all acclaimed her the greatest tragic actress of her day, and Kean declared her superior to any actress on the English stage.

Although there had been many native-born actors before his time, Edwin Forrest (1806–1872) was the first American performer to win lasting fame. On the stage from the age of fourteen, Forrest gained much of his early experience in frontier theatres. He made his New York debut in 1826 and by 1828 was the major attraction at the Bowery Theatre. Thereafter, he was considered America's leading actor. Following the Astor Place Riot of 1849 and his sensational divorce, his popularity diminished somewhat and after 1852 he appeared infrequently. He retired in 1872.

Forrest established an "American" school of acting (sometimes called the "physical" or "heroic" school). A man of powerful physique and great vocal strength, he disliked the repressed acting of the Kemble and Macready schools. His athletic and uninhibited performances made him the idol of unsophisticated theatregoers, but he won only grudging admiration from others. Forrest was always more vigorous than most of his contemporaries, many of whom sought to emulate him.

The first native-born actress to win international fame was Charlotte Cushman (1816–1876). Originally an opera singer, she turned to drama when her singing voice failed. After serving as a utility actress at the Park Theatre from 1837 to 1840, she played leading roles in Philadelphia and New York. Appearing with Macready in 1843, she was much affected by his methods. In 1845 she went to London, where she won immediate and lasting fame, soon being considered the finest tragic actress of the English-speaking world. After 1852 she appeared only sporadically and confined herself to a restricted repertory, notably Lady Macbeth, Queen Katherine in

FIG. 13.17

Edwin Forrest in the role of Virginius. Courtesy Hoblitzelle Theatre Arts Collection, University of Texas at Austin.

Henry VIII, and Meg Merrilies in *Guy Mannering.* In some ways, Cushman's acting style was not unlike Forrest's, for it depended upon energy and constant motion, but her intelligent line readings and emotional control won her a much wider following among sophisticated audiences.

Between 1815 and 1850, a number of American dramatists achieved limited fame. James Nelson Barker (1784–1858) wrote ten plays, of which five survive. The first to be acted was *Tears and Smiles* (1807), a comedy of manners, not unlike *The Contrast,* about Philadelphia society. His *The Indian Princess* (1808), a romantic drama about Pocahontas, was the first play about Native Americans to reach the stage. His best play, *Superstition* (1824), treats witchcraft in New England. Samuel Woodworth (1785–1842) wrote a number of domestic dramas, such as *The Deed of Gift* (1822) and *The Widow's Son* (1825), but is remembered now primarily for *The Forest Rose* (1825), which introduced the popular Yankee character Jonathan Ploughboy. Several playwrights were encouraged by Edwin Forrest, who after 1828 offered prizes for plays by American authors. Robert Montgomery Bird (1806–1854) began his playwriting career in 1827 with *The City Looking Glass,* one of the first American plays of local color and low-life. He subsequently supplied Forrest with some of his most lasting vehicles, *The Gladiator* (1831), *Oralloosa* (1832), and *The Broker of Bogota* (1834). John Augustus Stone (1801–1834) is remembered primarily for *Metamora* (1829), a play about a noble Native American chief in which Forrest performed throughout his career.

Between 1800 and 1850 the percentage of American plays in the repertory increased from about 2 percent to about 15 percent. As elsewhere, melodrama was the most important dramatic type. Its emphasis on suspenseful plots, theatrical effects, and moral preaching made it especially appealing to the unsophisticated audiences that flocked to the theatre increasingly. It was also a medium into which commentary about current concerns (such as slavery, the rights of workers, and slum life) could be inserted, so that despite its oversimplifications it served to reflect contemporary conditions, while its happy endings reassured audiences that their faith in justice and democracy was justified.

American plays of the early nineteenth century popularized two important native types: the Native American and the Yankee. The Native American was presented sympathetically, following the romantic tradition of the "noble savage," and provided strong roles for serious performers. The Native American had been introduced in American drama as early as 1766 in Robert Rogers's *Ponteach,* but Barker's *The Indian*

FIG. 13.18

Charlotte Cushman as Meg Merrilies in an adaptation of Sir Walter Scott's *Guy Mannering.* This was one of Miss Cushman's most popular roles. Courtesy Hoblitzelle Theatre Arts Collection, University of Texas at Austin.

Princess sketched the outline that was to be followed by others. The vogue for Native American dramas was given its major impetus by George Washington Parke Custis's (1781–1857) *The Indian Prophecy* (1827) and *Pocahontas* (1830). Between 1825 and 1860, more than fifty plays about Native Americans were seen in the United States, many performed by Forrest. The type was dealt a serious blow by John Brougham's burlesque, *Po-ca-hon-tas* (1855), but not until after 1870 was the "noble savage" tradition abandoned.

The Yankee character was the province of the comic actor or "specialty" performer. Although the Yankee had appeared in many plays after his introduction in *The Contrast* (1787), the idea of making him the central character seems to have stemmed from Charles Mathews's *A Trip to America* (1824), a work satirizing various American types. (With his "At Homes," Mathews also did much to popularize the "specialty" performer in America.) After 1825, the Yankee became a favorite character, and a number of "specialists" appeared. The Yankee was the symbol of the American common man, simple and naive on the surface, but upholding democratic principles and despising pretense and sham. The first important American actor of Yankee roles was James H. Hackett

(1800–1871), who conceived the character Solomon Swap in *Jonathan in England* (1828), the first important Yankee play. Hackett gave up Yankee roles in 1836, but continued his distinguished career as manager and actor, being especially noted for his portrayal of Falstaff. Hackett was succeeded by George Handel Hill (1809–1849), by 1832 considered the best of the Yankee specialists. In addition to monologues and skits, Hill performed full-length plays, such as J. S. Jones's *The Green Mountain Boy* (1833) and *The People's Lawyer* (1839). With Hill, the Yankee became more sympathetic and sentimental. Other Yankee specialists included Dan Marble (1810–1849), Joshua Silsbee (1813–1855), and John E. Owens (1823–1886). Ultimately, the vogue for the Yankee, which reached its height between 1830 and 1850, is perhaps most important for its role in establishing a native American comedy. A variation on the Yankee was the backwoodsman or frontiersman, the most famous example of which is found in *Davy Crockett* (1872) by Frank H. Murdoch (1843–72).

The African American, another important native type, also fell to specialists. The African American is present in American drama from the beginning as a faithful servant or comic caricature, but the popularity of the type dates from about 1828 when Thomas

D. Rice (1808–1860) introduced his "Jim Crow" song and dance. (The popularity of this song gave rise to the practice of using the label "Jim Crow" for any law or regulation designed to keep African Americans segregated). Soon a major star, Rice spawned a host of imitators, most notably Barney Williams, Jack Diamond, Barney Burns, and Bob Farrell. Rice's success also helped to create the Minstrel Show. In an effort to enlarge his repertory, Rice began to offer "Ethiopian Operas" around 1833. Building upon these, Dan Emmett (1815–1904) put together a full-length entertainment, "Virginia Minstrels," in 1843, and in 1846 the Minstrel Show was given its distinctive form by E. P. Christy (1815–1862).

The Minstrel Show was divided into two parts. In the first, the performers were arranged in a semicircle, the tambourine player at one end and the "pair of bones" player at the other. These "end" men came to be called Tambo and Bones. The "middle" man, or Interlocutor, served as master of ceremonies and exchanged jokes with the end men between musical numbers. The second part, or "olio," consisted of specialty acts and songs. In the Minstrel Show, whites acknowledged and appropriated the potential of African American music and dance, even as they exploited racial stereotypes. Beginning in 1865 with a company

FIG. 13.19
Charles Mathews the Elder as the various characters in one of his "at homes," *Invitations*. From Anne J. Mathews, *Memoirs of Charles James Mathews*, 3 (1842).

FIG. 13.20
George Handel Hill, a leading Yankee specialist, in *The Yankee Pedlar*. An aquatint published in 1838.

(1807–1867) with his first acting experience. Unable to pursue a theatrical career in America, Aldridge went to London, where he made his debut in 1825; within a few years he was known throughout England as "the celebrated African Roscius." In 1852 he undertook his first European tour and aroused such an enthusiastic response that he spent much of his time thereafter on the continent. Noted for his performances of Othello, Shylock, Macbeth, and Lear, he was decorated by the rulers of Prussia, Russia, and Saxe-Meiningen. He died while performing in Poland. By all indications, Aldridge was one of the great actors of his age, but racial barriers prevented him from ever exercising his mature power in the land of his birth.

Another native type, the city boy, came into prominence in the 1840s, perhaps to give the increasing urban population its own folk hero. City low-life had appeared on the stage occasionally since Pierce Egan's *Tom and Jerry, or Life in London* was adapted in the 1820s as *Life in Philadelphia, Life in New York,* and so on. The city boy was not popular, however, until Benjamin Baker's *A Glance at New*

headed by Charles Hicks, there were also Minstrel troupes made up entirely of African Americans, who "blacked up" in the manner of the white companies. The Minstrel Show reached the peak of its popularity between 1850 and 1870. After 1870, companies began to increase in size, some including more than one hundred performers. The popularity of the form declined, nevertheless, and by 1896 only ten companies remained. By 1919 there were only three, and soon the Minstrel Show was a mere curiosity.

Such appropriations of African American performance did not keep African Americans from making their mark in other ways. In 1821 the first known company of African American actors in the United States was assembled in New York by William Henry Brown, who presented occasional theatrical performances at the African Grove, an outdoor tea garden, and later at an indoor theatre. The repertory included *Richard III, Othello,* and other plays, and starred James Hewlett, a native of the West Indies. It also included the first known American play written by an African American author, Brown's own *King Shotaway,* which dealt with an insurrection on the island of St. Vincent. Unfortunately, the company was plagued by white thugs, and perhaps because of these difficulties it fades from surviving records after 1823.

The African Company left one important legacy, however, for it seems to have provided Ira Aldridge

FIG. 13.21
Thomas D. Rice as Jim Crow. Courtesy the Albert Davis Collection, Hoblitzelle Theatre Arts Collection, University of Texas at Austin.

FIG. 13.22
Frank Chanfrau as Mose the Bowery Boy and volunteer fireman. Courtesy Hoblitzelle Theatre Arts Collection, University of Texas at Austin.

York (1848) introduced the volunteer fireman and good-natured roughneck, Mose the Bowery Boy. The phenomenal success of this play led to many sequels in which Mose visits various countries and becomes embroiled in new situations. Frank S. Chanfrau (1824–1884) spent much of his career acting this role. The Bowery Boy faded in popularity after the 1860s, but was assimilated into other plays about city life.

By the 1840s American writers and actors were no longer novelties. For example, Anna Cora Mowatt (1819–1870) won immediate and widespread acceptance with *Fashion* (1845), a comedy of manners about New York social life. Of a well-to-do family, Mrs. Mowatt turned to writing around 1840 when her husband lost both his fortune and his health. Since playwriting paid little, Mrs. Mowatt went on the stage in 1845. With no previous experience, she was a star from the first. In such roles as Juliet and Rosalind, she won fame in both the United States and England before retiring in 1854.

Between 1815 and 1850 spectacle began to be given greater emphasis. For the most part, plays continued to be staged in stock settings, but occasionally an effort was made to provide more specific and elaborate backgrounds. Interest in historical accuracy is first found in John J. Holland's Gothic settings at the Park Theatre in 1809. Archeological detail did not make a deep impression, however, until 1845–1846, when Charles Kean staged *Richard III* and *King John* at the Park Theatre. Thereafter, accuracy was gradually accepted as an ideal.

Panoramas and dioramas were introduced in an attempt to gain greater realism. Nontheatrical panoramas had been seen in New York since the 1790s, and in the 1820s Daguerre's dioramas were regularly shown there. Perhaps as a result, Dunlap was commissioned by the Bowery Theatre in 1827 to write *A Trip to Niagara,* in which a journey by steamboat up the Hudson River was depicted. During her tour in 1838, Vestris allegedly attracted attention to more detailed settings and properties, and it is possible that she introduced the box set into the United States at that time.

In 1816 the Chestnut Street Theatre in Philadelphia became the first in the world to light its stage with gas. This new medium had been demonstrated in England by William Murdoch in the late eighteenth century but it had not then been sufficiently perfected as an illuminant. It was adopted for exterior lighting at Covent Garden in 1815 and may have been installed in the auditorium of the Lyceum in the same year. It was first used for lighting the stages of Covent Garden and Drury Lane in 1817. By the early 1820s, gas was being used experimentally in most countries of the Western world.

Gas did not win immediate acceptance, however, for it presented many problems. Since there were as yet no gas mains, each theatre had to install and maintain its own plant, an expensive undertaking. Furthermore, gas gave off unpleasant fumes and oppressive heat; the danger of fire was always great. It was not until the 1840s, when a dependable, centralized supply became available in many cities, that gas was widely adopted.

Gas eventually triumphed because of its advantages over candles and oil. For the first time, the stage could be lighted as brightly as desired. Since the burners did not have to be trimmed, as did the wicks of candles and lamps, they could be distributed more advantageously. As a result, border lights were used more extensively. Furthermore, complete control over intensity was now possible. At first each gas line was controlled separately, but in the 1840s the "gas table," comparable to the modern control board, made it possible for an operator to control all lights from one position. After 1850 many of the objections to gas were eliminated by the "fishtail" burner, which increased efficiency and reduced fumes by controlling the relationship of the fuel to oxygen. In the 1880s an incandescent mantle made gas even safer, but by this time electricity had begun to replace it.

The limelight (or calcium or Drummond light) was to be of special importance during the nineteenth century. Invented by Thomas Drummond in 1816, it required, in addition to gas, one cylinder of compressed hydrogen and one of oxygen, all of which were directed against a column of lime so as to heat it to incandescence. Placed inside a hood and fitted with a lens, the limelight was the prototype of the spotlight. Macready was the first to recognize its potential for the stage, but after using it for a time in 1837 he gave it up as too expensive. Nevertheless, by the 1850s it had been adopted widely and played a prominent role in productions thereafter. Its mellow and brilliant rays were first used for creating such atmospheric effects as sunlight or moonlight; only gradually was its potentiality for lighting the acting area developed. Eventually it came to be used primarily as a "follow" spot to emphasize starring performers. The major disadvantage of the limelight was its need for constant supervision: since the lime had to be kept in proper alignment with the gases and flame, it required a separate operator for each instrument.

These innovations—gas, gas table, limelight, and the various refinements on each—revolutionized stage lighting in Europe and North America between 1815 and 1880, although the artistic principles needed to guide usage were yet to be formulated.

Between 1800 and 1850, then, the theatre underwent many changes. During this time the last vestiges of neoclassicism almost wholly disappeared under the onslaught of romanticism. In England, the United States, and Canada the melodramatic and pseudo-Shakespearean mode in playwriting, local color, historical accuracy in settings and costumes, and emotional and psychological realism in acting had made themselves felt and had combined to create a theatre in 1850 quite unlike that of the late eighteenth century. But by 1850 the romantic outlook itself had come to pall, and new forces, destined to lead to realism, were already coming to the fore.

LOOKING AT THEATRE HISTORY

In theatre history there is a tendency to judge an era by the excellence of its drama. In most instances the best plays come to be treated as typical, while lesser works and other types of performance are swept aside as unimportant. This approach results in considerable distortion, for it suggests that "popular culture" is insignificant. As Lawrence W. Levine writes in *Highbrow/Lowbrow*, an impression is given that "culture is something created by the few for the few, threatened by the many, and imperiled by democracy; the conviction that culture cannot come from the young, the inexperienced, the untutored, the marginal." Yet the entertainments of the masses are more apt to represent the norm of the age than is the elitist art of "high culture." As Leo Lowenthal says in *Literature, Popular Culture and Society*, "By studying . . . the mass media, we learn about typical forms of behavior, attitudes, commonly held beliefs, prejudices, and aspirations of large numbers of people." In recent times, as Susan Sontag has noted in *Against Interpretation,* "the distinction between 'high' and 'low' culture seems less and less meaningful. . . . It is important to understand that [this] is not a new philistinism . . . or a species of anti-intellectualism or some kind of abdication from culture. . . . It reflects a new, more open way of looking at the world. . . . The new sensibility is defiantly pluralistic."

Concern for "popular culture" is especially pertinent in studying nineteenth-century theatre history, since the repertory was dominated by melodrama and minor forms usually scorned until recently by literary critics. Thus, nineteenth-century drama and theatre have often been treated condescendingly or passed over lightly as unworthy of serious attention. David Grimsted has sought to counter the typical approach by demonstrating how melodrama can be a key to understanding aspects of nineteenth-century culture:

The aesthetically poor quality of its plays has encouraged stage historians to view the period's theatrical history as a strange interlude either preparatory to twentieth-century

improvements or simply full of quaint plays, practices,
and anecdotes. Seen as a product of particular intellectual
and social preconceptions . . . the melodrama becomes
less an inexplicable monstrosity and more an emotionally
valid attempt to dramatize an era's faith. [x]

At the end of his study, Grimsted concludes:

[Melodrama's] conventions were false, its language
stilted and commonplace, its characters stereotypes, and
its morality and theology gross simplifications. Yet its
appeal was great and understandable. It took the lives of
common people seriously and paid much respect to their
superior purity and wisdom. . . . And its moral parable
struggled to reconcile social fears and life's awesomeness
with the period's confidence in absolute moral standards,
man's upward progress, and a benevolent providence that
insured the triumph of the pure. [248]

David Grimsted, *Melodrama Unveiled: American Theatre
and Culture, 1800–1850* (Chicago: University of
Chicago Press, 1968).

The introduction of gas, with its brilliance and ease
of control, gave stage lighting previously unknown
potential. Here is an account of the inauguration of
gas lighting at Drury Lane in London in 1817:

Gas lights . . . are introduced not only in front of the
stage, but at the various compartments on each side:
Their effect, as they appear suddenly from the gloom, is
like the striking of daylight; and indeed it is in its
resemblance to day that this splendid light surpasses all
others. It is as mild as it is splendid—white, regular,
and pervading. . . . If it is managed as well as we saw
it on Friday [it] will enable the spectator to see every
part of the stage with equal clearness. If the front light
could be thrown, as daylight is, from above instead of
below (and we should like to hear the reasons why it
cannot) the effect would be perfect.

Review by Leigh Hunt in *The Examiner,* September 7,
1817.

14
English-Language Theatre in the Late Nineteenth Century

The last half of the nineteenth century brought many changes to Western Europe. When the revolutions of 1848 demonstrated the working classes' overwhelming desire for political, social, and economic reform, governments initially were frightened into promising change, but after the violence abated most declined to implement their pledges. The republic established in France in 1848 gave way to another empire under Napoleon III from 1852 until 1871, and throughout Europe it was not until late in the century that the demands made in 1848 began to be met. England was probably the most compliant: in 1867 it greatly extended the franchise; in 1872 it introduced the secret ballot; and in 1884 it finally extended the vote to all adult males; in 1870 Parliament also made government appointments dependent on examination rather than patronage. But all such reforms were bitterly opposed by those who championed a benevolent despotism of the privileged over the working classes, and none of these reforms extended to women.

During the late nineteenth century the United States was involved in the same movements then underway in Europe. It too was extending its territories and consolidating its power, although most of its energies were expended on preserving the nation and filling up the continent over which it had won control. The most important event of the half-century was the Civil War, which brought an end to slavery and the influence of the rural South; it ensured the preservation of the union, but at great human and financial sacrifice. The empty reaches of western land, however, always held out the lure of wealth and security; consequently, adventurers and settlers streamed westward in search of mining strikes and free homesteads, displacing the Native Americans as they went.

This westward movement and the needs of commerce and industry motivated the development of networks of railroads, which by the end of the century extended throughout the land. The first transcontinental railroad was completed in 1869, and by the 1880s there were others. This expansion of the transportation system was paralleled by a race to gain control over the country's resources and to exploit them. During this era the United States was looked upon by many Europeans as a brawling giant lacking in refinement and culture, but to the commoners everywhere it was the "land of opportunity," and immigrants streamed in, contributing to the labor force and slum population, but also bringing diversity and talent. As in Europe, the United States government was not prepared to deal with such complex developments, and consequently the rapacious made enormous fortunes at the expense of others. But the cry for reform grew—in labor conditions, women's rights, education, civil rights, and protection against exploitation by "robber barons"—although it was not to be answered effectively until the twentieth century.

THEATRE IN THE UNITED STATES, 1850–1870

During this period the theatre continued to expand. In the cities, companies often resembled their European counterparts, but elsewhere they retained their pioneering quality as actors who could not find steady employment in urban centers tried their luck in mining camps and small towns. Thus, like the country itself, the theatre was diverse.

As the westward movement accelerated, especially after the discovery of gold in California in 1848, the theatre kept pace. In California the first professional performances in English were given in 1849, when Sacramento's Eagle Theatre began to offer three programs each week to the miners. In San Francisco the first theatre was opened in 1850 and throughout the following decade there were usually four in operation. After this time, San Francisco was to be the major theatrical center of the far West. From 1853 to 1856, Catherine Sinclair (1817–1891), Edwin Forrest's divorced wife, ran the Metropolitan Theatre with the first outstanding company seen in that area. All these early efforts, however, were eclipsed by the California Theatre, one of the best in the entire country when it was opened in 1869 by John McCullough and Lawrence Barrett.

Despite tedious journeys overland or by sea, stars began to visit the new territory almost immediately. Among the first were Junius Brutus Booth, Frank Chanfrau, and J. W. Wallack, Jr. Most stars came from the East, but one native performer, Lotta Crabtree (1847–1924), was to gain national fame. On the stage from the age of eight, she was a major star and had embarked on her first eastern tour by the age of seventeen. In vehicles written especially for her, she usually played several characters to demonstrate her versatility. In many of the plays she portrayed a ragged waif who regenerates drunken miners. All allowed her to display her talents for singing, dancing, and playing the banjo.

New mining strikes led to still further expansion of the western theatre. The Comstock Lode, discovered in 1859, had by the mid-1860s spawned five legitimate theatres and six variety houses in Nevada City, Nevada. Similarly, mining towns attracted actors to Idaho, Montana, and Colorado. In the late 1850s touring groups began to appear in Oregon, where a theatre was established at Willamette in 1861. Washington state saw its first professional

FIG. 14.1

An unpopular actor pelted with fruit and vegetables at Baldwin's Theatre, San Francisco, c. 1870. From the Albert Davis Collection, Hoblitzelle Theatre Arts Collection, University of Texas at Austin.

troupe in 1862, but no permanent theatre was established there until 1879.

In Utah the Mormons began to produce plays as early as 1850, and in 1862 they erected the Salt Lake Theatre, the first major structure built in Salt Lake City. Performances were at first given by amateurs, but in 1863 professional actors began to be added and a permanent company was maintained after 1865. The theatre in all these western areas was considerably strengthened with the opening of transcontinental railroads beginning in 1869.

Between 1850 and 1870 the number of resident companies increased throughout America. The thirty-five of 1850 had grown to about fifty in 1860, and remained constant until after 1870. Countless itinerant groups played in less populous areas. The dependence upon visiting stars continued, although a number of managers sought to counteract its adverse effects. Among these the most important were Burton and Wallack. William E. Burton (1804–1860) had been a low comedian in the English theatre before coming to the United States in 1834. A popular actor and successful manager in Philadelphia until 1848, he then opened Burton's Chambers Street Theatre in New York, where between 1848 and 1856 he maintained the most respected company in America. Because the Chambers Street Theatre seated only 800, in 1856 Burton moved to the Metropoli-

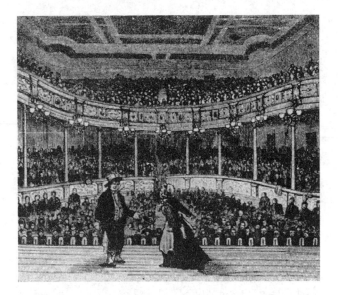

FIG. 14.2
Burton's Chambers Street Theatre, New York, in the late 1850s. Burton is on stage. Note the numerous posts used to support the balcony, since cantilevering had not yet been perfected. Courtesy Hoblitzelle Theatre Arts Collection, University of Texas at Austin.

tan Theatre, one of the largest in the world. Success did not follow him, and he soon had to import stars. He gave up management in 1858 and retired in 1859. With his excellent company and broad-ranging repertory Burton demonstrated at the Chambers Street Theatre that success did not require stars. He also gained much prestige with his productions of Shakespeare's plays in historically accurate settings and costumes.

Before Burton retired, his preeminence had already been seriously challenged by James W. Wallack (1791–1864), who in 1853 had taken over the Lyceum Theatre and renamed it Wallack's Lyceum. From 1855 until the 1880s, Wallack's was the leading theatre in the United States. He was succeeded as manager by his son, Lester Wallack (1820–1888), a fine romantic leading actor, who continued his father's policies until 1887. Also prominent in the troupe was James W. Wallack, Jr. (1818–1873), a performer of tragic roles. Maintaining a high standard of production, Wallack's presented a repertory made up primarily of standard works.

Another outstanding company was assembled by Laura Keene (c. 1820–1873), an English actress who had worked for Vestris. Following her American debut in 1852, she played for Wallack before going on tour. Between 1855 and 1863, she ran her own theatre in New York, serving as manager and leading actress in a series of lavishly mounted productions in the style of Vestris. After 1863 she toured

and was playing at Ford's Theatre in Washington on the night of President Lincoln's assassination.

Not all of the major troupes were located in New York. The Boston Museum, one of the finest in the country, owed much of its prestige to William Warren, Jr. (1812–1888), who performed there from 1847 until 1883. Because of his wide range, Warren is considered by many critics the finest comic actor of his age. Philadelphia's Arch Street Theatre, under the direction of Mrs. John Drew (1820–1897), became famous throughout the United States for its fine company and the training it gave young actors. Born Louisa Lane, Mrs. Drew was on stage as a child, came to the United States in 1827, and in 1850 married John Drew (1827–1862), an actor of Irish roles. Although she retained the management of the Arch Street from 1860 until 1892, the theatre's reputation was made during the 1860s. After 1870 Mrs. Drew toured widely, especially in the role of Mrs. Malaprop. In Chicago, James H. McVicker (1822–1896), who had worked for Ludlow and Smith and starred in Yankee roles, formed his own company in 1857. Until his death, his Chicago theatres were among the finest outside of New York. In St. Louis, Ludlow and Smith were succeeded by Ben DeBar, who dominated the theatre there from 1853 until the 1880s.

While the resident stock company continued to be the standard theatrical organization between 1850 and 1870, it was gradually undermined by several innovations. One of the most damaging was the introduction of the long run. Before 1850 successful new plays had usually been given no more than fifteen times and then placed in the repertory to alternate with other plays. In 1852–1853 *Uncle Tom's Cabin* was played for 300 consecutive performances. Although atypical, this run is symptomatic of the new trend toward extended engagements even in well-established stock companies. At the Boston Museum, for example, the average run for new plays in the 1860s was 14 to 40 performances, in the 1870s, 20 to 50, and in the 1880s, 50 to 100.

The increase in the length of runs brought a decrease in the size of the repertory. In 1851–1852 the Boston Museum gave 140 plays (68 full-length and 72 afterpieces), but by 1875 the number had declined to 75 and by 1893 to 15. At Wallack's Theatre in 1855–1856, 60 plays were performed, but by the mid-1870s only 15 to 25, and in the mid-1880s only 5 to 10. Although some of the decrease can be attributed to the gradual abandonment of the afterpiece around 1870, it is indicative as well of a new approach to repertory playing under which a series of plays was given for long runs, while the older scheme of alternating plays was retained merely in the intervals between successful productions.

With the extended run came greater emphasis upon new plays. Although between 1850 and 1870 Shakespearean and other standard works continued to make up a sizable portion of the repertory, the majority of long-running plays were new works. Adaptations of recent novels, melodramas, extravaganzas, and burlesques were prominent. Probably the most popular play of the period was *Uncle Tom's Cabin,* based on Harriet Beecher Stowe's novel. Although it was adapted many times, the most popular version was George L. Aiken's, first played in Troy, New York, in 1852 as two separate plays and then combined into a single six-act work. It was written for the Howard family (George C. Howard as St. Clare, Mrs. Howard as Topsy, and their daughter, Cordelia, as Little Eva), who played it until 1887. Although the craze for *Uncle Tom's Cabin* died down before 1860, it revived in the 1870s, when about fifty traveling companies were performing it. In 1927 there were still twelve touring companies who performed only this play.

It is ironical that Mrs. Stowe's tale should have been so phenomenally popular while *The Escape* (1858),

the oldest extant American play by an African American author, William Wells Brown (c. 1816–1884), a historian and former slave, never reached the stage. Brown had to content himself with reading his work about the dilemma of the slaves Glen and his wife Melinda to literary societies and abolitionist meetings.

Even more ironical, African American performers were permitted on the American stage during the last half of the nineteenth century only as caricatures of a caricature—that is, as members of African American troupes of minstrels. The first of these companies was formed in 1852, but many others followed. Circumstances forced them to imitate their white counterparts, even to blacking their faces, reddening their lips and wearing wigs, but they managed nevertheless to introduce many new specialty numbers. Furthermore, beginning in the 1890s African American musical plays were to evolve out of this form.

As in England between 1850 and 1870, burlesque-extravaganza was one of the most popular dramatic types. Parodying well-known plays, performers, or

FIG. 14.3
Uncle Tom's Cabin as produced by William Brady in 1901. Eliza is about to cross the frozen river. The use of horses and dogs had become usual by this time. Note the cut wings used to represent trees. Courtesy Harvard Theatre Collection.

FIG. 14.4
A ballet-extravaganza at Niblo's Theatre, 1855. Courtesy Hoblitzelle Theatre Arts Collection, University of Texas at Austin.

topical events, and featuring songs and dances, it appealed to the taste for broad comedy and spectacle. Probably the most successful writer of burlesque was John Brougham (1810–1880), an Irishman who had worked for Vestris before coming to the United States in 1842. A popular comic actor, Brougham tried his hand unsuccessfully at management several times, adapted many popular novels for the stage, and wrote numerous original works. Of all his plays, perhaps the most famous was *Po-ca-hon-tas,* or *The Gentle Savage* (1855), a burlesque of the "noble savage" tradition, popular especially after the 1820s. Many others also wrote and performed in burlesques. George L. Fox (1825–1877), one of the most talented comic actors of the nineteenth century, was famous for his travesties of *Macbeth, Richard III,* and *Hamlet.* He also revitalized pantomime with his *Humpty Dumpty* (1868), in which he played Clown more than 1,200 times. Mrs. John Wood (1831–1915) was probably the best burlesque actress of the day, winning special acclaim in *The Sleeping Beauty* and *The Fair One with the Golden Locks.*

Of the serious dramatists of this period, the best perhaps was George Henry Boker (1823–1890). Son of wealthy parents, he began to write plays about 1848. His first work, *Calaynos,* was produced in London by Phelps in 1849. His *Francesca da Rimini* (1855) is considered by many the finest poetic tragedy of the nineteenth century. Boker worked hard to secure more adequate legal protection for dramatists. Although probably not due to his efforts, a copyright act was passed in 1856. Unfortunately, it failed to give effective protection, because it merely provided for the registration of works in local courts. The transfer of registration to the Library of Congress in 1870 did much to correct the weaknesses, but reasonable protection of the American playwright was not to come until the acceptance by the United States of the International Copyright Agreement in 1891 and the passage of a revised American Copyright Act in 1909.

THEATRE IN THE UNITED STATES, 1870–1895

The years between 1870 and 1895 brought enormous changes to the American theatre as the resident company was undermined by touring groups, as New York became the major center of production, and as the long run superseded the repertory system. By 1870, the resident stock company was at the peak of its development, but thereafter was steadily weakened. While the causes of this decline are numerous, among the most important were the depression of 1873 and the rise of the "combination" company (that is, one that travels with stars and full company). Sending out a complete production was merely a logical extension of touring by stars. By the 1840s many major actors were already taking along a small group of lesser players, for they could not be sure that local companies could supply adequate support in secondary roles.

There is much disagreement about the origin of the combination company. Boucicault claims to have initiated it around 1860 when he sent out a troupe with *Colleen Bawn,* but this was in England and a book published in the United States in 1859 speaks of combination companies as already established. The practice may have begun with the Howard-Aiken company's production of *Uncle Tom's Cabin* in 1852. Further development of the combination company was interrupted by the Civil War, but it accelerated in the 1870s, as the rapid expansion of the railway system made transporting full productions increasingly feasible. In 1872 Lawrence Barrett took his company, but no scenery, on tour; by 1876–1877 there were nearly 100 and by 1886 there were 282 combination companies traveling with full companies, scenery, and properties. The combination company did not end the emphasis upon stars, but now they traveled with full productions. Henry Irving toured America eight times between 1883 and 1902; Salvini five times between 1872 and 1889; Coquelin three times between 1889 and 1900; and Sarah Bernhardt nine times between 1880 and 1918. Foreign

FIG. 14.5
Boucicault's *Colleen Bawn.* From an acting edition of the play, *c.* 1865.

As a young man, Edwin Booth (1833–1893) accompanied his father, Junius Brutus Booth, on his tours and made his own acting debut in 1849 in Boston. From 1852 to 1856 he played with various companies and toured in California, Australia, and the southern United States before appearing at Burton's Theatre in New York. From 1856 until his death, he was one of the country's major stars. In 1863, he leased the Winter Garden Theatre in New York and gave a number of Shakespearean productions which surpassed in quality any yet seen in America. His *Hamlet* ran for 100 nights, a record for that play not broken in the United States until the twentieth century. When his brother killed President Lincoln, Booth retired for a time.

In 1869 Booth returned to the stage and introduced several innovations. At Booth's Theatre, which had been built to his specifications, the stage floor was level and had no grooves. Several hydraulic elevators were used to raise set pieces from the 50 feet of working space below the stage, and flying machinery raised other pieces into the 76 feet of overhead space. Thus,

FIG. 14.6
Backstage at Booth's Theatre, 1870. Note the use of traps (hydraulic lifts) to raise and lower heavy props and pieces of scenery. This was perhaps the first stage to have a level floor and to dispense with grooves. Note the stage braces used to support scenery now that grooves were no longer available for that purpose. From *Appleton's Journal* 3 (May 28, 1870).

stars usually played a small repertory; American troupes most frequently performed a single play.

During the early years of the combination system, local managers maintained companies to perform during the intervals between traveling productions. Often the local company toured small towns in the vicinity while the visitors occupied its theatre. But, as local support was withdrawn from the resident troupes and given to touring productions, many managers dismissed their actors and became mere landlords. In the late 1880s, in some areas a more modest form of the resident company began to present a winter season of varied plays for short runs to neighborhood audiences at ticket prices less than half those charged for touring attractions. About 40 of these companies were formed during the 1890s, and by World War I there were about 120. Little known outside their own immediate areas, they posed no threat to large touring attractions.

Several of the major resident companies held out against the new system for many years. Nevertheless, Wallack's closed in 1888, as did the Arch Street Theatre in 1892 and the Boston Museum in 1893, by which time virtually all of the major resident troupes had been disbanded. Still, most of the significant contributions of the years between 1870 and 1895 came from those managers who maintained permanent troupes. Of these, the most important were Edwin Booth, Augustin Daly, and Steele MacKaye.

FIG. 14.7

The "ghost scene" from Act 1 of *Hamlet* in Edwin Booth's production at Booth's Theatre. Sketch by Thomas B. Glessing, c. 1870. Courtesy the Walter Hampden-Edwin Booth Theatre Collection and Library, New York.

Booth introduced "free plantation" of scenery many years before it was adopted by Irving in England. Booth's Theatre also had no apron, and box settings were used extensively to increase the illusion of reality. Booth produced on such a lavish scale that by 1874 he was bankrupt. From then until his retirement in 1891, he played starring engagements in the United States and abroad.

Booth believed that the theatre should confine itself to the best drama and that the actor's function is to reveal the beauty and wisdom contained in great plays. He studied his roles tirelessly and executed them with infinite care. He was noted for his elegant and graceful movements, the use of vocal tone to reveal mood and meaning, the combination of emotional intensity with clarity of interpretation, the consistency of his characterizations, and his freedom from mannerisms. Not having great physical strength, he depended much upon his flexible and expressive voice. At his best in serious roles, notably Hamlet, Iago, Othello, and Richelieu (in Bulwer-Lytton's play), Booth is considered by many historians the greatest actor the United States has produced.

Augustin Daly (1836–1899) was a critic before winning fame with *Leah the Forsaken* (1862), adapted from a German play, Mosenthal's *Deborah*. His first original work, *Under the Gaslight* (1867), also saw his

debut as a producer. In 1869 he leased the Fifth Avenue Theatre and formed his own company. From that time until his death he was one of the most influential figures in the American theatre. His most important work was done after 1879, when he opened Daly's Theatre, his company's third home. After playing in London several times successfully, he acquired his own theatre there in 1893 to supplement his American activities.

Daly's significance derives from several sources. He contributed much to the development of realism. Many of his works are adaptations of plays by Dumas and Sardou. Some of his original plays introduced realistic special effects that became legendary (the hero tied to the tracks in the path of an approaching train; the heroine locked in the stateroom of a burning steamboat). He also popularized new subject matter. *Horizon* (1871) was among the first works to present the Native American as villain (rather than noble savage) and to emphasize differences in codes of conduct in America's East and West. More important, Daly helped to establish the director as the major force in the theatre. He retained absolute control over every element of his production. In many ways, he was comparable to Saxe-Meiningen in Germany, and to Irving and the Bancrofts in England. Daly assumed the right to coach his actors in interpretation, stage business, and blocking, and he abandoned the traditional practice of casting according to lines of business.

FIG. 14.8

Daly's Fifth Avenue Theatre, New York. Note that all but a few boxes have been replaced by open balconies. Note also the chair seating in the orchestra and the center aisle. The apron has virtually disappeared. Courtesy Albert Davis Collection, Hoblitzelle Theatre Arts Collection, University of Texas at Austin.

FIG. 14.9

Daly's production of Shakespeare's *The Merchant of Venice* (Act I). Note the attempt to reproduce actual places in Venice. At left is the Grand Canal, with boats. Courtesy Harvard Theatre Collection.

Because of his working methods, Daly usually attracted young performers, many of whom he raised to stardom. Consequently, he was one of the earliest "star makers." The stars he promoted included Agnes Ethel (1852–1903), Fanny Davenport (1850–1898), and Clara Morris (1846–1925), all of whom soon left him to pursue their careers elsewhere.

Daly's mainstays after 1879 were "the big four": Ada Rehan (1860–1916) and John Drew II (1853–1927), players of leading roles; James Lewis (1840–1896) and Mrs. G. H. Gilbert (1822–1904), chief comic actors. Between 1879 and 1892 they helped Daly create the finest ensemble in America. Both Drew and Rehan had been trained by Mrs. Drew and continued to perform together until 1892, when Drew left Daly's company. For Daly, Rehan played more than 200 roles, of which her best was Katherine in *Taming of the Shrew.* Her personal magnetism and beautiful voice made her one of the most popular actresses of her day. Unable to adapt to other working conditions after Daly's death, she retired in 1905.

Steele MacKaye (1842–1894), actor, playwright, director, inventor, designer, and teacher, was more versatile than Daly but probably less influential, because few of his enterprises were sustained long enough to establish their worth. As an actor and teacher, he is remembered primarily for introducing the Delsarte method into the United States. After studying with Delsarte in France, MacKaye came to believe that Delsarte's system could reform the stage, and he promoted it through a series of acting schools. In 1872–1873 he created a short-lived training program, probably the first in North America, at his St. James's Theatre in New York. His greatest contribu-

tion, however, came in 1884, when at his Lyceum Theatre he began another training program which was to become the American Academy of Dramatic Art. Two of MacKaye's students founded other schools, both in Boston: Samuel S. Curry created the Curry School of Expression, and Charles W. Emerson the Emerson School of Oratory. As the most important of the early acting schools in the United States these three spread MacKaye's and Delsarte's system.

MacKaye also wrote or adapted nineteen plays, three of which were especially successful: *Won at Last* (1877), *Hazel Kirke* (1878–1880), and *Paul Kauvar* (1887). After achieving an initial run of 486 performances in New York, *Hazel Kirke* was taken on the road by fourteen different companies in 1884. It is also significant in the development of realism, for although essentially melodramatic, it contained no villain and all the characters were drawn with sympathy and fidelity. *Paul Kauvar* was noted for its crowd scenes staged in the manner of the Meiningen company.

MacKaye was one of the most fertile inventors of the late nineteenth century. His Madison Square

FIG. 14.10

Sectional drawing of the Madison Square Theatre, opened in 1879. Note the two stages, one above the other, mounted on elevators and operated by counterweights. From *The Scientific American* (April 5, 1884).

Theatre, opened in 1879, had two elevator stages, each 22 feet wide by 31 feet deep, which permitted complete scene changes in forty seconds. His Lyceum Theatre in 1885 was one of the first to use electric lighting and to emphasize safety devices. At Madison Square Garden, in a play on the westward movement written and staged for "Buffalo Bill" Cody, MacKaye created a realistic cyclone and stampede. But many of MacKaye's grandest schemes were never realized. For the Chicago Exposition of 1893 he designed a "Spectatorium" with twenty-five stages on which to portray Columbus's voyage to the New World and the subsequent story of America's development. A financial panic prevented its completion, but the surviving plans show that his conception was feasible. Few American producers have been so inventive, and few have been dogged by so many misfortunes.

As the emphasis shifted to new works, playwriting emerged as a full-time profession in the United States. Bronson Howard (1842–1908), America's first professional dramatist, began his playwriting career in 1864, but did not attract wide attention until his *Saratoga* (1870) ran for 101 nights. Of his eighteen plays, *The Banker's Daughter* (1878), *Young Mrs. Winthrop* (1882), and *Shenandoah* (1888) are the best known. Howard was one of the first dramatists to receive regular royalty payments, and in 1891 he founded the Society of American Dramatists and Composers, the forerunner of the present-day Dramatists' Guild.

Much of the drama of this period illustrates the trend toward realism. While fidelity of spectacle had been increasing throughout the century, realism of character and situation were slower in arriving. One step toward more daring subject matter was taken in 1857 with the production of *Camille*. Considered by many too bold, the play had first been presented by Laura Keene as a terrible dream from which the heroine awakens. Matilda Heron (1830–1877), on the other hand, translated the play faithfully and played it without idealizing the characters. It ran for one hundred nights, and Miss Heron was hailed for her naturalistic acting.

But realism was usually confined to local color. Building upon the popularity of Bret Harte and Mark Twain, such works as Bartley Campbell's (1843–1888) *My Partner* (1879) exploited frontier life. Local color was also emphasized in Augustus Thomas's (1857–1934) plays, *Alabama* (1891), *In Mizzoura* (1893), and *Arizona* (1897).

Local color of a quite different sort appears in the plays of Edward Harrigan (1845–1911), a comic writer who extended the "Bowery Boy" tradition and whose early fame was gained in variety houses in partnership with Tony Hart (1857–1891). Harrigan began by writing sketches and went on to full-length plays about life among various immigrant groups in New York. Combining knockabout farce and realism, most of the plays end with some outrageous denouement, such as the explosion of a fireworks factory followed by bodies falling though the ceiling. Harrigan performed in his own works and mounted them with absolute fidelity of background and dress. After 1895 Harrigan performed only rarely. Little appreciated by contemporary critics, he is now recognized as a faithful observer of his milieu.

In this period, realism was developed most extensively in the plays of Gillette and Herne. William Gillette (1855–1937), on the stage after 1875, wrote his first play, *The Professor*, in 1881. Of his twenty works, the most important are *Held by the Enemy* (1886), the first major play on a Civil War theme, *Secret Service* (1895), and *Sherlock Holmes* (1899). Gillette's most realistic drama, *Secret Service*, also has a Civil War background. Built around minutiae, the play's stage directions take up more space in print than does the dialogue. One act requires an authentic telegraph office, complete with a working telegraph key. Although Gillette's plays are essentially melodramas, they create the illusion of real life through the accumulation of external details. Gillette was also one of the finest actors of his day. By concentrating on the moment-by-moment development of the action, he sought to create the "illusion of the first time" regardless of how often he had performed a role.

James A. Herne (1839–1901) began his career in 1859 as an actor. During the 1870s while serving as a stage manager in San Francisco, he adapted several plays, some in collaboration with David Belasco. He first attracted favorable critical attention with *Drifting Apart* (1888), a work about the evil effects of drink on a Massachusetts fishing village. Encouraged by William Dean Howells and other realists, Herne thereafter consciously sought fidelity to life in writing, staging, and acting. His most important play, *Margaret Fleming* (1890), is usually considered the most realistic American drama of the nineteenth century. It tells the story of a woman who, upon learning of her husband's infidelity, takes his illegitimate child to rear with her own. While it includes much realistic visual detail, its major emphasis is upon psychological conflicts. Its subject matter made it unacceptable to commercial managers, and Herne had to present it in halls and out-of-the-way theatres. After suffering heavy financial losses, he recovered his fortunes with *Shore Acres* (1892), a play about a quiet, lovable, New England character. Although in the realistic mode, it did not offend moral sensibilities and was soon a popular favorite. Not a great playwright, Herne nevertheless did more than any other

FIG. 14.11
Miss Whitlock, who played the leading role in the original production of *The Black Crook* at Niblo's Garden, 1866. This costume, modest enough by today's standards, was considered shocking in the 1860s. From the Albert Davis Collection, Hoblitzelle Theatre Arts Collection, University of Texas at Austin.

ularity just prior to World War I, but it was not until around 1929 that the "striptease" became a feature that placed burlesque on the fringes of legality.

Modern vaudeville grew out of the same movement. In the 1880s Tony Pastor (1837–1908) reshaped the burlesque to make it suitable for the family audience. From about 1890 until 1930, vaudeville was one of the most popular of theatrical entertainments. Essentially a collection of variety acts, it also featured sketches and short plays in which leading actors often performed.

Most of the major actors of the period have already been mentioned, but a few others deserve attention. Joseph Jefferson III (1829–1905), one of the most beloved actors of the nineteenth century, was on the stage from the age of four. He early established a reputation for comic playing, but *Rip van Winkle* was to be the mainstay of his repertory after 1865. Noted for ease, expressive action, and inventive byplay, he mingled pathos and humor in a unique combination. John McCullough (1832–1885) came to the United States from Ireland at the age of fifteen. From 1861 to 1866 he played secondary roles to Forrest, whose approach he adopted. After playing in San Francisco from 1866 until 1875, McCullough came under MacKaye's influence and altered his acting style. By the time he died, he was considered second only to Booth as a

American dramatist of his day to establish the realistic mode.

Despite the trend toward realism, the majority of theatres continued to emphasize more popular fare. After 1870, minor dramatic forms were combined with variety acts to create new conceptions of burlesque and vaudeville. Burlesque began to change in 1866 when a troupe of ballet dancers, stranded in New York, were incorporated into *The Black Crook*. The resulting combination of spectacular scenery, lightly clad girls, music, dance, and song was so popular that it ran for sixteen months and spawned many imitations. This vogue was given further impetus in 1869 by the appearance of Lydia Thompson and her "British Blondes" in burlesques that emphasized feminine charms more than parody, the previous domain of burlesque. Soon burlesque had assumed its modern form: a collection of variety acts mingled with musical numbers featuring beautiful women. With its sexual overtones it came to appeal primarily to male audiences. Burlesque reached the height of its pop-

FIG. 14.12
Joseph Jefferson III as Rip van Winkle, a role he played for some forty years. Courtesy the Albert Davis Collection, Hoblitzelle Theatre Arts Collection, University of Texas at Austin.

tragic actor. Lawrence Barrett (1838–1891) had few attributes to recommend him for the stage. Accepted into Burton's company in 1857, he worked his way up slowly. Illiterate when he began, Barrett perfected his knowledge until he came to be known as the "scholar" of the American theatre. In the 1880s he became Booth's partner and co-star. Noted for his clarity of conception, he was somewhat faulty in execution because of his self-consciousness and artificial elocution. Richard Mansfield (1854–1907) went on the stage in 1880 and achieved his first success in 1883 as Baron Chevrial, a doddering lecher in *A Parisian Romance*. After 1886, he maintained his own company and each year added a new role to his repertory, alternating long runs of new works with his repertory of past hits. Best in melodramatic and eccentric parts, his lack of subtlety limited his success in major tragic roles. With his lavishly mounted productions, Mansfield was often compared to Irving as actor and manager.

By 1895 the actor's position in the theatre had changed radically. Benefits had been abandoned in the 1870s in favor of straight salary payments. With the triumph of the traveling company, most actors had to go to New York to seek employment. Furthermore, they were hired for the run of a play rather than by the season, and since there was as yet no union to protect their rights, they received no salary during rehearsal periods and were often stranded when productions closed on the road. From the position of dominance they had held for some 200 years, actors were now subordinate to both the director and the producer.

THEATRE IN CANADA

Canada had experienced the same large-scale emigration from English-speaking countries that the United States had experienced in the first half of the century, but its expansion into the western territories was slower. Since 1791 Canada had been divided into the largely French Catholic Lower Canada (now Quebec province) and the British loyalist Upper Canada (now Ontario). Attempts by the United States to annex Upper Canada in the War of 1812, and later conflict over borders in Oregon, had given emphasis to the need for a political system that would better provide for its defense. Reorganization into East and West Canada in 1841 did not provide the political authority needed to manage the expansion into the western territories, however, so in 1867 the Federation of Canada, which included Ontario, Nova Scotia, New Brunswick, and Quebec, was es-

tablished. By 1949 all the territories we now know as Canada had entered that federation, and it became a fully sovereign country in 1982.

During the second half of the nineteenth century Canada developed its first resident repertory companies (each with its own local touring circuit) and a chain of theatres in cities from the Atlantic to the Pacific coast. The companies played a season of thirty weeks, with the bill changing weekly. Actors were generally recruited from New York, but the star performers were often English. Still, the companies had close connections with the cities they resided in, and as local apprentice actors moved up in the companies more and more of the actors were Canadian. Thus, the potential for a national drama was there, but it failed to be realized primarily because of the rapid and unexpected success of the single-show touring companies. Since touring shows had to be successful in the larger cities of the United States, economics did not allow for the development of a distinctly Canadian theatre. As the resident repertory system was abandoned, Canadian theatres became more dependent on the New York theatrical "syndicate," ensuring the dominance of American shows and leaving plays by local talent to receive only occasional regional presentation.

For this reason the vast majority of plays written by Canadian authors during the late nineteenth century were published but not performed. Charles Heavysege's poetic drama *Saul* (1857), for example, was highly regarded but did not receive more than a public reading. The French comedies of Pierre Petitclair (1813–1860) were produced by amateur societies, but generally not for a decade or more after they were published. Political satires were quite popular but were generally by anonymous authors and were intended for a reading public. The first exception to this was Graves Sinco Lee's (1828–1912) *Fiddle, Faddle, and Foozel* (1853), which was a great success at the Royal Lyceum, Toronto. Two Gilbert and Sullivan–inspired pieces, *HMS Parliament* (1880), a biting satire on Canadian government by W. H. Fuller, and *Bunthorne Abroad* (1883), J. W. Bengough's caricature of his fellow Canadians, were also notable stage successes and rare examples of Canadian touring shows. Winnipeg author Charles W. Handscomb's (1867–1906) *The Big Boom* (1886) was another play on a Canadian subject to be produced, but other Canadian authors saw their plays performed only when they wrote dramas with no particular connection to Canada.

When Canadian actors became famous, as William Burke Wood (1779–1861) did at the start of the century, and as a whole host of Canadian actors did right down to Julia Arthur (1876–1958) at the very end of the century, it was for their work in U.S. or British markets, not for their work in Canada. One of the most noted exceptions to this was Charlotte Morrison (1832–1910). She became a star in Toronto, toured Canada as a star performer, and became the first manager of the Grand Opera House, Toronto, which she ran from 1874 to 1878. Eugene A. McDowell (1839–1913), Harry Lindley (1839–1913), and Ida Van Cortland (1854–1924) were among the other well-known actor-managers who chose to spend most of their careers in Canada.

By the mid-nineteenth century Halifax had become the summer home for companies from Boston and New York City. The Academy of Music was built there in 1877 but Halifax generally stayed outside the main Canadian touring circuits. Montreal, on the other hand, had become the largest city in Canada and was at the center of theatrical activities. It acquired its first resident repertory company, the Theatre Royal Stock Company, under John Willington Buckland (1815–1872) in 1852. By the 1870s Montreal was the home for companies that toured throughout Canada. The Academy of Music opened there in 1875, the Crystal Place and the Victoria in 1884, and five additional theatres by 1900. The Roman Catholic Church took an increasingly strong stand against theatre starting in 1859, and this had a chilling effect on French-language theatre both there and in Quebec City. Visiting French companies tended to restrict themselves to noncontroversial operettas. It was not until Sarah Bernhardt's visits in 1880, 1891, 1896, and several more times in the next decades that French dramas were able to attract a substantial audience.

Toronto acquired its first resident company at the Royal Lyceum in 1853 under the management of John Nickinson (1808–1864). Nickinson had started in garrison theatre but bought out his military commission to go into professional acting. The Grand Opera house, Toronto (1874; capacity 1,323), quickly took over from the Lyceum as the home of standard drama, and when it burned down in 1879 it was immediately rebuilt with an increased capacity (1,751). The Royal Opera house produced melodrama and the Queen's Theatre specialized in variety. Both burned in 1883 but the Toronto Opera House (with a capacity of 1,900) soon replaced them. The Princess Theatre was added in 1896 with a capacity of 1,815.

Resident companies and theatre buildings appeared in cities all over Quebec and Ontario, most notably at Ottawa where a theatre was built in the governor general's residence in Rideau Hall in 1873, the Grand Theatre in 1875, and the Russel Theatre in 1897. As the population moved west, theatre moved with it.

Winnipeg was in many ways typical of what happened in towns throughout the West. The Red River Hall, on the second floor of a saloon, was built as a theatre there in 1866. The Theatre Royal replaced it in 1870. A professional minstrel company made its way to Winnipeg in 1877, and when the rail link was made with Minneapolis in 1879, Winnipeg became a thriving city and a regular stop on the touring circuits. By 1883 the Princess Theatre had to be built with a capacity of 1,300. On the Pacific coast the garrison at Victoria performed plays on warships in the harbor until the gold rush of 1858. George Chapman's Pioneer Dramatic Company arrived the following year and built the 360-seat Colonial Theatre (1860). Three theatres were built in Vancouver by 1900, and dozens of tiny mining communities built "opera houses" for the use of touring companies.

THEATRE IN AUSTRALIA AND NEW ZEALAND

The first colony on the continent of Australia was the British penal colony at Port Jackson, now Sydney, founded in 1788. By 1829 England had laid claim to the entire continent, dividing it into the colonies of New South Wales, Victoria, Queensland, South Australia, Western Australia, and Tasmania. These colonies were formed into a federation under a unified constitution in 1901.

The aboriginal peoples of Australia and New Zealand encountered by the Europeans had developed sophisticated narrative dances telling stories of the history and myths of their cultures. Some stories were told as part of initiation rites while others served religious purposes and still others were primarily for entertainment. Each of the over 200 different aboriginal groups had its own distinctive form of dance narratives, but body painting and decoration with plants and feathers were common characteristics. Protestant missionaries, unlike the Catholic missionaries of Latin America and French Canada, did not use theatre as a tool for teaching religious doctrine, so there was less interaction between these native traditions and the techniques of Western theatre than was found in colonies elsewhere.

The first European play to be performed in Australia was a production of Farquhar's *The Recruiting Officer* staged with a few yards of stained paper and a dozen candles in a convict's hut in 1789. (The first continental European play, Kotzebue's *The Stranger*, was not performed there until 1833.) Robert Sidaway (1757–1809) opened a theatre in Sydney Town in 1796, but little is known of it beyond its unusual policy of accepting goods in place of money for entry. It was "dismantled" by order of the governor in 1778 but seems to have been in operation again from 1799 to between 1804 and 1808, when the government began to enforce the order that all theatrical activity should cease. Nonetheless, a convict theatre was started at Emu Plains, west of Sydney, in 1825 and managed to operate successfully for five years before it too was ordered closed.

Such government restrictions on the theatre meant that the first play written on an Australian topic, *The Bushrangers* (1828) by David Burn (1799–1857), had to be performed in Burn's hometown of Edinburgh. The play featured an outlaw hero based on a real person and a tyrannical British lieutenant-governor. It also featured savage aboriginals who, when they were not out to murder "honest" settlers, were dancing the *corraboree,* an authentic aboriginal dance that, when depicted on the stage, was made to look as foolish as were the dances of Americans of African descent in the minstrel shows of the United States. The first play on a local theme to be performed and published in Australia was also called *The Bushrangers* (1834), by Henry Melville (1800–1873). In this play the outlaws are not heroic and the main aboriginal character, Murrahawa, actually helps to rescue a settler family. By 1832 a system for licensing plays had been established and plays on local topics were discouraged. Charles Nagel (*fl.* 1837–1846) became Australia's first comic playwright with the burletta *The Mock Catalani* (1842) and the burlesque *Shakespiriconglommorofunnidogammonae* (1844). David Burn returned to Australia and to playwriting with *Our First Lieutenant* (1844) and *The Queen's Love* (1845), which were performed in both Sydney and Melbourne. But *The Currency Lass* (1844), by Edward Geoghegan (1813–?), was the first play on a local topic to get a license.

Professional theatre arrived in Sydney in 1832 when local businessman, music hall operator, and self-proclaimed father of the Australian stage Barnett Levey (1798–1837) brought a company there to perform in his hotel in December and opened the Theatre Royal, George Street, the following fall. His license stipulated that he could produce only plays already staged by the licensed theatres in London. He produced the first professional productions of Shakespeare's plays there, but was best known for short London farces adapted with a good deal of local color and called "at homes." Levey's theatre was supplanted by the Royal Victoria Theatre and its professional company, managed by Joseph Wyatt, in 1838. This company produced a large number of actor-playwrights including Conrad Knowles (*c.* 1810–1844) with *Salathiel* (1842), Francis Nesbitt McCron (1809–1853) with *Ravenswood* (1843), and Joseph Simmons (1810–1893) with *The Duellist*

(1844). Their plays were, however, adaptations of novels and pirated translations of French melodramas that were so common in this half of the nineteenth century. Two other theatres were built in Sydney in the 1840s, but the Royal Victoria dominated the market until 1880. Many of the Sydney-trained actors became actor-managers and stars in Australia, but only Eliza Winstanley (1818–1882) went on to become a success in London. She was followed by Nellie (Eleanor) Stewart (1858–1931), who started acting at five and went on to have a successful career in Australia, England, and the United States.

During the 1830s and 1840s theatre followed the colonization of other parts of the continent, which was often motivated by the discovery of gold and a subsequent gold rush. A Theatre Royal was built at Hobart in Tasmania in 1837 (which still stands, much altered, today). The free colony at Adelaide (founded 1836) opened its first theatre in 1838 and added two more before the Queen's Theatre opened in 1841. The Queen's became the Royal Victoria when English actor-manager George Selth Coppin (1819–1906) took it over in 1843. By 1850 he owned another theatre in Port Adelaide and four theatres in the free colony of Melbourne (founded 1835), including the prefabricated Olympic Theatre (1855, called the "Iron Pot") sent by ship from Manchester. Melbourne had an active theatre scene before Coppin arrived, however, having built the Pavilion Theatre in 1841 (later renamed the Royal Victoria) and the Theatre Royal in 1845, both managed by former members of the Sydney company.

Coppin introduced Australia to the star system and brought most of the important stars to tour there over the next twenty years. Among the British stars were Barry Sullivan (toured 1862–1866), Charles Kean and Ellen Tree (toured 1863), and Charles Mathews the younger (toured 1870–1871). Among the American stars were Edwin Booth (toured with Laura Keene, 1854) and Joseph Jefferson (toured 1861–1865). By the 1870s Australia was part of the international touring circuit and the American James Cassius Williamson had replaced Coppin as the foremost producer in the country. Williamson formed a "triumvirate" with Arthur Garner and George Musgrove and their firm, in various manifestations, dominated the Australian market for the next hundred years (until 1976). The Italian tragic actress Adelaide Ristori toured in 1875, Dion Boucicault in 1885 (his son stayed to found an important company in Melbourne), and Sarah Bernhardt in 1891. Janet Achurch brought the highly controversial *A Doll's House* to Australia in 1889, just after its London staging. Unfortunately Williamson had no interest in indigenous Australian drama and his control of the theatres stultified its development. A few playwrights did find success with Australian plays in spite of this, however; these included George Darrell (1841–1921) with *The Sunny South* (1882), the highly regarded actor Alfred Damper (*c.* 1847–1908) who wrote plays like *Robbery Under Arms* (1890 with Garnet Walch), and Charles Reade, who wrote, among other plays, *It's Never Too Late To Mend* (1893), which included "forty Queensland Aboriginals."

Australia's most successful actor-manager of this period was the Englishman Bland Holt (1851–1942). Holt had secured what amounted to a monopoly on the most recent successes from Drury Lane and the Adelphi Theatre in London and mounted them with meticulous attention to spectacle and detail. He was able to operate without assistance from the Williamson organization, but he remained skeptical of turning to the kind of local stories that George Darrell had made so popular. In 1899, however, he began to "localize" English and American melodramas into Australian settings. *The Breaking of the Drought* (1902) was his most successful such production.

New Zealand was governed from New South Wales until it became a separate colony in 1840. In 1907 it became completely self-governing, and in 1947 it became fully independent. Theatre there followed the pattern seen in Canada and Australia of garrison companies, followed by amateur companies, then by professionals, both resident and touring. New Zealand's touring companies were extensions of Williamson's Australian circuit. The most distinctive feature of theatre in New Zealand was that, because it was established so late, its railway system only started to facilitate theatrical touring about the time moving pictures arrived to undermine it. George Darrel's *Transported for Life* (1876) and George Leitch's (1842–1907) *Land of Moa* (1895) were the most successful plays on the New Zealand circuit.

ENGLISH DRAMA, 1850–1890

In England, drama was at a low ebb during the second half of the nineteenth century, although a number of writers achieved contemporary fame with melodramas, light comedies, burlesques, and musical dramas. Among the popular dramatists of this period were Taylor, Byron, and Boucicault.

Between 1844 and 1878, Tom Taylor (1817–1880) wrote more than seventy plays ranging through almost every type, but he was at his best in comedy and domestic drama. Among his most famous works were *Masks and Faces* (1852), based on the life of Peg Woffington; *Still Waters Run Deep* (1855), which cre-

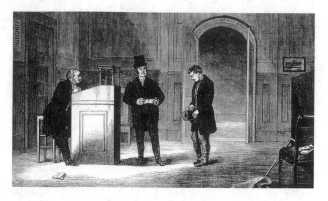

FIG. 14.13

Tom Taylor's *The Ticket-of-Leave Man* as produced at the Olympic Theatre, London, 1863. At center, Horace Wigan as Hawkshaw, perhaps the first stage detective. Courtesy Theatre Museum, Victoria and Albert Museum, London.

ated a stir because of its discussion of sex; *Our American Cousin* (1858), made famous by Edward Askew Sothern's (1826–1881) playing of the elderly rake, Lord Dundreary; and *The Ticket-of-Leave Man* (1863), a story of low life featuring the detective Hawkshaw.

Between 1857 and 1882 Henry James Byron (1834–1884) wrote nearly 150 plays ranging from sentimental comedy to burlesque-extravaganza. *Our Boys* (1875) achieved a run of 1,362 performances, a record that stood for many years. Byron's plays epitomize the general level of dramatic entertainment in the late nineteenth century, for they seldom penetrated beneath the surface of conventional ideas or stock characters.

Perhaps the most successful dramatist of the period was the comic actor Dion Boucicault (1822–1890), who began his writing career in 1841 with *London Assurance,* a sprightly comedy of manners, and continued to write prolifically thereafter. From 1844 to 1848 he lived in France, where he mastered the techniques of French romantic drama and melodrama. He spent the years between 1853 and 1860 in the United States where he wrote and produced plays, acted, and managed theatres. Thereafter he divided his time between the United States and England, traveling to Australia in 1885. During the 1850s Boucicault perfected the basic ingredients of his melodramas—sentimentality, wit, sensationalism, and local color—and seldom varied them thereafter except in details. His major works, such as *The Corsican Brothers* (1852), *The Sidewalks of New York* (1857), *The Octoroon* (1859), *The Colleen Bawn* (1860), *Arrah-na-Pogue* (1864), and *The Shaughraun* (1874), all tell suspenseful and melodramatic stories set in picturesque locales, and most are resolved through scenes of sensational spectacle, such as fires, explosions, snow-storms, or avalanches. Not only was Boucicault one of the most skillful playwrights of his age, his penchant for making the latest scientific inventions important elements in his plots exerted considerable influence on theatrical production.

Not until the 1860s did a dramatist interested in the realistic mode appear. Thomas William Robertson (1829–1871), son of a provincial actor, was originally a performer and for a time Vestris's stage manager. He began writing in 1851 but had little success until 1864 when *David Garrick* was produced. The plays upon which his reputation rests—*Society* (1865), *Ours* (1866), *Caste* (1867), *Play* (1868), and *School* (1869)—all tell stories of contemporary life and take place in highly particularized locales, every detail of which is meticulously described in the scripts. Furthermore, many important points are made primarily through pantomime and stage business which re-create everyday domestic events, such as making, serving, and drinking tea. As produced by the Bancrofts, these plays also popularized several innovations in performance. Robertson cannot be labeled a great dramatist but among his contemporaries he was unique. Unfortunately, he had no immediate successors, and consequently the realistic vein was not exploited by English writers until the 1890s.

In terms of popular appeal, the most favored forms between 1850 and 1900 were pantomime, burlesque-extravaganza, and musical entertainments. During these years pantomime underwent significant change as the traditional short form was enlarged into full-length entertainments. This transformation owed most perhaps to the playwright E. L. Blanchard (1820–1889) and to the Vokes family of performers at Drury Lane

FIG. 14.15
Puss in Boots, a pantomine at Drury Lane Theatre in 1887. Script by E. L. Blanchard, setting by Wilhelm. From *The Graphic* (7 January 1888).

FIG. 14.14
Slave auction scene in Boucicault's *The Octoroon,* first performed in 1859. A contemporary engraving.

between 1869 and 1879. Then, during the 1880s Augustus Harris (1851–1896) made still other changes when he began to import music hall performers to Drury Lane to play the "principal boy" (a breeches role) and the "dame" (played by a man) and to present numerous specialty acts as a part of the pantomime. After this time comedy gained the ascendancy, and the fairy tale element became merely a skimpy framework holding together the comic routines, dances, and spectacle. It is in this form that the English Christmas pantomime was to survive (with some modifications) down to the present.

At mid-century the most popular of all dramatic types was burlesque-extravaganza. Almost all theatres performed it, and a few built their repertory around it. By this time Planché's light touch and delicate irreverence had given way to broad travesties of popular plays, operas, myths, and fairy tales, all filled with topical allusions, low comedy business, and anachronisms. Puns appeared in almost every line of the doggerel verse in which they were written. Numerous songs set to already existing music and elaborate spectacle, including a magical transformation scene, completed the appeals. In addition to H. J. Byron, other masters of the genre were William Brough (1826–1870) and F. C. Burnand (1836–1917).

By the 1870s burlesque-extravaganza had begun to decline in popularity, although it continued to be performed until the end of the century. As it declined, its place was taken by comic opera, especially that of Gilbert and Sullivan. William S. Gilbert (1836–1911), encouraged by Robertson to take up dramatic writing, was the author of some forty plays, mostly comedies, quite independent of Sullivan's music. Several of these—most notably *Pygmalion and Galatea* (1871), *Sweethearts* (1874), *Broken Hearts* (1875), and *Engaged* (1877)—enjoyed considerable success. But Gilbert is now remembered primarily for the comic operas he wrote with Arthur Sullivan (1842–1900). Their first important work, *Trial by Jury* (1875), also brought an alliance with Richard D'Oyly Carte (1844–1901), who in 1881 built the Savoy Theatre to house their plays. Among their many collaborations, some of the best are *H. M. S. Pinafore* (1878), *The Pirates of Penzance* (1879), *The Mikado* (1885), and *The Gondoliers* (1889). Eventually a quarrel between Gilbert and Sullivan disrupted their partnership, but their comic operas have continued to hold the stage. With their lighthearted melodies and whimsical humor, the partners turned extravaganza into a form of satire sometimes said to be the nineteenth-century equivalent of Aristophanic comedy.

The success of Gilbert and Sullivan prompted still other developments in musical drama, most notably in the work of George Edwardes (1852–1915). Business manager of the Savoy Theatre for a time, in 1885 Edwardes became manager of the Gaiety Theatre. There, beginning with *In Town* (1892) and *The Shop Girl* (1894), Edwardes established a type of musical comedy in which a sketchy plot provided an excuse for songs, elaborate production numbers performed by beautiful chorus girls, and specialty acts. In this form, musical comedy was to flourish without significant change until the First World War.

The music hall also prospered in the late nineteenth century as regular drama was separated from the incidental entertainment that had accompanied it since around 1700. Music halls developed out of the "music rooms" attached to taverns, but it was not until about 1850 that Charles Morton (1819–1904) took the significant step of erecting a separate adjacent building to house entertainment. Other tavern owners followed his example, but it was many years before the link with taverns was broken. Gradually, however, the separation came, and the entertainment was made acceptable to middle-class audiences. Sketches and short plays were added to the bills, and famous actors and concert artists were induced to appear in the music hall theatres that sprang up throughout England. A number of circuits were created—the most famous being that of Edward Moss and Oswald Stoll. This form of variety entertainment remained a favorite with the British public until after World War I, when the motion picture began to replace it.

ENGLISH THEATRICAL CONDITIONS, 1843–1860

When the Theatre Regulation Act was passed in 1843, the London stage seemed at a low ebb. Many persons assumed that the new law would bring rapid change and that many new theatres would be built. However, the period between 1843 and 1860 was to be one of reassessment and gradual recovery. Unlike the years between 1810 and 1843, when many new buildings were erected, no new theatre was built in London until after 1860. Yet in retrospect, out of the years 1843–1860 grew unprecedented prosperity and prestige.

After 1843, Drury Lane and Covent Garden rapidly lost their positions of dominance. Covent Garden soon became the home of opera, while Drury Lane turned increasingly to spectacle and musical drama; both have continued these specialties to the present. Of the patent theatres, only the Haymarket retained its stability, becoming London's foremost home for regular drama between 1843 and 1850. From 1837 to 1853 it was managed by Benjamin Webster (1797–1882), a former member of Vestris's

FIG. 14.16
The Haymarket Theatre that in 1821 replaced the older structure, torn down in 1820. It is still in use. The ground plan is seen at bottom. From Wilkinson, *Londina Illustrata* (1825).

FIG. 14.17
Samuel Phelps as Macbeth, Act II, scene 1, just before the murder of Duncan. Courtesy Hoblitzelle Theatre Arts Collection, University of Texas at Austin.

pectations, not only was Phelps financially successful but also he made Sadler's Wells the principal home of poetic drama in London between 1844 and 1862. Phelps's significance lies in his demonstration—at a time when it was almost universally believed that only popular entertainment could attract a large audience—that fine drama could bring success. The source of Phelps's popularity was unmistakable, for his repertory was composed almost entirely of poetic drama. Except for six of the minor works, Phelps produced all of Shakespeare's plays in versions more complete than any since Shakespeare's time.

Although he mounted his productions with care, Phelps's lack of funds precluded sumptuous costumes and settings and, while he sought historical accuracy, he never sacrificed dramatic values. His most famous production, *A Midsummer Night's Dream* with settings by Frederick Fenton, used a moving diorama to shift the scene from one part of the forest to another and a scrim, behind which much of the action took place, to create a misty atmosphere. Phelps suffered most from the lack of first-rate actors. For the first two season, Mrs. Warner played leading roles; she was followed by Isabella Glyn and several lesser actresses. Perhaps because of their inexperience, the actors were coached extensively by Phelps, who also played many

troupe, who in 1844 also acquired the Adelphi, which specialized in melodramas, most notably those of J. B. Buckstone. In 1853 Webster ceded the management of the Haymarket to Buckstone, who retained it until 1876. Under Buckstone, the Haymarket maintained its reputation for comedy, but it lost its privileged position in serious drama except when visiting stars performed there. Webster rebuilt the Adelphi in 1858 and remained at its head until 1874.

Webster and Buckstone were both continuers of tradition rather than innovators. Major new developments were to come at Sadler's Wells and the Princess's Theatre. In 1844 Sadler's Wells was a remote house noted for its bloodthirsty melodramas. Since about 1730 it had been offering theatrical entertainments, and it had been the principal target of the bill of 1752, which required the licensing of all places of entertainment. In the early nineteenth century it had gained renown for its aquatic dramas and later as the summer home of Joseph Grimaldi (1778–1837), the most famous clown of pantomime.

It is unclear why Samuel Phelps (1804–1878), an actor since 1826 and Macready's principal support since 1837, chose this out-of-the-way, rundown theatre for his experiment in management, but it is probably explained by the low rent. Contrary to ex-

FIG. 14.18
Lord Byron's *Manfred* at Drury Lane, 1863. Shown here is the Steinbach Waterfall, haunt of the Witch of the Alps. Samuel Phelps appeared in this production after leaving Sadler's Wells. From *The Illustrated London News* (1863).

leading roles ranging from Lear to Bottom. As a performer, Phelps was universally praised for his judgment, taste, absence of tricks, and faultless elocution (which Macready and Charles Kean were slighting in their attempts to achieve greater realism). His faults were monotonous pace and slow delivery. Despite its mediocre company, Sadler's Wells had the most devoted audience of any theatre in London.

It is sometimes said that as a manager Phelps merely continued Macready's work. While this is partially true, Phelps succeeded where Macready failed, and it was he who reestablished that faith in poetic drama which Macready's financial troubles had helped to undermine. After he gave up Sadler's Wells in 1862, Phelps toured widely, and for a time in the 1860s restored Drury Lane to its former glory with a series of Shakespearean productions. He continued on the stage until 1877, by which time he was considered old-fashioned.

If Phelps revived poetic drama, Charles Kean (1811–1868) perfected pictorial realism and brought the fashionable audience back to the theatre. Son of Edmund Kean, he went on the stage in 1827 but, lacking his father's powers, he gained little recognition until 1838. In 1842 he married Ellen Tree (1806–1880), his leading lady thereafter. His first experience as a director came in 1841, when he staged *Romeo and Juliet* for Webster. During his third tour of America between 1845 and 1847, he pro-

duced *King John* and *Richard III* in New York, following Macready's prompt books closely. The most detailed productions yet seen in North America, their success probably encouraged Kean to go into management, and in 1850 he leased the Princess's Theatre in London.

The Princess's was the last theatre opened in London before the passage of the Theatre Regulation Act. During the 1840s it was noteworthy primarily because it presented the American actors Edwin Forest, Charlotte Cushman, and Anna Cora Mowatt. Its period of glory, however, was to come with Kean's management between 1850 and 1859.

Kean's work is significant for several reasons. First, it brought fashionable audiences back to the theatre, although much of the credit should go to Queen Victoria, who in 1848 revived the office of Master of Revels and appointed Kean to it. Queen Victoria requested from Kean many theatrical performances for Windsor Castle and also began to attend the Princess's Theatre. The combination of her prestige and the respectable tone of Kean's management soon made his theatre a fashionable resort.

Second, Kean influenced changes in the evening's bill. Because fashionable playgoers tended to dine late, Kean opened some productions with a short piece to offset the effect of late arrivals. Gradually this practice caught on, and the curtain-raiser replaced the afterpiece in many theatres. Furthermore, he dispensed with all incidental entertainment. Thereafter, variety acts were increasingly relegated to the music halls, and each theatre began to specialize in a limited range of theatrical entertainment.

Third, Kean continued the trend toward "gentlemanly" melodrama begun by Macready. Although now remembered primarily for his Shakespearean productions, Kean presented fewer than half of Shakespeare's plays, and his greatest success as an actor came in such melodramas as Boucicault's *The Corsican Brothers* and *Louis XI,* both adapted from French works blending romantic drama and melodrama. Such plays were to enjoy enormous popularity through the remainder of the century.

Fourth, and probably most important, Kean developed antiquarianism farther than any English producer. His first significant attempt to ensure accuracy in every detail came in 1852 with *King John.* Beginning with *Macbeth* in 1853, he provided the audience with a printed list of the authorities he had consulted in his search for authenticity. Kean considered his election in 1857 to the Society of Antiquaries one of his greatest honors. Despite his care for details, however, Kean could never induce Ellen Tree to abandon the hooped petticoats she wore under garments of every period.

FIG. 14.19
One of the witches scenes from Charles Kean's production of *Macbeth* in 1853 at the Princess's Theatre, London. Courtesy Hoblitzelle Theatre Arts Collection, University of Texas at Austin.

Often called the "illustrator" of Shakespeare's texts, Kean cut many of the finest descriptive passages and replaced them with spectacle and pantomime, and he often rearranged texts so as to avoid scene changes. For settings, Kean had the services of such gifted designers as Thomas Grieve, William Telbin, and Frederick Lloyds. About 400 water-color sketches of Kean's productions have survived to provide one of the most complete records of any nineteenth-century producer's work.

Finally, Kean helped to establish the director as the primary artist in the theatre. Other than himself and his wife, he employed no stars. He gained his effects primarily through care for details and the coordination of the whole. Despite his fame, Kean was not financially successful, for he always spent more than he made. Any deficit, however, can be attributed to his high standards rather than to lack of patronage, for his theatre was always well attended. After their retirement from management, the Keans toured throughout the world in starring engagements.

ENGLISH THEATRICAL CONDITIONS, 1860–1880

By 1860 the major work of both Phelps and Kean was over, and the theatre was well on its way to recovery. For the first time since 1843, new theatres began to be built, and by 1870 the twenty-one theatres of 1860 had increased to thirty. The population of London also grew from 3,316,932 in 1864 to 4,766,661 in 1881. This growth brought a number of changes in theatrical production, as can be seen in the work of Fechter, Boucicault, and the Bancrofts.

Charles Fechter (1824–1879), born in London to a German father and French mother, made his debut at the Comédie Française in 1844. Soon dissatisfied, he left to play for a time in Berlin and London before returning to Paris in 1848. He was soon regarded as the foremost stage lover of his day (he was the original Armand Duval in Dumas' *Camille*), and for a time was joint manager of the Odéon. Resigning after a disagreement, he decided to go to London.

Fechter opened at the Princess's Theatre in 1860 and there in 1861 created a sensation with his production of *Hamlet*. Unfamiliar with the English tradition, Fechter's interpretation of Hamlet was markedly different from any previously seen. Playing in the familiar style of gentlemanly melodrama and in settings furnished like ordinary rooms, he made the play seem contemporary. From 1863 to 1867 Fechter managed the Lyceum Theatre, where he featured translations of French plays and won a reputation as one of the finest actors of his time. In

1870 he went to the United States, but failed to gain a wide following because by then his powers were fading. In 1876 he retired.

Fechter's influence was considerable. First, he extended the vogue for gentlemanly melodrama begun by Macready and Kean. Second, he popularized a more realistic acting style, for he played the classics in precisely the same manner as he did contemporary drama. Thereafter, poetic drama grew in favor largely because it was merged with the nineteenth-century taste for spectacular melodrama. Third, Fechter revived interest in the box set, which he used for most interiors. He gave up the practice of entering between the wings, which English actors had done since the proscenium arch doors had gone out of fashion early in the century, even when the wings represented solid walls. While Fechter did not bring about a revolution in theatrical practice, he encouraged more rigorous concern for illusionism.

After Dion Boucicault returned to England in 1860, he helped to gain acceptance for several innovations. He contributed to the vogue of the "out-of-town tryout" when *Arrah-na-Pogue* was played in the provinces before opening in London in 1865. He was also one of the first to employ actors for the run

FIG. 14.20

Charles Fechter as Hamlet. Graveyard scene, Act V, scene 1. Courtesy Hoblitzelle Theatre Arts Collection, University of Texas at Austin.

of the play rather than on a season's contract, for he seems early to have grasped the implications of a long-run policy. Additionally, Boucicault was the first English playwright to achieve financial security from his writing. During the early nineteenth century the traditional practice of paying authors through benefit performances had gradually been replaced by the payment of set sums (normally £100 for a five-act play and proportionately less for shorter works) on the third, sixth, and twentieth nights of the original unbroken run. Few playwrights between 1810 and 1860, however, had received even £300 for a single play. Jerrold testified that for *Black-Eyed Susan*, one of the most popular works of the nineteenth century, he had received a total of £70. By 1830 dissatisfaction with this situation had prompted the formation of the Dramatic Authors' Society, and largely because of its efforts Parliament in 1833 passed England's first copyright law relating to plays. But, while the act protected dramas written after 1823, it did not cover dramatizations of novels, and the force of the bill was further reduced by a court decision which declared that the acting rights to printed plays belonged to their publishers. Thereafter, many dramatists sought to keep their works out of print. Thus, the new bill gave authors some protection but did not greatly improve their lot.

Boucicault's innovation did not stem from any new legal sanction. Rather, the audiences' desire to see the plays was so great that managers vied for the right to present them, and Boucicault could demand a percentage of the receipts as a condition. Consequently, *The Shaughraun* is said to have earned him $500,000. In 1865 the Bancrofts began to pay Robertson a set fee for each performance of his works; thereafter, the royalty system gradually gained in favor. The playwright's legal position did not become secure, however, until near the end of the nineteenth century, for copyright did not extend beyond national boundaries. In 1886 an International Copyright Agreement, under which each subscribing nation pledged to uphold the copyright provisions of all others, was prepared, and by 1900 most of the world's major countries had accepted it. Loopholes in earlier national laws were also gradually eliminated. Largely for these reasons, playwriting at last became a profitable profession.

Probably the most significant management between 1860 and 1880 was that of the Bancrofts at the Prince of Wales's Theatre, for here many earlier trends came together. Although it is difficult to discover a practice that they initiated, the Bancrofts combined a number of innovations to create a theatre quite unlike any other of the period.

Mrs. Bancroft, born Marie Wilton (1839–1921), was on the stage as a child, appearing with both

FIG. 14.21

Boucicault's *The Corsican Brothers*, Princess's Theatre, London, 1852. Charles Kean is seen at left as the dying Louis dei Franchi. Kean also played Louis's twin brother, Fabien, who avenges his brother's death. Courtesy Theatre Museum, Victoria and Albert Museum, London.

Macready and Charles Kean. Her success as an adult actress began in burlesque-extravaganza in 1856. Then, at the age of twenty-six, she decided to manage her own company. The only theatre she could afford to rent was the out-of-the-way Queen's Theatre, so run-down that it was known as the "dust hole." Nevertheless, after indemnifying him against loss, she induced the popular dramatist H. J. Byron to join her as co-manager and to supply the theatre with plays. Renamed the Prince of Wales's, the theatre opened in 1865. In securing Byron's services, Wilton obviously intended to present a repertory composed primarily of burlesques and light comedy. It was at Byron's urging that she produced Robertson's *Society*, a play previously refused by several other managers. Its run of 150 nights began an association that soon made Byron superfluous, and in 1867 he withdrew from the management. In the same year Wilton married Squire Bancroft (1841–1926), her leading man. Bancroft had made his debut in 1861 and had played in the provinces until he joined Wilton's company in 1865. From 1867 to 1879 the Bancrofts were joint managers of the Prince of Wales's Theatre, and from 1880 until they retired in 1885, of the Haymarket.

It is difficult to distinguish the Bancrofts' contributions from those of Robertson, for not only was he their major playwright, he also directed the plays during the formative years. On the other hand, Robertson had little success with any other troupe. Consequently, it would appear that their joint success stemmed from compatibility.

FIG. 14.22
Robertson's *Caste* as produced by the Bancrofts at the Prince of Wales's Theatre, 1879. Courtesy Enthoven Collection, Victoria and Albert Museum, London.

The distinctive Robertson-Bancroft style—a form of domestic realism—first appeared with *Caste* (1867). While several earlier producers had emphasized realistic visual detail, they had used spectacle primarily as embellishment. In Robertson's plays, on the other hand, character and stage business are inseparable, for the attitude and emotions of his personages are revealed primarily through the minutiae of everyday life. Without spectacle Robertson's plays scarcely exist, and the printed versions require lengthy and detailed stage directions to be comprehensible. They marked the advent of a new kind of realism in England.

Robertson worked with the actors of the Bancroft troupe on every detail; he substituted understatement for bravura acting and emphasized ensemble effects. Lines of business, still dominant in other companies, were ignored. The company had no stars, and even the Bancrofts often played small roles. Perhaps fortunately, most of the actors were young and welcomed these breaks with tradition.

The Bancrofts' contributions came primarily in contemporary drama. Only two of their productions were of classics and these were unsuccessful, for the company's acting style was not suited to period plays. Nevertheless, the prestige of the Bancroft company was comparable to that enjoyed earlier by Charles Kean, and contemporary drama was raised considerably in critical esteem.

The Bancrofts embraced the long run. In their twenty years of management they produced only thirty long plays, and almost half of all performances were of Robertson's works. After they began to present a series of plays for extended runs, they employed many of their actors on a "run of the play" contract. They abandoned benefits for actors, then still prevalent in most theatres, and raised salaries markedly. When other managers were paying actors £5 to £10 weekly, the Bancrofts were offering £60 to £100.

The Bancrofts also helped to establish several other important innovations. Their production of *Caste* in 1867 was among the first in England to tour with a full company and with all scenery and properties. Thereafter touring increased rapidly and by 1880 provincial resident companies were beginning to disappear. The Bancrofts also helped to establish the single-play bill by dropping the curtain-raiser and afterpiece. Although some theatres retained the longer bill, audiences no longer demanded it. Additionally, the Bancrofts aided in establishing matinee performances. Used occasionally after the 1850s, matinees became usual with the Bancrofts during their production of Sardou's *Diplomacy* in 1878. Matinees were adopted for Gilbert and Sullivan's comic operas in the 1880s and were standard in most theatres by 1900.

Many of the Bancrofts' contributions involved spectacle and theatre architecture. More than any other British management of the nineteenth century, they won acceptance for the box set. Because of their example, most theatres after 1875 devoted as much care to accuracy in modern as in period plays. The Bancrofts also firmly anchored acting behind the proscenium arch. The retreat from the forestage had begun with Garrick, but, despite several attempts to abandon the proscenium doors, they were not removed at Drury Lane until 1822 and at Covent Garden until 1823. In 1831 the Olympic became the first minor house to dispense with them. The apron persisted, however, and actors continued to use it. But after 1867, the "fourth wall" was always respected at the Prince of Wales's Theatre. When the Bancrofts moved to the Haymarket in 1880, they extended the gilded proscenium arch across the bottom of the stage to emphasize the picture frame. By 1900 the use of the apron had been seriously curtailed in virtually all of London's theatres.

The Bancrofts were also instrumental in establishing the orchestra level as the favored seating area. In 1800 the pit still consisted only of backless benches. The King's Theatre, which was used for opera, converted some of its benches into seats with backs in the 1820s, and in 1822 the Drury Lane added a few of these "stalls." Gradually other theatres accepted the change, although the stalls were restricted to a few rows at the front, and the pit continued to occupy the remainder of the ground floor. In 1863 the Haymarket replaced its stalls with upholstered chairs, and the last pit benches were removed when the Bancrofts took over in 1880. Other theatres eventually followed this example. With the introduction of chair-style seating came the numbering and reservation of places. In turn, the ability to reserve seats reinforced the long run, since popular plays encouraged the booking of seats in advance, and advance sales encouraged the extension of runs.

These changes are representative of many others in auditorium design. Since the Restoration, the pit had been surrounded by boxes only slightly raised above it. Around 1820, however, the Adelphi Theatre established a new trend when the boxes were raised sufficiently to permit the extension of the pit to the outside walls. Other changes came after 1860. Probably most important was the movement away from large houses. The Criterion, opened in 1874, held only 660, and the Prince of Wales's seated only 600. Few theatres built after 1875 held more than 1,500. This reduction in size meant fewer galleries, while the growing prestige of stall seating motivated the replacement of boxes with open balconies, usually called the Dress Circle, Upper Circle, and Gallery.

Furthermore, the balconies were foreshortened on the sides so that they no longer extended to the proscenium wall. As a result, the proscenium arch could be lowered. The cantilevering of balconies, made possible in the late nineteenth century by the introduction of structural steel and concrete, permitted the removal of visible supporting posts in the auditorium. All these changes did much to improve sight lines and comfort. Many of these innovations were made by C. J. Phipps (1835–1897), architect of about forty theatres in England.

ENGLISH THEATRICAL CONDITIONS, 1880–1900

Between 1880 and 1900 the English theatre was dominated by the actor-manager Henry Irving (1838–1905). Born John Henry Brodribb, Irving played in the provinces from 1856 to 1866 and then in London with several leading actors before going to the Lyceum Theatre in 1871 as leading man and stage manager. At that time, the Lyceum was under the management of H. L. Bateman (1812–1875), an American who had leased the theatre to star his daughters, Kate (1843–1917), Virginia (1853–1940), and Isabel (1854–1934). Kate and her sister Ellen (1844–1936) had achieved acclaim in the United States as child prodigies in such roles as Richard III, Macbeth, and Shylock. Ellen had retired at the age of sixteen, but Kate had won considerable fame as an adult performer before the family came to London. After Bateman died in 1875, his wife continued as manager until 1878, when the Lyceum passed to Irving. Under Irving's management from 1878 to 1898, the Lyceum became the foremost theatre of London. Irving also played throughout England and made eight tours of the United States. He retired in 1902.

As an actor, Irving gained his first outstanding success in 1871 as Mathias in *The Bells,* a thrilling melodrama about a man who confesses under hypnosis to the murder of a Jewish peddler. This role remained one of Irving's most popular throughout his career. He continued to build his reputation in such melodramas as W. G. Wills's (1828–1891) *Charles I* (1872) and *Eugene Aram* (1873). In 1874 his *Hamlet* ran for 200 nights, a new record for a Shakespearean play. By the time he became a manager in 1878, he was considered the finest serious actor in London. His success had been won only through long and diligent work. Irving had few natural attributes upon which to build, and throughout his career critics voiced grave reservations about his playing. He mispronounced many words; walked, as one critic put

FIG. 14.23
Henry Irving (foreground) as Mathias in *The Bells* seeing a vision of the Polish Jew he has murdered. Irving played this role for more than thirty years. A contemporary engraving.

it, like a man trying to get over a plowed field hastily; and at times interpreted roles in a bizarre fashion. On the other hand, he was a master of byplay which clarified every reaction and thought. His roles were boldly conceived and carefully portrayed. Like Charles Kean, Irving was at his best in melodrama, for though he is now remembered chiefly as a Shakespearean actor, the only Shakespearean role in which he was consistently successful was Shylock. Irving promoted no new playwrights and never appeared in the new realistic drama.

Irving's fame is bound up with that of his leading lady, Ellen Terry (1847–1928), who came from a large family of actors, two others of whom were well known. Kate (1844–1924), on stage with Ellen as a child in Charles Kean's company, went on to perform Ophelia to Fechter's Hamlet before retiring in 1867. She was to be the grandmother of John Gielgud. Fred Terry (1863–1933), outstanding in romantic roles in the Lyceum company, managed his own troupe from 1900 to 1930. As an adult, Ellen Terry had played in the provinces, for the Bancrofts, and at the Court Theatre before joining Irving in 1878. She remained Irving's leading lady until he retired. She then managed the Imperial Theatre for a time, where she allowed her son, Gordon Craig, to try out many of his ideas. After 1907 she performed only occasionally, although she did not retire fully until 1925. At her best in such roles as Beatrice in *Much Ado About Nothing,* Olivia in *Twelfth Night,* and Portia in *The Merchant of Venice,* Terry had an excellent sense of timing and a masterful command of movement and speech. To all of her roles she brought freshness and vitality.

Despite the personal fame of Irving and Ellen Terry, the reputation of the Lyceum rested upon the total effect of its productions. Building upon the tradition of Macready and Charles Kean and stimulated by the London appearance of the Meiningen Players in 1881, Irving's work climaxed the trend in England toward pictorial realism. Although never the stickler for accuracy that Kean had been, Irving often employed archeologists to aid him, as in *Cymbeline* (1896) and *Coriolanus* (1901), for both of which the costumes and scenery were by Sir Lawrence Alma-Tadema (1836–1912). At other times he commissioned designs from such famous painters as Edward Burne-Jones (1833–1898). In addition, he had on his staff the finest scenic artists of the day, Hawes Craven (1837–1910) and Joseph Harker (1855–1927). Craven had worked in London since 1857 for such producers as Fechter and the Bancrofts, and to him probably should go much of the credit usually given Irving. Craven was later to open a scenic studio which supplied many theatres with settings. Harker began his career as an assistant to Craven and later took major responsibility for many of Irving's productions. After leaving Irving, he became Herbert Beerbohm Tree's principal designer. Continuing to work into the 1920s, Harker was one of the major links between Victorian and modern scenic practices. But if Irving employed the finest artists available, he had no consistent policy. Sometimes a single artist designed the scenery and costumes for a production, but more frequently the tasks were divided among a number of designers.

Many of the innovations at the Lyceum resulted from changes in the method used to shift scenery. In 1881 Irving decided to copy the revolutionary steps taken at Booth's theatre in New York in 1869. He abandoned the grooves that had been the standard method of shifting scenery for more than 200 years. By adopting "free plantation," Irving could place scenery wherever he desired and achieve complete flexibility. Irving's solution was the culmination of many earlier trends. Since the beginning of the century, heavy set pieces had proliferated and many of them had been shifted by means of large elevator traps located upstage. Thus, while a "short scene" occupied the forward part of the stage, a "set scene" could be arranged behind a drop and revealed when needed. In this way, heavy pieces could be shifted without the necessity of closing the front curtain. Other complex changes were often made while the "act drop" was serving as a background for the entr'acte entertainment. Irving was the first English producer consistently to use the front curtain to mask major changes of scenery, although he too continued the alternation of shallow and deep scenes to avoid breaks in the action.

FIG. 14.24

Section drawing showing the operation of a star trap. The flexible parts of the trap opening, here displaced by the actor's body, conceal the opening when it is not in use. From Georges Moynet, *La Machinerie Théâtrale* (1893).

During the nineteenth century, as the requirements of spectacle increased, the layout of the stage floor grew ever more complex. Thus, after 1850 the stage was usually constructed in the following manner. The supporting joists, which ran parallel to the footlights, were arranged in groups of three or four set about 1 to 2 inches apart. The spaces between the joists could be covered with narrow strips of wood or left open to form "cuts," through which pieces of scenery, such as ground rows, might be raised or lowered. Occasionally, a vertical moving panorama ran from overhead through a cut to aid the illusion, for example, of climbing a cliff or falling from a height. The groups of joists were spaced about four feet apart. Between them were laid floorboards, some of which could be removed for the insertion of traps or all to form "bridges" the width of the

proscenium through which large set pieces could be raised or special effects manipulated.

Many traps were required by nineteenth-century plays. The "vampire" trap, named for Planché's *The Vampire* (1820), consisted of two spring-leaves that parted under pressure and immediately reclosed. It could be set into the floor to permit an actor seemingly to sink into the earth or set into a flat to permit the illusion of walking through a solid wall. The "Corsican" trap (so-called because of its use in *The Corsican Brothers*) or "ghost glide" was more complex. For it, a "bridge" was removed the full width of the stage. The flooring removed to create the bridge was replaced by a covering like that of a roll-top desk. Beneath the bridge an inclined track was installed. As a wheeled platform moved up this track, the actor standing on it was forced up through a "bristle" trap (an opening covered with bristles colored to match

FIG. 14.25

An English stage of the late nineteenth century. Note how the stage floor is divided; note also the sinking trap, the overhead grooves, and the strong beam of light (either a limelight or carbon arc). Footlights are visible in the extreme lower right corner, as is a row of vertical lights immediately back of the proscenium arch. From *The Magazine of Art* (1889).

FIG. 14.26
A horserace on stage, using a moving panorama and treadmills run by electric motors, the speed of which was controlled by the man at upper right. Union Square Theatre, New York, 1889–1890. From Georges Moynet, *La Machinerie Théâtrale* (1893).

the floor). The roll-top covering over the bridge was geared to move with the platform so that no opening in the floor was ever seen by the audience. Thus, figures appeared to rise from or sink into the earth while gliding through space.

A number of nineteenth-century innovations were brought together around 1890 to create some of the most spectacular productions ever seen on an indoor stage. Treadmills were installed in the stage bridges and coupled with moving panoramas to create such scenes as the chariot race in Ben Hur, for which the stadium was painted on the panorama and moved past the galloping horses, which were kept on stage by the treadmills, whose speeds were controlled by recently developed electric motors.

As the desire for complete illusion grew, so did the use of three-dimensional scenic elements. Charles Kean had still depended primarily on two-dimensional painted pieces, and it was not until the 1870s that steps, platforms, and similar three-dimensional units were common. It was probably Irving's desire to make more effective use of three-dimensional pieces that motivated his removal of the grooves,

which were suited only to flat wings. Since he then had to depend primarily upon manual shifting, Irving employed about 135 persons to "arrange and conduct the scenes," and he rehearsed them as thoroughly as he did his actors. Irving's innovation was soon to outmode the raked floor, on which it was difficult to handle scenery not mounted parallel to the footlights.

Irving also paid careful attention to costumes, but his chief improvement over his predecessors lay in the care given to minor characters. Even Kean had dressed the supernumeraries in armor made of zinc and tinfoil and had substituted glazed cotton for satin. Irving reputedly applied the same standard to all costumes and consequently achieved a more unified effect.

Irving was probably the first English producer to make an art of stage lighting, for while the many technical advances (such as the introduction of gas, the gas table, and limelight) had created new potential for stage lighting, few directors had explored the artistic applications. Irving's improvements were gained through care for details. He broke up the footlights and borders into short sections, each of which was equipped with different colors and controls. He experimented with transparent lacquered glass to achieve varied hues and with several means of distributing light more effectively. Critics almost always commented on his lighting, although many termed it arbitrary and distracting because each moment had obviously been contrived for beauty and effectiveness. Irving also introduced black masking pieces at the front of the stage to prevent "light spill" and was the first English producer consistently to darken the auditorium during performances. It required thirty "gas men" to mount and operate the lights at the Lyceum.

Until the end of his career, Irving used gas, even though by that time he was in the minority. In 1879 Edison's invention of the incandescent lamp had made it possible to light the entire stage electrically, and almost immediately the changeover began, in part because several disastrous theatre fires made managers anxious to adopt the first illuminant yet developed that did not require an open flame. In 1881 the Savoy Theatre became the first in London to be lighted throughout with electricity, and by 1900 almost all English theatres had followed its example. Because early incandescent lamps could be made only in very low wattages, limelight continued to be an important supplement. To this was added the carbon arc, which served much the same purpose.

The carbon arc was first demonstrated in 1808 by Sir Humphrey Davy, but the lack of a satisfactory source of power left its theatrical uses unexplored until the 1840s. By 1860 it had been placed in a housing and equipped with a lens to create a spotlight. It was not widely used, however, until after 1880, when electricity began to replace gas. To create a carbon arc, each electrical pole was attached to a stick of carbon; when the carbons were brought into close juxtaposition, the current leaped between them, creating an incandescence. Giving off a rather harsh light, the carbon arc also tended to be noisy and to flicker. Many of the drawbacks were eliminated with the invention in 1876 of the Jablochkoff Candle, which kept the carbon in proper alignment without the aid of an operator.

Beginning in 1905, significant improvements in the filaments of lamps made higher wattages possible and, as the potential intensity of lamps increased thereafter, the carbon arc and limelight were used less frequently. The limelight went out of use around World War I, but the carbon arc has continued in use, although primarily as a follow spot.

Irving's care with each element of production was crowned by even greater care for coordinating them into an integrated whole. It was for this reason that Irving's work was superior to that of his English contemporaries. His practices as a director pointed the way toward the future, even if his emphasis on pictorial realism was merely the culmination of the nineteenth-century tradition.

In 1895 Irving became the first performer in English history to be knighted, an indication that actors had at last achieved social acceptance and that Irving was considered preeminent in his profession. In 1897 Squire Bancroft was knighted, and by 1914 such performers as John Hare, Johnston Forbes-Robertson, and Herbert Beerbohm Tree had been similarly honored. Comparable awards were not given to women until 1925, when Ellen Terry was named Dame Commander of the British Empire.

LOOKING AT THEATRE HISTORY

One way of studying theatre history is through an examination of the technology available for creating the effects desired by playwrights, directors, and designers. All ages, from the Greek to the present, have made use of technological devices, and an understanding of the available means and how they were used can do much to clarify the stylistic and visual qualities of theatrical art in any era. Few periods have been as self-conscious as the late nineteenth century about the application of scientific knowledge to stage production. Perhaps the most obvious results were in stage machinery, but in all areas of production a major goal was to create illusion so true to nature that it could withstand the scrutiny of the most demanding observer. Stage technology became a frequent subject in periodicals, perhaps most notably in *The Scientific American*. Albert A. Hopkins, for many years editor of that magazine, drew heavily on articles first published there for his *Magic: Stage Illusions and Scientific Diversions* (1897), a section of which is devoted to

"Science in the Theatre." It is a valuable source of information about the theatre technology of that time.

Among the devices described in *Magic* is the elevator stage installed in MacKaye's Madison Square Theatre (see Fig. 14.10):

The shaft through which the huge elevator moves up and down measures one hundred and fourteen feet from the roof to the bottom. . . . The whole construction is fifty-five feet high and twenty-two feet wide and thirty-one feet deep, and weighs about forty-eight tons. . . . Only about forty seconds are required to raise or lower the stage in position, and the entire structure is moved by four men at the winch. The movement is effected without sound, jar or vibration, owing to the balancing of the stage and its weight with counterweights. . . . The borders and border lights are supplied to each of the movable stages, and each stage has its own trap floor. . . . [271]

Hopkins also describes MacKaye's Spectatorium, Lautenschläger's revolving stage, the horse race illustrated in Fig. 14.26, and various other devices, including many required by Wagner's operas (such as floating the Rhine Maidens in *The Rhinegold* and making and operating the dragon in *Siegfried*). One technological milestone of the period was the development of electricity as a motive force for stage machinery and lighting. Here is a report concerning the Savoy Theatre, built to house Gilbert and Sullivan's comic operas:

An attempt will be made here for the first time in London to light a theatre entirely by electricity. The system used is that of the "incandescent lamp." . . . About 1,200 lights are used, and the power to generate a sufficient current for these is obtained from large steam engines, giving about 120 horse power, placed on some open land near the theatre.

The new light is used not only in the audience part of the theatre, but on the stage for footlights, side and top lights, etc. . . . What is being done is an experiment, and may succeed or fail.

The Times, 3 October 1881.

The nineteenth century also sought to apply scientific (that is, precise) knowledge to the design of scenery and costumes so as to ensure their authenticity. Charles Kean sometimes even supplied his audiences with an account of the sources he had consulted and the reasoning that had led to his decisions. Such an account (some parts of which follow) were first used by Kean for his production of *Macbeth* in 1853:

The very uncertain information . . . which we possess respecting the dress worn by the inhabitants of Scotland in the eleventh century, renders any attempt to present this tragedy attired in the costume of the period a task of very great difficulty. . . . In the absence of any positive information I have borrowed materials from those nations to whom Scotland was constantly opposed in war. . . . I have introduced the tunic, mantle, cross gartering, and ringed byrne of the Danes and Anglo-Saxons. . . . The coats of mail appear to have been composed of iron rings or bosses, sewn upon cloth or leather, like that of the Anglo-Saxons. . . . The . . . architecture previous to the Norman conquest has been adopted throughout the play. . . . On this subject I have availed myself of the valuable knowledge of George Godwin, Esq., F. R. S. of the Royal Institute of Architects, to whose suggestions I take this opportunity of acknowledging my obligation.

Shakespeare's Tragedy of Macbeth, . . . Arranged for Representation at the Princess's Theatre, with Historical and Explanatory Notes by Charles Kean (London, 1853), v–ix.

15

Continental European and Latin American Theatre in the Late Nineteenth Century

While the early nineteenth century was marked by a loss of colonial power and the rise of nationalism in the Americas, the late nineteenth century was the heyday of nationalism and imperialism in Europe. On the continent the number of independent states declined markedly as they were brought into the German empire, the kingdom of Italy, the Austro-Hungarian empire, and the Russian empire. This trend toward centralization at home was paralleled by overseas expansion, motivated in part by the need for raw materials and markets to support rapid industrialization. Much of Africa and Asia came under the direct control of European nations. Britain acquired the largest empire, but it was followed closely by France and Germany.

Industry and trade encouraged technological advances, and each new invention increased faith in science and engineering to solve human problems. Nevertheless, benefits were not evenly distributed, and the working classes had to fight for every increase in their rights. Unionization and strikes became their principal weapons, especially after the 1860s, but even then success came only through costly work stoppages and violence. Trade unions were not legalized in France until 1884. It was a time when the working classes began to assert themselves through programs of nonrevolutionary action and to demand that their worth and dignity be recognized and respected.

Though anarchists became a powerful political force late in the century, most reformers no longer expected to achieve changes overnight. In search of pragmatic solutions, they rejected the idealistic and utopian visions of the romantics. It was out of this pragmatism that a new artistic movement—realism—emerged.

THE BEGINNINGS OF REALISM

Realism owed much to the "positivism" of Auguste Comte (1798–1857), author of *Positive Philosophy* (1830–1842) and *Positive Polity* (1851–1854). Comte classified the sciences according to their relative simplicity, placing sociology at the apex as the most complex and important of the sciences. Since to him the ultimate aim of all knowledge was the betterment of society, Comte argued that all the sciences must contribute to sociology, which, when it rigorously applied scientific methodology, would be able to discover the causes of social problems and the remedies needed to bring about desirable change. Above all, Comte demanded that metaphysical explanations of events and behavior be abandoned in favor of material explanations based in observation and analysis. Comte's arguments fell on willing ears, not only among scientists and philosophers, but also among

FIG. 15.1
Europe in the late nineteenth century.

many artists, who sought to make art "scientific" and "realistic."

The realistic mode in art had been attempted sporadically since the time of the Greeks. From the Italian Renaissance on, pictorial illusion dominated the theatre; melodrama and romanticism had accelerated the demand for a realism of appearances. Almost all the approaches before 1850, however, had emphasized "beautiful" nature, norms, picturesque local color, or pleasing contrasts. Even Hugo, who had demanded the inclusion of the grotesque in art, avoided the sordid in his own practice. Around 1850, however, some critics began to advocate a close and objective observation of life, no matter how squalid or elevated. Out of these demands came a movement called realism. As a conscious movement, realism is first discernible around 1853 in France. By 1863 the theoretical foundations had been fully expressed there in such periodicals as *L'Artiste, Le Figaro, Réalisme* (first published in 1856), and *Le Présent*. The main

tenets of the new movement were: Art must depict truthfully the real, physical world, and, since only the contemporary world can be observed directly, truth can be attained most fully through impersonal, objective observation and representation of the world around us.

Because old notions continued alongside these new demands, several types of productions were often labeled "realism" in the late nineteenth century: Any production that used actualistic visual detail might be called realistic; melodrama was often labeled realistic when it presented stories of ordinary people and daily life supported by detailed realistic spectacle and special effects, even though its metaphysical and moralistic stance led inevitably to happy endings; productions of nonrealistic historical and poetic drama that used spectacular scenery and historically accurate clothing and properties were often called realistic; and productions that sought to represent scientifically observed actions in physical spaces that demonstrated the interdependence of character and environment were almost always said to be examples of realism. The realism discussed here is confined to the last of these approaches.

RUSSIAN THEATRE TO 1900

During the late nineteenth century Russia wavered between reform and harshness. Alexander II (ruled 1855–1881) initiated a series of changes, including loosening censorship, freeing the serfs (in 1861), and extending the educational system. But after an attempt on his life in 1866, he lost his zeal for reform, and his assassination in 1881 led Alexander III (ruled 1881–1894) to reinstitute strict censorship and to strengthen the power of the aristocracy.

It is surprising, therefore, to find that realism appeared in Russian drama earlier than it did in the rest of Europe and that it was more uncompromising. It was first fully realized by Ivan Turgenev (1818–1883). Most of his plays were written between 1843 and 1852, but their influence on other dramas came much later since his finest work, *A Month in the Country* (1850), was not produced until 1872. Turgenev's major concern in this play is the inner life of the characters. He renders the daily routine of a country estate faithfully, but he does so only as a means of showing the permanent psychological changes wrought in several characters by the presence of a young tutor. Turgenev's contribution to realism comes from his use of domestic detail to reveal inner turmoil. Chekhov was to build upon his work. After 1863 Turgenev lived abroad, where he became the best known of all Russian authors.

Before Turgenev's plays appeared on the stage, realism had already been popularized through the work of Alexander Ostrovsky (1823–1886), Russia's first professional playwright and the first Russian writer to confine himself exclusively to drama. Ostrovsky wrote his first play in 1847, and from 1853 until his death completed at least one new drama each year. Working primarily from observation, Ostrovsky is often credited with creating a peculiarly Russian drama free from Western influence. Although he wrote in a variety of forms and used a wide range of subjects, his major works draw on the life he knew best, that of the middle class. He sought to eliminate Gogol's penchant for caricature and to avoid stage tricks and irrelevant spectacle by concentrating upon characters and their relationships to each other and to a particular milieu. Ostrovsky is perhaps best known for *Enough Stupidity in Every Wise Man* (1868, sometimes called *The Diary of a Scoundrel*) and *The Thunderstorm* (1859). The former is the comic

chronicle of a man's rise through his manipulation of other people's vanities, while *The Thunderstorm,* which shows the tragic outcome of parental tyranny, is noteworthy for its use of the storm as a symbol of turmoil in human affairs. In his use of symbolism, Ostrovsky anticipates Chekhov.

Ostrovsky was instrumental in founding the Russian Society of Dramatic Authors and Composers in 1866. Until this time, the dramatist usually received no pay for work beyond a set fee from the state troupes; provincial companies did not pay at all. After 1866, playwrights gradually won full copyright protection.

Of Ostrovsky's contemporaries, the most important were Pisemsky, Sukhovo-Kobylin, and Saltikov-Shchedrin. A. F. Pisemsky (1820–1881) wrote many kinds of plays but is now remembered primarily for one of the most naturalistic works of the nineteenth century, *A Bitter Fate* (1859), which antedates by many years the naturalist movement in France. The story is simple: A peasant learns that his wife has been seduced by a wealthy landowner; he kills the child born to her and turns himself over to the authorities. A masterfully written work, it more nearly realizes the aims of the French naturalists than does any of their own dramas. Alexander Sukhovo-Kobylin (1817–1903) is noted primarily for a trilogy of plays treating the Russian legal and bureaucratic systems, with which he was personally entangled. *Krechinsky's Wedding* (1854) is relatively lighthearted, but *The Case* (1861) and *Tarelkin's Death* (not produced until 1917) seem intended to arouse shudders rather than laughter. The work of Mikhail Saltikov-Shchedrin (1826–1889) is related to that of Sukhovo-Kobylin, for he too gives a satirical picture of corruption in his *The Death of Pazukhin* (1857, banned until 1900).

Near the end of the nineteenth century Leo Tolstoy (1828–1910), already famous as a novelist, turned to playwriting. Of his dramas, the most important is *The Power of Darkness* (1886, first performed in Russia in 1895), a story of greed and murder among Russian peasants. Like *A Bitter Fate,* it is one of the most effective of naturalistic plays.

Although the major Russian plays of the late nineteenth century fall into the realistic school, they were by no means the standard fare of the public theatres, which continued to favor melodrama, farce, musical drama, and romantic spectacles. Of the writers outside the realistic trend, probably the most important was Alexey K. Tolstoy (1817–1875), whose plays idealized the Russian past and emphasized the clash of strong personalities against picturesque historical backgrounds. His trilogy, *The Death of Ivan the Terrible, Tsar Fyodor Ivanovich,* and *Tsar Boris* (written between 1865 and 1870) are among the finest of their genre.

Thus, during the late nineteenth century Russia produced a number of outstanding playwrights, many of them still little known in the West. It is difficult to avoid speculating about the heights that might have been reached had censorship been less strenuous and theatrical conditions more favorable.

Perhaps because it did not arouse official displeasure, Russian ballet reached a peak of perfection during the last half of the century under the influence of Marius Petipa (1822–1910). Born in France, Petipa came to Russia in 1847 and was appointed ballet master of the Imperial Schools in 1862. After 1870 he was the virtual dictator of ballet in Russia. He choreographed seventy-four long works (among them *Swan Lake, Sleeping Beauty,* and *The Nutcracker,* with music by Tchaikovsky), in which considerable emphasis was placed on sets and costumes as well as upon storytelling dance. By the time he retired in 1903, Russian ballet had assumed the characteristics for which it is still noted.

THEATRICAL CONDITIONS IN RUSSIA TO 1900

Russian theatrical conditions changed little until after 1882, when the monopolies on performances in Moscow and St. Petersburg, held by the state theatres, were abolished. In actuality these monopolies had been violated for many years by performances disguised as private entertainments. The Nobility Assembly, the Painters Club, the Merchants Club, and others had regularly scheduled "dramatic evenings" and "family reunions" which often featured theatrical entertainment. By 1875 about twenty-five such groups offered performances regularly in Moscow and St. Petersburg.

After the monopolies were rescinded, the public theatre expanded rapidly, although the state troupes continued to command the greatest prestige. The quality of the provincial theatres also improved. Prior to the 1880s, even the best of them had to tour and felt it necessary to import stars to increase their appeal. Costumes and scenery were meager, and amateurs were often employed as stagehands. By the 1870s permanent buildings had been built in eight provincial cities, but not until about 1890 were any companies able to cease touring. In 1897 the first All-Russian Convention of Theatrical Workers was held to discuss common problems.

The trend toward accuracy in settings and costumes, which in Western Europe had preceded the development of realism in character and situation, was slow to develop in Russia. In 1853 one of Ostrovsky's plays is said to have startled audiences with its simple and accurate spectacle when the heroine appeared in a cotton dress and with natural hair rather than the usual fashionable garments and coiffure. Thereafter, realism of detail increased, especially at the Maly, upon which Ostrovsky exerted considerable influence. In 1885, the final year of his life, Ostrovsky was made head of the theatre, but he died before he could implement the reforms he envisioned.

It was not until the 1880s that managers began to be much concerned about accurate settings. Until then, most theatres used conventionalized settings devoid of national or period flavor. Such decor had been popularized by Andreas Roller (1805–1891), a German designer who dominated Russian scenic practices, since he and his pupils or disciples held the major posts in the state theatres. Nevertheless, archeologically correct settings began to appear sporadically after the 1860s. In 1865 the Alexandrinsky Theatre employed an archeologist to assist with historically accurate settings and costumes for Tolstoy's *The Death of Ivan the Terrible,* and after 1870 such major Russian painters as Mikhail Bocharov and M. A. Shishkov organized a special class in theatrical design at the Art Academy. By the 1890s a number of prominent painters were working for the private theatres. Nevertheless, Ostrovsky's response to the Meiningen Players (then universally admired for realism) when they played in Moscow in 1885 tells much about Russian attitudes of the time: He labeled them a talented group of amateurs who placed far too much emphasis upon spectacle except in the admirable

FIG. 15.2
Setting by Andreas Roller for a ballet. From Syrkina, *Russkoe Teatralne Dekoratsione Iskusstvo.*

FIG. 15.3

Setting by M. A. Shishkov for Griboyedov's *Woe from Wit*. From Syrkina, *Russkoe Teatralne Dekoratsione Iskusstvo*.

crowd scenes. On the other hand, Stanislavsky was deeply impressed by the Meiningen troupe's attention to pictorial values, which contrasted so sharply with the typical Russian approach. Stanislavsky states that in Russia around 1890 costumes from three periods were considered sufficient for all plays, and that, since these were used repeatedly, they were usually old and dirty. He adds that leading actresses still insisted upon wearing stylish (often inappropriate) clothing and that the secondary characters could always be identified by their drabness.

In acting, the troupe at Moscow's Maly continued to be superior to those in St. Petersburg. Shchepkin's major successor at the Maly was Prov Sadovsky (1818–1872), who was so effective in Ostrovsky's plays that the theatre came to be called "the House of Ostrovsky." Discovered in the provinces by Shchepkin, in 1839 Sadovsky came to the Maly, where he played minor roles until Ostrovsky's plays offered him parts suited to his style of performance. While Shchepkin had excelled at external detail, Sadovsky's ability to project both internal and external realism created more fully rounded characterizations than any previously seen in Moscow.

Until the 1860s, actors were trained either in service or at the state dramatic schools, which combined the course of study for actors, dancers, and singers. After the private Russian Musical Society opened a conservatory in St. Petersburg in 1862 and another in Moscow in 1866, the state schools reevaluated their approach. Training for opera and ballet were separated from acting, and graduates were no longer automatically eligible for employment in the imperial theatres. In 1882 lines of business were abandoned as the basis of employment in the state troupes. Although typecasting continued, greater flexibility became possible.

But true ensemble effects of the type exemplified by Saxe-Meiningen's company in Germany were not to be achieved in Russia until after 1898, when the Moscow Art Theatre was founded. Prior to this time, however, a few Russian companies had pointed the way. Especially important was the troupe founded in Moscow in 1882 by F. A. Korsh (1852–1921). Korsh maintained a high standard of production, introduced many significant plays from Western Europe, established matinee performances in Russia, and trained a number of actors later to be famous. The company continued until 1932, many years after Korsh's death. In Korsh's theatre the early productions achieved a consistent style and all roles were cast and prepared with care. By the 1890s, this meticulousness had begun to fade. Nevertheless, by 1898 the conditions and possibilities of a new theatre had been created. It remained for Stanislavsky and Nemirovich-Danchenko to consolidate the gains and to inaugurate a new era in the Russian theatre with the Moscow Art Theatre.

GERMAN AND AUSTRIAN THEATRE TO 1900

Germany produced few dramatists of note in the second half of the nineteenth century. The major playwrights of the 1850s were Otto Ludwig (1813–1865) and Gustav Freytag (1816–1895). Ludwig sought a middle ground between idealism and realism. He opposed the political and social stance of Young Germany and sought to substitute a realism lacking in tendentiousness. His best plays are *The Hereditary Forester* (1850), a middle-class tragedy which reflects *Othello* in its treatment of a misunderstanding between friends, and *The Maccabees* (1854), which treats the revolt of Judas Maccabeus against Antioch. Freytag is remembered primarily for *The Journalists* (1853), a good-humored view of politics in a small town. In addition, his *The Technique of Drama* (1863) was long considered to be a major treatise on playwriting.

Following the death of Hebbel in 1863, German-language drama entered a state of decline from which it did not recover until the 1890s. The general level of serious drama in this period is indicated by the works of Ernst von Wildenbruch (1845–1909), an ardent admirer of the Hohenzollern rulers and of the Teutonic heritage. His plays gained wide popularity following the unification of Germany in 1871. Wildenbruch had a considerable gift for writing crowd scenes and for depicting picturesque working-class life, but much of his drama, such as his two-part *Heinrich and Heinrich's Dynasty* (1896), now seems merely derivative.

In Austria, the peasant play was kept alive by Ludwig Anzengruber (1839–1889), who gave it a serious turn by using it to present a faithful picture of rural life. *The Priest of Kirschfeld* (1870) reflects the controversy over the recently promulgated doctrine of papal infallibility, while his *The Double Suicide* (1875) is reminiscent of *Romeo and Juliet*. But Anzengruber was not always serious; *He Who Signed With a Cross* (1872), for example, is a variation on *Lysistrata*. Because of his realism, Anzengruber was little appreciated until the end of his life, when the rise of naturalism called attention to his depiction of characters rooted in particular environments. His fame aroused new interest in peasant drama, as a result of which a theatre was founded in Bavaria in 1891 especially to produce and tour folk plays.

During the late nineteenth century, variety theatres, cabarets, summer theatres, and pleasure gardens flourished. Operetta also became increasingly popular, especially in Vienna. The vogue began around 1858 with the importation of Offenbach's works. The first important native composer was Franz von Suppé (1820–1895) with such pieces as *Fatinitza* (1872) and *The Devil on Earth* (1878), but he was soon surpassed by Johann Strauss (1825–1899) with *Die Fledermaus* (1874), *A Night in Venice* (1883), *The Gypsy Baron* (1885), and many others. Operetta was long to be one of Vienna's major attractions.

The lack of significant new dramatists was not keenly felt, since the plays of Shakespeare, Lessing, Goethe, and Schiller were prominent in the repertory and those of Kleist began to assume the status of classics. Following Grillparzer's death in 1872, directors vied in giving his works lavish productions. After 1850, foreign plays, especially those of Scribe, Sardou, Augier, and Dumas *fils,* also made up an increasingly large part of the German and Austrian repertory and helped to compensate for the lack of good new native plays. The period of stagnation was ultimately broken around 1890 with the emergence of the "modern" school.

In contrast to changes then underway elsewhere, in Germany resident companies did not decline markedly in number or prestige during the last half of the nineteenth century, probably because the major troupes were supported by state or municipal governments. By 1871 there were about 200 theatres in Germany with about 5000 artistic employees. By 1896, the number of such employees had tripled. Until German unification (1871), classics could only be performed by state theatres, but after that time any licensed theatre could perform any work passed by the censor.

During the late nineteenth century the major German-language theatre was Vienna's Burgtheater, in large part because of Laube and Dingelstedt. Heinrich Laube (1806–1884) was a well-known playwright of the Young Germany school before he was appointed director of Vienna's Burgtheater, a post he held from 1849 until 1867. Laube placed primary emphasis on the text and especially on diction and characterization. Under his direction, the Burgtheater regained the preeminence it had enjoyed under Schreyvogel. Its ensemble was the finest of any German-language company, including among its members Bogumil Dawison; Adolf Sonnenthal (1834–1909), who portrayed a wide range of serious and comic roles but was especially admired for his elegance and seeming normality in drawing room comedy; and Charlotte Wolter (1833–1897), one of the great international stars of the age and an exponent of "naturalistic" acting. Laube was opposed to elaborate historical settings because he thought them distracting and "operatic." On the other hand, he was the first German producer consistently to use the box set, which he adopted because it increased the sense of immediacy and intimacy. Nevertheless, he never permitted more furniture on stage than was demanded by the action. His was a rather austere realism aimed at riveting attention on the actor rather than on the spectacle. In the history of German directing, Laube holds a position comparable to Montigny's in France.

FIG. 15.4

Interior of the Burgtheater, Vienna, in the late nineteenth century. From *Die Theater Wiens* (1899).

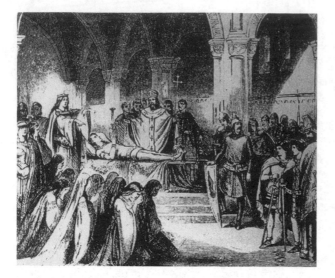

FIG. 15.5
Franz Dingelstedt's production at Weimar in 1861 of Hebbel's *The Niebelungen*. Seen here is the final scene in the second play of the trilogy. From *Leipziger Illustrierte Zeitung* (1861).

Laube was followed at the Burgtheater between 1870 and 1881 by Franz Dingelstedt (1814–1881), who, unlike his predecessor, emphasized lavish and historically accurate decor. Dingelstedt had become well known throughout Germany because of his work in Munich between 1851 and 1857 and in Weimar between 1857 and 1867. In Munich in 1851

FIG. 15.6
Friedrich Haase as Hamlet in his own production at Leipzig. The play-within-the-play scene. Woodcut by Knut Ekwall, 1871. Courtesy Theatermuseum, Munich.

he staged Sophocles' *Antigone* with the assistance of some of the most respected scholars, artists, and musicians of his day. The high point of his work in Munich probably came in 1854 with a festival (held in conjunction with the Munich Industrial Exposition) during which outstanding German actors presented plays by Goethe, Schiller, Lessing, and others. This venture aroused such enthusiasm that thereafter festivals began to appear elsewhere. At Weimar, Dingelstedt restored the reputation of the company, which had been in decline. He was especially noted for his staging there of Schiller's Wallenstein trilogy in 1859, Hebbel's Niebelungen trilogy in 1862, and almost all of Shakespeare's plays during a single week in 1864 (which motivated the formation of the German Shakespeare Society). In 1870 he became director of the Burgtheater, where, with his costume designer Franz Gaul (1837–1906) and scene designer Herman Burghart (1834–1901) he presented some of the most lavish productions of the age. Perhaps his major achievement came in 1875 with the presentation of Shakespeare's history plays as a connected cycle.

Another major director of the period was Friedrich Haase (1825–1911), especially at Coburg-Gotha's theatre from 1866 to 1868 and at the Leipzig Municipal Theatre from 1870 to 1876. Through his work at these theatres and elsewhere he came to be especially noted for his staging of such Shakespearean plays as *Hamlet* and *The Merchant of Venice* in the manner of Charles Kean, whose influence he freely acknowledged. As a major star, Haase extended his own influence through engagements with other companies.

By 1875 historical accuracy was accepted as an ideal by almost all German-language troupes. Nevertheless, the same settings were still reused for different plays of the same historical period, and inconsistencies abounded. Perhaps the greatest needs were for ensemble playing and for a controlling artistic consciousness. It was to these problems, above all, that the two major innovators of the period—Wagner and Saxe-Meiningen—addressed themselves so effectively that they would lay the foundations for the modern movement.

FRENCH DRAMA TO 1900

It was in France that dramatists first consciously sought to implement the realists' program. Among these pioneering playwrights, the most important were Dumas *fils* and Augier. But they owed much to their predecessors and perhaps most to Eugène Scribe (1791–1861), for he had popularized the structural pattern they were to appropriate. Between 1811 and

FIG. 15.7
Scribe's *A Glass of Water,* Act V, scene 7, first performed at the Comédie Française, 1840. From *Oeuvres Complètes de M. Eugène Scribe* 5 (1847).

1861, Scribe contributed over 300 pieces to Parisian theatres, twenty-three of them to the Comédie Française. He ranged through *comédies-en-vaudevilles,* opera libretti, comedies, and serious drama. Perhaps the best of his works were *Marriage for Money* (1827), *A Glass of Water* (1840), and *Adrienne Lecouvreur* (1849). Today, Scribe is remembered primarily as the popularizer of the "well-made play" formula. Often used as a term of derision, "well-made play" can perhaps best be understood as a combination and perfection of dramatic devices common since the time of Aeschylus: careful exposition and preparation, cause-to-effect arrangement of incidents, building scenes to a climax, and the skillful manipulation of withheld information, startling reversals, and suspense. Because they sacrifice depth of characterization and thought to intrigue, Scribe's plays now seem shallow. To theatregoers of the nineteenth century, however, they appeared more substantial, probably because they manipulate so effectively the attitudes and prejudices of the time. Although Scribe was not associated with the realistic

movement, his well-made play formula, emphasizing as it did the seemingly logical development from cause to effect, supplied Dumas *fils* and Augier with a suitable form for their ideas.

Alexandre Dumas *fils* (1824–1895) came to public attention with a dramatization of his own novel, *The Lady of the Camellias* (now usually referred to as *Camille*). Although today *Camille* (performed 1852) seems merely an idealized treatment of the "prostitute with a heart of gold," it was forbidden production for three years because of its realism. Set in Paris in the 1840s, the play used prose dialogue and depicted a protagonist based upon a well-known courtesan of the time.

Dumas soon underwent a change of attitude and in *The Demi-Monde* (1855) treated unsympathetically the same kind of characters that were presented sentimentally in *Camille*. He now set out to show that "women with a past" must be prevented from marrying into good families. After this time, Dumas wrote "thesis plays" about current social problems, utilizing Scribe's well-made play formula to create suspenseful and entertaining stories. His works are marred by didacticism, for in most a message is clearly stated by an articulate *raisonneur,* or author's mouthpiece. In spite of this lack of objectivity, Dumas considered himself a realist and his duty the betterment of society. In an open letter to the critic Francisque Sarcey, he wrote: ". . . if I can exercise some influence over society . . . if I can find some means to force people to discuss the problem, and the lawmaker to revise the law, I shall have done more than my duty as a writer, I shall have done my duty as a man."

FIG. 15.8
Final scene from *The Lady of the Camellias* by Alexandre Dumas *fils,* first performed in 1852. From *Le Théâtre Contemporain Illustré* (1867).

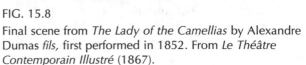

FIG. 15.9

Augier's *Giboyer's Son,* Act IV, scene 6, at the Comédie Française, 1862. Courtesy Bibliothèque de l'Arsenal, Paris.

Emile Augier (1820–1889) was a more versatile writer than Dumas *fils.* He began his career in 1844 as an adherent of the "theatre of common sense" but, after seven verse plays, adopted the realistic style. One of his first prose works, *Olympe's Marriage* (1855), was intended as a direct reply to Dumas' *Camille,* for it shows the disastrous results of a courtesan's marrying into an aristocratic family. It is Augier's most didactic play. His more characteristic works are comedies of manners, such as *M. Poirier's Son-in-Law* (1854) in which Augier depicts the struggle for supremacy between the impoverished but proud nobility and the well-to-do and ambitious middle class. Others of his plays treat the power of money, the influence of the church on politics, and numerous additional problems.

Although they occasionally shocked audiences, Dumas and Augier were viewed not as extremists but as sane citizens seeking to raise the moral tone of their times. Their plays treated subjects of concern to the middle-class citizenry of Napoleon III's materialistic and conservative Third Empire. Thus, Dumas and Augier were rapidly assimilated into the mainstream of drama not only in France but throughout Europe. It would be left to their more uncompromising successors to bring hitherto unacceptable topics onto the stage. Furthermore, perhaps because they used Scribean techniques, Dumas and Augier did not seem at the time to differ markedly, except in tone, from their less serious contemporaries, such as Sardou and Labiche.

Victorien Sardou (1831–1908), Scribe's true heir, was one of the world's most popular playwrights between 1860 and 1900. Like Scribe, Sardou used the well-made play formula and adapted it to almost every dramatic type. His early successes included comedies, such as *A Scrap of Paper* (1860) and *Our Intimates* (1861), and satires on contemporary life, such as *The Family Benoîton* (1865). He later wrote a number of plays for Sarah Bernhardt, including *Fedora* (1882) and *Tosca* (1887), and some of the most lavish historical spectacles of the nineteenth century, such as *Fatherland!* (1868) and *Theodora* (1884). The latter works elicited praise even from the naturalists for their faithful recreation of particular milieus. To George Bernard Shaw, however, Sardou's shallow dramas seemed to epitomize the decadence and mindlessness into which the late nineteenth-century theatre had descended, a state he labeled "Sardoodledom."

Eugène Labiche (1815–1888) was one of the finest writers of farce in the nineteenth century. Uninterested in theories, Labiche wrote for the popular audience and only reluctantly agreed to the publication of his plays. Most of his works, of which *The Italian Straw Hat* (1851) is representative, appear delightfully irresponsible, but others, such as *M. Perrichon's Journey* (1860) and *Dust in the Eyes* (1861), make penetrating observations on human nature. Many of his plays have worn better than those of his more self-consciously serious contemporaries.

Of the minor forms, the most popular in France during the late nineteenth century was operetta, which as a distinct form emerged around 1848. A mixture of song and speech, fantasy, buffoonery, and irreverent subject matter, operetta made its mark above all through the work of Jacques Offenbach

FIG. 15.10

Sardou's historical spectacle, *Fatherland!,* directed by Sardou at the Théâtre de la Porte Saint-Martin in 1868. Setting by Cambon. Courtesy Bibliothèque de l'Arsenal, Paris.

(1819–1880), especially *Orpheus in the Underworld* (1858) and *La Belle Hélène* (1865).

THEATRICAL CONDITIONS IN FRANCE TO 1900

The playwrights discussed here are only a few of those who sought to fill Parisian theatres, which sometimes numbered as many as fifty during the last half of the century. Until that time most of the stable minor houses specialized in one of five genres: melodrama, comedy, vaudeville, spectacle drama, or operetta, and therefore assembled companies best at performing one kind of play and sought authors who wrote that type. In 1864, a new law removed all remaining strictures on genre (except censorship of plays) and eased most other controls (among them one that since 1814 had forbidden women to manage theatres). These changes coincided with many others. Among the most important was the increase in the length of runs. By 1880 no play was considered successful unless it was given at least 100 performances; many were given 300 or more times. In turn, length of run as a standard of success led managers to search for works likely to attract large audiences; it also led them to replace the resident company with performers hired only for the run of a play to which their talents were especially fitted. The long run meant as well that each theatre needed to produce only a few works each year to fill out its season. Furthermore, the provincial theatre was so undermined by touring companies that by 1900 Paris was the only important theatrical center in France. Near the end of the century, one writer complained that about twenty-five authors had come to monopolize the market, since the demand for new plays had been so much reduced and since managers favored works by proven authors. Censorship (which was not done away with until 1905) encouraged conservatism in the choice of plays.

The theatre also had a formidable rival in the *café-concert,* a form somewhat analogous to the British music hall and American vaudeville. By 1894 there were as many *café-concerts* as there were theatres in Paris. The *café-concert* had originated in the eighteenth century with cafes that offered musical entertainment. In the late nineteenth century it still retained its table seating and did not charge admission, but it did demand that spectators order drinks and food. The entertainments became increasingly varied; in addition to music, song, and dance, there were stand-up comedians, well-known actors performing scenes from famous plays, and other diversions.

Overall, the theatre in Paris during the last half of the century was prosperous. After 1875 matinee performances were added, and by 1900 ticket agencies had appeared and were being accused of buying up seats to popular plays so they might resell them at inflated prices.

During this period, then, the French theatre was characterized by conservatism motivated in part by material prosperity but also by taste. It was this conservatism that would stimulate concern for reform and eventually give rise to the "modern" era in French theatre.

Throughout the last half of the century, two demands—for increased realism (and a consequent need for greater control over production) and for virtuosity (which tended to encourage defiance of control)—were evident and often in conflict. Of the two, the trend toward realism is perhaps most apparent, for it can be seen clearly in every aspect of production. It was certainly one of the decisive elements in the development of directing.

Both Sardou and Dumas *fils* credit Adolphe Montigny (1805–1880), director of the Gymnase, with first treating directing as an art in France. According to Dumas, Montigny, beginning around 1853, placed a table downstage center in order to prevent the actors from taking up the semicircular formation then common. Next, he put chairs around the table, seated the actors, and made them speak to each other rather than to the audience, as had been typical in the past. Finally, he furnished his settings like real rooms and placed properties, such as cigar boxes, handkerchiefs, or letters, about the stage to motivate movement from one place to another. In this way, he gradually arrived at an illusion of real life. According to Sardou, Montigny's success encouraged others to adopt his innovations.

Most of Montigny's work was done with contemporary plays written in the realistic mode. Thus, it was left to Sardou, who supervised the production of his own plays, to perfect historical spectacle, which he insisted be absolutely faithful to fact. By the end of the century practically all companies employed a director and gave him two or three assistants to oversee the various aspects of staging and performance.

The movement toward realism was also evident in scenery and costuming. In terms of archeological accuracy, it reached its peak in Sardou's spectacles. For *Hatred* (1874), set in medieval Siena, unprecedented sums were spent on armor, costumes, and scenery. *Theodora* (1884), laid in Byzantium, was given an even more elaborate mounting; in their reviews of this piece, some critics spoke of almost nothing except the scenic marvels.

Realistic details from daily life also proliferated. For example, *My Friend Fritz,* produced at the

FIG. 15.11
Setting by Philippe Chaperon for *Oedipus Rex*. From *Revue des Arts Decoratifs* (1881–1882).

Comédie Française in 1876, featured a farmyard in which real water flowed from a pump and real cherries were picked from trees; in another scene, real food and drink were served and consumed on stage.

The visual style and favored motifs differed little from those of earlier years, because the major designers were those who had begun their careers before 1850 or their students: A. A. Rubé, Philippe Chaperon, C. A. Cambon, J. B. Lavastre, Edouard Despléchin, Jean Daran, and Eugène Lacoste.

By the end of the nineteenth century, methods of obtaining scenery had become relatively standardized. The director, after consultation with the playwright, gave a summary of requirements to the scenic designers, who then made cardboard models of the sets. When these were approved, scale drawings were made to guide the theatre's carpenters, who built the settings. After completion, the scenery was sent to one of Paris's five or six scenic studios for painting. Each theatre hired a relatively small number of stagehands, for since French plays almost never changed place within acts, shifting was usually confined to intermissions when haste was not of major concern.

For costumes, theatres began after 1850 to employ special designers for historical plays and to increase their staffs of tailors and seamstresses to construct and maintain garments. Special supply houses were founded to meet the growing demand for armor and other articles too difficult to be made by the theatres. Professional wig makers supplied wigs, and several hairdressers were hired to assist the actors. By the late nineteenth century, Racinet's *Le Costume Historique* (completed 1888) had become the standard guide for the design of historical costumes.

In acting, realistic touches also increased. Actresses began to knit, actors to smoke or perform other fa-

miliar business on stage. One performer at the Comédie Française in the 1870s consulted toxicologists in order to make a death scene more convincing (it was judged one of the most realistic ever seen on the French stage); in 1890 a seemingly authentic blood transfusion was performed on stage. Such instances could be extended almost indefinitely.

There was also at least one important attempt to revolutionize training so that acting might become a more precise mode of communication. At this time most French actors still received their training while in service, although study at the Conservatoire became increasingly important as the repertory system began to decline. But even at the Conservatoire students learned primarily by imitating their teachers, and thus they perpetuated earlier acting techniques and styles. Given the temper of the nineteenth century, it was probably inevitable that someone would try to approach acting analytically and "scientifically." François Delsarte (1811–1871) took on this task when he set out to demonstrate that the laws of stage

FIG. 15.12
Backstage at a theatre in the late nineteenth century. Note the division of the floor and the poles supporting the wings. From Pougin, *Dictionnaire du Théâtre* (1884).

expression are discoverable and that these laws can be formulated as precisely as mathematical principles.

Delsarte sought to analyze emotions and ideas and to determine how they are outwardly expressed. He divided human experience and behavior into the physical, mental, and spiritual, and he related these to each action, thought, and emotion. He also divided and subdivided the body into parts and related each to the physical, mental, and spiritual. Eventually he arrived at an elaborate scheme whereby he sought to describe how the feet, legs, arms, torso, head, and every other part of the body can be used in communicating particular emotions, attitudes, or ideas.

Although Delsarte's system as applied by others eventually came to seem overly mechanistic, it remains important as the first significant attempt to reduce every aspect of the actor's training to method. By the end of the nineteenth century it was being taught nearly all over the world and, though it is now usually treated derisively, it has contributed to most subsequent attempts to formulate training programs for actors.

FIG. 15.13
Constant-Benoît Coquelin as Cyrano de Bergerac, a role written for him by Edmond Rostand. The original production in 1898. From *Le Théâtre* (1898).

If many forces encouraged realism in late nineteenth-century French theatrical production, perhaps an equal number worked against it. In scenery, for example, the same settings were still being used for several different plays. Thus, while a company might have many more settings than in the eighteenth century, it usually did not have specially designed scenery for each play. Furthermore, since the various settings for a single production were often designed by different artists, unity was lacking. Similarly, in costume many actors continued to supply their own wardrobes, and actresses were often outfitted by couturiers. Even when a manager employed a costume designer, the leading actors felt free to supply their own dress and were often praised by critics for their novel touches. Although consistency was most nearly achieved in historical spectacles, even here it was seldom complete. As with scenery, the same costumes were used for many different plays.

But earlier practices were probably most evident in acting. Until near the end of the nineteenth century, actors were employed according to lines of business, and thus they tended to build up a repertory of tricks and business which they drew on in every role. Contrarily, supernumeraries were almost always recruited amateurs, and they rarely rehearsed with the company before performing. Most theatres employed someone to secure and rehearse the supernumeraries and to provide leadership on stage during performances. The composition of the group might differ each night.

But most significant, the late nineteenth century glorified starring performers. Consequently, most productions were built around them. If the stars had strong artistic consciences, this practice could lead to excellent results, but all too often it brought the subordination of everything to their whims. Even the Comédie Française did not escape this trend, and bickerings and jealousies there did much to undermine that company's ensemble.

Stars were legion during the late nineteenth century, but among the most important were Got, Coquelin, Mounet-Sully, and Réjane. Edmond Got (1822–1901), who performed at the Comédie Française after 1844, was noted for his excellent characterizations in classical and, especially, contemporary comedy. Constant-Benoît Coquelin (1841–1909) performed at the Comédie Française from 1860 to 1886, after which he toured throughout the world before returning to Paris. In the early 1890s Coquelin created a major scandal when he defied the rule that forbade any actor who left the Comédie Française to perform elsewhere in Paris. (Bernhardt had also defied this rule, but she had been such a troublemaker at the Comédie that no one wished her to remain in the company.) Coquelin's example tended to undermine the Comédie's discipline by making it easy for any disgruntled actor to leave its ranks. In 1897 Coquelin became manager of the Porte-Saint-Martin, where he created the role of Cyrano de Bergerac, written especially for him. At his best in Molière's comic roles or in flamboyant romantic parts, Coquelin was noted for his technical proficiency, about which he wrote extensively in such works as *The Art of the Actor* (1880). Mounet-Sully (1841–1916) had been trained at the Conservatoire and had played at the Odéon before he entered the Comédie Française in 1872. He was soon acknowledged as the finest tragic actor of his time. With his striking physique, beautiful voice, and fiery temperament, he brought considerable originality to all the great tragic roles in both the classical and romantic repertory. Gabrielle Réjane (1857–1920) made her first appearance in 1875 and soon was considered the finest player of comedy of her age. She seldom ventured outside light contemporary drama, but in that she was unsurpassed. She appeared with considerable success in London, New York, and elsewhere before she retired in 1915.

But the most famous French star of the late nineteenth century was Sarah Bernhardt (1844–1923). She made her debut in 1862 and, after performing in several minor theatres and at the Odéon was engaged at the Comédie Française in 1872, where she soon became a great attraction and a source of controversy. After considerable unpleasantness, she left the company in 1880. The rest of her career was devoted to starring tours throughout the world and to the management of a series of Parisian theatres. Noted for her slim figure, dark eyes, "golden" voice, and portrayals of seductiveness, pain, tearful rage, and death, she achieved her greatest success as Camille, Tosca, Adrienne Lecouvreur, Phaedra, Dona Sol in *Hernani,* and the title role in Rostand's *The Eaglet.* Her technical skill and her magnetic personality combined to create the image of the "grand actress." Many still consider her the greatest actress of her age.

FIG. 15.14
Sarah Bernhardt (at center) in Sardou's *Theodora* in a 1902 revival in Paris.
From *Le Théâtre* (1902).

FIG. 15.15

Sectional plan of the Paris Opéra, opened in 1874. The stage house is at right. Note the many levels below the stage. Note also the great amount of space given over to lobbies and other audience uses. From *Monde Illustré* (6 February 1875).

The tension between tradition and change, so evident in every area of production, was also reflected in theatre architecture. During the 1860s, many new theatres were built as Napoleon III's scheme for an elaborate network of "grand boulevards" took shape. In this process, the Boulevard du Temple, the original home of the boulevard theatres, was obliterated. The new theatres that replaced the old ones retained many traditional features but included some innovations. In the auditorium, the area immediately forward of the stage was fitted out with comfortable armchairs (a practice begun at the Opéra-Comique in the 1840s) but behind this area there continued to be, as in the past, a section (the pit or *parterre*) equipped only with benches. This ground level was surrounded by a row of boxes (or *baignoires*), above which rose two or three additional galleries. The first contained two or three rows of chairs and behind these a row of boxes; the second gallery was usually devoted entirely to boxes, and the third entirely to benches. The more fashionable theatres had a number of lavish *loges á salon,* fitted up like sitting rooms complete with bell cords so that the occupants could

ring for service during the performances. The seating capacity of the theatres averaged from 1,200 to 2,000. Not until near the end of the century was there much concern for safety. The aisles were narrow and often filled with folding chairs; fire exits were inadequate and ventilation poor. After 400 persons perished in the fire that destroyed the Opéra-Comique in 1887, attention was at last turned to achieving greater safety.

The proscenium arch was usually very high in order to provide adequate sight lines for spectators in the galleries, which not only rose to the ceiling but extended along the sides of the auditorium to the proscenium. The proscenium arch was also usually very thick, for in most theatres a box was set into it on the level of each gallery. This thickness created a wide apron that was much used by the actors, especially before realism was fully established. The prompter was housed in a compartment at the front of the apron. The floor of the stage raked upward toward the rear. The chariot-and-pole system remained the usual method of scene shifting, although it was supplemented by flying and the movement of set pieces by hand. During the nineteenth century, space above and below the stage was greatly enlarged to permit more effective handling of the increasingly detailed settings; in several theatres elevator traps were installed.

Perhaps no theatre summed up earlier tradition so thoroughly as did the Paris Opéra, completed in 1874. Designed by Charles Garnier and begun in 1862, the Opéra cost about 40 million francs. Enormous foyers and stairways led to the auditorium with its four levels of galleries and seating capacity of 2,100 persons. A proscenium arch 55 feet wide framed a stage 175 feet wide by 85 feet deep. The depth could be increased to about 150 feet by including the dance salon immediately behind the stage. The stage floor was raked upward two inches in every 40 inches. Above the stage there was 119 feet of space, and below it 50 feet. The stage floor was divided from front to back into ten sections, or *plans*, each of which was subdivided into (1) several slots about 1½ inches wide, (2) narrow traps about 18 inches wide, and (3) larger traps about 40 inches wide. An entire plan could be opened the width of the proscenium arch. This flexibility permitted the operation of almost any effect from beneath the stage. Scenery was shifted by chariots, each about 10 feet long and equipped with four upright poles upon which flats could be mounted. In addition, scenery could be flown or moved through the stage traps. When it was built, this was the most elaborate theatre in the world. Ironically, this enshrinement of past practices was completed just as Wagner's Festspielhaus at Bayreuth, which initiated a new ideal, was being built.

In France, then, the late nineteenth century brought increased attention to every aspect of theatrical endeavor. At the same time, an uneasy tension between innovation and tradition was evident. Still lacking was a theory of theatrical production capable of welding the diverse elements into a unified whole. During the last years of the century this need would begin to be met.

THE THEATRE IN ITALY AND SPAIN TO 1900

During the late nineteenth century, Italy made its greatest impact internationally through touring stars, especially Ristori, Salvini, and Rossi. Adelaide Ristori (1822–1906) was on the stage from the age of twelve and at fourteen was already playing leading roles in the company of Giuseppe Moncalvo (1781–1859). In 1838 she joined the Royal Theatre at Turin, where she received formal training in classical poetic drama. By 1850 she was famous throughout Italy for her studious and regal performances. In

FIG. 15.16
Interior of a Spanish theatre, *c.* 1855. A contemporary print.

1853 she took her company to Paris, and from that time until 1885, when she retired, she toured internationally. She made four visits to America and in 1874 went around the world. Although she made no striking innovations, she raised the received tradition to new heights.

Tommaso Salvini (1829–1915) began his career at the age of fourteen in the troupe of Gustavo Modena (1803–1861) at Padua. By 1848 he was in Adelaide Ristori's company in Rome, where he won his first fame as Alfieri's Orestes. Around 1860 he began a series of international tours. Salvini excelled as Macbeth, Lear, Alfieri's heroes, and, above all, as Othello. An actor of great passion and energy, he is said to have terrified his leading ladies. Throughout the world, Salvini's name became synonymous with fiery tragic acting. He retired in 1890.

Ernesto Rossi (1829–1896) entered the theatre in 1846, replacing Salvini in Modena's company. He later performed with Ristori, and in 1857 took his own troupe to Vienna. After that time, he toured all over the world in plays by Alfieri and Shakespeare. A polished performer, he was considered by many too studied, a reaction which probably explains his failure to rival the fame of Ristori and Salvini.

Italy's contribution to theatre and drama in the late nineteenth century, then, was minor, since for the most part, it merely followed traditions already established elsewhere.

In the Spanish theatre, conditions were by 1849 so chaotic that a state council was created to establish guidelines for its regulation. This council was to accomplish the first significant reforms since the seventeenth century. At this time, the Teatro del Príncipe was renamed the Teatro Español and made the Spanish national theatre, a position which it still holds. Its building was remodeled, gas lighting was installed, and its production methods modernized. (The Teatro de la Cruz was abandoned in 1856.) The use of theatres to support charities was discontinued so that the revenue might be used to raise the quality of production. All theatres were classified into three ranks, and each was restricted to particular dramatic genres.

Although the latter provision was never fully enforced, it encouraged the growth of minor dramatic types. In 1870 only eight of Madrid's thirty-two theatres were devoted to regular drama. Furthermore, the major theatres found it difficult to compete with the minor houses, which soon established the custom of offering an evening's bill composed of four distinct entertainments, thereby allowing considerable flexibility in the time when one could be admitted and greatly increasing the popularity of the minor houses. This custom handicapped theatres wishing to present full-length plays and consequently seriously affected playwriting.

During the nineteenth century, then, the theatre of Spain burgeoned, growing from a few companies in 1800 to more than fifty by 1875. From an antiquated institution, it had been brought more nearly into line with current practices in other European countries. Nevertheless, it retained much of its insularity, participating in major international movements only at a distance.

THEATRE IN LATIN AMERICAN TO 1900

Throughout the eighteenth century the Spanish colonies of the Caribbean and of North, Central, and South America had followed the theatrical traditions of Spain. Just over 500 Golden Age play scripts were sent to the Americas in 1713 for the use of the professional theatres. While most companies still maintained an extensive repertory, some producing over 140 plays in a season, these Golden Age plays, supplemented by translations of French neoclassical dramas, were able to meet the theatrical needs of the colonies for over a century, with only a few new plays added to the repertories from year to year. With little demand for new plays, local dramatists generally came from the ranks of successful poets, novelists, or government employees who wrote plays as a sideline.

Mexico City was the capital of New Spain, an area that extended from what is now the southwestern United States down to Panama. From the sixteenth through the eighteenth centuries it was home to the most extensive theatre operations in the colonies. Eusebio Vela (1688–1737) was the most noted actor-manager of the eighteenth century, and of his three surviving plays, the most interesting for a modern audience is *Apostleship in the Indies and the Martyrdom of a Chief,* because of its focus on Mexican history and its sympathetic treatment of native peoples.

The Corral of the Royal Hospital of the Indians, which had been built around 1602, was destroyed by fire in 1722. It was replaced in 1725 by the Coliseo de México, which was in turn replaced by the Coliseo Nuevo in 1752. The Coliseo Nuevo was probably the first stone theatre in the New World. Its patio had standing room for 350 with benches for 75. Surrounding the patio were three levels of galleries with eighteen boxes per level. There was a *cazuela* for the unaccompanied women and a city box above. Renamed the Teatro Principal in 1826, it was Mexico City's most influential theatre for most of the nineteenth century. The Principal was renovated in 1880, 1893, and 1895, but by the time it was destroyed by fire in 1931 it had become the home of musical entertainments.

The attempts by Spain to assert crown control over religion by banning religious drama in 1765 and expelling the Jesuits in 1767 generated considerable resentment throughout Latin America. When Napoleon conquered Spain in 1808, animosities grew until open rebellion broke out in New Spain in 1810. After eleven years of warfare the independent Empire of Mexico was finally declared in 1821. But the empire did not last; it lost its Central American holdings in 1823, Texas in 1836, California in 1845, and New Mexico and Arizona in 1848. The War of Reform (1858–1861) and the occupation by the French under Maximilian (1864–1867), followed by revolts in 1876 and 1880, left Mexico with few opportunities to develop its professional theatre in the nineteenth century. But this did not stop Luciano Corés from opening the Corral del Palenque de los Gallos in 1823. In 1841 this theatre was roofed and renamed the Teatro Provisional, which lasted until 1884.

Despite the political upheavals, theatrical activities expanded rapidly in the 1840s and 1850s. In response, three major theatres were built: the Teatro Nuevo México (1841), the Teatro de la Unión (1843, also called the Puente Quebrado), and El Grand Teatro de Santa Anna (1844, later called the National or the Imperial). El Grand Teatro was designed by Lorenzo Hidalga and was considered to be the finest theatre in Latin America. Even this was not enough

FIG. 15.17

Map of Mexico and Central and South America

to meet the growing demand, however, and five more theatres were added in the next decade, including the Teatro del la Esmeralda (1858, later called the Fama and then the Hidalgo). But musical and variety entertainments were becoming so popular that by the end of the century only the Hidalgo was still staging legitimate drama.

Important authors continued to write for the stage. José Joaquín Fernández de Lizardi (1776–1827), Mexico's first novelist, wrote several plays during the

1820s concerning events (some of them quite recent) in Mexican history. Manuel Eduardo de Gorostiza (1789–1851) wrote a number of neoclassical plays including *Bread and Onion with Thee* (1833), satirizing the exaggerations of romanticism. Ignacio Rodriquez Galván (1816–1842) wrote *Muñoz, Inspector General of Mexico* (1838), a history play modeled on the plays of the French romantics. And Fernando Calderón (1809–1845), who was known primarily for romantic dramas set in the Middle Ages, wrote *None of the*

Three (1839), a light comedy that was immensely popular. In mid-century, Juan A. Mateos (1831–1913), first in collaboration with Vicente Riva Palacio (1832–1896) and then on his own, was the dominant playwright, producing a long string of successful melodramas and comedies. But for the most part the rapid expansion of theatre in the 1840s and 1850s did not lead to an equivalent growth in local playwriting. That was not to come until the last quarter of the century when Alfredo Chavero (1841–1906), José Peón y Contreras (1843–1907), Manuel José Othón (1848–1906), and José Rosas Moreno (1838–1883) all wrote highly successful plays, several of which foreshadowed the realism that would enter Latin American theatre in the next century. *Zarzuela* and other forms of musical and variety entertainments still dominated the stages of Mexico.

All of Spanish South America was under the viceroyalty of Peru until its northern territories became New Granada in 1717, its southeastern territories became Rio de la Plata in 1776, and Chile was separated off in 1778. These territories all became independent of Spain by 1824, but it would be a number of years before the territories subdivided themselves into the countries we know today.

Lima was the capital of Peru and the center for its limited theatrical activities well into the nineteenth century. Pedro de Peralta Barnuevo (1664–1743) encouraged the adoption of neoclassical techniques there with his adaptations of Corneille and Molière in the early eighteenth century, while Fray Francisco del Castillo (1716–1770) became the most popular writer of *entermeses* (short comic interludes) at mid-century. Peru's first important play after independence was *The Fruits of Education* (1830) by Felipe Pardo y Aliaga (1806–1868), whose conservative views reflect the lack of enthusiasm Lima's citizens had for the independence that had been thrust on them. A neoclassical comedy about a matchmaker in Lima, *Missy Catita* (1856) by Manuel Ascensio Segura, is the best-known Peruvian play of the period. By the second half of the nineteenth century, Peruvian plays were done in a satiric, *costumbrismo* style (one that depends on regional customs, dialects, and local color for its effects). As a consequence, the plays are difficult to appreciate today. Outside of Lima the Chilean dramatist Daniel Barros Grez (1834–1904) was highly regarded for his critiques of the social-climbing middle-class in plays like *As in Santiago* (1875) and *The Almost Wedding* (1881).

Buenos Aires, Argentina, was the capital of the Rio de la Plata viceroyalty. A theatre for *zarzuela* was built there in 1757 and the Teatro de la Rancheria in 1783. *The Love of the Ranch Girl* (probably written between 1787 and 1792 by Juan Bautista Maciel but possibly of a later date by an unknown author) established the pattern for later "*gaucho* melodramas," but more serious plays continued to be influenced by French neoclassicism. Argentina produced few dramatists of note but it did produce a number of actors, most notably the actor-manager Luis Ambrosio Morante (1775–1837), who were among the most successful touring actors of the age. Of the ten theatres built in Argentina in the nineteenth century, the Teatro Colón (1857–1944) was the most significant.

Bogotá, Colombia, the capital of New Granada, did produce a large number of local dramatists including Luis Vargas Tejada (1802–1829), José Fernández Madrid (1789–1830), José Caicedo Rojas (1816–1897), Santiago Pérez (1830–1900), José María Samper (1828–1888), Constancio Franco (1842–1917), and Adolfo León Gómez (1858–1927). The Corral de Ramírez, later rebuilt as the Coliseo de Ramírez, was erected there in 1791; in 1892 it became the Teatro Colón. But for the most part theatre in Colombia was provided by local amateurs and touring companies from Argentina, Mexico, and Spain.

Brazil was a Portuguese colony, and in 1807 the king of Portugal fled Napoleon's troops and established Rio de Janeiro as the capital of the Portuguese Empire. When the king returned to Lisbon in 1821, he entrusted Brazil to his son, who promptly declared it an independent nation in 1822. Throughout the nineteenth century theatrical activities in this vast country were concentrated in São Paulo and Rio de Janeiro.

Gonçalves de Magalhães's (1811–1882) tragedy *Antonio José, or the Poet and the Inquisition* (1838) is said to be the first Brazilian play on a national theme, though its subject was a Portuguese playwright of the previous century. Magalhães was a romantic poet and, while this play was neoclassical, its theme and his poetry proved to be an inspiration for Latin America romanticism. The nineteen domestic comedies of Luís Carlos Martins Pena (1815–1848), especially *The Frontier Justice of the Peace* (1838) and *The Novice* (1845), became extremely popular after his death and are especially noteworthy for their depiction of contemporary life in Brazil. Later writers like Joaquim Manuel de Macedo (1820–1882) with *The White Phantom* (1850) and the important novelist José de Alencar (1829–1877) with *The Family Demon* (1858) exploited Pena's comic style. Pena's five serious plays were written under the influence of romanticism, which had come to dominate by the 1840s. His *Nero in Spain* (1841), along with Gonçalves Dias's (1823–1864) historic drama *Leonor de Mendonça* (1847), the strangely nightmarish *Macário* (1852) by Alvaress de Azevedo (1831–1852), and novelist Castro Alves' (1847–1871) antislavery masterpiece *Gonzaga,* or the *Minas Revolution* (1867), are the notable examples of Brazilian romanticism. The serious plays of Mecedo and Alencar, on the other hand, were thesis plays in the style of Alexander Dumas *fils*. Puerto Rico playwrights Alejandro Tapia y Rivera (1826–1882) and Salvador Brau (1842–1912) wrote similar kinds of social problem plays, concerned with racism and the unequal treatment of women. Such plays had been promoted by Joaquim Heliodoro Gomes, who created the Ginásio Dramático in 1855 to popularize the "theatre of common sense" and French realism in Brazil. The remarkable success of Artur Azevedo (1855–1908), however, undercut this movement. Azevedo wrote highly successful musical comedies that dominated the stage, the best known of which is probably *The Second-Rate Traveling Theatre* (1896).

Of the Caribbean colonies, Cuba had the most extensive theatrical activity. The first Cuban play in Spanish was *The Presumed Gardener Prince Cloridano* (1730), by Santiago Pita y Borroto (?–1755). But Francisco Covarrubias (1755–1850) is considered the father of Cuban theatre. As an actor-manager and author of over twenty plays, he developed the *negrito* (c. 1812), a farcical blackface character reminiscent of those to be seen later in the minstrel shows of the United States which toured Cuba in 1860–1865. Versions of this character became a mainstay of Cuban comedy, and late in the century José Martí (1853–1895) wrote independence plays that made the *negrito* character into a dramatic hero. The first Cuban romanticist was actually an exile from Santo Domingo, Francisco Javier Foxá (1816–1865), best known for *Don Pedro de Castillo* (1838). His lead was followed by such noted writers as Bartolomé José Crespo y Borbón (1811–1871), who also wrote comedies in an Afro-Cuban dialect, José Jacinto Milanés (1814–1863), and Gertrudis Gómez de Avellaneda (1814–1873), one of the most successful woman authors of the age. Joaquín Lorenzo Luaces (1826–1867) was the most nationalistic of the Cuban writers. His plays are critical of colonialism and ridicule foreign fashions. They probably helped inspire *bufos habaneros* (Havana bufo), which were burlesques of both Spanish melodrama and *zarzuelas*. The *bufos* became popular about 1866 but were quickly suppressed in the unsuccessful rebellion (1868–1878) against Spain. They were revived and performed extensively from 1879 until Spain lost Cuba to the United States in 1898.

A Coliseo was built in Havana in 1775. Remodeled in 1792 and called the Teatro Principal after 1803, it was finally abandoned in 1846. It had already been replaced by the Gran Teatro Tacón (1838). With a capacity of 2,287 and standing room for 700, it was the largest theatre in Latin America when it opened. Havana also acquired a Teatro Mecânico in 1794. Like DeLoutherbourg's "Eidophusikon" in London, this was a small-scale theatre designed to create moving pictures with special effects, but this teatro made one major improvement: it included "automated dolls." A diorama was built in Havana in 1829 and saw use as a theatre on an occasional basis.

Few cities in Latin America were able to support full-time acting companies in the nineteenth century. Professional theatre was largely provided by touring companies from Spain, Italy, and France. Troupes from Mexico, Argentina, and Cuba also traveled widely, but they generally featured European actors and performed a European repertory. Many local companies were, therefore, amateur, and many of the plays by local dramatists were written for these companies. But it was from the work of these groups that Native American, African, and European folk traditions found their way into theatrical performances. It was not until World War I prevented the steady flow of touring companies from Europe that Latin American theatre was able to establish its own identity, and when it did, those folk traditions would play a major role.

LOOKING AT THEATRE HISTORY

The psychological realism being developed in European theatres in the last half of the century depended on the audience giving its full attention to the subtleties of events depicted on stage. Scholars have noted, therefore, that there is a close interrelationship between the success of this kind of realism and the change from a tradition of keeping the auditorium well lighted during performance to one of darkening the auditorium, which began in the mid-1870s. F. W. J. Hemmings notes a possible economic impetus for this change. Here he quotes from a French complaint of the 1870s that when the curtain was down,

> . . . for the sake of not wasting gas, the house is plunged into a sort of artificial night. The contrary would be more logical—to maintain a half-light in the auditorium when the curtain is up and when the stage, well lit, [is] drawing everyone's attention.

Hippolyte Hostein, *Historiettes et souvenirs d'un homme de théâtre*, Paris, 1879, p. 279, quoted in F. W. J. Hemmings, *The Theatre Industry in Nineteenth-Century France*, Cambridge, 1993, p. 45.

Like so many things in the nineteenth century, acting was subjected to "scientific" examination. Francois Delsarte sought to reduce acting to a set of laws that would permit it to be taught with precision:

> I had learned how vain is advice dictated by the caprice of a master without a system. . . . I knew that certain laws existed. . . . I had the nucleus of the science . . . and I did not despair of formulating it.

One of his disciples sums up the basic assumptions on which the system rested:

> There is no science without principles which give a reason for its facts. Hence to teach and to learn [this subject] it is necessary: 1. to understand the general law which controls the movement of the organs; 2. to apply this general law to the movements of each particular organ; 3. to understand the meaning of the form of each of these movements; 4. to adapt this meaning to the various states of the soul.

The Delsarte System . . . with the Literary Remains of François Delsarte (New York, 1887).

The study of postcolonial theatre has been an important focus in theatre history. The romantics had wanted to find evidence of an idyllic pure culture in the native peoples they encountered, but modern scholars have been much more concerned with the ways in which the imposition of Western forms of self-expression and identity were resisted by indigenous populations. In "Transculturating Transculturation," Dianna Taylor observes:

> The deceptive familiarity of Latin American theatre, then, has led to errors in criticism. As no indigenous theatre survived intact after the century following the conquest, it goes without saying that all the dramatic forms currently used in Latin America are derived in some degree from Western drama. While certain dramatic forms were forcefully imposed during the colonial period, since then Latin American dramatists have tended to "borrow" models. . . . Nonetheless, they do not borrow indiscriminately. . . . What they did adopt were forms that could help change their positions with regards to their socio-political exploitation and marginalization [97].

Performing Arts Journal (May 1991), 90–104.

In considering performance traditions of Native Americans on the northern continent, Linda Walsh Jenkins warns of the difficulties in getting past the limits of our Western worldview.

> Where the European aesthetic draws large distinctions between secular theatricality (the production of a Shakespeare play) and sacred theatricality (a church service), indigenous peoples, who see everything as sacred, might distinguish the two as public and private, both of spiritual and aesthetic importance to the tribe, and both incorporating performers, spectators and a predetermined oral text [400].

The World Encyclopedia of Contemporary Theatre, The Americas, edited by Don Rubin and Carlos Solórzano. London, 1996.

16
The Beginnings
of Modern Realism

For the most part, the theatre during the late nineteenth century was merely a logical outgrowth of what had gone before. But after 1875 several writers and directors made a marked break with the past. Nevertheless, in the beginning the changes were essentially intensifications of trends already underway. Saxe-Meiningen demonstrated the value of the all-powerful director who can weld all the elements of production into a unified whole. In playwriting, Ibsen was the first to realize fully the goals set forth by the realists and to make the public aware that a new era in the theatre had begun while Zola provided the theoretical framework that was to take realism to its most extreme form in naturalism.

SAXE-MEININGEN

Perhaps the most important of the new forces, the Meiningen Players, came to the fore in the 1870s and demonstrated the value of unity to the growing tendency toward realism in the theatre. Although plays had been performed in the Duchy of Meiningen since the late eighteenth century, a permanent court theatre was not opened until 1831, and the productions there remained commonplace until Georg II (1826–1914) succeeded to the throne in 1866. Georg II, Duke of Saxe-Meiningen, had received extensive

art training, had been at the Prussian court in Berlin when Tieck worked there, and had seen Charles Kean's Shakespearean productions in London, Friedrick Haase's in Coburg-Gotha, and the superior ensemble of the Burgtheater. Thus, his intense interest in the theatre was well developed before a Prussian invasion of Meiningen forced his father to abdicate in his favor.

Upon succeeding to the throne in 1866, Georg II immediately began to change the repertory of the court theatre and to take a personal interest in its affairs. In managing the troupe, the duke at first depended heavily on Friedrich von Bodenstedt (1819–1892), and after 1871 on Ludwig Chronegk (1837–1891). Trained as a singing comedian, Chronegk had been employed at Meiningen in 1866 as a comic actor. His appointment as director came as a surprise to the company, for there seemed little in his background to justify it. Nevertheless, the fame of the troupe probably owes as much to Chronegk as to Saxe-Meiningen, since not only was he an indefatigable worker, but he also conceived and arranged the tours which made the company famous. A third major influence was Ellen Franz (1839–1923), an actress who in 1873 became the duke's third wife. After this time she assumed responsibility for proposing the repertory, adapting the texts, and supervising stage speech. Thus, it is difficult to assign credit for the company's accomplishments, although it is now typical to allot it solely to the duke.

From 1866 until 1874 the company played entirely in Meiningen, and when it appeared in Berlin in 1874 it took the astonished spectators completely by surprise. After its initial success, the company began a long series of tours. Between 1874 and 1890, it played in thirty-eight cities in nine countries, including Russia, Sweden, Austria, Denmark, Belgium, Holland, and England, giving about 2,600 performances of forty-one plays. By 1890, when it gave up touring, the Meiningen commanded the greatest respect of any company in the world.

The repertory of the Meiningen Players, composed primarily of works by Shakespeare, Schiller, Grillparzer, and nineteenth-century romantic playwrights, was not unlike that of other companies except in its inclusion of more plays of high merit. Ibsen's *Ghosts* was presented for a few performances, but the other contemporary plays in the repertory were mostly poetic, romantic works.

Although the duke's productions are often considered the most historically accurate of the nineteenth century, historical accuracy was not for him an end in itself. His primary goal was to do full justice to the scripts he chose. It was his perception of what this goal demanded that led him to pursue a pictorial illusionism which excelled all previous standards because of its great accuracy. The duke divided each century into thirds and further distinguished among national differences within each time period. As a result, his productions attained unprecedented authenticity. Accuracy was further ensured by the duke's refusal to permit actors to tamper with their costumes. In most theatres of the times, the stars either supplied their own garments or altered as they saw fit those provided by the theatre. Actresses often wore crinoline petticoats under dresses of all periods. Furthermore, the duke insisted upon authentic materials in place of the usual cheap substitutes. He used heavy upholstery fabrics, many imported from France and Italy and some made to his specifications; he introduced genuine chain mail, armor, swords, axes, halberds, and other instruments. Authentic period furniture was always used. The success of the Meiningen Players led to the establishment of theatrical supply houses which manufactured furniture, properties, costume materials, and armor to meet the new demand from other troupes.

Saxe-Meiningen designed all of the costumes, scenery, and properties used by his troupe. The settings were usually painted by the Brückner brothers of Coburg, who also designed Wagner's and Haase's settings. Strong colors were used in scenery for the first time, reversing the former practice of having ac-

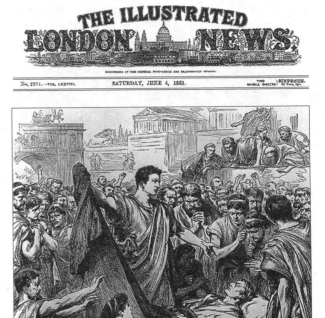

THE ILLUSTRATED LONDON NEWS

No. 2194.—VOL. LXXVIII. SATURDAY, JUNE 4, 1881. TWO WHOLE SHEETS | SIXPENCE.

FIG. 16.1
Saxe-Meiningen's production of *Julius Caesar* as performed at Drury Lane, London, 1881. Antony's oration over the body of Caesar. From *The Illustrated London News* (1881). Courtesy Theatre Museum, Victoria and Albert Museum, London.

tors play against pastel scenery. This innovation probably accounts for the adverse comments by critics on the "garishness" of the Meiningen settings. The duke was opposed to sky borders and used foliage, beams, banners, or other devices as overhead masking. He avoided symmetrical balance, for he thought this unnatural, and was careful to keep each detail in correct proportion and to blend painted and three-dimensional elements convincingly. He was also one of the first artists consistently to treat the stage floor as part of the design, breaking it up with fallen trees, rocks, hillocks, steps, and platforms.

While its use of scenery and costumes was probably superior to that of other troupes, the company's principal sources of power were totality of effect and, especially, ensemble acting. The duke maintained as complete authority over his actors as over the scenic investiture. Because he could not afford major performers, his company was composed either of beginners or of older actors who had not attained outstanding success. Guest actors sometimes performed with the troupe, but they had to conform to the company's rules against stars. Perhaps to discourage any tendency toward the "star complex," Saxe-Meiningen required all actors not cast in leading roles to appear as supernumeraries. This, in turn, made possible the effective crowd scenes for which the company was noted. Saxe-Meiningen used no supernumeraries who were not permanent members of the troupe. While this limited the number of persons available for crowd scenes, the effect of large masses was achieved by settings kept sufficiently small to force many of the actors into the wings (thus suggesting that great numbers were out of sight offstage) and by diagonal and contrasting movements to create effects of confusion and agitation. In rehearsing crowd scenes, the duke divided his actors into small groups, each under the charge of an experienced performer who aided in training those under him. Furthermore, each member of a mob was given individualizing characteristics and specific lines; then all were carefully coordinated. The results obtained

in this manner, contrasting sharply with the usual mob scenes, were considered revolutionary.

Fortunately, the duke could depend upon long rehearsal periods. Since Meiningen had a population of only 8,000, the theatre was open only twice a week for six months of the year. This schedule and the duke's authority made it possible to rehearse in a way quite different from the usual practice elsewhere. Each work was rehearsed from the first with full settings, furniture, and properties. Costumes were not always available from the beginning, but were always used for some time prior to the premiere. Actors were required to "act" from the first day rather than merely "walk through" the part as was typical in many theatres. Rehearsals, held in the evening after the duke's state duties were completed and often lasting five or six hours, continued until the play was judged ready for performance, even if this required several months. Because he did not work against a deadline, the duke conceived many details as he went along, and rehearsals were frequently delayed while furniture was rearranged or new plans made.

The impact of the Meiningen Players came from the complete illusion attained in every aspect of the

FIG. 16.2
Saxe-Meiningen's sketch for Act II of Julius Winding's *Pope Sixtus V.* Courtesy Theatermuseum, Munich.

production. Thus, the company stands as the culmination of trends that had begun in the Renaissance. More important, it stands at the beginning of the new movement toward unified production, in which each element is carefully selected because of its contribution to the total effect. The actor had given way to the director as the dominant artist in the theatre. Saxe-Meiningen's example influenced such men as Antoine and Stanislavsky, who were to figure significantly in the formation of the modern theatre. By the time the Meiningen Players discontinued touring in 1890, the theatre was already entering the new era which they had helped to inaugurate. By that time the public had also become aware of a new direction in playwriting, primarily through the work of Ibsen.

IBSEN

Henrik Ibsen (1828–1906), after publishing his first play in 1850, was appointed resident dramatist and stage manager at the newly created Norwegian National Theatre in Bergen in 1851. By 1857 he had assisted in staging 145 plays, and had written seven of his own. Between 1857 and 1862, he worked at the Norwegian Theatre in Christiania (now Oslo), and after 1864 he lived abroad until 1891.

Ibsen wrote twenty-five plays. Most of the early works are verse-dramas about the Scandinavian past. These include *Lady Inger of Ostraat* (1855), *The Vikings at Helgeland* (1858), and *The Pretenders* (1864). The most important early works, however, are *Brand* (1866) and *Peer Gynt* (1867). *Brand,* a dramatic poem, depicts an uncompromising idealist who sacrifices everything, including his family, to his vision. It established Ibsen's reputation, and the financial security which it brought made it possible for him to work as he pleased. *Peer Gynt* contrasts sharply with *Brand,* for its protagonist is a man who avoids issues by skirting them. A skillful blending of fantasy and reality, *Peer Gynt* was interpreted by many as a satire on the Norwegian character.

In the 1870s Ibsen made a sharp break with his past when he announced his intention of abandoning verse because it was unsuited to creating an illusion of reality. The future direction of his work first became apparent with *Pillars of Society* (1877), but it was with *A Doll's House* (1879), *Ghosts* (1881), and *An Enemy of the People* (1882) that Ibsen established his reputation as a radical thinker. Above all, it was *A Doll's House* and *Ghosts* that shocked conservative readers and served as a rallying point for supporters of a drama of ideas. Unlike Dumas *fils* and Augier, who also wrote about controversial subjects, Ibsen did not resolve his plays in ways that confirmed re-

FIG. 16.3
Ibsen's *Rosmersholm* at the Norwegian National Theatre, Oslo, 1906. Eleanora Duse is seen at left. From *Bühne und Welt* (1906).

ceived ideology. Rather, he made ideology the cause of problems and suggested the need to change it.

In *A Doll's House,* Nora, upon realizing that, as a woman, she has always been kept ignorant of the practical world and treated as a plaything, chooses to leave her husband and children in order to learn about the world so she can make decisions for herself. Contrarily, in *Ghosts,* Mrs. Alving, conforming to traditional morality, has remained with a depraved husband only to have her only son go mad, presumably from inherited syphilis. Thus, both plays were greeted as attacks on family and home, the bedrocks of civilized society, while the allusions to venereal disease and sexual misconduct in *Ghosts* were considered so offensive to standards of public decency that the play was forbidden production in most countries.

Ibsen soon turned in new directions. In *The Wild Duck* (1884), *Rosmersholm* (1886), *The Master Builder* (1892), *John Gabriel Borkman* (1896), and *When We Dead Awaken* (1899) he made increasing use of symbolism and of subjects more concerned with personal relationships than with social problems. In actuality, the basic theme of Ibsen's plays remained relatively constant: the struggle for integrity, the conflict between duty to oneself and duty to others. Mrs. Alving of *Ghosts* discovers too late that she has destroyed her life by overvaluing duty to others, whereas in many of the late plays the protagonists, while pursuing some private vision, destroy the happiness of others and finally their own.

Much of Ibsen's work contributed to the development of realism. In the prose dramas he refined Scribe's "well-made play" formula and made it more fitting to the realistic style. Ibsen discarded asides, soliloquies, and other nonrealistic devices, and was careful to motivate all exposition. Most often characters who have just returned after a long absence elicit information in a manner that appears completely natural by asking questions about happenings while they were away. All scenes are causally related and lead logically to the denouement. Dialogue, settings, costumes, and business are selected for their ability to reveal character and milieu, and are clearly described in stage directions. Each character is conceived as a personality whose behavior is attributable to hereditary or environmental forces. Internal psychological motivations are given even greater emphasis than external visual detail. In these ways, Ibsen provided a model for writers of the realistic school.

Ibsen's late plays were to influence nonrealistic drama as extensively as the earlier prose plays did realistic works. In them, ordinary objects (such as the duck in *The Wild Duck*) are imbued with significance beyond their literal meaning and enlarge the implications of the dramatic action. Furthermore, many of the works border on fantasy. In *Rosmersholm* a phantom white horse is significant, and in *When We Dead Awaken* the mountain heights exert an irresistible pull. This sense of mysterious forces at work in human destiny was to be a major theme of symbolist drama.

Whether realistic or nonrealistic, almost all drama after Ibsen was influenced by his conviction that art should be a source of insights, a creator of discussion, a conveyor of ideas, something more than mere entertainment. He gave playwrights a new vision of their role. Almost everywhere Ibsen's plays came to epitomize the break with the past and to be a rallying point for producers seeking new paths.

ZOLA AND THE FRENCH NATURALISTS

Even as Ibsen was writing his prose plays, the French naturalists, working quite independently, were also demanding a new drama. The naturalists considered heredity and environment to be the major determinants of human fate. This doctrine was grounded (at least in part) in Charles Darwin's *The Origin of Species* (1859). Darwin set forth two main theses:

(1) All forms of life have developed gradually from a common ancestry; and (2) the evolution of species is explained by the "survival of the fittest." These theories had several important implications. First, they implied that heredity and environment are the primary causal factors. Second, human behavior, when viewed (as it soon was) as a product of hereditary and environmental forces, came to seem determined by factors largely beyond any individual's control; thus, at least partial responsibility for undesirable behavior had to be accepted by the society that has allowed adverse hereditary and environmental factors to exist. Third, Darwin's theories strengthened the idea of progress since, if human beings had evolved from an atom of being to the complex creatures they now were, increasing complexity and improvement appeared to be inevitable. Nevertheless, it was argued, progress could be hastened by the consistent application of scientific method and new technology. Fourth, human beings were absorbed into nature. Prior to the nineteenth century humans had been set apart from the rest of nature as superior to it. Now they lost their privileged status and, like animals or plants, were often considered subjects to be studied and controlled like the members of any other biological species.

Naturalism also attracted many adherents because of contemporary political and economic conditions. The Franco-Prussian War of 1870–1871 was a severe blow to French pride, for not only was France defeated, but it lost Alsace and Lorraine to Germany and brought an end to Napoleon III's empire. In Paris a commune was established, but this was soon overthrown and France once more became a republic. The war and its aftermath served to emphasize that the working man enjoyed few privileges, and during the last quarter of the nineteenth century socialism began to gain support throughout Europe as many came to believe that only this form of social organization could ensure equality for all. Such pressures motivated several European governments to adopt constitutions at last; by 1900 every major country in Europe except Russia had some degree of constitutional government. This interest in the lot of the working classes and the rights of the common people was to provide a major focus for naturalism. As means of dealing with contemporary problems, science and technology were considered the major tools, and the naturalists argued that all social problems could be solved if only the scientific method were applied to them systematically.

Naturalism as a conscious movement first appeared in France in the 1870s. Its primary spokesman was Emile Zola (1840–1902), an admirer of Comte and an advocate of the scientific method as the key to all truth and progress. Believing that literature must either become scientific or perish, Zola argued that drama should illustrate the "inevitable laws of heredity and environment" or record "case studies." He wished the dramatist, in his search for truth, to observe, record, and "experiment" with the same detachment as the scientist. Zola compared the writer with the pathologist, who seeks the causes of a disease so it may be cured, not glossing over infection but bringing it out into the open where it can be examined. Similarly, the dramatist should depict social ills so they may be corrected. In addition, Zola argued that on stage the events should be reproduced with sufficient exactness to demonstrate the relationship between cause and effect.

Zola's first major statement of the naturalist doctrine came in 1873 in the preface to his dramatization of his novel *Thérèse Raquin;* he expanded his views in *Naturalism in the Theatre* (1881) and *The Experimental Novel* (1881). Some of Zola's followers were even more radical than he in their demands for theatrical reform, arguing that a play should merely be a "slice of life" transferred to the stage. Thus, in their zeal to approximate scientific truth, they often obliterated virtually all distinctions between art and life.

Naturalism, like many movements before it, was handicapped by a lack of good plays embodying its principles. Although a few plays, such as *Henriette Maréchal* (1863) by Edmond and Jules Goncourt and *L'Arlesienne* (1872) by Alphonse Daudet, were produced, they made little impact. Even *Thérèse Raquin* failed to live up to Zola's critical precepts except in the setting, for rather than a slice of life it was more nearly a melodrama about murder and retribution.

Ironically, it was Henri Becque (1837–1899) who most nearly captured the naturalist ideal in France, even though he and Zola were equally contemptuous of each other. Becque's *The Vultures* (1882) shows the fleecing of a family by their supposed friends following the death of the father; there are no sympathetic characters, the ending is pessimistic and ironical, and there are no obvious climaxes, merely a slow progression toward the cynical outcome. *La Parisienne* (1885) depicts a wife who considers her infidelity an asset to her husband's advancement in business. In these plays Becque raised French naturalism to its highest point.

That *The Vultures* was presented by the Comédie Française, a bastion of conservatism, would on the surface suggest that by the 1880s naturalism had been fully accepted in Paris. But Becque's play was ineffectually produced because he refused to comply with the company's request for revisions that would have brought the work more nearly into conformity with contemporary tastes. Because virtually all naturalist

FIG. 16.4

Zola's *The Earth* as dramatized by Ménessier and directed by Antoine at the Théâtre Antoine, 1902. Note the many naturalistic details, including the chickens in the foreground. From *Le Théâtre* (1902).

dramas that received a hearing were inadequately staged, the prevailing attitudes of both the public and theatrical workers remained unchallenged. Something more was needed if significant change was to come. This new element was to be added by Antoine at the Théâtre Libre, where after 1887 naturalistic staging and writing were united for the first time.

ANTOINE AND THE THÉÂTRE LIBRE

André Antoine (1858–1943) seemed a most unpromising source of revolution in 1887, for he was merely a clerk in a gas company, and his theatrical experience was limited to supernumerary acting with Parisian professional companies and occasional appearances with an amateur group (of which there were many in Paris). When Antoine sought to produce a program of new plays, including a dramatization of Zola's *Jacques Damour*, his amateur circle refused its sanction and Antoine set off on his own. In search of a name for his company, he adopted Théâtre Libre (or "Free Theatre"). The success of his first program won him the endorsement of Zola and other influential figures. His second program was attended by major theatrical critics, who wrote lengthy reviews. Before the end of 1887, Antoine had given up his clerk's job and thereafter until 1914 devoted himself to theatrical production.

Organized on a subscription basis, the Théâtre Libre was open only to members and therefore was exempt from censorship. As a result, many of the plays available to Antoine were those that had been refused licenses, and most were naturalistic. Much of the notoriety of the Théâtre Libre stemmed from its *comédies rosses* (plays in which the usual principles of morality are reversed), many so extreme that they repelled even Antoine's tolerant audience. It was largely because of these works that naturalism gained a reputation for depravity, but the publicity they attracted also gradually paved the way for greater freedom in established and conservative theatres.

In 1888 Antoine also began to produce one foreign work each year. After Tolstoy's *The Power of Darkness,* he went on to Ibsen's *Ghosts* and *The Wild Duck.* In this way, controversial foreign as well as domestic plays were given their first Parisian performances.

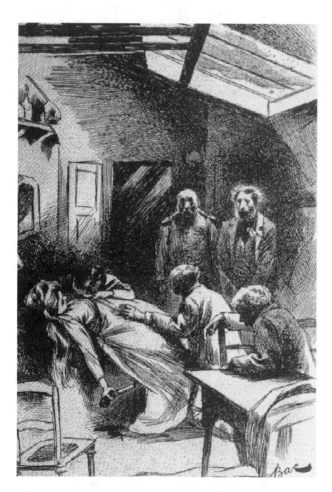

FIG. 16.5
Antoine's production of Iben's *The Wild Duck* at the Théâtre Libre. The final scene. From a contemporary lithograph.

In addition to serving as a showcase for new dramas, the Théâtre Libre became the proving ground for production techniques. Although Antoine had used a realistic approach from the beginning, he intensified his search for authenticity after witnessing the Meiningen Players and Irving's company in 1888. He then sought to reproduce environment in every detail. In *The Butchers* (1888), for example, he hung real carcasses of beef on the stage. The "fourth wall" was observed consistently; in designing settings, he arranged rooms as in real life and only later decided which wall should be removed. Often furniture was placed along the curtain line, and actors were directed to behave as though there were no audience. Through his belief in the importance of environment, Antoine helped to establish the principle that each play requires its own setting quite distinct from that of any other work. After witnessing the Meiningen company, Antoine also gave special attention to ensemble acting. Although most of his performers were amateurs, he coached them carefully and autocratically. He discouraged conventionalized movement and declamatory speech, seeking natural behavior instead.

Antoine's success worked against him, for as soon as playwrights or actors established their worth, they were employed by a major company. Furthermore, Antoine's high standards of production kept him constantly in debt. Even at the height of its popularity, the Théâtre Libre gave no production for more than three performances. By 1893, the company began to weaken and in 1894 Antoine left it. By then he had presented sixty-two programs composed of 184 plays. In addition to playing in Paris, he had toured in Belgium, Holland, Germany, Italy, and England. The example he had set was to be followed in several other countries.

Antoine did not stay away from the Parisian theatre long. In 1897 he opened his Théâtre Antoine, run as a fully professional theatre, and in 1906 he was appointed director of the state-subsidized Odéon, which he completely modernized. Although he practiced it less assiduously, realism still dominated his work. Probably his most famous productions of this era were of French classical dramas, for which he attempted to re-create the theatrical conventions of the seventeenth century. Costumed actors served as onstage audience, chandeliers were hung over the stage, and candle footlights were conspicuous. Through this approach, he helped to establish a realism based upon past theatrical conventions rather than upon architecture and dress, as had been usual with other producers. Antoine also directed several outstanding productions of Shakespeare's plays. Near the end of his tenure at the Odéon, he staged a few works in which stylization (based on visual sources) was clearly evident, but he resigned his post before this new trend was fully explored. By 1914 he had presented a total of 364 works. No one else had influenced the French theatre of the period so profoundly as had Antoine.

After 1890, most of the major new French dramatists were realists and many of these were given their first hearing by Antoine. Among these the most important were Porto-Riche, Curel, and Brieux. Georges Porto-Riche (1849–1930) was noted for subtle characterizations which emphasized internal conflicts. Probably his best play is *Infatuated* (1891) in which a husband tries to rid himself of his wife by arousing her interest in another man, only to discover that he cannot give her up. François de Curel (1854–1928) had his first play produced by Antoine in 1892. He made few concessions to popular taste, and his disregard for ordinary principles of dramatic construction often obscured his intentions. His concern for internal psychological conflicts, however, did much to forward realistic subject matter. Among his best works are *The Fossils* (1892), depicting a decaying aristocracy, and *The Lion's Feast* (1897), in which the protagonist attempts to improve the lives of workers. Eugène Brieux (1858–1932) was said by George Bernard Shaw to be the most important dramatist in Europe after the death of Ibsen. Given his first production by Antoine in 1892, Brieux went on to write *The Red Robe* (1900), showing the difficulty of obtaining justice from judges concerned primarily with promotion, *Damaged Goods* (1902), concerning syphilis and its transmission to a child, and *Maternity* (1903), in which a blistering attack is launched on a society that does not permit legal birth control. Controversy over *Damaged Goods* led to the abolishment of censorship in 1905. Thus, a subject that had been unacceptable to censors when Ibsen wrote *Ghosts* in 1881 was allowed in French commercial theatres by 1905.

THE FREIE BÜHNE AND GERMAN REALISM

The pattern that emerged in France was repeated in Germany. The first step toward theatrical reform came in 1883, when the Deutsches Theater was opened in Berlin by Adolf L'Arronge (1838–1908) and Ludwig Barnay (1842–1924), with a company headed by Josef Kainz (1858–1910), the major exponent of the new realism, and Agnes Sorma (1865–1927), later to be Germany's leading actress. Here a repertory of old and new plays was produced in the manner of the Meiningen Players. In 1888 Barnay left the Deutsches Theater to found the Berliner Theater, and in the same year Oskar Blumenthal (1852–1917) founded the Lessing Theater. Thus, by 1890 Berlin had several private companies of excellent quality. Nevertheless, their choice of plays was severely restricted by censorship.

Meanwhile, a group calling itself "Youngest Germany" had begun to advocate a new art based upon an objective observation of reality, while another calling itself *Durch* (or "Through") went even further than Zola in its demands for a naturalistic drama. Both groups found inspiration in Ibsen's plays, sixteen of which had been translated into German by 1890.

As in France however, the new movement lacked focus until an "independent" theatre was formed. Taking its inspiration from the Théâtre Libre, the Freie Bühne (or "Free Stage") was organized in Berlin in 1889. Unlike Antoine's company, however, the German group was a democratic organization with officers and a governing council. Otto Brahm (1856–1912), a dramatic critic, was elected president and became its guiding spirit. In order to secure the services of professional actors, the Freie Bühne gave its performances on Sunday afternoons since its actors and most of its personnel were regularly employed by established theatres, especially the Deutsches, Berliner, and Lessing. Each production usually involved different actors, over whom Brahm had little control. Thus, the Freie Bühne exerted little influence on theatrical production. Its major contribution was made by giving a hearing to plays forbidden by the censor. The opening production of *Ghosts* was followed with plays by the Goncourts, Zola, Becque, Tolstoy, Anzengruber, and Strindberg. After the season of 1890–1891, regular performances were discontinued, although occasionally programs were arranged when a worthy play was forbidden a license. The Freie Bühne came to an end in 1894, when Brahm was named director of the Deutsches Theater.

At the Deutsches Theater between 1894 and 1904 and at the Lessing Theater from 1904 until 1912, Brahm perfected the realistic mode. He had little success with the classics and increasingly concentrated on developing an ensemble of actors and designers attuned to the demands of contemporary drama, especially that of Ibsen, Hauptmann, Schnitzler, and Sudermann, in the presentation of which the company was unexcelled.

The only truly important German dramatist introduced by the Freie Bühne was Gerhart Hauptmann (1862–1946). The furor that greeted his *Before Sunrise* (1889), the story of a Silesian family that sinks into viciousness after the discovery of coal on their land, established Hauptmann as a major new playwright. During the next fifty years he wrote about thirty plays. Of the early works, the best is *The Weavers*

(1892), remarkable for its group-protagonist of desperate workers driven to revolt. Like Ibsen, Hauptmann went on to write plays in a more symbolic vein, notably *The Assumption of Hannele* (1893) and *The Sunken Bell* (1896). After 1912, his plays became increasingly nonrealistic. Before his death, Hauptmann lost much of his prestige because of his passive acceptance of Hitler's regime. All of Hauptmann's work shows great compassion for human suffering, but his protagonists, who are victims of circumstances beyond their control, are more pitiable than heroic.

The Freie Bühne stimulated the formation of several other stage societies in Germany. Although none achieved the fame of the original group, they helped to pave the way for a new drama. Perhaps of equal importance, a "people's" theatre was organized by socialist groups (the ban on which was lifted in 1890) interested in raising the cultural standards of the working classes. Using the Freie Bühne as a model, the Freie Volksbühne was organized in Berlin in 1890 to produce plays at Sunday matinees, for which season tickets were distributed by lot at a nominal price. Beginning with 1,150 members, the organization included 12,000 by 1908. In 1892 the Neue Freie Volksbühne, founded by the former director of the original group, began a similar program. By 1905, it was offering its subscribers a choice among productions at several major theatres. Before World War I the two groups had amalgamated, and with a combined membership of 70,000 it was sufficiently stable that it could build one of the most modern theatres in Germany and employ its own permanent company. The workers' theatre movement flourished throughout Germany and Austria. To it must go considerable credit for creating a broad-based theatre-going public in those countries.

Before 1900, the new realistic drama was being accepted almost everywhere. At the Burgtheater in Vienna a wide selection of recent works was presented between 1890 and 1898, when Max Burckhardt (1854–1912) was director of the theatre. His successor, Paul Schlenther (1854–1916), a friend and admirer of Hauptmann and a founding member of the Freie Bühne, continued his policies between 1898 and 1910. A somewhat similar pattern was followed elsewhere, for as public interest in the new plays grew the repertory expanded to include them.

In addition to Hauptmann, other important new dramatists include Sudermann and Schnitzler. Hermann Sudermann (1857–1928) was even more instrumental than Hauptmann in making realism acceptable to the public, for he tended to retain the well-made play techniques and to conform more nearly to accepted morality while writing about "provocative" subjects. His most popular play, *Magda*

(1893), concerning a singer whose bohemian life brings her into conflict with her father, became a favorite vehicle of such actresses as Bernhardt and Duse. Sudermann continued to write until well into the twentieth century. The most important Austrian dramatist of this period was Arthur Schnitzler (1862–1931), a recorder of the melancholic world-weariness that characterized the turn of the century, and of the shallow sexual attitudes that accompanied it. The most famous of his works is *Anatol* (1893), a series of short plays, each of which records a different love intrigue. Even in the midst of happiness, Anatol knows that his momentary pleasure will dissolve into jealousy and boredom. A similar work is *Reigen,* variously translated as *Hands Around, La Ronde,* and *Round Dance* (1900, but not performed in Germany until 1920), with its ten characters engaged in a series of sexual encounters. Schnitzler, a friend of Sigmund Freud, was much concerned with the centrality of sexual behavior, but was also convinced that love cannot be built upon pure ego satisfaction. While he seldom strayed from this theme, Schnitzler wrote on other subjects, as in *Professor Bernhardi* (1912), a play about anti-Semitism.

THE INDEPENDENT THEATRE AND REALISM IN ENGLAND

After the death of Robertson in 1871, the English theatre was given over largely to works in the tradition of Boucicault and Sardou or to lavish productions of the classics. A new direction was not evident until the 1890s, with Jones and Pinero. These writers hold a place in English drama comparable to that of Dumas *fils* and Augier in French theatre, for both were sufficiently provocative to be slightly scandalizing, yet both were conventional enough to be acceptable to the censor and the theatre-going public.

Henry Arthur Jones (1851–1929) began his playwriting career with a successful melodrama, *The Silver King* (1882), and did not turn to more serious drama until after 1890 with *The Dancing Girl* (1891), *The Liars* (1897), and *Mrs. Dane's Defence* (1900). His most unusual play, *Michael and His Lost Angel* (1896), treats a love affair between a minister and one of his parishioners. Although Jones had high ideals for drama, he was not an original thinker. He aroused suspense and titillation without giving any significant new insights.

Arthur Wing Pinero (1855–1934) began his career in 1874 as an actor and turned to writing in 1877. His first major success came with a farce, *The Magistrate* (1885), a form in which he excelled. Although Pinero never professed interest in a "drama of ideas," it was his *The Second Mrs. Tanqueray* (1893), the story of a "woman with a past," that brought the first change in public attitudes, for when it proved a popular hit, producers began to look more favorably upon "Ibsen-esque" drama. Pinero continued to write for another thirty years, turning out such successful plays as *The Notorious Mrs. Ebbsmith* (1895), *Iris* (1901), and *Mid-Channel* (1909), but his popularity declined steadily after 1910.

While Jones and Pinero paved the way for public acceptance, the development of a more significant drama owes most to Ibsen. By 1880, William Archer and others had begun to translate Ibsen's plays and by 1890 all those then written were available in English. In 1889, two actresses, Janet Achurch (1864–1916) and Elizabeth Robins (1862–1952), both began to appear in Ibsen's plays. Achurch made a strong impression in *A Doll's House,* the first unadapted version of a play by Ibsen seen in England. Robins first produced *Pillars of Society,* and subsequently appeared in seven of the plays. These early productions, by reminding the English how far behind the continent their own drama had fallen, supplied one motivation for founding the Independent Theatre.

Modeled on the Théâtre Libre and the Freie Bühne, the Independent Theatre was headed by J. T. Grein (1862–1935), a Dutch-born critic who had lived in London for many years. Like its predecessors on the continent, the Independent Theatre was organized on a subscription basis to avoid censorship, and like the Freie Bühne, it gave its productions on Sundays in order to gain the cooperation of theatre managers and actors. The opening play in 1891, *Ghosts,* prompted more than 500 articles, most of them vituperative. The second program, Zola's *Thérèse Raquin,* created almost as great a storm. This publicity began to make the general public aware of the new drama for the first time.

Between 1891 and 1897, the Independent Theatre presented twenty-six plays, mostly translations. It did little in the way of mounting the plays. Thus, like the Freie Bühne, it served primarily as a rejuvenator of drama rather than as an influence on production. Grein had hoped to produce new English plays, for he was convinced that the low state of English drama was attributable to the conservatism of producers. He soon found, however, that no significant plays were available. His disappointment prompted George Bernard Shaw to complete *Widower's Houses,* the production of which in 1892 launched Shaw's career as a dramatist.

George Bernard Shaw (1856–1950), previously a novelist and critic, wrote regularly for the theatre from 1892 until his death. Unlike most of the new writers, who tended to be gloomy and intensely serious as a

FIG. 16.6
Pinero's *The Second Mrs. Tanqueray.* Act I of the original production with Mrs. Patrick Campbell and George Alexander. From *The Graphic* (1893).

reaction against the shallowness of their predecessors, Shaw wrote primarily in the comic form. This choice may be explained in part by Shaw's belief in the perfectibility of human beings and his interest in persuasion, which was best served by having characters arrive at perceptions that remove the barriers to a happy resolution. Shaw also delighted in using paradoxes to make both characters and audiences reassess their values. Thus, *Arms and the Man* (1894) punctures romantic notions about love and war, while *Major Barbara* (1905) upholds a munitions manufacturer as a greater humanitarian than an officer in the Salvation Army, because the Salvation Army prolongs an inequitable system by caring for victims whereas the manufacturer provides his workers with the means whereby to help themselves. Many of Shaw's plays, notably *The Doctor's Dilemma* (1906) and *Getting Married* (1908), are essentially extended discussions of specific problems. Other works, such as *Man and Superman* (1901) and *Back to Methuselah* (1919–1921), show Shaw's interest in "creative evolution" and the "life force," which he believed were striving to create a "superman" by working through superior individuals. In still other plays, like *Caesar and Cleopatra* (1899) and *Saint Joan* (1923), Shaw sought to question popular misconceptions of historical figures and events.

Perhaps his least characteristic work is *Heartbreak House* (1914–1919), a parable about the failures of Europe at the time of World War I.

Although Shaw is related to the realistic movement through his concern for ideas and social problems, he differs markedly from most of the writers of this school. While acknowledging the importance of heredity and environment, Shaw always implies that human beings have freedom of choice. Furthermore, although his characters often speak in dialect, they are always articulate and seldom follow closely the patterns of everyday speech. Shaw was not objective, for he chose his characters and invented his stories to illustrate a point of view. His comic method eventually won a wide audience for the drama of ideas.

Shaw was not immediately successful, however, for at first his unconventional ideas and paradoxical situations only puzzled or irritated audiences. His reputation was built slowly through the efforts of organizations that succeeded the Independent Theatre. The first of these was the Incorporated Stage Society, founded in 1899 to present modern plays. At first its programs were given on Sunday afternoons but, as its membership grew from the original 300 to 1,500 by 1914, it added Monday matinees as well. By the time the group disbanded in 1939 it had presented about 200 works, many of which would otherwise not have been seen. It served as an experimental theatre which kept the English theatrical world abreast of the latest movements both at home and abroad.

Among the most significant companies in this period was the Royal Court Theatre, where between 1904 and 1907 Harley Granville Barker (1877–1946) and John Vedrenne (1863–1930) gave the new drama its first full hearing in an English public theatre. Barker had begun his career as an actor in 1891, had worked with several organizations, including the Incorporated Stage Society, and had established himself as a dramatist before being invited to assist Vedrenne with a production of *Two Gentlemen of Verona*. This beginning soon developed into a permanent arrangement, under which one play was offered each evening for several weeks while another little-known or seldom-performed work was given at matinees. If the matinees engendered enough enthusiasm, the play was moved to evening performances. Even successes, however, were not played consecutively for more than a few weeks. Between 1904 and 1907, the Court presented thirty-two plays by seventeen different authors, including Euripides, Hauptmann, Ibsen, Galsworthy, and Yeats. The mainstay of the theatre, however, was Shaw, eleven of whose plays were presented in productions directed by Shaw

FIG. 16.7

Shaw's *Caesar and Cleopatra* at the Savoy Theatre, London, 1907. Forbes-Robertson as Caesar, Gertrude Elliott as Cleopatra. From *Play Pictorial,* 10 (1907).

himself. These productions established Shaw's popularity with the British public.

The Court made other important contributions. It was noted for ensemble acting by a company that included some of the best actors of the period: Lillah McCarthy, Edith Wynne Matthison, Louis Calvert, Lewis Casson, and Godfrey Tearle. There were no stars. Since Barker believed that it is the director's primary task to give a thoughtful interpretation of the playwright's script, he sought to find in each work the style suited to it. Nevertheless, the dominant style was a subtle realism which avoided bravura. Simplicity and suggestion were the keynotes of both the acting and scenery. In 1907 Barker and Vedrenne moved to the much larger Savoy Theatre, but closed after one season because of lack of attendance and trouble with the censor. When Charles Frohman established a repertory company at the Duke of York's Theatre in 1910, he employed Barker to head it. After presenting seventeen plays in seventeen weeks and incurring a sizable deficit, Barker resigned.

In spite of these failures, the Barker-Vedrenne experiments engendered several imitators, especially in the provinces, where repertory companies began to be opened once more. The first important company was established by Miss A. E. F. Horniman (1860–1937) in 1907 at the Gaiety Theatre in Manchester. Until it was discontinued in 1917, this was to be one of the best companies in England, offering a wide variety of English and continental plays. Its encouragement of local writers gave rise to the "Manchester School," of which Stanley Houghton (1881–1913), author of *Hindle Wakes* (1912), and Harold Brighouse (1883–1958), author of *Hobson's Choice* (1916), were the most important. Other vigorous repertory companies were founded at Liverpool

FIG. 16.8

Shaw's *Mrs. Warren's Profession* in its original English production, a private performance by the Incorporated Stage Society in 1902. Granville Barker is at left. Courtesy Enthoven Collection, Victoria and Albert Museum, London.

THE CONTINUING TRADITION IN ENGLAND, 1900–1914

Despite these "modern" trends, pictorial realism continued to be the principal goal in England until World War I. Furthermore, most of the major figures of the London stage between 1900 and 1914 had been trained in the Bancroft-Irving tradition, and they made few innovations. Of the actor-managers, the most important were Forbes-Robertson, Martin-Harvey, and Tree.

Johnston Forbes-Robertson (1853–1937) differed from most of the major actors of his day in being an excellent speaker of verse, an art which he had learned from Samuel Phelps. On the stage from 1874, Forbes-Robertson acted with Phelps, the Bancrofts, and Irving. He also served as leading man to Helena Modjeska (1844–1909), the Polish actress who appeared with great success in England and the United States between 1877 and 1905, and to Mary Anderson (1859–1940), an American actress who won fame in England between 1883 and 1889 for her Shakespearean performances. Occasionally Forbes-Robertson undertook management, but his reputation rested primarily upon his acting. Some critics (including Shaw, who wrote *Caesar and Cleopatra* for him) consider him the finest Hamlet of all time. He was knighted in 1913, the year in which he retired.

John Martin-Harvey (1863–1944) made his debut in 1881 and after 1882 played for Irving, whom he succeeded as manager of the Lyceum Theatre. In his first independent production, an adaptation of Dickens's *A Tale of Two Cities,* he won such popularity that he was condemned to play the role of Sidney Carton through most of his remaining career. He gained new fame in 1912 for his performance in Max Reinhardt's London production of *Oedipus Rex.* Until about 1910, Martin-Harvey continued Irving's practices, but gradually accepted modern trends and after World War I abandoned pictorial realism altogether. More than any other producer, he successfully bridged the Victorian and the modern stage.

The most famous actor-manager between 1900 and 1914 was Herbert Beerbohm Tree (1853–1917). On the stage from 1878, he assumed the management of the Haymarket in 1887. From the profits made there on melodramas and light contemporary plays he built Her Majesty's Theatre in 1897. Although he had had little previous experience with Shakespearean drama, Tree's new theatre was to be the principal home of Shakespeare in London between 1900 and 1914. Tree continued, and even extended, the trend toward actualistic detail. His *A Midsummer Night's Dream* in 1900 featured live rabbits and a carpet of

in 1911 and at Birmingham in 1913. The Birmingham Repertory Company, under the direction of Barry Jackson (1879–1961), was to be especially influential after the First World War.

In addition to Shaw, a number of other dramatists in the realistic vein appeared after 1900. John Galsworthy (1867–1933), already one of England's most successful novelists, turned to playwriting in 1906 with *The Silver Box,* in which the justice meted out to a poor and a rich man for the same crime is contrasted. His later plays, *Strife* (1909), *Justice* (1910), and *Loyalties* (1922), were in the same vein. All are objective treatments of social problems and demonstrate Galsworthy's considerable gift for creating dramatic dialogue and clear-cut conflicts. Harley Granville Barker won fame as a dramatist with such plays as *The Marrying of Ann Leete* (1902), *The Voysey Inheritance* (1905), *Waste* (1907), and *Madras House* (1910). Similar to Shaw in his interests, Barker lacked Shaw's sense of the comic. After being ignored for many years, Barker's plays began to be performed again in the 1980s.

FIG. 16.9
Beerbohm Tree's production of Shakespeare's *A Midsummer Night's Dream* at Her Majesty's Theatre, London, 1900. Oberon stands in front of the tree center; Titania is at left surrounded by fairies. Courtesy Enthoven Collection, Victoria and Albert Museum, London.

grass with flowers that could be plucked; although the scene changes added 45 minutes to the playing time, the production's literal realism attracted more than 220,000 spectators, perhaps the largest number to witness any Shakespearean play in London up to that time. Beginning in 1905, Tree annually held a festival of Shakespeare's plays in which many other companies took part.

Although not a very good actor, Tree often starred in his own productions. On the other hand, he surrounded himself with the best performers available, and he worked on every production with unbounded enthusiasm. As the repertory system declined, Tree became concerned about the lack of effective training for young actors, and in 1904 he established the acting school which was to become the Royal Academy of Dramatic Art, still the most prestigious in England.

Following the outbreak of the war in 1914, Tree gave up his theatre. Before the hostilities ended, he was dead. With him died much of English tradition, for after the war the actor-manager system, the dominant type of organization since the sixteenth century, was largely abandoned, and pictorial realism, long the standard of perfection, had come to seem old-fashioned.

THE MOSCOW ART THEATRE AND REALISM IN RUSSIA

Russia also had to await the "independent theatre" movement before needed reforms were to come. Although such Russian dramatists as Turgenev, Ostrovsky, and Pisemsky had already inaugurated a realistic school of writing, theatrical production still preserved conventions inherited from the eighteenth century, and the visit of the Meiningen Players in 1885 and 1890 had revealed to many Russian producers how far behind they were. Little significant progress was made, however, until the formation of the Moscow Art Theatre by Konstantin Stanislavsky (1863–1938) and Vladimir Nemirovich-Danchenko (1858–1943) in 1898.

The Moscow Art Theatre (MAT) differed from the other independent theatres in being a fully professional organization from the beginning and in emphasizing theatrical production rather than neglected plays. Its first program, Alexei Tolstoy's *Tsar Feodor Ivanovich*, created a sensation because of its painstaking re-creation of the Russia of 1600, its ensemble acting, and its absence of stars. Public interest waned, however, until the production of Chekhov's *The Sea Gull* established the originality of both the author and the company.

Anton Chekhov (1860–1904) began his dramatic career with vaudeville sketches and short plays in the comic-pathetic vein and then went on to long plays. When *The Sea Gull* (1896) was performed at the Alexandrinsky Theatre in St. Petersburg, it was a failure because the actors did not understand their roles and had not learned their lines. As a result, Chekhov was determined to give up playwriting. After reluctantly permitting the Moscow Art Theatre to revive *The Sea Gull,* he went on to provide it with three other plays: *Uncle Vanya* (1899), *The Three Sisters* (1901), and *The Cherry Orchard* (1904). Chekhov's reputation rests primarily upon these four plays.

Each of Chekhov's four major plays is set in rural Russia and depicts the monotonous and frustrating life of the landowning class. All of the characters aspire to a better life, but do not know how, or have the initiative, to achieve their goals. The plays are composed of infinite detail, the connections among which are not always obvious. Yet gradually a unifying mood, clearly delineated characters, and a complete and simple action emerge.

The methods of the MAT were well adapted to the demands of Chekhov's plays. Stanislavsky always undertook a long study of each play before rehearsals began. He insisted upon careful attention to detail from each actor, and he sought to recreate the milieu only after visiting the site of the play's action, or after extensive research.

Despite its success with *The Sea Gull,* the MAT ended its first season in debt and was saved only by the generosity of patrons. With the new support, it was able in 1902 to build its own theatre, with workshops and such up-to-date equipment as a revolving stage, and increase its acting company from 39 to 100 members. Thereafter, it staged from three to five new plays each year, while keeping successful works in the repertory. The influence of the MAT was soon felt throughout Russia, and by 1906 it was sufficiently well known abroad to undertake a foreign tour.

Stanislavsky is now remembered above all for his attempts to perfect an approach to acting. He became fully aware of the need in 1906 and made the first outline of his ideas in 1909. In 1911 he founded the First Studio to train students and work out problems as they arose. Stanislavsky did not begin to publish his ideas until *My Life in Art* (1924) and *An Actor Prepares* (1936). The overall plan was not revealed extensively outside of Russia until the appearance of *Building a Character* (1949) and *Creating a Role* (1961). It is now acknowledged that neither the English-language nor the Russian-language version of Stanislavsky's writings were reliable. Since the USSR did not subscribe to the International Copyright Agreement when Stanislavsky's works were published in the West, they were copyrighted under the name of the American translator, Elizabeth Reynolds Hapgood. Thus, she, and subsequently her estate, controlled the international rights. Unfortunately, her versions considerably distorted Stanislavsky both through many mistranslations and through considerable cutting and rearrangement. Similarly, the Soviet versions altered the texts to make them conform to official ideology. Only recently, through the cooperation of the Hapgood estate and Soviet authorities, have new and apparently accurate translations of Stanislavsky's writings appeared.

Still, no summary of Stanislavsky's system can claim to be entirely accurate or hope to please all of Stanislavsky's admirers and critics. Nevertheless, the main outlines can be sketched. (1) The actor's body and voice should be thoroughly trained so they may respond efficiently to all demands. (2) Actors should be schooled in stage techniques so they can project characterization to an audience without any sense of contrivance. (3) Actors should be skilled observers of reality as a basis for building a role. (4) Actors should seek inner justification for everything done on

FIG. 16.10
Chekhov's *The Sea Gull* (Act I) at the Moscow Art Theatre, 1898. Setting by V. A. Simov. From *Moscow Art Theatre, 1898–1917* (Moscow, 1955).

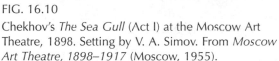

stage. In doing so, actors depend in part on "the magic 'if'" (that is, the actor says, "If I were this person faced with this situation, I would . . . .") and "emotion memory" (a process by which actors relate the unfamiliar dramatic situation to some analogous emotional situation in their own lives, although Stanislavsky was eventually to reject this approach). (5) If actors are not merely to play themselves, they must make a thorough analysis of the script and work within the "given circumstances" found there. The actor must define a character's motivations in each scene, in the play as a whole, and in relationship to each of the other roles. The character's primary "objective" becomes the "through line" of the role, around which everything else revolves. (6) On stage, actors must focus attention upon the action as it unfolds moment by moment. Such concentration will lead to the "illusion of the first time" and will help actors to subordinate their own egos to the artistic demands of the production. (7) Actors must continually strive to perfect understanding and proficiency.

Various aspects of this method have been emphasized by different interpreters. Taken as a whole, it is an attempt to analyze each phase of the actor's work and to make it as efficient as possible. Stanislavsky was never fully satisfied with his system and continued to refine it up to the time of his death. He also cautioned others against adopting it without making changes required by different artistic needs and cultural backgrounds.

The MAT discouraged the star system. Nevertheless, a number of outstanding actors came to the fore. In addition to Stanislavsky, these included Moskvin, Kachalov, and Knipper. Ivan Moskvin (1874–1946), a small man, was best suited to self-effacing characters such as Epikhodov in *The Cherry Orchard*. His was the art of understatement in which a few subtle touches brought out the emotional values of a scene. Vassily Kachalov (1875–1948), a tall, handsome man with a beautiful voice, was at his best in the roles of romantic heroes, rebels, or intellectuals. Olga Knipper (1870–1959), Chekhov's wife, played a wide variety of roles, but was best known as Madame Ranevskaya in *The Cherry Orchard*.

In addition to Chekhov, the MAT also encouraged Maxim Gorky (1868–1936), already famous as a writer of realistic stories. *The Lower Depths* (1902), set in a flophouse and featuring a collection of characters defeated by life, became one of the troupe's greatest successes. Other plays by Gorky include *Summer Folk* (1904) and *Enemies* (1907). Gorky was much involved in the political struggles of the day, including the Revolution of 1905, which though largely unsuccessful won a small measure of representative government. Gorky's activities caused him to be exiled, but his reputation as a champion of the proletariat would eventually make him head of the Soviet writers' union.

THE THEATRE IN ITALY AND SPAIN, 1875–1915

Between 1875 and 1915, both Italy and Spain were more emulative than innovative. Italy's major creative energies continued to be poured into opera. In drama, realism arrived first in the works of Paolo Ferrari (1822–1889), a writer in the vein of Dumas *fils*, and then through the "Verist" (or naturalistic) school. Neoromanticism found its major exponent in Gabriele D'Annunzio (1863–1938), who, under the influence of Maeterlinck, wrote such plays as *The Dead City* (1898), *La Giaconda* (1898), and *Francesca da Rimini* (1902).

The strong Italian acting tradition was continued by Eleanora Duse (1859–1924). On the stage from the age of four, she became Rossi's leading lady in 1879. After touring South America in 1885, she formed her own company and played throughout the world. She retired in 1909, but returned to the stage in 1921 and died in Pittsburgh while on tour. Duse played an extremely wide range of roles, many of them favorites of Bernhardt, with whose flamboyance her quiet style contrasted sharply. Noted for subtlety, she used simple means to convey complex conceptions. She scorned makeup and prided herself on her ability to make the physical adjustments required by each role unaided by external means. To many discerning critics, she was the greatest of modern actresses.

In Spain, the realistic drama found its first important exponent in José Echegaray (1848–1927), notably in *The Son of Don Juan* (1892), patterned on Ibsen's *Ghosts*, and *The Great Galeoto* (1881), a play about the power of gossip to ruin lives. After the war of 1898 had stripped Spain of her last shreds of glory, a new movement, "the Generation of '98," sought to revitalize literature. The most famous of the new writers was Jacinto Benavente (1866–1954), a versatile dramatist who composed nearly 300 works ranging through many styles and forms. Of his realistic plays, the best is probably *The Passion Flower* (1913), the story of a man's love for his stepdaughter, while of the nonrealistic works *The Bonds of Interest* (1907),

FIG. 16.11
Eleanora Duse in the title role of D'Annunzio's *Francesca da Rimini* at the Teatro Constanzi, Rome, 1902. From *Le Théâtre* (1902).

a philosophical work using *commedia dell'arte* conventions, is the best known.

The modern movement in Spain was helped considerably by the Teatro Intim, an independent theatre founded by Adria Gual (1872–1932) in 1898 at Barcelona. Here a cross section of drama from Aeschylus to the present was offered for some thirty years. Through his experiments in production styles, Gual brought many of the new trends to Spain.

THEATRE IN THE UNITED STATES, 1895–1915

The new trends made little impact on the American theatre prior to 1915. By 1895, the touring company had become the usual source of theatrical entertainment in the United States. In New York, the principal theatrical center, the long run hit was the goal. For managers outside of New York, booking productions became a major problem, since they usually had to go to New York to arrange a season of attractions. If they wished to schedule a forty-week season, they often had to deal with forty different producers, each of whom was negotiating with many other local managers. Furthermore, producers often defaulted on their agreements, leaving local theatres to deal with sudden cancellations. To remedy these ills, new procedures evolved. Theatres in a restricted area joined together to form circuits, and booking agents began to serve as middlemen between managers and producers.

In this confusion, a small group of men saw the possibility of gaining control of the American theatre. In 1896 Sam Nixon and Fred Zimmerman of Philadelphia, and Charles Frohman, Al Hayman, Marc Klaw, and Abraham Erlanger of New York formed what came to be called "The Syndicate." The new organization began by offering a full season of stellar attractions, on the condition that local managers book exclusively through it. This arrangement was welcomed by many managers, for it permitted them to deal with a single agent and to obtain outstanding productions. Managers who refused to deal with the Syndicate were systematically eliminated through simple, if ruthless, maneuvers. The Syndicate did not seek to gain direct control over all theatres in the country; rather, it concentrated on key routes between large cities, for unless productions could play along the way, touring was not financially feasible. Where it could not gain control over key theatres, the Syndicate encouraged the building of rival houses and booked into them the finest productions at reduced prices until the competing theatres were bankrupt. New York producers who refused to cooperate were denied bookings, and many actors were "blackballed," since the Syndicate would not send on tour any production in which they appeared. By 1900, the Syndicate was in effective control of the American theatre. Now in a position to influence the choice of plays, it refused to accept works not likely to appeal to a mass audience and favored productions that featured stars with large personal followings. As a result, between 1900 and 1915, the American theatre remained a conservative, largely commercial venture.

Of the Syndicate members, Charles Frohman (1854–1915) was by far the most important, since he was the only one directly involved in theatrical production. Working his way up from program seller to business manager and agent, Frohman entered management in 1889, and in 1893 opened the Empire Theatre in New York, where he maintained a fine stock company for many years. In 1896, he extended his interest to London and later controlled five theatres there. As an entrepreneur, Frohman was guided by two convictions: public taste is infallible, and stars are necessary to attract audiences. After Frohman was killed when the Lusitania was torpedoed in World War I, the Syndicate found it difficult to continue and disbanded in 1917.

Despite the Syndicate's strength, it did not go unopposed. James A. Herne, Mr. and Mrs. Harrison G. Fiske, James O'Neill, David Belasco, Maxine Elliot, and others held out, although with the exception of the Fiskes all eventually came to terms with the Syndicate. Minnie Maddern (1864?–1932) was on the stage from the age of three and had achieved considerable fame by 1889, when she married Harrison Grey Fiske (1861–1942), a dramatist and editor of the most influential theatrical newspaper of the day, *The New York Dramatic Mirror.* After she returned to the stage in 1893, Mrs. Fiske championed the new realistic drama and was the first American to give Ibsen an extensive hearing through her productions of *A Doll's House, Hedda Gabler, Rosmersholm, Pillars of Society,* and *Ghosts.* When the Syndicate closed its theatres to her, she and her husband leased the Manhattan Theatre, where from 1901 to 1907 they produced many outstanding plays in which they sought to subordinate stars to ensemble effect. As a performer, Mrs. Fiske relied upon direct observation of life and a close study of psychology. She moved away from lines of business and encouraged actors to play as wide a range of roles as possible. She probably did more than any other American performer of her day to pave the way for the modern theatre.

James O'Neill (1847–1920), now remembered as the father of Eugene O'Neill, was one of America's most popular actors from the 1880s until World War

I. Despite great promise, he became identified with the leading role in *The Count of Monte Cristo,* which he first played in 1883, and rarely appeared in others.

But the most significant opposition to the Syndicate came from David Belasco (c. 1854–1931), a producer and dramatist who shared many of Frohman's ideals. Born in San Francisco, he was on the stage as a child and by the time he left California in 1882 had written or adapted over 100 works and had staged some 300. In New York he served as manager of the Madison Square Theatre after MacKaye left it, and later was MacKaye's stage manager at the Lyceum. He also continued to build his reputation as a dramatist with such hits as *The Heart of Maryland* (1895), *Madame Butterfly* (1900), and *Girl of the Golden West* (1905). Although he had produced plays occasionally during the 1890s, it was not until 1902 that he acquired his own theatre. In 1907 he opened the Stuyvesant Theatre (renamed the Belasco in 1910), where every modern improvement was installed. Here he continued his work until 1928. Belasco never maintained a stock company and always worked on the single-play principle.

As a producer, Belasco is now remembered for three reasons: his power as a star-maker, his realism in staging, and his opposition to the Syndicate. Like Frohman, Belasco depended much on stars, many of whom he coached carefully and for whose capabilities he tailored plays. Among his stars were Mrs. Leslie Carter (1862-1937), Blanche Bates (1873–1941), Frances Starr (1886–1973), and David Warfield.

FIG. 16.12

Mrs. Fiske and Holbrook Blinn in Edward Sheldon's *Salvation Nell,* 1908. Courtesy Hoblitzelle Theatre Arts Collection, University of Texas at Austin.

Above all, Belasco is now remembered for his staging. Like Daly and MacKaye, Belasco insisted on controlling every aspect of his productions. With him, naturalistic detail reached its peak in America. For *The Governor's Lady* (1912), a Childs Restaurant was reproduced on stage and the Childs chain stocked it daily with food which was consumed during the performance. For Eugene Walter's *The Easiest Way* (1909), Belasco bought the contents of a boarding-house room, including the wallpaper, and had it transferred to his stage. His crowd scenes were famous for their authenticity and power. In collaboration with Louis Hartman, Belasco experimented extensively with stage lighting. In *Madame Butterfly,* the passage of night was shown in a twelve-minute sequence that moved through sunset to night to dawn. Around 1915, Belasco replaced footlights with spotlights mounted in the auditorium and developed new color media. In his search for perfection, however, Belasco remained firmly within the nineteenth-century tradition, for he sought merely to bring the maximum of illusion to a repertory in the Boucicault tradition.

Belasco first came into conflict with the Syndicate when he sought to take a production on the road in 1902. Further difficulties led to a court battle in 1906. By 1909 Belasco's productions were in such demand that the Syndicate agreed to Belasco's terms, even though he refused to book exclusively through it. Its concessions to Belasco marked the first important break in the Syndicate's power.

The willingness of the Syndicate to make concessions had been hastened by the rise of the Shuberts. Three brothers, Sam (1876–1905), Lee (1875–1954), and Jacob J. (1880–1963), after beginning in Syracuse, New York, leased a theatre in New York City in 1900. When the Syndicate closed its theatres to their productions in 1905, the Shuberts began to establish a rival chain. Unlike the Syndicate, which was always merely a cooperative arrangement among independent businessmen, the Shuberts created a corporation (a new organizational form at that time) and used its financial base to buy or build its own theatres throughout the country. By this time, the high-handed methods of the Syndicate had created much dissatisfaction, and the Shuberts were welcomed by many local managers as allies. The struggle between the Shuberts and the Syndicate reached its peak in 1913, after which the Syndicate's grip was broken. Further weakened by the death of Charles Frohman in 1915, the Syndicate ceased to be an effective force after 1916. Unfortunately, the Shuberts became as dictatorial and monopolistic as the Syndicate had been. As producers, they were noted for lavish musicals with little substance. They continued to control "the road" until 1956, when an antitrust ruling forced them to sell many of their theatres. Despite this divestiture, the Shubert organization remains a powerful force in the American theatre.

Under the conditions that governed the American theatre between 1895 and 1915, it is not surprising that significant playwriting did not flourish. Probably the most successful dramatist was Clyde Fitch (1865–1909), who, after being commissioned by Richard Mansfield to create *Beau Brummel* (1890), wrote about sixty plays, of which the most important were *Barbara Frietchie* (1899), *Captain Jinks of the Horse Marines* (1901), *The Girl with the Green Eyes* (1902), *The Truth* (1907), and *The City* (1909). During the season of 1900–1901, ten of Fitch's works were being played in New York or on the road. A careful observer, Fitch reflected the life of his times. Noted for his quiet, intense scenes, he probably failed to achieve true depth because of the haste with which he wrote. As the first American playwright to publish his works regularly, he established a pattern continued until the present.

During the first decade of the century William Vaughan Moody (1869–1910) seemed the dramatist with greatest promise. Moody was a professor at the University of Chicago and a poet of stature when he began writing closet dramas about 1900. His first produced work, *The Great Divide* (1906), performed by Henry Miller and Margaret Anglin, was considered a landmark because it combined considerable literary merit with an exciting action which dramatized the "great divide" between the effete and self-conscious East and the rough and open-hearted West. Moody's only other play to reach the stage, *The Faith Healer* (1909), was not well received, perhaps because of its rather unconvincing title character. Moody's early death blighted the hopes of those who saw in his work the potential for a truly significant American drama.

During the early twentieth century, American female playwrights began to make their presence felt, although today most have long been ignored. Perhaps the most important of these was Martha Morton (1865–1925), author of some thirty-five plays and sometimes called America's first female professional playwright. Among her plays are *The Merchant* (1891), *Her Lord and Master* (1903), and *The Movers* (1907). She is also significant for founding the Society of Dramatic Authors in 1907 when female writers were denied admission to the American Dramatists Club (the forerunner of today's Dramatists Guild). Josephine Preston Peabody (1874–1922) won international fame with her *The Piper* (1910), a poetic drama based on the story of the Pied Piper of Hamelin. It won the Shakespeare Memorial Prize in worldwide competition with more than 300 other writers, and was translated and performed in several languages.

FIG. 16.13

David Belasco's production of *The Governor's Lady,* 1912, showing the replica of Childs Restaurant. From *Le Théâtre* (1912).

By 1915 the theatre was beginning to decline in popularity. While increased ticket prices were partially responsible, effective competition, most notably from spectator sports and motion pictures, was also appearing. Soon after Thomas A. Edison demonstrated the "kinetoscope" in 1894, "penny arcades" began to show short motion pictures. Only one person at a time could be served, however, until George Eastman's flexible film and Thomas Armat's projector made it possible to show movies to an assembled audience.

In 1905 the first movie theatre was opened, and by 1909 there were 8,000. The early theatres seated only about 100 and offered only short films. Then in 1914, the Strand Theatre in New York, with its 3,300 seats, began the trend toward large houses. But it was not until D. W. Griffith's *The Birth of a Nation* (1915) surpassed Belasco's realism and melodramatic power that films became a serious competitor to the theatre. With their superior ability to capture spectacle and their markedly lower admission costs, motion pictures began to draw away that audience that had sought illusionism and thrills in the theatre. The competition from films did not bring an overnight revolution. In 1915 there were still about 1,500 legitimate theatres outside of New York and the number of theatrical productions on Broadway continued to increase until the season of 1927–1928. The invention of sound motion picture in 1927 and the depression of 1929 dealt serious blows, however, and by 1930 only 500 theatres remained outside of New York. Thereafter, the number steadily declined.

Although these new directions were not readily apparent in 1915, it was already clear to many that

FIG. 16.14
William Vaughan Moody's *The Great Divide,* Princess's Theatre, New York, 1906, with Henry Miller and Margaret Anglin. Act I. Courtesy Hoblitzelle Theatre Arts Collection, University of Texas at Austin.

the old production methods were outmoded and that commercialization had gradually reduced the repertory to works calculated to appeal to the mass audience. Reassessment, new methods, and changing ideals were in the offing.

MAJOR TECHNICAL INNOVATIONS, 1875–1915

Between 1875 and 1915 several important technical innovations were introduced, the majority in Germany. Many were motivated by the need to shift the heavy three-dimensional settings which were replacing the wings and drops designed for movement by the chariot-and-pole system. One of the most important of the new devices was the revolving stage. The first was installed at the Residenz Theatre in Munich in 1896 by Karl Lautenschläger (1843–1906). Its ability to accommodate several settings and to change them merely by revolving a turntable, led to its wide adoption after 1900. Another solution, the rolling platform stage, was introduced by Fritz Brandt (1846–1927) at the Royal Opera House in Berlin around 1900. With it, settings could be mounted on a large platform offstage and then moved on stage by means of rollers set in tracks. The elevator stage also was widely adopted. The first fully developed elevator system (the Asphaleian stage) was installed in the

Budapest Opera House in 1884. The entire stage was divided into sections, each of which could be lowered, raised, or tilted to create a variety of acting levels or used to raise or lower scenic elements. The elevator stage was subsequently used at the Munich Art Theatre, the Burgtheater, and elsewhere. A still more complex arrangement was installed in the Dresden State Theater by Adolf Linnebach (1876–1963) in 1914 by combining sliding platforms with elevators. These complex mechanical devices were supplemented with flying, manual shifting, and with small wagons mounted on casters. The new stage machinery was adopted more widely in Germany than elsewhere probably because of two factors: the expense, absorbed in Germany by government funding; and the decline of realism before the devices were widely adopted elsewhere, for the growing emphasis upon simplified settings made complex machinery less essential.

Many German theatres of this period also installed a plaster dome (or *kuppelhorizont*) which curved around and above the stage to give the effect of infinite space and eliminated the need for many overhead and side masking pieces. To fulfill the same function, other theatres used a cloth cyclorama hung from a pipe which curved around the stage.

Many experiments with stage lighting also were conducted. Light bridges and other new mounting positions were tried. After 1907, improvements in the filaments of incandescent lamps made it possible to increase wattage and to create the first spotlights (other than the limelight and carbon arc). By 1913, 1,000-watt lamps were available in Europe, and color media and spotlights were beginning to be common. Consequently, footlights were gradually replaced by spotlights mounted in the auditorium.

One of the most ambitious lighting systems of the period was devised by Mariano Fortuny (1871–1949), who directed strong light against colored silk panels, which reflected the light onto a *kuppelhorizont* and then onto the stage to create realistic ambient light. With elaborate machinery for changing the panels and controlling the light, the system gave the most subtle variations of any then known, but its complexity and cost prevented its widespread adoption. Nevertheless, it is indicative of the growing interest in lighting as an important element of design.

Auditoriums also underwent considerable change, largely under the influence of Wagner's theatre at Bayreuth. Boxes tended to disappear, the number of balconies to decrease (sometimes there were none), and center aisles to be eliminated, thereby improving sight lines. As the interest in breaking down the barriers between performers and audience grew, the apron stage returned to favor and in a few instances

FIG. 16.15
The first revolving stage in Europe, installed in the Residenz Theater, Munich. At right, the floor plan for two settings for Mozart's *Don Giovanni:* the Commandant's Garden, and a street in Seville. At left, the design for the Commandant's Garden. Courtesy Theatermuseum, Munich.

the proscenium arch was eliminated. Thus, the Italianate theatre, dominant since the seventeenth century, was challenged for the first time.

By 1915 the standards of production that had been accepted almost universally in 1875 had begun to seem outmoded. Although pictorial realism still dominated the popular theatre, it had been undermined by a host of experiments. A common theme ran through all of the experiments: the need for unified production, a strong director, and artistic integrity, so that the theatre might once more assume the role it had played in ancient Greece as a source of insight and place of communion. Although the war interrupted developments, it also provoked reassessments, out of which new conventions and renewed vigor came in the postwar years.

LOOKING AT THEATRE HISTORY

A study of critical responses to plays and production styles can be very helpful. For example, such responses suggest that in the late nineteenth century Saxe-Meiningen's approach was readily accepted because it was essentially an intensification of trends with which the audience was already familiar and of which it approved. When the company appeared in London in 1881, reviewers were not impressed by all aspects of the productions, since they thought that in some areas the English did as well or better, but they especially admired the crowd scenes. Here are portions of a review of *Julius Caesar* (see Fig. 16.1):

> *It may . . . be maintained that no spectacular play of Shakespeare, such as "Julius Caesar" may claim to be considered, has ever been put upon our stage in a fashion equally effective . . . the principal gain is in the manner in which those who are little or nothing more*

than supernumeraries wear the costumes of a bygone age, and take intelligent part in actions and movements of which they can have had no experience in real life. . . . The openly manifested desire to obtain an ascendancy over his fellows, which has been the disgrace of the English actor, is kept out of sight. . . .

In the case of "Julius Caesar" the most noteworthy features consisted of the arrangement of the tableaux and the disposition of the supernumeraries when as in the case of the oration of Antony over the body of Caesar, strong and growing emotion has to be expressed. From the picturesque standpoint these things were perfect.

The Athenaeum, June 11, 1881, 796.

A study of critical responses can also help us understand the great uproar caused by scripts or productions that now seem uncontroversial. As a playwright, Ibsen was a special focus for contention. Here are some of the responses of Clement Scott, one of London's foremost theatre critics, to *Ghosts* when it was first produced in London:

If people like the discussion of such nasty subjects on the stage . . . if it is desirable to drive decent-minded women out of the playhouse, and to use the auditorium as a hospital-ward or dissecting-room, let it be so. . . . But in our hurry to dramatize the Contagious Diseases Act let us first set about writing a good play. Who in their sense can say that Ghosts is a good play? . . . If, by the examples we have seen, Ibsen is a dramatist, then the art of the dramatist is dead indeed. . . .

The Illustrated London News, 21 March 1891.

During this period, Stanislavsky began to evolve his system of acting. *In My Life in Art,* he tells how his system took shape over many years, beginning in 1906 when he became concerned over his inability to remain fresh in his roles:

How was I to save my roles from bad rebirths, from spiritual petrifaction, from the autocracy of evil habit and lack of truth? There was the necessity not only of a physical make-up but of a spiritual make-up before every performance. [460–461]

As he experimented with a system capable of meeting the actor's problems, his ideas began to attract others:

For the young people who came to seek my help I founded a Studio [in 1911] . . . here we gathered all who wanted to study the so-called Stanislavsky System. . . . I began to give a full course of study in the shape in which I had at that time formed it. Its aim was to give practical and conscious methods for the awakening of superconscious creativeness. [531]

About his system, Stanislavsky warned:

My system cannot be explained in an hour or in a day even. It must be systematically and practically studied for years. It does good only when it becomes the second nature of the actor, when he stops thinking of it consciously, when it begins to appear naturally, as of itself. [529]

Constantin Stanislavsky, *My Life in Art,* trans. J. J. Robbins (New York: Theatre Arts Books, 1948).

17
Modern Alternatives to Realism

Although the "modern theatre" is often said to begin with Ibsen, Zola, and Saxe-Meiningen, "modernism" is now usually thought to have begun with the symbolists. In the late nineteenth century, both realists and nonrealists questioned the views that had dominated Western thought and art since the Renaissance and that were summed up in the "humanist ideal" (which posited a set of universal, unchanging values as the very basis of civilization). The belief that truth should be depicted representationally—that there should be a direct relationship between reality as normatively perceived and its artistic representation—had dominated artistic theory and practice since the time of the neoclassicists. The realist/naturalist attempt to reduce truth to what is scientifically knowable revealed just how much human values are based on the scientifically unknowable. Modernists, abandoning both the scientific and the humanist ideal, substituted their own subjective visions and esthetic modes (often abstract and usually departing drastically from objective appearance) for the traditional approach that had allowed the audience to compare the subject with its artistic rendering. The rejection of this long-accepted relationship between perception and representation, beginning with the symbolists, is often considered the true beginning of modernism.

WAGNER AND THE NONREALISTIC THEATRE

Richard Wagner (1813–1883) may be thought of as one of the significant forerunners of modernism. He was brought up in a theatrical family (his stepfather and four of his brothers and sisters were employed in the theatre). His first opera, *Die Feen,* was written in 1831, but he did not achieve critical success until 1842 with *Rienzi,* which also brought him an appointment as conductor at the Dresden opera house. Banished for his part in the revolution of 1848, he spent twelve years in exile, during which he formulated those theories that were to influence the course of the modern theatre.

Wagner rejected the contemporary trend toward realism, arguing that rather than a recorder of domestic affairs the dramatist should be a mythmaker—that he should portray an ideal world through the expression of the inner impulses and aspirations of a people as embodied in its racial myths and so unite them as a "folk." (This idea would later endear Wagner to the Nazis.) To him, true drama was concerned with the ideal world, which is left behind as soon as spoken dialogue is admitted. He suggested that drama should be "dipped in the magic fountain of music" to combine the greatness of Shakespeare and Beethoven. He

409

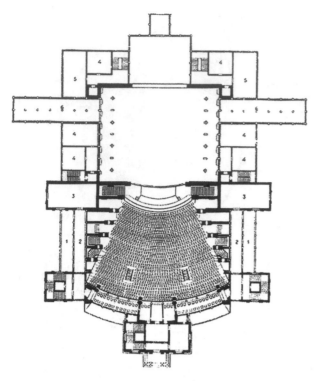

FIG. 17.1
Plan of Wagner's Festival Theatre at Bayreuth. From Sachs, *Modern Opera Houses and Theatres* (1896–1898).

also argued that music, through melody and tempo, permits greater control over performance than is possible in spoken drama, in which interpretation is subject to performers' personal whims. Thus, for Wagner the effectiveness of music-drama depended upon performance as well as upon composition, and he argued that the author-composer should supervise every aspect of production in order to unify all the elements into a *Gesamtkunstwerk,* or "master art work." These ideas undergird much of modern theory about the need for a strong director and unified production.

In addition to his theories, Wagner's practice also exerted considerable influence, especially on theatre architecture, since to house his idealized music-drama, Wagner demanded a new type of theatre structure. Begun in 1872 and opened in 1876, the Festival Theatre, originally planned for Munich but built in Bayreuth, was soon famous throughout the world and was to inspire many reforms in architectural design. Since Wagner wished to create a "classless" theatre, he abandoned the box, pit, and gallery arrangement. The main part of the auditorium had thirty stepped rows of seats; there were no side boxes or center aisle, and each row led directly to a side exit. At the rear of the auditorium was a single large box surmounted by a small gallery. The total seating capacity was 1,745. To ensure good sight lines, the auditorium was shaped like a fan, measuring 50 feet across at the proscenium and 115 feet at the rear of the auditorium. Since all seats were said to be equally good, a uniform price was charged. The orchestra pit was hidden from view, much of it extending underneath the apron of the stage. This feature helped to create a "mystic chasm" between the "real" world of the auditorium and the "ideal" world of the stage, an effect reinforced by darkening the auditorium during performances and by framing the stage with a double proscenium arch.

The arrangement of the auditorium was the theatre's greatest innovation, since the stage was essentially conservative in design. The stage floor was raked upward toward the back, and the chariot-and-pole system of scene shifting was retained. The principal innovation was a system of steam vents to create realistic effects of fog and mist and a "steam curtain" to mask scene changes. The proscenium opening, about 40 feet wide, gave onto a stage 80 feet deep by 93 feet wide. About 100 feet of overhead space and 32 feet of below-stage space were provided. The building also included ample workshops, storage, dressing rooms, and rehearsal space.

Although Wagner's theories later inspired several nonillusionistic approaches, his own productions aimed at complete illusion. He forbade the musicians to tune their instruments in the orchestra pit

FIG. 17.2
Auditorium and stage of the Bayreuth Festival Theatre. On stage is a setting for *Parsifal* designed by Max Brückner. From *Le Théâtre* (1899).

and allowed no applause during performances or curtain calls at the end. He sought precise historical accuracy in scenery and costumes and employed such devices as moving panoramas. His taste for minute detail may be seen in *Siegfried,* for example, in which he used a dragon with realistic scales and movable eyes and mouth. To Wagner, the ideal was to be reached through total illusion. Thus, Wagner's theatrical practice was grounded solidly in the nineteenth-century tradition. Nevertheless, his conceptions of the master artwork, unified production, and theatre architecture were to inspire many pioneers of the "modern" theatre.

NONREALISTIC THEATRE IN FRANCE

The realistic and naturalistic outlook that dominated the late nineteenth century did not go unchallenged. Although the intellectual climate between 1850 and 1900 was largely anti-idealistic, the sweeping claims made for science at this time brought several protests. The most significant of these came from the symbolists, who launched their counterattack in 1885 in a "manifesto." Taking its inspiration from the works of Edgar Allan Poe, Charles-Pierre Baudelaire's poems and criticism, Fyodor Dostoevsky's novels, and Richard Wagner's music and theory, symbolism attracted representatives from all the arts. The unknowable and relative were the bedrocks of antirealism (and for many critics "modernism"). Artists, no longer shackled to the natural world, could now be valued for novelty and experimentation with form rather than for accurate renditions of recognizable subjects. To the symbolists, subjectivity, spirituality, and mysterious internal and external forces were the sources of a truth more profound than that derived from the mere observation of outward appearance. This truth, they argued, cannot be represented directly but can only be evoked through symbols, legends, myths, and moods.

The principal spokesman for the movement was Stephane Mallarmé (1842–1898), whose views of drama—as an evocation of the mystery of existence through poetic and allusive language, performed with only the most essential and atmospherically appropriate theatrical aids, for the purpose of creating a quasi-religious experience—set the tone for the antirealistic works of the 1890s.

As with naturalism, symbolism made no marked impression in the theatre until an "independent" group, modeled on the Théâtre Libre, appeared. In 1890, Paul Fort (1872–1962), a seventeen-year-old poet, founded the Théâtre d'Art, where by 1892 he had presented works by 46 authors, ranging from readings of poems and adaptations of portions of the *Iliad*

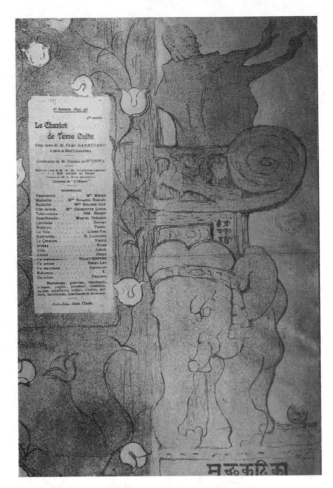

FIG. 17.3
Program for *The Little Clay Cart,* an adaptation of the Sanskrit drama made by Victor Barracund for Lugné-Poë's Théâtre de l'Oeuvre, 1894–1895. The program and some of the settings were designed by Toulouse-Lautrec. Courtesy Bibliothèque de l'Arsenal, Paris.

and the Bible to new plays. Most of the programs were given only one performance, and the actors, primarily amateurs, were often inadequate. Unlike Antoine, Fort received predominantly hostile critical notices, perhaps because his productions seemed incomprehensible to those accustomed to illusionism.

When Fort left the theatre in 1892, his work was carried on by the Théâtre de l'Oeuvre, headed by Aurélien-Marie Lugné-Poë (1869–1940). An actor and stage manager at the Théâtre Libre for a time, Lugné-Poë was converted to the idealist outlook after seeing and appearing in some of the productions at the Théâtre d'Art and while sharing an apartment with the symbolist painters Edouard Vuillard, Maurice Denis, and Pierre Bonnard. The Théâtre de l'Oeuvre gave its first performance in 1893. From that time until 1897 Lugné-Poë used a similar style for virtually all of his productions. Guided by the motto "the word creates the decor," he reduced scenery to simple compositions of lines and color painted on backdrops. Using settings by Toulouse-Lautrec, Denis, Vuillard, Bonnard, Odilon Redon, and others, Lugné-Poë sought to create a unity of style and mood rather than of milieu.

The opening production, Maeterlinck's *Pelléas and Mélisande,* was typical. Few properties and little furniture were used; the stage was lighted from overhead and most of the action passed in semidarkness; a gauze curtain, hung between the actors and the audience, gave the impression that mist enveloped the stage; backdrops, painted in grayed tones, emphasized the air of mystery; costumes were vaguely medieval, although the intention was to create draperies of no particular period. The actors spoke in a staccato chant like priests and, according to some critics, behaved like sleepwalkers; their gestures were strongly stylized. Given this radically new approach, it is not surprising that many spectators were mystified.

Lugné-Poë's repertory was made up primarily of French plays but with these he mingled some works by Ibsen, Hauptmann, Sanskrit dramatists, and others. Of the French dramas, those by Maeterlinck were the best. Maurice Maeterlinck (1862–1949), after coming to Paris from Belgium, turned to playwriting in 1889 and by 1896 had written *The Intruder* (1890), *The Blind* (1890), and *The Death of Tintagiles* (1894). Of his early work, the best known is *Pelléas and Mélisande* (1892), in which a young woman, after marrying a prince who has found her in a forest, falls in love with his brother and dies of grief after her husband kills his brother. The interest does not reside in the triangular relationship, however, but in the mood of mystery which envelops it and which is evoked through a multitude of symbols, such as a wedding ring dropped into a fountain, doves that fly away from a tower, subterranean pools and grottoes, enveloping shadows, and blood stains that cannot be washed away. In the early 1890s Maeterlinck argued that the most dramatic moments are those silent ones during which the mystery of existence, ordinarily obscured by bustling activity, makes itself felt. After 1896, Maeterlinck revised his view and modified his style to include more straightforward action. The most famous of his later plays is *The Blue Bird* (1908), an allegory about childrens' search for happiness, eventually found in their own backyard.

In 1896 Lugné-Poë presented Alfred Jarry's (1873–1907) *Ubu Roi,* sometimes called the first absurdist drama. Jarry's play is related to symbolist works in being antirealistic but its moral topsyturvydom more nearly resembles that of the naturalists' *comédies rosses,* although it completely avoids their scientific bias and realistic techniques. *Ubu Roi* shows in all its grotesqueness a world without human decency. Its central figure, Ubu, violent and totally devoid of moral scruple, is the epitome of all that Jarry found inane and ugly in bourgeois society and of all that is monstrous and irrational in human beings. The action of the play shows how Ubu usurps the throne of Poland and keeps his power by killing and torturing all those who oppose him; eventually he is driven from the country but he promises to continue his exploits elsewhere. Jarry wrote two other plays about Ubu, *Ubu Bound* (1900) and *Ubu the Cuckold* (published 1944), but these were not produced during his lifetime. At first Jarry's influence was negligible, but in the 1920s he attracted a following among the surrealists and after World War II his grotesque vision of man won him a place of honor as a major prophet of the absurdist movement.

The first major phase of the antirealistic movement came to an end in 1897 when Lugné-Poë broke with the symbolists after concluding that most of their plays were immature and that his commitment to a single style of production was too limiting. His decision was influenced by his admiration for Ibsen, whose plays he found unadaptable to the extreme stylization favored by the symbolists.

The Théâtre de l'Oeuvre closed in 1899, but Lugné-Poë was to revive it in 1912 and again after World War I until 1929. Nevertheless, it is his symbolist productions of the 1890s that constitute his most significant contribution to the theatre. Through tours with his company and articles written about

FIG. 17.4

Jarry's *Ubu Roi* at the Théâtre Antoine, 1908. Gémier directed the play and appeared as Père Ubu. From *Figaro* (16 February 1908).

his work, Lugné-Poë influenced almost every departure from realism between 1893 and 1915.

APPIA AND CRAIG

At about the time Lugné-Poë was closing the Théâtre de l' Oeuvre in 1899, two other men, Appia and Craig, working independently of each other, were beginning to lay the theoretical foundations of modern nonillusionistic theatrical practice. Adolphe Appia (1862–1928), born in Switzerland, first came into contact with the theatre through his musical studies. Deeply impressed by Wagner's music-dramas and theoretical writings, Appia recognized that the usual mounting (including Wagner's) of the operas did not properly embody Wagner's theories. After years of thought, he published *The Staging of Wagner's Musical Dramas* (1895), *Music and Stage Setting* (1899), and *The Work of Living Art* (1921). In these, he set forth ideas about theatrical production that were eventually accepted almost everywhere.

Beginning with the assumption that artistic unity is the fundamental goal of theatrical production, Appia sought to analyze failures to achieve it. He concluded that stage presentation involves three conflicting visual elements: the moving three-dimensional actor; the perpendicular scenery; and the horizontal floor. He considered painted two-dimensional settings to be one of the major causes of disunity and recommended that they be replaced with three-dimensional units (steps, ramps, platforms) that enhance the actor's movement and provide a transition from the horizontal floor to the upright scenery. Above all, however, Appia emphasized the role of light in fusing all of the visual elements into a unified whole. Since to him light was the visual counterpart of music, which changes from moment to moment in response to shifting moods, emotions, and action, Appia wished to orchestrate and manipulate light as carefully as a musical score. Attempts to implement this theory, which require control over the distribution, brightness, and color of light, have led to much of modern stage-lighting practice. Appia also argued that artistic unity requires that one person control all of the elements of production. Thus, his ideas strengthened the role of the director.

In 1906 Appia met Emile Jacques Dalcroze (1865–1950), who, next to Wagner, was to be the greatest influence on Appia's work. Dalcroze was the deviser of "eurythmics," a system under which students were led to experience music kinesthetically by responding physically to the rhythms of musical compositions. Under Dalcroze's influence, Appia came to believe that the rhythm embedded in a text provides the key to every gesture and movement to be used on the stage and that the proper mastery of rhythm will unify all the spatial and temporal elements of a production into a satisfying and harmonious whole. In 1910 Appia designed the first theatre of modern times to be built without a proscenium arch and with a completely open stage, for Dalcroze's school at Hellerau, where he also designed a series of productions for the 1912 and 1913 seasons.

In the 1920s Appia began to win his long-delayed recognition. In 1923 he staged Wagner's *Tristan and Isolde* in Milan and in 1924–1925 two parts of the *Ring* cycle in Basel. Nevertheless, it was not through practice but through theory that Appia was to exert lasting influence on the modern theatre.

Gordon Craig (1872–1966), son of Ellen Terry and Edward Godwin, began his career as an actor in Irving's company. His first important practical experience as a designer was gained in his mother's company at the Imperial Theatre in London in 1903. An exhibit of his work in 1902 and the publication of his book, *The Art of the Theatre* (1905), created such controversy that within a few years he was well known throughout Europe. In 1904 he designed a play for Brahm in Berlin, in 1906 one for Eleanora

FIG. 17.5
Adolphe Appia's design for the sacred forest in Wagner's *Parsifal*.

FIG. 17.6
Craig's set for *Hamlet* at the Moscow Art theatre, 1912. The screens were supposed to be sufficiently mobile to change configurations quickly and without closing the front curtain, but they never functioned as envisioned. From *Moscow Art Theatre, 1898–1917* (Moscow, 1955).

Duse in Florence, and in 1912 one for the Moscow Art Theatre. Everywhere controversy followed him. He continued to set forth his provocative and original ideas in *On the Art of the Theatre* (1911), *Towards a New Theatre* (1913), *The Theatre Advancing* (1919), and *The Mask,* a periodical issued sporadically between 1908 and 1929. In 1908 he settled in Florence, where he ran a school for a time. Although Appia had voiced many of the same ideas, it was Craig who publicized them. To many conservative producers, Craig seemed as dangerous as Ibsen had in the 1880s.

Craig thought of the theatre as an independent art and argued that the true theatre artist welds action, words, line, color, and rhythm into a product as pure as that of the painter, sculptor, or composer. He acknowledged the kind of theatre in which a craftsman-director, beginning with a literary text, coordinates the work of several other craftsmen, but he sought a higher form in which the master-artist, without the medium of a literary text, would create every part of a wholly autonomous art.

Craig's influence was felt most heavily in design, perhaps because he conceived of the theatre primarily in visual terms. He argued that the public goes to see rather than to hear a play. His own drawings show a marked predilection for right angles and an obsession with parallelism. Their most notable fea-

ture, however, is height and the resulting sense of grandeur. Perhaps Craig's favorite project was the mobile setting. Throughout most of his life he experimented with screens, out of which he hoped to create a setting that by invisible means, could move in ways analogous to the actor and to light.

Craig always refused to assign a hierarchy to the theatrical elements and blamed many faults of the past on the dominance of one or another part. Thus, he often denounced the dramatist, upon whom he blamed the overemphasis on the spoken word. Similarly, he often blamed starring actors for the low state of the theatre, since they sought to aggrandize themselves and to interject their own conceptions between those of the director and the public. Consequently, he once suggested that ideally the master-artist should use an *Ubermarionette,* a superpuppet without any ego but capable of carrying out all demands. No idea voiced by Craig aroused a greater storm.

Although Appia and Craig arrived at many of the same ideas, they also differed on important issues. Appia's artist was to be primarily an interpreter of the composer-dramatist's work; Craig's was a full-

FIG. 17.7
Craig's design for *Electra,* 1905. From City of Manchester Art Gallery, *Exhibition of Drawings and Models by Edward Gordon Craig* (1912).

fledged artist in his own right. Appia assigned a hierarchy to the theatrical elements; Craig refused to do so. Appia thought in terms of successive settings (a different setting for each locale); Craig sought a single setting capable of expressing the spirit of the entire work or of reflecting changes through mobility.

Appia and Craig were often denounced as impractical men who knew little of the workaday theatre and whose ideas were useless in practice. But they championed ideals and goals that practical men of the period could not provide. Together they forced their contemporaries to reconsider the nature of the theatre as an art, its function in society, and its elements (both separately and in combination). They influenced the trend toward simplified decor, three-dimensional settings, plasticity, and directional lighting—toward evocation rather than literal representation. At first highly controversial, their theories were to prevail after World War I.

STRINDBERG AND FREUD

The first decade of the twentieth century also brought works of another type that were to be a major influence on modern drama: the nonrealistic plays of the Swedish dramatist, August Strindberg (1849–1912). Strindberg had already established his reputation as a realistic dramatist with *The Father* (1887) and *Miss Julie* (1888), both of which demonstrate his preoccupation with what he considered to be the elemental and inevitable conflict between men and women. *Miss Julie* especially won high praise for its emphasis upon heredity and environment, its unusual setting (a triangular view of one corner of a kitchen), and its use of pantomimes to replace intermissions. Many critics considered it an excellent exemplar of naturalistic principles.

Powerful as these plays are, they were not to be as influential as those Strindberg wrote after undergoing a bout with insanity during the 1890s. Partially because of his recent experiences and partially under Maeterlinck's influence, Strindberg now began to write "dream plays," of which he said: "The author has tried to imitate the disconnected but seemingly logical form of the dream. Anything may happen; everything is possible and probable. Time and space do not exist. On an insignificant background of reality, imagination designs and embroiders novel patterns, free fancies, absurdities and improvisations. The characters split, double, multiply, vanish, solidify, blur, clarify. But one consciousness reigns above them all—that of the dreamer; and before it there are no secrets, no incongruities, no scruples, no laws." In such plays as *To Damascus* (a trilogy, 1898–1901)

and *The Dream Play* (1902) Strindberg reshaped reality according to his own subjective vision. Time and place shift frequently and without regard for logical sequence, the real and the imaginary merge, and the seemingly commonplace is invested with a sense of significance. In these late works Strindberg treats with great compassion alienated human beings, lost and rootless, seeking meaning in an incomprehensible universe, trying to reconcile disparate elements: lust and love, body and spirit, filth and beauty.

From 1907 to 1910 Strindberg was associated with August Falck (1882–1938), an actor and producer, at the Intimate Theater in Stockholm. Seating only 161, this theatre was intended as a home for Strindberg's plays, and for it he wrote five "chamber plays," of which the best known is *The Ghost Sonata* (1907), a work which echoes many of the ideas found in *The Dream Play*.

By the time Strindberg died in 1912 he was one of the most famous writers in the world. Although his plays have never been widely popular in the theatre, they have never ceased to be a source of controversy and inspiration. His vision of human beings as tortured and alienated was to attract many later writers, and his dramatic devices were to show others how psychological states and spiritual intuitions might be externalized. As the first dramatist to make extensive use of the unconscious, he was to be a major influence on subsequent playwrights.

Strindberg's acceptance was probably aided by widespread interest in the psychoanalytic theories of Sigmund Freud (1856–1939), who in such books as *The Interpretation of Dreams* (1900) and *Three Contributions to the Theory of Sex* (1905) sought to analyze the structure of the mind, to describe its functionings, and to suggest means for dealing with abnormal behavior. Freud's explanation of human behavior, with its revolutionary emphasis on the unconscious, dreams as a key to understanding suppressed desires, and the human propensity for telescoping experience, gave strong authority to Strindberg's dramaturgy. Unlike Comte, Zola, and others who had placed primary emphasis on external environment as a determinant of human behavior, Freud emphasized internal, unconscious, psychological causality. His interest in aggression and sexuality as basic human instincts also did much to break down taboos against using these subjects in drama. Additionally, the idea that culturally unacceptable instincts, feelings, and behavior are sublimated and buried in the subconscious opened infinite possibilities for disparities between surface appearance and suppressed realities. Truth became extremely complex, perhaps unknowable, since not only is it difficult to penetrate the masks of others but our own as well. The unspoken and unacknowledged (the subtext) became as important as the stated and conscious (the text). Freud's conception of reality, intermingling as it did the rational and irrational, the conscious and unconscious, the objective and subjective, the real and the fantastic, was to become a means of bridging many of the divisions that had previously existed between realistic and nonrealistic drama.

NONREALISTIC THEATRE AND DRAMA IN GERMANY

In Germany, a number of dramatists, most notably Hauptmann and Sudermann, eventually were to write alternately in realistic and nonrealistic styles. But others, among them Hofmannsthal and Wedekind, fall more clearly into the antirealist camp. Hugo von Hofmannsthal (1874–1929) is usually considered an exponent of neoromanticism, a movement which in Germany roughly parallels symbolism in France. His early plays are mostly short, as in *The Fool and Death* (1893) and *The Adventurer and the Singing Girl* (1899), and written in a verse that led many critics to praise him as the finest poet since Goethe. Around 1900 he underwent a crisis during which he came to believe that words are meaningless. Although he moved beyond this belief, he thereafter reworked existing materials, as in *Elektra* (1903), *Everyman* (1912), and *The Great World Theatre* (1922), and wrote opera librettos, such as *Der Rosenkavalier* (1911) and *Ariadne on Naxos* (1912), in collaboration with Richard Strauss. Some of his plays continue to be mainstays of the Salzburg Festival.

Benjamin Franklin Wedekind (1864–1918) is more nearly related to Strindberg than to the French symbolists. After working as a journalist, publicist, and actor, Wedekind toured Germany in a repertory of his own plays, which were never widely appreciated during his lifetime. Wedekind's first important play, *Spring's Awakening* (1891), is the story of adolescent struggle with sexual awareness. One dies from a botched abortion, another commits suicide, and still another is saved from a similar fate only by the mysterious "Man with the Mask." The play is interesting in part because of its intermingling of naturalism and symbolism, of brutal frankness and lyrical expression. Wedekind's interest in sexual themes continued in *Earth Spirit* (1895) and *Pandora's Box* (1895), both treating the same protagonist, Lulu, the eternal temptress. In the first play, a series of admirers seek to impose their own vision on Lulu and die when they fail. In the second, Lulu descends into prostitution and ultimately is murdered by Jack the Ripper. In these plays, Wedekind suggests a relationship between commercialized art (seen as a form of pros-

titution which caters to the public's taste for disguised sexuality) and commercialized sex (prostitution). Many of Wedekind's later plays also reveal his preoccupation with sexual themes, but in such late works as *Samson* (1914) and *Herakles* (1917) the treatment sometimes borders on lunacy. Wedekind's plays are of such uneven quality that it is difficult to judge them fairly. But after 1900 his reputation grew steadily and he exerted considerable influence on the expressionists, who were attracted both by his rebellion against conventional values and by his experiments with stylistic elements.

After 1900 German producers also came to be increasingly interested in nonrealistic staging. Some of the most important innovations were made at the Munich Art Theatre, founded in 1907 and headed by George Fuchs (1868–1949), a critic and theorist, with Fritz Erler (1868–1940) as designer. In two books, *The Theatre of the Future* (1905) and *Revolution in the Theatre* (1909), Fuchs expressed the need for a theatre to meet the needs of modern humanity and declared pictorial illusionism outmoded. Under the slogan "retheatricalize the theatre," he sought to unite all the arts in a new kind of expression.

For the project, Max Littmann (1862–1931) designed a theatre with an auditorium and sunken orchestra pit similar to those at Bayreuth. The stage, however, differed markedly from that at Bayreuth. The acting area could be extended into the auditorium by covering over the orchestra pit, while an adjustable inner proscenium, containing a door at stage level and a balcony above, made it possible to adjust

FIG. 17.8

Munich Art Theatre production of Shakespeare's *Twelfth Night*, 1908. Design by Julius Diez, directed by Albert Heine. Courtesy Theatermuseum, Munich.

the size of the stage opening. The stage floor was broken into sections, each of which was mounted on an elevator, permitting the floor to be arranged into levels. The stage was backed by four cycloramas, each of a different color, which could be changed electrically. The most controversial aspect of the productions was the acting, which typically was confined to the plane outlined by the inner proscenium, while the area back of this plane was reserved for scenery or for crowd scenes. The aim was to keep performers close to the audience so as to establish a sense of community and to emphasize the actors' plasticity by framing them against a simplified background. Erler sometimes used the adjustable proscenium as the principal scenic element; sometimes he used it in combination with other pieces, but often he employed it merely as a frame for the area behind it. His effects were achieved primarily with simple forms, painted drops, and the play of colored light.

Like Appia and Craig, Fuchs believed that rhythm fuses all the elements of production. Unlike them, however, he placed the actor in front of the setting rather than within it and so tended to mute the three-dimensionality they so avidly sought. Still, as the work of the Munich Art Theatre became widely known, Fuchs's theories reinforced those of Appia and Craig and helped to establish the trend toward stylization in all theatrical elements.

Ultimately, virtually all of the ideas and innovations introduced between 1875 and 1900—whether realistic or nonrealistic—came together in the work of Max Reinhardt (1873–1943). On stage as an actor from the age of nineteen, Reinhardt was brought to the Deutsches Theater by Otto Brahm in 1894. While acting with Brahm's troupe, Reinhardt experimented with staging at a cabaret and developed a strong appreciation for its intimate atmosphere. His first experience as a producer was gained between 1902 and

FIG. 17.9
Reinhardt's production of Wedekind's *Spring's Awakening* at the Kammer-spiele, Berlin, 1906. Act III, scene 6. Design by K. Walser. Courtesy the Max Reinhardt Archive, State University of New York, Binghamton.

FIG. 17.10
Reinhardt's production of Friedrich Freska's pantomime, *Sumurun,* at the Kammerspiele, Berlin, 1910. Design by Ernst Stern. Courtesy Harvard Theatre Collection.

Reinhardt's conception of theatrical style included the physical arrangement of the theatre and the spatial relationship of the audience to the performers. In his view, some plays required intimate surroundings, others large spaces; similarly, some needed a proscenium, others an open platform. For example, he staged *Oedipus Rex* in a circus building, because, of all modern structures, the physical configuration of the circus seemed most like that of ancient Greek theatres. He was to extend such experiments with production and theatre architecture after World War I.

Reinhardt believed that the director must control every element of production. For each play he prepared a *Regiebuch* (or prompt book) in which he recorded each detail of movement, setting, properties, sound, lighting, and costume. Some critics charge that Reinhardt's actors were mere puppets that he manipulated, while others maintain that Reinhardt was so sensitive that he knew exactly how to help each performer. In any case, Reinhardt worked closely with his actors to achieve performances that became world-famous for their stylistic excellence. Among his actors, the best known were Alexander Moissi

1905 at the Kleines Theater, where he presented nearly fifty plays drawn from many countries and styles. His major work began in 1905, when he succeeded Brahm as director of the Deutsches Theater. In 1906 he opened the Kammerspiele, a small theatre, in conjunction with the larger house. The flexibility in programing and style of production which this arrangement permitted was to influence almost all state theatres in Germany and eventually America and elsewhere.

Reinhardt's major contribution was his recognition that no single approach is appropriate to the staging of all plays. Until the twentieth century, directors in each era staged all plays in much the same style. Despite widespread experimentation in the late nineteenth century, each director had adopted a distinctive approach and applied it to all plays. With Reinhardt, each new production became a problem to be solved, not through the employment of proven formulas but through clues found within the work itself. Unlike his predecessors, he could embrace antirealism without denying realism. He developed eclecticism into an artistic creed. His was to become the most common approach to directing in the twentieth century.

FIG. 17.11
Reinhardt's production of Sophocles' *Oedipus Rex* at Covent Garden, London, 1912. John Martin-Harvey as Oedipus. Courtesy the Max Reinhardt Archive, State University of New York, Binghamton.

(1880–1935), noted especially for his Shakespearean and Greek roles; Max Pallenberg (1859–1934), a versatile comic actor; Albert Bassermann (1867–1952), famous for his performances in Ibsen's plays and later as an actor in U.S. films; Werner Krauss (1884–1959); and Emil Jannings (1887–1950).

Reinhardt also worked closely with his scene designers, notably Ernst Stern (1876–1954), Alfred Roller (1864–1935), Oscar Strnad (1879–1935), and Emil Orlik (1879–1932). Often his productions centered around a motif, a ruling idea, or the staging conventions of a past period; overall, they ranged through many styles. Reinhardt has been accused of debasing the ideas of others, but more so than anyone else he made new movements and techniques acceptable to the general public through his eclectic approach.

NONREALISTIC THEATRE IN ENGLAND

In England, few playwrights departed markedly from the realistic mode. Oscar Wilde (1854–1900), a member of the "Art-for-Art's Sake" or "Aesthetic" movement that paralleled French symbolism, rejected the idea that drama should be utilitarian or that the popular audience is a suitable judge of merit. He suggested that we should seek to turn life into a work of art rather than to make art imitate life. Nevertheless, of Wilde's plays only *Salomé* (1893) resembles French symbolist drama. His phenomenally popular comedy, *The Importance of Being Earnest* (1895), illustrates his best-known work through its parody of the stock devices of comedy and its epigrams that puncture the conventional sentiments of his time. Others of his plays, among them *Lady Winderemere's Fan* (1892), *A Woman of No Importance* (1893), and *An Ideal Husband* (1895), resemble Pinero's social dramas.

J. M. Barrie (1860–1937), after beginning as a journalist and novelist, turned to drama in 1892 and wrote regularly for the stage until 1936. Through all of his work shines an optimistic, whimsical view of life in which humor is infused with sentiment. His most popular play, *Peter Pan* (1904), is a sentimental fantasy which romanticizes childhood and the child's view of reality. Other popular works by Barrie include *The Admirable Crichton* (1902), *What Every Woman Knows* (1908), and *Dear Brutus* (1917).

Although few English plays departed from the realistic mode, several innovations in staging were to depart from illusionism. Many of these stemmed from interest in staging Shakespeare's works. An early step toward more simplified staging was taken by Frank Benson (1858–1939), who, after acting with Irving, founded his own troupe in 1883 and continued to tour

FIG. 17.12
Barrie's *Peter Pan*. The original production at the Duke of York's Theatre, London, 1904. The pirate's ship. Courtesy Theatre Museum, Victoria and Albert Museum, London.

the provinces in a Shakespearean repertory until 1933. Benson produced almost all of the plays seen at the annual festival at Stratford-on-Avon (instituted in 1879) between 1886 and 1913, and after 1900 gave a few performances in London each year. Benson began by producing plays in the style of Irving, but by 1900 he had reduced the scenic background to a few stock settings and was placing primary emphasis upon the actors. Although his solution was at best a compromise, Benson helped to make simplified staging acceptable to the public, as well as providing a training ground for a whole generation of Shakespearean actors.

A more drastic reform was sought by William Poel (1852–1934). After his debut as an actor in 1876, Poel worked for Benson and others before undertaking those experiments with staging Shakespeare's plays for which he is now remembered. In this work, Poel had, between 1894 and 1905, the support of the Elizabethan Stage Society, of which he was the guiding spirit. In staging Elizabethan drama, Poel did not always use the same solution, but he is now considered noteworthy almost entirely because of his attempts to reconstruct the Elizabethan public stage. He also popularized several conventions: dressing the actors in Elizabethan garments to reflect Shakespeare's own day rather than the historical epoch of the dramatic action; using costumed pages to draw the curtains of an "inner stage" and to arrange properties and furniture; and employing an on-stage audience to emphasize the audience-actor relationships of the Elizabethan era. But, above

FIG. 17.13
Poel's production of Shakespeare's *Measure for Measure* in 1893. Act II, scene 2. Note the Elizabethan public stage (complete with costumed spectators) erected on a picture-frame stage. Courtesy Theatre Museum, Victoria and Albert Museum, London.

all, Poel desired continuity of action, integrity of text, and lively pace. Although his productions were not always successful, they demonstrated the advantages of unbroken playing and of concentrating attention upon text and performers. Poel's approach represents another form of antiquarianism, one that sought to substitute the theatrical conditions of a past era for historical accuracy in performance.

Poel's work is representative of similar approaches then being tried in several countries. At the Royal Court Theatre in Munich in 1889, Karl von Perfall and Jocza Savits had attempted to approximate the Elizabethan plan on a picture-frame stage by using a deep apron behind which a playing space was enclosed by an architectural facade with several doors and, at center back, a curtained inner stage where furniture and realistic scenic pieces could be set up and revealed as needed. This and a similar attempt made in Munich in 1909–1910 by Julius Klein and Eugene Kilian differed little from the solution used in 1840 by Immermann. In a somewhat similar vein, Antoine staged a number of seventeenth-century French plays at the Odéon between 1907 and 1910 for which he sought to reproduce the playing conditions and conventions used in the original productions. In Russia, Nikolai Evreinov undertook similar "historically authentic" productions of plays of the Middle Ages and the Spanish Golden Age between 1907 and 1912.

Many of the earlier experiments in staging Shakespeare's plays were synthesized by Granville Barker in productions at the Savoy Theatre in London be-

tween 1912 and 1914. Barker, who had worked for Poel before going to the Royal Court Theatre, amalgamated Poel's continuous staging with the visual simplicity advocated by Craig and others. He remodeled the Savoy Theatre by adding an apron and doors forward of the proscenium. Back of the proscenium the stage was divided into a main acting area and a modified inner stage, raised a few steps and equipped with curtains. This division of the stage into three parts allowed a continuous flow of action and eliminated the extensive cutting and rearrangement of the scripts usual in illusionistic staging. Barker employed such artists as Norman Wilkinson (1882–1934) and Albert Rutherston (1884–1953) to design scenery and costumes. Settings were composed primarily of painted, draped curtains, while the costumes were of no certain period. Such colors as magenta, scarlet, and lemon replaced the somber tones usual in Shakespearean productions. The forest of *A Midsummer Night's Dream* (presented in 1914) contained no three-dimensional trees; rather, it was suggested by foliage painted on drapes that hung in folds. Similarly, Titania's bower was made of gauze suspended from a crown of flowers. The fairies were gilded and directed to move like

FIG. 17.14
Harley Granville Barker's production of *A Midsummer Night's Dream* at the Savoy Theatre, London, 1914. The forest is represented by trees painted on draperies, and Titania's bower is formed of gauze hanging from a wreath. Courtesy Theatre Museum, Victoria and Albert Museum, London.

marionettes in order to set them off from the mortals. Although many conservative critics were deeply offended by Barker's productions, his approach pointed the way toward the future.

THE IRISH RENAISSANCE

Around 1900 Ireland began to assert its artistic independence from England. Since the sixteenth century, England had ruled Ireland, although it had never been able to suppress Roman Catholicism or to command the full loyalty of the people. As elsewhere in Europe, in Ireland nationalistic sentiment became especially strong during the nineteenth century, and the increased interest among the Irish in their Gaelic and Celtic heritage inevitably found its way into the theatre.

Although Dublin had been one of the major British theatrical centers since the seventeenth century, it saw no significant attempt to create an indigenous Irish drama until 1898, when the Irish Literary Society was established. Between 1899 and 1902, this group produced seven short plays and demonstrated the possibility of creating an Irish theatre. The leaders of the Society were William Butler Yeats (1865–1939), Lady Augusta Gregory (1863–1935), George Moore (1853–1933), and Edward Martyn (1859–1923).

Meantime, another organization, the Ormond Dramatic Society, headed by W. G. Fay (1872–1947) and Frank Fay (1870–1931), was also presenting plays with an Irish flavor, and soon the two united to form the Irish National Theatre Society. An appearance by this new group in London in 1903 won the support of Miss A. E. F. Horniman, who acquired a building for the company and remodelled it into the Abbey Theatre, which opened in 1904. Until 1910 Miss Horniman also provided the troupe with a subsidy. Originally the group gave only three performances a month, but after it obtained a permanent home it began to present a different play each week. Not until 1908, however, was it able to pay royalties or actors' salaries. Nevertheless, its finest achievements came before 1910, after which many of its best authors and actors began to defect.

Of the Abbey's playwrights, three—Yeats, Lady Gregory, and Synge—were most important. Yeats wrote about thirty plays between 1892 and 1938. Much of his early work resembled that of the French symbolists, many of whom he had known in Paris. Of these early plays, the best known is probably *Cathleen ni Houlihan* (1902), in which the spirit of Ireland, incredibly old but forever lovely, is embodied in the figure of an old woman who is transformed into a young girl. Around 1910 Yeats ceased to write specifically for the Abbey and soon afterwards came under the influence of Japanese Noh drama. Thereafter he

FIG. 17.15
William Bulter Yeat's *The Hour Glass*. Design by Gordon Craig. From Yeats, *Plays for an Irish Theatre* (1911).

made increasing use of masks, dance, music, and chant. Among the late works, one of the best is *At the Hawk's Well* (1917), in which a chorus describes the action as two characters await the appearance of waters that will confer immortality. Yeats disliked realistic drama and sought to arouse a community of feeling and ideals among spectators through poetic plays based on Celtic myth or legend.

From the first there were two conflicting styles at the Abbey: the poetic-mythic (best represented by Yeats) and the realistic-domestic (best represented by Lady Gregory). Most of Lady Gregory's dramatic writing was done between 1902 and 1912, although she did not cease altogether until 1926. She was most at home in one-act peasant comedies, such as *The Spreading of the News* (1904), which shows how the account of an event is distorted as it passes from one person to another. But she also virtually invented the Irish folk-history play based primarily on oral tradition, as in *Kincora* (1905), which centers around a legendary Irish king. Only rarely did she venture into the fully serious realm, as in *The Gaol Gate* (1906). Though she does not rank in critical stature with Yeats, she was far more successful than he with audiences, perhaps because she wrote about familiar subjects and in a familiar style.

It remained for John Millington Synge (1871–1909) to fuse the two styles represented by Yeats and Lady Gregory, for he made the mythic seem familiar and the familiar mythic; he also created his own distinctive language, a lilting, poetic prose. Synge was also the most controversial of the Abbey's writers. *In the Shadow of the Glen* (1903) was denounced as a slander on Irish womanhood because it showed a wife happily leaving home to go away with a tramp after her husband has ordered her from the house. Here as in others of his plays Synge is concerned with the conflict between a repressive life and the urge toward joy and freedom. *The Playboy of the Western World* (1907) aroused even greater wrath, for its story, in which a young man becomes a village hero after boasting of killing his father, was considered an insult to the national character. Wherever it played, riots occurred. Not all of Synge's plays were controversial. Many critics consider *Riders to the Sea* (1904) to be the finest short play in the English language. In it, Maurya loses the last of her six sons to the sea, but achieves a new peace, since fate can do no more to her. Although Synge is now considered the finest Irish dramatist of his day, at the time his plays did much to create dissension in the company and motivated many actors and playwrights to desert the Abbey. Consequently, although in the 1920s the Abbey was to recapture some of its former glory with the plays of Sean O'Casey, its major contribution had been made by 1915.

RUSSIAN MODERNISM

In Russia, the antirealistic impulse at first centered around *The World of Art,* a periodical begun in 1898 by Sergei Diaghilev (1872–1929). In addition to keeping Russians abreast of events in the artistic centers of Europe, the magazine sought to encourage Russian artists and composers. Diaghilev's major contribution, however, was to involve ballet. After Petipa retired, Prince Sergei Volkonsky, Director of the Imperial Theatres, and Mikhail Fokine (1880–1942), choreographer at the Mariinsky Theatre, introduced several innovations. Fokine disliked the long narrative works that Petipa had favored, and sought more limited subjects that offered greater opportunity for novel choreographic design. Using music by such composers as Igor Stravinsky, he emphasized complex rhythms and an overall harmony of mood.

Meanwhile, Diaghilev had been arranging exchanges of art with other countries, and in 1909 he took a ballet company to Paris for a six-week season. The ecstatic response led Diaghilev to form his Ballets Russes, which then toured throughout Europe. Everywhere it was praised both for its dancing and for its scenic design. When the Revolution came, the company elected to remain in the West.

The scenic style of the Ballets Russes did not depend upon any new technical devices, for it relied on painted wings and drops. Nevertheless, it departed markedly from illusionism, since line, color, and decorative motifs were considerably stylized to reflect moods and themes rather than specific periods or places. Costumes also emphasized exaggerated line,

FIG. 17.16
Leon Bakst's design for the Ballet Russes' *Tamar,* 1912. From the souvenir program.

color, and mass. Thus, although the artists drew on familiar forms and decorative motifs, they created a sense of exoticism and fantasy through stylization. The influence upon European scenic art of the Ballets Russes' designers—among them Leon Bakst, Alexandre Benois, Alexander Golovin, Mstislav Dobuzhinsky, and Natalie Gontcharova—was incalculable. Bakst and Benois later settled in Paris and continued to work there.

During the 1890s the symbolist ideal began to be championed in Russia and after 1900 became a major literary movement. Stanislavsky, after presenting a bill of Maeterlinck's short plays in 1904–1905, decided that his company needed to supplement its realistic approach, and in 1905 he established a studio to experiment with nonrealistic styles. To supervise the work, Stanislavsky employed Vsevelod Meyerhold (1874–1940), a founding member of the Moscow Art Theatre who had left in 1902 to form his own troupe. A number of productions were planned for the new studio, but Meyerhold's subordination of the actors to his directorial concepts displeased Stanislavsky so much that he discontinued the experiment.

Nevertheless, the Moscow Art Theatre went on to produce other nonrealistic works, including Maeterlinck's *The Blue Bird* in 1908 and *Hamlet* in 1912, the latter with scenery by Gordon Craig. It also encouraged Leonid Andreyev (1871–1919), Russia's foremost symbolist dramatist. After beginning in the realistic mode, Andreyev was converted to symbolism in 1907, the year in which he wrote his most famous play, *The Life of Man,* an allegory which dramatizes the major stages in human existence. Stanislavsky staged it against black curtains, on which windows, doors, and walls were outlined in white rope. Although the production was popular, Stanislavsky withdrew it because he felt the acting was too abstract. In 1911 the Moscow Art Theatre established the First Studio, under the direction of Leopold Sullerzhitsky (1872–1916), primarily to give training in the Stanislavsky system but also to encourage nonrealistic approaches. Here a number of future leaders, notably Richard Boleslavsky, Mikhail Chekhov, and Yevgeny Vakhtangov, received their training. But, if Stanislavsky experimented with nonrealistic approaches, any marked departure from realism was ultimately unacceptable to him since all tended to "dematerialize" the actor.

The most important early experiments with nonrealistic staging in Russia were undertaken in the company maintained by Vera Kommissarzhevskaya (1864–1910). On the stage from 1891, she attracted an enormous following and opened her own theatre in St. Petersburg in 1904. Interested in new approaches, she employed Meyerhold when he left Stanislavsky.

For his production of Ibsen's *Hedda Gabler* for her theatre, Meyerhold ignored Ibsen's stage directions and realistic detail. Each character wore a distinctively colored costume devoid of realistic detail. Furthermore, each character was restricted to a limited number of sculpturesque gestures and always returned to the same pose. The setting and furniture were greenish-blue and white; Hedda, seated on a white, fur-covered throne at center stage, dominated the action. For Wedekind's *Spring's Awakening,* Meyerhold placed everything to be used in the production on stage at once and spotlighted each area as needed. His favorite work, which he would direct several times, was Alexander Blok's (1880–1921) *The Fairground Booth* (1906), a combination of *commedia dell'arte* and the grotesque, which dispensed with the proscenium arch and exposed all the mechanisms of the theatre.

When audiences did not respond favorably to these and other experiments, perhaps because Kommissarzhevskaya's considerable talents were not adequately exploited, Meyerhold was asked to leave. Immediately afterward he was employed as a director in the Imperial theatres where he continued his experiments. When he staged Molière's *Don Juan* at the Alexandrinsky Theatre in 1910, he removed the front curtain and footlights, extended the forestage into the auditorium, kept the house lights on throughout the performance, used visible stagehands to change properties and scenery, and set the actors' movements to Lully's music. After the enormous success of this production, he went on to stage several operas, among them Wagner's *Tristan and Isolde.*

Between 1910 and 1914 Meyerhold also established studios where he experimented with circus and *commedia dell'arte* techniques. In one studio the entire auditorium was treated as a performance space which intermingled actors and spectators. Actors evolved their own scripts and experimented with geometrically patterned movement, improvisation, and rhythm. Meyerhold also began to turn the scenic background into a mere apparatus for acting—a collection of steps and levels. Meyerhold was the first important director to believe that the director is the major creative force in the theatre and that a script is simply material to be molded and reworked as the director wishes. His was the most persistent exploration of the possibilities and limitations of the theatre as a medium of expression to be found anywhere at that time. He would continue his experiments after the Revolution.

At Kommissarzhevskaya's theatre, Meyerhold was succeeded by Nikolai Evreinov (1879–1953). Although equally opposed to realism, Evreinov sought to enlarge the actor's place in the theatre by emphasizing theatricality and the grotesque. Evreinov is probably most famous for his "monodramas," the basic principle of which was first set forth in his "Apology for Theatricality" in 1908. He suggested that an in-born theatrical instinct leads humans into "role playing" and makes them seek to transform reality into something better. Consequently, he argued, the theatre should not imitate life, but life should seek to become like theatre at its best. In his "monodramas," he aimed to help the audience achieve its desires by making it the alter-ego of the protagonist. Through identification, the audience was led to participate in the theatrical experience through which it came to perceive an existence more satisfying than that of ordinary life. The most famous of the monodramas was *The Theatre of the Soul* (1912). Evreinov was also a director and, considering illusionism mistaken, he sought to provide alternatives, some of which he demonstrated in seasons of works from the past, one devoted to works from the Middle Ages and another to plays of the Spanish Golden Age. Additionally, he conducted experiments with *commedia dell'arte,* and ran two of the most noted cabaret theatres of the time.

Theodore Kommissarzhevsky (1874–1954) worked with his sister, Evreinov, and others before opening his own theatre in 1910. Probably the most balanced Russian producer of his day, he adopted an eclectic approach out of his desire to remain faithful to each playwright's intention. His eclecticism extended farther than Reinhardt's, however, for he adopted what might be called "internal eclecticism," in which, rather than choosing a historical period or single style for a play and then staying consistently within it, he sought for each character and action a meaningful visual metaphor that would evoke the appropriate associations within the mind of the spectator. Thus, his productions often combined elements from many periods and styles (thereby anticipating postmodernist techniques). Kommissarzhevsky was associated with numerous theatres between 1910 and 1919 (when he emigrated to the West); at one time he was head of four theatres and a training school. He later was to continue his work in France, England, and America.

Alexander Tairov (1885–1950) worked for a number of producers before opening his own theatre, the Kamerny (or Chamber) Theatre in Moscow in 1914. Tairov argued that there is no relationship between art and life and that the theatre must be viewed as analogous to the sacred dances of an ancient temple. Like Meyerhold, he viewed the text as an excuse for creativity, although he objected to Meyerhold's suppression of the actor, who, according to Tairov, is the basic creative force in the theatre. Because he was concerned with rhythmical movement, Tairov's settings were essentially architectural, being composed

FIG. 17.17
Tairov's production of Wilde's *Salomé* at the Kamerny Theatre, 1917. Costumes and settings by Alexandra Ekster. Each costume combined materials of varying color and texture to create the effect of figures from stained glass windows.

primarily of sculptural elements, steps, and levels. Productions were approached as if they were musical compositions; speech was a compromise between declamation and song, and movement always tended toward dance. The effect was nearer to ritual than to the usual dramatic performance. By the time of the Revolution, Tairov had staged fourteen plays drawn from a wide variety of countries and dramatic types. Most productions featured his wife, Alice Koonen (1899–1974), his ideal interpreter. Tairov was to continue his work after the Revolution.

By 1917, Russian directors had experimented with techniques far removed from those employed by Stanislavsky in 1898. Some methods were as determinedly nonrealistic as any ever devised. One of the least advanced countries of Europe at the end of the nineteenth century, Russia had by the Revolution witnessed some of the most daring theatrical experiments of the time, although, with the exceptions of the Ballets Russes and the Moscow Art Theatre, the work had made little impact outside its borders.

THE REVIVAL OF IDEALISM IN FRANCE

After the closing of the Théâtre de l'Oeuvre in 1899, Paris settled once more into its somewhat complacent conviction that it was the artistic capital of Europe. Antoine's productions became the standard, and nonrealistic experiments were few and sporadic. Thus, the appearance of the Ballets Russes in 1909 came almost as a revelation. A new wave of experimentation was given further impetus by the publication in

1910 of *Modern Theatre Art* by Jacques Rouché (1862–1957). After describing the work of Fuchs and Reinhardt in Germany, of Meyerhold, Stanislavsky, and Kommissarzhevskaya in Russia, and the theories of Appia and Craig, Rouché went on to call for similar experiments in France. Not only was his book widely read and discussed, Rouché himself set out to implement his ideas at the Théâtre des Arts between 1910 and 1913. Rouché did not aim at extreme stylization, but sought a simplicity in which color and line characterize a milieu and mood without calling attention to themselves. Working with his designer Maxime Dethomas (1867–1929), Rouché was the first French producer to be truly eclectic. He went on to become director of the Opéra, where between 1914 and 1936 he renovated the repertory and brought to it a new generation of designers.

Rouché's work had important consequences. Lugné-Poë revived the Théâtre de l'Oeuvre, where he presented a series of plays with designs by Jean Variot. More important, Rouché inspired Jacques Copeau (1879–1949) to open his own theatre. A dramatic critic, Copeau gained his first practical experience at the Théâtre des Arts when his adaptation of *The Brothers Karamazov* was produced there in 1911. Copeau was convinced that Rouché's suggested reforms put too much emphasis on visual elements and that no significant progress could come except through the drama itself.

In 1913 Copeau published a manifesto for a new theatre. In it, he adopted a position almost opposite to that of Meyerhold, for he argued that the director's

FIG. 17.19
Copeau's adaptation of Dostoyevsky's *The Brothers Karamazov* at Rouché's Théâtre des Arts, 1911. At center Charles Dullin as Smerdiakov. Setting by Maxime Dethomas. From *Le Théâtre* (1911).

primary task is the faithful translation of the dramatist's script into a "poetry of the theatre." Furthermore, he stated that the actor, as the "living presence" of the author, is the only essential element of theatrical production, and that a rejuvenation of the drama depends upon a return to the bare platform stage.

Copeau assembled a company of ten actors, including Louis Jouvet and Charles Dullin, both of whom were to be significant in the postwar theatre, and retired to the country to perfect his first productions. Meanwhile, with the assistance of Francis Jourdain, Copeau converted a small hall into the Théâtre du Vieux Colombier, seating only 400. It had a forestage forward of the proscenium, but no machinery except for a set of curtains and asbestos hangings which could be moved on rods to effect rapid changes of locale. To these curtains were added only the most essential furniture and set pieces. In 1913–1914, before the war forced him to stop, Copeau presented fifteen plays, including works by Shakespeare, Molière, Heywood, Claudel, and others. In 1917 Copeau was asked to revive the troupe and take it to New York. There between 1917 and 1919 he presented plays for American audiences before returning to Paris to reopen his theatre. It is impossible to overrate the importance of the Théâtre du Vieux Colombier, for with its formation the leadership of the French theatre passed from Antoine to Copeau, who was to dominate the interwar years in France.

FIG. 17.18
Hamlet at the Théâtre de l'Oeuvre, 1913. Directed by Lugné-Poë and Gémier. The structure in the foreground remained throughout and set pieces were changed behind the central opening. From *Le Théâtre* (1913).

LOOKING AT THEATRE HISTORY

One of the most persistent features of the period between 1875 and 1915 was the attempt to redefine the "art of the theatre." In this effort, the leaders were Appia and Craig. Here are some excerpts from one of Appia's essays. After pointing out the weaknesses of the nineteenth-century theatre (which he blames on the disparity between the static, two-dimensional painted scenery, the flat stage floor, and the three-dimensional, moving actor), he goes on to ask:

What would happen if we begin with . . . the plastic, moving human body? . . . An object is three-dimensional to our eyes only because of the light that strikes it. . . . [Furthermore] human movement . . . requires obstacles if it is to be fully expressive. Therefore, the actor's mobility cannot be used to artistic advantage except when it is integrally related to objects and the floor. Thus the two basic conditions required for the artistic use of the human body on the stage are: light that reveals its plasticity, and its harmonization with the setting so as to enhance its attitudes and movements. . . .

The effects of lighting are limitless. . . . [When it is used properly] the actor no longer walks about in front of painted light and shade; he is enfolded in an atmosphere destined for him. . . . Scenic illusion may be defined as the living presence of the actor. . . . [If we are to create the appropriate scenic illusion] we must greatly simplify [the setting] . . . completely rearrange the stage floor, and above all make adequate provisions for lighting. . . .

"Comment Reformer Notre Mise en Scène," *La Revue,* 50 (June 1, 1904), 342–349.

Craig saw theatre as an autonomous art created by a master artist, rather than as an assemblage of other arts put together by craftsmen:

The Art of the Theatre is neither acting nor the play, it is not scene nor dance, but it consists of all the elements of which these things are composed: action, which is the very spirit of acting; words, which are the body of the play; line and colour, which are the very heart of the scene; rhythm, which is the very essence of dance. . . .

When [the director] interprets the plays of the dramatist by means of his actors, his scene-painters, and his other craftsmen, then he is a craftsman—a master craftsman; when he will have mastered the uses of actions, words, line, colour, and rhythm, then he may become an

artist. Then we shall no longer need the assistance of the playwright—for our art will then be self-reliant.

On the Art of the Theatre (Chicago: Browne's Bookstore, 1911), 138, 148.

When Granville Barker attempted to do away with illusionistic scenery in his Shakespearean productions, he met considerable derision. Here are portions of a review of *A Midsummer Night's Dream* written in 1915 (for an illustration of one setting, see Fig. 17.14):

Let it be said that it represented the last cry in the new stage decoration. . . . The. . .changes of scene were indicated by curtains that waved, to the loss of all illusion. . . . No human being . . . can be expected to be anything but worried and annoyed by pink silk curtains that are supposed to be the roofs of houses, or green silk curtains that are supposed to be forest trees. . . . I hope this is not indicative of what will happen when stage setting ceases to be scenery and becomes only decoration.

Review by G. C. D. Odell, reprinted in his *Shakespeare from Betterton to Irving,* 2 (New York, 1920), 467–468.

Probably the most extreme departure from the realistic mode, and a clear example of "modernism," was seen at Paris' Théâtre de l'Oeuvre, where more startling than the abandonment of illusionistic scenery was the highly stylized acting:

The most simple and sensible things take on a different appearance in passing through the mouths and gestures of the l'Oeuvre's actors under the direction of Lugné-Poë. They have a continual ecstatic air of perpetually being visionaries. As if hallucinatory, they stare before them, far, very far, vaguely, very vaguely. Their voices are cavernous, their diction choppy. They seem to be attempting to give the air that they are fools.

Moniteur Universel, 5 March 1894.

Sets of binary relationships are often used to help distinguish key aspects of premodernist and modernist approaches: rules/freedom; nature/artificiality; tradition/novelty; convention/innovation. Modernist approaches rapidly gained adherents and came to dominate much of twentieth-century art. Eventually it would be challenged, if not replaced, by "postmoderinism."

18

Continental European and Latin American Theatre in the Early Twentieth Century

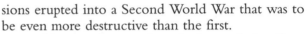

The period between 1915 and 1940 was bounded by the two most destructive and costly wars of modern times. World War I utilized not only the largest armies ever assembled up to that time, but new and improved instruments of destruction—tanks and other mechanized vehicles, airplanes and bombs, submarines and torpedoes. Some 8,300,000 people died and more than $337 billion were spent. To many, the war seemed an exercise in madness.

Nevertheless, the war ended in a wave of optimism as republics replaced monarchies, as small ethnic groups were allowed to form their own nations, and as a League of Nations and a World Court were established to arbitrate national disputes. But optimism soon declined because of the great economic problems created by human and material destruction and because of the vindictive treatment of the losing nations. Rampant inflation in the 1920s was followed by severe economic depression in the 1930s. In several countries conditions became so chaotic that dictators were able to gain complete control: Mussolini of Italy in 1922, Stalin of the USSR around 1928, Vargas of Brazil in 1930, Hitler of Germany in 1933, and Franco of Spain in 1939. During the 1930s, conflicts—over ideology, territorial claims, trade, and imperialistic designs—increased steadily. When the League of Nations proved ineffective, the great powers set about rearming. In 1939 the ten-

sions erupted into a Second World War that was to be even more destructive than the first.

World War I seems to have had a catalytic effect, however, in many realms, perhaps most notably those involving moral standards, codes of dress and behavior, women's and worker's rights, and artistic experimentation.

THEATRE AND DRAMA IN RUSSIA, 1917–1940

The most drastic changes brought by World War I were felt in Russia, where the czar's policies had been unpopular for many years. The economic hardships created by the conflict fed the unrest, which in early 1917 broke into open rebellion and ended more than 300 years of rule by the Romanovs. Moderate socialists controlled the government at first, but in late 1917 the Communists seized power. Civil war continued, however, until the early 1920s, by which time more than twenty million people had died and Russia's economic resources were severely depleted. For several years thereafter the government was so preoccupied with rebuilding the nation that the theatre was left relatively free to experiment with new forms.

The Communists viewed the theatre as a national treasure, formerly reserved for the middle and upper classes, to be made available to the proletariat. It was also considered a major tool of instruction and, as such, was placed under the authority of the Commissar of Education, Anatole Lunacharsky (1875–1932). Not only was attendance at professional productions encouraged, but amateur groups were organized among peasants, workers, and soldiers. By 1926, there were about 20,000 dramatic clubs among the peasants alone. Between 1918 and 1922, amateurs also figured prominently in the many mass spectacles that re-created major events in the Revolution. The most famous of these was *The Taking of the Winter Palace,* staged in 1919 by Evreinov on the site of the actual event with a cast of about 8,000 soldiers, sailors, and workers.

The new regime proceeded slowly in its nationalization of the theatre. By 1922–1923, only 33 percent of the theatre buildings belonged to the state. By 1925–1926, the percentage had increased to 63, but the process was not to be completed until 1936. Similarly, it was long before theatrical personnel were subjected to political domination.

Many of the most enthusiastic supporters of the Revolution were members of the *avant-garde,* who saw in the new regime the opportunity to break with the past and to create new theatrical forms. Meyerhold soon emerged as the leader of this faction. In 1920 he was appointed head of the theatre section in the Commissariat of Education, a position that made him nominal head of the theatre in Russia. At the same time, he continued his own work as a director, staging *The Dawns* (written in 1898 by the Belgian symbolist, Emile Verhaeren) as a Soviet propaganda piece, in which real news bulletins were read

FIG. 18.2

Meyerhold's adaptation of Gogol's *The Inspector General,* 1926. Shown here is the "bribery" scene. The set opened at the back to allow wagons to move in and out.

FIG. 18.1

Constructivist setting by Lyubov Popova for Meyerhold's production of Crommelynck's *The Magnanimous Cuckold,* 1922. The action occurs in and around a mill, suggested by various wheels, all of which turned at speeds that varied according to the rhythmical and emotional demands of the action.

from the stage and a public meeting was held with the audience taking part. When this production was denounced by the Central Committee of the Communist Party as foreign to the needs of the proletariat, Meyerhold resigned his government post, but later that year he was appointed head of the state's workshop for directors, and in 1922 he acquired a theatre of his own. This series of events is indicative of the power of the *avant-garde* even in the face of official disapproval.

Between 1921 and 1930, Meyerhold perfected techniques with which he had experimented before the Revolution. He now developed more conscious and systematic methods, to which he applied such terms as *biomechanics* and *constructivism.* Biomechanics referred primarily to Meyerhold's approach to acting, intended to create a style appropriate to the machine age. His performers were trained in gymnastics, circus movement, and ballet in order to make them as efficient as machines in carrying out "an assignment received from the outside." Basically what Meyerhold had in mind is a variation on the James-Lange theory: particular patterns of muscular activity elicit particular emotions. Consequently, actors, to arouse within themselves or the audience a desired emotional response, need only to enact an appropriate kinetic pattern. Thus, Meyerhold sought to replace Stanislavsky's emphasis on internal motivation with one on physical and emotional reflexes. To create a feeling of exuberant joy in both performer and audience, Meyerhold thought it more efficient for actors to plummet down a slide, swing on a trapeze, or turn a somersault than to restrict themselves to behavior considered appropriate by traditional social standards.

Constructivism was a term taken over from the visual arts, where it had first been applied about 1912 to sculpture composed of intersecting planes and masses without representational content. Similarly, Meyerhold frequently arranged nonrepresentational platforms, ramps, turning wheels, trapezes, and other objects to create a "machine for acting," more practicable than decorative.

Meyerhold applied his theories about biomechanics and constructivism most thoroughly in the years between 1922 and 1925, but he steadily softened them. His most famous production of the 1920s was Gogol's *The Inspector General,* presented in 1926. Meyerhold transferred the locale from a remote village to a large city, reshaped all of the characters and invented several new ones. Costumes, scenery, and properties were based on stylized nineteenth-century motifs, and the action was accompanied by period music. The most striking scene was one in which Meyerhold arranged fifteen doors around the stage, and an official emerged simultaneously from each door to offer the inspector a bribe.

Next to Meyerhold, the most influential Russian director of the 1920s was Tairov, who continued the methods he had introduced before the war. Following the Revolution, Lunacharsky had divided theatres into two groups: the well-established or "academic" theatres, which the government subsidized and allowed relative autonomy; and the unproven theatres, which were permitted to exist but given little encouragement. Thus, the government favored pre-Revolutionary groups, a practice bitterly opposed by Meyerhold. Under this scheme, the Kamerny Theatre was classified as an "academic" theatre. Until 1924, Tairov took little notice of the Revolution, producing such works as Wilde's *Salomé,* Scribe's *Adrienne Lecouvreur,* and Racine's *Phèdre* in the style he had always followed. Unlike most producers of the period, who clothed actors in uniform-like garments similar to those worn by the spectators, Tairov sought to lift audiences above the drabness of everyday life. After 1924, Tairov occasionally produced Russian classical and contemporary plays, but his theatre remained the principal link with the West. In addition to its predominantly Western repertory in which Shaw and O'Neill figured prominently, the troupe also toured in Western Europe in 1923, 1928, and 1929. When Tairov turned to contemporary Russian works, he often ran into difficulties. In 1929 his production of Mikhail Levidov's *Plot of the Equals,* a play about the degeneration of the French Revolution into the "reign of terror," was removed after one performance. Thereafter, Tairov's influence declined.

Another important innovator in these early years was Yevgeny Vakhtangov (1883–1922), who had become the artistic leader of the First Studio of the Moscow Art Theatre after Sullerzhitsky died in 1916. Vakhtangov's reputation rests primarily upon four productions: Maeterlinck's *The Miracle of Saint Anthony,* Strindberg's *Erik XIV* (both staged in 1921), Ansky's *The Dybbuk,* and Gozzi's *Turandot* (both staged in 1922). All were done at the First Studio except *The Dybbuk,* which was done at the Habima theatre).

Vakhtangov began as a faithful follower of Stanislavsky, but his strength came from his effective blending of the Moscow Art Theatre's realistic approach with Meyerhold's theatricalism. From Stanislavsky he preserved the emphasis upon concentration, each character's biography, and exploration of hidden meanings; to this he added a heightened and stylized use of movement and design not unlike that of the German expressionists. In *Erik XIV,* for example, which was conceived as a death knell for monarchy, all of the courtiers and bureaucrats were played as automatons while the proletariat were treated realistically. Vakhtangov's greatest achievement came with *Turandot,* throughout which the actors seemed to be improvising effortlessly. This production was retained in the repertory as a memorial to Vakhtangov, who died shortly after it opened. Because he worked with several student groups and trained so many actors, Vakhtangov's influence was considerable. His approach was continued by such associates and students as Yuri Zavadsky (1894–1977), Boris Shchukin (1894–1939), Reuben Simonov (1899–1968), Boris Zakhava (1896–1976), Nikolai Akimov (1901–1968), and Alexander Popov (1892–1961). Most of these men were to be important leaders into the

FIG. 18.3
Vakhtangov's production of Gozzi's *Turandot,* 1922. Setting by I. Nivinsky.

1960s. In the post-Stalinist era, Vakhtangov's methods were to offer the most acceptable alternative to Soviet realism.

In 1924 the First Studio became an independent organization, the Second Moscow Art Theatre, headed by Mikhail Chekhov (1891–1955), a nephew of Anton Chekhov. After entering the Moscow Art Theatre in 1910, Chekhov soon found the Stanislavsky method inadequate and later worked closely with Vakhtangov, winning considerable fame for his portrayal of *Erik XIV.* Chekhov thought that Stanislavsky's system restricted the actor to copying nature instead of emphasizing what might be. Thus, he came to stress inspiration above analysis as the actor's primary tool. His conceptions were always somewhat mystical, however, and in 1927 seventeen of his associates resigned from the troupe and published a denunciation. Chekhov then left Russia and ultimately settled in the United States, where he ran an acting school for many years and published *To the Actor.* The Second Moscow Art Theatre was dissolved in 1936.

Although the innovators of the 1920s attracted most attention, the conservative groups, notably the Maly Theatre in Moscow and the Alexandrinsky Theatre in Leningrad, were favored by political leaders and most of the public. Meyerhold disliked the Maly Theatre's realistic productions so much that in 1921 he recommended that the troupe be liquidated. In response, Alexander Yuzhin, the Maly's director, launched an attack on "formalism" that began a struggle not to be resolved until the 1930s.

Between 1917 and 1925, the Moscow Art Theatre played only a minor role in Russian theatrical life. It mounted only two new productions and its troupe was decimated in 1919 by the defection of several actors to the West. In 1922 it was granted permission to tour abroad, and in 1923–1924 the troupe performed in the United States to universal praise. When the company returned to Russia in 1924, it was at its lowest ebb. Its studios were alienated, and the company was so depleted that Stanislavsky had to add eighty-seven new members. Then the process of rebuilding began. In 1926 it achieved its first postwar success with Ostrovsky's *The Burning Heart,* and in 1927 presented Vsevelod Ivanov's *Armored Train 14–69,* its first important Soviet play. From this time, the company's fortunes steadily improved.

Around 1927 the Soviet attitude toward the theatre also began to change. After Lenin died in 1924, Stalin had gradually gathered power into his hands and in 1928 began his campaign to industrialize Russia and to collectivize farming. Concessions formerly granted dissident elements were withdrawn and the central government extended its power over all aspects of Soviet life. In 1927 a training program to equip party members to manage theatres was initiated and "artistic councils" within each theatre were given considerable power over repertory, style, and policy. Nevertheless, attacks on nonconformists in the theatre came primarily from the Russian Association of Proletarian Writers (RAPP), a radical group that sought to abolish everything not deriving directly from the proletariat. Its violence sufficiently alienated party leaders that it was disbanded in 1932 and replaced by the Union of Soviet Writers, headed by Gorky. At first, greater freedom seemed to be in store, but in 1934 "socialist realism" (realistic in form, socialistic in content) was declared the proper style for all art, and pressure began to be exerted to discourage "formalism" (any type of nonrealism). In 1936 all theatres were placed under the Central Direction of Theatres, and after 1938 the "stabilization" of companies made it almost impossible for workers to change jobs without specific government approval.

The new policies meant the gradual suppression of the *avant-garde* troupes and greater prestige for the Maly, Alexandrinsky (now renamed the Pushkin Theatre), and the Moscow Art Theatre, which after 1932 was called "the House of Gorky." The nonrealistic groups attempted to adapt to the new demands. Tairov began to alternate Soviet plays with productions in his older style. In 1933 he won considerable praise for his staging of Vishnevsky's *The Optimistic Tragedy,* but by 1937 he was so out of favor that his company was merged for a time with that of the Realistic Theatre. Reopening in 1939, the Kamerny gained approval for some productions but was sent to Siberia during the war years. Meyerhold adopted a style usually called "impressionistic," exemplified in his productions of Dumas' *Camille* in 1934 and Tchaikovsky's *Queen of Spades* in 1935. He did not alter the text or use biomechanics in either of these productions. Both were given lavish, if stylized, decor and both were popular successes. Nevertheless, Meyerhold's completely apolitical interpretations displeased officials even more than his formalism, and in 1938 his theatre was closed. In 1939 he made his last official appearance; in a speech to the First All Union Congress of Directors he is reported to have admitted errors, but to have added: "The pitiful and wretched thing called socialist realism has nothing in common with art. . . . Where once there were the best theatres in the world . . . in hunting formalism, you have eliminated art." Despite these repressions, stylization received official approval when it was used to convey acceptable political messages.

The most significant experiments of the 1930s were those of Nikolai Okhlopkov (1900–1966) at the

FIG. 18.4

Okhlopkov's Realistic Theatre, Moscow, 1932. Note the two levels of action and the placement of the audience for this production of *The Beginning,* adapted from a novel.

Realistic Theatre. Originating as the Fourth Studio of the Moscow Art Theatre in 1921, the Realistic Theatre attained independent status in 1927. Okhlopkov, who had worked with both Meyerhold and Tairov, was appointed its director in 1932. He eliminated the platform stage and placed all action in the auditorium. Although he often used a central playing area, Okhlopkov also staged scenes around the periphery of the auditorium or on a bridge overhead. Realistic set pieces might be placed almost anywhere, and sound effects from many directions made the audience feel at the center of events. Okhlopkov preferred to work with dramatizations of novels, and all of his productions were "cinematic" in their rapid cutting from one scene to another. But while his selection of plays was acceptable, his production approach was considered too anarchic. For a time his theatre was merged with Tairov's. In 1943 he was named head of the Theatre of the Revolution, where he was to be one of the most important directors of the postwar period. Yuri Zavadsky's career followed a similar path. After Vakhtangov's death he operated a studio for a time, and in 1932 was appointed director of the Red Army Central Theatre. Here he did several fine productions, but in 1935, after refusing to merge his studio with the larger troupe, he was exiled to the provinces until 1939. Zavadsky was succeeded at the Red Army Central Theatre by Alexei Popov, who was more responsive to official demands.

Considering the uncertainties of the early years and the political pressures of the 1930s, it is not surprising that few significant playwrights emerged. Gorky was the only pre-Revolutionary author who played an important role under the Communists and

even he was alienated from the regime for many years. Consequently, his plays were little performed until 1927, after which they came to be considered models of appropriate style. After Gorky was named head of the Union of Soviet Writers in 1932, his works came to be almost obligatory parts of each theatre's repertory. After the Revolution, Gorky wrote only two plays and these not till the 1930s—*Yegor Bulichev and Others* (1932) and *Dostigayev and Others* (1933)—and even these concern life before the Soviet regime began.

In the years immediately following the Revolution, leadership passed to the futurists, militant enemies of old forms and strong advocates of a utilitarian art suited to the needs of a machine age. The major playwright of the movement was Vladimir Mayakovsky (1894–1930), a close friend of Meyerhold, who staged all of his plays. Mayakovsky's *Mystery-Bouffe* (1918) parodied the Bible and ended with the proletariat entering the promised land, while *The Bedbug* (1929) and *The Bath-house* (1930) satirized Soviet bureaucracy. His last two plays were received so adversely that Mayakovsky committed suicide in 1930.

Most Soviet plays were either farces or melodramas upholding the Revolution or denouncing its opposers. Perhaps the best of the early dramatists was Mikhail Bulgakov (1891–1940), whose *The Days of the Turbins* (1925) depicted sympathetically the White Army faction during the civil war that followed the Revolution. Among the most popular of Soviet plays, it made Bulgakov suspect by the government, and thereafter his plays were often withdrawn from production. His *A Cabal of Hypocrites* (1929), about

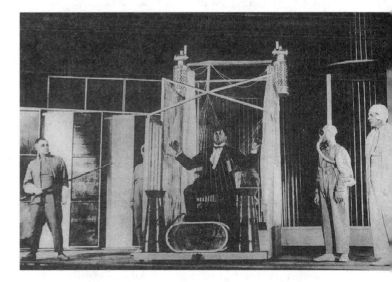

FIG. 18.5

Mayakovsky's *The Bedbug* as produced by Meyerhold in 1929.

FIG. 18.6
Trenyov's *Lyubov Yarovaya* at the Maly Theatre, Moscow, 1926.

Molière and the censorship of *Tartuffe,* eventually led to a ban on all his plays. Beginning in the late 1970s, Bulgakov's popularity would mushroom once more.

Other significant dramatists included Vsevelod Ivanov (1895–1963), with *Armored Train 14–69* (1927); and Constanin Trenyov (1884–1945), with *Lyubov Yarovaya* (1926). Of the later writers, the best were Nikolai Pogodin (1900–1962), with *Aristocrats* (1934) and *Kremlin Chimes* (1942); Alexander Afinogenov (1904–1941), with *Far Taiga* (1935) and *On The Eve* (1941); Alexander Korneichuk (1905–1972), with *Truth* (1937) and *The Front* (1942); and Vsevelod Vishnevsky (1900–1951), with *The Optimistic Tragedy* (1932) and *At the Walls of Leningrad* (1941). Most of these plays praise life under Communism, glorify Lenin and Stalin, or show the courage of the Soviets under siege from the Nazis.

By the beginning of World War II, the Russian theatre had been subjugated to political pressures. Nevertheless, no country in the world took its theatre more seriously as a medium of ideas and as an integral part of society.

GERMAN THEATRE AND DRAMA, 1915–1940

During World War I the German theatre continued without interruption and, unlike its English, French, and American counterparts, did not turn primarily to popular entertainment. When Germany became a republic at the end of the war, the former "royal" theatres were rechristened "state" theatres, but there were few changes in organization or policy, for they continued to offer seasons composed of varied plays performed by permanent companies. After 1920, as economic conditions worsened and inflation skyrocketed, nonsubsidized groups found it increasingly difficult to survive except by abandoning the repertory system in favor of new works tailored to popular tastes. Eventually most of the private theatres were taken over by municipalities, thereby increasing governmental involvement in theatre.

Of the prewar producers, Max Reinhardt remained the most important. While continuing his management in Berlin of the Deutsches Theater and the Kammerspiele, he also remodeled the Circus Schumann into the Grosses Schauspielhaus (seating more than 3,500), where between 1919 and 1922 he presented a series of monumental productions, most notably the *Oresteia, Julius Caesar,* and Romain Rolland's *Danton* (1900). The venture ultimately failed, perhaps because the theatre's great size discouraged subtlety and because the compromises demanded by the combined open and picture-frame stages were never entirely satisfactory.

From 1922 to 1924 Reinhardt moved his headquarters to Austria, where he annually produced von Hofmannsthal's *Everyman* (beginning in 1920) and *The Great Theatre of the World* (beginning in 1922) at the Salzburg Festival, which he had founded in 1918 along with Hugo von Hofmannsthal and Richard Strauss. In 1922 he became director of Vienna's Theater in dem Redoutensaal, converted from an imperial ballroom of the 1740s, where against a background of screens he presented plays and operas of the eighteenth century. The intimacy of this theatre contrasted markedly with the immensity of the Grosses Schauspielhaus. Although he retained and extended his Austrian enterprises, in 1924 Reinhardt returned to Berlin where he continued his manifold activities until Hitler's rise to power forced him to give up his German theatres in 1933. Between 1905 and 1933 Reinhardt had personally directed 136 plays and through his experiments with production styles and theatre architecture had exerted a pervasive influence on the German stage. In the United States in the final years of his life, Reinhardt directed a few plays and films, but he never fully adjusted to his new situation.

Reinhardt's postwar activities were essentially continuations of practices he had begun before 1914. But other directors championed a new mode—expressionism—which for a few years dominated the German stage. The term *expressionism* first gained currency in France around 1901 as a label used to distinguish the kind of painting done by Van Gogh

FIG. 18.7
Europe, c. 1925.

and Gauguin from that of the impressionists, who sought to capture the appearance of objects as seen under a certain light at a particular moment. In contrast, expressionism was thought to project strong feelings into objects and to portray them as modified and distorted by the painter's own vision.

Around 1910 expressionism as a term was introduced into Germany, where shortly afterward it was picked up by critics and popularized as a label for tendencies already underway in literature and the arts. Since almost any departure from realism soon came to be labeled "expressionism," the movement is difficult to define. Nevertheless, its basic premises may be outlined. An anthropomorphic view of existence led expressionists to project human emotions and attitudes into inanimate objects, and to seek truth in humanity's spiritual qualities rather than in external appearances. Expressionists opposed realism and naturalism on the grounds that those movements focused attention on surface details and implied that the observ-

able phenomena of contemporary materialistic and mechanistic society represent fundamental truth. Rather, the expressionists argued, external reality is alterable and should be changed until it is brought into harmony with humanity's spiritual nature, the only significant source of value. Many expressionists sought merely to focus attention upon these inner qualities, but others took a more militant view and worked to transform social and political conditions so that they would no longer mechanize and distort the human spirit and thereby prevent attainment of happiness.

Since the expressionists' "truth" existed primarily within the subjective realm, it had to be expressed through new artistic means. Distorted line, exaggerated shape, abnormal coloring, mechanical movement, and telegraphic speech were devices commonly used to lead audiences beyond surface appearances. Often everything was shown through the eyes of the protagonist, whose view might alter emphases and impose drastic interpretations upon the events. Most

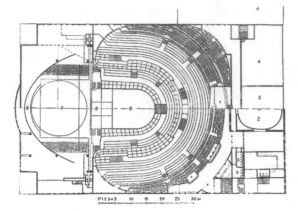

FIG. 18.8
Plan of Reinhardt's Grosses Schauspielhaus, remodeled from a circus building. At left, note the full proscenium stage with its revolving stage. Forward of the proscenium are a platform and arena. The theatre seated about 3,500. From Barkhin, *Architectura Teatra* (Moscow, 1947).

expressionist plays were structurally episodic, deriving their unity from a central idea or argument, often holding out the promise of a future Utopia.

The Beggar (1912) by Reinhard Johannes Sorge (1892–1916) is often considered to be the first true expressionist play. It shows the struggle between established conventions and new values, between the older and younger generations, and the attempt of a visionary poet to achieve fulfillment in a materialistic and insensitive society. Much the same idea is found in Walter Hasenclever's (1890–1940) *The Son*

FIG. 18.9
Reinhardt's Redoutensaal Theater, Vienna, 1922, created within the ballroom of an eighteenth-century palace. The stage was erected without harming the walls of the ballroom. There was no proscenium arch or front curtain. From *Le Théâtre* (1922).

(1914), in which the protagonist threatens to kill his father because his freedom to experience life in all its glory is restricted by his puritanical and hypocritical parents; it was probably intended as a symbolic treatment of the need to rid the world of those old values and social forms standing in the way of the "new man."

With the coming of World War I, expressionism began to change as its emphasis moved from personal concerns to warnings of impending universal catastrophe or pleas for the reformation of humanity and society. For example, Hasenclever's antiwar play *Antigone* (1916) suggests that love is the only path to happiness but that it cannot be followed until unjust and autocratic rulers are overthrown. Similarly, Fritz von Unruh's (1885–1970) *One Race* (1918) shows how mistaken values and deeds (especially war) have dehumanized people, and it ends with a plea to storm "the barracks of violence" as a prelude to a better world.

In 1918 widespread revolution overthrew the German government and brought an end to the war and the monarchy. Until that time few expressionist plays had been produced in Germany because of the strict censorship. Beginning in 1913 a few private readings and dramatic performances had been presented by Herwarth Walden (1878–1941) under the sponsorship of his periodical *The Storm*. But no professional performance of an expressionist play was given until 1916, and when the war ended only a few plays had been seen and these only by limited audiences. When peace came, however, expressionism flourished. For example, the ten German-language expressionist periodicals of 1917 had grown to forty-four in 1919. Similarly, beginning in 1919 theatres began to take expressionist plays into their repertories and until 1924 the new mode was to dominate. But the optimism that accompanied the end of the war (and that seemed to promise the possibility of achieving the expressionists' ideals) soon gave way to disappointment and disillusionment. By 1924 expressionism was virtually dead. This shift from optimism to pessimism is especially evident in the work of the two major expressionist playwrights—Kaiser and Toller.

Georg Kaiser (1878–1945) began his playwriting career in 1911 but his first important work in the expressionist vein was *From Morn to Midnight* (1916), in which a machine-age Everyman searches for the meaning of life only to become a martyr to callousness and greed. But, though the world is not yet ready for transformation, Kaiser seems to believe that his protagonist has pointed the way. Kaiser's trilogy of plays—*Coral* (1917), *Gas I* (1918), and *Gas II* (1920)—show the movement toward despair. In the first, the protagonist gradually comes to recognize the primacy

FIG. 18.10
Hasenclever's *The Son* at Kiel in 1919. Setting by Otto Reigbert. Courtesy Theatermuseum, Munich.

FIG. 18.11
Jessner's production of Shakespeare's *Richard III* at the Berlin State Theater in 1919. Setting by Emil Pirchan. Courtesy Theatermuseum, Munich.

of the soul, and in the second his son sets out to regenerate society. Though in neither play is the protagonist successful, both works are essentially optimistic about the future. But in *Gas II* Kaiser seems to have despaired of humanity, and when the play ends, the world is undergoing a cataclysmic destruction. After this time Kaiser abandoned the expressionist mode, though he continued to write until his death.

Ernst Toller (1893–1939) wrote his first play, *Transfiguration* (1918), while serving a prison term for antiwar activities. It shows the gradual evolution of its hero from a naive patriotic soldier to ardent antiwar revolutionary seeking to help fight oppressors. Toller's most influential work was to be *Man and the Masses* (1921), the story of a woman's struggle to aid workers, and her defeat by those who place ideological above humanitarian principles. By the time Toller wrote *Hurrah, We Live!* (1927) his disillusionment was complete. This play shows former idealists, now settled into comfortable lives, repeating the mistakes they once rebelled against. In protest against such madness, the protagonist commits suicide.

Between 1919 and 1924 expressionism also became a major style of production, especially as applied by Jessner and Fehling. Leopold Jessner (1878–1945) had worked in Hamburg and Königsberg before becoming director of the Berlin State Theatre from 1919 until 1933. Here he won international fame for his imaginative use of flights of steps (*Jessnertreppen*) and platforms as the major compositional elements in his productions. His principal designers, Emil Pirchan and Cesar Klein, discarded representational scenery for stylized pieces which, along with costumes and lighting, were selected primarily for their emotional and symbolic qualities. Jessner's production of *Richard III* is typical of his approach; the blood-red costumes and light used at the peak of Richard's power dissolved into white costumes and light as Richmond's forces came to the fore. Despite his fame as an expressionist director, Jessner worked primarily with the classics. In 1933 he emigrated to the United States.

Unlike Jessner, Jürgen Fehling (1890–1968) made his reputation with expressionist drama, beginning with Toller's *Man and the Masses* at Berlin's Volksbühne in 1921. Fehling sought to arouse intense emotional response in spectators. In his production, bankers fox-trotted to the sound of jingling coins; the workers did a wild dance, which, set to the tune of a concertina and accompanied by constantly shifting colored lights, gave the impression of a witches' sabbath; throughout, the masses were used to create striking effects with movement and sound. Fehling was more eclectic than Jessner, both in the kinds of plays he directed and in the devices he used. He remained in Germany under the Nazis, serving as director of the Berlin State Theatre.

As expressionism declined, a more militant approach, eventually to be called "Epic Theatre," arose. Its first major practitioner, Erwin Piscator (1893–1966), after working with some minor theatres was appointed director at Berlin's Volksbühne, where

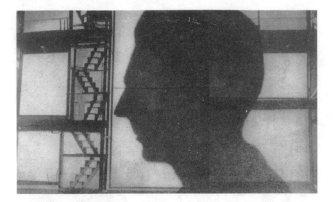

FIG. 18.12
Piscator's setting for Toller's *Hurrah, We Live!* From *Theatre Arts* (1932).

between 1924 and 1927 he sought to create a "proletarian drama," as opposed to merely producing standard plays for a working-class audience. His ideological reshaping of texts, however, aroused such controversy that he resigned in 1927 to found the Piscator Theater. There in 1927–1928 he perfected many of the techniques later associated with Epic Theatre. For Toller's *Hurrah, We Live!*, a reworking of Alexei Tolstoy's *Rasputin,* and an adaptation of Jaroslav Hacek's novel, *The Good Soldier Schweik,* Piscator used filmed sequences, cartoons, treadmills, segmented settings, and other devices to draw strong parallels between the dramatic events and recent European history, thus arguing the need for social and political reforms. Piscator left Germany in 1933 and in 1939 went to the United States, where until 1951 he taught at the New School for Social Research and staged a number of plays in New York and elsewhere.

Despite Piscator's pioneering work, Epic Theatre is now associated primarily with Bertolt Brecht (1891–1956), the movement's major theoretician and dramatist. Brecht entered the theatre as a director in Munich and later worked as a *dramaturg* for Reinhardt in Berlin. As a playwright, he experimented with dada and expressionism in such early plays as *Baal* (1918) and *Drums in the Night* (1922) before arriving at his more characteristic style with *Man is Man* (1926). His first major success came with a play he co-wrote with Elizabeth Hauptmann, *The Three-Penny Opera* (1928). With music by Kurt Weill (1900–1950) and settings by Caspar Neher (1897–1962), it ran for 400 performances. In 1933 Brecht went into exile, during which he wrote most of his major works: *Mother Courage and Her Children* (1938–1939), emphasizing both the endurance and the callousness of a woman during the Thirty Years' War; *Galileo* (1937–1939); *The Good Woman of Setzuan* (1938–1940); and

The Caucasian Chalk Circle (1944–1945), Brecht's last major play. Because of his exile, Brecht's works were little produced until he returned to Germany in 1947, but subsequently they became increasingly important throughout the world. Noted Brecht scholar John Fuegi has argued that while Brecht was a remarkable director, most of the dramatic writing for which he took credit was actually done by Elizabeth Hauptmann, Margarete Steffin, Ruth Berlau, or Martin Pohl, but this is an accusation that is still being debated.

Regardless of the outcome of the debate over the authorship of these highly regarded plays, Brecht's theory of theatre has been enormously influential in its own right. Brecht called his approach "epic" in order to indicate its broad sweep and its mixture of narrative and dramatic techniques. He wished to assign audiences an active role in the theatre by making them watch critically rather than passively. Consequently, he arrived at the concept of "alienation" *(verfremdungseffekt),* or making stage events sufficiently strange that the spectator will ask questions about them. To create this thoughtful contemplation and to prevent the spectator from confusing stage events with real-life events, Brecht wanted theatrical means (such as lighting instruments, musicians, scene changes) to be visible and as simple as possible. He also deliberately separated episodes by inserting songs, captions, or narrative passages between them. Brecht hoped to lead the audience to relate what they saw on the stage to socioeconomic conditions outside the

FIG. 18.13
Brecht's *Drums in the Night* at the Kammerspiele in Munich, 1922. Directed by Otto Falckenberg, setting by Otto Reigbert. Courtesy Theatermuseum, Munich.

FIG. 18.14
Brecht's *Threepenny Opera,* first production, at the Theater am Schiffbauerdamm. Berlin, 1928. Directed by Erich Engel, setting by Caspar Neher. Courtesy Theatermuseum, Munich.

theatre; ultimately, he wished the audience to apply its new perceptions by working for change in their own world.

Unlike Appia and Craig, Brecht did not believe that a unified effect should be sought from all the theatrical elements. Calling such unity redundant, he argued that each element should make a different comment on the action. He also rejected Stanislavsky's approach to acting and advised performers to think of their roles "in the third person" and through their acting comment on the characters' motivations and actions. Brecht's theory and practice have profoundly influenced directors throughout the world.

Still another experiment of the 1920s—the Bauhaus—was to have considerable international impact. In 1919, Walter Gropius (1883–1969) established at the Staatliches Bauhaus in Weimar a School of Fine Arts and of Arts and Crafts in which he attempted to break down the traditional barriers between the artist and the craftsman and to unite architecture, painting, sculpture, and other arts into a communal expression. Ultimately the Bauhaus

wished to shape daily surroundings into a "master art work" in which everything from the landscaping to the house, its furnishings, decorations, and even its kitchen utensils are conceived as parts of a total design for living. It sought to make the functional artistic and the artistic functional. It wished to end the elitist status of art, under which it had been confined primarily to museums or the homes of the wealthy, and to make it a part of daily life.

From 1923 until 1929 the Bauhaus's stage workshop was under the direction of Oskar Schlemmer (1888–1943), who was concerned primarily with three-dimensional figures in space. Rather than trying to adjust stage space to the natural human form, he sought to unify the human body with the abstract stage space, and consequently he altered the human shape through three-dimensional costumes that transformed actors into "ambulant architecture" and controlled their movement with mathematical precision. Schlemmer ignored the verbal element, but he systematically analyzed each visual element (empty space, the human figure, movement, light, and color) both in isolation and in various combinations. Like much of the Bauhaus's work, Schlemmer's can probably best be viewed as a form of basic research, the results of which might be applied in various ways to practical problems. Beginning in the 1920s his experiments were especially influential on dance. A painter, Schlemmer also designed scenery for a number of German directors.

In theatre architecture, the Bauhaus's most important work was done by Gropius, who in 1927 designed a "total theatre" for Piscator. Although never built, its design has continued to influence thinking about theatre architecture. According to Gropius, there are only three basic stage forms—arena, thrust, and proscenium—and in his total theatre he sought to accommodate all. He mounted a segment of seats and an acting area on a large revolvable circle forward of the proscenium. When this acting area was moved to a position contiguous with the proscenium, it formed a thrust stage, and when rotated 180 degrees it became an arena. From the wings of the proscenium stage ran an open platform which continued completely around the outer edge of the auditorium, and could be used as an acting area or for scenery shifted on it by means of wagons. A wide stage house also permitted rolling platforms to move horizontally. Spaced around the perimeter of the auditorium were twelve columns between which projection screens could be mounted. A translucent cyclorama at the rear of the proscenium stage also provided a surface for projections, and other screens were mounted in the auditorium above the heads of the spectators. Gropius declared that he wished to place

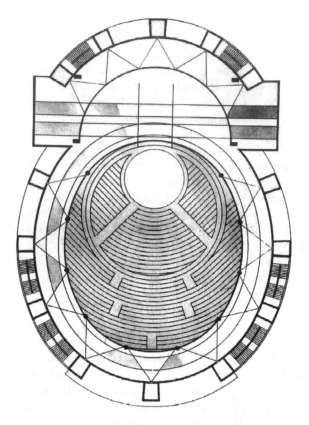

FIG. 18.15

Gropius's "total theatre." Note the gray circle which joins the mainstage to form a thrust stage. This circle, along with the seating shown on the larger circle, could be revolved to place the acting area in the middle of the auditorium to create an arena stage. Note the ramp surrounding the auditorium which also could be used for acting. The triangles represent the beams of projectors which made it possible to surround the audience with projected settings or moving pictures. From Barkhin, *Architectura Teatra* (Moscow, 1947).

the audience in the midst of the action and "to force them to participate in experiencing the play."

The Bauhaus was always controversial, and when the Nazis came to power it was forced to close. Its members dispersed throughout the world, but their influence upon design and architecture (especially furniture, interior decor, and the steel and glass buildings of our cities) became so pervasive that its source is now often unrecognized.

Although Epic Theatre and the Bauhaus now seem the major German contributions of the 1920s, at the time another movement—usually called *Neue Sachlichkeit,* neorealism or new objectivity—dominated the theatre. It came into being around 1923 in reaction to the excesses of expressionism and concentrated in documentary fashion on such mundane problems as the difficulties of adjusting to peacetime, the overly

rigid legal system, and the traumas of adolescence and school life. Unfortunately, though many neorealistic plays were written, few now bear reading. Among the best writers were Friedrich Wolf (1888–1953), with *Cyanide* (1929), an attack on abortion laws, and *The Sailors of Cattaro* (1930), a documentary drama about an uprising in the Austro-Hungarian navy during World War I; and Ferdinand Bruckner (1891–1958), with *The Malady of Youth* (1926), about the disillusionment of young people, and *The Criminals* (1928), which showed a cross-section of an apartment house, whose varied inhabitants break various moral laws. (Bruckner later won international fame with his plays about historical figures, such as *Elizabeth of England.*) The best of the neorealistic writers was Carl Zuckmayer (1896–1977), whose *The Merry Vineyard* (1925), an earthy comedy set against the background of a wine festival, was a resounding success. His most enduring work has been *The Captain of Kopenick* (1931), a satirical treatment of Prussian bureaucracy, showing how a petty criminal takes over a town merely by putting on a military officer's uniform and thereby commanding unquestioning obedience.

With the advent of Hitler in 1933, many important theatre artists left Germany. Many of those who remained underwent what has been called an "inner emigration"—writing or staging historical works or deliberately distancing their work from the contemporary scene. The Nazis encouraged plays about the Teutonic past, enormous outdoor spectacles, and a production style calculated to evoke a grandiose, larger-than-life picture of an all-powerful Nordic world. Theatrical personnel were seldom overtly required to comply with Nazi ideology, and several were able to retain relative independence. For the most part, however, the German theatre between 1933 and 1945 was subordinated to political demands.

THEATRE AND DRAMA IN FRANCE, 1915–1940

World War I severely curtailed theatrical activities in France. Practically all able-bodied actors were inducted and others spent much of their time performing for the armed forces. The Parisian companies were so depleted that even the Comédie Française had to fill out casts with students from the Conservatoire. The wartime mood turned the theatre toward popular entertainment, a direction which continued to dominate the "boulevard theatres" after the war. Of the boulevard producers, the most successful was Sacha Guitry (1885–1957), author of about 150 plays, most of which he produced, directed, and starred in.

At the opposite extreme, a series of revolts against tradition—fauvism, cubism, futurism, constructivism, dada, and surrealism—helped to break the hold of realism and to turn attention to new forms. During the war many artists and political dissenters sought refuge in Switzerland, where dada, the most extreme of the revolts, was launched in 1916 by Hugo Ball, Emmy Hemmings, Richard Hulsenbeck, and others. The principal spokesman for dada was Tristan Tzara (1896–1963), who published seven manifestoes between 1916 and 1920. Dada was grounded in a thoroughgoing skepticism about a world that could produce a global war. Since insanity seemed the world's true state, the dadaists sought in their actions to replace logic and reason with calculated madness, and in their art to substitute discord and chaos for unity, structure, and harmony. They presented a number of programs composed of recitations, "chance" (words arranged in chance order) or "sound" (wordless) poems, dances, visual art, and short plays. Often several things were going on simultaneously. As the war drew to a close, the dadaists dispersed. For a time, the movement thrived in Germany, but it received its greatest support in Paris. But everywhere it had begun to decline by 1920 and shortly afterwards disappeared. Much of what it stood for was to resurface in the 1960s under other names.

In France, dada was absorbed into surrealism, which drew much of its inspiration from the works of Jarry and Apollinaire. Guillaume Apollinaire (1880–1918), friend to almost all *avant-garde* writers and painters after 1900 and the principal spokesman for cubism, influenced surrealism largely through his play, *The Breasts of Tiresias* (1903, revised and produced in 1917), subtitled a "drame surréaliste." Purporting to be a plea for the repopulation of France, the play concerns Thérèse, who after releasing her breasts (balloons, which float away) is transformed into Tiresias. Her husband, now forced to take over her functions, eventually discovers the means of creating children (sheer willpower) and becomes the parent of more than forty thousand offspring. This work exemplifies many of Apollinaire's theories in which he rejected everyday logic and suggested that comedy, tragedy, burlesque, fantasy, acrobatics, and declamation should be mingled with music, dance, color, and light to create a form of expression free from everyday logic.

André Breton (1896–1966) was the acknowledged leader of the surrealists and issued the movement's first "manifesto" in 1924. Freud's considerable influence upon Breton is evident in his definition of surrealism as "pure psychic automatism, by which is intended to express, verbally, in writing, or by other means, the real process of thought. Thought's dictation, in the absence of all control exercised by the reason and outside all esthetic or moral preoccupation." Thus, the subconscious mind in a dreamlike state represented for Breton the source of artistic truth. After his conversion to communism in 1926, Breton sought to make surrealism more militant, and his second manifesto (1929) denounced many of the movement's former members. Thereafter, surrealism declined, although its crowning achievement did not come until 1938, when an international exhibition of painting demonstrated the movement's considerable accomplishments.

Surrealism's impact on the theatre was essentially indirect. The most effective uses of its techniques were made by Jean Cocteau (1892–1963), who began his theatrical work with *Parade* (1917), a ballet staged by the Ballets Russes, and *The Ox on the Roof* (1920), a pantomime performed by the Fratellini family of circus clowns. His finest plays, *Antigone* (1922), *Orpheus* (1926), and *The Infernal Machine* (1934), based on the Oedipus legend, are reworkings of myths. Cocteau's power came in part from his ability to make the mythic seem familiar and the familiar seem mythic. For example, in *Orpheus* the Orpheus and Eurydice of Greek mythology are depicted as a modern married couple, but this commonplace situation soon takes on an air of mystery when a glazier remains suspended in mid-air when a chair on which he has been standing is removed and when a horse speaks oracular messages. Associational patterns create relationships which illuminate both ancient myth and modern values.

Many of the new movements in the visual arts came into the theatre through the Ballets Russes, which after 1915 replaced its Russian designers with such major painters as Picasso, Matisse, Juan Gris,

FIG. 18.16

Cocteau's surrealistic version of *Antigone,* as produced by Charles Dullin at the Atelier, Paris, 1922. From *Le Théâtre* (1923).

Marie Laurencin, and Braque. The Ballets Suédois, which performed in Paris between 1920 and 1925 under the direction of Rolf de Maré (1888–1964), also commissioned settings from Léger, de Chirico, and Picabia. This company extended the traditional conceptions of ballet as well through such works as Cocteau's *The Marriage Party on the Eiffel Tower* (1921), in which dance was accompanied by dialogue and narrative spoken by actors costumed as phonographs.

Of all the *avant-garde* figures between the wars, Antonin Artaud (1896–1948), originally a surrealist, was to be the most important. Associated with the theatre from 1921, Artaud had worked with Lugné-Poë, Dullin, and Pitoëff before founding the Théâtre Alfred Jarry in 1926 in association with Roger Vitrac, a surrealist playwright. Devoted entirely to nonrealistic drama, this theatre lasted only two seasons. Artaud's most significant contributions were to be made after 1931, when the stimulation of a Balinese dance troupe motivated him to formulate his theory of the theatre, published in 1938 as *The Theatre and Its Double*.

According to Artaud, the theatre in the Western world has been devoted to a very narrow range of human experience, primarily the psychological problems of individuals or the social problems of groups. But to Artaud, the more important aspects of existence are those submerged in the unconscious, those things that cause divisions within people and between people and lead to hatred, violence, and disaster. He believed that if given the proper theatrical experiences, people can be freed from ferocity and can then express the joy that civilization has forced them to repress, for the theatre can evacuate those feelings that are usually expressed in more destructive ways. Or, as Artaud put it, "the theatre has been created to drain abscesses collectively."

Artaud was certain that his goals could not be reached through appeals to the rational mind. Rather, it would be necessary to operate directly upon the senses and break down the audience's defenses. Artaud sometimes referred to his as a "theatre of cruelty," since in order to achieve its ends it sought to force the audience to confront itself. Thus, the cruelty he advocated is not primarily physical but moral or psychological.

Artaud's intention to operate directly on the nervous system led him to suggest many innovations in theatrical practice. Among these was the substitution of new myths for outworn dramatic "masterpieces," replacement of the traditional theatre building with remodeled barns, factories, or airplane hangars. He wished to place the audience in the center of the action by locating acting areas in corners, on overhead catwalks, and along the walls. In lighting, he called

for a "vibrating, shredded" effect, and in sound he favored shrillness, abrupt changes in volume, and the use of the human voice to create harmonies and dissonances. Thus, Artaud wanted to assault the audience, to break down its resistance, to purge it morally and spiritually, and he sought to do this through devices "addressed first of all to the senses rather than to the mind," for "the public thinks first of all with its senses."

Like Appia and Craig, Artaud was a visionary rather than a wholly practical man, and like them he was at first little appreciated. But Artaud differed drastically from Appia and Craig in his conception of the theatre's ultimate purpose. Appia and Craig tended to value art for its own sake, whereas Artaud saw in it the salvation of mankind. Theirs is a world of idealized beauty, his a region of cruel torment. Consequently, as the post–World War II view of humanity darkened, the influence of Appia and Craig declined as that of Artaud increased.

Somewhere between the commercial and *avant-garde* figures of France were Gémier, Hébertot, and Copeau. Firmin Gémier (1869–1933) began his acting career with Antoine in 1892 and later worked with groups ranging from the Théâtre de l'Oeuvre to melodrama troupes. Perhaps for this reason, Gémier was to follow an eclectic approach not unlike that of Reinhardt. From 1906 until 1922 he served as director of the Théâtre Antoine, and from 1922 until 1930 as director of the Odéon. Under Gémier, the Odéon became almost an *avant-garde* theatre, in part because his designer, René Fuerst, drew upon practically all of the recent movements. Despite Gémier's fine work as a director, his major contribution probably was his ongoing attempt to bring the theatre to all the people.

The desire to make cultural activities available to the common people had led in the 1890s to the Volksbühnen of Germany and the less ambitious "people's theatres" of France. In 1903 Romain Rolland's *The Theatre of the People* outlined a program under which local groups would write and perform plays for their fellow citizens as in Greek times. Attracted by this movement, Gémier sought to make the best professional productions available to provincial audiences through his Théâtre Ambulant, which between 1911 and 1913 toured through France with a tent theatre. In 1920 Gémier persuaded the government to create the Théâtre National Populaire. Given only a token subsidy, Gémier had to rely on other companies to contribute occasional productions to the TNP. Although it never became a significant force during Gémier's lifetime, the TNP was to become one of France's finest theatres after World War II. Gémier's interests in a popular theatre also led him into other experiments. In 1919 he took over the Cirque d'Hiver, where he staged *Oedipus, King of Thebes* by Bouhélier and *The Great Pastoral,* a Provençal nativity play. In this and other ways, Gémier's work in France paralleled that of Reinhardt in Germany.

Jacques Hébertot (1886–1971) exerted his primary influence as an entrepreneur. In his three contiguous theatres, the Théâtre des Champs-Elysées, the Comédie des Champs-Elysées, and the Studio des Champs-Elysées, between 1920 and 1925, he employed the most imaginative directors of his age. Furthermore, he imported such companies as the Moscow Art Theatre, the Kamerny, and others. Thus, Hébertot made the best of both domestic and foreign theatre available to the Parisian public.

The most pervasive influence on the theatre between the wars was exerted by Jacques Copeau, who reopened the Vieux Colombier in 1919 and rededicated himself to the ideals he had set forth before the war. Unlike Gémier, Copeau thought it impossible to maintain high standards while appealing to the masses. Consequently, he was often accused of snobbery and of treating the theatre as a religion. Eventually, Copeau found it difficult to reconcile his high standards with a full schedule of public performances, and in 1924 he left Paris to open a school in Burgundy, where he hoped to perfect his ideas.

Although Copeau's company performed for only five years after the war, its ideals were to be continued by four other producers—Jouvet, Dullin, Pitoëff, and Baty—who dominated the Parisian theatre until World War II. In 1927 they formed an alliance, commonly called the Cartel des Quatre, under which

FIG. 18.18
Jouvet's production of Molière's *School for Wives,* 1937. Setting by Christian Bérard. From *Décor de Théâtre dans le Monde depuis 1935.*

they agreed to counsel each other, to share publicity, and to negotiate jointly with theatrical unions.

Louis Jouvet (1887–1951) began his career in Rouché's Théâtre des Arts where he met Copeau, for whom he acted minor roles in 1913–1914. Accompanying Copeau to New York in 1917, he remained with him until 1922 when Hébertot employed him as a director. After achieving a major success with Romains' *Dr. Knock* in 1923, Jouvet formed his own company in 1924, taking into it many members of Copeau's recently disbanded troupe. Jouvet did not prosper, however, until 1928, when he began his collaboration with playwright Jean Giraudoux. In 1934 he moved his company to the Théâtre de l'Athénée, a boulevard house, where he remained until 1941, after which he went into voluntary exile until 1945. Jouvet, like Copeau, put primary emphasis on the text. Above all, he respected language and its nuances. He demanded lucid analysis and careful attention to detail from his actors. In the early years he designed his own scenery, which was always tasteful without being innovative. At the Athénée, he usually worked with Christian Bérard (1902–1949), one of the finest designers of the period.

Charles Dullin (1885–1949) had played at many minor theatres before joining Rouché and then Copeau. After returning to Paris in 1919, he worked for Gémier before establishing his own theatre, l'Atelier, in 1922. He remained in this small, out-of-the-way theatre until 1939. Dullin was extremely eclectic, presenting works ranging from the Greeks to the

FIG. 18.17
Stage of the Vieux Colombier as adapted for Shakespeare's *Twelfth Night.* From *Theatre Arts Magazine* (1924).

present and from tragedy to farce. Through painstaking analysis of the text, he sought to let each play dictate the proper approach to it. His aim was to capture the "inner poetry" through honesty and unity. He refused to do any play that he thought depended upon machinery or upon a director's tricks. Nevertheless, he put considerable emphasis on visual design and employed some of the best artists of his time: Louis Touchagues, Lucien Coutaud, Georges Valmier, Jean-Victor Hugo, Michel Duran, and André Barsacq. Music, dance, and mimed spectacle also figured prominently in practically all of his productions. Dullin's perennial hope of attracting a wider audience led him in 1941 to become director of the Théâtre Sarah Bernhardt, a very large house, where he struggled along until 1947. His last years were spent in Geneva as director of the theatre section of the Maison des Arts. Ultimately, Dullin's impact on the theatre was to come in large part through his school, in which such significant later figures as Barrault and Vilar received their early training.

Georges Pitoëff (1884–1939) had performed widely in his native Russia before emigrating to Switzerland in 1914. He and his wife, Ludmilla (1896–1951), who had studied at the Conservatoire, came to Paris in 1922 and worked for Hébertot until 1925, after which they formed their own company, played in a number of Parisian theatres, and toured abroad. Pitoëff was noted for his knowledge of foreign drama, of which he was the principal producer in France. As a director, Pitoëff placed primary emphasis upon the text. For him, the most powerful element was perhaps rhythm, which he sought to find and project for each character and scene. He designed his own scenery, which ranged stylistically from the abstract to the realistically pictorial. Characteristically, however, he used a few indispensable set pieces which he invested with symbolic significance. Of all the members of the Cartel, Pitoëff was probably the most versatile and experimental.

Gaston Baty (1882–1951) was the only member of the Cartel who was not an actor and who did not place primary emphasis on the text. He began his career under Gémier in 1919, managed the Studio des Champs-Elysées from 1924 to 1928, and then settled in the Théâtre Montparnasse in 1930. After 1935, Baty became extremely interested in marionettes, as a result of which his productions became increasingly stylized. Through much of his career Baty was assisted by Marguerite Jamois (1903–1964), who starred in many of his productions and directed others. To Baty, the director was the major theatrical artist. In his productions, a mysterious and poetic world, created by the skillful manipulation of mood, seemed to lurk behind a realistic surface. His emphasis on costumes, scenery, properties, music, and lighting was sometimes criticized, but he was also known as the "magician of the *mise-en-scène*."

In 1930 students from Copeau's school formed the Compagnie des Quinze under the direction of Michel Saint-Denis (1897–1971), Copeau's nephew, and from 1931 to 1933 they played at the Vieux Colombier. After the company disbanded, Saint-Denis opened the Theatre Studio in London, which, in combination with his directing work at the Old Vic and elsewhere, served to carry Copeau's influence into the British theatre. Copeau returned to a more active role in the theatre during the 1930s. In addition to directing both in Paris and abroad, he was associated with the Comédie Française after 1936 and served as its director in 1939–1940 until dismissed by the Vichy government.

Three other directors, Barsacq, Dasté, and Jacquemont, were also to be of considerable importance. André Barsacq (1909–1973) had studied at the School of Decorative Arts and with Dullin before becoming one of Paris's leading scene designers. In 1937, he joined with Dasté and Jacquemont to form the Compagnie des Quatre Saisons, but left in 1940 to assume control of the Atelier when Dullin relinquished it. Barsacq continued to direct that theatre until his death, maintaining Dullin's high standards.

FIG. 18.19

Pitoëff's production of *Romeo and Juliet*. Note the strong emphasis on triangular shapes and converging lines, giving an expressionistic effect. From *Theatre Arts* (1935).

Jean Dasté (1904–), Copeau's son-in-law and pupil, was a member of the Compagnie des Quinze before joining the Compagnie des Quatre Saisons. In 1940 he went with Barsacq to the Atelier, where he was one of the theatre's principal directors. Maurice Jacquemont (1910–) was trained by Chancerel and had worked with several companies before the formation of the Compagnie des Quatre Saisons, with which he continued until 1942. In 1944 he became head of the Studio des Champs-Elysées, a position he was to hold until 1960.

Under Emile Fabré's direction between 1915 and 1936, the Comédie Française had steadily declined, in large part because of low subsidy and political interference. After 1936, the new director, Edouard Bourdet (1887–1945), was able to make many improvements. Not only was the subsidy doubled, Bourdet imported Copeau, Dullin, Jouvet, and Baty to direct several revivals. For the first time in its history, the Comédie Française began to list each play's director on its programs. By the time the war began, the prestige of the company was fully revived.

Although France produced few truly outstanding playwrights between the wars, a number achieved considerable renown. Henri-René Lenormand (1882–1951) was one of the first French writers to emphasize the subconscious mind and the relativity of time and space through such works as *Time Is a Dream* (1919) and *The Eater of Dreams* (1922). Henri Ghéon (1875–1944) sought to revive religious drama and for many years toured with his Compagnons de Notre-Dame. Of his approximately one-hundred plays, the best known are *The Poor Under the Stairs* (1921) and *Christmas in the Market Place* (1935). André Obey (1892–1975) was associated with the Compagnie des Quinze, which produced his first plays, *Noah* and *The Rape of Lucrece,* in 1931. Perhaps his best work is found in *Man of Ashes* (1949), a retelling of the Don Juan story.

Of the satirical writers, the best were Jules Romains (1885–1972), whose *Doctor Knock, or the Triumph of Medicine* (1923) shows the exploitation of people's anxieties about their health, and Marcel Pagnol (1895–1974), whose *The Merchants of Glory* (1925) satirizes the business schemes built around the war dead. Pagnol is now better known for his romantic trilogy about Marseilles waterfront life, *Marius* (1929), *Fanny* (1931), and *César* (1937). Surrealistic farce was exploited by Fernand Crommelynck (1888–1970), whose *The Magnificent Cuckold* (1921) tells of a man who, upon becoming suspicious of his wife's fidelity, insists on testing it endlessly but never to his satisfaction; and Roger Vitrac (1899–1952) who derided all traditional values in *Victor, or Children in Power* (1928). Marcel Achard (1899–1974) excelled in stylized ro-

FIG. 18.20

Baty's production of his own adaptation of *Madame Bovary,* 1936. The set shows a box at the opera. The actors are Lucien Nat and Marguerite Jamois. From *Theatre Arts* (1936).

mantic comedy, notably *Voulez-Vous Jouer avec Moi?* (1923), *Jean de la Lune* (1929), and *The Pirate* (1938), in which, typically, a devoted lover subdues the frivolity of a coquette.

The plays of the Belgian dramatist Michel de Gheldcrode (1898–1962) resemble those of Jarry, the surrealists, and the expressionists, and his theories recall those of Artaud. Throughout his more than thirty plays runs his vision of humans as creatures whose flesh overpowers spirit. Corruption, death, and cruelty are always near the surface, although behind them lurks an implied criticism of degradation and materialism and a call to repentance. Like Artaud, Gheldcrode downgrades language in favor of spectacle. Place is apt to shift rapidly and unexpectedly; characters are usually exaggerated and many are descended from the clowns of music hall, circus, and fair. His scorn for traditional dramaturgy is shown by the labels he applied to his work: "tragic farce," "burlesque mystery," "tragedy for the music hall," and so on. Of his many dramas, the best known are *Escurial* (1927), *Chronicles of Hell* (1929), *Pantagleize* (1929), and *Hop, Signor* (1935). After 1949, when he came to the attention of the absurdists, Gheldcrode's reputation rose considerably.

Probably the most important French dramatist between the wars was Jean Giraudoux (1882–1944), a novelist and member of the Foreign Service, who in

FIG. 18.21
André Barsacq's setting for Dullin's production of
Volpone, 1929. From *Décor de Théâtre dans le Monde
depuis 1935.*

1928 began his theatrical career with a dramatization
of his novel *Siegfried.* In Jouvet, Giraudoux found his
ideal interpreter and he wrote most of his important
works for him: *Amphitryon 38* (1929), *Judith* (1931),
The Trojan War Shall Not Take Place (1935), and *Ondine* (1939). Giraudoux often took his subjects from
familiar sources but gave them novel interpretations,
for he delighted in pointing out the simple in the complex and the surprising in the familiar. His works turn
on antitheses—peace and war, fidelity and infidelity,
life and death, liberty and destiny—and their reconciliations. His dramas take place at the moment when
people are faced with a choice between two contradictory positions; he explores the contradictions and
usually suggests means whereby they can be reconciled, often through some novel perception. Language,
which he considered the highest expression of human
reason, is Giraudoux's primary means. Writing at a
time when the playwright had been subordinated to
the director, Giraudoux sought to reaffirm the literary worth of drama. He wrote in a euphonious and
highly expressive prose, with a marked disposition for
fantasy, irony, and humor. Throughout all his work
runs a deep faith in humanity.

Giraudoux's position of preeminence was to be
challenged after the war by Jean Anouilh (1910–
1987), who began as Jouvet's secretary and turned
to writing in 1932 under Giraudoux's inspiration.
His first success came in 1937 with *Traveller Without
Baggage,* presented by Pitoëff. Most of Anouilh's later
works, such as *Carnival of Thieves* (1938) and *Antigone*
(1943), were produced by Barsacq. Anouilh divided
his plays into the serious, or "black" pieces, and the
comic, or "red" pieces. In the former, typically young,
idealistic, and uncompromising protagonists are able
to maintain their integrity only by choosing death.
Antigone is perhaps the best-known example. In the
"red" plays, although the characters are in many ways
similar, a fairy-tale atmosphere permits a happier resolution. Anouilh was to be one of France's most prolific writers after World War II.

With the coming of war in 1939 and the surren-
der of Paris to the Nazis, theatrical activities were at
first seriously curtailed. Some major figures went into
exile and those who remained were subject to close
surveillance. For the most part, the theatre was reduced to politically inoffensive plays or popular entertainments, but a few productions were to attain
true eminence despite all strictures.

ITALIAN THEATRE
AND DRAMA, 1915–1940

Many major Italian artists during the interwar years
were adherents of futurism, a movement launched in
Italy in 1909 by Filippo Tommaso Marinetti
(1876–1944). Like the expressionists, the futurists rejected the past and wished to transform humanity.
But, whereas the expressionists associated the past
with soul-destroying materialism and industrialism,
the futurists deplored the veneration of the past as a
barrier to progress. Consequently, they glorified the
energy and speed of the machine age and sought to
embody them in artistic forms. From 1910 onward
they gave performances during which they read their
manifestoes, gave concerts, read poems, performed
plays, and exhibited works of visual art—at times several of these simultaneously. Sometimes they moved
about among the spectators, using various parts of a
room sequentially or concurrently. They especially
outraged audiences with their demand that libraries
and museums be destroyed as the first step toward
creating a more dynamic future.

Among the art forms championed by the futurists were "picture poems" (or concrete poetry), kinetic sculptures, collages, and *bruitisme* (or "dynamic
music," based on the sounds of everyday life). As
for theatre, they denounced past practices and declared music halls, nightclubs, and circuses to be better models on which to base future forms. They
found earlier drama too lengthy, analytic, and static
and proposed instead a "synthetic drama" which
would compress into a moment or two the essence
of a dramatic situation. In 1915–1916 they published
seventy-six of these short plays.

During World War I futurism lost many followers because it glorified war as the supreme example

FIG. 18.22
Giraudoux's *The Trojan War Shall Not Take Place,* directed by Jouvet, who is seen at right. From *Theatre Arts* (1936).

of energy. After the war it received new vitality, perhaps because many of its tenets were compatible with Mussolini's program of aggressive action. The principal exponent of futurism in the 1920s was Enrico Prampolini (1894–1960), who demanded that the painted scene be replaced by "stage architecture that will move." He also wished to substitute luminous forms for human actors. He conceived of the stage as a multidimensional space in which spiritual forces (represented by light and abstract forms) would play out a drama of semi-religious significance.

After 1930 interest in futurism declined. Though it never became a major theatrical movement, it pioneered innovations that would be revived and extended in the 1960s: (1) the attempt to rescue theatrical art from a museum-like atmosphere; (2) direct confrontation and intermingling of performers and audiences; (3) the exploitation of modern technology to create multimedia performances; (4) the use of simultaneity and multiple focus; (5) an antiliterary and alogical bias; and (6) the breaking down of barriers between arts.

During World War I, a new school of writing, usually called "the theatre of the grotesque," appeared in Italy. Its name was derived from *The Mask and the Face* (1916), "a grotesque in three acts," by Luigi Chiarelli (1880–1947). Turning upon the contrast between public and private role-playing, this comedy tells the story of a man who, after confessing to the murder of his wife because he thought her unfaithful, is tried and acquitted, although in actuality she is merely locked up at home.

Luigi Pirandello (1867–1936) was by far the greatest Italian playwright of the period. After winning fame with his novels and short stories, Pirandello turned to playwriting in 1910 and after 1915 devoted himself increasingly to the theatre. From 1924 to 1928 he headed the Art Theatre of Rome, where he presented many significant Italian and foreign plays. Here he was assisted by Marta Abba (1906–1988), who played leading roles, and a company which included Ruggero Ruggeri (1871–1954), one of Italy's most respected actors.

Pirandello's plays, of which the best are *Right You Are—If You Think You Are* (1916), *Six Characters in Search of an Author* (1921), *Henry IV* (1922), *Naked* (1922), *Each in His Own Way* (1924), *Tonight We Improvise* (1930), and *As You Desire Me* (1930), usually turn upon a question of fact that cannot be resolved because each character has his own version of the truth. Thus, Pirandello raises doubts about the validity of the scientific approach to truth—the direct observation of reality. He seems to suggest that "truth" is necessarily personal and subjective.

Pirandello was also concerned about the relationship between art and nature. Since nature demands continual change and since a work of art is fixed forever, he found the theatre the most satisfying form of art, for it necessarily differs at each performance. Thus, he likened the theatre to a living statue. Since for him even the most realistic play could only give a travesty of truth, he thought the only remedy lay in writing philosophical plays that show reality as ever changing. Pirandello made a profound impression on his age. Perhaps no other writer did so much to popularize the philosophical view that was to be espoused by dramatists of the post-World War II period.

Italy's most eclectic director between the wars was Anton Guilio Bragaglia (1890–1960), who from 1922

FIG. 18.23
A futurist pantomime, *The Merchant of Hearts,* by Enrico Prampolini. Théâtre de la Pantomime Futuriste, Paris, 1927. Note the mingling of performers with various nonhuman shapes and forms.

to 1936 ran the Teatro degli Independenti in Rome, where on a tiny stage he presented a wide-ranging program of works by Strindberg, Wedekind, Jarry, Maeterlinck, Pirandello, and others, including the futurists. He strongly opposed the star system and sought to create an integrated ensemble. From 1937 to 1943 he was director of the Teatro della Arti, where he presented a repertory of modern world drama.

For the most part, however, the Italian theatre was made up of touring companies playing the latest hits. A step toward improvement was taken in 1936 with the formation of the Academy of Dramatic Art in Rome under the direction of Silvio D'Amico (1887–1955). Here the principles of Stanislavsky, Copeau, and Reinhardt were taught. The coming of the war interrupted the academy's work, however, and its impact was not to be felt until after 1945.

THEATRE AND DRAMA IN SPAIN, 1915–1940

In the years between 1915 and 1940 the most significant Spanish drama of the immediate postwar years was written by Unamuno and Valle-Inclán. Miguel de Unamuno (1864–1936), one of Spain's most respected philosophers, first expressed his theory of drama in *The Tragic Sense of Life* (1913). His declaration that tragedy stems from a conflict between the human desire for immortality and skepticism about its possibility was to contribute much to existentialist drama following World War II. Because of censorship, Unamuno's eleven plays, among them *Fedra* (1918) and *Dream Visions* (1920), were not widely produced until after 1950. Similarly, the plays of Ramón del Valle-Inclán (1866–1936), perhaps because of their similarity to absurdist drama, only later came to the fore. Valle-Inclán, noted primarily as a novelist, wrote several verse plays, satirical dramas, and farces, of which the best are probably *Divine Words* (1913), *The Horns of Don Friolera* (1921), and *Bohemian Lights* (1929). Valle-Inclán labeled his method *esperpento,* or a systematic deformation designed to show the grotesque reality beneath the surface of Spanish life.

A new spirit began to enter Spanish literature with the "Generation of '27," a group which blossomed especially after censorship was eased under the second Republic, proclaimed in 1931. Of the new dramatists, the most significant were Lorca and Casona. Federico García Lorca (1899–1936) wrote his first play, *The Butterfly's Crime,* in 1920. After its failure, he cultivated his interests in symbolism, surrealism, music, painting, and Spanish folklore, and wrote a number of puppet plays. Following the performance of his *Mariana Pineda* in Barcelona in 1927 by Margarita Xirgu

(1888–1969), one of Spain's leading actresses, Lorca resumed an active interest in the theatre.

But Lorca's major plays were written only after he had worked closely with a theatre group, La Barraca, a troupe composed of university students and subsidized by the government under its program to bring cultural events to the people. Formed in 1932, La Barraca played Golden Age dramas to rural audiences, and it was the enthusiastic response of these unsophisticated spectators that influenced Lorca to turn to similar themes of love and honor. The results are seen in *Blood Wedding* (1933), *Yerma* (1934), and *The House of Bernarda Alba* (1935). Blending poetic imagery with primitive passions, these plays are usually considered the finest Spanish works since the Golden Age.

In many ways, the career of Alejandro Casona (1903–1966) paralleled that of Lorca. Between 1931 and 1936, he too directed a government-sponsored troupe, The People's Theatre, which toured Spanish villages. Casona's troupe played primarily short, humorous plays, but like Lorca, Casona was inspired by his experiences to write for this audience. *The Siren Washed Ashore* (1934) and *Next Time the Devil* (1935) show that blend of realism and fantasy for which Casona was to be noted. In all his works an air of optimism suggests that human problems can be solved.

The Civil War of 1936 brought profound changes. Lorca was killed and Casona emigrated. During the war, the theatre served primarily as an instrument of propaganda for both sides of the conflict, and following the victory of Franco's forces it suffered from severe censorship. The plays of Lorca, Casona, and Unamuno were forbidden, and the Spanish theatre entered another period of isolation.

THEATRE AND DRAMA IN LATIN AMERICA

Throughout Latin America, commercial theatres in the early twentieth century continued to be dominated by late nineteenth-century Spanish and French traditions of light comedy, musicals, and melodrama. They were also dependent on tours by European acting companies. The First World War brought these tours to an end and opened the way for an independent theatre movement much like that seen in Europe a generation before. It was mid-century, however, before most countries in Latin America could claim the beginnings of a distinctive national theatre of their own.

Argentina was one of the first to lay the foundations for an identifiable national theatre. Over 200 shows by local writers, ranging from short farce comedies to serious full-length plays, were produced in its "glorious decade" of 1904–1914. But the period was best know for the triumph of *género chico* and naturalism. *Género chico* dramas were short plays, often with musical scores, which presented a sentimental view of the life of the lower classes. These plays lent themselves to a focus on local color and were therefore popular throughout Latin America, especially in Argentina where, by 1914, they took on their own distinctive form as *sainete orillero* and dominated the commercial theatre market. The best-known writer of this form was Alberto Vacarezza (1888–1939). The naturalist plays were full length and far less sentimental. Florencio Sánchez (1875–1910), born in Uruguay but working mostly in Argentina, became the most highly regarded naturalist dramatist in Latin America during this period. He wrote more than twenty full-length plays. His best-known works, *My Son the Lawyer, The Immigrant Girl, The Newspaper Boy* (all 1904), *Down the Gully* (1905), *Evicted* (1906), and *The Tigress* (1907), are examinations of the conflict between the old rural system, which was rapidly being destroyed by accelerating immigration, and urbanization, with its resultant poverty and degradation of the human spirit. He was surrounded by a host of lesser writers in Buenos Aires, the most accomplished being Alfonsina Storni (1892–1938), who with plays like *Cimbelina* (1900) showed herself to be the most *avant-garde* dramatist of her day, and Gregorio de Laferrère (1867–1928), author of such important satiric plays as *Summer Lunatics* (1905) and *The Barranco Women* (1908). The most versatile and prolific Argentine author of the period, however, was Enrique Garcia Velloso (1880–1938), who is credited with over 200 plays in a variety of styles, the best known of which are *Gabino the Tram Conductor* (1898) and *Eclipse of the Sun* (1904).

Around the time of the First World War, theatres were started by immigrant communities, unions, and social welfare organizations. Out of the experiences of these people came *grotesco criollo,* a form that blended the short comic *sainete orillero* with the lack of sentimentality found in the plays of the naturalists. Armando Discépolo (1887–1971) is credited with initiating this form with *Mateo* (1923), in which he looks at the destroyed dreams of an immigrant community where the dominant social order ceases to function.

El Teatro del Pueblo (The People's Theatre), founded by Leónidas Barletta in 1925, soon became the leading independent theatre of the time, producing such plays as *Saverio the Cruel* (1936), *The Creator of Ghosts* (1936), and *The Desert Island* (1938), all experiments in expressionism by the famous novelist Roberto Arlt (1900–1942). Independent theatres also introduced the country to the works of Cocteau, Pirandello, and O'Neill. Eventually over 50 such theatres were created in Argentina, and many similar companies could be found all over Latin America. As the Depression came to South America during the early 1930s, governments began to subsidize some theatres, and Argentina's Teatro de la Comedia (1936), which became the Teatro Municipal de Buenos Aires in 1943, was an early model for the effective partnership of government and the arts in Latin America.

The development of a national theatre in Brazil was hampered by its continued dedication to French cultural inspiration. This was epitomized by the Amazon Theatre at Manaus, the provincial capital of Amazonia. There, 900 hundred miles into the Amazon jungle, a spectacular French opera house was built by wealthy local rubber plantation owners in 1896. To underscore its French inspiration, the ceiling of the auditorium was painted to represent a vision of the heavens being viewed from beneath the Eiffel tower. The theatre had 250 seats at orchestra level and 450 seats distributed among its 90 boxes, arranged in three tiers. Many of the best touring shows of the time were brought to this frontier mecca until the rubber boom ended in the early 1920s, but it did nothing to encourage the development of an indigenous theatre. (Nonetheless, the Amazon Theatre became a national treasure in 1965.) Because of this strong French influence, reviews (*revistas*) were enormously popular. They contained considerable political satire until the Vargas dictatorship began censoring them in 1937.

Although in other areas of the arts Brazilians were in the forefront of experimentation with expressionism, futurism, surrealism, and other antirealist forms, such experiments had little impact on the nation's theatre. Independent theatres like the Teatro de Brinquedo, founded by Álvaro Moreyra in the early 1920s, and the Colméia (1922) struggled on without much immediate effect. Oswald de Andrade's (1890–1954) *King of the Candle* was perhaps the most highly regarded modernist script of its day, but it was not performed even by these independent groups. *May God Recompense You* (1932) by Joracy Camargo (1898–1973), by contrast, was the most successful Brazilian play of the period. It evoked a strongly leftist examination of bourgeois values that was extremely popular throughout South America at this time, but it was in all other respects a very traditional thesis play. Pedro Bloch (1914–) was equally conventional though heavily influenced by Pirandello, but his plays were performed on Broadway in the early 1950s and some became the basis for early soap operas on Brazilian television.

It was not until 1940, with the establishment of Os Comediantes, that nonrealistic techniques of staging, design, and dramaturgy began to meet with some success. When the Polish director Zbigniew Ziembinski joined the company in 1941, he was able to bring first-hand experience with German expressionism to the Brazilian stage. His production of *The Wedding Gown* (1943) by Nelson Rodrigues (1912–1980), now considered Brazil's greatest dramatist, is generally said to mark the beginning of modern Brazilian theatre. The production innovations of the Os Comediantes were reinforced by other early independent theatres such as the Teatro de Amadores de Pernambuco, Teatro Universitário, Teatro do Estudante do Brazil, and Teatro Experimental do Negro, the first black theatre in the country. As in Argentina, these were followed by a whole host of others, the most influential of which was the Teatro Brasileiro de Comédia (TBC), which opened in São Paulo in 1948, then opened a second company in the much more conservative market of Rio de Janeiro in 1954.

The development of theatre in Mexico was delayed by the revolution of 1910, which was followed by a succession of reformist governments that were unable to bring any real stability to the political situation until the election of Lázaro Cárdenas in 1934, though the worst of the turmoil was over by 1920. The Teatro National in Mexico City was a perfect symbol of this arrested development. In 1900 it was torn down as part of a major urban renewal project. Rebuilding began in 1905, but political unrest delayed its completion until 1934 and it was not to house a resident national theatre company until 1974. The venerable Teatro Principal was renovated in 1900 but by the late 1920s was reduced to being open only on weekends, and when it was destroyed by fire in 1931 it was not rebuilt. Several smaller theatres were constructed both in the capital and in the provinces before the revolution, including the state-of-the-art Teatro-Circo Xicoténcarl (1912), which was the only one to open during the revolutionary years. But the most noticeable trend in the first half of the twentieth century was for theatres to be converted into cinemas, and this was true worldwide.

Zarzuela and short comedies continued to dominate the commercial theatres both before and during the protracted revolutionary period. As in the other countries of Latin America, naturalistic plays were the most successful form of legitimate drama. Marcelino Dávalos (1871–1923) was the naturalistic playwright who was most dedicated to using Mexican settings. His plays, from *Guadalupe* (1903) to *So They Go By* (1908) to *The Old* (1911) and *Eagles and Stars* (1916), are all social critiques of Mexican life. But it was *The Revenge of the Soil* (1904), by Federico Gamboa (1864–1939), that most highlighted the grievances of the lower classes which lay at the heart of the coming revolution.

In the 1920s there was a revival of interest in pre-Columbian and folk performance in Mexico. Both the Teatro Folklórico and the open-air theatre at San Juan Teotihuacán, used for the staging of pre-Columbian dance, were established in 1921. The Teatro del Murciélago (Theatre of the Bat) was created in 1923 to foster indigenous dance and music. Under the Secretaría de Educación Pública, additional open-air theatres were built in the provinces for the educational programs of its Misiones Culturales, which promoted folk drama for teaching purposes. But the legitimate stage of the 1920s was generally recognized as being at a very low ebb.

A number of companies set themselves the task of reforming Mexican theatre during this time. As early as 1923, the well-known actor-manager María Tereza Montoya (1898–1974) secured a municipal subsidy to stage a season of Mexican plays. In 1925 seven Mexican dramatists known as the *Grupo de los Siete Autores* dedicated themselves to writing plays inspired by the European *avant-garde*. Most of the plays of this group were produced by Comedia Mexicana, founded by playwright Amalia González Caballero de Castillo Ledón in 1922 (though it did not become a significant producing organization for several years.) The group of seven were not the most successful dramatists produced by the Comedia Mexicana, however. Its production of *Father Merchant* (1929), by Carlos Díaz Dufoo (1861–1941), was its greatest success, becoming the first Mexican play to achieve a run of 100 performances.

The most influential work in experimental theatre in Mexico was started in 1928 by the Teatro de Ulises, founded by Xavier Villaurrutia (1903–1950) and Salvador Novo (1904–1974), both extremely important playwrights, directors, and educators, with the financial support and inspiration of the heiress and playwright Antonieta Rivas Mercado (1900–1931). It was followed, after Mercado's suicide, by the Teatro de Orientación, founded by Celestino Gorostiza (1904–1967) in 1932. This organization produced a great many plays of the European *avant-garde* in Mexican Spanish translation. It also secured significant state subsidy for a training program that taught many of the theatre artists who were to dominate the next generation. The two most important figures involved in this theatre, however, were Villaurrutia, and Rodolfo Usigli (1905–1979), who both wrote and directed for the company. Villaurrutia and Usigli had studied at Yale with George Pierce Baker. Villaurrutia returned to write plays that focused on the *avant-garde's* concern with the subconscious mind and complex human relationships. He wrote his five *Profane Acts* (1933–1937) while working for the Teatro de Orientación, along with a number of middle-class comedies including *The Absent One, The Moment Has Arrived,* and *Be Brief* (all 1934). But his most important works, *Invitation to Death* (1940) and *The Ivy* (1941), were written between the closing of that theatre and the opening of his own Teatro de Mexico (1943). Villaurrutia was the most experimental antirealist of his day but he also, with plays like *The Ivy,* an adaptation of Euripides' *Hippolytus,* began a vogue for adaptations of Greek classics among Latin American authors. Usigli was less experimental but more aggressively independent as a writer-director. He was concerned with the social problems that he believed arose out of the nation's lack of confidence, a lack he blamed on Mexico's colonial past. The subjugation of women was an especially egregious consequence of that past and led to a kind of sexual hypocrisy that was the focus of much of his sardonic wit. His play, *The Gesticulator* (sometimes called *The Imposter,* written in 1937 but not produced until 1947), deals with a second-rate history professor who pretends to be an important revolutionary leader long presumed dead. It is an indictment of the inability of people to live life without playing a role but was interpreted by many of his contemporaries as a criticism of the revolution and was therefore banned shortly after it opened. Today it is considered one of the most important of modern Mexican plays. Another of his plays to be produced in 1947, *The Crown of Shadows* (1943), is also considered to be a classic of Mexican theatre. In it, he examines the theme of history's influence on the present by looking at the downfall of the Emperor Maximilian. He took up this theme again with *Crown of Fire* (1960), dealing with the Aztec emperor Cuahutemoe, and *Crown of Light* (1963), concerning the Virgin of Guadalupe. He wrote thirty-nine plays in all, including *The Apostle* (1931), *Women Don't Work Miracles* (1939), and *Another Spring Time* (1945). He founded the Teatro de Medianoche in 1940, with the declared purpose of operating without a subsidy, but the experiment failed after one season. Usigli was also an important drama critic, an influential university professor, a diplomat, and the author of several important histories of theatre in Mexico.

Another dominant figure of the 1930s was Julio Bracho, who formed a series of experimental theatres and managed not only to secure one of the first state subsidies for such an organization but also to tour the provinces with the first experimental company to be seen there. In the 1940s the major figure was Seki Santo (1905–1966), a young Japanese director who had studied with Stanislavski and worked with Meyerhold for five years before immigrating to Mexico in 1939. He founded the Teatro de la Reforma (1948) dedicated to "theatre of the people for the people," which inspired a number of imitators. Santo inspired and helped to train many of those who would lead Mexican theatre in the second half of the century.

The theatres in other Latin American countries generally followed similar patterns of development to those outlined here, though many of them progressed more slowly and were still focused on naturalism and light comedy well into the 1950s.

LOOKING AT THEATRE HISTORY

One of the ways of studying theatre history is through the theories of art that lie behind practice. Perhaps for no period is this more helpful than the twentieth century, which has seen artistic movements come and go with bewildering rapidity. The proliferation was especially evident between 1910 and 1925, and many movements of that time introduced ideas and techniques that were to resurface in the 1960s. Because they are often based on unfamiliar premises, modern artistic movements have frequently seemed merely perverse, bizarre, or incomprehensible to those unaware of their goals. If we are to understand artistic movements, therefore, we must explore the theoretical premises that underlie them. Only then will we see why they depict human experience as they do and why the techniques they employ are consistent with their intent. Understanding may not cause us to admire the artistic products, but it will prevent us from reaching uninformed judgments. It will also help us understand the forces that have given rise to the extreme variety in modern theatre, where "newness" often seems an artistic principle and major goal.

Immediately following World War I, the movement with the greatest impact on theatre was expressionism. An excellent overview of the movement can be gained from John Willett's *Expressionism* (New York, 1970), but little of the theory has been translated into English. Here are some excerpts from a statement written by Yvan Goll in 1918 about his vision of a new "superdrama":

[Expressionism will depict] man's battle against everything that is thinglike and animallike around and within him. . . . The writer must recognize that there are realms quite different from that of the five senses. . . . His first task will be to destroy all external form. . . . Man and objects will be stripped as clean as possible and looked at through a magnifying glass for greater effect. . . . The theatre must not restrict itself to "real" life; it will become "superreal" when it learns what lies behind things. Pure realism was the worst mistake ever made in literature. . . . Art, if it wishes to educate, improve, or be effective in any way, must destroy everyday man . . . to make him become once more the child he once was. The easier way to do this is through the grotesque. . . . Consequently, the new theatre must use technological means that are equivalent to the ancient mask . . . the phonograph to distort the voice, masks . . . which typify through . . . physical distortions [equivalent to] the inner distortions of the plot. . . . We are searching for the Superdrama.

Yvan Goll, Preface to *The Immortal Ones* (Cologne, 1920).

The futurists made less immediate impact than the expressionists, but in their manifestoes they set forth ideas that were harbingers of future developments. Here are some excerpts from a manifesto that glorifies the variety theatre.

Futurism exalts the Variety Theatre because: . . .
4. The Variety Theatre is unique today in its use of cinema which enriches it with an incalculable number of visions and otherwise unrealizable spectacles. . . .
5. The Variety Theatre . . . naturally generates what I call "the Futurist marvelous," produced by modern mechanics [which includes] all the new significations of light, sound, noise, and language, with their mysterious and inexplicable extensions into the least-explored part of our sensibility. . . .
8. The Variety Theatre is alone the audience's collaboration. It doesn't remain static like a stupid voyeur. . . . The action develops simultaneously on the stage, in the boxes, and in the orchestra.
16. The Variety Theatre destroys all our conceptions of perspective, proportion, time, and space. . . .

"The Variety Theatre," September 29, 1913. From *Marinetti, Selected Writings*, edited and with an introduction by R. W. Flint (New York: Farrar, Straus and Giroux, 1971), 116–122.

The most influential theoreticians of the theatre between the two world wars were Bertolt Brecht and Antonin Artaud. They were united in their dislike for conventional, realistic theatre, but divided in their conceptions of the ideal theatre. Brecht's theories took shape over many years. (His theoretical writings have been collected in John Willett's *Brecht on Theatre*.) Perhaps the most systematic statement of his views is found in "A Short Organum for the Theatre." In it, Brecht states his dislike for the traditional theatre which lulls the spectator into a belief that social conditions are fixed, and he proposes to replace it with one which distances ("alienates") the audience from the stage events in such a way as to make it judge them critically:

42. . . . A representation that alienates is one which allows us to recognize its subject, but at the same time makes it seem unfamiliar . . .
43. . . . The new alienations are only designed to free socially-conditioned phenomena from that stamp of familiarity which protects them from our grasp today.
47. In order to produce A-effects the actor has to discard whatever means he has learnt of getting the audience to identify itself with the characters which he plays. . . .
48. At no moment must he go so far as to be wholly transformed into the character played. . . . He has just to show the character. . . .
74. So let us invite all the sister arts of the drama, not in order to create an "integrated work of art" in which they all offer themselves up and are lost, but so together with the drama they may further the common task in their different ways; and their relations with one another consist in this: that they lead to mutual alienation.

"A Short Organum for the Theatre," *Brecht on Theatre*, trans. by John Willett (New York: Hill and Wang, 1964), 179–205.

Brecht later sought to clarify his position on alienation in acting with this note:

The contradiction between acting (demonstration) and experience (empathy) often leads the uninstructed to suppose that only one or the other can be manifest in the work of the actor (as if the Short Organum concentrated entirely on acting and the old tradition entirely on experience). In reality it is a matter of two mutually hostile processes which fuse in the actor's work. . . . His particular effectiveness comes from the tussle and tension of the two opposites, and also from their depth.

"Appendices to the Short Organum," *Brecht on Theatre*, 276–281.

Artaud's major essays on theatre were collected in *The Theatre and Its Double* (1938). Here are some excerpts from one of the essays, "Theatre of Cruelty, First Manifesto":

The theatre will never find itself again . . . except by furnishing the spectator with the truthful precipitates of dreams, in which his taste for crime, his erotic obsessions, his savagery, his chimeras, his utopian sense of life and matter, even his cannibalism, pour out, on a level not counterfeit and illusory, but interior. . . .

Every spectacle will contain . . . cries, groans, apparitions, surprises, theatricalities of all kinds, . . . costumes taken from certain ritual models; resplendent lighting, incantational beauty of voices, . . . physical rhythm of movements whose crescendo and decrescendo will accord exactly with the pulsation of movements familiar to everyone. . . .

We abolish the stage and the auditorium and replace them by a single site, without partition or barrier of any kind. . . . A direct communication will be reestablished between the spectator and the spectacle, . . . from the fact that the spectator placed in the middle of the action, is engulfed and physically affected by it.

There will not be any set. . . .

We shall not act a written play, but we shall make attempts at direct staging, around themes, facts, or known works. . . .

Without an element of cruelty at the root of every spectacle, the theatre is not possible. In our present state of degeneration it is through the skin that metaphysics must be made to re-enter our minds. . . .

Antonin Artaud, *The Theatre and Its Double*, trans. M. C. Richards (New York: Grove Press, 1958).

19

English-Language Theatre in the Early Twentieth Century

World War I brought many changes to the English theatre. The actor-manager system all but disappeared, to be replaced by the commercial producer and the long run. Tree's theatre, for example, the home of Shakespeare since 1900, was by 1916 given over to *Chu Chin Chow,* a musical version of *Ali Baba and the Forty Thieves,* which ran for 2,238 performances. After World War I, the United States began to establish itself as an international power. It also began to produce playwrights and other theatre personnel who won widespread respect in Europe for the first time. The theatres of Canada, Australia, and New Zealand, on the other hand, continued the search for their own identities.

ENGLISH THEATRE AND DRAMA, 1915–1940

Probably the most significant occurrence of the war years was the emergence of the "Old Vic" as the principal producer of English classics. Built in 1818 as the Royal Coburg and later renamed the Royal Victoria, the Old Vic was taken over in 1880 by Emma Cons, a social reformer, who converted it into a "temperance music hall." In 1897 Miss Cons' niece, Lilian Baylis (1874–1937) came to assist her aunt and became manager of the Old Vic when Cons died in

1912, the same year in which the Old Vic was licensed as a theatre (rather than a music hall), and thereafter it presented both plays and operas. It was not until 1914, however, that Shakespeare's plays became the focus of the dramatic repertory. During the war years, the mounting of plays was under the direction of Ben Greet (1857–1936) who, in the tradition of Frank Benson, had long been touring Shakespearean works in highly simplified settings to both English and American audiences.

After the war, Greet was succeeded by Robert Atkins (1886–1972) from 1920 to 1925, Andrew Leigh (1887–1957) until 1929, and Harcourt Williams (1880–1957) until 1934. During these years, all of Shakespeare's plays were presented, some several times. In 1931 the Old Vic acquired the Sadler's Wells Theatre, and a ballet company was formed under the direction of Ninette de Valois (Edris Stannis, 1898–2001), who had been trained in the Diaghilev company and had later established her own school. Between 1931 and 1935, the opera and ballet company and the dramatic company alternated between the Old Vic and Sadler's Wells. When this arrangement became too cumbersome, drama was confined to the Old Vic, and opera and ballet to Sadler's Wells. The Sadler's Wells Ballet Company was to become the finest in England and was rechristened the Royal Ballet after World War II, and its opera

452

troupe developed into the present-day English National Opera.

When Miss Baylis died in 1937, it was feared that the Old Vic would close, but Tyrone Guthrie (1900–1971) was appointed administrator and operated it with distinction until 1945. Guthrie had made his debut as an actor in 1924, but had soon turned to directing. His first London production came in 1931, but his finest prewar work was done with the Old Vic. As a director, Guthrie was noted for his novel interpretations of standard works (sometimes considered merely bizarre by critics), and for the restless but vital quality of stage movement in his productions. By 1939 the Old Vic was the most respected troupe in England. With its own theatre, a permanent company, and a policy of producing the finest plays at reasonable prices, it set a standard for the entire country.

Several other producers in London helped to raise the level of performance between the wars. Among these, the most important were the Lyric Theatre and the Gate Theatre. The Lyric Theatre, Hammersmith, one of the many houses built in the suburbs during the heyday of music halls, had fallen upon hard times when Nigel Playfair (1874–1934) leased it in 1918. Although Playfair presented many kinds of plays, his reputation rests upon his productions of Restoration and eighteenth-century works, most notably *The Beggar's Opera* (which opened in 1920 for a run of 1,463 performances), *The Way of the World* (1924), *The Rivals* (1925), *The Beaux' Stratagem* (1927), and *Love in a Village* (1928). Most of his productions were decorative, stylized caricatures. For a time, the Lyric was the most fashionable theatre in London, but as Playfair's approach hardened into a formula, popularity declined, and in 1932 the company was dissolved. The Lyric was noted above all for its sense of style, first established by Claud Lovat Fraser (1890–1921), whose sensitive use of color and period motifs profoundly influenced others.

The Gate Theatre was opened in 1925 by Peter Godfrey (1899–1971), a former circus clown and Shakespearean actor. Unable to secure a license for the only hall he could afford, Godfrey ran his theatre as a private club. In nine years, he produced over 350 plays. His most characteristic productions were of expressionist plays or those with a psychoanalytic bias. Using set pieces against black drapes, unusual lighting effects, and stylized acting techniques, Godfrey was the principal exponent of expressionism in London. In 1934 the Gate Theatre passed to Norman Marshall (1901–1980), who presented many works forbidden by the censor. He also did much to reestablish the intimate revue, which had declined since the 1920s.

FIG. 19.1
The Norwich Players in *As You Like It* (1921), the inaugural production at The Maddermarket Theatre, Norwich, England. Walter Nugent Monck director.

Of the several important groups outside of London, perhaps the best was the Birmingham Repertory Company, which, under Barry Jackson's (1879–1961) direction between 1913 and 1935, produced about 400 plays ranging through the entire history of drama. Between 1922 and 1934, Jackson also presented 42 plays in London, many remarkably successful despite their departure from commercial formulas. Through his productions of *Hamlet* (1925), *Macbeth* (1928), and *Taming of the Shrew* (1928), Jackson began the vogue for playing Shakespeare in modern dress. When Jackson transferred ownership of his theatre to the City of Birmingham in 1935, it became England's first civic theatre.

Jackson also founded the Malvern Festival in 1929, thereby giving considerable impetus to the summer festival movement. Operated primarily by the Birmingham Repertory Company until 1939, the Malvern Festival had no clear policy, some seasons being devoted to plays of a particular era, others to plays by specific authors, especially Shaw. All, however, were of high quality. The festival was discontinued between 1939 and 1949.

The Norwich Players (1910–) were perhaps the most influential of the many amateur experimental groups that developed during these years (known as "little theatres" in the United States). They were led by Walter Nugent Monck (1878–1958), a professional

FIG. 19.2
The Old Vic's production of *The Tempest,* 1934. At rear, Charles Laughton as Prospero; front left, Elsa Lanchester as Ariel. Courtesy Debenham Collection, British Theatre Museum, London.

FIG. 19.3
Lyric Theatre, Hammersmith, production of *The Beggar's Opera.* Setting by Claud Lovat Fraser. The arch unit remained throughout and set pieces were changed behind it. Courtesy Theatre Museum, Victoria and Albert Museum, London.

director who had trained with William Poel and had worked for W. B. Yeats at the Abbey Theatre in Dublin, from 1911 through 1913. In 1921 Monck built the Maddermarket Theatre in Norwich, the first theatre to be modeled on an Elizabethan indoor playhouse. In it, he successfully applied Poel's theories on staging to a remarkable variety of plays, influencing such directors as W. Bridges-Adams, Nigel Playfair, Barry Jackson, and Tyrone Guthrie. By 1929, when the Norwich Players presented *Everyman* at the first Canterbury Festival, they were internationally famous. Hugh Hunt (1911–1993) directed the Norwich Players for the 1933 and 1934 seasons before going to the Abbey Theatre in 1935, the Bristol Old Vic in 1946, and Old Vic in 1949. (In 1955 Hunt became the first director of the Elizabethan Theatre Trust in Sydney Australia.) By the start of World War II, however, the period of greatest influence for amateur groups like the Norwich Players was over.

Two provincial troupes—the Cambridge Festival Theatre and the Oxford Repertory Company—were also outstanding. The Cambridge Festival Theatre was established by Terence Gray in 1926 with the avowed purpose of undermining realistic acting and production, a policy that was followed consistently. The theatre had no curtain, proscenium arch, or orchestra pit. Scenery normally consisted of ramps or other constructions set against a cyclorama, upon

FIG. 19.4
Gate Theatre production of Kaiser's *From Morn to Midnight,* 1928. Directed by Peter Godfrey. Courtesy Enthoven Collection, Victoria and Albert Museum, London.

which patterns of light were projected. The actors' movement was often described as "choreographic" and was always highly stylized. Gray thought the text an excuse for a director's improvisations. He performed *Romeo and Juliet* in flamenco costumes; put some characters in *Twelfth Night* on roller skates; and had the Judge in *Merchant of Venice* play with a yo-yo. Gray's productions generated much controversy but had little immediate influence. The theatre closed in 1933.

The Oxford Repertory Company, headed by J. B. Fagan (1873–1933) from 1923 to 1929, presented twenty-one plays a year drawn from many countries and periods. The schedule meant that productions were often rough, but all had vitality and clear interpretations. Little scenery was used, for the theatre had only a small stage fronted by a large apron, upon which most of the action transpired. The importance of this company rests in part on the many young actors, most notably Tyrone Guthrie, John Gielgud, Raymond Massey, Flora Robson, and Glen Byam Shaw, who received their first major experience under Fagan.

The Stratford–upon–Avon seasons of Shakespeare's plays also gained in prestige after they resumed in 1919. Until 1934, most of the plays were directed by W. Bridges-Adams (1889–1965), who worked under extremely adverse conditions. There were no shop or storage facilities, the Festival Committee controlled policy, and Bridges-Adams was required to open six plays on six successive evenings. After the old theatre burned in 1926, the company played in a motion picture house until the present building was completed in 1932. Although the new auditorium was largely satisfactory, the stage was a conventional picture-frame structure; its sliding platform stages could not move entirely out of sight and the elevator stages only sank 8 feet. Such blunders would require several remodelings. Bridges-Adams resigned in 1934 and was succeeded until 1942 by B. Iden Payne (1881–1976), whose most characteristic productions were in the style of Poel—using a reconstructed Shakespeare stage and Elizabethan costumes. Other directors, most notably Theodore Kommissarzhevsky, brought novel conceptions to the plays. Kommissarzhevsky's production of *Merchant of Venice* utilized *commedia dell'arte* conventions and his *The Merry Wives of Windsor* was set to Viennese waltzes. London critics largely ignored the Stratford company, which did not achieve high critical stature until after World War II.

During this period there were many performers of high merit. Of the actresses, the best were probably Sybil Thorndike (1882–1976) and Edith Evans (1888–1976). Thorndike began her career in Ben Greet's

FIG. 19.5
Malvern Festival production of *Gammer Gurton's Needle*. Setting by Paul Shelving. From *Theatre Arts* (1933).

company and after 1914 acted often with the Old Vic troupe. She was especially noted in the 1920s for her portrayal of Shaw's *Saint Joan,* although her performances ranged from Greek tragedy to modern comedy. Evans began her career with Poel and gained fame as Millamant in the Lyric Theatre's production of *The Way of the World*. She also appeared frequently

FIG. 19.6
Cambridge Festival Theatre production of *Henry VIII*, 1931. Directed by Terence Gray. Note the abstract setting and the playing-card costumes.

FIG. 19.7

Laurence Olivier as Romeo, Edith Evans as the Nurse, and John Gielgud as Mercutio in Gielgud's production of *Romeo and Juliet,* 1935. From *Theatre Arts* (1936).

with the Old Vic, at the Malvern Festival, and in many London commercial theatres. Other outstanding actresses included Lilian Braithwaite (1873–1948), Marie Tempest (1864–1942), Flora Robson (1902–1984), Gertrude Lawrence (1898–1952), and Peggy Ashcroft (1907–1991).

Of the actors, the most important was John Gielgud (1904–2000), who made his debut in 1921 and won major acclaim with Hamlet in 1934. He soon became one of England's major directors as well. In 1937–1938 he leased the Queen's Theatre, assembled a company that included Peggy Ashcroft, Michael Redgrave, and Alec Guinness, and produced a repertory of classics. By the time the war began, Gielgud was accepted as England's finest actor and director. Other outstanding performers included Cedric Hardwicke (1893–1964), who worked closely with Barry Jackson after 1922, Donald Wolfit (1902–1968), who played at the Old Vic, Stratford, and with his own company, and Maurice Evans (1901–1986), who played for Terence Gray and the Old Vic before emigrating to the United States in 1935. A number of young men, who would be of greater importance after the war, also established their promise: Laurence Olivier (1907–1989), who played with the Birmingham Repertory Company, Gielgud, and the Old Vic; Michael Redgrave (1908–1985), on the stage after 1934; Ralph Rich-

ardson (1902–1983); Alec Guinness (1914–2000), who made his debut in 1934; Anthony Quayle (1913–1989), on the stage after 1931; and Glen Byam Shaw (1904–1986), who played with the Oxford Repertory Company and Gielgud.

Few major dramatists emerged between the wars, although a number of older ones, such as Shaw, Barrie, Galsworthy, and Pinero, continued to write. During the 1920s three authors—Maugham, Lonsdale, and Coward—excelled in sophisticated comedy. Somerset Maugham (1874–1965) wrote his first play in 1904 and until 1933 was one of England's most prolific playwrights. His major achievement came with his comedies of manners, *Our Betters* (1917), *The Circle* (1921), *The Constant Wife* (1927), and *The Breadwinner* (1930), in which sardonic humor and unusual personal outlooks avoided trite happy endings. Often compared with Maugham, Frederick Lonsdale (1881–1954) drew a wide following with his amusing situations and effective dialogue in *The Last of Mrs. Cheyney* (1925), *On Approval* (1927), and *The High Road* (1929). Noel Coward (1899–1973) captured the spirit of the postwar era with such works as *Fallen Angels* (1925), *Hay Fever* (1925), *Bittersweet* (1929), *Private Lives* (1930), and *Design for Living* (1932), in which unconventional behavior was combined with sophisticated wit.

Of the serious writers, J. B. Priestley (1894–1984) gained the greatest prestige. He began his dramatic career in 1932 with *Dangerous Corner* and went on to *Time and the Conways* (1937) and *An Inspector Calls* (1946). Although he wrote many kinds of plays, Priestley is most noted for his compression or distortion of time to illuminate characters and ideas. Of the sentimental and melodramatic school, Emlyn Williams (1905–1987) was perhaps the most successful. After writing two sensational plays, *A Murder Has Been Arranged* (1930) and *Night Must Fall* (1935), he presented *The Corn Is Green* (1938), a sentimental story about a Welsh teacher and her star pupil.

This period also brought several attempts to revive poetic drama. Gordon Bottomley (1874–1948) wrote *King Lear's Wife* (1915), *Britain's Daughters* (1922), and *Laodice and Danae* (1930), and W. H. Auden (1907–1973) and Christopher Isherwood (1904–1986) collaborated on *The Dog Beneath the Skin* (1935) and *The Ascent of F6* (1936). The most lasting achievement was that of T. S. Eliot (1888–1965) with *Murder in the Cathedral* (1935), the story of Thomas à Becket's martyrdom. Eliot went on to write *The Family Reunion* (1939) and, after the war, several other verse plays. In general, however, the attempt to revive poetic drama was ineffective, primarily because of shortcomings in the plays rather than because of opposition to poetry.

FIG. 19.8
T. S. Eliot's *Murder in the Cathedral* at the Mercury Theatre, London, 1935. Directed by E. Martin Browne. Robert Speaight at right as Becket. Courtesy Debenham Collection, British Theatre Museum, London.

The revue was one of the most popular theatrical forms between the wars. C. B. Cochran (1873–1951), its most famous producer, began his work with "intimate revues" in 1914 and then turned to large-scale, lavish productions between 1918 and 1931. André Charlot (1882–1956) also presented many revues between 1916 and 1923, bringing Beatrice Lillie (1895–1989) to fame. The intimate revue was revived at the Gate Theatre in the 1930s, especially through the writing of Herbert Farjeon (1887–1945) and the performances of Hermione Gingold (1897–1987).

To Ireland, England's deep involvement in World War I offered the chance to throw off British rule. Consequently, in 1916 it began a rebellion which was put down after much bloodshed. But the demand for independence grew, and in 1919 Ireland declared itself a republic. Three years of armed conflict ensued before a treaty was signed in 1923 which granted independence to all but six northern counties.

This struggle provides the context for the early plays of Sean O'Casey (1884–1964), Ireland's most important postwar playwright. O'Casey turned attention away from folk and legendary subject matter to the urban life of his time. The plays that established his fame—*The Shadow of a Gunman* (1923), *Juno and the Paycock* (1924), and *The Plough and the Stars* (1926)—were realistic in tone and dealt with the effects of the rebellion on the lives of ordinary people. After this time O'Casey adopted expressionistic techniques in such works as *The Silver Tassie*

(1928), *Within the Gates* (1934), *Red Roses for Me* (1943), and *Purple Dust* (1945). His change of style precipitated a break with the Abbey Theatre in 1928, after which O'Casey lived in England. Many of O'Casey's works have been more widely read than produced, largely because, in spite of many powerful scenes, the dramatic action is sometimes obscure. Nevertheless, his characterizations, vivid use of language, and human compassion make him one of the finest writers of modern times.

THEATRE AND DRAMA IN THE UNITED STATES, 1915–1940

The United States was able to remain aloof from World War I until 1917, when it was drawn into the conflict. Not only was it decisive in the outcome of the war, it was a leader in founding the League of Nations and in establishing independent states for the ethnic and language groups of Europe. Following the war, however, the United States entered another period of isolationism, during which it sought to divorce itself from foreign affairs and imposed tariffs to reduce imports. The economic results were disastrous for farmers and workers and ultimately were instrumental in bringing on the Great Depression of the 1930s. It was during the interwar years that women won the right to vote and that mass production and new developments in transportation and communication revolutionized American life.

During the 1930s the energies of the nation were devoted to overcoming economic problems. For the first time, the government assumed a key role in social planning and began such programs as social security and public works. By 1940, U.S. life was vastly different from what it had been in 1915. The United States had become one of the world's great powers and an industrial giant. It had also won a measure of respect in artistic and cultural affairs for the first time.

Not until around 1915 did the United States begin to be aware of artistic innovations that had long been underway in the European theatre. This awareness came about in large part through nonprofessional groups. Around 1912 several "little theatres" were established in emulation of the independent theatres of Europe. Among the most important of these were the Toy Theatre, Boston (1912), the Chicago Little Theatre (1912), the Provincetown Players (Massachusetts, 1915), the Neighborhood Playhouse and Washington Square Players in New York (both 1915), and the Detroit Arts and Crafts Theatre (1916). By 1917 there were at least 50 of these groups. Generally these theatres had full-time directors but used amateur actors, designers, and staff. This was both an economic and an esthetic choice. Because these theatres were building new audiences they could not afford professional actors. But many also believed that professionals were too dependent on the melodramatic tricks they learned in the commercial theatre to stage a more challenging repertory effectively, and they argued that amateurs were more open to new approaches. Little theatres produced a series of plays for a subscription audience each year, using techniques already widely accepted in Europe. The little theatre movement made its greatest contributions between 1912 and 1920 by preparing audiences to accept new drama and production methods.

After 1920, the little theatres began to be indistinguishable from community theatres. Originating like its European counterpart in attempts to revive the spirit of ancient Greece, the community drama movement had begun in the United States around 1905. Its most ardent supporter was Percy MacKaye (1875–1956), whose *The Civic Theatre* (1912) and *Community Drama* (1917) outlined a program and whose outdoor pageants provided texts designed to involve several thousand participants. Interest in mass spectacles soon declined, however, and after 1920 most local groups turned to the performance of recent Broadway hits. By 1925, nearly 2,000 community or little theatre companies were registered with the Drama League of America, an organization which encouraged local interest in drama.

The primary competition for these community theatres came from the traveling tent theatres. From the first traveling tent theatre introduced by Fayette Lodawick "Yankee" Robinson (1818–1884) in 1857 at Rock Island, Illinois, the movement reached its peak in the 1920s when over 400 companies were on tour to over 16,000 cities, generating more productions and greater attendance than all the legitimate theatres in the country combined. While the repertory of these companies was little different from that of the community theatres, they did employ large numbers of professional theatre artists and contributed greatly to building audiences. Few of these companies survived the combination of the Depression followed by World War II, after which fixed summer stock companies, which had existed in small numbers since the founding of Elitch's Garden Theatre of Denver in 1890, became dominant.

Drama programs also began to be introduced into colleges and universities. Although plays had been produced by students since the seventeenth century, no courses in theatre were offered until about 1900. The first important change came in 1903 when George Pierce Baker (1866–1935) began to teach playwriting at Radcliffe College. Later opened to Harvard University students, the course was enlarged in 1913 to include a workshop for the production of plays. Baker attracted many of America's most talented young people, including Eugene O'Neill, S. N. Behrman, Hallie Flanagan, and Robert Edmond Jones, instilled in them high standards, and helped them to acquire skills. In 1925 Baker moved to Yale University where he established a drama school which was to provide professional training for many later theatre workers across America and Mexico. In 1914 at the Carnegie Institute of Technology, Thomas Wood Stevens (1880–1942) instituted the country's first degree-granting program in theatre, where many of the outstanding leaders of university theatres across the country were trained. In 1918 Frederick Koch (1877–1944) founded the influential Carolina Playmakers. Many other programs soon followed. By 1940 theatre education was an accepted part of many U.S. universities.

Stevens left Carnegie Tech in 1925 to found the Goodman Theatre and school in Chicago, one of the first major regional theatres, which he ran until 1930. In 1934 he had a reproduction of Shakespeare's Globe built as part of the Century of Progress Exhibition in that city, where he and English director B. Iden Payne produced one-hour versions of Shakespeare's plays at a rate of seven per day. The project proved so successful that identical Globe theatre reconstructions were built in San Diego, Cleveland, and Dallas, and over the next three years they generated more than 5,000 productions of eighteen Shakespeare plays which were seen by more than 2 million people. These Globes inspired multiple Shakespeare festivals

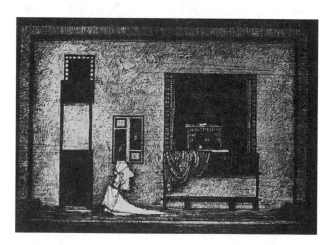

FIG. 19.9
Robert Edmond Jones's design for *The Man Who Married a Dumb Wife,* 1915; directed by Harley Granville Barker. This setting is usually said to be the first important native example of the "new stagecraft" in the United States. From *The Theatre* (1915).

FIG. 19.10
Robert Edmond Jones's setting for the banquet scene, *Macbeth,* 1921. Directed by Arthur Hopkins. Note the expressionistic elements, including the masks above the stage. From *Theatre Arts Magazine* (1924).

across the United States and Canada which became a dynamic component of the theatre industry in the second half of the century.

In the years following 1910, the "new stagecraft," as the European trends were called in America, began to find its way into the commercial theatre. Winthrop Ames (1871–1937), who had gone to Europe in 1907 to study new developments there, was employed in 1909 to manage the New Theatre in New York, an ambitious nonprofit repertory company. The large theatre soon proved both financially and artistically unsatisfactory, however, and Ames then built the Little Theatre, seating only 300, where in the years preceding World War I he presented a number of plays in the new style. In 1912 he imported Reinhardt's production of *Sumurun,* which also aroused much interest in European ideas.

In 1912 the Boston Opera Company hired Joseph Urban (1872–1933), a well-established Viennese designer of the new school, to mount its productions. Urban later worked in New York (most notably for Florenz Ziegfeld), where he was famous for the fresh coloring and simplicity of his settings. In 1915 the New York Stage Society invited Harley Granville Barker to direct a series of plays for its members. For Barker's production of *The Man Who Married a Dumb Wife,* Robert Edmond Jones (1887–1954) provided settings usually considered the first native expression of the "new stagecraft." Jones was one of several young men, including Lee Simonson and Sam Hume, who had studied in Europe between 1912 and 1915 and had been impressed by the changing theatrical trends. In 1914 Hume arranged an exhibit of continental scene design which was shown in New York, Detroit, Chicago, and Cleveland. Hume later was associated with the Detroit Arts and Crafts Theatre; there his associate, Sheldon Cheney, in 1916 launched *Theatre Arts Magazine,* which until 1948 was to be the principal disseminator of new ideas in the United States. Visits of the Abbey Theatre in 1911, the Ballets Russes in 1916, and Copeau's troupe from 1917 to 1919 also helped to stimulate interest in foreign

FIG. 19.11

Norman Bel Geddes project for staging Dante's *The Divine Comedy*, 1921. The Norman Bel Geddes Collection, Theatre Arts Collection, Harry Ransom Humanities Research Center. University of Texas at Austin. By permission of The Estate of Norman Bel Geddes, Edith L. Bel Geddes, Executrix.

movements. Nevertheless, when the war ended in 1918 the U.S. theatre was only beginning to be aware of European practices.

The triumph of the new ideal owes most to the Provincetown Players, the Theatre Guild, and Arthur Hopkins. After presenting a few programs on Cape Cod, the Provincetown Players moved to New York in 1916. In its early years the company concentrated upon plays by U.S. playwrights and by 1925 had presented ninety-three plays by forty-seven authors. After 1923, the group split into two branches. One continued the older practices, while the other, under Eugene O'Neill, Robert Edmond Jones, and Kenneth Macgowan, performed foreign and period plays along with the noncommercial works of O'Neill and others. Although it succumbed to financial pressures in 1929, the Provincetown Players had served an important role as an experimental theatre both for new plays and for new production techniques.

In 1918 the Washington Square Players was disbanded, but some of its members then formed the Theatre Guild, a fully professional company, with the avowed purpose of presenting plays of merit not likely to interest commercial managers. After an

uncertain beginning in 1919, it soon became the United States' most respected theatre, presenting a number of plays each year to an audience of subscribers. In 1928 it also began a subscription series in six other cities. The Guild was governed by a board of directors, and for a time maintained a nucleus company of actors. It adopted an eclectic approach to staging; its principal director, Philip Moeller (1880–1958), and its principal designer, Lee Simonson (1888–1967), drew upon several European movements, although their most typical style was a modified realism. During the 1930s the company gradually curtailed its activities because of financial problems and by World War II was merely another commercial producer investing in long-run hits.

In 1918 Arthur Hopkins (1878–1950) began a series of productions that were to mark him as the most adventurous of New York's commercial producers. Working with Robert Edmond Jones, Hopkins presented plays by Tolstoy, Ibsen, Gorky, Shakespeare, O'Neill, and others. In 1921 his production of *Macbeth* created a sensation with its expressionistic use of tilted arches, and in 1922 *Hamlet,* starring John Barrymore (1882–1942), was declared one of the best productions of the century. After Hopkins and the Guild demonstrated the commercial viability of the "new stagecraft," it was adopted by others, and by 1930 had become the standard approach.

The "new stagecraft" was primarily a visual movement, but the total effect of most productions might best be described as "simplified realism." In addition to Jones and Simonson, the major influence on scene design was Norman Bel Geddes (1893–1958), a visionary not unlike Appia. Geddes' plan (published in 1921) for staging Dante's *The Divine Comedy* on a series of terraces is still considered one of the most brilliant conceptions by a U.S. designer. His penchant for steps, platforms, and imaginative lighting was also seen in his productions of *Hamlet* (1931) and Werfel's *The Eternal Road* (1936), in which the platforms soared to a height of 50 feet. Other important designers included Cleon Throckmorton (1897–1965), Mordecai Gorelik (1899–1990), Boris Aronson (1900–1980), Aline Bernstein (1882–1955), Howard Bay (1912–1986), Donald Oenslager (1902–1975), and especially Jo Mielziner (1901–1976), who was to be the United States' most prolific and respected designer after 1945. While all did not follow the same style, they shared a respect for simplicity and a desire to capture the spirit of a text.

Continental influence continued to be felt in the 1920s through a series of visitors: the Moscow Art Theatre toured the United States in 1923–1924; Reinhardt presented *The Miracle* (with designs by Geddes) in 1924 and staged a season of plays in 1927–1928;

FIG. 19.12
Norman Bel Geddes's setting for *The Miracle* as staged by Max Reinhardt at the Century Theatre, New York, 1924. This sectional plan shows the arrangement of the scenery and machinery in this theatre after it was converted to look like a medieval cathedral. From *The Scientific American* (1924).

its excellent repertory and wide following, the company was always in debt and could not survive the Depression.

The most distinguished troupe of the 1930s was the Group Theatre, launched in 1931 by Lee Strasberg (1901–1982), Harold Clurman (1901–1980), and Cheryl Crawford (1902–1986) on the model of the Moscow Art Theatre, whose methods and ensemble approach it emulated. With a company including Stella Adler (1904–1992), Morris Carnovsky (1898–1992), and Elia Kazan (1909–), it presented plays by Paul Green, Maxwell Anderson, Sidney Kingsley, Irwin Shaw, William Saroyan, and others, although its reputation rests especially upon its productions of Clifford Odets' dramas. Ultimately the troupe foundered because of disagreements over policy. In 1941 it was disbanded. Its influence continued, however, through the work of many former members, several of whom were instrumental in popularizing the Stanislavsky system in the United States.

The Depression motivated the creation of a unique experiment, the Federal Theatre Project, which was established in 1935 to combat unemployment. Headed by Hallie Flanagan Davis (1890–1969), at its peak it employed 10,000 persons in 40 states. About 1,000 productions of all types were mounted, 65 percent of them free. In spite of its diversity, it is now remembered primarily for developing the "Living Newspaper," a cinematic form which integrated factual data with dramatic vignettes. Each script

and Copeau directed *The Brothers Karamazov* for the Theatre Guild in 1927. Two of Stanislavsky's actors, Richard Boleslavsky (1889–1937) and Maria Ouspenskaya (1881–1949), were induced to head the American Laboratory Theatre between 1923 and 1930. Here the Stanislavsky system was taught in a version later popularized by Boleslavsky's book *Acting, the First Six Lessons* (1933). Among the more than 500 students who studied at the American Laboratory Theatre were Stella Adler, Lee Strasberg, and Harold Clurman.

Between 1925 and 1940 several groups tried to escape the commercial pattern. From 1925 to 1930 Walter Hampden (1879–1955) revived the actor-manager system with his repertory company. Although the Depression forced him to give up his theatre in New York, Hampden continued to tour with his troupe for many years. Between 1926 and 1933 Eva Le Gallienne (1899–1991) managed the Civic Repertory Theatre, produced thirty-four plays and built up a subscription list of 50,000. Despite

FIG. 19.13
A "living newspaper," *One Third of a Nation,* staged by the Federal Theatre Project in 1938. Tenement house setting by Howard Bay. From *Theatre Arts* (1939).

FIG. 19.14
Orson Welles's adaptation of *Macbeth* to a Haitian setting. Produced for the Federal Theatre Project. Design by Nat Karson. From *Theatre Arts* (1936).

centered around a problem: *Triple-A Plowed Under* (1936) dealt with agriculture, *Power* (1937) with rural electrification, and *One-Third of a Nation* (1938) with slum housing. Most of the plays had as a central character the "little man" who, upon raising questions about a current problem, was led through its background, human consequences, and possible solutions. Much of the dialogue was taken from speeches, newspaper stories, or other documents. Many of the techniques were borrowed from Epic Theatre. The political tone of many works eventually alienated Congress, which in 1939 refused to appropriate funds for its continuance.

The Federal Theatre motivated the formation of the Mercury Theatre in 1937, when Orson Welles (1915–1985) and John Houseman (1902–1988) decided to present Marc Blitzstein's *The Cradle Will Rock* after it was withdrawn from production by the Federal Theatre. Welles had already established a reputation as an actor with his portrayal of Doctor Faustus and as an imaginative producer with *Macbeth,* which he set in Haiti and performed with an African American cast. Between 1937 and 1939 the Mercury Theatre presented works by Büchner, Dekker, Shaw, and Shakespeare. Its greatest success came with *Julius Caesar,* played as a comment upon fascism, then rampant in Europe.

The Federal Theatre also promoted African American theatre, which, though not extensive between the wars, was laying the foundations for later developments. In the years between 1890 and 1915 several musicals had been written for African American casts, a few stock companies had performed sporadically in New York and elsewhere, and (after 1910) one African American performer—Bert Williams (1876–1922)—had won stardom on Broadway in musical pieces.

An important step was taken in 1915 when Anita Bush (*c.* 1883–1974) organized a stock company, which soon metamorphosed into the Lafayette Players, to perform a weekly repertory in Harlem. The company took most of its plays from Broadway, but it gave African American actors their longest continuous employment in regular drama to that time. A few dramatists also began to write sympathetically about African Americans. The first serious plays for African American actors to be seen on Broadway were Ridgely Torrence's *Three Plays for a Negro Theatre* (1917), which not only marked a turning away from the stereotyped treatment of African Americans but also the first time that African Americans were welcomed into Broadway audiences. There followed such works as O'Neill's *The Emperor Jones* (in which the African American actor, Charles Gilpin, played the leading role in a serious American play on Broadway for the first time), DuBose and Dorothy Heyward's *Porgy,* Marc Connelly's *The Green Pastures,* and Paul Green's *In Abraham's Bosom,* all by white authors.

There were as well several African American authors, although they were given relatively little encouragement. Among the best of the plays were Willis Richardson's (1889–1977) *The Chipwoman's Fortune,* Frank Wilson's *Sugar Cane,* Hall Johnson's *Run Little Chillun,* Langston Hughes' (1902–1967) *Mulatto,* Georgia Douglas Johnson's (1880–1966) *Plumes* and *A Sunday Morning in the South,* and Zora Neale Hurston's (1891–1960) *Mule Bone* (written with Langston Hughes). There were also a number of musical plays, among the most successful of which were Noble Sissle (1889–1975) and Eubie Blake's (1883–1983) *Shuffle Along, Chocolate Dandies,* and *Runnin' Wild.* All of these plays helped such African American performers as Richard Harrison (1864–1935), Frank Wilson, Rose McClendon, and Abbie Mitchell to demonstrate that they could compete with the best actors of the period. Of all African American actors of this period, Paul Robeson (1898–1976) is probably the best known, both in America and abroad. Among the plays in which he appeared were O'Neill's *Emperor Jones* and *All God's Chillun Got Wings, Porgy and Bess, Showboat,* and *Othello* (in which he played the title role in three productions).

African American theatre received a major boost from the Federal Theatre, which in several cities established African American units that presented seventy-five plays in four years. Unfortunately, most of the hopes were dashed when the project ended in 1939. Since the archives of the Federal Theatre Project were rediscovered, considerable attention has been paid to the African American dramas found there.

By World War II many plays about African American life had found their way onto the stage. Perhaps the most disturbing of these was *Native Son,* Paul Green and Richard Wright's adaptation of Wright's novel, which showed the terrible effects of social evils on the life of the protagonist. But, if there was still a long way to go, there had been much improvement since 1915. The African American theatre artists had made their presence felt, even if they had not yet been permitted to demonstrate their full potential.

The Depression also gave impetus to the "worker's theatre" movement, which had begun in 1926 with the Worker's Drama League. In 1932, a national organization was formed, later called the New Theatre League. Most of the member groups were amateur, but in 1933 a fully professional organization, the Theatre Union, was formed in New York and provided leadership for the entire movement. After the failure of the Theatre Union in 1937, the League declined and by 1942 had virtually ceased to exist. For the most part, the worker's theatres presented socialist propaganda plays designed to arouse protest.

These dissident groups had little effect upon the basic pattern of the commercial theatre. The length of runs steadily increased, reaching a peak with *Tobacco Road* (1933), which played for seven years. The number of new productions also grew each season until 1927–1928, when about 300 plays were mounted, but rapidly declined after 1930, having fallen to eighty by 1939–1940. Theatrical production was complicated in these years by the emergence of powerful labor unions. The stagehand's union, the National Alliance of Theatrical Stage Employees, had achieved full recognition during the season of 1910–1911, and in 1918 the United Scenic Artists was formed. Actors Equity Association, founded in 1912, was recognized in 1919; it became a "closed shop" in 1924 and was able to establish a minimum-wage scale in 1933. The Dramatists' Guild, formed in 1912, became the bargaining agent for all playwrights in 1926. As each group bettered working conditions, it also demanded considerably higher pay for its members and thereby added to the economic problems of the theatre.

Between 1915 and 1940, American dramatists began to command international respect for the first time. Few were members of any particular movement, but most shared a dislike for romantic melodrama with realistic trappings. Only one American dramatist—O'Neill—achieved genuine stature. Eugene O'Neill (1888–1953), son of James O'Neill, turned to playwriting around 1912, attended Baker's playwriting classes at Harvard for a time, and in 1915 had his first works presented by the Provincetown Players. The group continued to encourage him through the 1920s by performing those works rejected by commercial producers. His first full-length play, *Beyond the Horizon,* brought him to Broadway in 1920. After 1934, although he continued to write, no new works were performed until 1946.

O'Neill wrote about 25 full-length plays of uneven quality. Many were seriously flawed, and even the best often suggest that more was intended than achieved. But despite all shortcomings, the plays, with their compelling characters in search of meaning and fulfillment in human existence, achieve a stature surpassed by few modern dramatists. O'Neill also experimented with many novel theatrical devices and dramatic techniques. In *The Great God Brown* (1926), *Lazarus Laughed* (1926), and *Days Without End* (1934) he made use of masks; in *Strange Interlude* (1928) he employed lengthy "interior monologues" to express the characters' inner thoughts; in *Mourning Becomes Electra* (1931) he gained scope by adopting the trilogy form. O'Neill also ranged through many styles. The devices of expressionism were adopted for *The Hairy Ape* (1922) and *The Great God Brown;* those of symbolism for *The Fountain* (1922) and to a lesser extent for almost all the plays; those of realism for *Beyond the Horizon, Anna Christie* (1921), and *Desire Under the Elms* (1924), as well as in those plays that would be produced following World War II.

Probably O'Neill's greatest rival was Maxwell Anderson (1888–1959), who after achieving renown for his antiromantic war play, *What Price Glory?* (1924), turned to blank verse drama in *Elizabeth the Queen* (1930), *Mary of Scotland* (1933), *Winterset* (1935), and other plays. Although dramatically effective, Anderson's plays offered few new insights, being merely skillful retellings of familiar stories. Other serious playwrights included Elmer Rice (1892–1967) with *The Adding Machine* (1923), an expressionistic drama about the dehumanization of modern life, and *Street Scene* (1929), a naturalistic play set in the New York slums; Sidney Howard (1891–1939), with *They Knew What They Wanted* (1924), an antiromantic comedy about three people who get their wishes by accepting compromises, *The Silver Cord* (1926), about a mother's attempt to retain her control over her newly married son, and *Yellow Jack* (1934), a semi-documentary play about the fight to control yellow fever; and Paul Green (1894–1981), with his tragedies, *In Abraham's Bosom* (1926) and *The House of Connolly* (1931), and the expressionistic antiwar play, *Johnny Johnson* (1936).

The comedy of manners was well represented by Phillip Barry (1896–1949) with *Paris Bound* (1927) and *The Philadelphia Story* (1939), both treating divorce among the upper classes; and S. N. Berhman (1893–1973), with *Biography* (1932), *Rain from Heaven* (1934), and *End of Summer* (1936), all of which contrast tolerance with inhumanity. Among the writers of farce, the best was George S. Kaufman (1889–1961), who worked with a number of collaborators, most successfully with Moss Hart (1904–1961), on *You Can't Take It With You* (1936) and *The Man Who Came to Dinner* (1940). William Saroyan (1908–1981) glorified the simple life in such plays as *My Heart's in the Highlands* (1939), *The Time of Your Life* (1939), and *The Beautiful People* (1941), all of which depict eccentric characters who find beauty and redemption while living on the fringes of society.

The drama of social consciousness was most persistently practiced by John Howard Lawson (1895–1977), whose *Roger Bloomer* (1923), *Processional* (1925), and *Internationale* (1928) were experimental in form and militantly propagandistic in theme. Clifford Odets (1906–1963) called for group action in his early plays, *Waiting for Lefty* (1935) and *Awake and Sing* (1935), while his later works, *Paradise Lost* (1935) and *Golden Boy* (1937), took a more complex view of social conditions. Odets was essentially a chronicler of family relationships; his strength lay in his ability to create believable characters struggling to achieve more than life will give them.

Two of the finest dramatists of the 1930s were Sherwood and Wilder. Robert E. Sherwood (1896–1955) in *The Petrified Forest* (1935) created an allegorical cross-section of U.S. life, in *Idiot's Delight* (1936) depicted through melodramatic farce the horrors of war and the spiritual bankruptcy which gives rise to it, and in *Abe Lincoln in Illinois* (1938) sought to remind Americans of the high ideals upon which their country had been founded. Thornton Wilder's (1897–1975) reputation was created primarily by three plays, *Our Town* (1938), which stresses the archetypal patterns of human experience which undergird seeming change, *The Skin of Our Teeth* (1943), a testimonial to humanity's ability to survive all disasters, and *The Merchant of Yonkers* (1938), later rewritten as *The Matchmaker* (1954), and then adapted into the musical *Hello, Dolly* (1963). Wilder's frank theatricality and simplicity won him a wide following both at home and abroad.

America also produced an unusually large number of female playwrights during this period, among them Rachel Crothers (1876–1958), author of *He and She* (1920), *When Ladies Meet* (1932), and *Susan and God* (1937); Zona Gale (1874–1938), whose *Miss Lulu Bett* (1920) was the first play by a woman to win the Pulitzer Prize; Susan Glaspell (1876–1948), whose *Alison's House* (1931), also won a Pulitzer Prize; Zoe Akins (1886–1958), whose *Declassée* (1919) was a major vehicle for Ethel Barrymore and whose *The Old Maid* (1934) won the Pulitzer Prize; Lulu Vollmer (1898–1955), whose *Sun-Up* (1923) began a vogue for folk plays; Edna Ferber (1885–1968) who adapted her own novel into the musical *Showboat* (1927) and wrote several successful plays with George S. Kaufman, including *Royal Family* (1927) and *Stage Door* (1936); and Sophie Treadwell (c. 1885–1970), whose expressionistic *Machinal* (1928) depicts a woman eventually driven to murder by her machine-like world. Despite the accomplishments of these women during the interwar years, they were, unlike their male contemporaries, subsequently relegated to oblivion. Only recently, under the influence of the women's movement, has interest in them revived. The only female playwright to escape this amnesia was Lillian Hellman (1905–1984), author of *The Children's Hour* (1934) concerning teachers whose lives are ruined by a student who maliciously accuses them of being lesbians, and *Little Foxes* (1939), a story of rapacious greed among the rising industrialists of the new South around 1900.

Much popular entertainment between the wars took the form of musical comedy and revues. Every year between 1907 and 1931, Florenz Ziegfeld (1869–1932) mounted a new edition of *Ziegfeld Follies*, each more lavish than the last. Musical comedy, long merely the excuse for presenting beautiful chorus girls, began to move in a new direction after 1928, when Jerome Kern and Oscar Hammerstein II shifted major emphasis to coherent story in *Showboat*. This new direction reached its culmination in Richard Rodgers's and Oscar Hammerstein's *Oklahoma* (1943), in which music, story, dance, and setting were fully integrated to tell a semi-serious story. With the triumph of the new approach, the old type of musical largely disappeared.

Of the United States' many outstanding performers, only a few can be mentioned: Jane Cowl (1884–1950), on the stage from 1903 and most famous for her portrayals of Juliet, Cleopatra, and the heroines of Sherwood; Pauline Lord (1890–1950), especially remembered for her performances in *Anna Christie* and *They Knew What They Wanted*; Laurette Taylor (1884–1946), one of the most versatile actresses of her day, whose last major appearance was as Amanda in Tennessee William's *The Glass Mena-*

gerie; Ina Claire (1895–1985), who appeared in many *Ziegfeld Follies* before playing the heroines of Behrman's comedies; Helen Hayes (1900–1993), noted especially for her appearances in Barrie's plays, Anderson's *Mary of Scotland,* and Housman's *Victoria Regina;* Katherine Cornell (1898–1974), who gave outstanding portrayals in *Candida, The Three Sisters, The Barretts of Wimpole Street,* and many other plays; Lynn Fontanne (1887?–1983), an English actress, who came to the United States in 1910 and whose later career was tied up with that of her husband, Alfred Lunt (1893–1977), with whom she appeared in *The Guardsman, Reunion in Vienna, Amphitryon 38,* and many other works.

THEATRE IN CANADA TO 1940

From 1902 to 1910 Harold Nelson Shaw (1865?-1937) ran the only successful "all Canadian" touring company. Except for A. J. Small's Great Lakes Circuit, the Canadian market for touring shows was dominated by New York's Theatrical Syndicate. To combat this, the British-Canadian Theatrical Organization was formed in 1912 to import British touring companies and stars. This organization was able to show some success, especially after the demise of the Syndicate in 1917, but growing competition from film made that success short-lived. With the advent of radio drama in the 1920s and the Great Depression of the 1930s, Canadian touring would be abandoned by both British and U.S. companies. Canadian theatre was finally left to develop on its own.

The foundation for a distinctively Canadian theatre was being laid during this period by its own "little theatre" movement. Toronto's Arts and Letters Club of 1908 was the first of these organizations, but it was not until its founding director, Roy Mitchell (1884–1944), took over the Hart House Theatre in 1919 that the production of Canadian plays became a goal. Of the dramatists Hart House encouraged, Merrill Denison (1893–1975) was the first to be successful. An anthology of his Hart House plays was published in 1923 under the title *The Unheroic North,* but he is best known for *Contract* (1929). The most famous actor to have started a career with Hart House was Raymond Massey (1896–1983), brother of the theatre's main financial supporter, Vincent Massey. But the actress Elizabeth Sterling Haynes (1897–1957) was the more important Hart House actor for the future of Canadian theatre as she went on to establish several theatres in Alberta.

A large number of Canadian playwrights appeared in the years between the wars, especially after Canada was given autonomy from England in 1931. Some were cultivated by theatre groups like the women's collective Playwrights Studio Group (founded 1932) and the experimental Play Workshop (founded 1934). Others were inspired by the competitions set up by the Dominion Drama Festival (founded 1932) and the Barry Jackson Trophy (1934). Of these many dramatists, Herman Voaden (1903–1991), John Coulter (1888–1980), Gwen Pharis Ringwood (1910–1984), and Robertson Davis (1913–) are still considered important today, and the latter three did most of their best work after World War II. Plays were also developed collectively in this period, the most famous example of which was the Toronto Worker's Theatre production of *Eight Men Speak* (1933), a highly controversial drama in support of the Communist party. Working for little theatres did not pay well, so when the Canadian Broadcasting Company was established in 1936 much of the best writing and acting talent of Canadian theatre began working in radio drama, an art form that had been growing in importance since 1925.

From 1890 to 1914, the theatre in French-speaking Montreal experienced its greatest period of growth. The number of theatres increased from three to ten, and the number of professional resident companies grew from one to eight, three of which did English-language drama. In 1902 the city's first independent theatre, the Société Anonyme des Théâtre, opened at the Théâtre des Nouveautés. Like its European counterparts, it was dedicated to modern production methods and a repertory of plays that went beyond the standard commercial fare of melodrama and musical reviews. But it showed little interest in Canadian authors and closed in 1908. French-Canadian playwrights from Julien Daoust (dates unknown) to Yvette Mercier-Gouin (1895–1984) would make their careers writing unchallenging drama for the commercial stage. The Community Players, founded in 1921, was the city's first little theatre. When it disbanded in 1925 one of its founders, Martha Allan, joined the Pasadena Playhouse before returning to establish the Montreal Repertory Theatre in 1929. But as early as the start of World War I, the French-Canadian theatre was entering a decline from which it would take three decades to recover.

THEATRE AND DRAMA IN AUSTRALIA AND NEW ZEALAND, 1915–1940

The movement towards realism manifested itself in "bush drama" at the turn of the century. These plays were not concerned with the colonial past but rather focused on the virtues and ingenuity of Australians as they faced the hardships of their difficult environment with good-natured humor and fortitude. Independent women were often the central characters; Australian English rather than British English was used; and upper-class characters tended to be villains, not heroes. *On Our Selection* (1907–1910) was by far the most successful representative of this type. It was the most popular play of its day and seems to have been in performance somewhere in the country constantly from 1912 to 1929. The play was a series of individual sketches focused on Dad, Mum, Dave, Joe, and Sarah Rudd, based on a collection of short stories by Steele Rudd (who was one of the several adapters). It became the model for a number of other plays including *Possum Paddock* (1919) by Kate Howard, which held the stage for twenty years. There were also more serious versions of this type, like Jo Smith's *The Bushwoman* (1909) and *The Girl of the Never Never* (1910). In the 1920s detective dramas, starting with *The Flaw* (1923), by Emelie Polini and Frank Harvey, came into vogue. In the 1930s historic dramas, like Allan Wilkie's *Governor Bligh* (1930), were most popular. But in general the commercial repertory was dominated by productions of comedies, reviews, melodramas, and lightweight realism imported from the United States and Great Britain.

As the Theatrical Syndicate dominated the theatre of the United States and Canada in the first years of the twentieth century, JCW, the management firm founded by American actor James Cassius Williamson (1844–1913), dominated the market in Australia and New Zealand. The theatrical boom that had started in Australia in 1870 continued right up to World War I, but the theatre remained conservative. To counterbalance the standard commercial fare, Leon Brodsky (1883–1973) established The Australian Theatre Society at Melbourne in 1904. It was modeled after the Independent Theatre in London but its members soon lost interest in experimental work and chose to become a playreading group. It was followed, however, by the Melbourne Repertory Theatre Company, founded in 1911 by Gregan McMahon (1874–1941), which proved to be a "little theatre" of outstanding quality. The Adelaide Literary Theatre (1908), founded by Bryceson Treharne (1879–1948), was even more successful. It exposed its audiences to the works of many of the more controversial European playwrights of the time as well as to the works of New Zealand dramatist Arthur H. Adams (1872–1936). This group became the Adelaide Repertory Theatre in 1911, perhaps the most influential little theatre of the era. The clearest indication of the success of these companies came when J. and N. Tait Ltd. (the equivalent of the Shubert brothers in the United States) hired McMahon to establish the Sydney Repertory Theatre Society in 1918 in a unique marriage of the independent theatre spirit with a dominant commercial operation of the time. (This operation became even more dominant when it bought JCW in 1920.) Mutual suspicion brought an end to this project in 1928, but McMahon continued to direct and influenced many of the best theatre artists of the next generation.

Large numbers of little theatres sprang up all over Australia between the wars, and several even appeared in New Zealand, but few outlasted the energy of their original founders. This energy could last a long time, as it did with Doris Fitton (1897–1985), one of McMahon's former students who started the Independent Theatre in Sydney in 1930 and ran it for forty-seven years. But the Ab Intra Studio Theatre in Adelaide, founded in 1931 by Alan Harkness (1908–1952) and Kester Baruch (1903–1992), was more typical. It produced some of the most experimental and visually spectacular productions ever seen in Australia, but when its founders left for England in 1935, the theatre closed. The New Theatre Sydney, founded in 1932, and the New Theatre Melbourne, founded in 1935, are exceptional in having continued to the present day. Of the numerous other little theatres, Melbourne's Dolia Ribush Players, named for the Russian immigrant who founded it in 1932, deserves special mention. Through this theatre, Ribush (1896–1947) popularized the Stanislavsky system in Australia and was probably second only to McMahon in his influence on young directors. In 1937, the Australian Drama League was established to provide mutual assistance and communication among the many diverse groups that made up the little theatre movement.

Despite the rapid expansion of little theatres, the commercial theatre in Australia and New Zealand was collapsing under the onslaught of film, the Depression, and radio drama. Governments imposed taxes on "entertainment," making it even harder for commercial theatre to be competitive. In 1929, the tax records report 2,460,000 tickets sold at theatres in Australia; five years later that number was down to 166,000. Of the ten theatres used for live performances in Sydney in 1929, only two were still used for that purpose in 1935, and one of those was used only for musical reviews. The strength of the little theatre movement was a testimony to people's interest in the art of the theatre, but they were no longer in a position to support it commercially.

The Second World War, like the first, interrupted the theatre's normal patterns. The war also raised serious doubts about a world that had created such horrors as the Nazi extermination camps and such destructive weapons as the atomic bomb. Out of the questioning would come many innovations in theatre and drama.

LOOKING AT THEATRE HISTORY

Following World War I, the American stage began to show the influence of Europe. American scene designers transformed the kinds of setting that had been typical on the New York stage. The results came to be labeled the "new stagecraft," although essentially it was new only in America, since for the most part it was merely an adaptation of scenic practices that had long dominated European stages. In writing about the transformation, Kenneth Macgowan noted:

> No art was so thoroughly conventionalized as was scenery-making when the new stagecraft began its reforms. The flat scenery and those large color cut-outs that ornamented the Christmas extravaganzas were all a flimsy pretense of reality [as were the landscapes and paneled rooms]. . . . It was against all of these unreal and unbeautiful conventionalisms that the new stagecraft "made war."

Kennneth Macgowan, "The New Stagecraft in America," *Century Magazine* 87 (Jan. 1914), 416–21.

Perhaps the most controversial American production of the 1920s was Arthur Hopkins' presentation in 1921 of *Macbeth*, starring Lionel Barrymore with settings by Robert Edmond Jones. (See Fig. 19.10.) Even though the new stagecraft had been welcomed by many critics, Jones's symbolic setting offended many, and their disparaging (even insulting) reviews frightened many contemporary designers, with the result that most Broadway designers subsequently seldom deviated from a style best described as modified realism. Kenneth Macgowan described Jones's vision of *Macbeth*:

> [Jones] saw the dominant element of Macbeth as the abnormal influence of the power symbolized . . . in the witches. He tried to visualize the superhuman nature of these mystic forces in gigantic masks appearing high in the air above the blasted heath. Through the rest of the play, he placed upon the stage very simple and abstract forms to carry the mood induced by the supernatural influences which seize and dominate the characters constantly throughout Macbeth.

Kenneth Macgowan, *Theatre of Tomorrow*. New York, 1921.

Eugene O'Neill quickly became the American playwright most admired at home and abroad. His adoption of several styles ranging through realism, expressionism, symbolism, and other modes marked him as a writer constantly experimenting. Among his plays, *Mourning Becomes Electra*, a play heavily influenced by Aeschylus' *Oresteia*, was one of the most ambitious. In his review, Hiram Motherwell wrote:

> to write three good acts which hang together is at least ten times as difficult as to write one. To write fourteen is a hundred times as difficult. . . . O'Neill has here proved himself the foremost playwright of our generation. . . . O'Neill has acknowledged that he sought in this play to render in terms intelligible to moderns the Greek "sense of fate." . . . The conflict of compulsions which O'Neill presents is not political, or even ethical. It is psychological. It is genuinely modern. O'Neill owes little to the Greek tragedy save the outline of his story. . . . The play pretty much sums up all that we moderns know about the deepest springs of human behavior.

Hiram Motherwell, *Theatre Guild Magazine* (December 1931), 15–17.

Orson Welles and John Houseman, as director and producer, made a strong impact through their productions with the Federal Theatre, but after they were forbidden to give public performances of Marc Blitzstein's *The Cradle Will Rock*, they founded their own company, the Mercury Theatre. In 1937 their production of Shakespeare's *Julius Caesar,* with its depiction of a fascist Europe, won wide critical praise and laid the groundwork for Welles' subsequent career in film:

> this is a Julius Caesar in modern clothes, with the players clad in Fascist costumes and the work transformed into a parable of current dictatorships. . . . Here a Fascist dictator is struck down by an alliance of his foes, and never once does it seem . . . that anything new is written into Shakespeare's original intent. . . . On a bare stage, with bricks of the back wall in evidence, shafts of light pick out the actors and the mobs, emphasizing the action, setting the mood and establishing the atmosphere of the scenes. . . . You will find no more thrilling stage pictures in many seasons than those of the two funeral orations. . . . there can no longer be a question of [Welles's] skill as a player.

Richard Watts, Jr., review in the New York *Herald Tribune,* November 12, 1937.

20
Continental European and Latin American Theatre in the Mid Twentieth Century

World War II was the most extensive war ever fought in terms of people killed, property destroyed, and the number of countries involved. It made use of the most deadly weapons yet devised, including bombers, ballistic missiles, and atomic bombs. The causes of the war were numerous, including problems left unsolved by World War I, the rise of totalitarian governments with their denial of civil liberties and, in some instances, programs of genocide, and the territorial ambitions of such countries as Germany, Italy, and Japan. The German extermination camps are one of the great blots on human history. At the end of the war Europe was divided into sectors, with the east dominated by the Soviet Union and the west dominated by the United States. There followed a "cold war" as the two nations sought to maintain or extend their influence. As a result, during the 1950s the world seemed under the threat of an atomic holocaust capable of ending life on earth. It was an age of anxiety and stress. A major stabilizing force was the United Nations, which provided a forum for debate and international cooperation, but it was often ineffective, since a few major powers had the right to veto its decisions.

Latin American countries, for the most part, sided with the Allies during World War II. Many, like Brazil, Mexico, and Peru, declared their allegiances quite early, while others, like Argentina, maintained a pro-Axis "neutrality" for several years before joining the Allied cause in 1945. Following the war these countries continued to struggle with the interrelated problems of political and economic instability. This instability often made them battlegrounds for the competing political models of communism, democracy, and totalitarianism, and thus became important parts of the Cold War strategies of the two super powers.

INTERNATIONAL DEVELOPMENTS

At the end of World War II, international cooperation was sought in every aspect of life. The formation of the United Nations was followed by many other organizations designed to promote international understanding. The International Theatre Institute (ITI) was founded in 1947 under the auspices of the United Nations Educational, Scientific, and Cultural Organization (UNESCO), which provided it with a yearly subsidy. From 1950 until 1968 the ITI published *World Theatre,* a periodical designed to disseminate information. The ITI also held frequent international meetings, and after 1954 sponsored an annual festival, the Théâtre des Nations. Other organizations also promoted the exchange of ideas. Among these were the International Organization of Architects, Scenographers, and Theatre

Technicians; the International Association of Theatre Critics; and the International Federation for Theatre Research.

International cooperation also encouraged the development of the theatre throughout the world. Consequently, theatres were established in parts of the world that formerly had few or none. In geographical scope, the theatre became more extensive after 1945 than at any time in the past.

FRENCH THEATRE AND DRAMA, 1940–1968

During World War II, the theatre in Paris was relatively prosperous after France capitulated to Germany. Productions were numerous and well attended, although with the exceptions of those by Dullin, Baty, Barsacq, and the Comédie Française, few were outstanding. The end of the war brought many stresses, as production costs rose and films and television drained away audiences. The postwar government, attempting to play a more decisive role than its predecessors, took steps to aid the theatre. In 1946 the Ministry of Arts and Letters began to subsidize productions of selected new plays and a few new companies; an annual competition was also inaugurated among the new troupes for the best production and direction. Furthermore, the state theatres were reorganized. The Opéra and Opéra-Comique were placed under a single management, and the Comédie Française and Odéon were merged, the Odéon being called the Salle Luxembourg and the main house the Salle Richelieu. At first, the Salle Luxembourg was restricted to new or recent plays, but this scheme proved impractical and both branches came to present similar repertories. When Pierre Dux, Administrator of the Comédie Française from 1944 to 1947, instituted new regulations designed to reduce his actors' film appearances and other outside commitments, many of the leading *sociétaires*, including Jean-Louis Barrault, Madeleine Renaud, Marie Bell, and Aimé

FIG. 20.1
Europe after World War II.

Clairond, resigned. As a result, the troupe lost much of its strength, and, although it slowly rebuilt under the administrations of Pierre-Aimé Touchard (between 1947 and 1953) and Pierre Descaves (between 1953 and 1959), its prestige suffered seriously.

The government also encouraged decentralization of the theatre, which by 1945 was restricted primarily to Paris. Consequently, in 1947 subsidized regional dramatic centers began to be established. The first, the Dramatic Center of the East, was based at Strasbourg, and a second was opened almost immediately at St. Etienne; in 1949, Le Grenier, a troupe which had been performing since 1945, was designated the Dramatic Center for Toulouse, and in the same year a fourth center was established at Rennes. Other centers were inaugurated at Aix-en-Provence (1952), Tourcoing (1960), and Bourges (1963). By the late 1960s the number of Dramatic Centers had grown to twelve. In addition to performing in its home theatre, each Center typically toured towns in its region or developed schemes to bring audiences to its theatre from outlying areas. Furthermore, both national and local authorities aided the many dramatic festivals founded after 1945, most notably at Avignon (beginning in 1947) and Aix-en-Provence (beginning in 1948). By the 1960s more than fifty festivals were being held annually.

Despite these steps toward decentralization, Paris continued to be the principal theatrical center. For a few years after the war, three members of the Cartel continued their work: Dullin remained in Paris until 1947, Baty until 1951, and Jouvet from 1945 until his death in 1951. But by 1952 all of the members of the Cartel were dead. Of the younger prewar leaders, André Barsacq (at the Atelier from 1940 until his death in 1973) and Maurice Jacquemont (at the Studio des Champs-Elysées until 1960) were probably the most important. To this group should be added Marcel Herrand and Jean Marchat, who, after acting with Pitoëff's company, had formed the Rideau de Paris in the 1930s. Upon Pitoëff's death in 1939, they took over his Théâtre aux Mathurins. Until 1953, they presented excellent productions of foreign works, as well as many new French plays.

The major leaders in the postwar years were Barrault and Vilar. Jean-Louis Barrault (1910–1994), after studying with Dullin and working with Artaud and the mime artist Etienne Decroux, had attained an enviable reputation as an actor in both theatre and film before the war began. In 1940 he became a *sociétaire* at the Comédie Française, where in 1943 his production of Claudel's *The Satin Slipper* popularized what came to be called "total theatre." Claudel's play, written between 1919 and 1924, had previously been considered unplayable because of its length and complexity, for the events span a century and occur in Spain, Italy, Africa, America, and at sea. At one point, the hemispheres converse, and at another the earth is represented as one bead on a rosary. A drama of love and salvation, *The Satin Slipper* was shaped by Barrault into a powerful theatrical experience that influenced other directors for many years. Although Barrault was later to refine his ideas, in 1943 he had already formulated his basic outlook. He declared that the text of a play is like an iceberg, since only about one-eighth is visible; it is the director's task to complete the playwright's text by revealing the hidden portions through the imaginative use of all the theatre's resources. Barrault sought a synthesis of elements from both Copeau's and Artaud's approaches.

In 1946, after resigning from the Comédie Française, Barrault (with Madeleine Renaud, whom he had married in 1940) formed the Compagnie Madeleine Renaud-Jean-Louis Barrault. With such major actors as André Brunot, Edwige Feuillère, and Pierre Brasseur, Barrault produced about forty plays ranging from the *Oresteia* to contemporary *avant-garde* works before he gave up his Théâtre Marigny in 1956.

Jean Vilar (1912–1971), a fellow student of Barrault at Dullin's school, was much slower in achieving recognition, and had worked in a number of companies before being employed to organize the festival at Avignon in 1947. His work there and his own performances in Paris (most notably as Pirandello's Henry IV in Barsacq's production) led in 1951 to his appointment as director of the Théâtre National Populaire (TNP), then on the verge of collapse. He assembled a company that included Maria Casarès, Georges Wilson, and Daniel Sorano, and was most fortunate in attracting Gérard Philipe

FIG. 20.2
Barrault's production of Claudel's *Christophe Colombe* at the Théâtre Marigny, 1953. Courtesy Agence de Presse Bernand.

FIG. 20.3
Vilar's production of Marivaux's *Triumph of Love* at the Théâtre Nationale Populaire, 1956. Setting by Leon Gischia. Courtesy Agence de Presse Bernand.

(1922–1959), who, after a brief career in the theatre, had become one of France's major film stars. Although not immediately successful, by 1954 the TNP was one of the most popular troupes in France. Vilar's productions always placed major emphasis upon the actor, reinforced by costume and lighting, and he usually restricted scenery to platforms or a few set pieces. Vilar was the first producer to achieve wide popularity with the approach advocated by the Cartel (whose following had always been limited). Although the TNP's principal home was at the Palais de Chaillot in Paris, it also played at the Avignon Festival and toured throughout France. It soon commanded greater popular support than any of the other state troupes, all of which played almost exclusively in Paris.

After General DeGaulle came to power in 1959, his minister of culture, André Malraux, retained many of the previous government's policies but also made a number of reforms. He continued to subsidize promising new dramatists and companies and sought to extend decentralization. In addition to founding several new dramatic centers, the Gaullist regime also promoted municipal cultural centers (*maisons de la culture*) and supplied 50 percent of the funds to finance them. The first of the cultural centers was opened in 1962; eventually there were about twenty. In addition to theatrical performances, these centers included facilities for films, music, dance, visual arts, and public lectures. Some of these *maisons* (as well as some dramatic centers) were located in the suburbs of Paris, for it became clear that the residents of those areas were too far removed from the center of the city to benefit adequately from its resources.

Malraux also reorganized the state theatres. He removed the Odéon from the control of the Comédie Française, renamed it the Théâtre de France, and installed Barrault's company in it. Similarly, the Théâtre National Populaire was elevated to a rank equal to that of the other state theatres. Jean Vilar continued to head the TNP until 1963, when he was succeeded by Georges Wilson (1921–), a long-time member of the company.

Many changes in the postwar theatre were intimately connected with experiments in dramaturgy, notably those of the absurdists. This movement did not come to the fore until the 1950s, however, and much of the major writing of the postwar period was to come from dramatists well known before 1940. Among these, the most prolific was Jean Anouilh, with such works as *Invitation to the Chateau* (1947), *Waltz of the Toreadors* (1952), *The Lark* (1953), *Becket* (1960), *Dear Antoine* (1970), and *The Pants* (1978). In these plays Anouilh continued to explore the problem of maintaining integrity in a world based upon compromises. Other prewar dramatists who made important contributions after 1945 include Marcel Achard, with *Patate* (1957) and *Eugene the Mysterious* (1964); and Armand Salacrou, with *Nights of Wrath* (1946) and *Boulevard Durand* (1960).

Among the most respected of the new dramatists was Henry de Montherlant (1896–1972), whose novels had won a wide following before the war. Although he had written a few minor plays, Montherlant's first produced work was *The Dead Queen* (1942), directed by Barrault at the Comédie Française. Its success led Montherlant to write *The Master of Santiago* (1948), *Port-Royal* (1954), *The Cardinal of Spain* (1960), and *The Civil War* (1965). *The Master of Santiago* is often considered Montherlant's most characteristic work because of its simple external action, complex psychology, and elevated style. The motif of sacrifice and the harsh rejection of all mediocrity runs through it. In all of Montherlant's work, the interest resides as much in the intellectual positions taken up by the characters as in their psychological traits and actions.

Postwar French drama exerted its greatest influence through existentialist and absurdist plays. Following the war, existentialism as a philosophical outlook attracted considerable attention, especially through the essays and plays of Jean-Paul Sartre (1905–1980), a philosopher and novelist who turned to drama in

1943 with *The Flies,* and went on to write *No Exit* (1944), *Dirty Hands* (1948), *The Devil and the Good Lord* (1951), and *The Condemned of Altona* (1959). All illustrate Sartre's existentialist views. Denying the existence of God, fixed standards of conduct, and verifiable moral codes, Sartre argued that human beings are "condemned to be free." Thus, people must choose their own values and live by them, for "man is only what he does. Man becomes what he chooses to be." Sartre's plays show characters faced with choices which require them to reassess their outlooks, forge their own standards, and then live by them uncompromisingly. In the uncertainty that followed the war, Sartre attracted a wide following, for he cast doubt upon the conformism that had made possible the Nazi atrocities. Sartre also believed that it is necessary for people to be politically "engaged," even though the choices open to them are seldom ideal. In *Dirty Hands* he argues that to participate in political action invariably means that one's hands will get dirty, but that refusing to become politically engaged merely means that others will make the choices that determine events.

The work of Albert Camus (1913–1960) was to be of comparable importance. Before turning to drama, Camus had been a theatre worker in his native Algeria, a journalist, and the editor of a clandestine newspaper during the German occupation of France. His dramatic output was small: *Cross-Purposes* (1944), *Caligula* (performed 1945), *State of Siege* (1948), *The Just Assassins* (1949), and a few adaptations. His influence on the theatre came in part from his essay, "The Myth of Sisyphus" (1943), in which his discussion of the "absurd" was to supply the name for the absurdist movement. In this essay, Camus argues that the human condition is absurd because of the gap between people's hopes and the irrational universe into which they are born. For Camus, the only remedy lies in each individual's search for a set of standards (admittedly without any objective basis) that will allow her or him to bring order out of this chaos. Although Camus denied being an existentialist, his conclusions were similar to those of Sartre.

Camus and Sartre differed most in their ideas about "engagement," for Camus rejected the conclusion advocated by Sartre in *Dirty Hands* and denied the validity of choosing between two immoral positions. Their difference on this point led to a prolonged and bitter debate. Between them, nevertheless, they supplied the philosophical basis for the absurdist movement which began to emerge in the early 1950s.

Although Sartre and Camus rejected rationalistic views of the universe, their plays were cast in traditional dramatic form. Since they began with the assumption that the world is irrational and then went on to create order out of chaos, their plays had dramatic actions that developed linearly through cause and effect. On the other hand, the absurdists, while for the most part accepting Sartre's philosophical outlook, tended to concentrate upon the irrationality of human experience without suggesting any path beyond. By employing a succession of episodes unified merely by theme or mood instead of a cause-to-effect arrangement, they arrived at a structure paralleling the chaos which was their usual dramatic subject. The sense of absurdity was heightened by the juxtaposition of incongruous events producing seriocomic and ironic effects. Because they viewed language as the major rationalistic tool, the absurdists often demonstrated its inadequacy and subordinated it to nonverbal devices. Of the absurdists, four—Beckett, Ionesco, Genet, and Adamov—were to be most important.

Samuel Beckett (1906–1989) was the first of the absurdists to win international fame—with *Waiting for Godot* which in 1953 brought absurdism its first popular attention both in France and elsewhere. Irish by birth, Beckett first went to Paris in the 1920s and settled there permanently in 1938. He began writing

FIG. 20.4

Original production of Beckett's *Waiting for Godot,* Théâtre de Babylone, Paris, 1953. Directed by Roger Blin, seated at left. Courtesy Pic, Paris.

around 1930 but did not turn to drama until after World War II. His plays include *Endgame* (1957), *Krapp's Last Tape* (1958), *Happy Days* (1961), *Play* (1963), *Come and Go* (1966), *Not I* (1973), *That Time* (1976), and several other short pieces. In many ways, Beckett seems the characteristic dramatist of the 1950s, a decade made anxious by the threat of atomic holocaust. In fact, Beckett's characters often seem to have been set down in a world already ravaged by some disaster which threatens human survival. Beckett is not so much concerned with people as social and political creatures as with the human condition in a metaphysical sense. His spiritual derelicts are usually isolated in time and space; they torment and console themselves and others, raise questions which cannot be answered, and struggle on in a world that seems to be disintegrating around them. Probably more than any other writer, Beckett expressed the postwar doubts about the human capacity to understand and control the world.

Eugène Ionesco (1909–1994), a Roumanian by birth, labeled his first work, *The Bald Soprano* (1949),

an "anti-play" to indicate a rebellion against conventional drama. The early works, which include *The Lesson* (1950) and *The Chairs* (1952), attracted little attention at first, but steadily grew in reputation after 1953, when Anouilh published an article praising *Victims of Duty*. These early plays, as well as *Amedée* (1954) and *The New Tenant* (1957), are mainly negative, for they concentrate upon the clichés of language and thought and the irrationality of materialist values. Later works, such as *The Killer* (1959), *Rhinoceros* (1960), *Exit the King* (1962), *Hunger and Thirst* (1966), *Macbett* (1972), and *The Man with the Suitcases* (1975), took a somewhat more positive view by showing protagonists who hold out against conformity, although they cannot offer any rational explanation for their actions.

Unlike Beckett, Ionesco is concerned primarily with social relationships, typically those of middle-class characters in family situations. Two themes run through most of his work: the deadening nature of materialistic, bourgeois society, and the loneliness and isolation of the individual. Perhaps ultimately his

FIG. 20.5
Genet's *The Screens,* Théâtre de France, 1966. Directed by Roger Blin. Madeleine Renaud is at center. Courtesy Pic, Paris.

vision of the human condition differs little from Beckett's, but it is conceived in more domestic terms. All of his plays seek to discredit clichés, ideologies, and materialism. His characters tend to be unthinking automatons oblivious of their own mechanical behavior, just as material objects tend to proliferate and take over the space that should be occupied by people. Ionesco is especially antipathetic to the notion that drama should be didactic. To him truth means the absence of commitment, for commitment involves a fatal step toward conformity.

Jean Genet (1910–1986) spent much of his life in prison, a background that figures prominently in much of his writing. His first plays, *The Maids* (presented by Jouvet in 1947) and *Deathwatch* (produced by Herrand in 1949), were at first unsuccessful, and his reputation was to be made with *The Balcony* (1956), *The Blacks* (1959), and *The Screens* (1961, not produced in France until 1966). Genet's characters rebel against organized society and suggest that deviation is essential if human beings are to achieve integrity. The plays also imply that nothing has meaning without its opposite—law and crime, religion and sin, love and hate—and therefore that deviant behavior is as valuable as the accepted virtues. Genet, viewing all systems of value as entirely arbitrary, transforms life into a series of ceremonies and rituals which give an air of stability and importance to otherwise nonsensical behavior.

Arthur Adamov (1908–1971), born in Russia and educated in Switzerland, was attracted early to surrealism, a movement that influenced most absurdist drama. Turning to playwriting in 1947, Adamov's first work was produced in 1950. The early plays, for example *The Invasion* (1950), *Parody* (1952), and *All Against All* (1953), show a seriocomically cruel world of moral destructiveness and personal anxieties in which the characters are condemned to eternal failure by their inability to communicate with each other. Time and place are usually indefinite, as in dreams. Adamov's later plays became progressively more socially oriented, especially after 1956, when he denounced his earlier work and adopted a Brechtian form. This new outlook was reflected in *Paolo Paoli* (1957), a commentary upon the materialism and hypocrisy which preceded World War I, and *Spring '71* (1960), which idealizes the men who created the Paris Commune in 1871. Adamov's late plays, staged by Roger Planchon's company, are indicative of the decline of interest in absurdism around 1960 and increased concern for plays of social action. Many critics now consider that Adamov's conversion marked a major turning point in postwar French theatre.

As a label, absurdism was popularized by Martin Esslin's *The Theatre of the Absurd* (1961) but, since it

FIG. 20.6

Arrabal's *The Automobile Graveyard* at the Théâtre des Arts, Paris, 1967. Directed by Victor Garcia. Courtesy Agence de Presse Bernand, Paris.

was never a conscious movement, it is difficult to specify those authors who should be considered among its ranks. Absurdism did not encompass all of the experimental dramatists of the time, of whom there were many in France. Among those who probably should not be labeled absurdists, some of the best were Jacques Audiberti (1899–1965), whose *Quoat-Quoat* (1946), *The Black Feast* (1948), and *The Sentry-Box* (1965) stress the power of evil and sex over human affairs; and Jean Tardieu (1903–1995), who concentrated upon one-act "chamber" plays, such as *The Information Window* (1955) and *The ABC of Our Life* (1959), treating human enslavement to social conventions.

After 1960, the best known of the *avant-garde* dramatists was Fernando Arrabal (1932–) who, born in Spain, moved to Paris in 1955. His early plays, such as *Fando and Lis* (1958), emphasize a childish, thoughtless cruelty couched in a form similar to that used by the absurdists. Around 1962 Arrabal became interested in what he called *théâtre panique,* "a ceremony— partly sacrilegious, partly sacred, erotic and mystic, a putting to death and exaltation of life, part Don Quixote and part Alice in Wonderland." Among his later works are *Solemn Communion* (1966), *The Architect and the Emperor of Assyria* (1967), *And They Handcuffed the Flowers* (1970), and *Young Barbarians Today* (1975). Of these, the second is perhaps most characteristic. It includes only two characters, who enact a series of ritualized human situations: master and slave, judge and criminal, mother and child, male and female, sadist and masochist, and so on.

Eventually one decides that he must be punished and asks the other to kill and eat him. When this is done, they seem somehow to merge. But now a new figure appears, apparently beginning the whole cycle over again. Through such plays, Arrabal not only challenged all values, he ferreted out the hidden corners of the human psyche. Following the death of Franco, Arrabal spent much of his time in Spain, where he continued to write plays, among them *The Mad Laughter of the Lillputians* and *Orangutan Opening.*

Most of the *avant-garde* drama was first produced in small, out-of-the-way theatres by adventurous directors, many of them heavily influenced by Artaud and later to be among France's most respected directors. Of these, perhaps the most important was Roger Blin (1907–1984), a disciple of Artaud, who, after working with Dullin and Barrault, was closely associated with the absurdist movement after 1949. He is especially noted for his staging of Beckett's and Genet's plays. Other important directors include André Reybaz (1922–), who introduced Audiberti,

FIG. 20.8

Planchon's production of Adamov's adaptation of Gogol's *Dead Souls,* 1960. Setting by René Allio. Théâtre de la Cité, Villeurbanne. Courtesy Pic, Paris.

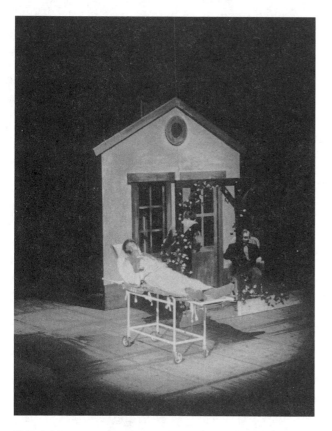

FIG. 20.7

Armand Gatti's *The Imaginary Life of the Scavenger August Geai* as produced by Roger Planchon's company in 1964. Directed by Jacques Rosner; designed by René Allio. Photo by Agence de Presse Bernand, Paris.

Ghelderode, and Ionesco to Parisian audiences and worked with a number of *avant-garde* theatres before becoming director of the Dramatic Center at Tourcoing in 1960; Georges Vitaly (1917–), who worked with Reybaz before founding the Théâtre LaBruyère in 1953; and Jean-Marie Serreau (1915–1973), a pupil of Dullin, who directed the first productions of Adamov's plays before opening the Théâtre de Babylone with Blin in 1952 and going on to direct at many other theatres. Beginning as members of the *avant-garde,* most of these directors were later to work regularly with such established troupes as the Comédie Française, the Théâtre de France, and various Dramatic Centers.

After 1960, several French playwrights treated political and socioeconomic themes. Aimé Cesaire (1913–), a black writer born in Martinique, in *The Tragedy of King Christophe* (1963), *A Season in the Congo* (1966), and *A Tempest* (1969), was especially concerned with the problems of postcolonialism. These plays, all directed by Serreau, made a deep impression on French audiences. Gabriel Cousin (1918–) wrote in the Brechtian vein, although with a Christian rather than a Marxist slant. In such plays as *Ordinary Love* (1958) and *Cycle of the Crab* (1969), he dealt with major world problems, such as hunger, racism, and nuclear threat, but always from the viewpoint of working-class characters. Armand Gatti

(1924–) also wrote a variation of Brechtian drama in which he advocated a humanitarian socialism and expressed hope for the exploited people of the world. Among these plays were *The Imaginary Life of the Scavenger August Geai* (1956), *A Single Man* (1966), and *V as in Vietnam* (1967). Beginning in the late 1960s, Gatti worked directly with ordinary people in writing plays, as in *The Lion, Its Cage and Its Wings* (1975), a series of six programs in which immigrant workers expressed their views of France.

Among the directors who came to the fore in the early 1960s, the most important was Roger Planchon (1931–), after 1957 head of the Théâtre de la Cité in Villeurbanne, an industrial suburb of Lyons, where he was successful in attracting the working-class audience he sought. In his productions, Planchon borrowed many techniques from film (since he considered this medium most familiar to his unsophisticated theatregoers) and from Brecht. He made liberal use of projections (captions, commentaries, and pictures) and often utilized turntables to show the action from different angles, as in the cinema. He presented plays by Molière, Marivaux, Shakespeare, Kleist, Marlowe, Racine, Brecht, and other major writers, but he usually gave them working-class interpretations. Consequently, his productions were often controversial. But their liveliness, richness, clarity, and novelty won Planchon one of the largest followings in France. Planchon was to be even more important after 1968.

SOVIET THEATRE AND DRAMA, 1940–1968

During the war years the Russian theatre was devoted primarily to building morale. Since governmental strictures were considerably relaxed, many thought that the end of the war would bring still greater freedom. Instead, restrictions even more severe than those of the 1930s were imposed in 1946, and in 1948 all subsidies, except those granted to a few favored theatres, were stopped. The loss of governmental financial support was a severe blow, since 450 of Russia's 950 theatres had been destroyed during the war. By 1953 only about 250 were left.

Artistic restrictions made socialist realism the only acceptable style and the Moscow Art Theatre's methods standard. Political control was strengthened in 1949 when party-appointed administrative directors were placed in complete charge of each theatre. Most Western plays were removed from the repertory, and new Russian works were expected to uphold government policy. A large number of plays, such as Anatoly Safronov's (1911–) *The Muscovite Character* (1949), show the reeducation of persons who have stood in the way of party goals, while Konstantin Simonov's *Alien Shadow* (1949) and Nikolai Pogodin's *The Missouri Waltz* (1950) are typical of the numerous anti-American plays. Other postwar dramas, such as Vsevelod Vishnevsky's *1919—The Unforgettable Year* (1949) and A. Stein's *Prologue* (1952), glorify Stalin's role in the development of Communism.

Following Stalin's death in 1953 many changes occurred. Although periods of freedom and restrictions alternated thereafter, in general there was a relaxation of the former strictures, especially after Khrushchev's denunciation of Stalin in 1956. Censorship in the sense of prior judgment was no longer practiced, although many pressures were still exerted on drama, most notably through the governing boards of theatres. Realism remained the dominant style and didacticism the dominant aim, but neither was systematically enforced and both declined in popularity. In new plays, individual concerns were treated more frequently, as in Pogodin's *Sonnet of Petrarch* (1957), about a middle-aged married man's affair with a young girl, while the theme of vindication from unjust charges, typified by Alexander Volodin's (1919–) *Factory Girl* (1957), became common. The conflict between generations, exemplified in Victor Rozov's (1913–) *The Unequal Struggle* (1960), also became a popular subject. By 1960 anti-American plays had largely disappeared from the repertory, while many previously banned Russian plays became acceptable. The penchant for reshaping classics to bring out propagandistic themes also had lessened.

One result of relaxed strictures was the presentation of many foreign plays for the first time in the

FIG. 20.9
Pogodin's *Sonnet of Petrarch* at the Mayakovsky Theatre, Moscow, 1957. From Komissarzkevsky, *Moscow Theatres*.

USSR. For example, in 1960 Brecht's works began to be introduced into the repertory, and soon plays by Miller, Osborne, Williams, and others were being performed with some frequency. On the other hand, few absurdist dramas were produced, being considered too "formalistic."

The changes brought a loss of prestige for the Moscow Art Theatre, although it continued to be the most favored company in terms of subsidies, salaries, and other government standards. Nevertheless, by the 1960s the Moscow Art Theatre was looked upon by the public as something of a museum. As the MAT declined in prestige, others rose. Some of the changes can be attributed to the abandonment in 1956 of the fixed pay scales, ranks, and prohibitions against changing companies which had hampered actors since the 1930s. Other changes can be attributed to shifts in taste. Of the older theatres, the Vakhtangov, under the direction of Reuben Simonov, became the most popular, for Vakhtangov's methods provided the most acceptable alternative to socialist realism. The Theatre of Satire, under Valentin Pluchek, also grew in esteem after it created a sensation in 1954 with productions of Mayakovsky's *The Bedbug* and *The Bathhouse* in a style not unlike Meyerhold's. At the Mayakovsky Theatre (formerly the Theatre of the Revolution), Nikolai Okhlopkov returned to his prewar experimentation with performer-audience relationships. In the late 1950s he restaged Pogodin's *Aristocrats,* with the audience surrounding the playing area as in his prewar productions. The most famous of Okhlopkov's postwar productions was probably *Hamlet* (1954), in which the compartmentalized setting created a prison-like world from which Hamlet wishes to escape. Two other prewar directors, Yuri Zavadsky at the Mossoviet Theatre and Alexei Popov at the Central Theatre of the Soviet Army, also linked the prewar and postwar theatres.

In Leningrad, the Pushkin Theatre occupied a prewar position comparable to that of the Moscow Art Theatre in Moscow and during the 1950s its prestige suffered similarly. The most admired theatre in Leningrad was the Gorky, after 1956 under the direction of Georgi Tovstogonov (1915–1989), noted for giving classics contemporary significance. Using realistic set pieces, Tovstogonov often dispensed with walls, ceilings, and similar details, and employed such cinematic techniques as moving the action forward on platforms for "close-up" effects. At the Leningrad Comedy Theatre, Nikolai Akimov (1901–1968), as both director and designer, also maintained high standards, but Akimov's official standing was probably reflected by the theatre in which he worked, a large room over a grocery.

The most innovative postwar company was Moscow's Sovremennik (Contemporary) Theatre, founded in 1957, the first new company to be authorized in Russia since the 1930s. Under the leadership of Oleg Yefremov (1927–2000), the Contemporary drew most of its personnel and methods from the Moscow Art Theatre or its training school. The principal departures of the new company lay in its concentration on plays (such as those by Brecht, Osborne, Shatrov, and Rozov) thought to be relevant to present-day life and in its use of simplified settings rather than the elaborate mountings typical at the MAT. By the late 1960s, the Russian theatre had moved away from the restrictions and standards imposed during the Stalinist era. But pressure to conform to party needs was still evident, and the government continued to make its presence felt when deviations became more than it wished to countenance.

FIG. 20.10
Okhlopkov's production of *Hamlet* at the Mayakovsky Theatre, Moscow, 1954.

THEATRE AND DRAMA IN CZECHOSLOVAKIA, 1940–1968

Following World War II, most of Eastern Europe came under the domination of Russia. As a result, theatre in these countries was subjected to restrictions similar to those imposed in the USSR. Following the break with Stalinism in 1956, however, strictures were considerably relaxed and experimentation flourished, especially in Czechoslovakia.

Czechoslovakia made its greatest international impact in the field of technology and design and above all through the work of Josef Svoboda (1920–2002). Although he began his career around 1945, Svoboda was unable to demonstrate his great versatility until the late 1950s when socialist realism was no longer the standard mode. Much of his work was an extension of experimentation begun with multimedia in the 1930s by E. F. Burian (1904–1959) and Miroslav Kouril (1911–). It was also heavily indebted to the Prague Institute of Scenography, founded in 1957 and headed by Kouril, for its staff and facilities did much of the experimentation.

The turning point in Svoboda's career came in 1958 when he began collaborating with the director Alfred Radok on two projects—Polyekran and Laterna Magika, both using a number of screens on which still and moving pictures were projected. Laterna Magika also integrated live actors into the performance. Both of these forms were shown at the Brussels World's Fair in 1958 and elicited enormous excitement. In 1959 Svoboda began to carry over many of the technical devices into his stage work. Subsequently, he experimented continuously with means to create a completely flexible stage which could change from scene to scene as the needs of the action changed. In addition to screens and projections, he also developed platforms and steps that could move vertically, horizontally, and laterally to alter rapidly the spatial relationships and size of the acting area. He also explored the potentials for stage use of such materials as mirrors, plastic, and various kinds of netting, and used most of these as surfaces on which to project images (or in some instances to reflect the action as seen from above, behind, or at an angle). He designed settings in almost every style and after 1960 was among the best known and most influential designers in the world. Svoboda's work did much to call attention to the high quality of the Czech theatre as a whole. In the 1960s there were about fifty-six companies in Czechoslovakia, but those best known abroad (aside from the Prague National Theatre) were a group of small theatres in Prague, most of which came into existence after 1962 when the government created the State Theatre Studio to assist experimental companies. Of these, three were especially outstanding. The Theatre Behind the Gate, founded in 1965 by Otomar Krejca, shared its 435-seat theatre with the Laterna Magika, for both of which Svoboda was principal designer. It was noted for its imaginative staging and thoughtful interpretation of Czech and foreign plays. The Cino-

FIG. 20.11

Svoboda's setting for *Their Day* by Josef Topol at the National Theatre, Prague, 1959. This was Svoboda's first attempt to apply Laterna Magika techniques to theatrical design. Photo copyrighted by Jaromir Svoboda.

herni (Actors' Club), founded in 1965 and headed by Jaroslav Vostry, performed in a theatre seating 220. Its primary emphasis was on ensemble acting (probably the best in Czechoslovakia) and a wide-ranging repertory drawn from world drama. The Theatre on the Balustrade, founded in 1958 and headed from 1962 until 1969 by Jan Grossman, seated about 200. This company was the primary home of absurdist drama in Czechoslovakia and had as its resident playwright Václav Havel (1936–), usually considered the leading contemporary Czech dramatist. His bitingly satirical treatments of bureaucracy, *The Garden Party* (1963), *The Memorandum* (1965), and *The Conspirators* (1974) came to be known and admired throughout the world. During later years, when he was imprisoned or refused productions, he continued to write. Among his later plays are *Largo Desolato* (1984) and *Temptation* (1985).

In 1968 the vitality of Czech theatre was severely curtailed following the invasion by Warsaw Pact troops sent to end the liberalization that had been underway in Czechoslovakia. Many theatre directors were removed from their posts and many plays were forbidden publication or production. Václav Havel was subsequently imprisoned several times for his continued resistance to government violations of human rights. These repressive measures were to continue until 1989, when within a few weeks' time not only were the restrictions removed but Havel was also named president of Czechoslovakia.

GERMAN THEATRE AND DRAMA, 1940–1968

When Germany surrendered to the Allies in 1945, all theatres were closed for a time but soon began to reopen under the surveillance of occupation forces. After 1945, the German theatre recovered rapidly and by the 1960s was one of the most stable in the world. Although Germany was divided into East and West after 1945, the theatre in the two areas shared many common characteristics. In both, the system of state-supported resident companies was reinstated. By the 1960s, there were 175 professional theatres in West Germany, of which 120 were government-owned, and in East Germany there were about 135 theatres, all state-owned. Almost every city had a dramatic company and many had an opera and ballet troupe of good quality. Typically, all of the subsidized troupes in a single city were under one manager (or Intendant), appointed by the city or state, and shared

physical facilities and a staff of directors and designers. In large cities, such as Berlin, there were multiple facilities, each with its own Intendant and company. A *dramaturg* (with a sizable staff) worked with each company on its choice of plays and other artistic matters.

Although more than a hundred theatre buildings were destroyed during the war, a phenomenal rebuilding program after 1950 replaced most of them. In the new buildings, sight lines were considerably improved, boxes were eliminated, and the number of balconies reduced. The prewar emphasis upon complex stage machinery continued. For example, the Schiller Theater, opened in West Berlin in 1951, had a revolving stage, elevators, and rolling platform stages. Most of the theatres were of the conventional proscenium-arch type. A few small theatres intended as second houses were more flexible, but there was little experimentation with audience-performer spatial relationships.

In addition to permanent resident troupes, festivals were of considerable importance in postwar Germany. The most famous was still the Bayreuth Festival, revived in 1951 under the direction of Wieland Wagner (1917–1966) until his death and then under his brother Wolfgang Wagner (1919–). After the war, Wagner's operas were performed for the first time at Bayreuth with simple scenic investiture and atmospheric lighting, much like that advocated by Appia, instead of the historical realism that had been used since Wagner's time. Bitterly opposed by traditionalists, the new methods won wholehearted approval from others.

In Austria, the pattern of postwar reconstruction paralleled that in Germany. By the 1960s there were thirty-six theatres in Austria, twenty of which were located in Vienna. Four of these were state theatres, the Staatsoper and the Volksoper for opera, the Burgtheater and the Akademietheater for drama, while the Theater-in-der-Josefstadt and the Volkstheater were subsidized by the city of Vienna. The festival at Salzburg, reopened in 1946, also resumed its position as one of the finest in the world.

Among postwar German directors, perhaps the most important were Kortner, Gründgens, and Hilpert. Fritz Kortner (1892–1970) was considered the leading expressionist actor of the 1920s. After spending the Nazi years in exile, he returned to Germany in 1949, working primarily in Berlin and Munich. His total dedication, long rehearsal periods, and detailed attention to the emotional lives of characters made him perhaps the most influenial director of the postwar period. Gustav Gründgens (1899–1963), Intendant of the Berlin National Theater under the Nazis and Hitler's favorite actor, known

FIG. 20.12
Wieland Wagner's production of *Tannhäuser*, Bayreuth, 1954. Note the absence of three-dimensional scenery and the dependence on light and projections. From *Décor de Théâtre dans le Monde depuis 1935*.

especially for his portrayal of Mephistopheles, served after the war as Intendant in Düsseldorf and later in Hamburg, coming to be seen as the primary preserver of German theatrical tradition. Heinz Hilpert (1890–1967), a leading actor who served as Intendant of the Deutsches Theater under the Nazis, after the war worked primarily in Göttingen. He was noted especially for his Shakespearean productions and for directing the premieres of Zuckmayer's postwar dramas. Both Gründgens and Hilpert justified their cooperation with the Nazis as a desire to preserve German culture in a time of barbarism. In 1951, Erwin Piscator returned to Germany and directed for numerous companies before being named Intendant of the Freie Volksbühne in West Berlin in 1962. He was especially instrumental in popularizing the documentary drama that emerged in the 1960s. Other major directors in Germany included Harry Buchwitz, Hans Schalla, Boleslag Barlow, Rudolf Sellner, Wolfgang Langhoff, Wolfgang Heinz, and Walter Felsenstein.

Of all German companies the most famous was the Berliner Ensemble, located in East Berlin and devoted primarily to the plays of Brecht. After Brecht returned to Europe in 1947, his plays rapidly found their way into the repertories of most German troupes and his theory was soon known throughout the world. His fame was confirmed through the work of the Berliner Ensemble. Opened in 1949 with *Mother Courage,* the Berliner Ensemble for a time shared the Deutsches Theater with another troupe. In 1954 it was given the Theater-am-Schiffbauerdamm, the house in which Brecht's *Threepenny Opera* was first produced in 1928. With its appearances in Paris in 1954 and 1955, the Berliner Ensemble became internationally famous and thereafter was considered one of the world's finest troupes. After Brecht's death in 1956, the company continued under the direction of Helene Weigel (1900–1971), Brecht's wife, who had been its official director from the beginning. Brecht's methods were also retained by the company's principal directors.

Upon returning to Germany, Brecht reestablished associations with several persons with whom he had collaborated before 1933: Erich Engel (1891–1966), who had directed the original production of *Threepenny Opera* in 1928, staged many of the Berliner Ensemble's plays; major German actors, among them Therese Giehse (1898–1975), Lionel Steckel (1901–1971), and Ernst Busch (1900–1980), appeared in Berliner productions; and Teo Otto (1904–1968) and Caspar Neher (1897–1962), Germany's most influential designers, did a number of productions for Brecht. Along with Karl von Appen, the Berliner's principal designer after 1954, Otto and Neher moved

FIG. 20.13
Gustav Gründgens's production of Goethe's *Faust* at the Neue Schauspielhaus, Hamburg. At left, Will Quadflieg as Faust; at right, Gründgens as Mephisto. Courtesy Theatersammlung, Universitat Hamburg.

postwar German stage design toward the frank manipulation of stage means. Through a few architectural elements, set pieces, projections, and lighting, they achieved settings both functional and beautiful.

Brecht also trained a number of directors who were to play a significant role in German theatre. Benno Besson (1922–) worked at the Berliner Ensemble from 1949 until 1958, then at the Deutsches Theater until he became Intendant of the Volksbühne in 1969; he came to be considered one of East Germany's most important directors. Manfred Wekwerth (1929–), with the Ensemble after 1951, was one of the company's mainstays after Brecht's death and eventually became its head. Peter Palitzsch (1918–) and Egon Monk (1927–), after working with the Ensemble, emigrated to West Germany, where they were highly influential directors.

Much of the Berliner Ensemble's achievement stemmed from its long and careful rehearsals, sometimes extending over several months. When each production was ready, a *Modellbuch* containing 600 to 800 action photographs was made. The published *Modellbücher* have influenced many producers who have never seen the company perform. The Berliner Ensemble demonstrated the validity of Brecht's theories, while the humanitarian and social emphases of his plays suggested an alternative to the absurdists (who concentrated on personal anxieties).

If Germany and Austria rebuilt one of the best systems of subsidized theatres in the world, they were less successful in developing significant new dramatists, for until the late 1950s the major German

FIG. 20.14
Brecht's production of his *The Caucasian Chalk Circle* at the Berliner Ensemble, 1954. Setting by Karl von Appen. From *Décor de Théâtre dans le Monde depuis 1935.*

dramatist was Brecht, all of whose major works were written before 1946. Zuckmayer also returned to Germany. His *The Devil's General* (1946) introduced the theme that was to dominate German drama until the 1960s—public guilt and responsibility, especially

FIG. 20.15
Duerrenmatt's *The Physicists* at the Kammerspiele, Munich, 1962. Directed by Hans Schweikart. Courtesy *World Theatre.*

under the Nazis. Wolfgang Borchert (1921–1947) won fame with one play, *The Man Outside* (1947), about a returning soldier trying to adjust to civilian life, but died before he could fulfill the promise shown by that work. Fritz Hochwalder (1911–1986) found a wide audience at home with *The Holy Experiment* (1943), *The Fugitive* (1945), and *The Public Prosecutor* (1949), all of which pose questions of individual responsibility and public guilt, but he never won a following outside of German-speaking territories.

The major drama in German during the 1950s was written by two Swiss playwrights, Frisch and Duerrenmatt, both of whom were encouraged by Kurt Hirschfeld (1902–1964) and Oskar Walterlin (1895–1961) of the Zurich Schauspielhaus, one of the best in Europe during the Nazi regime because so many refugees settled in Switzerland. Max Frisch (1911–1991) was trained as an architect but turned to writing in 1944. His reputation rests primarily upon *The Chinese Wall* (1946), *Biedermann and the Firebugs* (1958), and *Andorra* (1961), all of which treat questions of guilt. In each play the past is reviewed and the characters construct elaborate rationalizations for their actions; none is really willing to accept responsibility. Although it is clear that Frisch longs for a world of integrity, he seems to suggest that it is unattainable because human beings do not learn from their mistakes. Through techniques influenced by Wilder, Strindberg, Brecht, and others, he embodied his search and disillusionment in symbolic and nightmarish fantasy.

Friedrich Duerrenmatt (1921–1990) began writing plays in 1947. Of his many works, the most successful were *The Visit* (1956), *The Physicists* (1962), and *Play Strindberg* (1969). Like Frisch, Duerrenmatt was concerned with moral questions, which he suggested will not be solved satisfactorily because people are so readily corrupted by promises of power or wealth. Duerrenmatt was much more detached than Frisch. He emphasized the grotesqueness of the human condition, which he expressed through a rather dark comedy. Although he was concerned with moral dilemmas, he showed the human instinct for good corrupted either by power and greed or by chance. He avoided bitterness by standing at a distance and viewing events sardonically.

Because the majority of significant postwar German drama dealt with questions of guilt related to larger political and social issues, it differed considerably in tone from the French absurdist drama, which attracted few German exponents. Germany's major plays in the 1960s took the form of "documentary drama" or the "theatre of fact" in which actual events, often quite recent, were used to explore the by-then characteristic concern for guilt and responsibility in public affairs and morality. The best-known writers of the form were Hochhuth, Weiss, and Kipphardt, although all wrote other types of plays as well.

Rolf Hochhuth (1931–) came to prominence with *The Deputy* (1963), which seeks to place much of the blame for the extermination of Jews on Pope Pius XII's refusal to take a decisive stand against Hitler's policies. This accusation made the play controversial wherever it was performed, and in many countries it was forbidden. *The Soldiers* (1967) also aroused considerable consternation because of its suggestion that Winston Churchill conspired in the death of General Sikorski, president of the Polish government in exile, because Sikorski endangered the Anglo-Russian alliance. In the late 1960s Hochhuth seemed to tire of factual material. After writing a number of less provocative plays, Hochhuth returned to controversy with *Wessies in Weimar: Scenes from an Occupied Land* (1993) concerning the murder of an official whose job it is to sell off businesses previously owned by the East German state; the play implies that the murder was justified considering what was being done to a defenseless population. Almost all of Hochhuth's plays are long and diffuse and must be cut severely in production. Because he uses recent historical figures, to whom he attributes questionable motives and thereby raises serious ethical questions about the limits to which a dramatist may go without becoming libelous, Hochhuth was one of the most controversial playwrights of postwar Germany.

Peter Weiss (1916–1982) worked as a graphic artist, filmmaker, and journalist before winning fame as a playwright. Although he began writing in the 1940s, his first play was not produced until 1962. His international reputation dates from 1964 with the production of *The Persecution and Assassination of Jean-Paul Marat as Performed by the Inmates of the Asylum of Charenton Under the Direction of the Marquis de Sade* (usually shortened to *Marat/Sade*). Set in 1808 in the asylum at Charenton where the Marquis de Sade is confined, it shows the presentation of a play written by de Sade for performance by the inmates before a fashionable audience from nearby Paris. The play that de Sade has written is Brechtian in form, and is intended by Weiss to provoke thought about political and social justice. The asylum serves as a metaphor for the world, and the play's ending (in which the inmates get out of hand) suggests what happens when the sensual and anarchistic outlook of a de Sade is given full rein. Peter Brook's production of *Marat/ Sade* (seen first in London and then in New York) was to be one of the most influential of the decade, combining as it did devices of the "theatre of cruelty" with Brechtian social and political arguments

FIG. 20.16
Weiss's *Marat/Sade*. Premiere production; Schiller Theater, Berlin, 1964. Directed by Konrad Swinarski; designed by Peter Weiss. Photography by Heinz Köster.

embedded within the Artaudian swirl of visual and aural effects.

Marat/Sade is only partially factual, but in his next play, *The Investigation* (1965), Weiss passed over fully into documentary drama. Set in a courtroom, *The Investigation* utilizes dialogue taken from the official hearings into the extermination camp at Auschwitz. Weiss' subsequent documentary plays include *The Song of the Lusitanian Bogey* (1967), about the suppression of native Africans by the Portuguese in Angola, and *A Discourse on the Previous History and Development of the Long War of Liberation in Vietnam as an Example of the Necessity for the Armed Fight of the Suppressed Against Their Suppressors as Well as the Attempt of the United States of America to Destroy the Foundations of the Revolution* (1968).

Like Hochhuth, Weiss in the late 1960s began to retreat from documentary drama, although his work continued to be based on historical sources. *Trotsky in Exile* (1970) uses material from Trotsky's life to stimulate thought about his ideas and to raise questions about our own political perspectives. *Hölderlin* (1971) is based on the life of the nineteenth-century German poet who spent much of his time locked away from the world. It shows the protagonist in flight from a society he considers deranged, and through his plight Weiss suggests that we have a tendency to destroy our visionaries.

Heinar Kipphardt (1922–1982) first won international renown with *In the Case of J. Robert Oppenheimer* (1964), all the dialogue for which is excerpted from the United States Senate's hearings into the loyalty of Oppenheimer after he resisted development of the hydrogen bomb. Kipphardt's primary concern, however, is with the conflict between a scientist's responsibility to his country and his duty to humanity at large—a familiar issue in postwar German drama. In *Joel Brand* (1965) Kipphardt treats the attempt of the Germans during World War II to exchange one million Hungarian Jews for 10,000 Allied trucks and the failure of the attempt because the Allies could not be convinced that the offer was made in good faith. After a number of years in retirement, Kipphardt returned to documentary drama in 1983 with *Brother Eichmann,* about the man who carried out Hitler's plan to exterminate the Jews.

The success of documentary drama in Germany seems to have stimulated playwrights in other countries to adopt the form. Consequently, many contemporary events were dramatized, among them various aspects of the Vietnam war. But by the early 1970s, interest in the "theatre of fact" was on the wane, above all in Germany.

Other playwrights continued the earlier concern with collective guilt. Among the most important of these writers was Martin Walser (1927–) in such plays as *Oak and Angora* (1962) and *The Black Swan* (1964). The latter contrasts the younger generation, who seem overly sensitive about the Nazi period, with the older generation, who lead seemingly placid lives despite their own involvement in Naziism. Most of Walser's subsequent plays, such as *The Battle of the Bedroom* (1967) and *Children's Game* (1971) treated more private subjects. But in *The Pig Play—Scenes from the Sixteenth Century* (1975) and *In Goethe's Hand* (1982), he made historical events reflect the political fears and lack of certainty among today's workers and intellectuals.

Tankred Dorst (1925–) was representative of German playwrights concerned with political subjects. His early plays were in the absurdist vein. A representative play, *Freedom for Clemens* (1961), shows how an imprisoned man gradually realizes that freedom is an internal state independent of external circumstances. Dorst's later plays are more straightforward. In *Toller* (1968) he used material about the expressionist playwright to explore the relationship of the artist to political action, and followed it with *Ice Age* (1973), in which he examines

the Nobel-Prize-winning Norwegian author Knut Hamsun's defense of his collaboration with the Nazis. Subsequently, Dorst announced his intention to write a series of plays about the German middle class from the 1920s to the present. One of these, *On Chimborazo* (1975), is set on a hill near the border with East Germany where the characters reminisce and come to understand themselves as they wait to light a signal fire to friends on the other side of the border. This series also includes *The Villa* (1984). More recent plays include *Herr Paul* (1994), about the inability to change, and *The Shadow Line* (1995) about the decline of tolerance and enlightenment as seen through the powerlessness of intellectuals.

THEATRE AND DRAMA IN ITALY, 1940–1968

After World War II the position of the Italian playwright remained as difficult as it had been a century earlier, for there was still a conflict between the demand for realism (which required the use of some regional dialect) and for universality (which required a more literary speech). Consequently, playwrights normally wrote with one specific region in mind. Occasionally a dramatist was able to attract a national following, but only a few achieved international stature in the postwar years. Ugo Betti (1892–1953) began writing plays in 1927, but his reputation rests primarily upon his late works, *Corruption in the Palace*

FIG. 20.17
Giorgio Strehler's production of Goldoni's *Servant of Two Masters* at the Piccolo Teatro, Milan. Setting by Ezi Frigerio. From *Scene Design Throughout the World Since 1950.*

of Justice (1948), *The Queen and the Rebels* (1951), and *The Burnt Flower Bed* (1953). All of Betti's plays are concerned with crises of conscience, especially among those who have gained influence through questionable means. His preoccupation with guilt and power struck a responsive chord in the postwar consciousness.

Two other dramatists, Fabbri and de Filippo, also won international recognition. Diego Fabbri (1911–1980) upheld the teachings of the church through dramas of traditional form, such as *Christ on Trial* (1955), showing the difficulties created by Christ's presence in the world. Eduardo de Filippo (1900–1984) began writing around 1930. Although set in Naples and written in the Neapolitan dialect, his plays achieve universality because they show characters struggling to survive in the face of poverty, disease, and strained family relationships. They mingle the serious, comic, and pathetic with closely observed local detail. Among his best works are *Naples' Millionares* (1945), *Filumena* (1946), *Saturday, Sunday, and Monday* (1959), and *The Boss* (1960). De Filippo, also a fine actor, worked for many years with his brother, Peppino de Filippo (1903–1980), one of Italy's most popular performers.

In production, touring companies continued to dominate, but a few permanent resident companies were founded. The most important of the resident troupes was the Piccolo Teatro, established in Milan in 1947 by Giorgio Strehler (1921–1997) and Paolo Grassi (1919–1981). Given a rent-free theatre by the city of Milan and later the first dramatic company in Italy to receive a governmental subsidy, the Piccolo Teatro was a self-contained organization with a permanent troupe of twenty to thirty actors and a training school. Strehler directed about three-fourths of the plays (the majority by Goldoni, Brecht, and Shakespeare) but invited well-known foreign directors to stage others. He leaned heavily toward Brechtian techniques, as did his designers, Luciano Damiani (1923–) and Ezio Frigerio (1930–). Partially because of its foreign tours, the Piccolo Teatro came to be considered not only Italy's finest troupe but one of the best in the world. Permanent theatres were also established elsewhere in Italy. Perhaps the best of these were the Teatro Stabile in Genoa, founded in 1952 and headed by Luigi Squarzina (1922–), and the Teatro Stabile founded in Turin in 1955 and headed by Gianfranco de Bosio (1924–). By the 1960s there were ten of these resident companies in Italy.

Nevertheless, most cities had to depend on touring companies. Of these, three were especially important. Vittorio Gassman (1922–2000), who won an international reputation as a film star but was known in Italy as a major classical actor, from time

FIG. 20.18
Vittorio Gassman in his own production of Alfieri's *Oreste*, 1957. Setting by Gianni Polidori. Courtesy *World Theatre*.

to time assembled companies with which he presented outstanding works from the past. The Compagnia deLullo-Falk—with Giorgio deLullo (1921–) as leading man and director and Rosella Falk (1926–) as leading lady—was after 1955 the best of the touring groups. Its preeminence was later challenged by the Compagnia Proclemer-Albertazzi, run by the actor-directors, Anna Proclemer (1923–) and Giorgio Albertazzi (1923–), perhaps Italy's most famous acting team. These companies, in which most of the leading actors were veterans of Strehler's theatre, toured throughout Italy.

Two Italian directors won international fame in the postwar years. Luchino Visconti (1906–1976) was one of the originators of the neorealism that gave Italian film much of its renown during the 1950s; and he brought the same stylistic quality to his stage productions. His best-known work was done in opera, especially in a series of productions starring Maria Callas. Franco Zeffirelli (1923–) began his career as a designer for Visconti, perhaps the greatest influence on his work. He turned to directing in 1953, at first primarily in opera, and by 1958 was being invited to direct abroad. He built a reputation for bringing classics down to earth (his productions of *Romeo and Juliet* and *Hamlet* were especially well received). In most of his productions (which he also designed), Zeffirelli used neorealistic settings and business, an approach which led on the one hand to accusations that he swamped the text with visual details and on the other to praise for bringing a sense of concreteness to works that all too often remain inaccessible to audiences.

THEATRE AND DRAMA IN LATIN AMERICA, 1940–1968

Commercial theaters after the war reestablished the traditions of providing a well-produced classical repertory and hosting touring shows from Europe. The independent, experimental theatres, meanwhile, continued to grow, building new theatres, reclaiming those that had been taken over by cinema, and converting found spaces to theatrical uses. By 1950 Argentina, Brazil, and Mexico, and to a lesser extent Chile, Cuba, Puerto Rico, and Uruguay, had developed distinctive experimental theatres that were serving as training grounds for young artists throughout South America. Acting styles were generally based on some version of the Stanislavsky system, taught by those who had trained at the Moscow Art Theatre (like Hedy Crilla and Galina Tolmacheva in Argentina, or Seki Sano in Mexico), or by those who had trained with Stanislavsky's former students in Europe or had worked with the Actors Studio in the United States. Production methods were increasingly influenced by Brecht's ideas on epic theatre, however, while playwrights took their inspiration from Lorca, Miller, O'Neill, Pirandello, Tennessee Williams, and the absurdists. The proliferation of international festivals that grew up during the 1950s ensured that new ideas and approaches were shared throughout Latin America.

The Bridge (1949) by author-director Carlos Gorostiza (1920–) marked a turning point in Argentinean theatre when it became the first "independent theatre" play to receive a commercial run. This was a complex play in which the first and fifth acts duplicate the action of the second and fourth in order to show the same events from different points of view. Gorostiza continued to be influential in Argentine theatre well into the 1980s, with over twenty plays, including *Bread of Madness* (1958), *The Neighbors* (1966), *Beloved Brothers* (1978), and *Papi* (1984). Other successful authors of this period included Samuel Eichelbaum (1894–1967), who had written important dramas in the 1920s, the best of which was probably *The Bad Thirst* (1920), about hereditary sexual impulses like those explored by Ibsen and

Wedekind. He returned to playwriting with *A 1900s Dandy* (1940) and *Divorce Nuptial* (1941) and remained a dominant figure in Argentine theatre until his last play, *Underground* (1966). Uruguayan playwright Conrado Nalé Roxlo (1898–1971) wrote the lyrical *The Mermaid's Tale* (1941), while Juan Oscar Ponferrada (1907–) wrote the *Devil's Carnival* (1943) and Bernardo Canal Feijó (1893–1971) wrote *The Tales of Juan* (1954), two plays that revived an interest in folklore.

After Juan Perón was deposed in 1955 the country experienced a period that, although it was politically unstable, was relatively liberal when it came to the treatment of theatre. Professional theatres outside Buenos Aires expanded, especially in the province of Córdoba where a number of theatres were built and subsidized by the government. Independent theatres, too, spread to the provinces, though their major concentration was always in the capital. Groups El Galpó, from Uruguay, attracted Argentine playwrights for collaborative projects that inspired many imitators in Buenos Aires.

Agustín Cuzzani (1924–1990) was an advocate for individual liberty and lampooned the pettiness of state bureaucracy in plays like *The Center Forward Died at Dawn* (1955) and *Sempronio* (1958). *Stories to be Told* (1957), developed by Osvaldo Dragún (1929–) with the Teatro Popular Fray Mocho, achieved international recognition for its expressionistic treatment of the exploitation of the individual in the interest of economic survival (the issue that had caused Dragún disillusionment with Perón's government). This play was first performed at the Independent Theatre Festival in Mar del Plata, one of a growing number of influential provincial festivals of the period. Dragún's other 1957 play, *Those at Table 10,* was the most performed play of its day, and he continued as a successful writer into the 1980s. Andrés Lizárraga (1919–1982) led the epic theatre movement with his three-part revisionist history of the 1810 War of Independence, *Trilogy about May* (1960).

In response to the political turmoil of the 1950s, the "new realists" came to the forefront. These writers, including Roberto Cossa (1934–) and Ricardo Halac (1935–), wrote about the frustrations of the young who were growing increasingly cynical in a culture that seemed incapable of solving its political problems. Plinio Marcos (1935–), on the other hand, wrote about the degradation of life in slums. When General Ongania took control of the government in 1966, repressive policies were put in place and the theatre struggled to find a way to respond.

Brazil's Teatro Brasileiro de Comédia (TBC) was the most highly regarded of the independent theatres in that country until it closed in 1964. It was primarily noted for its European repertory and its imported Italian directors, who brought the highest artistic standards to its productions. On the occasions when TBC produced plays by Brazilian authors like Jorge Andrade (1922–1984), Dias Gomes (1922–1999), and Gianfrancesco Guarnieri (1934–), however, its reputation ensured that those authors received international attention. Nelson Rodrigues, meanwhile, continued to be a major force, adding such plays as *The Kiss on the Asphalt* (1961) and *All Nudity Shall Be Punished* (1965) to his work of the 1940s.

The far more radical Teatro de Arena was founded by José Renato in São Paulo in 1953. This was a politically committed company dedicated to finding an authentic Brazilian theatre. Augusto Boal (1930–), after studying in the United States, joined this company as a director in 1956, and his early play, *Lean Husband, Boring Wife,* was produced there in 1957, as was his most important political protest play, *Revolution in South America* (1960). Boal teamed up with Guarnieri in 1962 to produce a famous series of open-stage productions that combined epic theatre techniques with Brazilian folk theatre and music to tell stories of important figures from Brazil's past, drawing parallels with events in the present. After the military coup of 1964, Boal's outspoken Marxism began to get him into trouble, and following the crackdown of 1968 he was imprisoned. Boal was released and went into exile in Argentina when the Teatro de Arena was closed in 1971. While in exile, he developed his concepts of *teatro jornal,* a production approach reminiscent of the "Living Newspaper" productions of the Federal Theatre Project in the United States in the 1930s, and *teatro invisível,* a highly controversial technique in which performances are presented in a public space for an audience that is not aware that what they are seeing is staged. While in exile Boal also dedicated himself to writing books explaining his approach, the most popular of which, *Theatre of the Oppressed* (1975), brought him international recognition. His later books, *Rainbow of Desire* (1994) and *Legislative Theatre* (1998), represent his later rethinking of the uses of theatre in society.

Numerous other theatres were inspired by the radicalism of the Teatro de Arena, and among the most important of those was the Teatro Oficina, directed by José Celso Martinez Corrêa and known for its commitment to street theatre. In 1967 Teatro Oficina gave the first performance of Andrade's 1929 masterpiece, *King of the Candle,* which was hailed as one of the most innovative productions in Brazilian theatre history. The Teatro Oficina, like so many other theatres of the time, was closed (1973) by the political repression of the 1970s. When the Living Theatre arrived in Brazil in 1970, they discovered just how effective a government could be at repressing dissent as they, too, were arrested and expelled.

The poorer northern sections of Brazil saw little theatre but inspired writers like Ariano Suassuna (1920–) to write *The Rogue's Trial* (sometimes called *The Ceremony of the Compassionate,* 1956), an adaptation of the traditional *auto* which incorporated aspects of mysticism and local humor to depict human beings as the puppets in God's puppet show. It became one of the most produced shows in Brazil and won international recognition.

Theatre in Mexico expanded rapidly in the 1950s, and much of the more experimental work being done was supported by the government through both the Instituto Nacional de Bellas Artes (INBA, founded 1947) and the Universidad Nacional Autónoma de México (UNAM, the National University), which ran its own professional theatre. The dramatic activity they funded encouraged a building boom, and between 1953 and 1958 no fewer than twenty-two new theatres were constructed in Mexico City, including the Teatro del Granero, the country's first theatre in the round. In 1960 the government committed itself to making theatre accessible to everyone and through the Instituto Mexicano del Seguro had forty theatres built across the country. It also established a touring system under the direction of José Solé (1934–) and José Ignacio Retes (1918–), who provided a wide-ranging repertory of plays for this circuit. In 1977 this forty-theatre circuit was designated the Teatro de la Nación.

Under the continuing influence of Rodolfo Usigli, a new generation of playwrights came into prominence in Mexico. The first of the new playwrights was José Revueltas (1914–1976), whose play *The Quadrant of Loneliness* (1950) was an evocation of the psychologically devastating effects of the massive overcrowding already overtaking Mexico City— a theme later taken up by Sergio Magaña (1924–) in *The Signs of the Zodiac* (1951), the first major success of his long career. Mexico's most versatile and widely known dramatist, Emilio Carballido (1925–), began his career in 1950 with *Rosalba and the Llaveros,* a comedy in which the world of a conservative provincial family is turned upside down by a visit from their city cousin. His many other plays range from the existential *Medusa* (1958) to the satiric *The Watchmaker of Córdoba* (1960) to the hauntingly desolate *I Too Speak of the Rose* (1966). Carballido's later plays, like *Rose of Two Aromas* (1992), lacked the innovative energy of his earlier dramas.

Luisa Josefina Hernández (1928–), whose early work dealt with the frustrations of provincial life, especially for Mexico's women, went on to write plays that challenged the existing political and social system. Her plays include *The Royal Guest* (1957), a study of incest; *Popol Vuh* (1966), based on the sacred book of the Maya; and *The Festival of the Mulatto's* (1979), her most nonrealistic piece. She was given Usigli's chair in theatre at the National University when he entered diplomatic service.

Héctor Mendoza (1932–) was a successful playwright when he joined a group of artists that included the actor-playwright Juan José Arreola (1918–2001), whose play *Everybody's Time* (1963) dealt with the crash of an airplane into the Empire State Building, and the poet Octavio Paz to create the Poesia en Voz Alta (Poetry Out Loud) series. From 1956 to 1963, this was the most experimental theatre venture in Mexico and made Mendoza the most highly regarded director since Seki Sano. Many of the most important directors of the next generation began their careers under Mendoza's tutelage. Among the many successful Mexican playwrights who began their careers in the years between World War II and 1968 were Carlos Solórzano (1922–), a writer of expressionistic plays; Elena Garro (1922–), a surrealist; Hugo Argüelles (1932–), one of the first to be linked to the concept of "magic realism"; and Oscar Villegas (1943–), whose works were early examples of what was to become known as postmodernism. Felipe Santander (1934–) had only moderate success in this period, but his later musical review, *The Extension Agent* (1978), was the most popular play of that decade.

The Mexican theatre of this period challenged a great many established norms of the country but rarely made the kind of attacks on the national government that were so common in other parts of Latin America. This may be because the government was so supportive of theatre or may only explain the government's willingness to support it. In 1968, however, Mexican students joined the protest movements that had been sweeping the United States, France, and other nations. On October 2 they were fired on by the military, leaving over 300 dead and hundreds more injured. The relationship between the government and the theatre was never the same thereafter.

By the 1960s, then, the theatre had fully recovered from the destruction of the war years. For the most part, however, it had continued along lines that had been established earlier, although there were a few notable exceptions, especially in France and England. But during the 1960s, new tensions and outlooks gathered strength, and by 1968 the theatre was entering a period of enormous controversy and, in most countries, a period of enormous vitality. Repressive governments, political unrest, and economic crisis in many of the Latin American countries through the 1970s and 1980s, however, delayed any vibrant revival of theatre there until the 1990s.

LOOKING AT THEATRE HISTORY

In studying theatre history we need to be concerned about the "ideological climate" of an age. Is it a period in which there is strong agreement or sharp division? If so, about what? What is being defended or attacked? What is so taken for granted that it need not be questioned or discussed? What is privileged and what marginalized? What heirarchies of power (church/state, rank/class, male/female, nature/culture, individual/society, and so on) are evident? In no period is there total agreement on values and goals, but in most there is a discernible dominant ideology that is used to provide cohesiveness and a measure of stability. In others, there is sufficient disagreement to produce disarray. Whatever the case, the theatre reflects the ideological stances and tensions of its time.

After World War II, conflicts among ideologies were especially evident: capitalism/communism; equal rights/privilege established by custom or law; individual right/law and order; developed world/third world; and so on. Immediately following World War II, a crisis in belief, attributable in large part to the Nazi extermination camps and the threat of world destruction from atomic warfare, fueled interest in existentialism and absurdism. This crisis in belief was perhaps most clearly defined by Albert Camus:

A world that can be explained even with bad reasons is a familiar world. But, on the other hand, in a universe suddenly divested of illusions and lights, man feels an alien, a stranger. His exile is without remedy since he is deprived of the memory of a lost home or the hope of a promised land. This divorce between man and his life . . . is properly the feeling of absurdity. . . . I said that the world is absurd, but I was too hasty. This world in itself is not reasonable, that is all that can be said. But what is absurd is the confrontation of this irrational and wild longing for clarity whose call echoes in the human heart. . . . The absurd is born of this confrontation between the human need and the unreasonable silence of the world.

Albert Camus, "The Myth of Sisyphus," *The Myth of Sisyphus and Other Essays,* trans. Justin O'Brien (New York: Alfred A. Knopf, 1967), 6ff.

It was Martin Esslin who in 1961 first invented a label, "theatre of the absurd," for plays that seemed to stem from the position set forth by Camus:

The hallmark of [the theatre of the absurd] is its sense that certitudes and unshakable basic assumptions of former ages have been swept away, that they have been tested and found wanting, that they have been discredited as cheap and somewhat childish illusions. . . .

This sense of metaphysical anguish at the absurdity of the human condition is, broadly speaking the theme of the plays of Beckett, Adamov, Ionesco, Genet, and the other writers in this book. But it is not merely the subject-matter that defines what is here called the Theatre of the Absurd. . . . [That theatre also] strives to express its sense of the senselessness of the human condition and the inadequacy of the rational approach by the open abandonment of rational devices and discursive thought. . . . [It seeks] to achieve a unity between its basic assumptions and the form in which they are expressed.

Martin Esslin, *The Theatre of the Absurd,* revised and updated edition (Woodstock, N.Y.: The Overlook Press, 1973), 4–6.

Eugène Ionesco was not only one of the most successful but also one of the most argumentative of absurdist playwrights, often taking issue with the directors of his plays and with critics. (Many of his comments are collected in *Notes and Counter Notes.*)

Here are some reactions motivated by the American production of *Rhinoceros* in 1961:

Some critics blame me for denouncing evil without saying what good is . . . but it is so easy to rely on a system of thought that is more or less mechanical. . . . An unworkable solution one has found for oneself is infinitely more valuable than a ready-made ideology that stops men from thinking. . . .

One of the great critics of New York complains that, after destroying one conformism, I put nothing else in its place, leaving him and the audience in a vacuum. That is exactly what I wanted to do. A free man should pull himself out of vacuity on his own, by his own efforts and not by the efforts of other people.

Notes and Counter Notes, Writings on the Theatre, trans. Donald Watson (New York: Grove Press, 1964), 207–211.

By the 1960s, all the technological means of the space age were being adapted to theatrical purposes, barriers between the arts were being broken down, and multimedia events of all sorts were flourishing. Josef Svoboda is probably the best known of those who sought to extend the theatre's range of expression through technological devices. Here are some excerpts from his statements about the production of Luigi Nonno's opera *Intoleranza* (produced in Boston in 1965):

Instead of film I used television techniques in such a way as to project a TV image onto many screens placed on the stage. . . . We were able to transmit parallel actions that were performed in adjoining studios, in fact in studios as far as three miles from the stage. All these studios were joined with each other by audio and visual monitors, so that the actors could see the conductor in relation to themselves, the actors in the studio could see what was being played on the stage, and . . . the actors on the stage see what was played in the studios. In this way, the conductor was absolute master of the rhythm of the performance. . . .

Jarka Burian, *The Scenography of Josef Svoboda* (Middletown, Conn.: Wesleyan University Press, 1971), 103.

21

English-Language Theatre in the Mid Twentieth Century

With the coming of the war in 1939, the English theatre was soon at a virtual standstill. At the height of the German blitz, only one theatre remained open in London. The Old Vic retreated to the provinces, Donald Wolfit (1902–1968) organized lunchtime programs, and a few others attempted to keep the theatre alive, but for the most part English theatrical life was almost completely disrupted.

Every attempt was made to return to normal immediately following the war, but the economies of Europe had been devastated and it seemed that everything in England was in need of rebuilding. The English theatre did little more than try to pick up where it had left off before the war. But by the mid-1950s, frustration and cynicism were setting in, especially among the young, and a new generation of playwrights, directors, actors, and designers stepped in to express this frustration, setting in motion a dynamic reinvigoration of theatre. By 1968 this new theatre had forced the abandonment of the play-licensing system that had existed since the reign of Elizabeth I and thus set off yet another period of change.

In the United States, Canada, Australia, and New Zealand, theatre suffered less interruption during the war, but with many theatre artists involved in the war effort and rationing limiting the resources available, it could do little more than maintain the status quo. At war's end the economies of these countries re-

covered more quickly than did those of the European nations, and this made it easier for theatre artists to return to what they had done before the war and gave them less motivation to change. The Cold War with its ever-present threat of nuclear annihilation, McCarthyism and the civil rights movement in the United States, the Korean War, and the Vietnam War were among the many troubling events that caused profound uncertainties about the directions in which the governments of these countries were going. By the late 1950s the theatre had begun to reflect those uncertainties.

ENGLISH THEATRE AND DRAMA, 1940–1968

Following World War II, the English commercial theatre was largely innocuous. The leading dramatist was Terence Rattigan (1911–1977), who began to write plays in 1933, achieved his first popular success with *French Without Tears* (1936), and after the war turned to more serious subjects in *The Winslow Boy* (1946), *The Browning Version* (1948), *Separate Tables* (1955), and *Ross* (1960). Although Rattigan created compelling situations and interesting characters, the "drawing room" atmosphere of his plays perpetuated familiar traditions.

490

The commercial theatre also took poetic drama under its wing for a time during the 1950s, after E. Martin Browne generated considerable enthusiasm with his productions at the Mercury Theatre. With *A Phoenix Too Frequent* (1946), Browne called attention to Christopher Fry (1907–), and this led John Gielgud to produce *The Lady's Not for Burning* (1949), which established Fry's reputation and revived interest in poetic drama. Fry went on to write *Venus Observed* (1949), *The Dark Is Light Enough* (1954), *A Yard of Sun* (1970), and several adaptations. T. S. Eliot also returned to playwriting with *The Cocktail Party* (1949), which enjoyed considerable popular success following its production at the Edinburgh Festival. He went on to write *The Confidential Clerk* (1953) and *The Elder Statesman* (1958). All of these plays by Eliot were modernized and adapted versions of ancient Greek dramas. But by 1955 interest in poetic drama was on the wane, for it too had come to seem merely familiar fare dressed up in poetic dialogue.

After the war, the Old Vic was the most respected company in England. It returned to London in 1944, having spent the war years in the provinces. At first it played in the New Theatre, for its own building had been partially destroyed by bombing. At this time, the management passed from Tyrone Guthrie to Laurence Olivier, Ralph Richardson, and John Burrell, who presented a series of brilliant productions (among them *Oedipus Rex, Richard III, Love for Love,* and *Peer Gynt*) that made the Old Vic one of the most admired companies in the world. In 1946 the Old Vic also established a theatre school under the direction of Michel Saint-Denis, assisted by George Devine and Glen Byam Shaw, who utilized principles drawn primarily from Copeau. Closely

allied with this school was a company—the Young Vic, under the direction of George Devine—that performed for young audiences. After 1946 the Old Vic also had a second branch in Bristol.

Unfortunately, after 1948 the Old Vic began to decline, as Olivier and Richardson began to devote increasing amounts of time to outside commitments. In 1949 the management passed to Hugh Hunt (1911–1993), who had served as director of the Bristol Old Vic since its formation. The return of the company to the repaired Old Vic Theatre in 1950 created considerable conflicts between the school and the Young Vic troupe, and in 1952 both of the latter were dissolved. Hunt resigned and made his way to Australia to run the Elizabethan Theatre Trust, leaving Michael Benthall (1919–1974) in charge of the Old Vic, which he ran from 1953 to 1958. The company was still good though relatively young (the leading players were John Neville, Barbara Jefford, and Paul Rogers). But the days of greatness were over, although they were recaptured briefly in 1960 with Franco Zeffirelli's brawling, lusty production of *Romeo and Juliet*. In 1963 the Old Vic was dissolved and its building became the first home of the National Theatre.

As the Old Vic declined, the Stratford Festival Company gained in prestige, largely because of several reforms made by Barry Jackson, head of the theatre between 1946 and 1948. Under Jackson's management, the company became a self-contained producing organization with its own technical staff providing costumes and scenery; storage space was added and the stage was remodeled. Jackson also

FIG. 21.1
T. S. Eliot's *The Cocktail Party,* premiere production, 1949. At center, Rex Harrison as Harcourt-Reilly. Photo by Anthony Buckley.

FIG. 21.2
Zeffirelli's production of *Romeo and Juliet* at the Old Vic, 1960. From *Scene Design Throughout the World Since 1950*.

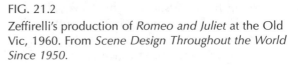

gained control over the entire festival so that its activities could be coordinated, and he enlivened the troupe by the addition of such vital young directors and actors as Peter Brook (1925–) and Paul Scofield (1922–). Between 1948 and 1956 the management was assumed by Anthony Quayle (1913–1989), who was joined in 1953 by Glen Byam Shaw. Such outstanding actors as Gielgud, Olivier, Redgrave, and Peggy Ashcroft appeared often, and in 1951 the number of productions given annually was reduced to permit more careful preparation. For the first time, London's critics attended the performances regularly and soon Stratford was being elevated in their reviews above the Old Vic. During the 1950s, novel interpretations also came to be accepted as the norm rather than as aberrations.

Festivals—such as those at Edinburgh, Chichester, Malvern, Glyndebourne, Canterbury, and Aldeburgh—also added considerably to the vitality of the English theatre during the 1950s. Nevertheless, by 1956 the English theatre seemed to many observers to be living on its past reputation. Then, quite unexpectedly, a "renaissance" occurred. The change can be attributed to two producing organizations, the English Stage Company and the Theatre Workshop, and to the dramatists with whom they worked.

The English Stage Company, founded in 1956, was placed under the artistic management of George Devine (1910–1966), who began his career as an actor in 1932, taught at Michel Saint-Denis's London Theatre Studio from 1936 to 1939, and directed the Young Vic Company after the war. Playing at the Royal Court Theatre, once the home of Granville Barker's troupe, the English Stage Company intended to emphasize new English plays and foreign works not yet seen in England. Failing to uncover a backlog of unproduced English dramas, Devine placed a notice in *The Stage,* which induced John Osborne (1929–1994) to submit *Look Back in Anger.* The production of Osborne's play in 1956 is usually considered the turning point in postwar British theatre.

Osborne's break with the past is not to be found in his dramaturgy (*Look Back in Anger* is straightforwardly realistic), but in his attack upon class distinctions and upon the complacency and inertia of all classes. Its protagonist, Jimmy Porter, seems to have no positive solution to suggest for the long list of moral, social, and political betrayals he denounces. Although essentially negative in tone, the play caught the contemporary rebellious mood so well that Jimmy came to represent an entire generation of "angry young men." Osborne's next play, *The Entertainer* (1957), has as its protagonist a disintegrating music hall performer (originally played by Laurence Olivier). Here England's progressive decline in vigor

FIG. 21.3

Osborne's *Look Back in Anger* at the Royal Court Theatre, 1956. The actors are Kenneth Haigh, Alan Bates, and Mary Ure. Directed by Tony Richardson. Photo by Houston Rogers.

and values is symbolized in three generations of the Rice family of entertainers. Osborne seems to have been influenced by Brecht in his alternation of realistic scenes with vaudeville routines. Olivier's great critical success as Archie Rice rejuvenated his career and forged a bridge between the old and new theatres. Thereafter, major established actors appeared increasingly in the new dramas.

Osborne's work after 1960 was very uneven in quality. Among his successful plays were *Luther* (1961), a psychological study of the religious reformer, and *Inadmissible Evidence* (1965), a moving evocation of the wasted life of an outwardly successful, middle-aged lawyer. But Osborne also wrote a number of lesser works, among them *A Patriot for Me* (1965), *Hotel Amsterdam* (1968), *West of Suez* (1971), *Watch It Come Down* (1976), and *Déjàvu* (1992). Despite the critics' fondness for declaring that he failed to live up to his early promise, Osborne must be considered one of the most important of postwar dramatists.

Next to Osborne, the Royal Court's most important dramatist of the early years was probably John Arden (1930–), author of *Live Like Pigs* (1958), *Sergeant Musgrave's Dance* (1959), *The Happy Haven* (1960), *Armstrong's Last Goodnight* (1964), and several other plays. Arden's work was both praised highly and said to be confused. Because he treated contemporary problems but did not seem to take sides, audiences found it difficult to decide what he intended. But practically all of the plays pursued the same themes—the conflict between order and anarchy, between conformity and freedom, between those who wish to impose some pattern or principle and those who resist such efforts. After 1967 Arden wrote most of his plays in collaboration with his wife, Margaretta D'Arcy, who was concerned above all with conveying messages and effecting social change. Consequently, Arden's work became increasingly polemical, as in *Island of the Mighty* (1972), which used the King Arthur legend to comment on English political and social problems.

The Theatre Workshop was founded in 1945 by a group of young people dissatisfied with the commercial theatre on both artistic and social grounds. Joan Littlewood (1914–) soon became its leader. Having few financial resources, the company toured England and the continent before settling in 1953 in a London suburb, Stratford East, a working-class district. It did its most important work between 1955, when it gained international recognition through an appearance at the world festival in Paris, and 1961, when Littlewood resigned.

Two playwrights, Behan and Delaney, were especially associated with the Theatre Workshop. Brendan Behan's (1923–1965) first play, *The Quare Fellow*, written in 1945, was presented by the Theatre Workshop in 1956. A mixture of the comic and serious, it shows a cross-section of prison life on the eve of a prisoner's execution. Similarly, *The Hostage* (1958) is built around varying attitudes toward the impending death of an I.R.A. agent and the hostage who is to be killed in reprisal. Many diversions (song, dances,

and character vignettes) enliven the play. Shelagh Delaney's (1939–) *A Taste of Honey* (1958) is the story of a young girl and her slatternly mother set against a closely observed background. The charge that Littlewood had a strong hand in reshaping the plays of both Behan and Delaney is supported in part by the failure of both to produce significant drama except with the Workshop.

The Theatre Workshop was also noted for its production style, perhaps best exemplified in *Oh, What a Lovely War!* (1963), a biting satire on the First World War. As the director of more than 150 of its productions, Littlewood was responsible for establishing the company's approach. She drew heavily on Brechtian and music hall conventions, but also on Stanislavsky, especially by emphasizing "through lines" of action and improvisation. Her ultimate aim was to create a theatre to which the working classes would go with the same regularity and enthusiasm as to fun palaces or penny arcades. Within a framework of conventions borrowed from popular entertainments, she sought to imbed some lasting message or significant content.

Several of the Theatre Workshop's successful productions were moved to commercial theatres, and this practice so weakened the company that Littlewood eventually resigned. Subsequently, she returned occasionally to direct productions for the Workshop, although it was no longer the vital force that it unquestionably was during the years between 1955 and the early 1960s.

Arnold Wesker (1932–), perhaps England's most socially conscious playwright of the late 1950s, is best known for his trilogy—*Chicken Soup with Barley* (1958), *Roots* (1959), and *I'm Talking about Jerusalem* (1960)—which trace the declining sense of purpose in the socialist movement and seek to show that workers have settled for too little and have chosen the wrong paths in seeking to remedy ills. In *The Kitchen* (1958) Wesker explores working-class conditions through the microcosm of a kitchen in a large restaurant, and in *Chips with Everything* (1962) he uses an air force camp to show that enlisted men are exploited and systematically deprived of all that is best in entertainment, art, and living conditions.

In 1962 Wesker became the leader of a working-class art movement, Center 42 (so named from the Trades Union Congress resolution number 42 which in 1961 called for the popularization of the arts among workers). With Center 42 Wesker intended to supply plays and music of high quality for festivals throughout the country, but after a brief burst of energy in 1962 the movement subsided, and from 1966 to 1970 it was almost wholly confined to the Roundhouse, a converted railroad shop located in

FIG. 21.4
Joan Littlewood's production of *Oh, What a Lovely War!* at the Theatre Workshop, 1963. Design by John Bury. Photo courtesy *The Report*.

north London. In 1971 Center 42 was disbanded. After 1962 Wesker wrote little, and such works as *The Four Seasons* (1966), *The Friends* (1970), and *Love Letters on Blue Paper* (1978) had little success, perhaps because they were so unlike Wesker's early work, upon which his reputation primarily rests.

Another popular dramatist, Peter Shaffer (1926–), also began his career during the 1950s. Shaffer wrote quite diverse plays, ranging through the realistic *Five Finger Exercise* (1958) to such absurdist comedies as *The Private Ear* and *The Public Eye* (1962) and *Black Comedy* (1965). He is most admired, however, for *The Royal Hunt of the Sun* (1964), a story about the Spanish conquest of Peru which Shaffer has described as "an attempt to define the concept of God"; *Equus* (1973), a psychological study of a boy who has blinded several horses and of the psychiatrist who treats him; and *Amadeus* (1979), which shows the destruction of the naive and clumsy genius, Mozart, by his mediocre, urbane, and jealous rival Salieri. His later plays include, *Yonadab* (1985), *Lettice and Lovage* (1988), and *The Gift of the Gorgon* (1992), but only *Lettice and Lovage* was viewed as significant.

Of the many other dramatists, those who attracted favorable attention include Graham Greene (1904–1991) with plays about moral and religious questions as in *The Living Room* (1953), *The Potting Shed* (1957), and *The Complaisant Lover* (1959); and Robert Bolt (1924–1995), with *The Flowering Cherry* (1957), a quasi-Chekhovian study of self-deception and failure, *A Man for All Seasons* (1960) based on the life and martyrdom of Sir Thomas More, and *Vivat, Vivat Regina* (1970), treating the story of Elizabeth I and Mary of Scotland.

But the playwright who achieved the greatest international reputation was Harold Pinter (1930–), who, after beginning his career as an actor, turned to playwriting in 1957 with *The Room*. Thereafter he wrote regularly for the theatre, television, and films. His stage works include *The Dumb Waiter* (1957), *The Birthday Party* (1958), *The Caretaker* (1960), *The Homecoming* (1965), *Old Times* (1970), *No Man's Land* (1975), *Betrayal* (1978), *A Kind of Alaska* (1982), *Moonlight* (1993), and several others. Although there is much variety among them, almost all of Pinter's plays have in common a few characteristics: everyday situations that gradually take on an air of mystery or menace; unexplained, unrevealed, or ambiguous motivations or background information; and authentic, seemingly natural though carefully wrought dialogue. With Pinter silence is an integral part of language, which he treats as a stratagem used by characters to cover their psychological nakedness. Thus, "unspoken subtext" is often as important as dialogue. In Pinter's plays everything may at first seem amusing or pleasantly ambiguous, but gradually the tone changes to anxiety,

FIG. 21.6
Pinter's *The Homecoming* at the Royal Shakespeare Company, 1965. Michael Craig as Teddy, Terence Rigby (seated) as Joey, and Ian Holm as Lenny. Directed by Peter Hall. Courtesy Royal Shakespeare Company.

FIG. 21.5
Peter Shaffer's *Royal Hunt of the Sun* at the National Theatre, London, 1964. Courtesy National Theatre, London.

pathos, or fear as the characters confront some pre-
dicament and seek to defend themselves against some
unknown, often undefined danger from outside or
within the room in which the action occurs. As a
dramatist, Pinter falls somewhere between Beckett
and Chekhov. Like Beckett, he isolates characters and
lets them wrestle with their anxieties in an unverifiable universe; like Chekhov, he creates a realistic texture of background and dialogue in which surface act
and speech are merely evasions or disguises of deeper
conflicts and uncertainties.

Much of the English theatre's postwar accomplishment was made possible by a change in attitude
toward subsidies. Until World War II, no direct governmental aid had ever been given the arts. Then, in
1940, the Council for the Encouragement of Music
and the Arts (CEMA) was given £50,000 to assist
in wartime work. In 1946 CEMA became the Arts
Council, an independent organization financed by
government funds. It never had much money (in the
1960s it had only about one million dollars annually
for drama), but it used it to encourage organizations
that seemed capable of providing leadership. In 1948
Parliament also authorized local governments to allot
a percentage of their revenues to support the arts.
As a result, several municipalities began to provide
subsidies for local resident companies, of which by
the 1960s there were more than fifty in Great Britain,
most performing a mixed repertory of classics and
recent works. Among the best of these were the com-

panies in Bristol, Birmingham, Manchester, Notting-
ham, Coventry, and Glasgow.

After 1960, two companies, in addition to the
English Stage Company, were especially important
in English theatrical life: the Royal Shakespeare
Company and the National Theatre. In 1961 the
Shakespeare Memorial Theatre was given a new
charter and a new title, the Royal Shakespeare Company (RSC). Its new status owed most to Peter Hall
(1930–) who, after beginning his directing career in
1955, had worked at Stratford since 1957 and had
been named head of its company in 1960. Upon
assuming the new post, Hall at once set out to overcome one of the troupe's principal problems: the inability to hold a company together and build an
ensemble because the season at Stratford lasted only
about six months each year. To remedy this situation, Hall took a lease on the Aldwych Theatre in
London and transformed the organization into a
year-round operation. Thereafter, the company divided its efforts between Stratford and London. Hall
also broadened the repertory to include plays other
than those by Shakespeare so that actors would have
diversified experience.

By 1962 the RSC's activities had been so enlarged
that Peter Brook and Michel Saint-Denis were added
to the management. The RSC also began an experimental program, and in 1963–1964 Peter Brook, in
collaboration with Charles Marowitz, produced a series of programs under the overall title, "Theatre of

FIG. 21.7
Henry VI, one part of the cycle, *The War of the Roses,* 1964. Directed by
Peter Hall; designed by John Bury. From the Tom Holte Theatre Photographic
Collection. Courtesy the Shakespeare Birthplace Trust, Stratford-upon-Avon.

Cruelty." Out of this season came Brook's production of Weiss' *Marat/Sade,* one of the most influential productions of the decade and the one that did most to draw attention to Artaud's theories. By the mid-1960s the RSC was London's major *avant-garde* troupe, noted both for its innovative techniques and for its wide-ranging repertory, with plays by Hochhuth, Pinter, and numerous continental and British dramatists of the past and present. The Aldwych also became the home of the World Theatre Season, an arrangement under which each spring from 1964 to 1975 major companies from throughout the world came to London for limited engagements.

Under Hall, the RSC's most characteristic productions used a simplified realism that owed much to Brecht. Verse was spoken in a measured downbeat. The visual style owed much to John Bury (1925–2000), Hall's principal designer after 1963. Bury avoided decorative and illustrative scenery; rather, his settings were functional skeletal structures. Costumes and props usually looked long-used. The high point of Hall's work was probably the cycle of Shakespeare's history plays, which he presented in 1963–1964 under the overall title of *The War of the Roses.*

Of the directors associated with the RSC, Peter Brook (1925–) was the most influential. He began directing while still in his teens and first worked at Stratford in 1946. During the 1950s he built an enviable reputation with productions starring such actors as Olivier, Paul Scofield, and the Lunts, and with plays by such authors as Shakespeare, Fry, Anouilh, Eliot, Duerrenmatt, and Genet. But he is now best known for a series of productions after 1960, including *King Lear* (1962), *Marat/Sade* (1964), *A Midsummer Night's Dream* (1970), and *Mahabharata* (1985). As a director, Brook was not so much an innovator as an eclectic who transformed borrowings from many sources into his own vital expression. For example, for *A Midsummer Night's Dream* he borrowed from Meyerhold, *commedia dell'arte,* circus, and radical theatre groups of the 1960s, but the results were uniquely his own. For this production, Brook sought to divest the play of its romantic aura of fairies and haunted woodlands and to make it more immediately relevant to his time. He interpreted the script as an exploration of love, and consequently he used the same pair of actors as Theseus and Hippolyta and Oberon and Titania, and treated the enchanted scenes as lessons on love for the betrothed royal couple. The stage was enclosed on three sides by white, unadorned walls broken only by two nearly invisible doors at the rear. The forest was suggested by loosely coiled metal springs attached to fishing rods. The flying was accomplished with trapezes lowered and raised to varying heights within the setting. Most

FIG. 21.8
Peter Brook's production of *A Midsummer Night's Dream,* 1970. Oberon and Puck (on trapezes) watch Titania and Bottom. Design by Sally Jacobs. Courtesy Royal Shakespeare Company.

of the performers wore a kind of coverall, but there was a sprinkling of *commedia dell'arte,* circus, and other costumes. Despite all these distinctive features, the text was given its full poetic value. Such novel and imaginative approaches made Brook one of the most effective and respected directors of the age.

Beginning in the 1960s the RSC had a powerful rival in the National Theatre. England was one of the last European countries to establish a national theatre, though it had long contemplated such a move. Parliamentary approval for the company was given in the late 1940s but it was not implemented until 1963, when the Old Vic company was dissolved and its building assigned to the new troupe. Laurence Olivier was named director and Kenneth Tynan (1927–1980) literary advisor. The National Theatre rapidly built a reputation for excellence through its extremely eclectic choice of plays and production styles. It sought to assemble for each production the team best suited to that script. Consequently, it uti-

FIG. 21.9
The National Theatre's production of Strindberg's *The Dance of Death*, 1967. The actors are Geraldine McEwan, Robert Stephens, and Laurence Olivier. Photograph by Zoë Dominic.

lized numerous English and foreign directors (among them Brook, George Devine, Jonathan Miller, Franco Zeffirelli, Ingmar Bergman, and Victor Garcia) and designers (among them Motley, Sean Kenny, Josef Svoboda, and René Allio). It also from time to time staged seasons of experimental plays. It was often said that the National Theatre was an actors' theatre, whereas the RSC was a director's theatre, and the English Stage Company a playwrights' theatre.

THEATRE AND DRAMA IN THE UNITED STATES, 1940–1968

After World War II the most influential figures in U.S. theatre were probably the director Elia Kazan and the designer Jo Mielziner, for through their joint work on such plays as Williams' *A Streetcar Named Desire* (1947) and Miller's *Death of a Salesman* (1949) they established the approach to production that was to remain dominant into the 1960s. Under Mielziner's influence, stage settings eliminated nonessential features, thereby creating a "theatricalized realism." On the other hand, acting moved increasingly toward a psychological truth rooted in the characters' inner motivations. It was an extension of the Group Theatre's approach as taught at the Actors Studio.

Founded in 1947 by Robert Lewis (1909–1997), Elia Kazan, and Cheryl Crawford, the Actors Studio was designed to permit selected actors to work and develop by applying the Stanislavsky method, with special emphasis on intention and action. But in 1948 Lewis resigned and Lee Strasberg became the dominant force and shifted the emphasis to emotion memory and exploration of the actor's psyche as the key to truth in acting. Marlon Brando (1924–), with his characterization of the inarticulate and uneducated Stanley Kowalski of *A Streetcar Named Desire*, came to epitomize in the popular mind the Actors Studio ideal, although Brando gives primary credit to Stella Adler for his training. The novelty of serious acting using substandard speech, untidy dress, and boorish behavior captured the public imagination and popularized an image of the Studio as being concerned only with inner truth while ignoring the skills needed to project character and dramatic action. In 1956 the Studio added a program designed to assist playwrights, and in 1960 a workshop for directors. By the 1960s, however, the influence of the Actors Studio had begun to decline as interest turned toward nonrealistic and period drama, for which the Studio's approach came to seem too limited. Nevertheless, it remained a powerful force.

After the war, the theatre was seriously threatened by the rapid development of television. In 1948 there were only 48 stations, but by 1958 there were 512 and over 50 million television sets. The free entertainment provided by the new medium came at just the time when production costs in the theatre were rapidly increasing. Between 1944 and 1960 the price of tickets doubled, and the costs of mounting a show increased at a still faster rate. Under these circumstances, Broadway producers tended to seek vehicles with broad appeal, and to avoid both plays and production styles that might offend or confuse spectators. Nevertheless, the Broadway theatre continued the decline that had begun before the war. It reached a low point in the season of 1949–1950, when only fifty-nine new productions were mounted, but then slowly climbed to about seventy, a number that could not be greatly increased because of the relatively small number of available theatres (about thirty in the 1950s).

In the late 1940s the reduction of U.S. theatre to a small number of Broadway productions served to motivate several attempts to diversify. One of the most important results was the off-Broadway movement. By playing in out-of-the-way theatres or improvised auditoriums, production costs could be cut considerably, and works which would not appeal to a mass audience could be played for smaller groups. The off-Broadway movement can properly be traced back to the little theatres of the World War I era. The little theatre movement had declined markedly during the 1930s but began to revive during World War II. In

FIG. 21.10
Tennessee Williams' *A Streetcar Named Desire.* At center, Jessica Tandy as Blanche; second from right, Marlon Brando as Stanley. Directed by Elia Kazan; setting by Jo Mielziner. Courtesy Graphic House, Inc.

1943 the city of New York acquired the Mecca Temple on 55th Street and converted it into the City Center, where opera, musical comedy, ballet, and drama were played for limited engagements at moderate prices. Under the general direction of Jean Dalrymple (1910–1998), the City Center was to build enviable ballet and opera troupes that would be transferred to Lincoln Center in 1966. Another significant effort came in 1946–1947 when Eva Le Gallienne, Margaret Webster (1905–1972), and Cheryl Crawford established the American Repertory Company (modeled on Le Gallienne's earlier Civic Repertory Company), which performed a season of six plays before being forced by financial difficulties to close.

The more typical off-Broadway groups, however, were begun by relatively unknown directors. A major upturn in prestige came in 1952, when the Circle in the Square presented to high critical praise Williams' *Summer and Smoke,* a failure on Broadway. Soon off-Broadway was viewed as a workable alternative to Broadway's commercialism. By 1955–1956, there were more than ninety off-Broadway groups, and they, rather than Broadway companies, gave the first performances in New York of works by such authors as Brecht, Ionesco, and Genet.

Of the off-Broadway groups, two—Circle in the Square and the Phoenix Theatre—were of special importance during the 1950s. The Circle in the Square was opened in 1951 by José Quintero (1924–1999) and Theodore Mann (1924–1999). In this former nightclub, the actor-audience relationship was entirely flexible, although spectators normally were seated around three sides of a rectangular acting area. Here such performers as Geraldine Page, Jason Robards, Jr., George C. Scott, and Coleen Dewhurst came to prominence. After his triumph with O'Neill's *The Iceman Cometh* in 1956, Quintero was asked to direct the Broadway production of *Long Day's Journey into Night.* Its cumulative record made the Circle in the Square one of the most respected of off-Broadway theatres.

The Phoenix Theatre was inaugurated in 1953 by Norris Houghton (1909–2001) and T. Edward Hambleton (1911–) in an out-of-the-way but fully equipped conventional theatre. It presented a diverse program of plays by such authors as Aristophanes, Shakespeare, Turgenev, Ibsen, Shaw, Pirandello, Ionesco, and Montherlant. It also attempted to use a different director for each play and frequently included well-known actors among its casts. Beginning in the late 1950s, the Phoenix employed a permanent acting company, which under the direction of Stuart Vaughan presented a series of plays each season. This arrangement lasted until the early 1960s, when Houghton and Hambleton formed a liaison with the Association of Producing Artists and thereafter became primarily presenters of that company's offerings.

For the most part, off-Broadway theatres in the 1950s were little concerned with experimentation in

FIG. 21.11
Jo Mielziner's setting for Arthur Miller's *Death of a Salesman*. Photograph by Peter A. Juley & Son. Courtesy Mr. Mielziner.

staging except in their use of arena and thrust stages. They were most interested in repertory, seeking to present a more challenging drama than that favored by Broadway. Their goals were essentially artistic. These goals were also promoted by the director Alan Schneider (1917–1984), who introduced Beckett in the United States (beginning with *Waiting for Godot* in 1956) and went on to direct the plays of Albee and other major playwrights through the remainder of his life.

During the 1960s the New York theatre continued to be enlivened by off-Broadway. Of the many off-Broadway groups, probably the most influential was the Living Theatre, founded in 1946 by Judith Malina (1926–) and Julian Beck (1925–1985). Originally interested in poetic drama and nonrealistic production techniques, during the 1950s they came under the influence of both Artaud and Brecht. A major turning point in their work came in 1959 with their production of Jack Gelber's *The Connection,* a drama in which the audience supposedly is being allowed to watch the making of a documentary film about dope addicts. The overall effect was that of a naturalistic slice of life. The production won a number of awards in New York and subsequently at the Théâtre des Nations in Paris. Another important production was Kenneth Brown's *The Brig* (1963), which

re-creates the repetitive and senseless routine of a day in a Marine prison. In 1964 the company went abroad after losing its theatre for failure to pay taxes. By the late 1960s it would be one of the world's most controversial companies.

By 1960 the off-Broadway theatre was beginning to undergo many of the same economic pressures felt by Broadway, and consequently it began to be less adventurous than in earlier years. As it declined, it was supplemented by off-off-Broadway. It is usual to date off-off-Broadway from 1958 when Joe Cino began to use his Café Cino as an art center. By 1961 plays were a regular part of his offerings, and others had begun to take up the idea. Soon plays were being presented wherever space could be found. Most of the participants were unpaid and budgets were infinitesimal, but by 1965 some 400 plays by more than 200 playwrights had been seen off-off-Broadway.

The most influential of the off-off-Broadway producers of the 1960s was Ellen Stewart (1920?–), who began to present plays in a basement room in 1961. After trouble with fire inspectors, she created the LaMama Experimental Theatre Club (ostensibly a private organization and therefore exempt from many regulations governing public performances). By 1969–1970 LaMama alone produced more plays than

FIG. 21.12
O'Neill's *The Iceman Cometh* at Circle in the Square, 1956. Directed by
José Quintero. Photograph by Jerry Dantzic.

were seen on Broadway that season. In 1969 the
LaMama organization acquired its own building with
two theatres, and in 1974 it quadrupled its space
through the acquisition of an annex.

Beginning in 1964, Stewart also took productions
abroad, where her freewheeling experiments attracted
such favorable attention that she was invited to found
branches in several countries. Thus the LaMama organization came to be known throughout the world.
Stewart considered LaMama to be a playwright's
theatre intended to nourish talent. Her tolerance of
innovation meant that many LaMama plays were amateurish, but it also meant that many talented writers were given a hearing they might otherwise have
been denied. Nevertheless, LaMama illustrates well
two basic characteristics of off-off-Broadway in the
1960s—the determined pursuit of novelty and the
lack of standards by which to judge it.

Other important off-off-Broadway groups of the
1960s included the Judson Poets' Theatre, founded
in 1961 by Al Carmines and especially important
for promoting small-scale musicals, many of them
written by Carmines and Cuban-born playwright
Maria Irene Fornes (1930–); the American Place
Theatre, founded in 1964 by Wynn Handman to re-

juvenate the American theatre by encouraging outstanding authors to write plays, and later housed in
one of the mid-Manhattan skyscrapers which, owing
to tax incentives, included theatres; and Theatre
Genesis, established in 1964 by Ralph Cook and
housed in St. Mark's in the Bowery.

Another attempt to diversify New York's theatre
brought the foundation of Lincoln Center for the Performing Arts (with facilities for opera, ballet, concerts, and plays). In anticipation of the Center's
completion, a repertory company was formed in 1963
under the direction of Elia Kazan and Robert Whitehead (1916–). Expectations were high, since at that
time Kazan was considered the finest director in
America and since he was promised new plays by
Arthur Miller (*After the Fall* and *Incident at Vichy*) and
S. N. Behrman (*But for Whom, Charlie*). The results
were so disappointing that after one season Kazan and
Whitehead resigned. They were replaced by Herbert
Blau (1926–) and Jules Irving (1924–1979), who had
been outstandingly successful at the Actors' Workshop in San Francisco. In 1965 the company moved
into its newly completed home (the Vivian Beaumont
Theatre, designed by Eero Saarinen and Jo Mielziner)
at Lincoln Center. But Blau and Irving soon ran into

difficulties, and in 1967 Blau resigned. Thereafter Irving continued slowly to build a company, but eventually the artistic and financial problems became so great that in 1973 he resigned. The search for success was to continue.

For a time New York also had a second repertory company, the Association of Producing Artists (APA). Founded in 1960 by Ellis Rabb (1930–1998), the APA formed a liaison in 1964 with the Phoenix Theatre, which thereafter served as its producer. The APA won high critical praise but because of financial difficulties had to be disbanded in 1970. Its repertory was eclectic, ranging through works by Shaw, Chekhov, Pirandello, Shakespeare, Ionesco, and others. The company was sometimes accused of being too conservative because it only produced already proven works, but for a time it provided the most impressive cross-section of drama to be seen in the United States.

After the war there were also a number of attempts to decentralize the theatre. One leader in this area was the American National Theatre and Academy (ANTA), which had been chartered by Congress in 1935 to stimulate the rejuvenation of the theatre outside of New York and to form an academy to train personnel. Owing to lack of funds, little was accomplished, although ANTA became the principal American center for collecting and exchanging information about the theatre. After the war, the attempt to found regional theatres was given its first important impetus by Margo Jones (1913–1955), who successfully established an arena theatre in Dallas in 1947. Other pioneering groups include the Alley Theatre, founded in Houston in 1947 by Nina Vance (1914–1980); the Arena Stage, opened in Washington in 1949 by Edward Mangum (1914–2001) and Zelda Fichandler; and the Actors' Workshop, begun in 1952 in San Francisco by Jules Irving and Herbert Blau. At first, most of the groups struggled along with semiprofessional personnel while gradually building audiences.

The 1960s saw the greatest expansion of the U.S. theatre outside of New York since the nineteenth century. The first important impetus came in 1959 when the Ford Foundation made sizable grants to a number of small companies that had managed to gain footholds in cities scattered throughout the country. The financial boost permitted such groups as the Alley Theatre, the Arena Stage, and the Actors' Workshop to become fully professional and relatively stable. The movement toward resident companies was further strengthened when Tyrone Guthrie announced his intention of founding a theatre in Minneapolis. When this theatre was opened in 1963 the favorable publicity motivated other cities to seek similar companies. By 1966 the regional theatres had so burgeoned (to about thirty-five) that for the first time in the twentieth century more stage actors were employed outside of than in New York. These troupes resembled European subsidized theatres in presenting a repertory of classics and recent successes and in relying little on new plays. To aid cooperation and communication among these not-for-profit theatres, the Theatre Communications Group was established in 1961.

Summer festivals also added diversity. The success of the Shakespeare Festivals at Ashland, Oregon (1935), and San Diego (1949) inspired Joseph Papp to establish the New York Shakespeare Festival in 1954. Beginning in 1957 it gave free performances each summer in Central Park where the municipally owned Delacorte Theatre (seating 2,263) was inaugurated in 1962. This was followed by the American Shakespeare Festival, Stratford, Connecticut (1955), the Colorado Shakespeare Festival, Boulder (1958), Utah Shakespeare Festival, Cedar City (1961), the Great Lakes Shakespeare Festival, Lakewood, Ohio (1962), and the New Jersey Shakespeare Festival (1963), and many more. Summer theatres, most of them in resort areas, also steadily increased in numbers. Additionally, by the early 1960s approximately 1,500 colleges and universities were offering theatre courses and productions.

For a time after the war, the United States seemed to be rich in playwrights. Its stature increased considerably with the return of O'Neill's plays to the repertory following the success of *The Iceman Cometh* in 1956. *A Long Day's Journey into Night* (written 1939–1941 and first produced 1957) was one of the most impressive plays of the 1950s; subsequently other previously unproduced works by O'Neill were performed to critical acclaim. Although he declined in power, Maxwell Anderson also continued to write. Among his postwar plays, *Joan of Lorraine* (1946) and *Anne of the Thousand Days* (1948) were especially popular. Clifford Odets regained some of his former strength with *The Country Girl* (1950) and *The Flowering Peach* (1954); William Saroyan returned with *The Cave Dwellers* (1957), Lillian Hellman with *The Autumn Garden* (1951) and *Toys in the Attic* (1960), S. N. Behrman with *The Cold Wind and the Warm* (1959) and *But for Whom, Charlie* (1962), and Thornton Wilder with *The Matchmaker* (1954).

The most outstanding new writers were Williams and Miller. Tennessee Williams (1911–1983) achieved his first success in 1945 with *The Glass Menagerie* and rapidly consolidated it with *A Streetcar Named Desire* (1947), *Cat on a Hot Tin Roof* (1955), *Sweet Bird of Youth* (1959), and *Night of the Iguana* (1961). But by the late 1950s Williams was being accused of repeating himself and thereafter his critical stature declined, although he continued to write up until his death. His later work includes *The Milk Train Doesn't Stop*

FIG. 21.13

The Guthrie Theatre, Minneapolis. Note the thrust stage and steeply banked seating. Tyrone Guthrie's production of Chekhov's *The Three Sisters,* 1963. Courtesy the Guthrie Theatre.

Here Anymore (1962), *Slapstick Tragedy* (1966), *This Is [an Entertainment]* (1976), and *Vieux Carré* (1978).

Williams's strength lay in his ability to create interesting characters caught in critical or violent situations as they seek to recover a past or create a future more satisfying than the vulgar and materialistic present. As the dramatic action progresses, the protagonist is usually forced to abandon his/her illusions, often after physical or moral degradation at the hands of callous or vicious characters. Williams's sensational situations often obscured his concern for the survival of love and beauty in a materialistic world. To achieve his effects, Williams used theatrical means imaginatively, manipulating them, sometimes quite obviously, to focus attention on the inner truth of character and situation. No American playwright commanded so wide an audience as did Williams between 1945 and 1960.

Arthur Miller (1915–) achieved his first success with *All My Sons* (1947), an Ibsenesque play about a manufacturer of airplane engines who has put profit above the safety of wartime pilots. Miller's reputation now rests primarily upon *Death of a Salesman* (1949), *The Crucible* (1953), and *A View from the Bridge* (1955). That reputation declined somewhat with *After the Fall* (1964) and *Incident at Vichy* (1964), but rose again with *The Price* (1968). His later works, among which have been *The Creation of the World and Other Business* (1973), *The Archbishop's Ceiling* (1986), *The Ride Down Mount Morgan* (1991), *The Last Yankee* (1993), and *Broken Glass* (1994) have not met with the critical acclaim of his early plays. Through most of Miller's plays run the same ideas. His characters stray because of overly narrow (often materialistic) values and find peace in some more meaningful understanding of themselves and of their roles in society. Miller is often called a "social" dramatist, but his interests have always been moral, for in his plays, though society may encourage false values, it remains the individual's responsibility to sort out the true from the false. Miller clearly implies that it is possible to maintain one's integrity within the framework of society. Of Miller's work, *Death of a Salesman* is usually considered most significant, perhaps because it dramatizes so successfully the conflict in the American consciousness between the desire for material success and for adventure and happiness.

Few other new playwrights lived up to their initial promise. William Inge (1913–1973) gained a considerable following with such works as *Come Back, Little Sheba* (1950), *Picnic* (1953), *Bus Stop* (1955), and *The Dark at the Top of the Stairs* (1957), but his work now seems essentially a more naive version of Williams's. Other popular dramatists of the time include Robert Anderson (1917–), with *Tea and Sympathy* (1953) and *You Know I Can't Hear You When the Water's Running* (1966); and Paddy Chayefsky (1923–1981) with *The Tenth Man* (1959) and *Gideon* (1961).

After 1960 production costs continued to soar with the result that Broadway ticket prices became ever higher. The need to attract large audiences led New York's producers to restrict their offerings primarily to musicals, comedies, and plays that had proven popular elsewhere. Broadway gradually gave up the out-of-town tryout and increasingly imported productions from America's resident theatres or from London. Thus, it lost its significance as a presenter of new plays while remaining the primary center of the American commercial theatre.

The most successful playwright on Broadway after 1960 was Neil Simon (1927–), who after a somewhat tentative beginning with *Come Blow Your Horn* (1961) turned out a string of hits, among them *Barefoot in the Park* (1963), *The Odd Couple* (1965), *The Last of the Red Hot Lovers* (1970), *The Sunshine Boys* (1972), *Chapter Two* (1979), *Biloxi Blues* (1984), *Broadway Bound* (1986), *Lost in Yonkers* (1991), *Laughter on the 23d Floor* (1993), and *Proposals* (1997), all combining zany humor, eccentric characters, and hints of pain and desperation beneath the comic surface.

The most prestigious American playwright of the 1960s was Edward Albee (1928–), whose first four plays, all short, were produced off-Broadway in 1960–1961. These early works, especially *The Sandbox* (1959) and *The American Dream* (1960), were thought to ally Albee with the absurdists, but with *Who's Afraid of Virginia Woolf?* (1962), his first full-length play and first Broadway success, Albee, through his exploration of tortured psychological relationships, demonstrated an affinity to Williams and Strindberg. In *Who's Afraid of Virginia Woolf?*, the

FIG. 21.14
Albee's *A Delicate Balance* as performed by the Royal Shakespeare Company, 1967. Courtesy Royal Shakespeare Company.

facades of the characters are gradually stripped away during the course of an all-night drinking bout, revealing people who create hells for each other through their inability to accept weaknesses. Most of Albee's subsequent work has been concerned with values. *Tiny Alice* (1964), a puzzling parable, seems to suggest that human beings reconcile themselves to their lot by constructing unverifiable systems to explain why they have been martyred by life; *A Delicate Balance* (1966) shows several characters seeking to escape anxieties; and *Seascape* (1974) suggests that human beings have lost their vitality and that the future belongs to other creatures (here two amphibians who crawl out of the water onto the beach) as they discover love and consideration. In these complex plays, Albee became increasingly abstract and for a time he fell from favor but would regain much of his following in the 1990s.

In the early 1960s Arthur Kopit (1937–) was often ranked with Albee. He first came to prominence in 1960 with *Oh, Dad, Poor Dad, Mama's Hung You in the Closet and I'm Feeling So Sad,* a parodistic work reminiscent of Tennessee Williams's more bizarre creations but using absurdist conventions. In it, Mme Rosepettle, whose household includes piranhas, Venus's-flytraps, and the stuffed body of her dead husband, tries to protect her son from life's harsh realities only to have him break free from her domination. Kopit had little further success until *Indians* (1968), in which he used Buffalo Bill's Wild West Show as a framework for suggesting how the betrayal of Native Americans has been transformed into entertainment, thus permitting us to ignore the reality. It is a variation on the by-now familiar theme of the American dream gone awry.

FIG. 21.15

Leonard Bernstein's *Candide,* directed by Harold Prince. For this production, designers Eugene and Franne Lee altered the interior of a Broadway theatre to integrate the performance-audience spaces. Photo by Martha Swope Photography, Inc.

The period between 1940 and 1968 was something like a golden age of musical comedy. The pattern was established by Richard Rodgers and Oscar Hammerstein with *Oklahoma* (1943), *Carousel* (1945), *South Pacific* (1949), and *The King and I* (1951). It was followed, with many variations, by Alan Jay Lerner and Frederick Loewe with *Brigadoon* (1947), *My Fair Lady* (1956), and *Camelot* (1960); Frank Loesser with *Guys and Dolls* (1950) and *Most Happy Fella* (1956); Leonard Bernstein with *Candide* (1956) and *West Side Story* (1957); Jule Styne with *Funny Girl* (1964); Jerry Bock with *Fiddler on the Roof* (1964); Jerry Herman with *Hello, Dolly!* (1964) and *Mame* (1966); and John Kander with *Cabaret* (1966) and *Zorba* (1968). All were large-cast, multiple-set productions with lavish (often athletic) dance sequences, tuneful songs, and easily understood plots.

CANADIAN THEATRE TO 1968

In the years following the war, all the elements that would lead to the modern Canadian theatre were put into place, including the reestablishing of professional theatres, large-scale government support for the arts, the establishing of summer festivals and year-round regional theatres, and the advent of the alternative (often called the alternate) theatre movement.

While amateur theatres remained important, many, like the New Play Society (NPS, 1946–1971), were making the transition to becoming fully professional. Established by Dora Mayor Moore (1888–1979), one of the most important figures in Canadian theatre, NPS succeeded when many others failed, largely because of the success of its musical review, *Spring Thaw.* From 1948 until NPS disbanded, *Spring Thaw* brought in much-needed revenues and provided an early showcase for many of the most talented theatre artists in Toronto. But the real influence of the New Play Society came through its theatre school (established in 1950) where many leading actors and directors of the modern Canadian theatre got their start in the days before the National Theatre School opened in Montreal in 1960.

In contrast to NPS, Vancouver's influential Everyman Theatre (1946–1953), founded by Sydney Risk (1908–1985), was professional from the start, as was

Montreal's Théâtre du Rideau Vert, founded in 1948 by Yvette Brind'amour (1918–1992). The latter was the first of the important French-speaking professional companies which, until the late 1950s, outnumbered the English-language theatres in Canada. By far the most influential of those French-speaking companies, however, was Le Théâtre du Nouveau Monde (Theatre of the New World) founded in 1951 by Jean Gascon (1921–1988) and Jean-Louis Roux (1923–). The success of its European tours in the 1950s made it the Canadian theatre best known outside of North America. Gascon went on to become the first Executive Director of the National Theatre School (1960–1967), with Michel Saint-Denis as Artistic Director, and the first Canadian Artistic Director of the Stratford Festival (1967–1974).

Government funding for theatre, led by the Saskatchewan Arts Board of 1948, became a major influence on modern Canadian theatre during these years. A Royal Commission on National Development in the Arts, Letters and Sciences, known as the Massey-Lévesque Commission, was established in 1949 to determine what the country needed to do in order to establish a cultural identity. The commission made a series of recommendations in 1951 that led to the formation of the Canadian Council/Conseil des Arts du Canada in 1957. One of the commission's most significant findings was that theatrical development in Canada was being hampered by a lack of theatre facilities. Few theatres had been built since the turn of the century, while many old theatres had been converted to cinemas. The Canadian Council immediately encouraged government funding for the building of new multipurpose theatres. When these multipurpose theatres proved unsatisfactory, the Council began to promote arts centers with multiple venues, best exemplified by the National Arts Center (1969) in Ottawa, which included an opera house, a thrust stage, and a studio theatre. By the mid-1970s, the Canadian Council was also promoting the restoration of many older theatres. But perhaps the commission's most important finding was that professional theatres need government subsidy. The Council began by providing such funding for three companies in 1957. By the end of the century, despite over a decade of low-growth budgets, it would be providing subsidies to nearly 250 theatres with awards equaling from 10 to 40 percent of their budgets.

Summer festival and year-round regional theatres were soon established, offering a repertory of classical and contemporary European and U.S. plays. Such a repertory was thought both to acknowledge Canada's cultural heritage and to establish its place among modern nations. New Canadian plays were encouraged by such companies, but they were expected to fit into an international repertory. Toronto's Jupiter Theatre (1951–1954) tried to sustain a more experimental repertory but soon failed. The Crest Theatre (1953–1966) lasted longer with a mix of new Canadian plays, experimental plays, and plays from the standard repertory, but it was always in financial difficulties.

The Stratford Festival, established by Tom Patterson at Stratford, Ontario, in 1953, was immediately successful with a standard repertory almost completely dedicated to Shakespeare for its classical component. Tyrone Guthrie was hired as artistic director for the 2,262-seat Greek-style auditorium that was set up within a large tent (the permanent theatre was erected in 1956). Designer Tanya Moiseiwitsch (1914–) created a permanent stage that was to be a modern expression of the essential elements of the stages used in Shakespeare's day. This was the first thrust stage in Canada, and it became the prototype for the highly successful Chichester Festival Theatre in England (1962) and the equally successful Guthrie Theatre in Minneapolis (1963). But while this theatre has long been the most internationally respected theatre in Canada, it has also been a target of criticism by Canadian nationalists. They see little value for Canada's national aspirations in the Festival's repertory and in its approach to production. The highly regarded Shaw Festival (founded 1962) in Niagara-on-the-Lake, is dedicated to European drama written in Shaw's lifetime but has attracted less criticism. The Charlottetown Festival (founded in 1965) is admired for its commitment to original Canadian musicals.

John Hirsch (1930–1989) and Tom Hendry (1929–) were co-founders of the Manitoba Theatre Center in 1958, which was created from the merger of two amateur theatre companies. Together they coordinated a highly successful standard repertory of classical plays interspersed with contemporary plays, predominantly light comedies. They also developed an effective touring program for taking plays into area schools. This was the first professional regional theatre in Canada, and it served as a model for the twelve others that would join it by 1984.

By 1959, Toronto's Workshop Theatre (TWT, 1959–1989) had started mounting a challenge to everything the festivals and regional theatres would come to represent. Founded by George Luscomb (1926–1999) and modeled after Joan Littlewood's Workshop Theatre in London, TWT was the first of what would, in the 1970s, become known as an alternative theatre. Alternative theatres, like the earlier independent theatres, set themselves against the existing theatre establishment. But the alternative theatres were opposed to the European and U.S. text-based, director-focused theatre that the independent theatres had championed and that both the festival theatres and the regional theatres came to embody. Those who led the alternative theatre movement argued that regional theatres had no real identity because all of them performed the standard repertory. Such a repertory might be part of Canada's cultural heritage, they conceded, but it was a colonial heritage and therefore should not be the foundation of a modern cultural identity for the nation. Alternative theatres rejected the standard repertory and championed community-based performance pieces. They also insisted on a return to theatre that was actor-focused, and therefore they emphasized collective creation. The Theatre Passe Muraille (theatre beyond walls), founded in 1968 by Jim Garrard (1939–), rapidly became Canada's premier alternative theatre, embodying much of what the movement stood for in its dedication to new Canadian plays (it would eventually produce over 300), to community-based theatre, and to collective creation. The most influential of the French-Canadian alternative theatres (le jeune théâtre) was the Grand Cirque Ordinaire (1969–1978), whose focus on nonverbal "sociopoetic" theatre became the inspiration for some of the most innovative Canadian theatre of the 1980s and 1990s. When the Festival of Underground Theatre was held in Toronto in 1970, it established the legitimacy of the alternative theatre movement, which then became the dominant force in Canadian theatre.

Numerous playwrights had come to prominence in the 1950s and 1960s. John Coulter (1888–1990) continued the trend of dramatizing stories from Canadian history with his epic-style play, *Riel* (1949), about the leader of a nineteenth-century Canadian rebellion against the British. Robertson Davis (1913–1995) wrote plays poking fun at the lack of culture among his fellow Canadians, beginning with *Fortune My Foe* (1948). Félix Leclerc (1914–1988) wrote a series of comedies on life in Québec starting with *Ring the Morning Bells* (1954). But it was the dramatists of the 1960s who received the greater international recognition. These include Françoise Loranger (1913–), whose first play, *A house . . . one day* (1965) focused on the breakdown of the middle-class family, and whose second play, *Five More Minutes* (1967), was the first major drama to address feminist issues. George Ryga's (1932–1987) *The Ecstasy of Rita Joe* (1967) took on the issue of racism in a story about a Native American woman's struggle to comprehend white urban society. Finally, John Herbert (1926–2001), founder of the influential Garret Theatre Stu-

dio (1965–1970), became internationally known for *Fortune in Men's Eyes* (1967), a play dealing with homophobia in the prison system.

The alternative theatres that would come to prominence after 1968 would be inspired first by Canadian determination to establish an identity separate from England—a determination most clearly represented by the introduction of the maple leaf flag in 1963—and second by a determination to establish an identity separate from that of the United States, a determination made more urgent by the desire of Canadians to distance themselves from the Vietnam War.

AUSTRALIA AND NEW ZEALAND THEATRE TO 1968

Though Australia and New Zealand had active little theatres that produced a number of plays by local dramatists, theatre remained dominated by vaudeville, reviews, and a commercial theatre largely imported from England and the United States. With the introduction of television in 1956, even the vaudeville houses and review theatres began to close. The best actors and writers continued to turn to radio drama or seek careers abroad.

In 1943 the Australian Council for Music and the Arts was created to promote the arts in the schools. In 1947 Tyrone Guthrie was asked to consider the feasibility of creating a National Theatre for Australia. When he reported that such a project would be premature, he set off a nationalistic debate on Australia's postcolonial identity. Tours by the Old Vic Company in 1948 and by the Stratford Memorial Theatre (featuring several expatriate Australian actors) in 1949 and 1952 were inspirations, but they were also forceful reminders of how much needed to be done if theatre in Australia or New Zealand was to achieve world-class standards.

The first steps to improve the situation in Australia were taken in 1954 with the formation of the Australian Elizabethan Theatre Trust. Though it was named in honor of Queen Elizabeth II's visit to Australia and headed by a British director, Hugh Hunt, it was charged with the task of making theatre as vital a force in Australia as it had been in the London of Shakespeare's day. The Trust immediately leased the abandoned 1500-seat Majestic (1917) and renamed it the Elizabethan Theatre. It got off to a rather inauspicious start by mounting two plays by the English playwright Terrence Rattigan, with casts dominated by English actors. The nationalists were outraged, but these productions did establish the quality of performance the Trust was aspiring to. The Trust then set out to hire the Australian theatre artists who could meet this standard.

Australia's greatest expatriate actress, Judith Anderson (1898–1992), was lured back to Sydney by the Trust in 1955 to star in a production of *Medea*—with a remarkable cast of Australian actors including the young Zoë Caldwell (1934–) as a member of the chorus. The Trust also sponsored a tour of *Summer of the Seventeenth Doll* (1955) by Ray Lawler (1921–), which rapidly became Australia's best-known and most loved play. Over time the Trust supported important productions of a large number of plays by Australian authors. In 1958 the Trust established its first playwriting award, adopted the Young Elizabethan Players (founded 1955), founded the National Institute of Dramatic Art on the campus of University of New South Wales, and began to identify and support the most promising semiprofessional companies in each of the six states. In 1958–1959 they formed the Elizabethan Trust Opera (which became the autonomous Australian Opera in 1969), the Australian Ballet, and the Trust Players (1959–1962). The Trust also assisted in the establishment of the Marionette Theatre of Australia (1965–1988) and in 1967 funded the Elizabethan Trust Orchestra, divided into Sydney and Melbourne ensembles. Thus, by the time the Australian Council for the Arts was established in 1968 (it became the Australian Council in 1974), the Trust had achieved its primary objectives. In trying to avoid duplicating the system of subsidizing theatre companies which the Australian Council began to undertake in 1968, however, the Trust lost its focus and ran into trouble with a series of poor investments in commercial productions. By 1991 it was bankrupt and after reorganization became little more than a friends of the arts organization for Sydney.

The Trust had promoted Shakespeare as a vital component of any English-language theatre, and this inspired the University of Western Australia at Perth to build the New Fortune Theatre quadrangle in 1964. This was the first attempt to build a space that followed the dimensions provided in the contract for London's original Fortune Playhouse of 1600. This was not a reconstruction; like the Stratford Festival in Canada it was an attempt to recreate the fundamental spatial relationships of the Elizabethan playhouses. The New Fortune did not stop with the stage, however; it also recreated the auditorium. The theatre was instrumental in moving Australian thinking about theatre away from naturalism. Dorothy Hewett (1923–), one of Australia's more successful playwrights of the 1970s and 1980s, got her start in this theatre before she scored her first real success with *The Chapel Perilous* (1971). In the meantime the university built the 600-seat Octagon Theatre (1969), the most successful of the numerous thrust stages it inspired throughout Australia.

But by the time the New Fortune was built, Australia's first alternative theatre was already underway. The Emerald Hill Theatre in South Melbourne (1961–1966), co-founded by one of Melbourne's most successful directors, Wal Cherry (1932–1986), and actor-director George Whaley, was committed to an *avant-garde* repertory and high standards of production. But it never really found an audience and closed after five years. By this time Australia was caught up in the controversies that surrounded its participation in the Vietnam War, and a more politicized theatre was coming to the forefront. La MaMa, established by Betty Burstall in 1967, was, like its namesake in New York, a resource center for anyone who could persuade Burstall that they had a project worth doing in Melbourne. For the first three years the resources of La MaMa included a resident acting company, and in the first two years La MaMa staged or provided space for productions of twenty-five plays by Australian authors, many of them plays of protest.

In New Zealand, little theatre groups from the Unity Theatre, Wellington (1944–1978), to the Globe Theatre, Dunedin (1961–), were still the only outlet for plays by local authors. The Community Arts Service Theatre at Auckland (1947–1962) provided the only equivalent to a regional theatre as it performed a standard repertory of classics and modern European plays throughout the North Island, but it showed no interest in the work of local writers. The most significant attempt to start a National Theatre in New Zealand came with the formation of New Zealand Players in Wellington in 1953. Founded by Richard and Edith Campion, who had received their training at the Old Vic, this company performed an excellent repertory with high production standards, but they were unable to attract a subsidy and finally closed in 1960. After the Queen Elizabeth II Arts Council of New Zealand was established in 1964, subsidies became available for the first time and a number of professional and semiprofessional theatres were established. Of these the most important were the fully professional Mercury Theatre, founded at Auckland by Anthony Richardson (1926–1982), who trained many of New Zealand's most influential theatre artists (it closed in 1992); and the semiprofessional Downstage Theatre, Wellington (1964–), which did more than any other theatre to promote works by New Zealanders.

LOOKING AT THEATRE HISTORY

During the 1950s, dissatisfactions were not expressed solely through absurdist drama. In England, the most powerful impact was made by the "angry young men" who expressed themselves in relatively traditional dramatic forms. Although it is now usual to suggest that Osborne's *Look Back in Anger* was recognized immediately as a turning point in English drama, most reviewers of the time voiced serious reservations about it. Here are some excerpts from one of the most negative reviews:

> We should be very frank about this. If more plays like tonight's Look Back in Anger *are produced, the "Writer's Theatre" at the Royal Court must surely sink. I look back in anger upon a night misconceived and mis-spent. . . . The principal character is self-pitying, uncouth, cheaply vulgar. . . .*
>
> J. C. Trewin in *The Birmingham Post*, 8 May 1956.

Fortunately, others were more perceptive:

> *Of course,* Look Back in Anger *is not a perfect play. But it is a most exciting one, abounding with life and vitality and the life it deals with is life as it is lived at this very moment—not a common enough subject in the English theatre. . . . Don't miss this play. If you are young, it will speak to you. If you are middle-aged, it will tell you what the young are feeling. . . .*
>
> T. C. Worsley in *The New Statesman*.

Between 1945 and 1960, the dominant production style in the United States was exemplified in the combined work of Elia Kazan (as director) and Jo Mielziner (as designer). Here, in his review of Tennessee Williams's *Cat on a Hot Tin Roof* (1955), Eric Bentley gives a good description of their work:

> *Jo Mielziner's setting consists of a square and sloping platform with one of its corners, not one of its sides, jutting towards the audience. A corner of a ceiling is above, pointing upstage. On the platform are minimum furnishings for a bed-sitting room. Around the room, steps and space suggest the out of doors. The whole stage is swathed in everchanging light and shade. . . .*
>
> *Such is the world of Elia Kazan, as we know it from his work on plays by more authors than one. The general scheme is that not only of* Streetcar *but also of* Salesman: *an exterior that is also a view of an interior—but, more important, a view of man's exterior that is also a view of his interior, the habitat of his body and the country of his memories and dreams. A theatre historian would probably call this world a combination of naturalism and expressionism. . . .*
>
> *It is one of the distinctive creations of American theatre. . . . With the means of the new American theatre (school of Lee Strasberg and Harold Clurman) it does reach the cherished end of the older theatre (true grandeur of performance) at a time when the older theatre itself . . . is failing to do so. . . .*
>
> *I do not think the reason for this resides in the formality itself. The effectiveness of this grandeur results . . . from the interaction between formality in the setting, lighting, and grouping and an opposite quality . . . in the individual performances. The externals of the physical production belong . . . to the old theatre, but the acting is internal, "Stanislavskyite." Within the formal setting, from the fixed positions in which they are made to stand, the actors live their roles with that vigilant, concentrated, uninterrupted nervous intensity which Mr. Kazan always manages to give. . . .*
>
> *The New Republic*, April 4, 1955.

22

Continental European and Latin American Theatre in the Late Twentieth Century

By 1968 enormous stresses had developed in almost every country. Protests moved away from the nonviolent tactics favored by civil rights advocates to confrontations. Such patterns of protest and violence were symptomatic of deep-seated doubts about the validity of long-accepted conventions of behavior and traditional values and about the ability of social institutions to deal effectively with changing needs. Individuals and groups began to elevate their own ideals above existing laws, to assert their obligation to live by their own standards, and to demand the alteration or destruction of anything contrary to their views. The result was a fragmented society lacking agreement about both goals and means.

The theatre could not remain aloof from the stresses of the time. It was caught in a struggle between those who wished to maintain tradition and those who championed innovation and change. This conflict provoked much controversy over the nature and function of theatre. The old conception of art as detached contemplation (or as the pursuit of some superior beauty and order) was challenged by those who wished to use it to provoke thought and action about pressing social and political issues.

Throughout the 1960s, prosperity gave the theatre considerable economic stability, for it was possible to gain financial support both for traditional and innovative work. The old and the new coexisted, sometimes in uneasy alliance, but often in radical opposition. By the 1980s, however, conservatism, both political and economic, reasserted itself and the exuberance of earlier years faded. By the end of the decade, as the Soviet empire collapsed and ethnic conflicts increased, uncertainty was once more apparent.

SOVIET AND RUSSIAN THEATRE TO 1990

The turn away from Stalinism that began in 1956 was sporadic thereafter. But the policies of *glasnost* introduced by Mikhail Gorbachev in the 1980s were to bring profound changes that would ultimately lead to the breakup of the Soviet Union. Still, from 1968 until the time of that breakup in the late 1980s, Soviet theatre enjoyed a popularity probably unsurpassed anywhere in the world. Moscow's approximately 30 theatres were usually filled each night. Soviet government statistics indicated that attendance in the late 1980s was high throughout the Soviet Union, with some 110 million people attending more than 600 professional theatres, including over 60 for children and youth.

During the 1960s, growing dissatisfaction with socialist realism led to a revival of interest in Meyerhold, Tairov, and Vakhtangov. Exhibitions were devoted to their productions; a complete edition of Meyerhold's writings was finally published; and in

FIG. 22.1

Yuri Lyubimov's production of Albert Camus' adaptation of Dostoyevsky's
The Possessed, 1985. Design by Lazaridis Stefanos. Photo by Agence de
Presse Bernand, Paris.

1974 the centenary of Meyerhold's birth was celebrated with performances, articles, conferences, and
commemorative stamps. But Vakhtangov's methods
were the most widely adopted as they provided the
most readily acceptable alternative to socialist realism.

The Moscow Art Theatre continued to command
the greatest official prestige after 1968, and its actors
the highest salaries of any theatre in the USSR. By
1973 its programs had become so extensive and its
company so large that a new and lavish theatre was
built to augment its facilities. In 1987 the complexities of the organization (exacerbated by operating in
two separate theatres located in different parts of
Moscow) led to the division of the company into two
parts, one headed by Oleg Yefremov, the other by
Tatyana Doronina. Rivalries among the two divisions
considerably tarnished the company's public image.

The Contemporary (Sovremennik) Theatre, meanwhile, continued to gain in prestige, especially after
1970 when one of its founders, Oleg Yefremov
(1927–2000), was named head of the Moscow Art
Theatre. Oleg Tabakov (1935–) became director of
the Contemporary, and in 1974 it too was given a
new theatre (a remodeled cinema with rehearsal
rooms and workshops) to augment its facilities.
Tabakov left two years later to pursue an independent career. He established his own highly regarded
Tabakov Studio Theatre, became director of the
Moscow Art Theatre's Studio-School, and also created the American Studio of the Moscow Art The-

atre. The Contemporary Theatre, meanwhile, under
the direction of Galina Volchek, had expanded its activities to include touring and visited the United
States in 1996 and 1998.

The most controversial and experimental theatre
was the Moscow Theatre of Drama and Comedy (usually called the Taganka after the suburb in which it
was located). Headed after 1964 by Yuri Lyubimov
(1917–), it made liberal use of dynamic movement,
dance, mime, masks, puppets, and projections, and reshaped scripts or adapted novels from a critical perspective. Its tendency to produce works considered
to be on the edge of permissibility and its "formalistic" production techniques (influenced by Meyerhold, Vakhtangov, and Brecht) kept the Taganka
highly visible and controversial. A number of its productions were censored or forbidden, but it was especially popular with young audiences. Among its
most noted productions were *Tartuffe* (1970), *Hamlet*
(1974), and *The Inspector's Recounting* (1978). At the
Congress of the All-Union Society of Theatre Workers in 1970, the Taganka was the only company sin-
gled out for censure. Nevertheless, in 1977 it was
permitted to make a foreign tour, and thereafter Lyubimov was occasionally permitted to direct in Western Europe. While in the West, he harshly condemned
Soviet opposition to his work, and in 1984, while
abroad, he was removed from his post at the Taganka
and stripped of his citizenship. Subsequently, he directed throughout Europe and the United States, stag-

ing a number of highly acclaimed productions, most notably adaptations of Dostoyevsky's *Crime and Punishment* and *The Possessed,* the latter for the Théâtre de l'Europe in 1985. Lyubimov was succeeded at the Taganka in 1984 by another of Russia's controversial directors, Anatoly Efros (1925–1987), several of whose productions at other theatres had been withdrawn from the repertory or censored.

Other innovative directors included Vasilyev, Sturua, and Dodin. Anatoly Vasilyev (1942–) began directing in the 1960s and came to international attention in the 1980s when his productions of Viktor Slavkin's *Cerceau* and Pirandello's *Six Characters in Search of an Author* played at various international festivals. *Cerceau,* which treats a reunion of old acquaintances in an isolated country house, was developed through improvisational techniques reminiscent of Grotowski's. Pirandello's mingling of life and art in *Six Characters* was mirrored in Vasileyev's intermingling of audience and performers and frequent switching of roles among the actors.

Robert Sturua (1938–), working at the Rustaveli Theatre in Tbilisi, gained international recognition in the 1980s, especially with his productions of Shakespeare's *Richard III* and *King Lear,* both of which were given political interpretations. In *Richard III,* Richmond followed Richard everywhere, taking notes and observing, apparently to ready himself to take over the role of ruler. In *King Lear,* the action occurred in a police state which seemed literally to disintegrate around the characters. He continued his productions of Shakespeare with *Macbeth* in 1996, which shows love giving way to desire for power.

Playwriting also underwent several ups and downs after 1968, for although strictures were relaxed, prior to the late 1980s the price for overstepping the bounds could be severe. Vasili Aksyonov (1932–), for example, had won considerable success with such plays as *Always for Sale* (1966), a commentary on popular culture using song, dance, masks, and film to depict a conformist society, and *Your Murderer* (1977), which drew on absurdist techniques reminiscent of Ionesco's *Rhinoceros* and its protagonist who refuses to go along with the crowd. But because of his involvement with a banned book, Aksyonov was forced to emigrate to the United States in 1980. Other writers—such as Chingiz Aitmatov (1928–) and Kaltai Mukhamed-zhanov (1928–) in *The Ascent of Mount Fuji* (1973) and G. Baklanov in *Fasten Your Seat Belts* (1975)—though they treated the problem of maintaining integrity in the face of authoritarian demands for conformity, stopped short of criticizing the Soviet system. A greater number of dramatists continued to write traditional dramas. Among the most successful playwrights were Aleksandr Vampilov (1937–1972),

FIG. 22.2
Askyonov's *Always for Sale* at the Contemporary Theatre, Moscow. Directed by Oleg Yefremov.

whose *Last Summer in Chulimsk* (1972) presents a gallery of characters in a Siberian village but concentrates on a young girl who, rejected by a visitor, is condemned to a life of disappointment; Mikhail Roshchin (1933–), whose extremely popular *Valentin and Valentina* (1971) treats young lovers caught in a generational conflict; and Aleksei Arbuzov (1908–1986), one of the most popular and prolific of Russian dramatists. Arbuzov began writing plays in the 1930s but was especially successful after 1968 with such plays as *Old Fashioned Comedy* (1976, produced on Broadway in 1978 as *Do You Turn Somersaults?*), which treats awakening love between two older people, and *Remembrances* (1981), about the pull between family loyalty and extramarital temptations.

Two of Russia's most admired playwrights were Radzinsky and Petrushevskaya. Edvard Radzinsky (1936–) first gained popularity with *104 Pages about Love* (1964), a work that helped to establish a trend toward plays about personal lives. Originally directed by Anatoly Efros, it was subsequently performed in more than 120 theatres before being made into a ballet and a film. His later work, especially his trilogy composed of *Conversations with Socrates* (1978), *Lunin* (1981), and *Theatre in the Time of Nero and Seneca* (1981), uses historical subjects to stir up thought about oppressive authority and its inability to enslave the human spirit. Ludmilla Petrushevskaya (1938–) won considerable fame with short, realistic, seemingly plotless plays filled with wry humor. Two of the most popular were *Cinzano* (1975) and *Smirnova's Birthday* (1975), a pair of related plays, one about men and the other about women, in which the characters discuss life as each group simultaneously but in separate locations consumes the Cinzano they bought with the money that was supposed to cover the expenses of a funeral. Other notable playwrights included Maria Arbotova, Sergei Kokovkin, Alexander Galin, and Olga Mukhina.

THEATRE IN POLAND AND CZECHOSLOVAKIA TO 1990

Like the rest of Eastern Europe, Poland came under Soviet domination following World War II, but it was the first to ease restraints after 1956. In 1968, when Poland's participation in the invasion of Czechoslovakia led to protests at home, new strictures were imposed. These restrictions gradually eased, but in 1982 fear of the Solidarity movement led the government to impose martial law. In 1989, after democratic reform ousted the Communists, almost all restraints were removed. Thus, the degree of government control varied drastically after 1945.

For several years after 1956 the dominant dramatic mode was absurdism, although it took a more satirical and didactic turn than in France. The vogue was initiated with the plays of Stanislaw Ignacy Witkiewicz (1885–1939), a previously neglected surrealist writer of the interwar years, whose theoretical work, *Pure Form in the Theatre* (1920), along with such plays as *The Water Hen* (1921), *The Madman and the Nun* (1923), and *The Mother* (1924), won increasing acceptance. The plays of Beckett were also popular and helped to establish the taste for absurdist drama.

Soon several new dramatists appeared, of whom the most important were Rósewicz and Mrozek. Tadeusz Rósewicz (1921–), already famous as a poet, began writing plays in 1960. His *The Card Index* (1960) and *He Left Home* (1964) did much to establish the pattern that would be followed by subsequent writers, with whom the most common theme was the search for a lost order even as the concept of absolutes was rejected. He continued to explore this theme in such plays as *The Laocoon Group* (1974), *White Marriage* (1975), and *The Trap* (1982).

Although within Poland Rósewicz was perhaps the most respected of contemporary dramatists, abroad he was overshadowed by Slawomir Mrozek (1932–), whose plays depended rather heavily on caricature. For example, *The Police* (1958), one of Mrozek's numerous short plays, shows how the secret police, having been so successful that they are in danger of being abolished, order one of their own men to become an enemy agent so they may survive. Mrozek also wrote full-length plays, of which the best known is *Tango* (1964), one of the most popular of all new plays in Europe during the late 1960s. *Tango* is a parable about the decay of values, which has become so com-

plete that only brute force is truly effective; consequently those who are most willing to exercise power, ruthlessly and without regard for humanistic principles, become the rulers. Mrozek continued this vein in *A Happy Event* (1971), in which he depicts left-wing anarchist youth in the form of a grown-up baby who tyrannizes his parents, blows up their house, and ends up helpless in the ruins; and in *The Emigrés* (1974), a two-character play which suggests that the left-wing intellectual and the worker depend on each other to give their lives significance. His later plays include *The Ambassador* (1981) and *Alpha* (1984). *Love in the Crimea* (1994) is a satirical history of Russia in the twentieth century. Using Chekhov-like characters and situations, its first act takes place in 1910 (Czarist Russia), the second in 1928 (Communist Russia), and the third in the 1990s (marketplace Russia). Mrozek, who left Poland in 1963, returned after spending his exile in France and Mexico.

Among later dramatists, Janusz Glowacki (1938–) was one of the most popular. He first began to write plays in the late 1970s. Because of his sympathy with the Solidarity movement, Glowacki came under increasing attack in the 1980s, and eventually fled to the United States. The best known of his early plays is *Cinders* (1979), which focuses on a girls' reformatory production of Cinderella and its leading actress, who chooses suicide rather than submit to the repressive circumstances in which she finds herself. The best known of the later plays, written after Glowacki arrived in the United States, are *Hunting Cockroaches* (1985), which shows a Polish emigré couple trying to adjust to their new environment and a new set of problems, and *Antigone in New York* (1993), in which emigrés bury a body in New York's Tompkins Square Park.

Internationally, Poland was perhaps best known for its innovative directors rather than for its dramatists. By far the best known was Jerzy Grotowski (1933–1999), who founded the Theatre of 13 Rows in Opole in 1959, which became the Polish Laboratory Theatre when they moved to Wroclaw (Breslau) in 1965. Grotowski gained an international reputation when his company began to tour and he began working with foreign troupes and lecturing widely on his methods. The collection of essays by and about him published under the title *Towards a Poor Theatre* (1968) became one of the most influential works of the period.

Ironically, Grotowski began to alter his interests just as he won international acceptance. Thus, the first phase of his work ended around 1970. During this phase, Grotowski began with the premise that the theatre has borrowed too heavily from other media, especially film and television, and thus has violated its own essence, which he sought to recover by elim-

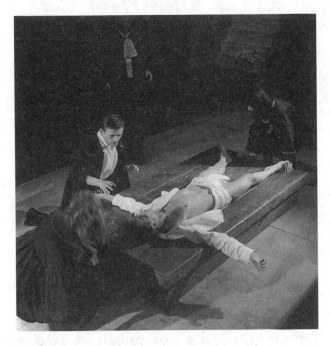

FIG. 22.3
Grotowski's production of *The Constant Prince,* adapted from Calderón's play. For this production, the space was arranged so that the spectators looked down on the acting space much as in a medical operating theatre; Grotowski suggested that in this performance symbolic "psychic surgery" took place. Photo by Agence de Presse Bernand, Paris.

inating everything except its two essential elements: the actor and the audience. He called his approach "poor theatre" (in contrast with technologically "rich" theatre) since it avoided all machinery and minimized all spectacle not created by the actor. His performers were not allowed to use makeup or change costume to indicate a change in role or within a character; all music had to be produced by the actors themselves; he used no scenery in the traditional sense, although a few functional properties might be rearranged or used in various ways as the action demanded; he abandoned the proscenium-arch stage in favor of a large room which could be rearranged for each production. In this way, actors were thrown back on their own resources.

During this period, actor training was the focus of Grotowski's concerns. His system required actors to gain absolute control over themselves physically, vocally, and psychically, so that during performances they might transform themselves as demanded by the production. Grotowski wanted his actors to arouse a sense of wonder because of their ability to exceed what the spectators can envision ever being able to do.

In this early phase, Grotowski looked upon the theatre as a secular ritual to which spectator-witnesses were admitted. He believed that the audience is the other essential ingredient of a performance and that it must be put in a position to play its role unselfconsciously. (He argued that attempts to involve the audience directly in the action only make it self-conscious.) Therefore, for each production he decided how the audience should respond psychologically and then arranged the space to create the appropriate psychic distance.

In preparing a production, Grotowski searched in a script to find archetypal patterns that have universal meaning for audiences today. Much of the script might be abandoned and the remainder rearranged. The ultimate aim was to make the actors and the audience confront themselves in something analogous to a religious experience. Among his most highly regarded productions from this period were *Akropolis* (first done in 1962), *The Constant Prince* (first done in 1965), and *Apocalypsis cum Figuris* (first done in 1968), all of which were restaged several times.

By 1970 Grotowski had come to believe that his group had reached the end of its search for technical mastery, and he decided to create no new productions. He realized that, while his actors had been able to eliminate the blocks that stood in their way as performers, they had not broken down the blocks that stood between performer and audience. He then set out to eliminate "the idea of theatre," in the sense of an actor playing for an audience, and to find a way of incorporating spectators into "a meeting, not a confrontation; a communion, where we can be totally ourselves." Consequently, he sought to develop means for leading participants back into the elemental connections between people and their bodies, the natural world, and each other.

The first major revelation of the new work came during the summer of 1975 when approximately 500 people from all over the world attended a "research university" organized by Grotowski at Wroclaw under the sponsorship of the Théâtres des Nations, which that year was held in Warsaw. The group included students, teachers, and journalists, as well as several famous directors—among them Peter Brook, Jean-Louis Barrault, Luca Ronconi, and Joseph Chaikin. Some of the activities involved groups going into the woods for 24 hours during which they were led through ritualized myths and archetypal experiences involving fire, air, earth, water, eating, dancing, playing, planting, and bathing. Through this process, participants were expected to rediscover the roots of the theatre in pure ritualized experience, as well as to discover their own true being.

After 1975, Grotowski began studying the diverse ritual performances of Japan, India, Haiti, Mexico,

FIG. 22.4
Tadeuz Kantor's *Wielopole, Wielopole* with the Cricot 2 Company. Photograph by Carol Rosegg.

Africa, and elsewhere, and used these experiences to enhance the work he had done earlier. He labeled this new phase the Theatre of Sources, and in 1983 he became head of an institute at the University of California, Irvine, devoted to continuing this research with a renewed concern for physical, vocal, psychological, and performance discipline. (In 1984 the Polish Laboratory Theatre was disbanded.) In 1985, a center to assist his work was established in Pontadera, Italy, and subsequently Grotowski spent most of his time there. Although Grotowski's work went through several phases after 1960, it is the work done before 1970 which continues to be of greatest interest.

Next to Grotowski, the best known of Poland's directors was Tadeusz Kantor (1915–1990). Originally an artist and designer, he founded his own company, Cricot 2, in 1955. It was Kantor who in 1956 reintroduced Witkiewicz's plays and initiated the interest in absurdist drama. Little known outside of Poland until after 1970, he subsequently appeared at major theatre festivals throughout the world. One of Kantor's best known productions was *The Dead Class* (1975), set in a school room where the characters, elderly corpse-like people, confront their younger selves, represented by effigies; the role of the teacher was played by Kantor, who remained on stage throughout, conducting the actors, music, and overall pacing. *Wielopole, Wielopole* (1980) evokes the suffering of the Polish people at the time of World War I, caught between the church and the army and subjected to mass murder and personal loss. In *I Shall Never Return* (1988), Kantor himself was the central character in a kind of summing up of his career with fragments from and allusions to many of his productions.

Andrzej Wajda (1926–), one of Poland's eminent film directors, also built an international reputation as a director in the theatre. In Poland much of his work was done for Cracow's Stary Theatre or Warsaw's Contemporary Theatre. His *Hamlet* (1982), staged just as General Jaruzelski was placing Poland under military rule, ended with Fortinbras, in uniform, taking charge. Not surprisingly, it was soon removed from the repertory, although Wajda restaged it in Rome in 1983. In 1989, two of Wajda's productions, *The Dybbuk* and *Hamlet IV,* were seen at the Pepsico Summerfare Festival in the United States. This *Hamlet* took place backstage and focused on an actor preparing to play the Danish prince and on the differences between public acts and behind-the-scene machinations.

In Czechoslovakia, the Soviet invasion in 1968 dealt a sharp blow to that country's theatre. Beginning in 1969 censorship was reimposed. In that year Grossman and Havel were removed from their posts at the Balustrade, Havel's plays were banned, and the Cinoherni was forced to change many of its policies. In 1971 Krejca was removed as director at the Gate and in 1972, reportedly because the actors remained loyal to him, the Gate was disbanded; in 1976 Krejca was permitted to leave the country for a permanent post in West Germany. The Prague Institute of Scenography was also closed. In 1977 Havel and several other writers were put on trial, and Havel was sent to prison, the first of six times. A number of writers and other theatre artists left the country. Perhaps because of his great international reputation, Svoboda was able to continue his work with little hindrance. With the fall of the Soviet Union, Czechoslovakia moved rapidly toward liberalization.

GERMAN THEATRE TO 1990

By the mid-1960s, German playwrights seem to have tired of preoccupation with guilt and were moving away from the postwar apolitical stance toward a leftist analysis of contemporary social problems. Many of the new dramas were related to the folk-play tradition through their choice of characters from everyday life, their use of dialects and colloquial speech (as opposed to the high German which had long been a standard on the German stage), and their concern for neo-naturalistic situations. They also were influenced by Odon von Horvath (1901–1938), whose plays such as *Tales of the Vienna Woods* (1930) and *Kasimir and Karoline* (1931), depicting the terror and repression that lies beneath the familiar and banal, had been banned in Germany since the 1930s but were revived in the 1960s to great acclaim.

Perhaps the most successful writer in this tradition was Franz Xaver Kroetz (1946–), whose most characteristic plays use the speech and behavior patterns of his native Bavaria to depict the brutalization of the proletariat. The best examples of this work are *Dairy Farm* (1972) and its sequel *Ghost Train* (1972), which develop the relationship of two misfits—an older farm worker and the mentally retarded adolescent daughter of the farm's owner. Many of the details are naturalistic, moving through rape, attempted abortion, and child murder, although the emphasis is upon the societal conditions which underlie the actions rather than on sensational events. In subsequent plays, such as *Upper Austria* (1973), *The Nest* (1975), and *Mensch Meier* (1978), Kroetz increasingly sought to clarify for working-class audiences the nature of society and their place in it. His *Fear and Hope of the Republic of Germany* (1983) and *I Am the People* (1994) are concerned with German youth, their discontents and neo-Nazi backlash. By arousing consciousness, he hoped to stimulate his viewers to take steps to change their situation. Kroetz was among the most controversial and popular of contemporary German-language dramatists. He also frequently directed productions.

Somewhat related to Kroetz's work was that of Martin Sperr (1944–), especially in his trilogy treating successively peasant life, small town life, and city life: *Hunting Scenes from Lower Bavaria* (1966), *Tales of Landshut* (1967), and *Munich Freedom* (1971). All depict human beings as selfish, corruptible, and cruel. Following an illness of several years, Sperr returned to the theatre in 1977 with *Spitzeder*, a street-ballad entertainment about an actual nineteenth-century trickster.

Botho Strauss (1944–) worked as a dramaturg for Peter Stein, Germany's most admired director, before beginning his playwriting career in 1971. His first success came with *Three Acts of Recognition* (1976), in which he questioned the relationship between life and art. In *Big and Little* (1978), perhaps his best-known work, the characters, isolated in cell-like cubicles, seek unsuccessfully to make contact with others, although the very search seems a delusion. Among his later plays, one of the best was *Visitor* (1989) which, using

FIG. 22.5

Kroetz's *Dying Farmer* at the Deutsches Schauspielhaus, Hamburg, 1985. Design by Wilfried Minks. Photograph by Roswitha Hecke.

rehearsal as a metaphor for role-playing, suggests that we live in the world like visitors at a play, denying the necessity for dealing with the problems that are presented to us. *Ithaka* (1996), based on Homer's *Odyssey,* is a contemporary story in which revenge is demanded for injustice. Strauss came to be one of the most produced of living German dramatists. Thomas Bernhard (1931– 1989), an Austrian writer, turned to playwriting in 1970 with *A Feast for Boris.* His subsequent dramas include *Minetti* (1976) and *Arrived* (1982). His plays use clichés, mechanical behavior, irony, and parody to comment on human behavior. Bernhard's pervasive misanthropy often led to protests against his plays, as it did with his final work, *Heroes' Square* (1989), in which he accused Austria of still being anti-Semitic and falling apart under an alliance of political parties and the Catholic Church. Despite his ongoing theme of the impotence of human striving, the German public remained fascinated by his plays.

Peter Handke (1942–) followed a different tack than most of his contemporaries, being concerned above all with language as ideology and manipulator of behavior. He began his playwriting career in 1966 with a group of short "speech plays" in which he abandoned plot, character, and environment. In one of these, *Offending the Audience,* four unnamed and undifferentiated speakers make, attack, and reformulate

FIG. 22.6
Botho Strauss's *Big and Little* at the Schaubühne am Halleschen Ufer, West Berlin, 1978. Directed by Peter Stein; design by Karl-Ernst Herrmann. Photo by Ruth Walz.

statements about theatregoing and the nature of theatrical illusion. One of Handke's best-known works is *Kaspar* (1968), in which a young man who has been brought up in total isolation (and therefore without speech) is gradually reduced to conformity and schizophrenia by making him accept behavioral codes. In these and other plays, *My Foot My Tutor* (1969), *The Ride Across Lake Constance* (1971), *The Unreasonable Are Dying Out* (1974), *Slow Homecoming* (1982), and *The Hour in Which We Knew Nothing of Each Other* (1992), Handke is preoccupied with the way human beings are reduced to or enact conformity.

The only East German playwright to achieve international fame was Heinar Müller (1929–1995), who began writing plays in 1956 with *The Scab,* a work about factory quotas written in the socialist realism mode. Later he turned to historical subjects, as in *Philoktetes* (1966), to provide a perspective on the present. Beginning in the late 1970s, his plays became increasingly indirect and allusive as in *Hamletmachine* (1977), a short work, most of it without designated characters or dialogue, using *Hamlet* as a reference point for a critique of the intellectual's position in the contemporary world. He subsequently wrote a trilogy of works similar to *Hamletmachine* but based in the Medea myth, and a number of other similar short pieces, among them *Description of a Picture* (1985), which he labeled "explosions of memory." His final play, *Germania 3* (about Hitler, Stalin, the failure of East Germany, and other aspects of twentieth-century German history), was produced posthumously in 1996. In all his late works, Müller is preoccupied with the contradictions and failures of our time as illuminated by allusions to our cultural heritage. Although for a time denounced in East Germany for his pessimism, in the 1980s, after being awarded major prizes in the West, Müller came to be recognized as one of East Germany's preeminent playwrights. In the 1990s, Müller's plays were among the most frequently produced throughout Germany. He also turned to directing in Berlin, Bayreuth, and elsewhere, and at the time of his death was director of the Berliner Ensemble.

Germany also produced a number of female playwrights, although few attained major recognition. Among these writers are Gerlind Reinshagen (1926–), whose *Sunday's Children* (1976), concerning a young girl in the Nazi era, was the first play by a German woman to receive wide recognition; Friederike Roth (1948–), whose *Piano Plays* (1980) explores the interplay of gender; and Kerstin Specht (1956–), whose *Little Red Hot-Man* (1990), influenced by the folk-play tradition, is set on the border between East and West and internalizes the uncertainties symbolized by that location. Since 1986 a Festival of Women, held every two years in Hamburg, has brought together female performers and artists from all over the world.

After 1968 Brecht's plays continued to grow in popularity, and by the 1970s had surpassed even those of Shakespeare in numbers of annual performances in Germany. Brecht's works and theory were also significant in the leftward trend that dominated German production until the 1980s. Brecht's own company, however, had to deal with a number of problems. By the time of Helene Weigel's death in 1971, the

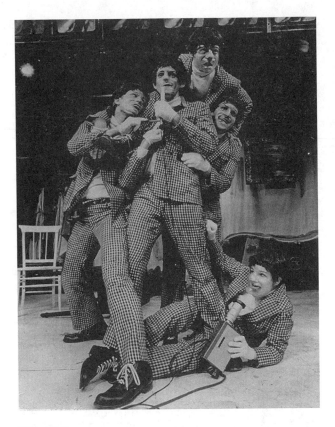

FIG. 22.7

Handke's *Kaspar* at the Chelsea Theatre Center, Brooklyn, 1973. Directed by Carl Weber; video by Video Free America. Photograph Amnon Nomis. Courtesy Chelsea Theatre Center.

Berliner Ensemble was considered by many to have become a museum. When Ruth Berghaus (1927–1996) was named director, she attempted to revitalize the company through highly experimental productions of such plays as Wedekind's *Spring's Awakening* and Strindberg's *Miss Julie*. Her efforts met with considerable opposition, being damned by many critics as "self-indulgent formalism." In 1977 she was replaced by Manfred Wekwerth (1929–), who had worked closely with Brecht. Under Wekwerth, the company regained much of it former vitality. After the reunification of Germany, however, the role of the Berliner Ensemble, like that of many other theatres, was questioned. In 1993 it was privatized, although it continued to receive some $16 million in subsidy. A five-person management—composed of Peter Palitzsch, Peter Zadek, Matthias Langhoff, Fritz Marquardt, and Heinar Müller—was installed in 1992. Brecht's heirs, having been removed from positions of power, for a time denied the theatre permission to present any of Brecht's plays. The Berliner Ensemble was left to seek a new artistic vision from a group of directors who had little in common, and

the management arrangement soon disintegrated. By 1994 only Müller was left. His death left considerable uncertainty, and the future of the Berliner Ensemble still remains in doubt.

The Festival Theatre at Bayreuth also underwent significant changes during the 1970s. In 1973 the Wagner family relinquished much of its control over the festival and archival materials when the Richard Wagner Foundation was formed. This foundation was created to maintain, but not run, the festival; it provided that a member of the Wagner family was to direct future festivals "if no better qualified applicants come forward." In 1976 the one-hundredth anniversary of the festival was celebrated with great fanfare and controversy over the innovative staging of the Ring by the French director, Patrice Chereau, who interpreted this cycle as a commentary on the Industrial Revolution and capitalism. These productions came to seem conservative alongside those of Harry Kupfer in 1988, in which the gods resembled gangsters in a nightmarish technological world nearing its end.

Another festival, the Berlin Theatertreffen, inaugurated in 1963, helped to give focus to the current state of German-language theatre. Each year ten productions, presumably the most significant, innovative, or provocative in Germany, Austria, or Switzerland, were invited to the festival. The choices, often controversial, provided a fair measure of theatrical trends in German-language theatre.

After 1968 the theatres of West Germany were plagued with dissension. As in other countries, there was much argument over the extent to which the repertory should be made relevant to the immediate social and political scene. Several critics charged that the typical season seemed more concerned with preserving the past than reflecting the present. The attempt of some directors to radicalize the repertory led to factionalism and dissension. The directors Peter Stein and Hansgünther Heyme played crucial roles in this controversy by staging German classics to reveal their disguised political and social ideologies and to comment on the social and theatrical realities of today. Increasing tensions and controversy led to a decline in attendance in the 1970s and some theatres began to experience financial difficulties even though subsidies covered about 80 percent of operating costs. Doubts were voiced that West Germany needed all of the subsidized stages then in existence. More typically, however, companies explored exchanging productions, lending sets and costumes, and combining publicity campaigns.

The stresses of the late 1960s also led to the formation of free theatres, cooperatives (which linked a number of small companies), and lunchtime theatres.

They seem also to have stimulated interests in children's theatre. Formerly, most theatres had performed one children's play each year (usually at Christmas and most often based on a fairy tale). During the 1970s, some companies were formed to play exclusively for children and youth. Of these, the best known was Grips in West Berlin. Like several other troupes, Grips abandoned fairy tales for material related directly to the children's own lives. This approach, usually referred to as "emancipatory theatre," aimed to free its audience from "false ideologies" and traditional repressions. A number of theatres also catered exclusively to adolescents. In 1976 the Alliance for Children's and Young People's Theatre was formed to help the companies deal with common problems and concerns. An annual festival of theatres for young audiences was also established.

Another significant controversy developed over managerial practices. Perhaps the greatest source of unhappiness was the almost unlimited decision-making power of the government-appointed theatre managers (Intendanten). The dissatisfaction came to a head in 1969 when in several cities actors interrupted performances to discuss the social realities reflected by their status in the theatre. Such crises were resolved in various ways. Cologne appointed a triumvirate of directors, each with a group of performers; Wuppertal turned to a six-person directorate under a supervisor; Frankfurt and Kiel attempted a participatory directorate in which every member of the company was involved; and in West Berlin a commune (in which Peter Stein was the most prominent figure) was established. Nevertheless, most companies continued under the old system, although many of the more conservative Intendants were replaced by less conservative directors. Many of the new organizational schemes were soon found too cumbersome and were abandoned or altered.

Among the important directors after 1968, some of the most innovative and influential were Heyme, Palitzsch, and Zadek. Hansgünther Heyme (1935–), once an assistant to Piscator, was named head of the Cologne company in 1968. In 1969 his production of Schiller's *Wallenstein* became one of the most influential productions of the time. Heyme reduced Schiller's trilogy to a single play and reshaped the text so as to illuminate the ideological forces that Schiller had glossed over. Many things in the production also echoed a major concern of the 1960s—the Vietnam conflict. In this and subsequent productions Heyme emphasized the subjugation of individual behavior to prevailing social and political ideologies. Along with Peter Stein, Heyme became a major influence on German approaches to staging in the 1970s. Later Heyme headed theatres in Essen and Bremen and was

director of the Ruhr Festival. Among his later productions, one of the most memorable was Gaston Salvatore's *King Congo* (1991), set in 1884 when a Congress of European rulers divided up Africa. Peter Palitzsch (1918–), Brecht's chief dramaturg, defected to West Germany in 1961 when the Berlin Wall was erected. In the West, his staging of Brecht's plays were extremely influential and motivated a number of young directors to experiment with and elaborate on Brechtian techniques in staging plays by other authors, including Shakespeare, Walser, Dorst, and Hochhuth. Largely through Palitzsch's influence Brechtian staging techniques came to dominate German theatre in the 1970s. Peter Zadek (1926–), though born in Germany, grew up in England and worked there until 1958. He directed many English plays and was often said to have infused an English influence into German staging. He headed the theatres in Bremen (1964–1967), Bochum (1972–1975), and, after a period of freelancing, Hamburg. Zadek often incorporated music hall and revue elements into his productions, and his innovative (sometimes seemingly perverse) interpretations of plays made him a figure of constant controversy and admiration.

By far the most respected director after 1968 was Peter Stein (1937–), eight of whose first twelve productions were included in the Berlin Theatertreffen. His staging of Goethe's *Tasso* at Bremen in 1969 was considered a watershed production. Goethe's play, a revered classic which had long been staged with loving respect, was radically altered by Stein to clarify the ideology underlying the play; ultimately the production became a critique of Goethe's failure to face the realities of his situation (and of theatre artists today) who, in accepting state subsidies and public patronage, place themselves in much the same kind of subordination as Tasso with his noble patrons in the Renaissance. When Stein and several of his actors insisted on reading political statements to the audience at intermission, they were fired. They then formed a theatre collective and eventually settled in West Berlin's Schaubühne. This collective, which included some of West Germany's most talented actors—among them Bruno Ganz, Edith Clever, Jutta Lampe, and Michael König—was soon considered the best company in the nation. Its productions, among them Ibsen's *Peer Gynt* (1971), Gorky's *Summer Folk* (1974), Shakespeare's *As You Like It* (1976), and Aeschylus' *Oresteia* (1980), were among the most praised of their time.

During the 1970s, Stein's interpretational approach came to dominate German directing. The entire company was involved in exhaustive explorations of the historical and ideological contexts of the plays and their authors. Scripts were reshaped to explore the ide-

FIG. 22.8
Peter Stein's production of Ibsen's *Peer Gynt* at the Schaubühne am Halleschen Ufer, West Berlin, 1971. Design by Karl-Ernst Herrmann; Werner Rehm in the role of Peer. The scene shows Begriffenfeldt's asylum under the Sphinx. Photo by Ruth Walz.

ological relationships obscured by the text's form and to clarify those relationships by revealing their contradictions and the determinants that had shaped them. In other words, a production became simultaneously a performance of a script and a critique of that script's ideological limitations, as well as an indication of its pertinence today. Productions also increasingly treated the theatre (rather than some fictional locale) as the scene of the action and the stage as a place where reality is to be examined rather than presented. Thus, Stein's and many other German theatres in the 1970s and 1980s were essentially dialectical.

In 1981, West Berlin completed a $30 million new theatre, the Schaubühne am Lehniner Platz, for Stein's company. Departing from the proscenium-arch mode that had dominated postwar German theatre architecture, it was a long, open space which could, by activating metal walls, be divided into three separate performance spaces. Its 76 floor sections could be raised, lowered, or tilted to create almost any configuration, both for staging and seating.

During the 1980s, the German theatre retreated from its leftist biases and ideological critiques, and many directors, among them Stein, turned to "text-true" productions. Stein's 1984 staging of Chekhov's *The Three Sisters*, astonishingly realistic and meticulously true to the text, became the company's most popular production. In 1985 Stein resigned as director of the Schaubühne, although he returned to direct regularly. He began to stage opera, earning especially high praise for his work with the Welsh National Opera. In 1988, Jurgen Grosch, an East German who had emigrated to the West, was named director of the Schaubühne.

During the 1980s, Jurgen Flimm emerged as a major director who staged plays from the past in ways that commented on the human condition today. For example, his *Uncle Vanya* made no attempt to evoke Russia but concentrated instead on time as the destroyer of hopes and illusions. This interpretation was made concrete by Erich Wonder's set with a back wall in which a narrow opening moved slowly but continuously—three centimeters per second—to reveal views beyond the neutral room in which the action occurred. Similarly Flimm's production of *Platonov* suggested that we cannot begin a new life because we do not know what to do with the one we have. As head of the Thalia Theater in Hamburg, Flimm made it one of the most adventurous companies in Germany. It became noted especially for producing a number of Robert Wilson's pieces.

One of Germany's best-known artists is Pina Bausch (1940–), creator of the Wuppertal Dance Theater. Trained in dance, she transformed her ballet company into one that broke down the barriers between dance and spoken or musical theatre by combining movement, speech, singing, spectacle, and other elements into nonlinear, nonliterary performances that expressed anxieties, obsessions, conflicts, and hopes ranging through the everyday and comic to the epic and terrifying. Since the 1980s hers has been one of the most honored theatre companies in the world and has served as a model for those who wish to break down the barriers among the arts and create a nontraditional theatre.

THEATRE AND DRAMA IN ITALY TO 1990

After 1968, Giorgio Strehler continued to be Italy's most respected director. When the Piccolo Teatro failed to get the new building it had been seeking and was not named a national theatre as had seemed likely, Strehler resigned as its head in 1968. The company continued under the direction of Paolo Grassi (with Strehler as occasional guest director) until 1972 when Grassi was named head of the LaScala opera company. Meantime, Strehler founded the Gruppo Teatro e Azione, the first professional theatre cooperative in Italy. All of this company's productions were successful, with Brecht's *Saint Joan of the Stockyards* (staged in 1970) being especially outstanding. In 1972, Strehler resumed the directorship of the Piccolo Teatro, which he retained until 1992.

In 1983 Strehler also became director of the Théâtre de l'Europe, which he founded with the cooperation of the French government as a company in which outstanding theatres from all over Europe would participate. The primary home of the Théâtre de l'Europe was the Odéon in Paris, but its membership included major companies in Barcelona, Berlin, Budapest, Düsseldorf, Stockholm, Milan, Paris, and elsewhere. Strehler inaugurated the Théâtre de l'Europe with his production of Shakespeare's *The Tempest* (subsequently seen at the Olympic Arts Festival in Los Angeles in 1984 and elsewhere). Strehler treated *The Tempest* as a play about the theatre with Prospero as director-magician who calls up the characters and events. At the end, Prospero, now in the auditorium, breaks his staff and the stage collapses; he asks the public to release him, as he is releasing them, from the world of illusion so they can return to the real world with the perceptions they have gained in the theatre. This production was one of the most praised of its time. Strehler contributed several other productions to the Théâtre de l'Europe, among them works by such dramatists as Lessing, Corneille, and Strindberg.

Other innovative directors include Fo, Ronconi, and Bene. Dario Fo (1926–) began to write and perform in the late 1940s, first in radio and subsequently in theatre. With his wife, Franca Rame (1929–), he later formed a company which produced satirical topical plays, most of them by Fo, who was also the principal actor. Following the major political upheavals of 1968, Fo adopted a more radical stance and sought to attract a working-class audience with agit-prop plays satirizing capitalism, the Italian Communist party, the Italian state, the church, and other enemies of the idiosyncratic communism he championed. His satire was so wide-ranging that he offended every political faction. Nevertheless, by the late 1970s Fo had become so popular that he was invited to present some of his plays on Italian state television. He also came to be increasingly in demand internationally both as playwright and performer.

Among Fo's most popular plays are *Mistero Buffo* (1969), which combines elements from medieval religious drama, mime, and contemporary life (and makes extensive use of his own made-up language, *grammelot,* rendered intelligible by Fo's expressive pantomime), and *We're All in the Same Boat—But That Man Over There, Isn't He the Boss* (1971), based on Italian political events between 1911 and 1923, when Mussolini came to power. In England and America, Fo's *Can't Pay? Won't Pay* (1974), in which housewives rebel against economic exploitation, and *Accidental Death of an Anarchist* (1970), concerning a man's attempt to discredit the police's version of how a political rebel died while in custody, were especially popular. Fo also wrote a number of feminist plays with Franca Rame under the collective title, *Female Parts* (1981). All of Fo's productions were bitingly satirical

FIG. 22.9
Dario Fo's *Accidental Death of an Anarchist* as produced at the Arena Stage, Washington, 1984. Directed by Douglas C. Wager; scenic design by Karl Eigsti; costumes by Marjorie Slainman; lighting by Allen Lee Hughes. Photo by Joan Marcus.

and theatrically imaginative, making use of devices drawn from practically all forms of popular entertainment. Fo has been one of the few modern Italian playwrights to attract an international audience.

Luca Ronconi (1933–) was an actor before turning to directing in 1963. He developed a distinctive, highly theatrical style in productions of Renaissance English dramas, but he first gained international prominence in 1968 with his production of *Orlando Furioso*, seen first at the Spoleto Festival and later in Belgrade, Milan, Paris, New York, and elsewhere. The text was adapted by Edoardo Sanguineti from Lodovico Ariosto's sixteenth-century epic poem, an enormously long work about chivalric adventures involving mythical creatures, enchanted castles, sorcerers, and other fanciful beings. Rather than performing the episodes in strict sequence, two or more progressed simultaneously in different parts of the theatrical space, since Ronconi believed that this achieved the same effect of disorder and fantasy in-

duced by reading the poem. About fifty wheeled wagons were used in a large open space, which was also occupied by the audience, who moved about choosing what to watch.

Ronconi's subsequent productions are less known but several were equally imaginative. For the Spoleto Festival in 1982, Ronconi adapted Ibsen's *Ghosts* for presentation in the crypt of a church which had been converted into a glass-covered conservatory encompassing both acting and audience space. Expressionistic and slow-moving, the four-hour production treated the characters, all dressed in black and gray, as literal ghosts.

The actor-director-dramatist Carmelo Bene (1937–) was among the major *avant-garde* figures of Italy after 1968. He was especially noted for deconstructing well-known plays (among them *Hamlet, Romeo and Juliet,* and *Edward II*) to reveal those themes and ideas he found most significant. His *Othello* reduced Shakespeare's cast to eight, all dressed in white and all atop a giant bed, to explore jealousy and the pattern of dominance and male bonding in the play.

FIG. 22.10
Ronconi's *Orlando Furioso*, first performed at the Festival of Two Worlds, Spoleto, 1969. Note the wheeled wagons on which the performers stand surrounded by the audience. Photography by Pic, Paris.

Beginning in the 1970s, a number of Italian companies rejected traditional dramatic texts in favor of electronic media, surrealistic visual imagery, pantomime, and music. Among the more popular of these companies were La Gaia Scienza, Falso Movimento, Krypton, and Trademark.

Italy was less fortunate in writers than directors. Virtually no contemporary playwright other than Fo won international acceptance, although a number were well known within Italy. Among these were Franco Brusato, Guiseppe Patroni Griffi, Luigi Squarzina, and Umberto Marino.

THEATRE IN FRANCE TO 1990

In May 1968 an uprising of students and workers virtually paralyzed France and prompted President DeGaulle to retire in 1969. These events also motivated a reevaluation of the role of theatre in French life and resulted in a number of changes. In the early 1970s, the government reorganized the national theatre system. In 1968, Barrault had resigned as head of the Théâtre de France and, since the troupe was under contract to him, the Odéon was left without a troupe. The Odéon was assigned to the Comédie Française, which used it primarily as a home for new and *avant-garde* works or for visiting companies. (In 1983, it became the home of the Théâtre de l'Europe.) In 1975, the rules governing the Comédie Française were revised to increase the number of *sociétaires* (there are now thirty-four), to reduce the length of contracts from twenty to ten years, and to grant greater freedom for actors to perform elsewhere. All of these changes were intended to make the Comédie more attractive to major actors. The company's theatre was also extensively remodeled in preparation for the celebration of the troupe's three-hundredth anniversary in 1980 (and refurbished again in 1994).

As a part of its reorganization of the national theatre system, the government for the first time designated some companies other than those in central Paris as national theatres. Those raised to this status were the Théâtre National de Strasbourg (a former dramatic center); the Théâtre de l'Est Parisien (located in a working-class suburb of Paris); and Planchon's troupe in Villeurbanne, which was assigned the title Théâtre National Populaire. (The Parisian-based troupe that had held that title was renamed the Théâtre National de Chaillot.)

For a time the program of decentralization also continued. By 1975 there were some fifteen Maisons de la Culture, eighteen Centres Dramatiques, and about two dozen other provincial companies, all competing for subsidies. But, because many subsidized companies, both in Paris and in the provinces, had been sympathetic to the demonstrators in 1968 and had permitted their theatres to be used as forums for debate, the government treated many companies with suspicion. Throughout the 1970s subsidies tended to be small for those companies that supported left-wing causes. Inflation also resulted in subsidies being eaten up by administrative costs and building maintenance. Some provincial groups virtually gave up producing their own productions and depended on touring groups, a practice which the French called "garaging."

During the 1970s the government was often accused of being interested primarily in institutionalizing culture. Many critics also charged that the crisis of 1968 had arisen because the government had lost touch with the common people, a charge also leveled against many theatres. Some established directors tried to respond. Upon leaving the Théâtre de France, Jean-Louis Barrault conceived and directed *Rabelais* (1968), a three-hour adaptation of material drawn from Rabelais's writings and intended as a timely commentary on repression and revolution. Drawing liberally on practically all recent trends in staging, the production was originally presented in a sports arena in Paris before being seen in London, New York, and elsewhere. In 1970 Barrault attempted to duplicate this success with a project based on Jarry's life and writings, *Jarry sur la Butte,* but the results were disappointing. In 1971 Barrault became director of the Théâtre des Nations, an international festival which until 1976 was always held in Paris. (Thereafter it was held in a different country each year. In addition to productions from various countries, the festival featured workshops, lectures, and discussions designed to provoke thought and to encourage understanding and innovation.) Barrault also continued his own company, which after 1974 performed at the Théâtre D'Orsay and subsequently at the Théâtre Rond-Point.

Roger Planchon (1931–) was among those most interested in reshaping the French theatre. Long considered Brecht's major champion in France, he continued, after assuming the directorship of the Théâtre National Populaire in 1972, to seek ways of making his productions accessible to the working class. He wrote a number of plays, among them *The Black Pig* (1972) and *Gilles de Rais* (1976), all of which begin with actual historical events of a violent nature and then search for adequate explanations. His staging of these works mingled Brechtian and Artaudian devices to create rich stage imagery designed to surprise audiences with unexpected reflections of its own world. Despite the great power of Planchon's productions, he was never able to attract the large

FIG. 22.11
Planchon's production of Michel Vinaver's *Overboard* at the Théâtre Nationale Populaire, 1974. Photo by Agence de Presse Bernand, Paris.

working-class audience he sought, a situation he declared inevitable until society itself changes.

In 1972, Planchon chose Patrice Chereau (1944–) to be co-director of the TNP. Chereau, an advocate of popular theatre who had established a company in one of Paris' communist-dominated suburbs, believed, as Planchon did, that although one should not compromise standards in order to appeal to the working class, one should seek to make theatre available and understandable to the masses. At the TNP he directed Marlowe's *Massacre in Paris,* Ibsen's *Peer Gynt,* and Dorst's *Toller* to considerable acclaim but attracted greatest international attention in 1976 when he staged Wagner's Ring cycle at Bayreuth so as to link it with a debasement of values stemming from the Industrial Revolution. From 1982 to 1990 he was director of the Théâtre des Amandiers in Nanterre, a working-class suburb of Paris, where in 1984 he created a sensation with his staging of Genet's *The Screens* as a reflection of the racial tensions created in France by the influx of African workers. Almost all of Chereau's major productions were done in collaboration with one designer, Richard Peduzzi. After leaving Nanterre, Chereau devoted much of his efforts to directing opera both in France and elsewhere, but he has returned to the theatre often.

Another approach to reaching a broader audience involved creating plays dealing with the experiences

of the theatre's own audience. Among the groups to follow this path was the Théâtre Populaire de Lorraine (under the direction of Jacques Kraemer), which after 1968 gave up the practice it had followed since 1963 of presenting a repertory composed primarily of the classics. After 1968, it created works about Lorraine, especially the iron and steel industry which dominates that area. It offended most of the leaders of the region, but it built strong support among the audiences it most sought.

Some of the most determined attempts to change the French theatre came from those more concerned with cultural issues than economic gain. In place of "establishment" theatre—using traditional theatre architecture, long-accepted conventions, and scripts written by individuals—they urged a return to popular forms (*commedia dell'arte,* circus, vaudeville) or collectively created pieces performed in the streets, parks, and other spaces that made theatre readily available to everyone and encouraged interaction among performers and audiences.

One of the most innovative of these groups was the Grand Magic Circus, headed by Jerome Savary (1942–), who argued that if the theatre's failure had resulted from attempts to make the working classes accept "high" culture, the remedy must lie in using "low" culture to alter accepted art forms. His company began

FIG. 22.12
Patrice Chereau's production of Genet's *The Screens,* 1984. Design by Richard Peduzzi. Théâtre des Amandiers, Nanterre. Photo by Agence de Presse Bernand, Paris.

to attract wide favorable attention in 1970 with the collectively-created *Zartan,* about "Tarzan's deprived brother" and described by Savary as the "marvelous story of colonialism from the Middle Ages to the present." Others of the company's pieces included *The Last Days of Solitude of Robinson Crusoe* (1972), *Adventures in Love* (1976), and *1001 Nights* (1978). The company, performing on beaches, in hospitals, parks, and other comparable spaces, won a considerable following with productions that had the zest of children's theatre, circus, and carnivals created by extensive exchanges between audience and performers, improvisations, acrobatic feats, satirical thrusts, and stunning effects of all sorts. Savary stated his dislike of Grotowski and the Living Theatre (both of which he labeled "cerebral") and sought to appeal to all types of audiences in a very direct manner. Around 1980, Savary began to direct already-existing scripts, including classics, using many of the techniques he had developed earlier. In 1989, his success in making theatre accessible to the general public was recognized with his appointment as director of the Théâtre National de Chaillot, where he has come to be noted for the extravagant visual spectacle and frenetic energy of his productions.

The most significant of the post-1968 companies was the Théâtre du Soleil, formed in 1964 with Ariane Mnouchkine (1940–) as its driving force. The company first gained recognition in 1967 with Wesker's *The Kitchen.* During the uprisings of 1968, it performed this production in factories where it received overwhelmingly favorable response from the workers. It decided then to become a theatre collective in which all members would receive the same salary. The collective's first production was *The Clowns* (1969), based on the belief that the clown is the best representation of the artist in society. Its first major success came in 1970 with *1789,* about the beginnings of the French Revolution and suggesting that the Revolution was subverted by those more concerned about property than justice. Staged on platforms surrounding a standing audience (which was treated as the mob), it was highly praised and extremely successful. First performed in Milan, *1789* was subsequently presented in France at the Cartoucherie (an abandoned cartridge factory) in the Parisian suburb of Vincennes, which was thereafter the company's home. It was followed by *1793* (1972), a much less successful treatment of later phases of the Revolution. Despite its great critical reputation, the company was so destitute that between 1973 and 1975 most of its members had to go on unemployment (a practice still common with the company when it is not performing). It began to recover in 1975 with *The Age of Gold,* which dealt with various aspects of materialism and

perverted values as seen through the experiences of an immigrant worker. In the early 1980s, Mnouchkine reorganized the company and mounted a series of Shakespearean productions—*Richard II*, both parts of *Henry IV,* and *Twelfth Night*—all incorporating liberal borrowings from Kabuki or Sanskrit conventions. When performed at the Olympics Art Festival in Los Angeles in 1984, these were the most highly praised of all the offerings. In 1985, the company applied its expertise in combining Eastern theatrical devices and Shakespearean history plays to its production of *The Terrible but Unfinished History of Norodom Sihanouk, King of Cambodia,* an eight-hour epic by Hélène Cixous, France's best known feminist writer, covering the years between 1955 and 1979 in Cambodian history. This production was followed by a somewhat similar work by Cixous, *The Indiade, or the India of Their Dreams* (1987), dealing with the efforts to create an Indian state to succeed British colonialist India. Among the theatre's most successful productions was *Les Atrides,* composed of Euripides' *Iphigenia at Aulis* and Aeschylus' trilogy *The Oresteia.* It was mounted over a period of two years (1990–1992) and was performed in France, Italy, Germany, England, Canada, and the United States. Drawing on Asian forms, most clearly Kathakali, its integration of dance, music, spectacle, and gripping drama was a major achievement. In 1994, the company staged Cixous' *The Forsworn City, or the Awakening of the Furies,* concerning the French government allowing the use of blood it knew to be

FIG. 22.13

The chorus in Ariane Mnouchkine's production of Euripides' *Iphigenia at Aulis* with the Théâtre du Soleil in 1990. It was the first play in a tetralogy of plays, the remainder of which was made up of Aeschylus' *The Oresteia.* The four plays were presented under the overall title, *Les Atrides* (The House of Atreus). Photo © Martine Frank-Magnum. Courtesy Magnum Photos, Inc.

contaminated with the HIV virus. Their 1995 production of Molière's *Tartuffe* was given an Algerian flavor with overtones of the restrictions demanded by Muslim fundamentalists. By the 1990s, the Théâtre du Soleil was one of the most respected companies in the world. With actors from twenty-one countries, it was also one of the most multicultural.

The Avignon Festival also played an important role in French theatre after 1968. As early as 1966 it had begun to increase its playing spaces, and eventually included about twelve official spaces and countless "fringe" spaces. Consequently, Avignon became increasingly diverse, accommodating major French groups, companies from various French-speaking areas of the world, numerous alternative theatres, and major artists and companies from foreign countries. Thus, it came to provide a representative cross-section of theatre work in France and elsewhere, offering about 50 official events and about 500 fringe events during a one-month period. By the 1990s, under the direction of Bernard Faivre d'Arcier, it was the premier cultural event for French-language theatre in the world.

Important new directors came to the fore after 1980. Among the most important of these was Jean-Pierre Vincent (1942–) who, as director of the Théâtre National de Strasbourg from 1975 to 1983, converted it into one of the most influential theatres in France because of his work with new playwrights and use of innovative working methods. An admirer of Brecht and Peter Stein, Vincent initiated working procedures adapted from major German companies. He also encouraged a group of young dramatists, among them Michel Deutsch and Jean-Paul Wenzel, whose work resembled that of Kroetz in its emphasis upon characters and themes drawn from the working class. Vincent's accomplishments were acknowledged in 1983 when he was appointed administrator of the Comédie Française. But that company's role as conservator of French culture proved incompatible with Vincent's goals, and Vincent left the post in 1986. In 1990, he succeeded Chereau as head of the Théâtre des Amandiers in Nanterre where his productions have been known for their high quality and experimentation.

Another important director was Antoine Vitez (1930–1990), director of the Théâtre National de Chaillot from 1981 until 1988, when he became director of the Comédie Française. His most notable productions were radical reinterpretations of plays by Racine, Molière, Hugo, and Claudel. In his productions, he worked closely with his designer, Yannis Kokkos, and his actors to break down and reshape realistic conventions. Settings were usually composed of a few elements that could be moved about by the actors; pieces treated in the script as scenery, such as

sailing ships on which the characters were supposedly located, were sometimes models which could be picked up and moved about by the actors; strong lateral lighting often divided the stage into planes of action; the actors shifted from naturalistic to nonrealistic conventions, emphasizing discontinuities. Vitez did not seek to impose unity but rather to let the audience be aware of the complexities, contradictions, and multiple possibilities for interpretation. Upon his death, he was succeeded at the Comédie Française by Jacques Lassalle (1936–), who brought in a number of foreign directors and emphasized new plays. Accused of having subverted the company's cultural role, Lassalle was replaced in 1993 by Jean-Pierre Miquel (1940–), who adopted a more conservative approach. The Comédie Française also managed the much smaller Théâtre du Vieux Colombier (once Jacques Copeau's theatre). In the late 1990s, the two houses together were presenting more than twenty productions each year. Other important French directors include Daniel Mesguich, Jorge Lavelli, Stephane Braunschweig, Stanislas Nordey, and Alain Francon.

Although few French playwrights who came to the fore after 1968 were able to win an international following, several achieved high critical standing at home. Perhaps the most important of these were Grumberg and Vinaver. Jean-Paul Grumberg (1939–) began to write for the stage in the mid-1960s but did not achieve success until 1971 with *Amorphe d'Ottenburg*, a parable about the Nazis. One of his best-known

FIG. 22.14

Antoine Vitez's production of Hugo's *Hernani* at the Théâtre National de Chaillot, Paris, 1985. Design by Yannis Kokkos. Photo by Agence de Presse Bernand, Paris.

FIG. 22.15
Jean-Paul Grumberg's *Comings and Goings at the Expo*, Théâtre de l'Oédon, Paris, 1975. Directed by Jean-Pierre Vincent. Design by Yannis Kokkos. Photo by Agence de Presse Bernand, Paris.

works is *Dreyfus* (1974), set in a Jewish ghetto in a Polish town around 1930 where amateurs, while rehearsing a play about the Dreyfus affair, explore the phenomenon of anti-Semitism. It won the critics award as the best play of the 1974–1975 season. *Comings and Goings at the Expo* (1975) takes place at the time of the Universal Exposition in 1900 and points up the banality of the forces that would lead to World War I. Much of it is set against the music of a *café concert*. *The Workshop* (1979), a naturalistic play about survival, shows Jewish survivors of the Occupation coping with their guilt about being survivors when so many others perished. *The Free Zone* (1989) shows the everyday life of Jews as they seek to avoid detection in the French "free zone" during World War II.

Michel Vinaver (1926–), though he wrote some plays in the 1950s, did not come to prominence until 1973 with Planchon's production of *Overboard*. This play is far more complex than Planchon's version might suggest. Its primary concern is with how American marketing strategies have altered European busi-

ness, but through numerous discontinuous and seemingly unrelated plot strands, it ultimately suggests the interconnectedness of everything that makes up a society, including how the corporate world displaces the world of myth and personal integrity. Vinaver's subsequent plays, including *Bending Over Backwards* (1980) and *The Usual* (1983), include no punctuation and almost no stage directions, thus remaining open to multiple interpretations since both what the characters are doing or what is meant by what is said remain ambiguous. Other significant playwrights include Bernard-Marie Koltès (1948–1989), Hélène Cixous, Olivier Py, and Xavier Durringer.

Under the leadership of Jack Lang, Minister of Culture during the 1980s and early 1990s, France continued to increase its support for the arts. In 1992, it appropriated $2.3 billion for cultural projects, and subsequently government officials pledged to devote 1 percent (about $3 billion) of the national budget to cultural projects. The allocation of support to theatre was about $500 million annually.

LATIN AMERICAN THEATRE TO 1990

Brazilian theatre did not begin to recover from the political oppression that followed the crackdown of 1968 until a new regime came to power in 1979. During those difficult years dramatists who wanted their plays produced avoided social commentary or at least disguised it behind a mask of humor as in *Miss Margarida's Way* (*Apareceu a Margarida*, 1973) by Roberto de Athayde (1949–). Groups like "Asdrubal Brought His Trombone" Theatre (*Asdrubal Trouse Seu Trombone*, 1974), meanwhile, resorted to irreverent productions of classic plays. With the lifting of restrictions in 1979, plays that had been banned in the 1960s and 1970s were quickly brought to the stage with *Break the Heart* or *Heart Stopping* (*Rasga Coração*, 1974), by Luis Vianna Filho (1936–1974), as perhaps the most important of this rather large group that included plays of feminist writers Leilah Assunção (1943–) and Consuelo Castro (1947–). But it was the Center for Theatrical Investigation (Centro de Pesquisa Teatral), established in 1978 under the direction of José Antunes Filho (1929–), that set the tone for the new direction Brazilian theatre was about to take. Antunes Filho's production of *Macunaíma* (1979), which told the story of a Native American's journey from his idyllic home in the forests to the degenerate city and back again, made eclectic use of nudity, spectacular athleticism, and highly evocative visual elements to create scenes of remarkable beauty. It also established a vogue for adapting plays from novels. This production was such an international success that the Grupo Pau, which had produced it, changed its name to the Grupo Macunaíma and quickly became the most influential company in Brazil. From this point on, Brazilian theatre became dominated by a style of theatre of images not unlike that being developed in Canada. Directors who trained under Antunes Filho, like Bia Lessa (1952–), best known for her production of *Orlando* (1992), and Ulysses Cruz (1952–), best known as the founder of the Flying Bull Theatre (O Boi Voador, 1985), took the lead in this new theatre. But Gerald Thomas (1954–) may best exemplify its tendencies. He is acclaimed as an imaginative director who, along with Daniela Thomas (1959–), his usual scene designer, creates remarkable visual images. But he is equally well regarded as an adapter of works by Kafka and author of such plays as *Flash and Crash* (1992). Because of adaptations and director-written scripts, few Brazilian playwrights have been able to achieve real success in recent years, and among those who have, problems getting their works translated have made them little known outside Brazil.

In Argentina, political turmoil and economic instability worked against major new developments after 1968. Throughout the 1970s and into the 1980s a great deal of experimentation of all kinds was carried out, but it seems to have had no definable direction beyond reflecting the disorientation felt generally within the society. When companies like the Open Theatre (Teatro Abierto, 1981) showed signs of becoming too political, their theatres were mysteriously burned down, sometimes on several occasions. But after Argentina's disastrous war with Great Britain over the Falklands in 1982, a less-repressive government came to power. Except for a burst of plays from noted dramatist Osvoldo Dragün (1929–) and Carlos Gorostiza (1920–), however, this did not lead to a release of pent-up theatrical energies like that seen after liberalization in Brazil. The new government favored decentralizing theatre to take the focus off of Buenos Aires, and while Argentina continues to have a very active theatre community, it no longer exerts the influence it had in Latin America prior to 1968.

In Mexico, the forty theatres that were linked into the National Theatre touring circuit in 1977 continued to provide a high-quality standard repertory of classical and modern European plays supplemented with the best work of Latin American writers and, from time to time, new plays by local playwrights like Oscar Liebra (1944–1990). The National Theatre company, however, was disbanded in 1982, and after that most of the actual theatres were increasingly used for musical reviews and, in the case of the largest theatres, as touring houses for the large-scale American or British musicals being staged in the commercial theatres by producers like Manolo Fábregas (1921–1996) and Silvia Pinal (1931–).

The *avant-garde* theatre faded in the 1980s, but director Héctor Mendoza (1938–) continues to do innovative work with his updatings of classical texts, while Juan José Gurrola (1935–) highlights elements of the text that might otherwise go unnoticed in his productions. The truly experimental work, however, is now being done at festivals starting with the Garden Day (*Jornadas Alarconianas*) festivals and the Mexico City Festival, both established in 1989. These festivals attract companies from around the world, giving audiences in Mexico the chance to see works by other Latin American dramatists, including Bolivian authors like Adolfo Mier Rivas (1939–) and Luis Ramiro Beltrán Salmón (1930–); Chilean dramatists, Jórge Díaz (1930–), Ariel Dorfman (1942–), Juan Radrigán (1937–), Antonio Skarmeta (1940–), and Ines Margarita Stranger (1957–); Colombian playwright, Guillermo Maldonado (1945–); Albio Paz (1950–) and Joel Cano (1966–) from Cuba; and finally, from Puerto Rico, Roberto Ramos-Perea (1956–).

LOOKING AT THEATRE HISTORY

Perhaps not surprisingly, a major goal in the 1960s was to create a new, superior unity by eliminating those things standing in the way of a more truthful vision. Thus, several theatre theorists and practitioners sought to arrive at the essence of theatre by identifying and eliminating accretions that divert us from its fundamental nature. These attempts are probably best articulated in Grotowski's concept of the "poor theatre":

By gradually eliminating whatever proved superfluous, we found that theatre can exist without make-up, without autonomic costume and scenography, without a separate performance area (stage), without lighting and sound effects, etc. It cannot exist without the actor-spectator relationship of perceptual, direct, "live" communion . . . . when rigorously tested in practice it undermines most of our usual ideas about theatre. It challenges the notion of theatre as a synthesis of disparate creative disciplines. . . . This "synthetic theatre" is the contemporary theatre, which we readily call the "Rich Theatre"—rich in flaws.

Jerzy Grotowski, *Towards a Poor Theatre* (New York: Simon and Schuster, 1968), 19.

Contemporary theatre has seen considerable borrowing and adaptation of conventions from other cultures. About this transculturalism or interculturalism, Carl Weber writes:

Whenever a society's stage was ripe for a change because its traditional performance codes had become obsolete, i.e., no longer responded to a perceived social reality, experimentation with ideas and forms lifted from other cultures was conducted. Emerging new modes of performance were frequently evolved from a transculturation of foreign structures and ideas . . . . The growing number of international festivals is breaking down the barriers between the world's theatre cultures. An international community is emerging where those who make and those who consume theatre become increasingly familiar with the multitude of forms and issues presented on the stages of all nations. Foreign performance modes are welcomed not in spite of but because of their Otherness.

"AC/TC Currents of Theatrical Exchange," *Interculturalism and Performance,* eds. Bonnie Marranca and Gautam Dasgupta (New York: PAJ Publications, 1991), 36.

23
English-Language Theatre in the Late Twentieth Century

The stresses that affected theatre throughout Europe were felt even more in the United States, where they were focused around the Vietnam War and the struggle for civil rights and equality. The concern for aesthetic values was largely replaced by the demand that theatre serve as a weapon in exposing and fighting outmoded values and practices both political and civil. The focus increasingly centered around issues of gender, race, and class.

BRITISH THEATRE TO 1990

An event of great significance to British theatre occurred in 1968, when the censorship that had been in effect since 1737 was abolished, making it possible to address topics and show behavior that had been forbidden. A number of plays previously banned were produced immediately, among them *Hair!* (banned because of nudity and obscenity), Osborne's *A Patriot for Me* (forbidden because of homosexual scenes), Hochhuth's *The Soldiers* (banned because it was considered offensive to Churchill's memory), and Edward Bond's plays (forbidden because they were considered immoral).

The change in law also gave impetus to small groups (comparable to American off-off-Broadway companies) which up to that time had made little impact.

After 1968 these "fringe" groups increased rapidly in number. They performed at universities, pubs, playgrounds, meeting halls, or almost anywhere an audience could be assembled, and at lunchtime or late at night, as well as at more traditional hours. Their great flexibility (in approach, place, time of performing, subjects, and desired audiences) did much to bring variety to the English theatre. Among the fringe groups, some of the most effective were Interaction, the People Show, the Pip Simmons Theatre, the Freehold, the Portable Theatre, Triple Action, Soho Poly, Joint Stock, King's Head, Bubble Theatre, Monstrous Regiment, 7:84 Theatre Company, and Tricycle Theatre. Such companies contributed enormously to the vitality of the English theatre, especially through their appeal to audiences that had previously ignored the theatre. Most were also highly critical of British social and political institutions. Many generated their own scripts or worked closely with playwrights. They appealed especially to young audiences and those who were alienated from the established companies. By the 1970s, the fringe companies, which had become common throughout Britain, were sufficiently accepted to begin receiving grants from the Arts Council and local authorities.

Perhaps the company most affected by the abolishment of censorship was the English Stage Company (ESC), which since 1956 had been the principal

FIG. 23.1
Edward Bond's *Saved* as produced by the English Stage Company at the Royal Court Theatre, London. Photo by John Haynes.

producer of works by new playwrights. After 1968, the proliferation of fringe companies, most of which presented new scripts only, made the ESC's contribution seem less crucial. Nevertheless, the ESC continued to play an important role, in part because it gave unknown writers fully mounted productions on its main stage, whereas most groups offered only minimally mounted productions.

The ESC was the principal cause for the abolishment of censorship. After George Devine's retirement in 1965, the new managers (William Gaskill, Lindsay Anderson, and Anthony Page) wished to produce Bond's *Saved* and Osborne's *A Patriot for Me,* and when denied licenses reconstituted the ESC as a private club open only to members, a practice that had long been used to gain exemption from censorship. Nevertheless, the Lord Chamberlain brought and won a suit against the ESC. The resulting controversy became so heated that Parliament was persuaded to abolish censorship. In 1969 the ESC enlarged its program by opening the Theatre Upstairs, devoted to short runs of new plays, and by giving readings of plays on Sunday evenings.

In 1980, the management of the ESC passed to Max Stafford-Clark, who sought various means of stemming the company's decline. He added a Young Writers' Festival devoted to the plays of teenaged dramatists, arranged exchanges of productions with Joseph Papp's Public Theatre in New York, and formed an alliance with the Joint Stock Company (presenting plays, such as those by Caryl Churchill,

that had been developed by that fringe group). Nevertheless, its activities steadily eroded during the 1980s, going from sixteen productions a year in the early 1980s to four in 1989, when the Theatre Upstairs had to be closed.

In 1968, the Royal Shakespeare Company (RSC) also entered a period of change when Peter Hall, Peter Brook, and Michel Saint-Denis resigned as its directors. Trevor Nunn (1940–), a young director with little managerial experience, succeeded them. Working closely with the designer Christopher Morley (until 1974), Nunn moved the company away from the Brechtian neorealism that Hall had favored. Morley's minimalist settings often resembled large empty boxes, but they served to focus attention on the acting which was far more flamboyant and stylized than under Hall. This approach also characterized Brook's *Midsummer Night's Dream* in 1970, a production which toured extensively to enormous critical acclaim and did much to relieve the company's financial stresses. In 1974, the RSC opened a small theatre, The Other Place, in Stratford, and in 1977 a similar space, The Warehouse, in London,

FIG. 23.2
The Royal Shakespeare Company's production of *Nicholas Nickleby,* adapted from Charles Dickens's novel by David Edgar. Directed by Trevor Nunn and John Caird (1980). Photo by Martha Swope.

both devoted to new plays and experimental productions. In 1978, Terry Hands (1941–), who had been directing for the company for several years, was named joint artistic director with Nunn. During the late 1970s, the company gained added acclaim with its monumental productions of *Nicholas Nickleby* (an eight-hour adaptation of Charles Dickens's novel), *The Greeks* (an adaptation of ten Greek plays), and a cycle of Shakespeare's history plays.

In 1982, the RSC moved into its long-awaited new home in London, the Barbican, with its two playing spaces. The Pit, a flexible space which replaced the Warehouse, seated approximately 200. The large Barbican theatre held 1,166. Its stage was 73 feet wide by 48 feet deep with a 30-foot-high opening. Above the stage, 109 feet of flyspace permitted the storage of scenery at two levels to facilitate the presentation of the rotating repertory. In 1986, the company opened a new theatre in Stratford, the Swan, a 400-seat open-stage facility intended primarily for non-Shakespearean plays written between 1570 and 1750. During the 1980s, the RSC also produced several musicals, among them *Les Miserables,* and this, along with Nunn's involvement in outside activities, provoked considerable criticism of his management. In 1987, he resigned and Terry Hands became sole artistic director. In turn, Hands left his post in 1991, and was succeeded by Adrian Noble (1951–), long one of RSC's major directors.

With its multiple theatres, large and varied repertory, and enormous size (some 700 employees), the RSC was one of the world's major companies. Its reputation depended much on its directors (among them John Barton, Clifford Williams, David Jones, Ron Daniels, Howard Davies, Barry Kyle, and Adrian Noble); its actors (among them from time to time Derek Jacobi, Alan Howard, Judi Dench, Ben Kingsley, Helen Mirren, Roger Rees, Ian Holm, Norman Rodway, Patrick Stewart, and Antony Sher); and its designers (especially John Napier, Nunn's usual collaborator after 1974; and Farrah, Hand's usual collaborator).

Those who had headed the RSC before 1968 continued their careers elsewhere. Michel Saint-Denis spent his remaining years (he died in 1971) with the actor-training programs at the Juilliard School in New York and the National Theatre School of Canada, thereby extending a tradition reaching back to Copeau. Peter Brook, after staging *A Midsummer Night's Dream* for the RSC in 1970, became director of the International Center for Theatre Research in 1971. Based in Paris, the Center included actors from all over the world. There Brook sought to discover means for transcending the barriers created by differing languages and cultures. The Center gave its first performance, *Orghast,* in 1971 at the Persepolis Festival in Iran; this production had a mixed reception, in part because it used an entirely invented language in an attempt to transcend any specific language. Subsequently, the company traveled in Africa, worked with the National Theatre of the Deaf and El Teatro Campesino in America, with aborigines in Australia, and with groups in many other parts of the world in an attempt to understand various communicative processes.

In Paris, Brook's company created a number of its own works as well as performing such well-known plays as *The Cherry Orchard.* It made its greatest impact with adaptations done in collaboration with the writer Jean-Claude Carrière, especially *Carmen* and *Mahabharata. The Tragedy of Carmen* (1982), based partially on Merimée's novel and partially on Bizet's opera, reduced the complex story to its essentials. It was staged in a sand-covered circle with a few essential properties and a cast of six. The simplicity of this production contrasted sharply with the richness of *Mahabharata,* Carrière's adaptation of the Indian epic, on which he and Brook had started working in 1976. It was first performed in 1985 in an abandoned quarry as a part of the Avignon Festival. Using a cast from sixteen countries (among them Ryszard Cieslak, formerly the principal actor in Grotowski's company), and elaborate costumes, music, and dance, it offered nine hours of spectacular and absorbing drama.

FIG. 23.3
Peter Brook's production of Jean-Claude Carrière's adaptation of the Sanskrit epic, *Mahabharata.* First performed at the Avignon Festival, 1985. Design by Chloe Oblensky. Photo by Agence de Presse Bernand, Paris.

FIG. 23.4
National Theatre, London. Auditorium and stage of the Olivier Theatre. Courtesy National Theatre. Photograph by Reg Wilson.

Subsequently it was performed in many European and American cities. Through his various productions, Brook probably did more than any other director to examine the nature of theatre and cross-cultural performance conventions.

After leaving the RSC, Peter Hall served as director of the Royal Covent Garden Opera Company before being appointed to succeed Laurence Olivier as head of the National Theatre in 1973. (Olivier's service to the theatre was recognized in 1970 when he became the first English actor to be elevated to the nobility.) In addition to administering a complex organization and directing several plays, Hall had to cope with numerous problems related to the company's new home. Scheduled to open in 1974, the building was not ready until 1976, by which time its cost had escalated to some $32 million. When completed, it housed three performance spaces: the 890-seat Lyttleton proscenium theatre; the 1,160-seat Olivier open-stage theatre with a revolving stage 40 feet in diameter divided into two parts that could be lowered to workshops 45 feet below; and the 400-seat Cottesloe laboratory theatre. There were more than 100 dressing rooms, several stage-sized rehearsal rooms, and numerous workshops. The delays and costs aroused considerable hostility, especially among fringe groups who argued that the great sums spent on the National could more productively be assigned to the many small companies that had sprung up throughout Britain. This hostility increased when in 1975–1976 one-quarter of the Arts Council's drama budget went to the National;

opposition was not quieted by statements that the largest percentage of this amount went for operating and maintaining the new building. Hall found himself besieged, and after 1976 much of his energy was spent in promoting the "national" role of his theatre. After 1980 productions were sent on tour in Britain for an average of twenty weeks annually. Nevertheless, the privileged status of the National continued to make it a ready target for rivals.

The stated goal of the National was to present a diverse repertory of classic, new, and neglected plays selected from the whole of world drama. Its repertory ranged through *The Oresteia, Coriolanus, The Way of the World, The Inspector General,* and Chekhov's *Wild Honey* to new plays by such contemporary authors as Peter Shaffer, Tom Stoppard, and David Hare. Such a complex organization depended on many persons. Among the National's directors, some of the most important were Peter Wood, Peter Gill, Richard Eyre, Bill Bryden, Michael Bogdanov, and David Hare. Its large and constantly changing acting company included from time to time Maggie Smith, Joan Plowright, Irene Worth, Fiona Shaw, Ian McKellan, Michael Gambon, Anthony Hopkins, Alan Bates, Albert Finney, and many others. Its design staff, headed by John Bury, included John Gunter, Hayden Griffen, Alison Chitty, and Dierdre Clancy. By the mid-1980s, Hall, like Nunn at the RSC, came under heavy criticism for his outside activities and he too resigned. Leadership of the National passed in 1988 to Richard Eyre (1943–), who had worked in both the fringe and regional theatres before coming to the National in 1981. In 1988, to honor its twenty-fifth anniversary, the company received a new name: the Royal National Theatre. By that time it had presented more than 300 productions and was acknowledged to be one of the world's major theatrical companies.

Outside of London, local resident companies continued to play an important role, and during the 1970s they were joined by numerous provincial fringe companies, many of which toured. Additional diversity was provided by festivals, especially the Edinburgh Festival, which steadily increased its number of offerings to become the largest and most diverse festival in Europe.

As elsewhere, in Britain increased costs and inflation created ongoing financial crises for the theatre. Subsidized theatres made frequent appeals for supplementary grants to avoid serious deficits. Regional arts associations were also formed throughout Britain to deal with financial crises, encourage cooperative ventures, and promote the arts in their areas. Beginning in the late 1970s, private corporations assisted

FIG. 23.5
Peter Hall's production of Shakespeare's *Coriolanus* at the National Theatre,
1984. Designed by John Bury. Ian McKellen down center as Coriolanus
and behind him Irene Worth as Volumnia. Photo by John Haynes.

some organizations by underwriting productions. The cost of production tripled between 1983 and 1993 and ticket prices rose 24 percent between 1991 and 1993. Ticket prices were still considerably less than for Broadway productions

After 1968, one of Britain's strengths continued to be its playwrights. Many of those who had begun their careers earlier continued to be productive, among them John Osborne, Peter Shaffer, and Harold Pinter. Of the new playwrights, perhaps the most controversial was Edward Bond (1935–), who achieved overnight notoriety in 1965 with a private performance by the ESC of *Saved,* in which a baby is stoned to death in its carriage by its father and his roustabout friends. Equally shocking was *Early Morning* (1968), a surrealistic farce about Victorian life in which Florence Nightingale and Queen Victoria are involved in a lesbian relationship and virtually all the characters indulge in cannibalism. Bond's first play to receive

a public performance, *Narrow Road to the Deep North* (1968), is set in Japan and avoids the more shocking features of the earlier works, although it too emphasizes the callousness of human beings. *Lear* (1971) uses many of the characters and situations from Shakespeare's play but alters them to make a despairing statement about human brutality and inhumanity. Selfishness, callousness, and violence continued to be preoccupations in Bond's later works: *Bingo* (1973), *The Fool* (1975), *The Woman* (1978), and a trilogy presented under the collective title, *War Plays* (1985). Bond was denounced by many critics as sensational, decadent, and overly preoccupied with violence, but ultimately his plays were based on moral (even self-righteous) concerns about a world in which the lack of love and compassion breeds a callousness that accepts the horrible as normal.

David Storey (1933–) began his career as a novelist and turned to playwriting in 1967 with *The*

FIG. 23.6
David Storey's *The Contractor* at the Royal Court Theatre, London, 1970. Directed by Lindsay Anderson. Photo by Tom Murray.

Restoration of Arnold Middleton. His subsequent plays include *The Contractor* (1970), *Home* (1970), *The Changing Room* (1971), and *Stages* (1992). Stylistically, Storey's plays bear a distant resemblance to those of Pinter and Chekhov in their surface realism and their absence of clear-cut meaning, but they lack the sense of menace found in Pinter's works. Storey is concerned above all with various kinds of alienation: class from class, person from person, person from self, the reality from the ideal, and so on. These various forms of alienation are perhaps most fully developed in *Home,* set in an asylum where the four main characters, through seemingly random dialogue, point up the ironic implications about alienation contained in the multiple meanings of the play's title. Storey also often gave focus to his concerns through detailed physical activity. In *The Contractor* a group of working men put up a tent for a wedding in the first act and take it down in the last act; during this process a cross-section of attitudes and relationships are demonstrated by workmen and their employers. Few writers have so precisely re-created the detail of real-life activities or used them to imply so much about modern society and its conventions.

Tom Stoppard (1937–) came to prominence in 1967 with *Rosencrantz and Guildenstern Are Dead,* a play reminiscent of Beckett's works, in which Stoppard makes protagonists of two attendant lords from *Hamlet* who sense that important events are going on around them but are killed without understanding anything about the events of which they have

been a part. Stoppard continued this highly theatrical exploration of the nature of reality in such plays as *The Real Inspector Hound* (1968), *Jumpers* (1972), *Travesties* (1974), *The Real Thing* (1982), and *Hapgood* (1988).

Peter Nichols (1929–) achieved his first stage success with *A Day in the Death of Joe Egg* (1967), which deals with the attempts of a schoolteacher and his wife to cope with their spastic child, whom they view as a joke played on them by life but who ultimately serves as a catalyst to bring to the surface their suppressed anxieties and frustrations. This mixture of humor, compassion, and astringent observation is continued in *The National Health* (1969), a play about elderly patients who drag out their lives in a hospital ward against a background of television programs which romanticize medical practice. Song and dance and music hall devices are prominent elements in Nichols' *Forget-Me-Not Lane* (1971), *Privates on Parade* (1977), *Born in the Gardens* (1979), *Passion Play* (1981), and *Poppy* (1982), but they are used to illuminate the ironies and deceptions that plague and often irrevocably alter the characters' lives.

David Hare (1947–) began his career with Portable Theatre, a fringe group. Among his plays are *Slag* (1969), *Teeth'n'Smiles* (1975), *Plenty* (1978), and *A Map of the World* (1983). Most of these plays develop the same basic themes: how the desire to gain and maintain power and wealth undermine and destroy personal integrity, shared values, and concern for the common good. The early plays tend to focus

FIG. 23.7
Tom Stoppard's *The Real Thing* (1982) as directed by Mike Nichols at the Plymouth Theatre, New York, 1984. Setting by Tony Walton, costumes by Anthea Sylbert, lighting by Tharon Musser. The performers are Glenn Close and Jeremy Irons. Photo by Martha Swope.

on working-class characters, whereas the later plays focus on intellectuals. Among his plays, *Plenty* (1979) is one of the best known. It moves through two decades following World War II, during which the British Empire disintegrates. The disintegration is paralleled in the protagonist, who sees her vision of collective endeavor for the common good become corrupted. As her despair grows, she disrupts the lives of all those around her and eventually drifts into drug-induced oblivion.

Hare often collaborated with Howard Brenton (1942–). Their best known joint work is *Pravda* (1985), in which a newspaper tycoon gains almost unchallenged control over public information. Brenton also wrote a number of controversial plays on his own, including *The Churchill Play* (1974) and *Romans in Britain* (1980). The latter, which drew parallels between the Roman occupation of England and the British presence in Ireland, was especially controversial, in part because of its treatment of violence as humorous but also because a play so critical of the British government was performed at the National Theatre.

Caryl Churchill (1938–) wrote many of her plays for the Joint Stock Company and the ESC. Like Hare and Brenton, her plays were primarily about power, powerlessness, and exploitation, but with a strong feminist perspective. She first gained wide recognition with *Cloud 9* (1979), which with great humor (and cross-gender casting) explores how stereotyping social forces determine gender roles. *Top Girls* (1982) contrasts famous women of the past (who recall the prices they had to pay for asserting themselves in a man's world) and a group of contemporary women (still caught in the rat race of a male-dominated society). *Fen* (1983) treats female farmworkers in East Anglia seeking to cope with low wages and impossible lives, while *Mad Forest* (1990) explores life in Romania before and after the fall of dictatorship in that country.

Alan Ayckbourn (1939–) has been one of England's most popular and prolific playwrights (in 1975, he had five plays running in the West End). Nearly all his plays are developed at the Stephen Joseph Theatre in Scarborough, where he has served as artistic director since 1970. His numerous plays include *How the Other Half Loves* (1970), *The Norman Conquests* (1973), *A Chorus of Disapproval* (1985), and *A Small Family Business* (1987). Ayckbourn is known for his wit, his innovative manipulation of space and time, and for the sense of desperation that underlies even his most farcical works.

Other well-known playwrights include Michael Frayn (1933–) with *Noises Off* (1982) and *Benefactors* (1984); and Stephen Poliakoff (1952–), with *City*

FIG. 23.8
Caryl Churchill's *Cloud 9* at the Royal Court Theatre, London, 1979. Photo by John Holmes.

Sugar (1976), *Strawberry Fields* (1977), and *Breaking the Silence* (1984). Still others that deserve mention are Trevor Griffiths, Howard Barker, Christopher Hampton, David Mercer, David Halliwell, Barrie Keefe, Peter Barnes, Pam Gems, Simon Gray, and Timberlake Wertenbaker.

One of the best English-language playwrights is Irish. Brian Friel (1929–) first came to prominence with *Philadelphia, Here I Come* (1964), concerning a young man's attempt to emigrate to America and the complications it creates. Numerous plays followed, among the most successful of which were *Translations* (1981), which parallels a British map-making unit who are changing Gaelic to English names in 1833 and the British military presence in Northern Ireland in the 1970s and 1980s; and *Dancing at Lughnasa* (1990), in which an adult man recalls his childhood with his mother and aunts for whom dancing ultimately becomes a means of release from their narrow existence. Friel was also one of the founders of the Field Day Theatre Company in 1980.

THEATRE IN THE UNITED STATES AFTER 1968

In many ways, 1968 was a watershed in U.S. theatre. In that year nudity and obscenity were introduced on Broadway in the musical *Hair!* In 1969, *Che!* brought explicit sexual acts on stage, and later that year *Oh, Calcutta* included a large number of scenes performed entirely in the nude. Although protests against obedience to authority, unquestioning patriotism, and accepted codes of behavior and dress had been increasing since the late 1950s, the introduction of nudity and obscenity seemed to accelerate these trends, and by 1970 almost all previously accepted standards were under attack. To traditionalists, it was a disturbing time since all they valued seemed endangered; to iconoclasts, it was a heady time, since innovation seemed unending and liberating. After 1968, theatrical practices altered rapidly and substantially.

Hair! (written by Galt McDermot, Gerome Ragni, and James Rado) was also significant for popularizing a new type of musical. Almost all of its elements were derived from the youth-oriented culture of the day: its antiestablishment stance, lifestyle, and dress; its highly amplified rock music; and its dance forms. Eventually it was performed throughout the world and almost everywhere became a focal point for those wishing to throw off behavioral restraints. Although the older form of musical continued in such works

FIG. 23.9

Hair! as produced on Broadway in 1968. Directed by Tom O'Horgan. Photo by Martha Swope.

as Charles Strouse's *Annie* (1977), Jerry Herman's *La Cage aux Folles* (1983), and Cy Coleman's *City of Angels* (1989), the musical after 1970 seemed to lack any clear direction. Stephen Sondheim (1930–) was by far the most successful and experimental writer of musicals after 1968. His *Company* (1970) had no chorus, instead using the principal performers in song-and-dance sequences; *Pacific Overtures* (1976) drew on conventions of the Japanese theatre; *Sweeney Todd* (1979) approached opera in its use of music throughout; *Sunday in the Park with George* (1984) explored artistic creation; and *Into the Woods* (1987) exposed the darker side of fairy tales. All Sondheim's works offered ironic views of human behavior and social values and avoided the happy endings of earlier musicals; most were organized around a concept rather than a story. Michael Bennett's *A Chorus Line* (1975) also contributed to the concept musical through its focus on multiple characters as revealed in auditions and its presentational style. It played on Broadway until 1990.

Ironically, some of the most popular musicals after 1968—*Jesus Christ, Superstar; Evita; Cats; Phantom of the Opera;* and *Sunset Boulevard*—were by the English composer Andrew Lloyd Webber (1948–), while others—*Les Miserables* and *Miss Saigon*—were by the French team Alain Boublil and Claude-Michel Schönberg, challenging the conviction that musicals were primarily an American form.

The year 1968 was also significant because it saw the return of the Living Theatre to the United States. Between 1964 and 1968 the company had toured throughout Europe, becoming increasingly committed to anarchy and revolution and serving as a kind of magnet for disaffected and radical groups. Although it performed Genet's *The Maids* and a version of *Antigone,* its major productions after 1964 were works of its own creation: *Mysteries and Smaller Pieces, Frankenstein,* and *Paradise Now,* all advocating freedom from restraints. Its best-known production was *Paradise Now* (1968), in part because it coincided with and mirrored the great unrest then evident in Europe and America. The action of the piece was divided into eight parts designed to increase the audience's political perceptions and to move ever nearer the present; at the end the audience was urged to move into the streets to continue the revolution. All barriers between actors and spectators were eliminated and both roamed the stage and auditorium indiscriminately. The performers were intensely aggressive, confronting spectators, and seeking to overcome, through insults and obscenities, all opposition. The overall effect was that of an inflammatory political meeting.

When the Living Theatre returned to the United States in 1968 it toured throughout the country and everywhere aroused bitter controversy and debate

536 CHAPTER 23

www.ablongman.com/brockett9e

FIG. 23.10
Stephen Sondheim's *Sweeney Todd,* 1979. Directed by Harold Prince. The actors are Angela Lansbury and Len Cariou. Photo by Martha Swope.

over the nature of theatre and the role of art in society. After returning to Europe, it split into three groups in 1970. The Becks took their contingent to Brazil, where they were jailed for several months before returning to the United States in 1971. Subsequently, they went back to Europe where the Living Theatre still commanded a considerable following. In 1984, when it presented a repertory of four works in New York, U.S. critics found its work amateurish and lacking in significant content. After Beck's death in 1985, Malina continued the company, although on a much reduced scale.

Despite its later decline in popularity, the Living Theatre's significance during the 1960s and 1970s cannot be denied. For a time the disaffected almost everywhere echoed its attitudes and practices: denigration of any text that could not be transformed into an argument for anarchy or social change; downgrading language in favor of Artaudian techniques; athleticism in performance; insistence on confronting and over-riding audiences; evangelical tone; and freewheeling lifestyle. Its work influenced not only theatre, but also the development of rock concerts in the 1970s, which in turn influenced theatre artists in the 1990s.

The theatre groups most closely related to the Living Theatre were the so-called radical companies. Of these, the most important were The Bread and Puppet Theatre, the San Francisco Mime Troupe, El Teatro Campesino, and the Free Southern Theatre.

The Bread and Puppet Theatre was founded in 1961 by Peter Schumann. Using puppets of varying sizes (some over 20 feet tall), live actors, and stories based on myths, the Bible, and well-known tales, it sought to promote love, charity, and humility and to denounce the evils of materialism and deception. The San Francisco Mime Troupe was founded in 1959 by R. G. Davis to perform silent plays, but after 1966 it turned to agit-prop spoken plays about current issues which it performed in a broad caricature style. El Teatro Campesino, founded in 1965 by Luis Valdez to dramatize the plight of agricultural workers in California, subsequently devoted itself to plays designed to encourage Mexican-Americans to take pride in their heritage. The Free Southern Theatre, founded in 1963 by Gilbert Moses and John O'Neal as an extension of the civil rights movement, sought to raise the consciousness of Southern African Americans. With the exception of the Free Southern Theatre, all of these groups continue to perform, although they command greatly reduced attention. After 1968 there were also a number of "guerrilla" theatre groups that seized on a gathering or occasion to present unscheduled, brief, pithy, attention-getting skits as a means of arousing interest in some issue. As the mood of the country changed in the late 1970s, guerrilla theatre declined.

In New York, the off-off-Broadway groups were those most concerned with innovation. One of the most important, the Open Theatre, was founded in

FIG. 23.11
The Living Theatre's *Paradise Now.* From the film *Paradise Now: The Living Theatre in Amerika* by Marty Topp; produced by Universal Mutant; Ira Cohen, producer. Courtesy Mark Hall Amitin.

FIG. 23.12

The Bread and Puppet Theatre's *Domestic Resurrection Circus,* as performed in Vermont, 1974. Photo by Craig Hamilton.

1963 by Peter Feldman and Joseph Chaikin (1935–), an actor with the Living Theatre who chose not to go into exile with that company. The Open Theatre was more nearly a workshop than a producing organization, and showed its work publicly only at irregular intervals. It was concerned especially with exploiting those aspects of the theatre that distinguish it from films and television—the sense of direct human contact and its constantly changing components. It drew heavily on "role playing" and "games" theories of human behavior, especially as they relate to "transformation" (that is, the idea that reality constantly shifts as people take on and discard roles in relation to the changing context). The Open Theatre utilized many techniques reminiscent of Grotowski's "poor theatre": the actors wore rehearsal clothes which remained unchanged throughout a performance; they used no makeup and few properties; scenery was almost nonexistent, and lighting was minimal; actors performed in a large open space and moved freely out of one role into another in a series of transformations.

The relationship between the Open Theatre and its playwrights was close. Typically, the writer supplied an outline, scenes, situations, or motifs; working from this base, the actors explored the possibilities through improvisations, metaphorical associations, and other techniques; the playwright then selected and sharpened those results that seemed most effective. Some of these experiments came to nothing, but other yielded outstanding results, especially in collaboration with Terry and Van Itallie. Megan Terry (1932–) was probably best known for *Viet Rock* (1966), a play about the horrors of war in Vietnam. She also used transformational techniques in works not written for the Open Theatre, most notably in *Approaching Simone* (1970), which traces the life of the French philosopher and mystic Simone Weil. Jean-Claude Van Itallie's (1936–) best-known work is *The Serpent* (1969), which mingles material from the Bible with more recent events, such as the assassinations of John F. Kennedy and Martin Luther King, Jr., and suggests that the serpent is that impulse within people that makes them break the limits set on them, whereas God is an idea invented by people to set limits on themselves.

In 1970 the Open Theatre was reconstituted as a collective and thereafter performed primarily for university and prison audiences. It was dissolved in 1973. Chaikin subsequently worked as a director and actor until a stroke in 1984 forced him to cease, although he was able to return to limited performing and directing beginning in the late 1980s.

The La MaMa organization continued to play a major role in off-off-Broadway after 1968. In addition to assisting new playwrights, it hosted other companies, American and foreign (including Growtowski and Kantor), and developed its own ensembles, some of which specialized in plays of interest to particular ethnic groups (Puerto Rican, African American, Native American, and others). La MaMa's influence also continued strong abroad. Few organizations served so many beginning artists and *avant-garde* companies.

There were a number of other significant off-off-Broadway companies. The Circle Repertory Company (founded in 1969 with Marshall Mason as artistic director) emphasized the development of new plays by its own closeknit working group, of which the best-known member was Lanford Wilson. In 1986, Mason was succeeded by Tanya Berezin as artistic director. The company eventually declared bankruptcy and ceased to exist in 1997. Between 1965 and 1980, the Chelsea Theatre Center, under the direction of Robert Kalfin, presented an outstanding series of foreign plays by such authors as Genet, Witkiewicz, Handke, and Bond. The Manhattan Theatre Club (under the direction of Lynne Meadow) after 1970 sought to assist playwrights through readings and productions in its three theatres. By 1990 it had become one of the most successful of the off-Broadway companies. Other important off-Broadway theatre companies include Roundabout Theatre, founded in 1965 and now headed by Todd Haimes, with some 30,000 subscribers for its repertory of established plays; The Vineyard Theatre, a small company founded in 1981, with an enviable record of highly successful productions of new and recent plays; and Second Stage, founded in 1979, headed by Carole Rothman. By the mid-1990s there were approximately 150 off-off-Broadway theatre groups of varying quality. Many were linked through the Off-Off-Broadway Alliance, formed in 1972 to assist members with common problems.

Of all the off-Broadway groups, the New York Shakespeare Festival was perhaps the most important. It was the creation of Joseph Papp (1921–1991), who in 1954 founded the New York Shakespeare Festival, which each summer after 1957 gave performances free of charge in Central Park, where the municipally owned Delacorte Theatre was inaugurated in 1962 to accommodate it. In 1964 Papp began to take some of his productions into New York's neighborhoods, since one of his goals was to reach unsophisticated audiences and prove to them that theatre could be both entertaining and relevant. In 1967 Papp persuaded the City of New York to acquire the Astor Library and lease it to him for a token fee. He con-

verted it into the Public Theatre with five auditoriums. It opened with *Hair!* (which after its initial run was restaged on Broadway to become one of the greatest hits of the decade). Subsequently, Papp ran an increasingly complex program and supplied Broadway with several hits, among them *Chorus Line*. In addition to producing many new plays and classics, Papp hosted many other groups. From 1973 to 1977, Papp also headed the Beaumont Theatre at Lincoln Center. By the time Papp died in 1991, he had presented more than 400 works.

After Papp resigned at Lincoln Center in 1977, the Vivian Beaumont Theatre remained unused for some time. Then in 1980 Richmond Crinkley began another unsuccessful attempt to establish a resident troupe. After still another hiatus, a new start was made in 1985 with Gregory Mosher (1952–) as artistic director. With a repertory made up primarily of U.S. plays, the theatre at last found success, although Mosher was criticized for blurring the distinctions between not-for-profit and Broadway theatre.

Broadway continued to be the heart of the commercial theatre in the United States, and acceptance there continued to be the mark of success. In the 1920s, Broadway had 80 theatres and presented about 218 productions each year. About 150 of these were new plays; only about 45 were new musicals. By 1990, Broadway had 35 theatres and presented just over 30 productions each year. New plays accounted for only about one-third of the total.

Much of the vitality of U.S. theatre after 1968 came from the nonprofit theatres, most of them located outside of New York. By the 1990s there were more than 250, and among them they were mounting more than 3,000 productions each year. They varied considerably in size, facilities, total program, and quality, but they offered live performances throughout the United States.

Of these companies, only a few can be mentioned. The Yale Repertory Theatre, established in 1966 by Robert Brustein (1927–) and after 1978 headed by Lloyd Richards (1923–), owed its distinction in part to its close association with the Yale Drama School, then the most influential U.S. theatre training program. Richards established a special working relationship with the South African playwright Athol Fugard and gave the premiere performances of some of his plays, including *Master Harold and the Boys* (1982) and *The Road to Mecca* (1984). Subsequently, he also established a similar relationship with August Wilson. In addition, Richards served as artistic director of the Eugene O'Neill Theatre Center, which each summer hosts the National Playwrights Conference, where writers are assisted in developing their plays. In 1992, Richards was succeded at

FIG. 23.13
New York Shakespeare Festival production of Shakespeare's *King John*,
1967, in the Delacorte Theatre in Central Park. Photo by George E. Joseph.

the Yale Reportory and Drama School by Stan Wo-jewodski, Jr.

The American Repertory Theatre, Brustein's company at Harvard University after 1979, was noted for its repertory, perhaps the most adventurous in America as staged by some of the most innovative directors, among them Andrei Serban, Liviu Ciulei, JoAnne Akalaitis, Ron Daniels, and Robert Wilson. It achieved international stature through its appearances at numerous festivals at home and abroad.

The Actors Theatre of Louisville, under the direction of Jon Jory (1938–), played a significant role in developing new playwrights through its annual festival (beginning in 1976–1977) of new plays and its annual "Classics in Context," which included productions, symposia, and films related to a particular period or writer. The Guthrie Theatre in Minneapolis, a leading regional company since its formation in 1963, was especially innovative after 1981 under the direction of Liviu Ciulei (1923–),

FIG. 23.14
Yale Repertory Theatre's production of August Wilson's *Ma Rainey's Black Bottom*. Directed by Lloyd Richards. The actress is Theresa Merritt. Photo by George G. Slade. Courtesy Yale Repertory Theatre.

portant Chicago companies included Wisdom Bridge, the Organic Theatre Company, Victory Gardens, the Body Politic, and the St. Nicholas Theatre Company where David Mamet got his start. The major companies of Los Angeles and the southern California area, in addition to the Mark Taper Forum, included the South Coast Repertory Company, the LaJolla Playhouse, and San Diego's Old Globe Theatre. Seattle's companies included A Contemporary Theatre, Intiman Theatre Company, Seattle Repertory Theatre, and several others.

The regional theatres derived much of their support from federal, state, and municipal agencies, but increasingly depended on grants from foundations and corporations. Government support of the arts began in 1965 when federal legislation established the National Endowment for the Arts as an agency to make grants of appropriated funds to groups or projects for artistic merit or for potential growth in excellence and service. The federal government also encouraged each state to establish an arts council, and consequently most states now have an official body charged with assisting and encouraging the arts. Many of these groups provide at least some financial support to theatres. In addition, some regional councils linked member states in an effort to coordinate plans for promoting the arts, and within states numerous communities formed arts councils to deal with local

a Romanian director noted for his provocative interpretations of standard works and under his successors, Garland Wright (1946–1998) and Joe Dowling (1948–). Other outstanding regional companies included the Arena Stage in Washington under the direction of Zelda Fichandler (1924–) and the Mark Taper Forum in Los Angeles under the direction of Gordon Davidson (1933–).

Beginning in the 1980s, Chicago, Los Angeles, and Seattle became increasingly important theatre centers. In 1979 Chicago had twenty-two companies, but by 1990 the number had grown to 110, although not all were fully professional. Among these, perhaps the best known was the Steppenwolf Theatre (established in 1976) which included among its members Gary Sinise, John Malkovich, Laurie Metcalf, and Glenne Headley, all of whom went on to stardom in New York and Hollywood. The Goodman Theatre (founded in 1925) gained national recognition through its work after 1978 under Gregory Mosher, especially the U.S. premieres of such plays as David Mamet's *Glengarry Glen Ross* and David Rabe's *Hurlyburly* and with Mosher's appointment in 1985 to head the Lincoln Center company. Mosher was succeeded at the Goodman Theatre by Robert Falls (1954–). Other im-

FIG. 23.15
Beckett's *Endgame* as directed by JoAnne Akalaitis at the American Repertory Theatre, Cambridge. Changes made in the setting and casting from those demanded in the script brought objections from Beckett. Photo by Richard Feldman.

FIG. 23.16
Liviu Ciulei's production of Shakespeare's *The Tempest* at the Guthrie Theatre, Minneapolis, 1981. In this production, the stage was surrounded by a
trough of blood in which floated artifacts representative of Western civilization. Photo by Bruce Goldstein. Courtesy Guthrie Theatre.

concerns and needs. Despite these advances, few theatre groups had any assurance of continuing financial
assistance (unlike European companies) and consequently they seldom could make long-range plans.

After 1968, a number of new and significant dramatists appeared. One of the most respected was Sam
Shepard (1943–), who began his playwriting career
in 1964 in the off-off-Broadway theatre. His extremely
large output includes *Mad Dog Blues* (1971), *The Tooth
of Crime* (1972), *Curse of the Starving Class* (1976),
Buried Child (1978), *True West* (1980), *Fool for Love*
(1982), and *A Lie of the Mind* (1985). Although there
is much variety in his work, a number of themes recur:
attempts to escape or deny the past; the cowboy and
the West as basic American myths; the family as a battle zone; and characters caught between empty dreams
and insubstantial reality. In the late 1980s, as Shepard
turned increasingly to film work, his output of plays
diminished markedly.

Lanford Wilson (1937–) wrote numerous works,
among them *Balm in Gilead* (1965), *Hot L Baltimore*
(1973), *Talley's Folly* (1979), *The Fifth of July* (1980),
and *Burn This* (1987). The story line of the plays is
minimal; the focus is on character relationships and
the eventual revelation of hidden feelings, hopes, and
disappointments. Wilson's compassionate treatment
of the misfits and rejects of society marks him as one
of the most humane of contemporary playwrights.

David Rabe (1940–) wrote most of his early plays
in response to the war in Vietnam. *The Basic Training of Pavlo Hummel* (1971) shows the gradual dehumanization of a naive and patriotic young soldier,
while *Sticks and Bones* (1971) concerns a veteran
blinded in Vietnam and the effect of his return home
on his family. *Streamers* (1976), which takes place just
as the Vietnam War is beginning, derives much of
its power from the veteran soldiers who in recalling
the Korean conflict make us recognize the price ex-

FIG. 23.17
Sam Shephard's *True West* with John Malkovich (left) and Gary Sinise. Directed by Gary Sinise. Photo by Martha Swope.

acted by all wars. Rabe's later play, *Hurlyburly* (1984), treats characters in Hollywood who seemingly are unaware of the casual cruelties they practice on each other to keep ahead in the Hollywood game; its sequel, *Those the River Keeps* (1993) explores how the chaos of contemporary life drives people apart.

David Mamet (1947–), who began his career in Chicago, has written primarily about the debasement and distortion of human beings by the materialistic goals of American society. Most of his characters are preoccupied with power or money, which they pursue through the manipulation of others. Reiterative speech (often scatalogical) reveals characters trapped by stereotyped attitudes and insubstantial values. Among Mamet's plays, some of the best known are *American Buffalo* (1977), *Glengarry Glen Ross* (1983), and *Speed-the-Plow* (1988). Like Shepard, Mamet has increasingly turned to film work.

Terrence McNally (1939–) had his first play produced in 1964 and wrote steadily for the theatre thereafter. Although some of his early plays, such as *Next* (1969) and *The Ritz* (1975) won considerable praise, it was not until the late 1980s that he became truly successful with *Frankie and Johnny at the Claire de Lune* (1987) and *The Lisbon Traviata* (1989). His plays deal primarily with the gaps between people and the importance of trying to bridge them. Other male playwrights deserving mention include John Guare, A. R. Gurney, Richard Nelson, Jon Robin Baitz, Donald Margulies, Robert Schenkkan, Horton Foote, and John Patrick Shanley.

After 1968 female playwrights achieved greatly increased acceptance. Among the best known of these

were Norman, Fornès, Henley, and Wasserstein. Marsha Norman (1947–), who wrote primarily about existential dilemmas, first gained recognition with *Getting Out* (1977), dealing with a woman leaving prison; the protagonist is represented by two personae, before and after prison, to show how she remakes her life. Norman's most successful play, *'night Mother,* the Pulitzer Prize winner of 1983, concerns a woman who prepares for and ultimately commits suicide. Other plays include *The Laundromat* (1978) and *Traveler in the Dark* (1984). She also wrote the book for the musicals *The Secret Garden* (1991) and *Red Shoes* (1993). Marìa Irene Fornés (1930–), a versatile and prolific Cuban-born writer, was best known in the 1960s for the small-scale musicals she wrote with Al Carmines. After virtually giving up writing for a time, she returned with such works as *Fefu and Her Friends* (1977), which reunites eight women on a weekend retreat, where they look back over their lives and seek to understand themselves within a patriarchal society, and *The Conduct of Life* (1985), set in Latin America, which draws parallels between the subjugation of women and political subjugation. Beth Henley (1952–) wrote about complex and bizarre relationships in small Southern towns. Among her plays, which include *The Miss Firecracker Contest* (1984), *The Lucky Spot* (1986), and *Abundance* (1990), the best known is *Crimes of the Heart* (1977, the Pulitzer Prize winner of 1980), in which three sisters, faced with charges of attempted murder and the death of their grandfather, eventually recognize the ways in which they have shortchanged themselves. Wendy Wasserstein (1950–)

FIG. 23.18
Lanford Wilson's *Burn This,* 1987. Directed by Marshall Mason. Joan Allen is in the foreground. Photo by Martha Swope.

FIG. 23.19
David Rabe's *Streamers.* Directed by Mike Nichols. Photo by Martha Swope.

made her first impact with *Uncommon Women and Others* (1977), a collage about the struggles of young college women, but her reputation rests primarily on *The Heidi Chronicles* (1988, the Pulitzer Prize play of 1989), in which the action, ranging over some twenty years, traces the protagonist's awakening feminist consciousness and her eventual sense of betrayal. Other female playwrights include Paula Vogel and Naomi Wallace.

A number of feminist theatres also were founded. Among the most important of these were Women's Experimental Theatre, WOW Cafe, Spiderwoman Theatre, the Women's Project of the American Place Theatre, and Split Britches, all in New York; Double Edge in Cambridge, Massachusetts; the Rhode Island Feminist Theatre; At the Foot of the Mountain in Minnesota; Lilith Theatre in San Francisco; and Omaha Magic Theatre. During the 1980s, more than ten national festivals of women's theatre were held.

Another positive development was the reemergence of a strong African American theatre. It began in 1963 with the Free Southern Theatre and received additional impetus in 1965 when LeRoi Jones and others founded the Black Arts Repertoire Theatre

School in New York, although this organization soon came to an end. Other organizations sprang up throughout the country, and by the late 1960s there were more than forty groups. Three were of special importance. Spirit House was founded in 1966 by LeRoi Jones, who breaking with the past, took the name Imamu Baraka, then changed it to Amiri Baraka and returned to his home in Newark, where he wrote and produced plays denouncing whites and promoting a wholly black society. The New Lafayette Theatre, founded in 1967 by Robert Macbeth, served as a cultural center for Harlem. It also served as a clearinghouse for African American groups throughout the country through an information service and through *Black Theatre Magazine.* Unfortunately, dissension within the company brought its dissolution in 1973. The Negro Ensemble Company (NEC), founded in New York in 1968 and directed by Douglas Turner Ward, produced a wide range of plays meaningful to African Americans but not necessarily written by African Americans. The longest lasting of the three groups, the NEC was by the mid-1990s only sporadically active. Other African American companies were formed throughout the United States. In 1988, the inaugural National Black Arts Festival was held to celebrate the artistic achievements of African Americans. It was followed in 1989 by the

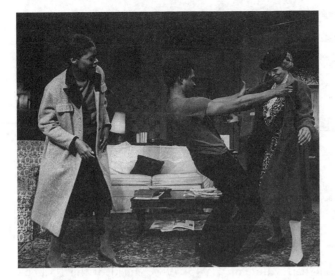

FIG. 23.20

The Negro Ensemble Company's production of Joseph Walker's *The River Niger*, 1972. Photo by Bert Andrews.

first National Black Theatre Festival with attendance by representatives of nearly 200 African American theatre groups (professional and nonprofessional) from throughout the United States. These organizations have continued to meet biannually to witness performances and to discuss common issues.

The upsurge in African American theatrical activity brought a corresponding increase in opportunities for actors and directors. Furthermore, the number of African American dramatists increased markedly. Among the early dramatists, the most important were Hansberry, Baraka, and Bullins.

Lorraine Hansberry (1930–1965) won recognition with *A Raisin in the Sun* (1959), a compassionate drama about a hardworking black family in Chicago whose dreams are shattered but whose values mature in the process. Before her untimely death, Hansberry completed only one other play, *The Sign in Sidney Brustein's Window* (1964), concerning a naive idealist who is too busy to recognize the problems within his own family. Some of Hansberry's uncompleted works were later assembled and staged by her husband, Robert Nemiroff. Amiri Baraka (LeRoi Jones, Imamu Baraka, 1934–) in such early plays as *The Toilet* (1964) and *Dutchman* (1964) treated black–white relationships as confrontational and violent, but his contempt for misguided blacks and whites was well-balanced. After 1965, he depicted all whites as devils incarnate. One of the best of these plays, *Slave Ship* (1969), traces the black experience from Africa to the present in America, and shows the unremitting and sadistic treatment of blacks by whites. Baraka

eventually abandoned his black nationalism in favor of revolutionary socialism, and his late plays show this shift. *Boy and Tarzan Appear in a Clearing* (1983), for example, shows the leaders of present-day black Africa as greedy and corrupt, and suggests the need to overcome this behavior, learned from white colonists. Ed Bullins (1935–) was resident dramatist and associate director of the New Lafayette Theatre and editor of *Black Theatre Magazine*. All of Bullins' plays, among them *Clara's Old Man* (1965), *The Electronic Nigger* (1968), *The Pig Pen* (1970), *The Taking of Miss Jamie* (1975), *Daddy* (1977), and *Boy x Man* (1997), are united by his concern for pride in blackness and contempt for blacks who seek to deny their blackness.

Two of the most effective African-American playwrights are Wilson and Wolfe. August Wilson (1945–) won his first success with *Ma Rainey's Black Bottom* (1984), about the humiliations, small victories, and defeats of African American musicians working for exploitative whites in Chicago in the 1920s. Wilson announced his intention of writing a play about the African American experience in each decade of the twentieth century. Of these, the most praised have been *Fences* (1985), winner of the Pulitzer Prize in 1987, and *The Piano Lesson* (1988), the 1990 Pulitzer Prize winner. Set in Pittsburgh in the 1950s just before the civil rights movement gained force, *Fences* reveals the psychological and economic wounds inflicted on an African American family by social and employment barriers. *The Piano Lesson* takes up the decade of the 1930s and the conflict that arises when a family's cultural heritage (represented by an heirloom piano) is thrown into conflict with their economic future (represented by land the family has worked since slave days). Others of his plays include *Joe Turner's Come and Gone* (1986) and *Two Trains Running* (1990). Wilson's plays, unlike those of several earlier African American dramatists, do not exploit themes of rage about whites but concentrate on African American identity and quests for fulfillment and dignity. George C. Wolfe gained wide recognition with *The Colored Museum* (1986), a sometimes satirical and always insightful commentary on African American life and art, but would become best known as a director and as the Managing Artistic Director of the Public Theatre. Other African American playwrights include Charles Fuller, Ntozake Shange, Adrienne Kennedy, Alice Childress, Leslie Lee, Lonne Elder III, Joseph Walker, Charles Gordone, Richard Wesley, Ron Milner, Philip Hayes Dean, and Vinette Carroll.

Other ethnic and minority groups also won increased acceptance. The first Asian American dramatist to gain national prominence was David Henry Hwang (1957–), who intermingled Asian and Western theatrical conventions. He began his playwriting career in 1979 and had his first major success with *M. Butterfly* (1988), about a French diplomat who declared that he did not know that the Beijing Opera star he had lived with for twenty years was a man. Hwang uses this story to suggest that the West has always looked upon the East as a submissive female accepting domination by the macho West. Other works by Hwang include *F.O.B.* (1980), *Face Value* (1992), *Golden Child* (1996), and a number of collaborations with the composer Philip Glass. Other Asian American playwrights include Frank Chin, with *Chickencoop Chinaman* and *Year of the Dragon;* Philip Kan Gotanda (1950–), with *The Wash* (1987), *Yankee Dawg You Die* (1987), and *Day Standing on Its Head* (1993); and Ric Shiomi, with *Yellow Fever* (1982). Asian American theatre was nourished by the East-West Players founded in Los Angeles in 1965; the Northwest Asian American Theatre, founded in Seattle in 1973; the Asian American Theatre Company, founded in San Francisco in 1973; the Pan Asian Repertory Theatre founded in New York in 1977; and several others.

After 1968, Hispanic American theatres also gained strength. A 1985 survey found 101 groups: 29 Chicano, 24 Cuban, 28 Puerto Rican, and 20 with a variety of allegiances. Some performed only in Spanish, some only in English, and some were bilingual. Some of the best known groups were INTAR, Repertorio Espagnol, and the Puerto Rican Traveling Theatre, all in New York, and El Teatro Campesino and the Bilingual Foundation of the Arts in California. An international festival of Chicano and Latino theatre was held beginning in 1970, at first annually and then biannually, under the auspices of TENAZ (Teatros Nacionales de Aztlan), the oldest artistic organization of the Chicano and Latino theatre community.

Along with Maria Irene Fornes, the best-known Hispanic American playwright was Luis Valdez (1940–), who, after his work in support of the United Farm Workers Union, turned to writing plays about Aztec myth and Mexican-American life. His *Zoot Suit* (1978), concerning a notorious murder trial of Mexican-Americans in Los Angeles during World War II, was also made into a movie. His folk musical, *Corridos* (1983), is a series of vignettes based on traditional songs. Each year, Valdez's company presents *La Pastorela,* his adaptation of the shepherds' visit to the newborn Christ. Milcha Sanchez-Scott is best known for *Roosters* (1987), a play of family relationships built around the metaphor of cockfighting. Other plays by Sanchez-Scott are *Dog Lady, Latina,* and *El Dorado.* Cherríe Moraga offers a Latina lesbian perspective on relationships in such plays as *Giving Up the Ghost* and *La Ofrenda.* Other Hispanic American playwrights include Estela Portillo Trambley, Omar Torres, Miguel Piñero, José Rivera, and Eduardo Machado.

Native American theatre groups have been few in number. The first all-Native American repertory company, the Native American Theatre Ensemble, was founded by Hanay Geiogamah (1945–) in 1972. With the support of La MaMa it presented plays based on myths and contemporary life with the aim of building pride in the Native American heritage. Geiogamah's own plays include *Body Indian* (1972) and *49* (1982). Spiderwoman Theatre, founded in 1975 by three Native American sisters, took their group's name from the Hopi goddess of creation. Its productions, which are multimedia interweavings of narrative, include *Lysistrata Numbah* and *Sun, Moon, and Feather.*

Gay and lesbian theatre also made considerable impact. One of its best known exponents was Charles Ludlam (1943–1987), head of the Ridiculous Theatrical Company after 1967 and author of several plays, among them *Bluebeard* (1970), *Camille* (1973), and *The Mystery of Irma Vep* (1984), which parodied familiar genres and the absurdities of life and art. Ludlam also acted in the plays, often playing several roles, many of them female. After Ludlam's death, the company was continued by Everett Quinton. Harvey Fierstein (1954–) won mainstream acceptance with *Torch Song Trilogy* on Broadway in 1981 and with the book of the musical *La Cage aux Folles* (1983). The AIDS crisis generated numerous plays, among the first of which were Larry Kramer's *The Normal Heart* (1985) and William Hoffman's *As Is* (1985). Later AIDS plays include Cheryl West's *Before It Hits Home,* Paula Vogel's *Baltimore Waltz,* and Paul Rudnick's *Jeffrey* and *The Naked Truth.*

Lesbian plays failed to make their way into the mainstream, but were numerous. Jane Chambers' *Last Summer at Bluefish Cove* (1980) and Holly Hughes' *The Well of Horniness* (1985) were among the best known. Several theatres, scattered throughout the country, were devoted to producing gay or lesbian drama.

Much that happened in the theatre after 1968 reflected a cluster of ideas and practices that came to be called "postmodernism"—an imprecise label, but one that suggests a significant break with "modernism." Under modernism a variety of styles had flourished, but within any one, the artist usually sought unity by adhering consistently to the set of conventions associated with that mode. If there were disparate elements, they were ultimately harmonized into a unified whole. Postmodernists, on the other hand, were undisturbed by lack of consistency or continuity. They allowed disparities to exist without seeking to mask them, and they juxtaposed styles and moods that previously would have been considered incompatible or inconsistent. They collapsed categories which under modernism had been treated as distinct; boundaries were breached between the sexes, the arts, cultures, dramatic forms, and performance styles.

Postmodern art was often reflexive, calling attention to the fact that it was being made and how it was being made. It might include overt references to other works. It tended to value popular and high culture equally and to intermingle them. Postmodernism was reinforced by poststructuralism (or deconstruction). Poststructuralists argued that it is impossible to think about any subject without language, that language makes consciousness and thought possible. Additionally, meaning can never be fully present because, during the process of communication, it is always being modified by what has gone before and deferred by what is yet to come. Statements and categories are also haunted by what they suppress or ignore; therefore a supplement of meaning is always left over, and if we examine the supplement it begins to call into question the adequacy of the original statement or the boundaries of the category and to suggest modifications which lead to still other modifications in an endless chain of deferred and differing meanings. This analytical process came to be known as deconstruction. It demonstrates that there can be no closure of meaning because additional possible meanings are always being uncovered, often ones of which the playwright may have been unaware. This led to distinctions between a "work" (the physical document written by the author) and a "text" (what individual readers find when they interrogate a script), and to the idea that the author has no more right than anyone else in the text, since no one (including the author) can dictate how a work can be interpreted. In effect, audiences became partial authors of the text they perceive. This idea, along with the principle of no closure of meaning, provided justification, if any were needed, for directors to depart drastically from dramatists' instructions. Sometimes, it was argued, works (especially classics) have become so enshrined within accepted interpretations that we can see them afresh only upon being subjected to a radically different (even "blasphemous") interpretation. Much theatre of the 1970s and 1980s intermingled elements of postmodernism and poststructuralism in highly innovative productions.

Such interminglings were foreshadowed in "happenings," which themselves harked back to concepts and conventions introduced by the futurists, dadaists, and surrealists. One key figure was Allan Kaprow (1927–), a painter and art historian, who in the 1950s became interested in "environments" (that is, the extension of the concept of art to include the entire setting in which it is exhibited or in which it occurs); believing that all those who attend an exhibit become a part of the total experience, he began to give the spectators things to do. In 1959 he published an outline for an artistic event that he labeled a "happening" because he considered the term to be neutral. Later that year he gave the first public showing of such an event—*18 Happenings in 6 Parts.* For it, the gallery was divided into three compartments; different activities went on in each but simultaneously, and images were projected onto a variety of surfaces while music and sound effects provided a background. All those who attended became a part of the event as they carried out instructions given them when they entered.

Many persons other than Kaprow were interested in happenings, and the term eventually came to be used to designate any event in which improvisation and chance played a large role. Though happenings were not strictly theatrical, many of their characteristics were carried over into theatre in several ways. First, as "institutionalized" art came under attack, there were many attempts to move it outside the confines of theatres, museums, or concert halls and to put it into more accessible and familiar surroundings—parks, playgrounds, nightclubs, etc. Second, emphasis was shifted from passive observation to participation—from the product to the process. Sometimes the spectators and the performers were the same. Third, emphasis shifted from the artist's intention to the participant's awareness. Each participant-spectator thus became partial creator of the piece and could derive whatever meaning he or she could from the experience. Fourth, simultaneity and multiple focus tended to replace orderly sequence and cause-to-effect arrangement; usually there was no pretense that everyone could see and hear the same things at the same time or in the same order. Fifth, happenings were multimedia events, breaking down the barriers between the arts and intermingling them.

Many of these ideas were carried over into *environmental theatre,* a term popularized by Richard Schechner (1934–), editor of *TDR (The Drama Review)*. In 1968 Schechner published six "axioms" designed to clarify environmental theatre. First, he declared that events may be placed on a continuum with "Pure/Art" at one end and "Impure/Life" at the other, extending from traditional theatre at one pole through environmental theatre to happenings and ending with public events and demonstrations at the other pole. Thus, he located environmental theatre somewhere between traditional theatre and happenings. Second, in environmental theatre "all the space is used for performance; all the space is used for the audience." Spectators are both "scene-makers" and "scene-watchers," for, as in a street scene from daily life, those who watch are part of the total picture, even when they consider themselves to be mere spectators. Third, "the event can take place either in a totally transformed space or in a 'found' space." In other words, space may be converted into an "environment," or a place may be accepted as it is and the production adapted to it. Fourth, "focus is flexible and variable." Fifth, "all production elements speak their own language" rather than being mere supports for words. Sixth, "a text need be neither the starting point nor the goal of a production. There may be no text at all." Thus the site of a performance is made an integral part of the whole, encompassing both actors and spectators so they may interact as an entity. Such an attempt demands that traditional theatre architecture be abandoned in favor of places already suitable as environments or that may easily be converted. Furthermore, focus tends to become multiple or variable. Schechner considered the Polish Laboratory Theatre, the Living Theatre, the Open Theatre, and several other groups to be environmental.

In 1968 Schechner formed his own company, the Performance Group. Its theatre was a converted garage with towers and platforms scattered about, all

FIG. 23.21
The Performance Group's *Commune,* 1970. Photo by Elizabeth Le Compte.

of which could be used by both actors and spectators. The company's first production was *Dionysus in 69,* a reworking of Euripides' *The Bacchae* into a series of rituals, most of them relating to sexuality, freedom, or repression. Overall, the production became a plea for greater freedom coupled with a warning against blindly throwing off restraints. Subsequently, the group presented *Commune* (1970), a company-created work about American ideals and failures to realize them; Sam Shepard's *The Tooth of Crime* (1973), a play about rivalries in the pop music world treated in terms of gangsterism; and, in 1975, Brecht's *Mother Courage.* In 1980 Schechner left the company.

The performance space was then taken over by The Wooster Group, which since 1975 had existed as a unit within Schechner's company. Under its artistic director, Elizabeth LeCompte (1944–), it developed its own pieces, several of them based on the autobiographical recollections of Spalding Gray (1941–), one of its principal members. It won high critical praise and international recognition through appearances at festivals abroad. It also applied deconstructionist techniques more fully than any other U.S. company, especially in *Route 1 & 9* (1981) and *L.S.D.* (1983). In the former, portions of *Our Town* were juxtaposed with a blackface vaudeville routine and a pornographic film, thereby showing what is marginalized or ignored in Wilder's idyllic picture of America: ethnic groups, sex, and the industrial wastelands through which run the highways referred to in the piece's title. Somewhat similarly, *L.S.D.* borrowed portions of Miller's *The Crucible* and used them reflexively to illuminate parallels between colonial witchcraft and present-day witch-hunts as they relate to induced visions and violations of accepted behavior. Because of Miller's violent opposition to the use of passages from his play, the piece was never performed as planned.

The Wooster Group's conflict with Miller, along with another at the American Repertory Theatre—Samuel Beckett threatened legal action when JoAnne Akalaitis set Beckett's *Endgame* in an abandoned subway station—aroused heated debate over long-simmering issues about the rights of authors to have their works performed as they had been written versus the rights of directors to interpret scripts however they thought most effective. The debate brought to the fore many issues (still unresolved) central to postmodernism and poststructuralism.

Similar controversy was evoked by virtually every production directed by Andrei Serban (1943–), a Romanian director who came to the United States in 1969, although he worked with scripts whose authors were no longer alive. In such productions as *The Cherry Orchard* at Lincoln Center in 1977, Handel's *Alcina* at the New York City Opera in 1983,

FIG. 23.22
The Wooster Group's *L.S.D.* Photo by Nancy Campbell.

Uncle Vanya at La MaMa in 1983, *King Stag* for the American Repertory Theatre in 1984, and *Figaro* on Broadway in 1985, Serban used iconoclastic visual imagery to create contemporary resonances and at the same time comment on the dramatic situations, characters, and ideas in ways intended to break through received ideas about the plays so they might be seen afresh. Perhaps familiarity eventually reduced controversy, for in recent years Serban's productions have ceased to arouse outrage.

Peter Sellars (1957–) worked in comparable ways. His Handel's *Orlando* at the American Repertory Theatre transformed the adventurers of Handel's opera into astronauts; his *Mikado* at the Chicago Lyric Opera was set in the boardroom of a contemporary Japanese corporation; his production of Shakespeare's *Pericles* used a jive-talking black performer as narrator; and his production of Sophocles' *Ajax* used a deaf actor in the leading role. In the late 1980s, he turned his attention primarily to opera, especially operas by Mozart. In 1993 his production of Aeschylus's *The Persians,* staged for the Los Angeles Festival and subsequently seen in Paris and Berlin, included a dancing messenger telling of a battle that takes place during the recent Gulf War, Sudanese music, and a ghost who speaks in sign language.

Lee Breuer (1937–) worked with the Actors' Workshop in San Francisco, studied Grotowski's theatre and the Berliner Ensemble, and directed Beckett's *Play* in Paris before joining with several others to create Mabou Mines, of which he was artistic director from 1970 to 1976, when it became a "theatre collaborative"—nine people who worked both within and outside the group. By 1990, Mabou Mines had presented some thirty-eight works and had performed widely in America, Europe, Asia, and Australia. Although it performed some works by others (especially Beckett), it generated most of its pieces within the company. Those written by Breuer were often partially autobiographical, relying heavily on verbal-visual puns, esoteric references, and electronic devices. His *Prelude to Death in Venice* (1979), which he stated he had written to help him understand his own clinging to youth, interwove a puppet as alter ego and recorded voices that metamorphosed from mother to girlfriend, from father to agent; quotations from Thomas Mann's novel and images from Dracula films. These seemingly disjointed elements were ultimately related through associations with the Oedipal impulse, youth, aging, and death. His *Gospel at Colonus* (1984) blended Sophocles' *Oedipus at Colonus* (which Breuer thought reflected the Greek ecstatic impulse) with the gospel service of a black church in today's America. In 1990 he presented *Lear,* his transposition of Shakespeare's play to Georgia in the 1950s with gender-reversed roles. Breuer also directed for companies other than Mabou Mines. One of his best-known productions was of Wedekind's *Lulu* (which he transposed to contemporary America complete with punk-rock band) at the American

Repertory Theatre in 1980. Another member of Mabou Mines, JoAnne Akalaitis, was also well known for experimental pieces and as a director, especially of *Endgame* for the American Repertory Theatre in 1984 and of Genet's *The Screens* for the Guthrie Theatre in 1989. Although Mabou Mines continues, it had by the early 1990s lost some of its best-known members and its work no longer aroused the interest it once had.

Many aspects of postmodernism and poststructuralism came together in the pieces of Robert Wilson (1942–), among them *Deafman Glance* (1971), *The Life and Times of Joseph Stalin* (1972), *A Letter to Queen Victoria* (1974), *Death, Destruction and Detroit* (1979), and *CIVIL warS* (1983–1984). In these pieces, Wilson borrowed eclectically from several media, cultures, and historical periods and juxtaposed seemingly unrelated images in ways reminiscent of surrealism. Movement often created a hypnotic effect through its slow pace (crossing the stage might take an hour). Most of the pieces were very long—from four to twelve hours, and one continued for seven days and nights. He usually began with some striking image or perception, which he then allowed to expand through a chain of associations. *CIVIL warS,* intended for the Olympic Arts Festival in Los Angeles in 1984 but never performed in its entirety for lack of funding, was created in segments, one each in West Germany, the Netherlands, France, Italy, and the United States. It included such disparate figures as Lear, Voltaire, Frederick the Great, Karl Marx, Abraham Lincoln, and a Native American tribe; it was intended to reflect all types of conflicts that interfere in human relationships. Utilizing twelve languages, it was not meant for an audience from a single culture. According to Wilson, there is in his pieces nothing to understand, only things to experience. Spectators are left to construct their own interpretation from the evocative, indeterminate, discontinuous, time-warped images and sounds.

While continuing to create his own pieces, Wilson began to stage works by others or to collaborate with others both in Europe and America. In his staging of Euripides' *Alcestis,* at the American Repertory Theatre in 1986, he intermingled the original text with Heiner Müller's *Description of a Picture* (used as a prologue), a Japanese kyogen play (which parodied many of *Alcestis's* themes) set to music by Laurie Anderson, and a number of laser projections. Despite the seeming incongruities of these varied elements, all were linked by the theme of death and rebirth. Others of Wilson's staging of classics include Wagner's *Parsifal,* Ibsen's *When We Dead Awaken,* Gertrude Stein's *Doctor Faustus Lights the Lights,* Büchner's *Danton's Death,* and Debussy's *Péllèas and Melisande.* His

FIG. 23.23
Robert Wilson's *CIVIL warS*. A segment presented at the American Repertory Theatre, Cambridge. Photo by Richard Feldman.

collaborative works include *Einstein on the Beach* (1976) with Philip Glass, and *The Black Rider* (1989), an adaptation of von Weber's opera *Der Freischutz*, with Tom Waits and William S. Burroughs. Wilson always has several projects underway at the same time, many of them not due for completion until several years in the future. Because Wilson's productions are so expensive to mount, he has worked most often in the subsidized theatres of Europe, where he is generally considered one of the most significant artists of his time. Probably no other artist so fully embodied the postmodern vision.

Many postmodern and *avant-garde* productions, both American and foreign, are presented at the Brooklyn Academy of Music (BAM), which since 1982 has mounted annually the Next Wave Festival. It offers in brief engagements productions by contemporary artists and companies that probably would not otherwise have been seen in New York, among them the Théâtre du Soleil, Pina Bausch's dance-theatre company, several productions by Robert Wilson, Peter Brook, Lee Breuer, Peter Sellars, and many less well known artists on the "cutting edge."

During the 1980s, performance art and the type of theatre presented by the Wooster Group, Mabou Mines, and Wilson began to intersect. In the 1970s, performance art, a successor to happenings, was usually brief, minimally rehearsed, and given one time only. Because most champions of performance art thought pieces should avoid impersonation and emphasize personal, near-improvisatory elements, they were bitter opponents of theatre. But in the 1980s performance art and theatre began to overlap, creating what was often called "interarts" or "new theatre," labels that could cover a wide spectrum of performers and performance modes. Some of its best known practitioners were solo performers. Spalding Gray, after leaving the Wooster Group, presented after 1979 some fifteen autobiographical monologues, among the most successful of which were *Swimming to Cambodia, Monster in a Box, Gray's Anatomy,* and *It's a Slippery Slope.* Eric Bogosian (1953–), in his monologues *Drinking in America* (1986) and *Sex, Drugs & Rock and Roll* (1987), created multiple male characters addicted to profanity and power. Other significant practitioners of this new theatre were Meredith Monk, Laurie Anderson, John Kelly, and Ping Chong. Tim Miller, John Fleck, Holly Hughes, and Karen Finley should also be added, since it was their work, with its frank treatment of sex, gender, and power, that precipitated the NEA funding crisis in 1990 and began the attacks in Congress on the NEA.

This new theatre also valued popular culture and often integrated it with "high art." A group of performers, among them Bill Irwin, David Shiner, Michael Moschen, the Flying Karamazov Brothers, and Avner ("the Eccentric") Eisenberg, came to be called "new vaudevillians" because they wove clowning, juggling, acrobatics, dance, and magic into their performances. Several also appeared in plays, both new and from the standard repertory.

CANADIAN THEATRE TO 1990

Just as a national identity came into focus for Canada in the 1960s, a radical separatist movement arose in French-speaking Quebec Province, giving that identity a dual focus. When the referendum on independence for Quebec failed in 1980, Canada was also entering an economic recession. The combination of these two events seems to have inspired theatre artists to move beyond the exploration of Canada's national identity in order to examine things like race, gender, and ethnicity as foundations for identity.

The 1970s were best known for the collective creations of the alternative theatres like *The Farm Show* (1972) by Theatre Passe Muraille, *Not Working, She's Got Too Much to Do* (1975) by Théâtre des Cuisines, and *They Club Seals, Don't They* (1978) by Newfoundland's Mummers Theatre. They also included highly ritualistic, dream-like imagistic productions such as *The Purple Room of the Archbishop* (1978), created by L'Eskabel Théâtre.

The experimental work of troupes like L'Eskabel was carried into the 1980s by such groups as Carbon 14, Omnibus, Primus, and Théâtre Repére (where Robert Lepage began his career). These theatres developed a highly visual style that became known internationally as Theatre of Images. Other innovations came from groups like Necessary Angel (1978), whose production of *Tamara* (1980) by John Krizanc became an international phenomenon. This production asked audience members to select one of nine characters to follow as the story progressed into a variety of locations.

The 1980s opened with the Edmonton Fringe Festival, which marked another turning point in Canadian theatre. Modeled after the fringe festival started in Edinburgh, Scotland, in 1947, the Edmonton festival inspired so many imitators that Canada now has the largest concentration of fringe festivals in the world. Canadian fringe theatres are much like the off-off-Broadway theatres of New York in terms of their scale of operation and variety of goals. Like the off-off-Broadway theatres, they tend to favor comedy and parody, but they also tend to be activist theatres, advocating social or political causes. The fringe festivals soon became the most visible venues for theatres representing the concerns of native peoples, gays and lesbians, feminists, ethnic groups, and labor movements. With government support for the arts dwindling after 1984, fringe theatres with small, clearly targeted audience bases proliferated.

The explosion of small theatres dedicated to new Canadian plays that started with the alternative theatres in the 1970s and expanded further with the fringe theatres of the 1980s brought with it a determination to promote those works both nationally and internationally. In 1971 the Playwright Circle was established. It sought to win an agreement that all theatres receiving government subsidy would dedicate at least 50 percent of each season to Canadian plays. No regional theatre would agree to this, but many of the smaller theatres did. Today this organization, which became the Playwrights Union of Canada in 1984, provides a catalogue and Web site featuring over 2,000 works by Canadian dramatists. The Association Québécoise des Auteurs Dramatiques (founded in 1965) provides a similar service for over 3,000 plays by French-Canadian dramatists.

Of the hundreds of dramatists represented by these organizations, several have won both national and international acclaim. Among those are Michel Tremblay (1942–), who had his first major success with *The Sister-in-law* (1968), a play set in a working-class neighborhood of Montreal, written in "street French." Tremblay has had a long list of successful plays, including *Like Death Warmed Over* (1970), *Hello There, Hello* (1975), *Albertine in Five Times* (1984), and *For the Pleasure of Seeing Her Again* (1998). David French (1939–) provided a romanticized view of life in Newfoundland in a series of plays starting with *Leaving Home* (1972) and running through *That Summer* (2000). He is best known, however, for *Jitters* (1980), in which the rehearsal of a Canadian play becomes a forum for critiquing the pervasive influence of U.S. culture in Canada. Canada's most successful dramatist, however, has been George F. Walker (1947–), who began playwriting in 1970. Walker's plays have been heavily influenced by the nonlinear rhythms of electronic media. *Gossip* (1977) was the first of his plays to be commercially successful, and it has been followed by a long list of others, including *Criminals in Love* (1984), *Escape from Happiness* (1992), and *Heaven* (2000). Judith Thompson has become known for her complex and highly emotional dramas from *The Crackwalker* (1981) to *Sled* (1995).

THEATRE IN AUSTRALIA AND NEW ZEALAND TO 1990

In the years after 1968, the six state theatres of Australia became the mainstay for the standard repertory.

While these theatres were not the primary venue for new Australian work, they did begin to have foreign plays translated by Australian writers rather than depending on existing English translations. Australia also took a major step in attracting the attention of the world to its commitment to the arts by building the Sydney Opera House, with its trademark sail-like design, in 1973. Since that time, major arts complexes have been opened in Adelaide (1973), Melbourne (1984), and Brisbane (1985). J. C. Williamson Ltd. rebuilt Her Majesty's theatre in 1973, but by 1976, after over a century of dominance, the venerable company was bankrupt. Harry M. Miller (1934–) took over as the premier producer in the country, having already brought *The Boys in the Band* (1968), *Hair!* (1969), and *Jesus Christ Superstar* (1972) to Australian audiences, but his empire was short lived as he was convicted of fraudulent misappropriation of funds in 1978. British producer Cameron Mackintosh soon filled the void by bringing his productions of *Cats* (1981), *Les Miserables* (1985), and *Miss Saigon* (1995) to Australia. But Sydney did not have adequate theatres to house such productions, and this prompted developer David Marriner to buy up a number of old theatres and cinemas and have them lavishly renovated. Across the nation old theatres were torn down or renovated and new ones built, not just to house the state theatres, but to provide modern innovative spaces for a growing number of alternative theatres that were thriving under the new system of Australian Council funding.

Melbourne's La MaMa Theatre continued to produce up to forty plays a year in the 1970s and 1980s, but it no longer had a resident company. In 1970 the La MaMa company decided to strike out on its own. Its members moved into the old Pram Factory and changed their name to the Australian Performing Group (APG). APG was known for its political activism and its collective productions such as *Betty Can Jump* (1972) and its most successful effort, *The Hills Family Show* (1975). But it is remembered now for its championing of Australian playwrights. Its resident playwright was Jack Hibberd (1940–) who was best known for his audience participation dramas like *Dimboola* (1969), in which the audience is treated like guests at a wedding. Though he continued to write such plays through *Liquid Amber* (1982), he has been one of Australia's most versatile dramatists, writing everything from social critiques of sexism in *Peggy Sue* (1974) to monodramas, of which the best is probably *Stretch of the Imagination* (1972). Among the most successful of the other dramatists were John Romeril (1945–), who wrote the highly political *The Floating World* (1974) about trade relations with Japan, and David Williamson (1942–), who has become Australia's most popular and most internationally known dramatist since his first success with *The Removalist* (1971), a play about abusive policemen which went on to a successful run in London in 1973. Seven of his plays have been widely produced outside Australia, including *The Club* (1977), about the tensions within a sports team as old loyalties give way to commercialism, which went on to play on Broadway in 1978, and *Money and Friends* (1992), which had a successful run in Los Angeles. Despite its success APG closed in 1980, but not before two of its members had gone on to found the equally influential Playbox Theatre Center in 1976.

Rex Cramphorn (1941–1991), one of Australia's most successful directors, created the Performance Syndicate in Sydney in 1969. The Syndicate's unique contributions to Australian theatre were its introduction of performance techniques from Asia and, after Cramphorn went to study with Grotowski in 1972, its introduction of the concepts of "poor theatre" to Australia's theatre artists. Just as the Performance Syndicate was getting underway, *The Legend of King O'Malley* (1970), a political satiric review by Michael Boddy (1934–) and Bob Ellis (1942–), became the most successful alternative theatre piece in the country. Its director, John Bell (1940–), was inspired by this success to establish the Nimrod Street Theatre (1970). The Nimrod quickly became the most innovative and influential alternative theatre in Australia, inspiring the formation of a number of other troupes, including the Black Theatre Group (founded by Betty Fisher), Griffin Theatre Company, the Sydney Theatre Company, and Company B. The Nimrod became famous for *Hamlet on Ice* (1972), but it also produced work by many of Australia's best playwrights. Peter Kenna (1930–1987), who had his first success when the Trust Players produced his *The Slaughter of St Teresa's Day* in 1959, gave the Nimrod one of its best successes with *A Hard God* (1973). Alex Buzo (1944–), whose play *Norm and Ahmed* (1968) was at the heart of the battle over censorship, had already had *Rooted* (1969) produced in the United States when Nimrod did his play *Tom* (1972). But most of the Nimrod writers, like the prolific Alma De Groen (1941–) and the equally prolific Louis Nowra (1950–), were early in their careers. The Nimrod eventually became too successful to maintain its alternative theatre identity, lost its focus, and closed in 1987. Bell, however, went on to form the Bell Shakespeare Company in 1990.

Through the 1980s, fringe theatres in Australia, like those in many other countries, became less interested in nationalistic politics and more interested in issues of race, ethnicity, and gender. The Woman's Theatre Group of Melbourne (1974–1976) had already stim-ulated interest in women writers and directors. The Gay Theatre Company of Sydney and the In the Pink company at Melbourne promoted gay and lesbian writers. Companies like The Deck Chair Theatre Company at Perth, along with Doppio Teatro and the Gilgul Theatre at Adelaide, produce plays for ethnic communities. Perth's Black Swan Theatre, founded in 1991 under director Andrew Rose, is the country's first multiethnic theatre and works to develop aboriginal actors, directors, and writers. But it is at Australia's four major international arts festivals—at Perth, Sydney, Melbourne (all annual), and Adelaide (biennial)—along with Sydney's Gay and Lesbian Mardi Gras, that most such work is seen.

By the end of the 1980s, directors like Jim Sharman (1945–) and Gale Edwards (1955–) had become international successes without having to leave Australia. Playwrights and actors who in earlier years would have left the country to find a career, were now finding success and staying home. This was also the time when aboriginal theatre, led by the playwright-activist Jack Davis (1917–2000), came into its own.

In New Zealand, Downstage received a new theatre space in 1974 and continued to be one of the strongest producers of new plays in the country. It had passed up the opportunity to produce a play by Roger Hall (1939–) called *Glide Time* (1976), however. That civil service comedy was produced by a Wellington actor's cooperative called Circa, and the play went on to be the most successful in New Zealand's history. Hall's second play, *Middle Aged Spread* (1978), became an award-winning comedy in London's West End, and Hall continues to be New Zealand's most prolific and most highly regarded dramatist. Meanwhile, the government funding that had started in 1964 had led to the creation of nine semi-professional theatres which formed themselves into the Association of Community Theatres (ACT). Of those, the Court Theatre at Christchurch was the first to become known for its adventurous repertory. Among its most successful productions were *Foreskin's Lament* (1980) by Greg McGee (1950–), a play which uses a rugby team as a symbol of New Zealand's postcolonial struggle to find its place in the world; Michelanne Forster's *Daughters of Heaven* (1991) about a murder involving lesbian schoolgirls; and the "songplays" of its co-founder Mervyn Thompson (1936–1992). Other important members of the community theatre group were Centerpoint Theatre at Palmerstone North, the Fortune at Dunedin, Bats at Wellington, and the Auckland Theatre Company. Declining government subsidies reduced ACT membership to five active theatres by 1986; by 1994 there would be only three.

As in other countries, fringe theatres have developed to replace the independent theatres. Taki Rua was founded in Wellington in 1983 to promote Maori performance, which has had a profound influence on New Zealand's theatre. They have produced works by Maori writers Harry Dansey (1920–1979), Rori Hapipi (1935–), and John Broughton (1947–) among others. Pacific Theatre, founded at Auckland by Justine (1961–) and Paul Simei-Barton (1958–), focuses on plays that express the immigrant experience of Pacific Islanders. While there have been no theatres specifically dedicated to gay or lesbian plays, the socialist lesbian playwright Renée (1929–) has seen a large number of her plays produced, as has feminist dramatist, Lorae Parry (1953–). Vincent O'Sullivan has been New Zealand's most postmodern dramatist with plays like *Shuriken* (1983), which incorporates expressionism with music hall and Noh drama and inserts of newsreel footage.

LOOKING AT THEATRE HISTORY

Challenging the dominant culture was a hallmark of the 1960s. In this, the Living Theatre played a leading role. Its challenge reached a climax in *Paradise Now* (1968), described by the company as "a vertical ascent toward Permanent Revolution." The production's most notorious feature, direct confrontation with audiences, was little understood, for in actuality the audience was cast as obstacles to successful revolution. Here is a passage from the printed version of the work:

> The Confrontations are an attempt to define and thereby understand the characteristics of the stumbling block at each [phase], and of the form of action that can overcome it. Thus at the beginning the stumbling block is The Culture which is overcome by Aesthetic Assault; and at the end the stumbling block is Stasis which is overcome by Impetus. The Confrontations are guides to the relationship between the actor and the public at each stage of the trip. The Resistance to the Revolutionary Change is treated as the obstacle. The energy form designed is an appropriate strategy for the actor to use to transform the obstacle.

> Paradise Now, Collective Creation of the Living Theatre, written down by Judith Malina and Julian Beck (New York: Vintage Books, 1971), 11–12.

By the mid-1970s, much that had been intended as an attack on the dominant ideology had been absorbed into it. Hilton Kramer interpreted this absorption as a rejection of the attack, although it might equally well be seen as an absorption of both old and new into an altered dominant mode:

> The appetite for assaults on the audience and on the medium, has clearly diminished. . . .
>
> Does this mean that the innovations of the 60s have disappeared without trace? Not at all, but where they survive . . . they have been . . . co-opted by the establishment, and put to eminently more benign use.

> "A Yearning for 'Normalcy'—The Current Backlash in the Arts," *The New York Times*, May 23, 1976, sec. 2, 1, 25.

That Kramer's perception was not entirely adequate is suggested by Elinor Fuch's observations on postmodernism:

> These characteristics—the collapse of traditional boundaries, an absorption with the theatre's own artifacts and techniques and styles—are the best reason we have for calling such theatre postmodern. . . . Some such perception of the inversion and breakdown of historical cultural values in the past two decades has bred the sense of "postness" that has invaded virtually every human enterprise in Western society. We are post-industrial, post-capitalist, post-humanist, post-apocalyptic, even post-cognitive.

> "The Death of Character," *Theatre Communications*, 5 (March 1983), 2.

24
Contemporary Theatre

By the late 1980s, several world events suggested new directions that would affect the development of theatre in the coming years. Among the most important of these was the collapse of the Soviet Union and the destruction of the Berlin Wall in 1989, both of which helped to mark the end of the Cold War that had dominated European and American policies since the end of World War II. In Czechoslovakia dissident groups rose up against the Communist regime and installed a multiparty government in 1989, and in 1990 Communist dominance of Poland came to an end when Solidarity leader Lech Walesa was elected president. Also in 1990 the United States became involved in the Gulf War, which seriously affected worldwide relations with the Middle East. These and other indications of change would be reflected in theatre in the following years.

THEATRE IN RUSSIA

The collapse of communism, the breakup of the Soviet Union, and the removal of censorship around 1990 raised hopes that the arts would blossom, but many of these hopes were dashed by economic problems. When state subsidies that had supported most theatres were reduced by about three-fourths (or in many instances stopped altogether) and inflation diminished the purchasing power of what was left, most companies struggled just to remain active. A large number of theatre artists emigrated, and many well-known companies toured internationally in an attempt to earn foreign currency. Several prominent Russian directors and theatre companies entered into exchange programs with European and American theatres and universities. After ten years of decline, the Russian theatre began to recover. Outside of St. Petersburg and Moscow, there are now 400 to 600 theatres, many of which receive government subsidies; about 100 theatres in Moscow are subsidized by the city government. The Cultural Ministry of Russia announced that it would increase its budget by 25 percent to $350 million in 2002.

In the 1990s, Moscow used festivals to increase interest in its theatrical life. One of the most important of these was the Chekhov Festival, founded in 1992 and held every two years with participation from several countries. The annual Golden Mask Festival (founded in 1995) honors the top achievements in drama, musical theatre, dance, and puppetry by theatres from throughout Russia. The Third National Theatre Olympics was held in Moscow in 2001. (The first was held in Greece in 1995, the second in Japan in 1999.) It included 150 productions from thirty-five countries presented over a period of seventy days.

Among the participants were Robert Wilson, Tadashi Suzuki, Declan Donellan, and many other foreign and Russian directors.

The management of several companies changed during the 1990s. Oleg Yefremov (1927–2000), who had headed the Moscow Art Theatre for thirty years, died in 2000 and was succeeded by Oleg Tabakov (1935–). Tabakov had been a founder of the Sovremennik Theatre, was head of the Moscow Theatre-Studio (which had been granted official status in 1987), and was the creator of more than 760 roles. Anatoly Smeliansky succeeded Tabakov as director of the Theatre-Studio.

The Taganka Theatre underwent several changes in management. Following Anatoly Efros' death in 1987, Nikolai Gubenko (1941–) was named head of the Taganka. The changed status of this company was perhaps most clearly indicated when in 1989 Gubenko was named Minister of Culture, the first professional artist to hold that position since the 1920s. With the breakup of the Soviet Union, he lost that post and returned to the Taganka. After Gorbachev proclaimed the policy of *glasnost,* Lyubimov's citizenship was restored, and he returned to the Taganka. Among his most successful productions there were *Boris Godunov* (1993) and *Medea* (1995). Eventually Gubenko (who had been one of Lyubimov's staunchest supporters) became alienated from Lyubimov, and the animosity that developed led to the theatre's being divided into two rival companies, much as the Moscow Art Theatre had been earlier. One of Lyubimov's most successful recent productions was a circus-like *Marat/Sade* performed in Prague in 2000.

During the 1990s, new plays were not highly valued in Russia. This situation led to the establishment of the Playwright and Director Center and the Debut Center, which have developed a cooperative relationship with the Royal Court Theatre in London. A few playwrights, however, champion innovation in playwriting, among them Maxim Kurochkin (1970–), whose *Kitchen* (2001) was commissioned, directed, and starred in by Oleg Menshikov, Russia's top stage and screen actor. This very popular play interweaves contemporary life with the German Nibelung saga, social satire, and bitter irony. Another of Kurochkin's plays, *Steel Will,* concerning the invention of a new Slavic mythology, won an award in 1998 for innovative writing.

Among the leading directors of Russia, in addition to those already mentioned, are Victor Fomenko, Galina Volchek, Kama Ginkas, Henrietta Yanovskaya, Valery Fokin, and Lev Dodin. Fomenko (1932–) has rejected large-scale theatre. His *Innocent as Charged* (a reworking of a play by Ostrovsky) concerning a long-lost child, has been playing in Moscow since it was

FIG. 24.1

Vakhtangov Theatre production of *Innocent as Charged* (1993), Victor Fomenko adaptation of a play by Ostrovsky. Photo of the New York tour by Stephanie Berger © 2001.

first produced in 1993; it began a vogue for plays written for small spaces with action on a more-human scale. Some critics praised it as the end of ideological drama. Formerly with the Vakhtangov Theatre, he now heads his own Fomenko Studio. Galina Volchek, one of the founders of the Sovremennik, long considered one of Moscow's leading theatres, is now its director. This theatre has also won much praise abroad, including in New York, to which she brought productions of plays by Chekhov in 1996 and 1997. Kama Ginkas (1941–) is noted for his small, intense, and highly personal productions. His *The Room of Laughter* was named the best production at the Gold Mask Festival in 2000. He is married to Yanovskaya, artistic director of the Young Spectators Theatre in Moscow since 1987, considered one of the top five directors in Russia. Her productions have been seen at several European festivals. Valery Fokin (1946–) gained wide recognition after 1994 for his *A Hotel Room in the Town of NN,* written to be performed in a completely enclosed setting; it won several awards (including a Golden Mask) and has toured in seven countries. He is also the founder of the Meyerhold Arts Center, one of the few companies to have a new theatre built especially for it, signaling the renewed acceptance of Meyerhold.

Lev Dodin (1944–) began his professional career in 1967 and became artistic director of the Maly Drama Theatre in St. Petersburg in 1983. He gained national and international recognition with his seven-hour dramatization of Fedor Abramov's novel *Brothers and Sisters* (1985), about life on a collective farm between the end of World War II and 1949; in it the characters' initial optimism gradually gives way to

FIG. 24.2
Maly Theatre Production of *Brothers and Sisters* (1985).
Seven-hour dramatization of Fedor Abramov's novel
directed by Lev Dobin. Photo of the New York tour
by Stephanie Berger © 2001.

disillusionment. It has been performed in more than
fourteen countries and won the Europe Theatre
Prize in 2000 (previous winners were Peter Brook,
Giorgio Strehler, and Robert Wilson). Other productions by Dodin include *Stars in the Morning Sky*
(1988) about prostitutes and others rounded up before the 1980 Moscow Olympics, *Gaudeamus* (1991)
concerning humiliations and violence among army
conscripts, and *Chevengur* (2000), a dramatization of
an antiutopian novel by Andrei Platonov, for which
Dodin won a Golden Mask award.

By the early twenty-first century, Russian theatre
had begun to recover from the setbacks it had endured during the 1990s, but it still had many obstacles to overcome. After the dissolution of the Soviet
Union, theatre achieved considerably more freedom
but paid for it through economic hardships.

THEATRE IN POLAND AND
THE CZECH REPUBLIC

As in Russia, the triumph of Poland's Solidarity
movement in 1989 led to greater freedom in society
but worsened the economic situation. In seeking to
cope with these problems, the government discontinued subsidies to all but eight theatres, leaving many
struggling to survive. This struggle continued through
the 1990s.

The triumph of Solidarity also permitted playwrights and other theatrical personnel to return to
Poland. Slawomir Mrozek returned to a strong welcome of his plays, as did Janusz Glowacki, whose *The
Fourth Sister* (referring ironically to Chekhov's play)

was a mixture of the grotesque and the realistic in a
tale about sisters in today's Moscow who long to escape that world. The work of Witold Gombrowicz
(1904–1969) also gained renewed popularity after his
novel *Ferdydurke* was adapted for the stage and presented in Lublin in 1998. This play, in an English
translation by Allen Kuharski, has been performed
in several American cities since 2000.

Perhaps the major event was the death of Jerzy
Grotowski in 1999. He had labeled the final phase
of his work, which was concerned with the transformation of the individual, "art as vehicle." These
explorations took place primarily at the Fondazione
Pontadera Teatro in Italy, supported by the Italian
government and administered by Thomas Richards.
Disciples came there in an attempt to understand
Grotowski's concept of "Action"—how an actor creates precise movements with the body as a way to
communicate character, story, and the actor's intentions. Beginning in 1996 a separate research center called the Workcenter of Jerzy Grotowski and
Thomas Richards was opened to participants from
around the world. The work done there was based
in part on Stanislavsky's theories of physical actions.
Grotowski's work at Pontedera continues under the
guidance of Richards.

In Czechoslovakia in 1989 the overwhelming desire for democratic reform brought an end to the
Communist regime. Vaclav Havel, only recently released from prison, became the country's president,
and censorship was discontinued. Unfortunately, de-
pressed economic conditions led to a severe reduction in subsidies for theatres, while attendance
declined. Many theatres had to reduce personnel by
30 to 40 percent.

Under the new government, theatres rushed to
produce Havel's plays, as well as those of other dissident writers. Many of the small theatres that had
been so active prior to 1968 were reestablished, and
their former directors, such as Otomar Krejca and
Jan Grossman, were returned to their posts. A sense
of political inequity among the regions of the nation soon led to the division of Czechoslavkia into
two new states, the Czech Republic (with Havel as
president) and Slovakia.

In 1992 the Alfred Radok Awards were established
in the Czech Republic to honor the outstanding
Czech production of each calendar year. During the
first decade of the awards, three directors stood out:
Hana Buresova, Jan Antonin Pitinsky, and Petr Lebl.
Hana Buresova (1959–) worked in various theatres
before joining the Labyrint in 1992. She first won the
Radok Award for her production of Grabbe's *Don Juan
and Faust,* a play usually considered unstageable. It remained in the repertory for several years. She also

staged an adaptation of *The Barber of Seville,* using *commedia* elements and frank theatricality. She went on to direct *Murder in the Cathedral* and several Czech plays. J. A. Pitinsky (1956–) won consecutive Radok awards in 1995 and 1996 and a third in 2000. He is probably best known for an adaptation of Thomas Mann's *The Magic Mountain* in 1997.

Petr Lebl (1965–1999) became head of the Theatre on the Balustrade upon Jan Grossman's death in 1993. He established his reputation with a radical adaptation of Genet's *The Maids* in 1993 and a controversial production of Chekhov's *The Seagull* in 1994. He followed these with *The Inspector General* (1995), *Cabaret* (1995), and Chekhov's *Ivanov* (1997) and *Uncle Vanya* (1999); during the run of the last of these he committed suicide. His death puzzled and saddened many, for he was considered by most critics to be the best Czech director of his time.

The Alfred Radok Awards also include an annual prize for the best new unproduced script. A New Wave Festival in 2000 featured new Czech work, and the Theatre on the Balustrade initiated monthly readings of new, unproduced Czech plays. Foreign plays dominated the Czech stage in the 1990s because, some have speculated, the loss of strong political opposition provided no focus for dissent. For whatever reason, native playwriting did not flourish. Havel largely gave up playwriting, and no one took his place. Among contemporary playwrights, Arnost Goldflam and Jan Kraus are perhaps the best known.

The Prague Quadrenniel, at which designers, technicians, and theatre architects from around the world exhibit their work and discuss issues that affect their profession, continues to be the preeminent gathering in its field. It also acknowledges the strong role that Czech designers and technicians have played (and continue to play) both nationally and internationally.

THEATRE IN GERMANY

The destruction of the Berlin Wall and the reunification of East and West Germany brought new opportunities, but also posed new challenges because the financial cost of reunification was so great. East and West Berlin, for example, had duplicate arts institutions, and how to maintain, merge, or abandon some has remained a major problem. In 1999 Berlin was subsidizing 100 cultural institutions despite serious doubt that all were needed. In Germany, there is little federal subsidy of the arts. Rather, each of Germany's sixteen states establishes its own arts budget, which is supplemented by municipal budgets. Though after 1989 subsidies decreased and left some

theatres stranded, Germany's support for the arts was still among the highest in the world, about $1.9 billion per year, although governments were hard-pressed to continue their past commitments. In 2001 Germany had some 150 publicly owned theatres (plus about 280 private theatres).

Some well-established theatres underwent major changes. Despite strong objections, Berlin's Schiller Theater was closed, and in 1993 the Berliner Ensemble was privatized, although it continued to receive $16 million in subsidies. A five-person management—composed of Peter Palitzsch, Peter Zadek, Matthias Langhoff, Fritz Marquardt, and Heinar Müller—was installed. Brecht's heirs, having been removed from positions of power, for a time denied the theatre permission to present any of Brecht's plays. The managerial arrangement soon collapsed. By 1994 only Müller was left and after he died in 1995 the theatre was adrift for a time. Celebrations in 1998 of the centennial of Brecht's birth revived much of his former prestige, and the Berliner Ensemble's reputation recovered considerably after 1999 when Claus Peymann, who since 1986 had headed Vienna's Burgtheater (considered by many the best German-language theatre), assumed direction of the company.

Within Germany, the Schaubühne in Berlin, founded in 1970 by Peter Stein and a group of actors, was considered to be Berlin's most important company. When Stein left the company in 1985, he was succeeded by Luc Bondy, then Jurgen Grosch from 1988 to 1992 and Andrea Breth from 1992 to 1998. Problems within the company led to its dissolution in 1999. It was reconstituted in 2000 by Thomas Ostermeier and Jens Hilje, who invited Sasha Waltz, head of one of the most respected Tanztheaters in Germany, to join them as a full partner. They are struggling to revive the reputation of the theatre.

After leaving the Schaubühne, Stein directed in Italy and France, and from 1992 to 1997 was supervisor of dramatic performances at the Salzburg Festival, one of the richest and most prestigious in Europe. Its director from 1989 to 2001, Gerard Mortier, however, did not like Stein's monumental stagings and replaced him with Frank Baumbauer, artistic director of the Deutsches Schauspielhaus in Hamburg. During Mortier's tenure as head of the Salzburg Festival, many of the world's most famous directors—Robert Wilson, Patrice Chereau, Luc Bondy, Christoph Marthaler, Robert Lepage, and Peter Sellars—staged productions there. Peter Ruzicka became director of the festival in 2002. Mortier has been named head of a new festival, the Ruhr Triennale, which has at its disposal fourteen remodeled spaces in abandoned factories. The festival got underway in 2002 but will not be fully activated

FIG. 24.3
Peter Stein's fifteen-hour production of the full text of Goethe's *Faust,* Hannover, Germany. Photo courtesy of Ruth Walz Fotografin © 2000.

until 2003. In 2004 Mortier is to become artistic director of the Paris National Opera.

Other important festivals include the Berlin Theatertreffen, which each year hosts the ten best German-language productions of that season; the Bonn Biennale, inaugurated in 1992 with a focus on new plays from throughout Europe; and the Vienna Festival, which since World War II has hosted not only German-language productions, but also others from

Eastern Europe, Russia, and elsewhere. The Bayreuth Festival continued to be one of the best known in the world, but for several years has been bogged down in controversy over who will succeed Wolfgang Wagner (now past eighty years old) as director.

Stein directed the two parts of Goethe's *Faust* after leaving Salzburg. The finished work, produced in 2000, took fifteen hours to perform. This was the first time the play had ever been presented in its entirety (with no cuts and faithfully following the script and its stage directions). While the production was admired by many, Stein was denounced by others for betraying the "director's theatre" he had helped to establish at the beginning of his career.

Germany has a number of well-known and admired directors. In the early 1990s, Thomas Langhoff at the Deutsches Theater in Berlin and Dieter Dorn at the Kammerspiele in Munich staged productions that rivaled those at the Burgtheater in Vienna. Frank Baumbauer (1946–), after serving as director of the Bavarian State Theater in Munich and the Basel (Switzerland) Schauspielhaüs, became director of the Schauspielhaüs in Hamburg in 1993. This theatre was named Germany's best three times by critics before Baumbauer left to become head of the theatre section of the Salzburg Festival.

Frank Castorf (1952–), as director of the Berlin Volksbühne after 1992, became known for his irreverent treatment of texts and his unusual casting. Often called a "text destroyer" because of his anarchic, antirealistic, and grotesque mountings of scripts, he was

FIG. 24.4
Christoph Marthaler's 2000 revival of *The Beautiful Prospect* (1926) by the influencial Hungarian playwright Ödön von Horváth (1901–1938), at the Schauspielhaus, Zürich. Photo courtesy of Ruth Walz Fotografin ©.

FIG. 24.5
Elfriede Jelinek's play *Him Nothing but Him* (1998).
Photo courtesy of Ruth Walz Fotografin ©.

especially popular with young audiences. Christoph Marthaler (1952–) also valued production over text, although he is best known for composing his own theatre pieces. He became head of Schauspiel Zurich in 2000. Einar Schleef (1945–), known for his antiliterary, antirealist productions, was especially interested in choral performances, as seen in his production of Elfriede Jelinek's *Sports Play* at the Burgtheater in 1998. Other important directors include Leander Haussmann, Matthias Hartmann, and Klaus Bachler.

Perhaps the best known of contemporary German-language playwrights is Elfriede Jelinek (1947–). Her *Illness, or Modern Women* (1987) contrasts the blood men have spilled in battle with the blood women shed as part of their nature. Many of her plays have been very controversial. *The Farewell* (2000) was an attack on Jorg Haider, the right-wing leader of Austria, mixed with passages from the *Oresteia*. It used thirteen identically dressed actors who served as a chorus, much as in her 1998 *Sports Play*. Other of her plays include *Service Area, or Cosi fan Tutte* (1994), *Stechen, Stab und Stangl* (1997), and *Him Nothing but Him* (sometimes called *He Not as Himself,* 1998). Other recent playwrights include Theresia Walser (1968–) with *King Kong's Daughters* (1999), David Gieselmann with *Herr Kolpert* (2001), Marius von Mayenburg (1973–), and Moritz Rinke (1967–).

THEATRE IN ITALY

Giorgio Strehler continued to play a major role in Italy. In 1989 he relinquished the directorship of the Théâtre de l'Europe in Paris to Lluís Pasqual (1951–), head of Madrid's Teatro Maria Guerrero, and returned to the Teatro Piccolo in Milan, where he was involved in a project based on Goethe's *Faust* (in collaboration with Josef Svoboda). Called *Faust Frag-*

ments, the first part opened in 1989 and was followed by three more parts, each three hours long. Strehler himself played the role of Faust in what he called "contaminations," with some scenes fully staged and others read by actors standing behind lecterns. In 1992–1993 Strehler turned his attention to productions honoring the two-hundreth anniversary of Goldoni's death, as did almost all of Italy's professional companies, and in 1995 he staged a much-praised production of Pirandello's *Mountain Giants.* Strehler was also successful in getting new facilities for his company. The Teatro Studio, seating 423, was opened in 1986. A large theatre (begun in 1979) was finally completed in the 1990s after an expenditure of $66 million. By the time he died in 1997, Strehler had directed more than 250 productions.

Following Strehler's death, Luca Ronconi (1933–) was appointed director of the Piccolo Teatro. Ronconi had been highly praised for his adaptation of Ibsen's *Peer Gynt* under the title *Toward Peer Gynt* and for O'Neill's *Mourning Becomes Electra,* both staged at the Teatro di Roma, which Ronconi had made second only to Strehler's company since joining it in 1994. He was noted for both the artistic impact and the gigantic cost of his productions. Upon taking his post at the Piccolo Teatro, he staged Hugo's *Ruy Blas* in 1997 and an adaptation of *The Brothers Karamazov* done in three parts, each four hours long.

Mario Martone, a Neapolitan director, succeeded Ronconi at the Teatro di Roma. There he oversaw the conversion of a former industrial complex into a theatre center, the first phase of which opened in 1999. One of its most striking offerings was a monumental production of Wagner's *Parsifal,* which used several different spaces in the complex simultaneously.

In 1998 Italy's cultural minister, Walter Veltroni, persuaded Parliament to enact the first national legislation concerning theatre in Italy. It recognized spoken drama as a fundamental aspect of national culture and acknowledged the state's responsibility for sustaining and promoting it. Much of that responsibility was assigned to regional and local authorities, but it recognized two theatres—the Piccolo Teatro in Milan and the Teatro di Roma—as national theatres. According to the legislation, each region will be expected to maintain at least one central theatre, which must produce at least four productions each year and host touring groups.

Dario Fo continued to be recognized as Italy's major playwright and director, especially after he was awarded the Nobel Prize for Literature in 1997. His recent plays include *Johan Padan and the Discovery of the Americas* (1995), *Sex? Thanks, Just for the Hell of It* (1995), *The Devil with Boobs* (1997), and *Coppia Aperta, quasi Spalancate* (2001), a satire on marriage.

Fo, in his more than seventy plays, has continued to be primarily concerned with the corruption of power and the inept bureaucracy of state and church. In 2001, to celebrate the fifthieth anniversary of the writing and performing career of Fo and his wife, Franca Rame, the Italian Cultural Institute in New York sponsored a Fo festival which divided its performances among several northeastern cities in the United States.

THEATRE IN FRANCE

Festivals flourished in France, especially after 1990. Among the more than fifty, the one held in Avignon, under the direction of Bernard Faivre d'Arcier since 1992, has continued to be the most prestigious. In 2001 it mounted its fifty-fifth season, presenting more than fifty works in some thirty spaces over a one-month period. Long considered a major showcase of French culture, the festival began to feature theatre from other cultures beginning in 1994. Japan was the first to be welcomed, followed by Russia, Taiwan, Korea, Latin America, and Eastern Europe, although French-language companies remained the primary focus. Fringe performances at the Avignon Festival Off, administered by Alain Leonard, have grown steadily, since no would-be participants are turned away. Typically, it now attracts more than 550 productions each year.

The Festival d'Automne in Paris has grown considerably both in size and reputation since 1990. Begun in 1972, it originally lasted four weeks. Now it begins in late September and continues for three months. This festival seeks to present the best contemporary creations from beyond France and often commissions productions. It has been especially interested in American artists, inviting Robert Wilson, Richard Foreman, Laurie Anderson, Merce Cunningham, the Wooster Group, and many others to participate. It was the co-sponsor, with New York's Lincoln Center, of the production of *The Peony Pavilion,* which created international outrage when cultural authorities in Shanghai sought to forbid its performance in the West. Although the festival has a small budget, it has been very successful in persuading other Parisian arts groups to stage or sponsor experimental works.

France has about 400 theatres that receive some subsidy from the government. There are 5 national theatres, 43 dramatic centers (10 of them regional), and 63 theatres classified as National Stages, all subsidized by the Ministry of Culture. Taken all together, these theatres serve every region in France. In the mid-1990s, government officials pledged to devote 1 percent (about $3 billion) of the national budget to cultural projects. Though that goal has yet to be realized, France does allocate about $500 million to theatre annually,

The Comédie Française remained the primary national theatre. When Antoine Vitez, its administrator, died in 1990, he was succeeded by Jacques Lasalle (1937–), who employed a number of foreign directors and increased the number of recent plays in the repertory. Accused of having subverted the company's role of preserving French culture, Lasalle was replaced in 1993 by Jean-Pierre Miquel (1940–), who returned to a more conservative approach. In 1998 the Comédie Française, for the first time in its existence, staged a play by a living foreign dramatist—Tom Stoppard's *Arcadia.* In 2001 Miquel was succeeded by Marcel Bozonnet, former director of the Conservatoire National Superieur d'Art Dramartique, France's most prestigious theatre training school. The Comédie Française also manages the much smaller Théâtre du Vieux Colombier (once Jacques Copeau's theatre). By 2000 the two houses were presenting more than twenty productions each year.

The company with the greatest international reputation continued to be the Théâtre du Soleil, headed by Ariane Mnouchkine. Her first major production in the 1990s was *Les Atrides,* composed of Euripides' *Iphigenia at Aulis* and Aeschylus' trilogy *The Oresteia.* It was mounted over a period of two years (1990–1992) and was performed in France, Italy, Germany, England, Canada, and the United States. Drawing on Asian forms, most clearly Kathakali, its integration of dance, music, spectacle, and gripping drama was a major achievement. In 1994 the company staged Hélène Cixous' *The Forsworn City, or the Awakening of the Furies,* concerning the French government's allowing the use of blood it knew to be contaminated with HIV. Mnouchkine's 1995 production of Molière's *Tartuffe* was given an Algerian flavor with overtones of the restrictions demanded by Muslim fundamentalists. *Drums on the Dike* (1999), written by Cixous, concerns characters in an unspecified Asian country who live under the threat of a flood that will destroy half of the kingdom. Which half is to be spared—the district of artists or the district of factories? Mnouchkine's actors were given travel grants to observe theatre in Vietnam, Taiwan, Japan, and Indonesia. In the production, some scenes used conventions borrowed from Vietnamese water puppets, but for the most part actors played puppets based on Japanese Bunraku and were manipulated by other actors playing their handlers. In the final scene, the flood annihilates all life. Then the puppet master wades through the water, retrieves small, inanimate puppets, and lines them up to dry on the edge of the stage. This highly praised production, after its debut

FIG. 24.6
Yasmin Reza's *The Unexpected Man* (1995), directed by Luc Bondy. Photo courtesy of Ruth Walz Fotografin ©.

in France, was seen in Canada, Australia, and Korea, and was scheduled to be seen elsewhere.

Next to Mnouchkine, Oliver Py (1966–) is perhaps France's most admired director. After starting his own theatre at the age of nineteen with a government grant, he first came to prominence in 1995 with *La Servante,* made up of five pieces dealing with spreading an angel's message, staged continuously over twenty-four hours. As the play ended, its epilogue dovetailed into the play's prologue, ready to start all over again. His *Face of Orpheus* (1997) was four hours long, during which a young masked man is dismembered alive and the pieces of his body auctioned. At the end, when the mask is removed, the auctioneer discovers that the young man is his son. In 1998 Py was named director of the Centre Dramatique National in Orleans. He wrote and directed *Requiem for Srebrnica,* in 1999, a series of journalistic pieces about the war in Bosnia. Other important French directors include Daniel Mesguich, Stephane Braunschweig, Stanislas Nordey, Georges Lavaudant, Jerome Savary, and Jorge Lavelli.

Few recent French playwrights have won wide recognition. Yasmin Reza (1959–) is probably the best known, and she was at first only grudgingly admired in France because she wrote for the Boulevard theatres. She drew wide attention, however, when *Art* (1994) was produced in more than thirty countries and won major awards in London and New York. This was followed by productions of *The Unexpected*

Man (1995), later translated and produced in England by the Royal Shakespeare Company; *Conversations after a Burial* (written in 1987 but best known through a revival by the Almeida Theatre in London); and *Life × 3* (2000), which was premiered almost simultaneously in Paris, Vienna, Athens, and London. All of her plays use small casts and take place in very restricted spaces. The gradual and subtle unveiling of unacknowledged feelings that characterizes her plays has won her a wide and enthusiastic audience.

THEATRE IN BRITAIN

Several theatres in England were beneficiaries of the National Lottery Fund, a percentage of whose receipts was allotted to the Arts Council of England beginning in 1995. One beneficiary, the Royal Court Theatre, after a $43 million renovation, reopened in 2000 with a season that included sixteen world premieres. Since 1992 the Royal Court has enlarged its influence by working with theatres in several countries in programs designed to encourage new playwrights. These cooperative endeavors have extended to France, Germany, Israel, Palestine, Romania, Bulgaria, Russia, Spain, Uganda, and the United States. The programs include residencies by playwrights, a new-writers festival, partnerships with specific theatres, and co-productions of single newly commissioned plays.

Another beneficiary of lottery funding is Shakespeare's Globe Theatre—a reconstruction of the first Globe Playhouse of 1599—created by American actor-director Sam Wanamaker (1919–1993). The Globe received $18.5 million from the lottery fund in 1995 and was able to open for its first season in 1997. This open-air, galleried theatre, which seats 1000 and has a standing audience of 600 to 700, sells more tickets per performance than any other theatre in London. Under the artistic direction of Mark Rylance (1960–), the company attempts to mix "original practices" productions (in which they explore the production methods of the period in which the play was written), with modern and postmodern stagings of Shakespeare, his contemporaries, and modern authors commissioned to write for the Globe. It has also hosted Shakespearean productions from Brazil, Cuba, India, Japan, and South Africa. Among the company's most notable "original practices" productions have been *Henry V* (1997), which opened the theatre, *Antony and Cleopatra* (1999), with Mark Rylance as Cleopatra, and *Twelfth Night* (2002) performed by an all male cast in Middle Temple Hall, where the play was first staged in 1602. Its more unusual productions have been *The Tempest* (2000) with

FIG. 24.7
The Almeida Theatre production of *Celebration* (2000), by Harold Pinter. Photo of the New York tour by Stephanie Berger © 2001.

Vanessa Redgrave as Prospero, *It's a Mad World My Masters* (1998) set in the 1950s, and *Cymbeline* (2001) staged with only five actors in neutral costuming.

Covent Garden also benefited from the National Lottery. It reopened in 1999 after a $360 million redevelopment. The only part of the 1858 structure that was not torn down and rebuilt was the auditorium. The building now includes a new studio theatre, additional rehearsal and dressing rooms, and expanded backstage facilities. In 2001 Tony Hall became director of the company, succeeding Michael Kaiser, who returned to the United States to head the Kennedy Center. In 1999 the Sadler's Wells Theatre also reopened after extensive renovation partially funded by the lottery.

Concern about the decline of regional theatres in Britain led the Arts Council to commission a report covering fifty theatres. "Roles and Functions of the English Regional Producing Theatres," completed in 2000, concluded that all of the theatres were underfunded, with the result that they were concentrating on "safe" plays and avoiding innovation. It concluded that not only was more funding needed, but also more risk-taking.

A few companies within London achieved enviable reputations and were often considered models for other independent companies. The Almeida Theatre, under the joint direction of Jonathan Kent and Ian McDiarmid beginning in 1990, mounted an average of five plays a year to high critical praise. Among their most successful productions were Racine's *Britannicus* and *Phaedra* (1998) with Diana Rigg and Toby Stephens; *Medea,* for which Rigg won a Tony; *Hamlet,* for which Ralph Fiennes won a Tony; *Richard*

II and *Coriolanus* (2000) with Fiennes playing the title role in each; and an adaptation of Frank Wedekind's Lulu plays (2001). Many of the Almeida's productions also played in the United States. In 2001 Kent and McDairmid announced that they would resign from their positions in the summer of 2002. The Théâtre de Complicité was founded in 1983 as a collective, but Simon McBurney has dominated this experimental physical theatre company, which combines movement, design, and text to create a multi-layered expressiveness. Among its highly praised productions, some of the best were *Street of Crocodiles* (1992), a depiction of provincial Polish life in the early twentieth century; *The Three Lives of Luci Cabrol* (1994); Ionesco's *The Chairs* (1997); *Mnemonic* (1999), which intermingles a story about the discovery of a 5000-year-old body on a glacier in the Alps with another about a couple in the twenty-first century; and *The Noise of Time* (2000), a contemplation of Shostakovich which involved the Emerson String Quartet, four actors, and multimedia.

Cheek by Jowl was founded by Declan Donellan (1953–) and Nick Ormerod (1951–) in 1981. Among its many highly praised productions were *Measure for Measure* (1994) and *As You Like It* (1995), with an all-male cast, including Adrian Lester, who won special acclaim as Rosalind. Donellan and Ormerod have also staged a number of plays for the National Theatre and other companies. They sought to make theatre accessible through performances of classic plays using the simplest of means. Beginning in 1985, their

FIG. 24.8
Théâtre de Complicité 1998 revival of *Street of Crocodiles: A Dance of the Mind* (1992), based on the autobiographical works of Bruno Schulz (1892–1942), the influential Polish-Jewish writer slain by a Gestapo officer. Photo of the New York tour by Stephanie Berger © 1998.

productions were nominated for major awards each year. As a permanent company, Cheek by Jowl was abandoned in 1998, although Donellan and Ormerod have continued to work together on such productions as Tony Kushner's *Homebody/Kabul* (2001).

England's two major companies continued to be the Royal National Theatre and the Royal Shakespeare Company. In 1988 leadership of the National Theatre (Royal was added to its title in 1988 to mark its twenty-fifth anniversary) passed to Richard Eyre (1943–), who had worked both in the fringe and regional theatres before coming to the National in 1981. As director of the company, Eyre sought to keep it vital by making room for more experimental productions and by bringing in young directors, among them Deborah Warner, Sam Mendes, Katie Mitchell, Phyllida Lloyd, and Stephen Daldry, all among England's most successful directors during the 1990s. In 1997, like the Royal Court, the National underwent extensive renovations, financed by proceeds from the National Lottery. In 1997 Eyre was succeeded by Trevor Nunn, who is to be replaced by Nicholas Hytner in 2003. In seeking to convince the public that the company was national in more than name, Nunn imported some regional theatre productions and toured some of its own to other English cities.

Adrian Noble (1951–), long one of the Royal Shakespeare Company's major directors, became its head in 1990. In 1997 he significantly shortened the RCS's seasons at the Barbican Theatre in London to allow the company to tour England during the summer months. (The Barbican has replaced the RSC summer season with the Barbican International Theatre Event or BITE.) In 2001 Noble announced that the RSC would cease to play at the Barbican at the end of the 2001–2002 season and that the company would undertake its first major restructuring in forty years. Instead of hiring actors on long-term contracts which often required them to split their time between Stratford-on-Avon and London, he proposed to use short-term contracts; create several small companies that would premiere plays in different cities throughout the year; and expand the company's work abroad. The RSC also expects to renovate its headquarters in Stratford-on-Avon including tearing down its Festival Theatre (1932) and replacing it with a new one. (The Arts Council has authorized $71 million in matching funds for this undertaking.) The company is also considering the acquisition of the Round House Theatre for its operations in London. During the 2000–2001 season the RSC presented, in chronological order, eight of Shakespeare's history plays about England in the 15th century.

After he resigned as director of the National Theatre in 1988, Peter Hall founded his own company

FIG. 24.9

Shakespeare's Globe Theatre 1998 production of *Merchant of Venice,* with Mark Rylance as Bassanio and Norbert Kentrup as Shylock. Courtesy of Shakespeare's Globe, London. Photo by John Tramper © 1998.

designed to bridge the gap between the British and American theatres and to move productions between London and New York. His first two offerings—Tennessee Williams' *Orpheus Descending* with Vanessa Redgrave, and Shakespeare's *The Merchant of Venice* with Dustin Hoffman—played in both cities, but the exchange then stopped. In 1997 Hall's company settled into the Old Vic, where it performed a repertory of classic plays that included *Waiting for Godot, The Seagull, The Provok'd Wife, King Lear,* and others. When the Old Vic was put on the market in 1998, Hall's company moved to a series of theatres in the West End. In 2000 Hall returned to directing in both London and New York, and in 2001 he rejoined the RSC company for a specially developed production of *Tantalus* at the Denver Arts Center.

For a time after Hall's company left it, the future of the historic Old Vic Theatre seemed in jeopardy. But in 1998 it was sold to the Old Vic Theatre Trust 2000, which has booked a series of successful transfer productions into the building. They have also mounted a number of London premiers including Matthew Bourne's *Car Man* (2000) which combined the music of the opera *Carmen* with a story adapted from *The Postman Always Rings Twice.* Bourne first achieved popular acclaim with his all-male *Swan Lake* (1998), noted for breaking down the boundaries between dance and theatre.

Peter Brook continued his work with the International Center for Theatre Research in Paris. In 1992, on the hundredth anniversary of Maeterlinck's *Pelléas and Mélisande,* Brook presented a reworking of Debussy's operatic setting of the play, *Impressions of Pelléas,* in which the action, a combination of myth and hothouse passion, swirled around two grand pianos in a stripped-down nineteenth-century drawing room. Later works included *The Man Who* (1994) based on Oliver Sachs's case studies of the deranged, and *Who's There?* (1995), a work which looks at how a play is transformed into a performance by viewing rehearsals of *Hamlet* through the eyes of some of the most important theatrical visionaries of the twentieth century: Stanislavsky, Meyerhold, Craig, Brecht, and Artaud. His own adaptation of *Hamlet, The Tragedy of Hamlet* starring Adrian Lester, opened in Paris in 1999, and then toured several European and Asian countries as well as several cities in the United States in 2001.

Several of England's established playwrights continued to be active after 1990. Caryl Churchill's *The Skriker* (1994) intermingles the natural and supernatural as a "shape changer" leads other characters into the dark world of the unconscious. Her *Blue Heart* (1997) is made up of two short plays, "Heart's Desire" and "Blue Kettle"; in the second of which, the use of conventional language is gradually lost until only the words *blue* and *kettle* are left. *Far Away* (2000) is an end-of-the-world vision in which human response to suffering is deadened. Churchill usually works with Max Stafford-Clark, director of Out of Joint, a company he founded in 1993 after the Joint Stock Company was abandoned. Tom Stoppard continued to be praised for such plays as *Arcadia* (1993) and *The Invention of Love* (1997), and David Hare remained prolific with *Skylight* (1995), *Amy's View* (1997), *Via Dolorosa* (1998), and *My New Zinc Bed* (2000). Harold Pinter, in addition to writing new plays such as *Moonlight* (1993), *Ashes to Ashes* (1996), and *Celebration* (2000), was honored with a festival devoted to his works in New York in 2001. Michael Frayn won critical praise and major awards with *Copenhagen* (1998), about Werner Heisenberg's (father of Germany's nuclear program) visit to Niels Bohr (a Danish physicist who had been Heisenberg's mentor) during the Second World War. This was followed by a popular comedy, *Alarms and Excursions* (1999), about characters who become victims of their electronic devices.

Alan Ayckbourn continued his success with plays that cleverly manipulate time, space, and misunderstandings. *Communicating Doors* (1994) moves from 1978 to 1998 to 2018 in an effort to alter history; *Comic Potential* (1998) has as its focus a robotic actor;

FIG. 24.10
Copenhagen (1998), by Michael Frayn. Photo of the New York production by Joan Marcus © 1999.

and *The Things We Do for Love* (1999) suggests that despite desperate efforts, few people find the love they hope for. *House* and *Garden* (1999) are two plays written to be staged simultaneously on two separate stages using the same actors.

Among England's young playwrights, Sarah Kane (1971–1999) attracted the most attention, perhaps because she committed suicide just as she was being critically recognized. Her first important play was *Blasted* (1995), which in the beginning shows an abusive sexual relationship between a middle-aged journalist and a young female family friend, but widens out to include various atrocities. Eventually the man is raped; his eyes are sucked out; and he tries to eat a dead baby. Many audience members were outraged. *Phaedra's Love* (1996) is based on Seneca's version of Phaedra and Hippolytus. *Crave* (1998) is made up of poetic exchanges without stage directions among four characters who are identified only by letters of the alphabet. *4.48 Psychosis* (staged in 2000) refers to 4:48 A.M., the darkest hour, and concerns suicidal despair.

In 1999 *The Color of Justice* by Richard Norton-Taylor became one of England's most popular plays. Composed primarily of excerpts from a hearing into an apparent racially motivated murder that was largely ignored by the police, it was performed originally in the fringe Tricycle Theatre, but response to the play led to its transfer to a large West End theatre.

Other recent playwrights include Patrick Marber with *Closer* (1997); Mark Ravenhill with *Shopping and Fucking* (1996), *Some Explicit Polaroids* (1998), and *Mother Clap's Molly House* (2001), about male prostitution in the eighteenth century and the present; David Grieg, whose *Victoria* concerns three women who try to escape economic bonds in 1936, 1974, and 1996; and Joe Penhall with *Blue/Orange,* about race and class in a power struggle between two psychiatrists and a black patient.

Although the English musical seemed to lose its strong appeal, Andrew Lloyd Webber was able to use $145 million of the profits from his earlier works to acquire ten of London's leading theatres and variety halls in 2000. Cameron Mackintosh also secured ownership of seven theatres, and SFX Entertainment, the organization that dominates touring in the United States, bought twenty-three theatres scattered throughout England. Lloyd Webber argued that a dangerous situation is created when theatres are not owned by theatre professionals. Neither he nor Mackintosh gave up producing musicals, but they were unable to duplicate their successes of the past.

THEATRE IN IRELAND

As Ireland became a major European computer center, its new prosperity encouraged the growth of theatre. A plan was approved to build a new home for the Abbey, Ireland's national theatre. Ben Barnes, director of the Abbey, was faced with a debate over whether to move the Abbey, especially since the Dublin Docklands Development Authority offered prime real estate on Dublin Bay that would become the cornerstone of a new waterfront neighborhood. Others wanted the Abbey to stay where it was but to enlarge and renovate the present site. Although all seem agreed on the importance of the Abbey to Ireland, the squabbling has left the problem unresolved.

The Gate, Dublin's second most important theatre, devoted so much attention to filming all of Samuel Beckett's plays under the overall supervision of its director, Michael Colgan, that many thought it had entered a state of serious decline; responding to these accusations, the company has made an effort to restore its former reputation. Other important theatres in Ireland include Rough Magic, which staged a festival of international new plays in 2000; and the Druid Theatre in Galway, directed by Garry Hynes, who has won considerable international attention, especially for her productions of Martin McDonagh's plays. (She won the Tony Award for best director for her production of McDonagh's *The Beauty Queen of Leenane* in 1998, making her the first woman to win that award.)

As elsewhere, there are many festivals in Ireland. The Gate used a festival in 1991 to do all of Beckett's plays. There have also been festivals devoted to the works of William Butler Yeats, Brian Freil, John Millington Synge, and Oscar Wilde. The Galway Arts Festival takes place in July, the Limerick festival in January, the Dublin Fringe in September, the Dublin Theatre Festival in October, and the Queens Festival in Belfast in November.

Ireland is known above all for its playwrights. Martin McDonagh (1970–) had his first production in 1996 at the Druid Theatre. His grotesque and ironic stories of life in rural Ireland soon attracted a wide audience. They include *The Cripple of Inishman* (presented by the National Theatre in London), *The Beauty Queen of Lenane, A Skull in Connemara,* and the *Lonesome West* (all presented first by the Druid Theatre), and *The Lieutenant of Inishmore* (2001), written for the Royal Shakespeare Company.

Conor McPherson (1971–) is a prolific playwright, many of whose plays are made up of alternating monologues. His dramas include *This Lime Tree Bower* (1996), which shows three men discussing sex and robbery and ending in public nudity; *The Weir,* in which four men and a woman exchange stories in a pub; *The Good Thief* in which an underworld Dublin man roughs up people for a living; and

FIG. 24.11

Lonesome West (1999) by Martin McDonagh. Photo of the New York tour by Joan Marcus © 1999.

Dublin Carol, three short scenes about a man estranged from his family at Christmas.

Other recent playwrights include Mark O'Rowe (1970–) with *Howie the Rookie* (1999), two interrelated monologues about two nights that lead to savage deaths; Sebastian Barry (1955–) with *The Steward of Christendom,* set in a mental home, where the last police chief before Ireland's independence relives and tries to justify his opposition to the Irish rebels; Marie Jones (1951–), whose *Stones in His Pockets* (1999), about the impact of a film company on an Irish village, became an international favorite as two actors portray numerous characters; and Marina Carr (1964–), considered to be Ireland's leading female writer, with *On Rafferty Hill* (2000), in which a young woman is raped on stage by her father.

THEATRE IN CANADA

While the social and political activism of the works of Brazil's Augusto Boal were the inspiration for a great many of Canada's fringe groups of the 1980s, the corporal mime training of the French master, Jacques Lecoq (1921–), as adapted by Richard Pochinko (1946–1989), has inspired a major movement in "physical theatre" in the 1990s. The aim of this movement has been the retheatricalization of theatre and, for many companies, the depoliticizing of it. This movement has been energized by three of Canada's most successful exports of the 1990s: Robert Lepage (1957–), the Cirque du Soleil (Circus of the Sun), and Theatresports.

Lepage has become an international celebrity for highly imagistic works inspired by his early experience with rock concerts that were given a story line in the 1970s and 1980s. Along with his controversial adaptations of Shakespeare, Lepage has received considerable acclaim for productions of *Vinci* (1986), *Polygraph* (1988), *The Seven Streams of the River Ota* (1996), *Zulu Time* (1999), and *The Far Side of the Moon* (2000). Cirque du Soleil (founded in 1984) produces circuses without animals in which highly unusual and visually stunning acts are organized around an impressionistic story line. Starting with *Cirque Réinvente* (1987), the group began to tour outside Canada. Among their most successful shows have been *Mystére* (1994), a resident show for a Las Vegas hotel; *Quidam* (1996), their most scripted production; *La Nouba* (1998), which was developed for Disney World; *"O"* (1998), for which a special theatre was built in Las Vegas; and *Dralion* (1999), the first show by the company's new creative team headed by Gilles Ste-Croix. Theatresports is an improvisational organization founded by Keith Johnstone in Calgary, Alberta, in 1978. It has now be-

FIG. 24.12
Jonathan Larson's *Rent* (1996). Photo of the New York tour by Joan Marcus © 1996.

come a franchise with "teams" on five continents, all following a precise set of regulations for the improvisational competitions they sponsor.

Tremblay and Walker have continued to be among Canada's most visible dramatists, but the search for a national cultural identity undertaken by the alternative theatres in the 1970s led to the development of fringe theatres that looked for a cultural identity independent of nationalism in the 1980s. In the 1990s those fringe theatres brought attention to a number of dramatists, many of whom wrote on racial, ethnic, or gender themes, including Ron Chambers, Marty Chan, Brad Fraser, Tomson Highway, M. J. Kang, Stewart Lemoine, Daniel MacIvor, Clem Martini, Rick Miller, Andrew Moodie, and a long list of others.

Canada's two major theatre production companies, Mirvish Productions and Livent, have probably had the greatest impact on Canadian theatre in recent years, however. The father-and-son team of Ed Mirvish (1914–) and David Mirvish (1947–) have produced everything from Royal Shakespeare Company productions to the latest fringe theatre successes. But they are best known for producing already successful mega-musicals from *Les Miserables* and *Miss Saigon* to *The Lion King, Rent,* and *Mamma Mia.* Since buying the Royal Alexandra Theatre (1907) in Toronto in 1962, they have built the spectacular Princess of Wales Theatre (1993), the first privately built theatre in Canada in eight-five years, and acquired the Canon theatre (formerly the Pantages) in 2001. (Ed Mirvish bought the Old Vic in London in 1982, painstakingly restored it, and ran it successfully until selling it in 1998.) Livent, run by Garth Drabinsky (1948–) from 1992 to 1998, generated a long list of awards and even greater profits from a series of musical revivals and adaptations from *Kiss of the Spider Woman* (1993) to *Show Boat* (1994), *Barrymore* (1997), *Fosse* (1998), and *Ragtime* (1999). Drabinsky also undertook the renovations of historically important theatres from the Apollo (New York), to the Oriental (Chicago), to the Pantages (Toronto) before he was indicted in the United States for securities fraud in 1999.

The success of these commercial producers has brought significant attention to the Canadian theatre, and Toronto is now said to be the third largest English-language theatre market in the world. But these productions have also taken Canadian theatre back to a focus on a colonial repertory, drained away audiences and resources from the smaller theatres, and caused many political figures to argue that the theatre in Canada is no longer in need of government subsidies.

FIG. 24.13

Brazil's Grupo Galpão is one of many that tours to international festivals each year. This production of *Romeu & Julieta,* in a translation by Onestaldo de Pennafort, has been one of their great successes. Courtesy of Shakespeare's Globe, London. Photo of the London tour by Sheila Burnett © 2000.

THEATRE IN THE UNITED STATES

As in other countries, one of the most notable developments in the United States after 1990 was the proliferation of festivals. The bringing together of companies (often from places widely separated geographically and culturally) came to seem in its variety more attractive than long-run, stand-alone productions. Festivals offer opportunities to see in rapid succession and in a concentrated period of time events that, were they to be seen on their home ground, might require extensive and expensive travel. With festivals, productions were, in effect, brought to the spectator and demanded prompt decisions to attend before the opportunity vanished. Such festivals have had a long tradition as places where theatre artists can share new ideas and where audiences can be exposed to a wide range of approaches to performance. There is a growing concern that the sheer number of festivals, however, might be encouraging a lack of diversity as theatre artists develop a festival style that focuses on visual images.

Festivals became so numerous in the United States after 1990 that only a few can be named. Each summer Lincoln Center hosts a festival of theatre, dance, and music that presents outstanding companies from across the world. Some of its productions have included *The Peony Pavilion* (from China, performed for the first time ever in its entirety), Vietnamese water puppets, the opera *White Raven* by Philip Glass and Robert Wilson (which had been commissioned by the Portuguese government to commemorate its fifteenth-century explorers), a two-week festival devoted to the plays of Harold Pinter, and numerous other events from throughout the world. In 2001 the New York International Fringe Festival (founded in 1997) offered 180 productions in twenty performance spaces utilizing 2000 artists from twelve countries. The Asian Performing Arts Festival held in New York in 2001 included companies from Indonesia, Thailand, Vietnam, Japan, and elsewhere. The Henson International Festival of Puppet Theatre (founded in 1991 and held every two years) attracted twenty-six companies in its tenth-anniversary year. The International Hispanic Theatre Festival held in New York in 2001 included productions from Mexico, Brazil, Bolivia, Ecuador, and elsewhere. The National Black Theatre Festival celebrated its twelfth anniversary in Winston-Salem in 2001 with more than 100 performances over six days. In 2000 the Magic Theatre in San Francisco staged a week-long Playwrights in Danger Festival featuring plays by authors who have risked their lives to write about things they believe in; it included plays from Nigeria, Singapore, Egypt, Algeria, and Argentina. By far the greatest number of festivals (too numerous to count) are devoted to Shakespeare.

Despite the appeal of festivals, Broadway remained for many the measure of acceptance, even though by the mid-1990s only about 10 percent of the productions it offered originated there. The rest came from London or non-Broadway theatres, or were revivals. The cost of mounting a production on Broadway increased between 350 and 400 percent between 1967 and 1997. Ticket prices increased at a slower rate, but by 1997 some musicals were charging $75 for tickets, and by 2001 the price had increased to $100 or more. In the 1990s, Broadway's thirty-five theatres presented an average of about thirty productions each year (compared to fifty or sixty in the 1970s). Few of these were of spoken drama. In the late 1980s and 1990s, Broadway was most hospitable to the English musicals of Andrew Lloyd Webber, and in 1996 *Cats* became the longest running production in Broadway's history with 7485 performances and earnings of more than $400 million. The popularity of new imported musicals seemed to decline during the 1990s, although *Miss Saigon* did not close until 2000 after some 4100 performances. Many of the musicals that replaced imports were revivals, such as *Carousel, Cabaret,* and *Kiss Me Kate*. Through the early 1990s, Stephen Sondheim continued to be the most popular American composer of musicals, but his output dropped off considerably thereafter. Probably the most popular American musical of the late 1990s was Jonathan Larson's *Rent* (1996), partly based on Puccini's *La Bohême,* but transposed to New York's Lower East Side and brought up-to-date (sadly, the author died shortly before the show opened). In the late 1990s, many musicals—among them *Contact, Swing, Fosse, Tap Dogs, Riverdance,* and *Stomp*—were more nearly dance entertainments than traditional musicals. After 2000 popular musicals—such as *The Full Monty* (with book by Terrence McNally, music and lyrics by David Yazbek) and *The Producers* (book, music, and lyrics by Mel Brooks)—returned to the story-based form, but they also marked a new trend—adapting popular movies for the stage. Harold Prince, America's most successful director of musicals, devoted his energies to rejuvenating the American musical by helping writers develop their works at his Prince Music Theatre in Philadelphia.

The image of Broadway was brightened by the 42d Street Development Project, (a city and state sponsored plan approved in 1984), which was created to transform an area of urban blight into something resembling the showplace that Broadway had been early in the twentieth century. Using this plan, several decrepit theatres in the Times Square area were reclaimed. The Livent Corporation remodeled and linked two theatres to create the Ford Center for the Performing Arts; the New Victory Theatre (opened in 1995) was devoted to limited runs of productions from throughout the world intended for young audiences. The Selden Theatre was transformed into the American Airlines Theatre and became home to the Roundabout Theatre, the second-largest nonprofit company in America. The Disney Corporation took over the renovated New Amsterdam Theatre (formerly the Ziegfeld Theatre) as home for *The Lion King*. A new ten-story building, the 42nd Street Studios, housing fourteen rehearsal studios, the offices of several nonprofit arts organizations, and a 200-seat theatre, was opened in 1999. The project also included a hotel, restaurants, shops, a wax museum, and movie theatres.

This rejuvenation encouraged similar changes in the neighboring Theatre Row, made up of off-Broadway and off-off-Broadway theatres. The best known of these theatres, Playwrights Horizons, devoted to developing new plays, razed its building in 2001 to make way for a new $24 million, five-story complex. Five other new theatres were also being built, one with 199 seats and four with 99 seats; in addition, a 499-seat house, to be used for productions on their way to Broadway, began construction in 2001.

The distinctions between Broadway, off-Broadway, and off-off-Broadway theatres are primarily contractual. According to Actors Equity standards, Broadway theatres have a seating capacity of 500 or more; off-Broadway theatres seat 100 to 499; and off-off-Broadway 99 or fewer. Most of the spoken dramas produced in New York appear in off-Broadway or off-off-Broadway theatres. It is difficult to specify how many there are (there were more than 400 not-for-profit theatres in New York in 2001). Some of the best known of these—including ones that pioneered off-Broadway—went bankrupt in the 1990s. Among these were Circle in the Square (1951–1997), the most important off-Broadway house in the 1950s and the one usually associated with the revival of interest in Eugene O'Neill's plays; the Circle Repertory Theatre (1969–1996), supporter of new plays and playwrights, perhaps most notably Lanford Wilson; and the Ridiculous Theatrical Company (1967–1999), founded by Robert Ludlum, who wrote, directed, and acted in most of the gender-bending productions the theatre was known for.

Other established off-Broadway theatres continued to be leaders. Perhaps the most important of these was the Public Theatre (New York Shakespeare Festival), which was headed for thirty-seven years by Joseph Papp before he turned over the artistic direction to JoAnne Akalaitis (1937–) shortly before his death in 1991. The choice of a director noted primarily for her postmodern productions with the *avant-garde* collective Mabou Mines and a few resident theatres came as a surprise, since it seemed to place the Public Theatre on a path quite different from the one Papp had cultivated. Unfavorable response to her productions led to her replacement in 1993 by George C. Wolfe (1955–), who was much more successful, especially in attracting a youthful and diversified audience. Wolfe's success as head of the company, as a director, and as a playwright made him one of the most influential figures in the New York theatre, but by 2001 the most powerful members of the theatre's board of directors had resigned in protest over Wolfe's financial management.

The La MaMa organization also continued to be active, offering a crowded season of plays in New York each year, and since 1990 running the La MaMa Umbria International, a cultural center and artists' residence in Italy. Other important off-Broadway and off-off-Broadway theatres included the Manhattan Theatre Club, under the direction of Lynne Meadow, noted for its productions of new plays; the Drama Department; the Pearl Theatre Company; the Atlantic Theatre Company; Target Margin; Tectonic Theatre Company; the New York Theatre Workshop; and many others.

The *avant-garde* continued to flourish in New York. The Wooster Group, in keeping with its past practice, borrowed portions of well-known plays, reconfigured their structure, and combined them with other materials, as in *Brace Up!* its 1991 reimagining of Chekhov's *Three Sisters,* which made considerable use of video cameras and interaction among live actors and video images; it also borrowed the Stage Manager from *Our Town* who interviewed characters from Chekhov's play. In 1999 the Wooster Group presented *House/Lights* at the Festival d'Automne in Paris; it is working on a piece based on Phaedra and another project drawing on William Faulkner's novel, *As I Lay Dying.* Richard Foreman continued to write and produce plays at his Ontological-Hysteric Theatre. In 2001 he wrote and directed his fiftieth play, *Maria del Bosco,* about three fashion models and their

attraction to a race car. In addition to local *avant-garde* companies, numerous U.S. and foreign troupes were presented each year by the Brooklyn Academy of Music in its Next Wave Festivals, which sought to keep Americans abreast of the best and most provocative recent work being done elsewhere.

In the 1990s *avant-garde* theatre took on new shapes as it melded with other art forms. "Theatre" was used less often than earlier to describe these new works, which instead were more often associated with performance art (or just performance) than with traditional theatre. One of the principal homes of this type of performance was P.S. 122 (an abandoned public school building in the East Village). Originally it merely rented space to various groups, but it later became a producing organization as well. By 2000 it had presented more than 5000 artists and had commissioned a large number of new plays and dance works. By then it was presenting more than 150 productions each year (10 to 20 of which it had commissioned). The emphasis was always on the new and provocative, and productions were aimed primarily at an audience in their mid-twenties to mid-thirties.

In addition to the blending of art forms, dramatic forms themselves underwent considerable change. Monologues and narrative became dominant devices in many plays, and subject matter was often autobiographical or biographical. Many plays were performed by a single actor or a very small cast. Most required little scenery and few props or costumes, but lighting effects (and sometimes multimedia) were occasionally complex. Among their attractions for producers were the limited resources required to mount them. Some of the better known of these works are Anna Deveare Smith's (1951–) *Fires in the Mirror* and *Twilight: Los Angeles* about issues of race and class as revealed in neighborhood riots; John Leguizamo's (1964–) semi-autobiographical sketches of Latino life, *Mambo Mouth, Freak,* and *Sexaholix;* Eve Ensler's *The Vagina Monologues,* and Danny Hoch's *Jails, Hospitals and Hip-Hop.*

Gaining renown as a playwright became much rarer for Americans after 1990, perhaps because success on Broadway had always been the major indicator of acceptance. David Mamet, who wrote *Oleanna* (1992), *Cryptogram* (1994), *The Old Neighborhood* (1995), and *Boston Marriage* (1999), was the most recognized contemporary American dramatist, in part because his work in films gained him much prominence. Terrence McNally also continued to achieve and maintain a high level of success with such plays as *Lips Together, Teeth Apart* (1991), *Love! Valor! Compassion!* (1994), and *Master Class* (1995), as well as the books for the musicals *Kiss of the Spider Woman, Ragtime,* and *The Full Monty.* Edward Albee, after years of neglect, returned to prominence after his *Three Tall Women* won the Pulitzer Prize in 1994. His more recent plays include *The Play about the Baby* and *I Think Back Now on André Gide.*

Among new playwrights, Tony Kushner (1956–) was the most praised American dramatist of the 1990s, almost entirely for *Angels in America: A Gay Fantasia on National Themes* (1991–1993), presented in two parts: *Millennium Approaches* and *Perestroika.* This epic play, which required more than six hours to perform, was not only about the AIDS crisis in the 1980s but also about the moral crisis in the United States as concern for self leads to rejection of the needs of others, even loved ones. But the possibility of change is also suggested by the titles of the two parts. Others of Kushner's plays include *Slavs* (1994) and *Hydriotaphia* (written as a one-act play in 1987; rewritten in three acts in 1997). *Homebody/Kabul* (2001), another epic play, concerns Islam and a daughter's search for her missing mother in both London and Afghanistan.

Another playwright whose recognition greatly increased during the 1990s was Charles L. Mee (1939–), a magazine editor and historian before turning to playwriting. His first play to have a major production in New York was *The Imperialists at the Club Cave Canem* (1988), one of a series of political plays that questions U.S. foreign policy. He later turned to Greek plays; after deconstructing them, he used their themes as foundations for contemporary plays, transformed into the language and people of America today. His *Orestes* is set on the White House lawn following the Gulf War and seeks to explore American society's malfunctions. *Big Love* was inspired by Aeschylus's *The Suppliants,* and *True Love* is based on Euripides' *Hippolytus* and Racine's *Phèdre. First Love* is about an elderly couple who fall in love for the first time. These three plays were presented in New York in 2001 and were sometimes spoken of as a trilogy. *Bobrauschenbergamerica,* meant to emulate the style of Rauschenberg's assemblages as well as to comment on the evolution of culture in the twentieth century, was first performed at the Actors Theatre of Louisville's Humana Festival in 2001.

Paula Vogel (1951–) began writing plays in the 1980s with such works as *And Baby Makes Seven* (1984). Her best known plays are *Baltimore Waltz* (1992), a tribute to her brother who died of AIDS, and the Pulitzer Prize winning *How I Learned to Drive* (1997), in which the protagonist tells how as a teenager she was seduced by her uncle (who is treated sympathetically). Others of her plays include *Desdemona:*

FIG. 24.14
Final scene of Tony Kushner's *Angels in America: Millennium Approaches* directed by George C. Wolfe. The actors are Stephen Spinella and Ellen McLaughlin. Photo by Joan Marcus © 1993.

FIG. 24.15
How I Learned to Drive (1997), Pulitzer Prize winning play by Paula Vogel. Courtesy of Center Stage, Baltimore, Maryland. Melissa Leo and Dennis Parlato are on stage. Photo by Richard Anderson © 1998.

A Play about a Handkerchief; Hot 'n' Throbbing (1994), and *The Mineola Twins* (1996). All of these plays have a strong feminist point of view. Other significant American playwrights included David Auburn (who won the 2001 Pulitzer Prize for *Proof*), Kenneth Lonergan, and Neil LaBute.

August Wilson continued to be the best-known African American playwright. During the 1990s, his plays included *Seven Guitars* (1995) and *King Hedlley II* (2000), the latter about the constricted lives of black characters in Pittsburgh during the 1980s. Aside from his plays, Wilson made his greatest impact with an impassioned speech in 1996 to the Theatre Communication Group national conference; it concerned the lack of financial support for African American professional theatres, which he declared essential if African Americans are to explore their own culture and history in a context not dominated by white society. This speech led to a heated and extended debate and to a plan for six regional meetings about the issues that had been raised. These meetings are expected to culminate in a national convention in 2002–2003.

Another prolific African American playwright is Suzan-Lori Parks (1963–), who began writing plays in 1989 with *Imperceptible Mutabilities in the Third Kingdom*, and went on to *Death of the Last Black Man in the Whole Entire World, The America Play, Venus, In the Blood* (based on *The Scarlet Letter*), and *Topdog/Underdog* (2001). Most of her plays have been discontinuous, postmodern ruminations on the black experience in American society. *Topdog/Underdog,* more linear and naturalistic than her earlier plays, depicts a world of hustlers and victims. It concerns two brothers, Lincoln (who now impersonates Abraham Lincoln in a side show), and Booth (who seeks to master three-card monte, at which Lincoln formerly excelled), and the struggle for dominance between the two.

The American theatre continued to achieve considerable diversity in the 1990s. In addition to those already mentioned in earlier chapters, Latino writers proliferated. Migdalia Cruz's *Miriam's Flowers* concerns a boy killed in an accident who watches over his family, and Edwin Sanchez's *Unmerciful Good Fortune* is about a woman arrested as a serial killer because of information she has as a clairvoyant. Among the best-known Latino writers were Jose Rivera (1955–) and Eduardo Machado (1950–). Rivera completed *Marisol* (1992), an apocalyptic fantasy, when he was a writer in residence at the Royal Court Theatre in London; he followed with *References to Salvador Dali Makes Me Hot,* a story that juxtaposes the literal and the surreal, and *Giants Have Us in Their Books* in which a runaway tiger is blamed for the sexual chill that has settled over New York. Machado was greatly influenced by Maria Irene Fornes, with whom he worked closely. He is especially noted for his *Floating Islands* trilogy (*The Modern Ladies of Guanabocoa, Fabiola,* and *Broken Eggs*). The first of these plays is set in Cuba in the 1920s and 1930s, the second in Cuba in the 1950s and 1960s, and the third in California in 1979. They trace the fortunes of a formerly wealthy family that attempts to adjust to new conditions in Cuba and the United States. *Havana Is Waiting* (first performed at the Humana Festival in 2001 under the title *When the Sea Drowns in Sand*) is a semi-autobiographical play about a Cuban American who returns to his original homeland for the first time since he was eight years old.

Similarly, new Asian American playwrights gained critical acceptance after 1990. Han Ong (1967–), with *The L.A. Plays* (1993), *Middle Finger* (2000), and *Watcher* (2001), became in 1997 the youngest artist and the first Filipino American to be given a MacArthur Foundation "genius" grant. Jessica Hagedorn (1950–) won critical praise for the adaptation of her novel *Dogeaters* (1998), about life in Manila under Ferdinand Marcos's presidency. Naomi Iizuka (1965–), born in Japan, lived in several countries but received much of her schooling in the United States, including law school at Yale University, before she turned to theatre. Her plays include *Carthage* (1993), which transfers the story of Dido and Aeneas to the rough streets of Los Angeles; *Tattoo Girl* (1994), about a young female trumpet player seeking meaning in her life; *Skin* (1995), which blends Büchner's *Woyzeck* with the lives of contemporary rootless Californians; *Polaroid Stories* (1997), about homeless young people (first produced

FIG. 24.16

Proof, by David Auburn, the Pulitzer Prize winning play in 2001 directed by Daniel Sullivan. Actors Johanna Day and Mary-Louise Parker are on stage. Photo of the New York production by Joan Marcus © 2000.

at the Humana Festival); and *36 Views* (2001), which examines authenticity in art and human relationships. Her plays are free-form, but combine great emotional intensity and lyricism with cutting humor and a concern for the rougher aspects of life.

Almost 350 not-for-profit theatres in the United States are affiliated with the Theatre Communications Group (TCG). Many of them are more solidly established than they formerly were, and more were breaking even financially in 2000 than ever before. Several of them have stated their intentions to expand their facilities and programs. The Guthrie Theatre in Minneapolis announced that it will build a $100 million, three-theatre complex on the shore of the Mississippi River to be completed by 2004–2005. The company has about 30,000 subscribers and presents about twelve plays each year, but looks forward to expanding its programs. In 2001 Chicago's Goodman Theatre, under the direction of Robert Falls, opened a new complex built with substantial assistance from the City of Chicago. Its main auditorium (with a proscenium stage) seats 856 people, and its second stage is an intimate, three-tiered arena accommodating 200 to 400 persons. It is one of the 150 members of the League of Chicago Theatres, among which some of the most prominent are Steppenwolf, Victory Gardens, and Second City. About two dozen of the theatres are permanent professional ensembles. In 2001 the Arena Stage in Washington, under the direction of Molly Smith, celebrated its fiftieth year and is planning a renovation that would double the size of its building. Anchored by the Kennedy Center, Arena Stage, and the Shakespeare Theatre (directed by Michael Kahn), the Washington area now has more than eighty professional theatres. Tina Packer and her Shakespeare and Company, in its twenty-third year in 2000, acquired a new home with twenty-two buildings on sixty-three acres in Lenox, Massachusetts, into which it expects to move over a period of five years. It also announced plans to build a replica of London's Rose Theatre of 1587. The California Institute of the Arts stated its intention of building a $20 million state-of-the-art experimental theatre in Los Angeles, meant to make its productions more visible. (They now are seen only in Valencia, a relatively small town considerably removed from Los Angeles). In 2000 the Denver Theatre Center produced *Tantalus,* a ten-and-one-half-hour production based on Greek myths, written by John Barton (of the Royal Shakespeare Company) and directed by Peter Hall. In New York, the not-for-profit Lincoln Center has announced a major overhaul, for which the City of New York pledged $240 million over ten years. (It should be recognized, however, that, in the aftermath of the attack on the World Trade Center

FIG. 24.17

Peter Hall's production of John Barton's ten-hour Trojan War epic *Tantalus* (2001), at the Denver Center of the Performing Arts. Greg Hicks (as Priam, black costume) with the Chorus. Photo by P. Switzer © 2001.

in New York, it is uncertain whether Lincoln Center's plans or any others mentioned at various places in this chapter, will be able to proceed.)

The large number of resident companies scattered throughout the United States offered opportunities for directors to work with many different theatres, most of which employ visiting directors for at least

FIG. 24.18

Wendy Wasserstein's *The Sisters Rosenweig*. The actors are Madeline Kahn, Jane Alexander, and Frances McDormand. Photo by Martha Swope © 1993.

some of their productions. Among these directors, Daniel Sullivan (1940–) is much in demand. After serving as director of the Seattle Repertory Company for 18 years, he became well known for directing plays that were developed through a series of regional theatre productions before they opened in New York. He directed most of Wendy Wasserstein's plays as well as *Dinner with Friends* by Donald Marguiles (the Pulitzer Prize winning play of 2000), *Proof* by David Auburn (the Pulitzer Prize winning play in 2001), and numerous important revivals including O'Neill's *Moon for the Misbegotten* and Shaw's *Major Barbara*.

Julie Taymor (1952–) became one of America's best-known directors with her production of *The Lion King,* for which she became the first woman to win a Tony Award for directing a musical in 1998. Building on an extremely varied background that included studying mime in Paris and living in Indonesia, she brings a wide range of theatre practice from various countries to her work, perhaps most notably the puppetry of Bali. Working with various companies in New York and elsewhere, Taymor won sufficient recognition that the MacArthur Foundation rewarded her with a "genius" award in 1991. In New York she directed several of Shakespeare's plays, including *The Tempest* and *Titus Andronicus* (later made into a film) for the Theatre for a New Audience, and in resident companies she designed costumes and

FIG. 24.19

Julie Taymor's production of *Green Bird* on Broadway (2000). Photo by Joan Marcus © 2000.

masks for several productions, perhaps most notably for Andrei Serban's *King Stag* at the American Repertory Theatre. She was highly praised for *Juan Darién* (the dramatization of a Uruguayan story) at Lincoln Center, but her major triumph came with the production of *The Lion King* on Broadway (which she directed and for which she designed costumes and masks) for the Disney Corporation. In 2000 she directed and designed *The Green Bird* on Broadway, a production she had worked on elsewhere for many years. Her multiple talents have placed her in the forefront of American theatre artists.

Robert Wilson continued to be one of America's best-known directors, even though most of his work was done in Europe. After 1990, he averaged eight to twelve premieres throughout the world each year at almost every major festival and opera house in Europe. Many of these productions were of well-known works, such as Büchner's *Danton's Death* in Houston in 1993, Bela Bartók's *Bluebeard's Castle* (1995), Strindberg's *A Dream Play* at Stockholm's Stadsteater in 1998, and Brecht's *Flight over the Ocean* at the Berliner Ensemble in 1998 in honor of the hundredth anniversary of Brecht's birth. Some of his original works after 1990 include *Alice* (1992) an adaptation of *Alice in Wonderland,* with Tom Waits and Paul Schmidt, and *Time Rocker* (1996), a collaboration with Darryl Pinckney and Lou Reed based on H. G. Wells's *Time Machine.* He often works with Philip Glass, as in *White Raven,* performed at the Lincoln Center Festival in 2001. Wilson has established a school called the Watermill Center on Long Island, where he develops many of his productions. Currently it is open only in the summer, but the finished center will operate year round, will serve as a site for international conferences, and will house Wilson's archives.

Anne Bogart (1951–) is one of America's most controversial directors. She sometimes surrounds a script with a "play within a play" framework that forces audiences to see the play in a new light, as in *South Pacific,* which she set in a clinic for emotionally disturbed war veterans. For a time, she created plays that examined American entertainment forms, as in *American Vaudeville* (1993) and *Marathon Dancing* (1994). She directed frequently for the American Repertory Theatre and for one season was director of the Trinity Repertory Theatre in Providence, but her approach proved incompatible with that company. In 1993 she co-founded with Tadashi Suzuki, the Japanese director and acting theorist, the Saratoga International Theatre Institute (SITI), where acting workshops and symposia are held, and where Bogart develops productions in collaboration with her students. Whenever she directs at other theatres, she insists that at least some members of her SITI company be employed, since they are familiar with her working methods. She has directed several of Charles L. Mee's and Naomi Iizuka's plays.

Bogart is also noted for her rejection of the Stanislavsky system of actor training in favor of Viewpoints, many of whose features are adapted from postmodern dance and focus on formal elements such as movement and space. Instead of emphasizing one method, Viewpoints seeks to create new theatrical languages by borrowing from a variety of sources. It favors "sampling"—juggling many dramatic techniques and combining them with almost any aspect of contemporary culture. Bogart has argued that since we live in a fragmented world, acting itself needs to be fragmented.

The 1990s saw a rapid expansion of experimentation with computer technologies and the ways in which they can be used to enhance live performance. George Coates' Performance Works in San Francisco was in the forefront of this experimentation with productions such as *Desert Music* (1992), *Box Conspiracy* (1993), *Nowhere NowHere* (1994), *Wittgenstein on Mars* (1998), and *Crazy Wisdom* (2001). In all of these, computer-generated images interacted with live actors on stage. The expense of such work has forced Performance Works to limit its experimentation, but several university theatres have continued to work along these lines. Computer controls have long since changed the way lights, sound, and sets are designed in the theatre, but more recent innovations have focused on the ways in which computer sensors and motion detectors can allow actors to interact with set pieces, props, lights, sound, computer-generated images, and real-time animations. Productions have also made use of the Internet to allow actors on different continents to perform in the same play at the same time. In such productions the audience sees live actors interacting with video projections of actors from other locations, all performing their roles as if they were on the same stage. Complete plays have been produced on the World Wide Web using a wide variety of approaches, and the proliferation of Webcam monitoring of public spaces has inspired a new form of guerilla theatre in which actors produce short plays in view of these cameras after notifying potential audience members to watch for their performance on the relevant World Wide Web site. Just as the introduction of film at the turn of the twentieth century caused artists to undertake a reevaluation of what makes theatre a distinctive art form, computer technology has encouraged a similar reevaluation at the turn of the twenty-first.

After 1990, one of the most controversial issues involved subsidization of the arts, which since the 1960s had played a major role in the impressive increase in theatres throughout the United States. The issues that arose at the end of the 1980s centered around the National Endowment for the Arts (NEA) and the appropriateness of the government's subsidizing any of the arts, especially if standards of decency were not adopted and enforced. Although it had always had powerful opponents, the NEA had also commanded considerable support and had received small annual increases in appropriations through 1992, when federal budgetary support reached its high point of $175.9 million, about 70 cents per capita. Toleration for the NEA both inside and outside of Congress began to erode in 1990, however, when four performance artists, all noted for works that openly and frankly treated sex, gender, and power, were awarded NEA grants in a category reserved for individual artists. An intense and ongoing controversy followed over whether the government should be allowed to spend citizens' tax dollars to subsidize art considered by many to be indecent and counter to community standards. A law designed to ensure that grants would not be approved if they did not take into account "general

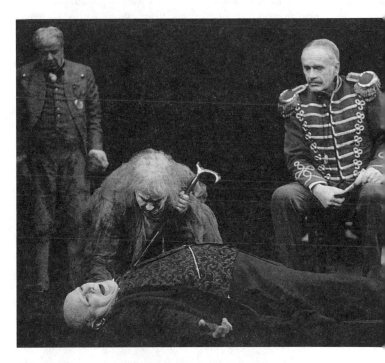

FIG. 24.20

Ghost Sonata by August Strindberg, directed by Ingmar Bergmann (1918–). Since the 1950s Bergman has been one of Sweden's most highly acclaimed stage directors. He was better known in Europe as a filmmaker than a stage director until his tax exile in Germany from 1976 to 1985, when he did a series of notable productions. He is now especially admired as an interpreter of Strindberg's plays. Photo of the New York tour by Stephanie Berger © 2001.

standards of decency and respect for the diverse beliefs and values of the American public" was passed into law by Congress in 1990. This provision was challenged in court but eventually was upheld (in 1998) by the Supreme Court. The Court left unsettled the issue of who was to define what constituted "general standards of decency" or who was to decide when these had been violated. The grants to the four artists were retracted, and it was decided that in the future grants would not be made to individual artists. Con-

gressional controversy over the NEA continued, and its budget was reduced substantially, reaching only about $98 million in 2000. Although many expect that the NEA's budget will increase, the future of the agency and the amount of government support it can expect remain uncertain. Some of the retrenchment was offset by state, municipal, foundation, and corporate financial support, but the combined support remains slight in comparison with that given the arts in many European countries.

LOOKING AT THEATRE HISTORY

Contemporary practitioners have sought in various ways to sharpen the audience's perceptions about both the theatre and the world in which we live. Some have offered ironic critiques of social, religious, and political institutions. Others have sought to reach us by drawing on theatrical traditions from other cultures. Still others have forced us to see, as if new, plays that had become so familiar that we no longer were moved by them. Some have sought to forge a new theatre by imaginative integration of existing forms with new technology. These and other practices are indications of the vitality of the theatre that challenges us to consider both the accomplishments of the present and the potential of the future.

Long one of Italy's favorite playwrights, Dario Fo's reputation was solidified after 1997 when he won the Nobel Prize for Literature. He is said to be the most frequently translated living writer, his plays having been performed in thirty languages. The Vatican pronounced one version of Fo's *Mistero Buffo* (it is altered each time it is performed) "the most basphemous show in the history of television." About his work, Fo has said:

I have tried to make it clear to young people that a writer should be linked to his times and that the writer who is linked to his times should put his hands into the awful things of life. You have to plunge into the muck. . . . There is no such thing as living comedy unless it has its roots in things that are tragic.

Dario Fo, comments at Barnard College, September 2000.

Ariane Mnouchkine is often said to be France's most accomplished director. Her productions, cre-

ated through work with a collective, take shape over several months. About the foundations of her work, Mnouchkine has said:

[Working with a collective] is very important. I always said that when I would not be able to do it anymore like that . . . I would stop. . . . I'm like a midwife. I help to give birth. . . . Our sources, our tools at Théâtre du Soleil are traditions. . . . Our inspiration comes from traditional theatres, real traditional theatres. . . . My love for Asia and for Asian theatre has determined much of my work. My theatrical parents are India, Japan, and China.

In Contact with the Gods? Directors Talk Theatre. Edited by Maria M. Delgado and Paul Heritage. Manchester: University of Manchester Press, 1996. From an interview conducted by Delgado in 1995.

Peter Brook believes that many audiences attend productions of classics with preconceived notions of what they will see based upon their knowledge of the play and past productions. To undermine this tendency, Brook has altered many well-known plays and operas, including *Carmen, Pelléas and Melisande,* and most recently *Hamlet* (retitled *The Tragedy of Hamlet*). Here is Brook's response to a suggestion that audiences are shocked by his cutting and rearrangement of Shakespeare's text.

I would say that is good news if it's a shock. That's part of the aim. The reason for doing Hamlet *is for people to receive it as a new experience. The first thing was to break the disastrous habit that exists with a play like* Hamlet*—the fact that people come to the play humming the tune, as they say on Broadway, before* *they enter the theatre. . . . The first thing I had to do was cut through the enormous superstructure of prejudices and do away with the various conceptions of* Hamlet. *If this production broke through expectations, that is already good news.*

Margaret Croyden, "A Certain Path; an Exclusive Conversation with Peter Brook," *American Theatre* (May/June 2001), p. 18.

The Canadian writer–actor–director Robert Lepage is in the forefront of those seeking to expand the theatre's ability to communicate on several levels. He calls *Zulu Time,* on which he began working in 1999, a techno-cabaret. About it, he has said:

We were wondering how to connect poetics and dramaturgical ideas and heartfelt emotions with the new tools we have around. Technology comes in with a new vocabulary, and we're still stuttering, trying to figure out exactly how to use it.

[In Zulu Time] We're working with letters of the alphabet, so the show has 26 scenes. Each letter refers to the international radio transmission code that aviators use. . . . Zulu Time is the military's universal clock. . . . The show reflects this idea, that the notion of time and space have been unified.

From an interview with Robert Lepage by Don Shewey. *The New York Times,* September 16, 2001.

25
The Theatre of Africa

Because Africa had little performance that resembled the theatrical forms they knew, Europeans, when they began to colonize Africa, were convinced that it was devoid of theatre. Nevertheless, the continent was teeming with performance activities—ceremonies, festivals, religious rites, storytelling, and various kinds of celebrations, all interwoven into the daily life of the various African cultures. The Europeans brought with them their own form of theatre and sought to naturalize it throughout much of the continent. The tension between this colonialist heritage and indigeneous forms has created a vigorous and dynamic spectrum of performance in contemporary Africa, only a small portion of which can be treated here.

SOME BASIC ISSUES AND PROBLEMS

Two of the basic and intertwined problems of theatre in Africa (and of writing about it) are language and colonialist influence. More than 800 local languages are spoken on the continent, and while this clearly makes for immediacy of communication and performance on the local level, it can limit cross-communication and accurate perception of performance and theatre beyond its own language-specific area. Most of these languages had no written form

when colonialism began in earnest—after a congress of European leaders in 1884–1885 agreed on spheres of influence in Africa. By around 1900 Europeans had divided among themselves the whole of the African continent, with the exception of Liberia and Ethiopia, and colonial rule continued in most areas until around 1960.

When it established control, each colonial power, faced with multiple language and ethnic groups within a single administrative territory, made its own European language the official language of that territory. (Most of the internecine conflicts in Africa today are attributable to the geographic divisions, made by Europeans and preserved when independence came, that place rival tribal groups within the same country.) Schools were established; at the lower levels, teaching was often conducted in the local language, which had been converted into written form, often first by missionaries who wished to translate the Bible for local use. Both the missionaries and the colonial authorities discouraged local religions and indigenous performances, which were perceived as barbaric or as potentially subversive. Nevertheless, both religious practices and performances continued, though often in disguised forms, sometimes even incorporating colonial officials as characters into performances. At the upper levels, education was most commonly conducted in a European language, in part

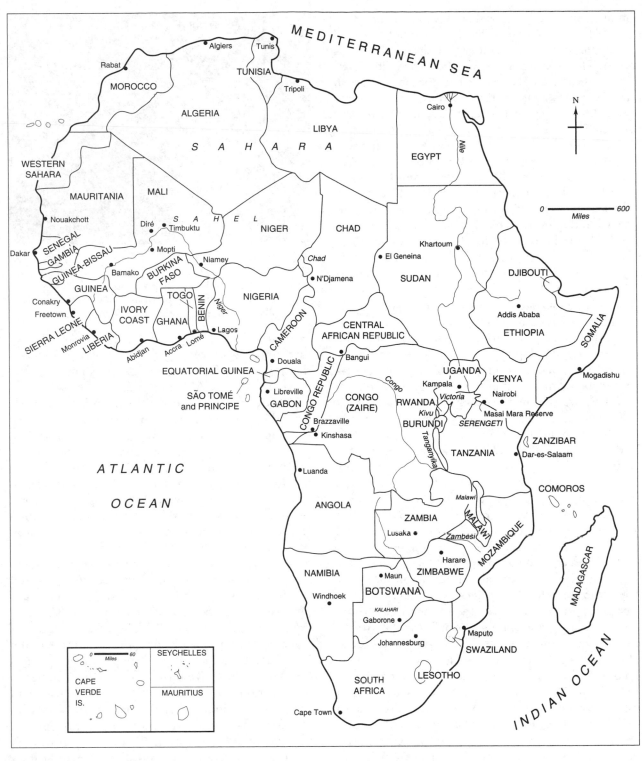

FIG. 25.1
Map of Africa today.

to create a supply of lower-level bureaucrats and clerks, but also because colonial authorities considered local languages useful only for the most elementary purposes. These upper schools taught a largely European curriculum, including the classics of European drama, and sometimes encouraged performances of the plays on proscenium-arch stages, which were built as part of many schools.

The most common languages were French and English, and in many areas one of these was the only language that local groups shared, although it is questionable how many of those who had not attended the upper schools (the majority) understood the language. Those Africans who aspired to be writers usually chose the language of their colonial rulers, in large part because it was the only way to reach a large audience, since local-language audiences were very limited. Because large areas of Africa were dominated either by the English or the French, writing in those languages promised not only a potentially large African audience but also an international one.

When African nations gained independence, they typically retained the colonial language and governmental and educational structures as means of coping with the problem of local languages and ethnic rivalries. Thus began what is often referred to as neocolonialism, for colonial power had in many instances merely been exchanged for native versions of it. Only Tanzania has adopted an African language, Swahili, as its official language, although in many other countries African languages have semi-official status, and the pressure to adopt African languages for official purposes is growing. (Ethiopia, which was never colonized, uses Amharic as its official language, and most North African countries recognize Arabic as their official language.)

The struggle for independence, which intensified following World War II, and the achievement of independence, for most countries around 1960, served as catalysts for dramatists and for performance. The output, both in European and local languages, increased markedly. Several African playwrights, writing in English or French, gained international reputations. Furthermore, several of the new nations constructed buildings on European lines (and usually named them the National Theatre). On the other hand, the use of local languages and indigenous performance modes also gained in popularity, often serving as a protest against colonialist and neocolonialist values and practices. Especially since about 1980, a struggle has intensified between the neocolonialists, often those who are in power and seek to maintain the status quo, and those who wish to establish an independent African identity and to overcome class distinctions. Many in the latter group encourage writing (or improvising) in African languages and using African performance traditions (including spatial arrangements); they also attack the power structures inherited from colonialism and those who use position for their own aggrandizement and acquisition of wealth without regard for the well-being of the people as a whole. In 2000 the first conference ever held in Africa on the problem of languages was convened in Eritrea under the title "Against All Odds: African Languages and Litera-

FIG. 25.2

A *Hira Gasy* performance in Madagascar showing colonialist influence. Courtesy N. Brian Winchester, Department of African Studies, Indiana University.

tures in the 21st Century." The delegates concluded that the use of African languages is essential for the decolonization of African minds.

Another problem in discussing African performance is the complexity of performance elements. In indigenous forms, words are often the least important element. Other "languages," especially those of drumming and dance, often communicate more to African audiences than words do. To these can be added visual imagery, symbolism, gesture, mask, and costume, all of which may convey specific meaning and resonance difficult to describe or explain. Even when words are included, they are often used in ways quite different than in Western drama. Frequently songs and anecdotes are incorporated or improvised that seemingly have little to do with narrative structure. Performances are seldom organized like traditional European drama, and they usually occur in spatial arrangements quite different from those of the European theatre. Audience behavior also differs from that in most Western theatres. Direct audience participation is expected. The dancing, music, and song have a communal character, and audiences respond by clapping in rhythm, singing refrains, repeating phrases, or making comments. Although written texts may include no directions indicating the use of dance and music, those elements are very frequently added in performance and provide another level of symbolic meaning. Perhaps most important, indigenous performance is so embedded in its specific culture that outsiders may be baffled by what is transparently clear to insiders. African ritual and performance are not rigidly fixed, for although the function of a ritual or ceremony may be constant, in its

FIG. 25.3
A traditional Tanzanian dance performed by the original National Dance Troupe (1963–1976). From the private collection of Louis A. Mbughuni. Courtesy Mr. Mbughuni.

execution there is almost always room for improvisation and adaptation. Consequently, indigenous performance is always in flux.

Storytelling, which may take many forms, is an important African performance mode. In part because when they arrived most African cultures had no written language, Europeans declared that Africa had no history. They failed to recognize that much of what Africans considered to be of historical importance was embodied and preserved in their performances. Especially important in several cultures was the *griot,* the storyteller and sometimes "living archive" of the society, who committed to memory and passed on to successors a record of the tribe. In other societies, storytellers were primarily entertainers, but almost every African society had some form of storytelling as a cultural tradition. Storytellers usually accompanied themselves on a musical instrument, such as the zither, lute, or harp-guitar, but might be accompanied by one or more musicians or singers. Storytellers told stories both as education and entertainment, in a tradition analogous to the Homeric epics of ancient Greece and the *scops'* tales of Teutonic Europe, both of which in oral form preceded written records of them. Storytelling remains a vital form and a major influence on much African drama, in which the storyteller often appears as narrator or as a character.

It seems especially ironic that Europeans should have thought Africa to be without a history since scientific opinion now holds that the human species probably originated in Africa. Many kingdoms existed in sub-Saharan Africa before the Europeans arrived, and in some, especially in what are present-day Ghana, Nigeria, Benin, and Mali, visual art of great beauty was created between 800 and 1500 C.E. and would eventually exert a major influence on twentieth-century sculpture and painting. Ruins of sizable cities have been uncovered in some parts of sub-Saharan Africa. Nevertheless, to Europeans Africa was barbaric and lacking in history because everything that did not fit their own cultural usages was discounted. Africa was denoted the "heart of darkness," and Europe's task was to bring it light. The supposed contrast between African barbarity and Christian enlightenment was even evoked to rationalize the slave trade, which between 1450 and 1865 brought as many as 10 million enslaved persons from West Africa to the Americas. There was as well an East African slave trade with other parts of Africa and with Arab countries. The attitude of African rulers who supplied the slaves was much like that of the Greek and Roman world—enemies captured in wars or raids became property to be owned or disposed of.

Colonial attitudes made it all too easy to think of Africa in monolithic terms, as many people still do. But Africa is quite diverse in geography, climate, language, and politics. It is also quite diverse in performance and theatre, only some of the most characteristic or significant aspects of which can be treated here.

NIGERIA

Nigeria is Africa's most populous and densely populated country. It includes some 250 different ethnic groups, the largest of which are the Hausa in the north, the Yoruba in the southwest, the Ibo in the southeast, and the Fulani in the north. The first Europeans, the Portuguese, arrived in 1472. The British began occupying Nigerian territory in 1861 and continued encroachment thereafter, but did not unify all of present-day Nigeria until 1914. Nigeria became fully independent in 1960.

Nigeria was the site of several kingdoms prior to the coming of the Europeans. One of these was centered around Ifa, a sacred Yoruba city, in the thirteenth century, and another in Benin in the fifteenth century. Both produced ceremonial art objects that are now valued internationally. Since public performance was the usual medium of expression and communication in indigenous Nigerian cultures, one kind or another of performance went on throughout the year's cycle. One of the major Yoruba festivals was (and is) the *egungen,* which can be traced back at least to the fourteenth century, when it was already fully established. *Egungen* refers to ancestors and establishes a spiritual link between the living and the dead, the present and the past. The festival was performed annually at the beginning of the planting season. On the night before the festival, in an all-night ceremony, sacrifices were offered and petitions for blessing and prosperity were addressed to the dead in the sacred *egungen* grove. On the day of the festival, the masked and costumed *egungen,* along with priests and other members of the cult, emerged from the sacred grove dancing to the accompaniment of drummers and made their way toward the house of the chief. The masqueraders continued until a "carrier" appeared whose function it was to gather up the accumulated evil of the community and carry it away in a canoe. *Egungen* masqueraders may also dance at funerals and on other occasions. Joel Adedeji has traced the development of Alarinjo theatre out of *egungen* masquerades in the seventeenth century. This kind of theatre, with its masked actors, was performed at the court of the Oyo Yoruba kingdom, and a guild system developed around it to make sure that the secrets and skills of the art did not pass to others. There were separate guilds for musicians, carvers of masks, and actors. During the first part of the nineteenth century, internecine warfare led to the breakup of the kingdom and the guilds, and thereafter performances passed to professional traveling companies. The performances of the traveling groups took the form of a variety show, mainly improvised and therefore capable of endless change. They also depended much on audience participation. Some remnants of this form survive to the present day, especially in Yoruba opera. The influence of *egungen,* as well as numerous other masquerades, festivals, and ceremonies from various areas of Nigeria, is significant on other contemporary theatrical forms as well.

FIG. 25.4
Masked dancers at an Owuru Festival in Nigeria. Originally seven performers were used in the dance, but the number has dwindled to two. Photo courtesy Phil Peek.

Another influence is storytelling. The Ijo of southern Nigeria, for example, had sagas that required several days to complete. This storytelling was usually accompanied by musicians, and the audience was expected to participate by repeating phrases or joining in "call and response." Other traditional forms include dance theatre and puppetry.

In the late nineteenth and early twentieth centuries much of the entertainment presented for colonial audiences was patterned after English music halls. Christian churches presented dramatized Bible stories and religious plays. It was partially from these that the most popular contemporary theatrical form, Yoruba opera (now usually called Yoruba traveling theatre), emerged, although Alarinjo was also an influence. Yoruba opera was first developed by Hubert Ogunde (1916–1990), who had participated in *egungen* masquerades and an Alarinjo-type company. He wrote his first piece, *The Garden of Eden and the Throne of God,* in 1944, and staged it to benefit his church. In 1945, his *Strike and Hunger,* concerning the plight of workers, turned to more political concerns, and in 1946 he established a professional company (the first in modern Nigeria) with which he toured thereafter wherever there were concentrations of Yoruba-speaking populations, even outside of Nigeria. By 1947, the form of his work had taken shape: an opening glee (or rousing musical number), followed by a topical and satirical story with dialogue, songs, and dances, ending with another glee. Although the emphasis was upon entertainment, there was always a clear moral message. After independence, Ogunde sought through such plays as *Yoruba Awake* (1964) to encourage national unity. Between 1944 and 1972, Ogunde created and performed some thirty-eight different operas. Many of his anticolonial pieces were censored or forbidden and at one time he was imprisoned. Ogunde worked hard to remain in touch with popular feelings and grievances, and his plays always concerned problems or issues of current interest. His company was tremendously popular. In the 1980s, Ogunde further enhanced his status by making and appearing in films.

So many others came to emulate Ogunde that by 1981 there were some 120 companies with about 3,600 full-time employees. To serve their needs, Ogunde founded the Association of Theatre Practitioners of Nigeria.

Another important figure in Yoruba opera was Duro Ladipo (1931–1978), who found his inspiration in Yoruba oral tradition, music, myth, and masquerade, perhaps influenced by Alarinjo theatre. Unlike most Yoruba opera companies, Ladipo used traditional Yoruba musical forms and instruments. His first opera, *The Ghost Catcher* (1962), opened his Mbari-Mbayo Center, which he founded to train performers and visual artists. His most famous opera, *The King Did Not Hang* (1964), concerning the Yoruba god of lightning, was performed with great success on international tours by the Duro Ladipo Theatre. Overall, his operas are usually considered to be literarily superior to those of his contemporaries, and in 1969 *The King Did Not Hang* became the first Yoruba opera to be published. Ladipo was also an accomplished musician and visual artist. In addition to operas, Ladipo also wrote *Eda,* an adaptation of *Everyman.*

Another popular Yoruba company, the Alawada Theatre, was headed by Moses Alaiya Adejumo (1936–), who performed under the name Baba Sala. Adejumo was the most popular comic actor in Nigeria, and he eventually extended his activities into the ownership of hotels, production of records and magazines, and the management of musical groups, as well as appearing on television and making films. By 1990, he had virtually abandoned live performance. He founded his theatre in 1963 and performed throughout Nigeria and coastal West Africa. His plays were improvised satirical comedies centering on the figure of Baba Sala, an ingenious poor man who exposed, accidentally or on purpose, those seeking to prosper through dishonest means.

Yoruba traveling theatre has proven to be a very adaptable form. It may use traditional music, dance, and myth, or it may incorporate the latest styles in music and comment on the latest fads in behavior. It may use a variety of playing spaces, most of them simple so they can be prepared quickly. The costumes are colorful. The language is Yoruba (and sometimes pidgin English) and is mostly sung; there is constant musical accompaniment, either of drumming or various instruments or of singing. The songs are rehearsed but the dialogue is mostly improvised. There is always strong interaction with the audience. Since the 1980s, Yoruba opera has increasingly appeared on television and in films and videos, so much so that live performance is seriously threatened except within universities.

English-language plays also came to play a significant role in Nigeria's theatrical life. The Glover Memorial Hall, which served the needs of Europeans and certain black elite clubs, opened in Lagos in 1899. Such theatres were intended to promote European culture. In 1904, D. A Oloyede's *King Elejigbo and Princess Abeje of Kotangora* was the first play written by a Nigerian to be presented there (under the auspices of a church-sponsored drama group). Church and government schools usually had assembly halls with raised stages and proscenium arches, and Nigerian students who attended those schools

FIG. 25.5

Wole Soyinka's *The Beatification of Area Boy* as performed at the West Yorkshire Playhouse, Leeds, England, in 1995. Photo by Eckhard Breitinger. Courtesy Mr. Breitinger.

were taught that this was the appropriate arrangement for theatrical presentations. School productions of plays by such authors as Shakespeare and Molière were encouraged. After World War II, the British Broadcasting Corporation also beamed European radio dramas into Nigeria. This was how most of Nigeria's future playwrights were educated. Thus, English-language playwriting, which began to flourish around the time of independence in 1960, reflected a tension between European and indigenous forms.

The best-known Nigerian playwright is Wole Soyinka (1934–), son of an Anglican priest but familiar with the *egungen* masquerades and other traditional performance. He attended university in both Nigeria and England, and then worked at London's Royal Court Theatre in 1959–1960 when that company was at its peak as a promoter of new plays. He returned to Nigeria in 1960 and founded the 1960 Masks, a company that presented his first major play, *A Dance of the Forests* (1960), for the celebration of independence. It was also a warning about the future. In it, tribes assemble for a great feast and petition the gods for well-being, but instead the gods send two accusers who suggest that a dreadful future can be avoided only by sacrifice and self-knowledge, a frequent idea in Soyinka's plays. Soyinka also wrote light-hearted plays, among them *The Trials of Brother Jero* (1964), a satire on a religious huckster, and *The Lion and the Jewel* (1964), about a teacher who, in rebellion against tradition, refuses to pay a bride price for the woman he wishes to marry and loses her to the village chief—an obvious commentary on the tension between tradition and change. Other plays include *Kongi's Harvest* (1967), a satire on power seekers who lose sight of the people's need in their search for dominance; and *Madmen and Specialists* (1970), a bitter play written after Soyinka had been detained by government authorities for two years, showing the healer having been turned into a killer, although at the end his sister is taught another art of healing by the earth mothers. After his release from detention, Soyinka went into exile until 1976, during which time his *The Bacchae of Euripides* (1973) was presented at England's National Theatre, and during which he wrote *Death and the King's Horseman* (1975), concerning an episode in Nigeria's colonial past. After he returned to Nigeria, he produced his *Opera Wonyosi* (1977), an adaptation of Brecht's *Threepenny Opera,* treating an African tyrant and those who benefit from cooperating with him. *A Play of Giants* (1985) parodies some of Africa's worst modern tyrants, among them Idi Amin, Jean-Bedel Bokassa, Francisco Macias Nguema, and Joseph Mobutu, and attacks Western powers for sitting idly by.

In his plays, Soyinka draws on the symbolism, masks, and imagery of his Yoruba heritage. He also shows the potential for Yoruba traditions to recall the people to their responsibilities in the face of those who all too often are concerned only with power and wealth. Nevertheless, his plays are not propagandistic; his messages are fully integrated into the action. In 1986, Soyinka won the Nobel Prize for Literature, the first African to be so honored. Under the military rule of General Sani Abacha after 1993, Soyinka was condemned as an enemy of the state but managed to escape from the country. In 1997 he was convicted in absentia of treason but continued his criticism of the military regime. His *Beatification of Area Boy* (1994) is a satire on life under Abacha seen through the vendors and homeless who pass their days in a Lagos square. After Abacha was removed as ruler, Soyinka returned to Nigeria in 1998. Since then he has written only one drama, *Document of*

Identity (1999), a play for radio. Soyinka now devotes most of his time to human rights.

John Pepper Clark-Bekederemo (1936–) won international recognition with plays that reflect Ijo life and folktales. His *Song of a Goat* (1964), first produced by Soyinka's company, tells the story of a man whose wife betrays him with his brother, whom he kills. He then walks into the sea; his wife subsequently dies in childbirth. A chorus creates an atmosphere resembling that of Greek tragedy. *Masquerade* (1964) has as its main character Tufa, the now grown-up son born at the

FIG. 25.6

A scene from John Pepper Clark-Bekederemo's *The Raft,* directed by Martin Banham, University of Leeds Workshop Theatre. Courtesy Mr. Banham; photo by Trevor Faulkner.

end of *Song of a Goat*. When his past is revealed, his father-in-law insists that his daughter leave Tufa, and when she refuses, he kills her; Tufa revenges her death before he himself is killed. *The Raft* (1964) shows four men adrift on a raft in the Niger delta, each of whom tells his own story. In *Ozidi* (1966) the title character, helped by the magic of his grandmother, avenges the death of his father and the humiliation of his brother. It is an encapsulation of a major Ijo saga. In one version of this saga a storyteller took all the roles, usually to musical accompaniment. In another version, it involved the entire community and used music, dance, and mime. The performance of the saga required several years to prepare and about seven full days to perform. It was long one of Nigeria's major traditional forms. Clark-Bekederemo, however, had great difficulty finding anyone who could still recall the saga in its entirety, but he transcribed what could be recalled and published it in 1977. During much of his playwriting career, Clark-Bekederemo was a professor of English at the University of Lagos. He resigned this position in the early 1980s and founded a professional theatre devoted to African plays in English. For this company he has written several pieces, among them *The Bikoroa Plays* (1981, a trilogy) and *The Wives' Revolt* (1985).

Ola Rotimi (1936–), after studying at Yale University, returned to Nigeria and founded the Ori Olokun Acting Company in 1968. Its first production was of Rotimi's *The Gods Are Not to Blame* (1968), an adaptation of Sophocles' *Oedipus Rex* into a Yoruba background. This remains one of Rotimi's best-known works. Rotimi later turned to Nigerian history in *Kurunmi* (1969), concerning the struggle for the Oyo crown of the Ijaiye people; a highly theatrical piece making extensive use of singers, musicians, dancers, and a chorus, its noble title character and his people are ultimately destroyed. *Ovonramwen Nogbasi* (1971) concerns the Oba of Benin who surrendered to the British in 1897. *If . . . : The Tragedy of the Ruled* (1979) concerns the collective protest of renters against their landlord (a politician); their protest fails and the young boy, who represents the promise of the future, dies during the police raid that evicts the renters. *Hopes of the Living Dead* (1988) uses leprosy as a metaphor for social and political problems which, despite their difficulties, can, it is implied, be addressed constructively. Like most other Nigerian playwrights, Rotimi has held academic appointments throughout most of his career. From 1991 to 1993 he headed a professional theatre company in Lagos.

Femi Osofisan (1946–) is the best known of a new generation of playwrights who have been critical of their predecessors for being too little concerned with issues of class and socioeconomic structures. These new writers have attracted a wide following among students and others who feel that Nigerian economic and power structures need to be revolutionized to make them more equitable for the masses. *No More the Wasted Breed* (1982) and *Another Raft* (1989) are direct critiques of plays by Soyinka and Clark-Bekederemo. Osofisan's best known play is *The Chattering and the Song* (1976) which concerns the underground Farmers Movement. In it, the rehearsal of a play, about a nineteenth century rebel, serves metaphorically as a rehearsal for revolution which promises equity and sharing. Others of his plays include *Once upon Four Robbers* (1980), which suggests that it is the Nigerian military who are the thieves; *Morountodun* (1982), in which actors and a director enact a play which combines elements of a Nigerian myth and a farmers' uprising; and *Yungba Yungba and the Dance Contest* (1993) with an all-female cast. Other playwrights in this vein include Wale Ogunyemi (1939–) with *Ijaye War* (1970) and *Langbodo* (1980); Zulu Sofola (1935–1995), one of the few published female Nigerian playwrights, with *The Sweet Trap*

FIG. 25.7
Femi Osofisan's *Nkrumah ni . . . Africa ni.* The scene shows Nkrumah celebrating his birthday in exile. Photo courtesy Eckhard Breitinger.

FIG. 25.8
A dramatization of Amos Tutuola's popular Nigerian novel, *The Palm Wine Drinkard*. Courtesy Department of African Studies, Indiana University.

(1977) and *Song of a Maiden* (1991); Bode Sowande (1948–) with *Tornadoes Full of Dreams* (1990) and *Monkey's Gold* (1993); and Ken Saro-Wiwa (1941–1995), with *The Transistor Radio,* but best known for a television series, *Basi and Company* (mid-1980s), and his execution on a trumped-up charge of treason for his political activism. Still other contemporary playwrights include Kole Omatoso, Olu Obafemi, Tess Onwueme, and Emeka Nwabueze.

Among the greatest influences on contemporary Nigerian theatre and performance are the government and the universities. Around 1970, after the end of a brutal civil war (a direct result of colonial inclusion of antagonistic ethnic groups within the same country), Nigeria became a federation of states, almost all of which established a state arts council, a university, and a television channel. By 1985 there were twenty-three universities, of which eight offered graduate training in theatre and performance. Several of these also supported theatre companies, many of which traveled with productions. All of the states gave support for preserving traditional performance, and several universities encouraged and documented traditional performance. Beginning in the 1980s, some established centers to promote theatre for development, which work with communities to develop plays and performance designed to raise consciousness about local problems or national issues and to seek solutions for them. Although financial support for all these endeavors declined somewhat in the 1980s with the downturn in the price of oil, one of Nigeria's major sources of wealth, the national commitment to theatre and performance remained firm. Its support is probably indicated best by the MUSON Center in Lagos, opened in 1994, that includes a conference hall, concert hall, music school, and theatre. An annual MUSON arts festival was initiated in 1997.

GHANA

Like other African countries, Ghana has many languages, the principal ones being Akan, Dagbani, Fanti, Ewe, Ga, Hausa, and Moshi. English is the official language. When the Portuguese visited Ghana, first around 1450, they found so much gold that thereafter it was referred to by Europeans as the Gold Coast. Later it figured prominently in the slave trade. In 1874, England made part of it a British colony and in 1901 extended control over the remainder. In 1957, when Britain granted the Gold Coast and British Togoland (previously a German protectorate) their independence, the two territories combined to create present-day Ghana; it was the first black African colony to become independent.

Also like other African countries, Ghana has a rich heritage of indigenous performance, especially dance-drama, storytelling, and ceremonies. Most of the traditional forms incorporate music, dancing, masks, and costumes, and some include short dramatic scenes. All of them are community based and emphasize the importance of community over individuality. Several, including the storytelling tradition of *Anansesem* (spider stories), have exerted considerable influence on contemporary drama.

One major type of theatre—the Concert Party—parallels Yoruba opera and may have influenced it. The Concert Party is sometimes traced from the work of Mr. Yalley, the headmaster of an elementary school who began in 1918 to give concerts (a mixture of jokes, singing, and dancing for which he wore various disguises, including minstrel makeup) for Empire Day celebrations. But it is Ishmael (Bob) Johnson, a pupil of Yalley's, who is credited with giving the Concert Party its distinctive form by intermingling elements from many sources, including Yalley's performances, American black vaudeville, silent films, and spider storytelling conventions. In 1930, Johnson created the first of his "trios," *The Two Bobs and Their Carolina Girl* (consisting of Johnson, J. "Bob" Ansah, and C. B. Hutton). As developed by Johnson, the Concert Party began with an opening section which included a musical number sung and danced by the trio; a ragtime song by one of the Bobs; and a joking duet between the two Bobs. This was followed by a comic play about one hour in length. The plays, parts of which were always improvised and always used music and dance, were sometimes given in English, sometimes in a local language, and sometimes in pidgin English. In addition to being entertaining, most

Concert Parties dealt with contemporary topics and sought to provoke their audiences to think about them. By 1960, when Johnson formed the Musicians' Union of Ghana, there were about twenty-eight trios but the number has declined in recent years. The Concert Party was the first fully professional theatre in Ghana. It was also a popular form in the neighboring Republic of Togo.

A more literary drama can be traced through Kobina Sekyi's *The Blinkards* (1915) and J. B. Danquah's (1895–1965) *The Third Woman* (1943), both of which dealt with the relationship between native and colonial influences. Written drama did not begin to flourish, however, until after independence in 1957.

Two of Ghana's major playwrights—Sutherland and Aidoo—were women. Efua Sutherland (1924–1996) was the most important figure in Ghanaian theatre after independence. Associated with President Nkrumah until his overthrow in 1966, she sought to create a theatre that would embody the social ideals of the state. She founded an open-air theater, the Ghana Drama Studio, in Accra in 1957, and helped to establish the School of Music and Drama at the University of Ghana in Lagon, where she encouraged research about traditional performance. She also sought to strengthen the storytelling tradition through the establishment of the *Kodzidan* (Story House) in Ekumfi-Atwia and by organizing its space to fit the storytelling tradition rather than using the colonialist proscenium-arch structure. She

FIG. 25.9

A joint performance by the National Dance Company of Ghana and Abibigromma (the Resident Theatre Company of the School of Performing Arts, University of Ghana, Legon) during a residency at the University of Texas. Both companies are now part of the National Theatre of Ghana. Photo by Robert Pandya. Courtesy Performing Arts Center, University of Texas at Austin.

helped to encourage children's theatre through some of her own plays, such as *Vulture! Vulture!* and *Tahinta*. She was also a major director.

Sutherland's best-known plays are *Edufa*, *Foriwa*, and *The Marriage of Anansewa*. In *Edufa* (1962), the title character seeks through divination and ceremonies to manipulate his wife into the death predicted for him by oracles. *Foriwa* (1962) concerns the attempt to bring change to a backward village in which the elders refuse to consider new ways. It illustrates the need for cooperation among rival groups and openness to ideas favored by Ghana's new rulers. *The Marriage of Anansewa* (1975) draws on the *Anansesem* spider tales tradition to create a structure that Sutherland called *Anansegoro*. It shows how Ananse schemes to get money by setting off a bidding war among four chiefs for the hand of his daughter. The storyteller is the most prominent feature, not only setting the scene but commenting on the action and directing audience attitudes. The actors not directly involved in a scene also serve as stage audience responding to the action with comments and responses, thereby forging a link with the real audience. There are also numerous musical numbers, and a property master who visibly resets the scenes. This is usually considered to be Sutherland's most important play.

Ama Ata Aidoo (1942–) is noted for two plays. *The Dilemma of a Ghost* (1964) concerns a man who returns from America with a black American wife, and the tensions this creates within the man's family, who have deep-rooted prejudices about slave ancestry. As the wife, unable to adjust, turns to drink, the husband isolates her. The play puts much of the blame on the man for failing to face and prepare his wife for his family's probable reactions, and ultimately it is his mother who must take charge. It includes a chorus, who expresses fear of outsiders, whispers rumors, and spreads gossip. It is noted for being told from a woman's point of view and for its concern with male-female relationships. *Anowa* (1970) is set in the nineteenth century and concerns the conflict that develops between husband and wife after the husband decides, over the wife's objections, to buy slaves. The husband becomes impotent, which the wife believes is connected with slave ownership. Eventually, both husband and wife commit suicide. Once again, Aidoo is concerned with the lack of positive male-female communication, and she uses a chorus in a way that reminds the audience that the implications of the action reach beyond the particular situation. Aidoo worked with Sutherland's Drama Studio and was later the Minister of Education. In recent years she has lived abroad.

Joe C. de Graft (1924–1978) was another of Ghana's major writers. His *Sons and Daughters* (1964) concerns a self-made African who seeks to force his youngest son and daughter to follow the path of their older siblings into professions other than art and dance, which the younger ones have chosen. A strong commentary on contemporary values and education, this play was very popular throughout English-speaking Africa. In *Through a Film Darkly* (1966), an educated young African man rejects his black fiancée to go away with a white English woman, only later to be rejected by her (she considers him merely an anthropological specimen). When he returns home, now bitterly antiwhite, he is confronted by his former fiancée who feels disgraced; she then commits suicide, as the young man subsequently does. This play, which treats both black-white relationships and the demand that newly educated Africans play roles in multiple cultures, was also popular throughout Africa. *Muntu* (1975), commissioned by the All Africa Council of Churches, uses mythology to comment on modern Africa and the dictatorial tendencies of governments.

Another influential playwright is Mohammed Ben-Abdallah (1944–). His early works include plays based on *Anansesem* stories, *Ananse and the Magic Drum* and *Ananse and the Rain God*. Among the best-known of his later plays are *The Trial of Mallam Ilya* (which makes extensive use of puppets) and *The Land of a Million Magicians* (1991), an adaptation of Brecht's *The Good Woman of Setzuan*. Ben-Abdallah has also played a major role in Ghanian theatre by holding a variety of government posts, including head of the National Commission on Culture. He also played a prominent role in the creation of the National Theatre and the construction of its modern building, along European lines, which includes facilities both for a professional dance company and a professional theatre company, Abibigromma, the only professional companies (other than Concert Parties) in Ghana.

Other Ghanaian playwrights include Kwesi Kay with *Maama* (1968) and *Laughter and Hubbub in the House* (1972), Asiedu Yirenkyi with *Kivuli* (1972) and *Blood and Tears* (1973), Martin Owusu with *The Mightier Sword* (1973) and *The Sudden Return* (1973), and Jacob Hevi with *Amavi* (1975). As in Nigeria, the theatre was greatly assisted in Ghana by universities and government programs. Although there is still little fully professional theatre in Ghana, aside from the Concert Party and the new national theatre, performance in its various guises is pervasive and dynamic. There has also been increasing emphasis upon festivals.

SIERRA LEONE

Sierra Leone became a British colony in 1896 and was granted its independence in 1961. Its population is composed of fourteen main groups. The Mende is the largest, with the Temne next in size. Creoles (descendants of returned enslaved Africans) make up only about 1 percent of the population, but their language, Krio, is the most widely spoken. English is the official language.

Storytelling is especially important among the Mende. There are two major types, historical and fictional. The historical, called *Ngawovei*, are spoken documents which preserve the past. They may be narrated, chanted, or sung, but are presented without any attempt at dramatization. The goal is historical fidelity. The fictional stories, *Domei*, are usually the creations of the storytellers, although they draw on an accumulated body of tales which each storyteller can borrow or alter. Storytelling is most popular in the time after the harvest season has ended. A performance usually takes place in the evening, and may last until well after midnight. Most storytellers are amateurs, but there are a few accomplished professionals who move from one village to another. Though the narrative may provide a framework, other elements tend to dominate. The storyteller may begin with a song, riddle, or joke that establishes the theme of the story. There are many digressions, some caused by voiced skepticism from the audience. The performance usually occurs in a large open space, typically a circle, and the narrator may move about so as to include all the audience. He also takes on the role of various characters. Songs are numerous and contribute to mood. Dance may also be used but is less important. Costume is usually minimal. The audience is fully involved. The musician and singing chorus are drawn from the audience, but any spectator is free to join in, and the audience almost always provides rhythmic hand-clapping. Sometimes the storyteller assigns roles to audience members. Consequently, the entire performance has the air of spontaneous improvisation.

The Temne believe that adulthood cannot be reached without going through the ritual and ceremony of initiation. These include performances combining singing, dancing, instrumental music, costuming, and makeup. Initiation is thought to induce a metamorphosis as a prerequisite to adulthood. There are separate initiation ceremonies for boys and girls, the entire process of which may extend up to one year. These and other rituals and ceremonies, in addition to their intrinsic value, constitute a repertory of performance symbolism and "language" frequently drawn on in contemporary theatre.

Freetown, the capital of Sierra Leone, has a number of small theatre groups, most associated with the University of Sierra Leone, the National Theatre League, or schools. Only a few writers of importance have emerged. Raymond Sarif Easmon (1913–) is probably the best known. His *Dear Parent and Ogre* (1965) is unusual in being set in the elite world of the ruling class, the members of which flaunt their wealth and power. The plot revolves around a politician, who is seeking to become prime minister, and his daughter who, against his wishes, wants to marry a musician. After many intrigues and shady dealings, everything works out satisfactorily for all. *The New Patriots* (1965) is set in the same milieu and includes some of the same characters, who are scrambling for power and illicit wealth. It involves complex love affairs and intrigues, but also makes a strong statement against corruption.

Thomas Decker campaigned for many years for a theatre using Krio, the language of some 60 percent of the population. His work came to fruition after the success of his translation of *Julius Caesar* in 1964 and subsequently *As You Like It*. Juliana John furthered the process by writing original works in Krio. This trend was accelerated through the work of Yulisa Amadu Maddy (1936–), one of Africa's most radical dramatists, concerned with exposing the hypocrisy of those in positions of power, especially when religion figures in the deceptions. An anthology of his plays, including *Alla Gbah, Obasai, Yon-kon, Life Everlasting,* and *Gbanda-Bendu,* was published in 1971. All deal with problems of the masses and demand social reform. Maddy left Sierra Leone to become Director of the Zambian National Dance Troupe and then spent a few years in Europe working as a director and writing novels. Upon returning to Sierra Leone, he produced *Big Berrin* (1976), which in Krio, the language of the play, means "big death." The title apparently refers to the living death of the urban poor as seen in their plight and thwarted dreams. A highly theatrical play with much stylized music (including a chorus) and mime, it suggests the ritual of a funeral. Maddy was subsequently imprisoned, illustrating the dilemma of the African dramatist who wishes to use the theatre in the cause of social reform, and has lived abroad since his release in the late 1970s.

Other playwrights include Dele Charley (d. 1994), author of some 25 plays; Juliana John (1938–) with *Nar Mami Born Am* (1968) and *E Day E Nor Do* (1969); one of the popularizers of the use of vernacular languages, Akmid Kabarr, author of some dozen plays, of which the most popular is *The Great Betrayal;* and John Kolosa Kargbo (d. 1994), author of ten plays, the best known of which is *Let Me Die Alone* (1979), about the tensions between a colonial power and a local ruler as well as about a woman who wishes to establish her right to rule.

Krio theatre is very popular, especially with urban audiences. Much of it is based in storytelling, mime, music, and dance, and depends especially on a narrator and chorus. Performances can be found in the streets, bars, and other public places. Most productions originate in Freetown, the capital, but many tour to other areas. In recent years, a devastating civil war has greatly reduced theeatrical activity.

KENYA

Kenya, located in East Africa, is quite different from the tropical West African countries. Much of it is dry, bush-covered plains, but there are fertile strips along the coast and in the southwestern part (where about 80 percent of the population lives). There are about forty indigenous groups, of which the Kikuyu, Kamba, Luhya, Luo, Kisii, Kalenjin, and Maasai are the most prominent. The British first arrived in 1887, and by 1903 the entire area was under British control. Britain urged Europeans to settle in Kenya, and many did, establishing large plantations, farms, or businesses. The goal was to create a European-style country. The refusal of the settler population to share or yield control explains why, unlike most of Britain's other colonies, independence was gained only after several years of terrorist activity and warfare by the Mau Mau. Independence was won in 1963. A large proportion of the settlers remained, and much of the wealth and power continued under their domination even after the government was in the hands of Africans. The official language of Kenya is Swahili, but English is used for many official proceedings.

Prior to independence, much of the theatre activity in Kenya was of the English community theatre type or was performed by English touring companies. In 1952, the colonial government established in Nairobi a national theatre, which primarily served the settler population and those Africans who had allied themselves with colonial power. After independence, it continued along the same lines, and not until 1968 was an African, Seth Adagala, named head of the theatre, although this did little to change the theatre's program. He established the National Theatre Drama School, which supplied the National Theatre with a trained company that performed in Nairobi and toured widely. After 1964, the Chemchemi Company, founded by Ezekial Mphahlele, a South African in exile, performing both in English and Swahili, also sought to provide a repertory aimed at a wide audience.

Only the schools and universities encouraged black students to participate in theatre. Under the colonial government, a Drama Festival brought schools together in competition with productions of set plays from the curriculum (at first, always European and judged by Europeans). As African plays began to be

FIG. 25.10

Scene from *Afadhali Mchawi (Better Than the Witch)*, a performance created and directed by Graham Hyslop in Nairobi, Kenya in 1964. From the private collection of Louis A. Mbughuni. Courtesy Mr. Mbughuni.

published after independence, they gradually began to be included in the festivals. The University of Nairobi also expanded its theatre and drama program beyond the European canon and performance modes. It encouraged explorations of indigenous forms and experiments in new modes of writing and performance. African plays from other countries were also studied and produced. These influences combined to provoke nationalistic concerns and to produce a number of Kenyan playwrights of importance.

The first full-length play by an East African, *The Black Hermit* (1962), was written by Ngugi wa Thiong'o (1938–). It deals with an educated African who must decide whether to return to his tribe or to follow other paths. *This Time Tomorrow* (1968), concerning the indifference of the rich for the poor (epitomized in the bulldozing, in the interest of tourism, of shanties built by the poor), sets the tone for much of Ngugi's subsequent work with its strong anticapitalist stance. *The Trial of Dedan Kimathi* (1975), written with the female playwright Micere Githae Mugo, is based on incidents which took place twenty years earlier. Kimathi, the leading rebel general, is the focus of this largely symbolic play, which through song, dance, and mime reviews the coming of the Europeans, slavery, colonialism, and struggle against oppression, along with the four trials of Kimathi. Though Kimathi is ultimately sentenced to death, the struggle is not over. At its premiere at the National Theatre for a predominantly working-class audience, the end of the performance was followed by a freedom song as the actors and audience (with the exception of whites and the military) danced out of the theatre into the streets. This production created considerable debate about the role of a national theatre.

In 1976 Ngugi reluctantly agreed to assist a local group in creating the Kamiriithu Community Educational and Culture Centre at Limuru as an integrated rural development program, using theatre to raise consciousness, stimulate thought, and provoke action. This project is significant in being the first Theatre for Development program that was initiated by a community rather than being imposed by university students or other outsiders. At Kamiriithu, the project was the conception of the community, and it was community members who persuaded Ngugi to join them. They built an open-air theatre entirely with volunteer labor. The first production was *I'll Marry When I Want* (1977), a collaborative effort between Ngugi wa Thiong'o, adult-educator Ngugi wa Mirii, and the local people. Performed in the Kikuyu language, it incorporated traditional ritual, song, and dance in a work essentially concerned with the betrayal of the masses by those Kenyans who had allied themselves with foreigners. The Kenyan government suppressed the play after seven weeks, detained Ngugi wa Thiong'o for a year, and fired Ngugi wa Mirii from his university appointment. After his release, Ngugi wa Thiong'o returned to work at the Centre, where in 1982 he was denied permission to perform his *Mother Sing to Me,* concerning resistance to colonial oppression by various Kenyan peoples (the play used multiple African languages and included some eighty songs from eight Kenyan ethnic groups). The government closed the Centre and razed the theatre. Nevertheless, the work of the Centre came to be seen throughout Africa as a model for a true people's theatre. Ngugi wa Thiong'o went into exile and, after working for a time in Zimbabwe, has taught at New York University. He also published *Decolonizing the Mind* (1986) and *Moving the Center* (1993), important critiques of colonialism and neocolonialism.

The Kamiriithu experience gave rise to a populist political (sometimes radical) theatre movement in Kenya. The Tamaduni Players in Nairobi, for example, developed their own plays about street life and performed *The Trial of Dedan Kimathi* in Swahili. Other theatres were founded in townships and working-class suburbs. In 1986 these groups held a four-day festival in Nairobi. Nevertheless, the government kept a close watch, using laws that required every theatre group to register and each script to be read and approved prior to production. The large gap between the privileged and the masses, which Ngugi had brought to consciousness, increasingly became the basis for theatrical works.

Other playwrights of importance include Micere Mugo (1942–), author of *The Illness of Ex-Chief Kiti* (1976) and co-author of *The Trial of Dedan Kimathi;* Kenneth Watene with *My Son for My Freedom* (1973),

The Broken Pot (1973), and *Dedan Kimathi* (1974); and Francis Imbuga (1947–) with *Betrayal in the City* (Kenya's entry in the Second World Festival of Arts and Culture held in Nigeria in 1976) and *Aminala* (1985), concerning a woman who refuses to be bound by cultural taboos without any of the predicted curses befalling her.

Kenyan theatre is still caught in a confrontation between the neocolonialist theatre favored by the government and theatre (often harassed by the government) which depicts the marginalization and repression of the common people. In the 1990s, a professional theatre began to emerge with the formation of such companies as Sarakasi Ltd. and the Miujiza Players that also demonstrated a greater concern for Kenyan issues.

UGANDA

Uganda followed much the same pattern as other areas of Africa that came under British domination. It has some fifty ethnic groups with their own languages, but the most important are Niolitic and Bantu. It became a British protectorate in the late nineteenth century and was granted independence in 1962. It uses English as its official language.

Uganda has a rich heritage of indigenous performance (ritual initiations, celebrations, storytelling, etc.) in which dance and music are essential for observing major community occasions and creating communal emotional experiences. Historically, Uganda's royal courts retained groups of musicians and dancers, and remnants of these still remain in traveling individuals and groups who are often invited to perform at weddings and other traditional celebrations. With the coming of Europeans, missionary and colonial schools sought to replace indigeneous with European forms. Interest in Western-style theatre increased during the twentieth century, especially as the desire for independence grew. After 1946, theatre was promoted by officially sponsored competitions among schools, youth, and adult groups.

In Uganda, Makerere University, long the only university in East Africa, played a major role. Its dramatic society mounted the first production of *The Black Hermit* by Ngugi wa Thiong'o in 1962. In 1971 the university developed a department of music, dance, and drama, which offered undergraduate and graduate programs, along with productions. After independence, the taste for theatre became nationwide, and both local and traveling companies proliferated. In 1965, Makerere University started its Free Traveling Theatre, and soon most theatre groups felt the need to tour. This attempt to take theatre to the people

was at least in part a rejection of elitist colonial theatre. A national theatre was built in 1959, and in 1963 it added a drama school. Nevertheless, most companies are amateur, although the Ugandan theatre has been fully Africanized. (Many socialist artists in Africa consider professional theatre to be a legacy of colonial capitalism best avoided.) During the repressive regimes of Obote and Amin between 1966 and 1978, many prominent theatre people were killed or exiled, but the theatre recovered rapidly after 1986 under Yoweri Museveni as semi-professional and amateur groups flourished. The best work was done in musical satire and dance drama (perhaps because it did not pose a language problem). One of the countries most devastated by AIDS, Uganda has made considerable use of theatre in its campaigns against it.

Uganda has produced some important playwrights, among them Serumaga, Ruganda, and Rugyendo. Robert Serumaga (1939–1982), after graduating from Trinity College, Dublin, and gaining some theatre experience in England, returned to Uganda in 1966 and founded the semi-professional Theatre Limited in 1968. This theatre later participated in international festivals in Manila, Belgrade, and elsewhere. Serumaga subsequently headed the Abafumi Players which, owing to political upheavals, later settled in Nairobi. Serumaga was concerned with finding a form for an authentic African theatre, and consequently in his

FIG. 25.11
Robert Serumaga's *Majangwa* as performed by the Pride Theatre, Kampala, Uganda. Photograph by Eckhard Breitinger. Courtesy Mr. Breitinger.

FIG. 25.12
A woman pleads for religious tolerance in Alex Mukulu's *The Wounds of Africa*. Photo by Eckhard Breitinger. Courtesy Mr. Breitinger.

plays he used music, song, imagery, and dance to enhance or replace words. One of his earliest works, *Renga Moi* (1972), which he toured widely, is focused around a chief who must defend his village and way of life. Serumaga extended his use of indigenous techniques in *A Play* (1967), *The Elephants* (1970), and *Majangwa* (1971), but later moved into dance drama. The best known of his plays is *The Elephants,* which concerns characters in an East African university who manipulate each other to maintain their own self-esteem; the play implies that they may be elephants on the outside but are no more than mice on the inside.

John Ruganda (1941–), unlike most of his contemporaries, wrote in the realistic mode. His major plays include *The Burdens* (1972), *Black Mamba and Covenant with Death* (1973), *Music without Tears* (1982), *Echoes of Silence* (1987), and *The Floods* (1988). *The Burdens,* which brought Ruganda to prominence, deals with a disgraced politician now living in poverty with his wife and children, and drowning his disappointment in drink and adultery; the wife seeks to help him recover his dignity and position, but his drive is gone and ultimately she is driven to kill him. *The Floods,* apparently commenting on the regime of Idi Amin, explores the psychology behind such brutality. Ruganda later taught at the University of Nairobi in Kenya.

Similarly, Mukotani Rugyendo worked outside of Uganda (as an editor in Tanzania). His plays, including *The Barbed Wire, The Contest,* and *And the Storm Gathers* (all published 1977), argue the need for a socialist African state. Of these, *The Barbed Wire* is typical in showing how a rich man tries to acquire the communal land of a peasant community for his

FIG. 25.13
A Theatre for Development AIDS play, *Mutabani,* played by Nthuuha Cramactors in Bundibuyo, Uganda. Photo by Eckhard Breitinger. Courtesy Mr. Breitinger.

FIG 25.14
Street theatre in Kampala, Uganda, 1994. Photo by Eckhard Breitinger. Courtesy Mr. Breitinger.

own gain. *The Contest* makes use of storytelling traditions in the contest for a wife between two heroes (one representing capitalism, the other socialism). The drummer is the master of ceremonies, and the audience is the final arbiter.

Other important theatrical figures include Wycliffe Kiyingi-Kagwe (1934–) who wrote *The One You Despise* (1963) and *Lozio, Cecilia's Husband* (1972) but who is most famous for his radio and television dramas; Cliff p'Chong Lubwa (1946–) with *The Last Safari* (1975) and *Kinsmen and Kinswomen* (1986); and Alex Mukulu, with *The Wounds of Africa* (1990) and *Thirty Years of Bananas* (1993), a popular musical with political overtones.

The theatre in Uganda has worked with the Royal Court Theatre in London since 1994 in seeking to develop new playwrights. Six Ugandan writers and directors have attended the International Residency program in London, and in 1996 a series of play development workshops led to a National Playwriting Network based at the National Theatre in Kampala. Its members meet throughout the year and at intervals present a festival of new plays. The most successful of the new writers is Charles Mulekwa, whose play *A Time of Fire* was produced by the Birmingham Repertory Company in 1999. He has also been commissioned to write a play for the Royal Court.

TANZANIA

Tanzania encompasses some 120 ethnic groups. It was a German protectorate from the late nineteenth century until after World War I, when it was ceded to the British. As Tanganyika, it achieved independence in 1961, and was united with Zanzibar (another British protectorate granted independence in 1963) in 1964 to become Tanzania. Its official language is Swahili.

As do other African countries, Tanzania has a rich heritage of traditional performance modes, including initiation rites, celebration dances related to such events as weddings, harvests, and other social events, storytelling, and recitations. Also as in other African countries, colonial powers sought to discourage these native expressions until the late 1940s. This change in policy led to the rapid proliferation of dance groups. Colonial schools introduced European-style theatre in the 1920s and in the late 1950s inaugurated competitions among the schools.

Many changes came with the Arusha Declaration in 1967, a blueprint for socialism which discouraged production of foreign plays and encouraged writing in Swahili. Almost all of Tanzania's major playwrights emerged after 1967. Most supported the call

FIG. 25.15
Scene from *Mafuta (Oil),* devised and performed by the Paukwa Theatre Group at the University of Dar es Salaam. Photo courtesy Paukwa Theatre Group.

to socialism, but after 1978 many also expressed disillusionment over corruption among the ruling elite. One of the most important of these playwrights was Ebrahim Hussein (1943–), whose plays include *Kinjeketile* (1970), *The One Who Got What She Deserved* (1970), *The Dock in the Village* (1976), and *Wedding* (1980). *Kenjeketile* is sometimes considered to be one of Africa's finest plays. It deals with the Maji Maji uprising in Tanganyika against German oppressors in 1904. Kenjekitile, seen as the agent of the god Hongo, heals the divisions among the Tanganyikans by convincing them that the holy water he anoints them with makes them invincible but, while this gives them united strength, it also makes them walk fearlessly into hails of German gunfire and so lose the battle their common effort might have won. The play raises consciousness about the necessity of united struggle against oppression as well as the need to act in accordance with reason.

Traditional dance changed after 1967 to accommodate the call of socialism. Its popularity gave rise to some thirty dance companies in the capital, Dar es Salaam. A new performance type, *Ngonjera,* was created after 1967, consisting of recitations of poetry enriched by the use of costumes, props, movement, and gesture. Performed especially at national festivals and on other official occasions, it became one of the most popular of theatrical forms, especially in the schools. Among the common people, the most popular form was *Vichekesho,* composed of improvised sketches, music, and dance. The universities involved themselves in trying to discover appropriate forms for Tanzanian theatre through study and experimentation with indigenous performance, as well as with contemporary domestic and foreign practices.

After the 1970s, concern for "theatre for development" became increasingly important in Tanzania. Workshops and long-term projects were conducted in villages by faculty connected with universities. Leading figures in this work were Penina Muhando Mlama (1948–) and Amandina Lihamba. Their theatre for development projects differed from those elsewhere in Africa in stressing the use of indigenous performance techniques rather than spoken drama. Mlama was also a playwright especially concerned with women's rights in such works as *My Respect* (1974), *I Divorce You* (1976), and *Mother the Main Pillar* (1982), but she largely abandoned writing her own plays when she began her theatre for development work. She has also been head of the Department of Art, Music, and Theatre at the University of Dar es Salaam.

Tanzanian dramatists have published many plays, but since they are written in Swahili and since few have been translated into European languages, they remain little known outside of Africa. These include Godwin Kaduma (1938–) with *Pledge* (1980) and Emmanuel Mbogo (1947–) with *The Dawn of Darkness* (1980) and *The Last Drop* (1985). Since 1990, the emphasis on theatre for development has continued, and increased emphasis has been placed on training teachers to produce theatre for children and youth. As a part of this program, an annual festival was created. The merging of African and European performance modes also became very common, especially under the leadership of the University of Dar es Salaam and the Bagamoyo College of Arts.

ZAMBIA AND ZIMBABWE

Zambia, which under the British was called Northern Rhodesia, gained its independence in 1964. It has six major language groups: Bemba, Nyanja, Lozi, Tonga, Lunda, and Kaonde, but there are also many others. English is the official language.

Like other African countries, Zambia has traditions of performance that stretch back into prehistory. These include dance, dance-drama, and rituals that deal with seasonal changes, initiations, funerals, puberty rites, accessions of rulers, games, storytelling, and victory celebrations. Many of these were adapted into works performed by the National Dance Troupe, established in 1965, and by the professional Zambia Dance Company, founded in 1969 with Yulisa Amadu Maddy as its director.

As elsewhere, colonizers imported European theatre. In Zambia, this type of theatre flourished especially in the 1950s, when the copper-mining companies, seeking to keep their European employees happy, built a number of well-equipped theatres that staged European plays. Eventually these theatres were linked through the Northern Rhodesia Drama Association (later Theatre Association of Zambia). Until independence, these theatres catered mostly to whites. Some interest in European-style theatre also developed among blacks, encouraged by the schools and leading in the 1950s to an annual drama festival. In 1963, a desire to promote African drama led to the formation of the Zambia Arts Trust, which toured productions both in English and in Zambian languages. It also organized theatre festivals.

The University of Zambia began to offer drama courses in 1969 and established the Chikwakwa Theatre in 1971. This open-air theatre was deliberately temporary in feeling, being refurbished each season. It aimed to approximate performance touring conditions under which a performance space had to be prepared at each stop. Not only did Chikwakwa develop plays, many drawing on indigenous forms, it also took them on tour to all parts of the country. The plays were rehearsed in English but performed in the language of the audience. Students and staff also went into communities and helped the people develop their own performance projects. One goal was to create the conditions for a new indigenous theatre. Chikwakwa became one of the greatest influences on the development of theatre in Zambia and spawned several imitators, which eventually were united in the Zambian Theatre Arts Association, with membership drawn from schools, colleges, and community theatres. It also held annual festivals. Other theatres were also influential. The Theatre Circle, founded by David Wallace, developed plays based on traditional storytelling. Community-based theatres in working-class areas also mushroomed in the 1980s, and one, the Kanyama Theatre, became Zambia's first full-time professional theatre, touring both in Zambia and Zimbabwe. Developmental theatre, as a means of helping the people recognize, analyze, and formulate courses of action, was also introduced. This form of theatre became so popular that it was given a special category for competition in the Zambian National Theatre Festival, and in 1991 a separate organization, the Zambia Popular Theatre Alliance, was formed to meet its needs. In 1994, the government created the National Arts Council to encourage the arts.

Zambia's best-known playwrights are Kasoma, Chifunyise, and Phiri. Kabwe Kasoma was especially interested in creating local audiences as a step in national development. Consequently, most of his plays deal with Zambian subjects. His best-known works are the *Black Mamba* trilogy (completed 1971), based on the ideas of Kenneth Kuanda, head of the Zambian government; the trilogy traces Zambia's struggle for freedom up to independence. The plays make considerable use of dance and song, and Kasoma requests in accompanying instructions that the language of the performance be modified to fit the particular audience. After their initial performance, the plays were forbidden. Others of Kasoma's plays include *The Long Arm of the Law, Fools Marry,* and *Katongo Chala.*

Stephen Chifunyise (1948–) was educated in the United States as well as in Zambia, and has held government posts related to the arts. His plays deal with the plight of the poor in rural areas, or the way the fight for a new society is undermined by neocolonial forces. *I Resign* shows an African submanager resisting the plan of the white manager to import machines that will replace black workers, leaving them destitute. In *The District Governor Goes to the Village,* the corruption of public officials is exposed. Chifunyise's plays are very popular both in Zambia and Zimbabwe.

Masautso Phiri (1945–) has been active in the theatre since 1963, and was the founder in 1975 of Tikwiza Theatre, out of whose experimental workshop came *Soweto: Flowers Will Grow* (1979). A collage of songs, poetry, music, testimonies, and history by prominent indigenous South African writers, it seeks to arouse intense emotion and raise consciousness about the evils of apartheid. The company toured extensively in Zambia. Others of Phiri's plays include *Things Fall Apart* (an adaptation of Chinua Achebe's novel) and *Nightfall.*

In Zimbabwe, the pattern is much like that in Zambia. The major language group is Shona; others include Ndebele, Tonga, Kalanga, and Venda. The official language is English. Like Zambia, Zimbabwe had a long tradition of indigenous performances, especially dance-dramas celebrating initiation rites, marriages, harvests, and many other occasions. The British sought to suppress these ceremonies by condemning them as witchcraft. As independence approached Zimbabwe, the white-settler minority, seeking to avoid having control turned over to blacks, seceded from Britain in 1965 and struggled to maintain white rule until forced to capitulate to black-majority rule in 1980. Until that time, theatre was largely segregated. The white settlers had established numerous theatre clubs which were linked in 1958 in the Association of Rhodesian Theatrical Societies with its annual festivals. Theatre for native Africans was relegated to churches, schools, and amateur clubs. During the 1970s, the struggle for liberation turned attention to indigenous forms. In the struggle to overthrow the white government, the freedom fighters used the *pungwe,* an all-night performance that incorporated songs, dances, poetry, and skits, as a means of mobilizing the people's support. After 1980, segregation as a policy was abandoned, and native African groups

began competing in the previously all-white annual National Theatre festival. Similarly, Zimbabwe's National Dance Company, founded in 1981, was devoted to the performance of indigenous dance.

In 1982 Ngugi wa Mirii and Kimani Gecau (who had been involved in the Kamiriithu project in Kenya) were employed by the Ministry of Education and Culture to develop a community-based theatre. As a beginning, they staged *The Trials of Dedan Kimathi* and toured it in English and Zimbabwian languages. In 1983 an international workshop on theatre for development was held in Zimbabwe under the auspices of UNESCO, and after that time considerable emphasis was placed on community-based theatre. Groups involved in development were linked through the Zimbabwe Association of Community Theatre, founded in 1987. By 1995, 200 groups belonged to this association. The University of Zimbabwe also began to play a larger role after 1984, when a drama program was introduced. In addition to training students, it took a leading role in the community-based theatre movement.

Zimbabwe has yet to produce playwrights of stature, although Stephen Chifunyise has served as Director of Arts and Crafts in the Ministry of Youth, Sport, and Culture, and his plays, among them *Jekesa* (1994) and *Strange Bedfellows* (1995), are frequently performed. Two playwrights that have made an impact are Thompson Tsodzo (1947–) with *The Storm* (1982) and *Changes* (1983), and Ben Sibenke (1945–) with *My Uncle Grey Bhonzo.* There are also a few women's companies, among them Just for Women and Glen Norah's Women's Theatre.

The most successful theatre in Zimbabwe is the Amakhosi Company, headed by Cont Mhalanga. Founded in 1982, when the group was essentially a karate club, it gained nationwide attention in 1985 when its *Here Comes the Man* won the award for the best production in the National Theatre Organization's Winterfestival. In the 1990s, it became a professional theatre and began to receive a subsidy. Its popularity led many other companies to imitate it. One such group, Township Artists, established in 1991, is typical of the booming community theatre movement.

ANGOLA, MOZAMBIQUE, GUINEA-BISSAU, SÃO TOMÉ AND PRINCIPE, AND CAPE VERDE

Portugal was the first European country to explore the Atlantic coast of Africa, beginning in the fifteenth century when it was searching for a sea route to India. Eventually it controlled five colonies: Angola,

Mozambique, Guinea-Bissau, São Tomé and Principe, and Cape Verde. In all, there were extensive indigenous rituals and performances, and in all the Portuguese sought to suppress them. The theatre brought by the Portuguese was used as a tool for promoting and imposing Catholicism. Little more was done to promote theatre. The Portuguese exercised strict censorship over all forms of communication, including theatrical activity, which remained minimal prior to the armed struggle for independence in the 1960s and the granting of independence to all five colonies in 1975. At that time, the literacy rate among the native populations was only about 10 percent. Thus, there was not a great market for literary drama. The most common fare was vaudeville-like programs intended purely for entertainment. From the 1960s onward, serious plays were used as mediums of propaganda by various contending factions.

A potentially important breakthrough came in 1971 when a young Portuguese director, Norberto Barroca, staged *The Engagement or the Dramatic Discourse about the Purchasing of a Bride* by Lindo Lhongo (1940–) in Mozambique. This drama, about tribal customs in transition, made considerable use of traditional music and dance; it played to packed houses in two separate theatres, one primarily for Europeans, the other for Africans. In Angola in 1972, Domingos Van-Dúnem (1925–), who had headed a short-lived theatre in the 1940s, staged *Christmas Play,* a musical piece, to racially mixed audiences. But in both countries the Portuguese clamped down on such performances through the remainder of their rule.

After independence, a few theatre groups were founded in Luanda (capital of Angola). In 1977, the theatre group Xilenga-Teatro began staging dramas based on the oral traditions of the Tchokwe people. Among the more notable productions of this time in Luanda was *Bombo's Chalk Circle* (1979), written under the influence of Brecht, by Henrique Guerra. In other theatres, there were a number of experiments with productions using puppets. In São Tomé and Principe, Guinea-Bissau, and Cape Verde, plays based on indigenous forms but with political themes were popular after independence. These were especially well developed in Cape Verde, where Francisco Fragoso (1940–) founded the Korda Kaoberdi ("Awaken, Cape Verde") theatre. There he collaborated with Kaoberdiano Dambará on folk musicals and social dramas.

These five colonies were depleted to a far greater degree than most English and French colonies. Unsettled conditions, especially in Angola, have not been conducive to theatrical development, although a foundation for more extended work was established in most of these former colonies beginning in the 1980s.

SENEGAL

During its precolonial history, Senegal was included within a number of successive African empires from the eighth century C.E. onward. Europeans began to establish stations there as early as the fifteenth century, and it eventually became a French colony. All of Senegal was under French rule by 1895, when it became the headquarters of the French West African Federation, which included several colonies. It gained full independence in 1960. Senegal has many language groups, of which the most important are the Wolof, Serer, Fulani, Tukuler, Diola, and Mandingo. French is the official language.

As with other colonial powers, the French sought to discourage indigenous performance and ritual, but with little success, since those performances were based in religious beliefs about the origin of the world, human relationships to the gods, and the necessity of maintaining continuity between the dead and the living.

Perhaps the greatest influence on the development of theatre in French was the William Ponty School, a teacher-training college established in Senegal in 1930 to educate teachers from all over French West Africa. Between 1933 and 1948, stories from the various cultural groups of West Africa were dramatized and presented as end-of-the-year projects. The spoken part, rather stiff and elementary, was in French, while the sung text was in an African language. The play was further filled out with African songs and dances. In making these dramatizations, the French never forgot their "civilizing" mission, for though African life, customs, and history were included in the plays, the perspective was French. Teachers were encouraged to perform the Ponty plays in their schools or to evolve their own plays according to the Ponty formula when they returned to their countries. Students were also encouraged to tour West African colonies with these plays during the holidays. In 1937 a troupe was sent by the school to the International Exhibition in Paris, where it performed two plays to considerable acclaim.

In 1948, the colonial school systems were overhauled and emphasis shifted from the Ponty school to the French Cultural Centers established in all the French African colonies. In these centers between 1951 and 1958, a drama competition was held each year, and the winning group in each colony was sent to a competition among colonies. Almost all of the plays produced in the French colonies during these years were first mounted for this contest. After independence, which came to most colonies around 1960, the former French colonies adopted a comparable scheme for their Youth Festivals, held annually or biannually. Each country was divided into regions, within which a competition was held, and the winning production was sent on to the national festival. Out of these festivals, some individual participants were selected for specialized theatrical training, often in France or some other European country.

The first theatre to be built in Dakar, the capital of Senegal, was opened in 1954. Perhaps the most successful play staged there was a dramatization of a work by Birago Diop, *Sarzan* (1955), based in the story-telling tradition. Following independence, Senegal in 1965 established the Daniel Sorano National Theatre. Its first director was Maurice Sonar Senghor (1927–), nephew of the Senagalese president. The Daniel Sorano Theatre also included a Theatre Arts Department charged with training theatrical personnel. In 1966, Senegal hosted the First Festival of Negro Arts (later called The World Festival of African Arts and Culture, FESTAC), and in 1969 it won first prize at the First Panafrican Cultural Festival held in Algiers. Productions from the Daniel Sorano Theatre also toured in France as well as in Africa and won prizes in Lagos (1977), Lyon (1979), and Carthage (1987 and 1995). Despite this record, state support for its national theatre drastically decreased during the 1980s, cutting in half the size of the company and leading to the closing of its training school for six years.

After independence, theatre training in all of French-speaking Africa was enhanced by the French government's ongoing interest in its former colonies. Partially out of the desire to ensure the continued importance of French language and culture in Africa, France, through its Ministry of Cooperation, sent companies to Africa to set a standard for performance. This program was supplemented by another under which France sent major practitioners to give workshops to enhance skills. In addition, it sponsored a few African directors each year to attend festivals at Avignon and elsewhere in France. Among the more far-reaching of its efforts, France after 1966 organized and sponsored through its state radio network an Inter-African Radio Theatre annual competition in playwriting open to all French-speaking Africans. Five prizes were awarded each year, the fifth being chosen by listeners. After 1978, a company from the author's country was commissioned to produce the grand prize-winning play and take it on tour to neighboring countries. Archival recordings of the plays were made and the five prize-winning plays each year were published.

In 1983, Senegalese television instituted its own annual drama competition open to plays presented on national television stations in Africa, but since ownership of television sets was still restricted, a far smaller audience was reached than through radio. All of these efforts helped to encourage and promote theatre in Africa, although they also served to support neocolonialism.

Despite all the efforts from various sources, Senegal produced few outstanding playwrights. Perhaps the best-known is Cheik Aliou Ndao (1933–). His first play, *Le Marabout,* was produced in 1961. He is best known for *The Exile of Albouri* (1968), the prize-winning play in Algiers in 1969. It concerns the first contacts between European powers and Senegalese rulers. Albouri, ruler of the Djoloff kingdom between 1875 and 1890, realizing that he cannot win, chooses to go into exile rather than live under foreign domination. It draws on the storytelling tradition by using the *griot* as a narrator and commentator. One of Ndao's goals was to rehabilitate African history which had been distorted under the French by teaching that the French had "pacified" a chaotic and violent territory, rather than conquering it. This French perspective was the one shown in the Ponty plays, which Ndao sought to counteract. Most of Ndao's other plays, which were very popular in Africa, deal with historical subjects concerning African conflicts with colonizers. They include *The Almany's Son* (1973), and *Blood for a Throne* (1983). The last of these is set in the 1860s, when Senegalese were being threatened by whites. Attempts to unite various groups end in fratricidal war. The role of the *griot* is important in the play as narrator, genealogist, moderator, and entertainer. Another well-known dramatist is Abdou Anta Ka (1931–), whose plays include *The Amazulus* (1972), one of several plays by African dramatists concerning Shaka and the Zulus of South Africa; and *Pinthioum Fann* (1972), about life in a Senegalese mental hospital. Other important writers include Thierno Bâ (1926–) with *Lat Dior or the Path of Honor* (1971); Mamadou Traoré Diop (1944–) with *The Native Land or Death* (1986); and Ibrahima Sall (1949–) with *The Republic* (1987).

It should also be noted that Senegal was the center in Africa of *négritude,* a concept set forth in the 1930s and promoted especially after 1945. Negritude involved a sense of the common inheritance and destiny of French-educated black intellectuals in Africa and the Caribbean. It advocated revolt against colonialist values, and glorified the African past and the beauty and harmony of traditional African society, which was seen as being founded on black emotion and intuition as opposed to white reason and logic.

Its main African exponent was L.-S. Senghor, the first president of Senegal. Its influence was considerable in several African countries.

THE IVORY COAST (CÔTE D'IVOIRE)

The Ivory Coast received its name in the late fifteenth century when the French began to trade there for ivory. It became a French colony in 1893 and gained its independence in 1960. Its people fall into four main groups—the Akan, the Kru, the Mandé, and the Voltaic—but these groups are made up of more than sixty smaller ones. Several kingdoms of importance, each with diverse performance and ritual modes, preceded the coming of Europeans.

The Ivory Coast shared in the establishment of European-style theatre in French primarily through its Ecole Primaire Superieure at Bingerville, which was closely linked with the William Ponty School in Senegal. In 1938, two Ponty graduates, Amon d'Aby (1913–) and Cioffi Gadeau (1915–), founded the Théâtre Indigène de la Côte d'Ivoire, the only independent troupe of this period. Between 1938 and 1946, they produced plays that had first been done at the Ponty school, as well as others in the same vein which they themselves wrote. In 1953, d'Aby and Gadeau, joined by another Ponty graduate, Bernard Dadié (1916–), founded the Cercle Culturel et Folklorique de la Côte d'Ivoire, whose productions placed first for two consecutive years in the competitions held by the French Cultural Centers of Africa. In 1956 and 1960, the Cercle performed in Paris at the Théâtre des Nations, where each time it won the award as the best indigenous troupe. It also toured within France. Other companies began to appear in the 1950s and 1960s, and the University of Abijdan, which was founded in the 1960s, also began to play a major role in the development of theatre. It was the only francophone university to develop a traveling theatre. A conference held at the university in 1970 initiated a debate over the relationship of traditional African modes to European theatre, as well as about what audience the theatre was reaching or ought to reach. Several experiments followed. Porquet Niangoran, attempting to break away from European models, sought to develop "griot" theatre using storytelling, music, song, mime, and dance. Among Niangoran's *griot* plays, *Soba or Great Africa* (1978) is perhaps the best known. Souleymane Koly based his Koteba Ensemble on the *koteba* performances of the Bambara peoples of Mali, which combine social comedy with mime, gesture, and dance forms based on the spiral pattern of the snail, which was thought to symbolize the whirl-

wind and divine thought. Koly's performances were essentially mimed dance, through which, with occasional additions of local languages, he sought to reflect the preoccupations of ordinary people. Sidi Bakaba (1949–) also drew on storytelling to create performances composed of a sequence of scenes evolved through collective creation and performed on a stage that broke with the proscenium arch; on separate levels, different kinds of scenes were played, while some performers were in the audience. These and other attempts were made to create a theatre better suited to African urban audiences.

The major dramatist of the Ivory Coast, and some say of French Africa, is Bernard Dadié, a graduate of the Ponty school, for whom he wrote his first plays. One of these, *Assémien Déhylé, King of the Sanwi,* was performed by the Ponty school in Paris in 1937. Dadié worked in Paris from 1936 to 1947, when he returned to the Ivory Coast and subsequently held a number of important government posts. After giving up writing plays for many years, he returned to that form in the 1960s. Among his plays, the best known is probably *Beatrice of the Congo* (1970), produced at the Avignon Festival in 1971. It spans almost three centuries, from 1415 to the death of Beatrice in 1706, and uses liberty and domination as its unifying theme. It is concerned essentially with the relationship between Europe (as seen in the Portuguese) and Africa (represented by the Congo). It focuses on the process of cultural, economic, and political domination. It also suggests parallels with postcolonial relationships. As the play progresses, its satire of Africans who attempt to imitate European customs, dress, and manners gradually gives way to the more serious story of the attempt of Beatrice, daughter of the King of the Congo, to make her people realize the mistakes of accepting white values. Eventually she is burned at the stake but her final cry suggests that the elemental forces of the continent will reassert themselves. *Monsieur Thôgô-gnini* (1967), or the opportunist, is a comedy set in 1840. It concerns a man who seeks to exploit for his own gain his relation with white traders. Ultimately, Dadié is concerned with how colonialism served as a force to divide Africans, and how its influence continues to do so. *The Voice in the Wind* (1970) concerns a poor man who believes that if he were in power he could institute rule based on justice and peace; when he magically comes to rule, he finds that he can only be the despotic head of a police state. Dadié also wrote a number of one-act plays.

Other Ivory Coast dramatists include d'Aby, Nokan, Koffi, and Zaourou. Amon d'Aby was the Ivory Coast's most prolific dramatist, writing first in the Ponty school mode and then serious plays about social customs with an eye to reform. His plays, among them *Kwao Adjoba* and *The Crown of Auctions*, have rapidly dated. Charles Zégoua Nokan (1936–) wrote left-wing political plays on historical subjects. *The Misfortunes of Tchakô* (1968) concerns the growing division between the masses and an elite ruling class, while *Abrah Pokou or a Great African Woman* (1970) concerns the migration of a group of Baoulés led by Queen Pokou around 1717 and the legend that grew up around this event (treated here from a Marxist perspective through storytelling devices). Rafaël Atta Koffi, whose best-known play is *The Golden Throne* (1968), set in precolonial times, depicts the king of Abron surrendering without a struggle his golden throne to one of his Ashanti vassals, only to be embroiled in war when his sister has a still finer throne made. Eventually the sister kills her brother and then commits suicide. The theme of the play concerns precolonial values relating to the defense of freedom and suggests lessons for today. Zadi Zaourou (1938–) is noted for his distinctive style based on an ancient tradition called *didiga,* which challenges the familiar world with the irrational so as to create a new awareness. Through the use of language, symbolism, rhythm, and music, Zaourou denounces political practices in such plays as *The Eye* (1974), *The Anthill* (1981), and *Secret of the Gods* (1984).

MALI AND CAMEROON

Mali is a large country partially in the Sahara, where the population is made up primarily of Taureg and Arabic nomadic herders. The central region is inhabited primarily by Peuls, while the major population, in the south, is composed of Bambara, Malinke, Sarakole, Songhai, Bozo, Bamana, and Dogon. Mali was the center of a series of empires in West Africa between the seventh and sixteenth centuries. Between the thirteenth and sixteenth centuries, the Mali empire was the greatest of all the African black empires. When France entered Mali around 1850, it encountered the greatest resistance anywhere in Africa. In 1895, Mali (known as Soudan) became a French colony. Independence was granted in 1960. It is a strongly socialist state. Its official language is French.

There are many indigenous performance traditions in Mali. One of these among the Bambara people is known as *koteba,* which combines a style of dance (based on the spiral shape of the snail which is considered symbolic of the whirlwind and divine thought) with mime, gesture, and social comedy. It involves a chorus of female singers enclosed by five circles of dancers and musicians. This form has been very influential on theatre both in Mali and elsewhere in West Africa. Puppetry was also highly developed in Mali and continues today with such groups as the Bamana Youth Theatre. The Bamana puppet performances, which are given twice a year, once before planting and again prior to harvest, are organized and executed by a youth association that includes all men from ages fourteen to forty and young unmarried women over the age of fourteen. The performers may construct their own puppets and masks or pay others to do so. They are always careful to retain some puppets from previous celebrations, preserving a balance between tradition and change. They compose their own songs and devise their own movement and dances, although the rhythm is controlled by the drummers or female singers. This activity is considered to be entertainment provided by the young, who will move on to more serious ceremonies when they become elders.

Many students from Mali attended the William Ponty school in Senegal during the 1930s and brought back to Mali a taste for historical plays which continued even after independence, giving the Mali theatre a strong nationalistic bias. Among these is Sory Konaké's (1922–) *The Great Destiny of Soundjata* (1971), a reworking of a popular epic using a *griot* to introduce and comment on the unfolding story, calling up characters to act out the scenes. The magical elements are restricted to the narrated portions. The story is presented as an illustration of the exemplary African virtues of selflessness, courage, and patriotism.

At the time of independence, there were approximately twenty theatre companies of various sorts in Mali. These were merged to form the Théâtre du Mali. The National Institute of the Arts, with a Theatre Arts department to train theatre personnel, was founded in 1964. It was headed by G. Diawara, who had been trained in Moscow and who had worked with the Berliner Ensemble. Diawara sought to draw on precolonial indigenous forms, especially *koteba* mime and dance, in shaping the Malian theatre. As one of Mali's leading playwrights, Diawara has also drawn on *koteba* in his *Moriba Yassa* ("goat's dance," 1983), in which the characters are such animals as Hyena, Deer, Goat, Crocodile, and Lion. It is made up of six tableaus filled with light-hearted repartee and many proverbs. Others of his plays, such as *Dawn of Sheep* (1975), are allegorical. Other Malian playwrights include Seydou Badian, whose *The Death of Chaka* (1975), based on a favorite subject with African playwrights—the Zulu king Shaka (who by the time of his death in 1828 ruled a kingdom of more than 200,000 square miles)—has been performed throughout French Africa. (Shaka served

FIG. 25.16
A worshipper of Dionysus in *The Bacchae Inspired by Euripides* as performed by La Troupe d'Ébène in Cameroon. Photo by Eckhard Breitinger. Courtesy Mr. Breitinger.

throughout Africa as a symbol of cultural validity, vitality, and value in the face of European treatment of Africa as backward and uncivilized. He also served as a symbol of a united African consciousness.) Other playwrights raised questions about traditional tribal customs. A. Kone, in *From Chair to Throne* (1975), treats the Bozo custom of strangling the king every seven years, and his *The Respect for the Dead* (1980) questions the custom of child sacrifice.

The Republic of Cameroon includes more than 250 different ethnic groups, the most important of which are Bamiléké, Fulani, Kirdi, Bassa, Pahouin, and Douala. Historians know little about its early history, but it is clear that people living there after the tenth century produced now-valued distinctive cast-bronze objects. The Portuguese arrived in the fifteenth century, and from 1884 until 1919 Cameroon was a German colony. After World War I, the territory was divided among the English and French. At the time of independence in 1961, a small part of Cameroon joined Nigeria, and the remainder was united as the Federated Republic of Cameroon. The official languages are French and English.

Neither the colonial nor the postcolonial governments did much to encourage theatre. Restrictions were many and censorship was severe between 1961 and 1982, when the country was governed by a dictator. The forms that prospered most were traditional dances. The Cameroon National Traditional Dance Ensemble (founded in 1963) was used to represent Cameroon throughout the world. Most theatre in Cameroon is amateur. The only government support has come through the drama department of Yaoundé University. The most important dramatist is Guillaume Oyônî-Mbia (1939–), who has taught at Yaoundé University and served as a government minister. He makes both French and English versions of his plays, which are among the most popular in Africa and which have also been performed in France and England. He uses comedy to treat conflicts—concerning marriage, education, social standing, etc.—in a time of societal change. His plays include *Three Suitors, One Husband* (1964), *Until Further Notice* (1970), *Our Daughter Must Not Marry* (1971), *His Excellency's Special Train* (1979), and *Le Boubier* (1989). He eventually abandoned playwriting and turned instead to short stories.

Werewere Liking (1950–), who now works in the Ivory Coast, developed a form of drama based on Bassa rituals. Her plays, which include *The Power of Um* (1979), *The Sleep of Injustice* (1980), and *The Rainbow Measles* (1987), must be seen in performance to be appreciated since the written text cannot convey the power added by imagery, music, dance, mime, and gesture. Liking insists that her plays are of therapeutic use to those who witness them; she wishes to draw the entire audience into the action, in order to make each person question his/her own existence and seek an explanation for what has gone wrong. For this to happen, spectators must allow themselves to be spellbound as in a mystical cult so they may cooperatively search for the origin of the evil that threatens unity.

Victor Eliame Musinga is one of Cameroon's major English-language playwrights. He also heads a very popular theatre company, the Musinga Drama Group, which has performed his more than twenty plays, which deal with characters in the lower ranks of society who seek, sometimes with the help of magic and spells, to reach their goals, often involving sex, marriage, wealth, or status. His plays include *Madame Magrano* (1968), *Colofanco* (1970), *The Trials of Ngowo* (1973), *The Tragedy of Mr. No-Balance* (1975), and *The Director* (1978). Another major Anglophone playwright is Bole Butake, who writes scathing plays on contemporary social life in Cameroon that draw large audiences. Among his works, some of the best are *Lake God* (1986), *And Palm*

Wine Will Flow (1990), and *Shoes and Four Men in Arms* (1995).

THE CONGO POPULAR REPUBLIC AND CONGO (ZAIRE)

The Congo Popular Republic lies immediately north of the Congo River. Its people belong to four main groups, the BaKongo, the Batéké, the M'Bochi, and the Sangha, although each of these has many subgroups. The area became a French colony in 1903 and achieved independence in 1960. French is the official language.

The theatre of this country has been limited. The Théâtre National Congolais was formed in 1965 and has since produced the plays of Congolese playwrights, who are among the best in French-speaking areas of Africa. They include Menga, Letembet-Ambily, U Tam'si, and Bemba. In *The Oracle* (1968), Guy Menga (1935–) humorously condemns arranged marriages and reveals a fetishist, who is involved in making such an arrangement, to be a fake. This play became a favorite with school groups and was frequently produced throughout French-speaking Africa. In *Koka-Mbala's Pot* (1968), Menga uses a fetishist's claim to have gathered all the tribal spirits of the Koko-Mbala people in a clay pot to question the traditional awe of spirits, which stands in the way of change. This play uses dance as added entertainment. Antoine Letembet-Ambily (1929–) is noted primarily for *Europe Indicted* (1969), an allegorical verse play in which Europe is put on trial before Humanity as judge, with Asia as the prosecutor and Oceania as the defense attorney. Tchicaya U Tam'si (1931–1988), a major African poet, also wrote plays, of which *The Zulu* (1977) is perhaps the best known. It has as its central figure Shaka, the Zulu leader, but unlike many other Shaka plays, it shows Shaka's tyrannical use of power, and issues a warning about dictatorial power in contemporary Africa. It was later produced in France. U Tam'si's other plays include *Vwene the Founder* (1977), and *The Glorious Destiny of Marsal Nnikon Nniku* (1979). Silvain Bemba (1934–1995) is usually considered to be the Congo's most important dramatist. His plays include *Hell Is Orfeo* (1970), *The Man Who Killed the Crocodile* (1972), *Black Tarantula and White Devil* (1976), and *A Rotten World for an Over-Honest Laundryman* (1979). The last of these plays uses the *griot* to provide a framework and to link scenes in this biting satire on corruption so prevalent that it seems to have infected the entire population except for the laundryman. In *The Man Who Killed the Crocodile,* the rich N'Gandou (whose name means crocodile) tyrannizes and exploits the whole district until a teacher rebels and turns the tables on him. At the end, the storyteller warns people to be wary, for new crocodiles can appear any day. In his plays, Bemba seeks to reconcile standard French with the language of everyday life.

Congo (formerly Zaire), which occupies territory south of the Congo River, is among Africa's largest countries, especially known for its tropical rain forests, copper mines, and industrial diamonds. More than 200 languages are spoken, with French as the official language. One of Africa's major empires, the Kingdom of the Kongo, flourished there during the fifteenth and sixteenth centuries, and was followed by other powerful states before it became the personal property of the King of Belgium in 1885. Following international protests about the brutal treatment of native populations, the area was made a Belgian colony in 1908, although this did little to prevent the repressive treatment of the African population. It achieved independence in 1960, but political upheaval, including the assassination of the prime minister, Patrice Lumumba (an event that has been the subject of many poems and plays both in Africa and elsewhere), kept the country in upheaval for many years before power was seized by General Joseph Mobutu Sese Seko. The name of the country was changed from Congo to Zaire in 1972. Mobutu maintained his power until 1997, when he was ousted by rebels under the leadership of Laurent Kabila. At that time the name of the country was changed once more to Congo.

The Belgians paid little attention to education or theatre until after World War II. Among colonial playwrights, the most successful was Albert Mongita (1916–1985), a very popular author of works on historical, traditional, and social themes, among them *Thanks to Stanley* (1954), concerning the British explorer H. M. Stanley, and *Ngomba* (1957), based on traditional stories and customs. Mongita was also associated with several theatre companies and organized popular theatre festivals and tours by foreign companies.

Following independence, a National Institute of the Arts, which provided professional training, was founded in 1967, as was a National Theatre. The universities also aided theatre, especially Lubumbashi University, which studied and recorded traditional performances and techniques. Its company, Catharsis, created some of its own plays. Theatre for development also flourished. In the 1990s, Wembo Ossako (1946–) was championing Augusto Boal's Theatre of the Oppressed through programs called *Love and Prejudice.*

Zaire produced a relatively large number of dramatists but few are known outside of the country. Under

Mobutu it was unsafe to write overtly political plays, since censorship or detainment was a constant threat. Writers sometimes chose non-Zairean subjects, especially South African, to voice indirect comment, as in *They Are Crying in Soweto* (1978) by N. Musangi. Traditional performances still thrive and are frequently being amalgamated with spoken drama, but unsettled conditions in the Congo during the past several years have left the theatre in an uncertain state.

SOUTH AFRICA

The Republic of South Africa occupies the southern tip of Africa. Most of the population is concentrated in the eastern half, which has fertile farmland, whereas the western half is primarily grassland or desert. The indigenous peoples were Khoisans, Zulus, Basutos, Xhosas, Swazi, Ndebele, Pondos, and other smaller groups. (Several of these are often grouped together as Bantus.)

The history of theatre in South Africa is bound up in the complexities of its colonial and recent past. Because of its strategic location and resources, South Africa began early to be coveted by Europeans. Beginning around 1652 the Netherlands encouraged Dutch immigrants to settle there. Around 1814 the British seized part of the territory and soon encouraged English settlement. Not wishing to live under British rule, the Dutch settlers (the Boers, now called Afrikaners) moved inland and established their own states. During all this, the indigenous peoples were seeking to defend their territory, and for approximately 100 years, beginning in the 1770s, there was frequent fighting. It was during this time that the Zulu king, Shaka, was killed (1828). By the 1880s, most of the native people were confined to territories not unlike Native American reservations in the United States.

The discovery of diamonds (1867), and later gold (1886), in Boer territory, began a struggle with the British which by 1902, after two wars, left Britain in possession of the entire territory. Reconciliation between the English and the Afrikaners led in 1910 to the formation of the Union of South Africa. The Union won independence from Britain in 1931 but remained a member of the British Commonwealth until 1961, when it became the Republic of South Africa. The latter change came largely in response to international controversy over South Africa's policy of apartheid, which had gradually evolved, especially after the 1920s, but had intensified after 1950, when a law requiring separate white and nonwhite residential areas was passed. As a result of this law, much of the black population was moved to town-ships, best described as shantytowns, isolated but near enough to cities or industrial facilities to allow blacks to work in mines, factories, offices, and homes as ill-paid laborers. Separate homelands, always the least desirable land, were set up for blacks, who were considered to be citizens of those homelands; when black men left the homelands to work elsewhere, they were not allowed to bring their families, thus disrupting family life. These men usually lived in all-male hostels, and over a period of time, some scholars have argued, created a new kind of urban culture. All black men had to carry "passes," a provision that made it possible to control black movement and employment. For blacks, South Africa became a police state. Separate black schools provided minimal training, and it was protests over education that led in 1976 to black student riots, beginning in Soweto and spreading throughout the country. This was one of the crucial events in recent South African history and a major boost for the Black Consciousness movement. The African National Congress, beginning in the 1950s, was the chief internal oppositional force to apartheid, but owing to government suppression and the detainment of ANC leaders, not until 1990 did the government finally agree to start dismantling apartheid after international boycotts made a change in policy inevitable. In 1994 the country's first democratic elections brought the selection of Nelson Mandela, a black lawyer, as president. In 1995, South Africa rejoined the British Commonwealth. The process of reforming African civil and economic rights is still under way.

Under apartheid, it was not only blacks who suffered discrimination. Two other groups, coloreds (mixed race) and Asians (primarily Indians), also lived under separate government-established sets of restrictions, though not as severe as those that governed blacks. The many divisions within South Africa have made for a complex theatre.

As in other African countries, indigenous performances were numerous and of long standing before the arrival of Europeans. These included storytelling, religious ritual, initiation ceremonies, and various other kinds of performance that depended on music, dance, masks and costumes, visual symbolism, and speech. Some of these are still performed, especially among those Zulus who, living in their own homeland, were able to preserve certain of their rituals and ceremonies, although in altered or shortened form. These include coming-of-age ceremonies, prewedding celebrations, and the installation of chiefs. Storytelling has also survived in altered forms. Men who had left their homelands to work in urban areas brought with them elements of their traditional practices and, in intermingling with men from still other areas, they developed mixtures of traditional and modern ceremony and dance to create new types of indigenous performance. Many black Christian churches, among them the Zionist and Nazareth Baptist, also retained elements of traditional African religious beliefs in their ceremonies, which are often quite elaborate. Peter Larlham has described many of the ceremonies and performances among the Zulus, in the churches, and in urban working-black cultures. In recent times, as protest against white domination increased, traditional practices frequently were invoked as models for contemporary black performance modes and many plays sought to recover indigenous history and culture.

The first performance of a European play in South Africa came in the 1780s, and after 1801, when the African Theatre was founded in Cape Town, theatrical performances were available occasionally through visiting companies from England and elsewhere. During the last part of the nineteenth century, the discovery of diamonds and gold brought an influx of new immigrants, whose presence, especially in urban areas, motivated the building of theatres based on European models in which European plays could be performed.

Afrikaners were in a somewhat different situation than the English settlers. The latter could draw on a long tradition of plays in their own language, so there was little incentive for them to write plays in English. Their attention was focused more on providing facilities and making arrangements for the foreign companies who found it profitable to tour South Africa. I. W. Schlesinger's African Theatres, founded in 1913, was a major builder of theatres and manager of tours until about 1930. But there was no tradition of writing plays in Afrikaans, a language that had evolved out of Dutch (with influence from English and several other languages). After about 1880 Afrikaners became especially concerned to establish the validity of their language and culture, and they placed high priority on creating a literature of their own and seeking international acceptance of it. The first Afrikaans play, *Magrita Prinslo* by S. J. du Toit (1847–1911), was produced in 1897. It antedated any South African play in English.

Unlike the English-speaking South Africans, Afrikaners also had to create their own productions. In 1907, the first Afrikaans theatre group, the Afrikaans-Hollandse Toneelvereniging, was founded, and plays of emerging Afrikaner dramatists, among them Melt Brink (1842–1925) and C. J. Langenhoven (1873–1932), were toured by amateur groups through the mostly rural areas where the majority of Afrikaners lived. The Afrikaners were to remain essentially rural and conservative, distinguishing themselves from the English, who were primarily urban and liberal. Afrikaans theatre expanded through a growing network of essentially amateur companies and organizations, among them the Hendrik Hanekom Afrikaanse Toneelspelers, founded in 1925; the Kaapstadse Afrikaanse Toneelvereniging, founded in Cape Town in 1934; and the Johannesburgse Afrikaanse Amateur-Toneelspelers, founded in 1942. The first professional Afrikaans company was established by Paul de Groot in 1925. Afrikaans playwrights also increased in number. Among the best known were Louis Leipoldt (1880–1947) with *The Witch* (1923), J. W. F. Grosskopf with *If the Halter Chafes* (1926), and Gerhard Beukes (1913–) with *Let the Candles Burn* (1945). In 1925, the struggle for acceptance of Afrikaans succeeded when it, along with English, was declared the official language of South Africa.

Touring companies from England declined in number in the 1930s, but a mixture of professional and amateur South African companies remained. The work of amateur theatres received greater recognition and was better coordinated after the formation of the Federation of Amateur Theatrical Societies of South Africa in 1938. This was followed in 1947 by the first state-funded agency intended to assist professional theatres, the National Theatre Organization. This organization did much to encourage both Afrikaans and English professional theatre for white audiences between 1947 and 1963.

Around 1960, South African theatre began to enter a new phase, precipitated in large part by internal and external conflict over apartheid. Withdrawal from the British Commonwealth and the formation of the Republic of South Africa were in large part motivated by this conflict, and international censure began to increase consciousness and protest about apartheid at home. In 1963, foreign playwrights refused to allow their plays to be staged in South Africa, and in 1966 British Equity forbade its members to act in segregated theatres (mixed audiences were forbidden by South African law between 1966 and 1977). These decisions deprived South African theatres of a large proportion of their repertory and virtually eliminated English touring companies, thereby creating an increased market for both South African plays and performers. In 1963, the National Theatre Organization was replaced by Performing Arts Councils, one for each of the provinces that made up South Africa, and support for the theatre was channeled through them. Because of constraints imposed by the government, these councils had to be conservative in what they supported, and thus they did little to encourage innovative drama at a time when the need for change was being felt. They did eventually build impressive theatres, however, such as the Nico Malan Theatre in Cape Town (1975), the Pretoria State Theatre (1981), the Playhouse in Durban, and an arts complex in Bloemfontein (in the Orange Free State). The councils also offered training and experience to theatre practitioners.

The people best served by the councils were Afrikaans, who tended not to oppose government policies, and it was during the 1960s and 1970s that some of the best Afrikaans playwrights were active. Bartho Smit (1924–1986), perhaps the best of these writers, frequently had trouble with censors. *The Maimed* (1960) suggests the absurdity of South Africa's race laws, while *Bacchus in the Highveld* (1974) shows Bacchus switching the roles of a white winemaker and his nonwhite workers. *Christine* (1971) focuses on events in Nazi Germany and their effects on the title character as seen in her younger and older selves, played by two actresses simultaneously. Others of his plays include *Mother Hanna* (1959), *Well without Water* (1962), and *The Emperor* (1977). P. G. du Plessis (1934–) began his playwriting career with *Night of Legion* (1969), which deals with religious experience set against the background of a men's ward in a mental hospital. His *Seer in the Suburbs* (1971), concerning family life in the suburbs of Johannesburg, was one of South Africa's most popular plays and was made into a film after a long run and two literary prizes. Adam Small's (1936–) *Kanna Comes Home* (1962) concerns a man who, returning from Canada upon his mother's death, recalls through flashbacks the ups and downs of the family. Pieter Fourie treated life in the plateau region of South Africa in his *Faan de Trein, Faan se Stasie,* and *Mooi Maria* (1980). Pieter-Dirk Uys (1945–) has alternated writing plays and writing and performing in cabarets and revues. He has appeared thousands of times both at home and abroad as his satirical drag character Evita Bezuidenhout, an Afrikaans grand dame (often called "the most famous white woman in South Africa"), who prior to the abandonment of apartheid helped to reveal its ridiculousness and who after 1994 interviewed numerous prominent government officials on television (thereby helping South Africans understand figures who under apartheid had been demonized by the white government). He is one of the best known and most popular performers in South Africa. His plays include *Paradise Is Closing Down* (1977), *Beyond the Rubicon* (1986), and *Just Like Home* (1988). In recent years he has performed one-person shows primarily seeking to make young people and politicians more aware of the dangers of AIDS. The best known of these shows is *Foreign AIDS* (2001). Other Afrikaans dramatists of note are Chris Barnard (1939–) and André P. Brink

FIG. 25.17
Shakespeare's *Othello* as performed at the Market Theatre, Johannesburg. Directed by Janet Suzman. The actors are Joanna Weinberg, Richard Haines, and John Kani. Photograph by Ruphin Coldyzer. Courtesy Market Theatre.

(1935–). Afrikaans drama is also promoted by the Klein Karoo Festival, begun in 1994 with the goal of nation-building through art.

Because of government restrictions, many white English-language and virtually all black playwrights worked outside the subsidized theatre. Black interest in theatre, other than traditional performance, can be traced back to at least the 1920s. In 1927, G. B. Sinxo's *Debeza's Baboons* became the first play in the Xhosa language to be performed. The first drama in English by a black person to be published, H. I. E. Dhlomo's (1903–1956) *The Girl Who Killed to Save: Nongquase the Liberator* (1935), concerns a Xhosa seer whose prophecies led to mass killing of cattle in the late nineteenth century. Dhlomo interpreted the discrediting of the seer as a triumph for Christianity. Dhlomo had already founded the Bantu Dramatic Society in 1933 with the goal of developing black African drama, although the society also performed European drama.

Other far-reaching work came by way of another path. In 1927, Esau Mthethwa founded the first company of black actors, the Lucky Stars, with which he performed for audiences using the Zulu language. Although the material came from Zulu daily life and included a great deal of song and dance, the goal seems to have been to teach lessons through satire and humor. This company performed throughout the country until 1936. The next major development in black performance came around 1952, when Alf Herbert, a Johannesburg promoter, began to assemble and tour popular entertainments called African Jazz and Variety. The Union of South African Artists (usually called Union Artists), formed in 1953 to protect the rights of black artists, developed Herbert's idea further and in 1959 created and staged the musical, *King Kong,* based on the life of the heavyweight boxing champion, Ezekial Dhlamini. This was the first example of what came to be called the "township musical," a fusion of urban working-class culture, popular forms of entertainment, jazz, and other forms of township music. Using the money made from *King Kong,* the Union Artists founded the African Music and Drama Association and sponsored a theatre workshop and drama school in Johannesburg. In 1961, they opened a theatre, the Rehearsal Room, where a large number of persons, both black and white, who would later play significant roles in South African theatre (including Athol Fugard and Gibson Kente) worked together.

After the law forbidding mixed casts and mixed audiences was passed in 1965, Gibson Kente (1932–) broke away from the Union Artists and in 1967 formed his own company. By 1970, he had presented

FIG. 25.18
Student performing in the Laboratory, the Market Theatre's educational wing. Courtesy Market Theatre, Johannesburg.

three musical works, *Sikalo, Lifa,* and *Zwi.* Kente's was merely the best of the black companies that were springing up to play in the townships. These township performance modes went far to replace the traditional performances that had been destroyed by displacement and urbanization. Township theatre was commercial. It was created and performed in the townships and reflected township life. Music and dance were the essential ingredients; the dialogue was largely improvised by the performers. Since there were no township theatres, these pieces were staged in a variety of spaces, usually for no more than one night in the same location. Casts were large and, consequently, pay was low. Most performers held day jobs. Kente's plays were only indirectly political, except for *How Long?* (1973), which treated the "pass" laws and the effect they had on families and communities. This play was a great success, and a film of it was being made in 1976 when Kente was detained for an extended period. After his release, he returned to his theatre work but usually avoided overtly political subjects, although some, like *Too Late* (1981), are clearly political. It concerns a young boy who, imprisoned for defending his handicapped cousin from a menacing black policeman and being abused by other prisoners, becomes an embittered, violent man. Political or not, Kente's company continued throughout the 1980s to be the most popular in South Africa.

In the 1970s, black political theatre grew out of the Black Consciousness movement, which had originated in the universities. Not being able to act politically, this movement chose theatre as a means of uniting blacks, reminding them of their history and lost culture, and building resistance. Out of this movement came the People's Experimental Theatre (PET), founded in 1973. PET's best known production was *Shanti,* a play about a relationship between an African man and an Indian woman during a guerilla struggle for independence in South Africa. It was written by Mthuli Shezi, a leader in the Black Consciousness movement and a founder of PET, who recently had been killed. The members of PET and several other companies associated with Black Consciousness were detained in 1975 but, despite this setback, their cause was greatly enhanced in 1976 when students in Soweto rebelled against the educational system. In seeking to put down the demonstrations, soldiers fired on and killed a large number of students. Demonstrations quickly spread to other parts of the country. Thereafter, no one could be unaware of Black Consciousness. The influence of the militant Pan Africanist Congress, whose slogan was "One settler, one bullet," also grew.

Because of raised consciousness and unhappiness over government policies, the most vital theatre in South Africa in the 1970s was a committed theatre, whether white or black, which explored new ways of working and new modes of performance. In many instances blacks and whites worked together. The major alternative theatres were the Space Theatre, opened in Cape Town by Brian Astbury, Yvonne Bryceland, and Athol Fugard in 1972, and the Market Theatre in Johannesburg which came into being in 1976 when The Company, under Mannie Manim and Barney Simon, took over a converted fruit market. Works that had their first productions at the Space include Athol Fugard, John Kani, and Winston Ntshona's *Sizwe Bansi Is Dead, Statements after an Arrest under the Immorality Act,* and *The Island;* and works by other major South African playwrights, among them Pieter-Dirk Uys's *Pity about People, Selle ou Storie,* and *God's Forgotten;* Geraldine Aron's (1941–) *Bar and Ger;* and Fatima Dike's (1948–) *The Sacrifice of Kreli* and *The First South African.* (Dike was the first black South African woman to have a play published. She has been commissioned by the Robben Island Museum to write a play about the political activists, including Nelson Mandela, who were imprisoned on Robben Island.) The Market Theatre's long roll of important plays includes works by Fugard, Uys, and such black writers as Matsemela Manaka, Maishe Maponya, and Zakes Mda. Other alternative theatres included The Glass Theatre in Cape Town; The Junction Avenue Theatre Company, the Box Theatre, and the Nunnery Theatre in Johannesburg; the Window Theatre in East London; the Serpent Players in Port Elizabeth; and several churches, institutes,

FIG. 25.20

Woza Albert! by Mbongeni Ngema, Percy Mtwa, and Barney Simon. The performers are Ngema and Mtwa. Courtesy Market Theatre, Johannesburg.

FIG. 25.19

Starbrites as directed by Barney Simon at the Market Theatre. Photo by Ruphin Coldyzer. Courtesy Market Theatre, Johannesburg.

and universities. Most of these were run by whites, but they included black performers and writers, and most used subterfuges to get around the prohibition against mixed casts and audiences prior to the removal of this restriction in 1977. Many black performers were criticized for their "whiteness," but it was virtually impossible for whites to work in the townships. Black, white, and mixed groups produced works of considerable importance.

Between 1971 and 1973, Fugard and the black actors Winston Ntshona and John Kani, experimenting with collective creation, produced *Sizwe Bansi Is Dead* and *The Island.* The former play, concerning obtaining a "pass" by taking on a dead man's identity, was very successful not only in Africa but also in the United States and elsewhere. Others also began to use this experimental approach to creating a performance. One of the most successful was the Workshop '71 production of *Survival* (1976), commissioned by the Space Theatre and created by a company of four actors and its director. A play about prison, it focuses on the experiences—some comic and satirical, some terrifying—of four people with the South African police, and calls for oppressed people to join hands and change the system. The piece made extensive use of song and dance. It was performed not only at the Space but also in the black urban areas around Cape Town, and subsequently in Soweto, East London, and Johannesburg, as well as on tour in the United States. Conceived before but originally presented almost simultaneously with the Soweto riots, its impact was great.

Barney Simon (1934–1995) who had worked with Joan Littlewood in London, was involved at the Market Theatre with several plays growing out of group collaboration. One of these, *Cincinatti* (1979), subtitled "Scenes from City Life," had as its focus the police closing of a night club called Cincinatti. Developed in a workshop by Simon and ten actors, it enjoyed great popularity. *Born in the RSA* (1986) was the collaborative work of Simon and a multiracial cast of eight persons. The characters, who on the surface seem to have little connection, are all eventually caught up in investigations which stem from the security-police recruitment of a university student to be a campus spy and his infiltration of a multiracial activist group. Simon was also involved in the creation of *Woza Albert!* (1980), which originated with Mbongeni Ngema (1955–) and Percy Mtwa who, while performing in a Gibson Kente production, began work on a play about what would happen if Jesus were to come back to South Africa, including questions about what blacks would think about him and how the white government would react. Eventually Simon became the director and joint author of this work, one of the most popular plays ever to come out of Africa. It later toured the United States

and elsewhere and won the Edinburgh Festival Fringe First Prize and some twenty other awards. It was performed by the two black actor-authors, who shifted rapidly among multiple roles, using a few props and costumes pieces on a sparsely furnished stage. To play white characters, they placed half a pink squash ball over their noses.

Both Ngema and Mtwa went on to create other pieces. Mtwa's *Bopha!* (1985) looks at apartheid through its effect on a black family. It sets an activist son against his policeman father, whose job it is to enforce the laws of apartheid. Eventually the policeman realizes that he has become an enemy of his own people and quits his job. Like other black plays, this one makes use of storytelling narration, music, dance, humor, and anger. It was made into a film in 1993. In 1982, Ngema founded a theatre group, Committed Artists, out of which came a number of international successes. His *Asinamali* (1985) is set in a South African jail, where five male characters recount, through words, song, dance, satire, humor, and outrage, what has led to their imprisonment. Each has come a different route—murder, unemployment, mistaken identity, violation of the Immorality Act, political activism—all resulting from apartheid. The title—"we have no money"—is the cry against rent increases of township demonstrators, whose leader, Msizi Dube, was killed by police but whose death led to the formation of a group dedicated to ending racial inequality. Ngema had even greater success, including international tours, with *Sarafina* (1986), which emphasizes the importance of women in the Soweto uprising, especially that of Sarafina who emerges as the most committed activist, and the female schoolteacher, who teaches her students the history of blacks that is not in the history books. It was eventually made into a Hollywood movie. The money made on these musicals allowed Ngema to provide employment to increased numbers of theatrical personnel and to offer them training. *Township Fever* (1990), a fusion of township musical with serious drama and dance, was based on a transport strike in 1987 during which several strikers were charged with murdering "scab" workers.

Maishe Maponya (1951–) began writing in 1975. He subsequently founded the Bahumutsi Drama Group of Soweto and received an award that took him to England to observe theatre there. *The Hungry Earth* (1979), which presents a somewhat Brechtian lecture-demonstration about working conditions of blacks in South Africa, was first presented in Soweto and later toured Britain and West Germany. Others of his plays include *Peace and Forgive* (1977), *Umongikazi* (1982), and *Dirty Work* (1984). One of his best-known plays is *Gangsters* (1984), with which he became the first

FIG. 25.21

Bopha! by Percy Mtwa and Cast. Photo by Ruphin Coudyzer. Courtesy Market Theatre, Johannesburg.

black playwright of note to include a role for a white actor. Reflecting the notorious incident of the prison death of the young black activist Steve Biko, in *Gangsters* a black policeman, under orders from his white superior, tortures to death a black poet.

Matsemala Manaka (1955–), founder of the Soyikwa Theatre Group, began writing with *The Horn* (1977) and won international attention with *Egoli—The City of God* (1979), which toured Europe and was voted Play of the Year in London. It deals with the destruction of a family caused by the labor system under which men must leave their homelands to find work. Despite its grim story, it ends on a note of promise as workers declare their freedom. In 1983, two of his one-act plays, *Imbumba* (1979) and *Pula* (1982), won first prize in the Edinburgh Festival's fringe. *Children of Asazi* (1984) is set against the government's order to remove people from the Alexandra township in Johannesburg and focuses on a young activist caught between personal ties and his need to protest the government's action. Songs and the music of a jazz saxophonist play key roles in the performance. Manaka worked primarily in the townships, although he occasionally presented work at the Market Theatre.

Most black playwrights concentrated on contemporary problems, but occasionally dealt with their historical and cultural heritage. Perhaps the best of such plays was *uNosilimela* (1973) by Credo Mutwa (1921–), developed in part in collaboration with Workshop '71. It was subsequently presented in Soweto and elsewhere. The staging demands made it so difficult to move from one venue to another that the production, though still popular, closed in 1975. The play draws on the history, legends, aspirations, and various indigenous performance traditions of the Bantus in its narrative, ritualistic, satirical, and allegorical sequences as the title character seeks to discover who she is, ultimately becoming the proud inheritor of African history and culture. It suggests the need for blacks to give up imitating foreign cultures and return to their own.

By far the best known among South Africa's white playwrights is Athol Fugard (1932–), often mistakenly considered by those outside the country to be South Africa's only playwright of note. Fugard began his playwriting career with *No-good Friday* (1959), written and staged while working with the Union Artists in Johannesburg between 1958 and 1961; *The Blood Knot* (1961), which shows two brothers struggling to maintain their relationship in the face of racial laws that threaten to separate them, was the first production of the Rehearsal Room there. After a few years of theatrical experience in Europe, Fugard set-

FIG. 25.22

Athol Fugrad's *Boesman and Lena* as directed at the Manhattan Theatre Club (New York) by Fugard in 1992. The actors are Tsepo Mokone, Lynn Thigpen, and Keith David. Photo by Gerry Goodstein.

tled in Port Elizabeth, where he wrote a series of plays about the effects of South Africa's laws and social attitudes on working-class characters. These include *Hello and Goodbye* (1965), *People Are Living There* (1968), and *Boesman and Lena* (1969). Between 1971 and 1973, as indicated earlier, he developed plays in collaboration with John Kani and Winston Ntshona. Subsequently, Fugard returned to writing alone. *Master Harold and the Boys* (1982) is a play often considered to be autobiographical about a white boy's friendship with a black worker who serves as a surrogate father and how, through attitudes learned from apartheid, the boy destroys that relationship. *My Children, My Africa* (1989) is set in a school where a rivalry for achievement between a black boy and a white girl develops toward friendship but is interrupted by a boycott in which the boy feels compelled to participate and which leads to the death by a mob of the black teacher who has attempted to bring them together. In *Playland* (1992), two men—one black, one white—with violent pasts meet in an amusement park (playland) and in the course of the action confront each other, their pasts, and themselves. It suggests a microcosm of South Africa in which an exorcism of white-black experience and guilt is played out, a theme he takes up again in *Sorrows and Rejoicings* (2001). Others of his plays include *A Lesson from Aloes* (1978), *Road to Mecca* (1984), *A Place with Pigs*

(1987), and *The Captain's Tiger* (1997). In recent years, Fugard has been attacked by some of his countrymen for his stance as a passive observer, who depicted but did little to change life in South Africa.

Among South Africa's other white playwrights—which include Lewis Sowden, Basil Warner, James Ambrose Brown, Guy Butler, H. W. D. Manson, Deon Opperman, and Ian Ferguson—Slabolepszy and Akerman stand out. Paul Slabolepszy (1948–) is among the most prolific and popular of South Africa's playwrights. He is especially noted for his multilingual and comic representatons of ordinary characters which do not address directly but suggest a great deal about African politics. His many plays include *Saturday Night at the Palace* (1981), *Making Like America* (1986), and *Victoria Almost Falls* (1993). Anthony Akerman (1949–) began writing plays while in exile, but returned to South Africa in 1992. His plays, which include *A Man out of the Country* (1985), *A World Elsewhere* (1987), and *First Loves* (1993), reflect the conflict in what it means to be South African. Another major playwright is Reza de Wet, who writes both in Afrikaans and English and in 1994 won the Herzog Prize, the highest honor in Afrikaans literature. Wet's experimental pieces use various theatrical metaphors to deal with sexual and psychological taboos. Her plays, which have been especially popular with younger audiences, include a trilogy, *Trits,* and *A Worm in the Bud.*

Since the late 1980s, South African theatre has been caught up in uncertainty and transition. In 1987 the performing arts councils changed their rules to permit blacks to serve on their boards of directors. They also decided to create outreach programs. By 1990, much of what had been thought of as alternative theatre in the 1960s and 1970s had entered the mainstream. Among developments of the 1980s was the emergence of a workers theatre under the sponsorship of trade unions. In these performances, workers presented plays intended to educate other workers about the hidden structures that control their professions. Theatre was also used in the fight against AIDS, among the most effective programs being "Puppets against AIDS," a project of the African Research and Educational Puppetry Program, which performed skits while a narrator described the action and supplied information. Johannesburg's Handspring Puppet Company, founded in 1981 by Adrian Kohler and Basil Jones, is the most internationally famous puppet theatre in South Africa. Kohler and Jones write the plays and manipulate the puppets in full view of the audience, as in Bunraku. They often work with William Kentridge, one of South Africa's best-known painters, printmakers, and filmmakers. Their joint pro-

ductions have toured widely and include *Woyzeck on the Highveld* (1992), an adaptation of Buchner's play with a black migrant worker as the principal character; *Faustus in Africa* (1995), adapted from Goethe; and *Ubu and the Truth Commission* (1997), a satirical view of the Truth and Reconciliation Commission which probed into apartheid's worst crimes.

Changes were also felt in the universities. The drama department at the University of Zululand began shifting its curriculum away from Western forms to indigenous South African forms and popular theatre. Its classes increasingly focused on workshops and playmaking. Other universities also reexamined their programs and sought to adapt to new conditions. Almost everywhere the question of language was raised (under the new government there are eleven official languages, although English dominates), and dance became increasingly important. That South African theatre today is vigorous is attested by the annual Grahamstown Festival to which productions are brought from all over the country. Founded in 1970 and formerly primarily a festival of white theatre, since the late 1980s the number of black entries has increased each year. In the late 1990s, approximately 500 theatre events were being seen annually in the festival's main and fringe venues. The primary issue being discussed and dramatized was how to define and realize a just society and a genuinely South African theatre.

NORTH AFRICA

Some aspects of North African history are discussed in earlier chapters. As has been indicated, ancient Egyptian ritual-drama is among the oldest performance modes of which we have knowledge. Subsequently, those portions of North Africa that bordered the Mediterranean became parts of the Hellenistic, Roman, and Byzantine worlds and participated in the theatre of those times. In the seventh and eighth centuries C.E., all of northern Africa was conquered by Moslems, and Arabic gradually became the official language and Islam the official religion. Since that religion was antipathetic to it, theatre was of little importance. Storytelling, sometimes with enactment of portions, was common from the ninth century onward, and shadow puppetry, imported from Persia or Turkey, was long the most popular form of theatrical entertainment.

Egypt has played the largest role in North Africa's theatre. During much of the nineteenth and early twentieth centuries, Egypt was under English domination or occupation. During the nineteenth century theatrical companies began to appear. The first

Western-style production dates from 1870. In this and subsequent productions, singing and dancing were the primary attractions, with story of secondary concern. Men played all the roles.

Theatre in Egypt has flourished primarily in the twentieth century. The most important troupe in the early years was that of Jurj Abyad, established in 1910 with the encouragement of the minister of education. It performed entirely in Arabic, presenting comedy and tragedy and both European and Arabic works. In 1914 it merged with another company headed by Salama al-Hijazi. Several other companies soon followed its lead. Among the most popular of these was the one headed by Naguib al-Rihani (1892–1949), noted especially for his portrayal of the character Kishkish Bey, who always outsmarted the Europeanized tricksters he encountered. During the 1930s he turned to less conventionalized comedy in *The Egyptian Pound* (1931) and *Quaraqush's Rule* (1935). In the 1940s he made a number of films.

Egypt's first important playwright was Ahmad Shauqi (1868–1931), author of six historical plays and one comedy. His serious plays include *The Fall of Cleopatra* and *Qambiz (Cambyses)*, retellings of stories that had been dramatized in Elizabethan England and whose views of their subjects Shauqi sought to amend. Of still greater importance was Tawfiq al-Hakim (1898–1987), sometimes called the father of modern Egyptian drama, who wrote some eighty plays which deal with philosophical and religious issues, and explore such social questions as the position of women and the search for happiness in a world of war, poverty, and disease. Among his early dramas, one of the most important (in part because it was the opening production in 1935 of the newly-formed Egyptian National Theatre Troupe) was *The Sleepers in the Cave*, based on a parable from the Qur-an. Others of his plays include *The Sultan Who Could Not Make Up His Mind* (1960), *The Tree Climbers* (1962), *Fate of the Cockroach* (1966), and *The Donkey Market* (1975). Al-Hakim's plays were intended primarily to be read. In contrast, Ashad Rushdy wrote with the stage in mind. Surprisingly, Rushdy largely escaped censorship despite the social and political criticism contained in his plays, some of the best-known of which are *The Butterfly* (1959) and *Egypt My Love* (1967).

After 1967, the theatre in Egypt began to decline because of poor economic conditions, the increase in Islamic fundamentalism, and the introduction of television. Egypt's role as the primary source of drama in the Arab world metamorphosed into that of primary source of Arabic television programs and films. Since the early 1990s, Egypt has hosted the Cairo International Festival of Experimental Theatre, financed by the government. In twelve days each September, more than fifty companies from the Middle East, Europe, Australia, North and South America, Japan, and elsewhere present plays. There are also symposia and wide-ranging discussions of theatre.

Other North African countries—Morocco, Algeria, and Tunisia—were long dominated by France. Algeria was annexed as a province of France in 1830 and became an independent country again only in 1962. Much of its theatre prior to 1962 came from Egypt (in Arabic) or France (in French). Allâlû did much to promote an Algerian theatre between 1926 and 1931 by writing seven plays in colloquial Arabic and by seeking to make theatre accessible to all types of audiences. After independence, Algeria established a conservatory (under the direction of Bachtarzi Mahiedine) to train actors, and a National Theatre (under the direction of Mustapha Kateb). Both of these men were interested in developing a theatre that could serve all the people. Mahiedine was also one of Algeria's major playwrights. Among his works are *The Traitors, The Yes-Men,* and *They Have Awakened,* all of which achieved considerable popularity with working-class audiences. The best-known of all Algerian dramatists is Kateb Yacine (1929–), whose *The Encircled Corpse* (1958), a strong attack on French colonialism, aroused so much hostility in France (produced there in the midst of the Algerian war for independence) that performances had to be moved to Brussels. A second play, *The Ancestors Redouble Their Ferocity,* created almost as great a furor. His *Mohamed, Take Your Suitcase,* concerning Algerian immigrants in France, achieved considerable success, especially among French immigrant audiences. In recent years, theatre in Algeria has encountered increased opposition from Islamic fundamentalism.

Both Morocco and Tunisia regained independence in 1956, and both have since established national theatres, although neither has produced playwrights or directors of more than local significance. In Tunisia, Izz al-Din al-Madani (1938–) and in Morocco Tayyib al Siddiqui (1938–) have both sought to create a specifically Arab form of drama.

In addition to the countries discussed above, there are many others which have not been covered. These include Mauritania, Guinea, Gambia, Burkino Faso, Liberia, Togo, Benin, Equitorial Guinea, Niger, Chad, Central African Republic, Gabon, Sudan, Ethiopia, Somalia, Djibouti, Rwanda, Burundi, Malawi, Namibia, Botswana, Lesotho, Swaziland, the island of Madagascar, Libya, and Western Sahara. All deserve attention, but few have played a major role in documented African theatre.

LOOKING AT THEATRE HISTORY

In studying African theatre, most of us soon become aware of its "otherness"—its unlikeness to the traditions with which we are most familiar. In studying Western theatre, we are in a position to examine it from an "insider's" point of view, for we are looking at our own inherited or created traditions and conventions, many of them so familiar that we have ceased to be conscious of them. When most of us see or hear the words *play, theatre,* or *performer,* we almost automatically form images based on experience with Western theatre. When we turn to African theatre, we may at first be inclined to impose on it Western assumptions and associations, thereby seriously misperceiving it. Although Westerners are unlikely ever to be able to experience African theatre from the "inside"—that is, as someone does who has grown up within African traditions—they can improve their perceptions by ceasing to consider Western notions of theatre as "normative," "commonsensical," or "valid," as opposed to the "aberrational," "exotic," or "flawed" notions of cultures with which they are unfamiliar. Although theatre can always be better understood by viewing it within its cultural context, this is especially true of African modes that have existed since pre-colonial times, few of which fit easily into Western concepts of "theatre" and most of which were integrated into the life of the society rather than being discrete "events." In societies that did not have a written language, performance had ramifications larger than those usually associated with theatre in Western culture. The term *performance* (as understood in the emerging field of "performance studies") more nearly encompasses the wide variety of behavior and activity involved. Margaret Thompson Drewal says of "performance":

> *Performance is . . . a fundamental dimension of culture as well as the production of knowledge about culture. It might include anything from individual agents' negotiations of everyday life, to the stories people tell each other, popular entertainments, political oratory, guerrilla warfare, to bounded events such as theater, ritual, festivals, parades, and more.*

"The State of Research on Performance in Africa," *African Studies Review,* 34, 3 (December 1991), 1.

It is difficult for non-Africans to gain an understanding of indigenous African performance as a total experience because those who write about it often take it out of its cultural context or tend to divide it into its components, each of which is studied in isolation from the rest, a practice which disrupts the totality forged by the several "languages" of performance as they work off each other, often improvisationally. Additionally, those who write about performance have a tendency to ignore much of the improvisation, repetition, and elaboration in order to present an orderly account:

> *. . . while [African] performers often specialize in certain performance genres—drumming, dancing, singing—these activities rarely happen in isolation. Meanwhile, as drummers, dancers, singers, and others are communicating and negotiating with each other in the process of performance, scholars isolate them from each other in their representations by focusing on one genre to the exclusion of others. . . .*
>
> *. . . Performance is then reduced to a linear, unidimensional structure organized sequentially and normatized—not by performers—but by social scientific procedures.*

Ibid., p. 16.

Colonial authorities tried to forbid or control indigenous performance, in part because they considered it pagan and in part because they feared its potential for subversion. They were seldom fully successful in their attempts:

> *Since public performance is the usual medium adopted by the arts in indigenous African as in other societies, it was not difficult to find one kind or another going on throughout the year's cycle. Drama, dance, poetry, storytelling, music, and the creation of sculpture lent themselves readily to performance, which naturally exploited contemporary religious and social realities. . . . the Christians raided ancestral shrines and forbade African converts to participate in their cultural association's activities, or even play their musical instruments. . . . To . . . pronounce their practices evil or barbaric was the best way to stamp out the art forms and politics engendered by them.*

. . . The reaction of the indigenous theater to colonial efforts to gag it was similar in many African countries. The Igbo in Nigeria created new plays featuring British colonial officers—administrators, police, missionaries—and their families as characters to replace the banned traditional characters.

J. Indukaku Amankulor, "English-Language Drama and Theater," *A History of Twentieth-Century African Literatures,* ed. by Oyekan Owomoyela (Lincoln: University of Nebraska Press, 1993), 139–40, 141.

Among the major issues in contemporary African theatre has been the intended audience. For whom is theatre being done? This questioning leads inevitably to language. In what language should the dramatist write? Ngugi wa Thiong'o poses the issue clearly:

The moment you write in English you assume a readership who can speak and read English, and in this case it can only mean the educated African élite or the foreigners who speak the language. This means that you are precluding in terms of class the peasantry, or the workers in Africa who do not read or understand these foreign languages.

Ngugi wa Thiong'o, Interview, *Kunapipi,* 1 (1981). Quoted in Ingrid Björkman, *"Mother Sing For Me": People's Theatre in Kenya* (London: Zed Books, 1989), 3.

Another major issue in African theatre concerns the nature and function of theatre. Is it intended to entertain and give esthetic pleasure, or should it be an instrument of social change? Even those who do

research about African theatre are sometimes challenged by those primarily concerned with "theatre for development," and in turn practitioners of "theatre for development" may be chastised for failing to proceed beyond performance to engage in the political action needed to bring about change.

The academic observer of a people's traditional performances, or serious theatrical experimentation, who goes away and presents the analysis of these "objective" observations in a foreign place, is in fact something of a thief . . . [The research benefits the traditional performers] not at all whilst providing the researcher with academic honours, high salary and international travel. Some African activists now maintain that recording a traditional performance, even preserving it "live" in some form or other, is less relevant to the peasant owners of that art than a growing ability by them to make it contribute to a better society for them. . . . We have been told time and time again by the peasant farmers that they would . . . want us to help them regain land taken from them for speculative purposes instead of making plays about how they lost their lands. . . . For those at the bottom of the social heap, and ultimately for the intellectuals and creative artists who seek to engage with them, the art of drama cannot be separated from the greater political task, and, in its function, from social reality.

Michael Etherton, *The Development of African Drama* (London: Hutchinson University Library for Africa, 1982), 26–27.

26
The Theatre of Asia

Asian theatrical traditions are strong and of long standing. Eastern theatrical developments remained almost completely distinct from those of the West well into the twentieth century. Furthermore, Asian theatre developed and changed at a pace quite different from that of the West. Its conventions have in many instances remained relatively fixed for considerable periods of time, unlike the West, where conventions changed more rapidly. Thus, it is difficult to trace the two strands simultaneously. The delay in treating Asian theatre is not meant to marginalize it but rather to respect its own distinctive patterns of development. According to the *Cambridge Guide to Asian Theatre,* the theatrical arts in Asia and the western Pacific have taken on as many as 700 or 800 distinct forms or genres and are performed by perhaps as many as 25,000 theatre troupes. Only a few of these can be discussed here. What follows is a discussion of some of the best-known and most characteristic of Asian forms and theatrical conventions.

INDIA

Civilization in India can be traced back almost as far as in Egypt and the Middle East. But our knowledge of it is slight until the Aryans arrived from central Asia around 1500 B.C.E. In the centuries that followed, those features that were to be most significant in Indian life and art emerged. Perhaps the most important of these influences on drama were Hinduism, the caste system, and Sanskrit literary conventions.

Hinduism teaches that the essence of all things is spirit or soul and that the ultimate goal is to achieve union with the Supreme World-Soul, or Brahman, who is infinite, eternal, indescribable, and perfect. In all creation, only Brahman is unchanging, and since only what is permanent is real, Brahman is also the ultimate reality from which all else emanates and to which all else seeks to return. Although it emphasized oneness of spirit, Hinduism sanctioned the worship of hundreds of gods or spirits, since all are merely aspects of Brahman. Nevertheless, Hindus tended to honor three principal gods who personify different aspects of Brahman: Brahma, the creator; Siva, the destroyer; and Visnu, the preserver. Hindus also believed it impossible to achieve spiritual perfection during one lifetime and posited the necessity of successive reincarnations.

The early Hindus encouraged the representation of living beings in literature, drama, and art as manifestations of spirit. Thus, Hinduism was almost the opposite of Mohammedanism, which denied all gods except Allah and forbade the representation of living beings in art. Hinduism was as hospitable to theatre as Islam was antipathetic.

Before the beginning of the Christian era, India had evolved a caste system based partly on social, economic, and racial concepts but also on notions of spiritual development. Although the number of castes eventually became numerous, there are four traditional ones: Brahmins, the priests and intellectuals; Kshatriyas, the warriors and rulers; Vaisyas, the artisans and farmers; and Sudras, the unskilled laborers. These castes were considered to be hereditary and binding, and each was assigned specific duties, rites, tasks, and diets. In addition, there were the Untouchables, who performed the most menial tasks and with whom any contact was considered to defile members of the other castes.

The language of Indian drama was primarily Sanskrit. Originally, Sanskrit was the commonly spoken language, but by the early Christian era it was primarily a medium of written expression, and most people spoke one of the Prakrits, or dialects.

A Sanskrit literature began to emerge in India sometime between 1500 and 1000 B.C.E. The *Rigveda*, a collection of prayers or hymns, is usually considered the oldest literary piece in any Indo-European language. It was followed by other religious works. But most important for drama are two great epics, *Mahabharata* and *Ramayana*, which may have originated as early as 1000 B.C.E. but did not assume their final form until about 250 C.E. These two epics are to Sanskrit literature what the *Iliad* and *Odyssey* are to Greek and were to be the major sources of material for Sanskrit dramatists. As Hinduism spread

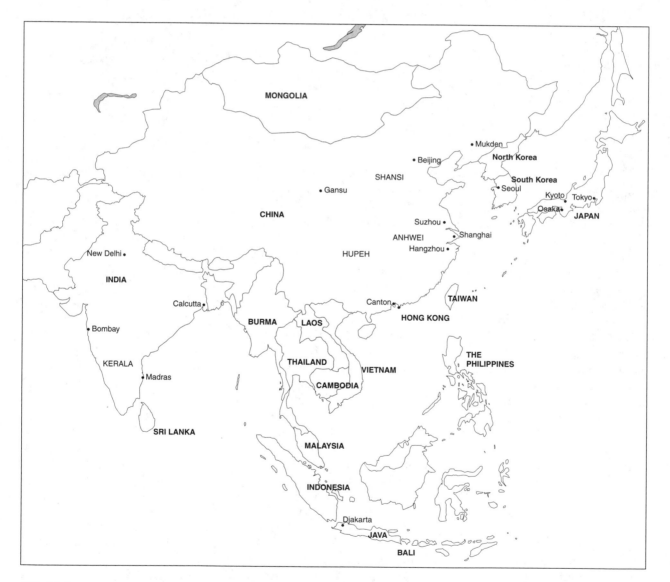

FIG. 26.1
Asia, showing theatrical centers.

throughout Southeast Asia, these epics also inspired (and continue to inspire) much drama in those areas.

Both the *Mahabharata* and *Ramayana* are compounds of history, legend, and myth. The former deals primarily with the struggle between various members of two ruling families and with the tales of love, war, and adventure that revolved around them. The *Ramayana* tells of the expulsion of Prince Rama and his wife Sita from their kingdom because of the machinations of Rama's stepmother, their wandering during a period of fourteen years, Sita's abduction by a demon king, her rescue through the help of a monkey king, and their triumphant return to their kingdom. These epics, Hinduism, and the society summed up in the caste system undergird most Indian drama.

A "golden age" of Indian culture began around 120 C.E. and lasted until about 500. It reached its peak during the fourth and fifth centuries when the Gupta Empire of northern India was a major center of art, learning, and medicine. Beautiful cities arose there, universities were founded, and a great and graceful civilization flourished. Another high point came during the first half of the seventh century under the rule of King Harsa, who was also the major playwright of that time. During Harsa's reign India's influence spread through Southeast Asia, laying the basis for future developments in drama in those areas.

SANSKRIT DRAMA

Rituals and entertainments of various sorts seem to have been common in India from earliest times. Although it is difficult to determine when drama first appeared in India, it is evident that plays were being written there by the beginning of the Christian era. Our major source of information about both dramatic writing and performance is the *Natyasastra* (The Art of Theatre), attributed to Bharata (although perhaps the cumulative work of many persons). It dates from around the second century C.E.

Dating the beginnings of Sanskrit drama is difficult because of Indian indifference to chronology and recordkeeping. Because the evidence is vague, modern scholars have assigned a wide range of dates to surviving dramas. Most agree, however, that the earliest fragments date from approximately 100 C.E. About twenty-five plays have survived, some from perhaps as late as the ninth century, although the best come from the fourth and fifth centuries C.E.

Sanskrit plays are not categorized according to such Western forms as tragedy, comedy, or melodrama; and, rather than action, character develop-

ment, or philosophical issues, the central goal of Sanskrit drama is the appropriate *rasa* (variously translated as aesthetic delight, fundamental mood, or joyful consciousness). The *Natyasastra* states: "nothing has meaning in the drama except through *rasa*." There are eight *rasas* (erotic, comic, pathetic, furious, heroic, terrible, odious, and marvellous), and these in turn are related to the eight basic human emotions (*bhavas*) which can be portrayed on the stage (pleasure, mirth, sorrow, wrath, vigor, fear, disgust, and wonder) to make possible the realization of the appropriate *rasa*. There are also thirty-three transitory emotional states and eight types of character temperament. Basically, the *Natyasastra* is concerned with how emotional states (the *bhavas*) are to be presented on stage through words, actions, costume, and makeup in the manner required to induce the appropriate *rasa*. Although a play may include elements related to more than one *bhava* and *rasa*, one *rasa* must dominate, for the final aim is to induce a sense of harmony and composure. For that reason, all plays end happily. Death and violence do not occur on stage, and right and wrong are clearly differentiated. During a play, joy and sorrow may be mingled, but at the conclusion all must be resolved into harmony with good triumphant over evil.

Because they intermingle so many elements, the plays are complex. The heroic and domestic, the exalted and the commonplace exist side by side. The mixture is exemplified in the typical practice of making the hero's confidant a bald, dwarfish, gluttonous clown, who provides considerable comic relief in a basically serious story. The diversity may also be seen in the dialogue, a mixture of verse (used for heightened expression in scenes of intense emotion) and prose (used for more ordinary scenes) and of Sanskrit (the learned language, spoken by gods, kings, ministers, generals, and sages) and Prakrit (the everyday dialect, used for women, children, servants, peasants, and persons of low birth). Considerable variety is also achieved by grouping subsidiary plots, ranging from the farcical to the serious, around the main story.

Sanskrit plays vary in length from one to ten acts. According to the accepted rules, the events of a single act should be confined to a twenty-four-hour period, while no more than one year should elapse between successive acts. Events not represented on stage but necessary for understanding the plot are made known in interludes preceding acts. The place of the action may shift often and may range through both heaven and earth.

The *Natyasastra* describes ten major kinds of plays, of which the most important are the heroic and the social. The heroic is based on mythology or history and has an exemplary hero who defends a righteous cause; there is usually a love story in which the lovers are kept apart by some evil force until the end of the play. The social play resembles the heroic but its plot and hero are entirely imaginary, and a king is never the leading character. The surviving Sanskrit plays are mostly of these two types.

Among the oldest surviving Sanskrit plays are thirteen works by Bhasa (second or third century C.E.). The best known of these are *The Vision of Vasavadatta* and *Carudatta,* the latter based on the same story that King Sudraka (considered by many to be a wholly legendary person) was to use for *The Little Clay Cart* (*c.* fourth-eighth century), one of the most famous of all Sanskrit dramas. A social play, according to the traditional Hindu classifications, *The Little Clay Cart* tells of the love of a Brahmin for a courtesan. Written in ten acts, it has a number of subplots which come together in the resolution in which the true prince, previously aided by the courtesan, recaptures his throne and unites the courtesan and Brahmin, who have narrowly escaped death at the hands of an evil prince.

Kalidasa's (late fourth-early fifth centuries) *Shakuntala,* a heroic drama in seven acts, is generally considered the finest of all Sanskrit dramas. It tells of King Dushyanta's meeting with Shakuntala (the foster daughter of a hermit), their love and separation (prolonged by a curse pronounced by a holy man to whom Shakuntala has denied hospitality), and their eventual reunion. Renowned in part for its beautiful descriptive passages evoking the forest, stream, and other natural phenomena, it moves freely between heaven and earth, forest and court, from the serious and romantic to the comic. The lyrical and the fantastic mingle with the everyday as the play moves through a wide range of human experience.

Other Sanskrit dramatists include King Harsa (seventh century C.E.), with *The Pearl Necklace, The Lost Princess,* and *Delight of Snakes;* Bhavabhuti (late seventh century), with *The Story of the Great Hero, The Later Story of Rama,* and *The Stolen Marriage;* and Visakhadatta (seventh century?), with *The Signet Ring of Rakshasa.*

The *Natyasastra* also lists eighteen kinds of "lower" drama. What these were is not entirely clear. There is evidence that farce was being performed in the seventh century C.E., but lesser types of drama must have existed before that time. The shadow puppet play is among the oldest of these, for it was probably invented by the Indians several centuries before the Christian era began. It seems to have spread both east and west from India to become a popular entertainment in many areas that had few other types of theatrical entertainment.

Beginning in the late seventh century India was subjected to political upheaval, and the lack of stability probably contributed to the decline of Sanskrit drama. After the assumption of power by Muslims in the twelfth and thirteenth centuries, dramatic entertainments lost their position of honor. Nevertheless, some Sanskrit traditions were preserved in a few temples. Such forms as shadow plays, folk dramas, and incidental entertainments continued to flourish, but the great era of Indian drama was over. Nevertheless, between the second and seventh centuries, Sanskrit drama was more sophisticated and highly developed than that being written or produced anywhere else in the world at that time. In the twentieth century scholarly and production interest in Sanskrit drama has revived and continues to grow. In 1957 a Kalidasa festival was established, and in 1987 another was devoted to Bhasa.

SANSKRIT PERFORMANCE

Performances seem to have been given on many occasions and for all types of audiences. Those most written about and praised were given at religious festivals, marriages, coronations, victory celebrations, or other special occasions. Each type of play was thought to be most appropriate to particular hours of the day or night, and consequently plays might be performed at almost any time.

Since Hindu drama was most concerned with the emotional and spiritual, rather than the external and material, it avoided realistic production practices. Its spiritual inspiration was always recognized in an elaborate preliminary ceremony preceding the play to acknowledge the gods and to prepare performers and spectators for the drama to come.

The *Natyasastra* describes three shapes of playhouses (square, rectangular, and triangular) and three sizes of each (large, medium, and small)—a total of nine theatres. The rectangular theatre of medium size is most fully described and idealized. It was 96 feet long by 48 feet wide and divided into two equal parts (auditorium and stage). The auditorium was shaped like a cave for acoustical purposes and had four pillars (white, red, yellow, and blue), probably intended to symbolize not only the four castes (and where each was to sit) but also geographical regions and compass points. The theatre in its totality symbolized the entire universe.

The half of the theatre devoted to the stage was further divided into two equal parts, one to be used as acting area, the other as backstage space. Two doors led from backstage to the acting area; between them was the place reserved for the vocal and instrumental musicians.

No scenery was used (but the stage was decorated with paintings or carvings as a decorative or symbolic background). At the beginning of the play, a preliminary section established the time, place, and situation. In each scene, descriptive passages and pantomime evoked place as needed. The actors used stylized movement and gestures to suggest such actions as climbing a hill, picking flowers, crossing a stream, riding a horse, or driving a chariot. A walk around the stage indicated a long journey; each part of the stage may have been associated with types of places or with different atmospheres or moods. Because no scenery was used, place could shift rapidly as one scene flowed into the next. Indoor and night performances were lighted with torches or lamps.

The primary emphasis in performance was on the actor, who was said to have four basic resources at his disposal: movement and gesture; speech and song;

costume and makeup; and psychological insight. Movement and gesture, although based upon natural behavior, were codified into a system of prescribed signs as described in the *Natyasastra* and in other Hindu writings. Classified according to the parts of the body and inner feelings, gestures were codified (at least for some of the traditional performance forms) into thirteen movements of the head, six of the nose, six of the cheek, seven of the eyebrows, nine of the neck, seven of the chin, five of the chest, thirty-six of the eyes, thirty-two of the feet, and twenty-four of the single hand. Gait and stance also were prescribed. All these movements and gestures were combined (according to character type, emotion, and situation) to create a sign language as complex as speech.

There was a similar classification of verbal speech and music in which elaborate patterns of intonation, pitch, and tempo were mingled according to the emotion, character, and situation. Each play was accompanied by music, for which the instruments varied according to the type of play but might include stringed instruments, flutes and woodwind instruments, cymbals and drums. There usually were also vocal musicians. The drum was considered most essential, for it followed the dialogue closely and enhanced rhythmic effects. The vocalists provided information about the situation or characters through entrance or exit songs; other songs indicated changes in mood or bridged gaps in the action.

Costume and makeup for each character were also strictly prescribed. The makeup indicated the character's caste, social position, and place of birth, as well as the historical period. Color was used symbolically: the Sun and Brahma were golden, lesser gods orange, high-caste characters red, low-caste characters blue, and so on. Ornaments such as earrings, bracelets, belts, necklaces, and headgear differentiated characters within categories. Properties were used symbolically: as examples, the presence of an elephant was indicated by the use of a goad, a horse by a bit, and a chariot by a whip.

Characters were divided into clearly differentiated categories. There were four basic types of heroes, eight basic types of heroines, and numerous lesser types. Overall, each actor sought to weld conventionalized gestures and movements, speech and intonation, costume and makeup, emotion and character type into a performance capable of arousing the appropriate *rasa*. In sum, the Sanskrit theatre demanded a discipline and a knowledge of conventions probably equaled only in certain later forms in China and Japan.

There seem to have been many kinds of theatre companies. Each was headed by a director and each

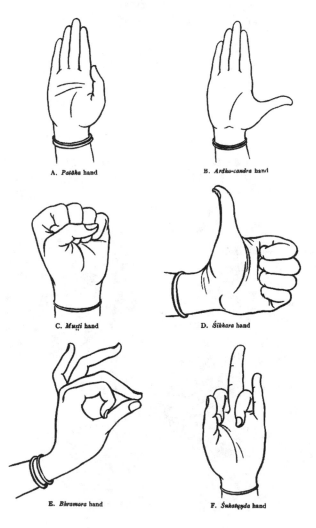

A. *Pataka* hand

B. *Ardha-candra* hand

C. *Musti* hand

D. *Sikhara* hand

E. *Bhramara* hand

F. *Sukatunda* hand

FIG. 26.2
Some of the many hand positions used in Sanskrit drama and dance. From *The Mirror of Gesture* (1917).

included the actors, musicians, and craftsmen required for the company's work. Some companies were entirely male, some entirely female, and some (the most admired) included both male and female performers. At times there were competitions among companies at which prizes were awarded by judges.

As with the Greek and Roman theatres, we can reconstruct a reasonably clear, though very general, overview of the Sanskrit theatre. Still, there is much that we do not (and probably will never) know about it. Obviously the Sanskrit theatre was highly developed, widespread, and sophisticated. Like its Greek and Roman counterparts, it too flourished for a time and then ceased to be vital.

MODERN INDIA

The production of Sanskrit plays ceased in the thirteenth century, but a regional form, apparently (but not definitely) derived from this tradition, *kutiyattum,* continued to be given in the southwestern Indian state of Kerala by actors and musicians who were part of a hereditary temple-service caste. Until the 1960s, these performances were given only at temple festivals. Then, a series of public performances was arranged,

and eventually a systematic study of these dramas began. The traditions can be traced back to at least the tenth century. The temple-theatres in which *kutiyattum* is performed vary in size, proportion being more important than dimensions, since each part of the whole is symbolic. There is a good deal of sculptural decoration, the most elaborate reserved for the stage. The square stage is equipped only with stools, a single bronze lamp, a removable curtain, and drums set between the two doors that lead to the dressing room back of the stage. The characters, who are representatives of the cosmic world, wear colorful costumes and makeup with strong visual patterns.

In modern India the folk play tradition has been far more popular than the Sanskrit. Its definite history can be traced no further back than the fifteenth or sixteenth centuries, although it probably existed earlier. Each area of India has its own characteristic folk plays, and thus the variations are extremely numerous. In some locales they assume operatic form and feature legendary heroes or themes of love and chivalry; in others they are light farces, dance-dramas, or devotional plays. Regardless of type, almost all have common characteristics. A narrator usually sets the scene, calls out each character as needed, and describes events not shown on stage. All are performed

FIG. 26.3
Purulia chhau dancer of northeastern India. Courtesy Performing Arts Program of the Asia Society.

on an open stage surrounded on three sides by the audience. No scenery is used. The acting is stylized, but uses conventions fully understood by the audiences of the area. Music accompanies the entire performance. Most plays continue all night in the light of flickering torches. Such folk plays kept Indian traditions alive during the centuries of Muslim and English domination.

Similarly, early dance traditions were preserved by temple dancers. When Indian nationalism began to reassert itself in the 1890s, one traditional dance form, now called the *Bharatanatyam*, came into prominence once more. Although originally probably performed by more than one dancer, it is now a woman's solo dance noted for its grace. Classical dance also survived in the Kathak, characterized by intricate footwork and precise rhythms; the Manipuri, noted for its swaying and gliding movements; and in innumerable local variants throughout India. Two of the most interesting variants are the chhau and Kathakali.

The purulia chhau masked dances are found in northeastern India, where for centuries they have been a part of the spring festival given in honor of the god Siva. Encompassing solos, duets, and dance-dramas which interpret mythology, sacred history, legend, and nature subjects, they are performed throughout four nights, usually in a courtyard lighted by torches and lanterns. Purulia chhau makes use of the conventions described in *Natyasastra* but adds many of its own. The dancers wear gold and silver brocaded costumes in rich colors, elaborate headdresses, and intricate molded and painted masks made of cloth and wood. The dances are performed entirely by men to the precise rhythms of drums.

Kathakali, now about 300 years old, is restricted to Kerala in southwestern India. Its subject matter is taken primarily from the Hindu epics. Perhaps because it is pantomimic, Kathakali has exaggerated many of the features found in Sanskrit drama and has brought violence and death onto the stage. Its stories center around the passions and furies of gods and demons, or the loves and hates of superhuman characters; the forces of good and evil clash in desperate struggles, but good always wins. The actors rely entirely upon dance, mime, costume, and makeup, although musicians also help to tell the story through narrative and instrumental accompaniment. The gestural language includes more than 500 separate signs. Characters fall into about seven basic types, each with its own elaborate and layered costume and symbolic makeup, which takes hours to apply. Kathakali uses boys or men to perform female roles. The Kathakali dancer must begin his training as a child and is not considered mature until he has performed a role for about twenty years. Kathakali tradition-

FIG. 26.4

Kathakali performers. Note the heavily stylized makeup and costume, especially on the figure at left. From Gargi, *The Theatre in India*. Courtesy Theatre Arts Books.

ally has been presented in a family or temple courtyard or other open space, upon a stage about 20 feet square covered with a flower-decked canopy and lighted by torches, but in recent times it has frequently been seen on proscenium stages. Performances last all night.

Western-style drama also became common in modern India. Western plays were first introduced by the British when they arrived in India in the eighteenth century. In the nineteenth century Indian plays written in the Western style began to appear. Of the modern playwrights, Rabindrinath Tagore (1861–1941) was the most successful in blending Indian and Western traditions in such plays as *Chitra* (1894), *King of the Dark Chamber* (1914), and *The Cycle of Spring* (1917).

Present-day India has many successful dramatists, although relatively few are known outside of India, and even within India fame is difficult to achieve because most dramatists write in one of the regional languages. (India has 17 major languages and some 22,000 dialects.) Some of the best-known of contemporary Indian playwrights are Adya Rangacharya (1904–1985), Utpal Dutt (1939–), Mohit Chattopadhyaya (1934–), Kavalam Narayana Panikkar (1928–), Girish Karnad (1938–), Mahesh Elkunchwar (1939–), Mahesh Dattani, and Vijay Tendulkar. There is much interest in contemporary plays. In Bombay, the Prithvi Theatre has held sixteen festivals since its founding in 1978 to showcase modern drama, both Indian and international. Such interest is not confined to Bombay. In 2000–2001, a six-month-long festival of German plays was staged in fourteen cities. The performing arts are also taught and promoted by the National Academy of Music, Dance, and Drama, founded in 1953 and located in New Delhi. It works in cooperation with its counterparts in the various states and with voluntary organizations throughout India.

The Indian theatre today is extremely diverse, ranging through productions of Sanskrit plays, dance dramas, and folk dramas to modern realistic works. The influence of India on other countries, nevertheless, continues to derive primarily from its classical forms.

CHINA

Records of performance within the vast territory that is contained within present-day China are scant until 1767 B.C.E., when the Shang Dynasty assumed power. From this time onward, dance, music, and ritual (relating to fertility, success in war, and the prevention of disease or disaster) played an important role in Chinese life, and some early rulers considered them crucial to a harmonious state. By the eighth century B.C.E. some temples may have had performers associated with them. Historians have sought to draw a parallel between such practices and the dithyrambic choruses of Greece. After 1000 B.C.E. there are references to secular entertainments at court banquets, where dwarfs, buffoons, and court jesters performed mimes, dances, and songs. One reference to a raised stage also survives. By 206 B.C.E. a large portion of China was united under a single ruler who had built the Great Wall to keep out invaders. By this time we also hear of emperors who kept thousands of entertainers at court; often these accounts associate such practices with debauchery and license.

The first great period of Chinese art and literature came under the Han Dynasty (206 B.C.E.–220 C.E.), during which China came to equal the Roman Empire in size. All sorts of entertainments seem to have flourished, so many in fact that they came to be called the "hundred plays." They included tightrope walking, pole climbing, athletic displays, con-

juring, juggling, sword and fire swallowing, music, dance, and mime. Many of these entertainments were presented at fairs and markets as well as at court. The Han emperors actively encouraged the arts and in 104 B.C.E. established the Imperial Office of Music to organize entertainments and to promote music and dance. Many of the instruments still used in Chinese theatre orchestras date from this period. The Chinese also trace the origin of the shadow play to about 121 B.C.E. when it was first used by wizards to materialize departed souls or gods. Not until later did it become a form of entertainment. (Most historians credit the Hindus with originating this form.)

The Han Dynasty was followed by some 400 years of conflict and unrest, but entertainments seem to have continued. We hear of marionettes between 265 and 420 C.E. and of impersonations of historical personages in the fourth century. After China was reunified under the Sui Dynasty (581–618 C.E.), the forms of entertainment were conglomerations of native traditions with elements imported from India and central Asia. The emperor Yang-Di became so interested in this new version of the "hundred plays" that he set up a training school to encourage its development. Before his reign ended in 618, he is said to have staged a festival involving 18,000 to 30,000 performers in an area extending over four miles.

During the succeeding Tang Dynasty (618–907) great progress was made toward a distinctive theatrical form incorporating music, dance, dialogue, and acrobatics. In 714 Emperor Xuan Zong (also transliterated as Hsuan Tsung and sometimes called Minghuang) established a school to train singers, dancers, and other court entertainers. It differed from earlier schools in its stress on popular and innovative (rather than traditional) forms and in its scope (at one time it included 11,409 students and entertainers). This school underwent several changes but it is usually known as "The Pear Garden." To the present day Chinese actors trace their descent from this school. "Student of the Pear Garden" has roughly the same meaning in China as "thespian" does in the West. Stories of considerable length that would become a fertile source for future dramatists also began to appear in abundance in this era.

The Tang Dynasty was followed by a period of unrest before the Song Dynasty (960–1279) brought China another of its great cultural eras. Not only did the arts flourish during this time, but its scientists produced such inventions as the magnetic compass, gunpowder, and movable type. Storytelling also reached a new peak. Two of the most famous Chinese novels, *Romance of the Three Kingdoms* and *The Water's Edge,* both of which evolved over many centuries, took definite shape. These and other tales were narrated by

FIG. 26.5
Chinese shadow puppets made of skin. They are manipulated by rods attached to the back of the puppet. Courtesy the Performing Arts Program of the Asia Society, New York.

professional storytellers at teahouses and were dramatized for puppet and shadow-play theatres, two of the most popular entertainments of the common people.

At this time innovations were made in poetry that were to affect drama thereafter. Previously, Chinese verse had used an identical number of written symbols in each line; but when these were sung they often did not fit existing melodies, many of which had been imported from other countries. Efforts to eliminate these incongruities led to a new type of poetry in which the number of symbols could differ in each line. By 1000 C.E., this new form had been combined with dance and pantomime, and subsequently a number of different verses were grouped to tell a sustained story. Nevertheless, the form remained more nearly narrative than dramatic.

A fully developed drama began to emerge during the Song Dynasty. Our knowledge of these works was very slight until 1920 when three plays from that era were discovered. Since then more than 150 additional titles and several play fragments have been recovered. *Zhang Xie* (also *Chang Hsieh*), *The Doctor of Letters* is the most important of the surviving plays, since it is considered the oldest extant Chinese drama. Like the others, it includes a prologue (which

FIG. 26.6
A Chinese theatre used for a festival of the twelfth century C.E. at Kaifeng, the northern capital of the Song dynasty. A silk scroll of the twelfth century, recopied in the eighteenth century. Courtesy John Hu and the Taipei Museum.

summarizes the action) and a main story told through dialogue and songs.

During the Song Dynasty the best performers were recruited for the court, where elaborate celebrations were given on such occasions as the emperor's birthday. Other performers played wherever they could. They banded together into troupes of five to seven members and played in villages or cities, in teahouses, or improvised theatres. In the cities, playhouses were situated in special areas called "tile districts." There are said to have been fifty or more theatres in Kaifeng, the northern Song capital. In Hangzhou, there were seventeen "tile districts." According to contemporary accounts, these theatres were fenced enclosures, above which flags and banners flew; the stage was a roofed platform open on three sides; at ground level there was a large area where people might stand, and around this there might be raised stands or balconies.

THE DEVELOPMENT OF CHINESE LITERARY DRAMA

Ironically, it was not until the Mongols conquered China in the thirteenth century that drama began to flourish. The Mongols, whose empire stretched across Asia into Europe, established the Yüan Dynasty, which was to rule China from 1279 until 1368. (It was during this time that Marco Polo visited China and alerted Europeans to the marvels of this rich and highly sophisticated country.)

Historians often say that advances in literature under the Yüan rulers are explained by the exclusion of native Chinese intellectuals from government posts, the traditional outlet for their talents. Supposedly, intellectuals then began to practice and perfect native folk arts, including drama. Especially attracted to earlier forms of music-drama, these writers created works usually considered the foundation of the classical Chinese theatre. Thus, despite political and social repression, China enjoyed something of a golden age in drama.

Yüan dramatists drew their stories from history, legend, novels, epics, and contemporary events. The characters ranged through the entire spectrum of humanity, although the most important roles usually were those of emperors, scholars or students, government officials, generals, rebels, wives, daughters, or concubines. The plays advocated the virtues of loyalty to family and friends, honesty, and devotion to work and duty. They often showed a world out of joint, but one in which poetic justice usually prevailed, and even plays that ended unhappily for the protagonists often

showed the villains being discovered and punished. In the final scenes, lovers or long-separated relatives were reunited or reconciled, deserving officials rewarded, and wealth or honor restored. Overall, the plays provided a wide and rich panorama of Chinese life, much of it based on the past but always made relevant to the contemporary scene.

Through most of the Yüan period the best dramatists lived in northern China, especially Beijing, where they developed a style usually labeled "northern" or *zaju*. Each play in this style usually (but not invariably) consisted of four acts with from ten to twenty songs or arias, all sung by the protagonist. The rest of the characters spoke or recited their lines. No

FIG. 26.7
A wall painting from northwestern China, 1324, showing that many features of the traditional Chinese theatre were already established by that date. Note the hangings at the rear of the stage, the character entering at rear left, and the costumes and accessories of the figures in the foreground. Courtesy Professor Wu-chi Liu.

scores for Yüan plays have survived. The writers were governed by strict rules which demanded that all songs in a single act use melodies from the same mode and that all lyrics make use of the same rhyme scheme; the mode and rhyme used for one act could not be used for any other act of the same play.

If the dramatic action could not be represented in four acts, one or more wedges (*chieh jie*) could be added as prologues or interludes. A wedge was short, with no more than two arias, which might be sung by a character other than the protagonist. At the end of the play a rhymed couplet or quatrain summed up the story. One of these final lines also served as the title for the piece.

The simple, unadorned accompaniment used a seven-tone scale and was usually played by an orchestra consisting of gong, drum, clapper, flute, and p'i p'a (a four-stringed plucked instrument similar to a lute). The action typically extended over months or years, only rarely was it confined to one place, and it occasionally ended unhappily, although poetic justice usually prevailed.

The many stage directions included in the texts, contemporary references, and a still-extant wall painting (dated 1324) indicate that many of the now-traditional staging practices of the Chinese theatre were already in use by the fourteenth century. The stage was essentially bare, with one door on either side at the rear for entrances and exits. Between the two doors hung an embroidered, purely decorative wall piece (the extant picture shows this in two pieces which meet at the center). In the painting the performers wear colorful costumes, some with long and extremely wide sleeves, makeup, and beards. Properties—such as fans, swords, and belts—are also in evidence. Both male and female performers were included in the companies, many of which were named for the leading actresses of the time.

It is unclear how many plays were written during the Yüan period, but about 700 titles are recorded; about 170 of these plays have survived. Some 550 dramatists are known to have written at this time, but little information about them (often not even life dates) has come down to us. One of the best of these authors was Guan Hanqing (or Kuan Han-ch'ing, *c.* 1245–*c.* 1322), often called the father of Chinese drama. He wrote sixty-seven plays, of which eighteen survive. Perhaps the best known of these plays is the domestic tragedy, *The Injustice Done to Ngo Tou,* based on a real-life murder and trial. It shows the suffering, courage, and virtue of a chaste widow wrongfully accused of murder by a wicked rejected suitor. After she has been executed, her spirit appears to her long-lost father, now a judge, who reopens the case and

punishes the villain. The moral courage of Ngo Tou, who epitomizes the virtuous Chinese woman, is intended to provide a lesson for everyone.

The most popular of Yüan dramas is *Romance of the Western Chamber* by Wang Shifu. Unique among northern dramas, it is composed of twenty acts, although the traditional form is preserved by casting it into five parts, each with four acts. Based on a novel, it traces the trials and joys of a pair of ideal lovers, the beautiful Ying Ying and the talented Student Yang, and shows their reunion after long separation. It is noted especially for its characterizations and its poetic excellence, variety, and beauty.

Another well-known play of this period is *The Orphan of the House of Zhao,* probably by Qi Zhun Xiang (or Chi Chün-hsiang), which concerns a

FIG. 26.8
A scene from *Romance of the Western Chamber* showing a rendezvous between Ying Ying and Student Yang as the maid Hung Niang keeps watch. From an edition published during the Ming dynasty. Courtesy Professor Wu-chi Liu.

child who is saved at great sacrifice to his rescuers so that he can grow up to avenge his family, who has been exterminated by a corrupt general. This was the first Chinese play widely known in the West, although only through Voltaire's adaptation of it as *The Orphan of China* (1755). An even more influential play in the West has been *The Story of the Chalk Circle* by Li Xingdao (or Li Hsing-tao). It tells of two women who both claim to be the mother of a young child and family heir; the judge places the child inside a chalk circle and orders the women to pull him out; he awards the child to the one who shows her love by refusing to hurt him. This drama was to serve as a basis for A. H. Klabund's *The Circle of Chalk* (1923) and Bertolt Brecht's *The Caucasian Chalk Circle* (1944). Other plays of this period deal with the religious and supernatural (as in Zhi Yüan's *Dream of the Yellow Millet*), bandit heroes (as in Gao Wenxiu's *The Black Whirlwind*), and many other topics.

During the Yüan period, several large cities had theatre districts, each with many theatres offering both standing room and stall seating for patrons. Surviving records from the period suggest that performers, both male and female, often served as both actors and prostitutes.

Before the middle of the fourteenth century, another school of drama, the "southern," began to gain in popularity in the area around Hangzhou, where the northern style was little understood or appreciated. Of the Yüan dramas from this area, the best known is *Lute Song* (c. 1350) by Gao Ming. Its forty-two acts tell the story of Zhao Wu Niang (or Chao Wu-niang), a virtuous wife who stays at home when her scholar husband, Cai Bojie (or Ts'ai Po-chieh), sets off for the emperor's court. There he succumbs to the allure of fame and wealth and marries the daughter of a prime minister. After Cai Bojie's parents die, Zhao Wu Niang makes her way to the court, where she recalls her husband to his duty. They are reconciled, and he places her on an equal footing with his second wife. *Lute Song* is noted especially for its pathos, poetry, and songs of great beauty. The founder of the Ming dynasty (1368–1644), who ousted the Mongol rulers, admired *Lute Song* so much that he demanded to see it often. His patronage increased the prestige of the southern drama and helped to make it the dominant style.

Important innovations in southern drama were made in the early sixteenth century by Wei Liang-fu who, after studying earlier operas and their music for some ten years, introduced changes based on the music of K'un-shan (the region near Suzhou). These changes were so popular that by 1600 they dominated the stage. By that time the southern style had

also assumed its characteristic features, markedly different from those of the northern style.

A southern play may have as many as fifty or more acts, each with its own title. In the opening act, usually called the argument or prologue, a secondary character sets forth the author's purpose and explains the story. Succeeding acts introduce many plot strands, all of which are happily resolved by the final scene. Any of the characters may sing, and there are solos, duets, and even choruses. The music is composed from a five-tone scale (except for those tunes borrowed from northern drama). The melodies are usually soft and slow (four or five times as slow as in northern drama). The basic accompaniment is played on a horizontal bamboo flute (*di ci* or *ti tzu*), noted for its lingering and emotionally evocative effects. The orchestra also includes other (especially percussion) instruments.

For the most part this later southern drama followed the traditions established by Gao Ming in *Lute Song*. The main changes lay in greater harmony between words and melody, more elaborate and standardized musical scores, and the exclusive use of the Suzhou dialect (noted for its sweet, liquid sounds) in the dramatic songs. This dramatic form was known as *chuanqui*, and it became the dominant drama for elite audiences. Although northern dramas continued to be written after 1600, they were mainly poetic exercises, and the earlier northern dramas ceased to be performed. A new musical mode, with a delicate, languorous quality, was developed in the mid sixteenth century, after which the form was referred to as *Kunqu* and became the dominant dramatic form for the next 200 years.

The best of the Ming dramatists was probably Tang Xianzu (or Hsien-tsu, 1550–1616) whose four plays, collectively called the "Four Dreams," all develop the theme that life is but an illusion. *The Peony Pavilion* is the most admired of the four. In fifty-five acts it tells a complex story of a girl who pines her life away for a lover she has seen only in a dream; later, when he actually appears at her grave she is resurrected. Her father, believing that a deception is being practiced on him, has the lover arrested and beaten before harmony is restored. The play has great variety—a trial in Hades, combats, farcical episodes, suspense, and rescues—but it is most renowned for its love scenes and poetry. (This play became the focus of an international incident in 1998 when New York's Lincoln Center commissioned a production for its annual festival. Mounted in Shanghai with Chinese actors, the production was forbidden by cultural censors, but was remounted in the United States in 1999. This was the first time the work, in fifty-five scenes taking nineteen hours to perform had ever been mounted in its entirety.) Tang Xianzu's greatest rival was Shen Jing (1553–1610), an expert in prosody whose most lasting contribution was a treatise on the musical patterns of southern drama, long the standard work on the subject.

Although in the beginning southern drama was a vital theatrical form, it too gradually became mere closet drama. The scripts often became too long to be produced in their totality; the language became too formal and filled with allusions to be understood by anyone other than scholars; and the writers came to follow prescribed rules of prosody so slavishly that spontaneity suffered. Nevertheless, the southern style continued to dominate literary output until well after the Manchu invaders from the north established the Qing (also Ch'ing) or Manchu Dynasty (1644–1912). The most important dramatists of the Qing period are Kong Shang Ven (1648–1718), whose *Peach Blossom Fan* shows a series of tragic episodes during the closing years of the Ming dynasty, and Hong Sheng (*c.* 1646–1704), whose *The Palace of Long Life* deals with the love of a Tang emperor for his concubine.

Alongside these literary works there were others intended primarily for theatrical performance. The best of the popular writers was Li Yu (1611–*c.* 1680), noted especially for his intricate comedies of situation, such as *Ordained in Heaven* and *Be Circumspect in Conjugal Relations*. He was a master craftsman who invented his own plots based on the ludicrous situations of everyday life. Although extremely effective, these works were largely ignored by literary people of the time. It is ironic, therefore, that Li Yu, through his *A Temporary Lodge for My Leisure Thoughts* (1671), came to be known as China's first dramatic critic.

Unfortunately neither Li Yu nor his more literarily inclined contemporaries could stem the decline of southern drama, although it continued to be the principal type until 1853, when Suzhou, its primary home, was destroyed during a rebellion. Still, southern drama must be admired for the resiliency that permitted it to survive for some 500 years. Even after 1853, its theatrical traditions and texts were to influence its principal successor, the Beijing Opera.

BEIJING OPERA

Beijing Opera, the dominant theatrical form in China after the mid nineteenth century, came to the fore only gradually. It was an amalgamation of several regional forms, of which there were more than 300, distinguished from each other by musical mode, dialect, and performance traditions. In the eighteenth century the most highly developed regional forms were found in the provinces of Hebei and Anhui (in central China), and Gansu and Shaanxi (in the west). In 1790, to celebrate the eightieth birthday of Emperor Qian Long (or Ch'ien-lung), the best performers from various regions were brought to Beijing. Many of these performers remained in the capital where features from various regional styles were gradually amalgamated to form Beijing Opera. By the mid nineteenth century this new style had become dominant, and since that time it has remained the most widely known Chinese theatrical form.

Unlike its predecessors, Beijing Opera is primarily a theatrical rather than a literary form; its emphasis is upon rigidly controlled conventions of acting, dancing, and singing rather than upon the text. Instead of a single work, an evening's program in Beijing Opera is usually made up of a series of selections, many of them acts or portions of longer works intermingled with acrobatic displays. There are no intermissions and usually the scenes are arranged to ensure that the best actors are saved for the final episodes.

The plays of Beijing Opera are usually classified under two headings: civil plays (dealing with social and domestic themes) and military plays (involving the adventures of warriors or brigands), although the two are often mingled. The dramas are derived from earlier literary plays, novels, history, legend, mythology, folklore, and romance. All end happily. The text of a work is seldom strictly followed, for all great actors make changes at certain points, and each troupe has its own version of standard works. The dramatic action is often obscure because the selections are chosen to emphasize the high points of a story. A text, however, is merely an outline for a performance, and the audience goes to see a production rather than to hear a play. The names of the dramatists usually are not even listed on the programs.

Above all, Beijing Opera is characterized by conventions inherited from earlier periods and developed into a strict system. Since they differ so markedly from Western practices, these conventions need to be described in some detail. Many are related to the architectural features of the playhouse. The earliest stages were probably the porches of temples—simple platforms with an ornate roof—and the influence of the temple stage was to continue into the twentieth century. The stage of the traditional Chinese theatre was an open platform, often almost square, covered by a roof supported by lacquered columns. Raised a few feet above the ground and surrounded by a wooden railing about 2 feet high, the stage was equipped only with a carpet, two doors in the rear wall (the one on stage right for all entrances and that on stage left for all exits), between which hung a large embroidered curtain. The only permanent properties were a wooden table and a few chairs.

This simplicity allowed for rapid changes of place, which were indicated through speech, action, or properties. In addition to statements about place, actors might pantomime knocking at gates, entering rooms, or climbing stairs. Circling the stage indicated a lengthy journey. The table and chairs might symbolize a law court, banqueting hall, or other interior scene, for each of which furniture was arranged according to a prescribed formula. The significance of the table and chairs was further extended through their combination with other simple properties: an incense tripod on the table indicated a palace; paper and an official seal indicated an office; an embroidered, divided curtain hung from a bamboo pole signified a general's tent, an emperor's chamber, a drawing room, or a bride's bedroom, depending upon the other properties with which it was combined. The table and chairs might also be used less representationally. Two chairs back to back indicated a wall; chairs placed with backs to the end of a table formed a bridge; a chair might represent a tree or the door of a prison; a table might stand for a hill, cloud, or other high place.

Other properties served to clarify setting and action. A wall painted upon a blue cloth represented a fort, city gate, or mountain pass; a whip indicated that an actor was riding a horse; two yellow flags with wheels painted on them signified a chariot or wagon; four pieces of cloth carried by an actor running across the stage represented the wind; a banner with a fish design indicated water; a stylized paddle was used to mime rowing. A rolled water banner on a tray became a fish, while a corpse was represented by a paddle wrapped in a garment. Weapons, although modeled after real ones, were made of bamboo, wood, or rattan and were decorated. Thus, the audience's imagination was stimulated, but much was left to be filled in. The overall conventionalization is well illustrated by the presence on stage throughout the performance of assistants who helped the actors with their costumes and brought on, removed, or rearranged properties as needed. No attempt was made to disguise their presence; in contrast with the gaudily attired actors, they wore ordinary street clothes, often of an extremely informal type.

Traditionally, the musicians also remained in full view throughout the performance and were dressed in the same style as the stage assistants. They came and went freely and were never considered part of the stage picture. (In contemporary China, where the traditional stage has largely been supplanted by the proscenium stage, musicians are usually seated in the wings rather than onstage.) Music was and remains an integral part of every performance. It provides an atmospheric background, accompanies the many sung passages, controls the timing of movements, and

FIG. 26.9

The orchestra of Beijing Opera. Note the variety of stringed and percussion instruments. From *Peking Opera* by Rewi Alley (Beijing, 1957).

welds the performance into a rhythmical whole. Since Chinese musical notation is very imprecise, theatre musicians learn their parts by rote. Most music used in Beijing Opera has been worked out collaboratively between actors and musicians; most is borrowed from already existing sources and recombined according to the requirements of a particular play. Although they may be classified as string, wind, and percussion, the instruments of the Chinese orchestra have no counterparts in the West. The leader of the orchestra plays a drum which establishes the time and accentuates the rhythm. Gongs, cymbals, brass cups, flutes, stringed instruments, and more exotic items complete the orchestra. Songs are accompanied only by flute and strings, but entrances and exits are signaled by deafening percussion passages. Much of the onstage action is performed to a musical background.

The actor, however, is the heart of the Beijing Opera. On a bare stage furnished only with a few properties and served by drably clothed stage attendants and musicians, the lavishly and colorfully dressed actors speak, sing, and move according to rigid conventions. Acting roles are divided into four main types: male, female, painted face, and comic. The male roles (*sheng*) are subdivided into old men (*lao sheng*), young men (*xiao sheng*), and warrior types (*wu sheng*). Actors playing these roles wear simple makeup and, except for young heroes, beards. The female roles (*dan*) are subdivided into the quiet and gentle (*qing yi*), the vivacious or dissolute (*hua dan*), warrior maidens (*wu dan*), and old women (*lao dan*). Originally all *dan* roles were played by women, but from the late eighteenth century until the twentieth

FIG. 26.10
The contemporary Chinese actress Hu Hongyan in a *dan* role from Beijing Opera. Courtesy Performing Arts Program of the Asia Society.

tell their names and family background, and give other essential information. Such speeches clarify situation and character quickly and leave time to develop fully the moments of high interest.

The actor's delivery of lines is rigidly controlled by conventions. Each role has its prescribed vocal timbre and pitch, and syllables are often drawn out without regard for conversational usage in order to maintain the appropriate rhythm. Even spoken passages are governed by strict rhythms and tempos. Chanted and sung passages are freely inserted into spoken monologues or dialogues. Thus, the lines are rendered in an extremely stylized manner.

All stage movement is related to dance, since it is rhythmical, mimetic, and symbolic. Furthermore, each word is accompanied by movement intended to enhance or explain its meaning. Such stage gesture has been fully codified. There are seven basic hand movements, many special arm movements, more than twenty different pointing gestures, more than twelve special leg movements, and a whole repertory of sleeve and beard movements. Methods of walking or running vary with each role. The prescribed

century actresses were forbidden. Perhaps as a result, the *dan* roles were always considered secondary until Mei Lan-fang (1894–1961), the most famous of Chinese actors, raised them to prominence. After 1911, actresses returned to the stage and now have largely supplanted the male *dan* actors. The painted face (*jing*) roles are so called because of the brilliant and elaborate patterns painted on the actors' faces. They may be rough but frank and open-minded or crafty and treacherous characters. They include warriors, bandits, courtiers, officials, gods, and supernatural beings, but the basic attributes of all are their swagger and exaggerated strength. They are also subdivided according to whether they are principal or minor characters, civilians or warriors, and whether they emphasize fighting and gymnastics or singing and acting.

The comic actor or clown (*chou*) speaks in an everyday dialect, is free to improvise, tells many jokes, and is the most realistic of the characters. He may be a servant, businessman, jailer, watchman, soldier, shrewish mother-in-law, or matchmaker. He combines the skills of the mime and the acrobat.

Upon first entrance, each important character describes his or her basic nature and appearance in a half-spoken, half-chanted passage. This is often followed by other lines in which actors explain the story,

FIG. 26.11
A *wu sheng* (military role) character, noted for acrobatics and excellent physical coordination. From Alley, *Peking Opera* (Beijing, 1957).

FIG. 26.12
A bearded *lao sheng* (old man) role in Beijing Opera. The headdress, beard, and costume are those of a civil courtier. From Alley, *Peking Opera* (Beijing, 1957).

white and the eyes surrounded by a deep red, shading into pink. A similar makeup, although with less marked contrasts, is used for the unbearded *sheng* roles. The clown's distinguishing feature is the white patch around the eyes; the various types of clowns are differentiated by distinctive black markings. By far the most complex makeup is that of the *jing* roles, the entire face being painted in bold patterns symbolic of the particular character.

Such a complex and formalized system of performance requires long and rigorous training. Would-be actors enter a school between the ages of seven and twelve, where they undergo a period of strict discipline for six to twelve years. At first their training is generalized, but as a student shows suitability for a particular type of role, training becomes specialized. If actors are to achieve fame, they must remain within the prescribed conventions of their roles but somehow endow them with their own personalities.

The peculiar flavor of the Chinese theatre also owes much to the audience. In the seventeenth century actors began to perform in teahouses where customers sat at tables. Permanent theatres retained this arrangement, and the ground floor was fitted out with tables and stools at which spectators were served tea while watching the play. The permanent theatres also included a raised platform around the sides and back

gestures and movements are combined according to character, mood, situation, or other conditions.

Costumes, most of which are heavily patterned and gaudy in color, are also extremely important in the Chinese theatre. Each of the more than 300 standard items is designed to describe its wearer's character type, age, and social status through color, design, ornament, and accessories. Color is always used symbolically: red for loyalty and high position, yellow for royalty, dark crimson for barbarians or military advisors, and so on. The designs also have symbolic significance: the dragon is the emblem of the emperor; the tiger stands for power and masculine strength; the plum blossom indicates long life and feminine charm. Headgear is almost as varied as the garments, but the approximately one hundred variations are all used symbolically. Most costumes are made of rich materials regardless of the wearer's rank, but occasionally linen or cotton is used for very poor characters or clowns.

The visual appearance is completed by makeup. Bearded *sheng* actors and old women wear very little makeup. For other female roles, the face is painted

FIG. 26.13
Scene from a Beijing Opera, *The Wild Boar Forest*, showing the hero (center) and his companion (right) buying a sword. From Alley, *Peking Opera* (Beijing, 1957).

FIG. 26.14
Examples of face painting in Beijing Opera. From top left, clockwise: a heroic face; an unstable character; a dragon character; a fierce but stupid general. From *Peking Opera* by Alley (Beijing, 1957).

of the auditorium where poorer spectators sat on benches. A balcony, divided into sections much like the boxes of a Western theatre, was also added. In some periods the balcony was occupied by the wealthy class, but in others it was reserved entirely for women. After the Chinese Republic was formed in 1912, the traditional arrangement of the auditorium began to change and most urban theatres eventually were furnished

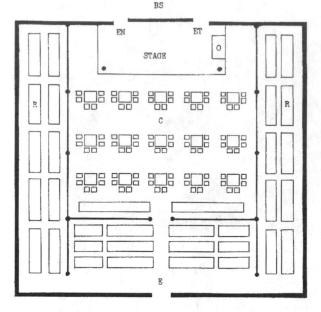

FIG. 26.15
Ground plan of a traditional Chinese theatre. BS = back-stage; EN = entrance to stage; ET = exit from stage; O = orchestra; E = main entrance to auditorium; R = raised side seats; C = tables and stools for audience. Drawing by Douglas Hubbell.

with Western-style chair seating. Until recently, audiences felt free to carry on conversations, to eat and drink, and to come and go during performances. They were usually familiar with the plays, having favorite passages to which they attended carefully while ignoring others.

TWENTIETH-CENTURY DEVELOPMENTS IN CHINESE THEATRE

Western-style drama made considerable headway in China after the empire was replaced by a republic in 1912. At first this form was called "new drama" or "modern drama," but since the late 1920s it has most often been labeled "spoken drama" to distinguish it from the essentially operatic mode of traditional forms. Originally many spoken dramas were translations or adaptations of foreign works, especially those by Shakespeare, Chekhov, Shaw, Galsworthy, and Ibsen. A number of native authors also attempted the new style, but the first to win wide critical and commercial success was Cao Yu (1910–1996), usually considered the finest Chinese dramatist of the twentieth century. His works, such as *Thunderstorm* (1933), *Sunrise* (1935), and *The Bridge* (1945), deal with contemporary social problems, especially the conflict between old and new standards.

After the Communists assumed control over the mainland in 1949, Beijing Opera underwent a number of changes. A committee was set up to revise plays to conform to Communist doctrine, and some plays were removed from the repertory altogether. Many new Beijing Operas on contemporary themes were also written and staged in the early 1960s. During the Cultural Revolution after 1966, there was an attempt to suppress the traditional forms altogether. For a time, the professional theatre almost ceased except for the performance of a few "model" plays. Not until around 1980 and the rejection of the Cultural Revolution were more traditional plays performed once more. Many regional theatrical forms were also revived. In the 1980s, more than 360 forms of traditional theatre, scattered throughout China, were still being performed. In the early 1980s there were 2,072 traditional theatre companies, and of the more than 2,500 productions performed in 1980, more than 2,200 were of traditional plays and only 176 of spoken drama. The greatest threat to traditional theatre has come from the decline in attendance, especially in the cities as the availability of television and movies has altered tastes and theatre-going habits.

Performance traditions also underwent change after 1949. Some use of scenery was at times permitted. The orchestra was removed from the stage altogether, enlarged, and some Western musical instruments accepted into it. After 1980 the voices of performers were electronically amplified. Audience behavior also altered somewhat. Spectators were forbidden to smoke, but refreshments were usually still available in the auditorium. In many theatres, noisy verbal response was replaced by applause.

After 1949 there was also much experimentation with forms other than Beijing Opera. The most popular of all Chinese dramas during this period was *The White-Haired Girl,* by Hi Jingchi (or Ho Ching-chih) and Ding Yi (or Ting Yi), which in its original form borrowed heavily from Western operatic conventions. It was subsequently transformed into a spoken drama, a Beijing Opera, several regional types, and a ballet (which during the Cultural Revolution was treated as a model work). It tells the story of a girl who, sold into slavery and raped by her master, flees to the mountains where she is mistaken for a goddess because her hair has turned white; she eventually joins the Communist rebels and with their help achieves an honored place in society. This ideologically based story is typical of many others.

Spoken drama continued after 1949. The majority of the plays were shaped by Party demands. In these melodramatic works, the characters were treated as heroes or villains primarily on the basis of their ideological positions; invariably the enemies of communism were exposed and routed. After the end of the Cultural Revolution, much greater freedom in theatrical subjects and conventions was permitted, but this trend was halted by the crackdown following the student "democracy movement" in 1989. Recently, restrictions have begun to lessen again.

Although little known outside of China, a number of playwrights have achieved recognition within China since 1949. Among these, some of the most prominent are Wu Han, Zong Fuxian, Cui Dezhi, Bai Hua, Sha Yexin, Gao Xingjian, Ma Zhongjun, Lao She, and Sun Huizhu. Two directors, Meng Jinghui and Lin Zhaohua, have been the major supporters of spoken drama. The China Theatrical School is the primary trainer of actors.

China has begun to build major theatrical complexes similar to those in the West. The new Grand Theatre in Shanghai, which cost $150 million and includes a main auditorium seating 1800 and two smaller halls (seating 600 and 200), is one of Asia's largest and most advanced theatrical structures. In the large auditorium, the main stage, rear stage, and two side stages can be rotated, raised, or lowered; its orchestra pit accommodates 120 musicians. Other Chinese cities, among them Shenzhen and Nanking, are also building opera houses. The new National Theatre Complex in Beijing (set to open in 2003) will cost $360 million. The egg-shaped building, 430 feet long and 135 feet high, will include an opera house, concert hall, and two theatres.

Despite twentieth-century developments, the traditional forms (or variations on them) remain those most fascinating to Westerners.

JAPAN

The early history of Japan and its theatrical forms are shrouded in mystery, since the first written account, *Records of Ancient Things,* was not compiled until 712 C.E. Before that time, however, there were numerous rituals, many of them related to Shintoism, which began in nature and ancestor worship. All these rituals are now usually grouped together under

FIG. 26.16
A *Bugaku* Dance of the Left, "The Music of Great Peace," in which the dancers represent warriors who return to the capital in time to prevent a revolt. From Robert Garfias, *Music of a Thousand Autumns.* Courtesy Mr. Garfias and the University of California Press.

the general label *kagura*; some have persisted to the present day. During this early period a form of rhythmic movement set to music—*sangaku,* "miscellaneous" or "scattered" music—was also being performed at court. In addition, jesters were common.

During the sixth century C.E. Japan began to undergo profound changes after Buddhism was introduced during the reign of Prince Shotoku (573–621). During the following 200 years continental culture, especially from Korea, China, and India, was enthusiastically embraced. Writing and numerous forms of music were among the imports, as were masked dances that soon became regular features of Japanese festivals. Of these masked dances, one—*bugaku*—has survived to the present day and is still performed on important state occasions at the imperial court and at certain shrines and temples. *Bugaku* now designates any dance performed to classical court music (*gagaku*) by dancers whose art has been passed down through generations of families with hereditary rights. Some of the dances are Japanese in origin, but most were imported from continental Asia, especially from Korea, China, Tibet, and India. The dances are usually divided into two categories: "Dances of the Right," from Korea; and "Dances of the Left," from China or South Asia. Despite these labels, the dances are now almost wholly Japanese in character. *Bugaku* performers are also divided into two groups: "Dancers of the Music on the Right," who are dressed predominantly in green and perform to accompaniment played primarily on percussion instruments; and "Dancers of the Music on the Left," who are dressed predominantly in red and perform to accompaniment played primarily on woodwinds. The rhythms vary from the stately to the lively. *Bugaku* is a symbolic representation of one part, the most interesting, of a whole story, and is structured in terms of *jo-ha-kyu* ("beginning, breaking from, fast," indicating tempo, mood, emotional intensity, and vitality of performance). It probably exerted considerable influence on the early development of Noh drama.

In 1955 the Japanese government recognized *bugaku* and *gagaku* as national treasures. Since then they have gained a much wider audience (sometimes even being televised) and have become objects of international scholarly research. The future of these art forms seems to be assured.

NOH THEATRE

Noh owes most to *sarugaku-no* and *dengaku-no.* *Sarugaku-no* probably originated when ritualistic elements, music, and dance from the continent were mingled with tumbling, dancing, and mimicry. The result was a kind of noisy merrymaking (*sarugaku* means "monkey music"). It was extremely varied, even circus-like. An early treatise, *New Notes on Sarugaku* (c. 1060), considers *sarugaku* to be an inclusive term for all kinds of comic entertainment. *Dengaku-no,* which may have been imported from Korea, came to be associated primarily with harvest rituals. It was both acrobatic and rural in character. The first reference to it as a dramatic performance (c. 1023) describes it as made up of rustic dances and songs.

Around the beginning of the twelfth century, *sarugaku-no* was adapted by Buddhists as a way of demonstrating their teachings. Thus, it was given a role similar to that of the medieval mystery and morality plays of Europe. At first the plays were acted by priests, but as performances came to attract large numbers of people to the temples, professional players began to imitate the temple performances at times other than festivals. As the skill of the professionals grew, some temples began to employ them to replace the actor-priests. *Dengaku-no* was developed in much the same way, but primarily at Shinto shrines.

After a time performers had so proliferated that controls were needed. As a result, guilds (*za*) were formed. *Dengaku* guilds can be traced back as far as 1150 and *sarugaku* guilds to about 1270. Most of these guilds were attached to some powerful shrine or temple which granted them a monopoly on performances in its area. In return, the players gave at least some free performances during ceremonies and festivals. By the beginning of the fourteenth century, then, there were numerous groups of well-organized players who mingled mimicry, song, and dance, although the results were probably not yet fully dramatic.

During the fourteenth century Japanese theatre underwent what was probably its most crucial change, a development that can best be understood within the sociopolitical context of the time. In 1192 the emperor ceded his secular powers to a *shogun* (military dictator), a post that became hereditary, although new families won possession of the title from time to time in civil wars. Under the shogunate, Japan developed a strict feudal system that lasted until the late nineteenth century. Within this rigidly organized society, the highest rank was accorded the *samurai* (warriors), with the *shogun* at their head. Beneath the *shogun* were *daimyo* (feudal chiefs), directly responsible to him; below the *daimyo* were the *hatamoto* (or lesser warriors), many with their own fiefs but all receiving an annual allowance of rice according to their ranks. The distinctive badge of the *samurai* was the right to wear two swords. A *samurai* followed a strict code of behavior which demanded that he always be ready to face death, fulfill his filial duty, and be absolutely loyal to his lord and his class. If a *samurai* lost his position because of disgrace or poverty, he and his followers became *ronin* (men adrift), common figures in Japanese drama. Below the *samurai* were the other ranks: *shonin* (merchants), *shokunin* (artists and craftsmen), and *hyakusho* (farmers and peasants)—all with numerous subdivisions. These lesser ranks were usually denied access to the pleasures of the *samurai*, a situation that was to have considerable effect on Japanese theatre.

In 1338 the Ashikaga family assumed the shogunate and held it until the late sixteenth century. It was during the Ashikaga shogunate that Japan, after centuries of domination by imported culture, rediscovered its own heritage. The result was an era of great creative energy during which foreign and native elements were mingled in new and distinctive ways. During this time, the shoguns patronized the arts and the *daimyo*, perhaps in emulation, sought to demonstrate their cultural sophistication.

It was within this context that the first great Japanese theatrical form, Noh, emerged in the late fourteenth century. In 1374 Kiyotsugu Kan'ami (1333–1384), a major performer of *sarugaku-no*, appeared before the *shogun* Yoshimitsu Ashikaga (1358–1408), who was so impressed that he took Kan'ami and his son Motokiyo Zeami (1363–1444) under his patronage and granted them privileges that placed them among the highest officials of the court. Within this rather refined atmosphere, Noh assumed its characteristic form.

Kan'ami was the great innovator, for he seems to have amalgamated elements of *sarugaku kuse* (a narrative song which he brought into Noh and set to dance), and Zen Buddhist ideals to create a form suited to the tastes of the *shogun* and his followers. It remained for Zeami to perfect the form. Its triumph was rapid. *Dengaku-no* quickly declined in popularity and eventually disappeared, and *sarugaku-no* came to be called merely *no* (Noh).

Zeami is considered the greatest of all Noh dramatists. He wrote more than 100 of the approximately 240 plays that make up the active Noh repertory today. Furthermore, it was Zeami who summed up Noh's aesthetic goals and described its practices in some twenty-six theoretical treatises. Consequently, Noh is above all a product of the fourteenth and fifteenth centuries; no play written during the past 400 years holds a permanent place in the Noh repertory.

The major influence on Noh's vision is Zen Buddhism, with its belief that ultimate peace comes through union with all being, through acceptance that individual desire must be abandoned and that

nothing in earthly life is permanent. The most typical Noh plays have as protagonists ghosts, demons, or obsessed human beings whose souls cannot find rest because in life they had been too much devoted to worldly honor, love, or some other goal that keeps drawing the spirit back to the physical world. Although Noh plays are extremely varied, all draw on these Buddhist views.

Noh dramas are classified into five types: *kamimono,* or plays praising the gods; *shuramono,* plays about warriors; *kazuramono,* plays about women; *zatsu,* miscellaneous plays, most often about deranged persons (usually women who have suffered grievous loss of a child or husband) or spirits but sometimes about unmasked "living persons"; and *kirimono,* plays about demons, devils, or other supernatural beings. Traditionally, a program is made up of one play of each type performed in the order listed above, making up a pattern which shows, first, the innocence and peace of the world of the gods; then human error, repentance, and possibility of redemption; and, finally, the glory of defeating those forces that stand in the way of peace and harmony. Since World War II,

FIG. 26.17
Scene from a Noh play. Note the audience seated at the front and side of the main platform. At upper center left is the *hashigakari* (bridge). The orchestra may be seen at the rear of the main stage; an actor stands by the *shitebashira* (upstage-right pillar). From Haar, *Japanese Theatre in Highlight.* Courtesy Charles E. Tuttle Co., Tokyo.

programs of five plays have been considered too lengthy, and now they are usually made up of two or three plays, although still chosen to provide some sense of the older scheme.

Zeami taught that beauty lies in suggestion, simplicity, subtlety, and restraint. Virtually all of his premises are summed up in the complex term *yugen,* which essentially means gentle gracefulness, the mysterious beauty of impermanence in which elegance is always accompanied with awareness of its fragility. It is the qualities summed up in *yugen* that Noh seeks to capture.

Because it relies on indirectness, suggestion, simplicity, and restraint, Noh makes great demands on its audience, for it is not easy to comprehend fully or to enter the realm it embodies. It is not present-time enactment so much as recollection and reenactment through retrospection of some past event which evokes an emotional state or mood. A musical dance-drama, the written script of a Noh play (typically shorter than the average one-act drama of the West) provides a framework for telling a story through choreography. All Noh plays culminate in a dance, and the dialogue and song that precede it serve primarily to outline the circumstances that motivate it. A chorus of six to ten sings the actor's lines while he is dancing and also narrates many of the events during the rest of the play. The chorus may take the lines, either in verse or in prose, of major characters (*shite* or *waki*). Those sections in verse are sung in a rhythmic fashion to instrumental musical accompaniment, while sections in prose are intoned without musical accompaniment. Ordinary speech is used only when a player comes on stage between the parts of a two-act piece to summarize what has happened during the first act.

A Noh performance requires the collaboration of three groups: the *shite* and his followers, the chorus members, and *kokata,* or children, who usually play child roles but also some adult characters or even gods; the *waki* and his followers, whose purpose it is to introduce the drama and lead the main character toward the climactic moment for which the play exists; and *kyogen* actors, who in addition to performing in *kyogen* plays appear in Noh in the roles of commoners and peasants or as narrators in plays in which there is a narrative summary between the parts. All Noh performers traditionally have been male, but many female amateurs learn Noh and perform in recitals. Professional Noh actors derive a substantial income from teaching amateurs.

The *shite* and his companions (unless they represent living humans, rather than ghosts or demons) wear masks of painted wood, many of which have been handed down for generations. Masks fall into five basic types—aged, male, female, deities, and monsters—but each has many variations. In addition, special masks are sometimes used. Only the *shite* characters wear masks.

Costumes, rich in color and design, are based on the official dress of Kan'ami and Zeami's time. Most are made of silk decorated with elaborate embroidery, but they are never as gaudy as those used in the Chinese theatre. The garments may be divided into four categories: the outer garments; garments worn indoors or without an overdress; lower garments, such as divided skirts; and headdresses and wigs. Each category has many variations, but the same garments may be combined (or layered) for use in different roles. Thus, costumes are less rigidly conventionalized in color and design than in the Chinese theatre. The chorus and orchestra wear a simple black kimono and divided overskirt.

Hand properties are few and conventionalized. The fan is by far the most important, for it can be used to suggest the blowing of the wind, the ripple of water, a rising moon, falling rain, and many subtle emotional responses. The meaning of the fan is determined by the actor's movement and the music. Occasionally the actor may use a sword or spear. Stage properties are simple. A miniature wooden or bamboo structure may represent a palace, mountain, bedchamber, or other place; a bamboo frame represents a boat. Usually no more than one or two stage properties are present at once. There is no machinery or scenery.

FIG. 26.18
The Noh stage and auditorium today. Note the Western-style seating. The bridge is at left.

A stage attendant is always present to assist the main actor in changing or adjusting costumes or masks, to set stage properties or remove them when no longer needed, to prompt if it should be needed, and in an emergency to assume the main role if the actor cannot continue. Thus, the attendant is usually a senior actor. He is never considered to be a part of the action or the stage picture.

The Noh stage has been standardized since about 1615. Its two principal areas, the stage proper (*butai*) and the bridge (*hashigakari*) are both roofed like the shrines from which they are descended. The stage roof is supported by four columns, each with its own name and significance. At the upstage right pillar, *shitebashira* (principal character's pillar), the *shite* pauses when he enters to announce his name and where he comes from. While reciting this speech, he faces the pillar at the downstage right corner, the *metsukebashira* (the gazing pillar). The pillar at the downstage left corner is called *wakibashira* because of its association with the secondary character. The upstage left pillar, *fuebashira* (flute pillar), indicates the flute player's position on stage.

The stage is divided into three principal areas, although none is marked off architecturally except by the pillars. The largest area, the main stage, is enclosed within the four pillars and is about 18 feet square. The floor of this area is specially constructed of polished cypress, and sounding jars are placed beneath it to make the rhythmic and emphatic stamping of feet, a distinctive feature of Noh, more effective. Back of the upstage pillars is the rear stage (*atoza*), occupied by the orchestra which is composed of a flute and either two or three drums (never more than four instruments). The musicians are seated so they may see both the main stage and the bridge, since they must always adapt what they do to the principal actor's performance. To stage left of the main stage is the *waki-za*, occupied by the chorus throughout the performance. The chorus sits in two rows, with the chorus leader in the center of the second row.

There are two entrances to the stage. The principal one, the bridge (*hashigakari*), is a railed gangway about 6 feet wide and from 33 to 52 feet long leading from the dressing room. In front of this bridge are three small pine trees symbolizing heaven, earth, and man. The bridge is used as an entrance for the musicians and for all important characters. The other entrance, the "hurry door," upstage left and only about 3 feet high, is used by the chorus, stage assistants, and for the exit of dead characters. The rear walls of the stage and bridge are made of wood. On the wall back of the orchestra is painted a pine tree (usually said to symbolize the Yogo pine tree, through which the god descended to sanctify the first Noh perfor-

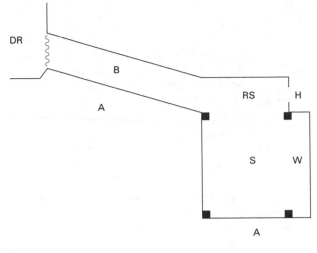

FIG. 26.19
Ground plan of a Noh stage: A = audience; B = bridge; DR = dressing room; H = hurry door; RS = rear stage; S = main stage; W = chorus area. Drawing by Douglas Hubbell.

mance) and on the stage-left side-wall bamboo, perhaps as a reminder of the natural scenery which formed the background of the earliest performances. The audience views the stage from two sides: from in front of the main stage and from the side in front of the bridge. Contemporary Noh theatres usually seat 300 to 500 persons.

There is usually only one rehearsal for a Noh performance. The performers have been trained in the same tradition and know the plays thoroughly. Any combination of actors and musicians occurs only once. In performance all the elements come together in a very dynamic way, for each participant must be able to adjust to the nuances created during that particular performance. Perfection comes not from the mere mastery of conventions and traditions but from the fusion of elements in a collective collaboration.

Noh is intimately bound up with *kyogen* (wild words), short farcical pieces used as interludes between Noh plays. Kyogen, like Noh, is descended from *sarugaku*, but unlike Noh it maintains the comic tone that characterized the earlier form. Again, like Noh, kyogen's conventions were probably set in Zeami's time.

By the sixteenth century there were three main schools of kyogen performers: Okura, Sagi, and Izumi. None of the plays was written down until 1638–1642, when Toraaki Okura (?–1662) recorded 203 of them. These have remained important in the kyogen repertory. In 1660 Okura also published the first treatise devoted wholly to kyogen.

Kyogen covers a wide range of comic subjects that place more emphasis on situation than character. It shows the unexpected dilemmas in which the drunkard, cowardly *samurai*, ignorant lord, sly servant, greedy monk, shrewish woman, and others find themselves. Sometimes the plays parody Noh; occasionally subjects are taken from folklore with animals, gods, or devils as characters. Two- and three-character plays are most common. Prose dialogue comprises the bulk of most kyogen texts. In many plays short songs and dances occur in climactic scenes, occasionally accompanied by the drums and flute of Noh. But though kyogen depends on humorous dialogue and pantomime, it is performed according to strict conventions. Its performers also appear in Noh plays as villagers, peasants, or commoners, thereby adding an earthy and occasionally humorous touch to otherwise stately plays.

Although during the Middle Ages Noh and kyogen were from time to time given publicly for "subscription" audiences, they were essentially aristocratic entertainments. The *shoguns* took Noh under their protection, accorded the performers *samurai* status, and granted them a stipend raised through a system of national requisitions. Five schools, or branches, of Noh were recognized and the headship of each made hereditary. These schools still exist.

When the shogunate fell in 1868 Noh lost its privileged position and survived through the difficult period immediately following primarily because of the patronage of societies organized for that purpose. Since World War II it has been recognized as a national treasure and has drawn devoted audiences. Furthermore, its prestige has been greatly enhanced by tours abroad and the growing interest of international scholars. Each of the five Noh schools owns its own theatres. At the National Noh Theatre opened in Tokyo in 1983, performances by all the schools can be seen. The actors of both Noh and kyogen have also established a strong economic base by teaching amateurs.

BUNRAKU

While Noh was assuming its role as a major aristocratic art form, other entertainments were being addressed to more plebeian audiences. At the beginning of the Tokugawa shogunate (1603–1867), major popular forms began to emerge. As with Noh, the new forms can best be understood within the sociopolitical context of the time. Through most of the Tokugawa era, Japan was at peace. As a result, the *samurai* declined in importance while the lesser ranks improved their economic position. Beginning in the early seventeenth century, the shoguns also expelled all foreigners and deliberately isolated Japan from outside influences. The resulting emphasis on native social and artistic forms encouraged the elaboration of ceremonies and entertainments of all kinds just when the increased wealth of the lesser classes permitted them to patronize the arts. This conjunction of events helps to explain why during the course of the seventeenth century there evolved two of Japan's most distinctive theatrical types—the puppet (or doll) theatre and Kabuki.

The puppet theatre (*ningyo shibai*) first came to prominence during the seventeenth century as an amalgamation of numerous earlier influences, although some types of puppet performances can be traced back to the Heian era (781–1185), during which Oe Tadafusa published his *Book of Puppeteers* (1100); thereafter some type of puppet theatre was always practiced by wandering entertainers.

Even before this puppet theatre came to the fore, there was another entertainment in which stories or legends were recited or chanted to the accompaniment of a stringed instrument, the *biwa*. After 1560 this form underwent a major change when another stringed instrument with quite different qualities, the *samisen*, was introduced from the Ryukyu Islands. By far the most popular work in this altered genre treated the love story of Joruri, the daughter of a wealthy family. It became so dominant that the form itself came to be called *joruri*.

The first major step toward a mature puppet theatre was taken sometime between 1596 and 1614 when puppet performances were combined with *joruri* narration. This combination became increasingly popular, especially after 1648 when Toraya Gendayu established a company in Tokyo. The perfection of the form, however, had to await Takemoto Gidayu (1650–1714), who founded a company in Osaka in 1685. His style was to dominate the doll theatre thereafter. Takemoto's popularity owed much to the plays of Chikamatsu Monzaemon (1653–1724), Japan's greatest playwright, who began writing specifically for Takemoto in 1686. Chikamatsu wrote many kinds of works but was noted especially for his five-act history plays and his three-act plays on contemporary life. Modern critics especially admire the sensitive characterizations and the beautiful language of his dramas about the double suicides of lovers. Among his best-known plays are *The Double Suicide at Sonezaki* (1703), *Drumming of the Waves at Horikawa* (1707), *Battle of Coxinga* (1715), and *The Love Suicide at Amijima* (1721).

Another important Bunraku dramatist is Takeda Izumo II (1691–1756), who worked with Chikamatsu and succeeded him as principal writer for the Osaka doll theatre. His masterpiece is *Chushingura*

(1748), written with the assistance of Namiki Sosuke and Miyake Shoraku. Based upon an actual event, it tells of forty-seven faithful *samurai* who avenge the wrongs done to their master. (This story was so popular that between 1748 and 1900 more than 100 full-length puppet and Kabuki plays were based on it.)

The puppets used in these performances underwent many changes, becoming ever more complex. Originally the puppeteers used a head only, but later hands and feet were added, and by 1678 rather complete figures were in use. In 1730 a mechanism was introduced that allowed the dolls to move their eyes; in 1733 jointed and movable fingers were added; later, the puppets were fitted with movable eyebrows. As the figures grew in complexity, the number of operators increased. Originally one handler, hidden from view, was sufficient, but after 1734 each doll was operated by three men, all visible to the audience. One person manipulated the head and right arm, a second the left arm, and a third the feet. In 1736 the figures were doubled in size to their present height of 3 to 4 feet.

The stage also grew in complexity. The use of movable stage settings after 1715 soon led to the invention of stage machinery which has since been adopted throughout the world. In 1727 elevator traps were introduced to raise scenery through the floor, and after 1757 they were used to create different stage floor levels.

The puppet theatre reached the height of its popularity in the eighteenth century. Its most successful playwrights at that time were Takeda Izumo (1691–1756) and Chikamatsu Hanji (1725–1783). Most of the conventions were also fixed at this time. Around 1780 the puppet theatre began to decline as it was overshadowed by Kabuki. Some of its vitality was restored after Uemura Bunrakuken (1737–1810) came to Osaka sometime between 1789 and 1800. The name Bunraku, used by the only present-day puppet theatre, was derived from him. Despite Bunrakuken's work, the puppet theatre was to lead a precarious existence throughout the nineteenth and twentieth centuries. Its future now seems secure, however, for in 1963 the Bunraku Association was formed to manage all phases of the art, and in 1984 the luxuriously equipped National Bunraku Theatre was opened in Osaka. The Bunraku troupe performs six to eight months a year, divided among their home theatre in Osaka, a small theatre in the National Theatre in Tokyo, and on tour both in Japan and abroad.

Like Noh, Bunraku has its own conventions. Its stage is about 36 feet wide by 25 feet deep and is divided into three levels from front to rear, each indicated by low partitions between which the han-

FIG. 26.20

Japanese puppets and their handlers. From Haar, *Japanese Theatre in Highlight.* Courtesy Charles E. Tuttle, Tokyo.

dlers work. All locales are represented scenically and changed as required by the story. Numerous properties are used. At the right side of the auditorium just forward of the stage is a platform for the narrator and *samisen* player. This platform is equipped with a turntable which is revolved to bring the narrator and *samisen* player into position. At the end of each act a new team replaces the earlier one.

A puppet performance begins with the appearance of an announcer, clad in black and wearing a hood (this costume is worn by all the stage assistants except the principal handlers, the musicians, and the narrator), who proclaims the title of the play and the names of the *samisen* player and the narrator, both of whom command greater prestige than the puppet handlers. The *samisen*, a three-stringed instrument related to the lute, has a skin-covered base and is played with a heavy ivory plectrum. Extremely varied in sound, it can follow the rise and fall of the voice, give special emphasis, and provide punctuations to the narration and action. Its accompaniment is considered essential in the puppet theatre. The narrator tells the story (the handlers do not speak) and expresses the feelings of each puppet. He smiles, weeps, starts with fear and astonishment.

The handlers and the puppets occupy center stage. The puppets vary somewhat in size and complexity according to their importance in the play. The female figures ordinarily do not have feet, although these are suggested by the way the kimono is handled. Minor puppets do not have movable mouths, eyes, and eyebrows. The handlers seek to become one with their puppets and to absorb themselves in

FIG. 26.21
Scene from a Japanese doll theatre performance. The principal puppeteer is seen at left and two others can be glimpsed at right. Courtesy Performing Arts Program of the Asia Society.

the drama. They undergo long and arduous training before appearing on stage, first learning to operate the feet (usually about ten years is spent mastering this operation), then progressing to the left hand (requiring another ten years), and then to the head and right arm. Their artistry has exerted considerable influence upon Kabuki.

KABUKI

Even as the puppet theatre was developing in the seventeenth century, Kabuki was taking shape. It is usually traced back to 1603 when Okuni, a female dancer from the Izumo Grand Shrine, began to give public performances on an improvised stage set up in the riverbed at Kyoto. Her programs were composed of playlets interspersed with dances. Kabuki was a genuinely new expression of an optimistic, hedonistic urban society. Most of the performers were women, although they sometimes dressed as men, and they were obviously erotic. The programs caught on rapidly, and by 1616 there were seven licensed the-

atres. They came to be associated with prostitution, however, and in 1629 local authorities forbade women to appear on the stage. Women's Kabuki was succeeded by Young Men's Kabuki, which was suppressed in 1652, for the boys proved to be as seductive as the women. Next, came Men's Kabuki, destined to be the permanent form, although the men were required to shave their foreheads and to avoid any emphasis upon physical charms.

Kabuki developed rapidly, and between 1675 and 1750 evolved most of its characteristic techniques. New methods of acting were introduced, fully developed plays replaced the former improvised entertainments, and artistry increased personal appeal. In mature Kabuki of the eighteenth century the repertory consisted in more or less equal measures of three general categories of plays: "pure" Kabuki plays written especially for the Kabuki stage; adaptations of major Bunraku dramas; and dance dramas. Many purists consider that true Kabuki ended in 1868, when the emperor resumed his authority from the shogunate and Western influence began. Since World War II ticket prices have made Kabuki something of a luxury, while the patronage of tourists has brought alleged debasements of the traditional practices. Nevertheless, Kabuki remains the most popular of Japanese theatrical forms, and its future now seems assured since the Japanese National Theatre was opened in 1966.

Kabuki drama has undergone many changes. It began as sketches about life of the urban commoner and dance scenes often improvised by the main actors, and gradually expanded to multiscene plays written by professional playwrights. The first multi-act play dates from 1664. In the 1670s the major playwright Chikamatsu Monzaemon began to write for a major Kyoto actor and troupe manager, Sakata Tojuro. Over a period of some twenty-seven years he wrote scores of plays both for the Kabuki stage and for the puppet theatre. Many of the domestic plays which he first wrote for the Kabuki stage in the late seventeenth century became models for the domestic lovers' suicide plays that he wrote for the puppet theatre in the early eighteenth century, and which Kabuki actors later readapted for their performances.

As drama increased in importance, the staff of each troupe came to include a playwright and a number of assistants who prepared each of the six annual productions of the season. After the 1860s playwrights were usually novelists, journalists, or literary figures who worked outside the professional system of the preceding era. Among the writers of the nineteenth century, two of the most famous are Kawatake Mokuami (1816–1893), famous for his domestic plays, especially those about thieves and other low-life characters, such as *Benten Kozo and His Gang of Thieves* (1862) and *Gorozo the Dandy* (1864); and Tsuruya Namboku (1755–1829), whose *The Ghost of Yotsuya* (1825) is still often revived.

Kabuki writers never thought in terms of Western dramatic forms, and no clear line was drawn between comic and serious works. Most Kabuki plays are made up of loosely connected episodes that bring together three or four separate dramatic worlds.

Kabuki programs have traditionally been lengthy. From around 1650 until after 1850 they usually lasted about twelve hours. In this period it was customary to arrange programs according to a four-part division: first came a historical play (*jidaimono*) that glorified the traditions and values of the *samurai*; a dance (either with or without a story but with a strong emotional flavor) either came next or was included within the *jidaimono*; then a domestic drama (*sewamono*) set in the milieu of merchants, traders, or artisans was presented; and the performance concluded with a striking one-act dance drama, often humorous. All parts of the performance were related thematically whenever possible. In 1868 the maximum length of

performances was reduced to eight hours a d[...] performances were not given until 1878, [...] lighting was introduced.) Since World W[...] length of performances has been reduced a[...] plete full-length plays are seldom performe[...] four-part arrangement, with as many as ten acts from a variety of plays, is usually followed. At commercial theatres today, it is customary to give two programs a day. Plays are performed every day from the second to the twenty-sixth day of the month.

Many critics consider dance to be the basis of Kabuki, although dance must be understood to include rhythmical movement, studied posture, and conventionalized gesture. Originally only the female roles were danced, but by the late eighteenth century dance was such an essential part of all performances that a professional choreographer was added to each company. Since then dance has grown more complex and new forms have been created. The choreographers founded hereditary schools. Many of the present schools date back to the eighteenth century. These choreographers also teach amateurs outside the Kabuki world.

Dance in Kabuki is always expected to reflect the verbal text. It seeks to distill the essence of real emotions and deeds into stylized gesture, movement, and posture. Thus, weeping becomes a rhythmical

FIG. 26.22
A Kabuki theatre in the eighteenth century. Note that the stage still retains some features of the Noh, although they have been modified, and that the *hanamichi* has been added. An eighteenth-century print. Courtesy British Museum.

movement of the head accompanied by precise hand gestures. Kabuki dance is accompanied by narrative and descriptive music that helps to establish its character but always remains subordinate.

Three types of music are heard in Kabuki, each identifiable by sound quality, theatrical function, and the placement of the musicians on stage. First, Kabuki's basic music is in Nagauta style (*samisen*, drums, flute, and singers). Because in Naguata the musicians are placed offstage, the music is known as *geza* ("lower seat"). This style of music may be augmented by special drums, gongs, bells, and cymbals. It underscores entrances, exits, dialogue, and fighting scenes. *Geza* musicians draw on a repertory of several hundred known melodies and rhythmic patterns; in each production the music is chosen for its appropriateness to season, location, and the emotional quality of individual scenes. Second, for dance plays, dance music of several kinds is played and sung; in addition to Naguata, several styles have developed within Kabuki specifically to accompany dances. Third, puppet-style music accompanies plays adapted from puppet theatre and some dance plays. The dance-play and puppet-play musical ensembles are placed on stage (at the rear or at stage left, depending on the type of play); for these plays the score is "through composed" and unique to each puppet or dance play as in a Western opera or ballet. Onstage musicians wear the ceremonial dress of the *samurai* (divided skirt, kimono, and stiff horizontal shoulder pieces). When not performing, they sit upright and motionless.

Song and narration are important in Kabuki, especially in dance plays or those taken from the puppet theatre. The actors never sing. In dance plays, the chorus sings lyrics which describe the scene or narrate the story; the chorus may also sing lines supposedly said or thought by the dancers. In puppet-derived plays, the narrator chants or sings the third-person descriptive and narrative passages, but the actors speak their own dialogue. Even the actor's spoken lines follow conventionalized intonational patterns.

Kabuki acting is a combination of speaking and dancing. Because it follows established rules, it requires long and diligent study. The actor begins his training at the age of six or seven, first studying dance and then proceeding to diction, intonation, and the wearing of costumes. Since there are many children's roles, the student is usually on stage from the beginning of his career and learns his profession at first hand. Most of the leading performers come from a few families for whom acting is a hereditary profession. Each family has an elaborate system of stage names, some of which are so honored that they are awarded only to those considered undisputed mas-

FIG. 26.23
Ichikawa Danjuro V in the role of Kagemasa Gongoro in the Kabuki play *Shibaraku* (1697). Depicted is one of the characteristic features of Kabuki acting, the pose struck and held *(mie)*. In this play the character exits along the *hanamichi* through a series of these poses. The popularity of the play and this exit were such as to motivate woodcuts of the type shown here. Woodcut by Katsu Shunsho (1770). Courtesy Rietberg Museum, Zurich.

ters of their art. An actor is almost never judged mature until after he has reached middle age.

The roles in Kabuki are divided into a few basic types: *tachiyaku,* loyal, good, and courageous men;

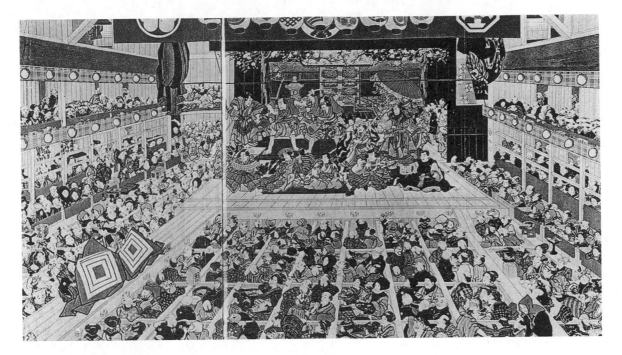

FIG. 26.24
The Nakamura-za in 1859 during a Kabuki performance. Note the two
hanamichi and the arrangement of the auditorium. A contemporary engraving.

katakiyaku, villainous men; *dokekata,* comic roles, including comic villains; *koyaku,* children's roles; and *onnagata,* women's roles of various kinds, all played by men. These basic types are subdivided into a score of subtypes.

Kabuki actors do not wear masks, but some roles require boldly patterned makeup to exaggerate the muscular conformation of the face. Red and black patterns are normally painted upon a white base, although demons and evil characters may use blue or brown. The *onnagata* draws in false eyebrows and adds rouging at the corner of the eye and to the mouth but otherwise leaves the face completely white. Married women blacken their teeth and obliterate their eyebrows. For some of the more athletic male roles, the musculature of arms and legs is outlined in a conventional pattern. The makeup of each role is symbolic of the character.

Every role also has its traditional costume. Most are based upon historical garments which have been altered for dramatic purposes. Dress from different periods is often seen in a single play, for historical accuracy is of no importance in Kabuki. Some costumes weigh as much as fifty pounds, and stage attendants assist the actors in keeping them properly arranged while on stage.

In visual style Kabuki lies somewhere between the conventionalism of Noh and the illusionism of Western theatre. This combination can be seen most clearly in the properties, stage, and scenery. Properties range from the symbolic to the relatively realistic. Especially in dance plays, the fan, as in Noh, can indicate riding a horse, shooting a bow and arrow, the rising of the moon, or opening a door. A scarf serves a multitude of similar purposes. On the other hand, many properties are representational although none is intended to be convincingly real. The Kabuki horse probably best exemplifies the degree of illusionism: a wooden framework shaped like a horse, covered with velvet, and ridden by an actor is supported by two actors, whose human legs clearly show. Many other properties—armor, swords, human heads, tigers, elephants, monkeys, household goods—are represented through similar conventions.

The stage also is a melding of convention and illusion. The earliest Kabuki performances were on temporary stages modeled after the Noh stage. When multi–act plays evolved in the 1660s, a curtain was added to conceal the stage; the bridge was also widened to provide more acting space. Mats suspended over the audience provided shade until 1724, when government regulations for the first time allowed theatres to be permanently roofed. After that time machinery began to be used for special effects. A small elevator trap was installed in 1736, and soon more elaborate devices were exploited. In 1753

Namiki Shozo invented the large elevator stage and in 1758 he introduced the revolving stage (first used at the Kado-za in Osaka). After 1827 the revolving stage was sometimes constructed in two sections, one revolving inside the other, and worked independently. A forestage had become a permanent feature of the Kabuki theatre by 1736 and was the principal acting area after 1745. Some scenic pieces began to appear in the late seventeenth century and grew ever more complex thereafter.

Some time between 1724 and 1736 one of the Kabuki's most distinctive features, the *hanamichi,* was introduced. A raised gangway which connects the stage with a small room at the rear of the auditorium, the *hanamichi* is used for all major entrances and exits, as well as for many important scenes. The *hanamichi* was so popular that a second had been introduced by the 1770s. By 1830, the Kabuki stage had achieved its characteristic form. The Noh roof had been abandoned, and the stage now occupied the full width of the auditorium and was equipped with re-

volving stage and elevator traps. The area between the two *hanamichi* was divided into numerous square enclosures, or floor boxes, in which spectators sat on mats. Two levels of boxes (*sajiki*) ran along each side of the auditorium.

After 1868 several changes were made as a result of Western influence. The proscenium arch was introduced in 1908 and became standard after 1923, as did Western-style seating. The second *hanamichi* was eliminated, although it is still installed temporarily when required for a particular play. Except for the introduction of flying machinery, electric lighting, and the proscenium arch, however, the stage has remained relatively unchanged. The proscenium arch of the present Kabuki-za in Tokyo is 93 feet wide but only about 20 feet high, and the auditorium is only 60 feet deep. Thus, the spatial relationship between stage and audience differs considerably from that of the typical Western theatre.

Unlike Noh, Kabuki uses a great deal of scenery, both for decorative and functional purposes. Every

FIG. 26.25

A Kabuki stage of the nineteenth century showing the revolving stage (first used in 1758) and a small elevator trap (first used in 1736). At center left is the *hanamichi.* Note also the screens at either side of the stage, the one at right raised like a venetian blind. A woodcut published in *Scribner's Magazine* 7 (1890).

locale in a Kabuki play is suggested scenically. When there is no intermission between scenes, settings are changed in full view of the audience by means of the revolving stage, elevator traps, grooves, or by visible stage attendants. More often, scenery is changed during intermissions behind the stage's striped front curtain. Kabuki emphasizes lateral composition; sets are never pie-shaped, and almost all scenery is placed parallel to the front of the stage. Painting is usually flat and is not intended to appear three-dimensional. Typically the stage is enclosed at the rear by flats painted with a distant view, but illusionism is avoided by letting the cracks between individual flats show and by using a black curtain to cut off the top of the scene.

Sometimes relatively realistic Japanese buildings are erected on stage, but the entry gates to houses are often removed by stage assistants when they are no longer needed, and other theatrical conventions constantly remind the audience of the contrivance. Many scenic pieces are used symbolically. White mats represent snow, blue mats water, gray mats the ground; different kinds of trees indicate changes of locales. This mingling of the familiar with the conventional makes Kabuki, among all the traditional Asian forms, most accessible to Westerners.

Like other traditional forms, Kabuki has gained considerable international fame through tours abroad and the interest of scholars. Kabuki has also been influenced by Western conventions and many productions have introduced innovations into Kabuki plays, acting, and scenery. But traditional practices still dominate.

MODERN JAPANESE THEATRE AND DRAMA

After the end of Japan's isolation and the fall of the shogunate in the late nineteenth century, many of the earlier restrictions on the theatre were removed. Women were now allowed to appear on the stage and entrepreneurs to open new theatres. The major novelty, however, was the introduction of Western-style drama and theatrical conventions. The earliest productions in this mode came in the 1880s, but *shimpa* (as this movement was called) reached its peak between 1904 and 1909, and then declined. Since World War II there have been attempts to revive *shimpa*. These plays have typically been sentimental, romantic, or melodramatic.

Still another offspring of the Western movement is *shingeki* (or new theatre). It began from two sources. First, in 1906, Tsubouchi Shoyo (1859–1935), a professor of English at Waseda University in Tokyo, founded the Literary Arts Society to train young am-

FIG. 26.26
Scene from a Kabuki play at the present-day Kabuki-za in Tokyo. Note the mingling of representational and conventionalized elements. From *Décor de Thèâtre dans le Monde depuis 1935.*

ateur actors in Western theatre and to stage plays by Shakespeare, Ibsen, Shaw, Chekhov, Strindberg, and others. Tsubouchi also established a theatre museum at Waseda University which has become a major center for theatre research. Second, in 1909, Osanai Kaoru and the Kabuki actor Ichikawa Sadanji established the Free Theatre to retrain professional theatre artists to perform Western drama. At first committed to realism and to the Stanislavsky method, *shingeki* has in recent decades become eclectic in outlook and experimental in approach.

Japan's best known post-World War II dramatists were Kobo Abe (1924–1993) and Yukio Mishima (1925–1970). An admirer of Brecht, Abe wrote a number of protest plays, among them *Slave Hunting* (1955), a denunciation of postwar traffic in the remains of the war dead. Others of his best known plays include *Friends* (1967), *The Green Stocking* (1974), and *Image Hunting* (1978). Mishima, an admirer of Japanese tradition, wrote about forty plays, including several Noh and Kabuki dramas. Among his *shingeki* works, perhaps the best known are *The Nest of the White Ant* (1955), about the hollow lives of Japanese emigrés in Brazil, and *Madame de Sade,* a play about the wife of the Marquis de Sade that achieved considerable popularity in Europe and America.

Contemporary dramatists include Juro Kara (1940–), author of *Virgin Mask* and *John Silver;* Seiichi Yashiro, author of *They Vanished at Dawn, Hokusai Sketchbooks,* and *Bewitching;* Minoru Betsuyaku (1937–), author of *The Elephant, The Move,* and *Buried Scenery;* Masakazu Yamazaki, author of *Zeami,*

The Boat Is a Sailboat, and *Hideyoshi and Ricky;* Oriza Hirata, author of *Tokyo Notes, Citizens of Seoul,* and *Citizens of Seoul 1919;* and Ryo Iwamatsu, author of *Tea and a Lecture, Romance Is Banned,* and *Futon and Daruma.* Unlike the plays of the 1980s, which tended toward apocalyptic spectacles, plays since the 1990s have become more naturalistic and analytic. They are often referred to as "quiet theatre" to distinguish them from the raw energy of plays that dominated the 1980s.

Among contemporary Japanese directors, by far the best known is Tadashi Suzuki (1939–), who began his work in the student theatre at Waseda University and eventually established his own theatre, the Suzuki Company of Toga. Suzuki developed a highly disciplined acting mode which synthesized martial arts, Kabuki, and Noh techniques. He also sought to build a bridge between Japanese and Western theatre; his most famous productions are adaptations of Greek myths, among them *The Trojan Women, The Bacchae,* and *Clytemnestra,* all of which were performed in the West to great acclaim. Many U.S. schools came to offer training in the Suzuki method, described in Suzuki's *The Way of Acting.* To Suzuki's theatre center in Togamura groups of professional actors came annually from many countries for training and to perform theatrical productions of international interest. In 1993, in collaboration with Anne Bogart, he established the Saratoga (New York) International Theatre Institute.

Yukio Ninagawa (1935–) is another internationally known director, especially noted for his productions of Western classics, among them *Peer Gynt, Macbeth,* and *A Midsummer Night's Dream,* although he has also directed many contemporary Japanese plays. He has received important artistic awards both in Japan and Britain (including an honorary doctorate from Edinburgh University).

Perhaps Japan's best-known cultural export is the *avant-garde* dance form, Butoh, which sets out to assault the senses. A theatre of protest, it uses full body paint (usually white), near or complete nudity, shaved heads, and grotesque costumes. Sankai Juku was the best known of the early Butoh companies, but the number has greatly increased and they now perform throughout the world.

Since 1989, Japan has built more than two dozen performance halls. Most are devoted to specialized uses, including opera, concerts, dance, and Western-style theatre. Contemporary forms of entertainment are now considerably more popular with audiences than are Noh, Bunraku, and Kabuki, although the traditional forms still command respect in Japan and are of special interest in Europe and America, where knowledge of Japanese contemporary theatre is slight.

OTHER ASIAN COUNTRIES

Each Asian country has its own dramatic traditions, often quite diverse and highly developed. Many of Korea's theatrical forms predate those of Japan and exerted considerable influence on Japanese performance traditions. Ritualistic performances in Korea can be traced back to the third century C.E., but they may be even older. Eventually Korea produced various types of dance-drama, puppet shows, farces, pantomimes, and, after 1908, a Western-style drama.

The most characteristic native form is Kamyonguk (masked dance-drama). Originally, masked dance-drama probably grew out of shaministic rituals (many of which are still performed) intended to exorcise evil spirits, to ensure a good harvest, and to honor the dead, but it is now valued as a source of national identity and as entertainment. There are many local variations, but most involve vigorous dancing, singing, and short skits. Most include satire and social commentary, which serve as vents for frustrations with authority and injustice. The costuming is colorful and the masks numerous and varied. The musical accompaniment is played on woodwind, string, and percussion instruments. The government has encouraged the preservation and development of the traditional performing arts through subsidies, a program of theatre building, and the establishment of a National Theatre. Western-style drama is also common.

The theatre of Southeast Asia is allied to that of India, perhaps because the people of that area share the heritage of Hinduism, the Hindu epics, and Buddhism. Dance-drama, especially, is highly developed in Indonesia, Thailand, Cambodia, Laos, and Burma.

FIG. 26.27
The masked dance-drama of Pongsan, Korea. In the background are the musicians. Courtesy Performing Arts Program of the Asia Society.

But there are as well many other theatrical forms in Southeast Asia—folk drama, operetta, spoken drama, pantomime, improvised plays, shadow puppet plays, doll puppet plays, and Western-style drama.

One of the most distinctive forms of Asian drama is the shadow play, widely performed in Indonesia and Malaysia in numerous local variations. This form seems to have been cultivated most fully on the islands of Java and Bali in Indonesia, where it is called *wayang kulit*. It is unclear when or where it originated. Some scholars argue that it is purely indigenous, others that it came from India, and still others that it came from China. Regardless of its origin, it had by the eleventh century C.E. developed into a highly complex art quite unlike the forms seen in India or China. Between the thirteenth and seventeenth centuries, the Indonesian and Malaysian shadow puppets evolved to their present size and shapes, and by the nineteenth century their visual features and the conventions of performance had become fixed.

The *wayang kulit* uses flat puppets made of leather that are cut and decorated to create intricate patterns

FIG. 26.29
Shadow puppet from Malaysia representing Seri Rama (the hero). From the private collection of Molly and Walter Meserve.

FIG. 26.28
Shadow puppet from Malaysia representing Hanuman (the money king). From the private collection of Molly and Walter Meserve.

of light and shadow when images of the figures are cast on a screen. The puppets, which range in size from 6 inches to more than 3 feet, are mounted on sticks of buffalo horn. The major characters in the dramas, most of whom are based on *Mahabharata* or *Ramayana*, are differentiated through size, shape, color, and costume, but minor figures are differentiated only according to type (ogre, clown, god, and so on). A complete set of *wayang kulit* puppets includes 300 to 400 figures. All the puppets used during a single performance (no more than about 50) are manipulated by one person (the *dalang*), who also speaks the dialogue (much of it improvised) and narrative passages, sings songs, provides many sound effects, and gives cues to the *gamelan,* a gong-chime musical ensemble composed of various kinds of xylophones, percussion and stringed instruments, flute, and singers. By tradition, performances begin at 8:30 P.M. and last until dawn (nine to ten hours). Only on special occasions (primarily for tourists) are performances given during daylight hours.

A *wayang kulit* nighttime performance is divided into phases related to the passing hours: first, a problem or situation is established; then an intrigue begins, usually in the stronghold of the hero's enemies; next, the hero appears, accompanied by clown-servants (this happens at midnight); the action reaches its climax in a battle fought between the hero and several powerful giants (this phase of the story usually begins about 3 A.M.); and the action is resolved at dawn with the triumph of the hero over the forces of evil. The drama is accompanied throughout by music, which also varies according to the phase of the story and the hour of the night. The performances are usually given in an open pavilion. The audience sits on both sides of the screen—those on one side see the puppets themselves, those on the other side the shadows cast by an oil lamp (or now often by an electric lamp).

FIG. 26.31
Performer in the *wayang topeng* masked dance theatre of Bali. Courtesy Performing Arts Program of the Asia Society.

A number of dramatic types have been derived from the *wayang kulit*. One variation (*wayang golek*) uses three-dimensional doll puppets. Another (*wayang orang*) uses human performers, as does *wayang topeng*, a masked dance-drama that makes use of stories from many different sources. The variations are numerous indeed. There are also many other performance traditions, especially in Bali, where they are traditionally associated with temple ceremonies, but where they are increasingly performed in shorter versions for tourist audiences. Another form of puppetry, found in Vietnam, uses brightly painted wooden puppets that perform on and in a pool of water. Manipulated with long poles from under the water by puppeteers (who remain unseen behind a bamboo screen), the puppets appear to act independently of any manipulator.

The Western world for the most part remained ignorant of the Asian theatre until the late eighteenth century. The Sanskrit plays were the first to be translated and read, but Asian theatrical conventions were

FIG. 26.30
Wayang topeng mask of wood for the role of Pandji, Prince of Djenggala. From Java, eighteenth century. Courtesy Rietberg Museum, Zurich.

unappreciated until Eastern companies began to appear in the West. A Chinese troupe played in Paris in 1895; a Japanese group appeared in London in 1900; and individual performers toured with some frequency thereafter. Nevertheless, it was not until such Western producers as Meyerhold, Vakhtangov, Brecht, and Artaud began to advocate them as alternatives to the Western emphasis on illusionism that Asian conventions began to affect Western practices. At first viewed as perverse or exotic, the innovations have been increasingly accepted since World War II, largely because of the influence of Brecht and Artaud. In recent years, Ariane Mnouchkine, through her highly acclaimed productions of Shakespearean and Greek plays in which she drew heavily on Sanskrit, Kathakali, and Kabuki conventions, and Peter Brook, with his adaptation of the *Mahabarata*, have intensified interest in Asian theatre. Although it is doubtful that many Westerners have fully mastered Asian theatre conventions, many have drawn inspiration from them, especially when seeking alternatives to the realism that has so long dominated Western theatre. Increased research and study of Asian theatre in Western universities has also contributed to greater familiarity.

LOOKING AT THEATRE HISTORY

In studying the theatre of other cultures, it is important to become familiar with the context out of which it has emerged, for otherwise it will seem merely quaint rather than a vital expression. Obviously, it is difficult to enter fully into another culture, which is a compound of elements often quite unlike those we know. It is possible to gain insight into other ways of life, however, by reading social and cultural histories and by examining the arts these cultures have produced. This kind of approach is especially important if Westerners are to understand Eastern theatrical forms more than superficially.

The complexity of the "visual language" of Sanskrit drama can be appreciated if the following descriptions are read in relation to the drawings of hand gestures shown in Fig. 26.2. Note that each gesture has several possible meanings, the specific meaning at any given time depending on how it is related to other elements in the performance:

Pataka (flag): *the thumb bent to touch the fingers, and the fingers extended. Usage: beginning a dance, cloud, forest, forbidding things, bosom, night, river, world of the gods, horse, cutting, wind, reclining, walking, prowess, graciousness, moonlight, strong sunlight, knocking . . . entering a street, equality . . . , taking an oath, silence, benediction . . .*

Ardha-candra (half-moon): *the thumb of the Pataka hand is stretched out. Usage: the moon on the eighth day of the dark fortnight, a hand seizing the throat, a spear, consecrating an image, origin, waist, anxiety, meditation, prayer, touching, greeting common people. . . .*

Musti (fist): *the four fingers are bent in to the palm, and the thumb is set on them. Usage: steadiness, grasping the hair, holding things, wrestling.*

Sikhara (spire): *in the same hand, the thumb is raised. Usage: the God of Love, bow, pillar, silence, husband, tooth, entering, questioning, the body, saying no, recollection, untying the girdle, lover, sound of a bell, pounding. . . .*

Bhramara (bee): *the second finger and thumb touching, the forefinger bent, the rest extended. Usage: bee, parrot, crane, cuckoo, union.*

Sukatundaka (parrot's beak): *the third finger of the Arala hand is also bent. Usage: shooting an arrow, throwing a spear, mystery, ferocity.*

From *The Mirror of Gesture*, trans. Ananda Coomaraswamy and Gopala Kristnayya Duggirala (Cambridge, Mass., 1917), 26–35.

The following brief passage points out the relationship between Chinese drama and the three great Chinese philosophies, Confucianism, Buddhism, and Taoism:

Whatever native ingredients and alien elements entered into the melting pot of Chinese civilization, its main component has been essentially Confucianism. . . . A practicable moral philosophy that teaches the rules of personal cultivation and virtues of human relationship, Confucianism has molded the Chinese national character and pervaded every aspect of Chinese society, the family, literature and the arts . . . but when the country was in disorder, Taoism and Buddhism took over [since] disappointments bred . . . a desire to wander astray in . . . otherworldliness. The majority of Chinese writers, however, have been conformists to the grand Confucian tradition. To them, literature has been a vehicle for the communication of the aim of Confucian doctrine: to teach and influence people to be good. . . . The three great Chinese doctrines merged in the common belief in retribution . . . [which] deterred the growth of anything like the Western concept of tragedy. . . . From the Chinese point of view it would be a blemish in the literary work not to give its readers a sense of satisfaction in the ultimate vindication and triumph of the good and virtuous.

Wu-chi Liu, *An Introduction to Chinese Literature* (Bloomington: Indiana University Press, 1966), 4–5.

Similarly, in his study of Kabuki, A. C. Scott points out the influence of Buddhism, Shintoism, and Confucianism on Japanese life and theatre. He also discusses domestic architecture, dress, food, social relationships, etiquette, and other aspects of daily life that have contributed to theatrical subjects and conventions:

Formerly, everything and everybody in Japan was bound by a strict code of etiquette. There were correct ways of eating, drinking, wearing clothes and moving about according to time and place. . . . This fact, coupled with their characteristic manner of living, such as for instance sitting, dining and sleeping on the tatami [reed mats] created gestures and movements which were individual in style, and these translated into terms of stage technique have developed a very special visual effect, both in the case of the single actor or group composition. . . . The legends, customs, habits, religion, loves and hates of the Japanese people are drawn upon freely and woven into the pattern of construction of this colorful drama.

The Kabuki Theatre of Japan (London: George Allen and Unwin, Ltd., 1955), 32–33.

Even with a knowledge of the intellectual and cultural context, a Western observer often has difficulty, at least in the beginning, with many conventions of the Asian theatre. Among these are the color symbolism and face painting of Beijing Opera. (For some examples, see Fig. 26.14.)

The more admirable characters are usually painted in relatively simple colors. Enemy leaders or very special people have more complicated designs on their faces—toughs, bandits, hardened soldiers, rebels. A lot of red indicates courage, loyalty, straightforwardness; more black denotes impulsiveness, while a blue face is a cruel one. A crook who is completely untrustworthy is given a white, often twisted face.

Musical modes are also apt to seem strange. To the Westerner the Chinese orchestra has "a superabundance of gongs, cymbals, and drums."

The accompaniment for the voice is played on the "chinghu"—the two-stringed fiddle . . . . Flutes are also used, the bamboo kind, held parallel to the face when played. The "sheng" or reed flute is really a small organ and has chords. Then there are the moon guitars and three-stringed guitars, a kind of Chinese clarinet . . . ; big and small drums, a bell, cymbals and the "pan" or wooden time-beater which does for the orchestra what the conductor does for his musicians in a Western performance. . . . Entrances and exits have a musical accompaniment. An actor, before breaking into song, will speak his last words in a certain way so that the orchestra knows the song is about to begin.

Rewi Alley, *Peking Opera* (Beijing, 1957).

In the advice he gave to Noh actors in his *Works*, Zeami emphasizes restraint, which is to be accomplished in part through the reconciliation of opposites:

In representing anger the actor should yet retain some gentleness in his mood, else he will portray not anger but violence.

When the body is in violent action, the hands and feet must move as though by stealth. When the feet are in lively motion, the body must be held in quietness.

Translated by Arthur Waley in his *The No Plays of Japan* (New York: Alfred A. Knopf, 1922), 26.

A number of works that give advice to actors or preserve anecdotes about acting in Kabuki have survived from the late seventeenth and early eighteenth centuries. In "The Words of Ayame" this passage appears about the *onnagata* (female) role, at that time always played by men:

The onnagata *role has its basis in charm, and even one who has innate beauty, if he seeks to make a fine show in a fighting scene, will lose the femininity of his performance . . . if he does not live his normal life as if he was a woman, it will not be possible for him to be called a skillful* onnagata.

From "A Sequel to 'Dust in the Ears'" comes this account of playwriting for Kabuki prior to the late seventeenth century:

The normal way of working was that after the discussion of a new play and a decision upon it, the construction of each scene was worked out. Then the actors in a scene were called together, placed in a circle, and taught the speeches orally. They stood there until they made their exit, and then either rehearsed it again . . . or the authors worked out the speeches for the next section, and got them fixed by repetition.

The Actors' Analects, ed., trans., and with an introduction and notes by Charles J. Dunn and Bunzo Torigoe (New York: Columbia University Press, 1969), 53, 118.

Bibliography

This bibliography lists authoritative or representative books. Except in rare cases, they are in English. For additional listings see the Web site at www.ablongman.com/brockett9e.

GENERAL WORKS

APPIAH, KWAME ANTHONY, AND HENRY LOUIS GATES, JR., eds. *The Dictionary of Global Culture.* New York, 1997.

BANHAM, MARTIN, ed. *The Cambridge Guide to Theatre.* Cambridge, 1995.

CHAMBERS, COLIN, ed. *Continuum Companion to 20th Century Theatre.* Leicester, 2001.

DUERR, EDWIN. *The Length and Depth of Acting.* New York, 1962.

GASSNER, JOHN, AND RALPH ALLEN, eds. *Theatre and Drama in the Making.* 2 vols. Boston, 1964 (rev. ed. vol. 1, 1992).

IZENOUR, GEORGE. *Theatre Design.* New York, 1977.

LAVER, JAMES. *Drama, Its Costume and Decor.* London, 1951.

LEACROFT, RICHARD, AND HELEN LEACROFT. *Theatre and Playhouse: An Illustrated Survey of Theatre Building from Ancient Greece to the Present Day.* New York, 1984.

NAGLER, ALOIS M. *Sources of Theatrical History.* New York, 1952.

RUBIN, DON, ed. *World Encyclopedia of Contemporary Theatre.* Vol. I *Europe;* Vol. 2 *The Americas;* Vol. 3 *Africa;* Vol. 4 *The Arab World;* Vol. 5 *Asia/Pacific.* New York, 1995–1999.

TIDSWORTH, SIMON. *Theatres: An Architectural and Cultural History.* New York, 1973.

CHAPTER 1: THE ORIGINS OF THEATRE

BROWN, IVOR. *The First Player: The Origin of Drama.* New York, 1928.

BUDGE, E. A. W. *Osiris and the Egyptian Resurrection.* 2 vols. New York, 1911.

ELSE, GERALD F. *The Origin and Early Form of Greek Tragedy.* Cambridge, 1964.

FRANKFORT, HENRI. *Ancient Egyptian Religion.* New York, 1948.

GASTER, THEODOR. *Thespis: Ritual, Myth and Drama in the Ancient Near East.* New York, 1950.

HAVEMEYER, LOOMIS. *The Drama of Savage Peoples.* New Haven, 1916.

HERINGTON, JOHN. *Poetry into Drama.* Berkeley, 1985.

HUIZINGA, JOHANN. *Homo Ludens: A Study of the Play Element in Culture.* Boston, 1955.

HUNNINGHER, BENJAMIN. *The Origin of the Theatre.* New York, 1961.

KIRBY, E. T. *Ur-Drama: The Origins of Theatre.* New York, 1975.

LÉVI-STRAUSS, CLAUDE. *The Savage Mind.* Chicago, 1966.

RIDGEWAY, WILLIAM. *The Drama and Dramatic Dances of Non-European Races.* Cambridge, 1915.

SCHECHNER, RICHARD. *Performance Theory.* rev. ed. New York, 1988.

TURNER, VICTOR. *From Ritual to Theatre.* New York, 1982.

WISE, JENNIFER. *Dionysus Writes: The Invention of Theatre in Ancient Greece.* Ithaca, NY, 1998.

CHAPTER 2: THEATRE AND DRAMA IN ANCIENT GREECE

ARNOTT, PETER D. *Greek Scenic Conventions in the Fifth Century, B.C.* Oxford, 1962.

————. *Public and Performance in the Greek Theatre.* London, 1989.

ASHBY, CLIFFORD. *Classical Greek Theatre: New Views of an Old Subject.* Iowa City, 1999.

BIEBER, MARGARETE. *The History of the Greek and Roman Theatre.* 2nd ed. Princeton, NJ, 1961.

CSAPO, ERIC, AND WILLIAM J. SLATER. *The Context of Ancient Drama.* Ann Arbor, 1995.

DEARDON, C. W. *The Stage of Aristophanes.* London, 1976.

EASTERLING, P. E., ed. *The Cambridge Companion to Greek Tragedy.* Cambridge, 1997.

ELSE, GERALD E. *The Origin and Early Form of Greek Tragedy.* Cambridge, 1964.

FLICKINGER, ROY C. *The Greek Theatre and Its Drama.* 4th ed. enlarged. Chicago, 1936.

GREEN, J. R. *Theatre in Ancient Greek Society*. New York, 1994.

HALLERAN, MICHAEL R. *Stagecraft in Euripides*. New York, 1985.

IZENOUR, GEORGE. *The Roofed Theatres of Classical Antiquity*. New Haven, 1992.

KITTO, H. D. F. *Greek Tragedy*. 2nd ed. London, 1950.

LAWLER, LILLIAN B. *The Dance of the Ancient Greek Theatre*. Iowa City, 1964.

LEVER, KATHERINE. *The Art of Greek Comedy*. London, 1956.

NICOLL, ALLARDYCE. *Masks, Mimes, and Miracles*. New York, 1931.

PICKARD-CAMBRIDGE, A. W. *Dithyramb, Tragedy, and Comedy*. 2nd ed. revised by T. B. L. Webster. Oxford, 1962.

———. *The Dramatic Festivals of Athens*. 2nd ed. revised by John Gould and D. M. Lewis. Oxford, 1968.

———. *The Theatre of Dionysus in Athens*. Oxford, 1946.

ROSSETTO, PAOLA C., AND GIUSEPPINA P. SARTORIO. *Greek and Roman Theatres*. 3 vols. Rome, 1994–1996. (In English, Italian, French, and German.)

SCODEL, RUTH. *Theater and Society in the Classical World*. Ann Arbor, 1993.

SCOTT, WILLIAM C. *Musical Design in Aeschylean Theatre*. Hanover, NH, 1984.

———. *Musical Design in Sophoclean Theatre*. Hanover, NH, 1996.

SIFASKIS, G. M. *Studies in the History of Hellenic Drama*. London, 1967.

SOMMERSTEIN, ALAN H. *Greek Drama and Dramatists*. London, 2002.

TAPLIN, OLIVER. *Comic Angels*. Oxford, 1993.

———. *Greek Tragedy in Action*. Berkeley, 1978.

VINCE, RONALD W. *Ancient and Medieval Theatre: A Historiographical Handbook*. Westport, CT, 1984.

WALTON, J. MICHAEL. *Living Greek Theatre: A Handbook of Classical Performance and Modern Production*. Westport, CT, 1987.

WEBSTER, T. B. L. *Greek Theatre Production*. 2nd ed. London, 1970.

———. *The Greek Chorus*. London, 1970.

WINKLER, JOHN J., AND FROMA I. ZIETLIN, eds. *Nothing to Do with Dionysus? Athenian Drama in Its Social Context*. Princeton, NJ, 1990.

WILES, DAVID. *Tragedy in Athens: Performance Space and Theatrical Meaning*. Cambridge, 1999.

———. *Greek Theatre Performance*. Cambridge, 2000.

CHAPTER 3: HELLENISTIC, ROMAN, AND BYZANTINE THEATRE

BEACHAM, RICHARD C. *The Roman Theatre and Its Audience*. Cambridge, MA, 1992.

———. *Spectacle Entertainments of Early Imperial Rome*. New Haven, 1999.

BEARE, WILLIAM. *The Roman Stage: A Short History of Latin Drama in the Time of the Republic*. 3rd ed. London, 1963.

BIEBER, MARGARETE. See under chapter 2.

DUCKWORTH, GEORGE. *The Nature of Roman Comedy*. Princeton, NJ, 1952.

GENTILI, BRUNO. *Theatrical Performances in the Ancient World: Hellenistic and Early Roman Theatre*. Amsterdam, 1979.

HANSON, J. A. *Roman Theatre-Temples*. Princeton, NJ, 1959.

HUNTER, R. L. *The New Comedy of Greece and Rome*. New York, 1985.

IZENOUR, GEORGE. See under chapter 2.

KONSTAN, DAVID. *Roman Comedy*. Ithaca, NY, 1983.

LAPIANA, G. "The Byzantine Theatre," *Speculum*, 11 (1936), 171–211.

MYRSIADES, LINDA S., AND KOSTAS MYRSIADES, *Karagozis: Culture and Comedy in Greek Puppet Theater*. Lexington, KY, 1992.

NICOLL, ALLARDYCE. See under chapter 2.

ROSSETTO, PAOLA C., AND GIUSEPPINA P. SARTORIO. See under chapter 2.

SEGAL, ERICH. *Roman Laughter: The Comedy of Plautus*. Cambridge, MA, 1968.

SLATER, WILLIAM J., ed. *Roman Theatre and Society*. Ann Arbor, 1995.

VINCE, RONALD W. See under chapter 2.

VITRUVIUS. *Ten Books of Architecture*. Trans. by Morris H. Morgan. New York, 1960.

ZAGAGI, NETTA. *The Comedy of Menander: Convention, Variation, and Originality*. Bloomington, IN, 1995.

CHAPTER 4: EUROPEAN THEATRE IN THE MIDDLE AGES

BEADLE, RICHARD, ed. *The Cambridge Companion to Medieval English Theatre*. Cambridge, 1994.

BEVINGTON, DAVID. *From Mankind to Marlowe: Growth in Structure in the Popular Drama of Tudor England*. Cambridge, MA, 1962.

BRYAN, GEORGE B. *Ethelwold and Medieval Music-Drama at Winchester: The Easter Play, Its Author, and Its Milieu*. Bern, 1981.

BUTTERWORTH, PHILIP. *Theatre of Fire: Special Effects in Early English and Scottish Theatre*. London, 1998.

CHAMBERS, E. K. *The Mediaeval Stage*. 2 vols. Oxford, 1903.

COHEN, GUSTAVE. *Histoire de la Mise-en-scène dans le Théâtre Religieux Français du Moyen Age*. Paris, 1926.

———. *Le Livre de Conduite du Régisseur et le Compte des Déspenses pour le mystère de la Passion, joué a Mons en 1501. . . .* Paris, 1925.

COLLINS, FLETCHER. *The Production of Medieval Church Music-Drama*. Charlotte, VA, 1971.

CRAIK, THOMAS W. *The Tudor Interlude: Stage, Costume and Acting*. Leicester, 1958.

CRAIK, THOMAS W., et al. *The Revels History of Drama in English*. Vol. 2: 1500–1576. New York, 1980.

DONOVAN, R. B. *Liturgical Drama in Medieval Spain*. Toronto, 1958.

ENDERS, JODY. *The Medieval Theatre of Cruelty*. Ithaca, NY, 1999.

EVANS, MARSHALL B. *The Passion Play of Lucerne*. New York, 1943.

FRANK, GRACE. *The Medieval Drama*. Oxford, 1960.

GARDINER, HAROLD C. *Mysteries' End: An Investigation of the Last Days of the Medieval Religious Stage*. New Haven, CT, 1946.

HARDISON, O. B. *Christian Rite and Christian Drama in the Middle Ages: Essays in the Origin and Early History of Modern Drama*. Baltimore, 1965.

HUNNINGHER, BENJAMIN. See under chapter 1.

KOLVE, V. A. *The Play Called Corpus Christi*. Stanford, CA, 1966.

MILLS, DAVID. *Recycling the Cycle: The City of Chester and Its Whitsun Plays*. Toronto, 1997.

NAGLER, A. M. *The Medieval Religious Stage: Shapes and Phantoms*. New Haven, 1976.

NELSON, ALAN H. *The Medieval Pageants and Plays*. Chicago, 1974.

NICOLL, ALLARDYCE. See under chapter 2.

OGDEN, DUNBAR H. *The Staging of Drama in the Medieval Church*. Madison, NJ, 2001.

POTTER, ROBERT A. *The English Morality Play: Origins, History and Influence of a Dramatic Tradition*. London, 1975.

Records of Early English Drama. Toronto, 1978–.

SALTER, F. M. *Medieval Drama in Chester*. Toronto, 1955.

SHERGOLD, N. D. *A History of the Spanish Stage from Medieval Times until the End of the 17th Century*. Oxford, 1967.

SIMON, ECKHARD, ed. *The Theatre of Medieval Europe: New Research in Early Drama*. New York, 1991.

SOUTHERN, RICHARD. *The Medieval Theatre in the Round*. London, 1957.

STERN, CHARLOTTE. *The Medieval Theatre in Castile*. Binghamton, NY, 1996.

STICCA, SANDRO. *The Latin Passion Play: Its Origin and Development*. Albany, 1970.

SUMBERG, S. *The Nuremberg Schembart Carnival*. New York, 1941.

TYDEMAN, WILLIAM, MICHAEL J. ANDERSON, AND NICK DAVIS, eds. *The Medieval European Stage 500–1550*. Cambridge, 2001.

TYDEMAN, WILLIAM. *The Theatre of the Middle Ages*. New York, 1979.

VINCE, RONALD W. *A Companion to the Medieval Theatre*. New York, 1989.

———. See under chapter 2.

WICKHAM, GLYNNE. *Early English Stages, 1300–1660*. 3 vols. New York, 1959–1980.

———. *The Medieval Theatre*. 3rd ed. Cambridge, 1987.

YOUNG, KARL. *The Drama of the Medieval Church*. 2 vols. Oxford, 1933.

CHAPTER 5: ENGLISH THEATRE TO 1642

ADAMS, JOHN C. *The Globe Playhouse: Its Design and Equipment*. 2nd ed. New York, 1961.

ASTINGTON, JOHN N. *English Court Theatre, 1558–1642*. Cambridge, 1999.

BALDWIN, T. W. *The Organization and Personnel of the Shakespearean Company*. Princeton, NJ, 1927.

BARROLL, J. L., et al. *Revels History of Drama in English*. Vol 3: 1576–1613. New York, 1975.

BECKERMAN, BERNARD. *Shakespeare at the Globe, 1599–1609*. New York, 1962.

BERGER, THOMAS L., AND WILLIAM C. BRADFORD, eds. *An Index of Characters in Early Modern English Drama: Printed Plays 1500–1660*. Cambridge, 1998.

BERRY, HERBERT, ed. *The First Public Playhouse: The Theatre in Shoreditch, 1576–1598*. Montreal, 1979.

———. *The Boar's Head Playhouse*. Washington, 1986.

BENTLEY, GERALD E. *The Jacobean and Caroline Stage*. 5 vols. Oxford, 1941–1956.

———. *The Profession of Dramatist in Shakespeare's Time, 1590–1642*. Princeton, NJ, 1971.

———. *The Profession of Player in Shakespeare's Time, 1590–1642*. Princeton, NJ, 1984.

BRADLEY, DAVID. *From Text to Performance in the Elizabethan Theatre: Preparing the Play for the Stage*. New York, 1992.

CALLAGAN, DYMPNA. *Shakespeare without Women*. New York, 2000.

CHAMBERS, E. K. *The Elizabethan Stage*. 4 vols. London, 1923.

COOK, ANN J. *The Privileged Playgoers of Shakespeare's London, 1576–1642*. Princeton, 1981.

DESSEN, ALAN C. *Recovering Shakespeare's Theatrical Vocabulary*. Cambridge, 1995.

DESSEN, ALAN C., AND LESLIE THOMSON. *A Dictionary of Stage Directions in English Drama, 1580–1642*. Cambridge, 1999.

DUTTON, RICHARD. *Mastering the Revels: The Regulation and Censorship of English Renaissance Drama*. Iowa City, 1991.

GILDERSLEEVE, VIRGINIA. *Government Regulation of the Elizabethan Drama*. New York, 1908.

GRAVES, R. B. *Lighting the Shakespearean Stage, 1567–1642*. Carbondale, IL, 1999.

GURR, ANDREW. *Playgoing in Shakespeare's London*. 2d ed. Cambridge, 1996.

———. *The Shakespearian Playing Companies*. Oxford, 1996.

HARBAGE, ALFRED. *Shakespeare's Audience*. New York, 1958.

HILDY, FRANKLIN J., ed. *New Issues in the Reconstruction of Shakespeare's Theatre*. New York, 1990.

HODGES, C. W. *The Globe Restored*. 2nd ed. London, 1968.

———. *Shakespeare's Second Globe*. London, 1973.

INGRAM, WILLIAM. *The Business of Playing: The Beginning of the Adult Professional Theater in Elizabethan London*. Ithaca, NY, 1993.

JOSEPH, BERTRAM. *Elizabethan Acting*. 2nd ed. London, 1962.

KING, T. J. *Shakespearean Staging, 1599–1642*. Cambridge, MA, 1971.

KNUTSON, ROSLYN LANDER. *Playing Companies and Commerce in Shakespeare's Time*. Cambridge, 2001.

———. *The Repertory of Shakespeare's Company 1594–1613*. Fayetteville, AR, 1991.

LIMON, JERZY. *Gentlemen of a Company: English Players in Central and Eastern Europe, 1590–1660*. Cambridge, 1985.

MACINTYRE, JEAN. *Costumes and Scripts in the Elizabethan Theatres*. Edmonton, 1992.

NELSON, ALAN H. *Early Cambridge Theatres: College, University, and Town Stages, 1464–1720*. Cambridge, 1994.

MCMILLIN, SCOTT, AND SALLY-BETH MACLEAN. *The Queen's Men and Their Plays*. Cambridge, 1998.

MULLANEY, STEVEN. *The Place of the Stage: License, Play, and Power in Renaissance England*. Chicago, 1988.

MULRYNE, J. R., AND MARGARET SHEWRING, eds. *Theatre and Government under the Early Stuarts*. Cambridge, 1993.

NICOLL, ALLARDYCE. *Stuart Masques and the Renaissance Stage*. London, 1937.

ORGEL, STEPHEN. *The Illusion of Power: Political Theatre in the English Renaissance*. Berkeley, 1975.

ORGEL, STEPHEN, AND ROY STRONG. *The Theatre of the Stuart Court; Including the Complete Designs . . . Together with Their Texts and Historical Documentation*. 2 vols. Berkeley, 1973.

ORRELL, JOHN. *The Human Stage: English Theatre Design, 1567–1640*. New York, 1988.

———. *The Quest for Shakespeare's Globe*. New York, 1983.

———. *The Theatres of Inigo Jones and John Webb*. New York, 1985.

PEACOCK, JOHN. *The Stage Designs of Inigo Jones, The European Context*. Cambridge, 1995.

REYNOLDS, GEORGE F. *The Staging of Elizabethan Plays at the Red Bull Theatre, 1605–1625*. New York, 1940.

RUTTER, CAROL, C., ed. *Documents of the Rose Playhouse*. Dover, NH, 1985.

Shakespeare Survey: An Annual Survey of Shakespearean Study and Production. Cambridge, 1948–present.

SHAPIRO, MICHAEL. *Children of the Revels*. New York, 1977.

SMITH, IRWIN. *Shakespeare's Blackfriars Playhouse: Its History and Its Design*. New York, 1964.

SOUTHERN, RICHARD. *The Staging of Plays before Shakespeare*. New York, 1973.

SPRAGUE, A. C. *Shakespearean Players and Performances*. Cambridge, MA, 1953.

STERN, TIFFANY. *Rehearsal from Shakespeare to Sheridan*. Oxford, 2000.

STRONG, ROY. *Splendor at Court*. Boston, 1973.

STURGES, KEITH. *Jacobean Private Theatres*. London, 1987.

THOMSON, PETER. *Shakespeare's Theatre*. 2nd ed. London, 1992.

VINCE, RONALD W. *Renaissance Theatre: A Historiographical Handbook*. Westport, CT, 1984.

WELSFORD, ENID. *The Court Masque*. Cambridge, 1927.

WICKHAM, GLYNNE. See under chapter 4.

WICKHAM, GLYNNE, HERBERT BERRY, AND WILLIAM INGRAM. *English Professional Theatre, 1530–1660*. Cambridge, 2000.

WHITE, MARTIN. *Renaissance Drama in Action*. London, 1998.

CHAPTER 6: SPANISH THEATRE TO 1700

ALLEN, JOHN J. *The Reconstruction of a Golden Age Playhouse: El Corral del Principe, 1583–1744*. Gainesville, FL, 1983.

CRAWFORD, J. P. W. *Spanish Drama before Lope de Vega*. rev. ed. Philadelphia, 1937.

GANELIN, CHARLES, AND HOWARD MANCING. *The Golden Age Comedia: Text, Theory, and Performance*. West Lafayette, IN, 1994.

MCKENDRICK, MELVEENA. *Theatre in Spain, 1490–1700*. London, 1989.

————. *Women and Society in the Spanish Drama of the Golden Age*. London, 1984.

RENNERT, HUGO A. *The Spanish Stage in the Time of Lope de Vega*. Philadelphia, 1909.

RUANO DE LA HAZA, JOSÉ M., AND JOHN J. ALLEN. *Los Teatros Comerciales del Siglo XVII y la Escenificación de la Comedia*. Madrid, 1994.

SHERGOLD, N. D. See under chapter 4.

VINCE, RONALD W. See under chapter 5.

WEBSTER, SUSAN VERDI. *Art and Ritual in Golden-Age Spain: Sevillian Confraternities and the Processional Sculpture of Holy Week*. Princeton, 1998.

WILSON, EDWARD M., AND DUNCAN MOIR. *A Literary History of Spain: The Golden Age, Drama, 1492–1700*. New York, 1971.

WILSON, MARGARET. *Spanish Drama of the Golden Age*. New York, 1969.

ZIOMEK, HENRYK. *A History of Spanish Golden Age Drama*. Lexington, KY, 1984.

CHAPTER 7: ITALIAN THEATRE TO 1700

ANDREWS, RICHARD. *Scripts and Scenarios: The Performance of Comedy in Renaissance Italy*. Cambridge, 1993.

BJURSTROM, PER. *Giacomo Torelli and Baroque Stage Design*. Stockholm, 1961.

BURCKHARDT, JAKOB B. *The Civilization of the Renaissance in Italy*. 3rd ed. New York, 1950.

CAIRNS, CHRISTOPHER, ed. *Scenery, Set, and Staging in the Italian Renaissance*. Lewiston, NY, 1996.

DI MARIA, SALVATORE. *The Italian Tragedy in the Renaissance: Cultural Realities and Theatrical Innovations*. Lewisburg, PA, 2002.

DUCHARTRE, PIERRE L. *The Italian Comedy: The Improvisation, Scenarios, Lives, Attributes, Portraits and Masks of the Illustrious Characters of the Commedia dell'Arte*. Trans. by R. T. Weaver. London, 1929.

HERRICK, MARVIN. *Italian Comedy in the Renaissance*. Urbana, IL, 1960.

————. *Italian Tragedy in the Renaissance*. Urbana, IL, 1965.

————. *Tragicomedy: Its Origin and Development in Italy, France, and England*. Urbana, IL, 1955.

HEWITT, BARNARD, ed. *The Renaissance Stage: Documents of Serlio, Sabbattini, and Furttenbach*. Coral Gables, FL, 1958.

KENNARD, JOSEPH S. *The Italian Theatre*. 2 vols. New York, 1932.

KERNODLE, GEORGE. *From Art to Theatre: Form and Convention in the Renaissance*. Chicago, 1943.

LEA, KATHLEEN M. *Italian Popular Comedy: A Study of the Commedia dell'Arte, 1560–1620*. 2 vols. Oxford, 1934.

MULLIN, DONALD C. *The Development of the Playhouse: A Survey of Architecture from the Renaissance to the Present*. Berkeley, 1970.

NAGLER, ALOIS M. *Theatre Festivals of the Medici, 1539–1637*. New Haven, CT, 1968.

NICOLL, ALLARDYCE. See under chapter 2.

OREGLIA, G. *The Commedia dell'Arte*. New York, 1968.

PALLEN, THOMAS B. *Vasari on Theatre*. Carbondale, IL, 1999.

SCHWARTZ, ISIDORE A. *The Commedia dell'Arte and Its Influence on French Comedy in the Seventeenth Century*. Paris, 1933.

STRONG, ROY. See under chapter 5.

VINCE, RONALD W. See under chapter 5.

VITRUVIUS. See under chapter 3.

WHITE, JOHN. *The Birth and Rebirth of Pictorial Space*. London, 1957.

WORSTHORNE, S. T. *Venetian Opera in the 17th Century*. Oxford, 1954.

CHAPTER 8: FRENCH THEATRE TO 1700

BJURSTOM, PER. See under chapter 7.

CLARKE, JAN. *The Guenegaud Theatre in Paris (1673–1680): The Accounts Season by Season*. Lewiston, NY, 2001.

DEIERKAUF-HOLSBOER, WILMA. *Histoire de la Mise-en-scène dans le Théâtre Français de 1600 á 1657*. Paris, 1933.

DOCKS, STEPHEN. *Costume and Fashion in the Plays of Jean-Baptiste Poquelin, Molière*. Geneva, 1992.

HERZEL, ROGER W. *The Original Casting of Molière's Plays*. Ann Arbor, 1981.

HOWARTH, W. D., JAN CLARKE, AND EDWARD FORMAN, eds. *French Theatre in the Neo-Classical Era, 1550–1789*. Cambridge, 1997.

JACQUOT, J., ed. *Les Fêtes de la Renaissance*. 2 vols. Paris, 1956–1960.

————. *Le Lieu Théâtral à la Renaissance*. Paris, 1964.

JEFFREY, B. *French Renaissance Comedy, 1552–1630*. Oxford, 1969.

LANCASTER, H. C. *A History of French Dramatic Literature in the Seventeenth Century*. 5 vols. Baltimore, 1929–1942.

LAWRENSON, T. E. *The French Stage in the XVIIth Century: A Study in the Advent of the Italian Order*. rev. ed. Manchester, 1984.

LOCKERT, LACY. *Studies in French Classical Tragedy*. Nashville, 1958.

LOUGH, JOHN. *Paris Theatre Audiences in the Seventeenth and Eighteenth Centuries*. London, 1957.

MAHELOT, LAURENT. *La Memoire de Mahelot, Laurent et d'autres Décorateurs de l'Hôtel de Bourgogne et de la Comédie Française au XVIIe siècle*. Edited by H. C. Lancaster. Paris, 1920.

MCGOWAN, M. *L'Art du Ballet de Cour en France*. Paris, 1963.

MITTMAN, BARBARA G. *Spectators on the Paris Stage in the Seventeenth and Eighteenth Centuries*. Ann Arbor, 1984.

MONGREDIEN, GEORGES. *Daily Life in the French Theatre at the Time of Molière*. London, 1969.

RAVEL, JEFFREY S. *The Contested Parterre*. Ithaca, NY, 1999.

SCOTT, VIRGINIA. *Molière: A Theatrical Life*. Cambridge, 2000.

————. *The Commedia dell'arte in Paris, 1644–1697*. Charlottesville, VA, 1990.

STRONG, ROY. See under chapter 5.

TURNELL, MARTIN. *The Classical Moment: Studies in Corneille, Molière, and Racine*. New York, 1948.

VINCE, RONALD W. See under chapter 5.

WILEY, W. L. *The Early Public Theatre in France*. Cambridge, MA, 1960.

CHAPTER 9: ENGLISH THEATRE TO 1800

BOOTH, MICHAEL, et al. *The Revels History of Drama in English*. Vol. 6, 1750–1880. London, 1975.

BURNIM, KALMAN. *David Garrick, Director*. Pittsburgh, 1961.

CIBBER, COLLEY. *An Apology for the Life of Mr. Colley Cibber*. London, 1740.

FISK, DEBORAH PAYNE, ed. *The Cambridge Companion to English Restoration Theatre*. Cambridge, 2000.

HIGHFILL, PHILIP H., JR., KALMAN BURNIM, AND EDWARD LANGHANS. *A Biographical Dictionary of Actors, Actresses, Musicians, Dancers, Managers, and Other Stage Personnel in London, 1660–1800*. Carbondale, IL, 1973.

HILL, ERROL. *The Jamaican Stage, 1655–1900: Profile of a Colonial Theatre*. Amherst, MA, 1992.

HOTSON, LESLIE. *The Commonwealth and Restoration Stage*. Cambridge, MA, 1928.

HUME, ROBERT. *Henry Fielding and the London Theatre, 1728–1737*. London, 1988.

JOHNSON, ODAI, WILLIAM J. BURLING, AND JAMES A. COOMBS. *The Colonial American Stage, 1665–1774: A Documentary Calendar.* Madison, NJ, 2002.

JOSEPH, BERTRAM. *The Tragic Actor.* New York, 1959.

KRUTCH, JOSEPH W. *Comedy and Conscience after the Restoration.* New York, 1949.

LEACROFT, RICHARD. *The Development of the English Playhouse.* Ithaca, NY, 1973.

LOFTUS, JOHN, et al. *Revels History of Drama in English.* Vol. 4: 1660–1750. New York, 1976.

The London Stage, 1660–1800. 11 vols. Carbondale, IL, 1960–1968.

LONDRÉ, FELICIA HARDISON, AND DANIEL J. WATERMEIER. *The History of North American Theatre: The United States, Canada, and Mexico: From Pre-Columbian Times to the Present.* New York, 1998.

LYNCH, JAMES J. *Box, Pit and Gallery: Stage and Society in Johnson's London.* Berkeley, 1953.

MILHOUS, JUDITH. *Thomas Betterton and the Management of Lincoln's Inn Fields, 1695–1708.* Carbondale, IL, 1979.

MOODY, JANE. *Illegitimate Theatre in London, 1770–1840.* Cambridge, 2000.

NICOLL, ALLARDYCE. *History of English Drama, 1660–1900.* 6 vols. London, 1955–1959.

———. *The Garrick Stage.* Athens, GA, 1980.

ODELL, G. C. D. *Shakespeare from Betterton to Irving.* 2 vols. New York, 1920.

PRICE, CECIL. *Theatre in the Age of Garrick.* Oxford, 1973.

RANKIN, HUGH F. *The Theatre in Colonial America.* Chapel Hill, NC, 1965.

ROSENFELD, SYBIL. *A Short History of Scene Design in Great Britain.* Oxford, 1973.

———. *Strolling Players and Drama in the Provinces, 1660–1765.* Cambridge, 1939.

SOUTHERN, RICHARD. *Changeable Scenery: Its Origin and Development in the British Theatre.* London, 1952.

———. *The Georgian Playhouse.* London, 1948.

STERN, TIFFANY. See under chapter 5.

STYAN, J. L. *Restoration Comedy in Performance.* Cambridge, 1986.

SUMMERS, MONTAGUE. *The Playhouse of Pepys.* London, 1935.

———. *The Restoration Theatre.* London, 1934.

VINCE, RONALD. *Neoclassical Theatre, A Historiographical Handbook.* Westport, CT, 1988.

WRIGHT, RICHARDSON. *Revels in Jamaica, 1682–1838.* New York, 1937.

CHAPTER 10: ITALY AND FRANCE TO 1800

BAUR-HEINHOLD, MARGARETE. *Baroque Theatre.* New York, 1967.

BRENNER, C. D. *The Theatre Italien: Its Repertory, 1716–1793, with an Historical Introduction.* Berkeley, 1961.

GOLDONI, CARLO. *Memoirs of Carlo Goldoni.* Trans. by John Black. New York, 1926.

GOZZI, CARLO. *The Memoirs of Count Carlo Gozzi.* Trans. by J. A. Symonds. 2 vols. London, 1890.

HEMMINGS, F. W. J. *Theatre and State in France, 1760–1905.* Cambridge, 1994.

KENNARD, JOSEPH S. See under chapter 7.

LANCASTER, H. C. *French Tragedy in the Reign of Louis XVI and the Early Years of the French Revolution, 1774–1792.* Baltimore, 1953.

———. *French Tragedy in the Time of Louis XV and Voltaire, 1715–1774.* Baltimore, 1950.

———. *Sunset: A History of Parisian Drama in the Last Years of Louis XIV, 1701–1715.* Baltimore, 1945.

LARSON, ORVILLE K. *The Theatrical Writings of Fabrizio Carini Motta.* Carbondale, IL, 1987.

LOUGH, JOHN. See under chapter 8.

MAYOR, A. H. *The Bibiena Family.* New York, 1945.

———. *Giovanni Battista Piranesi.* New York, 1952.

MELCHER, EDITH. *Stage Realism in France between Diderot and Antoine.* Bryn Mawr, PA, 1928.

MITTMAN, BARBARA G. See under chapter 8.

OGDEN, DUNBAR, trans. and commentary. *The Italian Baroque Stage: Documents by Giulio Trioli, Andrea Pozzo, Ferdinando Galli-Bibiena, Baldassare Orsini.* Berkeley, 1978.

VIALE FERRERO, MERCEDES. *La Scenografia del '700 e i Fratelli Galliari.* Turin, 1963.

VINCE, RONALD. See under chapter 9.

CHAPTER 11: NORTHERN EUROPEAN THEATRE TO 1800

AIKIN, JUDITH P. *German Baroque Drama.* Boston, 1982.

AIKIN-SNEATH, BETSY. *Comedy in Germany in the First Half of the 18th Century.* Oxford, 1936.

BAUR-HEINHOLD, MARGARETE. See under chapter 10.

BEIJER, AGNE. *The Court Theatres of Drottningholm and Gripsholm.* Trans. by G. L. Frolich. Malmo, 1944.

BRANDT, GEORGE W., ed. *German and Dutch Theatre, 1600–1848.* Cambridge, 1993.

BRUFORD, WALTER H. *Theatre, Drama and Audience in Goethe's Germany.* London, 1957.

CARLSON, MARVIN. *Goethe and the Weimar Theatre.* Ithaca, NY, 1978.

HEITNER, R. R. *German Tragedy in the Age of Enlightenment, 1724–1768.* Berkeley, 1963.

HILLESTROM, G. *Theatre and Ballet in Sweden.* Stockholm, 1953.

KARLINSKY, SIMON. *Russian Drama from Its Beginnings to the Age of Pushkin.* Berkeley, 1985.

LAMPORT, F. J. *German Classical Drama: Theatre, Humanity, and Nation, 1750–1870.* Cambridge, 1992.

LEACH, ROBERT, AND VICTOR BOROVSKY, eds. *A History of Russian Theatre.* Cambridge, 1999.

LIMON, JERZY. See under chapter 5.

MARKER, FREDERICK J., AND LISE-LONE MARKER. *A History of the Scandinavian Theatre.* Cambridge, 1996.

MCCABE, WILLIAM H. *An Introduction to the Jesuit Theatre.* ed. by Louis J. Oldani. St Louis, 1983.

PASCAL, ROY. *The German Sturm and Drang.* Manchester, 1953.

PATTERSON, MICHAEL. *The First German Theatre: Schiller, Goethe, Kleist, and Büchner in Performance.* New York, 1990.

PRUDHOE, JOHN. *The Theatre of Goethe and Schiller.* Oxford, 1973.

SENELICK, LAURENCE, ed. *National Theatre in Northern and Eastern Europe, 1746–1900.* New York, 1991.

SLONIM, MARC. *Russian Theatre from the Empire to the Soviets.* Cleveland, 1961.

VINCE, RONALD. See under chapter 9.

WILLIAMS, SIMON. *German Actors of the Eighteenth and Nineteenth Centuries: Idealism, Romanticism, and Realism.* Westport, CT, 1985.

CHAPTER 12: CONTINENTAL EUROPEAN THEATRE IN THE EARLY NINETEENTH CENTURY

ARVIN, NEIL E. *Eugène Scribe and the French Theatre, 1815–60.* Cambridge, MA, 1924.

BRANDT, GEORGE W. See under chapter 11.

CARLSON, MARVIN. *The French Stage in the Nineteenth Century.* Metuchen, NJ, 1972.

———. *The German Stage in the Nineteenth Century.* Metuchen, NJ, 1972.

———. *The Theatre of the French Revolution.* Ithaca, NY, 1966.

GIES, DAVID THATCHER. *The Theatre in Nineteenth-Century Spain*, 1994.

HEMMINGS, F. W. J. *The Theatre Industry in 19th Century France*. Cambridge, 1993.

KARLINSKY, SIMON. See under chapter 11.

KENNARD, JOSEPH S. See under chapter 7.

LACEY, ALEXANDER. *Pixérécourt and the French Romantic Drama*. Toronto, 1928.

LAMPORT, F. J. See under chapter 11.

LEACH, ROBERT, AND VICTOR BOROVSKY, eds. See under chapter 11.

MCCORMICK, JOHN. *Popular Theatres of Nineteenth-Century France*. New York, 1993.

MELCHER, EDITH. See under chapter 10.

MOYNET, JEAN-PIERRE. *French Theatrical Production in the Nineteenth Century*. Binghamton, NY, 1976.

PATTERSON, MICHAEL. See under chapter 11.

POLLAK, GUSTAV. *Franz Grillparzer and the Austrian Drama*. New York, 1907.

SENELICK, LAURENCE. *Serf Actor: The Life and Art of Mikhail Shchepkin*. Westport, CT, 1984.

————. See under chapter 11.

SLONIM, MARC. See under chapter 11.

WILLIAMS, SIMON. See under chapter 11.

CHAPTER 13: ENGLISH-LANGUAGE THEATRE IN THE EARLY NINETEENTH CENTURY

APPLETON, WILLIAM W. *Madame Vestris and the London Stage*. New York, 1974.

BAER, MARK. *Theatre and Disorder in Late Georgian London*. Oxford, 1992.

BAINS, YASHDIP S. *English Canadian Theatre, 1765–1826*. New York, 1998.

BENSON, EUGENE, AND L. W. CONOLLY. *English-Canadian Theatre*. Toronto, 1987.

————. *The Oxford Companion to Canadian Theatre*. Toronto, 1987.

BOGARD, TRAVIS, et al. *Revels History of Drama in English*. Vol 8: *American Drama*. New York, 1977.

BOOTH, MICHAEL. *English Melodrama*. London, 1965.

BOOTH, MICHAEL, et al. See under chapter 9.

CARSON, W. G. B. *The Theatre of the Frontier*. Chicago, 1932.

————. *Managers in Distress*. St. Louis, 1949.

CROSS, GILBERT. *Next Week "East Lynne": Domestic Drama in Performance, 1820–1874*. Lewisburg, PA, 1976.

DAVIS, TRACY C. *The Economics of the British Stage, 1800–1914*. Cambridge, 2000.

DAVIS, TRACY C., AND ELLEN DONKIN. *Women and Playwriting in Nineteenth-Century Britain*. Cambridge, 1999.

DONOHUE, JOSEPH W. *Theatre in the Age of Kean*. Oxford, 1975.

————, ed. *The Theatre Manager in England and America: Players of a Perilous Game*. Princeton, NJ, 1971.

DUDDEN, FAYE E. *Women in the American Theatre: Actresses and Audiences, 1790–1870*. New Haven, 1994.

DURHAM, WELDON B., ed. *American Theatre Companies, 1749–1887*. Westport, CT, 1986.

ENGLE, RONALD, AND TICE L. MILLER, eds. *The American Stage: Social and Economic Issues from the Colonial Period to the Present*. Cambridge, 2001.

GRIMSTED, DAVID. *Melodrama Unveiled: American Theatre and Culture, 1800–1850*. Chicago, 1968.

Irvin, Eric. *Theatre Comes to Australia*. Brisbane, 1971.

————. *Australian Melodrama*. Sydney, 1981.

JOSEPH, BERTRAM. See under chapter 9.

IRVING, ERIC. *Dictionary of the Australian Theatre 1788–1914*. Sydney, 1985.

LEACROFT, RICHARD. See under chapter 9.

LONDRÉ, FELICIA HARDISON, AND DANIEL J. WATERMEIER. See under chapter 9.

LOVE, HAROLD, ed. *The Australian Stage: A Documentary History*. Kensington, NSW, 1984.

MACREADY, WILLIAM CHARLES. *Macready's Reminiscences*. New York, 1875.

MATTHEWS, BRANDER, AND LAURENCE HUTTON. *Actors and Actresses of Great Britain and the United States from the Days of David Garrick to the Present Time*. 5 vols. New York, 1886.

MCCONACHIE, BRUCE A. *Melodramatic Formations: American Theatre and Society, 1820–1870*. Iowa City, 1992.

MAMMEN, EDWARD W. *The Old Stock Company School of Acting*. Boston, 1945.

MEISEL, MARTIN. *Realizations: Narrative, Pictorial, and Theatrical Arts in Nineteenth-Century England*. Princeton, NJ, 1983.

MOODY, JANE. See under chapter 9.

NICOLL, ALLARDYCE. See under chapter 9.

ODELL, G. C. D. *Annals of the New York Stage*. 15 vols. New York, 1927–1949.

————. *Shakespeare from Betterton to Irving*. 2 vols. New York, 1920.

PARSONS, PHILIP, ed. *Companion to Theatre in Australia*. Sydney, 1995.

PETERSON, BERNARD L., JR. *Profiles of African American Stage Performers and Theatre People, 1816–1960*. Westport, CT, 2001.

PLANCHÉ, J. R. *The Recollections and Reflections of James Robinson Planché*. 2 vols. London, 1872.

QUINN, ARTHUR H. *A History of the American Drama from the Beginning to the Civil War*. 2nd ed. New York, 1943.

REES, TERENCE. *Theatre Lighting in the Age of Gas*. London, 1978.

ROWELL, GEORGE. *The Victorian Theatre, 1792–1914*. 2nd ed. London, 1979.

SADDLEMYER, ANN, ed. *Early Stages: Theatre in Ontario, 1800–1914*. Toronto, 1990.

SCHOCH, RICHARD W. *Shakespeare's Victorian Stage: Performing History in the Theatre of Charles Kean*. Cambridge, 1998.

SHATTUCK, CHARLES H. *Shakespeare on the American Stage; From the Hallams to Edwin Booth*. Washington, DC, 1976.

————. *Shakespeare on the American Stage: From Booth and Barrett to Southern and Marlowe*. Washington, DC, 1987.

SOUTHERN, RICHARD. See under chapter 9.

SPEAIGHT, ROBERT. *Shakespeare on the Stage: An Illustrated History of Shakespearean Performance*. London, 1972.

STEPHENS, JOHN RUSSELL. *The Profession of the Playwright: British Theatre, 1800–1900*. London, 1992.

VARDAC, A. N. *Stage to Screen: Theatrical Method from Garrick to Griffith*. Cambridge, MA, 1949.

WILMETH, DON B., AND CHRISTOPHER BIGSBY, eds. *The Cambridge History of American Theatre*. Vol. I: *Beginnings to 1870*. Cambridge, 1998.

WITHAM, BARRY B., ed. *Theatre in the United States: A Documentary History*. Vol. I: *1750–1915, Theatre in the Colonies and the United States*. Cambridge, 1995.

WITTKE, CARL F. *Tambo and Bones: A History of the American Minstrel Stage*. Durham, NC, 1930.

YOUNG, WILLIAM C. *Documents of American Theatre History: Famous American Playhouses*. 2 vols. Chicago, 1973.

————. *Documents of American Theatre History: Famous Actors and Actresses on the American Stage*. 2 vols. New York, 1975.

CHAPTER 14: ENGLISH-LANGUAGE THEATRE IN THE LATE NINETEENTH CENTURY

BOGARD, TRAVIS, et al. See under chapter 13.

BOOTH, MICHAEL, AND JOEL H. KAPLAN, eds. *The Edwardian Theatre: Essays on Performance and the Stage*. Cambridge, 1996.

———. *Theatre in the Victorian Age.* London, 1991.

DAVIS, TRACY. *Actresses as Working Women: Their Social Identity in Victorian Culture.* New York, 1991.

———. See under chapter 13.

DURHAM, WELDON B., ed. *American Theatre Companies, 1888–1930.* Westport, CT, 1987.

ENGLE, RONALD, AND TICE L. MILLER. See under chapter 13.

FELHEIM, MARVIN. *The Theatre of Augustin Daly: An Account of the Late Nineteenth Century Stage.* Cambridge, MA, 1956.

FITZGERALD, PERCY. *The World behind the Scenes.* London, 1881.

FROW, GERALD. *Oh, Yes It Is: A History of Pantomime.* London, 1985.

GLASSTONE, VICTOR. *Victorian and Edwardian Theatre.* Cambridge, MA, 1975.

HAY, SAMUEL A. *African American Theatre: A Historical and Critical Analysis.* Cambridge, 1994.

HENDERSON, MARY C. *The City and the Theatre: New York Playhouses from Bowling Green to Times Square.* Clifton, NJ, 1973.

HODGE, FRANCIS. *Yankee Theatre.* Austin, TX, 1964.

HOPKINS, ALBERT A. *Magic: Stage Illusions and Scientific Diversions.* New York, 1897.

HUNT, HUGH, et al. *The Revels History of Drama in English.* Vol. 7: *1880 to the Present Day.* New York, 1979.

JOSEPH, BERTRAM. See under chapter 9.

LONDRÉ, FELICIA HARDISON, AND DANIEL J. WATERMEIER. See under chapter 9.

QUINN, A. H. *A History of the American Drama from the Civil War to the Present Day.* 2nd ed. New York, 1949.

SADDLEMYER, ANN. See under chapter 13.

TREWIN, J. C., AND T. C. KEMP. *The Shakespeare Festival: A History of the Shakespeare Memorial Theatre.* London, 1953.

CHAPTER 15: CONTINENTAL EUROPEAN AND LATIN AMERICAN THEATRE IN THE LATE NINETEENTH CENTURY

HEMMINGS, F. W. J. *Theatre and State in France, 1760–1905.* Cambridge, 1994.

———. *The Theatre Industry in Nineteenth-Century France.* Cambridge, 1993.

KENNARD, JOSEPH S. See under chapter 7.

LEACH, ROBERT, AND VICTOR BOROVSKY, eds. See under chapter 11.

MATTHEWS, BRANDER. *French Dramatists of the Nineteenth Century.* 5th ed. New York, 1914.

———. *The Theatres of Paris.* New York, 1880.

OSBORNE, JOHN. *The Naturalist Drama in Germany.* Manchester, 1971.

PELLETTIERI, O. *Cien años de teatro argentino, 1886–1990.* Buenos Aires, 1991.

SACHS, EDWIN O., AND E. A. E. WOODROW. *Modern Opera Houses and Theatres.* 3 vols. London, 1897–1898.

SCHULER, CATHERINE. *Women in Russian Theatre: The Actress in the Silver Age.* London, 1996.

CHAPTER 16: THE BEGINNINGS OF MODERN REALISM

ANTOINE, ANDRÉ. *Memories of the Théâtre Libre.* Coral Gables, FL, 1964.

BELASCO, DAVID. *Theatre through Its Stage Door.* New York, 1919.

BENTLEY, ERIC. *The Playwright as Thinker: A Study of Drama in Modern Times.* New York, 1946.

BERNHEIM, A. L. *The Business of the Theatre.* New York, 1932.

BRUSTEIN, ROBERT. *The Theatre of Revolt.* New York, 1964.

CARTER, LAWSON A. *Zola and the Theatre.* New Haven, CT, 1963.

COLE, TOBY, ed. *Playwrights on Playwriting: The Meaning and Making of Modern Drama from Ibsen to Ionesco.* New York, 1961.

COLE, TOBY, AND HELEN K. CHINOY, eds. *Directors on Directing.* Indianapolis, 1963.

GRUBE, MAX. *The Story of the Meiningen.* Trans. by Ann Marie Koller. Coral Gables, FL, 1963.

KOLLER, ANN MARIE. *The Theater Duke: Georg II of Saxe-Meiningen and the German Stage.* Stanford, 1984.

LEACH, ROBERT, AND VICTOR BOROVSKY, eds. See under chapter 11.

LUMLEY, FREDERICK. *Trends in Twentieth Century Drama: A Survey since Ibsen and Shaw.* 2nd ed. London, 1960.

MACCARTHY, DESMOND. *The Court Theatre, 1904–07.* London, 1907.

MARKER, LISE-LONE. *David Belasco: Naturalism in the American Theatre.* Princeton, NJ, 1975.

OSBORNE, JOHN. *The Meiningen Court Theatre, 1866–1890.* Cambridge, 1988.

SANDERSON, MICHAEL. *From Irving to Olivier: A Social History of the Acting Profession, 1880–1983.* New York, 1985.

STANISLAVSKY, KONSTANTIN. *An Actor Prepares.* Trans. by Elizabeth R. Hapgood. New York, 1936.

———. *Building a Character.* Trans. by E. R. Hapgood. New York, 1949.

———. *Creating a Role.* Trans. by E. R. Hapgood. New York, 1961.

———. *My Life in Art.* Trans. by J. J. Robbins. Boston, 1924.

WAXMAN, S. M. *Antoine and the Théâtre Libre.* Cambridge, MA, 1926.

WILLIAMS, RAYMOND. *Drama from Ibsen to Eliot.* London, 1952.

CHAPTER 17: ALTERNATIVES TO MODERN REALISM

APPIA, ADOLPHE. *The Work of Living Art and Man Is the Measure of All Things.* Coral Gables, FL, 1960.

———. *Essays, Scenarios and Designs.* Ann Arbor, 1989.

BABLET, DENIS. *Edward Gordon Craig.* New York, 1967.

———. *The Revolution of Stage Design in the Twentieth Century.* Paris, 1977.

BLOCK, HASKELL. *Mallarmé and the Symbolist Drama.* Detroit, 1963.

BOURGEOIS, MAURICE. *J. M. Synge and the Irish Theatre.* New York, 1965.

BRAUN, EDWARD. *The Director and the Stage: From Naturalism to Grotowski.* New York, 1982.

———. *Meyerhold on Theatre.* New York, 1969.

———. *Meyerhold: A Revolution in Theater.* Iowa City, 1995.

BROCKETT, OSCAR G., AND ROBERT R. FINDLAY. *Century of Innovation: A History of European and American Theatre and Drama since the Late Nineteenth Century.* 2nd ed. Needham Heights, MA, 1991.

BYRNE, DAWSON. *The Story of Ireland's National Theatre: The Abbey.* Dublin, 1929.

CRAIG, EDWARD GORDON. *On the Art of the Theatre.* 2nd ed. Boston, 1924.

DEAK, FRANTISEK. *Symbolist Theater: The Formation of the Avant Garde.* Baltimore, 1993.

FUCHS, GEORG. *Revolution in the Theatre.* Trans. by C. C. Kuhn. Ithaca, NY, 1959.

FUERST, WALTER R., AND SAMUEL J. HUME, *Twentieth Century Stage Decoration.* 2 vols. London, 1928.

GORELIK, MORDECAI. *New Theatres for Old.* New York, 1940.

INNES, CHRISTOPHER. *Avant-garde Theatre 1892–1992.* London, 1993.

———. *Edward Gordon Craig.* New York, 1983.

LABELLE, MAURICE. *Alfred Jarry: Nihilism and the Theatre of the Absurd.* New York, 1980.

LEHMANN, ANDREW G. *The Symbolist Aesthetic in France, 1885–1895.* Oxford, 1950.

MAXWELL, C. E. W. *A Critical History of Modern Irish Drama, 1891–1980.* New York, 1985.

MORASH, CHRIS. *A History of Irish Theatre, 1601–2000.* Cambridge, 2002.

PATTERSON, MICHAEL. *The Revolution in German Theatre, 1900–1933.* Boston, 1981.

RISCHBEITER, HENNING. *Art and the Stage in the Twentieth Century.* Greenwich, CT, 1968.

ROOSE-EVANS, JAMES. *Experimental Theatre: From Stanislavsky to Peter Brook.* New rev. ed. London, 1984.

SHATTUCK, ROGER. *The Banquet Years: The Arts in France, 1885–1918.* New York, 1961.

SPEAIGHT, ROBERT. *William Poel and the Elizabethan Revival.* London, 1954.

STEIN, JACK M. *Richard Wagner and the Synthesis of the Arts.* Detroit, 1960.

STYAN, J. L. *Max Reinhardt.* Cambridge, 1982.

———. *Modern Drama in Theory and Practice.* 3 vols. New York, 1981.

VALENCY, MAURICE. *The Flower and the Castle: An Introduction to Modern Drama.* New York, 1963.

VOLBACH, WALTER. *Adolphe Appia, Prophet of the Modern Theatre.* Middletown, CT, 1968.

WAGNER, RICHARD. *Opera and Drama.* Trans. by Edwin Evans. London, 1913.

WALTON, J. MICHAEL, ed. *Craig on Theatre.* London, 1983.

WILLIAMS, SIMON. *Richard Wagner and Festival Theatre.* Westport, CT, 1994.

CHAPTER 18: CONTINENTAL EUROPEAN AND LATIN AMERICAN THEATRE IN THE EARLY TWENTIETH CENTURY

BERGHAUS, GUNTHER. *Italian Futurist Theatre, 1909–1944.* Oxford, 1998.

BRAUN, EDWARD. See under chapter 17.

BROCKETT, OSCAR G., AND ROBERT R. FINDLAY. See under chapter 17.

GORDON, MEL. *Dada Performance.* New York, 1987.

KIRBY, MICHAEL. *Furturist Performance.* New York, 1971.

KURTZ, MAURICE. *Jacques Copeau: Biography of a Theatre.* Carbondale, IL, 1999.

LAMBS, RUTH. *Mexican Theatre in the Twentieth Century.* Claremont, CA, 1975.

LEACH, ROBERT, AND VICTOR BOROVSKY, eds. See under chapter 11.

MATTHEWS, J. H. *Theatre in Dada and Surrealism.* Syracuse, NY, 1974.

MELZER, ANNABELLE. *Latest Rage the Big Drum: Dada and Surrealist Performance.* Ann Arbor, 1980.

PATTERSON, MICHAEL. See under chapter 17.

PISCATOR, ERWIN. *The Political Theatre: A History, 1914–1929.* Trans. Hugh Rorison. New York, 1978.

RICHTER, HANS. *Dada: Art and Anti-Art.* New York, 1966.

RISCHBEITER, HENNING. See under chapter 17.

RITCHIE, J. M. *German Expressionist Drama.* Boston, 1976.

CHAPTER 19: ENGLISH-LANGUAGE THEATRE IN THE EARLY TWENTIETH CENTURY

BISHOP, B. W. *Barry Jackson and the London Theatre.* London, 1933.

BROCKETT, OSCAR G., AND ROBERT R. FINDLAY. See under chapter 17.

BRUSTEIN, ROBERT. See under chapter 16.

COLE, TOBY. See under chapter 16.

DOWNER, ALAN S. *Fifty Years of American Drama, 1900–1950.* Chicago, 1951.

ENGLE, RONALD, AND TICE L. MILLER. See under chapter 13.

FINDLATER, RICHARD. *Lilian Baylis: The Lady of the Old Vic.* London, 1975.

HUNT, HUGH, et al. See under chapter 14.

KRASNER, DAVID. *Resistance, Parody, and Double Consciousness in African American Theatre, 1895–1910.* New York, 1997.

LONDRÉ, FELICIA HARDISON, AND DANIEL J. WATERMEIER. See under chapter 9.

ROWELL, GEORGE, AND ANTHONY JACKSON. *The Repertory Movement: A History of Regional Theatre in Britain.* New York, 1984.

RYAN, TOBY GORDON. *Stage Left: Canadian Theatre in the Thirties.* Toronto, 1985.

SHAFER, YVONNE. *American Women Playwrights, 1900–1950.* New York, 1995.

STOWELL, SHEILA. *A Stage of Their Own: Feminist Playwrights of the Suffrage Era.* Ann Arbor, MI, 1992.

STUART, E. ROSS. *The History of Prairie Theatre.* Toronto, 1984.

CHAPTER 20: CONTINENTAL EUROPEAN AND LATIN AMERICAN THEATRE IN THE MID TWENTIETH CENTURY

ARTAUD, ANTONIN. *The Theatre and Its Double.* Trans. by Mary C. Richards. New York, 1958.

BEARDSELL, PETER. *A Theatre for Cannibals: Rodolfo Usigli and the Mexican Stage.* London, 1992.

BROCKETT, OSCAR G., AND ROBERT R. FINDLAY. See under chapter 17.

BURGESS, RONALD DAVE. *Mexican Theatre: The Generation of 1969.* Ann Arbor, 1985.

CLARK, FRED, AND ANA L. G. GARCIA, eds. *Twentieth Century Brazilian Theatre.* Chapel Hill, NC, 1978.

GADBERRY, GLEN. *Theatre in the Third Reich, the Pre-war Years: Essays on Theatre in Nazi Germany.* Westport, CT, 1995.

GARTEN, H. F. *Modern German Drama.* New York, 1959.

GORCHAKOV, NIKOLAI A. *The Theatre in Soviet Russia.* Trans. by Edgar Lehman. New York, 1957.

GORCHAKOV, NIKOLAI M. *The Vakhtangov School of Stage Art.* Moscow, n.d.

GORELIK, MORDECAI. See under chapter 14.

GROPIUS, WALTER, ed. *The Theatre of the Bauhaus.* Middletown, CT, 1961.

HOOVER, MARJORIE L. *Meyerhold: The Art of Conscious Theatre.* Amherst, MA, 1974.

HORTMANN, WILHELM. *Shakespeare on the German Stage: The Twentieth Century.* Cambridge, 1998.

HOUGHTON, NORRIS. *Moscow Rehearsals: An Account of Methods of Production in the Soviet Theatre.* New York, 1936.

INNES, C. D. *Erwin Piscator's Political Theatre.* New York, 1972.

KIENZLE, SIEGFRIED. *Modern World Theatre: A Guide to Productions in Europe and the United States since 1945.* Trans. by A. and F. Henderson. New York, 1970.

KNAPP, BETTINA. *Louis Jouvet, Man of the Theatre.* New York, 1958.

KNOWLES, DOROTHY. *French Drama of the Interwar Years, 1918–39.* New York, 1967.

KUHNS, DAVID F. *German Expressionist Theatre: The Actor and the Stage.* Cambridge, 1997.

LEACH, ROBERT. *Vsevelod Meyerhold.* Cambridge, 1993.

MACGOWAN, KENNETH, AND ROBERT E. JONES, *Continental Stagecraft.* New York, 1922.

RUDNITSKY, KONSTANTIN. *Russian and Soviet Theatre: Tradition and the Avant-Garde.* London, 1988.

SAINT-DENIS, MICHEL. *The Rediscovery of Style.* New York, 1960.

SCHMIDT, PAUL, ed. *Meyerhold at Work.* Austin, TX, 1980.

SCHOENBACH, PETER JULIAN. *Modern Brazilian Theatre: Art and Document.* New Jersey, 1973.

SEGEL, HAROLD B. *Twentieth-Century Russian Drama: From Gorky to the Present.* Updated ed. Baltimore, 1993.

SIMONOV, REUBEN. *Stanislavsky's Protegé: Eugene Vakhtangov.* Trans. by Miriam Goldina. New York, 1969.

SLONIM, MARC. See under chapter 11.

STANISLAVSKY, KONSTANTIN. See under chapter 16.

SYMONS, JAMES. *Meyerhold's Theatre of the Grotesque: The Post-Revolutionary Productions, 1920–1932.* Coral Gables, FL, 1971.

TAIROV, ALEXANDER. *Notes of a Director.* Trans. by William Kuhlke. Coral Gables, FL, 1969.

WILLETT, JOHN. *Expressionism.* New York, 1970.

———. *The Theatre of Bertolt Brecht.* New York, 1959.

———. *The Theatre of Edwin Piscator.* New York, 1979.

———. *The Theatre of the Weimar Republic.* New York, 1988.

WINGLER, HANS. *Bauhaus.* Cambridge, MA, 1969.

WORRALL, NICK. *Modernism to Realism on the Soviet Stage: Tairov, Vakhtangov, Okhlopkov.* London, 1989.

CHAPTER 21: ENGLISH-LANGUAGE THEATRE IN THE MID TWENTIETH CENTURY

ARONSON, ARNOLD. *American Avant-Garde: A History.* New York, 2000.

BROCKETT, OSCAR G., AND ROBERT R. FINDLAY. See under chapter 17.

CLURMAN, HAROLD. *The Fervent Years: The Story of the Group Theatre in the Thirties.* New York, 1957.

DAVIS, HALLIE FLANAGAN. *Arena.* New York, 1940.

DONOGHUE, DENIS. *The Third Voice: Modern British and American Verse Drama.* Princeton, NJ, 1959.

DURHAM, WELDON B., ed. *American Theatre Companies, 1931–1986.* Westport, CT, 1989.

ELAM, HARRY J., AND DAVID KRASNER. *African American Performance and Theatre History: A Critical Reader.* Oxford, 2000.

EYRE, RICHARD, AND NICHOLAS WRIGHT. *Changing Stages: A View of British and American Theatre in the Twentieth Century.* New York, 2001.

ENGLE, RONALD, AND TICE L. MILLER. See under chapter 13.

GIELGUD, JOHN. *Early Stages.* New York, 1939.

GOLDBERG, ROSELEE. *Performance Art from Futurism to the Present.* rev. ed. New York, 1988.

ISSACS, EDITH J. R. *The Negro in the American Theatre.* New York, 1947.

KIENZLE, SIEGFRIED. See under chapter 20.

LARSON, ORVILLE K. *Scene Design in the American Theatre from 1915 to 1960.* Fayetteville, AR, 1989.

LONDRÉ, FELICIA HARDISON, AND DANIEL J. WATERMEIER. See under chapter 9.

LUMLEY, FREDERICK. See under chapter 14.

MARSHALL, NORMAN. *The Other Theatre.* London, 1947.

MAXWELL, C. E. W. See under chapter 17.

O'CONNOR, JOHN, AND LORRAINE BROWN, eds. *Free, Adult, Uncensored: The Living History of the Federal Theatre Project.* Washington, DC, 1978.

QUINN, ARTHUR H. See under chapter 14.

ROOSE-EVANS, JAMES. See under chapter 17.

SANDERSON, MICHAEL. See under chapter 16.

SCHECHNER, RICHARD. *Public Domain: Essays on the Theatre.* Indianapolis, 1969.

SCHEVILL, JAMES. *Breakout! In Search of New Theatrical Environments.* Chicago, 1972.

STYAN, J. L. See under chapter 17.

TREWIN, J. C., AND T. C. KEMP. See under chapter 17.

USMIANI, RENATE. *Second Stage: The Alternative Theatre Movement in Canada.* Vancouver, 1983.

WEALES, GERALD. *American Drama since World War II.* New York, 1962.

———. *The Jumping Off Place: American Drama in the 1960s.* New York, 1969.

WILLIAMS, E. HARCOURT. *Old Vic Saga.* London, 1949.

WILLIAMS, RAYMOND. See under chapter 16.

CHAPTER 22: CONTINENTAL EUROPEAN AND LATIN AMERICAN THEATRE IN THE LATE TWENTIETH CENTURY

BARRAULT, JEAN-LOUIS, *The Theatre of Jean-Louis Barrault.* Trans. by J. Chiari. New York, 1961.

BOWERS, FAUBION. *Broadway, USSR: Theatre, Ballet and Entertainment in Russia Today.* New York, 1959.

BRADBY, DAVID. *Modern French Drama, 1940–1980.* New York, 1984.

BRAUN, KAZIMIERZ. *A History of Polish Theatre, 1939–1989.* Westport, CT, 1996.

BROCKETT, OSCAR G., AND ROBERT R. FINDLAY. See under chapter 17.

BURIAN, JARKA. *The Scenography of Joseph Svoboda.* Middletown, CT, 1971.

ESSLIN, MARTIN. *The Theatre of the Absurd.* rev. ed. New York, 1969.

FOWLIE, WALLACE. *Dionysus in Paris: A Guide to Contemporary French Theatre.* New York, 1960.

FREEMAN, E. *The Theatre of Albert Camus.* London, 1973.

FO, DARIO. *The Tricks of the Trade.* Trans. by Joe Farrell. London, 1991.

GARTEN, H. F. See under chapter 20.

GORCHAKOV, NIKOLAI A. See under chapter 20.

GRODZICKI, AUGUST. *Polish Theatre Today.* Warsaw, 1978.

GROTOWSKI, JERZY. *Towards a Poor Theatre.* New York, 1968.

GUICHARNAUD, JACQUES. *Modern French Theatre from Giraudoux to Beckett.* New Haven, CT, 1961.

HAINAUX, RENÉ, ed. *Stage Design throughout the World since 1935.* New York, 1956.

———. *Stage Design throughout the World since 1950.* New York, 1964.

———. *Stage Design throughout the World.* New York, 1972.

———. *Stage Design throughout the World, 1970–1975.* New York, 1976.

HAYMAN, RONALD, ed. *The German Stage.* New York, 1975.

HIRST, DAVID L. *Giorgio Strehler.* Cambridge, 1993.

HOUGHTON, NORRIS. *Return Engagement: A Postscript to "Moscow Rehearsals."* New York, 1962.

INNES, C. D. *Modern German Drama.* New York, 1979.

KUMIEGA, JENNIFER. *The Theatre of Grotowski.* London, 1985.

LEACH, ROBERT, AND VICTOR BOROVSKY, eds. See under chapter 11.

MITCHELL, TONY. *Dario Fo: People's Court Jester.* New York, 1985.

O'CONNOR, GARRY. *French Theatre Today.* London, 1975.

OSINSKI, ZBIGNIEW. *Grotowski and His Laboratory.* New York, 1986.

PATTERSON, MICHAEL. *German Theatre Today.* London, 1976.

———. *Peter Stein: Germany's Leading Theatre Director.* New York, 1981.

RISCHBEITER, HENNING. See under chapter 15.

ROUSE, JOHN. *Brecht and the West German Theatre: The Practice and Politics of Interpretation.* Ann Arbor, 1989.

SEGEL, HAROLD B. See under chapter 15.

SLONIM, MARC. See under chapter 11.

SMELIANSKY, ANATOLY. *The Russian Theatre after Stalin.* Cambridge, 1999.

TRENSKY, PAUL I. *Czech Drama since World War II.* White Plains, NY, 1978.

WILLET, JOHN. See under chapter 15.

Yarrow, Ralph, ed. *European Theatre 1960–1990.* London, 1992.

CHAPTER 23: ENGLISH-LANGUAGE THEATRE IN THE LATE TWENTIETH CENTURY

ADDENBROOKE, DAVID. *The Royal Shakespeare Company: The Peter Hall Years.* London, 1974.

ANSORGE, PETER. *Disrupting the Spectacle: Five Years of Experimental and Fringe Theatre in Britain.* London, 1975.

ARONSON, ARNOLD. *American Set Design.* New York, 1985.

———. *American Avant-Garde: A History.* New York, 2000.

BARTOW, ARTHUR. *The Director's Voice: 21 Interviews [with American Directors].* New York, 1988.

BETSKO, KATHLEEN, AND RACHEL KOENIG. *Interviews with Contemporary Women Playwrights.* New York, 1987.

BIGSBY, C. W. E. *A Critical Introduction to Twentieth-Century American Drama.* Vol. II and III. *Williams/Miller/Albee.* New York, 1984–1985.

BLAU, HERBERT. *The Dubious Spectacle: Extremities of Theater, 1976–2000.* Minneapolis, 2002.

BLUMENTHAL, EILEEN. *Joseph Chaikin: Exploring at the Boundaries of Theatre.* New York, 1984.

BORDMAN, GERALD. *American Musical Comedy.* New York, 1982.

BRADBY, DAVID, AND DAVID WILLIAMS. *Directors' Theatre.* [Littlewood, Planchon, Mnouchkine, Grotowski, Brook, Stein, Wilson.] New York, 1988.

BRATER, ENOCH, ed. *Feminine Focus: The New Women Playwrights.* New York, 1989.

BRECHT, STEFAN. *The Theatre of Visions: Robert Wilson.* Frankfurt am Main, 1978.

BROCKETT, OSCAR G., AND ROBERT R. FINDLAY. See under chapter 17.

BROOK, PETER. *The Empty Space.* New York, 1968.

———. *The Shifting Point: Forty Years of Theatrical Exploration, 1946–1987.* London, 1988.

BROWNE, TERRY. *Playwrights' Theatre: The English Stage Company at the Royal Court.* London, 1975.

BRUSTEIN, ROBERT. See under chapter 14.

———. *Revolution as Theatre: Notes on the New Radical Style.* New York, 1971.

BULL, JOHN. *New British Political Dramatists.* New York, 1984.

BYRD HOFFMAN FOUNDATION. *Robert Wilson: Theatre of Images.* 2nd ed. New York, 1984.

CALANDRA, DENIS. *New German Dramatists.* New York, 1984.

CHAMPAGNE, LENORA. *French Theatre Experiment since 1968.* Ann Arbor, 1984.

COHN, RUBY. *New American Dramatists, 1960–1980.* New York, 1982.

COOK, JUDITH. *The National Theatre.* London, 1976.

CROYDEN, MARGARET. *Lunatics, Lovers and Poets: The Contemporary Experimental Theatre.* New York, 1974.

DOTY, GRESDNA A., AND BILLY J. HARBIN, eds. *Inside the Royal Court Theatre, 1956–1981: Artists Talk.* Baton Rouge, LA, 1990.

ELSOM, JOHN. *Post-War British Theatre.* Boston, 1979.

ESSLIN, MARTIN. *The Peopled Wound: The Work of Harold Pinter.* New York, 1970.

EYRE, RICHARD, AND NICHOLAS WRIGHT. See under chapter 21.

FINDLATER, RICHARD, ed. *Twenty-Five Years of the English Stage Company.* London, 1981.

GOLDBERG, ROSELEE. See under chapter 17.

GOODMAN, LIZBETH. *Contemporary Feminist Theatres: To Each Her Own.* London, 1993.

GOORNEY, HOWARD. *The Theatre Workshop.* London, 1980.

GREEN, SUSAN. *Bread and Puppet: Stories of Struggle and Faith from Central America.* Woodstock, VT, 1985.

HART, LYNDA, AND PEGGY PHELAN, eds. *Acting Out: Feminist Performances.* Ann Arbor, MI, 1993.

HAYMAN, RONALD. *British Theatre since 1955: A Reassessment.* New York, 1979.

———. *Theatre and Anti-Theatre: New Movements since Beckett.* New York, 1979.

HILL, ERROL, ed. *The Theatre of Black Americans.* 2 vols. Englewood Cliffs, NJ, 1980.

HINCHLIFFE, ARNOLD. *British Theatre, 1950–1970.* Totowa, NJ, 1975.

HIRSCH, FOSTER. *A Method to Their Madness: The History of the Actors Studio.* New York, 1984.

ITZIN, CATHERINE. *Stages in the Revolution: Political Theatre in Britain since 1968.* New York, 1981.

JENKINS, RON. *Acrobats of the Soul: Comedy and Virtuosity in Contemporary American Theatre.* New York, 1988.

JOHNSTON, DENIS. *Up the Mainstream: The Rise of Toronto's Alternative Theatres.* Toronto, 1991.

KERENSKY, OLEG. *The New British Drama: Fourteen Playwrights since Osborne and Pinter.* New York, 1979.

KIRBY, MICHAEL. *Happenings.* New York, 1966.

KOLIN, PHILIP C., ed. *American Playwrights since 1945; a Guide to Scholarship, Criticism, and Performance.* Westport, CT, 1989.

KOSTELANETZ, RICHARD. *The Theatre of Mixed Means.* New York, 1968.

LESNICK, HENRY, ed. *Guerrilla Street Theatre.* New York, 1973.

LITTLE, STUART. *Enter Joseph Papp: In Search of a New American Theatre.* New York, 1974.

———. *Off-Broadway: The Prophetic Theatre.* New York, 1972.

LONDRÉ, FELICIA HARDISON, AND DANIEL J. WATERMEIER. See under chapter 9.

MAROWITZ, CHARLES, AND TRUSSLER, SIMON. *Theatre at Work: Playwrights and Productions in the Modern British Theatre.* New York, 1968.

MARRANCA, BONNIE, ed. *The Theatre of Images.* New York, 1977.

NOVICK, JULIUS. *Beyond Broadway.* New York, 1968.

PASOLLI, ROBERT. *A Book on the Open Theatre.* New York, 1970.

ROBERTSON, TIM. *Perambulations: The Australian Performing Group Recollected.* Melbourne, 2001.

SANDERSON, MICHAEL. See under chapter 16.

SAVRAN, DAVID. *In Their Own Words: Contemporary American Playwrights.* New York, 1988.

———. *The Wooster Group: Breaking the Rules.* Ann Arbor, 1988.

SEBALD, W. G., ed. *A Radical Stage: Theatre in Germany in the 1970s and 1980s.* Oxford, 1988.

SELLER, MAXINE SCHWARTZ, ed. *Ethnic Theatre in the United States.* Westport, CT, 1983.

SHANK, THEODORE. *American Alternative Theatres.* New York, 1982.

STRASBERG, LEE. *Strasberg at the Actors Studio.* New York, 1965.

TAYLOR, JOHN RUSSELL. *The Angry Theatre.* London, 1969.

———. *Second Wave: British Dramatists for the Seventies.* New York, 1971.

WILMETH, DON B., AND TICE L. MILLER, eds. *Cambridge Guide to the American Theatre.* New York, 1993.

ZIEGLER, JOSEPH. *Regional Theatre: The Revolutionary Stage.* Minneapolis, 1973.

CHAPTER 24: CONTEMPORARY THEATRE

BLAU, HERBERT. See under chapter 23.

BLUMENTHAL, EILEEN, AND JULIE TAYMOR. *Playing with Fire.* New York, 1999.

BOAL, AUGUSTO. *Legislative Theatre*. Trans. by Adrian Jackson. New York, 1998.

BRADBY, DAVID, AND ANNIE SPARKS. *Mise en Scène: French Theatre Now*. London, 1997.

BROOK, PETER. *Threads of Time*. Amsterdam, 1998.

BURIAN, JARKA. *Modern Czech Theatre: Reflector and Conscience of a Nation*. Iowa, 2000.

CHINOY, HELEN KRICH, AND LINDA WALSH JENKINS, eds. *Women in American Theatre*. 3d ed., fully revised. New York, 2001.

DELGADO, MARIA M., AND PAUL HERITAGE, eds. *In Contact with the Gods? Directors Talk Theatre*. Manchester, Eng., 1996.

EYRE, RICHARD, AND NICHOLAS WRIGHT. See under chapter 21.

GILBERT, HELEN. *Sightlines: Race, Gender, and Nation in Contemporary Australian Theatre*. Ann Arbor, 1998.

HERBERT, IAN, AND NICOLE LECLERCQ. *The World of Theatre 2000 Edition*. London, 2000.

HOLMBERG, ARTHUR. *The Theatre of Robert Wilson*. Cambridge, 1996.

KALINA, STEFANOVA, AND KALINA STEFANOVA-PETEVA. *Eastern European Theatre After the Iron Curtain*. Harwood, 2001.

LEACH, ROBERT, AND VICTOR BOROVSKY. See under chapter 11.

LEPAGE, ROBERT. *Connecting Flights*. New York, 1999.

LONDRÉ, FELICIA HARDISON, AND DANIEL J. WATERMEIER. See under chapter 9.

MULRYNE, J. R., AND MARGARET SHEWRING. *Shakespeare's Globe Rebuilt*. Cambridge, 1997.

PILKINGTON, LIONEL. *Theatre and the State in 20th Century Ireland*. New York, 2001.

QUADRI, FRANCO, FRANCO BERTONI, AND ROBERT STEARNS. *Robert Wilson*. New York, 1997.

ROBERTS, PHILIP. *The Royal Court Theatre and the Modern Stage*. Cambridge, 1999.

SHANK, THEODORE. *Beyond the Boundaries: American Alternative Theatre*. Ann Arbor: 2002.

TYTELL, JOHN. *The Living Theatre: Art, Exile, and Outrage*. New York, 1995.

WILLIAMS, DAVID. *Collaborative Theatre: The Théâtre du Soleil Sourcebook*. New York, 1999.

CHAPTER 25: THE THEATRE OF AFRICA

BAME, KWABENA N. *Come to Laugh: A Study of African Traditional Theatre in Ghana*. Accra, 1981.

BANHAM, MARTIN, AND CLIVE WAKE. *African Theatre Today*. London, 1976.

BANHAM, MARTIN, JAMES GIBBS, AND FEMI OSOFISAN, eds. *African Theatre in Development*. Bloomington, IN, 1999.

———, eds. *African Theatre: Playwrights and Politics*. Bloomington, IN, 2001.

———, ed. *The Cambridge Guide to Theatre*. Cambridge, 1995. [Entries on African theatre]

BANHAM, MARTIN, ERROL HILL, GEORGE WOODYARD, and advisory editor for Africa, OLU OBAFEMI, eds. *The Cambridge Guide to African and Caribbean Theatre*. Cambridge, 1994.

BARBER, KARIN. *The Generation of Plays: Yoruba Popular Life in Theater*. Bloomington, IN, 2001.

BJORKMAN, INGRID. *Mother Sing For Me: People's Theatre in Kenya*. London, 1989.

BOSMAN, F. C. L. *The Dutch and English Theatre in South Africa, 1880 till Today, and the Afrikaans Theatre*. Pretoria, 1951.

BREITINGER, ECKHARD, ed. *Theatre and Performance in Africa*. Bayreuth, 1997.

———, ed. *Theatre for Development*. Bayreuth, 1994.

CLARK, EBUN. *Hubert Ogunde: The Making of Nigerian Theatre*. London, 1979.

COLE, CATHERINE M. *Ghana's Concert Party Theatre*. Bloomington, IN, 2001.

CONTEH-MORGAN, JOHN. *Theatre and Drama in Francophone Africa*. Cambridge, 1995.

COPLAN, DAVID B. *In Township Tonight! South Africa's Black City Music and Theatre*. Johannesburg, 1985.

DAVIDSON, BASIL. *Modern Africa: A Social and Political History*. 2nd ed. London, 1983.

DREWAL, MARGARET THOMPSON. "The State of Research on Performance in Africa," *African Studies Review*, 34, 3 (December 1991), 1–64.

———. *Yoruba Ritual: Performers, Play, Agency*. Bloomington, IN, 1992.

ETHERTON, MICHAEL. *The Development of African Drama*. London, 1982.

FINNEGAN, RUTH. *Oral Literature in Africa*. Oxford, 1970.

FLETCHER, JILL. *The Story of South African Theatre, 1780–1930*. Cape Town, 1994.

GIBBS, JAMES. *Wole Soyinka*. London, 1986.

GOTRICK, KACKE. *Apidan Theatre and Modern Drama*. Stockholm, 1984.

GRAY, JOHN, comp. *Black Theatre and Performance: A Pan-African Bibliography*. Westport, CT, 1990.

HAUPTFLEISCH, TEMPLE, AND IAN STEADMAN, eds. *South African Theatre: Four Plays and an Introduction*. Pretoria, 1984.

JEYIFO, BOIDUN. *The Truthful Lie: Essays in a Sociology of African Drama*. London, 1985.

———. *The Yoruba Popular Theatre of Nigeria*. Lagos, 1984.

KARIN, BARBARA, et al. *West African Popular Theatre*. Bloomington, IN, 1997.

KAVANAGH, ROBERT MSHENGU. "Introduction," *South African People's Plays*. Johannesburg, 1981.

KERR, DAVID. *African Popular Theatre: From Pre-Colonial Days to the Present Day*. London, 1995.

———. *Theatre and Cultural Struggle in South Africa*. London, 1985.

———. *Theatre and Popular Culture in Southern Africa*. Bayreuth, 1997.

KIDD, ROSS. *From People's Theatre for Revolution to Popular Theatre for Reconstruction: Diary of a Zimbabwean Workshop*. The Hague, 1984.

KRUGER, LOREN. *The Drama of South Africa: Plays, Pageants, and Publics since 1910*. New York, 1999.

LARLHAM, PETER. *Black Theatre, Dance, and Ritual in South Africa*. Ann Arbor, MI, 1985.

MDA, ZAKES. *When People Play People: Development Communication through Theatre*. Johannesburg, 1993.

MLAMA, PENINA MUHANDO. *Culture and Development: The Popular Theatre Approach in Africa*. Sweden, 1991.

NDLOVU, DUMA, ed. "Introduction," *Woza Afrika! An Anthology of South African Plays*. New York, 1986.

NGUGI WA THIONG'O. *Decolonizing the Mind: The Politics of Language in African Literature*. Nairobi, 1986.

OBAFEMI, OLU. *Contemporary Nigerian Theatre: Cultural Heritage and Social Vision*. Bayreuth, 1997.

OGUNBA, OYIN, AND ABIOLA IRELE, eds. *The Theatre in Africa*. Ibadan, 1978.

OGUNBIYI, YEMI. *Drama and Theatre in Nigeria: A Critical Sourcebook*. Lagos, 1981.

ORKIN, MARTIN. *Drama and the South African State*. Johannesburg, 1991.

OWOMOYELA, OYEKAN, ed. *A History of Twentieth-Century African Literatures*. Lincoln, NE, 1993.

RACSTER, OLGA. *Curtain Going Up! The Story of the Cape Theatre*. Cape Town, 1951.

ROHMER, MARTIN. *Theatre and Performance in Urban Zimbabwe*. Bayreuth, 1999.

RUBIN, DON, et al. *The World Encyclopedia of Contemporary Theatre: Africa.* Vol. 3. New York, 1997.

SCHIPPER, MINEKE. *Theatre and Society in Africa.* Johannesburg, 1982.

TDR: THE DRAMA REVIEW, 32, 2 (Summer 1988). [Issue devoted to ritual performance in Africa today.]

THEATRE RESEARCH INTERNATIONAL, 9, 3 (1984). [Issue devoted to African theatre in the French language.]

TRAORE, BAKARY. *The Black African Theatre and Its Social Functions.* Trans. by Dapo Adelugba. Ibadan, 1972.

CHAPTER 26: THE THEATRE OF ASIA

The Actor's Analects, ed., trans., with an Introduction and Notes by Charles J. Dunn and Bunzo Torigoe. Tokyo, 1969.

ALLEY, R. *Peking Opera.* Beijing, 1984.

BAUMER, RACHEL V., AND JAMES R. BRANDON. *Sanskrit Drama in Performance.* Honolulu, 1981.

BHARATA. *Natyasastra.* Trans. by M. Ghose. Bengal, 1950.

BIRCH, CYRIL. *Scenes for Mandarins: The Elite Theatre of the Ming.* New York, 1999.

BOWERS, FAUBION. *Japanese Theatre.* New York, 1952.

BRANDON, JAMES R. *Theatre in Southeast Asia.* Cambridge, MA, 1967.

———, ed. *The Cambridge Guide to Asian Theatre.* New York, 1993.

CRUMP, JAMES I. *Chinese Theatre in the Days of Kublai Khan.* Tucson, 1980.

DOLBY, WILLIAM. *A History of Chinese Drama.* London, 1976.

ERNST, EARLE. *The Kabuki Theatre.* New York, 1956.

GARGI, BALWANT. *Theatre in India.* New York, 1962.

GUPTA, CHANDRA B. *The Indian Theatre.* New Delhi, 1991.

Half a Century of Japanese Theatre, edited by Japan Playwrights Association. Vol. I: *1990s, Part 1.* Tokyo, 1999.

———, *Vol. II: 1990s, Part 2.* Tokyo, 2000.

———, *Vol. III: 1980s, Part 1.* Tokyo, 2001.

HIRONAGA, SHUZABURO. *Bunraku, Japan's Unique Puppet Theatre.* Tokyo, 1964.

HOWARD, ROGER. *Contemporary Chinese Theatre.* Hong Kong, 1979.

INOURA, YOSHINOBU, AND TOSHIO KAWATAKE. *The Traditional Theatre of Japan.* New York, 1981.

IYER, K. B. *Kathakali: The Sacred Dance-Drama of Malabar.* London, 1955.

JACOB, PAUL. *Contemporary Indian Theatre: Interviews with Playwrights and Directors.* New Delhi, 1989.

KAWATAKE, SHIGETOSHI. *An Illustrated History of Japanese Theatre Arts.* Tokyo, 1956.

KEENE, DONALD. *Bunraku: The Art of the Japanese Puppet Theatre.* Tokyo, 1965.

KEITH, A. B. *The Sanskrit Drama: Its Origin, Development, Theory and Practice.* Oxford, 1924.

KOMPARU, KUNIO. *The Noh Theatre: Principles and Perspectives.* New York, 1983.

LEITER, SAMUEL L. *The Art of Kabuki: Plays in Performance.* Berkeley, 1979.

———. *New Kabuki Encyclopedia.* Westport, CT, 1997.

MACKERRAS, COLIN. *The Chinese Theatre in Modern Times.* Amherst, MA, 1975.

MATHUR, JAGDESH. *Drama in Rural India.* New York, 1964.

MELLEMA, R. L. *Wayang Puppets: Carving, Colouring, Symbolism.* Amsterdam, 1954.

MRAZEK, JAN, ed. *Puppet Theater in Contemporary Indonesia: New Approaches to Performance-Events.* Ann Arbor, 2001.

O'NEILL, P. G. *Early No Drama; Its Background, Character and Development, 1300–1450.* London, 1958.

———. *A Guide to No.* Tokyo, 1953.

ORTOLANI, BENITO. *The Japanese Theatre: From Shamanistic Ritual to Contemporary Pluralism.* rev. ed. Princeton, 1995.

PE-CHIN, CHANG. *Chinese Opera and Painted Face.* New York, 1979.

POWELL, BRIAN. *Japan's Modern Theatre: A Century of Change and Continuity.* London, 2002.

RICHMOND, FARLEY. *Kuttiyattam: Sanskrit Theater in India.* Ann Arbor, 2001.

RICHMOND, FARLEY, et al., eds. *Indian Theatre: Traditions of Performance.* Honolulu, 1990.

RILEY, JO. *Chinese Theatre and the Actor in Performance.* Cambridge, 1997.

SAKANISHI, S. *Kyogen.* Boston, 1938.

SASAYAMA, TADASHI, RONNIE MULRYNE, AND MARGARET SHEWRING, eds. *Shakespeare and the Japanese Stage.* Cambridge, 1999.

SCOTT, A. C. *The Classical Theatre of China.* New York, 1957.

———. *The Kabuki Theatre of Japan.* London, 1955.

SIU, WANG-NGAI, with PETER LOVRICK. *Chinese Opera: Images and Stories.* Vancouver and Seattle, 1997.

SUZUKI, TADASHI. *The Way of Acting: The Theatre Writings of Tadashi Suzuki.* Trans. by J. Thomas Rimer. New York, 1986.

TARLEKAR, G. H. *Studies in the Natyasastra, with Special Reference to the Sanskrit Drama in Performance.* Delhi, 1975.

TOITA, YASUJI. *Kabuki, the Popular Theatre.* New York, 1970.

TUNG, CONSTANTINE, AND COLIN MACKERRAS, eds. *Drama in the People's Republic of China.* Albany, NY, 1987.

WALEY, ARTHUR. *The No Plays of Japan.* London, 1921.

WINSATT, G. *Chinese Shadow Shows.* Cambridge, MA, 1936.

ZEAMI. *Kadensho.* Trans. by Chuichi Sakurai, Shuseki Hagashi, Rokuro Satoi, and Bin Miyai. Kyoto, 1971.

NOTE ON SOURCES OF INFORMATION

Information about recent developments must be sought primarily in periodicals, newspapers, and on the Internet through the World Wide Web. We have provided a list of periodicals which are most helpful for gathering information on contemporary theatre, and a separate list for those periodicals most helpful for locating additional information on theatre history, on our Web site at www.ablongman.com/brockett9e. You will also find a links page for each chapter and additional bibliographic information on that site.

Index

Caron, Antoine, 186–187
Carr, Marina, 567
Carrièr, Jean-Claude, 531
Carro (wagon), 140–141
Carros, 90
Cartel des Quatre, 441, 442, 471
Carter, Mrs. Leslie, 404
Casarès, Maria, 471
Casket, The (Ariosto), 159–160, 165–166
Casket, The (Plautus), 48
Casona, Alejandro, 446
Casson, Lewis, 398
Caste (Robertson), 361
Castelvetro, Lodovico, 161, 162, 184
Castillo, Fray Francisco de, 385
Castillo Ledón, Amalia González Caballero, 448
Castle of Perseverance, The, 97, 98
Castle Spectre, The (Lewis), 320
Castorff, Frank, 559–560
Castro, Consuelo, 526
Castro, Guillén de, 144, 191
Cathleen ni Houlihan (Yeats), 421
Catiline (Jonson), 112
Cato (Addison), 218, 234–235
Cat on a Hot Tin Roof (Williams), 501–502, 508
Cats, 569
Caucasian Chalk Circle, The (Brecht), 436, 482, 624
Caudi, José, 154
Cavea, 56
Cave art, 5, 6
Cazuela, 150, 151, 154, 383
Cecchini, Pier Maria, 182
Cenci, The (Shelley), 319
Cenodoxus (Bidermann), 268
Censorship, 118, 147, 220–223, 297, 299–300, 304, 313, 314, 319, 370, 371, 397, 446, 453, 477, 529–530, 557, 604
Center 42 (London), 493–494
Centlivre, Susanna, 218
Centunculus, 63
Cervantes, Miguel de, 143
Cesaire, Aimé, 476
Chaeremon, 33
Chaikin, Joseph, 513, 537–538
Chamberlain, Lord, 221, 318, 319, 324
Chamberlain's Men, 111, 115, 116, 118, 125, 126
Chambers, E. K., 136
Chambers, Jane, 546
Chambers, Ron, 567
Chambers of Rhetoric, 99–100, 121, 285
Chambers Street Theatre (New York), 342–343
Chambre à quartre portes, 207, 262
Champmeslé, Mlle, 203, 205, 257
Chan, Marty, 567

Chanfrau, Frank S., 338, 342
Chapelain, Jean, 192
Chaperon, Philippe, 378
Chapman, George, 112, 352
Chapman, William, 331
Chappuzeau, Samuel, 209
Characters
    comedia (Spain), 143, 150–151
    commedia (Italy), 248
    commedia dell'arte, 179–181, 270, 271
    Etruria, 45
    French farce, 189, 192–193
    Greece, 15, 27, 35
    liturgical drama, 79–80
    masque, 133
    Medieval, 79–80
    New Comedy, 37–38
    Rome, 48, 51
    Sanskrit drama, 617
Chariot-and-pole (scene shifting), 168–169, 197, 227, 243, 278–279, 381–382, 406, 410
Chariot races, 45, 52, 57, 66–67
Charles II (Payne), 330
Charles IX (Chénier), 303, 308
Charley, Dele, 589
Charlot, André, 457
Chaste Maid in Cheapside, A (Middleton), 122–123
Chattopadhyaya, Mohit, 620
Chavero, Alfredo, 385
Chayefsky, Paddy, 503
Cheek by Jowl, 563–564
Chekhov, Anton, 370, 400–401, 495, 519, 520, 558, 570
Chekhov, Mikhail, 423, 430
Chekhov Festival, 555
Chelsea Theatre Center (New York), 539
Chemchemi Company (Nairobi), 589
Cheney, Sheldon, 459
Chénier, Marie-Joseph, 303, 308
Chereau, Patrice, 517, 523, 558
Cherry, Wal, 507
Cherry Orchard, The (Chekhov), 400, 402, 531, 548–549
Chesnaye, Nicolas de la, 99, 187
Chester cycle, 83, 89, 107
Chestnut Street Theatre (Philadelphia), 328, 329, 332, 338
Chetwood, William, 233
Chiarelli, Luigi, 445
Chiari, Pietro, 247, 248
Chicago Exposition (1893), 349
Chicago Little Theatre, 457
Chifunyise, Stephen, 595
Chikamatsu Monzaemon, 636, 639
Chikwakwa Theatre (Zambia), 594
Child actors, 330, 362
Child Murderess, The (Wagner), 275
Children of Heracles, The (Euripides), 16

Children of the Queen's Revels, 117–118
Children's Hour, The (Hellman), 464
Children's theatre, 518
Chin, Frank, 546
China, 620–631, 647–648
Chionides, 18
Chips with Everything (Wesker), 493
Chitty, Allison, 532
Choregoi, 20, 21, 24, 26, 32, 42
Chorus
    Greece, 14–18, 18, 20, 22–24, 27, 34, 37, 42
    Italy, 161–162
    Rome, 50
Chorus Line, A, 539
Chorus Line, A (Bennett), 536
Christian opposition to theatre, 64, 67–68, 74, 146–147, 193–194, 452
Christine (Dumas *père*), 306
Christmas, 75, 78–79, 102–103, 109
Christmas Tale, A, 229
Christus Paschon, 67–68
Christy, E. P., 336
Chronegk, Ludwig, 388
Chryséide and Arimand (Mairet), 190
Chrysoloras, Manuel, 158
Chuanqui, 624
Church and theatre, 66, 67–68, 75–83, 99, 105, 110, 139–141, 146, 153, 182, 188, 193–194, 210, 267–268, 342, 352, 383, 582–583
Churchill, Caryl, 530, 535, 565
Cibber, Colley, 217, 224, 234, 236, 240
Cibber, Susanna, 236
Ciceri, Pierre-Luc-Charles, 312
Cicero, 59
Cid, Le (P. Corneille), 144, 191–194, 209, 313
Cid, Le Controversy, 191, 196, 206
Cinders (Glowacki), 512
Cino, Joe, 499
Cinoherni (Prague), 479
Cinthio, Giambattista Giraldi, 160
Cipriani, Giovanni Battista, 229
Circle in the Square (New York), 498, 569
Circle Repertory Theatre Company (New York), 539, 569–570
Circuses, 333, 567
Circus Maximus (Rome), 53–54, 57, 66
Cirque d'Hiver, 441
Cirque du Soléil, 567
Cirque Olympique, 304, 310
City Center (New York), 497–498
City Dionysia, 12–23, 33, 34, 42
City of Angels (Coleman), 536
City Theatre (Charleston), 329
Ciulei, Liviu, 540–541, 542

Civic Repertory Theatre (New York), 461

CIVIL warS (Wilson), 550

Cixous, Hélène, 526, 561

Claire, Ina, 465

Clairon, Mlle (Claire-Josèphe-Hippolyte Léris de la Tude), 258, 259–260

Clairond, Aimé, 470–471

Clancy, Dierdre, 532

Claques, 54, 307

Claramonte, Andrés de, 156

Clari (Payne), 330

Clark-Bekederemo, John Pepper, 584–585, 585

Claudel, Paul, 471

Cléopâtre Captive (Jodelle), 186

Clever, Edith, 518

Cliff p'Chong Lubwa, 593

Clitophon (Ryer), 190

Clive, Kitty, 236

Cloud 9 (Churchill), 535

Clouds, The (Aristophanes), 19, 27

Clowns, 269

Clurman, Harold, 461

Coates, George, 575

Cochran, C. B., 457

Cockpit-in-Court (London), 126, 135

Cockpit in Drury Lane, The (London), 127, 135

Cocktail Party, The (Eliot), 491

Cocteau, Jean, 439, 440

Cody, "Buffalo Bill," 349

Coelina (Pixérécourt), 304, 320

Cofradías (Spain), 147, 148–149

Cohen, Gustave, 107

Colclow, Thomas, 85

Coleman, Cy, 536

Coleridge, Samuel Taylor, 295, 319

Colet, John, 108

Colgan, Michael, 566

Coliseo, 154, 383

Colleen Bawn, The (Boucicault), 345, 346

Collier, Jeremy, 217

Colman, George the Elder, 221, 222–223

Colman, George the Younger, 222, 224

Colombia, 385

Colosseum (Rome), 53, 57, 59–60

Combination companies, 345–346

Comedia, 143–145

Comedia Himenea, 142

Comédie des Champs-Elysées, 441

Comédie des Comédiens, La (Gougenot), 193, 209

Comédie Française, 203–208, 249–259, 261–263, 276, 303–310, 312, 313, 375, 378–380, 393, 438–439, 442–443, 470, 472, 476, 522, 525, 561

Comédie Italienne, 248, 254–256, 258, 261–262, 304

Comédie larmoyante, 250–251

Comédiens du Roi, Les (The King's Players), 188, 193

Comédiens Ordinaires due Roi, 254–256

Comédies-en-vaudevilles, 254, 304, 314, 375

Comédies rosses, 394

Comedy
   France, 201–203, 249–251, 313
   Greece, 17, 18–19, 22, 26–27, 30, 33–34, 37–38
   Humours, 112, 216
   Italy, 158–161, 162, 246–248
   Manners, 216–217, 223, 250, 464
   Medieval, 80
   Rome, 47–49, 49, 58, 60–61, 61, 62, 109

Comedy, Satire, Irony, and Deeper Meaning (Grabbe), 296–297

Comedy-ballets, 198–199, 202

Comedy of Calisto and Melibea, The (Rojas), 142

Comedy of Errors (Shakespeare), 111

Comical Tale, A (Scarron), 192, 209

Comic opera, 219–220, 245, 253–257, 319, 327, 355–356

Comic Theatre, The (Goldoni), 248

Comic vision, 5

Comings and Going at the Expo (Gumberg), 526

Commedia dell'arte, 423
   Denmark, 287
   England, 218–219
   France, 188, 189, 196, 202, 203, 204, 252–254, 264
   Germany, 270, 271, 285
   Italy, 246–248
   origins of, 177–182
   Poland, 288
   Roman influence on, 51
   Russia, 423–424
   Spain, 402–403
   Sweden, 288

Commedia erudita, 177–179, 186

Commune, 548

Community theatres, 458, 553

Compagnia Proclemer-Albertazzi, 485

Compagnie des Quatre Saisons, 443

Compagnie des Quinze, 442–443

Compagnons de Notre-Dame, 443

Computers, 575

Comte, Auguste, 368–369

Concert Party (Ghana), 586–587

Condell, Henry, 111

Condemnation of the Banquet (Chesnaye), 99

Confidants, 162, 201

Confidenti troupe, 182

Confrérie de la Passion, 187–188, 189, 204

Confucianism, 647–648

Cong, Ping, 551

Congo, 601

Congreve, William, 216, 217–218, 223

Connection, The (Gelber), 499

Connelly, Marc, 462

Cons, Emma, 452

Conscious Lovers, The (Steele), 218

Conservatoire (Paris), 257, 438, 442

Constantinople, 63–68, 158–159, 161, 178

Construction of Theatres and Theatrical Machinery (Motta), 169

Constructivism, 428–429

Contemporary Theatre (Moscow), 510

Contest, The (Rugyendo), 592–593

Contractor, The (Storey), 534

Contrast, The (Tyler), 329, 330, 335

Cook, Ralph, 500

Cooke, George Frederick, 324, 329

Cooke, T. P., 325

Cooper, Thomas Abthorpe, 328, 329, 334

Copeau, Jacques, 425, 441, 442–443, 459, 461, 471, 491, 525, 561

Coppin, George Seth, 353

Copyright, 224, 345, 360, 401

Coquelin, Constant-Benoît, 345, 379–380

Coral (Kaiser), 434–435

Corés, Luciano, 383

Coriolanus (Shakespeare), 111, 322, 323, 363, 533

Corneille, Pierre, 190–194, 197, 200–201, 208, 210, 216, 269

Corneille, Thomas, 200–201

Cornish rounds, 90–91, 94–95

Corpus Christi, 82–83, 86, 88–89, 90, 140–141, 142, 143, 146, 153, 155

Corraboree, 353

Corral de la Cruz (Spain), 149, 151–152

Corral del Príncipe (Spain), 148, 149, 151, 152

Corrales, 145–146, 148–151, 153, 383

Corsican Brothers, The (Boucicault), 358, 360, 364

Cossa, Roberto, 486

Costantini, Angelo, 203, 204

Costenoble, Ludwig, 300

Costumbrismo style, 385

Costume
   China, 628
   England, 130, 134–135, 230–232, 241, 321–322, 326, 327, 365
   France, 205, 259–260, 308, 313, 377–379, 378, 379
   Germany, 279–280, 300–301
   Greece, 21, 24–27, 39
   Ireland, 421–422
   Japan, 634, 635, 640, 641
   liturgical drama, 79–80

Environmental theatre, 547–548
Ephesus, theatre at, 41
Epicharmus, 18
Epic theatre, 435–438, 462
Epidaurus, theatre at, 34
Episkenion, 40
Episodes, 50
Equestrian melodrama, 320, 322
Equus (Shaffer), 494
Erasmus Montanus (Holberg), 287
Eretria, theatre at, 40
Erik XIV (Strindberg), 429, 430
Erlanger, Abraham, 403
Erler, Fritz, 416–417, 417
Escossoise, L', 188
Esperpento, 446
Esslair, Ferdinand, 301
Esslin, Martin, 475, 489
Eternal Road, The (Werfel), 460
Ethel, Agnes, 348
Ethelwold, Bishop of Winchester
        (England), 76–77, 106
Etherege, Sir George, 216
Etherton, Michael, 612
Ethiopia, 580
"Ethiopian Operas," 336
Etruria, 43, 44–45, 49
Eubulus, 34
Eugène (Jodelle), 186
Eugene O'Neill Theatre Center, 539
Eugénie (Beaumarchais), 251, 262
Eumenides, The (Aeschylus), 15, 16, 22,
        25, 30
Eupolis, 18
Euripides, 15, 16–17, 21, 22–24, 25,
        30–31, 33, 37, 68, 185, 398, 524,
        548, 550, 561, 571, 600
Eurythmics, 413
Evans, Edith, 455, 456
Evans, Henry, 126
Events, conceptions of, 3
Everyman, 98–99, 416, 432, 454
Every Man in His Humour (Jonson), 112
Evil Spirit Lumpazivagabundus, The (Ne-
        stroy), 297, 298
Evreinov, Nikolai, 420, 423–424, 428
Ewald, Johannes, 288
Exile's Daughter, The (Pixérécourt), 310,
        316
Existentialism, 472–473
Exodia (afterpieces), 51
Exodos, 15
Expressionism, 433–435, 450, 463
Eyre, Richard, 532, 564

Fabbri, Diego, 485
Fabré, Emile, 443
Fábregas, Manolo, 527
Fabula atellanae, 45, 51, 62, 63, 176
Fabula crepidata, 49, 62–63
Fabula palliata, 49, 62

Fabula praetexta, 49, 50, 63
Fabula riciniata, 51–52
Fabula saltica, 52
Fabula togata, 49, 62
Fagan, J. B., 454
Fair theatres (Paris), 254–257
Faithful Shepherd, The (Guarini), 160
Faith Healer, The (Moody), 405
Faivre d'Arcier, Bernard, 525, 561
Falck, August, 415
Falk, Rosella, 485
Falls, Robert, 541, 573
False Antipathy (LaChaussée), 250
False Delicacy (Kelly), 222
False Prude, The, 204
Falstaff (Shakespeare), 231
Family Reunion, The (Eliot), 456
Farce, 37–38, 69, 95–97, 107–108, 109,
        143, 178, 188–190, 216, 349, 376,
        464
Farjeon, Herbert, 457
Farquhar, George, 217–218, 319, 352
Farrant, Richard, 126
Farrell, Bob, 336
Farren, Elizabeth, 236
Fashion (Mowatt), 338
Fashionable Prejudice, The (LaChaussée),
        250
Fate tragedy, 296
Father, The (Dunlap), 330
Father, The (Strindberg), 415
Fatherland! (Sardou), 376
Father of a Family, The (Diderot), 251
Faucit, Helen, 326
Faust (Goethe), 285, 295, 481, 558, 560
Favart, Charles-Simon, 254, 259
Favart, Marie-Justine, 259
Fay, Frank, 421
Fay, W. G., 421
Feast of Fools, 80, 96
Feast of the Boy Bishop, 80
Fechter, Charles, 359
Federal Street Theatre (Boston), 239,
        329, 332–333
Federal Theatre Project (United States),
        461–463, 487
Fehling, Jürgen, 435
Feldman, Peter, 537–538
Felsenstein, Walter, 481
Feminist theatre, 544, 553
Fences (Wilson), 545
Fennell, James, 328
Fenton, Frederick, 357
Ferber, Edna, 464
Ferguson, Ian, 609
Ferrari, Paolo, 402
Ferrex and Porrix (Sackville and Norton),
        109
Fescennine Verses, 44–45
Festival d'Automne (Paris), 561, 570

Festivals, 19–21, 34, 36–37, 44, 46–47,
        54, 55, 74–75, 104, 175–176,
        186–187, 480, 492, 501, 505, 506,
        507, 518, 544–545, 551–552, 555,
        558–559, 561, 564, 568–569. *See
        also specific festivals*
Feudalism, 74, 81–82, 84–85, 157, 182
Feuillère, Edwige, 471
Fiabe, 248, 295
Fichandler, Zelda, 501, 541
Fideli Company, 182
Field, Nathan, 118
Fielding, Henry, 220
Fiennes, Ralph, 563
Fierstein, Harvey, 546
Fiesko (Schiller), 275, 284
Fifth Avenue Theatre (New York), 347
Figueroa, Roque di, 146
Filippo, Eduardo de, 485
Filippo, Peppino de, 485
Film, 405
Finley, Karen, 551
Finney, Albert, 532
Fiorello, Tiberio, 204
First Studio (Moscow Art Theatre), 401,
        423, 429–430
Fischer, Franz, 283
Fisher, Betty, 553
Fisherman, The (Ewald), 288
Fiske, Harrison Grey, 403
Fiske, Minnie Maddern, 403
Fitch, Clyde, 405
Fitton, Doris, 466
Fitzball, Edward, 320
Five-act form, 50, 188, 203, 255
Flanagan, Hallie, 458
Flats, 312
Fleck, John, 551
Fletcher, John, 111, 112, 114, 215
Fleury, Abraham-Joseph, 308, 309
Flimm, Jürgen, 520
Floridor, 193
Flying Karamazov Brothers, 551
Flying machinery, 79, 93, 129–130, 135,
        141, 169, 174, 226, 346–347
Fo, Dario, 520, 521, 560–561, 576
Fokin, Valery, 556
Fokine, Mikhail, 422
Folk and peasant plays, 69, 297, 448,
        618
Folz, Hanz, 96
Fomenko, Victor, 556
Fontanne, Lynn, 465, 496
Fonvizin, Denis, 289
Fools, 143, 144, 269, 270, 326
Foote, Samuel, 221, 222, 224
Footlights, 313, 325, 365, 404
Forbes-Robertson, Johnston, 366, 399
Ford, John, 114
Ford Center for the Performing Arts
        (Broadway), 569

Ford Foundation, 501
Ford's Theatre (Washington, D.C.), 343
Foreman, Richard, 561, 570
Forest, Edwin, 333
Forest Rose, The (Woodworth), 335
Foriwa (Sutherland), 587
Formalism, 430
Fornés, Maria Irene, 500, 543, 546, 572
Forrest, Edwin, 326, 334–335, 335, 342
Forster, Michelanne, 553
Fort, Paul, 411
Fortune, The (London), 119, 124–125,
    131, 136, 211, 302, 507
Fortuny, Mariano, 406
Foster, J., 316
Four Elements, The (Rastell), 99
Fourth Studio (Moscow Art Theatre),
    430–431
Fourth Wall, 251, 362, 394
Fox, George L., 345
Foxá, Domingo Francisco, 386
Fragoso, Francisco, 596
France
    1500–1700, 185–210
    1700–1800, 248–263
    1789–1815, 303–304
    1800–1850, 303–313
    1850–1900, 374–382
    1875–1915, 392–395, 411–415,
        424–425
    1915–1940, 438–444
    1940–1968, 470–477
    1968–1990, 522–526
    1990–, 561–562
Francesca da Rimini (Boker), 345
Francesca da Rimini (D'Annunzio), 402
Francini, Tomaso, 190
Franco, Constancio, 385
Francon, Alain, 525
Franconi, Laurent, 310
Franz, Ellen, 388
Fraser, Brad, 567
Fraser, Claud Lovat, 453, 454
Frayn, Michael, 535, 565
Free plantation system, 346–347, 363
Free Southern Theatre, 537
Free theatres, 517–518
Free Traveling Theatre (Uganda), 591
Freie Bühne, 395–396, 397
Freie Volksbühne, 396, 481
French, A. B., 331
French, David, 552
French Academy, 191, 208, 209
French Theatre at Le Fevre's Riding
    Academy, 126, 129
Freska, Friedrich, 418
Freud, Sigmund, 396, 415–416, 439
Freytag, Gustav, 372
Friar Bacon and Friar Bungay (Greene),
    111
Friel, Brian, 535, 566

Frigerio, Ezio, 485
Fringe theatre
    Australia, 553
    Canada, 551–552
    England, 529–530, 563–564
    France, 561
    Ireland, 566
    New Zealand, 554
    South Africa, 605–608, 606–607
    United States, 536–537, 568–569, 570
Frisch, Max, 482
Frogs, The (Aristophanes), 19, 25
Frohman, Charles, 398, 403, 404
From Morn to Midnight (Kaiser), 434
Fronde, La, 192, 200
Frontier theatre, 331, 349
Fry, Christopher, 491
Fuchs, Elinor, 554
Fuchs, George, 416–417
Fuegi, John, 436
Fuerst, René, 440
Fugard, Athol, 539, 605, 606, 608–609
Fulgens and Lucrece (Medwall), 101, 108
Fuller, Isaac, 228
Fuller, W. H., 351
Fulton, Robert, 311
Furttenbach, Joseph, 170
Futurism, 444–445, 450, 547

Gadeau, Cioffi, 598
Gaiety Theatre (Manchester), 356, 398
Gale, Zona, 464
Galleries, 194. *See also* Box, pit, and
    gallery
Galliari family, 245
Gallienne, Eva Le, 461, 498
Galsworthy, John, 398, 399, 456
Gambler, The (Regnard), 250
Gamboa, Federico, 448
Gambon, Michael, 532
Game at Chess, The (Middleton), 113
Game of Love and Chance, The (Mari-
    vaux), 250
Gamester, The (Moore), 222, 251, 273
Gammer Gurton's Needle, 109
Ganz, Bruno, 518
Gao Wenxiu, 624
Garcia, Victor, 475, 497
Garcia Velloso, Enrique, 447
Garner, Arthur, 353
Garnier, Charles, 382
Garnier, Robert, 186
Garrard, Jim, 506
Garrick, David, 221, 224, 227, 229–236,
    240–241, 258, 321, 362
Garrison theatres, 333, 354
Garro, Elena, 488
Gascoigne, George, 109
Gascon, Jean, 505
Gas I and Gas II (Kaiser), 434–435
Gaskill, William, 530

Gaslight, 313
Gas lighting, 338–339, 340, 365–366,
    639
Gassman, Vittorio, 485
Gas table, 338, 365
Gaster, Theodor, 8–9
Gate, The (Ireland), 566
Gate Theatre (London), 453, 454, 457
Gatti, Armand, 476–477
Gaucho melodramas, 385
Gaul, Franz, 374
Gaultier-Garguille, 189, 193
Gay, John, 219–220
Gay and lesbian theatre, 546, 553
Geai, August, 476
Gecau, Kimani, 595
Geiogamah, Hanay, 546
Gelber, Jack, 499
Gellert, C. F., 273
Gelosi troupe, 182
Gémier, Firmin, 440–441
Gems, Pam, 535
Generation of '27 (Spain), 446
Generation of '98 (Spain), 402
Género chico dramas, 447
Genet, Jean, 474, 475, 476, 523, 550,
    558
Gentlemanly melodrama, 326, 358, 359
Geoghegan, Edward, 353
George, Mlle, 308, 309–310
German Stage, The (Gottsched), 272
Germany
    1648–1800, 265–285
    1800–1850, 294–303
    1850–1900, 372–374, 409–411
    1875–1915, 388–391, 395–396,
        406–407, 416–419
    1915–1940, 432–438
    1940–1968, 480–484
    1968–1990, 514–520
    1990–, 558–560
Gesticulator (Villaurrutia), 449
Ghana, 586–588
Ghelderode, Michel de, 443, 476
Ghéon, Henri, 443
Ghosts (Ibsen), 389, 391–392, 394, 395,
    397, 402, 403, 408, 521
Ghost Sonata, The (Strindberg), 415, 575
Ghost Train (Horvath), 515
Giehse, Therese, 481
Gielgud, John, 363, 455, 456, 491, 492
Gieselmann, David, 560
Giffard, Henry, 221, 239
Gigolo, 250
Gilbert, Mrs. G. H., 348
Gilbert, William S., 327, 356
Gill, Peter, 532
Gilleberts, Guillaume des, 193
Gillette, William, 349
Gillot, Charles, 262–263
Gilpin, Charles, 462

Gingold, Hermione, 457

Ginkas, Kama, 556

Giotto, 158

Giraudoux, Jean, 441, 443–444

Girl from Samos, The (Menander), 38

Girl of the Golden West, The (Belasco), 404

Gissey, Henri, 199

Gladiator, The (Bird), 335

Gladiatorial contests, 42, 44, 52–53, 57, 64, 66–67

Glance at New York, A (Baker), 337–338

Glaspell, Susan, 464

Glass, Philip, 546, 551, 568, 574

Glass Menagerie, The (Williams), 501–502

Glass of Water, A (Scribe), 375

Glengarry Glen Ross (Mamet), 541

Glinka, Mikhail, 315

Globe, The (London), 111, 119–120, 123, 124, 125, 127, 136, 302–303, 458–459

Globe Theatre (London), 562–563

Glowacki, Janusz, 512, 557

Gluck, Christoph Willibald, 245

Glyn, Isabella, 357

Gnapheus, 99

Godfrey, Peter, 453, 454

Godfrey, Thomas, 239

Gods Are Not To Blame, The (Rotimi), 585

Godwin, Edward, 413

Goethe, Johann Wolfgang von, 274, 275, 282–285, 291–292, 294, 295, 296, 300, 301, 302, 374, 416, 481, 518, 559, 560

Goetz von Berlichingen (Goethe), 275, 279, 280, 282

Gogol, Nikolai, 314, 315, 428, 476

Golden Apple, The, 242, 243, 267

Golden Fleece, The (Grillparzer), 297

Goldflam, Arnost, 558

Goldoni, Carlo, 247–248, 254, 255, 264, 484

Goldsmith, Oliver, 222–223, 252

Goll, Yvan, 450

Golovin, Alexander, 423

Gombrowicz, Witold, 557

Gomes, Dias, 487

Gómez de Avellaneda, Gertruda, 386

Goncourt, Edmond and Jules, 393

Gontcharova, Natalie, 423

Gonzáles de Eslava, Fernán, 153

Good Friday, 76

Goodman's Fields Theatre (London), 221, 235

Goodman Theatre (Chicago), 458, 541, 573

Good Natur'd Man, The (Goldsmith), 222–223

Good Soldier Schweik, The (Hacek), 436

Good Woman of Setzuan, The (Brecht), 436, 588

Gorboduc (Sackville and Norton), 109

Gorelik, Mordecai, 460

Gorky, Maxim, 402, 430, 431, 518

Gorky Theatre (Leningrad), 478

Gorostiza, Carlos, 527

Gorostiza, Celestino, 448

Gorostiza, Manuel Eduardo de, 384

Gosson, Stephen, 115

Got, Edmond, 379

Gotanda, Philip Kan, 546

Gotha Court Theatre, 276

Gottsched, Johann Christoph, 270–272

Gottsched, Johann Gottfried, 274, 280

Gougenot, Le Sieur, 193, 209

Government regulation of theatre, 54, 114–116, 140–141, 144, 146, 191–192, 213–214, 220–223, 237, 238, 252, 254–255, 299–300, 304, 307, 313–315, 318–319, 327–328, 353, 356, 358, 370, 371, 382–383, 395, 430, 466–467, 470–471, 518, 522, 529–530, 586

Governor's Lady, The, 404, 405

Gozzi, Carlo, 247, 248, 295, 429

Grabbe, Christian Dietrich, 296–297, 302, 557–558

Gradas, 149–150

Graft, Joe C. de, 587–588

Grand Cirque Ordinaire, 506

Grand Magic Circus, The, 523–524

Grand Theatre (Bordeaux), 262

Grandval, Charles-François de, 258

Grassi, Paolo, 485, 520

Gray, Simon, 535

Gray, Spalding, 548, 551

Gray, Terence, 454–455

Gray's Inn, 109

Great Divide, The (Moody), 405, 406

Greatest Enchantment is Love, The (Calderón), 153–154

Great Galeoto, The (Echegaray), 402

Great Theatre of the World, The (Hofmannsthal), 432

Great World Theatre, The (Hofmannsthal), 416

Greban, Arnoul, 84

Greece, 6, 9, 10, 11–35, 36–43, 70
classical theatre, 11–35
Hellenistic theatre, 36–43

Green, John, 268–269

Green, Paul, 461, 462, 463–464

Greene, Graham, 494

Greene, Robert, 110–111

Green Mountain Boy, The (Jones), 336

Green Pastures (Connelly), 462

Greet, Ben, 452, 455

Gregory, Johann Gottfried, 288

Gregory, Lady Augusta, 421, 422

Grein, J. T., 397

Grévin, Jacques, 186

Griboyedov, Alexander, 314

Grieg, David, 565–566

Grieve, John, 327

Grieve, Thomas, 359

Griffen, Hayden, 532

Griffith, D. W., 405

Griffiths, Trevor, 535

Grillparzer, Franz, 297, 300, 373, 389

Grimaldi, Joseph, 357

Grimsted, David, 339–340

Gringoire, Pierre, 96

Griot theatre, 581, 599

Gripsholm (Sweden), 288

Groot, Paul de, 603

Grooves (stage), 346–347, 365

Gropius, Walter, 437–438

Grosch, Jürgen, 519, 558

Gros-Guillaume, 189, 190, 193, 209

Grosses Schauspielhaus (Berlin), 432, 434

Grosskopf, J. W. F., 603

Grossman, Jan, 479, 514, 557, 558

Grotesco criollo, 447

Grotowski, Jerzy, 512–514, 524, 527–528, 538, 557

Ground Floor and the First Floor, The (Nestroy), 297

Group Theatre (New York), 461, 497

Grumberg, Jean-Paul, 525–526

Gründgens, Gustav, 480–481

Grüner, Karl Franz, 291–292

Gryphius, Andreas, 271

Gual, Adria, 403

Guare, John, 543

Guarini, Giambattista, 160

Guarnieri, Gianfrancesco, 487

Gubenko, Nikolai, 556

Guénégaud Theatre (Paris), 203–204, 206

Guérin, Robert, 189

Guérin d'Etriché, Isaac François, 205

Guerra, Henrique, 596

Guerrilla theatre, 537

Guéru, Hugues, 189

Guilds
Hellenistic, 39
Medieval, 81, 84–85, 85, 90, 103–104, 147
Spain, 147

Guillot-Gorju, 193

Guinea-Bissau, 595–596

Guinness, Alec, 456

Guitry, Sacha, 438–439

Gunter, John, 532

Gurney, A. R., 543

Gurr, Andrew, 111, 121

Gurrola, Juan José, 527

Guthrie, Tyrone, 453, 454, 455, 491, 501, 505, 506

Guthrie Theatre (Minneapolis), 502, 505, 540–541, 542, 573

Oh, What a Lovely War!, 493
O'Keeffe, John, 222
Okhlopkov, Nikolai, 430–431, 478
Oklahoma!, 464, 504
Okura, Toraaki, 635
Old Comedy (Greece), 18, 19, 24, 33–34, 37
Oldfield, Anne, 234, 235, 258
Oldmixon, Mrs., 328
Old Vic, The (London), 318, 442, 452–453, 490, 491–492, 496–497, 506, 564
Olivier, Laurence, 456, 491, 492, 496
Olivier Theatre, 532
Oloyede, D. A., 583
Olympic Academy of Vicenza (Italy), 171
Olympic Arts Festival (Los Angeles), 524, 550
Olympic Theatre (London), 327, 362
Olympic Theatre (New York), 332
Omai, or A Trip Around the World, 229
Omatoso, Kole, 586
Ondine (Giraudoux), 444
O'Neal, John, 537
O'Neill, Eliza, 324
O'Neill, Eugene, 403, 429, 458, 460, 462, 463, 467, 498, 501, 560
O'Neill, James, 403–404, 463
One Race (Unruh), 434
Ong, Han, 572
Onkos, 39
On the Razzle (Stoppard), 297
Onwueme, Tess, 586
Open Theatre, 537–538, 548
Opera
    ballad, 219–220, 221–222, 289
    Beijing, 625–630, 648
    comic, 219–220, 245, 253–257, 319, 327, 355–356
    England, 211, 215–216, 219–220, 234, 319, 452
    France, 196–199, 206, 263–264
    Germany, 266, 367, 406–407, 409–411, 410–411, 423, 480
    Italy, 173, 175, 245–246, 485–486, 560
    origins of, 163–164
    Russia, 289, 290, 315, 372
    Spain, 154
    Yoruba, 582–583
Opéra (Paris), 198–199, 204, 206, 207, 229, 252–256, 258, 260–263, 262, 304, 307, 312, 313, 381–382, 425, 470
Opera buffa, 245, 247
Opéra-Comique, Theatre National del', 304, 307, 381, 470
Opéras-comiques, 245, 253–257, 289
Operetta, 373, 376–377
Opperman, Deon, 609

Oralloosa (Bird), 335
Orange, theatre at, 56, 59
Orbay, François d', 206
Orbecche (Cinthio), 160
Orchestra
    England, 362
    Greece, 28, 29, 41, 42
    Rome, 56
Ordo Virtutum, 77
Oreste (Alfieri), 485
Oresteia (Aeschylus), 16, 24, 28, 467, 518, 524, 561
Orestes (Euripides), 16, 571
Orfeo (Monteverdi), 164
Orghast, 531
Origin of the Species, The (Darwin), 392
Origins of theatre, 1–10
Orlando Furioso, 521
Orleans Theatre (New Orleans), 333
Orlik, Emil, 419
Ormerod, Nick, 563–564
Ormond Dramatic Society (Ireland), 421
O'Rowe, Mark, 567
Orphan, The (Otway), 215
Orphan of China, The (Voltaire), 259–260, 262, 624
Orphan of the House of Zhao, The (Qi Zhun), 623–624
Orpheus (Cocteau), 439
Orpheus and Eurydice (Gluck), 245
Orpheus in the Underworld (Offenbach), 376–377
Orrell, John, 125, 135
Orthón, Manuel José, 385
Ortiz, Christobal, 146
Osborne, John, 492, 508, 529, 530, 533
Os Comediantes (Brazil), 447–448
Osiris, 7–8, 9
Osofisan, Femi, 585–586
Ossako, Wembo, 601
Ostermeier, Thomas, 558
Ostrovsky, Alexander, 370, 371, 372, 430, 556
O'Sullivan, Vincent, 554
Othello (Shakespeare), 111, 160, 305–306, 319, 337, 521, 604
Otto, Teo, 481
Otway, Thomas, 215
Our Boys (Byron), 354
Our Town (Wilder), 464, 548, 570
Ouspenskaya, Maria, 461
Out for a Lark (Nestroy), 297
Out-of-town tryouts, 359–360, 503
Ovid, 49
Owens, John E., 336
Owusu, Martin, 588
Oxford Repertory Company, 454, 455
Oyônî-Mbia, Guillaume, 600
Ozerov, Vladislav, 313
Ozidi (Clark-Bekederemo), 585

Packer, Tina, 573
Pacuvius, Marcus, 49
Pagan rites, 74–75, 80
Page, Anthony, 530
Page, Geraldine, 498
Pageant Master, 85–86
Pageant wagons, 85, 88–90, 91, 94, 100, 103, 107, 121, 167, 176
Pagnol, Marcel, 443
Palace of Long Life, The (Hong Sheng), 625
Palais à volonté, 207, 262, 278, 313
Palais Cardinal (Paris), 196
Palais Royal (Paris), 197, 202, 206, 260–261
Palitzsch, Peter, 481, 517, 518, 558
Palladio, Andrea, 128, 134, 171
Pallenberg, Max, 419
Palm Sunday, 76
Pammachius (Naogeorgus), 99
Pandora's Box (Wedekind), 416
Panikkar, Kavalam Narayana, 620
Panorama-Dramatique, 312
Panoramas, 311–313, 322, 338, 364, 365, 411
Pantomime, 5, 60–61, 62, 63, 70, 175, 218–219, 222, 240, 251, 254, 316, 355, 445
Paolo, Giovanni e, 173
Papp, Joseph, 501, 530, 539, 570
Parabasis, 19
Parade (Cocteau), 439
Parades, 255
Paradis (upper balcony), 194
Paradise Now (Malina and Beck), 536, 537, 554
Paradox of the Actor, The (Diderot), 258
Paraskenia, 40
Pardo y Aliaga, Felipe, 385
Parigi, Alfonso, 153, 170
Parigi, Giulio, 134, 135, 169, 170
Parisienne, La (Becque), 393
Parks, Suzan-Lori, 572
Park Theatre (New York), 329, 330, 332, 334, 338
Parodoi, 15, 31, 40, 56
Parry, Lorae, 554
Parsifal (Wagner), 560
Parterre, 194. *See also* Pit
Parthenon, 12
Pasos, 143
Pasqual, Lluís, 560
Passion Flower (Benavente), 402–403
Passion play, 7–8, 68, 82–95
Pastor, Tony, 350
Pastoral drama, 160, 188
Patents (England), 220, 318–319, 321, 356–357
Pater Noster plays, 97
Patient Grissell (Phillip), 102
Patin, Jacques, 187

Patio (Spain), 149–150, 151, 154
Patriot for Me, A (Osborne), 529, 530
Patroni-Griffi, Guiseppe, 522
Patte, Pierre, 246
Patterson, Tom, 505
Paul Kauvar (MacKaye), 348
Paul's Boys, 116, 117, 126
Paulsen, Carl Andreas, 269
Paulus (Vergerio), 158
Pavilions, 123–124
Pavoni, Giuseppe, 183–184
Paymann, Claus, 558
Payne, B. Iden, 455
Payne, John Howard, 330
Paz, Albio, 527
Paz, Octavio, 488
Peabody, Josephine Preston, 405
Peace (Aristophanes), 19
Peduzzi, Richard, 523
Peer Gynt (Ibsen), 391, 518, 523, 560, 644
Pegmata, 60
Peisistratus, 12
Pelléas and Mélisande (Maeterlinck), 412, 565
Penafiel, Damien Arias de, 147
Penhall, Joe, 566
Penny arcades, 405
Pensionnaires (France), 256, 257, 309
Peón y Contreras, José, 385
Peony Pavilion, The (Tang Xianzu), 561, 568, 624–626
People's Experimental Theater (South Africa), 605
People's Lawyer, The (Jones), 336
People's Theater, The (Spain), 446
People's theatre, 440
Peralta Barnuevo, Pedro de, 153, 385
Perez, Cosme, 147
Pérez, Santiago, 385
Perfall, Karl von, 420
Performance art, 551, 561
Performance Group (New York), 548
Performance Works (San Francisco), 575
Performative elements, 1, 3–5, 6
Pergolesi, Giovanni Battista, 245, 254
Periaktoi, 30, 42, 58, 135, 167, 168
Pericles, 12, 28, 31
Pericles (Shakespeare), 549
Pericles (Wilkins), 111
Perrucci, Andrea, 184
Persians, The (Aeschylus), 16, 549
Perspective scenery, 165–168, 242–245
Perspective setting, 186
Pertharite (P. Corneille), 192
Peru, 385
Peruzzi, Baldassare, 166
Peter Pan (Barrie), 419
Petipa, Marius, 371, 422
Petit Bourbon (Paris), 187, 197, 198, 202, 210

Petitclair, Pierre, 351
Petit-Jean, Pierre Regnault (Laroque), 193
Petrarch, 158
Petrushevshya, Ludmilla, 511–512
Phallic rites, 18
Phallus, 21, 26–27
Phantom Lady, The (Calderón), 145
Phèdre (Pradon), 201
Phèdre (Racine), 201, 308, 429, 571
Phelps, Samuel, 357–358, 399
Philander, 164
Philemon, 38
Philipe, Gérard, 471–472
Philips, Ambrose, 218
Philoctetes (Sophocles), 16, 25, 29
Phipps, C. J., 362
Phiri, Masautso, 595
Phlyakes, 33, 43, 45
Phoenician Women, The (Euripides), 16
Phoenix, The (London), 127, 135, 211, 212–213, 213–214, 225
Phoenix Theatre (New York), 498, 501
Phrynichus, 15, 27
Physical theatre, 567
Physician to His Own Honor, The (Calderón), 145
Physicists, The (Duerrenmatt), 482
Piano Lesson, The (Wilson), 545
Piccolo Teatro (Milan), 485, 560
Pickard-Cambridge, A. W., 30
Pictorial and Architectural Perspective (Pozzo), 268
Pierre Pathelin, 95, 96
Pietas Victrix (Nikolaus), 268
Pillars of Society (Ibsen), 391, 403
Pinakes, 30, 41
Pinal, Silvia, 527
Pinero, Arthur Wing, 396–397, 456
Pinter, Harold, 494–495, 533, 565, 568
Pirandello, Luigi, 445, 471, 511
Piranesi, Giovanni Battista, 246
Pirchan, Emil, 435
Pisarev, Alexander, 314
Piscator, Erwin, 435–436, 437, 481, 518
Pisemsky, A. F., 370
Pit, 173, 194
Pita y Borroto, Santiago, 386
Pitinsky, Jan Antonin, 557, 558
Pitoëff, Georges, 442, 444, 471
Pix, Mary, 218
Pixérécourt, René Charles Guilbert de, 304–305, 308, 316, 320
Pizarro (Kotzebue), 320
Pizarro (Sheridan), 322
Place, conceptions of, 3
Placide, Alexandre, 330
Plague, 131
Planché, James Robinson, 322–323, 327, 355, 364
Planchon, Roger, 476, 477, 522–523

Platea, 79, 91, 129
Plato, 21, 36–37
Platonov (Flimm), 520
Platter, Thomas, 136
Plautus, Titus Maccius, 48, 49, 54, 58, 62, 63, 109, 141–142, 158, 159, 160, 178, 185, 208, 286, 287
Playboy of the Western World, The (Synge), 422
Playfair, Nigel, 453, 454
Playhouse at Newington Butts (London), 119, 120
Play of Robin and Marion, The (Halle), 95
Play of the Greenwood, The (Halle), 95
Play of the Magi Kings, 82
Plays Confuted in Five Actions (Gosson), 115
Play Workshop (Canada), 465
Playwrights
 methods of paying, 21, 118, 223–224, 252, 307, 325, 349, 351, 360, 370
 See also Dramatists
Playwrights' Horizons, 569
Playwrights Studio Group (Canada), 465
Pleasures of the Enchanted Island, The, 200
Pléiade, 185–186
Plenty (Hare), 535
Plessis, P. G. du, 604
Pliny the Elder, 55
Plot of the Equals, The (Levidov), 429
Plowright, Joan, 532
Pluchek, Valentin, 478
Plutus (Aristophanes), 19, 33–34
Po-ca-hon-tas (Brougham), 335, 345
Pocahontas (Custis), 335
Pochinko, Richard, 567
Poel, William, 419–420, 453–454, 455
Poetic drama, 319–320, 357–358, 359, 491
Poetics (Aristotle), 13, 37, 45, 161, 164, 185
Pogodin, Nikolai, 432, 477, 478
Pohl, Martin, 436
Poland
 1968–1990, 512–514
 1990-, 557
Polevoy, Nikolai, 314
Poliakoff, Stephen, 535
Police, The (Mrozek), 512
Polini, Emelie, 466
Polish Laboratory Theatre, 512–514, 548
Pollux, 37–38, 167, 174
Polus, 34
Polyekran, 479
Polyeucte (P. Corneille), 194
Pompa (Roman festivals), 47
Pomponius, 51, 165
Ponferrada, Juan Oscar, 486
Ponsard, François, 307
Ponty, William, 596–597, 598
Poor theatre, 513, 527–528, 538